National Income and Related Statistics for Selected Years, 19...

1952	1953	1954	1955	1956	1957	1958	1959	1960	1961	1962	1963	1964	1965	1966	1967
							494.2	51_							
219.1	232.6	239.8	257.9	270.6	285.3	294.6	316.3	330.7				_.7	477.3	503.6	
53.5	54.9	54.1	69.7	72.7	71.1	63.6	80.2	78.2				_.2	128.6	125.7	
75.8	82.8	76.0	75.3	79.7	87.3	95.4	97.9	100.6	108.4	118.2	123.8	130.0	138.6	158.6	179.8
3.2	1.3	2.6	3.0	5.3	7.3	3.3	1.5	5.9	7.2	6.9	8.2	10.9	9.7	7.5	7.4
351.6	371.6	372.5	405.9	428.2	451.0	456.8	495.8	515.3	533.8	574.6	606.9	649.8	705.1	772.0	816.4
29.2	30.9	32.5	34.4	38.1	41.1	42.8	44.6	46.4	47.8	49.4	51.4	53.9	57.4	62.1	67.4
322.5	340.7	340.0	371.5	390.1	409.4	414.0	451.2	468.9	486.1	525.2	555.6	595.9	647.7	709.9	749.0
30.9	34.1	33.7	35.2	33.8	37.1	39.0	42.0	44.0	47.1	51.9	55.2	58.3	62.5	67.9	71.3
291.6	306.6	306.3	336.3	356.3	372.8	375.0	409.2	424.9	439.0	473.3	500.3	537.6	585.2	642.0	677.7
9.3	9.6	10.6	12.0	13.5	15.5	15.9	18.8	21.9	22.9	25.4	28.5	30.1	31.6	40.6	45.5
19.4	20.3	17.6	22.0	22.0	21.4	19.0	23.6	22.7	22.8	24.0	26.2	28.0	30.9	33.7	32.7
9.6	8.6	9.8	14.8	12.7	12.3	10.1	15.6	13.9	14.2	19.9	21.9	25.3	31.3	33.5	31.2
20.5	22.4	24.8	26.7	29.0	32.8	37.0	39.5	43.0	46.9	49.2	52.6	56.1	60.6	66.6	76.2
273.8	290.5	293.0	314.2	337.2	356.5	367.1	390.0	409.4	426.0	453.2	476.3	510.2	552.0	600.8	644.5
34.0	35.5	32.5	35.4					50.8	52.2	57.0	60.5	58.8	65.2	74.9	82.4
239.8	255.1	260.5						_.8	396.2	415.8	451.4	486.8	525.9	562.1	
1328.2	1435.3	1416.2						_.7	1799.4	1873.3	1973.3	2087.6	2208.3	2271.4	
$5,742	$5,964	$5,941						_06	$7,034	$7,182	$7,588	$7,954	$8,256	$8,470	
1.6	3.9	-0.4						1.4	3.7	2.1	5.7	4.8	3.8	2.6	
26.5	26.7	26.9						9.9	30.2	30.6	31.0	31.5	32.4	33.4	
1.9	0.8	0.7						1.0	1.0	1.3	1.3	1.6	2.9	3.1	
126.8	128.2	131.6						5.2	147.9	153.4	160.4	167.9	172.1	183.3	
157.6	160.2	163.0						3.7	186.5	189.2	191.9	194.3	196.6	198.7	
62.1	63.0	63.6						0.5	70.6	71.8	73.1	74.5	75.8	77.3	
1.9	1.8	3.5						4.7	3.9	4.1	3.8	3.4	2.9	3.0	
2.9	2.8	5.4						6.5	5.4	5.5	5.0	4.4	3.7	3.7	
19.2	18.1	18.8						1.1	33.1	35.7	40.5	42.9	46.6	49.5	
16.0	16.8	16.3						3.9	26.2	27.5	29.6	33.2	39.1	42.1	
66.2	69.6	69.7	65.5	74.6	80.0	79.6	79.2	92.5	94.4	99.7	107.0	112.6	116.8	130.8	148.8
67.7	76.1	70.9	68.4	70.6	76.6	82.4	92.1	92.2	97.7	107.0	111.0	118.5	118.2	134.5	157.5
-1.5	-6.5	-1.2	-3.0	3.9	3.4	-2.8	-13.0	0.3	-3.3	-7.1	-4.8	-5.9	-1.4	-3.7	-8.6

Source: Economic Reports of the President,, 1960-1992 ,and author calculations.

Economics

5th Edition

Ralph T. Byrns
The University of Colorado at Boulder

Gerald W. Stone, Jr.
Metropolitan State College of Denver

SPECIAL EDITION

HarperCollins *College Publishers*

Sponsoring Editor: Bruce Kaplan
Development Editor: Bob Nirkind
Project Editor: Bob Cooper
Design Supervisor: Dorothy Bungert
Text and Cover Design: Howard Petlack, A Good Thing, Inc.
Cover Illustration/Photo: Marc Yankus
Production Manager/Production Assistant: Kewal Sharma
Compositor: York Graphic Services, Inc.
Printer and Binder: R. R. Donnelley & Sons Company
Cover Printer: The LeHigh Press, Inc.

ECONOMICS, Fifth Edition

Library of Congress Cataloging-in-Publication Data

Byrns, Ralph T.
    Economics/Ralph T. Byrns, Gerald W. Stone, Jr. — Special
5th ed.
      p.   cm.
    Includes index.
    ISBN 0–673–46842–9
    1. Economics.   I. Stone, Gerald W.   II. Title.
HB171.5.B99 1993
330–dc20   92–31794
                                        CIP

93   94   95   9 8 7 6 5 4 3 2

Contents in Brief

A cross-reference to the chapters in *Economics* (hardcover edition) and in *Macroeconomics* and *Microeconomics* (the two paperback editions).

Contents

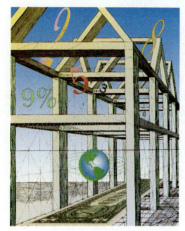

MACROECONOMICS

Part 2 Cornerstones of Macroeconomics 98

Part 3   Keynesian Macroeconomics 170

Chapter 8   Classical Macroeconomics and Keynesian Aggregate Expenditures 172

Part 5   Challenges to Macroeconomic Policymaking 334

Part 6 Core Concepts of Microeconomics 418

Part 8 Resource Markets 626

Part 9   Modern Microeconomic Issues 700

To the Instructor

Our fifth edition of *Economics* continues its tradition of "firsts." Our package for teaching economics was the first to augment standard supplements with (*a*) student software, (*b*) computerized testing, and (*c*) such unique items as *Great Ideas for Teaching Economics* and *The Hyperinflation Collection*. We were also the first to successfully use full-color production that capitalizes on familiarity with descriptive graphs from popular magazines and newspapers.

Our fifth edition of *Economics* ushers in more "firsts": it is the first text with a chapter on Strategic Behavior; it is the first with a microeconomic simulation that parallels *Macrosim*; it is the first accompanied by a laser disk that lets instructors use animated graphs with shifting curves and video clips to portray difficult concepts; and it is the first to provide a special edition of *The Economist* magazine, reporting recent developments in the world economy.

Key features that made our previous editions so successful have not been slighted to accomplish these "firsts." *Economics* uses a traditional organization to present:

1. clear and up-to-date coverage of core principles of economics, abundantly illustrated with graphs that set a standard unmatched by any competing text;

2. a lively writing style generously seasoned with intuitive examples;

3. sound pedagogy, from summary figures and tables stressing key concepts to expanded emphasis on interesting end-of-chapter problem sets that range from easy to challenging.

Virtually every paragraph drawn from the previous edition of *Economics* has been polished and refined.

Key Features in the Fifth Edition

Some of the most noteworthy of our extensive revisions to *Economics* include:

Macroeconomics

Intuitive foundations for the *Aggregate Demand/ Aggregate Supply Model* are now presented in the introductory macro Chapter 5 (much earlier than in most competing texts), and then applied to American business cycles in the 20th century so that students quickly recognize how this model can be used to interpret modern macroeconomics.

The *internationalization of economic activity* is a recurring theme in this text, including new material on developments in Eastern Europe, the USSR, and the Pacific Rim; Chapter 14 clearly describes the linkages between persistent federal budget deficits and persistent deficits in the U.S. balance of trade.

Our revised Chapter 8 contrasts and compares *Classical and Keynesian models*, providing students with a balanced and clearer historical sense of the disagreements about theory that now divide economists when they interpret major economic issues.

Chapter 12 explores in depth the *Federal Reserve's economic role*, and provides detailed coverage of financial intermediation processes, financial regulation, and how deregulation, swings in real estate markets, and the "moral hazards" created by deposit insurance all contributed to the *widespread collapse of Savings & Loans*.

Revisions to Chapter 16 stress current debates about *active vs. passive policymaking*, intuitively considering such theoretical issues as how expectations are formed (adaptively or rationally?) and real business cycles.

New Focus Boxes in the macro section cover such topics as Errors in International Comparisons of Per Capita GNP (Chapter 7), and the S&L crisis (Chapter 12).

Microeconomics

A new Chapter 26, "Strategic Behavior," addresses such topics from the New Industrial Organization as Game Theory, Asymmetric Information, Moral Hazard, Adverse Selection,

Screening and Signalling, Contestable Markets, and Predatory Pricing.

A new Chapter 21, "Theory of the Firm," explains why firms exist, the role of the entrepreneur, the forms firms may take and how they are financed.

Coverage of international economics has been expanded dramatically, and includes, for example, Focus boxes in Chapter 28 on how the globalization of world markets affects American workers and how tax rates affect labor supplies internationally, international mergers and acquisitions (Chapter 27), and the international scope of business in Chapter 37.

Chapters 28 and 29 now survey such issues as wage differentials and discrimination, comparable worth, and the changing roles of labor unions. Chapter 34 on environmental economics has expanded discussions of such topics as acid rain, recycling, and solid wastes.

Numerous new Focus Boxes consider such topics as Rational Ignorance and Artificial Intelligence (Chapter 20), The "Winner's" Curse (Chapter 26), The International Market for Corporate Control (Chapter 25), How Can You Cope in a Global Economy? and Are Exploitation and Discrimination Caused by Capitalistic Greed? (Chapter 28), The Airlines: Caveat Deregulator? (Chapter 33), and Solid Waste Recycling (Chapter 34).

Pedagogy

Each part of *Economics* opens with a broad introduction indicating how sequential chapters are related, and each chapter begins with an overview of the topics it covers. Numerous other instructional aids run through the text:

1. Major points are *italicized*, and **key terms** and **economic laws** are **bold-faced** when introduced, with

   Definitions *that are set off from the rest of the text.*

2. Analytical graphs are rendered simply, to efficiently convey economic concepts, and attractively, to pique student interest. Standardized notation in graphs and equa-

tions aids student comprehension. Descriptive and historical data are illustrated through modern techniques paralleling the graphical data presented in TV news broadcasts and in such newspapers as the *Wall Street Journal* or *USA Today*, and such magazines as *Newsweek* or *Fortune*.

3. Boxed Focuses (e.g., Will Social Security Absorb our National Debt?, Should We Export Pollution?, The Winner's Curse and Regional Economic Integration and Biographical Sketches give students a well-rounded introduction to economics.

4. Chapters conclude with (*a*) a comprehensive Chapter Review that covers Key Points, (*b*) a list of Key Concepts that students should be able to define, and (*c*) Problems and Questions for students to work. (Solutions are provided only in our *Instructors' Manual for Teaching Economics*.)

5. Selected legal cases reveal the linkages between Law and Economics.

6. Optional Materials covering selected analytical concepts (e.g., Graphing, the Mathematics of Multipliers, Indifference Curves, and Isoquants) are appended to some chapters for instructors who seek intensive coverage of these topics.

7. An extensive Glossary and thorough Indexes at the end of the book provide handy references for students.

Printed Supplements

Our *Economics* package provides a broader spectrum of quality teaching supplements than is available for any other text:

1. *Great Ideas for Teaching Economics* now includes more than 600 analogies, anecdotes, exercises, and general teaching tips, contributed by instructors from across the country.

2. Our *Student Guide for Learning Economics* uses a variety of techniques to facilitate student mastery of economic concepts. Each chapter includes a chapter review, matching problems, true-false questions, fill-in reviews, multiple-choice questions, and problems sets, and some have specialized exer-

cises as well. Step-by-step solutions to especially challenging problem sets are provided.

3. Timely and authoritative articles have been excerpted into special editions of *The Economist* magazine to provide students with current information about global economic issues.

4. The expanded *Hyperinflation Collection* contains brief histories and actual samples of currency and stamps from such hyperinflations as those experienced in Germany in the 1920s, Greece and Hungary in the 1940s, and South America in the 1980s.

5. The *Instructors Manual for Teaching Economics* contains chapter outlines, lecture suggestions, answers to end-of-chapter problems and questions, and analyses of the legal cases that conclude some chapters. Some supplementary materials can be reproduced as class hand-outs (e.g., selected legal cases).

6. The 8,500+ item *Test Bank for Economics* has been split into *Banks I, II, III,* and *IV* to allow you to alternate test banks between semesters. Software versions of this class-tested *Test Bank* are available for both Macintosh and IBM-PC computers.

7. Four-color overhead *Transparencies* are available for all important figures and tables from the text.

Software Supplements for Students

Each chapter of *Economics* is paralleled with interesting software exercises for Macintosh and IBM PCs. All programs (available shrink-wrapped with our texts) permit individual "print-outs" for each student at every step, including normalized scores (based on a standard of 100 percent) to facilitate comparisons of student performance. Students successfully completing all programs should understand most basic principles of economics. Schedules detailing the exercises appropriate for each week of a typical course are included in the Sample Syllabi provided on diskette to instructors who adopt our texts.

1. *Macro-Study* allows macro students to review concepts that include graphical analysis, production possibilities, demand and supply, GNP accounting, unemployment and inflation, classical vs. Keynesian theories, Aggregate Demand and Aggregate Supply, money and banking, active vs. passive macroeconomic policymaking, new classical economics, and international trade and finance.

2. *Macrosim*, a computer-based simulation now in its fifth revision, allows macro students in the last 5-7 weeks of a course to manipulate policy instruments (e.g., government spending, tax rates, and the money supply) in attempts to stabilize economic activity and stimulate growth. An Instructor's Edition, *CREATE*, allows instructors to tailor scenarios to reflect virtually any macroeconomic view of how the world works.

3. *Micro-Study* sequentially tests student mastery of graphical techniques, production possibilities, simple demand and supply analysis, elasticity calculations, consumer analysis, the theory of the firm, market structures for outputs and resources, applied topics, and international trade.

4. *Microsim* is a simulation for microeconomics with features similar to *Macrosim*. This program allows students to test their skills at business decisionmaking in market structures for outputs ranging from pure competition to pure monopoly. Elements of strategic behavior and simple game theory are extended to decisions about resources ranging from labor unions to international capital markets.

Software Supplements for Instructors

The TestMaster computerized testing system, available in both IBM and Macintosh versions, allows you to construct tests easily by choosing from test items specifically prepared to accompany this text. The TestMaster software lets you choose test questions randomly, by choosing a chapter, question type, and quantity, or manually, by choosing specific items numbers. Questions can also be selected by viewing them on screen or by doing computer searches for groups of questions that meet specific criteria. The TestMaster software allows you to select existing questions or add your own questions to the chapter disks. Tests can be printed in several different formats and can include figures such as graphs, charts and tables.

Economics Laser Disk

Our Byrns and Stone *Laser Disc* allows instructors to call up nearly a thousand images at the touch of a button, including all graphs from the text. It provides additional newsreels, video clips, and animated graphics (e.g., shifting demand and supply curves) to highlight complex economic principles.

Any principles text is always in process. Suggestions that aid us in making the next edition of *Economics* or its supplements clearer, more topical, or more complete will be deeply appreciated and gratefully acknowledged. Please send us your comments, c/o HarperCollins Publishers, 10 East 53rd Street, New York, NY, 10022-5299.

To the Student

Although economic problems are universal, roughly 90 percent of the world's population was relatively sheltered from distant events for over 95 percent of human history. Such isolation, however, is no longer possible — nor would it be desirable. A relatively quiet revolution has been sweeping the world — the globalization of economic activity. The prices of the food we eat, the types of transportation we use, and the occupations we pursue are among the myriad activities that may be powerfully affected by events a half a world away.

The basic economic problem confronting you, if you are typical, is that you would like far more than you can afford. Tuition and books probably absorb much of the income you would like to devote to clothes, cars, and entertainment. You would probably also like more time to study, a more gratifying social life, or more sleep. Your limited budget and time require decisions about how you will spend your hours and money. In a similar way, all societies must choose among alternatives. How individuals and societies choose, and the effects of their choices, are the focal points of economics.

Economics can be as fascinating as anything you will ever study and, if you are diligent, it will seem natural and logical. Understanding economics enables you to systematically address issues ranging from national policies to your professional and personal life. Insights gained from an economic perspective can provide you with advantages that most people lack.

How to Study Economics

Superficial cramming is unlikely to succeed in an economics course. Keeping up is crucial. Most people learn most effectively if exposed to concepts in several ways over a period of time. You will learn more economics and retain it longer if you read, see, hear, communicate, and then apply economic reasoning. This material is much more than a few facts and glib generalizations; understanding economics requires reflection.

Here is one strategy that students have found helpful for studying economics; many students have also adapted these techniques for other classes.

Visual Information

Don't let the extensive graphs in economics frighten you. There is a brief review of graphical analysis at the end of Chapter 1; our *Student Guide for Learning Economics* also opens with a set of helpful exercises. Avoid the agony of trying to memorize each graph by taking the time now to learn how graphs work. Proceed to Chapter 2 only after you quell your anxiety a bit. (Be sure that you also understand simple algebra. The elementary algebra used in this book should pose no problem if you remember the material from a basic course.) As you become familiar with graphs, you may be surprised to find yourself mentally graphing many noneconomic relationships, and even more amazed to find this process enjoyable.

Reading

Schedule ample time to read your assignments, and try to use the same quiet and cool (but not cold) room every day. Avoid drowsiness by sitting in a hard chair in front of a desk or table. Think about the material as you read. Many students spend hours highlighting important points for later study, for which they somehow never find time. Too frequently, busy work substitutes for thinking about economics. Try to skim a chapter; then go back and really focus on five or six pages. Don't touch a pen or pencil except to make margin notes cross-referencing related materials you already know.

Writing

After a healthy dose of serious reading, close your text and outline the important points with a half-page of notes. If you cannot briefly summarize what you just read, put your pen down and re-read the material. You have not yet digested the central ideas. Don't be surprised if some concepts require several readings. Be alert for graphs and tables that recapitulate important areas. When you finish each chapter, read its Chapter Review, and work through all Problems and Questions.

Listening

Most lectures blend your instructor's own insights and examples with materials from the text, but few students conscientiously work through assignments before lectures. Reading assignments before class will help you take lecture notes more selectively, giving you a major advantage over your classmates. Focus on topics that your instructor stresses but which are not covered in depth in the text. Notes from lectures should supplement, not duplicate, your text.

Teaching

Your instructors know that they learn their subject in greater depth every time they teach it. Teaching exposes you to previously unfamiliar aspects of a topic because you must conceptualize and verbalize ideas so that other people can understand them. Take turns with a classmate in reading the Key Points (in the Chapter Review) to each other. After one person reads a Key Point aloud, the other should explain it in his or her own words. Study groups work well in this way, but you may learn economics even more thoroughly if you simply explain economic concepts to a friend who has never studied it.

Applications

Working the parallel materials from (a) our *Student Guide for Learning Economics* and (b) our *Economic Software for Students* for each chapter of the text you study will make it easier to comprehend economic events regularly featured in the news. When this happens, you will be among the minority who truly understand economic and financial news. Use economic reasoning to interpret your day-to-day behavior, and that of your friends and relatives. This will provide unique insights into how people function and how the world works.

Examinations

Following the preceding suggestions should prepare you for minor tests and quizzes. To prepare for major exams and finals:

1. Read the Chapter Reviews for all material to be covered on the examination. Keep a record of any Key Points you could not explain to an intelligent friend who had never taken economics.

2. Return to each Key Point that you do not grasp adequately. Read the text material that covers it and rework the parallel parts of the accompanying chapter from your *Student Guide*.

3. Discuss any Key Point that is not clear to you with a friend.

4. Skim the Glossary at the end of the text for a last-minute refresher before your final exam.

We know that this is a tall order, but if you conscientiously follow these study tips, we guarantee you an enjoyable and enlightening course.

Careers in Economics

Many students find studying economics a pleasant surprise, but wonder if this interesting field is practical. Professors are often asked, "Could I get a good job with a bachelor's degree in economics?" We won't promise anything, but new economics graduates have job opportunities in such areas as public administration, operations analysis, management trainee and internships, sales, real estate appraisal, production management, insurance, or investment and financial analysis. What you might do as an economist depends on your specific areas of study, your minor, and how far you continue your training.

Economists are employed in most large business firms, government agencies, and non-profit organizations. Many economists teach because effective personal, business, and political decisionmaking increasingly requires economic literacy. Others find that there are substantial and remunerative demands for their services as consultants or researchers.

Business

Executives are increasingly aware that workable business strategies and policies require applied economic reasoning. Roughly one-third of economists are employed by private firms and trade associations. Most medium-to-large firms in manufacturing, transportation, energy, investment, communications, banking, insurance, retailing, utilities, finance, and mining, employ one or more economists. Many have staffs of economists. In 1990, the median income of business economists was above $60,000, with entry salaries exceeding $26,000. Most business economists have advanced degrees, but there are opportunities for bright, hard-working people with bachelor's degrees. Business economists with only bachelor's degrees averaged more than $42,000 in 1990.

Government and Non-profit Organizations

One economist in five works for a non-profit corporation or for government. For example, 15 different economists have filled seven different cabinet-level posts during the Carter, Reagan, and Bush administrations. Local, state, and federal agencies offer job opportunities for people with training in economics ranging from a bachelor's degree through post-doctoral training.

Teaching

Roughly half of all economists with advanced degrees are teacher/researchers employed by colleges and universities. At the university level, there are ample opportunities and rewards for economic research and consulting. Academic economists averaged annual incomes exceeding $48,000 in 1990. Many states have recently made economics a requirement for a high school diploma. People who are motivated to teach economics, but not to endure extended graduate training, are finding a growing demand for their services as teachers in secondary schools.

We hope you find this text helpful and enjoyable as you study economics. Many valuable improvements were suggested by students who used earlier versions of this book. If you have any comments, we would like to hear about them. Write us in care of HarperCollins Publishers, 10 East 53rd Street, New York, NY 10022-5299.

Our 1993 Special Edition

Three broad events motivated our revisions for this special edition of *Economics:*

1. **Ongoing changes in the world economy** — especially the collapse of the USSR and the turmoil in former Eastern bloc countries during their painful drives toward "privatization" and fuller integration into the world economy.

2. **The Recession of 1990–1992 and its effect on the 1992 Presidential election** — the longest U.S. economic downturn since the 1930s.

3. ***Gross Domestic Product*** (GDP) has replaced GNP in government accounts. Although GNP accounting techniques are regularly fine-tuned, the switch from GNP to GDP is an important change in nomenclature.

We also used this opportunity to update other material, and to correct some typos. The most important updates in this revision are **bold-faced** in our index.

Ralph T. Byrns
Gerald W. Stone, Jr.

Acknowledgments

Numerous economists and students have made suggestions that have improved this edition of *Economics*. Some reviewers of earlier editions offered comments that were not implemented until now. Among those who reviewed (in some cases, multiple) previous editions of our *Economics* teaching package are:

Scott Aguais *Wellesley College*

Dennis Appleyard *University of North Carolina, Chapel Hill*

Robert E. Arnold, Jr. *Henry Ford Community College*

John Baden *Southern Methodist University*

Dale Bails *Memphis State University*

J. Gregory Ballentine *University of Florida*

Bill Barber *Henry Ford Community College*

Andy H. Barnett *Auburn University*

Carl Biven *Georgia Institute of Technology*

David Black *University of Delaware*

Dudley Blair *Clemson University*

Bruce Bolnick *Northeastern University*

Michael Brand *University of Texas, El Paso*

William Brown *University of Puget Sound*

Jeffrey A. Buser *Murray State University*

Lou Cain *Loyola University*

Steven T. Call *Metropolitan State College, Denver*

Colleen Cameron *University of Southern Mississippi*

E. Ray Canterbery *Florida State University*

David Colander *Middlebury College*

Frank Curtis *Ferris State College*

Clinton Daniels *West Texas State University*

A. Edward Day *University of Central Florida*

Norbert Dorow *North Dakota State University*

Phil Duriez *University of Texas, El Paso*

Randall Eberts *University of Oregon*

Keith D. Edwards *California State University-Northridge*

John Elliott *University of Southern California*

Gordon Erlandson *North Dakota State University*

James Esmay *California State University, Northridge*

Patricia J. Euzent *University of Central Florida*

Ronald C. Fisher *Michigan State University*

Patricia Garland *Northeast Louisiana University*

Mark Gertler *University of Wisconsin, Madison*

Fred Glahe *University of Colorado, Boulder*

Joseph R. Guerin *Saint Joseph's University*

Robert Gustavson *Washburn University*

Dan Hagen *University of Western Washington*

Reza G. Hamzaee *Missouri Western State College*

Robert B. Harris *Indiana Univ.-Purdue Univ./Indianapolis*

Will Harris *University of Delaware*

Robert F. Hebert *Auburn University*

John S. Henderson *Georgia State University*

Stan Herren *University of Mississippi*

Thor Hertsgaard *North Dakota State University*

Jack High *George Mason University*

Janos Horvath *Butler University*

Hong Hwang *National Taiwan University*

E. Bruce Hutchinson *University of Tennessee, Chattanooga*

Thomas Ireland *University of Missouri, St. Louis*

Dilmus James *University of Texas, El Paso*

Robert Johnson *University of San Diego*

Jonathan Jones *Catholic University*

Monte Juillerat *Indiana University, Indianapolis*

Nicholas Karatjas *Indiana University of Pennsylvania*

Sol Kauffler *Los Angeles Pierce College*

Jerry J. Knarr *Hillsborough Community College*

Tom Koplin *University of Oregon*

Jerry Langin-Hooper *Rutgers University*

Stephen E. Lile *Western Kentucky College*

Kenneth Long *New River Community College*

Richard Long *Georgia State University*

Tony Loviscek *Indiana Univ.-Purdue Univ./Fort Wayne*

Rodney Mabry *Clemson University*

Hugh Macaulay *Clemson University*

Larry Mack *North Dakota State University*

Michael Maloney *Clemson University*

Denise Markovich *University of North Dakota*

Drew E. Mattson *Anoka Ramsey Community College*

Michael McElroy *North Carolina State University*

Charles E. McLure *Stanford University and the Hoover Institute*

Patrick H. McMurray *Missouri Western State College*

Tommy C. Meadows *Austin Peay State University*

Stephen Mehay   *San Jose State University*
Mostafa Mehdizadeh   *Miami University of Ohio*
Peter Meyer   *University of the Pacific*
Ed Morey   *University of Colorado, Boulder*
Ronald Moses   *University of Illinois, Chicago*
Panos Mourdoukoutas   *Long Island University*
William Nelson   *Indiana University Northwest*
Michael Nieswiadomy   *North Texas State University*
Dennis Olson   *Ferris State College*
James O'Neill   *University of Delaware*
G. W. Parker   *Mississippi State University*
Tim Petry   *North Dakota State University*
Joseph E. Pluta   *University of Texas at Austin*
Ronald G. Reddall   *Alan Hancock College*
Mason Russell   *Bentley College*
Edward Sattler   *Bradley University*
Donald Shadoan   *Eastern Kentucky University*
Michael Shelby   *Boston University*
David Shorow   *Richland College*
Timothy Smeeding   *University of Utah*
Gordon Smith   *Rice University*
George A. Spiva   *University of Tennessee, Knoxville*
Bruce Stecker   *North Hennepin Community College*
Dudley Stewart   *Stephen F. Austin State University*
Eugene Swann   *University of California, Berkeley*
James L. Swofford   *University of South Alabama*
Tom Rogers   *Southern Methodist University*
Victor Tabbush   *UCLA*
Claude A. Talley   *The Victoria College*
Tom Teitenberg   *Colby College*
F. Stephen Trimby   *Worcester State University*
Holley Ulbrich   *Clemson University*
Edwin F. Ulveling   *Georgia State University*
Jim Vincent   *University of St. Thomas*
Frank Vorhies   *University of Witwatersrand*
C. Richard Waits   *Texas Christian University*
Michael Watts   *Purdue University*
Steve Weiss   *University of Toledo*
Don Wells   *University of Arizona*
Leonard White   *University of Arkansas*
Allan Wilkens   *University of Wisconsin, Madison*
Richard Winkelman   *Arizona State University*
Peter A. Zaleski   *Villanova University*
Joseph Ziegler   *University of Arkansas*
George Zodrow   *Rice University*

A few ideas from reviewers of this edition were not implemented because of onrushing deadlines and so must await the next revision. Most, however, are reflected in these pages or in our supplements. We deeply appreciate the many useful suggestions provided for this (and, in many cases, previous) editions by:

John T. Addison   *University of South Carolina-Columbia*
James Alm   *University of Colorado-Boulder*
George Anayiotas   *International Monetary Fund*
Mark Arnold   *BRG Group*
Jim Aylsworth   *Lakeland Community College*
Gerry Babb   *Tulsa Junior College*
Lynn Bennett   *University of Colorado-Boulder*
Donna Bialik   *Indiana University-Purdue University/ Fort Wayne*
Brian Binger   *University of Arizona*
Scott Bloom   *North Dakota State University*
John Bockino   *Suffolk Community College*
John Booth   *Stetson University*
Kenneth Boulding   *University of Colorado, Boulder*
Josef M. Broder   *University of Georgia*
Maureen Burton   *Cal State Polytechnic University, Pomona*
Amelia Sue Cain   *Eastern Kentucky University*
Michael Carter   *University of Lowell*
Ann Carlos   *University of Colorado, Boulder*
Richard Chalecki   *Truman College*
Ted W. Chiles   *Pennsylvania State University*
John P. Cochran   *Metropolitan State College at Denver*
Mikel W. Cohick   *Collin County Community College*
Chip Condon   *College of Charleston*
Eleanor Craig   *University of Delaware*
Larry Daellenbach   *Univ. of Wisconsin at La Crosse*
Larry DeBoer   *Purdue University*
Pat Dumoulin   *Elgin Community College*
Harry Ellis   *University of North Texas*
Fred Englander   *Farleigh Dickinson University*
Don Evans   *Elizabethtown College*
Rudy Fichtenbaum   *Wright State University*
Ronald L. Friesen   *Bluffton College*
Gary Galles   *Pepperdine University*
Frank Giesber   *Texas Lutheran College*
Gary Gigliotti   *Rutgers University*
Rob Graham   *University of North Carolina, Charlotte*
Phillip Graves   *University of Colorado-Boulder*
Steven Greenlaw   *Mary Washington College*
Joseph M. Grens   *Elgin Community College*
James Grunloh   *University of Wisconsin-Oshkosh*
Ralph Gunderson   *University of Wisconsin-Oshkosh*
Harish C. Gupta   *University of Nebraska-Lincoln*
Michael Haynes   *Southern Oregon State College*

Gus Herring *Brookhaven College*

Elizabeth Hoffman *University of Arizona*

Joan Huckaby *University of Washington*

Beth Ingram *University of Iowa*

Ray Johns *Hagerstown Junior College*

Walter Johnson *University of Missouri at Rolla*

Janet Johnson *University of Colorado-Boulder*

Pat Joyce *Michigan Technological University*

John Kaatz *Georgia Institute of Technology*

William Kaempfer *University of Colorado-Boulder*

Veronica Kalich *Baldwin-Wallace College*

Jay Kaplan *University of Colorado-Boulder*

Ziad Keilany *University of Tennessee at Chattanooga*

Kishore Kulkarni *Metropolitan State College at Denver*

Kevin Klein *Illinois College*

Terry Knarr *Hillsborough Community College*

William Kordsmeir *University of Central Arkansas*

Jamie Brown Kruse *University of Colorado-Boulder*

Maureen Lage *Pennsylvania State University*

Daniel Lee *Shippensburg University*

Jane Lillydahl *University of Colorado-Boulder*

Tom Lorenzin *Davidson College*

Marjorie Mabrey *Delaware County Community College*

Don Mar *San Francisco State University*

Pete Mavrokordatos *Tarrant County Junior College*

Bruce McCrea *Lansing Community College*

John McCurin *North Dakota State University*

John McDowell *Arizona State University*

Mike McKee *University of New Mexico*

Robert McNown *University of Colorado-Boulder*

Mark A. McNulty *San Diego State University*

Steven G. Medema *University of Colorado at Denver*

Peter Mezer *University of Pennsylvania*

Ed Mills *Clackamas Community College*

J. Michael Morgan *College of Charleston*

Maggie Moore *Franklin University*

Richard Moss *Ricks College*

Steve Myers *University of Akron*

Tom Oberhofer *Eckerd College*

Allan Olsen *Elgin Community College*

Vincent Panzone *College of DuPage*

Dilip Pendse *Indiana University at Kokomo*

Diana Petersdorf *University of Wisconsin-Stout*

Maurice Pfannestiel *Wichita State University*

Hassan Pirasteh *Southern Oregon State College*

Wayne Plumly *Valdosta State College*

Joseph Pluta *St. Edward's University*

Tom Porebski *Triton College*

Barry W. Poulson *University of Colorado-Boulder*

Mark Prell *California State University-Northridge*

W. Robert Reed *Texas A&M University*

Delores K. Roman *Parks College*

Dwayne Rosa *West Texas State University*

Clark G. Ross *Davidson College*

Giovanni Ruscitti *University of Denver*

Mark E. Schaefer *Georgia State University*

Dean Schiffman *University of California-San Diego*

Richard Schimming *Mankato State University*

Walter P. Scott *Southwest Texas State University*

John Simonson *University of Wisconsin-Platteville*

Lynn A. Smith *Clarion University of Pennsylvania*

Abdul Soofi *University of Wisconsin-Platteville*

Richard Spivak *Bryant College*

James Stephenson *Iowa State University*

Danny Taylor *New Mexico State University*

Tony Uremovic *Joliette Junior College*

Percy Vera *Sinclair Community College*

Dale Warnice *College of Lake County*

Robert Welch *Midwestern State University*

Allison Wellington *Davidson College*

Arthur L. Welsh *Pennsylvania State University*

Jonathan Wight *University of Richmond*

William Zeis *Bucks County Community College*

Support from Susan Katz, publisher at Harper-Collins, and encouragement from Jack Greenman, one of our acquisitions editors, helped ensure the timely publication of our complete package for teaching economics. The superb skills of our sponsoring editor, Bruce Kaplan, have now been reflected in creative improvements across three editions. Dr. Willard W. Radell provided valuable help reviewing the art program. This edition also owes much of its polish and cohesiveness to the professionalism of Bob Nirkind, our developmental editor, and Bob Cooper, our project editor. Our distinctive design reflects the aesthetic sensibilities of Dorothy Bungert, assistant art director at HarperCollins, and Howard Petlack and J. Paul Kirouac of A Good Thing, Inc., who rendered the fine artwork for our program.

This book remains dedicated to Jennifer, Melissa, Rachel, Matthew, Sheila, and Trish for their support during this revision — we hope that seeing their names in print is still a thrill.

Foundations of Economics

People often refer to the financial aspects of business or their personal lives as *economics*, but the subject of economics encompasses a much broader spectrum of human behavior than money and business alone. Just as connecting the straight-edged pieces along its borders is a good way to start a jigsaw puzzle, this first part of this book introduces core concepts for an understanding of economics. These basic concepts are then applied to a variety of problems to provide a relatively complete picture of the scope of economics when you finish this course.

Core economic concepts are the themes of Chapter 1. *Scarcity* (the basic economic problem), which arises because human wants exceed the world's capacity to produce goods—if scarcity vanished, economics would be unnecessary. We then survey various resources, and examine how scarcity makes decisions necessary and *opportunity costs* unavoidable. Economists assume that people make rational decisions which they, sometimes incorrectly, expect to serve their own *self-interest*. Attempts to maximize self-interest tend to yield *economic efficiency* because costs are minimized.

Our second set of building blocks centers on methods economists use to study the way the world works, and the division of economics into *positive* (scientific) versus *normative* (prescriptive) components. We also distinguish *macroeconomics*, which focuses on national and international economic issues (e.g., exchange rates among currencies), from *microeconomics*, which examines choices by individual decision makers and patterns of exchange (e.g., international trade).

Chapter 2 opens with an overview of broad roles in a market economy by such institutions as *households*, *business firms*, and *governments*. Basic interactions among these social organizations are shown in a simple *circular flow model*. Then we explore how *comparative advantage* governs efficient exchange patterns and trade relationships within and between countries. This provides a background for the *production possibilities frontier* model. We also introduce several allocative mechanisms (such as socialism or the market system) that people use to deal with the problem of scarcity in a changing world.

These foundations of capitalism and its alternatives lead to Chapter 3, where *supply and demand* are introduced. Supply and demand analysis provides profound insights into how a market system determines prices and outputs, and allows us to interpret a wide range of human behavior. We also address some ways in which people tend to fine-tune their behavior based on how they expect *marginal* (small) changes to affect them. In Chapter 4, we apply supply and demand to a variety of public policy topics, ranging from agriculture to wage and price controls to the changes sweeping Eastern Europe and China.

Economics: The Study of Scarcity and Choice

Does aggressive foreign competition threaten American jobs and businesses? Why is the stock market so volatile? Can inflation and unemployment be controlled? Will most small firms be absorbed by multinationals if merger mania persists? Are deficits sapping U.S. power and prestige? Why do so many people seem trapped just working and paying their bills, but never really getting ahead? Is poverty inescapable for some while the rich few get ever richer? Such questions are only part of the puzzle as we strive toward the ultimate economic goal — high standards of living for people everywhere.

History books are filled with tales about politicians who lost power partially because of economic crises. Recent reform movements in the USSR, China, Eastern Europe, and South Africa sprouted from mixtures of despair about economic stagnation and desires for political freedom. Policies to foster prosperity have been key issues in every U.S. election from 1792 through 1992.

Before you get the idea that economics is relevant only for politics or business, we should mention that *economics focuses on* **all** *the choices people make as well as the personal and social consequences of these choices.* Some choices involve money, but even nonfinancial decisions fall within the realm of economics. Most decisions involve balancing costs versus benefits, which may or may not be measurable with money because many costs and benefits are primarily psychological.

Will you finish college? (Potential benefits include higher lifetime income, meeting people with shared interests, and the joy of learning; costs include outlays for tuition and books, the drudgery of dull classes, and income you could be making right now.) What will you choose for a major? (Will your enjoyment of subjects be as important as whether they are potentially lucrative?) Where will you live and work? Should you marry? If so, when? To whom? (Marriage involves both financial and psychological costs and benefits.) Should you have children? If so, how many? How will your limited income be spent? Decisions about these and other economic choices will shape the course of your life.

Economics is woven from concepts that currently may seem a mystery, but you have heard such terms as *costs, profit, prices,* and *supply and demand* used all your life. Other concepts may seem overly abstract at first, but most are merely precise descriptions of everyday events.[1] You may be skeptical about the *theories* and *graphs*

---

1. Our glossary (at the end of the text) and the reviews at the end of each chapter should help when you require reminders of meanings for terms previously defined.

economists use to interpret how the world works, but when you finish this book, we think you will join us in the view that the economic way of thinking offers valuable insights into people's everyday behavior—producing, consuming, voting, and striving for the good life.

Your study of economics is launched in this chapter by looking at core concepts that will help you understand why people make certain choices and avoid others. We first survey how scarcity emerges when relatively unlimited wants clash with limited resources. Scarcity implies that every decision involves opportunity costs, another key topic. You will also learn how people try to adjust to scarcity efficiently. Our final task in this chapter is an overview of methods economists use to study human behavior.

Scarcity

A world in which all human wants are instantly fulfilled is hard to imagine. Productive resources and time, and hence, production, are limited, while human wants are virtually unlimited. Pitting insatiable human wants against the immutable forces of limited time and resources, as shown in Figure 1, yields the basic economic problem—scarcity.

Scarcity *occurs because human wants exceed the amounts of production possible with the limited time and resources that are available.*

The pervasiveness of scarcity means that you face **trade-offs**; you can select only some things from all available alternatives. For example, if

FIGURE 1 The Origins of Scarcity

Scarcity occurs because our limited resources and time can only yield limited production and income, but people's wants are virtually unlimited. Output is produced by using knowledge (technology) to apply energy to a blend of resources. Production, in turn, generates the income people spend on the limited goods and services available.

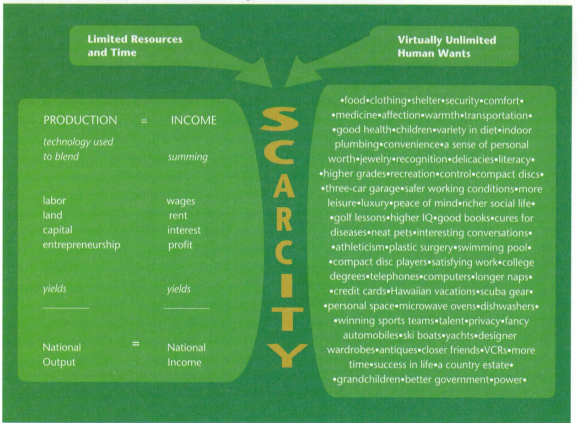

you have only three spare hours, you cannot go hiking, study for a test, and see a film. Thus, scarcity forces us to choose, a fact reflected in a broad definition of economics:

Economics *is the study of how individuals and societies allocate their limited resources to try to satisfy their unlimited wants.*

A **good** (anything that adds to human happiness) is scarce if the amounts people desire exceed the amounts freely available. Most people are individually or collectively (through taxes) willing to pay for scarce goods — public parks, an apartment, or a car are obvious examples, but services such as haircuts or police protection are also goods because they add to our happiness. Trash, an economic **bad** (anything that reduces happiness) is, unfortunately, not scarce, so garbage collection is a scarce good.

Desirable things that are not scarce are **free goods**, but limited time ensures that almost nothing is truly free — you could always be doing something else. For example, you can have all the seawater you want at roughly zero cost (but only if you are already on the beach), or freely breathe all the air your lungs will hold (accepting current pollution levels), or look at a sunset all you like (if you truly have nothing else to do). Even air is scarce for scuba divers, astronauts, and victims of flat tires.

That almost nothing that people enjoy is truly free is reflected in the cliche that "there ain't no such thing as a free lunch" (TANSTAAFL). Our limited time and resources allow only limited production that can never fully satisfy our insatiable desires for goods.

Production and Resources

VCRs and houses are, obviously, produced goods, but services also entail production.

Production *occurs when knowledge or technology is used to apply energy to materials in ways that make the materials more valuable.*

For example, pouring a cup of coffee is productive — the coffee is more valuable in your cup than in the coffee pot. Studying economics is also productive: Economic concepts on printed paper increase in value when integrated into your thinking processes.

Productive resources (*factors of production*) come in all types, shapes, and sizes, and all are limited. Economists conventionally refer to four broad categories of resources: **land, labor, capital**, and **entrepreneurship**. These resources provide the energy and materials that, combined through technology, make production possible.

Technology *is the "recipe" used to combine and reshape resources so that production occurs.*

The technology to grow roses is a simple example. If you know that roses need sunlight and moisture, you (being entrepreneurial and willing to bear the risk of failure in this case) find a sunny spot and apply energy (labor) to a shovel (capital) to dig a hole in the earth (land). Insert a rose bush, add fertilizer, dirt, and water (materials), and, with luck, roses will soon bloom — but never unlimited amounts of roses. How resources, technology, and production are related is summarized in Table 1.

Land Economists define "land" to include all natural resources, such as raw land, minerals, water, climate, and forests. Payments per time period for the use of land are called **rent**.

Labor Labor resources are the physical and mental talents that people can make available for production; labor is typically measured by the time available for work during a period. Farm hands, accountants, and NFL quarterbacks all provide labor services. Payments for labor services (including all salaries, commissions, fringe benefits, etc.) are called **wages**.

Capital Improvements that make natural resources more productive are capital, which includes such things as buildings, machinery, and roads. Production of new capital is **investment**. Some capital wears out each year; this decline in value is *depreciation*. A bulldozer, for example, becomes worth less as it ages and suffers wear and

Table 1 *Resources and Production**

Resources	Functions	Contributions	Production
natural resources land (*rents*)	acreage, minerals, and natural environment	materials and energy	tangible consumer goods (commodities) and services
human resources labor (*wages*)	productive talents (mental and physical) and energy	knowledge (technology) and energy	gross investment (new capital) *minus* depreciation *equals* net new capital
entrepreneurs (*profits*)	organize production, innovate new goods and technologies, and take risks		
produced resources capital (*interest*)	buildings, equipment, and other refined materials (e.g., or incomplete outputs)	technology, energy, and materials	

*Note that financial capital (e.g., stocks, bonds, and currency) is not economic capital, nor is it a resource.

tear. Total investment each year is *gross investment.* Subtracting depreciation leaves *net investment*—the change in the nation's capital stock.[2] If firms pay $900 billion for new capital while existing capital depreciates by $400 billion, society's net investment for the year is $500 billion.

Paper assets like currency or stocks and bonds are **financial capital**, which ultimately permits claims on finished goods or resources, including economic capital. People often fail to distinguish economic (physical) capital from financial capital, which is normally a document of some sort. A deed to a house is financial capital; the house itself is economic capital. Throughout this book, the term "capital" normally refers to economic capital. Payments for both types of capital services are called **interest**. Note that capital providers receive interest—not profit; all profit goes to entrepreneurs.

Entrepreneurship Entrepreneurs provide a special type of human resource; they combine labor, natural resources, and capital to produce goods and services while incurring risk in their quest for profits. After paying wages, rent, and interest for the use of other resources, entrepreneurs keep any money left over from their sales revenue. An entrepreneur's **profit** is a reward for organizing production, bearing business risks, and introducing innovations that improve the quality of life.

Risk of **loss** (negative profit) to an entrepre-

---

2. "Stock" in this context does not refer to the corporate stock traded on Wall Street. Instead, it refers to the amount of capital available to society at a point in time. Economists refer to "flow" variables and "stock variables." A flow variable makes no sense without a time reference. For example, if your salary is $100, it matters greatly whether it is $100 per hour or $100 per week. Thus, income is a flow variable. A sack of groceries is a stock; so is your bike. It makes no sense to refer, for example, to such stocks as your bicycle "per hour," but you can compute such flow variables as hourly income or hourly production. One subtle distinction is between "saving" (a flow—the amount you save per period) and "savings" (a stock—the accumulation of your past efforts to save).

neur is often enormous. Over half of all ventures fail within their first two years. Hundreds of small oil companies went bankrupt when oil prices plummeted in the 1980s. Coleco and Atari were among the many firms that lost fortunes trying to develop personal computers and software in the 1980s, while Bill Gates established Microsoft (a major software developer) and became the world's youngest self-made billionaire after dropping out of Harvard in 1979. Only prospects of profit can overcome fears of loss.

Constraints on resources and time are only one of two important dimensions of scarcity. The other dimension of scarcity stems from our unlimited wants.

Unlimited Human Wants

An economist is a man with an irrational passion for dispassionate rationality.

John Maurice Clark

Try to imagine consuming all the cars, clothes, or gourmet meals you would ever want if they were costless. Even if all desires for some goods were met, being so satisfied that you could think of nothing else that would add to your happiness is hard to imagine. You will always want more goods and pleasures for as long as you live. (If all wants could be met, economics would be irrelevant, because decisions would never be required. But most people thrive on a bit of adversity and would find this imaginary world boring.)

Rational Self-Interest Most economists follow the lead of Adam Smith, an eighteenth-century philosopher who laid the foundations for modern economics, by assuming that people act purposefully and rationally to maximize their satisfactions, given their limited time, information, resources, and budgets. This characterization of *homo sapiens* as *homo economicus* (not to be confused with home economists) views all human behavior as self-interested. Why Smith adopted this approach is addressed in Focus 1.

This assumption of self-interest does not imply that people are inherently sociopathically selfish. Personal values are powerful influences on perceptions of costs and benefits. No society could

function, for example, if everyone were willing to use a $1 bullet to gain a $99 profit by shooting a stranger flashing a $100 bill in a dark alley.

Fortunately, most of us consider other people's welfare to some extent — we enjoy feeling that our activities benefit society and try to avoid doing more harm than good. Thus, humanitarian acts are not exceptions to self-interested behavior. People's self-esteem and public reputation are boosted by picking up litter and contributing to charities. Many people share a "warm glow" feeling when stars induce audiences at benefit concerts to donate funds to support human rights, farmers, or victims of famine.

You may agree with the many philosophers who deny that behavior universally reflects attempts to maximize pleasure and minimize pain — an idea that seems to reduce motivation to its lowest common denominator. Nevertheless, theories based on individual "happiness maximization" or "wealth maximization" are usually more realistic than models based on humanitarian motives. Moreover, even people who view behavior as driven by loftier motives concede that personal interest is important at the margin. Otherwise, charities would not fight proposals to eliminate tax deductions for charitable contributions. (Museums across the country noticed severe declines in donations of art after donors' tax loopholes were closed by the Tax Reform Act of 1986.)

Self-interest need not condemn humanity to a state of constant conflict — you will learn in Chapters 3 and 4 why most economists view it as a powerful force that tends to coordinate people's plans and that commonly leads, indirectly, to a broad form of social cooperation. In fact, so-called selfish people and so-called altruists react to many events in similar ways. For example, if the price of fruit falls relative to the prices of other foods, both the selfish person and the altruist may buy more — the selfish person to personally devour the fruit and the altruist to distribute it to needy children.

Some Basic Choices

Scarcity occurs because limits on time and resources make it impossible to produce all that we want. We can have some things we want, but not

Is Self-Interest Immoral or Unavoidable?

If you sliced off a fingertip while buttering your toast just minutes after hearing on the "Today" show that an earthquake had swallowed China and its billion people, which event would dismay you more? In his first book, *Theory of Moral Sentiments* (1759), Adam Smith argued that loss of a little finger would keep the average European from sleeping that night, "but, provided he never saw them, he will snore with the most profound security over the loss of millions of his brethren, and the destruction of that immense multitude seems plainly an object less interesting to him than this paltry misfortune of his own."

Smith illustrated the power of self-interest with this example, arguing that disasters to others arouse sympathy only to the extent that you can imagine yourself in similar straits. Suppose inserting your pinkie into a crack in the space/time continuum would prevent the catastrophe in China, but you would lose your finger in the process. Would you make the sacrifice? Smith thought most of us would, not out of love for humanity, but rather because of ". . . love of what is honourable and noble, of the grandeur, and dignity, and superiority of our own characters." That is, you probably could not live with yourself if you failed to give up your finger.

Self-interest tends to limit, but not eliminate, charitable acts. Our personal senses of morality yield a spectrum of willingness to sacrifice for others. If you would surrender your pinkie for the lives of a billion anonymous Chinese, would you give up an arm? (Would whether others knew about your sacrifice matter?) Would you sacrifice your life? Only a saint could automatically answer this last question.

everything. Thus, scarcity forces every society to make choices in trying to resolve three *basic economic questions*:

1. *What* economic goods will be produced?

2. *How* will resources be used in production?

3. *Who* will get to consume economic goods?

All choices by all decision makers are ultimately related to these three basic questions.

What? Current resources and technology limit a society to choosing one combination from the innumerable mixes of goods producible during a given period. More of any one good means less of another. How much of each good would we like? Shall we have more guns and less butter? More health care and less housing? Cleaner air but fewer cars? More leisure and less work?

How? Many different mixes of resources can be used to produce most goods. Farm crops can be harvested by hand or by machine. A swimming pool can be excavated in 1 day with 1 bulldozer and 1 operator, by 30 people with shovels in 1 week, or by 300 people wielding teaspoons in 1 month. Thousands of Chinese push brooms through the streets of Beijing daily, while major U.S. cities use giant streetsweepers to rid our roads of debris.

Who? Even if we know what goods we want and how they will be produced, we still must address the question of *who* will get (*a*) income and wealth, and (*b*) specific goods. Every society faces hard questions about *equity* (fairness); wealth generates broad claims to control over goods and resources, but this is only one aspect of the "Who?" question. Some rich eccentrics, for example, happily drive rusty old pickups, while some poor eccentrics sacrifice almost everything else to drive sporty modern cars. Answers to the "Who?" question ideally accommodate differences in people's tastes and preferences.

These three basic questions — *what, how,* and *for whom* — seem simple, but each must be addressed almost countless times. For example, "What?" covers not only the types of goods to be produced from *a* to *z* (aardvark fodder to zithers?), but also how much of each good. And each basic question is faced at different levels by individuals, families, business firms, government agencies, and society as a whole.

For example, college administrators must decide *what* courses to offer, *how* they will be taught (huge lectures, computer labs, or small seminars), and *who* will receive admission and loans or scholarships. Students must choose *what* courses to take, *whom* to take them with, and *how* to study. (Will you attend class and do all homework, or party hearty and cram for your finals?) Families must choose. Shall family funds be used for extravagant vacations? . . . a new home? . . . your education? . . . or ballet lessons for Baby? Government also chooses. Should more or fewer resources be devoted to education? . . . national defense? . . . shelter for the homeless? . . . the war on drugs?

The economic fabric of a society is woven from the composite of all the answers to these three basic questions by all of its decision-making units. And our combined choices about what, how, and for whom automatically answer a related issue: *When* will goods or resources be used? Perishables such as ice cream or newspapers lose value relatively soon after their production, but durable goods such as stained glass windows or canned coffee can be stored for years. Similarly, some productive resources are perishable, while others last for centuries. For example, eight hours of labor are lost forever each day that a worker is unemployed, but a vein of silver or a barrel of oil can be stored indefinitely. Each generation decides how much capital to accumulate and how many natural resources to leave for use by future generations.

Different aspects of these basic questions recur throughout economics. Relative scarcities of various goods are indicated by their prices, which are vital information (another scarce good) when choosing among limited alternatives. This raises the question of what "price" or "cost" mean. The answer is less obvious than you might think.

Opportunity Costs

Choosing any scarce thing forecloses other options; such losses are economic costs. Suppose you drive a gas hog. Buying an extra gallon of gasoline per week may preclude an extra weekly milkshake, but buying the milkshake instead of the gas may force you to drive less and walk more. Economists view economic (opportunity) cost as the value of the next best option forgone because of a decision.

Opportunity cost *is the value of the best alternative surrendered when a choice is made.*

Most people think costs are measured solely by the money paid to produce or acquire goods, but opportunity costs are ultimately personal and involve far more than money alone. Have you ever estimated the cost of your education? Fill in the blanks in Table 2, which suggests that these costs extend far beyond payments for tuition and books. How about the value of your time? Instead of studying and attending class, you could be holding a full-time job (or maybe two). You may be sacrificing better food and clothes, a nice car, and a comfortable apartment. The values of all forgone alternatives are the true costs of education. But suppose you quit school. The costs of your nice car, apartment, food, and clothing would be the sacrificed enjoyment of learning and campus life, and the higher future income and consumption your degree might have made possible.

To show how broad the concept of opportunity cost is, suppose that Amy and Liz both love Ken. Ken, resigned to indifference from Iris, his true heartthrob, reciprocates both Amy's and Liz's love. Unfortunately, Amy threatens to find "someone new" if Ken does not quit seeing Liz. Soap opera fans might commiserate with Ken's

Table 2 *The Costs of a College Education — 1992**

	National Average (annual)	Your Costs
Tuition	$1,300 (public)	_____
	$8,500 (private)	_____
Books & misc. supplies	$900	_____
Forgone income	$9,700 (minimum wage)	_____
Annual total	$11,900 to $19,100	_____
Typical total for a four-year degree	$47,600 to $76,400	_____

*Sources: American Council of Education, Department of Education Estimates for 1990, and author estimates and updates.

dilemma, but economists view his situation as similar to that faced by a family that would really like lobster but can only afford either small steaks or big hamburgers, not both. Irrelevant alternatives (such as Iris) have no effect on the costs of the choices at hand — the real cost to Ken of a continued relationship with Amy is giving up Liz, and vice versa.

Occasional failures to recognize options may leave people feeling trapped: Despondent teenagers who lose "the only one I'll ever love," workers laid off when plants shut down, high-risk entrepreneurs bankrupted when market conditions change. In most situations, however, time and reflection disclose numerous alternative choices.

What people do often differs from what they say, so most economists concentrate on behavior instead of words alone. For example, Focus 2 suggests that most people exaggerate when describing something as "priceless" — implying that its value is so high that trying to estimate costs is futile. Fortunately, most people are incredibly ingenious in finding and selecting good alternatives.

Monetary (Absolute) Prices Opportunity costs are only loosely related to **monetary** (absolute) **prices** per se.

> **Absolute prices** *are prices in terms of some monetary unit.*

Prices in the United States are commonly stated in dollars and cents, but these absolute prices could also be stated in francs, pesos, inflated dimes, or solid gold dollars. For example, if dollars and francs were equally acceptable for purchases and $1 could be exchanged for 5 francs, just divide any price stated in francs by 5 to figure the dollar price. Tourists and decision makers in international trade quickly learn to make such adjustments and become indifferent about which currency is used to state absolute prices.

Relative Prices Opportunity costs as measured by **relative prices** shape most decisions — how many hot fudge sundaes must be sacrificed for a new compact disk? For a ski vacation to Aspen? Answers to such questions require comparisons of monetary prices.

> **Relative prices** *are the prices of goods or resources in terms of each other, and are computed by dividing their absolute prices by one another.*

Rational decision making focuses on relative prices, which embody tremendous amounts of information about sacrificed alternatives. If hot fudge sundaes are $2 while CDs are $14 and ski vacations are $560, then a CD costs 7 sundaes and a ski vacation costs 280 sundaes or 40 CDs. (14/2 = 7; 560/2 = 280; 560/14 = 40.)

Monetary prices are largely irrelevant for decisions until, perhaps unconsciously, we convert them to relative prices. Relative prices and most rational decisions are *not* affected if all absolute prices change on one-time, fixed-proportional basis. This mental experiment should prove our point: What would you do if your income, assets, liabilities, and the prices of all goods and re-

FOCUS 2

Is Life Priceless?

The cliche ". . . human life is priceless" is often heard in debates about public policies, but, in reality, people constantly assign prices to their own lives and those of others. Here are a few of the countless ways life is priced.

1. Choosing more dangerous over less dangerous activities. Every time you ride in a car without using a seat belt, you (subconsciously?) weigh the inconvenience of buckling up against the higher probability of death or injury. In so doing, you implicitly assign prices to your life and body parts. And parents assign prices for their children when they fail to buckle up the kids. Tobacco, skydiving, hitchhiking, swimming, or even taking a walk all involve risks that assign prices to life.

2. After adjusting for required training and the pleasantness of working conditions, higher wages are paid for riskier jobs.*

3. High prospective medical bills cause some people to forgo treatment that would prolong their lives or the lives of seriously ill relatives.

4. A few dollars each could save the lives of millions of starving children in famine-plagued countries.

5. Major wars are always fought with draftees, whose lives are

_____
*Numerous studies conclude that an annual wage premium of about $2,000 is paid for each additional 0.1% probability of dying on the job. This translates into roughly $2 million as the average value for the life of a U.S. worker.

implicitly priced by politicians and military strategists.

6. We could cut murder rates by surer and swifter law enforcement, but reforming or expanding our police forces, the judicial system, and prisons seems too costly.

7. The fees of paid killers range from $200 to $500,000.

8. The 1975–1986 drop in speed limits on interstate highways from 70 mph to 55 mph was estimated to save lives at a cost of from $2–5 million each (based on the value of time lost because travel was slower). Congress responded to widespread calls for more speed by raising the limit to 65 mph in 1986, suggesting that many people viewed the lives saved by 55 mph limits as too costly.

---

sources doubled on a one-time-only basis? *Answer:* You would handle twice as many dollars, but otherwise your behavior should not change.

Conclusion: Relative prices guide decisions; changes in absolute prices ultimately affect most decisions only to the extent that relative prices are distorted. Absolute price changes can, however, be a problem during inflation, which is harmful primarily because it warps relative prices and garbles information about relative

scarcity. (We deal with the inflation problem later in the book.)

Prices as Information Relative prices compress immense amounts of information about buyers' desires and sellers' costs. For example, farmers aware that grapes consistently sell for $2 per pound while limes sell for $1 per pound also know (perhaps unconsciously) that consumers want more grapes roughly twice as much as they want more limes. And consumers know that grapes cost roughly twice as much as limes to produce.

Information embedded in relative prices stimulates action. A tour of a shopping mall can provide thousands of prices to guide your purchases. Low-paying job openings are passed over when a job seeker scans the want ads, while more attractive wage offers are circled for follow-ups. And entrepreneurs are steered by expected prices and costs into types of production where they perceive profit opportunities.

Prices as Incentives Relative prices signal opportunities for pleasure and prospects of pain. Most people seek pleasure and avoid pain, but life is a series of trade-offs. You may want to rent one video tape, for example, but dislike having to pay for it because you've read good reviews about other taped films. A child's reluctance to do family chores may be overcome with either a reward (an allowance) or a punishment (no TV tonight). Grades can be thought of as prices. Prospects of an A may persuade you to forgo a fascinating film for 2 hours of study, while fear of failing drives your roommate to study 2 hours.

Sellers view relatively *high* prices for goods (relative to their production costs) as **incentives** that stimulate production, while *low* prices are **disincentives** that push resources into alternative types of production. High wage rates, for example, reward work, but an offer of only a low wage may cause a worker to opt for little work and much leisure.

Prices as Rationing Devices Goods that are especially scarce will ideally be reserved for their more important possible uses and, wherever feasible, people will tend to conserve relatively less on more abundant goods and resources. For example, daubing polish on shoes with designer silk scarves would be wasteful; using cotton rags instead seems to make sense. Relatively higher prices for goods or resources signal greater relative scarcity and discourage use. Thus, prices act as **rationing devices**. Buyers are encouraged to use lower-priced goods more and higher-priced goods less.

The information conveyed by relative prices and their incentive and rationing effects are central to our discussions of supply and demand in

Chapters 3 and 4, and explain why many economists refer to private transactions as **the price system**, which helps allocate goods and resources into economically efficient patterns.

Economic Efficiency

Physicists call a system efficient if it minimizes the energy expended in accomplishing some task, while environmentalists talk about efficiency as the absence of waste in an ecological system. Economists take a different approach to efficiency.

> **Economic efficiency** *for society as a whole is achieved when we produce the combination of outputs with the highest attainable total value, given our limited resources.*

Efficiency may seem an abstract concept, but it becomes more concrete when decomposed to parallel the three basic economic questions: (*a*) **allocative efficiency** addresses *what* things will be produced, (*b*) **productive efficiency** addresses *how* to produce them, and (*c*) **distributive efficiency** addresses *who* will use specific outputs.

Allocative Efficiency—What? Using all of society's resources to produce mustard and sawdust instead of a mix of more useful goods would obviously waste resources.

> **Allocative efficiency** *requires the pattern of national output to mirror what people want.*

The social value of output produced from given resources and costs is maximized in an allocatively efficient economy.

It is usually easier to describe *in*efficiency than to specify an efficient situation. Mountains of mustard and sawdust would be allocatively *inefficient* nuisances far exceeding anyone's ability to use these outputs. Another example: England's nationalized auto industry built taxis according to the same design from World War II into the 1970s, long after the rest of the world had abandoned unreliable 1940s engines and electronics, and ugly 1940s styles.

Productive Efficiency—How? Expending more resources than the minimum required to produce a given level of any specific product is also economically wasteful.

> **Production (technical) efficiency** *requires minimizing opportunity cost for a given value of output.*

This requirement also ensures maximum output for a given cost, or using given resources. Production is *technically* in*efficient* whenever production costs are unnecessarily high or if more output could be produced without raising costs or using more resources.

For example, the saying that "too many cooks spoil the broth" implies that excess company in the kitchen is economically inefficient. More good-quality food presumably could be produced at lower cost using fewer resources if some of the cook's helpers left. Society as a whole is also productively *in*efficient if excessive unemployment holds output below the maximum possible from the resources available.

Distributive Efficiency—Who? The question of "Who?" is divisible into issues of (*a*) the distribution of income and wealth, and (*b*) the distribution of goods. Suppose the distribution of income and wealth (discussed later in the book) is a settled issue, and our economy produces precisely what people want. Properly distributing goods among people may still be a problem.

> **Distributive efficiency** *requires that specific goods be used by the people who value them* **relatively** *the most.*

By *relatively*, we mean one person's preferences for certain goods relative to other goods, when compared to other people's preferences among goods. People's relative likes and dislikes are important in determining who will gain the most from which goods.

Suppose, for example, that you have gallons of orange soda (which nauseates you) but lack broccoli, your favorite food, while I have bushels of broccoli (which I despise), and I love orange soda. An exchange of your orange soda for my broccoli is obviously in order. Such exchanges are automatic when people buy and sell things.

Distributive efficiency to accommodate people's relative preferences requires that consumers *maximize* the satisfaction available from their individual budgets. (Relative budget sizes are a separate issue of distribution.) When this occurs, all individuals also *minimize* their outlays to obtain goods yielding a given total satisfaction. You currently consume inefficiently if you could gain by changing the mix of goods you now buy for a given cash outlay. Alternatively, you could cut your total spending and maintain the same satisfaction yielded by your inefficient purchasing pattern.

People try to act efficiently. You could always turn off all lights and adjust your thermostat when you leave home to prevent "wasting" electricity or gas, but many of us absentmindedly leave on lights and heat or cool empty buildings. Conscientiously "saving" energy may absorb time more valuably used in other ways, but recognition that a current buying pattern is economically inefficient prompts changes in behavior. An unexpected $700 utility bill might shock you into trying harder to conserve energy. But breaking habitual patterns can be difficult, as any ex-smoker will tell you.

Economy-wide Efficiency Certain standards govern an economy-wide state of efficiency. Opportunity costs must be minimized for all forms of economic activity. Consumption patterns and the production of goods are both efficient whenever any change from the current situation would unavoidably harm at least one person. This implies that resources are allocated so that they produce the most valuable combination of goods possible—every drop of potential net benefit must be squeezed from the resources available.

> **Economic efficiency,** *broadly considered, means that it is impossible for anyone to gain unless someone else loses.*

Alternatively, economic inefficiency exists if production could be changed or goods could be exchanged so that no one lost and at least one person gained. Thus, whenever there are potential but unrealized gains to someone entailing losses to none, the current situation is inefficient. Inefficiency means that appropriate corrections would enable society to cope better with scarcity.

The bargains people make usually represent moves toward greater efficiency. All direct parties to a voluntary transaction expect to gain or they will not bother. For example, you will not trade an apple for my orange unless you value the orange more than the apple, and vice versa. Trading your apple for my orange raises your satisfaction from a given outlay because you now have a subjectively (to you) more valuable orange. I gain in a similar fashion. Thus, efficiency is usually enhanced through trade, and a failure to trade when such gains are possible is inefficient. In fact, if only *one* of us would gain by a trade but no other party would be harmed, failure to trade is inefficient.

We have probed why scarcity makes opportunity costs and decisions unavoidable, and have suggested that people try, not always successfully, to cope with scarcity in efficient ways. Now that you know a bit about the economic problem, the rest of this chapter surveys methods economists have developed to try to understand economic behavior.

Economic Analysis

Good economic analysis blends both art and science and borrows ideas heavily from philosophers, behavioral scientists, legal scholars, and historians, all of whom offer alternatives to the economic way of thinking. Economics is an art because it requires qualitative judgments about seemingly contradictory evidence; it is also a science that requires organizing a maze of ideas and phenomena into a coherent whole. Understanding economics thoroughly can help you adjust to an ever-changing world.

Areas traditionally within the domain of economics include consumer and business behavior, taxes, international trade, inflation, and unemployment. More recently, economic analysis has been applied to areas ranging from marriage to criminal behavior and war, from how our political and legal systems operate to questions about education and environmental quality. No short description can cover all the varied concerns of economists.[3] One famous economist, John Maynard Keynes, summarized economics as "a method rather than a doctrine, an apparatus of the mind, a technique of thinking which helps its possessor to draw correct conclusions." Sound theory is a key to the scientific side of economics.

Common Sense and Theory

Everything should be made as simple as possible, but not more so.

Albert Einstein

Some people ridicule *theory*, believing that "theorists" cannot cope in the "real world" and find it hard to walk and chew gum simultaneously. These critics favor *common sense* as a practical guide for life. How can we judge theory or common sense? Good theories or common sense must correctly describe how the world works. In other words, we judge both theory and common sense by their accuracy!

In fact, most common sense is just a blend of useful theories that have been tested extensively. Progress occurs when new knowledge disproves old theories, causing better theories to be developed and absorbed, albeit slowly, into our common sense. But how do theories develop? And how may new theories become tomorrow's common sense?

The process of theorizing consists, first, of identifying a problem area. Then we collect facts that seem germane to the problem. Of course, we cannot gather all the facts, because some things cannot be sensed directly. For example, sophisticated equipment can discern microwaves, but subatomic particles cannot be viewed directly, even by using our most advanced technology — their existence is inferred. Moreover, we cannot concentrate on everything that can be

---

3. Evidence of the diversity of economics is that about half of all academic Economics Departments are in Schools of Business, with most of the rest being housed with Social Sciences or Liberal Arts.

sensed. Our senses are selective. (If you live near the tracks, after a while you don't hear the trains.) Finally, gathering all potentially helpful data is too costly, so we deal with incomplete information.

After we collect some data that seem relevant, we try to figure out how they are related. That is, we develop a theory that can be tested to see how well it explains how things work. New theory that passes this test replaces older theory and eventually becomes part of our common sense, a pattern illustrated in Figure 2.

Exceptions usually compel revision of scientific rules. For example, prior to Columbus's voyages, conventional European wisdom viewed Earth as flat — it looks irregular but relatively flat from your window. The flat Earth theory was gradually replaced by a better theory after ships sailed around the world, but some eccentrics still deny that Earth is spherical. (The British Flat Earth Society still meets regularly.)

Models are representations of theories; these two terms are synonyms for many purposes. Some models are physical, such as a watch, which models the passage of time. Others exist as mental images or mathematical equations. Still others are graphical, such as an architect's blueprints or the maps you consult on your vacation.[4] Many people are surprised to learn that their heads are filled with models. For example, most single people who ultimately plan to marry have imagined general models of their prospective spouses (appearance, intelligence, sense of humor, etc.).[5]

Theory necessitates *abstraction* (generalization); we try to focus on important relationships and to ignore insignificant tangents. High levels of abstraction cause many theories to be criticized as overly complicated, but abstraction usually simplifies analysis. In fact, most scientists prefer simple but accurate theories to complex ones.

Occam's Razor *is the idea that the simplest* **workable** *theories are also the most useful and the best.*

For example, Earth once was thought a fixed point about which all the universe spun. Incredibly complex equations were developed to trace movements of the then-observable planets and stars. Modern astronomy applies Occam's Razor to explain cosmic acts in a simpler fashion; all the universe is in motion, and Earth orbits the Sun, not vice versa.

A good model may be so simple that it is unrealistic except for its intended use. Simple models are usually less costly than complex ones. For

FIGURE 2 How a Theory Is Developed and Refined

The first step in any scientific theory is to identify the problem to be studied. (Asking the right questions is a sign of genius.) The second step is to collect some data and think about how they are related. Next, we formally develop a theory. Then we test it. This leads into a loop in which the theory is refined, more data are collected, and we test and retest our model. If the theory is an improvement over past theories, it eventually becomes a part of our common sense.

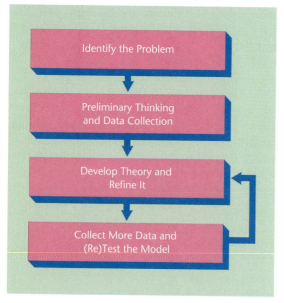

4. Economic models are often shown graphically, which makes many students uncomfortable. A first step in curing this problem is to study the optional material at the end of this chapter. Then spend time on the exercises at the beginning of our *Student Guide for Learning Economics* to relieve your anxiety.

5. These examples are drawn from articles by Donald Elliott, Joe Garwood, Regan Whitworth, and Salvatore Schiavo-Campo in Ralph Byrns and Gerald Stone, ed., *Great Ideas for Teaching Economics*, 5/ed. (New York: HarperCollins, 1992).

example, intricate plastic models can show how an airplane looks, but tossing a cheap balsa glider into the air will give you a better understanding of aerodynamics. Watches come in solar, quartz-crystal, and other varieties. Which is best? If all you care about is knowing the time, the best one most simply, accurately, reliably (and cheaply?) reflects the passage of time.

To summarize, a good theory or model as simply as possible predicts how the real world works. Common sense evolves as exceptions to old theories compel acceptance of better theories after they have been tested extensively and appear reliable.

Positive vs. Normative Economics

If you took all of the economists in the country and laid them end to end, they'd never reach a conclusion.

George Bernard Shaw

Shaw's famous line echoes a popular view that economists usually disagree, but 90 percent of economists would probably accept 90 percent of the theory in this book, with only nitpicking differences about which 90 percent to accept. How can the reputation for discord be reconciled with the fact of widespread agreement? Part of the answer is that economists may disagree sharply about how even widely accepted theory applies to a specific situation. Economists' differences about how to translate theory into policy receive wide publicity, while broad areas of agreement tend to be ignored by the media.

Even if economists reach consensus, politicians often reject their advice. For example, most economists favor freer international trade, but tariff barriers are standard responses when imports threaten many voters' jobs. Apparent discord also arises when economists in government agree publicly (but disagree privately) with politicians who appoint them, even if economic logic supports policies the politicos won't enact.

Economists tend to agree most about positive economics—which, ideally, generates ideas that are free of value judgments and which can be tested for accuracy.

Positive economics *addresses "what is" and predicts observable and testable tendencies in economic relationships.*

Positive statements may be either true or false. For example, the positive statement "U.S. per capita income is the highest in the world" sounds plausible. But is it contrary to the data? (To test this, look up data for the small island nation of Brunei.)

Disagreement is most common when value judgments are at the core of a problem.

Normative economics *depends on* value judgments *and addresses what "should be."*

Most statements containing the prescriptive word "should" are normative.

Positive and normative elements are often intertwined. For example, economists may differ sharply about the normative issue of whether government "should" ever execute murderers, but most economists agree that quicker, stiffer, and surer penalties deter crime, which is a value-free prediction drawn from positive economics.

Normative issues frequently turn on questions of equity and provoke debate among economists and the public alike. Policy is inherently more normative than theory. For example, the statement, "We should redistribute wealth from the rich to the poor," implies a value judgment that benefits to the poor would outweigh the harm done to the rich. There is little reason to suppose that an economist's value judgments are superior to those of other people, but economic reasoning can offer unique insights into the effectiveness of alternative policies in achieving specific normative goals.

Few normative issues are settled by looking at evidence, because value judgments involve faith and argument, not scientific proof. Disputes about positive economics can ultimately be settled by evidence, but even economists with shared values may disagree, because some areas of positive economics remain unsettled for generations. For example, virtually everyone favors price-level stability and high employment, but economists may disagree about how to cure economic instability because of difficulty in finding

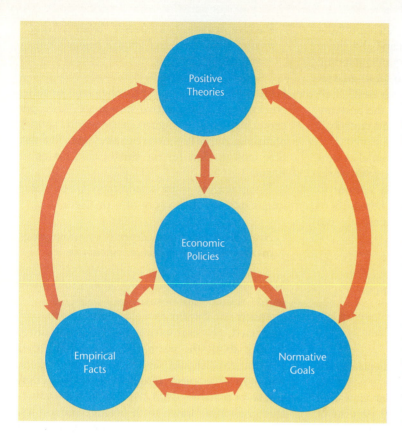

FIGURE 3 Positive Theories, Empirical Facts, Normative Goals, and Economic Policies

Positive economic theories are derived by applying logic to observed reality (*empirical facts*), but even positive theory is influenced by (*a*) the desires of the policymakers who provide funding for research, and (*b*) normative goals that help us decide which questions to examine. Some empirical observations are filtered through our sense of equity to shape normative goals, but most people want their goals to be attainable, which requires consistency with their positive theories. Normative goals, positive theories, and economic policies all cause us to focus on certain empirical data, and to ignore other real-world data. Directions for economic policies, in turn, are distilled from a mix of (*a*) observations of empirical reality, (*b*) normative goals, and (*c*) positive theories of economics.

the right evidence and then digesting and accurately interpreting it in changing circumstances.

Understanding economic reality is useful primarily because it helps society develop policies to resolve the problem of scarcity. All policies hinge on normative issues, but if economists design policies intended to achieve goals set by policymakers, then their quest is positive in nature. For example, if minimizing unemployment is a goal, then developing policies to accomplish this goal involves positive economics. We can evaluate policies by how well they accomplish our goals, but positive economics cannot determine whether any goal is good or bad. The complex interactions of positive theory, empirical (observable) facts, normative goals, and economic policies are indicated in Figure 3.

Macroeconomics and Microeconomics

Economics can also be divided into macroeconomics and microeconomics. (*Macro* and *micro* derive from Greek words for "large" and "small," respectively.) Macroeconomics involves study of the entire society and addresses *aggregate* variables — the sums of many smaller variables (e.g., the number of workers employed by a firm) yield aggregate variables (e.g., national employment). Microeconomics, on the other hand, focuses on the behavior of individual households, firms, or specific industries. By analogy, macroeconomic tools are telescopes, while microeconomic tools are microscopes.

Macroeconomics Macroeconomics considers how national income, unemployment, inflation, and economic growth are determined, and macro policy addresses the total effects of changing taxes and government spending, or growth in the money supply.

Macroeconomic analysis *focuses on large, economy-wide* **aggregate** *variables such as indicators of total economic activity.*

Commonly agreed-upon normative goals of macro policy include:

1. *High employment.* People suffer when many workers cannot find jobs and many manufacturing plants and much machinery sit idle.

2. *Price-level stability.* If average prices rise or fall rapidly, people may be uncertain about how much their wages will buy, or whether to consume now or invest in hopes of future returns.

3. *Economic growth.* People want higher incomes each year and most hope their children will be even more prosperous than they are.

4. *Economic security.* People want to retain their jobs and the good things they have. Security may be threatened by changes in what society wants (the birth of the auto put buggy-whip braiders out of work) or by such possibilities as nuclear war.

We mentioned earlier that absolute (monetary) prices influence economic behavior only when translated into relative prices. Thus, for example, inflation (increases in average monetary prices) is important only if it alters relative prices. This notion must be qualified, however, because inflation is unimportant only if relative prices and the income distribution are unchanged. But inflation always disrupts both, distorting economic activity and creating uncertainty, and so it is a major concern for *macro* policymakers.

Microeconomics Macro and micro differ more by degree than kind. In a sense, macro involves the study of the forest while micro involves the study of individual trees. Thus, micro addresses interactions among households, firms, and government agencies in more detail than macro.

> **Microeconomic analysis** *is the study of individual decision making, resource allocation, and how relative prices, outputs, and the distribution of income are determined.*

Our ability to achieve the macro goals discussed previously depends strongly on micro policy — how government regulations and taxes affect price and output structures, the numbers of firms in an industry, and the income distribution. Beyond ensuring that micro policies are

compatible with macro goals, three major goals dominate micro policy:

1. *Efficiency.* An inefficient economy wastes resources and fails to provide the highest possible standard of living for consumers.

2. *Equity.* Gaps between the "haves" and "have-nots" may leave most people impoverished while a privileged few live luxuriously.

3. *Freedom.* Maximum freedom requires people to have the widest possible range of choices available. As with equity, however, more freedom for some may leave less for others. I may be limited in how wildly I can swing my arms if your nose is in the way.

Efficiency is a generally accepted goal, but equity and freedom hinge on more controversial value judgments. Efficiency is also the micro goal most easily analyzed by economists. All economic goals are more easily achieved in an efficient economy. Excessive cost is one form of inefficiency. Lack of job opportunities is another. More generally, inefficiency implies that resources are wasted that could be used to enhance stability, growth, security, freedom, and equity.

Some economic goals involve trade-offs. For example, efficient policies might be widely viewed as inequitable. Granting patents for an AIDS vaccine might be efficient if potential profit stimulated research to control the disease, but it might seem unfair not to immunize those unable to afford the vaccine after its discovery. Alternatively, freedom and efficiency conflict if one person (a stickup artist) disrupts another's production (operating a gas station). Such trade-offs are among the reasons why all societies implement legal systems to govern people's relationships. Acceptably balancing freedom, efficiency, and equity is among society's major challenges.[6]

---

6. Conflicts between efficiency and equity occur frequently in this book. Efficiency is more easily analyzed with economic reasoning; issues of equity are unavoidable, inescapably normative, and a bit nebulous. Such conflicts are detailed in Arthur Okun's *Efficiency vs. Equity: The Big Tradeoff* (Washington, D.C.: Brookings, 1973).

Most early economists stressed microeconomics, believing that macroeconomics merely entailed summing micro variables and then tacking on changes in the money supply to account for changes in the price level. Inadequate analysis of macro phenomena may have contributed to the boom-bust cycles that culminated in the worldwide Great Depression of the 1930s. That slump forced us to realize that one decision maker's acts may yield a far different result than will be the case if all decision makers take the same action at once. For example, one person in the bleachers may see a ball game better by standing up, but when others also stand (as they will) this advantage is lost. It is now clear that reaching our micro goals depends on achieving our macro goals, and vice versa. Understanding both is essential for an accurate perception of how any economy operates.

You will repeatedly encounter the building blocks from this chapter when we investigate more advanced topics later in this book. If graphs make you queasy, you should study the optional material at the end of this chapter before you move on to Chapter 2. In Chapter 2, we explore *comparative advantage*, a concept that permits us to evaluate why different people and countries specialize in some types of production and exchange their outputs for goods produced by others. We also develop graphical devices called *production possibilities frontiers* to illustrate how scarcity limits our available choices, and examine some mechanisms that people use in trying to cope with scarcity.

Chapter Review: Key Points

1. *Economics* is concerned with choices and their consequences, and focuses on ways that individuals and societies allocate their limited resources to try to satisfy relatively unlimited wants.

2. *Scarcity* occurs because our relatively unlimited wants cannot be completely met from the limited resources available. A good is scarce if people cannot freely get all they want, so that the good commands a positive price. Scarcity forces all levels of decision makers, from individuals to society at large, to resolve three basic economic questions:

   a. *What* will be produced?

   b. *How* will production occur?

   c. *Who* will use the goods produced?

3. *Production* occurs when knowledge or technology is used to apply energy to materials to make them more valuable.

4. *Resources* (factors of production) include:

   a. *Land.* All natural resources. Payments for land are called *rents.*

   b. *Labor.* Productive efforts made available by human beings. Payments for labor services are called *wages.*

   c. *Capital.* Improvements that increase the productive potential of other resources. Payments for the use of capital are called *interest.* When economists refer to capital, they mean physical capital rather than financial capital, which consists of paper claims to goods or resources.

   d. *Entrepreneurship.* The organizing, innovating, and risk-taking function that combines other factors to produce. Entrepreneurs are rewarded with *profits.*

5. The *opportunity costs* of choices are measured by the subjective values of the best alternative you sacrifice. *Absolute prices* are monetary, and are useful primarily as indicators of *relative prices*, which are the prices of goods or resources in terms of each other, and which provide information and incentives to guide our decisions.

6. *Economic efficiency* occurs when a given amount of resources produces the most valuable combination of outputs possible. In an efficient economy, no transactions are possible from which anyone can gain without someone else losing.

   a. *Allocative efficiency* requires production of the things people want.

   b. *Productive (technical) efficiency* is obtained when a given output is produced at the lowest possible cost. Another way of looking at efficiency is that it occurs when the opportunity cost of obtaining some specific amount of a good is at its lowest.

c. *Distributive efficiency* requires consumers to adjust their purchasing patterns to maximize their satisfactions from given budgets.

7. *Common sense* is theory that has been tested over a long period and found useful. In general, good theory accurately predicts how the real world operates. *Occam's Razor* suggests that the simplest workable theories are the most useful or "best."

8. *Positive economics* is scientifically testable and involves value-free descriptions of economic relationships, dealing with "what is." *Normative economics* involves value judgments about economic relationships and addresses "what should be." Normative theory can be neither scientifically verified nor proven false.

9. *Macroeconomics* is concerned with aggregate (the total levels of) economic phenomena, including such items as Gross National Product, unemployment, and inflation. *Microeconomics* concentrates on individual decision making, resource allocation, and how prices and output are determined.

Key Concepts

Ensure that you can define these terms before proceeding.

scarcity	profit
production	opportunity cost
labor	relative prices
wages	allocative efficiency
land	productive efficiency
rent	distributive efficiency
capital	Occam's Razor
interest	macroeconomics vs.
investment	microeconomics
financial capital	positive vs. normative
entrepreneurship	economics

Problems and Questions

1. What opportunity costs do you face if you have just enough money to buy 1 T-shirt, 2 cassettes, or a tank of gasoline?

2. Suppose your tuition was $1,500 this semester; that you paid $225 for six textbooks (average = $37.50); and that your new calculator cost $15. What are the relative prices of the other two goods in terms of your calculator? Your texts? Your tuition?

3. Suppose the price of entry to your local swimming pool rises from $2 to $3 per day, while movie tickets rise from $5 to $7. Which of these forms of entertainment has become relatively more costly?

4. What are the basic differences between economic goods and free goods? Provide an example of an economic good, a free good, an economic resource, and a free resource. (This last one is tough.)

5. How do economic and financial capital differ? Provide three examples of each.

6. Whose lives are potentially assigned lower prices when a drunk decides to drive home without waiting to sober up?

7. Classify the following statements as positive or normative.

a. Relatively fewer people are poor under capitalism than under socialism.

b. Union wage demands and strikes cause inflation.

c. Federal budget deficits make business investors pessimistic and drive up interest rates.

d. American workers should not have to compete with cheap foreign labor.

e. Bad weather abroad benefits most American farmers.

8. Why is class attendance almost always higher on days when examinations are given?

9. Why is it probably accurate to believe that you can think of nothing better to do with your time right now than to study this book?

10. Truly free goods are almost inconceivable. Some alternative is nearly always forgone. Why are none of the following goods free, and who winds up paying for them?

a. A mother's love.

b. An all-expense-paid vacation to Paris, won on a TV game show.

c. Free popcorn at a theater.

d. A free school lunch program for poor children.

e. Leftovers dug from a fancy restaurant's garbage by a homeless family.

11. In an economic sense, can two ever live as cheaply as one? What are the opportunity (alternative) costs of marrying someone you love?

12. Does everything have a price? Are there some things you would not do regardless of price? (*Remember:* prices and money are not synonyms; prices may be nonmonetary.)

13. Which statements (whether true or not) are primarily macroeconomic and which are primarily microeconomic? Do some strongly involve blends of the two approaches?

a. Policymakers face a trade-off between high rates of unemployment and rapid inflation.

b. Equipment used in the U.S. steel industry is largely obsolete.

c. State and local governments increasingly rely on "sin" (e.g., alcohol and tobacco) taxes as revenue sources.

d. Medical care absorbed only 5% of all U.S. spending in 1955; by 1990, it absorbed 12% of all U.S. spending.

e. Excessive union wage demands in key U.S. industries cause inflation and reduce our ability to compete in international markets.

14. Why do people often let water run onto sidewalks and into the street when they water their lawns? Is this wasted water a sign of inefficiency?

15. Do you agree with the adage that "You can't get rich working for someone else"? Must successful entrepreneurs serve others to enrich themselves? Can wage earners achieve great wealth without investing? How might you test the correctness of your answers to these questions?

16. Explain why this type of federal farm policy creates inefficiency: U.S. farms must have allotments (legal permits) to grow certain crops. Smith's land, which lacks an allotment, is more suited to grow sugar beets than Brown's land, which is relatively more suited for alfalfa, but Brown has an allotment for sugar beets. Consequently, Brown grows sugar beets while Smith grows alfalfa.

17. Some critics of our economic system contend that self-interested behavior is not intrinsic, but that people are taught to be "selfish" by our society's stress on competition. These critics argue that if we encouraged cooperation as much as we now reward competitive behavior, children would be far less selfish when they became adults. Are people naturally selfish? If you agree with these critics, how might we restructure typical child-rearing practices and our education system to encourage more cooperation? Whether you agree or disagree that selfishness is a learned behavior, would the world be better off if people acted in less self-interested ways? Why, or why not?

18. Modern sociobiologists view perpetuation of one's gene pool as the basic human drive, and offer examples of behavior that apparently conflict with the economist's *homo economicus* assumption: Parents sacrifice their lives for their children, or invest in their kids' college educations so that the next generation will enjoy richer lives. On the other hand, people adopt other people's biological children and some childless people are voluntarily sterilized or join religious orders that require sexual abstinence. To what extent might perpetuation of one's gene pool conflict with self-interested behavior? Which assumption do you think more accurately predicts human behavior?

Optional Material: Graphical Techniques in Economics

Are you as likely to suffer nightmares after exposure to equations or graphs as you are after watching Freddy Kruger terrorize people in a horror film? We have a possible cure if you are afflicted with "math/graph-phobia." Try to subdue your anxiety and spend an hour or two studying this material and working the applications. Our *Graph-Tutor* software program and the parallel exercises in our *Student Guide For Learning Economics* can also help clarify analytical material in economics and may facilitate your work in other courses. In this section, we will show you how to read, interpret, and use graphs.

Graphical Analysis

[T]here is just no substitute for the [economic] intuition one acquires with lots of curve bending.

James P. Quirk (1976)

Words, graphs, tables, and equations are all useful in describing economic relationships. Familiarity with all four techniques is a key to understanding economics. Learning how **graphs** work is a lot easier than trying to memorize all the graphs in this book. Graphs are "snapshots" of information that can be used descriptively, as in maps and charts, or analytically, to gain insights into economic theory.

*A **graph** is a picture of a relationship between two or more **variables**, which are items that can be described by numbers and include such things as time, distance, income, prices, and outputs.*

You should gain confidence in dealing with graphs if you concentrate on understanding the figures described in the first few chapters of this text.

Maps are descriptive graphs that use grid systems called **Cartesian coordinates** to specify locations. A first step in locating Miami, for example, is to find it in the alphabetical index of a map of Florida. Miami's coordinates, J-7, help pinpoint where to look for Miami. Coordinate J at the side of the map tells you how far north or south Miami is. Coordinate 7 at the top indicates Miami's east-west orientation. Aha! — Miami!

Cartesian Coordinates

Just as maps plot geographic relationships, economic graphs use Cartesian coordinates to show relationships among variables. For example, how per capita income has changed over time is much easier to describe with a graph than with words. A Cartesian coordinate system is constructed by drawing two lines (or **axes**) perpendicular to each other. These axes, labeled **x** and **y**, are numbered and normally intersect at their respective zeros — the **origin**. The black lines in Figure 4 are axes for a standard set of Cartesian coordinates.

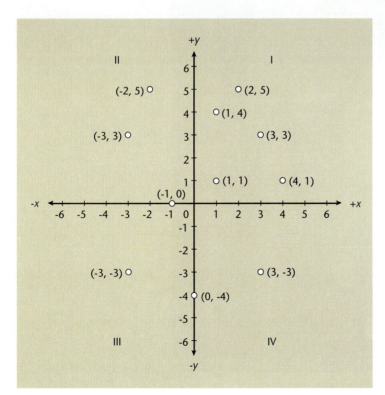

FIGURE 4 Cartesian Coordinates

This coordinate system is divided into four areas called *quadrants*; starting from the northeast, they are numbered I, II, III, and IV in a counterclockwise fashion. A point is located numerically by an ordered pair, denoted (*x*, *y*). Various ordered pairs are located on the graph. The *x* value represents a rightward movement from the vertical axis if the number is positive, and vice versa. The second coordinate (*y*) value is the vertical distance from the horizontal axis (upward movement if *y* is positive and downward if *y* is negative).

This coordinate system divides a "*space*" into four areas called **quadrants**, which are numbered **I** through **IV**, beginning from the northeast area and then moving in a counterclockwise direction.

Each point in this space is identified numerically by an **ordered pair**, denoted (x, y). The first coordinate, x, directs rightward movement if the number for x is positive, or leftward movement if x is negative. The second coordinate, y, governs upward movement if y is positive, or downward movement if y is negative. Thus, quadrant I contains pairs for which both x and y are positive, quadrant II shows pairs for which x is negative and y is positive, quadrant III shows situations where both x and y are negative, and quadrant IV depicts positive values of x paired with negative values of y.

The following points are placed on the coordinate system in Figure 4: $(1, 1)$, $(1, 4)$, $(3, 3)$, $(4, 1)$, $(2, 5)$, $(-2, 5)$, $(-3, 3)$, $(-1, 0)$, $(-3, -3)$, $(0, -4)$, and $(3, -3)$. Be sure you know how to locate these coordinates before proceeding. Remember, each pair gives two pieces of information: left-right for the value of x; then up-down for the value of y. Even though economists consider multidimensional problems, this technique allows us to deal with very complex issues by considering only two dimensions of a problem at a time.

Most economic analysis uses only the first, or positive, quadrant (quadrant I). Negative values of many economic variables do not make sense; examples of such nonsense include negative prices or negative unemployment rates.

FIGURE 5 Different Ways to Display the Same Economic Data

The sales data shown in the Macron advertisement are converted directly into the bar graphs, and then into the line graphs, using the Cartesian coordinate system.

Panel A

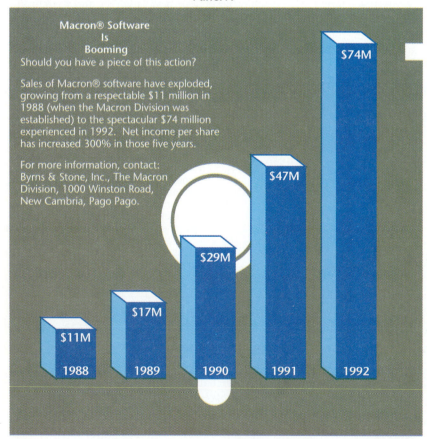

Macron® is a registered trademark of Byrns & Stone, Inc.

Descriptive Graphs

Computerized graphics allow economic data reported in news broadcasts and articles in magazines or newspapers to be imaginatively presented in numerous ways. The ad for *Macron* in Panel A of Figure 5, for example, dramatizes its growth during 1988–1992 with vertical bars; Panels B, C, D, and E superimpose grids on these data to help indicate their Cartesian coordinates. Revenues (on the vertical axis) are plotted against years (on the horizontal axis). Panels B and C are called **bar graphs** because they use bars to represent revenue in each year. **Line graphs** showing annualized sales data over time are shown in Panels D and E. All five panels illustrate the same information.

Bar Graphs

Line Graphs

Analytical Graphs

Economic concepts often hinge on how much one variable changes in response to a given change in another. Graphs can be used to present extremely complex relationships among variables, but reading them is easy if you concentrate on what a figure shows. Variables may be unrelated, or related to each other either positively or negatively. That is, higher values of x will be associated either with higher values of y (a **positive relationship**) or with lower values of y (a **negative relationship**).

The Slope of a Line   Graphically, such relationships are equivalent to the **slope** of the line depicting how the two variables are related. Slope is often described as "rise over run" — (*rise/run*).

The **slope** *of a line is the ratio of its vertical change* **(rise)** *to its horizontal change* **(run)** *as we move along it from left to right.*

Figure 6 depicts possible relationships between hours spent studying (x) and grade point average (y) for students with good, typical, and poor study habits. More study usually results in higher grade point averages, so these relationships are positive. But how much extra will you have to study to raise your grade point one full grade? The answer is found by determining the slope of the grade-point-average/study-hours line.

In this case, the grade (on the vertical axis) is the rise; study hours (along the horizontal axis) is the run. Suppose you have typical study habits and study each subject 30 hours a semester, so that your grade point average is 2.0, or C. In-

FIGURE 6   How Studying and Grade Point Averages Might Be Related

The slope of a line is defined as the ratio of the vertical change (rise) to the horizontal change (run). Curve *A* might reflect good study habits; each one-point improvement in your grade point average requires only an extra 7.5 hours of study per course. Curve *B* might depict average study habits; an extra 15 hours of study are required to raise your grade point average by a full point. Curve *C* shows the problem faced by someone with poor study skills; 30 hours of extra study time are required per course to raise the grade point average by one point.

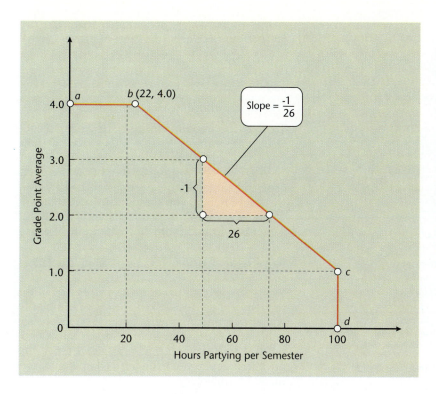

FIGURE 7   How Partying and Grade Point Averages Might Be Related

Slope can also be negative, zero, or infinite. Between points *a* and *b* the slope is zero, indicating that a little partying will not affect grades. Between points *b* and *c* the slope is $-1/26$, suggesting that each additional 26 hours of partying reduces your grade average by one point. Between points *c* and *d*, the slope is infinite, which means that a small change in partying may result in one point or more decline in your grade point average.

creasing your study time to 45 hours per subject (run = 45 − 30 = 15 hours) will raise your average to 3.0, or B (rise = 3.0 − 2.0 = 1.0). Fifteen extra hours of study per subject will raise your grade point average by one full point (*rise/run* = 1.0/15) if the middle line in Figure 6 corresponds to the relationship between your grade average and the hours you study.

Note that steeper lines yield higher values for slope and that the slope of each line reflects the efficiency of study. Students with good study habits raise their grade averages a full point with only 7.5 extra hours of study, but 30 extra hours are required for people with poor habits; the slopes of these relationships are 1/7.5 and l/30, respectively.

The slope of a line can also be negative. Excessive partying usually lowers grades, a negative relationship reflected in Figure 7. As the graph suggests, you can party for up to 22 hours per semester without harm to your grade point average (point *b*); there is no relationship between your recreation and your grades within this range. Beyond point *b*, however, each 26 hours of partying reduces your grade average by one

grade point until point *c* is reached (1.0 grade point average and 100 hours of partying).

Your grades drop to 0.0, or failing, when you party beyond 100 hours. Thus, between points *a* and *b*, the slope of the curve is zero (change in partying has no effect on grades or, alternatively, the two variables are unrelated). The slope of the line is −1/26 between 22 and 100 hours of party time (between points *b* and *c*); each 26 hours partied drops your grade average by one full point. The slope is infinite if you party 100 hours (between points *c* and *d*), so as little as one second may increase or decrease your average by a full grade point.

Intercepts   To simplify learning about economics, we often assume that the relationships studied are *linear*, which means that a graph of the relationship has a constant slope. The only information we need beyond slope to fully specify a linear relationship is its **intercept**, which is the value of the *y* variable when the *x* variable has a value of zero.

For example, Figure 8 shows a hypothetical relationship between lumber yields and annual

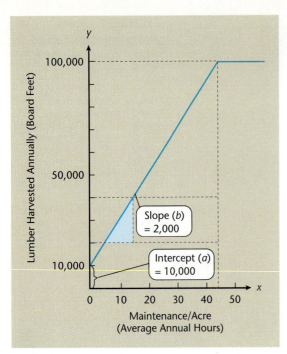

FIGURE 8 Forest Maintenance and Lumber Production

This figure shows that the sustainable number of board feet of lumber that can be harvested from a forest annually is 10,000 board feet if no one works to maintain the forest. As the number of hours that forestry experts devote to each acre of forest rises, the forest's yield rises by 2,000 board feet/hour.

maintenance per acre of forest to control tree diseases and clear debris (reducing fire hazards). Even with zero maintenance ($x = 0$) we may harvest some lumber ($y = 10,000$), and the harvest rate rises as maintenance increases. Each extra hour of maintenance per acre raises annual lumber yields by 2,000 board feet. This continues (given the linear relationship) until the ability to harvest lumber peaks when 45 hours of annual maintenance are devoted to each acre of forest.

The general algebraic formula for linear relationships is $y = a + bx$, where y and x are the variables considered, b is the slope of the relationship, and a is the intercept. For this forestry example, $a = 10,000$, $b = 2,000$, and the equation is:

$$y = 10,000 + 2,000x$$

where

y = annual yield of lumber in board feet
10,000 = the intercept (the value of y [board feet of lumber annually] when x [maintenance] is zero

and

x = hours of maintenance per acre, annually.

To find the harvest rate for each maintenance level, just multiply each possible value of x by 2,000 and add 10,000.

To ensure that you understand how the intercept and slope of a line are influenced by how variables interact, you should construct graphs of $y = a + bx$ where you select values of a and b as if you were blindly drawing them out of a hat.

Nonlinear Curves Some economic relationships (especially those in microeconomics) tend to swing from positive to negative, or vice versa, just as the temperature in Alaska varies from summer to winter to spring. Assuming constant slope for such **nonlinear** relationships is nonsensical. Our descriptions of some complex relationships later in this book will require you to understand a bit of mathematical terminology.

Slopes may change persistently along nonlinear curves, which may be *decreasingly positive* (curve segment *abc* in Panel A of Figure 9), *increasingly negative* (segment *cd* in Panel A), *decreasingly negative* (segment *ab* in Panel B), or *increasingly positive* (segment *bc* in Panel B). The slope at a point on a nonlinear curve is measured with the familiar "rise/run" formula for the slope of its **tangent** (a straight line drawn to barely touch the curve at that point). The slope at point *b* in Panel A, for example, is 0.5.

Note that both point *c* in Panel A and point *b* in Panel B have zero slope; tangents at these points are flat. Zero slope indicates that a relationship is either at its **maximum** (point *c* in Panel A) or its **minimum** (point *b* in Panel B). Nonlinear functions are especially necessary to illustrate parts of microeconomic analysis, which frequently involves maximization (e.g., of profits or satisfaction) or minimization (e.g., of risks or costs).

The Misuse of Graphs

Darrell Huff and Irving Geis wrote a popular book called *How to Lie With Statistics* that also shows how you can be misled by cleverly drawn

FIGURE 9 Nonlinear Relationships: Slopes, Maxima, and Minima

Along nonlinear curves, the slope may be *decreasingly positive* (segment *abc* in Panel A), *increasingly negative* (segment *cd* in Panel A), *decreasingly negative* (segment *ab* in Panel B), or *increasingly positive* (segment *bc* in Panel B). Slope is measured with the familiar "rise/run" formula for the *tangent* (a straight line that barely touches the curve). The slope at point *b* in Panel A, for example, is 0.5. Point *c* in Panel A and point *b* in Panel B have zero slope because these tangents are flat. Zero slope indicates a *maximum* (point *c* in Panel A) or *minimum* (point *b* in Panel B).

graphs. You should be alert for several pitfalls when graphs are used to illustrate, support, or prove an analytical point.

First, be sure the period selected for a graph is typical for the point made by the analysis. For example, during the 1980s, many aggressive financial investors bought Colorado real estate based on its performance in the 1970s. It seemed that property and land prices could only rise. But commercial real estate in Colorado crashed by roughly 60 percent in the 1980s, leaving widespread bankruptcy in its wake. This was not the first boom-bust cycle in real estate. Real estate buyers would have been way ahead if they had seen graphs depicting booms and busts, instead of the 1970s boom in isolation.

Second, be aware that the appearance of a graph depends on the choice of measurement units. One distortion caused by using different units on the axes is illustrated in Figure 10. Curve *A* appears to have a greater slope than Curve *B*, but both curves accurately portray the

same data, so this is impossible. The vertical axes are measured on different scales, accounting for the illusion that the two curves have different slopes.

Finally, the data used should be tightly linked to the analysis. Thus, comparing standards of living between countries cannot be done by simply looking at countries' total production or income; India is much bigger but far less prosperous than Dubai (one of the United Arab Emirates). Income per person or family is a much closer measure.

You will repeatedly be confronted with both analytical and descriptive graphs as you read through the rest of this book. We hope this section has helped ease your mind and that you will find graphs helpful in learning economics. You should return to these materials on graphs if you find yourself perplexed by some of our more advanced topics. The adage that one picture is worth a thousand words is especially true in economics.

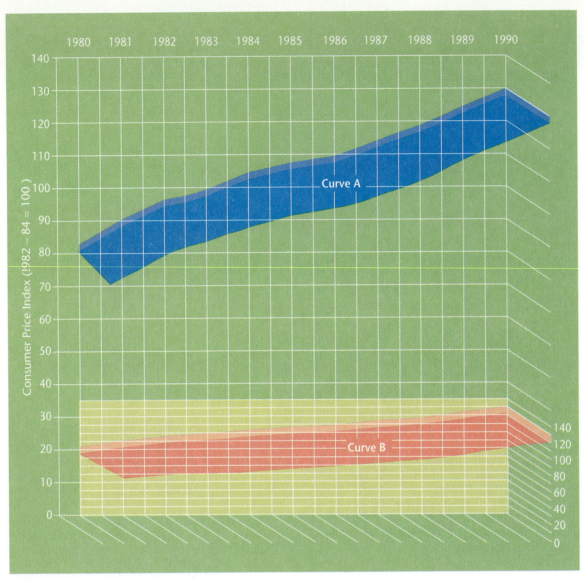

FIGURE 10 Consumer Prices

Units of measurement on the axes can make a line appear steeper (have a greater slope), even though its slope remains constant. Both curves *A* and *B* have the same slope; the units of measurement on the vertical axes have expanded in curve *A*.

Applications

Graph paper will make it easier to do a number of exercises in this course, including these, but you can use a ruler to do problems 1–7 on plain paper. For questions 5–7, you may need to approximate (guess) what some data might be like.

For each question:

A. Draw sets of Cartesian axes for each problem (a horizontal *x* axis and a vertical *y* axis that intersect at the origin where *x* =

0 and $y = 0$). Place appropriate measurement "ticks" at regular intervals along each pair of axes after you have read each problem.

B. Plot the relationship specified (questions 1–4) or a relationship you might expect (questions 5–7) between each pair of variables.

C. Specify whether each relationship is positive, negative, or nonexistent. (Slope = zero for unrelated variables.)

D. Identify each relationship as linear or nonlinear.

E. In questions 1–4 you have sufficient information to specify a and b. Calculate a and b and then write an equation for this line using the formula $y = a + bx$, where a = the y intercept and b = the slope. For example, if the intercept = 100 and the slope is -0.5, write $y = 100 - 0.5x$.

F. If a relationship is nonlinear, try to specify whether the curve representing it is increasingly positive, decreasingly positive, increasingly negative, or decreasingly negative, and try to identify the minimum or maximum if one exists.

1. Plot the ordered pairs $(-5, 0)$, $(-2, 7)$, $(0, 5)$, $(3, 2)$, $(5, 0)$, $(8, -3)$, $(10, -5)$. Connect these plotted ordered pairs with a line. Randomly select a point (e.g., $(5, 0)$) and call it (x_1, y_1), and then a second point, say $(-2, 7)$, and label it (x_2, y_2). Calculate the slope of the line by plugging these values into the formula $(y_1 - y_2)/(x_1 - x_2)$.

2. Repeat question 1, using the following ordered pairs: $(-5, -10)$, $(-2, -7)$, $(0, 5)$, $(3, -2)$, $(5, 0)$, $(7, 2)$, $(10, 5)$.

3. Suppose income tax rates were zero for the first $5,000 in annual income and 25% for each dollar of income over $5,000. Plot the relationship between people's **income** (up to a maximum of $100,000) on the horizontal (x) axis and their **income taxes** on the vertical (y) axis. How much income tax does an entrepreneur who gains $100,000 pay? How much income tax does a bus driver who makes $20,000 annually pay?

4. Each week has 168 hours. Any hours not worked are considered leisure. Put **hours of leisure** (nonwork) on the horizontal axis, and **total income** at $10 per hour worked on the vertical axis. Draw a graph showing alternative weekly income levels for hours of leisure ranging from 0 to 168.

5. Put adult women's **height** on the x axis, and their average **weight** for each possible height from 3'6" to 6'6" on the y axis. (*Hint:* Would an average woman 6' tall weigh only 20% more than an average woman who was 5' tall?)

6. For all possible automobiles with model years from 1930 through 1992, put the **average ages** of cars being traded in on a new car on the horizontal axis, and what you expect would be the **average trade-in allowance** in hundreds of dollars on the vertical axis. (*Hint:* Your curve should be "U"-shaped.)

7. Many supermarkets in big cities now operate 24 hours a day all year round. Suppose you operate the only store in a very isolated small town, and that you would sell $1,000 worth of groceries daily if you operated one hour each day. Put all possible numbers of **hours per day** you could be open on the x axis, and the resulting **expected weekly sales revenue** on the y axis. (*Hint:* People would try to ensure purchases of things they consider necessities but might skip frivolous and inconvenient purchases, or they might drive long distances to shop elsewhere if your service were too limited.)

CHAPTER

Scarcity in a Changing World

Modern communication and transportation networks now link markets everywhere—you can have a Big Mac in Boston, Paris, or Moscow. Old political regimes and alliances are crumbling because time and distance are compressed, while people all over the world have better information about how other people live—international news broadcasts are partially responsible for reform movements in China, Eastern Europe, and the USSR. Yet Americans seem largely oblivious to global events that profoundly affect our lives; a typical survey reveals that only 44 percent of high school seniors can locate Korea on a map.

A framework for understanding international economic developments is introduced in this chapter, which opens by discussing the *circular flow* of income across three types of institutions—households, firms, and government. Then we consider why efficiently maximizing the world's output requires: (*a*) cooperative production based on a *division of labor*, and (*b*) specialized production and exchange according to *comparative advantage*. This leads to *production possibilities frontiers*—graphic portrayals of a nation's productive capacity that, among other things, help explain why countries import some things and export others. We also examine some allocative mechanisms used to cope with scarcity: Shall economic questions be addressed by government, the market system, or some other de-

vice? Finally, we explore the different ways capitalism and socialism resolve economic issues, and discuss dramatic recent changes in the international economy.

Circular Flows of Income

People sometimes act collectively, but organizations do not breathe and cannot make decisions apart from those of the people who operate through them. Thus, although which individuals' choices count most depends on organizational structures, business and government exist primarily to channel interactions among people in *households*. Markets pivot on the decisions of households and businesses, which together are called the **private sector**. In our mixed economy, government (the **public sector**) takes a back seat only to the marketplace as a dominant allocative mechanism. A simple model of how households interact through firms and government is shown in the **circular flow** diagram in Figure 1.

Households

Roughly 255 million Americans now live in 90 million **households**, a catchall term covering groups ranging from individuals who live alone to extended families in which several adults and a flock of children share a home.

> **Households** *are centers for consumption and ultimately own all wealth, including resources that they make available to businesses or government in exchange for income.*

Labor is the major asset of most households, as indicated by the *functional distribution of income* in Table 1, which also presents the major uses of household income. Wages (including all salaries and fringe benefits) provide roughly three-fourths of income, with the rest being derived from rent, interest, and profit. Part of household income flows to government as taxes, with the rest being either spent on consumer goods or saved. Household saving is the primary source of investment funds for business firms.

Firms

Some of U.S. national output is produced by households (e.g., do-it-yourself projects), non-profit organizations (e.g., hospitals), or government-controlled industries (e.g., public schools),

FIGURE 1   Circular Flows of Income, Resources, and Goods

This circular flow model depicts flows of income, resources, and outputs among households, business firms, and government. Households provide resources to business firms or government in exchange for money income, which is used to purchase goods from business, or to pay taxes for provision of goods through government. Firms provide goods to households (indirectly in some cases, via government) and, in return, receive payments, which are conveyed to households as income. Tax revenues enable government to provide for collective wants and to redistribute incomes among households.

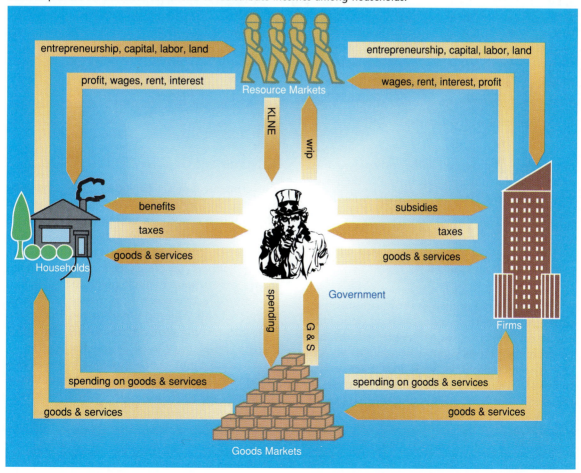

TABLE 1 *Sources and Uses of Income, 1929–1990*

| Year | $ Billions Total Income | Functional Distribution of Income (Percentage of Total Income) | | | | |
		Compensation of Employees	Proprietors' Income	Net Rents	Corporate Profits	Interest
1929	84.7	60.3	17.6	5.8	10.8	5.5
1933	39.4	73.9	14.5	5.5	−4.3	10.3
1940	79.6	65.4	16.2	3.4	10.9	4.1
1950	239.8	65.5	16.3	3.0	14.3	1.0
1960	424.9	71.6	11.4	3.3	11.3	2.4
1970	832.6	76.3	8.2	2.3	8.5	4.7
1980	2,203.5	75.5	5.7	3.1	8.6	8.9
1990	4,417.5	73.4	9.1	0.2	6.7	10.6

| Year | $ Billions Total Income | Uses of Income ($ Billions) | | |
		Consumption	Saving	Taxes
1929	84.7	77.3	2.6	3.8
1933	39.4	45.8	−0.9	4.0
1940	79.6	71.0	3.0	10.0
1950	239.8	192.1	12.6	41.2
1960	424.9	330.7	20.8	93.9
1970	832.6	640.0	57.7	207.8
1980	2,203.5	1,732.6	136.9	615.1
1990	4,417.5	3,658.1	179.1	699.8

Source: *Economic Report of the President,* 1991.

but the bulk is produced within privately owned *firms*. Figure 1 indicates that firms use their sales revenues to pay for the resources households provide.

> *A* **business firm** *is a privately owned and operated center for production.*[1]

Entrepreneurs and managers of firms interpret prices and profits as signals about individual wants or collective wants (expressed through government). Firms prompt households to provide specific resources with incentives in the forms of wage rates paid for specific labor skills, rental rates for land, or rates of return on capital.

Government

Government directly provides some goods and services, and indirectly channels resources and the production and consumption of other goods via taxes and regulations. Figure 1 shows that taxes are the primary sources of government revenue. Political processes transform this command over resources into governmental provision for collective wants (e.g., police protection, public schools, highways, and national defense), and into income redistributions that politicians view as reflecting voters' desires for equity.[2]

A critical point in the circular flow model is that firms are not the final owners of resources or products, because firms are owned by house-

---

1. The different legal guises that business firms may take (e.g., proprietorships, partnerships, and corporations) are discussed later in this book.

2. Possible economic roles for government are considered in depth later in this book.

holds. Nor does government ultimately own anything in a democratic society in which, ideally, it is responsive to the people — who bear the consequences of policies formulated within firms or government. Firms, for example, cannot bear tax burdens; only their resource suppliers, owners, or customers truly pay taxes. It is common to speak of government changing its economic policies, or of firms profiting, changing prices, or introducing new products, but such institutions only shape the flow of individual decisions. Activities that matter affect people, not organizations per se.

Standard circular flow models show how goods, resources, and incomes move among households through firms and government. But will resources be used in allocatively and productively efficient ways? And will goods and resources flow in distributively efficient ways to those who desire them relatively most?

Specialization and Trade

Imagine how miserable life would be if your family had to be totally self-sufficient — no cars or convenience foods, no ready-made clothing, and no electricity. If you consumed only what you produced, life would be "nasty, brutish, and short." Both living above bare subsistence and economic efficiency require (a) production entailing a *division of labor*, and (b) specialization and exchange according to *comparative advantage*.

Division of Labor

Romance may motivate most marriages, but mundane considerations also play a role. People wed, in part, to share gains from a division of labor. Household chores, for example, involve less drudgery if one spouse cooks and mows the lawn while the other pays the bills and buys the groceries. And cleaning a kitchen takes less than half the time when one person rinses crockery while the other loads the dishwasher.

> The **division of labor** *entails dividing the work required to produce a given good or accomplish a particular task.*

Gains from the division of labor arise because: (a) teamwork fosters productivity (no one could do heart transplant surgery alone), and (b) people develop expertise in particular jobs (practice improves quality and reduces error). A division of labor in firms occurs, for example, when one person on an assembly line installs car bumpers, another aligns headlights, a third balances tires, and so on.

Comparative Advantage

Specialization enhances production, but how should people specialize? All potential gains are realized if you concentrate on doing that which you can do at the lowest cost relative to other people. David Ricardo, a famous early economist, was focusing on international trade when he generalized this idea into an economic law in 1817.

> The **law of comparative advantage:** *Mutually beneficial exchanges are possible whenever* **relative** *production costs differ prior to trade.*

This law applies to all exchanges, whether between individuals or nations. Oranges are grown at relatively lower cost in Florida than in Iowa, for example, while Iowa excels in wheat production. Floridians and Iowans obviously share gains from exchange according to comparative advantage by trading Florida oranges for Iowa wheat. Similar gains are realized when Americans trade with foreigners; efficiency requires using all the world's resources in the relatively most productive ways.

Suppose Brazilians can grow coffee more easily than they can catch salmon, while Alaskans find it relatively easier to catch salmon than to grow coffee. Alaskans have a comparative advantage in salmon fishing, the Brazilians in coffee production. Trading Alaskan salmon for Brazilian coffee clearly yields gains to both parties. Table 2 shows how both parties to a trade can gain as long as their opportunity costs are not identical. If Alaskans and Brazilians each specialize in their areas of comparative advantage, and if 1 pound of salmon trades for, say, 1 pound of coffee, then Alaskans can consume an extra 4 pounds of coffee daily while Brazilians can consume an additional 4 pounds of salmon.

TABLE 2 *Opportunity Costs and Efficiency*

Before Specialization	Hours Worked		Production and Consumption
Alaskan	4		5 pounds of salmon
	4		*1 pound of coffee*
Brazilian	4		*1 pound of salmon*
	4		5 pounds of coffee
After Specialization	**Hours Worked**	**Production**	**Consumption**
Alaskan	8	10 pounds of salmon	5 pounds of salmon
			5 pounds of coffee
Brazilian	8	10 pounds of coffee	*5 pounds of salmon*
			5 pounds of coffee

Note that the Alaskan opportunity cost of producing 1 pound of coffee is 5 pounds of salmon before trade, while the Brazilian cost of 1 pound of coffee is only 1/5 of a pound of salmon. Thus, opportunity cost guides us to comparative advantage: *Individuals and nations gain by producing goods at relatively low costs and exchanging their outputs for different goods produced by others at relatively low cost.* All potential trading partners can gain enormously through appropriate specialization and exchange.

But what if Alaskans had *absolute advantages* in everything; that is, they could do every task faster and easier than Brazilians? You might think that Alaskans must lose if Brazilians gain from trade but, surprisingly, both sides can gain. Suppose, for example, that a lawyer whose fees run $100 an hour types twice as fast as her secretary, whose wage is $10 hourly. She still gains by hiring the secretary despite her absolute advantage as a typist — her time is worth more in court. Similarly, many professional athletes probably have absolute advantages in lifting and carrying compared to furniture movers. Nevertheless, few pro athletes move their furniture when traded between teams. Athletes and movers both gain by concentrating in their own areas of comparative advantage.

Roots of Comparative Advantage Relative resource abundance is often cited as a major source of comparative advantage. It seems natural for a nation with fertile soil to have comparative advantages in agriculture, that huge oil reserves give the

Middle East advantages in oil, and that hordes of low-wage workers yield advantages in labor intensive goods. But why is Mexico, which is so rich in resources, relatively poor, while Switzerland, with few natural resources, enjoys one of the world's highest standards of living? And why is India's economy stagnant while Singapore thrives despite even greater population density and fewer natural resources?

An emerging answer to such riddles is that comparative advantage is also molded by: (*a*) climate and location, (*b*) institutional and cultural factors, (*c*) government policies, (*d*) the skills and education of the populace, (*e*) the vigor of internal competition and size of domestic markets, and (*f*) the commitment of domestic entrepreneurs to innovate new technologies and cultivate global markets. How resources are combined is as important as the mix of resources available.

A recent study of ten major economies — directed by Michael Porter, a professor at the Harvard Business School — surprisingly concludes that many government policies intended to promote domestic industries (e.g., export subsidies or tariffs against imports) fail as often as they succeed.[3] In this view, government policy should be directed toward: (*a*) encouraging domestic rivalry (which rewards success in lowering costs and improving quality), (*b*) investing in human resource skills that enhance productiv-

---

3. Michael E. Porter, *The Competitive Advantage of Nations* (New York: The Free Press, 1990).

Is the United States at a Comparative Disadvantage?

One new car in four bought by Americans is foreign. U.S. imports exceeded exports each year from 1982 into the 1990s. We now import shiploads of oil and steel, many of our clothes, and most of our shoes. Such facts alarm people who worry that we are losing our ability to compete in world markets.

The growing internationalization of most economies is the first major explanation for concern that the United States has lost its ability to compete. Countries everywhere are both exporting and importing record shares of their production and income, so most societies have an increasingly international flavor—an alarming fact to traditionalists all over the globe who fear "foreign influence."

Second, some countries' exports have grown faster than U.S. exports. Signs are emerging, however, that rates of gain are shrinking for countries that have played "catch-up" in recent decades. For example, our average labor productivity grew more slowly than that of Japan and parts of Western Europe during much of 1950–1980. This pattern reversed during the 1980s, while wages in those countries grew faster than U.S. wages. Consequently, average U.S. labor costs per unit of output, which formerly exceeded those in other major industrial powers, have fallen to roughly average.

Third, the international value of the dollar was at record highs in the mid-1980s. Foreigners sought high prices by exporting goods to the U.S. and were discouraged from buying high-priced U.S. exports, partially accounting for huge imbalances of trade during 1983–1990. Combining the relative decline in U.S. labor costs with the fall in the dollar's value should encourage U.S. exports and discourage imports in the next few years.

The United States was once the world's dominant industrial exporter. Robust international competition has made it easy to forget that the U.S. continues to be the world's largest producer in most major industries, including aluminum and paper. Voracious national consumption may mean, however, that we sometimes import goods at which we excel as producers. For example, the United States imports steel even though we are the world's #2 steel maker.

Broad areas in which our comparative advantages remain overwhelming include advanced technology, entertainment, and agriculture. The United States continues to be the world's largest "high-tech" exporter if we lump together such things as aircraft, computers, instruments, petrochemicals, plastics, and semiconductors. We dominate exports of movies and music, and of agricultural products. (The topsoil in our farm belt and our agricultural technology are the envy of the rest of the world.) And even our auto industry is the #3 exporter in world markets. If you are in another country and see a new "foreign" car, chances are 1 in 9 that it was "Made in the U.S.A."

ity, and (c) emphasizing quality as a national priority.

U.S. exports have recently been swamped by imports. Does this mean that we are losing all comparative advantages? NO! Being comparatively disadvantaged in all areas is impossible, because relative magnitudes determine comparative advantage. Although many countries are expanding outputs in which the United States has traditionally enjoyed huge competitive advantages, Focus 1 identifies some continuing areas of comparative advantage for U.S. producers. The shapes of *production possibilities frontiers* (graphs of the limits to productive capacity) show how comparative advantages differ internationally.

Production Possibilities

Can you afford a flight in a hot air balloon if you already spend all your income each week? Of course, but only by buying less of something else. You can walk instead of filling your gas tank, eat peanut butter and jelly instead of having pizza delivered, watch TV instead of buying movie or concert tickets, and drive on bald tires till they go flat. But something has to give! Just as your budget constrains your purchases, scarcity forces society as a whole to make choices about the goods we produce and consume.

Production Possibilities Frontiers

A production possibilities frontier (**PPF**) is among the simplest models of an economy.

> A **production possibilities frontier** *describes the maximum combinations of goods a society can produce in a given period.*

This model relies on three critical assumptions[4]:

1. The amounts of land, labor, capital, and entrepreneurship are fixed, but can be allocated among different types of production.

2. Technology, which includes such things as the state of knowledge about production and the qualities of resources, is assumed constant.

3. All scarce resources are fully and efficiently employed.

---

4. If a lack of realism in these assumptions disturbs you, remember (from Chapter 1) that a model needs be no more realistic than is necessary for the purpose at hand. The PPF model yields valuable qualitative insights even if it lacks quantitative precision.

Suppose you live in Ruritania, a mythical empire ruled by the dictator Atilla. Ruritania contains 1,000 units of each resource. Atilla believes that "balanced" production requires all industries to use the same proportional mixes of capital, land, and labor. (In a moment, you will see how dopey this constraint on technology is.)

Some production possibilities for Ruritania using Atilla's technology are detailed in the table in Figure 2. Points *a*, *b*, *c*, *d*, and *e* in the figure denote five possible combinations of armaments and bread that can be produced during a given period. (For simplicity, we assume that only two goods are produced.) As resources are shifted from armaments to bread, weaponry output falls and bread output rises. When all resources are used to produce guns, no bread is produced, and vice versa.

Alternatives *a* through *e* are only five of many feasible combinations. Atilla can choose any point on the production possibilities frontier (PPF) graphed by connecting combinations *a* through *e* with a smooth line. The point he chooses (answering the basic question of *what* will be produced) depends on whether he wants Ruritanians better fed and less well defended, or vice versa. Atilla would never knowingly choose a point such as *x* because some resources would either be wastefully used or idle. Productive efficiency (addressing *how* production will occur) requires being somewhere on the PPF. Any inefficiency (e.g., underemployment of resources) could be eliminated by moving from *x* to a point between *c* and *d* so that more of both goods was produced.

Producing 1,250 units of each commodity at point *z* is clearly preferable to all points on the existing frontier. Resources cannot be stretched to attain point *z*, however, in part because Atilla's neurotic fixation on "balanced" production represents a limited technology. Remember that an economy produces efficiently, given its technology, when it operates on its production possibilities frontier.

What does bread cost in our example? If Ruritanians move from point *c* in Figure 2 to production possibility *d*, they gain 250 boxcars of bread but lose 250 machine guns; the cost of each extra boxcar of bread is one machine gun.

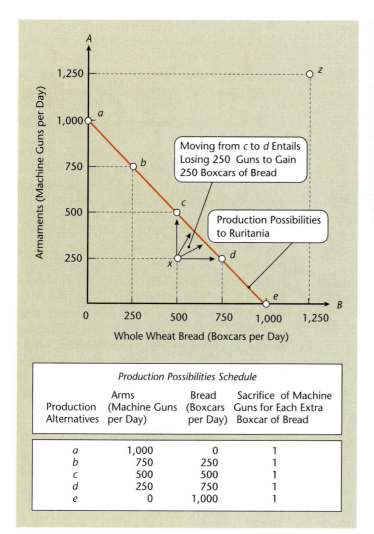

FIGURE 2   A Primitive Production Possibilities Frontier

This straight-line PPF reflects the availability of resources (1,000 units of capital, land, and labor) and the crude technology used (Atilla's "balanced" production formula). If production of both arms and bread is exactly proportional to the amounts of resources used and a maximum of 1,000 boxcars (or 1,000 guns) can be produced daily, then total production when all resources are employed will equal 1,000 total units of bread plus weapons. Each gun produced costs 1 boxcar of bread, and vice versa.

Moving from c to d Entails Losing 250 Guns to Gain 250 Boxcars of Bread

Production Possibilities to Ruritania

Production Possibilities Schedule			
Production Alternatives	Arms (Machine Guns per Day)	Bread (Boxcars per Day)	Sacrifice of Machine Guns for Each Extra Boxcar of Bread
a	1,000	0	1
b	750	250	1
c	500	500	1
d	250	750	1
e	0	1,000	1

The guns forgone for extra bread are the opportunity costs (in guns) of producing and consuming more bread, and vice versa. A straight-line *PPF* such as this one yields *constant costs* because producing an extra boxcar of bread costs one machine gun at every point along the curve. But constant cost is actually an unlikely case — in fact, because of *diminishing returns* in production, increasing costs are the norm.

Diminishing Returns

Here is a very general statement of the law of diminishing returns:

The **law of diminishing returns:** *As any activity is extended, it eventually becomes increasingly difficult to pursue the activity further.*[5]

For example, the faster you drive, the more gas your engine burns, and it becomes ever harder for your car to gain another 10 miles per

---

5. The law of diminishing *marginal* returns that economists apply to production is a narrow application of the much broader tendency described here, which, for math purists, is equivalent to the idea that all economic functions are bounded by a convex hull.

hour. Diminishing returns are encountered in many areas, including physics and biology, and the law of diminishing returns has wide and varied applications within economics: Expanding any type of production eventually becomes ever more difficult and costly. Increasing your total satisfaction from any good ultimately becomes harder the more of the good you have already consumed. Would four candy bars daily quadruple the enjoyment you got from eating the first?

Increasing Opportunity Costs   The inevitable occurrence of diminishing returns in all forms of production ultimately generates increasing opportunity costs.

> The **Principle of Increasing Costs:** *Repeatedly increasing output by some set proportion ultimately requires more than proportional increases in resources and costs.*

For example, your grades tend to improve the more you study — a C requires more effort than a D. But boosting a B to an A usually requires far more extra work than moving from a D to a C. Thus, there are increasing costs to raising your grade point average. Let's see how this concept applies to the production possibilities frontier.

Atilla's "balanced" technology naively mandated the same resource mix for all outputs. Suppose he appointed you minister of production. You might reason that, relative to arms, efficient bread output requires more land and less capital, while weapons should use capital relatively more intensively — a technological breakthrough that allows both outputs to grow! After experimenting to discover the appropriate resource mix, you will find that increasing costs are encountered as output of either good expands, causing the production possibilities curve to be concave (bowed away) from the origin. Here's why.

Ruritania's production possibilities frontier with this new technology is shown in Figure 3. When bread production is raised from zero to 100 boxcars daily, machine gun output falls only from 1,000 units to 995 daily (from point *a* to point *b*). Why does the first 100 boxcars of bread cost only 5 machine guns? Because the first re-

sources shifted into food production will be those relatively best suited for bread and least suited for weapons. Far more land than capital will be transferred to bread production. But as bread output is continually increased, the resources shifted are decreasingly suited for bread production relative to the production of armaments, and the cost of extra bread rises. Thus, moving from point *f* to point *g* yields an extra 100 boxcars of bread daily, but costs 66 machine guns, while moving from point *i* to point *j* also yields 100 extra boxcars of bread, but the cost is higher: 164 machine guns.

When bread output finally grows from 900 to 1,000 boxcars daily (point *j* to point *k*), the last few resources shifted from armaments are very suited for producing guns but not for producing food. Thus, 436 machine guns are sacrificed for the last 100 boxcars of bread. Less and less land is available for shifting, so more and more capital moves into farming. Note that the slope of the production possibilities frontier reflects relative production costs: As more and more bread is produced, the production possibilities curve becomes ever "steeper" and bread becomes increasingly costly relative to machine guns.

The ever-rising cost of extra bread in terms of forgone machine guns, as shown in the table in Figure 3, is graphed in Figure 4. You will learn in the next chapter that Figure 4 shows the typical shape of a society's long-run supply curve for bread.

To summarize, the production possibilities model illustrates scarcity, opportunity costs, choice, and diminishing returns. Desires for "more" are boundless but resources are scarce, so only limited amounts of goods can be produced. Scarcity forces every society to choose among competing goods, so we face opportunity costs. Finally, opportunity costs eventually rise if we repeatedly expand the production of any good.

Economic Growth

Allocating resources more efficiently allows movement from inside a production possibilities frontier to its border; output is expanded, but not productive capacity. **Economic growth** en-

	Production Possibilities and Increasing Costs			
(1)	(2)	(3)		(4)
	Average Daily Production			Average Opportunity Costs (Average Machine Guns Sacrificed per
Point	Arms	Bread		Extra Boxcar of Bread)
a	1,000	0		--
b	995	100		0.05
c	980	200		0.15
d	954	300		0.26
e	917	400		0.37
f	866	500		0.51
g	800	600		0.66
h	714	700		0.86
i	600	800		1.14
j	436	900		1.64
k	0	1,000		4.36

FIGURE 3   A More Realistic PPF that Reflects Increasing Costs

If the resources available (1,000 units each of capital, land, and labor) are used in the combinations that best fit the various forms of production, the PPF will be concave from the origin. In this example, arms are capital intensive (use more capital relative to land), and bread is land intensive. The differences in the appropriate mixes of capital/labor/land causes a society to encounter diminishing returns (increasing costs) as more and more boxcars of bread (or arms) are produced.

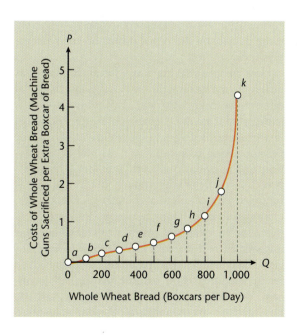

FIGURE 4   Rising Opportunity Cost of Bread

Diminishing returns cause the opportunity cost of bread to rise as production is increased. This means that more and more guns must be sacrificed as bread production grows.

tails outward shifts of production possibilities frontiers so that more of all goods can be produced, and requires either (a) advances in technology, or (b) the acquisition of more resources. Growth occurs when entrepreneurs implement new technology that enables given amounts of resources to produce more output. It may seem surprising, but technological advances in any active industry will expand production possibilities for all other industries.[6] The reason is that a technological advance in, say, the textile industry, would allow fewer resources to produce more textiles. Resources would be freed from textiles to produce more food, housing, and other goods.

In addition to technological advances as sources of growth, opening up new land is a possibility, but there is little unexplored land on Earth and settling other planets remains in the realm of science fiction. Another possibility is growth of the labor force through: (a) increases in the number of workers, or (b) improvements in their productivity. Investment in new capital requires *saving* and is an especially important source of growth.

Present vs. Future Consumption Scarcity forces us to choose between work and leisure, among various commodities, and between consumer goods and military goods. We also must choose between current and future consumption. Producing capital goods requires forgoing some of our potential current consumption. If almost all output is in the form of perishable consumer goods, society will acquire little new machinery and few new manufacturing plants, shrinking the amounts of goods available in the future.

National income that is not consumed, freeing resources for new investment, is called saving.

Consuming less than we produce is **saving,** *which allows resources to be channeled into the production of new capital goods* (**investment**).

Rapid investment directly updates technology

---

6. Trivial exceptions to this statement are cases of technological advances in industries not previously operational.

and boosts production possibilities; enhanced labor productivity and the availability of new products are common side benefits. But productive capacity is eroded if depreciation exceeds investment; failure to replace worn-out capital yields stagnation. In such cases, the production possibilities frontier shrinks toward the origin. Thus, choices between current consumption and saving (to allow investment) determine future prosperity, as shown in Figure 5.

Panel A indicates possible choices between consuming and investing in 1993, with point *a* reflecting greater consumption than point *b*, point *b* more consumption than point *c*, and so on. Curves PPF_a through PPF_e in Panel B show the production possibilities in the year 2000 that result from 1993 choices of *a*, *b*, *c*, *d*, and *e*, respectively. In sum, growth in an efficient economy is stimulated by higher investment, which requires more saving (less consumption). This analysis partially explains why, on average, U.S. economic growth since 1970 has been anemic compared to that in some other countries.

Only 4 to 6 percent of U.S. income has been saved since 1970, while the Japanese saved 20 percent of their income to promote capital investment. Many American industries consequently now try to compete with foreign firms that use better technology and more machinery. Our auto industry, for example, is reeling under competition from Japanese carmakers, who rely more heavily on industrial robots on their assembly lines.

How people's saving is used is as important as different saving rates in explaining international differences in growth rates. Economic growth is stimulated if saving is channeled into productive investments. But if, say, government uses most private saving to fund a war, capital accumulation and economic growth will both be hampered. Growth is also squelched when saving is funneled into obsolete and inefficient industries.

England's experience between 1945 and 1980 provides an example; most private saving was invested in nationalized industries in which England had lost its comparative advantage. The result was stagnation relative to the U.S. economy, despite relatively higher saving rates by the English than by Americans. Similar stagnation

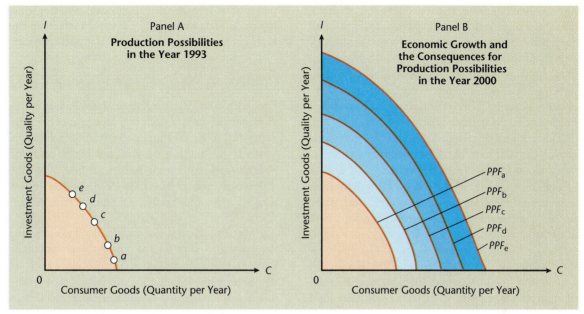

FIGURE 5 Economic Growth: Trade-Offs Between Consumption and Investment

Panel B illustrates that a movement from PPF_a to PPF_b (or even PPF_e) represents economic growth—more of both goods can be produced, and any two goods could be on these axes. Society must make choices between present and future consumption. If in 1993 this society selects a mix of production that emphasizes consumer goods (point a in Panel A) rather than investment (capital) goods (point e in Panel A), the 2000 PPF will be relatively smaller. Choice a in Panel A yields only enough investment to replace the capital that has depreciated, so PPF_a is the same in both panels. Moving from point a to point b in Panel A causes capital to grow somewhat, so in Panel B more of both consumption and investment are possible along PPF_b than on PPF_a. Moving to point c in Panel A enables still greater growth, yielding PPF_c in Panel B. And so on.

has prompted drastic reforms in Eastern Europe and the Soviet Union; economic growth was anemic despite suppression of consumption to create high rates of saving and investment.

One reason for weak U.S. economic growth during the 1980s may be that much of private saving was absorbed by a string of record federal budget deficits; many financial investors bought U.S. government bonds instead of making saving available to investors in new capital. High interest rates and recurring $100+ billion annual deficits in our federal budget discouraged investors and caused many to question coupling major cuts in tax rates (1982–1984) with vigorous expansion of defense spending. This is an example of the dilemma every society faces when it chooses between "guns" and "butter."

Unemployment, Inflation, and National Defense

Production possibilities analysis illuminates major differences between the World War II and Vietnam War eras. The deepest U.S. depression ever still lingered at the dawn of World War II. The unemployment rate had fallen from its 25% peak in 1933 to roughly 15–16% by 1939. (Unemployment averages 4–6% in prosperous times.) Some consumer goods (butter) and a few military goods (guns) were produced, but high unemployment held the economy well inside its production possibilities frontier. Mobilizing these idle resources when war erupted allowed acceleration of military production without cutbacks of consumer goods. In fact, as the economy approached its PPF in the early 1940s, consumption actually rose. Productive capacity also soared in the early war years, as new technology was introduced while patriotism pulled women into the work force and spurred worker productivity. Then, at the war's end, the economy moved along its PPF by retooling from military hardware to consumer goods.

This experience differs sharply from events during the Vietnam era. The economy was operating close to its PPF in the mid-1960s, with a jobless rate of around 4 percent. President Lyndon Johnson strove for "more guns and more butter," and escalated U.S. military resources in Vietnam while expanding domestic programs (e.g., the "War Against Poverty"). His goals required moving beyond society's PPF, which, unfortunately, is impossible. Although the economy grew strongly from 1964 to 1969, at least part of the persistent double-digit inflation during the 1970s was a hangover from stress on the U.S. economy exerted by the Vietnam conflict.

Production Possibilities and Trade

Specialization and exchange according to comparative advantage allows any society's consumption to exceed its PPF in isolation. Figure 6 portrays production possibilities for Alaska and Brazil drawn from a previous example. Note the relative shapes of the two PPFs, which reflect these two regions' respective comparative advantages.

If trade results in one pound of salmon costing the same as one pound of coffee, then both Alaskans and Brazilians can consume anywhere on the negatively sloped 45° line (which reflects the 1:1 price) that is just tangent to both PPFs. Peo-

FIGURE 6   Production Possibilities and Comparative Advantage*

Consumption in Alaska and Brazil without trade would be limited to choices along their respective PPFs. With trade, both Alaskans and Brazilians can consume along the negatively sloped 45° line just tangent to the two PPFs.

*These PPFs are based on simplifying assumptions that, if all resources were used in a single industry, Brazil could produce five times as much coffee as Alaska, which could produce five times as much salmon as Brazil; that maximum Brazilian coffee output just equals maximum Alaskan salmon output; and that maximum coffee output in Alaska equals maximum salmon output in Brazil.

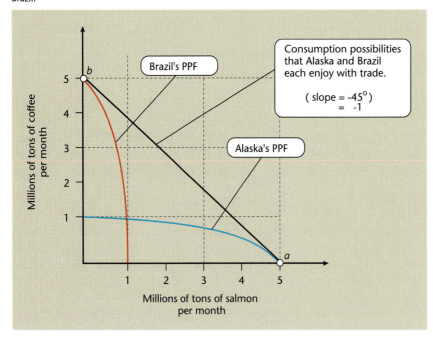

ple in both countries gain through trade-induced growth of their "consumption possibilities" frontiers; consumption options expand in both countries.

For any society to attain its PPF requires technical efficiency in production. Some methods for selecting what and how to produce may be so inherently inefficient that ever reaching true capacity is impossible. (Recall Atilla's formula for "balanced" production.) And even if production is efficient, neither nature nor human industry can provide everything we want; the choices we make automatically eliminate other options.

Some methods of choosing among goods or production techniques may inhibit allocative or distributive efficiency. (Would you like it if all restaurants forced you to select food by tossing darts at their menus?) Important insights into issues posed by scarcity and the need to choose are gained by examining various mechanisms used to resolve competition among people for scarce goods.

Allocative Mechanisms

Self-interested behavior combines with scarcity to yield competition for the good things in life. The form this competition takes is shaped by such **allocative mechanisms** as the market system or government. Some mechanisms alter overt behavior, but self-interest is a universal motive; whether it can even be reduced is dubious. For example, punishing a "selfish" child for not sharing toys may yield more sharing, but only because the child learns to see its self-interest in a different light. Policies intended to force people to ignore self-interest have uniformly failed in tragic ways (e.g., China since 1948, the Soviet Union from 1919 through the 1980s, and Kampuchea during the 1970s).

Every allocative mechanism we will discuss is used in some situations, and in all countries. Thus, societies everywhere have *mixed* economic systems. But people try to "beat the system" no matter which mechanism is used. Each mechanism may work well in certain circumstances, but improperly applying some mechanisms can be disastrous.

The Market System

The **market system** is the major device used in the United States and much of the industrialized world to address economic problems. **Markets** enable buyers and sellers to transact business so that people can share in the gains possible through specialization and exchange according to comparative advantage. Markets range from commodity exchanges where millions of bushels of grain change hands in thousands of daily trades to markets where one huge transaction requires years to complete (major construction contracts). Markets range from geographically limited (kids' lemonade stands) to global (international markets for petroleum engineers). Some deal in a single type of good (brickyards), while others offer thousands of products (shopping centers).

Every market is somewhat unique, but all share certain characteristics: (*a*) buyers who demand goods or the resources that produce them and (*b*) suppliers who make products or resources available if the price is right. Private buyers and sellers trade money for resources or goods in a market economy. Much of this book describes how markets allocate resources and distribute income and production. But before we introduce supply and demand in the next chapter to indicate how markets resolve economic issues, we will look at some nonmarket methods of choosing.

Brute Force

Brute force is a way to decide who gets what. You could lose your life, limbs, or loved ones if you refused to hand over your goods to a bully. Thugs might view brute force as a fine system — but parts I, II, and III of *The Godfather* films illustrate how violence may inspire unending cycles of violence (and how successful films inspire sequels).

Brute force also wastes resources. The arms race between the United States and the USSR from 1945 to 1990 absorbed mountains of resources that could have been used to expand standards of living in both countries and elsewhere. And why should people bother to produce if their output will just be seized?

Queuing

Queuing (lining up) is another way to decide who gets what. First-come, first-served systems operate for mining claims or purchases at bookstores. Queuing can sometimes be efficient. For example, there is a trade-off between time you spend in a checkout line at the grocery store and the time cashiers would wait for customers if there were always enough open checkout lines to provide instant service to everyone. (Your time is costly, but so is theirs.) But if queuing were the dominant allocation mechanism, so much time would be spent in lines that little production would occur—and you would be forced to be very selective about which long waiting line you chose. Should production then be oriented toward goods that have the longest queues? It's hard to say, because people's priorities change. Winter coats in July attract few buyers.

Random Selection

What would happen if all economic questions were decided by **random selection**? Once again little production is likely. For example, if your job were assigned by throwing dice, drawing straws, or other games based on pure luck, you probably would lack ambition, and most of the potential gains from specialization would be lost. Many of us would be round pegs in square holes. Young men are now required to register with the Selective Service. Is a lottery to determine who will serve in the Army fair? Is a draft efficient? Would you want all college educations, new cars, or medical care to be distributed by lottery?

Tradition

Tradition may also be used to resolve economic questions. Feudal European monarchies and the caste system in India operated largely on this basis. In our society, women and minority members have often been pushed into low-paying jobs because tradition has limited their access to better positions. Most of us reject the notion that only senators' children should become senators, or that garbage collectors' kids should necessarily haul tomorrow's trash. Resources and human talent are wasted when tradition alone rules.

Government

Government often plays a major role when basic economic issues must be resolved—but how should government decide? Even if everyone agreed that a democratic government should make all economic decisions, we would still confront the questions of who should be given what and how to produce the things to be distributed. Among the criteria that government might use to distribute production are *equal shares* and *need*.

Equal Shares An egalitarian approach entitling everyone to equal shares might seem a fair way to distribute goods, but equal amounts of food may be more than can be eaten by a person weighing 100 pounds, yet a starvation diet for a 250-pound all-pro linebacker. Should we all be issued equal paychecks and identical housing and clothing? Egalitarianism, moreover, offers few incentives for production. Why should an American farm family work hard to produce wheat if its share is only 1/90 millionth of farm production?

Another problem rises because policymakers are as self-interested as any of us. If you could decide what is equal or fair, you would probably give yourself and your friends the benefit of every doubt. Egalitarianism may regress to the state of George Orwell's *Animal Farm*: "All animals are equal, but some animals are more equal than others."

Need An alternative is for government to distribute goods according to *need*. Unfortunately, it is extremely difficult for anyone to judge someone else's needs. Distribution according to need is inherently costly and imprecise, and causes people to exaggerate their needs. For example, beggars in underdeveloped countries sometimes cripple their children so the children will appear more pathetic to compassionate strangers.

The 1950s TV game show "Queen for a Day" was a bit less brutal. Contestants told heartbreaking tales of children needing operations, unemployed husbands, and foreclosed mortgages. The woman drawing the loudest audience applause was crowned "Queen" and awarded a washer and dryer or trip to Las Vegas. Might you have stretched the truth a bit if you had been a contestant? Do you think that even well-intentioned decision makers might become calloused to the plights of the truly unfortunate and especially sensitive to their own material needs if all allocations were based on *need*?

Still another difficulty is that distribution by need causes special-interest groups to expend resources lobbying to make decision makers aware of their special needs. And what better way to make your needs known than through hefty campaign contributions? The potential for graft and corruption is enormous—few politicians can be expected to be Good Samaritans. Finally, only minimal production is likely. How many people would exert themselves to produce things only for redistribution to the "needy"?

Misallocation If government dictated production and consumption in detail, we could count on policymakers' preferences being reflected, but we should not be surprised if there were only two sizes of everything—too big and too little. The quality and amount of output suffers when rigid decisions from distant managers do not fit local conditions—a common failure in all *bureaucracies* (large organizations), including government.

Government decision makers also face an almost unsolvable dilemma even if they conscientiously try to mirror the varied desires of millions of consumers. People's subjective preferences are often idiosyncratic and tend to be poorly served when other people make decisions. A national vote to mandate what everyone will eat during Thanksgiving, for example, would ignore those who dislike turkey and prefer roast beef or ham. Such decisions are more efficiently left up to individuals and their families so that each family can have its first choice.

Another problem area is that most people work better when their expertise is valued and they are rewarded for good performance. Decisions within bureaucracies, including government, are often rigidly detailed and do not allow workers latitude to make intricate decisions that yield high-quality output. Workers who feel powerless tend to perform lethargically, and may indulge in sabotage. (As a youngster, were you ever tempted to break dishes in hopes that your parents would take over your chores?)

Landscaping an office building located on uneven ground, for example, requires adjusting for variations in soil quality and knowing how much moisture, sunlight, and fertilizer suit different plants and trees. These factors will not be reflected in blueprints intended for thousands of buildings and mandated by a "Landscape Architecture Commission" that never visits the specific site. The point here is that government decision making is often crude relative to the fine-tuning made possible through individual choice (*a*) in consumption, when people have differing preferences, and (*b*) in production, when policies specified centrally are not responsive to local conditions.

You can probably identify situations in which each of the preceding allocative mechanisms seems to work well. Most economic decisions in the United States, however, are made through markets in which prices and productivity largely determine what is produced and who gets it. One important exception is the family, whose decisions are based on varying degrees of command, tradition, and communal sharing, whether equally, by need, or based on some other criterion. The second most important mechanism for decision making in our society is government. In many countries, government is the dominant economic decision maker.

Converging Economic Systems

Every society attempts to cope with scarcity in certain basic ways: (*a*) use of money to convey information about relative prices, (*b*) specialization according to comparative advantage, and (*c*) division of labor. Which allocative mechanisms are used in which situations determines how efficiently a society produces and delivers goods to its members. Brute force, tradition, queuing, and other mechanisms play roles in every society. Economic systems are conventionally classified, however, by who makes decisions and who owns which resources. These issues are crucial in determining the importance of government relative to the market system.

Who Decides?

Some economies, including the United States, rely heavily on **decentralized decision making**. The basic economic questions are largely answered by the price system (as determined by interactions among many independent consumers and producers) in these market economies. At the opposite end of the spectrum are **command economies** in which important decisions rely primarily on **centralized decision making** by government. Elaborate production quotas and plans for distribution to consumers are drawn up and enforced. The command system was epitomized by the Soviet Union until recent reforms swept through many countries previously isolated behind the "Iron Curtain."

Who Owns?

Economic systems are also categorized by whether resource ownership is primarily private or public. Under **capitalism**, individuals own most resources, while most are owned by the state (acting as a trustee for its citizens) under **socialism**. But whether resources are privately or publicly owned is not rigidly linked to whether decisions are primarily centralized or decentralized. Table 3 summarizes the four basic types of economic systems and lists some countries where each system has dominated.

Relatively rapid transformations toward greater reliance on the price system are now being widely experienced in systems that previously operated by command, as described in Focus 2. Such dramatic changes historically have emanated from violent revolution or military conquest. But what elements of capitalist markets are being adopted, and why?

Foundations of Capitalism

Capitalism is not like it used to be, and never was.

Unknown

Capitalism is only a few centuries old, but its ideological roots began emerging when our early ancestors first started staking claims to territory. The hallmarks of "pure" capitalism are private property and laissez-faire policies by government.

Private Property Rights Things are often described as "owned" by someone. You probably own books, sports equipment, and perhaps a car, but what does ownership mean? Generally it means that you have certain rights to use these things in certain ways. **Fee-simple property rights**, the broadest of **private property rights**, include rights to: (a) use a good as you choose as long as no one else's rights are violated; (b) trade or give these

Table 3 *Economic Decision Making*

Every economy uses a mix of allocative resources, but the importance of different allocative devices has differed sharply between countries and, within some countries, across time. Virtually all economies now trying to modernize so that they can compete in an increasingly internationalized world market system are also increasingly relying on decentralized decision making and private ownership.

	Decision Making		
	Decentralized		**Centralized**
Private Ownership	**Capitalism**		**Wartime Capitalism or Fascism**
	United States	Poland (since 1990)	Japan (Tojo)
	Canada	Russia (since 1992)	Germany (Hitler)
	Western Europe	Czechoslovakia (since 1992)	Italy (Mussolini)
	Australia		
Public Ownership	**Decentralized Socialism**		**Communism**
	Yugoslavia		USSR (until 1990)
	Romania		East Germany (until 1990)
	Czechoslovakia (before 1968)		Czechoslovakia (until 1990)
	China (Deng Xiaoping) (since 1978)		China (Mao Zedong)

rights to other people; and (c) deny use of the good to others.

Many property rights, however, are much more limited than this. For example, you cannot shoot people or dogs for trespassing on your land, or burn rubbish in smog-filled cities. You cannot use leaded gas in most new cars. You cannot raise hogs in New York City (or Des Moines, Iowa, for that matter). You cannot abuse your children, burn your house for the insurance money, . . . the list goes on and on. The critical point is that most property rights are circumscribed.

How does a person acquire rights to property? John Locke, a seventeenth-century English philosopher, offered the labor theory of value to justify natural property rights. The *labor theory of value* assumes that all value is created by human labor. According to Locke, mixing your labor with "gifts of nature" makes land and the crops it produces valuable. Thus, he viewed improvements to natural resources as the ethical cornerstones of original property rights, which could then be legally transferred to others.

The idea that mixing labor with material resources creates property rights raises several moral and practical problems. Should those who encounter "gifts of nature" have property rights on a first-come, first-served basis? If you are the first to pour a pint of blood into the sea, should the oceans and all their riches be yours? And what about rules for transferring property? Who should have property rights to things produced by employees? . . . by slaves? Should you own a piece of land, not because of anything you have done, but because you inherited it from your parents who inherited it from their parents who bought it from the family who cleared the land? What if the family who cleared it murdered the previous owners? Should property rights be a matter of convention, so that property rights become ever stronger over time, regardless of whether a transfer of property long ago was legal or illicit? Difficulties posed by these and similar questions for Locke's "natural rights" theory suggest that we need more practical foundations for property rights.

A system of property rights based on brute force would be violent. If your claims were only valid to the extent that you had the muscle to enforce them, many resources would be devoted to aggressively protecting your rights and trying to take from others. Because of this inefficiency, we surrender to government the right to be violent, giving it a near-monopoly on the use of force. Most legal scholars would argue that your property rights are determined by law — what the law says is yours is yours; neither more nor less. Society can be viewed as specifying sets of rights by law and then redefining rights through changes in statutes or legal opinions.

Although most of us think of property rights only with respect to tangible goods, intellectual property rights (e.g., patents for inventions and copyrights for computer software and other written and artistic works) are increasingly important as our world relies ever more on technological advances to cope with scarcity. In fact, property rights and most legal rights are almost synonymous to many economists. For example, traffic laws define how we may use our cars; zoning ordinances, how we may use our land and buildings; and criminal laws, how we must treat our neighbors. We place ourselves in legal jeopardy if we abuse any of them. You do not have the right to slander your neighbor, litter, or to shout "Fire!" in a crowded theater. All laws can be viewed as establishing boundaries governing our uses of both our own and our neighbors' property. Naturally, changes in rights occur whenever laws change; just as laws create property rights, they can take them away. For example, before 1974, you could go 70 miles an hour on most freeways. Between 1974 and 1986, your rights were restricted to 55 miles an hour. Drivers lost some legal rights. When 65 mph speed limits were reestablished for many highways in 1986, some of drivers' legal rights were restored.

Thus, government's major role in a capitalist economy is to establish who owns what and how ownership rights can be transferred. Property rights are implicit in tariffs, welfare programs, and similar laws. Government sets property rights, and it can also change them. But frequent legal changes, even those that seem trivial, may create uncertainty and discourage production and investment.

The major challenger of capitalism is **socialism**, which holds that most resources should be

Are Economic Systems Converging?

[W]hen authoritarian regimes promote economic progress, they are likely to lose their authority, because students, intellectuals, and executives will demand greater civil and political freedom.

Gary Becker[*]

Markets are only one of several possible allocation mechanisms. People universally try to imitate successful behavior. Consequently, the expanding scope of international trade and modern telecommunications are shrinking the differences among people and countries. The successes and failures of different economic systems become obvious when radio and TV signals cross geographic boundaries. As a result, political leaders in less prosperous nations are pressured to adopt allocative mechanisms that have succeeded elsewhere. Widespread changes in fundamental national policies, especially for former Eastern Bloc countries, have been in the headlines for much of the past decade.

Communist regimes have been falling like dominoes. Drives for political freedom and economic reform have toppled communist regimes everywhere except China, Cuba, and North Korea.

A united Germany now dominates economic and political developments in Western Europe. Nationalists have splintered the former Soviet Union into 15 separate nations.

In the 1980s, television and magazines filtering through the "Iron Curtain" made it obvious that Soviet living standards were falling ever further behind those in more market-oriented economies.[†] Embarrassment to communist leaders rising from the success of growing numbers of "Pacific Rim" countries (e.g., Japan, Korea, Hong Kong, Singapore, and Taiwan) created irresistible pressure for economic reform in the former USSR and China, and in most of the countries that they dominated for decades.

From the onset of Premier Joseph Stalin's first "Five-Year Plan" in 1929 until Premier Nikita Krushchev's modest reforms in the early 1960s, the Soviet Union relied on an iron-fisted version of central planning. But Premier Brezhnev's regime was beset by cronyism, corruption, and economic paralysis through-

out the 1970s. Reforms to partially decentralize economic decisions accelerated in 1986, under President Gorbachev. When Boris Yeltsin became president of an independent Russia, the pace of reform accelerated. Yeltsin used broad powers of presidential decree to deregulate large segments of the Russian economy. Painful price increases have slowed the pace of reform in recent days, and there is no guarantee of success, but the direction is clear.

China began to slowly decentralize economic decisions early in the 1980s, with far more success than the former USSR in "decollectivizing" (privatizing) agriculture. Consequently, China has moved from being a net importer of rice and grain to being a net exporter. The former USSR was slow to privatize farming, and remains a net importer of food. Both of these countries increasingly rely on market forces in hopes of matching the economic growth common in Western Europe, North America, and Japan.

Rapid transitions from a familiar economic system to a radically different system invariably create chaos and outcries from some for a "return to the good old days," especially from those who were the beneficiaries of the old system. Consequently,

---

[*]*"Democracy is the Soil where Capitalism Flourishes Best,"* Business Week, 28 Jan 91, p. 18.

[†]*Testimony in July 1990 by Professor Abram Bergson (an expert on the Soviet economy) before a committee of the U.S. Senate indicated that per capita consumption in the USSR is, at most, 25 percent of the level enjoyed by typical Americans.*

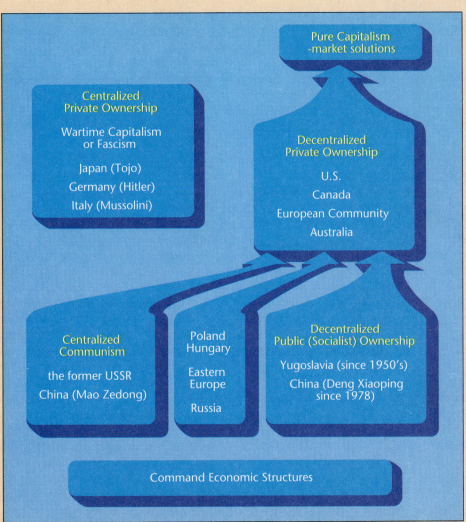

Pure Capitalism
-market solutions

Centralized
Private Ownership

Wartime Capitalism
or Fascism

Japan (Tojo)

Germany (Hitler)

Italy (Mussolini)

Decentralized
Private Ownership

U.S.

Canada

European Community

Australia

Centralized
Communism

the former USSR

China (Mao Zedong)

Poland
Hungary

Eastern
Europe

Russia

Decentralized
Public (Socialist) Ownership

Yugoslavia (since 1950's)

China (Deng Xiaoping
since 1978)

Command Economic Structures

official policies in China have vacillated while moving towards greater reliance on markets, reflecting changes in the relative power of supporters and opponents of reforms. Nevertheless, it appears that economic decentralization and political democratization are, in fact, the real "wave of the future" throughout the world.

When these changes are coupled with increasing government economic regulation in Western economies from the 1930s into the 1980s, it appears that "we" are becoming slightly more like "them" while "they" are becoming a lot more like "us." However, Western politicians, including Presidents Reagan and Bush and England's Prime Ministers Margaret Thatcher and John Major, have increasingly tried to steer their economies toward greater reliance on decentralized capitalism.

owned jointly by all people in society instead of by private individuals. Differences between capitalism and socialism also tend to be very pronounced when we try to specify appropriate roles for government.

Laissez-Faire Policies

That government is best which governs least.

Thomas Jefferson

Feudal monarchs ruled by "divine right," claiming they were chosen by God to lead their countries. Even so, their policies often failed. Vexed by the economic plight of seventeenth-century France, Louis XIV's finance minister asked for advice from a leading industrialist. Without hesitation, the manufacturer responded, *"Laissez-nous faire,"* meaning roughly, "Leave us alone." **Laissez-faire** has ever since been a rallying cry for those who believe that the market system works best with only minimal government.

But what specific roles should government play? Nearly everyone recognizes the need for national defense and police protection. In the economic sphere, a laissez-faire government only specifies property rights and enforces contracts. Under pure capitalism, private individuals own virtually all resources and decide their uses. Market prices determine the range of choices available to us, given our budgets, which are in turn determined by the resources we individually own. Most socialist economies replace the marketplace with central planning.

Private property and laissez-faire policies distinguish capitalism from alternative systems. Ideological battles between advocates of capitalism and socialism have raged for centuries. Capitalism's defenders cite many virtues of the price system, but the two most important are freedom and efficiency. Capitalism, it is argued, allows people maximum freedom because it requires only minimal government. A tradition predating the American Revolution views all "Big Brother" governments as enemies of freedom.

All societies blend elements of both capitalism and socialism, so people everywhere live in **mixed economies.** Thus, for years in the Soviet economy, most fruits, vegetables, and meats were produced for sale in private markets. These markets tended to be efficient relative to other sectors in the Soviet economy, encouraging the wave of recent reforms. In the United States, socialism appears in the form of government-provided education, highways, and medical care for the aged or poor.

Dissatisfaction with the political oppression and economic stagnation common in command economies has recently led to experimentation with the "price system" in many nations that, for decades, were avowedly socialist. A market system requires systems of property rights that, for centuries, have been condemned by socialists as leading to an unfair and exploitative class system. But socialism has not avoided this problem. Command economies traditionally disguised special privileges for elite groups. For example, stores exclusively for elite groups in communist countries typically had a wide variety of quality goods at low prices, while the stores open to the masses suffered frequent shortages, lower quality, fewer goods, and higher prices.

In capitalist countries, government policies often reflect attempts to achieve what some people perceive as greater equity. Where efficiency is our major goal, we tend to rely on the marketplace to provide most goods. The efficiency of capitalism depends on how well it meets consumer wants, given the resources available. A key element of capitalism is reliance on markets to allocate goods and resources. In the next chapter, we examine the forces of supply and demand, which are the devices determining *What? How?* and *For whom?* in a market system.

Chapter Review: Key Points

1. *Households* ultimately own all wealth and provide all resources to firms or government in exchange for income with which to buy goods. Interactions between households, business firms, and government are shown in *circular flow* models.

2. *Comparative advantage* is a guide to efficient

specialization: You gain by specializing in production where your opportunity costs are lowest and trading your output for things other people can produce at lower opportunity cost.

3. A *production possibilities frontier (PPF)* shows the maximum combinations of goods that a society can produce. The PPF curve assumes that (*a*) resources are fixed; (*b*) technology is constant; and (*c*) all scarce resources are fully and efficiently employed.

4. *Opportunity costs* are the values of outputs if resources were deployed in their next best alternatives. Opportunity costs are not constant because resources are not equally suited for all types of production. Increasing a particular form of production invariably leads to *diminishing returns* and *increasing opportunity costs*, so PPF curves are concave (bowed away) from the origin.

5. The idea that "a point of diminishing returns" has been reached is sometimes cited as a reason for ceasing an activity. This is usually a misuse of this phrase — people intend to say that a point of *negative* returns has been reached. An activity is often worth doing even though diminishing returns are encountered.

6. *Economic growth* occurs when technology advances or the amounts of resources available for production increase. Economic growth is reflected in outward shifts of the production possibilities curve; more of all goods can be produced.

7. The choices a society makes between consumption and investment goods affect its future production possibilities curve. Lower saving and investment restricts economic growth and PPF expansion.

8. The shapes of PPFs illustrate different countries' comparative advantages. Trade allows a country's people to consume far more goods than they could produce in isolation.

9. Alternative *allocative mechanisms* include: (*a*) the *market system*, (*b*) *brute force*, (*c*) *queuing*, (*d*) *random selection*, (*e*) *tradition*, and (*f*) *government*.

10. Many different economic systems have been used in attempts to resolve the problem of scarcity. They can be classified by who makes the decisions (*centralized* or *decentral-*

ized) and who owns the resources (*public* versus *private*).

11. Property is privately owned under pure *capitalism* and government follows *laissez-faire* (hands-off) policies. Thus, decisions that answer the basic questions of *what, how,* and *for whom* are decentralized and rely on individual choices in a market system. Under *socialism,* government acts as a trustee over the nonhuman resources jointly owned by all citizens, with many socialist economies also relying heavily on centralized production and distribution decisions.

Key Concepts

Ensure that you can define these terms before proceeding.

circular flow
division of labor
comparative
  advantage
production possibilities frontier (PPF)
law of diminishing
  returns
increasing costs
brute force

queuing
random selection
tradition
capitalism
markets
property rights
laissez-faire
socialism
central planning

Problems and Questions

1. Some health care professionals use the slogan "the best care for the most people" to defend the American medical system against critics. Suppose current levels of medical resources (12% of our total output nationally in 1990) yield the PPF curve going through points *a* and *b* in Figure 7. Complete the following questions and exercises.

   a. Point _____ must be attained to make this slogan true.

   b. Attaining this point would require either more _____ or an advance in _____.

   c. This PPF is concave from below because medical resources _____ in their _____ for different types of medical care.

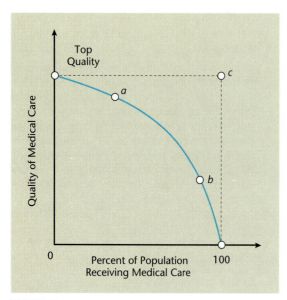

FIGURE 7

Source: J. Michael Swint, "Best Medical Care for the Most People Myth," in R. T. Byrns and G. W. Stone, eds., *Great Ideas for Teaching Economics*, 5/ed. (New York: HarperCollins, 1992).

    d. A PPF that conformed to this slogan would look unusual because it would _____. (This question is a bit tricky.)

2. Suppose Bruno can brew 50 barrels of beer or bake 800 pizzas per year while Gino can brew 100 barrels of beer or bake 600 pizzas. (We use Occam's Razor to assume, for simplicity, that only these two goods are produced.) How much beer is sacrificed for each pizza Bruno bakes? For each pizza Gino bakes? Assume that each initially devotes half of the time to beer brewing and half to baking and that they do not trade. What will be their respective consumption patterns? Demonstrate how both Bruno and Gino can gain through specialization and exchange.

3. Place fish and grapes on the axes of production possibilities curves you draw representing Atlantis, which has a comparative advantage in producing fish, and Vinlandia, which has a comparative advantage in grape production. How are the shapes of these countries' PPFs related to the relative opportunity costs of these goods?

4. Draw a PPF based on Table 4. How is this PPF for woven baskets and canoes shaped? What does this suggest about the opportunity costs of producing these goods? Place an X at point (300, 300) on your graph. What can you say about this point?

Table 4 *Baskets and Canoes (Millions)*

Baskets	Canoes
500	0
400	100
300	200
200	300
100	400
0	500

5. Use the data in Table 5 to construct a PPF. What shape does the PPF have? What does this suggest about the opportunity costs of producing additional mangoes or passion fruit? Draw an X at point (300, 300) on your graph. What can you say about this point given the PPF you just constructed?

Table 5 *Bushels of Mangoes and Passion Fruit (Millions)*

Mangoes	Passion Fruit
500	0
450	200
375	350
275	425
125	475
0	500

6. What would happen to our PPF if outlays (spending) on human capital were increased (human capital refers to the education and skills embodied in an individual)? What does this suggest about countries/cultures that place a high priority on education?

7. Draw five typical PPFs and label their *x* axes "Agricultural Goods" and their *y* axes "Consumer Durables." (Goods that provide services over a number of years; e.g., cars, appliances, and bicycles.) Show how the PPF changes when:

    a. Technological advances are achieved in agriculture.

    b. Technological advances are achieved in the production of consumer durables.

c. The median education level of all workers increases by three years.

d. Investment in capital goods steadily declines over the decade.

e. Millions of acres of arable land are claimed from the ocean.

8. One way to illustrate that an economic arrangement is inefficient is to show how, through some rearrangement, some people could gain with no one else losing. Use this approach to evaluate the following situations:

a. *Brute force.* The Soviet Union and the United States each devote valuable resources to national defense because each side fears attack by the other.

b. *Queuing.* A $100-per-hour lawyer is at the end of a 2-hour waiting line to renew driving licenses, and a vacationing college student is at the front of the line.

c. *Random selection.* A rock star who makes more than $10 million a year is drafted, while an unemployed 18-year-old high school dropout who would be willing to join the Army for a $9,000 salary is not drafted, and does not enlist because the pay is only $7,000 annually.

d. *Tradition.* Quota systems once limited the numbers of women, Jews, blacks, and Hispanic Americans admitted to medical school.

e. *Government.* Procurement procedures sometimes require that imported goods be used to fulfill government contracts only if American-made goods are not available.

9. Use the opportunity cost of time to explain why our welfare system involves long queues for people seeking food stamps, housing subsidies, or aid for dependent children.

10. In what kinds of goods do Americans enjoy comparative advantages over production by foreigners? Is this related primarily to the relative abundance of certain resources here in the United States compared to abroad, or are such influences as technological leads, government policies, highly skilled labor, or sophisticated consumers also powerful in shaping comparative advantage?

11. What mix of allocative mechanisms is used within most American families to decide which family members get what, given limited family income? How are different mechanisms used for different kinds of decisions?

12. Use three different pairs of goods to draw three separate PPFs when the pair of goods considered is produced under conditions of: (*a*) constant costs, (*b*) increasing costs, and (*c*) decreasing costs. Do you think it is possible for a "real-world" PPF to have a shape like this last one?

13. Evaluate the following argument: Grades and athletic medals should be allocated through a market system. The buyers would be the people who value such awards the most, so this would be more efficient than awarding according to merit. For example, if a C student could buy an A from a more diligent student, both could gain from the exchange without harming anyone else in the process.

14. Explain why a family with a fixed budget has a "purchasing possibilities" frontier that is a straight line. But a family's budget is seldom independent of the activities of family members. Suppose that different family members can work for different hourly incomes, and that they differ in their ability to do tasks for the family (e.g., cooking, cleaning, gardening, painting, and household repairs). Discuss whether production and the generation of income within the family is characterized by a family production possibilities frontier that is straight or concave from below.

15. Suppose that government could perfectly control the rate of interest, the rate of inflation, the level of taxes, and the relative levels of wages and prices. How could the government foster economic growth through low consumer spending and more saving and investment via each of these tools?

CHAPTER

Demand and Supply

Why is Bill Cosby paid more than the President? Why are gasoline prices so volatile? And why are frivolities such as jewelry so costly, while such necessities as water or salt are relatively cheap? These and similar questions about why prices are what they are, and why outputs rise and fall, are all answered by the phrase *"supply and demand."*

Supply and demand are as integral to economic analysis as saws and hammers are to carpentry. For simplicity, the analysis developed in this chapter assumes vigorous competition — every market is assumed to contain many potential buyers and sellers. But even if competition is weak, or when other mechanisms (e.g., brute force, tradition, or government) are used, market forces powerfully influence resource allocations. Your basic goal for this chapter is a tall order that requires only a short sentence: Learn how demand and supply interact in markets to determine prices and outputs.

We launch this chapter with a discussion of *marginalism* — the idea that most decisions entail weighing the relative costs and benefits of small changes in behavior (e.g., purchases or sales). Then we survey influences on the amounts of goods people buy or sell, and show how demand and supply are linked in markets. After you have worked through this chapter and the next, you should be able to use supply and demand to in-terpret price and quantity changes in the markets for such goods and resources as oil, cocaine, foreign currencies, professional athletes, real estate, air fares, or grand pianos.

Thinking at the Margin

All decisions are at the margin.

Unknown

Adjusting rational decisions to changes in relative costs and benefits tends to be a **marginal** (*incremental*) process. Just as a sheet of paper is bordered by margins, the last few bits or edges of something are its margins. Bankruptcy looms for marginal firms; marginally passing an exam means that you are in danger of failing.[1]

Even large changes can be treated as a series of small changes. For example, people seldom decide in advance to have three brownies. Suppose you just ate a brownie. You then weigh the cost of a second (market price, calories, etc.) against

---

1. Several of these examples are drawn from "The Relevance of Marginal Analysis," by Michael Behr, in *Great Ideas for Teaching Economics*, 5/ed., edited by Ralph T. Byrns and Gerald W. Stone (New York: HarperCollins, 1992).

its expected ability to satisfy your hunger. When the marginal benefits of extending any activity exceed the marginal costs, you proceed, but if marginal costs exceed marginal benefits, you stop (or even reduce the level of the activity slightly). If you eat the second brownie, comparable analysis determines whether you will eat a third. Similarly, firm managers usually adjust operations a bit (*marginally*) rather than deciding whether to shut down or hire 10,000 workers.

Economists often refer to a marginal unit of something as its *last* or *extra* unit, which is often incorrectly interpreted as a specific unit. For example, if there are 30 students in your class, who is the thirtieth? If any student drops the course, only 29 students would be enrolled. Thus, each of you is the thirtieth (marginal) student. (Does that make you uneasy?) Similarly, there is no way to detect the last (marginal) slice from a cherry pie until the rest are eaten, nor is there a way to detect the extra (marginal) worker hired by IBM.

Each unit of any grouping may, in a sense, be the marginal unit. (Marginal changes are commonly written by preceding the symbol for the changing variable with a Greek capital delta (Δ) – e.g., a price (P) change is written ΔP.)[2] Decisions about buying (demanding) or selling (supplying) are based on opportunity costs, which ultimately depend on the relative marginal benefits and costs of goods.

Demand

Buying goods is like voting with money. Firms view "dollar votes" as signals about how to most profitably satisfy consumer wants. Items with the highest prices relative to their production costs earn the greatest profits. Firms compete to provide these items so that the needs consumers

perceive as most pressing tend to receive top priority.

You may wonder if available resources can accommodate everyone's "needs," but "needs" are ambiguous. Most Americans find a car a "necessity," and many of us go through withdrawal symptoms when deprived of television for a day or two. And in a wealthy society like ours, even meals are often recreational and unnecessary.

What things are absolutely required for survival? Life could be sustained for $1,000 a year if, for example, you consumed soybean curd and vitamins, lived in a cardboard shack, and wore secondhand clothes to prevent sunstroke or frostbite. Most of us, however, would view people trying to live so meagerly as still needy. Economists stress consumer demand because "need" is both vague and normative.

> **Demands** *are the quantities of various goods that people are willing and able to buy during some period, given the choices available.*

Consider a typical consumption choice. You probably attend concerts, buy stereo tapes, and watch television. The market price of TV is roughly $0, tapes are about $8, and concert tickets range from $10 to $100 apiece. If you are typical, you probably spend the most time watching TV and the least going to concerts, with listening to tapes (or CDs) falling somewhere in between. This example suggests that the market prices of goods and the amounts consumers purchase are negatively related. Purchasing patterns depend on two sets of relative prices.

> **Market prices** *are the prices charged for goods whether we buy them or not;* **demand prices** *are the relative values subjectively placed on having a bit more or less of a good.*

You buy gum or a frisbee only if they are subjectively worth their market prices to you. Whether market prices and our demand prices are aligned is partially determined by our budgets. Porsches are "worth the money" to their owners, but the rest of us have demand prices for a Porsche far below their market price. Given

---

2. Economic "marginals" often refer to the ratios of changes in one thing in response to small changes in another. For example, the *marginal physical product of labor* is output generated by adding a worker to a production process (Δoutput/Δlabor), and the *marginal propensity to consume* is the proportion spent on consumer goods out of any extra income (Δspending/Δincome).

our budgets, a Porsche subjectively "is not worth the price" to us, and we drive cheaper cars, if we drive at all.

The Law of Demand

Most goods have many possible uses. How extensively a good is used depends on its price. When a good's relative price falls, it is advantageous to substitute it for other goods where possible, while substitutes are used to displace goods that become more expensive. This **substitution effect** of a change in relative prices is the foundation for the law of demand, a basic concept in the economics of consumer behavior.

> The **law of demand:** *All else equal, consumers buy more of a good during a given period the lower its opportunity cost (relative price), and vice versa.*[3]

Substitution is pervasive. For example, caviar is now a high-priced delicacy, but it might replace baloney on children's sandwiches if its price fell to $0.50 per pound. Were it free, we might use it for dog food, hog slop, and fertilizer. We would use diamonds as a base for highways if they were as cheap as gravel. On the other hand, if gasoline cost $10 a gallon, cities would be more compact and we would rely far more on bicycles, walking, or public transit; few people would waste fuel on meandering pleasure trips or hit-and-run shopping. If peanut butter were $50 per pound, gourmets might consider it a delicacy to be savored on fancy crackers at posh parties.

The critical point is that people find substitutes for goods that become relatively more costly, and wider uses for goods that become cheaper. Focus 1 indicates how even people's use of water changes as its price varies.

A facet of the law of diminishing returns partially explains why substitution occurs:

> The **principle of diminishing marginal utility (satisfaction):** *The more you have of any good relative to other goods, the less you desire and are willing to pay for additional units of that good.*

For example, you would probably not find a ninth chocolate chip ice cream cone as satisfying as the first you ate on a given day. This principle applies to demands for wind surfing, hair transplants, affection from your current heartthrob, or any other good.

Another reason purchases of a good rise when its price falls is that the purchasing power of your income increases—so you can buy more of the good while maintaining or even increasing your other purchases. This is the **income effect** of a price change, but income effects tend to be less direct and far less important than substitution effects.

Individuals' Demand Curves

The law of demand's negative relationship between the price of any good and the quantity consumed yields a negatively sloped demand curve.

> A **demand curve** *depicts the maximum quantities of a good that given individuals will purchase at various prices during a given period, all else assumed equal.*

An alternative perspective views demand curves as reflecting the maximum price people are willing to pay for an *additional* unit of a good, given their current consumption. Thus, demand curves reflect the subjectively determined marginal benefits of goods.

Figure 2 illustrates that lower market prices for paperbacks will induce Arlene to buy more books. She buys 30 novels annually when each is

---

3. Note that all influences on consumption of the good other than price are held constant! Throughout economic analysis, this "all else assumed equal" methodology is used so that we can examine, one at a time, the variables that affect human behavior. The Latin term *ceteris paribus* is used by many economists to refer to the idea that "all other influences" on some **dependent** variable are held constant while examining the effect of changing a single **independent** variable. Thus, the law of demand deals with the independent influence of price on the quantity demanded (the dependent variable), *ceteris paribus.*

Substitution and the Uses of Water as its Price Changes

How much purchases are affected by prices depends on the options available. If a good has *close substitutes* (cotton and wool are examples), we may readily switch from one good to another as their relative prices change. In other situations, substitution entails major losses of efficiency or quality (replacing light bulbs with candles, for instance). In extreme cases, adjusting to higher prices may require that we simply do without.

Figure 1 shows how water usage might be influenced by different prices. If water were incredibly scarce and costly because you were stranded in the desert, you might sip only a little to avoid feeling parched and trust your camel to make it to the next oasis without a drink. Once there, the subjective value of water decreases and you would find ever broader uses for water — brushing your teeth,

FIGURE 1   How Water Usage Expands as Its Price Falls

People use water sparingly when it is quite scarce and costly, confining its uses to those most necessary. As the price falls, more and more uses are considered economical.

washing, and so on. Water flows down city streets when people water their lawns only if its price is incredibly low.

$1, only 10 at $5, and none if the price rises to $7 (she might watch more TV or renew her public library card instead). Suppose she currently buys 14 books at an average of $4.20 apiece. Her demand price (the maximum she would pay) for a fifteenth book is $4 (point *a*). Figure 2 also includes Arlene's demand schedule. A *demand schedule* is a table that lists the maximum quantities of a good consumers will purchase at various prices during some period and summarizes points on a demand curve.

Market Demand Curves

Business firms and government policymakers are far more interested in market demands than in individual demands. Firms, for example, are much more concerned about how much they

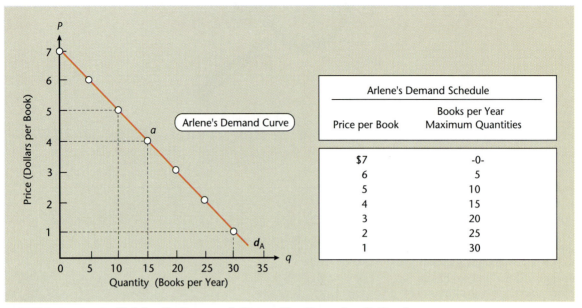

FIGURE 2   An Individual's Demand Curve for Paperback Books

Arlene's demand for paperback books can be shown as a demand curve or schedule. Demand reflects an individual's willingness to buy various quantities of a good at various prices. The demand curve's negative slope reflects the *law of demand*—at lower prices individuals will purchase larger quantities of a particular product. In this instance, more paperback books will be purchased at lower prices per book.

will sell at various prices than about which individuals buy which goods.

> A **market demand curve** *is the* horizontal summation *of the individual demand curves of all potential buyers*.

Figure 3 depicts the demand curves of Arlene and Bert, the market demand curve if they are the only paperback buyers, and the corresponding demand schedules. *Horizontal summation* involves summing the quantities per period that individuals buy at each price. At a price of $5, Arlene buys 10 paperbacks annually while Bert buys none. Thus, at $5, the quantity demanded in this market is 10 books (10 + 0). At $2, Arlene buys 25 books and Bert buys 15, so the quantity demanded is 40 (25 + 15), and so on.

Market behavior is a somewhat erratic process of discovery. Measuring actual demands is complex because markets are volatile and "all else" is seldom equal. (Most parents learn that whether a child is along may be as important as prices in

determining what winds up in the family's shopping cart.) Rapid changes in the many influences on buying and selling yield foggy information about prices and quantities. Economists who estimate market demands must unravel fragmentary data with sophisticated statistical methods beyond the scope of this book. Nevertheless, most influences on buying patterns are conceptually simple.

Other Influences on Demand

A good's relative price is joined by six other broad determinants of the amounts consumers purchase: (*a*) tastes and preferences; (*b*) income and its distribution; (*c*) prices of related goods; (*d*) numbers and ages of buyers; (*e*) expectations about future prices, incomes, and availability; and (*f*) government taxes, subsidies, and regulations.

Tastes and Preferences   People's preferences arise from individual idiosyncrasies (e.g., whether we try to conform or to differentiate ourselves from the crowd) and the styling, quality, and status traits of goods. Most advertising targets preferences among goods subject to consumers' whims, including cars, clothes, and music. "Knockoffs" of the latest fashions and the numerous clones of hit TV shows are evidence that business firms can react quickly to fads.

Consumer tastes and preferences cannot be measured with precision. You should, however, be able to evaluate whether a given change in preferences will raise or lower demand. For ex-

ample, what effect have "animal rights" campaigns had on the demand for fur coats? And what will happen to demands for gym mats and judo lessons if the 1996 Olympics popularize judo as a way for people to stay in shape?

Income and Its Distribution Demands for high-quality goods tend to rise sharply if income grows. Goods for which demand is positively related to income are **normal goods.** Most products and services are normal goods. Normal goods include luxuries that are especially responsive to

FIGURE 3 Individual and Market Demands for Paperbacks

A market demand curve is derived by horizontally summing a series of individual demand curves. That is, for each price we add the quantities that each individual will purchase. At a price of $2, Arlene is willing to purchase 25 books, while Bert demands 15 books. Thus, the quantity demanded in the market at a price of $2 is 40 books. To obtain market demand, this process is followed for each price.

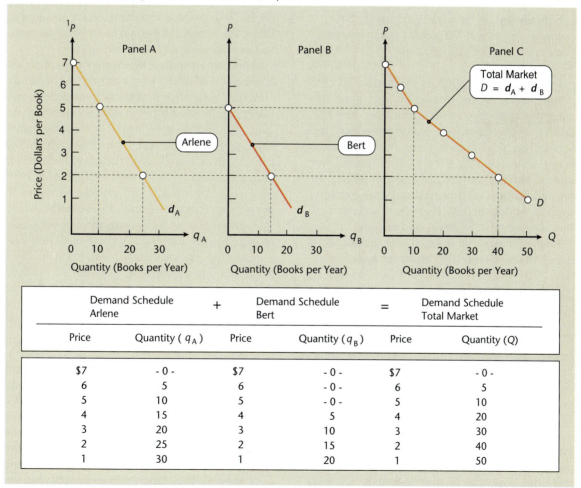

Demand Schedule Arlene		+	Demand Schedule Bert		=	Demand Schedule Total Market	
Price	Quantity (q_A)	Price	Quantity (q_B)			Price	Quantity (Q)
$7	- 0 -	$7	- 0 -			$7	- 0 -
6	5	6	- 0 -			6	5
5	10	5	- 0 -			5	10
4	15	4	5			4	20
3	20	3	10			3	30
2	25	2	15			2	40
1	30	1	20			1	50

changes in income, including resort vacations, jewelry, live entertainment, and yachts.

On the other hand, when a poor family's income rises, its demands fall for such **inferior goods** as lye soap, clunker cars, and pinto beans. When students graduate and get "real" jobs, their higher incomes typically cause them to buy fewer inferior goods. With all else equal, it follows that income redistribution alters the structure of demands: Transferring income from the rich to the poor causes declines in demands for both inferior goods and luxuries, while rising inequality stimulates the demands for both.

Prices of Related Goods
A good's own price is important, but prices of related products also influence demand. Most goods are at least weak **substitutes** for one another.

> **Substitutes** *are the items increasingly purchased in place of the good in question when its price rises, or vice versa.*

For example, if golf balls climbed to $5 each, you would golf less frequently, but your consumption of such substitute goods as tennis balls and racquets might rise. This is especially true for duffers who drop at least one golf ball in every water hazard. When coffee prices soar, sales of tea bags climb. Like golf and tennis, coffee and tea are *close* substitutes. Other examples include Acuras and BMWs; phone calls and letters; or hot tubs, Jacuzzis, and saunas.

Coffee, cream, and sugar are examples of goods that are typically consumed together.

> **Complementary goods** *generate more consumer satisfaction if consumed together.*

Other sets of *complements* are tuition and textbooks; microwave ovens and restaurants' "doggy bags;" gas, tires, and cars; or left shoes and right shoes. Demand for the good in question falls when its complements' prices rise, and vice versa.

Numbers and Ages of Buyers
Population growth expands the number of potential buyers and, therefore, the market demands for most

goods. The public's age structure is also a factor. Lengthened average life spans have swollen demands for golf courses, Ben-Gay, retirement communities, and medical services. Demands for baby products slumped when birth rates fell in the 1960s, but the incomes of orthodontists and producers of diapers and formula recovered somewhat when "baby boomers" began their families.

Expectations about Prices, Incomes, or Availability
Consumers who expect shortages or price hikes in the near future may race to buy storable products now, thus boosting current demands. The onset of the Korean War sent many Americans on buying sprees because shortages, spiraling prices, and rationing were common during World War II; memories of that era stimulated attempts to stockpile many goods, including sugar, flour, appliances, tires, and cars. Widespread shortages drove up prices. Today, some consumers react to news of killing frosts that clobber citrus crops by hoarding frozen orange juice concentrate.

People often splurge when they expect higher incomes. You might buy a car on credit before receiving your first paycheck from a new job; many people fall deeply in debt by spending income faster than they make it. On the other hand, people tend to delay purchases when they expect prices to fall, or if they fear losing their jobs. Expectations of economic downturns typically reduce consumption, causing decreases in overall demand throughout an economy.

Expectations about government actions also reshape buying patterns. A Food and Drug Administration proposal to ban saccharin in 1977 because it was suspected as a carcinogen resulted in shoppers stripping grocers' shelves. These consumers worried more about the hazards of "fat attacks" than about greater risks from cancer.

Taxes, Subsidies, and Regulations
We have focused on how private behavior shifts demands, but regulations and taxes or subsidies also influence demands. From a buyer's perspective, demand is a relationship between the quantity bought and the price *paid*. Sellers, however, view demand as the relationship between the quantity sold and the price *received*. These approaches normally yield the

same results, but taxes or subsidies can drive a *wedge* between the demand price that buyers are willing to pay and the price the seller receives. Figure 4 illustrates this.

Suppose a tax of $1 per paperback novel were imposed. Buyers perceive no change in their willingness to purchase, so they view their demand for paperback books as being stable at D_0. They are still willing to buy 200 million books annually at a demand price of $5. However, publishers view demand as having declined to D_2 because the after-tax prices they receive are reduced by $1 for each novel sold. They would receive only $4 per book if they priced books so that 200 million were bought.

Now suppose the government offered publishers a $1 subsidy per book sold to encourage national literacy. Buyers would view their demand curves as stable at D_0, but from the vantage points of publishers, demand would rise to D_1. They would receive $1 more per paperback at every output level. Regulation may either stifle demand, as it does for such illicit goods as narcotics, or bolster it, as the effect of compulsory education on demands for chalk and erasers demonstrates.

To summarize, demand grows if: (*a*) preferences change so that people are more inclined to buy a good; (*b*) consumer incomes rise (*fall*) in the case of a normal (*inferior*) good; (*c*) the price of a substitute (*complementary*) good rises (*falls*); (*d*) the population of consumers expands; (*e*) consumers expect higher prices or incomes, or they anticipate shortages of the good; or (*f*) favorable regulation is adopted, taxes are cut, or government subsidizes the good. Decreased demands would result if these changes were reversed.

Changes in Demand

A demand curve shows the negative relationship between the price and quantity of a good demanded during a given interval, holding all other influences constant. But what happens if influences on the demand for a good other than its own price change?

Most marketing strategies are aimed at tastes and preferences. Publishers often mail novels to reviewers gratis, hoping to promote a best seller. When male beer drinkers worried about their weight but viewed light beers as tasteless and unmacho, one brewer's ads featured retired jocks debating whether the beer is "less filling" or "tastes great." And the suds flowed and flowed.

Another ploy entails marketing linkages. Kids' lunch boxes, underwear, and toys regularly mirror the latest crazes, from Bart Simpson to Teenage Mutant Ninja Turtles. Firms often try to swell both book and box office receipts by tying

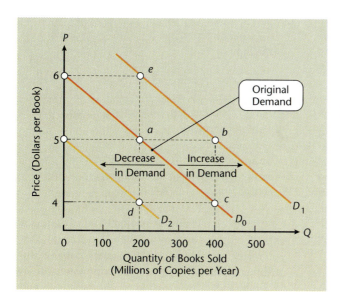

FIGURE 4   Changes in the Market Demand for Paperback Books

Movements along a demand curve (point *a* to point *c*, or point *b* to point *e*) occur when buyers respond to a change in the price of the good itself. It is important to distinguish such changes in quantity demanded (movements along a single demand curve) from changes in demand—a shift to the right (D_0 to D_1) represents an increase in demand, while a shift to the left (D_0 to D_2) is a decrease in demand. These shifts result from changes in influences other than the product price itself. For example, demand increases for most goods when consumer incomes grow; demand declines if consumers begin viewing a good with distaste.

film and books together in their advertising. Figure 4 shows how successful promotion can shift a demand curve to the right (from D_0 to D_1) so that more books are demanded at every price.

If paperbacks are normal goods, demand will increase if income rises. Beginning on D_0 in Figure 4, pay raises cause consumers to purchase more paperbacks at every price, moving demand to D_1. On the other hand, a drop in income normally causes demand to fall (a shift of the demand curve toward the origin — from D_0 to D_2). Naturally, such effects would be reversed if novels were inferior goods.

Now consider changes in the availability or prices of related products. Improved cable service, for example, might transform some readers into TV addicts, shrinking the demand for books (again in Figure 4, from D_0 to D_2). Or if ticket prices for movies fell, substitution could cause demands for books to fall. Take a moment to consider how demand would shift if illiteracy were eliminated, or if consumers' expectations changed.

Thus, *a change in demand means a* **shift** *in the demand curve.* Shifts to the left show falling demand, while rightwards shifts show growth of demand. These shifts result from changes in tastes, incomes, related prices, numbers of consumers, expectations, or government policies. Consumers may perceive no changes in their demands when taxes or subsidies are imposed, but sellers will. Demand rises when consumers become willing to purchase more of a good at every price, or to pay a higher demand price for a given quantity of the good, and vice versa. These relationships are summarized in Figure 5.

Changes in Quantity Demanded vs. Changes in Demand

Distinguishing **changes in demand** from **changes in quantities demanded** is crucial. Changes in the quantity of a good demanded are *movements along a demand curve* and are caused by only one thing — a change in its price. Changes in demand, on the other hand, involve *shifts* of demand curves.

A review of these differences using Figure 4 will help you avoid confusion. Suppose 200 mil-

lion books are now sold annually at a price of $5. How might sales be raised to 400 million novels? The demand curve could grow from D_0 to D_1 so that 400 million would be bought annually at $5 (point *b*); alternatively, 400 million copies would be sold if the price were cut to $4 (point *c*). Increased income is one way to increase *demand* (to point *b*), while simply reducing price yields an equivalent increase, but in *quantity demanded* (point *c*). Similar differences apply to decreases in demand versus a decrease in quantity demanded. A shift in the entire demand curve in Figure 4 from D_0 to D_2 represents a drop in demand. Given demand curve D_0, an increase in price from $3 (point *c*) to $5 (point *a*) reduces the quantity demanded from 400 to 200 million books.

You will spare yourself a lot of grief if you can clearly distinguish changes in demand from changes in quantity demanded. **Changes in demand** reflect influences other than a good's own price; **changes in the quantity demanded** follow changes in the price of the good. Thus, a price change for computer diskettes yields a change in the quantity demanded, but changes in the prices of personal computers or software, or in consumers' incomes will change the demand for diskettes. The importance of this distinction will become clear after we show how demand and supply are linked in markets.

Supply

Transactions require both buyers and sellers. Thus, demand is only one aspect of decisions about prices and the amounts of goods traded; supply is the other.

> **Supply** *refers to the outputs sellers will provide under alternative conditions during a given period.*

One critical condition is that producers must expect to gain by selling their outputs or they will refuse to incur production costs. This section outlines some influences on firms' decisions to produce and sell.

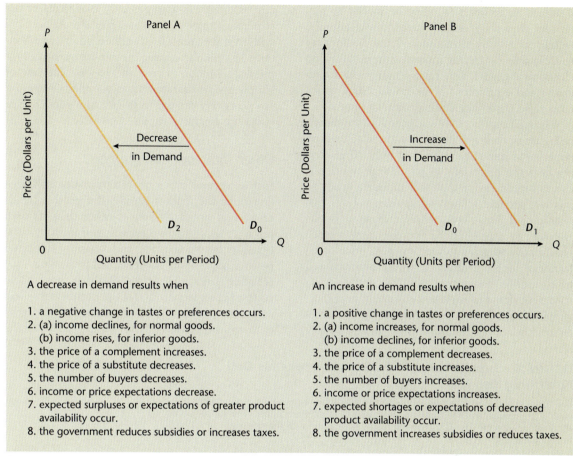

Panel A

Price (Dollars per Unit)

D_2 D_0

← Decrease in Demand

0   Quantity (Units per Period)   Q

A decrease in demand results when

1. a negative change in tastes or preferences occurs.
2. (a) income declines, for normal goods.
   (b) income rises, for inferior goods.
3. the price of a complement increases.
4. the price of a substitute decreases.
5. the number of buyers decreases.
6. income or price expectations decrease.
7. expected surpluses or expectations of greater product availability occur.
8. the government reduces subsidies or increases taxes.

Panel B

Price (Dollars per Unit)

D_0 D_1

Increase in Demand →

0   Quantity (Units per Period)   Q

An increase in demand results when

1. a positive change in tastes or preferences occurs.
2. (a) income increases, for normal goods.
   (b) income declines, for inferior goods.
3. the price of a complement decreases.
4. the price of a substitute increases.
5. the number of buyers increases.
6. income or price expectations increases.
7. expected shortages or expectations of decreased product availability occur.
8. the government increases subsidies or reduces taxes.

FIGURE 5 **Factors Causing Shifts in Demand**

The Law of Supply

Producers' decisions about the amounts to sell yield the law of supply.

> The **law of supply:** *All else equal, higher prices induce greater production and offers to sell more output during any given period, and vice versa.*

The law of supply occurs, in part, because higher prices provide incentives to expand production. More importantly, attempts to expand output ultimately succumb to diminishing returns; increasing costs occur when returns diminish because, as larger numbers of costly "doses" of resources are applied, output may grow, but less than proportionally. When this happens, higher prices are needed to induce suppliers to produce and sell their goods.

The Supply Curve Just as the law of demand yields *negatively* sloped demand curves, the law of supply generates *positively* sloped supply curves.

> A **supply curve** *shows the maximum amounts of a good that firms are willing to furnish during a given time period at various prices.*

A different perspective views the same supply curve as showing the minimum prices that will induce specific quantities supplied.

The positive slopes of supply curves reflect eventual increases in costs per unit when output grows because firms: (*a*) ultimately encounter diminishing returns; (*b*) may be forced to pay current workers overtime wages for extra hours; or (*c*) successfully attract more labor or other resources only by paying more for them. Working closer to capacity also causes more scheduling errors and equipment breakdowns. Such problems raise costs when firms increase output.

A typical supply curve and schedule are shown in Figure 6. Dell will produce and sell 40 million paperbacks annually at $6, but only 10 million books if the price falls to $3. A **supply price** is the minimum price that will induce a seller to increase production beyond its current level. For example, if Dell were selling 9 million books annually at a price of $2.95, the market price would have to grow to Dell's supply price of $3 (point *a*) before production would be expanded to 10 million books annually.

Market demand curves horizontally sum individual demands. Similarly, **market supply curves** entail horizontally summing all firms' supply curves. Figure 7 assumes only two firms in the paperback market, Dell and Bantam. At $3, Dell will produce and sell 10 million books, and Bantam, 15 million, making the annual quantity supplied 25 million books, and so on. The law of supply asserts that quantities supplied per period are positively related to prices; as a good's price rises, the quantity supplied grows.

Other Influences on Supply

Just as several types of determinants influence demands, the market supply of a good depends on several broad influences other than its own price. A supply curve reflects the positive relationship between price and quantity supplied per period, holding constant: (*a*) technology; (*b*) resource costs; (*c*) prices of other producible goods; (*d*) expectations; (*e*) the number of sellers in the market; and (*f*) taxes, subsidies, and government regulations. The supply curve shifts

FIGURE 6 Supply Curve of Paperback Books for Dell Publishing Co., Inc.

The supply curve and schedule represent the maximum amounts of a good firms are willing to produce and sell during a given period at different prices. The supply curve depicted reflects the *law of supply*—at higher prices, more of the good will be offered to the market.

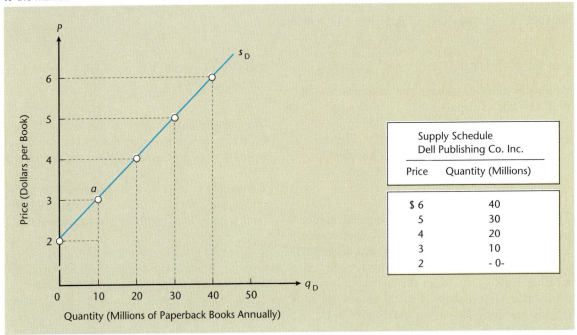

Supply Schedule Dell Publishing Co. Inc.	
Price	Quantity (Millions)
$ 6	40
5	30
4	20
3	10
2	- 0-

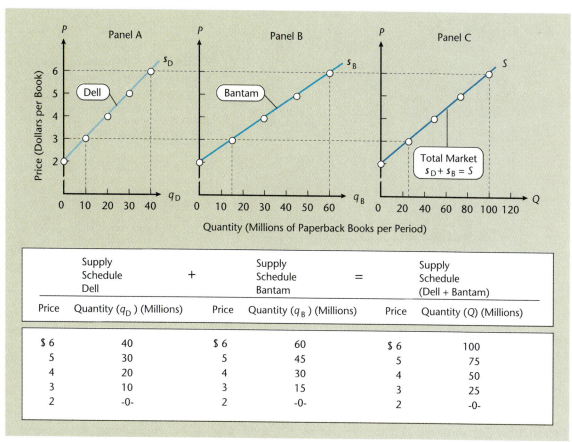

	Supply Schedule Dell		+		Supply Schedule Bantam		=		Supply Schedule (Dell + Bantam)	
Price	Quantity (q_D) (Millions)			Price	Quantity (q_B) (Millions)			Price	Quantity (Q) (Millions)	
$ 6	40			$ 6	60			$ 6	100	
5	30			5	45			5	75	
4	20			4	30			4	50	
3	10			3	15			3	25	
2	-0-			2	-0-			2	-0-	

FIGURE 7   Individual Firm and Market Supply Curves for Paperback Books

The supplies of all producing firms are added horizontally to obtain market supply. For example, at $6 per paperback, Dell will furnish 40 million and Bantam 60 million books. Thus, the quantity supplied at $6 per paperback is 100 million books. The same procedure is followed for all possible prices to obtain the market supply curve.

when there are changes in any of these influences, which operate primarily by altering the opportunity costs of producing and selling.

Changes in Supply

Figure 8 illustrates increases in supply by shifts of the supply curve outward and to the right, while movements upward and to the left reflect declines in supply. Along supply curve S_0, 50 million books are supplied at $5 per novel. If supply grows to S_1, 80 million are supplied at $5. If supply falls to S_2, only 30 million books will be offered at $5 each. Thus, an increase in the supply

of a good means that more is available at each price; the supply price required for each output level falls. On the other hand, decreases in supply raise supply prices (the minimum required per unit to induce extra production).

Caution: Supply curve movements may seem confusing; the shift from S_0 to S_1 is vertically downward even though supply is rising. Always think of horizontal movements *away* from the price axis as increases, and shifts *toward* the price axis as decreases. This rule also works for shifts of demand curves. After all, quantity is measured along the quantity axis.

Parallels between our development of supply

FIGURE 8 Changes in the Supply of Paperback Books

Movements along a supply curve occur when sellers respond to a change in a good's own price. It is important to distinguish such changes in quantity supplied (movements along a single supply curve) from changes in supply—the supply curve will shift if one or more of its determinants change. With the exception of the number of sellers in the market, these determinants operate by changing the costs of production and sales. For example, if the price of paper fell, supply would increase from S_0 to S_1. Or if translations of foreign novels became less costly for publishers to acquire, supply would grow; but if writers insisted on bigger royalty checks, supply would decline, shifting from S_0 to S_2.

and earlier discussions of demand may correctly have led you to expect that shifts in supply result from changes in one or more of the influences on supply. Supply shifts when the way these influences affect production costs change.

Production Technology Technology encompasses the environment within which resources are transformed into outputs. It includes such influences on production costs as the state of knowledge, the qualities of resources, and such natural phenomena as physical laws (e.g., gravity) and weather. Costs fall and supply grows when technology advances.

Consider innovations in markets for calculators and computers. Massive desktop calculators cost $400 to $2,000 in the 1960s. New technology enabled cheap microchip processors to displace mechanical calculators from the market, and computer capacity that once occupied huge rooms now fits in a briefcase. Supplies soared and prices fell, so $5 hand-held calculators are now common. If transportation technology had advanced as rapidly, you could now travel to Mars and back on a teacup of gasoline.

There are occasions, however, when technology regresses and drives up costs. For example, a plague of locusts might shrivel food output, or a nuclear war could blast us back to the Stone Age. Although technology is hard to quantify, you should be prepared to predict whether a given technological change will boost or inhibit supply.

Resource Costs Supply declines when resource costs rise. Higher wages, rents, interest rates, or prices for raw materials raise costs, squeeze profits, and shrink supplies. For example, higher coal prices raise the cost of steel and reduce incentives to produce. Conversely, falling resource prices cause supply to grow. Thus, lower fertilizer prices expand farm outputs.

Prices of Related Producible Goods Most firms can produce a variety of goods, so changes in the prices of other potential outputs can affect the supply of the current good. Price hikes increase the quantity of a good supplied by using resources that would be available for other types of production. Shirtmakers, for example, might switch to sewing parachutes if skydiving became more popular and profits from sewing parachutes grew. The supply of shirts would fall because their opportunity costs of production (the value of the parachutes sacrificed by producing shirts) would rise. Similarly, if corn prices rose, farmers might plant more corn and reduce the soybean supply. These sets of goods are examples of *substitutes in production*.

Iraq, Kuwait, and the Supply of Oil

The specter of a 1970's-style "energy crisis" is raised whenever major oil-producing countries become embroiled in conflicts. Iraq's 1990 invasion of Kuwait quickly pushed up oil prices; gasoline prices rose an average of 30 cents per gallon within days.

Most American drivers viewed this as clear evidence of unethical "profiteering" by major U.S. oil companies. After all, how can the cost of gasoline already stocked in a service station's storage tank be affected by events thousands of miles away? But firms dealing with storable goods have alternatives to sell now or later. Gasoline sold today is not available for sale at a later date at a potentially higher price. Thus, expected price hikes immediately raise the opportunity costs of goods sold today.

The Iraqi invasion of Kuwait created expectations of price hikes that immediately raised the opportunity cost of oil, and thus reduced the supply of gasoline. Many U.S. oil companies did gain from this conflict in the Middle East; their inventories increased in value immediately, just as homeowners gain when housing prices climb. But did consumers necessarily lose because of "profiteering"?

When dealers raised prices, the amount of gasoline consumers demanded was reduced. This conserved fuel, and consequently increased the supply of gasoline available at a later date when gasoline was expected to sell at a much higher price. This involuntary form of conservation, even though unpleasant from the short-run vantage points of drivers, undoubtedly contributed to cuts in gas prices in early 1991.

On the other hand, when goods are by-products (beef and leather, for example), an increase in the price of one **joint product** yields an increase in the supply of the other; production is complementary among such goods. For example, hikes in the price of honey will induce a greater quantity of honey supplied, and the supply of beeswax will grow automatically even if its price falls.

Producers' Expectations Firms that expect higher output prices in the near future usually increase production quickly. They may also expand their productive capacity by, for example, acquiring new buildings or investing in new equipment and machinery.

Durable goods are easily stored products. Producers of durables who expect prices to rise will try to temporarily stockpile their output, intending to sell their expanded inventories after prices rise. Short-term withholding of products from the market triggers higher prices that, in the longer term, generate larger supplies. Focus 2 illustrates, however, how such short-term reductions of supply often dismay consumers.

The longer term effect of expectations of rising prices is that supplies of durable goods grow when (a) swollen inventories are sold, and (b) new investments become productive. Such adjustments tend to reduce supply when prices are expected to rise, but if producers' expectations are correct, supply will be larger in the future to partially dampen upward pressures on prices. Conversely, expectations of lower prices often cause firms to sell much of their current inventory; the short-run supply grows and consumers enjoy lower prices temporarily, but smaller long-run supplies eventually drive up prices.

Adjustments of this type occur regularly when agricultural firms try to time their sales to obtain the highest prices. For example, ranchers increased breeding but reduced cattle shipments to the market temporarily in 1988. This lowered the beef supply and raised 1988 prices, but prices fell by 1990 when these extra cattle were finally marketed.

Nondurable goods are not easily inventoried. Adjustments to expected price hikes are very different if storage is impossible. For example, newspaper publishers who expected a booming market to soon justify higher prices could not store news, but would probably increase the supply of newspapers quickly, partially to justify expanding capacity and partially to hook more customers into reading the firm's paper each day.

Other types of expectations also sway production and sales. For example, a steel company may cut current supplies and try to expand output and inventories if it expects a strike. This allows the firm to serve some customers during the strike. Generalizing about how changing expectations affect supply is difficult, however, because these effects vary with the types of expectations, products, and technologies. A profitable market can attract a lot of new sellers. The evidence is the proliferation of clones whenever a particular new item sells well.

Number of Sellers   More producers generate more output. Thus, as the number of sellers in a particular market increases, the supply also increases (shifts to the right).

Taxes, Subsidies, and Government Regulation   Government policies affect supply as powerfully as they influence demand. From the sellers' vantage point, supply is the relationship between the price *received* and the units produced and sold. Buyers perceive supply as the relationship between the quantities available and the prices *paid*. Again, taxes or subsidies cause these prices to differ. In Figure 8, a subsidy to buyers of $1 per book yields no change in the original supply curve (S_0) from the perspective of sellers. But buyers would perceive an

increase in supply from S_0 to S_1, which is the same as a price cut of $1 for every quantity purchased. For example, 50 million paperbacks could now be sold for a $4 retail price (point *b*).

Taxes and subsidies provide simple examples of how government policies create differences between sellers' and buyers' supply curves. Regulations may either raise or lower supplies, depending on how they affect production costs. For example, policies to protect the environment drive up costs and reduce supply for production processes that generate pollution (e.g., tanning leather, which fouls water), while reducing the costs and increasing the supplies of certain other goods (e.g., fresh fish).

In sum, supply decisions are molded by several influences other than a product's price. Specifically, the supply of a good grows (the curve shifts rightwards) if: (*a*) costs decline because resource prices fall or technology improves; (*b*) substitute goods that firms can produce decline in price; (*c*) the price of a joint product rises; or (*d*) the number of suppliers increases. Expectations of higher prices normally reduce supplies in the short term and enlarge supplies in a longer term if goods can be inventoried, but results are uncertain for less durable goods. Subsidies tend to expand supply from buyers' perspectives, while taxes tend to shrink supply. The only determinant of supply that does not operate primarily by changing opportunity costs is the number of sellers.

Changes in Quantity Supplied vs. Changes in Supply

A *change in supply* occurs only when the supply curve shifts. A *change in the quantity supplied* (movement along the curve) is caused only by a change in the price of the good in question. Consider an adjustment in quantity supplied caused by a change in the market price. The supply curve stays constant because it is defined by the entire relationship between price and quantity. A change in supply (caused by a change in a nonprice determinant) shifts the supply curve because this price/quantity relationship is altered.

FIGURE 9   Factors Causing Supplies to Shift

(You will learn why this distinction is not trivial after we combine supply and demand curves in a market.) Figure 9 summarizes categories of things that shift supply curves.

Market Equilibrium

It's easy to train economists. Just teach a parrot to say "Supply and Demand."

Thomas Carlyle

Supply and demand go together like diapers and babies or the top and bottom blades of scissors — each seems incomplete without the other. Supply and demand jointly determine prices and quantities so that markets achieve *equilibrium*, a term meaning that all forces for change are balanced.

Buyers and sellers use prices as signals to communicate their wants, and then exchange money for goods or resources, or vice versa. You accept or reject thousands of offers during every trip to a shopping center or perusal of a newspaper. Prices efficiently transmit incredible amounts of information that is relevant for decisions to buy or sell, and make a lot of other information (or misinformation) irrelevant. For example, during the nineteenth century, Ghana exported cocoa to England, believing that the British used it for fuel. Their mistake was not a problem, however, because their decision to produce depended on the price of cocoa, not its final use.

Suppose that every potential buyer and seller of a good submitted demand and supply schedules to an auctioneer, who then calculated the price at which the quantities demanded and supplied were equal. All buyers' demand prices (the maximum they are willing to pay) and all sellers' supply prices (the minimum they will accept per unit for a given amount) are equal. There is market equilibrium, so the market *clears*.

Market equilibrium *occurs when the quantities demanded and supplied are equal.*

The amounts buyers will purchase at the *equilibrium price* exactly equal the amounts producers are willing to sell. Let's examine the sense in which this is an equilibrium.

Figure 10 summarizes the market supplies and demands for paperbacks. (Note that there are more buyers and sellers than in our earlier examples.) After studying the supply and demand schedules, our auctioneer ascertains that at $5 per book, the quantities demanded and supplied both equal 300 million books annually. Sellers will provide exactly as many novels as readers will purchase at this price, so the market clears.

But what if the auctioneer set a price of $6 per book, or $4 per book? First, let us deal with the problem of a price set above equilibrium.

A **surplus** *is the excess of the quantity supplied over quantity demanded when the price is above equilibrium.*

At $6 per book, publishers would print 400 million books annually, but readers would only buy 200 million books. The surplus of 200 million books shown in Figure 10 would wind up as excess inventories in the hands of publishers.

Most firms would cut production as their inventories grew, and some might cut prices, hoping to unload surplus paperbacks on bargain hunters. (Publishers call this "remaindering.") Other firms with swollen inventories would join in the price war. Prices would fall until all surplus inventories were depleted. Some firms might stop production as prices fell; others might permanently abandon the publishing industry.

How much the quantity supplied would decline is shown in the table accompanying Figure 10. When the price falls to $5 per book, consumers will buy 300 million books annually while publishers will supply 300 million books—the quantity demanded equals the quantity supplied. The market-clearing price is $5 per book. At this market equilibrium, any pressures for price or quantity changes are exactly counterbalanced by opposite pressures.

A shortage is created when the price is below equilibrium, so the quantity of a good demanded exceeds the quantity supplied.

FIGURE 10   Equilibrium in the Paperback Book Market

At a price of $6 per paperback, there is a surplus of 200 million books annually. (The surplus is the horizontal distance between the supply and the demand curves when the price is above $5.) At a price of $4, there is a shortage of 200 million books annually. (The shortage is the horizontal distance between the supply and demand curves when the price is below $5.) When the price is $5, quantity demanded equals quantity supplied and the market is in equilibrium.

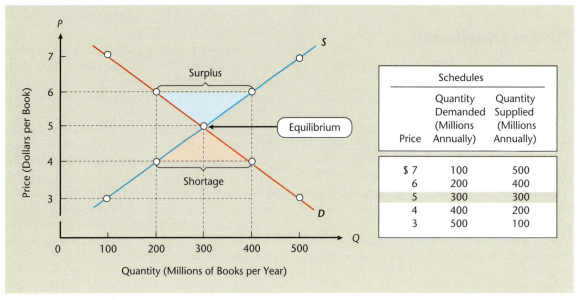

| | Schedules | |
Price	Quantity Demanded (Millions Annually)	Quantity Supplied (Millions Annually)
$ 7	100	500
6	200	400
5	300	300
4	400	200
3	500	100

*A **shortage** is the excess of quantity demanded over quantity supplied when the price is below equilibrium.*

At $4 per book, readers demand 400 million books, but firms only print 200 million; a shortage of 200 million books annually is depicted in Figure 10. Publishers will try to satisfy unhappy, bookless customers who clamor for the limited quantities available by raising the price until the market clears; then books will be readily available for the people most desperate to buy them. (Clearing occurs because quantity supplied rises as price rises while quantity demanded falls; they become equal at the equilibrium price.)

Equilibrium is not instantaneous. Firms experiment with the prices of their output in a process resembling an auction. Inventories vanishing from store shelves are signals that prices may be too low. Retailers will order more goods and, because the market will bear it, may also raise prices. If manufacturers' orders grow rapidly, prices also tend to rise at the wholesale level, quickly eliminating most shortages. People refer to "tight" markets or "sellers' markets" when shortages are widespread. Suppliers easily sell all they produce, so quality may decline somewhat while sellers raise prices. Many sellers also exercise favoritism in deciding which customers to serve during shortages.

When prices are above equilibrium, surpluses create "buyers' markets" and force sellers to consider price cuts. This is especially painful if production costs seem unyielding to downward pressures even though sales drop and inventories swell. (Most workers stubbornly resist wage cuts.) In many cases, firms can shrink inventories and cut costs only by laying workers off and drastically reducing production. The price system ultimately forces prices down if there are continuing surpluses. Evidence that this process may be long and traumatic includes huge losses by major manufacturers and sluggish economies in many industrial states during the recession of 1990–1991.

Price hikes eliminate shortages fairly rapidly, and price cuts eventually cure surpluses, but such automatic market adjustments may seem like slow torture to buyers and sellers. These self-corrections are what Adam Smith described as the *invisible hand* of the marketplace. Long-term shortages or surpluses are, almost without exception, consequences of governmental price controls. We will discuss price controls and other applications of supply and demand in the next chapter.

Supplies and Demands Are Independent

Although specific demands and supplies jointly determine prices and quantities, it is important to realize that they are normally independent of each other, at least in the short run. Many people have difficulty with the idea that demands and supplies are independent. It would seem that demand depends on availability — or that supply depends on demand. The following examples show that supplies and demands are normally independent in the short run.

1. Suppose that nonreusable "teleporter buttons" could instantly transport you anywhere you chose. Your demand price to go on the first, most valuable tour might be quite high, but it would decline steadily for subsequent journeys. Short shopping trips would be economical only if teleporters were very inexpensive. By asking how many buttons you would buy at various prices, we can construct your demand curve for such devices even though there is no supply.

2. Would you have made more mud pies when you were a kid if your parents had paid you a penny for each one? At two cents each, might you have hired some of your playmates to help you? If mud pies were worth $1 each today, might you be a mud pie entrepreneur? Our point is that supply curves can be constructed for mud pies even if there is no demand for them.

3. You might be willing to pay a little to hear some professors' lectures even if you did not receive college credit for gathering the pearls of wisdom they offer. Some professors, however, like to talk even more than you like to listen. A set of such demand and supply curves is illustrated in Figure 11. It is fortunate for both you and your professors that your demands for their lectures are supplemented by contributions

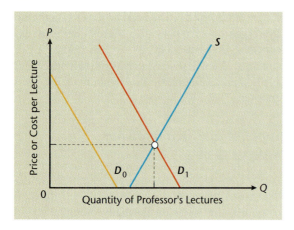

FIGURE 11 The Demand and Supply of a Professor's Lectures

This figure represents the supply of a professor's lectures and students' demand for them (D_0). Without supplementing their demand through lower tuition or contributions (D_1), this professor would have to lecture for free—and, at times, to an empty room (S and D_0 do not intersect at any positive price and quantity).

from taxpayers, alumni, and possibly your parents—because only later and upon mature reflection will you realize how valuable those lectures really were!

We hope these examples convince you that specific supplies and demands are largely independent of each other, and that they are relevant for markets only when they intersect at positive prices. Markets establish whether the interests of buyers from the demand side are compatible with the interests of sellers from the supply side, and then coordinate decisions where mutually beneficial exchange is possible. Keep this in mind as you study the applications of supply and demand in the next chapter.

Chapter Review: Key Points

1. Rational decision making is governed by evaluations of the relative benefits and costs of *incremental* or *marginal* changes.

2. The *law of demand*. People buy less of a good per period at high prices than at low prices. *Demand curves* slope downward and to the right, and show the quantities demanded at various prices for a good.

3. Consumers buy more of a good per period only at lower prices because of:

   a. The *substitution effect*—the cheaper good will now be used more ways as it is substituted for higher-priced goods.

   b. *Diminishing marginal utility*—consuming the additional units ultimately does not yield as much satisfaction as consuming previous units, so demand prices fall as consumption rises.

   c. The *income effect*—a lower price for any good means that the purchasing power of a given monetary income rises.

4. Changes in market prices cause changes in *quantity demanded*. There is a *change in demand* (the demand curve shifts) when there are changes in influences other than a good's own price. These determinants include:

   a. Tastes and preferences

   b. Income and its distribution

   c. Prices of related goods

   d. Numbers and ages of buyers

   e. Expectations about prices, income, and availability

   f. Taxes, subsidies, and regulations

   Taxes and subsidies shift demand curves from the perspectives of sellers, who are concerned with the price *received* when a good is sold, while buyers focus on the price *paid*. Taxes or subsidies make these two prices differ.

5. The *law of supply*. Higher prices cause sellers to make more of a good available per period. The *supply curve* shows the positive relationship between the price of a good and the quantity supplied. Supply curves generally slope upward and to the right because:

a. Diminishing returns cause opportunity costs to increase.

b. To expand output, firms must bid resources away from competing producers or use other methods (such as overtime) that increase cost.

c. Profit incentives are greater at higher prices.

6. In addition to the price paid to producers of a good, supply depends on:

a. The number of sellers

b. Technology

c. Resource costs

d. Prices of other producible goods

e. Producer's expectations

f. Specific taxes, subsidies, and government regulations

Changes in prices cause *changes in quantities supplied*, while changes in other influences on production or sales of goods cause shifts in supply curves that are termed *changes in supply*.

7. When markets operate without government intervention, prices tend to move toward *market equilibrium*, so quantity supplied equals quantity demanded. At this point, the demand price equals the supply price.

8. When the market price of a good is below the intersection of the supply and demand curves, there will be *shortages* and pressures for increases in price. If the market price is above the intersection of the supply and demand curves, there will be *surpluses* and pressures for reduction in price.

9. Supply and demand are largely independent in the short run.

Key Concepts

Ensure that you can define these terms before proceeding.

supply and demand	demand curves
demand price	normal goods
law of demand	inferior goods
income effect	substitutes
substitution effect	complements
diminishing marginal utility	supply
	law of supply

supply curves	surpluses
supply price	shortages
market equilibrium	

Problems and Questions

Use scratch paper to draw graphs illustrating the changes in supply or demand described in problems 1–7. If only one curve shifts, assume that the other is stationary.

1. What happens in the market for bananas if the Food and Drug Administration announces research results that eating 5 pounds of bananas monthly raises IQ scores by an average of 10 points? What would happen in the markets for apples or other fruit?

2. What happens to the demand for college professors in the short run if government raises its funding of graduate school educations? What happens to the supply of college professors over a longer time span? What will happen to their wages during the adjustment periods?

3. What happens if new "miracle" seeds allow grain to be grown in shorter periods and colder climates? If the world population mushrooms because starvation ceases to be so widespread?

4. What happens in the U.S. clothing market if freer trade with the People's Republic of China expands our imports of textiles? If, after two years, import tariffs and quotas are imposed? (Tariffs are special taxes on goods that cross international borders, while quotas are quantitative limits.)

5. Around the middle of every January, the annual crop of mink furs is put on the auction block. How will the following affect the supplies and demands for mink pelts?

a. Wearing fur in public increasingly elicits jeers and harassment from strangers.

b. More fur-bearing animals are classified as endangered species.

c. The price of mink food rises.

d. A sharp, worldwide (1929-type) depression occurs.

e. Higher income tax rates and a new wealth tax are imposed, and the added revenues are used to raise welfare payments.

6. If oil prices suddenly fell after rising rapidly for several years, what might happen to the:

a. Demand for small cars?

b. Demand for luxury sedans?

c. Demand for air travel?

d. Supply of synthetic fabrics?

e. Demand for wool and cotton?

(*Hint:* Many synthetic fabrics are made from petroleum products.)

7. What would happen in the market for lawyers if all civil laws were carefully rewritten in plain English so that contradictions and ambiguities were largely eliminated?

8. Use supply and demand curves to illustrate how the monetary price of color TVs could fall consistently over the past 30 years despite inflation that, on average, more than tripled the absolute prices of other goods.

9. Which of the following sets of goods tend to be substitutes in consumption, and which are usually complements?

a. VCRs and rental video cassettes

b. Salt and pepper

c. Yogurt and ice cream

d. Ballpoint pens and paper

e. Whiskey, beer, and wine

10. Which of the following sets of goods are substitutes in production, and which are either joint products or complementary in production?

a. Wool and cotton

b. Oranges and honey

c. Lumber and paper

d. Eggs and hash browns

e. Footballs and ham

11. Why will the demands for both inferior goods and luxury goods fall if income is redistributed from the rich to the poor? Name at least three goods for which sales would suffer if income were redistributed. Name three other goods for which sales would rise.

12. Is the law of demand refuted if snobs are willing to buy more mink coats only at high prices, or if some people buy more high-priced aspirin than low-priced aspirin?

13. Imports of oil rose during the 1970s even though prices skyrocketed over the decade. Is this an exception to the law of demand? Why or why not?

14. The law of demand asserts that the quantity of a good demanded will fall if the price rises because people will find substitute goods or will alter their behavior so that they do with less. Does the law of demand hold for people who rely on certain goods to continue living, such as: (*a*) insulin for a diabetic? (*b*) kidney dialysis? (*c*) heart transplants? If not, what would happen to most of these sick people if insulin rose to $800 per dose, kidney dialysis to $10,000 per session, and a heart transplant to $1,000,000? Can you think of substitutions that these consumers could make?

15. Why do some people pay premium prices for "brand-name" goods? All else equal, people will pay more for goods that they perceive as higher quality. And some people will pay higher prices for goods in certain stores than in others, even if they know the goods are physically identical. Does knowingly paying higher prices in fancier stores than in discount stores refute the law of demand?

16. How can a production possibilities curve be transformed into market supply curves for the two goods considered by the PPF?

17. When Cabbage Patch dolls were first marketed in 1983, shortages were widespread and they commonly sold at a premium of as much as 200 percent over the $35 recommended retail price. By 1986, they were frequently sold at a substantial discount. Use demand and supply to explain these price movements. Do shortages and premium prices stimulate or hinder a good becoming a fad?

18. The concepts of average and marginal occur in many areas other than economics. Describe the effects on averages of the following marginal events:

a. What happens to your average for this class if your score on the next (marginal) test is above your current average? Suppose that you do not do quite as well on the final exam as on the next test. How is it possible for your average to rise even though the marginal test score is falling?

b. Patrick Ewing, a 7'2" center for the New York Knicks basketball team, walks into your class. What happens to the average height of people in your classroom? To their average income?

c. Fill in the following table to show what happens to the average temperature in Denver in February if, as the month progresses, the following high temperatures are recorded. (A hand calculator will help.)

Is there a consistent relationship between changes in the marginal (observed) temperature for sequential days and the average? (NO!) What is the simple relation between the marginal (observed) temperature and the average for the month?

d. Explain how an increase in the rate of inflation might still reduce the average rate of inflation over a decade.

e. Can you specify a simple mathematical law governing the relations between marginals and averages, and identify five situations outside of economics where this law is important?

High Temperatures for the Month of February in Denver

Date	Temperature	Average	Date	Temperature	Average
Feb. 1	16°	_____	Feb. 15	31°	_____
2	18°	_____	16	16°	_____
3	23°	_____	17	15°	_____
4	23°	_____	18	23°	_____
5	20°	_____	19	42°	_____
6	26°	_____	20	34°	_____
7	29°	_____	21	14°	_____
8	37°	_____	22	24°	_____
9	24°	_____	23	24°	_____
10	14°	_____	24	48°	_____
11	12°	_____	25	50°	_____
12	22°	_____	26	39°	_____
13	35°	_____	27	40°	_____
14	30°	_____	28	55°	_____

Markets and Equilibrium

Every individual endeavors to employ his capital so that its produce may be of greatest value. He generally neither intends to promote the public interest, nor knows how much he is promoting it. He intends only his own security, only his own gain. And he is in this led [as if] by an **invisible hand** to promote an end which was not part of his intention. By pursuing his own interest he frequently promotes that of society more effectually than when he really intends to promote it.

Adam Smith, *Wealth of Nations* (1776)

How powerfully and efficiently the forces of demand and supply operate to determine prices and quantities depends on the particular goods or resources being exchanged, and on a host of other influences, including the quality of information available, the vigor of competition, and the extent of government regulation. Market forces are at work, however, even where allocative decisions seem dominated by nonmarket mechanisms. For example, laws may forbid certain types of activities (e.g., smuggling or pornography), but prices and quantities are still heavily influenced by the market forces of supply and demand.

We explore the ways prices and outputs move when supplies and demands fluctuate in this chapter. Then we examine how *transaction costs* prevent equilibration from being instantaneous,

and why these costs may cause apparently identical goods to have multiple prices. We also explore how firms acting as *intermediaries* help reduce transaction costs, facilitate equilibration, and stabilize markets. Our analysis then turns to how market forces may cause such policies as *price controls, minimum wage laws,* or the *war on drugs* to yield undesirable side effects that are incompatible with policymakers' stated goals.

There has been substantial disagreement (accompanied by wars and revolutions) over the past century about how efficiently and equitably demand and supply answer the basic economic questions of *"What?" "How?"* and *"for Whom?"* Nevertheless, government policies allowing market allocations are increasingly prominent around the globe — from the United States to the European Community, from the USSR to China, and from South Africa to Argentina. A brief survey of these developments is our final task in this chapter.

The Search for Equilibrium

Some markets are not very stable because consumers can be fickle, forever changing their minds. Changes in income, the prices of related goods, expectations, or taxes also shift demand curves. Fluctuations in the business climate dis-

Adam Smith (1723–1790)

Modern economics is by no means the product of a single mind, but no one has a better claim to the title of "Father of Economics" than Adam Smith, a Scottish philosopher who was internationally renowned even before he published *An Inquiry into the Nature and Causes of the Wealth of Nations* in 1776. This enduring work attracted widespread attention and helped establish economics as a field of study apart from moral philosophy.

The eccentric Smith was a lifelong bachelor who described himself to a friend as "a beau in nothing but my books." He burned sixteen lengthy unpublished manuscripts shortly before he died, but his published remains are literary classics. Smith's *Wealth of Nations* covered the spectrum of the then current knowledge of economics and was the starting point for virtually every major economic treatise until 1850.

This work provided: (*a*) an impressive array of economic data gleaned from his wide reading of history and keen insights into human affairs; (*b*) an ambitious attempt to detail how economic processes operate in an individualistic society; and (*c*) a radical critique of existing society and government. Smith advocated replacing government activities with laissez-faire policies in most economic matters.

Laissez-faire theory greatly differed from *mercantilism*, the conventional wisdom of Smith's era. Among other policies, mercantilism supported (*a*) imperialism in an era when European monarchs competed to colonize the rest of the world, (*b*) grants of monopoly by government to private firms, and (*c*) import restrictions, because it was erroneously thought that countries gained power by exporting goods in exchange for gold. Smith exposed the fallacy of protectionist trade policies by pointing out that the real "wealth of a nation" consists of productive capacity and the goods available for its people, and not shiny metal.

Smith strongly dissented from the interventionist policies prevalent in the eighteenth century and called for a minimal economic role for government. A major point of his argument is that economic freedom is an efficient way to organize an economy. The model of the marketplace was the centerpiece of Smith's inquiry. Decisions freely made by buyers and sellers are coordinated in the marketplace by what he called **the invisible hand** of competition. Competition harmonizes the driving force of self-interest with the public interest, yielding increases in real national wealth.

The freshest idea in Smith's argument is that the public interest is not served best by those who intend (or pretend) to promote it by government intervention, but rather by those who actively seek their own gain in disregard of the public interest. Self-interested merchants engaged in competition can gain advantages over rivals and increase their sales only by better serving consumers. Monopoly, on the other hand, harms the public interest because it restricts output and forces prices up. Smith thought that virtually all monopoly power would succumb to competitive forces if not for governmental protection of monopolies.

---

rupt the supply side; resource prices vary, and technology advances, altering costs and, thus, supplies. Changes in the prices of related products, producer expectations, or taxes and regulations also shift supply curves.

Let's examine in a general way how changes in supplies and demands affect prices and quantities. (You should use a pencil and paper to duplicate the graphing in this section.) We will use the wheat market to explore how Adam Smith's "invisible hand" accommodates changes in the forces that affect markets.

Changes in Supply

Suppose the initial supply and demand for American wheat are S_0 and D_0 in Figure 1; Q_0 bushels of wheat sell at price P_0 at equilibrium point a. If fantastic weather then yields a bumper crop, expanding supply from S_0 to S_1 in Panel A, the market now clears at point b. Price declines from P_0 to P_1, and the equilibrium quantity rises from Q_0 to Q_1. We conclude that growing supplies push prices downward and increase the quantities sold.

Now consider what happens if higher seed or fuel prices raise farmers' costs. Starting at the original equilibrium point a, now shown in Panel B of Figure 1, supply declines from S_0 to S_2. The equilibrium price rises from P_0 to P_2 at point c, while equilibrium quantity falls from Q_0 to Q_2. Thus, decreases in supply exert upward pressures on prices and decrease the quantities traded in the market.

We have held demand constant while shifting supply. We will now hold supply constant and review how shifts of demand curves affect equilibrium prices and quantities.

Changes in Demand

The original demand D_0 and supply S_0 from Figure 1 are duplicated in Figure 2. If rising oil prices stimulated gasohol production from grain, the demand for wheat would grow to, say, D_1 in Panel A. Equilibrium price would rise to P_1, and quantity to Q_1 (point b). Thus, increases in demand exert upward pressures on both prices and quantities.

Now suppose that new dietary findings recommend replacement of wheat bread by oatbran loaf, decreasing the demand for U.S. wheat from D_1 to D_0 in Panel B of Figure 2. The equilibrium price and quantity both fall (point c). Thus, de-

FIGURE 1   Price and Quantity Effects of Changes in Supply (American Wheat Market)

Panel A illustrates that increases in supply put downward pressures on prices. When supply increases from S_0 to S_1, prices fall to P_1 and quantities sold rise from Q_0 to Q_1 (equilibrium point a to point b). The opposite is true when supply declines, as depicted in Panel B. Supply declines from S_0 to S_2, causing prices to rise and quantity sold to fall (from point a to point c).

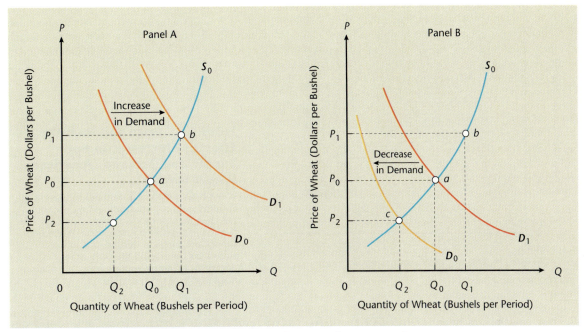

FIGURE 2 Price and Quantity Effects of Changes in Demand (American Wheat Market)

Increases in demand put upward pressures on price. In Panel A, when demand increases from D_0 to D_1, equilibrium price rises to P_1 and equilibrium quantity sold rises as well. As Panel B illustrates, declines in demand (from D_1 to D_0) cause prices to fall (from P_0 to P_2) and equilibrium quantity to decline (from Q_0 to Q_2).

creases in demand exert downward pressures on both prices and quantities.

In Chapter 3, we distinguished a change in demand from a change in the quantity demanded, and changes in supply from changes in the quantity supplied: Changes in demand (*supply*) refer to *shifts* of the curve, while changes in the quantity demanded (*supplied*) refer to movements *along* a curve. Compare the two equilibrium positions in Figure 1. Notice that changes in the quantities demanded result from changes in supply. It would be wrong to say that demand changed; it was supply that shifted. Similarly, Figure 2 shows that changes in quantities supplied are caused by changes in demand. Demand shifted; supply did *not* change. This illustrates how failing to keep your terminology straight in this area can lead to confusion and error.

Please review any of the preceding analysis that seems a bit murky before reading on because now we are going to shift supply and demand curves simultaneously.

Shifts in Supply and Demand

Markets are sometimes bombarded by multiple changes. For example, technology may advance during periods when consumer tastes are also changing. We need to fit each change into our supply/demand framework to assess net changes in equilibrium prices and quantities, which depend on the relative magnitudes of shifts in supplies and demands.

The wheat market is now shown in Figure 3, allowing us to examine what happens when supply and demand curves shift in the same direction. Demand and supply are originally at D_0 and S_0, respectively, with equilibrium price at P_0 and equilibrium output at Q_0 (point *a*).

Assume that the Soviet Union began buying more U.S. wheat in a year we experienced a bumper crop. These events would increase *both* demand and supply in Figure 3. This information by itself leaves us unsure whether the price at the new equilibrium (point *b*) is higher or lower than

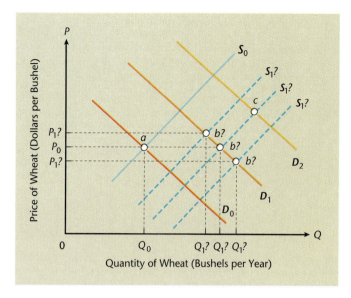

FIGURE 3 Price and Quantity Effects of Increases in Both Supply and Demand (American Wheat Market)

When both supply and demand increase, equilibrium quantity traded will always rise, but the change in price will depend upon the relative magnitudes of the two shifts. When both supply and demand decline, quantity will always fall, and again the price change is uncertain, being dependent upon the relative magnitudes of the two shifts.

P_0, but equilibrium quantity (now Q_1) is definitely higher than its old value of Q_0. The lesson here is that when both demand and supply grow, quantity increases but price changes are unknowable without more information.

You may have perceived that whether the new price of wheat will be above or below P_0 depends on the relative magnitudes of the two shifts. For example, if the Soviet Union's new demand were relatively large and drove market demand to D_2, equilibrium price would rise (point c). Symmet-

ric results occur if both demand and supply decrease, say, from D_1 and S_1 to D_0 and S_0: Quantity falls, but price changes cannot be predicted without more information.

What happens if supplies and demands move in opposite directions? The wheat market is again initially in equilibrium at point a in Figure 4. Equilibrium moves to point b if population growth boosts demand to D_1 while drought cuts supply to S_1. Price increases to P_1, but we need more information to be sure whether quantity

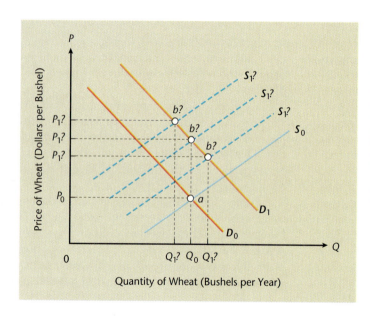

FIGURE 4 The Effects of an Increase in Demand and a Decrease in Supply (American Wheat Market)

How the price changes is predictable when demand and supply curves move in opposite directions, but the quantity adjustment is not. When demand increases and supply falls, price will rise, but the change in equilibrium quantity depends on the nature of the two shifts. When demand declines and supply increases, prices will fall, but again the change in quantity is uncertain without further information.

increases, decreases, or remains constant. In this case, quantity changes depend on the relative magnitudes of the shifts. Thus, if demand rises while supply falls, the price rises, but we cannot predict quantity changes without more information.

Similar results occur if demand falls and supply rises. Thus, declines in demand and increases in supply cause prices to fall, but predicting quantity changes requires more data. Figure 5 summarizes how changes in supplies and demands affect prices and quantities in the short run. A good review of this section is to match the relevant segments of Figure 5 with the possible adjustments listed in its caption.

Market economies are sometimes plagued by volatile prices and production. High prices and abundant profit opportunities cause existing firms to expand and new firms to enter the market, boosting supply and driving the high price down. Low prices and inadequate profits, on the other hand, cause some firms to exit an industry, while the survivors cut back on output and reduce their hiring. This pushes low prices up. There may be long lags between planning for production and selling output, so prices and outputs can swing wildly before finally settling at equilibrium.

Suppose, for example, that wheat prices rose sharply after a drought devastated a crop. The high price relative to cost could cause wheat farmers to overproduce in the next year, driving the price down. This low price could cause discouraged farmers to cut production back too much in the third year, causing the price to again rise far above production costs. And so on. Similarly cyclical price swings have been observed for engineering wages (it takes four years to get an engineering degree) and in other markets in which training and/or production take a long time.

Transaction Costs

Differences between market prices and opportunity costs occur because of *transaction costs*. We often refer to "the price" of a good, as if each good had only one price at a given time. But gas prices differ between service stations, and gro-cery stores commonly charge different prices for what seem to be the same foods. How can this be reconciled with economic models that arrive at a single price? The answer lies in transaction costs.

Transaction costs *are the costs associated with* (a) *gathering* information *about prices and availability, and* (b) mobility, *or transporting goods, resources, or potential buyers between markets.*

The value of the time you take reading ads and driving to a store to take advantage of a bargain is one form of transaction costs. Gasoline used and wear and tear on your car in gathering information and locating goods are also transaction costs. Would you drive 50 miles to save $5 by going from store to store, or would you simply go to a department store or shopping mall?

If transaction costs were zero, sellers would always sell at the highest possible price, and buyers would only pay the lowest possible price. The highest and lowest possible prices would therefore have to be identical, and only one price could exist for identical goods. Thus, transaction costs, in which the value of time plays an important role, account for ranges in the monetary prices of any single good. Paying a higher monetary price is often efficient if acquiring the good at a lower monetary price entails high transaction costs.

Transaction costs also help explain why prices sometimes move erratically towards equilibrium. If information were perfect and mobility instantaneous and costless, prices would be driven to equilibrium like arrows shot at a bull's-eye by an expert archer. Instead, prices may resemble basketballs — bouncing up, down, and sideways before finally "reaching equilibrium" by going through the hoop. The speed of equilibration is negatively related to the costs of mobility and information.

People search for bargains only to the extent that they expect the benefits from shopping (price reductions) to exceed the transaction costs they expect to incur. We live in an uncertain world and constantly make decisions based on incomplete or inaccurate information. Acquiring better market information is a costly process, as is moving goods or resources between markets.

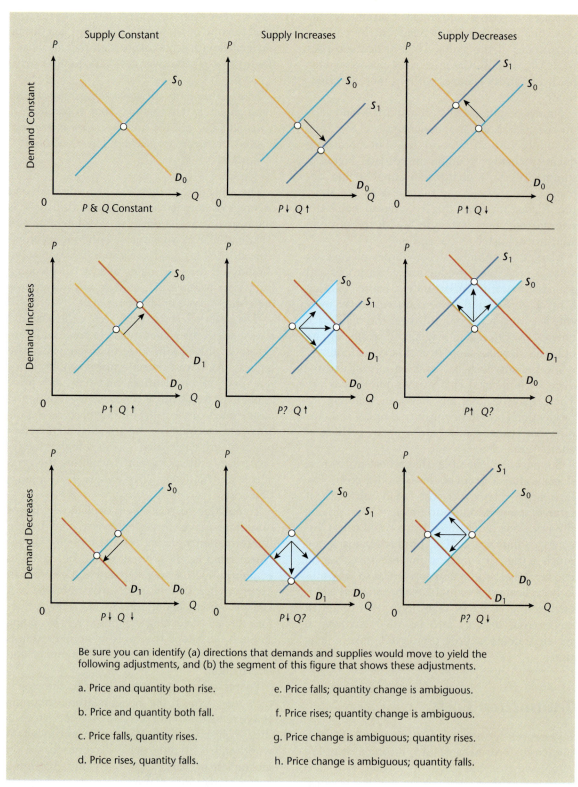

FIGURE 5 Summary of Price and Quantity Responses to Changing Demands and Supplies

Intermediaries help minimize these transaction costs.

Intermediaries

Retail stores and wholesalers are examples of operations that cut transaction costs.

> **Intermediaries** *specialize in reducing uncertainty and cutting the transaction costs of conveying goods from original producers to the final users, often transforming the good to make it more compatible with ultimate users' demands.*

Surprisingly, price swings are moderated by successful *speculators*, who are special types of intermediaries.

Intermediaries ("middlemen") are sometimes identified as villains who cause inflation, shortages, or a host of other economic maladies, but they actually absorb risks and help move prices towards equilibrium. This reduces transaction costs and facilitates getting goods to those who desire them most while boosting the incomes of the original suppliers. In fact, intermediaries reduce opportunity costs to consumers, and speculators tend to reduce both the volatility of prices and the net costs of products.

Have you ever paid more than you had to for anything? Your answer must be NO if you behave rationally. You might object that, say, buying apples from a grocery store costs more than buying them from an apple grower. But if you bought from a store, it must have charged less than if you had bought the apples directly from the orchard, after considering all information costs, travel, potential spoilage, and time entailed in going to the orchard. Otherwise, you would have bought directly from the apple grower.

Similarly, monetary prices at convenience stores are higher than at supermarkets. However, after we adjust for greater accessibility because of the longer hours typical of convenience stores and the frequent extended waits at supermarket checkouts, the customers of convenience stores must be paying less, or they would buy elsewhere.

One important way in which intermediaries reduce transaction costs is by absorbing risk. Quality is often somewhat variable. Apples, for example, range from rotten to those that would win prizes at county fairs. Consumers would be distraught if they bought a few apples to eat fresh, but wound up with fruit suitable only for applesauce. Orchard owners specialize in growing apples, but might not be geared to assuring top quality to every consumer of every apple. Another problem is that an individual customer may buy apples only at irregular intervals, while individual orchards have tons of apples available at some times, and none at others. Timing between individual purchases and harvesting at a given orchard may not be synchronous.

Apple wholesalers and grocers, however, purchase such large quantities that they are accustomed to dealing with a mix of good and bad apples. They also sell to so many customers that no sale to any single final buyer is crucial. This assures apple eaters high quality and allows orchard owners to concentrate on production. Thus, intermediaries absorb risks that ultimate producers and consumers want to avoid.

Transportation and information costs, time, and risk all contribute to transaction costs. No matter how hard you try, we doubt that you can come up with a single example where, after considering all transaction costs, you paid more than the lowest price possible for any good.

Arbitrage Profit is ensured if you can buy low and sell high.

> **Arbitrage** *is the process of buying at a lower price in one market and selling at a higher price in another, where the **arbitrager** knows both prices and the price differential exceeds transaction costs.*

For example, if gold is priced at $328 per ounce in London while the New York price is $337 per ounce, an arbitrager can make $9 per ounce (minus transaction costs) by buying in London and selling in New York.

Traders constantly seek riskless profits through arbitrage. When intermediaries buy in a market with a lower price, demand is increased, which drives up the price. When they sell in the market with the higher price, the greater supply pushes the price down. Thus, arbitrage reduces transaction costs and forces relative prices toward equality in all markets. This intermediary activity promotes economic efficiency by linking markets that are spread geographically, so goods are moved from areas where they have a relatively low value to markets where the goods are more highly valued.

Speculators

Speculation is unlike arbitrage, because profits are not guaranteed.

> **Speculators** *derive income by buying something at a low price and storing it in the hope of selling it* **later** *at a higher price.*

This time delay makes speculation risky. Speculators can make fortunes if they predict correctly, but they go broke and cease being speculators if they are frequently wrong.

If speculators believe that prices will soon rise, then they expect demands to grow faster than supplies. They respond by buying now, increasing the *current* demand and price. For example, expectations that bacon prices will soon rise cause speculators to buy and store pork bellies (the source of bacon) right now, driving up the current price. Does this cause prices to be higher later? NO! If speculators are more often right than wrong, they sell when prices are high and add to the supply at that time. When bacon speculators sell the stored pork bellies, the price of bacon will be reduced. Thus, successful speculation shifts the consumption of a good from a period in which it would have a relatively low value into a period when its value to consumers is higher.

Correct speculation reduces price peaks and boosts depressed prices, so successful speculators reduce price swings and, by absorbing some risks to others of doing business, raise the net incomes of the ultimate suppliers. Overall, costs fall, because speculators absorb risks and the prices consumers pay are lower and more predictable.

Markets and Public Policy

The level of the sea is not more surely kept than is the equilibrium of value in Society by supply and demand; and artifice or legislation punishes itself by reactions, gluts, and bankruptcies.

Ralph Waldo Emerson

No economic system distributes income and allocates resources to everyone's satisfaction. Our mixed economy relies most on the market system, with government coming in a close second — the list of regulations and governmentally provided goods and services ranges from police and fire protection to dog leash laws and financial regulations, from national defense to education and interstate highways, and on and on. In this section, we look at how some government policies may affect market outcomes.

Some regulations inefficiently raise costs. If production costs rise by more than the benefits of a regulation, this creates an inefficient wedge between buyers and sellers. Let's see how specific laws and regulations may cause inefficiency.

Price Controls

You can't repeal the Laws of Supply and Demand.

Anonymous

Influences on supplies and demands change continuously, so we might expect relative prices to bounce around like ping-pong balls. We all want low prices for the things we buy and high prices for the things we sell. When prices rise or fall, some people gain while others lose, but there is not much that any individual can do alone to directly control market forces. Special-interest groups, however, often succeed in persuading government to establish *price controls*.

Price Ceilings Regulatory attempts to control monopoly power or inflation often entail price controls.

> *A* **price ceiling** *is a* **maximum** *legal price.*

Price ceilings set above equilibrium prices are usually as irrelevant as laws limiting joggers to 65 miles per hour. Price ceilings below the equilibrium price, however, keep monetary prices, but not opportunity costs, from rising and, unfortunately, also create shortages. Shortages needlessly absorb resources, because less efficient mechanisms are used when the price mechanism does not operate. Severe shortages were the major result when President Nixon imposed a wage and price freeze in August 1971. This price freeze initially covered virtually all markets in the United States, although controls were phased out and then largely abandoned by 1976.

Suppose that a price ceiling of $1 per gallon is set in the market for gasoline depicted in Figure 6. The quantity of gasoline demanded will be 75 million gallons daily, but the quantity supplied will be only 30 million gallons. There will be an *excess demand* (or shortage) of 45 million gallons. Who will get gasoline? People who bribe service station attendants, or who are able to persuade government to give them priority access, or those who wait through long lines. Even people who waited for 2 to 4 hours in gasoline queues in 1974 and 1975 often went without because the pumps ran dry.

But ceilings keep average prices down, don't they? Unfortunately, the answer is NO! The people who most value the 30 million gallons of

gas available daily tend to get it. They are willing to pay at least $2 per gallon for gasoline; that is, an extra dollar per gallon in waiting time, lobbying efforts, bribery, or as a black market premium.

A **black market** *is an illegal market where price controls are ignored.*

Had the price ceiling not been imposed, the price of a gallon of gasoline would have been roughly $1.25. Although the monetary price of gasoline is held at $1 per gallon by this ceiling, its opportunity cost rises to $2 per gallon to typical customers.

The transaction costs of queuing, however, tend to be lower for poor people. Thus, the impoverished or jobless may gain from price ceilings because waiting in line secures gasoline that they might lack funds to buy if its monetary price rose. Some people view this redistributional effect as worth the inefficiency price controls create. Nevertheless, effective price ceilings create shortages so that opportunity costs — including money, time wasted in lines, and illegal side payments — unnecessarily exceed free-market prices. Only pump prices are controlled; real costs to average consumers are not.

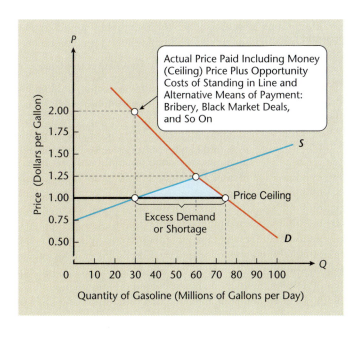

FIGURE 6 Governmentally Induced Shortages in the Gasoline Market

This figure depicts the effect of a $1-per-gallon ceiling on the price of gasoline. At $1 per gallon, 75 million gallons will be demanded but only 30 million will be supplied. Therefore, shortages will exist, and nonprice methods of allocating the shortages will emerge.

Price Floors Price controls of a different type are frequently aimed at redistributing incomes.

A **price floor** *is a minimum legal price.*

Price floors set below equilibrium tend to be as irrelevant as laws requiring pilots to fly above sea level, but floors set above equilibrium create artificial surpluses and raise costs. Price floors are most common in labor markets (minimum wage laws) and agriculture, where the government attempts to boost farm incomes by maintaining farm commodity prices above equilibrium. Figure 7 depicts the consequence of price floors in the cotton market.

Equilibrium price and quantity are 4 million bales annually at $0.60 per pound of cotton (point *e*). A floor set at $0.75 per pound yields a quantity supplied of 5 million bales, but only 3 million bales are demanded—*excess supply* (surplus) is 2 million bales annually. The government can ensure the $0.75 price by buying and storing excess supplies. (Government warehouses often hold mountains of surplus wheat, cotton, corn, beet sugar, peanuts, and soybeans.) Alternatively, the government can pay cotton farmers not to produce or limit the amount of planting. (It has done both.)

Inefficiency is a major problem. In our example, consumers view the 5-millionth bale as worth only $0.45 per pound, even though this last bale cost $0.75 per pound to grow and harvest. Worse than that, people do not get to use the surplus 2 million bales society buys from farmers. Hardly a bargain.

Price ceilings cause shortages and do not hold down the real prices paid by most consumers. Shortages drive up transaction costs, so the opportunity costs incurred in acquiring goods are actually raised by price ceilings. Some desperate buyers must go without even after enduring long queues or extended shopping trips intended to acquire information and locate goods. On the other hand, price floors cause surpluses. Production costs of the surplus goods are far greater than their values to consumers.

If price controls tend to be counterproductive, why are they so common? In some cases, price ceilings are enacted because voters favor them, mistakenly perceiving controls as a solution for inflation. Most of the time, however, controls are political responses to pressures from special-interest groups. Some beneficiaries of controls are obvious: Price floors in agriculture survive because of bloc voting by three generations of farmers. Even price supports have not prevented persistent crises in agriculture, however, as evidenced by rampant farm foreclosures from 1981 to 1987. Technological advances have made it

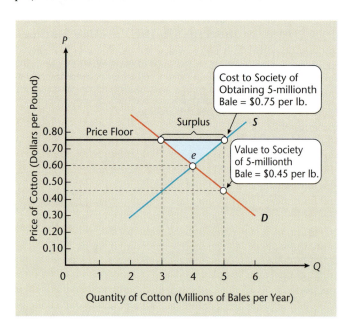

FIGURE 7 Surpluses in the Cotton Market

Price floors generate surpluses, as this figure illustrates. If the government maintains the price of cotton at $0.75 per pound, quantity supplied exceeds that demanded by 2 million bales. The surplus ends up in the hands of the government, which is forced to buy it up to maintain the price at $0.75. Furthermore, the cost to society to produce the 5-millionth bale is far greater than its value. Thus, such policies tend to waste scarce resources.

possible for ever smaller numbers of farmers to feed our growing population. Price supports have merely slowed the painful flow of people from agriculture into other work.

While most direct gainers from controls are very conscious of their gains, long-run losers from controls may not recognize their losses. For example, you might favor rent controls that bar your current landlord from raising the rent. But will you blame rent controls if you later decide to relocate and cannot find an apartment, because construction has been squelched and older rental units have turned into slums after landlords halt repairs? Shortages of rental property and inadequate maintenance are predictable consequences of rent controls.

The winners from price controls tend to be special interest groups who lobby for controls, and even their gains are eroded by lobbying costs and related inefficiencies. One lesson from price controls is that market forces often thwart policies that, on the surface, seem compatible with good intentions and intuition. Economic reasoning may be a far better guide in designing humane policies for areas ranging from minimum wage laws to illicit drugs. Minimum-wage laws, for example, may hurt far more workers than they help, with young workers and members of minorities being especially harmed.

Minimum Wages and Unemployment

The goal of ensuring workers a living wage implicit in *minimum wage laws* is achieved only if inexperienced and unskilled workers can find jobs. Figure 8 shows the effect of imposing a $5 minimum hourly wage in a competitive labor market for unskilled workers, where the equilibrium wage is $4 and equilibrium employment is 7 million workers. As Panel A illustrates, 2 million unskilled workers are laid off when a $5 legal floor is imposed on hourly wages. Another million enter the job market at this higher wage, so 3 million out of 8 million are now unemployed, and the unemployment rate among the unskilled rises from 0 to 37.5 percent.

Jobless workers adjust in several ways. The million who entered the market will seek work elsewhere, but lower wages elsewhere will cause most to leave the market. The two million disemployed workers will look for work in labor markets not covered by the minimum wage law (mowing lawns, delivering papers, etc.) shown in Panel B. The labor supply in this uncovered market consequently shifts rightward by 2 million workers, and wages fall to $3.50 per hour. A million workers find work, but a million do not. This model shows how legal wage floors create surpluses of workers and unemployment just as surely as price floors for goods cause surpluses of goods. Losses of opportunity caused by minimum wage laws may cause some unemployed workers to give up hope.

Our society has tried numerous cures for teenage unemployment. Asked if he was making progress while attempting to develop the light bulb, Thomas Edison replied, "Why certainly. I've learned 1,000 ways you can't make a light bulb."[1] Edison eventually developed a good light bulb, but he abandoned failed experiments. Society has not fared as well. In the 8 years before 1955, when minimum hourly wages first crept over $1, teenage unemployment rates hovered around 10 percent; in the 16 years after 1974, when the minimum wage first exceeded $2, teenage unemployment averaged over 18 percent.[2] Misguided policies probably contribute heavily to persistent teenage unemployment.

Figure 9 shows that between 1948 and 1955, black teenagers had lower average unemployment than whites. Black teenagers have lost steadily since 1955, and now suffer twice the unemployment rate experienced by white teenagers. Panel B suggests that many black teenagers may be so discouraged that decreasing proportions try to find work, while labor force participation rates among white teenagers have grown slightly over time.

---

1. This anecdote is related by Steven P. Zell in "The Problem of Rising Teenage Unemployment: A Reappraisal," *Economic Review*, March 1978, Federal Reserve of Kansas City, March 1978.

2. The dampening of this disemployment effect due to inflation over this era was probably offset by expanded coverage of the labor force by minimum-wage laws, which increase disemployment. Restaurant and grocery store employees, for example, are now covered by federal minimum-wage laws, but were not in the early 1950s.

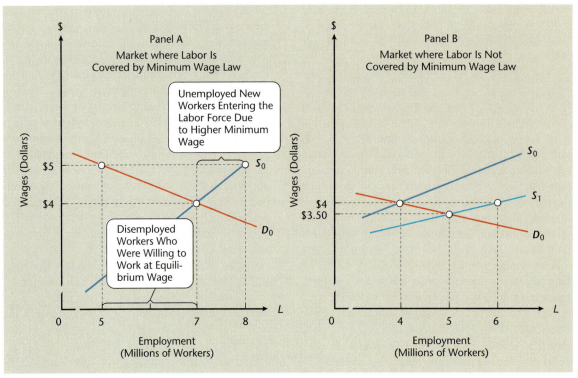

FIGURE 8   Minimum Wages and Unemployment

Minimum-wage laws cause the involuntary unemployment of many poor people with few marketable skills. This especially harms young people who are denied experience that would enhance their future employability. As workers are disemployed in the markets covered by minimum wages (Panel A), they move to uncovered markets that pay lower wages, such as delivering papers, mowing lawns, or odd-job self-employment (Panel B). But not all workers are absorbed in uncovered markets. Some may become "hard-core unemployed," while others drop out of the labor force. Still others become criminals.

FIGURE 9   Teenagers and the Minimum Wage

As minimum legal wages have risen (Panel A), black male teenagers apparently have lost jobs to white male teenagers. As a result, many black male teenagers have dropped out of the labor market (Panel B).

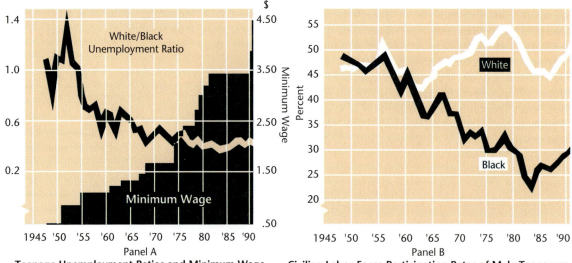

Panel A	Panel B
Teenage Unemployment Ratios and Minimum Wage	Civilian Labor-Force Participation Rates of Male Teenagers Age 16-17, by Race 1948-87

Minimum wage laws are examples of how regulations may subtly and indirectly benefit special-interest groups. These laws create surpluses of unemployed workers who are primarily young and unskilled. Why do labor unions lobby for higher minimum wage laws even though union workers invariably earn wages much higher than these floors? Misguided humanitarianism may play a role, but another reason is that wage floors limit the ability of unskilled workers to compete with skilled union workers. For example, if two unskilled workers willing to work for $3.50 hourly apiece can do the job of an $8-per-hour union worker, a $4.50 minimum wage eliminates their ability to compete.

Heroin Addiction

Drug addiction, once thought confined to ghettos, has become widespread in the past few decades. Standard approaches to the drug problem emphasize punishing users somewhat, but pushers much more harshly. This reduces demands for drugs but shrinks their supplies much more. The result is that illicit drug prices are much higher than free-market prices would be, and addiction poses more problems for the rest of society.

Suppose that S_0 and D_0 in Figure 10 represent the demand and supply of heroin if it were legal. The price of heroin, P_0, would probably fall somewhere between the prices of aspirin and penicillin, because its production is not complex, nor are presently legal narcotics very expensive. (Some estimates suggest that completely legalized and untaxed marijuana would sell for about $8 a bale — roughly the price of prime hay.)

Penalizing heroin users reduces demand to D_1, while the stiffer punishment of dealers reduces supply to S_1, boosting the price to P_1. This high price permits successful pushers to drive luxury cars and live in plush houses, but many users are pushed into prostitution, mugging, and other street crimes. Thus, higher crime rates are among the social costs of policies that reduce the supply of heroin more than the demand for it.

One alternative approach is complete legalization. Advocates of allowing heroin to be governed strictly by demand and supply argue that it

FIGURE 10   The Heroin Market

Prosecuting pushers reduces supply more than demand, but resulting price hikes from P_0 to P_1 makes selling heroin very profitable. Severe prosecution of addicts might reduce demand to D_2, eliminating much of this profit. Alternatively, giving heroin to addicts through government clinics might dry up both the demand and the supply of illegal heroin. Supply would shrink because catching and prosecuting pushers would be easier.

would be so cheap that few addicts would feel driven to commit crimes against others. Instead, they would spend a lot of time nodding off, bothering people no more than derelict alcoholics. Most people, however, are unwilling to let others waste away their lives in such a fashion.

What policies might slash heroin abuse below Q_0 (the free-market amount, shown in Figure 10) without pushing addicts to commit crimes? Punishing users far more than suppliers would reduce demand to, say, D_2, and could cut heroin prices, pushers' profits, and rates of addiction to Q_2. Most people, however, are reluctant to impose life sentences or the death penalty to punish drug users, especially when minors or experimenters are involved.

Paradoxically, allowing clinics to give heroin freely to proven addicts while enforcing stiff penalties against pushers might allow society to suppress both addiction and the crime it fosters. Such a policy would leave suppliers with only experimenters as potential customers and could, over time, reduce the illicit demand for heroin even below D_2. Pushers would be more vulnerable to undercover investigation, because they would not know their customers, and the illegal supply of heroin should dry up. A similar approach used in England for almost three decades appears to work reasonably well. It does not cure all addicts, however, which causes some people to view it as a failure.

Do simple solutions exist for such social problems as teenage unemployment and heroin addiction? Should supply and demand operate without controls? The answers probably depend on particular market conditions. Supply and demand exert considerable pressure regardless of which allocative mechanism is used to resolve any problem. We hope that these overviews of price controls, minimum-wage laws, and the market for heroin convince you that market forces cannot be ignored when structuring social policies, even in areas that are closely tied to people's views of morality.

The Market in Operation

You have now had an overview of supply and demand in action. It is time to address how efficiently and equitably market mechanisms answer the basic questions of *"What?" "How?"* and *"for Whom?"*

What?

Our exploration of how the price system operates has relied on two critical assumptions:

1. *Individuals are self-interested* and try to maximize their personal satisfaction through the goods they consume. If goods add less to your satisfaction (valued in terms of money) than they cost, you will not buy them. Consumer willingness to buy underpins the demands for goods.

2. *Firms try to maximize profits* when they sell goods to consumers willing to pay for them. The drive for profit underpins the supply side of the market.

Thus, market systems answer the "What?" question by producing the things people demand.

How?

Two things limit a firm's ability to exploit consumers. First, competition among sellers keeps prices from straying much above costs for long, because high profits attract new firms, increasing supply, so prices and profits fall. Second, suppliers strive to be efficient, because any firm that cuts costs or introduces a successful technology temporarily reaps higher profits. Before long, any firm not using the new technology will be trying to sell outdated products, or its costs will exceed its competitors' prices, and it will fail.

Competition among producers ensures that price is approximately equal to the opportunity cost (sacrifice to society) incurred in production. International competition exerts pressure for specialized production and exchange according to the principle of comparative advantage. Thus, competitive markets answer the "How?" question by using the least costly methods of production for most types of goods.

For Whom?

How markets answer this "for Whom?" question is relatively simple. Consumers who hold "dollar votes" and are willing to pay market prices purchase and consume goods. Those who do not own many resources cannot buy very much. It is this distributional side that seems to cause the most problems for critics of the market system.

Many people perceive the price system as impersonal and inequitable. However, the market offers some major compensating advantages. Decisions are decentralized: No government agency dictates what everyone must (or cannot) buy or produce. Moreover, markets tend to be efficient. Consumers usually pay prices for goods that roughly reflect the minimal costs of producing these goods. Finally, although markets may not provide perfect stability, the forces that drive markets toward equilibrium tend to yield more stability than most other mechanisms.

Global Markets in Transition

Firms compete for profits both domestically and internationally by trying to produce superior products at lower costs and prices. A different mode of competition pivots on how society will govern economic activity. Competition (in the form of war at times) between mixed capitalism and Marxist socialism has dominated international relations for much of the twentieth century. The past decade has witnessed a rising tide of disillusionment with central planning that has buoyed use of the market system throughout the world as indicated in Figure 11.

Transactions are guided primarily by supply and demand in a system of mixed capitalism. Dramatic advances in standards of living during the past four decades in western Europe, North America, and some Pacific Rim countries (e.g., Japan, Korea, Taiwan, Hong Kong, and Singapore) have helped publicize the gains available from allowing market forces to channel special-

FIGURE 11 The Changing International Economy—1992

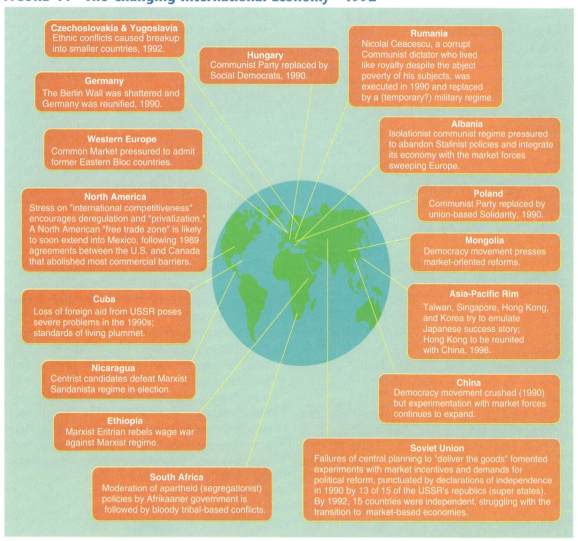

Czechoslovakia & Yugoslavia
Ethnic conflicts caused breakup into smaller countries, 1992.

Hungary
Communist Party replaced by Social Democrats, 1990.

Rumania
Nicolai Ceacescu, a corrupt Communist dictator who lived like royalty despite the abject poverty of his subjects, was executed in 1990 and replaced by a (temporary?) military regime.

Germany
The Berlin Wall was shattered and Germany was reunified, 1990.

Albania
Isolationist communist regime pressured to abandon Stalinist policies and integrate its economy with the market forces sweeping Europe.

Western Europe
Common Market pressured to admit former Eastern Bloc countries.

Poland
Communist Party replaced by union-based Solidarity, 1990.

North America
Stress on "international competitiveness" encourages deregulation and "privatization." A North American "free trade zone" is likely to soon extend into Mexico, following 1989 agreements between the U.S. and Canada that abolished most commercial barriers.

Mongolia
Democracy movement presses market-oriented reforms.

Asia-Pacific Rim
Taiwan, Singapore, Hong Kong, and Korea try to emulate Japanese success story; Hong Kong to be reunited with China, 1998.

Cuba
Loss of foreign aid from USSR poses severe problems in the 1990s; standards of living plummet.

China
Democracy movement crushed (1990) but experimentation with market forces continues to expand.

Nicaragua
Centrist candidates defeat Marxist Sandanista regime in election.

Ethiopia
Marxist Eritrian rebels wage war against Marxist regime.

Soviet Union
Failures of central planning to "deliver the goods" fomented experiments with market incentives and demands for political reform, punctuated by declarations of independence in 1990 by 13 of 15 of the USSR's republics (super states). By 1992, 15 countries were independent, struggling with the transition to market-based economies.

South Africa
Moderation of apartheid (segregationist) policies by Afrikaaner government is followed by bloody tribal-based conflicts.

ized production and exchange. The results are that:

1. Economic reforms in former Eastern Bloc countries (e.g., Czechoslovakia, Poland, China, and the USSR) are aimed at replacing the corruption and inefficiency of central planning with the efficiency of the market system.

2. National borders, which once were transformed primarily through military conquest, are increasingly open to facilitate international trade.

The drive for political freedom and economic modernization overthrew repressive regimes in many former Eastern Bloc countries during 1990, and compelled shifts towards more democratic policies in several South American nations and South Africa which reformed "apartheid" policies in 1992. Figure 11 indicates that many countries are being restructured by mounting pressure for economic efficiency, political freedom, and the globalization of international markets.

The Process of Worldwide Economic Integration

Modernization and sustained economic growth require information flows across all levels of society and between virtually all centers for production. (Shared information is vital, for example, in pushing out technological frontiers. Otherwise, isolated scientists would continually start by reinventing the wheel.) Secrecy is a feature of totalitarianism. Thus, closed societies tend to become stagnant and, all else equal, seldom compete successfully against more democratic nations.

The need for free flows of information also tends to favor decentralized market systems over centrally planned economies in the race for economic growth. Central planning tends to result in centralized instead of shared information. On the other hand, a decentralized market system fosters the spread of information. Anyone who has ever worked with the bulletin boards and data bases available on computer networks in the United States quickly realizes that far more information is available on any topic than anyone could completely digest and organize.

Isolation facilitates differentiation; exposure (communication and trade) facilitates homogeneity because of political and economic imitation. Thus, patterns that are successful in any society are increasingly rapidly adapted to local conditions in almost all other societies. International trade increasingly makes goods that are available anywhere available everywhere. The result is that our world is increasingly homogenous, although significant regional variation remains.

In the political sphere, countries once governed by rigid dictatorships are slowly evolving towards greater democracy in South America (Chile, Argentina, Nicaragua, and Brazil), Africa (Ethiopia and South Africa), and Asia (Mongolia, North and South Korea, and China), and throughout Eastern Europe. In the economic sphere, once devoutly socialistic countries are increasingly abandoning central planning, relying instead on market forces to resolve economic issues. Even relatively capitalistic countries have "privatized" many activities that have traditionally been the purview of government.

As you proceed through this book, you will constantly encounter the supply and demand analysis presented in this and the previous chapter. Prices that emerge from the forces of supply and demand are important information even when nonmarket mechanisms are used to settle economic issues. Markets, however, are the mechanisms that increasingly dominate economic activity everywhere. The directions in which the international economy is being swept along by market forces are powerful arguments that no tools of economics are more important than supply and demand.

Chapter Review: Key Points

1. Increases in supplies or decreases in demands tend to reduce prices. Decreases in supplies or increases in demands tend to raise prices. Increases in either supplies or demands tend

to increase quantities. Decreases in either supplies or demands tend to shrink quantities. If both supply and demand shift, the effects on price and quantity may be either reinforcing or at least partially offsetting. (You need to review this important material if these points make little sense to you.)

2. *Transaction costs* arise because information and mobility are costly. This allows the price of a good to vary between markets and to approach its equilibrium erratically.

3. *Intermediaries* prosper only by reducing the transaction costs incurred in getting goods from the ultimate producers to the ultimate consumers. *Speculators* facilitate movements toward equilibrium, because they increase demand by trying to buy when prices are below equilibrium, and increase supply by selling when prices are above equilibrium. This dampens price swings and reduces the costs and risks to others of doing business.

4. *Arbitrage* involves buying in a market where the price is low and selling in a market where the price is higher. If this price spread is greater than the transaction costs, arbitrage is risklessly profitable. Competition for opportunities to arbitrage dampens profit opportunities and facilitates efficiency by ensuring that price spreads between markets are minimal.

5. Government can set monetary prices at values other than equilibrium price, but *price ceilings* or *price floors* do not "freeze" opportunity costs; instead, these *price controls* create economic inefficiency and either shortages or surpluses, respectively.

6. The market system tailors production according with consumers' demands in answering the basic economic question of *what* will be produced. Competition tends to compel efficient forms of production in answering *how* production will occur. Markets answer the *who* question by producing for those who own valuable resources that secure income.

7. Although the market system has many persuasive critics, and other mechanisms (e.g., socialist governments) have dominated allocative decisions in many countries, powerful communications networks and the obvious prosperity of most mixed capitalist economies began to alter policies in nations everywhere toward greater reliance on market allo-

cations of resources and incomes during the 1980s. This trend is accelerating in the early 1990s.

Key Concepts

Ensure that you can define these terms before proceeding.

invisible hand	price ceiling
intermediaries	black market
arbitrage	price floor
speculators	minimum-wage laws
price controls	

Problems and Questions

Draw supply and demand graphs for the relevant markets to show the impact of the following changes on prices and quantities for questions 1–12. Be as explicit as possible about the market adjustment mechanisms.

1. There is a major technological breakthrough in producing natural gas from coal. What happens in the market for natural gas? The market for coal?

2. What happens to the world market for coffee if coffee blight destroys three-quarters of the crop in Brazil? The market for tea?

3. Gasoline prices soar. What happens in the markets for big cars? Bicycles? Tune-up shops? Rapid-transit systems?

4. The economy goes sour. What happens to the market for economists?

5. Tomorrow afternoon AT&T announces that oil has been discovered under every telephone pole. What happens to the market for AT&T stock? How rapidly would this occur? Do you think you could get rich buying AT&T stock the next day? (The answer is NO!) Who would get rich from this discovery?

6. What happens to quality and quantity if a legal maximum price is set at $10 per pair of denim jeans? To opportunity cost? Is the government doing jean wearers any favor?

7. A "miracle seed" for corn is developed. Analyze the markets for corn and wheat.

8. The birthrate suddenly increases enor-

mously. What would happen in the market for baby furniture? The market for baby-sitters? The market for nightclub entertainment or movies? Do the answers to these questions differ in the short run and in the long run? How?

9. In 1992, the government announces a major renewal of space exploration. In 1999, this program is discontinued. What will happen to the market for aeronautical engineers in 1992–1993? Between 1993 and 1999? During 1999–2001?

10. There is a radical overhaul and simplification of the income tax system. What happens to the market for accountants? Lawyers? Erasers?

11. The minimum legal wage is raised from $4.50 per hour to $6.00 per hour. What happens in labor markets for teenagers and other unskilled workers?

12. Researchers announce that aspirin reduces the risks of heart attacks. What happens to the market for aspirin? To the market for cardiologists? To their incomes?

13. Is the assertion that "everyone always buys everything at the lowest possible price" correct? Have you ever paid more than you had to for any good, after allowing for all transaction costs?

14. Ticket scalpers enable latecomers to avoid standing in line for tickets and allow people to wait until the last moment before deciding to attend concerts or athletic events. Are promoters of an event harmed by scalping? Should ticket scalpers' services be free? See if you can devise graphs to explain this form of speculation.

15. Financial institutions such as banks act as intermediaries. They lend their depositors' savings to ultimate borrowers, charging higher interest to borrowers than the banks pay to depositors, who are the ultimate providers of loans. How does this reduce the transaction costs incurred in making private savings available to borrowers?

16. Casual surveys of our students at the beginning of each semester reveal an amused but overwhelming support for a proposal to raise the legal minimum wages of college graduates to $50,000 per year. (They assumed our proposal was facetious.) After covering this chapter, student support for this idea evaporated. How might such a minimum-wage law be harmful to most new college graduates?

17. Senator Ernest Hollings (D–South Carolina), in advocating wage-price controls, asserted that "most people prefer shortages to higher prices." Is this true? Why or why not? Do you think advocates of wage-price freezes understand the cause of shortages?

18. Pharmaceutical companies have recently developed and tested drugs that reverse the influence of alcohol on the brain within a half hour. These pills enable drivers to sober up before driving and to reduce the severity of hangovers. In the past few years, many states have imposed stiff mandatory penalties for drunk driving convictions. How do you think these two separate events will interact to influence alcohol consumption?

19. Ceilings on rents for apartments and housing are in effect in several U.S. cities, including New York and Santa Monica, California. What effect do such controls have on the incentives of property owners to build residences for rent? To maintain rental property in top shape? Can you identify some groups that may gain from rent controls? Now identify several groups that lose.

20. Laws forbid or severely limit free-market transactions in atomic bombs, sex, cocaine, murder for hire, marijuana, surrogate motherhood, pornography, and a host of other activities. At the same time, minimal education and inoculations against communicable diseases are compulsory. Which of these or other illegal or mandatory goods do you think could be allocated more efficiently and equitably through the market system? Are there goods that are now bought and sold freely that you believe the government should control tightly? What are they? Why?

Cornerstones of Macroeconomics

The ultimate macroeconomic goal is ensuring prosperity so that people have op-portunities for good jobs and secure standards of living. Thus, the central concern of macroeconomic theory is erratic growth of national income. An overview of business cycles (ups and downs in national income and output) and the tools used to measure economic fluctuations are the central themes of Part 2. Business cycles are sometimes isolated within a country, but more often, prosperity or stagnation is internationally contagious. Cornerstones for macroeconomic models and policies designed to achieve high employment, price-level stability, and economic growth include consistent measures of such aggregate variables as Gross National Product and the price level (an index of average prices).

Chapter 5 provides a broad overview of the domain of macroeconomics, open-ing with a discussion of *business cycles* followed by a survey of various theories intended by early economists to explain macroeconomic instability. A simple *Aggregate Demand/Aggregate Supply* model is then introduced to describe historical swings in unemployment, inflation, and economic growth. The chapter concludes by using this powerful model to interpret the course of twentieth-century Ameri-can business cycles.

We examine how *unemployment* and *inflation* are measured in Chapter 6, and investigate weaknesses of current measurement techniques. We also lay the groundwork for understanding the causes and cures of unemployment and infla-tion. Achieving prosperity often requires policymakers to weigh trade-offs. For ex-ample, policies to curb inflation may temporarily push hordes of workers into un-employment lines, while attempts to boost employment can stimulate inflationary pressures.

Economic growth tends to ease excessive unemployment or inflation. Tracing growth or stagnation in an economy requires measurements of *National Income* and *Gross National Product*, which are the focus of Chapter 7.

The concepts presented in Part 2 should prepare you for the macroeconomic theory and policy in more advanced parts of this book. Every modern economy has suffered at times from inadequate growth, erratic price levels, and excessive unemployment. This international experience illustrates the ultimate challenge fac-ing policymakers—maintaining stable rates of healthy economic growth.

An Overview of Macroeconomics

Macroeconomic fluctuation is a recurring theme in history. Periods of famine alternated with periods of feast in primitive societies. Booms and busts in modern economies periodically uproot workers from their jobs, press business firms into bankruptcy, and oust politicians from power. The survival of firms and the success or failure at the polls of political incumbents are only a few of the many things that depend strongly on the state of the economy. Your job prospects upon graduation may shrink if the economy is in a recession; campus recruiting is one of the first areas cut by most business firms. And how much your wages will buy may depend on how much inflation the country experiences.

A knowledge of macroeconomics will enable you to evaluate the benefits and costs of different approaches to macroeconomic policy, which is intended to promote *economic growth* and high employment (and thus *low unemployment*) while keeping *inflation* in check. Figure 1 traces these "big three" macroeconomic variables for both the United States and the European Community (EC) over the past two decades. As this figure illustrates, unemployment, inflation, and growth in both economies tend to move in tandem — evidence that the world economy is increasingly interdependent.

Figure 1 also illustrates that unemployment

rates rose in the early 1980s in both economies, but high unemployment has lingered more persistently in Europe. The U.S. economy generated nearly 20 million new jobs during the 1980s, while Europe created fewer than 3 million. Sluggish economic growth in Europe has been blamed on a mix of problems ranging from militant labor unions to inefficient government bureaucracies, and from excessive monopoly in important industries to overly restrictive government policies intended to control inflation.[1] Panel B indicates that inflation spurted up internationally in the 1970s, but had largely abated in both economies (and most other economies) by the mid-1980s. Finally, Panel C shows that both the U.S. and EC economies continue to grow, but at erratic rates.

The ancestors of all modern macroeconomic theories were early theories intended to explain financial panics and cycles in agricultural and general business activity. This chapter begins with descriptions of business cycles and some of their consequences. Early business cycles theories, ranging from "external shock" theories to the Marxist approach, are surveyed to provide

---

1. See John Cornwall, *The Theory of Economic Breakdown: An Institutional-Analytical Approach* (Cambridge, MA: Basil Blackwell, Ltd., 1990), for a detailed discussion of this issue.

FIGURE 1 Unemployment, Inflation, and Economic Growth in the United States and the European Community (EC) — 1969–1990

Loosely parallel paths have been recorded recently in the United States and the European Community for the "Big Three" macroeconomic variables — unemployment, inflation, and economic growth. For example, unemployment rose in both economies during the early 1980s. High unemployment has, however, been more sustained in the EC in recent years.

Source: *Economic Report of the President*, 1991.

insights into some possible causes of macroeconomic instability. We then introduce an Aggregate Demand/Aggregate Supply model to interpret historical swings in unemployment, inflation, and economic growth.

This Aggregate Demand/Aggregate Supply framework is applied through the rest of our treatment of macroeconomics to interpret differences between modern classical and Keynesian macroeconomic theories. The foundations of Aggregate Demands and Supplies sketched in this chapter are elaborated in Chapter 15, after interactions between individual behavior and macroeconomic activity have been developed more completely.

Business Cycles

Unemployment rises when national output declines, while inflation climbs when productive capacity shrinks or pressures are exerted for output to exceed capacity.

Periods of economic expansion and contraction alternate over a **business cycle.**

Expansions seem to be lengthening, while contractions tend to be shorter than in earlier periods. Consequently, most economists are optimistic that improvements in our ability to measure and adapt to cyclic pressures may help us avoid the violent fluctuations of earlier times. Less traumatic disruptions, however, will undoubtedly continue to nag all societies.

A Typical Business Cycle The comparatively smooth business cycle extracted in Figure 2 shows how cycles are divisible into four subperiods: (*a*) the *peak* or *boom*, (*b*) a *recession* or *contraction*, (*c*) a *depression* or *trough*, and (*d*) a *recovery* or *expansion*. The specific terms applied depend on subjective perceptions of the severity of a cycle, but smooth fluctuations are rare. Ex-

pansions last from as little as 10 months to as long as 108 months, while contractions range from 7 to 65 months in length. Notice that long contractions (e.g., 1929–1940) may be associated with short expansions (1940–1944) or vice versa (e.g., 1981–1983 to 1984–1991).

Turning Points in Business Cycles

Methodical analyses of business cycles began when the *National Bureau of Economic Research* was founded in 1920. Tracing economic history is now a relatively systematic process, but forecasting remains relatively imprecise. Nevertheless, sophisticated statistical models are used to simultaneously forecast every major sector of the economy.

FIGURE 2 Business Activity, 1880–1990

The business cycle is divided into four distinct phases: the peak (boom), contraction (recession), trough (depression), and expansion (recovery). The intensity and timing of business cycles vary considerably, with expansions apparently lengthening in recent years while contractions seem to be growing shorter.

Source: AmeriTrust Company (Cleveland, OH), *American Business Activity from 1790 to Today*, 62/ed., January, 1991.

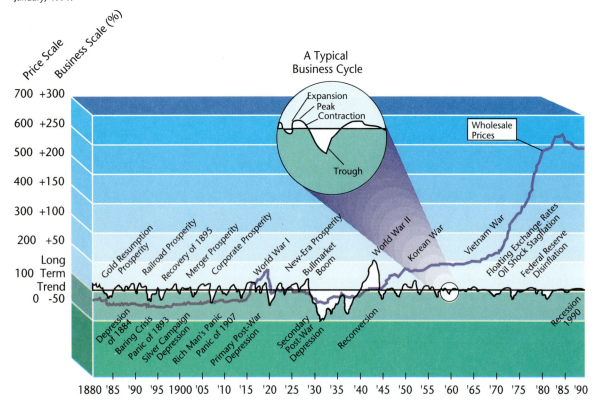

Unemployment rates and the Dow-Jones stock index are among the more than 5,000 data series now used to analyze and "date" U.S. business cycles. **Troughs** of the cycle occur when most measures of business activity indicate low points; **peaks** are dated when most data point to cyclic highs. These **turning points** are unofficial until the next peak or trough is past. For example, the latest trough, tentatively dated November 1982, was not official until the expansion that began in 1983 ended late in 1990.

Social Aspects of the Business Cycle

Emphasizing the losses of output and income during economic downturns sometimes causes analysts to lose sight of the losses associated with waves of crime, illness, and family breakdowns during recessions. Marriage and divorce are both positively related to economic swings. Hard times cause many couples to delay marriage. Rates of illegitimate birth soar, and unhappy couples postpone divorce. Changes in marital status seem to be "luxuries" demanded primarily when income is secure. Would you be as prone to marry if your job were threatened? Would couples with young children be as apt to divorce during hard times?

Protracted downturns trigger epidemics of such stress-related diseases as heart attacks, alcoholism, and mental illness. Suicide rates were 60 to 70 percent above normal during the depths of the Great Depression, reflecting the gloom caused by sharp income losses and forced idleness. One study indicates that roughly 240 more males aged 20 to 60 commit suicide annually with each 1 percent hike in unemployment rates.

Widespread unemployment tends to fill prisons. Prosperity reduces most crime rates, but shrinking legitimate income-earning opportunities during recessions cause fraud, robberies, and other property crimes to soar. Violent crime also becomes more common.

Policymakers feel forced to react to the ugly repercussions of severe downturns. Social Security, unemployment compensation, and other relief systems were enacted in the 1930s to aid the victims of the Great Depression. More recent recessions have been shorter and milder, but the social maladies of business cycles have not evaporated.

Early Business Cycle Theories

Accurately forecasting the next boom or bust offers substantial strategic advantages to business firms and can be an easy path to personal riches. (Perhaps you thought fortune-tellers were used only for romantic forecasts.) Even though the sparsity of reliable statistics limited early economists to impressionistic theorizing about changing levels of economic activity, their thoughts provide some important insights into the nature of macroeconomic fluctuations.

External Shock Theories

Many early business cycle theories focused on such external shocks as wars or weather.

> **External shocks** *are economic disturbances that originate outside an economy.*

Although parts of an economy may flourish during a war (e.g., weapons manufacturing), conflict wreaks havoc on both victorious and vanquished nations. Wars divert output away from capital investment and destroy equipment (e.g., factories), infrastructure (e.g., bridges and roads), and labor (e.g., soldiers). Today, agriculture dominates few economies, but weather cycles are still studied to help predict the effects of erratic crop yields. For example, a severe drought in the U.S. farm belt in 1988 drove up food prices internationally. Unless crop failures are global, however, countries are now buffered somewhat by their increasing ability to import from regions blessed by bumper crops.

The **sunspot theory** is an exotic external force theory developed in 1875 by W. Stanley Jevons, a pioneering English mathematical economist. Jevons reasoned that sunspots (nuclear storms on the sun's surface) affect weather and, hence, agriculture. Although Jevons' theory has been discredited, a new "sunspot theory" may develop if we ever depend heavily on solar energy.

Population Dynamics Theories

Early economists often pondered the long-term effects of such events as wars or the opening of new territory. Thomas Malthus (1766–1834) popularized a **population dynamics** approach, which concludes that bare subsistence is all that people can ultimately expect. A theory from biology illustrates why these early forecasts were pessimistic.

Subsistence and Population S-Curves Suppose that at Time 0 in Figure 3, a few rabbits are set loose in a new territory. With ample space and food, rabbits "prosper" and their population growth accelerates for some time. Competition for food and territory mounts, however, when rabbits reproduce excessively (as they will). Malnutrition and a parallel population explosion of predators "depresses" the rabbits and curbs population growth. "Survival of the fittest" causes rabbits that fail to secure territory to starve. An equilibrium population entails reduced average lifespans. This sequence is called a **population S-curve.**

FIGURE 3   An S-Curve for a Rabbit Population

Plentiful resources facilitate prosperity and rapid population growth. Scarcity becomes more onerous and population growth slows down as the carrying capacity of an environment is approached.

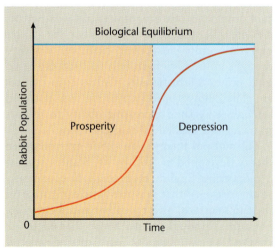

Malthus used a similar model to describe the growth of human population. He viewed our procreative urges as constant, but argued that birth rates depend primarily on maternal health. Population explodes in response to favorable circumstances; while birth rates rise, death rates fall for both infants and adults. But population pressures against available resources eventually stifle economic activity, leaving famine or war to impede population growth. Booms and then busts, according to this line of reasoning, should alternate across generations.

Early fans of Malthus's model failed to anticipate technological advances and generally opposed birth control programs; their speculations apply more to primitive economies than to modern industrial giants. Modernization in less developed countries is often offset by population growth that limits standards of living to subsistence levels; starvation is the ultimate population check in Malthus's theory. Small wonder that the historian Thomas Carlyle, a contemporary of Malthus, characterized economics as "the dismal science."

Marxian "Capitalistic Crises"

Contrary to popular stereotypes, Karl Marx was in awe of economic progress under the market system. In the *Communist Manifesto* (1848), he marveled that capitalism

. . . has created more massive and more colossal forces than have all preceding generations together. . . . It has accomplished wonders far surpassing Egyptian pyramids, Roman aqueducts, and Gothic cathedrals; it has conducted expeditions that put in the shade all former migrations of nations and crusades.

Nevertheless, Marx condemned markets as permitting the rich and powerful to exploit workers.[2] Describing his views as "scientific socialism," he predicted that capitalism would

---

2. An old Soviet joke: "Under capitalism, man exploits man. Under socialism, it's vice versa."

spasmodically expand and then contract, with each peak higher than its predecessor and each successive crash deeper than the last.

Marxists view business cycles as driven by increasing concentrations of wealth in the hands of capitalists. *Underconsumption* is inevitable when, because rapid investment and growth distribute income inequitably, workers lack income to buy all the goods they produce; glutted markets then plunge capitalism into depressions or imperialistic wars. An upswing emerges when new markets open, new raw materials are discovered, or a successful war yields plunder for capitalists to exploit. This plants the seeds for the next downswing, and so on. Finally, the working class will overthrow its exploiters, the spark of a revolution igniting during the abyss of a deep depression.

Marx's ideas inspired generations of radical critics of capitalism, and he provided a number of predictions (outlined in the last chapter of this book) about the course of history. Most have proven wrong. The ongoing collapse of communist governments, for example, is absolutely contrary to Marx's predictions.

Long Waves and Innovations

The recent rebirth of entrepreneurial instincts in the Eastern bloc might also have surprised Joseph Schumpeter, whose writings celebrated the creative vigor of capitalism. In 1911, he proposed a *long-wave* theory of business cycles in which development is fueled when entrepreneurs initiate such **innovations** as (*a*) discoveries of raw materials, (*b*) new goods or new quality in familiar products, (*c*) technological advances, (*d*) the opening of new markets, or (*e*) major reorganizations of industries.

Major innovations generate *spin-offs* — related inventions, mimicry of an original innovation, or the birth of new industries. Such advances as microelectronics, Teflon, and laser surgery, for example, were spin-offs of the space program. Economic growth peaks by the time society fully adapts to a major innovation; saturated markets cannot absorb further supply increases or emulation of technology. When firms retrench, the economy slumps while awaiting fresh innovations. The next long-wave process is sparked by a new wave of innovation. Of course, minor innovations might explain shorter cycles.

Schumpeter used railroads to illustrate major innovations.[3] Cars and airplanes have also driven U.S. economic development. More recently, computers have enabled some firms to grow to sizes that were impossible when information processing was primitive, and microprocessors have thrust an array of new consumer goods (e.g., garage door openers, electronic toys, and microwave ovens) into the realm of "necessities" for many Americans. Perhaps the most underrated innovation of the past century is the supermarket, which reduces transaction costs for an incredible variety of goods. Supermarkets provide outlets for specialized firms that would have been denied shelf space in old-fashioned general stores.

Kondratieff Long Waves Nikolai Kondratieff, a Russian economist, offered his own long-wave theory in the 1920s. He studied economic data for 1780 to 1920 and charted two complete long waves (40 to 60 years each), with a third beginning in the early 1920s. The Great Depression attracted some converts to his idea that the world economy will boom and then bust every 40 to 60 years, so that another worldwide depression should have begun between 1970 and 1990, but one has not arrived as he predicted.

Most economists view **Kondratieff long waves** as statistical accidents. Believers are convinced, however, that Middle East conflict and erratic oil

---

3. He noted: "Expenditures on, and the opening of, a new line has some immediate effects on business in general, on competing means of transport, and on the relative position of centers of production. It requires more time to bring into use the opportunities of production newly created by the railroad and to annihilate others. And it takes still longer for population to shift, cities to decay, and, generally, the new face of the country to take a shape that is adapted to the environment as altered by railroadization." Joseph A. Schumpeter, *Business Cycles: A Theoretical, Historical, and Statistical Analysis of the Capitalist Process* (New York: McGraw-Hill, 1939).

Joseph A. Schumpeter (1883–1950)

As a young man, Joseph Schumpeter expressed three life ambitions: to be the world's greatest economist, lover, and horseman. He later joked that he had achieved two of the three, confessing in a wry way that he never was much of an equestrian. The issue of his ambitions aside, he was undoubtedly a man of extraordinary energy and accomplishment.

Widely versed in economics, mathematics, statistics, history, and philosophy, Schumpeter was both a scholarly observer and a major participant in the world of affairs. At one time or another he was lawyer, banker, teacher, and public official, serving a stint as finance minister in his native Austria. Two books on economics, both published before he was 30 years old, are still highly regarded. In 1932, he became a professor of economics at Harvard University, where he taught until his death 18 years later.

Schumpeter's writings span the entire economic process: equilibrium, business cycles, and the survival prospects of capitalism. He viewed competition as a learning process and an ordering force. Somewhat paradoxically, he considered business cycles essential to economic progress. Cycles occur because equilibrium is destroyed by entrepreneurial innovations, but since innovation improves the economic conditions of society, this destruction of equilibrium is "creative."

Certain institutional features were identified by Schumpeter as essential to economic vitality. First, there must be broad scope for the operation of innovative entrepreneurs. Second, well-developed credit markets must allow entrepreneurs to capture income streams and use them in production even before actually contributing anything to national income.

Schumpeter distinguished three types of business cycles, naming the cycles for earlier pioneers in business cycle theory. The length of each depends on the kind of disturbance that causes it. The shortest (*Kitchin*) cycle is associated with inventory changes and usually lasts about 3 years. An intermediate (*Juglar*) cycle depends on fairly small innovations, such as microwave ovens or electronic calculators, and runs its course in 8 to 11 years. The long (*Kondratieff*) cycle lasts 40 to 60 years and is caused by sweeping innovations such as electrification or jet flight.

Schumpeter made one major prediction that extended beyond even his own long-wave theory (30 to 60 years). It seems strange, but Schumpeter, a devotee of capitalism, was almost as convinced as Marx was that capitalism might ultimately self-destruct. Schumpeter, however, hypothesized a very different mechanism. He thought that the prosperity created by capitalism (and not, as Marx thought, a capitalist depression) would ultimately create irresistible pressure for redistributions of income from the haves to the have-nots. This, in turn, would diminish incentives for entrepreneurs, draining capitalism's creative vigor. Thus, in essence, Schumpeter's most sweeping forecast was that capitalism would be a victim of its own success.

FIGURE 4 The Kondratieff Wave

Source: *The New York Times,* October 17, 1982. Copyright 1982 by The New York Times Company. Adapted by permission.

supplies are symptoms of Kondratieff's fourth wave. The 1989–92 recession reinforced expectations of a deep trough by year 2000 (see Figure 4).

Will the Bottom Drop Out in the 1990s?

Gloom-and-doom forecasts have found receptive audiences for generations, but cyclic regularities are not the only reasons cited for pessimism about the health of the world economy. Some modern analysts fear that policy errors from the 1930s will be repeated in the 1990s. One group blames the Great Depression on a trade war set off by the Smoot-Hawley Tariff of 1930. In their view, the 1929 stock market crash was precipitated when it became apparent that Smoot-Hawley, the highest set of U.S. tariffs ever, would be enacted.[4] The ensuing collapse of international trade then stimulated a worldwide

---

4. "The Trade Bill Fluffs Its Feathers," *The Economist,* March 19, 1988, pp. 21–22.

depression. This group views sentiment for protection against international trade as a threat that could collapse economies everywhere.

Psychological Theories

Predictions of collapse can prove prophetic because fear of a dismal future is often self-fulfilling. Psychological theories of cycles focus on how human herd instincts make prolonged optimism or pessimism contagious. These theories help explain the momentum of swings initiated by such shocks as wars or changes in agricultural yields, the expected profitability of investments, or natural resource availability.

Once a "real" disturbance (e.g., a rise in energy costs) occurs, decision makers' reactions set off secondary shock waves—the psychological part of a cycle. Information is costly, so decisions often rely on educated guesses (much as you sometimes answer multiple-choice questions on exams). Most business managers are loath to go it alone and operate from the same information bases, which include government and market research data. It is not surprising, therefore, that firms commonly move in the same directions.

Business cycles unfold when firms develop similar expectations about the future and adjust their plans accordingly. Once set off, waves of pessimism or optimism seem to have lives of their own. For example, pessimistic firms might slash output, lay off workers, and postpone investments. If workers then moderate their own spending, firms with shrinking sales lay off even more workers. Thus, expectations of a depression may be self-fulfilling. (With psychology involved, is there any wonder at the term "depression"?)

A wave of optimism operates in the opposite direction. Recoveries commence when firms begin expanding output. More labor is hired, bolstering household optimism and spending, creating more employment, and so on. Psychological theories explain inertia in a recovery or downturn but do not address turning points in business cycles.

A Prelude to Modern Macroeconomics

The preceding theories provide partial insights into some economic fluctuations, but most modern economists now focus on two general theories that compete in explaining broad cyclic activity: *classical theory* and *Keynesian theory*. Classical economics was not the creation of a single economist, but, rather, represents a conglomeration of the thoughts of mainstream economists dating back to Adam Smith.

Classical macroeconomic theory *stresses coping with scarcity from the supply side as the key to macroeconomic vitality, and supports market solutions to problems and laissez-faire (minimal) government policies.*

Classical economics relies heavily on the self-correcting power of automatic market adjustments (Smith's "invisible hand") to cure macroeconomic instability, including excessive unemployment. Recessions create pressures for wages and prices to fall that, in turn, lead to growth of sales and expanding demands for labor. Opposite adjustments help prevent a rapid boom from overheating the economy.

Persistent 15 to 25 percent unemployment rates during the worldwide Great Depression of the 1930s clashed with classical predictions. Could people wait for decades for the economy to self-correct? Or was the classical model flawed? John Maynard Keynes (1883–1946), the most influential economist of this century, concluded that capitalism might neither automatically nor quickly rebound from a depression.

Keynesian theory *views macroeconomic problems as emerging primarily from the demand side, and recommends actively adjusting government policies to ameliorate instability.*

The demand-oriented model Keynes developed in his 1936 book, *The General Theory of Employment, Interest, and Money,* dominated macroeconomics from the 1940s through the 1960s, but classical theory was refined and resurrected when Keynesian policies failed to cure economic atrophy and inflation in the 1970s. Some economists continue to favor demand-oriented Keynesian analysis; others view the supply-side orientation of *new classical macroeconomics* as the major recent advance in economic knowledge.

Aggregate Demand and Aggregate Supply

Demand and supply analysis describes not only movements of the prices and quantities of individual goods, but also movements of such broad macroeconomic aggregates as national income and the *price level* (using an index that averages changes in nominal prices relative to a specified base year). **Aggregate Demand** and **Aggregate Supply** curves are useful in tracing the symptoms of business cycles and describing the broad effects of changes in macroeconomic policies. The Aggregate Demand/Aggregate Supply framework we develop next also highlights critical differences between major modern macroeconomic theories, which are explored in depth in Parts 3 through 5 of this book.

Aggregate Demand Curves

Aggregate Demand for national output is underpinned by the purchases of four groups of ultimate buyers: (*a*) consumers, (*b*) investors, (*c*) government, and (*d*) foreigners. Their spending plans are interdependent,[5] and are combined in an Aggregate Demand curve. The amount of national output each group buys depends, in part, on the price level.

> An **Aggregate Demand** curve *depicts a negative relationship between the price level and purchases of national output.*

If the price level rises, purchases of our national output fall, and vice versa.

Foundations for the negative slopes of Aggregate Demand curves are variations on the substitution and income effects used to justify negative slopes of individual demands in Chapter 3. The Aggregate Demand curve is negatively sloped because of the *wealth effect*, the *foreign sector substitution effect*, and the *interest rate effect*. The negatively sloped Aggregate Demand curve in Figure 5 is based on these effects.

The Wealth Effect Will money in your checking account buy as much if the price level skyrockets? Of course not. A higher price level reduces the value of financial wealth. Assets such as stocks, bonds, cash, and checking account balances are worth less, which shrinks your purchases.[6] Thus, higher average prices reduce the amount of production sold along an Aggregate Demand curve.

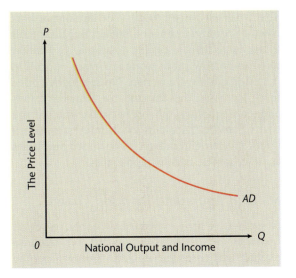

FIGURE 5 The Slope of the Aggregate Demand Curves

The Aggregate Demand curve is negatively sloped because an increase in the price level generates (*a*) *wealth effects*, (*b*) *foreign sector substitution*, and (*c*) *interest rate effects* that result in a lower level of aggregate output.

The Foreign Sector Substitution Effect Might buyers tend to switch from Plymouths to Hyundais if the prices of American cars rose relative to those for imports? Of course. Higher U.S. prices cause domestic consumers to buy more imports and fewer American goods. Foreign buyers respond similarly, which shrinks our exports. Investment is also affected. Increases in the price level drive up domestic production costs. If you were the president of a company considering a new manufacturing facility, you would be more likely to build it in Mexico if U.S. prices and costs rose. Thus, a higher price level shrinks investment in this country, and both foreign and U.S. firms would find it relatively more profitable to invest abroad.[7] Thus, trends toward imports and foreign investments reinforce the wealth effect in making Aggregate Demand curves negatively sloped.

---

5. Consumption, for example, depends on national income, which in turn depends on all sources of demand. These sorts of interdependencies (detailed in later chapters) preclude the type of horizontal summation used to calculate, for example, the market demand for a good.

6. Note that this wealth effect resembles the income effect discussed in Chapter 3 as a minor reason for the negative slope of a market demand curve.

7. Foreign sector substitution resembles the substitution effect introduced in Chapter 3.

The Interest Rate Effect The amount of borrowing required to finance a major purchase rises if the price level rises. For example, you might need to borrow more to finance your education if tuition costs were to rise. Thus, a higher price level increases the demand for loanable funds and, consequently, the interest rate, which is the cost of credit. This increase in interest rates reduces investment and such consumer purchases as new homes, cars, or appliances.[8]

Shifts of Aggregate Demand Curves

Now that we have explained why the Aggregate Demand curve slopes downward, we need to explore why these curves shift. National income is a major determinant of market demands for specific goods but, in conjunction with the price level, it only identifies a specific point on an Aggregate Demand curve. (Note that national income is treated as synonymous with the national output shown on the horizontal axis of Figure 5 — sales revenues from output are simultaneously receipts of income that can be divided among suppliers of productive resources.[9] Thus, the output on the axis of Figure 5 also measures national income.) Changes in national income and the price level reflect movements along the Aggregate Demand curve; they do not cause it to shift. Aggregate Demand curves shift when planned spending changes for consumption (C), investment (I), government (G), or net exports to foreigners (X − M, or exports minus imports).

Consumer Spending

Customary living standards and buying habits help shape consumption spending, which represents about two-thirds of Aggregate Demand.

---

8. The structure of purchases by consumers, investors, government, and foreigners is explored in more detail in Chapter 9. The interest rate mechanism may be the most powerful force causing Aggregate Demand curves to be negatively sloped, but it is not very intuitive. All of these mechanisms are elaborated more completely in Chapter 15.

9. The accounting differences between national output and income addressed in Chapter 8 can be ignored for simplicity in this simple Aggregate Demand/Aggregate Supply model.

Planned consumption is also influenced by (a) disposable income, (b) wealth, (c) average size and ages of households, (d) stocks of consumer goods on hand and household balance sheets, and (e) consumer expectations about future prices, incomes, and availability of goods.

Disposable Income Workers are often upset by how sharply withholding taxes shrink their take-home pay below their stated salaries. Your *disposable income* is the amount available to spend after subtracting federal and state taxes, and then adding any *transfer payments* (such incomes received but not earned as unemployment compensation or Social Security). Adjustments of this type cause aggregate disposable income to be less than national income.

Keynesian theory (detailed in Part 3) emphasizes disposable income as the primary determinant of consumer spending. Increases in disposable income stimulate saving somewhat, but most of it tends to be spent. Thus, changing relationships between national income and disposable income (e.g., new taxes or transfer payments) alter consumers' spending plans and shift Aggregate Demand.

Wealth or Expected Income Is a new car purchase more likely for a senior accounting major at your college, or one majoring in philosophy? Expected higher income after graduation makes the accountant the more probable buyer. Now consider relative spending by a retired tycoon and a retired postal employee. Even a tycoon suffering huge stock market losses this year is likely to spend significantly more. The point is that wealthy people or those who expect higher incomes typically spend more than poorer people with identical current incomes. Conversely, people who fear losing their jobs tend to decrease their consumption.

Household Size and Ages Big families spend proportionally more from income than small families. Young families busily acquire durables (e.g., cars and appliances), while established families tend to replace only worn-out or obsolete durables. Thus, societies full of young or large families spend proportionally more than societies composed of older or smaller families.

Household Balance Sheets A household's assets include such things as its productive resources, durable goods, and financial wealth; its debts are *liabilities*. Most families that are deeply in debt try to postpone spending to reduce their indebtedness. Financially secure families typically spend proportionally more from current income. Thus, shrinking debt stimulates spending. Families may also spend more if more money becomes available for their purchases.[10]

Consumer Expectations Consumer debt usually climbs when buyers stockpile goods to guard against inflation, but shaky confidence may reduce use of credit. In the late 1970s, soaring prices convinced many young couples they could never afford homes if they waited; panic buying pushed up housing prices even faster. When people expect widespread shortages, they hoard almost anything that can be stored. Outputs for consumers were limited during World War II and shortages were rampant. Most consumers had long "wish lists" and went on spending binges at the war's end. Opposite trends occur if people have recently been on buying sprees — large stocks of new durable goods alleviate the need to purchase more.

Investment

Economic investment enhances future consumption. (Remember that financial investments are merely specialized forms of saving.) Circular flow models identify firms as channels for investment, which falls into three basic categories: (*a*) new buildings and all other *construction*, (*b*) new *equipment*, and (*c*) *inventory accumulation*.

All investment spending is sensitive to business cycles, but inventory accumulation is especially volatile. Erratic customer purchases allow firms only partial control over their inventories. Firms invest in new inventories unintentionally if sales are unexpectedly low, but inventories dwindle and there is unintentional *disinvestment* when sales exceed forecasts. Unexpected inventory changes signal firms to adjust their orders to suppliers.

Expected Rates of Return Planned investment spending depends powerfully on expected rates of return. Firms invest only if the new capital's revenue stream is expected to exceed all costs.

*A **rate of return** is the annual percentage earned from an investment after all costs are considered.*[11]

Rates of return, the level of investment, and Aggregate Demand are positively related to the net revenues expected from investment across time. Like everyone else, investors prefer more income to less income and lower costs to higher costs. And, because time is valuable, they prefer current income to delayed income. (Would you prefer an extra $1,000 now or a year from now?) Similarly, they prefer to delay costs wherever possible. (Would you rather pay $1,000 to the Internal Revenue Service now or 10 years from now?) Another major influence on rates of return and investment decisions is *risk*, which, all else equal, investors try to avoid. Therefore, rates of return rise when expected revenues are greater, are expected sooner, or appear more certain, or when expected costs (including taxes) fall, are postponed, or involve less risk.

Investment is stimulated when technological advances are innovated. Innovations yielding high rates of return tend to arrive erratically and in waves. Consequently, investments to implement technological advances tend to be clustered over time.

Costs of Investment Expected returns rise when capital prices fall and shrink when construction or machinery costs rise. Demands for such capital as lathes or computers rise during upswings, boosting capital prices and inhibiting surges in investment. Conversely, investor pessimism during downturns reduces orders for new capital goods. Capital suppliers then cut prices for new equipment to liquidate their excess inventories, slightly dampening drops in investment.

---

10. How a government's central bank regulates the money supply is addressed in Part 4.

11. Computing rates of return is mathematically parallel to the process used when compounding interest rates.

Interest is the major cost of investment. Investors' opportunity costs rise when interest rates rise — investors with their own funds might make loans instead of buying investment goods, while higher interest rates make investment less attractive for potential investors who must borrow. Taxes on investment income are another consideration. For example, higher corporate taxes shrink after-tax rates of return. Investment tax credits, on the other hand, boost rates of return and demands for investment goods.

Higher expected rates of return boost both investment and Aggregate Demand, but investor pessimism shrinks both investment and Aggregate Demand (shifts it leftward).

Government

Expectations about government policies also affect investment. For example, firms that rely on exports or imports might cancel new capital orders if restrictions on foreign trade are expected. Defense contractors invest heavily when war clouds loom. But government affects Aggregate Demand most directly through its spending and tax policies.

Government Purchases Government purchases such as highways or education resemble private investment by yielding benefits over time. Other purchases immediately exhaust resources and resemble private consumption, e.g., police protection and Medicare. Both consumption and investment types of government purchases directly increase Aggregate Demand. Some outlays, however, do not entail direct spending. For example, cash transfer payments are only translated into Aggregate Demand when the recipients spend these funds on consumer goods. Thus, these payments are not lumped into government purchases.

The percentage of output absorbed by government purchases rose substantially but erratically over this nation's first two centuries, growing most rapidly during wars. The Civil War, World Wars I and II, the Korean conflict, and the Vietnam War were peaks for government demands. Government purchases tend to shrink when a

war ends, but rarely to earlier levels. One possible reason for this upward trend in government spending is that rising standards of living may make voters willing to devote ever larger shares of income to such publicly provided goods as education or parks.

Tax Rates Consumption depends on disposable income, investment depends on after-tax rates of return, how much (and what) we import depends on tariffs and import quotas, while how competitively we can produce goods for export depends, in part, on the burdens of taxation. Thus, higher tax rates generally decrease our Aggregate Demand.

Money When people have more money, they tend to spend it. A larger money supply, all else equal, allows a greater supply of loanable funds, so interest rates will be lower. Lower interest rates stimulate borrowing and spending by both consumers and investors. The central bank of the United States is the Federal Reserve System. How this arm of government regulates the supply of money is detailed in Part 4.

The Foreign Sector

Exports (X) reflect foreign demands for U.S. goods. Thus, they increase Aggregate Demand. Imports (M) are goods produced by foreigners but used by American consumers, investors, or government. In fact, the accounting categories of consumption, investment, and government spending include many goods produced abroad. These imports augment Aggregate Supply but may reduce Aggregate Demand for domestically produced goods, because (presumably) imports may replace some purchases of domestic output. This is one reason declining industries persistently lobby for protection from foreign competition. For example, the auto, clothing, and steel industries have advocated tariffs and quotas for decades; microchip makers have recently echoed similar pleas.

It is conventional to look only at the net effect of the foreign sector on Aggregate Demand. Our level of national income undoubtedly influences our imports. Domestic prosperity inspires imports of Mercedes-Benz cars, French wine, and Nikon cameras, and our vacations and booming industrial production require more foreign oil. On the other hand, our exports depend primarily on economic conditions abroad, which may be in the doldrums even if the American economy is prosperous.

Economic interdependence is, however, accurately characterized by the cliché, "When America sneezes, the rest of the world catches a cold."

Although the foreign sector is vital for the strength and health of our economy, its net effect on Aggregate Demand is relatively small. Exports and imports each average around 10 percent of GNP, so net exports $(X - M)$ are usually only a negligible percentage of Aggregate Spending.

Use Figure 6 to review how all these influences shift Aggregate Demand curves before reading our overview of Aggregate Supply.

FIGURE 6 Shifts of Aggregate Demand Curves

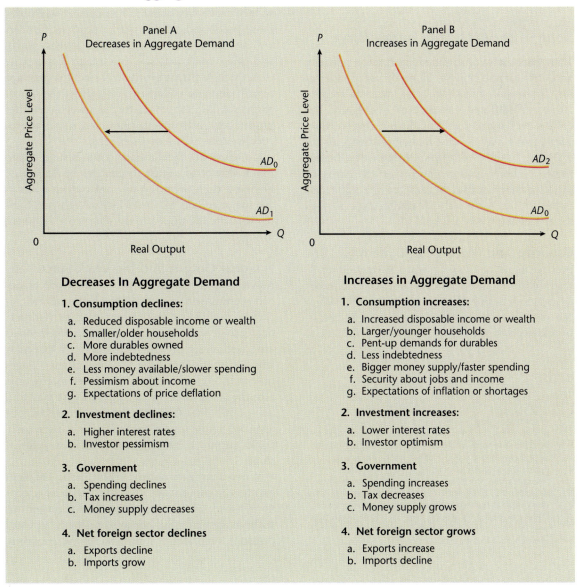

Decreases In Aggregate Demand

1. Consumption declines:
   a. Reduced disposable income or wealth
   b. Smaller/older households
   c. More durables owned
   d. More indebtedness
   e. Less money available/slower spending
   f. Pessimism about income
   g. Expectations of price deflation

2. Investment declines:
   a. Higher interest rates
   b. Investor pessimism

3. Government
   a. Spending declines
   b. Tax increases
   c. Money supply decreases

4. Net foreign sector declines
   a. Exports decline
   b. Imports grow

Increases in Aggregate Demand

1. Consumption increases:
   a. Increased disposable income or wealth
   b. Larger/younger households
   c. Pent-up demands for durables
   d. Less indebtedness
   e. Bigger money supply/faster spending
   f. Security about jobs and income
   g. Expectations of inflation or shortages

2. Investment increases:
   a. Lower interest rates
   b. Investor optimism

3. Government
   a. Spending increases
   b. Tax decreases
   c. Money supply grows

4. Net foreign sector grows
   a. Exports increase
   b. Imports decline

Aggregate Supply

Just as the negative slopes of Aggregate Demand curves resemble those of market demands, the positive slopes of Aggregate Supply curves mimic those of market supplies.

*The **Aggregate Supply curve** reflects a positive relationship between the price level and the real quantity of national output.*

The foundations of Aggregate Supply curves have some parallels with the foundations of market supplies, but there are also some major differences.

Slope of the Aggregate Supply Curve

The general law of diminishing returns partially accounts for the upward slope of supply curves for individual firms and for market supply curves. Additional production eventually becomes ever more costly as output levels grow. Thus, firms may require higher prices to justify expanding their outputs. Moreover, higher prices embody greater incentives for firms to produce more output because of the enhanced opportunities for profits. A similar logic applies for the economy as a whole.[12]

Capacity and Price/Cost Dynamics The positive slope of the Aggregate Supply curve illustrated in Figure 7 reflects the fact that prices adjust more rapidly than production costs. When the price level rises, the delay in cost increases provides profit incentives for greater production.

---

12. Classical theory relies on market forces to quickly and automatically drive an economy to full employment. In the long run, full employment levels of output depend on resources and technology, and not on the price level per se. Thus, classical theory predicts a vertical long-run Aggregate Supply curve. Keynesian theory, on the other hand, deals with depressed economies plagued by so many idle resources that the short-run Aggregate Supply curve is horizontal. An intermediate position that allows us to explore these two extremes is to view Aggregate Supply as positively sloped. The merits of these two positions are explored in much more detail in Parts 3 through 5 of this book.

Idle resources become less available when higher employment presses against a society's productive capacity. The prices a firm can charge in a growing economy tend to rise faster than its resource costs. Thus, profit per unit of output grows during a business upturn. Firms naturally respond by producing and selling more goods. But prices tend to fall faster than costs when business activity slows down, and profit per unit of output may even become negative. Firms facing declining profit margins may drastically cut back production and lay off workers to cut their costs.

For example, if demand for food from your local grocery store expands, movement along the supply curve will occur. The manager will order more goods and quickly mark up prices. Grocers will also hire more workers. Employees' wages and other costs will rise, but much less rapidly than prices, so total profits will swell. What happens if demand collapses? The prices the grocer charges will fall much faster than wages or other production costs. Profits plummet, so many grocery workers will lose their jobs.

Conclusion? Production costs per unit are much slower to adjust to changes in Aggregate Demand than are the prices of output. This is the major reason why a society's Aggregate Supply is positively sloped in the short run, as shown in Figure 7.

National Output and the Work Force National output expands when more workers become employed, but because of diminishing returns, beyond some point, extra workers decreasingly add to total output. Labor markets are based on supply and demand, much like markets for goods you have studied. Higher wages may induce greater effort or attract more people into the labor force, or the unemployed may find acceptable positions after shorter periods of joblessness. Thus, unless the economy is extremely slack, supply curves for labor have a positive slope.

When aggregate output is low and unemployment is high (output $< Q_0$ in Figure 7), economic slack allows most firms to expand output without incurring higher average costs; upward pressure on prices is minimal. As the economy

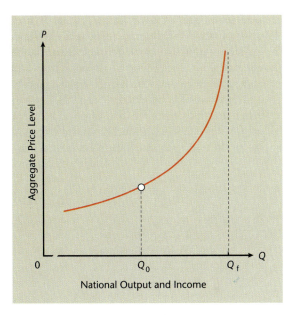

P

Aggregate Price Level

Q₀ Qf

0

Q

National Output and Income

FIGURE 7   The Slope of Aggregate Supply Curves

The Aggregate Supply curve is a positive relationship between aggregate real output and the price level in the short run. When the economy has substantial slack and unemployment is high ($Q < Q_0$), output can be increased without substantial increases in price. As the economy approaches full employment (Q_f), all prices and costs adjust rapidly and completely and the Aggregate Supply curve becomes vertical. This "capacity" level of output can be exceeded in the short run, but only through coercion (e.g., slavery), or by "fooling" workers (e.g., by paying wages that lack the purchasing power workers expected). The prices of outputs tend to adjust faster than production costs when economic conditions change. Thus, profit per unit rises during expansions, or falls during contractions. Aggregate Supply is positively sloped in the short run because firms hire more (*fewer*) workers to produce more (*less*) output when profit per unit rises (*falls*) during an expansion (*contraction*).

approaches its capacity (Q_f) additional output becomes increasingly costly, pushing prices up sharply. Classical theory relies on market forces to quickly and automatically drive an economy to full employment levels of output, which depend on resources and technology, not on the price level per se. Thus, classical economics predicts a vertical *long-run* Aggregate Supply curve. Keynesian theory, on the other hand, deals with depressed economies plagued by so many idle resources that the *short-run* Aggregate Supply

curve is horizontal. Consequently, the Aggregate Supply curve is positively sloped when the economy operates between the extremes of classical full employment and a severe Keynesian depression.

In summary, rising employment and output levels generate pressure for hikes in wages and prices, while falling employment and output create pressure for cuts in wages and prices. How the short-run and long-run adjustments differ will be explored thoroughly after we have surveyed classical and Keynesian macroeconomics in more depth.

Shifts in Aggregate Supply

Aggregate Supply is determined by how technology and government regulation interact with the quantities and qualities of labor, land, capital, and entrepreneurship to shape productive capacity and costs. Our discussion of shifts of Aggregate Supply curves begins with a quick review of the influences on market supply curves detailed in Chapter 3. In addition to price, the major determinants are (*a*) resource costs, (*b*) production technology, (*c*) expectations, (*d*) taxes or subsidies or regulations on producers, (*e*) the prices of other producible goods, and (*f*) the number of producers in the market.

Changes in influences other than its own price cause a good's market supply to shift. The economy's Aggregate Supply curve, however, encompasses all outputs, all producers, and an *average* of all domestic prices (reflected in the price level). Thus, because substitutions between domestic production of different goods tend to cancel each other, we will ignore changes in the prices of other producible goods. We are left with changes (*a*) in the costs and availability of resources, (*b*) technology, (*c*) expectations, and (*d*) government policies as the four major shifters of the Aggregate Supply curve.

Resource Costs   All production absorbs resources, so any shock boosting resource costs reduces Aggregate Supply. As resource costs (e.g., wages for labor) climb, Aggregate Supply falls (shifts to the left), and vice versa. Labor supplies depend on how individuals balance income from work against their enjoyment of leisure. Today, people increasingly opt for more leisure through shorter workweeks, part-time employment, or other forms of work sharing. Growing preferences for leisure over work cause leftward shifts of labor supply curves. Such reductions in labor supplies shift Aggregate Supply leftward, as shown in Panel A of Figure 8 by the shift from AS_0 to AS_1. Alternatively, if more people chose

to work or began working longer hours, Aggregate Supply might shift from AS_0 to AS_2 in Panel B. Another type of labor market disturbance would occur if the power of unions grew and organized labor negotiated higher wages; Aggregate Supply would shrink.

Other resource costs are also important. Most oil-importing countries endured painful leftward shifts in their Aggregate Supply curves during

FIGURE 8 Shifts of Aggregate Supply Curves

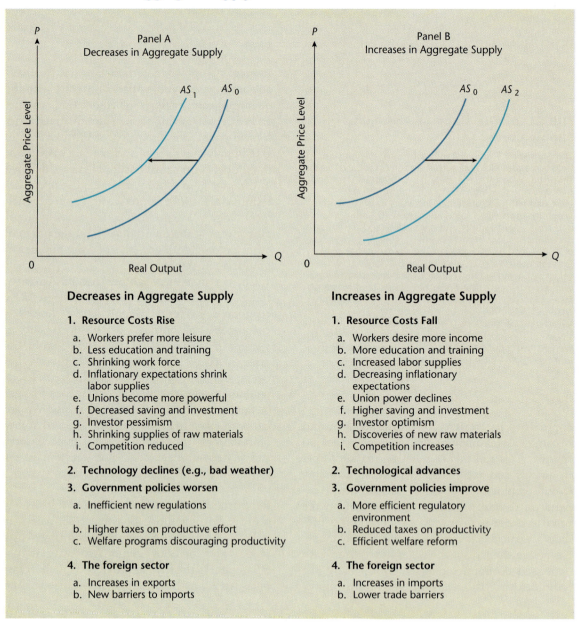

Decreases in Aggregate Supply

1. Resource Costs Rise

a. Workers prefer more leisure
b. Less education and training
c. Shrinking work force
d. Inflationary expectations shrink labor supplies
e. Unions become more powerful
f. Decreased saving and investment
g. Investor pessimism
h. Shrinking supplies of raw materials
i. Competition reduced

2. Technology declines (e.g., bad weather)

3. Government policies worsen

a. Inefficient new regulations

b. Higher taxes on productive effort
c. Welfare programs discouraging productivity

4. The foreign sector

a. Increases in exports
b. New barriers to imports

Increases in Aggregate Supply

1. Resource Costs Fall

a. Workers desire more income
b. More education and training
c. Increased labor supplies
d. Decreasing inflationary expectations
e. Union power declines
f. Higher saving and investment
g. Investor optimism
h. Discoveries of new raw materials
i. Competition increases

2. Technological advances

3. Government policies improve

a. More efficient regulatory environment
b. Reduced taxes on productivity
c. Efficient welfare reform

4. The foreign sector

a. Increases in imports
b. Lower trade barriers

1973–1975, after OPEC quadrupled oil prices. Rightward shifts occur when new resources are discovered and put downward pressure on prices. Discoveries of huge pools of oil in Mexico, Alaska, and Britain's North Sea during the late 1970s created a world oil glut that drove prices down in the 1980s, boosting the Aggregate Supply to the right.

Some "costs" are artificially raised if economic power is increasingly concentrated. Aggregate Supply shrinks when firms with excessive market power reduce output to extract higher prices and profits. Alternatively, Aggregate Supply grows if competition intensifies because of external firms' quests for shares of monopolists' profits, vigorous antitrust actions, or the invasion of a market by imports.

Technology New technologies increase productivity and shift Aggregate Supply curves rightward. A spin-off of the microchip from space programs, for example, has enhanced Aggregate Supplies internationally, in part because robots do boring or repetitive tasks with less physical and mental "burnout" than humans often suffer. Sophisticated software and cheap microcomputers also accelerated office automation, permitting huge firms to grow to sizes once thought hopelessly inefficient. Such innovations permit a society to get more from existing resources and talent.

Expectations Economic expectations about inflation or future prosperity can mold people's decisions in ways that acutely affect Aggregate Supply. For example, investors' willingness to buy new machinery or to plan new construction depends on their projections for future profits. New investments enhance productivity and, consequently, Aggregate Supply.

Inflationary expectations are especially powerful. For example, labor supply curves will shift leftward continuously if workers believe that inflation threatens the purchasing power of their earnings. If you were negotiating with management for your union, the wage increases you would accept would be closely tied to your estimate of how high inflation would be throughout the life of a contract. Expectations of inflation shift Aggregate Supply to the left. Naturally,

decreases in inflationary expectations stabilize labor supplies and shift the Aggregate Supply curve to the right.

Government Policies Work-leisure choices may be influenced by taxes and social welfare policies. Suppose, for example, that personal income tax rates rise. Some people might work harder in attempts to maintain their disposable incomes. However, even more workers would work less, and some might choose not to work at all. These leftward shifts of labor supply curves occur because higher taxes make earning additional income worth less. Workers base work-leisure decisions on take-home pay, not gross wages. Higher Social Security taxes or increases in unemployment compensation or welfare payments also tend to hinder labor supplies. More people try to draw unemployment compensation and labor supply curves shrink if these benefits become more generous.

Critics argue that massive growth of government regulation causes inefficiency. Some estimates suggest that between 5 and 10 percent of GNP is absorbed in complying with federal regulations.[13] If inefficient new regulations (e.g., rigid wage and price controls) smother private business activity, the Aggregate Supply curve shifts to the left (a movement from AS_0 to AS_1 in Figure 8). Abolishing burdensome regulations shifts Aggregate Supply rightward.

For example, airline deregulation in 1978 resulted in sharp declines in fares and the emergence of several new airlines; passenger volume almost doubled in the decade that followed.[14] On the other hand, new regulations that facilitate efficiency increase the Aggregate Supply curve. For example, the supplies of professional services were enhanced by Federal Trade Commission orders forbidding the American Medical Association and American Bar Association from setting medical or legal fees, and banning these organizations from prohibiting advertising by doctors and lawyers.

---

13. See Murray L. Weidenbaum and Robert DeFina, *The Rising Cost of Government Regulation* (St. Louis, MO: Center for the Study of American Business, 31 Jan. 1977).

14. U.S. Aviation Safety Commission, April 18, 1988.

Policies that dampen incentives to introduce new technologies or to accumulate capital hamper economic growth. If policies impede technological advances and investment, the economy declines (or fails to grow as fast as it could), and the Aggregate Supply curve shifts to the left (or is held back). Government policies encouraging capital accumulation (e.g., reduced capital gains taxation) or speeding introduction of modern equipment (investment tax credits) shift the Aggregate Supply curve to the right. The Reagan Administration engineered substantial cuts in corporate taxes, favorable tax treatments for savers, investment tax credits, and accelerated depreciation allowances in attempts to expand Aggregate Supply. Similar reasoning was behind President Bush's call for lower taxes on "capital gains" (which occur when investments grow in value), but concern about massive and growing federal deficits prevented their implementation.

Some changes that shift Aggregate Supply are grouped in the lists below Figure 8. Be sure that you understand why each influence shifts Aggregate Supply as it does.

Macroeconomic Equilibrium

Aggregate Demand and Aggregate Supply meet to yield a unique short-run equilibrium of the aggregate levels of prices and outputs. This is illustrated in Figure 9 with an equilibrium price level of P_e and equilibrium output equal to Q_e (point e). To see why this point represents equilibrium, consider the consequences of a lower price level such as P_1. When prices are below equilibrium, consumers will demand Q_2 level of output — more than is currently supplied (Q_1). Retailers will experience a rise in sales and a decline in inventories, and will order more from wholesalers and manufacturers.

Manufacturers react to growing orders by boosting both production and their own orders for raw materials and intermediate goods. Some may expand output by paying overtime wages to current employees, while others hire additional workers. Additional output will, however, be increasingly costly, raising the prices firms charge. The economy moves from Q_1 to Q_e as aggregate output and employment rise. Equi-

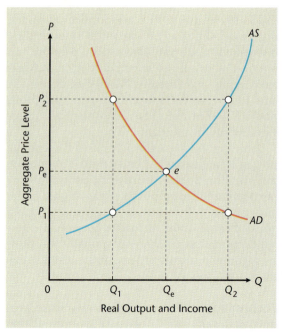

FIGURE 9 Macroeconomic Equilibrium

Macroeconomic equilibrium occurs where Aggregate Demand meets Aggregate Supply. If the price level deviates from this equilibrium (P_e), pressures on business and consumers will move the economy back toward point e. For example, if the price level is tentatively at P_1, excess demands for goods will result in greater sales, shrinking inventories, and new orders to manufacturers. These new orders cause manufacturers to hire additional workers, resulting in more output and employment, but at higher prices (diminishing returns partly explains this). Opposite pressures exist when the price level exceeds P_e.

librium is achieved at Q_e and P_e (point e), and economy-wide excess demands for goods evaporate.

Pressures in the opposite direction would occur if this economy were at a price level P_2. Sales fall and inventories rise, precipitating layoffs and declining aggregate output. Ultimately, these pressures again result in an economy-wide equilibrium at point e.

Comparing equilibrium points when Aggregate Demand and Supply curves shift provides immediate insights into problems faced by macroeconomic policymakers. All major American depressions before World War II were periods when the price level, output, and employment all declined. Note that in Panel A of Figure 10, if

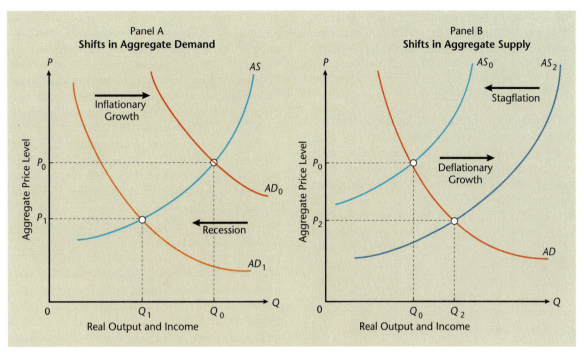

FIGURE 10   Macroeconomic Equilibrium and Shifts in Aggregate Demand and Supply

Employment, income, and the price level all fall if Aggregate Demand falls; society then suffers the hardship of recession or depression. Expansion of Aggregate Demand in Panel A from AD_1 to AD_0, on the other hand, precipitates booming employment and real growth of income accompanied by inflationary pressure. When Aggregate Demand is stable and Aggregate Supply increases, the economy experiences deflationary growth as real output rises but prices fall. When Aggregate Supply declines (AS_2 to AS_0 in Panel B), the economy is hit simultaneously with the twin evils of reduced employment and real output (or higher unemployment) plus inflation. This has been named *stagflation*.

Aggregate Demand falls from AD_0 to AD_1, both the price level (P) and the level of real national income (Q) decline. Thus, one explanation for recessions or depressions is a decline in Aggregate Demand. Conversely, if Aggregate Demand rises from AD_1 to AD_0 (Panel A), both the price level and real output rise. Thus, periods of mild inflation accompanied by real growth conform to expansion of Aggregate Demand relative to Aggregate Supply.

In a similar vein, changes in Aggregate Supply can lead to growth or stagflation. First, as Panel B of Figure 10 illustrates, growth that exerts negative pressure on prices (called *deflationary growth*) can occur if Aggregate Supply increases faster than Aggregate Demand. This pattern was common between 1865 and 1890. Alternatively,

if Aggregate Supply declines, rising prices accompany declines in output and increases in unemployment, a condition known as *stagflation*. This is illustrated in Panel B by a decline in Aggregate Supply from AS_2 to AS_0. Prices rise from P_2 to P_0 while real output falls from Q_2 to Q_0. This is an incumbent politician's nightmare.

The American Business Cycle

The basic Aggregate Demand/Aggregate Supply framework developed in the previous section opens important insights into macroeconomic problems and helps us interpret recent economic history. This section provides an overview of U.S. business cycles in the twentieth century.

Our discussion begins with the 1920s because the events of that decade and the 1930s profoundly changed American perspectives on capitalism.

The Prosperous 1920s

The 1920s were prosperous by any yardstick. Following a minor dip in business activity after World War I, the United States enjoyed a boom lasting until 1929. Prosperity was sparked by (*a*) rapid growth of technology, labor productivity, and productive capacity; (*b*) the popularity of such new and important goods as telephones, radios, and autos; (*c*) electrification of homes and industries; and (*d*) a wave of optimism lasting until 1929.

Rising auto production spurred such subsidiary industries as service stations and oil and rubber. Nationwide electrification also stimulated demands for business capital equipment and consumer goods. These key ingredients yielded record growth. Rapid technological advances allowed growth without inflation, because growth in Aggregate Supply kept pace with growing Aggregate Demand.

The Great Depression of the 1930s

The year 1929 began with widespread optimism that the boom would continue, but by October, a business slump was clearly under way. Almost everyone was shocked at how sharply the economy collapsed, not to recover fully until the eve of World War II. Real disposable income fell by more than 26 percent between 1929 and 1933, while unemployment rates mounted from 3.2 percent to nearly 25 percent. The 6- to 8-percent annual decline in average prices between 1929 and 1933 may sound great, but lower prices were almost meaningless to workers who lacked jobs. Family incomes and assets melted away. Even though consumption spending fell sharply, years of accumulated savings were eroded. Investment was insignificant.

Public welfare programs were meager, so the burden of relief fell primarily on private charities. But harsh times yielded sparse donations. People in other countries commonly suffered even more than Americans because the Great Depression was spread around the globe. Many families were evicted when they were unable to pay rent. The lucky ones would then move to another dwelling or live with relatives for as long as possible. It was as if a large segment of our population had been swept into the dark ages. Entire families spent their days prowling garbage dumps looking for scraps of food and clothing with which to stay warm and alive.

Hindsight provides explanations for the Great Depression that could not be derived from the supply-side emphasis of classical theory that had dominated economic thinking in the 1930s. In Figure 11, if the Aggregate Demand curve falls from AD_{1929} to AD_{1933}, the price level and real national income (Q) both decline. Employment is closely tied to national output, so employment also falls and unemployment rates tend to rise. Thus, recessions and depressions are almost uniformly periods when Aggregate Demand has plummeted.

War and Its Aftermath in the 1940s

The economy falteringly began to recover after the trough of 1933, but unemployment still hovered at 15 percent in 1940. Massive defense spending during World War II had snapped the economy out of the Depression in the early 1940s, apparently confirming John Maynard Keynes's ideas in his *General Theory* that recessionary trends could be overcome through government spending to boost Aggregate Demand.

The government imposed rationing to divert output to the war effort and price controls in attempts to defuse inflationary pressures. After World War II, most consumers had amassed huge savings because many goods had been tightly rationed or not produced at all. The price level jumped about 10 percent in 1946, after the war had ended and price controls were lifted. Aggregate Demand grew when families binged on new cars and appliances; manufacturing plants for these products had been restricted to war goods.

The Sluggish 1950s

The 1950s were a period of modest growth, with occasional doses of mild inflation. A short-term jump in inflation occurred, however, at the onset

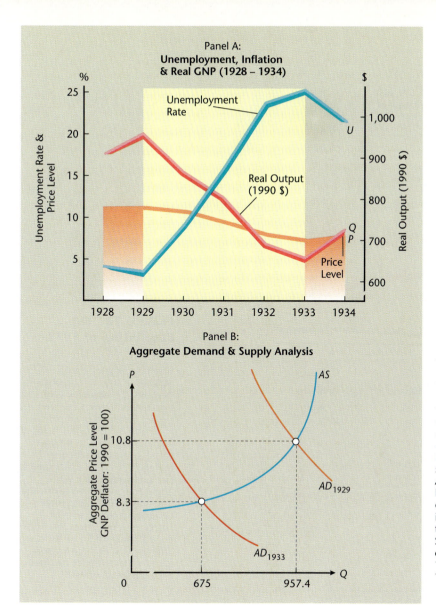

Panel A:
Unemployment, Inflation & Real GNP (1928 – 1934)

Panel B:
Aggregate Demand & Supply Analysis

FIGURE 11   The Great Depression

Employment, real output and income, and the price level all fell when Aggregate Demand shrunk from AD_{1929} to AD_{1933} while Aggregate Supply remained stable. The collapse of the economy resulted in extended hardships for nearly all Americans. Such movements also occurred during the severe recession of 1981–1983. Expansion of Aggregate Demand AD_{1933} to AD_{1929}, on the other hand, precipitates booming employment and real growth of income accompanied by inflationary pressure. The United States experienced movements of this sort throughout the 1960s, and from 1983 through 1990.

of the Korean conflict. Many consumers, remembering hassles associated with rationing and price controls during World War II, tried to stockpile commodities that they expected to be rationed. This panic buying caused a short burst of price hikes, but the price level was relatively stable over the rest of the decade, climbing at an average rate of only 1 to 2 percent annually. A mild recession followed the Korean War (1949–1952), and another ended the decade.

The Booming 1960s

John F. Kennedy was the first major U.S. politician to propose tax cuts to stimulate Aggregate Demand when the economy was not in a deep depression. Lyndon Johnson's administration followed through with sharp cuts in tax rates. The experiment worked, and the nation heralded an era of prosperity under the guiding hands of Washington economists.

Figure 11 helps show trends in the 1960s. Growth of Aggregate Demand from AD_{1933} to AD_{1929} increases employment, national income, and the price level. Many economists thought that macroeconomic "fine-tuning" could reduce an apparent trade-off between unemployment and inflation to a minor irritant. Then pressure from the Vietnam War began overheating our economic engine. Nevertheless, unemployment dropped to a low 3.2 percent, and the federal budget was last balanced in 1969.

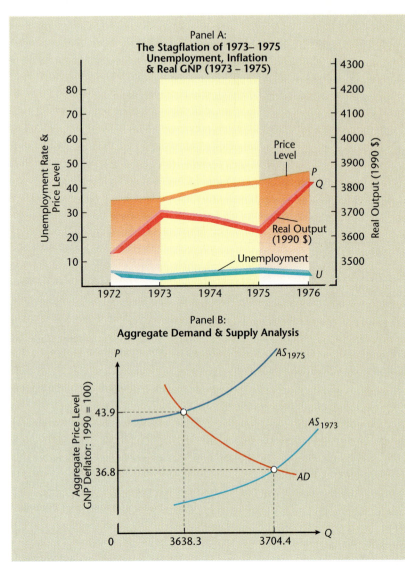

Panel A:
The Stagflation of 1973– 1975
Unemployment, Inflation
& Real GNP (1973 – 1975)

Panel B:
Aggregate Demand & Supply Analysis

FIGURE 12 The Stagflation of 1973– 1975

When Aggregate Supply declines relative to Aggregate Demand, the economy is hit simultaneously with the twin evils of increased unemployment and inflation. This is called *stagflation*, a malaise experienced in the U.S. economy during 1973–1975. If Aggregate Demand were stable while Aggregate Supply increased, the economy would experience *deflationary growth* as real output rose but prices fell. The period 1870–1895 was the last time the U.S. economy experienced sustained price declines and substantial growth.

Stagflation in the 1970s

Demand-side inflationary forces arising from escalation of the Vietnam War induced President Nixon to introduce peacetime wage and price controls on August 15, 1971. The mid-1970s saw our first brush with serious supply-side inflation. Lagging productivity growth and rising prices for energy and other raw materials erupted in rapid inflation and high unemployment that persisted through the decade. Real output grew slowly; on the average, unemployment rates rose, while the United States experienced its most persistent and severe inflation since the Civil War.

This "stagflation" is characterized in Figure 12. Although the economy as a whole grew in the 1970s, growth in Aggregate Supply remained below that of Aggregate Demand; the shift from AS_1 to AS_0 in Figure 12 reflects this relative movement. Thus, declines (or slower growth) in Aggregate Supply relative to Aggregate Demand may account for poor overall economic performance.

The Erratic 1980s

The Reagan Administration's attempts to shrink inflation and high interest rates triggered the deepest recession since the 1930s. (This is illustrated as a decline in Aggregate Demand in Figure 11.) "Supply-side" tax cuts enacted in 1981 eventually stimulated both Aggregate Demand and economic growth (the growth of Aggregate Demand in Figure 11). By the mid-1980s, inflation and unemployment were both relatively low, but federal deficits continued to mushroom into the 1990s. The national debt, which had tripled during the 1970s, tripled again between 1980 and 1990.

Competitiveness became a paramount issue when goods from Pacific Rim countries (especially Japan) and the European Community began flooding world markets, dislodging American products from markets in which they had been dominant. The dollar's status as the world's premier currency was eroded, and U.S. balances of payments and trade persistently experienced huge deficits. Remedying persistent deficits in the federal budget and our balances of trade and payments while adapting to the internationalization of economies everywhere in the world may be as formidable a task as curing the Great Depression seemed in 1933.

Our Aggregate Demand and Supply framework helps illustrate economic events and the major goals of macroeconomic policy — full employment, price stability, and economic growth. But before we can discuss macroeconomic goals and policy options knowledgeably, we need to understand more about unemployment and inflation. Chapter 6 addresses some reasons for unemployment and inflation, and describes how these important concepts are measured.

Chapter Review: Key Points

1. *Business cycles* consist of alternating periods of economic expansion and contraction. A business cycle is typically broken down into four phases: (*a*) *peak* (boom), (*b*) *contraction* (recession or downturn), (*c*) *trough* (depression), and (*d*) *expansion* (recovery or upturn). Business cycles are measured from peak to peak by the National Bureau of Economic Research, and have averaged roughly 4 years although some have been as short as 18 months, while others have lasted a decade. Reference dates are established by a detailed examination of data from past cycles.

2. Such things as mental and physical health problems, marital tensions, divorces, suicides, alcoholism, prostitution, illegitimacy, and both personal and property crime are closely related to changes in business conditions. Marriages and divorces alike tend to be positively related to the business cycle. Mental disorders and some physical diseases, suicides, crimes, and illegitimate births appear inversely related to business conditions. That is, they all rise when the economy turns down. Declines in income and the negative social effects of business slumps together have prompted policymakers to look for ways to keep the economy on a steady path.

3. Many early business cycle theories were *external shock* theories, focusing on sources of instability outside the economic system such as changing weather conditions and wars.

4. *Joseph Schumpeter* developed a business cycle theory around major innovations that may partially explain major long-term business fluctuations. He cited the development of railroads, automobiles, and similar innovations as generating significant investment leading to tremendous economic growth for a period of time.

5. *N. D. Kondratieff* suggested that long waves of economic activity (40 to 60 years) underlie minor reverberations that occur roughly every four to eight years. Economists tend to be skeptical about this *long-wave theory* and view it as a statistical coincidence.

6. *Psychological theories* of the business cycle use people's herd instincts to explain the effects of extended periods of optimism or pessimism. These theories may partially account for the cumulative nature of business cycle downturns or recoveries, but provide little insight into the reasons for turning points.

7. *Classical macroeconomics* focuses on resolving scarcity from the supply side. It relies on

market forces to automatically move the economy to full employment and views recessions as self-extinguishing without a role for government.

8. The persistence of the Great Depression seemed to refute classical theory, which was dominated by the demand-oriented theories of John Maynard Keynes from 1936 through the 1960s. *Keynesian macroeconomics* concludes that government can counter business cycles by adjusting Aggregate Demand through government tax and spending policies.

9. *Aggregate Demand* is based on spending by (*a*) consumers, (*b*) investors, (*c*) government, and (*d*) foreigners (i.e., net exports). The *Aggregate Demand curve* is negatively sloped because a higher price level causes reduced spending on our domestic output due to (*a*) the *wealth effect*, (*b*) the *foreign sector substitution effect*, and (*c*) the *interest rate effect*.

10. The single most important determinant of *consumer spending* is disposable income. Other important determinants of consumption and saving include (*a*) wealth and expectations of future income, (*b*) the average size and age composition of typical households, (*c*) household balance sheets and stocks of consumer goods, and (*d*) consumer expectations regarding prices and availability of products.

11. *Investment* in capital refers to purchases of new output that can be used in the future to produce other goods and services. There are three major components of investment: (*a*) new business and residential structures, (*b*) machinery and equipment, and (*c*) inventory accumulation.

12. The quantity of investment is determined primarily by expected returns from investment which, in turn, depend on (*a*) expectations about the business environment, (*b*) rates of technological change and innovation, (*c*) existing stocks of capital relative to total production, and (*d*) investment costs, which depend most on the interest rate.

13. *Exports* (*X*) add to Aggregate Demand and detract from Aggregate Supply. (Goods sold to foreigners are not available to Americans.) *Imports* (*M*) enhance Aggregate Supply and may reduce Aggregate Demand.

(Buyers of imported goods may spend less on American goods.) Exports and imports are reasonably balanced, so *net exports* (*X* − *M*) have a comparatively small net effect on Aggregate Demand. The foreign sector is vital to our economic strength, however, because it provides (*a*) markets for our production and (*b*) imported goods that would be much more costly if produced only domestically.

14. The *Aggregate Supply curve* is positively sloped, because when business conditions change, a firm can adjust its prices more rapidly than its production costs. Prosperity increases per unit profit, so firms hire more resources and produce more output.

15. Aggregate Supply curves shift in response to changes in (*a*) supplies of resources, (*b*) technology, (*c*) government policies that affect costs, or (*d*) net imports.

16. Increases in Aggregate Demand tend to increase national income and output, employment, and the price level. Increases in Aggregate Supply exert downward pressures on prices and facilitate growth of employment and national income and output.

Key Concepts

Ensure that you can define these terms before proceeding.

business cycle	Keynesian
turning points	macroeconomics
external shocks	Aggregate Demand
population dynamics	wealth effects
population S-curves	foreign sector
long-wave theory	substitution
of business cycle	interest rate effects
Marxian "capitalistic	consumption
crises"	investment
innovations	rate of return
psychological	government purchases
theories	net exports
classical	Aggregate Supply
macroeconomics	

Problems and Questions

1–8. Use up arrows (↑), down arrows (↓), zeros (0), or question marks (?) in the blanks to indicate how (*a*) Aggregate Demand and (*b*)

Aggregate Supply will be shifted by the economic changes described in questions 1 through 8, and how each change will affect (c) national income and output, (d) total employment, (e) employment rates, and (f) the price level. (*Note:* Both Aggregate Demand and Aggregate Supply may be affected in some instances, some reasonable arguments are debatable, and long-run consequences can differ from short-run effects.)

1. Twenty years after a new baby boom, millions of young workers begin to establish families and enter the work force.
   a. _____   b. _____
   c. _____   d. _____
   e. _____   f. _____

2. A nuclear power meltdown kills hundreds, and all nuclear plants are shut down while the accident is investigated.
   a. _____   b. _____
   c. _____   d. _____
   e. _____   f. _____

3. Investors pessimistically begin to expect lower rates of return because their consultants predict a recession.
   a. _____   b. _____
   c. _____   d. _____
   e. _____   f. _____

4. People become increasingly conscientious about recycling glass, paper, plastic, and aluminum and other scrap metals.
   a. _____   b. _____
   c. _____   d. _____
   e. _____   f. _____

5. Italian investors establish American plants to build Fiats, jewelry, and fine furniture.
   a. _____   b. _____
   c. _____   d. _____
   e. _____   f. _____

6. Record harvests in the Soviet Union reduce international demands for U.S. agricultural products.
   a. _____   b. _____
   c. _____   d. _____
   e. _____   f. _____

7. Widespread deregulation eliminates 7,000 pages of inefficient federal regulations.
   a. _____   b. _____
   c. _____   d. _____
   e. _____   f. _____

8. A Constitutional amendment is adopted requiring the federal budget to balance; tax rates are increased and government spending falls by $200 billion.
   a. _____   b. _____
   c. _____   d. _____
   e. _____   f. _____

9–11. Indicate whether the rates of return expected by most investors will rise or fall, and what will happen to the levels of investment and Aggregate Demand in response to the events described in questions 9 through 11.

9. Congress reduces quotas (maximums allowable) for foreign oil, textiles, steel, and automobiles, and enacts the highest U.S. tariffs since the 1930 Smoot-Hawley Tariff on most other imports.

10. President Bush's proposal to slash tax rates on "capital gains" from investments is finally enacted.

11. Stock markets crash in Tokyo, Hong Kong, London, Australia, and New York when a Martian fleet of starships signals its intention to invade Earth.

12. Draw several capital "S's" lying on their sides and connect them to represent reasonably smooth business cycles. (Time is on the horizontal axis; growth of national income is on the vertical axis.) Now identify periods of (a) boom, (b) expansion, (c) recession, (d) peak, (e) trough, (f) contraction, (g) recovery, and (h) depression.

13. Draw sets of Aggregate Demand and Aggregate Supply curves and show shifts to reflect the following circumstances.

    a. Increases in national income and output and reductions in the price level.

    b. Increases in national income and output and increases in the price level.

    c. Decreases in national income and output and decreases in the price level.

    d. Decreases in national income and output and increases in the price level.

    e. Increases in national income and output and a relatively stable price level.

    Identify periods when the American economy experienced each of these situations.

CHAPTER

Unemployment and Inflation

Being laid off or fired is a depressing event that some workers experience numerous times in their careers. Prolonged joblessness, which can become an epidemic during downturns of the business cycle, can be even more devastating. During severe recessions, many unemployed workers and their families are left destitute, unable to afford even the bare necessities of life. Thus, *unemployment* is a major macroeconomic problem.

Inflation is another crucial macroeconomic issue. Savers intent on buying new homes, paying for their children's educations, or retiring in comfort can have their plans shattered by runaway inflation (increases in most nominal prices). At very high rates of inflation, even simple exchanges become extremely difficult because uncertainty makes nominal prices seem almost meaningless. Fortunately for most Americans, the severe inflation experienced at times in some countries has been rare in the United States, although mild inflation has been a sporadic but nagging problem for decades.

We examine the meanings of the terms "unemployment" and "inflation" in this chapter, how each is measured, their possible causes, and their respective costs and benefits. Only after we understand inflation, unemployment, and the meaning of *economic growth* (which is usually measured by changes in Gross National Product — the subject of our next chapter), can we reasonably address how to reduce unemployment to tolerable levels, and how to dampen inflationary pressures that have persisted for a half century.

Unemployment

Friday began like any other morning. The shrill beep-beep-beep of the alarm, steam rising from a hot shower, and the smell of brewing coffee. Driving to work entailed the usual irritations. Morning conferences seemed standard fare, with most thoughts focused on the coming weekend's activities. The bomb dropped at 2 P.M. The plant manager announced the loss of a major contract. Layoffs would affect not only assembly line workers this time, but executives as well. Two months' severance pay and accrued vacation were in the final check. Firm handshakes accompanied sincere wishes for the best of luck. Then, out the door, lugging a cardboard box of personal effects. The trip home was a nightmare. "My skills are strong; some competitors may need my expertise. But are they hiring now? Recession has been in the news lately. How will the mortgage be paid? Will I have to move to find work?" The happily anticipated weekend has been enveloped by pure gloom.

This executive is experiencing a reaction typical for those who are cut adrift without a job. Massive unemployment during the Great Depression was extremely traumatic for many Americans, and ultimately led to the Employment Act of 1946, which specified "maintaining maximum employment" as one government goal. Weighing achievement of this goal usually begins with the overall unemployment rate—a statistic heard regularly on the nightly news. But this single measure is only a crude guide to policy because unemployment occurs for several reasons. Before examining the different types of unemployment, we must discover who the unemployed are.

The Concept of Unemployment

Half of the 250 million people in the United States are in the labor force, but this does not mean the rest are unemployed. (Any notion that homemakers are *not* working is quickly cured by a short stint up to your elbows in dish suds with a screaming 2-year-old tugging at your leg.) Adults can elect to be, or not to be, members of the labor force. Economists classify people as "employed" or "unemployed" only if they choose to be in the labor force.

> *Conceptually,* **unemployment** *occurs when people are able to work and would willingly accept the prevailing wage paid to someone with their skills, but either cannot find or have not yet secured suitable employment.*

Voluntary vs. Involuntary Unemployment

Unemployment can be viewed as either voluntary or involuntary.

> **Voluntary unemployment** *occurs when people could find work quickly, but choose to search for what they view as better jobs in terms of pay or working conditions.*

For example, you would be voluntarily unemployed if you turned down a night job that required a 50-mile commute, looking instead for 9-to-5 work closer to your home.

Some people believe that all unemployment is voluntary: If you really want a job and are willing to work for "what you're worth," you can find

work almost immediately. I am willing to hire you to paint my home, mow my lawn, or babysit as long as you accept a wage equal to what these activities are worth to me. My neighbor would do the same. Thus, if you are unemployed for more than a few hours, it *must* be voluntary.

The counterargument is that people should not be forced to accept just any job.

> **Involuntary unemployment** *occurs when people lack jobs, but they are willing and able to work at wages commensurate with their skills.*

Work should neither underemploy people's skills nor insult their human worth. And there may be times and places where wretched business conditions yield no job openings.

Neither position is unambiguously correct. Willingness to work at prevailing wages is impossible to ascertain, so any measure of involuntary unemployment is only an educated guess. In any event, published unemployment data rely on government surveys that use criteria only loosely related to our conceptual definition of unemployment.

Measuring Unemployment

The U.S. Department of Labor uses the following definitions to classify people as employed, unemployed, and in or out of the labor force.

> *The* **labor force** *consists of all employed or unemployed civilians over age 16 plus members of the Armed Forces stationed in the United States.*

A **labor force participation rate** is the proportion in the labor force from a specific group. The **employment–population ratio** is total employment relative to the population.[1]

Employed persons include (*a*) all civilians who worked for pay any time during the week that includes the 12th day of the month or who worked unpaid for 15 hours or more in a family-operated enterprise, and (*b*) those who were temporarily absent from their regular jobs be-

---

1. Source: U.S. Department of Labor, *Monthly Labor Review*, numerous issues.

cause of illness, vacation, industrial dispute, or similar reasons. Members of the Armed Forces stationed in the United States are also counted as employed. Persons working at more than one job are counted only in the job at which they worked the greatest number of hours.

Unemployed persons are those who did not work during the survey week but were available for work, except for temporary illness, and who looked for jobs within the preceding 4 weeks. Persons who did not look for work because they were on layoff or waiting to start new jobs within the next 30 days are also counted among the unemployed.

The overall **unemployment rate** *is the number unemployed as a percent of the total labor force.*

Our major source of unemployment statistics in the United States is a monthly Department of Labor survey of about 60,000 households. This survey (illustrated in Figure 1) asks detailed questions to determine the labor force status of each adult family member. This large sample ensures that the statistics collected are reasonably good.

Limitations of Unemployment Statistics

Unemployment statistics may fail to accurately reflect the true level of unemployment. One possibility is that published statistics understate

FIGURE 1   Determining Who Is Unemployed

A monthly questionnaire administered to roughly 60,000 families randomly selected by the Bureau of Labor Statistics uses the logical chains in this figure to ascertain the work force status of people aged 16 and over.

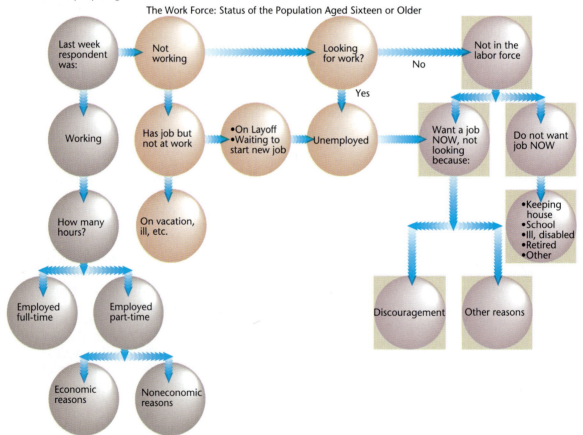

The Work Force: Status of the Population Aged Sixteen or Older

true unemployment—some workers who are truly unemployed may not be counted because they have given up looking for jobs.

Discouraged workers *are so pessimistic about their prospects that they do not look for jobs, although they would like to work.*

Figure 2 shows that the discouraged worker syndrome is most pronounced during recessions, when many people perceive that job openings are few and far between.

On the other hand, unemployment statistics may be overstated because of our unemployment compensation system. (Have you ever known people who drew unemployment checks even though they did not want a job?)

Dishonest nonworkers *claim to be available for work so they can draw unemployment benefits, even though they do not intend to work.*

Discouraged workers and dishonest nonworkers bias unemployment statistics in opposite directions. Which effect is stronger is a matter of continuing debate.

FIGURE 2   The Unemployment Rate and Discouraged Workers

This graph indicates how failure to include discouraged workers among the unemployed causes the measured unemployment to be understated. More workers become despondent and cease looking for a job during economic downturns. Obtaining an accurate count of discouraged workers is extremely difficult.

Sources: Bureau of Labor Statistics, *Handbook of Labor Statistics*, 1985, U.S. Department of Commerce, *Statistical Abstract of the United States*, 1991, *Economic Report of the President*, 1991, and updates by the authors.

Sources of Unemployment

Five different but overlapping forces generate five types of unemployment: *frictional, seasonal, structural, cyclical,* and *induced.* Each poses somewhat unique problems for government policy.

Frictional Unemployment   People enter or reenter the work force, are fired or permanently laid off, or voluntarily quit one job to look for another. Both firms and workers expend resources trying to match job applicants with job openings. Information about job openings and applicants is far from perfect, and mobility (e.g., relocating an employee or moving to get a job) is costly.

Frictional unemployment *arises from transaction costs incurred in matching workers with jobs.*

In a narrow sense, virtually all unemployment is frictional. Suppose transaction costs were zero. This would mean that every potential worker would know about all possible jobs, and that every firm would know about all potential workers. Moreover, mobility would be instantaneous and costless. In such a world, people willing and able to work could instantly move into the (relatively) best jobs available to them, and firms could instantly fill every available job with the worker having the greatest comparative advantage in that job. The fit between workers and jobs would be optimal.

However, it actually takes time for workers to move between jobs, and for firms to find suitable employees. Thus, many economists refer to frictional unemployment as *search* unemployment. This search process can be viewed as *investment in information.* Workers search for satisfying and remunerative employment, sometimes turning down several jobs before finding a position that suits them. They will continue to look for a better job until the expected marginal benefits from further search (e.g., higher wage offers) no longer exceed their expected marginal costs (wages forgone while looking).

Similarly, firms search for workers with skills that are honed to accomplish the work until their marginal benefits (better workers or lower wages) no longer exceed their marginal costs (e.g., forgone output and profit). Firms may make many job offers before finding someone acceptable who agrees to the job conditions. (Most fast-food restaurants post semipermanent HELP WANTED signs.) Unemployed workers often offer their labor ten or twenty times before landing a job that meets their own requirements. Thus, frictional unemployment is an unavoidable by-product of normal economic activity. Unemployment rates naturally increase as the average *duration* of search increases.

The employed and unemployed both experience considerable **turnover** (a term used when workers change jobs). For example, employment in 1990 averaged more than 125 million persons per month, but about 138 million different persons worked at some time during the year. While unemployment averaged around 7 million per month, nearly 24 million people experienced unemployment at some time during those 12 months.

Seasonal Unemployment Vacations, football, tomato harvests, and holidays are seasonal activities. Seasonal unemployment also varies systematically over the year. For example, most lifeguards are only employed during the summer months. Economic data published for activities that vary regularly over the year, including unemployment, must be seasonally adjusted to make them comparable.

> **Seasonal unemployment** *varies systematically over the year.*

Weather, for example, operates from the demand side to drive employment patterns in agriculture and construction. Department store Santa Clauses work only a few weeks annually. Beach towns and ski resorts also experience seasonal swings in employment. Seasonal influences emerge on the supply side as well. School vacations are the major reason that teenage unemployment rises in June and falls in September.

Structural Unemployment Some individuals lack significant marketable skills, a barrier that makes finding work an ordeal in the best of times.

> **Structural unemployment** *occurs when a worker's skills do not meet the requirements of virtually any job opening.*

Why are people who are structurally unemployed usually jobless for long periods? First, structural change may displace some workers. For example, technological innovation may make certain skills obsolete. Many typesetters found themselves jobless after computerized typesetting, which did the same job with less labor and at a lower cost, was introduced. Today, desktop publishing is replacing traditional paste-up and layout work. Second, some people have acquired few, if any, job skills. Examples include many high school dropouts and most ex-convicts. Firms may find it unprofitable to hire and train workers if they expect their training costs to exceed the benefits to the firm. This is especially a problem if employees commonly leave to find better jobs after being trained.

Cyclical Unemployment Employment and output both rise during economic booms and decline during downturns.

> **Cyclical unemployment** *coincides with downturns in business cycles.*

Many marginal firms shut down during recessions or are forced into bankruptcy, which pushes up unemployment rates. Figure 3 shows that joblessness has varied enormously over the past century. These swings are dominated by cyclical unemployment, which is a major target of macroeconomic policy.

Unless your family or friends are affected directly, unemployment rates may seem fairly abstract. Not all groups of workers are affected in the same way by a cyclical downturn. Table 1 shows unemployment rates for specific groups during selected periods of high and low employment. Cyclical unemployment is heavily borne by manufacturing and construction workers, and affects professional and technical workers less severely.

Cyclical downturns tend to increase the average *duration* of unemployment. The effects on official unemployment statistics are identical if 52 workers each lose a week of work or one

FIGURE 3   The Rate of Unemployment, 1900–1990

The unemployment rate has varied considerably over time. Unemployment reached a peak in 1933 when roughly one in four workers was out of work. Unemployment rates dropped to 1.2 percent, an all-time low, during World War II.

Sources: 1900–1928 derived from Stanley Lebergott, *Manpower and Economic Growth* (New York: McGraw-Hill, 1974); 1929–1990 derived from the Bureau of Labor Statistics and *Economic Report of the President*, 1991.

worker is jobless for a year, but the suffering associated with long-term unemployment is probably disproportionately higher. Families that rely on regular paychecks may endure minor discomfort if a primary breadwinner is jobless for a short period, but extended unemployment is likely to be a disaster.

Induced Unemployment   Finally, certain government policies induce some unemployment. Minimum-wage laws, for example, over-

price the labor of unskilled and inexperienced workers and limit their job opportunities. Unemployment compensation provides incentives for people who sincerely desire work to turn down some employment offers in the hope that they will find the perfect job if they keep looking. Laws requiring wages at the union scale on government contract work are another hindrance to full employment—they leave workers unemployed who would be willing to work for less on government contracts.

Table 1   *Percentage Unemployed by Industry and Occupation (Selected Periods of High and Low Unemployment)*

	(1973) Peak Low Unemployment	(1975) Trough High Unemployment	(1981) Peak Low Unemployment	(1982) Trough High Unemployment
Total unemployment	4.9	8.5	7.6	9.8
Professional and technical	2.2	3.2	2.8	3.3
Government	2.7	4.1	4.7	4.9
Blue-collar	6.2	14.7	12.2	17.7
Manufacturing	4.4	10.9	8.3	12.3
Service	5.8	8.6	8.9	10.6
Construction	8.9	18.0	15.6	20.0

Source: U.S. Department of Labor, *Monthly Labor Review*, 1991.

More than one type of unemployment may account for some joblessness. For example, a golf pro in Michigan who lacked other skills might find a job easily each May, but be both seasonally and structurally unemployed in the dead of winter. Simple frictional unemployment and seasonal unemployment are normal by-products of economic activity. These two types of unemployment pose relatively mild social problems when compared with structural, cyclical, or induced unemployment. Nevertheless, different government programs are broadly aimed at different types of unemployment:

1. State employment offices match job applicants with vacant positions to reduce transaction costs that lead to frictional and seasonal unemployment.

2. Government retraining programs are intended to provide marketable skills to the structurally unemployed, and firms that hire the "hard-core" unemployed receive tax subsidies.

3. Occasional reforms to the unemployment compensation system (e.g., tighter monitoring to prevent cheating) are aimed at reducing induced unemployment. A lower minimum wage rate that applies to trainees is aimed at reducing unemployment among teenagers.

4. Policymakers attempt to reduce cyclical unemployment by trying to dampen the frequency, intensity, and duration of economic downturns.

Although cyclical unemployment is a primary focus of macroeconomic policy, general prosperity tends to ease unemployment of all types, a fact reflected in the cliché, "A rising tide lifts all boats."

Costs and Benefits of Unemployment

Unemployment imposes costs on all of us. Unemployment compensation eases the burdens of missed paychecks on most people who lose their jobs, but the resulting higher payroll taxes spread the cost of lost production across all workers and employers. The aggregate costs of unemployment fall into two categories: lost income and social costs.

Losses of Aggregate Income

Production lost because of unemployment is not trivial.

> The **lost-income costs of unemployment** consist of the value of the output the unemployed could have produced.

Estimates of the income lost because of the recession of 1989–1992 range to $700 billion— almost 12 percent of potential annual Gross Domestic Product. Even if the unemployed are partially buffered by unemployment compensation, society as a whole suffers, because production falls when the jobless rate soars.

Social Costs of Unemployment

The social and psychic costs of unemployment may be even more tragic than the financial losses. Table 1 indicates that the burdens of unemployment are not spread evenly, but dry statistics may cloud our view of the people behind the numbers. Consider the memories of a woman who was a college student during the Great Depression:

When I attended Berkeley in 1936 so many of the kids had actually lost their fathers. They had wandered off in disgrace because they couldn't support their families. Other fathers had killed themselves, so the family could have the insurance. Families had totally broken down. Each father took it as his personal failure . . . so they killed themselves. It was still the Depression. There were kids who didn't have a place to sleep, huddling under bridges on the campus. I had a scholarship, but there were times when I didn't have food. The meals were often three candy bars.[2]

---

2. Source: Studs Terkel, *Working: People Talk About What They Do All Day & How They Feel About What They Do* (New York: Pantheon Books, 1974).

The self-confidence of workers who view their jobs as central to their lives may be crushed by extended unemployment. Joblessness also wreaks havoc with family structures. Families may exhaust their assets and go deeply in debt. Plans for college can go up in smoke. Teenagers suffer especially high unemployment rates, and some acquire criminal records. Table 2 provides estimates of some human costs of unemployment. The damage caused by long-term unemployment is a major reason why the Employment Act of 1946 emphasized promoting full employment.

Trauma from unemployment has been partially reduced by higher unemployment compensation benefits, and partly by having more than one breadwinner in many families. Both spouses worked full-time in 1960 in only one-quarter of all traditional families. More than half now have two wage earners. By 1990, in two-thirds of households where the husband was unemployed, another family member had a full-time job.

Benefits from Unemployment

The bad press unemployment receives largely derives from its economic, social, and psychic costs, while its *allocative* and *disciplinary* benefits go largely unpublicized.

Allocative Benefits Unemployment yields *allocative benefits* by facilitating match-ups between workers and jobs. Looking for a new job is easier if you are not working full-time. At the same time, pools of unemployed labor allow firms to interview more potential employees than if jobless rates were zero. This process, whereby firms search for suitable help while the unemployed search for work, represents investment in labor market information. This cuts transaction costs, enhancing economic efficiency. Unemployment also prompts some workers to return to school or to acquire new skills through on-the-job apprenticeships.

Some critics cite unemployment as an evil unique to capitalism. Unemployment was unacceptable when the tenets of Marxism ruled Eastern Europe, but guarantees of jobs at all times for all citizens resulted in artificial work for many. For example, rest room attendants who sold tickets and toilet paper have been fixtures in Eastern European railway stations, but their pay typically exceeds their receipts. (Siberia once beckoned Soviet citizens who objected to meaningless work.) Recent reform movements may signal growing acceptance that unemployment performs a valuable allocative function. One reason so many people in these previously socialist countries resist these reforms is the widespread unemployment that accompanies conversion from obsolete factory systems to the modern industrialization that should, ultimately, boost production and income.

Disciplinary Benefits We all know people who exaggerate the worth of their own work and who do not pull their own weight. Many make unwarranted demands for wages, vacations, coffee breaks, and other perks. Some economists view possible layoffs as curbs to excessive de-

---

TABLE 2 *Estimated Incidence of Some Social Traumas Caused by a 1 Percent Increase in Unemployment Rates Over a 6-Year Period*

Social Trauma	Incidence of Trauma Related to a 1% Rise in Unemployment (1990)
Total Mortality	46,466
Whites	
Males	15,571
Females	20,829
Nonwhites	
Males	4,824
Females	5,242
Cardiovascular Mortality	25,498
Cirrhosis of Liver Mortality	1,159
Homicide	817
State Mental Hospital First Admissions	
Males	3,853
Females	1,472
State Prison Admissions	4,207

Source: M. Harvey Brenner, "Influence of the Social Environment on Psychology: The Historical Perspective," in *Stress and Mental Disorder,* ed. James E. Barrett (NY: Raven University Press, 1979). Reprinted by permission. Updated to 1990 population by the authors.

mands for wages and fringe benefits. Threats of unemployment are also powerful work incentives for people who respond better to sticks than to carrots. These *disciplinary benefits* accrue to firms (and consumers) when there is slack in the labor market.

Evidence that the costs of unemployment generally outweigh its benefits includes the emphasis unemployment receives from policymakers. Excessive unemployment has been the death knell at the polls for numerous political incumbents. Unemployment statistics based on surveys only crudely measure real (conceptual) unemployment, but they provide gauges of the success of government policy. And differentiating between types of unemployment helps in tailoring policies to attack the types that are especially troublesome — structural, cyclical, and induced. We will now turn to another major macroeconomic issue — inflation.

Inflation

Whip inflation now.

President Gerald Ford, 1975
(Lost Reelection Bid in 1976)

Inflation is Public Enemy #1.

President Jimmy Carter, 1976
(Lost Reelection Bid in 1980)

Inflation is America's most pressing economic problem.

President Ronald Reagan, 1981
(Won Reelection Bid in 1984)

The earliest recorded antiinflation policies were price controls imposed by Egyptian pharaohs 4,000 years ago. In the United States, a battle against inflation begun during the 1960s escalated into the early 1980s, but inflation rates rose from 3.1 percent in 1967 to 13.6 percent in 1980. Finally, monetary growth was slashed during 1981–1982 to "cure" double-digit inflation. This shock therapy to growth of Aggregate Demand plunged the economy into its deepest slump (1981–1983) since the Great Depression, but by 1986, the economy had largely recovered,

while inflation fell to under 2 percent. Nevertheless, at the dawn of the 1990s, mild inflation persisted, with average prices rising 4 to 6 percent annually.

The drop in U.S. national income in response to these antiinflationary policies parallels international adjustments. Brazil's attempts to subdue inflation during 1989–1991, for example, imposed severe hardships on most Brazilians. Is defusing inflation worth the associated losses of employment and income? Before dealing with basic questions about inflation's costs and benefits, we need to specify what inflation is and how it is measured.

The Concept of Inflation

Most people view increases in any of the prices they pay for goods or services as inflationary. For the purpose of macroeconomic analysis, we are concerned with changes in the average level of *absolute* prices, because these changes represent inflation or deflation.

> **Inflation** *occurs when the average level of prices rises, while the average price level falls during* **deflation**.

Price hikes for a single good may not be inflationary. For example, a rise in the price of football tickets is not inflationary if it is offset by cuts in the prices of long-distance phone calls or domestic wine. Inflation occurs only when the average price level rises.[3]

Price Index Numbers

If the prices of houses, seafood, and leather jackets rise while prices for sweaters, frisbees, and gasoline fall, have we experienced inflation or deflation? Price indices allow this question to be answered systematically. Most readers of newspapers and magazines frequently encounter indices of one kind or another.

---

3. Not all economists accept this definition. Some argue that only continuous and prolonged increases in the price level should be termed inflationary, but it is often hard to distinguish between *continuing* inflation and *one-shot* increases in average prices because even one-shot general price hikes take time.

An **index** *is a series of numbers that summarize what has happened over time to prices (inflation or deflation), productivity, labor markets, construction, or some agglomeration of other items. An index is calculated as:*

$$\frac{\text{Value of variable in current period}}{\text{Value of variable in base period}} \times 100$$

Index numbers compress, sharpen, and simplify information. Comprehending these statistics is vital for interpreting economic changes.

If you wanted to develop an index of local job opportunities, you might count the help wanted ads reported monthly in your local newspaper. Suppose 38,510 ads appeared in your paper during April 1992, the month selected for a base period. (Note that the index equals 100 for the base month [(38,510/38,510) × 100 = 100].) If 47,230 ads appear in May 1992, the index of job opportunities (based on help wanted ads) would be

$$\frac{47,230}{38,510} \times 100 = 122.6$$

This index indicates that local job openings during May 1992 were roughly 122.6 percent of those available during April 1992, so your estimate suggests that work opportunities grew 22.6 percent. Index numbers are easier ways to interpret change than trying to digest the original (raw) numbers. As your job opening index developed a track record, you might notice it rising each November and December, reflecting Christmas employment, and falling each spring. This phenomenon is *seasonality*, or changes that recur each year. Most indices are seasonally adjusted to show comparable data over time.

Now that you understand how indexes work, we will examine the three principal indexes used to measure inflation: (*a*) the Consumer Price Index (CPI); (*b*) the Producer Price Index (PPI); and (*c*) the Gross National Product Deflator (GNP Deflator).

Measuring Consumer Prices (CPI)

The *Consumer Price Index* (CPI) estimates purchasing power by tracking changes in costs of a sample "market basket" that consists of over 650 products and services, including food, energy,

shelter, apparel, transportation, medical care, utilities, and insurance.

The **Consumer Price Index** *is a statistical measure of changes over time in the prices of a basket of typical goods purchased by typical consumers.*

Nearly 100 different major markets are sampled monthly by the Bureau of Labor Statistics (BLS) for the prices of the items in this sample market basket to regularly update the CPI.

The components of the CPI are *weighted* to reflect relative importance. For example, if typical families spend twice as much on syrup as on oatmeal, the weight for syrup prices will be twice that of the weight for oatmeal prices. The BLS conducts annual surveys of the prices paid and spending patterns of thousands of households in over 1,000 marketing areas to calculate weights for the CPI's components. The base period is changed every few years because spending patterns change, which requires updating weights for various goods. For example, personal computers were unknown 15 years ago. Their current popularity means that their prices should now be reflected in the CPI. In 1987, the BLS switched its base period from 1967 to the period 1982–1984. Table 3 summarizes the current methods used to compile the CPI.

How the CPI Is Used

The CPI is used to estimate changes in the purchasing power of money and as an *escalator* (cost-of-living adjustment) in some contracts calling for future payments. Unfortunately, problems are inherent in any economic index used to prescribe policy.

Moving from Nominal to Real Values Most economic variables are presented in their current dollar, or nominal, values.

Nominal *or* **monetary values** *are the dollar amounts received or paid.*

Nominal values lose comparability over time unless adjusted for inflation or deflation.

Table 3 *Summary of the Procedures and Methods Used to Compute the CPI*

Item	Methods and Procedures
Title	1. Consumer Price Index for All Urban Consumers (CPI-U) 2. Consumer Price Index for Urban Wage Earners and Clerical Workers (Revised Series) (CPI-W)
Population covered	CPI-U—All urban residents, including salaried workers, self-employed workers, retirees, unemployed persons, and urban wage earners. CPI-W—Urban wage earner and clerical worker families and single individuals living alone. At least one family member must be employed for 37 weeks or more during the year in wage or clerical worker occupations.
Geographic coverage	278 urban areas selected to represent all urban places in the United States, including Alaska and Hawaii.
Sample of items priced	Consumer expenditure survey (1982–1984) data classified into 68 expenditure classes covering roughly 650 goods.
Sample of stores	A sample of retail stores and other outlets was selected from the results of a point-of-purchase survey covering about 23,000 families across the country.
Number of price quotations obtained	About 650,000 food prices per year. About 70,000 rent charges per year. About 350,000 quotations per year for items other than food, rent, and property taxes. About 28,000 property tax quotations per year.

Source: Bureau of Labor Statistics.

Real values *are nominal values adjusted for changes in the price level.*

For example, suppose that your nominal income this year is $20,000. How does its purchasing power compare with your $10,000 income of 10 years ago? Are you better off or worse off? If all prices also doubled, it would take twice as much money now to buy the goods you bought ten years ago and you would be no better off. The purchasing power of your real income (Y_{real}) is current income ($Y_{current}$) adjusted for inflation or deflation according to the formula:

$$Y_{real} = \frac{Y_{current}}{CPI/100}$$

Using the preceding formula with a CPI of 200 for this year (the base index for 10 years ago is 100), your current real income is $10,000 ($20,000/2.00 = $10,000). Table 4 illustrates this conversion process for per capita income during selected years since 1929.

Just as we have adjusted nominal income to account for changes in the price level, we can adjust other nominal variables to see how relative prices are changing.

Deflating *is the process of ensuring the comparability of nominal values by adjusting them for inflation.*

The general formula for deflating any variable is:

$$\text{real value} = \frac{\text{nominal variable in dollars}}{\text{price index}/100}$$

For example, movie tickets rose from an average of $4 each in 1983 to an average of $6 in 1990. How much did real prices rise for movies? The CPI (based on 1983 prices) rose to 133. Thus, real 1990 movie prices (in 1983 prices) were $6/1.33, or around $4.50 per movie ticket. Similar calculations are used to deflate home prices, wages, or any other nominal variables.

A price index ideally estimates average losses from inflation for typical people. But averages

TABLE 4 *Converting Nominal Income (Before Taxes) to Real Annual Income*

Year	Aggregate Money Income ($Billions)	Population (millions)	Per Capita Income ($)	CPI (1982–84 = 100)	Real Per Capita Income (deflated $)
1929	$ 84.3	121.8	$ 692	15.5	$ 4,465
1933	46.3	124.8	371	11.6	3,198
1960	409.4	180.7	2,266	29.6	7,655
1970	831.8	204.9	4,060	38.8	10,464
1980	2258.5	222.3	10,160	82.4	12,318
1990	4,645.6	251.4	18,479	130.7	14,138

Source: *Statistical Abstract* 1990, *Economic Report of the President,* 1980–1991.

may not mean much if you are not typical. On the next test you take, other students' average grades will be far less important to you than how well you do personally. You might perform far below the class's average, but you also might be the "curve buster" at the top of your class. A price index is a similar average, and so may either overstate or understate the amount of inflation experienced by any given individual.

Inflation is especially harmful if the prices of the goods that dominate your purchases soar even faster than inflation, but you could actually gain during an inflationary period if prices drop for the goods you buy the most. For example, a pilot who enjoyed touring the country in a personal plane could be clobbered by inflation triggered by higher oil prices, while over the same period, a computer hacker would be delighted by lower costs for computer hardware, supplies, and software. Inflation also affects people less to the extent that they easily substitute among goods for which nominal prices change at different rates. For example, if you are indifferent between Coke and Pepsi, increases in Pepsi prices damage you far less than they do fans of Pepsi.

CPI as an Income/Payment Escalator Many monetary payments are directly tied to the CPI. For example, if a union wage contract has an escalator clause, wages rise by roughly the same percentage that the CPI climbs. Escalator clauses that buffer purchasing power from inflation are included in union contracts covering roughly 8 million workers. Our income tax system, many pension plans, and various transfer payment programs are also closely tied to the CPI.

CPI as an Economic Indicator The CPI is a major yardstick by which the success of economic policy is measured. Every president since George Washington has promised price-level stability. Macroeconomic policymakers keep a close watch on movements in price indices for indications of their success in controlling inflation. Their record since World War II has been erratic. Americans pay more attention to the Consumer Price Index today than in earlier periods when inflation seemed less persistent.

Problems with the CPI Estimating changes in consumer prices poses major conceptual problems for the Bureau of Labor Statistics. How can the BLS adjust the CPI to accurately reflect changes in (a) consumption patterns, (b) the availability of new products, (c) new qualities in older goods, and (d) the prices of major assets such as homes, which some families bought earlier at lower prices, while others must pay higher current prices to buy now?

The CPI is thoroughly revised about once a decade, and relatively constant consumption patterns are assumed in order to compute the CPI between revisions. The failure of a fixed, representative "market basket" to reflect changes in typical buying patterns reduces the accuracy of the CPI. Inflation tends to be overstated because consumers purchase more goods whose prices rise most slowly and cut back on items where prices rise most rapidly. For example, between 1972 and 1980, average energy prices rose 218 percent, but consumer outlays for energy only rose 140 percent.

The BLS began annual Consumer Expenditure

Surveys in 1986 to keep up with changing consumption patterns. Area and item samples are now updated regularly instead of once a decade as was done in the past. Annual surveys and phased updating now mitigate the fixed-market-basket limitations of the CPI.

Changes in quality may also distort the CPI. Quality changes in products *should not* cause changes in the price index, because it ideally measures consumers' costs of purchasing a *constant* "market basket." The CPI overstates inflation if prices rise to reflect quality improvements that the BLS ignores. Suppose, for example, that 1993 movies are superior to the films of 1992. If ticket prices rise only because better quality costs more, then the CPI might still reflect inflation because of these hikes. Ideally, dollar measures of how much consumers value improvements in quality should be deducted from any price increases. Similarly, deteriorating quality may cause inflation to be understated. Inflation occurs even though money prices stay constant if, say, fast food becomes less tasty because soy beans are substituted for ground beef in hamburgers.

Direct measurement of the values consumers place on quality changes is not possible, so the Bureau uses an indirect method — it estimates the costs of quality changes. When figures are available, cost differentials between new and old features are treated as proxies for the real values of quality changes. This approach poses many problems. For example, does the cost of installing pollution control equipment on cars represent an increase in the quality of an automobile? Or are we actually just buying cleaner air?

Another problem of measuring inflation is that some asset owners gain from higher prices. Thus, if inflationary pressures cause both wages and housing prices to rise, this does not mean that current homeowners who have fixed mortgage payments pay more for housing services. After adjusting for inflation, "real" mortgage payments fall. Before 1981, the BLS measured the costs of acquiring a house by the monthly mortgage payment, rather than the price of "housing services" consumed. As a result, when mortgage interest rates rose or fell and changed typical monthly payments, the CPI treated these changes as if all families bought new houses each month. The new approach of the BLS is to estimate rental values to represent the cost of shelter. These changes permit the CPI to more truly reflect inflation for established American households. Despite all these problems, the CPI is a reasonable estimate of changes in average consumer prices.

Other Price Indices

The CPI only tracks changes in prices consumers pay. Other prices are also important.

Producer Price Index The **Producer Price Index (PPI)** is a general-purpose index for non-retail markets. It averages price changes for over 2,800 primary products and such intermediate goods as flour, steel, and office supplies. Most prices used to compute this index are the wholesale selling prices of representative producers, but some prices come from specialized markets such as commodity exchanges. The prices used for imported products (e.g., coffee beans) are the prices paid by the original importer (e.g., Folger's). Your reaction may be, "Why should I care about this concept? I only consume. I'm not a producer." Be aware, however, that the PPI is often an indicator of future directions for consumer prices.

The GNP Deflator The **GNP Deflator** is used to deflate the nominal value of our Gross National Product. (GNP is the total market value of all goods and services produced in an economy in a year. GNP accounting is the subject of our next chapter.) The GNP Deflator is largely based on other price indices. For example, each component of consumer spending is adjusted using appropriate data from the Consumer Price Index. Business spending for capital equipment or raw materials is deflated with appropriate parts of the Producer Price Index. Parts of other indices are used to deflate the prices of items not included in the CPI or the PPI, such as government services, construction, and agricultural outputs.

The History of U.S. Inflation

Few Americans can remember when the price level fell. Average prices fell by roughly one-third between 1929 and 1933, while wages dropped by one-fourth, so wages after adjusting for deflation actually *rose*. Workers might seem to have gained, but remember that by 1933 the unemployment rate was almost 25 percent. There have been other periods when we experienced deflation, as you can see in Figure 4. For example, prices fell on average by roughly 40 percent between 1870 and 1895.

Before the creeping inflation of the 1960s, an annual inflation rate of 4 percent seemed outrageous. Nevertheless, we became habituated to annual inflation ranging from 6 percent to 14 percent during the 1970s. Most of us now view 2 to 4 percent inflation as price-level stability. To some extent, what you are accustomed to determines what you consider moderate or excessive inflation. Many South Americans view inflation rates of 40 to 50 percent as no big deal. Inflation in Argentina, Bolivia, and Brazil raged at annual rates as high as 400 to 800 percent at times between 1950 and 1990.

FIGURE 4 Inflation Since 1860

This figure highlights the various inflationary and deflationary periods experienced by the United States since 1860. The majority of these inflationary periods have occurred during extended military hostilities. Although the 1970s and early 1980s were relatively peaceful, the price level crept up briskly.
Source: Bureau of Labor Statistics, 1991.

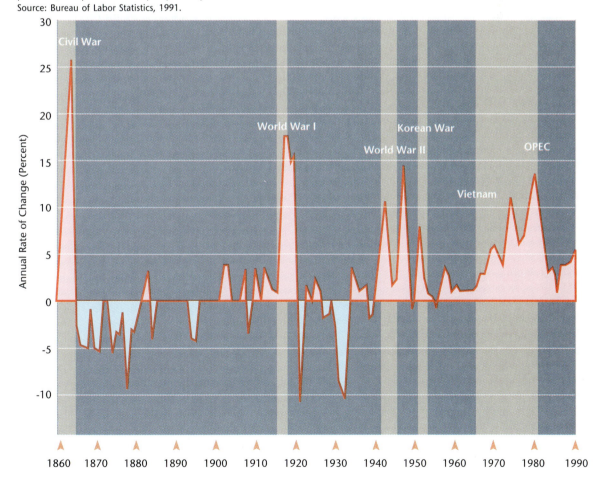

Types of Inflation

Now that we have seen how inflation is measured and when it has occurred, let's turn to analyzing the different types of inflation. Inflation can be classified by how rapidly average prices rise, or whether people expect it. Other distinctions pinpoint *causes* of inflation. This section addresses all three approaches.

Creeping or Galloping Inflation vs. Hyperinflation

The price level may rise for a number of reasons and at different rates over time.

Creeping inflation *occurs if average prices rise consistently but at fairly low rates.*

Average prices are described as **galloping** when inflation moves at double-digit annual rates. Inflation has persisted at creeping rates for decades in the United States, but it "galloped" briefly in the 1970s; other countries have not been so fortunate. Most economists accept the definition of

hyperinflation offered by Philip Cagan, a specialist in this area.

Hyperinflation *occurs when average prices rise more than 50 percent per month.*

Hyperinflations have occurred at rates that can only be described as astronomical. A kilogram of bread cost less than 1 German mark in 1919, and 9 marks would buy an American dollar. Between the onset of World War I and 1923, average prices in Germany rose 1,422,900 million percent. By the end of 1923, $1 exchanged for an incredible 4.2 trillion German marks, and a one-inch stack of 5 million mark notes would buy one egg. But even more remarkable inflations have occurred. Hungary experienced inflation of 8.28 octillion (8.28 followed by 22 zeros!) percent between 1945 and 1946. Figure 5 illustrates three twentieth-century hyperinflations.

Interestingly, studies by Philip Cagan indicate that a monetary system still functions reasonably well as long as inflation stays below 50 percent monthly. When inflation soars, however, bond markets collapse, and investment falters because of uncertainty. Creeping inflation clearly poses

FIGURE 5   Selected Episodes of Hyperinflation: China, Germany, and Hungary

Sources: For China: Shun-Hsin Chou, *The Chinese Inflation: 1936–1949* (New York: Columbia University Press, 1973), p. 261. For Germany: Fritz K. Ringer, *The German Inflation of 1923* (New York: Oxford University Press, 1969), p. 69. For Hungary: B. Nogaro, "Hungary's Monetary Crisis," *American Economic Review*, XXXVIII (1948), pp. 526–542.

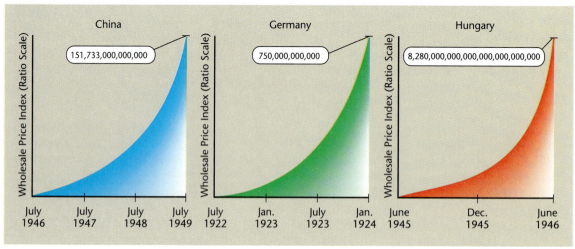

fewer problems than hyperinflation does for consumers, investors, and for macroeconomic policymakers. During periods of hyperinflation, people spend their money as fast as they can in order to beat constant price increases. People may even quit trusting in money. When this happens, *barter* takes over and goods and resources are traded directly for other goods or resources, and money becomes unacceptable.

Anticipated vs. Unexpected Inflation

A second way to categorize inflation or deflation is by whether people anticipate changes in the average price level. Unexpected changes in the price level do far more harm than anticipated ones. You can buffer yourself against losses of purchasing power by *hedging* against inflation that you predict accurately. For example, if you are convinced that virtually all prices will soon rise, you might hedge by buying a new car now, or by making reservations a year in advance for a resort vacation. Even stocks of canned food are suitable hedges against severe inflation.

Speculation is also stimulated by inflationary expectations; guessing correctly can be very advantageous. Buying real estate on credit before an inflationary boom, for example, often yields very high real rates of return. (Have you heard of the rule, ''Buy low and sell high''?) But overly generous forecasts can be as damaging as projections that underanticipate changes in the price level. For example, investors who speculated that real estate prices would continue to climb in energy ''boom towns'' in the 1970s commonly went bankrupt when oil prices plummeted in the 1980s, intensifying pressures that culminated in the collapse of hundreds of savings-and-loans during 1988–1991.

The lesson here is that the rate of inflation may be less harmful than its volatility. Price-level stability is desirable because consumers and investors can avoid unnecessary costs associated with hedging and speculating. A stable price level allows consumers to focus on buying the most satisfying goods, and investors to concentrate on capital expenditures that will help firms best serve the needs of consumers, instead of strategies to avoid inflation or profit from it.

Demand-Side Inflation

We can use the Aggregate Demand/Aggregate Supply model introduced in the previous chapter to help identify different sources and types of inflation. When a given price rises, then either: (*a*) demand increased, or (*b*) supply decreased, or (*c*) some combination of **a** and **b** occurred. This pattern offers parallels for the economy as a whole.

> **Demand-pull (demand-side) inflation** *occurs when average prices rise because Aggregate Demand grows excessively relative to Aggregate Supply.*

When Aggregate Demand expands from AD_0 to AD_1 in Figure 6, the price level rises from P_0 to P_1. Inflation is sustained only if Aggregate Demand continues to rise.

Economists are nearly unanimous in believing that inflation occurs when our demands for goods grow faster than our capacity to produce them. Indeed, a substantial minority of economists insist that this is the only realistic explanation for sustained inflation. Excessive demands

FIGURE 6   Demand-Side Inflation

If expansions of Aggregate Demand drive up the price level, the economy experiences demand-side inflation, shown here as the jump in the price level from P_0 to P_1.

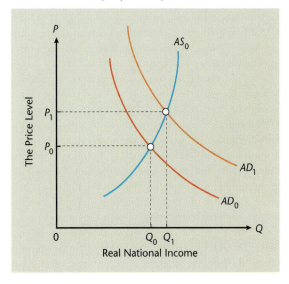

ripple through a fully employed economy when the money supply grows too rapidly or government spends far more than it collects in taxes.

Supply-Side Inflation

Creeping inflations in many industrialized economies during the 1960s and 1970s at least partially originated from shocks on the supply side.

> **Supply-side inflation** *results when Aggregate Supply shrinks (e.g., because of rising resource prices or technological reversals), causing the price level to rise and aggregate output to fall.*

Figure 7 illustrates a supply-side "shock" as a shift in Aggregate Supply from AS_0 to AS_1. Runaway energy costs, worldwide drought, monopolistic greed, and disputes between labor unions and management are only a few of the culprits that some people identify as causal factors. OPEC oil price hikes during the 1970s were clearly severe shocks to the supply side. Supply-side shocks can be grouped into the broad categories of *cost-push* and *administered-price* explanations for inflation.

FIGURE 7 Supply-Side Inflation

Inflation may originate from the supply side of the economy; when the Aggregate Supply curve shifts from AS_0 to AS_1, the price level rises from P_0 to P_1.

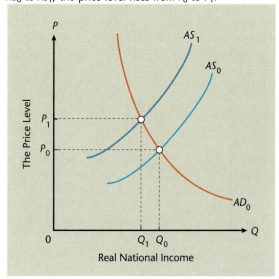

Cost-Push Inflation Exorbitant union wage hikes are often pinpointed as inflationary. This is one example of a **cost-push** theory of inflation. Powerful unions presumably demand wage increases not warranted by increased worker productivity. Increased labor costs are then passed forward to consumers as "pushed up" prices. This explanation points to unions as the villains causing inflation. Blaming unions is especially popular among some politicians and business leaders. Other cost-push theories point to rising prices for oil or to increases in the prices of imported goods or raw materials.

Administered-Price Inflation Some economists turn the mechanics of the union-based, cost-push inflation explanation upside down. According to the **administered-price** theory, firms with monopoly power may be reluctant to raise prices, because they fear adverse publicity, antitrust actions, or similar threats to their dominance in a market. They use hikes in wages or other resource costs as excuses to raise prices, generally by more than their higher costs would justify. Huge firms' failures to resist excessive wage demands, it is argued, tend to perpetuate inflationary momentum.

Mixed Theories of Inflation

Debates about whether inflation is caused only by shifts of Aggregate Demand or by shifts of Aggregate Supply parallel arguments about whether the top or bottom blade of a pair of scissors cuts a piece of paper. An accurate portrait of any episode of inflation usually requires considering influences from both sides. *Composition-shift* and *expectational* theories blend demand-side and supply-side pressures.

Composition-Shift Inflation The foundation of **composition-shift** inflation theory is the assumption that prices rise more easily than they fall. Thus, if demand rises in one sector of the economy, prices rise. But if there are offsetting declines in demands in other sectors, prices do *not* fall, at least in the short run. Instead, as sales shrink, firms reduce output and lay off workers. Thus, inflationary pressures emerge as the composition of demands and supplies changes. Growing sectors will typically experience increases in prices, while declining sectors suffer from stagnation and unemployment rather than long-term price cuts.

Expectational Inflation   Inflationary expectations may cause **expectational** inflation because prevalent forecasts are at least partially self-fulfilling—we create our own future realities by what we anticipate. Thus, producers who expect inflation build inventories by boosting output while cutting back on current sales. Why sell now when prices will soon be higher? Current sales are reduced by immediate price hikes and temporary decreases in supplies.

If, at the same time, buyers expect inflation, they will try to accumulate their own inventories of durable goods. This bolsters their current demands, as they attempt to beat the higher prices expected later. Thus, inflationary expectations quickly cause price hikes because they reduce supplies and increase demands. These adjustments explain why inflation may develop incredible momentum. Inflation causes expectations of inflation, which stimulates more inflation, and so forth. You may have heard people refer to the "wage-price inflationary spiral" or to the "vicious circle of inflation." Inflationary expectations are important in explaining why inflation is so difficult to suppress.

The preceding theories of inflation are not mutually exclusive; many inflations emerge from combinations of forces. For example, all European hyperinflations following World Wars I and II were triggered by political turmoil and supply-side disturbances followed by incredibly rapid growth in these countries' money supplies. Bolivian inflation in the 1980s was caused by a government policy that financed 15 percent of its spending by taxation and printed money to cover the other 85 percent. Aggregate Demand grows excessively if the money supply grows faster than real output. When we explore these sources of inflation in detail in Chapters 13 through 18, you will learn why inflation cannot be sustained for long without growth of the money supply.

Composition-shift, expectational, or other mixed theories of inflation entail combinations

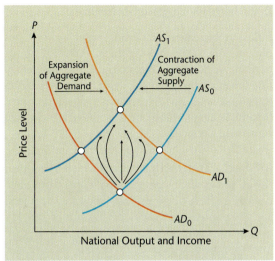

FIGURE 8   Aggregate Demands and Supplies in a Mixed Inflation

Aggregate Demand increases during a mixed inflation (a movement from AD_0 to AD_1), imposing pressure for higher prices and outputs. Aggregate Supply, however, decreases (e.g., from AS_0 to AS_1), generating pressure for higher prices but less output. Thus, without more information, we cannot ascertain whether national output grows or declines, but we can be sure that the price level will rise.

of declines in supply and expansion of demand. Thus, Aggregate Supply curves shift leftward, while Aggregate Demand curves shift to the right, as illustrated in Figure 8. You now have some ideas about how indices are calculated, various types of inflation, and how the forces at work in an inflationary process shift Aggregate Demands and Aggregate Supplies. We need to examine the effect of inflation on social welfare.

Inflation's Costs and Benefits

Surprisingly, some people "win" from inflation, while others lose. Losses from inflation are of two major types. First, inflation may reduce the efficiency of production and distribution. In either case, there will be declines in standards of living. These are the **real-income costs of inflation**. Second, inflation fractures the implicit and explicit agreements that bind people together. These are the **social costs of inflation**.

Real-Income Costs of Inflation

Inflation increases transaction costs and reduces real income (*a*) by making the information about market conditions summarized in monetary prices less certain, and (*b*) by unnecessarily shifting resources into the repricing of goods. Real income is also reduced because inflation distorts economic decisions.

Inflated Transaction Costs   Information about prices collected through expenditures of time and effort by producers, resource suppliers, and consumers becomes obsolete more quickly during inflation. Have you ever visited a store intending to buy a certain item, only to discover that you can no longer afford it because its price has risen? Workers are caught in a similar squeeze when they learn that price hikes have made it impossible for them to cover all the purchases they planned when they agreed to a wage offered by an employer. *Transaction costs* are increased, because perceptions about prices and purchasing power turn out to be mistaken far more frequently during inflationary periods than when average prices are stable.

Another way inflation increases transaction costs is that resources that could have been used productively elsewhere are used to reprice goods. Some repricing occurs at all times because relative prices change even when price levels are stable. During an inflationary period, however, it is not unusual to find that most items in your grocery cart have been marked up since they were first put on the shelf. Restaurant menus and airline ticket schedules must be reprinted, and candy and cold drink machines must be adjusted to accept new denominations of coins. Where government regulates prices (e.g., utility rates or bus fares), considerable time and effort may be absorbed in redesigning rate schedules. Such increases in information cost are called the *menu costs of inflation.*

Distortion Costs   Another major cost of inflation emerges from feelings of uncertainty among savers and investors. Saving and investing reflects faith in the future. Uncertainty caused by infla-

tion stifles investment and saving, which then hampers growth of Aggregate Supply. Funds that would normally flow into new capital may be diverted into real estate or inventories, so that growth and technological advances sputter well below the levels needed for a healthy economy. Firms also mark up price margins to compensate for increased risks. If so, over the long run, inflation causes Aggregate Supply to wither.

Relative prices are distorted if inflation artificially causes prices to rise at different rates; inefficient decisions about production and consumption result. For example, many people incurred huge mortgages in the early 1980s that required monthly payments they could afford only if double-digit inflation continued. An epidemic of foreclosures swept the country during 1984–1991 when inflation slowed down. Many buyers might have waited were it not for their fear that "if we don't buy now, we won't ever be able to afford a home." Inefficiencies in decision making caused by inflation are termed **distortion costs.**

Social Costs of Inflation

Inflation stimulates strife between buyers (who want low prices maintained) and sellers (who want prices raised to reflect rising production costs). Conflicts among consumers, producers, and regulatory agencies are accentuated during inflationary episodes. Ignoring menu and distortion costs for a moment, inflation is roughly what mathematicians call a *zero sum game.* For every loser during inflation (someone who must pay more for a given good), there is a winner (someone who receives a greater price for the things sold). The somewhat arbitrary income redistributions caused by inflation are a major source of inflation's *social cost.* Even though losses to some are offset by gains to others, the process seems capricious and erodes the trust we have in each other.

You gain during inflation if the prices of things you sell go up faster than the prices of things you buy. Some people lose because their incomes do not keep pace with the average prices of the goods they buy. Why all the furor over inflation if the gains and losses are roughly in balance?

One major reason is that most gains from recent inflation went to people who sell petroleum — many of whom are foreigners.

A basic problem is that inflation is often blamed for unfavorable circumstances that would have arisen because of shifts in *uninflated* demands and supplies. Most of us feel that increases in our paychecks are much-deserved rewards for hard work. Have you ever considered that your raise is an increase in the price of your services that is seen as inflation by purchasers of the goods you produce? If your neighbor's pay rises faster than your own, supply and demand may be at work, not inflation.

Even if our nominal income keeps pace with inflation, it erodes the value of money we have saved. A past irritant was that progressivity in our federal income tax system allowed inflation to bump us into higher tax brackets, a process called *bracket creep*. Federal income tax rates were indexed to inflation in 1985, reducing bracket creep, but it remains a problem where state or local governments use progressive taxes.

On the other hand, the prices of physical assets such as land and housing often rise even more rapidly than the rate of inflation. Homeowners gain during inflation; prospective home buyers lose. Borrowers are an important group of gainers from inflation. Homeowners with huge mortgages find repaying loans increasingly easy if inflation pushes up nominal income. (Would you like to borrow $1,000,000 today if inflation was going to be 1,000,000 percent next year before the loan was due?) Of course, borrowers' gains are almost exactly offset by losses in the real wealth of lenders.

Government, business firms, farmers, and young families tend to be net debtors/borrowers and often gain from unexpected inflation. Federal debt now exceeds $3 trillion. Holders of U.S. Treasury bonds are the losers in this exchange of wealth. Established households and mature people anticipating retirement are usually savers and lose from inflation. (The ultimate lenders are people with bank deposits, not bankers.) A related cost of inflation is that this redistributional effect of rewarding borrowing and penalizing saving provides substantial incentives for the use of credit. It is probably undesirable for most of us to become even more debt-ridden than we already are.

Still another consideration is that some people live on fixed incomes — their pensions or wage contracts are not adjusted for changes in the cost of living. The growing numbers of contracts containing escalator clauses illustrates how people adjust to inflation over time. Even so, there are people whose incomes are at least partially fixed; those living on life insurance annuities or who long ago contracted for long-term fixed-dollar payments to take care of their old age are examples. Many senior citizens are harmed by inflation to the extent that some portions of their incomes are fixed.

Redistributions caused by inflation are commonly seen as unfair and capricious, but many social ills blamed on it actually result from other forces. You may have seen news programs indicating that low-income people suffer most from inflation, a charge refuted by most studies of this problem. The difficulties faced by the poor result from poverty, not inflation per se. Joseph Minarik analyzed census data on income and concluded that the sustained but moderate inflation of the 1970s harmed people at the top proportionally far more than it did people at the lower end of the income spectrum.[4]

The income redistribution aspects of inflation generally do not affect the real level of national production, which Adam Smith (in 1776) rightly termed the *wealth of nations*. Rather, the redistributive properties of inflation are part of the larger problem of achieving and maintaining an equitable distribution of our real national income.

Benefits of Inflation

A little inflationary pressure may ease needed changes in relative prices. This is especially true if price reductions are resisted more vigorously than price increases. For example, in the 1970s

---

4. Joseph J. Minarik, ''Who Wins, Who Loses from Inflation,'' *The Brookings Bulletin*, 15, 1 (1980): 6.

the demand for college professors fell due to declines in enrollment, but the supply of professors increased. Market pressures to reduce professors' real wages were accommodated fairly easily by allowing their salaries' purchasing power to decline because of inflation. This process would have been far more traumatic if colleges had been forced to negotiate lower money wages for faculty, which might have been necessary had the price level been stable.

Inflation's effects on capital accumulation and economic growth may also be positive at times. If managers believe that equipment costs will rise in the near future, firms may invest more in capital equipment, boosting Aggregate Supply in the short run. Such planning can backfire, however; investment decisions made prematurely because of inflationary expectations can wipe out some investors.

A third possible benefit is that inflation may ease expanding government spending relative to private spending. Politicians may prefer to use inflation to finance more government spending instead of relying on an unpopular tax system — spending can grow without paying for it directly via taxes. For example, inflationary pressures were allowed to build during World War II. Tax hikes sufficient to finance the war without inflation might have posed severe disincentives for production. Of course, many people would argue that under most circumstances, inflationary growth of government is a cost, not a benefit, of inflation. This issue will be treated in more detail in Chapters 10 and 16.

The Discomfort Index

Arthur Okun, chairman of President Lyndon Johnson's Council of Economic Advisors, developed an index intended to summarize the general state of the economy.

> The economic **discomfort index** equals the inflation rate plus the overall unemployment rate.

In 1976, Jimmy Carter renamed this the **misery index** and used it to brand President Ford's economic policies as failures. Ronald Reagan then resurrected the misery index to condemn economic performance during President Carter's administration. The index was also featured in the 1984 political campaign.

The index for 4-year presidential terms (averaged to smooth short-run fluctuations) since 1950 is presented in Table 5. This index showed remarkable stability during the 1950s and 1960s but took a big leap upward during the 1970s and

TABLE 5 *The Discomfort (Misery) Index*

Term	President	Average Inflation Rate	Average Unemployment Rate	Discomfort Index
1949–1952	Truman	2.8	4.4	7.2
1953–1956	Eisenhower	1.4	4.2	5.6
1957–1960	Eisenhower	1.7	5.5	7.2
1961–1964	Kennedy-Johnson	1.2	5.8	7.0
1965–1968	Johnson	3.2	3.9	7.1
1969–1972	Nixon	4.6	5.0	9.6
1973–1976	Nixon-Ford	8.2	6.7	14.9
1977–1980	Carter	10.6	6.5	17.1
1981–1984	Reagan	5.2	8.6	13.8
1985–1988	Reagan	3.4	6.4	9.8
1989–1990	Bush	5.4	5.4	10.8

Source: *Economic Report of the President,* 1991.

early 1980s. By 1990, however, the discomfort index had returned to levels accepted as normal before 1970.

Macroeconomic policies focus on the goals of full employment, price-level stability, and economic growth. Implementing appropriate policies requires relatively accurate measures of unemployment and inflation. You should keep the various costs and benefits of unemployment and inflation, as well as their data limitations, in mind while you study the material in the next few chapters.

Chapter Review: Key Points

1. *Voluntary unemployment* occurs when people could find work quickly, but choose to look for what they view as better jobs in terms of pay or working conditions. *Involuntary unemployment* occurs when people lack jobs, but are willing and able to work at wages commensurate with their skills.

2. The *labor force* consists of all employed or unemployed civilians plus military personnel. A *labor force participation rate* is the proportion in the labor force from a specific group.

3. Unemployed people who are so discouraged about job prospects that they do not look for work are not counted in unemployment statistics. Some people who are not truly out of work indicate that they are to collect unemployment compensation. Thus, data for unemployment may either understate the true unemployment rate because of *discouraged workers* or overstate it because of *dishonest nonworkers*.

4. *Frictional unemployment* arises because of transaction costs associated with normal entry and exit from the labor market, voluntary job changes, or layoffs or firings. Both workers and firms "invest in information" by *searching* for jobs or screening applicants until their expected marginal benefits no longer exceed their expected marginal costs.

5. *Seasonal unemployment* arises from the annually recurring influences of weather, vacations, and the like on labor markets.

6. *Structural unemployment* results from mismatches between workers and jobs because of changes in the skill requirements of job openings or individuals lack marketable skills.

7. *Cyclical unemployment* results from recessions.

8. Government policies that reduce work incentives or that prevent workers from securing employment (e.g., minimum-wage laws) cause *induced unemployment*.

9. Unemployment causes both *economic* and *social costs*. Society as a whole suffers because of lost output that unemployed individuals could have produced. Individuals and their families suffer socially and psychologically when they are unemployed for long periods. Personal losses are, however, partially cushioned by such programs as unemployment compensation.

10. Unemployment is not distributed equally across all groups. Workers in manufacturing and construction are hit harder by cyclical unemployment during recessions than employees in most other lines of work.

11. *Index numbers* are used to compare particular variables over time. The *Consumer Price Index* (CPI) measures average price changes for a given bundle of consumer goods over time. The CPI is based on typical consumer patterns for approximately 80 percent of the urban population.

12. The CPI is used extensively as an escalator clause (cost-of-living adjustment) in many contracts. It is also an economic indicator and is used to convert nominal values to real values.

13. *Deflating* nominal variables means dividing their monetary values by (1 percent of) a price index.

14. Among the major difficulties in computing the CPI are the problems inherent in adjust-

ing the index for (a) new products, (b) changes in the qualities of existing products, (c) changes in the composition of consumer expenditures, and (d) already owned consumer durables such as housing.

15. The *Producer Price Index* (PPI) measures changes in the prices of goods in other than retail markets. The *GNP Deflator* adjusts GNP for changes in prices. It is composed of relevant portions of the CPI and the PPI, plus some additional prices covered by neither.

16. *Creeping inflation* occurs relatively slowly; *galloping inflation* occurs when average prices begin moving at double-digit annual rates. *Hyperinflation* entails average price hikes exceeding 50 percent monthly. Inflation is generally less harmful if it is anticipated than if it is a surprise to people.

17. Inflation increases *transaction costs* by making price information obsolete faster, and it causes resources that could be used productively elsewhere to be used for repricing. These are the *menu costs* of inflation.

18. Inflation also distorts relative prices and economic decision making, and depresses incentives to save. Capital accumulation may or may not be hampered by inflation, depending on business expectations and the availability of funds for investment. These are the *distortion costs* of inflation.

19. There are *social costs of inflation*, too, because people feel greater uncertainty during inflationary periods. People living on fixed incomes are hurt by inflation, but many transfer payments and wage contracts now have *escalator clauses* that adjust payments for price-level changes. Borrowers tend to gain from unexpected inflation, while the ultimate lenders (e.g., savers with bank deposits) lose. When inflation boosts income, meeting a fixed mortgage payment becomes easier, so heavily mortgaged homeowners tend to gain.

20. The *discomfort (misery) index* is the sum of the inflation rate and the unemployment rate. It averaged 6 to 7 percent during the 1950s and 1960s. During the late 1970s and early 1980s, the index ranged from 13 to more than 20 percent. By 1988, economic growth had pushed the index below 10 percent.

Key Concepts

Ensure that you can define these terms before proceeding.

unemployment
labor force
inflation
deflation
index number
Consumer Price Index (CPI)
Producer Price Index (PPI)

GNP Deflator
creeping inflation
galloping inflation
hyperinflation
discomfort (misery) index

Problems and Questions

1. Many payments are tied to the CPI through escalator clauses to adjust for inflation. Are such formal adjustments necessary for payments tied to sales prices, such as percentage commissions or percentage sales taxes?

2. Table 6 lists aggregate personal income in current dollars for selected years since 1929 and the CPI for the same years. (Use the "deflating" process described on page 136.)

   a. Compute real personal income in 1983 dollars for each year.

   b. How much did real income increase between 1929 and 1990?

   c. Convert the CPI to a base year of 1990 = 100. Adjust current dollar personal income for each year to 1990 dollars.

   d. What percent did prices fall between 1929 and 1933?

   e. If between 1991 and 1992, nominal personal income grew 6 percent and the in-

TABLE 6 *Personal Income (Billions of Dollars)*

Year	Current $B	CPI (1982–84 = 100)
1929	84.3	15.5
1933	46.3	11.6
1960	409.4	29.6
1970	831.8	38.8
1980	2258.5	82.4
1983	3290.0	100.0
1990	4645.6	130.7

TABLE 7

	Price Year 1	Price Year 2	Price Year 3	Units Purchased in Year 1		
				Jennifer	Melissa	Total
candy bars	$0.50	$0.75	$1.00	10	30	
gasoline	$1.00	$1.50	$1.80	10	8	
computer disks	$1.50	$1.00	$0.80	10	2	
Price Index/Year 1				____	____	____
Price Index/Year 2				____	____	____
Price Index/Year 3				____	____	____

flation rate was 4 percent, by how much did real personal income grow? What was the percentage growth?

3. The CPI uses spending on particular goods in the base year as a proportion of total spending that year to "weight" the price changes of particular goods. Spending by Jennifer and Melissa follows the patterns in Table 7. Use year 1 as the base year when you answer the following questions. (*Hint:* The simplest approach is to compute how much each would have to spend in years 2 and 3 to buy her "market basket" from year 1. Then divide these figures by what their nominal costs were in year 1.)

a. Compute personal price indices for the three years to fill in the blanks for Jennifer and Melissa.

b. Compute price indices that fill in the blanks to average the two women's purchasing patterns as if they were the total population.

c. Who is harmed relatively more by these changes in average prices? Does this depend on which year you consider?

4. In 1990, the U.S. population was 251,394,000, of whom 188,049,000 were age 16 or over. The labor force including the Armed Forces was 126,424,000, the civilian labor force was 124,787,000, and civilian employment was 117,914,000. Compute the following:

a. Employment/population ratio.

b. Labor force participation rate for ages 16 and over.

c. Total unemployment rate (including the military).

d. Civilian unemployment rate (ignore the military).

Why is the total unemployment rate lower than that for civilians?

5–10. Which of the individuals described in questions 5–10 would be counted as unemployed by the Bureau of Labor Statistics? Which would be considered unemployed by an economist? Why do these lists differ?

5. A Ph.D. in anthropology who works full-time as a cab driver while devoting three hours daily to searching for a job as a researcher or an assistant professor.

6. After quitting work as a cab driver, the anthropologist remodels her home six days a week, devoting only Monday mornings to looking for work as an anthropologist.

7. An eighth-grader who temporarily loses her job delivering papers when the printer's union at the local newspaper goes on strike.

8. A chef who chops off two fingers the day before the *Les Gourmands* restaurant closes forever draws disability pay while vacationing before looking for another job.

9. A novelist who has not written a page in months because he can't think of a good plot for his next book.

10. A building contractor who employs a crew of 30 workers, all of whom are idle while awaiting a big job that starts in three weeks.

11. Some absolute prices fall even though most

are rising during an inflationary period. How is it possible for the welfare of some people to increase during a mild inflation even if their income does not rise as fast as the Consumer Price Index? (Consider their assets, their liabilities, and the patterns of their purchases.)

12. Draw sets of Aggregate Demand and Aggregate Supply curves to illustrate demand-side inflation and supply-side inflation. List five events that could precipitate demand-side inflation, and five events that could generate supply-side inflation.

13. What improvements to official data on unemployment rates would make them better (negative) indicators of social welfare?

14. In October of 1982, the Reagan Administration faced political embarrassment: The unemployment rate had soared into the double-digit range (10.1 percent) for the first time since the 1930s. The White House implemented a proposal advocated by numerous politicians in the past—to base unemployment rates on the total (civilian plus military) labor force instead of on the civilian labor force alone. Our military force is between 2 and 3 million people. What effect did this change have on published unemployment rates? Why did several previous presidents favor this change?

15. Some critics believe that unemployment statistics tremendously underestimate unemployment, because so many potential workers have become discouraged. Other critics suggest that the published unemployment rate "measures with considerable lack of reliability the number of people in the labor force of this country who, if the pay were right and the hours were right, might be available for a little work once in a while." Which position do you think is correct? Why?

16. Changes in the Consumer Price Index are the most quoted measures of inflation, but the way the index is computed often has perverse consequences for public policy. For example, the index includes property, sales, and Social Security taxes, but not income taxes. If elected officials wanted to lower taxes and "cut" inflation at the same time, which tax rates would they prefer to cut? Does this method make any sense, or would we simply be the victims of a political con?

17. The CPI traditionally used fixed consumer budgets (expenditure categories) that were updated every few years. But when the price of one good rises relative to another, consumers do not wait to change their buying patterns. What kinds of adjustments will consumers make? Did the CPI consequently overstate or understate the true inflation rate? What was the effect of this over- or understatement on contracts containing cost-of-living adjustments? Could this inaccuracy fuel the fires of inflation? How was the CPI altered to remedy such problems? Do you suspect that implementing these changes was very costly?

CHAPTER 7

Measuring Economic Performance

Politicians, investors, union leaders, and business policy makers all eagerly await each government announcement of its latest estimates for unemployment, inflation, and Gross Domestic Product (**GDP**) or Gross National Product (**GNP**). Investments, wage demands, and national policies all hinge on trends in these numbers. You now know a bit about unemployment and inflation, but GNP and GDP probably seem a bit abstract. Economic analysts pore over these data the way fortune-tellers read tarot cards for hints about the future. How accurate are these data, and what do they mean?

Unemployment, inflation, and *economic growth* are our central macroeconomic concerns. Economic growth, as estimated by growth of GDP or GNP, can cure excessive unemployment or inflation pressure. Expansion of Aggregate Supply, for example, puts downward pressure on average prices, while boosting output (real GNP) and reducing unemployment. Increases in Aggregate Demand normally reduce unemployment and boost real output (GNP), but may stimulate inflation. After completing this chapter, you should understand what GNP and GDP represent, and be aware of some problems with national income accounting, developed roughly 50 years ago by Simon Kuznets (see his biography).

From Gross National Product to Gross Domestic Product

Published estimates of GNP rely on accounting data compiled by the Commerce Department.

> *Gross National Product (GNP) is the total market value of all goods and services produced annually **by U.S. residents**.*

GNP includes income earned by U.S. residents and U.S.-owned corporations abroad, but excludes income earned in the U.S. by residents of foreign countries. However, in 1992, the government began reporting Gross Domestic Product (GDP) as the principal measuring rod for the economy.

> *Gross Domestic Product (GDP) is the market value of all goods and services produced annually **within U.S. borders**.*

Gross Domestic Product, in contrast to GNP, includes the value of all goods produced inside the United States, without regard for where these organizations are headquartered. Thus, the income of all foreigners who work in the United States and the profits of all foreign-owned firms from U.S. operations are included in U.S. GDP.

Simon Kuznets (1901–1985)

Russian-born but American-educated, Simon Kuznets earned his Ph.D. from Columbia University in 1926 and began an association with the national Bureau of Economic Research that lasted for a half century. Kuznets developed and refined the concepts and measurements used in GNP accounting. When he began estimating economic aggregates, empirical data for many aspects of economic life were either crude or nonexistent. The concept of National Income was primitive.

Kuznets pioneered modern estimation techniques that sum expenditures by different classes of purchases over different classes of goods. Thus, he was responsible for providing the statistical foundations for modern studies of the relationships among income consumption, and investment, and well deserved the title, "Father of GNP." Without his work, quantitative methods to evaluate the Keynesian revolution in economic thought would have been impossible. This realization prompted one economist to declare that "we live in the age of Keynes and Kuznets." For his monumental achievements in empirical economics, Kuznets won a Nobel Prize in 1971.

His almost single-handed construction of the National Income accounts made him keenly aware of GNP's deficiencies as a measure of well-being. GNP ignores working conditions (e.g., stress and strain) and most nonmarket activities, so Kuznets strongly opposed reliance on National Income data as sole indicators of economic performance. Nevertheless, GNP is generally accepted today by economists, businesspeople, and politicians as a barometer of macroeconomic performance.

For example, the salary of a French chauffeur working at the French embassy would be considered as part of French GNP, but American GDP.

The U.S. switched to GDP in 1992 largely because most countries report GDP rather than GNP. The differences between GNP and GDP are not large for the United States. (See Focus 3 at the end of the chapter.) Therefore, the remainder of this chapter focuses on GNP, the measurement system in place as this text was being written.

GNP and GDP as Indicators

GNP and GDP provide fairly consistent gauges of economic activity over time so that we can estimate economic growth.[1] Measures of GNP and GDP are important indicators of the success or failure of policies, and forecasts help government policy makers time corrective policies. The level of economic performance is also important to business managers who must constantly re-view how macroeconomic growth or decline will affect their plans.

GNP, GDP and Economic Well-Being

GNP and GDP also provide crude yardsticks to estimate national well-being. Employment and income are related to aggregate output, so our individual incomes and spending tend to rise or fall with aggregate economic activity. A rough measure of well-being is obtained if we divide real values of both by population. Per capita GNP or GDP can be used to estimate how well off the average American is now compared to earlier times or with average people in other

---

1. Official estimates of GNP and GDP are reported in nominal (dollar) amounts. Thus, data series for both must be *deflated* to make these estimates truly comparable across time. (How to deflate nominal figures was described in Chapter 6.)

countries, and to compare growth rates among various countries.

The uses of these data as a measure of total production *and* as a measure of economic well-being sometimes conflict. Some numbers that should be included in national output if the intention is to measure economic welfare cause inaccuracies when we try to measure production, and vice versa. For example, when we bought weapons to reverse Iraq's 1990 invasion of Kuwait, were we better off than people in countries with lower per capita GDP that systematically avoid massive defense spending? Most of the choices made favor accurate measurement of production over accuracy and measuring the social well-being. This is why we include such things as inventory accumulation and exports in GDP and GDP.

Measuring GNP

There are two conceptually different ways of measuring Gross National Product: (*a*) the *expenditure* approach and (*b*) the *income* approach. Figure 1 illustrates these approaches with a version of the circular flow diagram you studied in Chapter 2. This shows that everything *bought* (expenditures) is *sold* by someone who receives income from the sale.

Both methods ideally yield the same numbers because spending on output results in income to producers. Neither approach is perfect, because available data reflect recording for accounting purposes and so are only roughly suited for economic analysis. Figure 2 illustrates the proportional makeup of GNP by major types of income and expenditures.

FIGURE 1   The Circular Flow and National Income Accounting

The two major approaches to GNP accounting are illustrated in this figure using the circular flow of income model. In this simple model, all goods are traded in the product market, and total expenditures equal the total value of output. Similarly, income is paid to owners of resources, and summing all of these payments will provide an estimate of GNP. Note that all expenditures on goods and services must necessarily equal all of the payments to resource owners to produce the output. That is, what is bought must have been sold. (*Note:* Clockwise arrows show money flow; counterclockwise arrows show flow of goods and resources.)

Net Exports (X - M)

Government Purchases (G)

Investment (I)

Consumption (C)

Gross National Product

Expenditures

Miscellaneous Corrections

Corporate Profits

Proprietors' Income

Interest

Rent

Employee Wages and Salaries

Income

FIGURE 2 Expenditure and Income Approach to GNP

Gross National Product can be estimated using either the expenditure approach or the income approach. As the figure illustrates, the sum of incomes paid to resource owners approximately equals total spending in the economy. (*Note:* Net exports have been consistently negative for the past decade.)

The Expenditure Approach

The *expenditure approach* to measuring Gross National Product leads us to the final buyers of all U.S. output.

> **Aggregate Expenditures** *are the sum of* (**a**) *consumer spending,* (**b**) *business investment,* (**c**) *government purchases, and* (**d**) *net spending by foreigners.*

Note that this breakdown precisely reflects the sources of Aggregate Demand described in Chapter 5. Figure 2 illustrates this division of the national pie into consumption (*C*), investment (*I*), government purchases (*G*), and net exports — exports − imports (*X* − *M*). (Foreigners provide outputs that we consume, invest, or use for government-provided services. As we noted in Chapter 5, imports boost Aggregate Supply.) Why the foreign sector is shown as a small contributor to our GNP will be explained after we examine spending by domestic purchasers in more detail.

Personal Consumption Expenditures (C)

Household spending includes outlays for *nondu-* *rable* goods (food and clothing), *durable* goods (appliances and cars), and *services* (e.g., medical care, haircuts, or legal advice).

> *Personal* **consumption** *expenditures* (**C**) *are the values of all commodities and services that households and individuals buy.*

This category is familiar because we all engage in consumption every day.

Business Investment (*I*) Remember that investment, as economists use the term, does not refer to the flows of money or documents that we term *financial investment.*

> **Economic investment** *refers to acquisition of new physical capital.*

GNP accountants refer to business spending for new capital as **Gross Private Domestic Investment**, or **GPDI**. *Gross* means that all purchases of *new* buildings, equipment, and the like are included. Whether investment replaces obsolete or worn-out capital does not matter. *Private* means that government investment is excluded. *Domestic* means that the new capital is bought from U.S. producers. We exclude foreign investments by American firms, but investment by foreign companies in the United States is part of our GPDI.

The major components of investment spending are

1. All new construction.
2. All final purchases of new equipment (e.g., machinery and tools).
3. Changes in inventories.

New production facilities, apartment buildings, and office space clearly fit the definition of investment, but why not treat construction of residential dwellings as consumer spending? One reason is that housing can be bought for rental purposes. In addition, the useful life of housing is quite long relative to most consumer goods. Consequently, it is regarded as a capital good, and newly constructed housing is included in investment. The rental value of owner-occupied housing is considered consumption because a home produces shelter year after year.

The second item, capital equipment, enhances the productive capacities of firms and also clearly fits the category of investment. But what about purchases of stocks and bonds? These are *financial* rather than *economic* investments. Financial investment may facilitate spending on real capital, but buying and selling securities merely transfers ownership from sellers of stock to buyers; our productive capability is not directly enhanced. Thus, transactions in financial instruments are not economic investments.

Inventory growth is also investment, while declines are **disinvestment.** Inventories include (*a*) raw materials or intermediate goods bought for use as productive inputs and (*b*) finished goods held in stock to rapidly meet customers' demands. Your customers would soon buy from other firms if they had difficulty getting prompt delivery.

Adjustments for inventory changes are needed because we use sales data to estimate production. If inventory growth were ignored, GNP would understate total production. Goods held as inventories should be counted in GNP in the year produced rather than the year sold. Since inventories vary from year to year, changes in inventories must be estimated to consistently measure total production and keep our national income accounts straight. Increases in inventories *add to* investment, and decreases *reduce* investment.

Government Purchases (G)   We consume commodities and services both as private individuals and collectively, through government. When the government provides goods, it may buy them in finished form from private firms, or it may buy resources or intermediate products and use them to produce the goods it provides. The most important resource government buys is the labor of its employees. *Government purchases of goods and services* (G), which include items ranging from pay for police officers to fire hydrants to cancer research, are then provided at zero or minimal prices to the people who use them. Because these items are seldom sold in markets, we do not know their value with any precision. Thus, all government goods enter the GNP accounts at the prices government pays for them. This means that, for GNP accounting purposes, government is assumed to add nothing to the value of the labor and other resources it uses.

An important point to remember is that transfer payments are excluded from government purchases. Transfer payments (welfare payments, Social Security, and others) are simply shifts in income from one set of households to another set and are not directly connected with production. Transfer payments only affect consumption and, consequently, Aggregate Demand when their recipients spend the funds they receive from the government.

Net Exports (X − M)   Net exports are defined as exports (X) minus imports (M).

> **Exports** *are goods manufactured in this country and bought by foreigners.*

We obviously need to include exports in GNP as a measure of the value of all production in a year. But what about imports? Do imports reflect American production? The answer is clearly "No."

Imports *are goods produced in foreign countries and consumed or invested in the United States.*

A Hyundai purchased in the United States is part of Korean production (and adds to Korean consumption when the owners of the resources that produce the car spend their pay). When Americans buy a Korean auto, the price paid to the Korean producers must be subtracted from U.S. consumption or it will appear that the car was produced in the United States. Similarly, if Swiss machinery is installed in an American factory, the purchase appears in the U.S. investment category and should be subtracted. Thus, imports are subtracted from exports to arrive at the net effect of foreign trade on GNP in our economy.

To summarize briefly: Using the expenditure approach, Gross National Product is the sum of consumer spending (C), business investment (I), government spending for goods and services (G), and net exports (X − M):

$$C + I + G + (X - M) = GNP$$

Table 1 shows these expenditures.

The Income Approach

All spending ultimately translates into income. Thus, national output calculated by the expenditure approach must equal National Income.

Table 1 *Components of Gross National Product: Expenditure Approach (1990 Billions of Dollars)*

Component	$Billions
Personal Consumption Expenditures (C)	$3,658.1
Gross Private Domestic Investment (I)	745.0
Government Purchases of Goods and Services (G)	1,098.0
*Net Exports of Goods and Services (X − M)	−38.0
Gross National Product	**$5,463.0**

*This negative number reflects a deficit in the U.S. balance of trade—beginning in 1982, we have consistently imported more than we exported each year.

Source: U.S. Department of Commerce, *Economic Report of the President*, 1991.

National Income (NI) *is computed by summing all payments to resource owners — wages, rents, interest, and profits.*

Conceptually, National Income is the sum of all income received by owners of the various resources (wages to labor, interest to capital, rent to land, and profit to entrepreneurship). In fact, however, limitations of accounting data cause NI to be measured as the sum of five slightly different categories: (*a*) wages and salaries, (*b*) noncorporate proprietors' income, (*c*) corporate profits before taxes, (*d*) rental income, and (*e*) interest. Table 2 presents the proportions and trends in these income payments for selected years.

Wages and Salaries This category includes not only wages, but also the monetary values of employees' fringe benefits, tips, bonuses, stock option plans, paid vacations, and firms' contributions to Social Security. As you can see from Table 2, wages and salaries are by far the largest category in National Income. Wages have consistently increased as a percentage of U.S. National Income, growing from less than half in 1900 to roughly three-fourths today.

Proprietors' Income National Income accountants separate accounting profit into two categories: proprietors' net income and corporate profits. *Proprietors' incomes* are incomes received by sole proprietorships, partnerships, professional associations, and (unincorporated) farms. Included in farm income is an estimate of the value of food grown and consumed on farms — although it is not marketed, this clearly represents production.

Much of this income category represents wages, interest, or rent that proprietors would have earned if they had not been operating their own firms. Dividing this category according to purely economic concepts (to distinguish opportunity costs) is not possible, however, given limitations of the accounting data available. Thus, we will term this "profit," but only for purposes of GNP accounting.

Over the last few decades, proprietors' income has declined relative to National Income, falling from 17.5 percent in 1929 to only 9 percent today. (Could a recent reversal of this trend be

Table 2 *National Income: Income Approach to GNP (Selected Years 1929–90)*

Category	1929 Billions $	1929 %	1933 Billions $	1933 %	1960 Billions $	1960 %	1980 Billions $	1980 %	1990 Billions $	1990 %
Wage and salaries	51.1	58.9	29.5	73.1	294.2	71.0	1,598.6	75.5	3,224.2	73.3
Proprietors' income	15.2	17.5	5.9	14.6	46.2	11.2	116.3	5.5	402.4	9.2
Corporate profits	10.5	12.0	−1.2	−3.0	49.9	12.0	181.6	8.6	297.1	6.7
Rental income	5.4	6.2	2.0	5.1	15.8	3.8	32.9	1.5	6.7	0.2
Interest	4.7	5.4	4.1	10.2	8.4	2.0	187.7	8.9	467.1	10.6
National income	86.8	100.0	40.3	100.0	414.1	100.0	2,117.1	100.0	4,397.5	100.0

Source: U.S. Department of Commerce, *Economic Report of the President*, 1991.
(*Note:* The declining share of rental income shown is a bit misleading because of rapid write-offs of depreciation for real estate in recent years.)

signaling a new era for entrepreneurs?) Part of the reason for shrinkage in proprietors' incomes and the growth in wages and salaries is that many people whose families once owned small farms have sold these farms and moved to urban areas where they could realize greater incomes through wages and salaries.

Corporate Profit Corporations use their accounting profit in three ways. First, they *must* pay corporate income taxes. Second, they *may* pay stockholders dividends from what is left after taxes. Finally, remaining profits are kept in the firm to help finance expansion, to be used as working capital, or for other purposes. Economists call the corporate profits kept within the firm *undistributed corporate profits*; to accountants they are *retained earnings*.

Much of the accounting category called *corporate profit* actually represents interest stockholders could have made had they bought bonds instead of stock. Again, because dividing the data is difficult, it is conventional to lump this figure in with corporate profits.

Proprietors' income has fallen as a percentage of National Income, so you might expect that the share accruing to corporate profit would be rising. A glance at Table 2, however, reveals that corporate profit as a percentage of National Income has been shrinking. What accounts for the increase in wages and salaries and the erratic declines in both corporate and proprietors' entrepreneurial profits? The explanation lies partially

in the fact that government outlays as a percentage of total output have risen markedly since the Great Depression. The bulk of government-provided services require substantial labor, so wages and salaries have been growing steadily.

Rental Income Accounting rents are usually associated with the leasing of real property (such as land, houses, offices), but can be obtained from renting any asset (e.g., a videotape or U-Haul trailer). Determining what part conforms to the economic definition of rent as a payment for the use of land is impossible, so again we use the accounting classification. As you can see in Table 2, rental income is the smallest category in National Income.

Interest Interest is also rather self-explanatory. Accountants include the payments made for the use of borrowed capital (usually, financial capital). These payments are made by borrowers to banks, or to holders of bonds, or by banks to their depositors. In the 1970s, rising interest rates caused interest income to be the most rapidly growing component of National Income. National Income accounting conventions treat interest paid to holders of government bonds as a transfer payment and exclude it from the interest component of National Income. If interest on government bonds were included, interest would have been roughly one-seventh of National Income in 1990.

Reconciling GNP and NI

Gross Private Domestic Investment (GPDI) overstates growth of the nation's stock of capital because some capital wears out each year.

Accountants refer to the decline in value of capital because of wear and tear or obsolescence as **depreciation**.

Accounting estimates of depreciation reflect rapid write-offs to exploit advantageous tax treatments. Economists label accounting depreciation as *capital consumption allowances*.

Subtracting depreciation from Gross Private Domestic Investment yields **Net Private Domestic Investment**, an estimate of annual growth in a nation's capital. All else equal, depreciation reduces capital owners' wealth. Thus, one step in reconciling GNP and NI requires subtracting depreciation from GNP, which yields Net National Product (NNP). Conceptually, NNP estimates how much we could consume in a given year and still have the same amount of productive capital at the beginning of the next year.

Net National Product *is the net value of annual output in the economy after adjustment for depreciation*.

Failing to consider depreciation would cause overstatement of the net value of our production. In a sense, depreciation represents a "death rate of capital" that must be subtracted from the "birth rate of capital" (GPDI) to arrive at net capital formation.

One more adjustment to our GNP is necessary before it equals National Income. The amounts you pay for goods and the amounts received by firms are not equal. Sales and excise taxes, collectively known as *indirect business taxes*, drive wedges between what consumers or investors spend and the amounts received by sellers. For example, sales and excise taxes must be subtracted from the buyer's payment for a new car before we arrive at the amount that auto workers or manufacturers will receive as income. Consequently, indirect business taxes must be subtracted from Net National Product. We obtain National Income only after these and other miscellaneous adjustments have been made. Table 3 shows the adjustments necessary to reconcile GNP and NI.

The Value-Added Technique What are the mechanics of computing GNP? Government statisticians could wait for households to file

Table 3 *Reconciling the Income and Expenditure Approaches to GNP (1990 Billions of Dollars)*

Expenditure Approach	$Billions
Gross National Product (GNP)	$5,463.0
minus: Capital consumption allowance (depreciation)	−575.7
equals: Net National Product (NNP)	4,887.4
minus: Indirect Business Taxes (IBT) and misc.	−440.4
equals: National Income (NI)	$4447.0

Income Approach	$Billions
Wages and salaries	$3,244.2
plus: Proprietors' income (business, professional, farm)	402.4
plus: Corporate profits before taxes	297.1
plus: Rental income	6.7
plus: Interest	467.1
equals: National Income (NI)	$4,447.0

Source: Department of Commerce, *Economic Report of the President*, 1991.
Note: Rounding may cause minor inconsistencies.

their income taxes. Calculating GNP would require summing all declared incomes and then adding indirect business taxes and depreciation, but this strategy depends crucially on people's honesty. Worse yet, revised figures would only be available in May or June, which would make them five or six months old because the income tax returns due on April 15 are for the preceding year. For these reasons and more, National Income is calculated primarily as a double check on GNP figures.

An alternative is to collect all sales figures for a year. Most firms are subject to sales and income taxes and to other government controls requiring extensive reporting, so sales figures are available on a regular and continuing basis. But what then? If we just total all sales figures, there will be a lot of *double counting*. For example, if U.S. Steel's sales are added to Ford's sales, we count steel output twice — once when it is sold to Ford and again when Ford sells the steel in, say, a new Bronco to the final customer.

For this reason, National Income accountants use the **value-added technique**. A firm's purchases of intermediate goods from other firms are subtracted from its sales, leaving only the value of its own production — its *value added*. Summing values added by all firms in an economy yields reasonably accurate GNP figures, after adjusting for such things as changes in inventories, the imputed (estimated) rental values of owner-occupied housing, and the imputed values of food grown and consumed on the farm.

Suppose that, while wandering in a forest one weekend, you find a gnarled piece of weathered wood. You haul it home and show it to an artist friend. Your friend wants to carve a figure from the piece of wood and offers you $20 for it. When you accept, measured GNP has grown by $20. Your friend carves the wood and sells the finished sculpture to a gift shop for $100, which then sells the carving to a customer for $150.

Has GNP increased by $270 ($20 + $100 + $150)? The answer is no. If we were to sum all these transactions, your original sale of the wood for $20 would be counted three times — in the original sale, in the sale to the shop, and then in the final sale to the customer. During the first two sales, the piece of wood is an *intermediate*

good — something used in the production of another good. The sale to the customer is the final sale, and the carving sold by the shop is the *final good*.

The value-added approach sums the value added at each stage of production. For our wood carving example, $20 in value was added by you in finding and selling the piece of wood to your friend, who generated $80 in value added by sculpting the wood. Then the store added value of $50 by putting the carving in the ultimate buyer's hands. (*Note:* The major taxes collected from business firms in most European nations are taxes on values added. Many American economists favor replacement of corporate income taxes by value-added taxes — a proposal that is being considered in Congress as one way to reduce huge federal budget deficits in the 1990s.)

Moving from GNP to Disposable Personal Income

Models used to explain how National Income is determined largely ignore the differences among GNP, National Income (NI), Net National Product (NNP), Personal Income (PI), and Disposable Personal Income (DPI). We already know that capital consumption allowances (depreciation) must be subtracted from GNP to compute Net National Product (NNP). Subtracting indirect business taxes from our NNP yields the total income earned by the suppliers of productive resources, which is known as National Income (NI).

More adjustments are needed, however, before arriving at household income before taxes (*Personal Income*, or *PI*) and the income households actually have left to spend after taxes (*Disposable Personal Income*, or *DPI*).

From NI to Personal Income (PI) National Income includes wages, interest, rent, proprietors' income, and corporate profit. Firms often act as tax collection points; in fact some households never see parts of the income attributed to them. For example, corporate taxes must be paid before stockholders have claims on corporate incomes, so these taxes must be subtracted from

National Income. Stockholders' dividends are parts of their Personal Income, but undistributed corporate profits must also be subtracted from National Income. Also, business firms are legally obligated to match employees' Social Security contributions. National Income accounts subtract both employer and employee Social Security taxes from NI on this journey toward Personal Income.

> **Personal Income (PI)** *is the money income received by households before they pay their personal taxes.*

In addition to household income that is earned but not received, two forms of income are *received* but *not earned*. A growing share of our National Income is devoted to government transfer payments (e.g., welfare payments). Many firms also engage in charitable activities. Funds transferred through either government or business to private individuals must be added to National Income. At this point, we have finally arrived at the total amount of personal money income that households receive.

From PI to Disposable Personal Income (DPI)

You might think that Personal Income is the amount available for personal consumption and saving, but direct taxes on individuals must be paid out of your Personal Income.

> **Disposable Personal Income (DPI)** *is income households can consume or save as they choose after subtracting income taxes from Personal Income.*

Table 4 details the breakdown from GNP to DPI for selected years.

Table 4 *Gross National Product and Related Data (Billions of Dollars)*

	1929	1950	1990
Gross National Product (GNP)	$103.1	$284.8	$5,463.0
minus: Capital consumption allowance (depreciation)	−7.9	−18.3	−575.7
equals: Net National Product (NNP)	$ 95.2	$266.5	$4,887.4
minus: Indirect business taxes	−3.4	−14.1	−440.4
equals: National Income (NI)	$ 91.8	$252.4	$4,447.0
minus: Corporate profits with inventory evaluation adjustment	−10.5	−37.7	−297.1
Contributions for social insurance	−.2	−6.9	−506.9
Net interest	−4.7	−3.0	−467.1
plus: Government transfer payments	0.9	14.3	659.5
Personal interest income	2.5	7.2	680.9
Dividends	5.8	8.8	123.8
Business transfer payments	0.6	0.8	35.0
equals: Personal Income (PI)	$ 86.2	$235.9	$4,675.0
minus: Personal taxes	−2.6	−20.7	−699.8
equals: Disposable Personal Income (DPI)	$ 83.6	$215.2	$3,975.2
minus: Consumer interest and personal transfer payments to foreigners	−1.9	−2.8	−108.7
Consumption expenditures	−77.2	−191.0	−3,658.1
equals: Personal saving	$ 4.5	$ 21.4	$ 208.4

Source: U.S. Department of Commerce, *Economic Report of the President*, 1991.
(*Note:* Totals may not add up because of rounding.)

Limitations of GNP Accounting

How well do estimates of GNP and National Income measure economic performance? Although the National Income accounts are fine for some purposes, they suffer from certain limitations. These limitations fall into four categories: (*a*) accuracy, (*b*) inclusion of only "legal" market transactions, (*c*) misclassification, and (*d*) measurement of government output.

Accuracy of GNP Figures

There is a tendency toward specious accuracy, a pretense that things have been counted more precisely than they can be — e.g., the U.S. Army published enemy casualties for the Korean war to 1/1000 of 1 percent, at a time when our own losses were not well known even to the thousands of men! The classic case is, of course, that of the story in which man, asked about the age of a river, states that it is 3,000,021 years old. Asked how he could give such accurate information, the answer was that twenty-one years ago the river's age was given as three million years.

Oskar Morgenstern
("Qui Numerare Incipit Errore Incipit")

Just how accurate must GNP accounts be to be useful to economic planners and business forecasters? Estimation errors are often clearly biased. For example, many people systematically understate the incomes reported on their tax forms. Statisticians commonly assume that errors of measurement are offsetting, but we have a bridge to sell anyone who thinks that as many people overreport income as underreport it.

Another problem is that most accounts are reported to the exact dollar. For example, per capita Personal Income for Utah in 1990 was reported as $12,893. Would it be just as useful (and less misleading) to learn that Personal Income in Utah was roughly $13,000? Social and economic statistics need be no more accurate than their use dictates. Further, social scientists should not report results from studying these numbers in a fashion that creates a false sense of precision.

Exclusion of Nonmarket Transactions

GNP is the total value of all production during a year, so it should cover all outputs. Our national accounts focus on market transactions because dollar sales figures are reasonably available, but not all productive activity goes through the marketplace. Some nonmarket transactions are included in GNP because estimates of their values are available (e.g., estimated rents for owner-occupied housing and estimates of the value of food produced and consumed on farms). But the values of housewives' services are excluded from GNP, because even crude estimates are almost pure guesses. This leads to the ludicrous situation where a maid hired to clean your home increases GNP, while the same work done by a family member does not enter our GNP accounts. The same is true of homemade haircuts, mowing your own lawn rather than hiring your neighbor's kid, and many other nonmarket activities.

Only crude estimates are available of the values of unrecorded activities such as cash or barter transactions, so the government traditionally excluded them, as well as all illegal activities (see Focus 1). Should legalization of gambling or marijuana lead to growth in measured GNP figures even if people's behavior doesn't change? Under current accounting practices, it would. Such problems mean that comparisons of GNP over time or among countries must be tempered by recognition that GNP accounts are affected by the relative importance of do-it-yourself production, by the frequency of barter, and by differences in laws and regulations.

Misclassification

Some GNP items seem misclassified. For example, individual spending on education is treated as personal consumption. Football games, parties, and some frivolous courses may qualify as consumption activities. But time and effort spent studying will increase your future productivity and should be considered investment, not consumption. (Should your body's deterioration as you age be considered "depreciation"?) Govern-

FOCUS 1

The Underground Economy

We all know people who cheat on their taxes by understating their income. Cosmetologists who report only half their tips, plumbers who give customers a break if they pay cash, and gamblers who keep no records are all part of the "underground economy." Estimates of its size range from a conservative 3 percent to an astounding 20 percent of GNP, which means that our official 1990 GNP of $5.4 trillion could easily have exceeded $6 trillion if everyone had reported all their income. Moreover, it means that underground participants may now cheat the U.S. Treasury out of as much as $300 billion in taxes annually. Figure 3 presents one set of estimates of the size of the underground economy.

Although researchers disagree on the size of the subterranean economy, all agree that it is growing roughly twice as fast as GNP. One piece of evidence is that the demand for the cash component in our money supply has grown sharply in recent decades. Large bills are the payment of choice in much of the underground economy.

Why is this happening? One part of the answer is that many Americans view high tax brackets as powerful incentives to cheat. Another aspect of this problem is the falling probability of an Internal Revenue Service audit. About 3 percent of all tax returns were audited in the late 1960s;

the proportion is now around 1.5 percent. Finally, tax evasion has become respectable in the eyes of some, who excuse their behavior with the argument that "everybody does it."

Cataloguing all the ways that people have discovered to cheat on their taxes would generate a book as thick as a New York City telephone directory. Legitimate businesspeople may not report cash income or may overstate their tax deductions and thus understate their incomes. If you

falsely claim that new drapes in your home are a business expense, you are involved in the underground economy. Barter is perfectly legitimate but it is a major avenue for tax evasion. When a dentist trades a root canal for brickwork on a backyard fireplace, both the dentist and the bricklayer should report as income the value of what they received.

Nearly 70 percent of the underground economy consists of income that, if reported, would

FIGURE 3 Sources of Underground Income, 1990

Source: Carl R. Simon and Ann D. Witte, *Beating the System: The Underground Economy* (Boston: Auburn House Publishing Co., 1981); updated by authors.

Unreported Income from Illegal Sources (Billions of Dollars)

Pornography $10
Fraud $21
Gambling & Loan Sharking $8
Bribery $28
Other Illegal $19
Prostitution $30
Stolen Goods $37
Drugs $93
Wages and Salaries* $151
Self-Employment* $240
Interest* $38
Corporate Profits* $35
Rents and Royalties* $25
Other Legal $13
*Partly included in recorded GNP accounts

Unreported Income from Legal Sources (Billions of Dollars)

Total Illegal $246 billion + Total Legal $502 billion
= Total Legal & Illegal $748 billion

be legitimate; 30 percent or so of the income flowing through untaxed channels is derived from criminal activities. Bank robbers, shoplifters, drug dealers, prostitutes, and loan sharks understandably try to minimize their contact with the Internal Revenue Service. Failure of the IRS to collect taxes is important because those of us who scrupulously pay our taxes suffer from higher tax rates.

Growth of self-employment in almost all economies during the past decade may signal a groundswell in entrepreneurial instincts, but it also triggers growth of underground economies in nations ranging from the United States to Sweden to Taiwan to the Soviet Union.* Tax evasion is far easier for the self-employed than for most other people.

What are the implications of the underground economy for economic statistics and public policy? For one thing, the slowdown of GNP growth during the 1970s may have been overstated to the extent that unreported income grew in importance nationally. In January 1986, the Department of Commerce began adjusting the GNP accounts to try to account for misreporting on tax returns. These adjustments totaled more than $220 billion for 1990.

Another consideration is that unemployment statistics may be

*"The Shadow Economy: Grossly Deceptive Product," The Economist, 19 Sept. 1987, pp. 25–28.

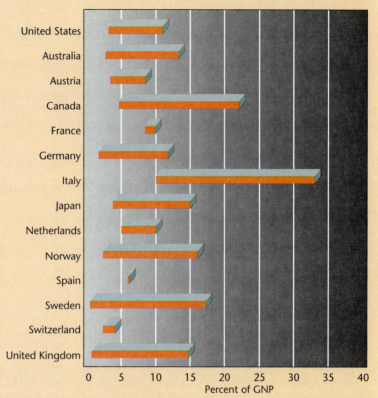

FIGURE 4   The Underground Economy
Source: U.S. Dept. of Commerce, Bureau of Economic Analysis; Carol Carson, "The Underground Economy: An Introduction," Survey of Current Business, May 1984, p. 33.

overstated (or labor force participation understated) if underground activity is not taken into account. Still another is that if poor people participate in cash or barter transactions proportionally more than high-income individuals, the degree of income inequality and the need for welfare programs may be overstated; conversely, if high-dollar, white-collar crime is rampant, income may be even less evenly distributed than we think. This list of reasons for the importance of accounting for underground

transactions could be extended considerably.

We can wish that compliance with tax laws were more widespread among Americans but, at the same time, we can be grateful that we do not suffer from the underreporting that appears common in parts of Europe. As Figure 4 shows, the underground economy is estimated to run as high as one-third of Italian GNP.†

†"Lies, Damned Lies, and Italy's GDP," The Economist, 27 Feb. 1988, pp. 4–9.

ment investments in flood control, research and development, transportation networks, and so on are treated similarly. These investments are reported as government spending instead of investment. Classification in this way tends to understate the extent to which present consumption is diverted to activities that enhance our future productivity, output, growth, and well-being.

Measuring Government Output

Measuring the value of government output poses special problems. Few government services are directly charged to final users, so valuing government output is ambiguous. Consequently, government accountants use the next best estimate — the cost of the inputs (primarily, government workers) used to produce the output.

Problems with GNP accounting cause some critics to assert that GNP and NI figures are worthless. It may be that parts of our measures of GNP and some of its relatives are a bit like the following example.

Imagine that all members of your class were transported back in time to around 1803. Each is assigned by President Thomas Jefferson to travel to various parts of North America and then return to Washington, D.C. with estimates of distances between certain points. To standardize measurements, everyone is to pace the distances. People walking to Philadelphia, New York, or Boston would cross-check each other, ensuring reasonable estimates for these short distances. But people's strides differ in length, some people might wander in circles, and others might guess at the distance while they rode in wagons. Still others might not even go to faraway destinations but would fill in travel vouchers as if they had. The mishmash of estimates turned in to President Jefferson might resemble parts of GNP accounting — far from perfect, but still better than no data at all.

GNP and Social Welfare

GNP accounts were created to measure economic performance. These accounts may be abused when they are used to make comparisons about the well-being of citizens in various countries. This is especially true if the relative amounts of self-production, barter, or the underground economy vary much among countries. Focus 2 addresses some serious problems for inferring that standards of living are roughly proportional to estimates of per capita GNP across different countries.

When our government reports that per capita GNP rose by 1 percent last month, this need not imply that your personal quality of life improved by 1 percent. There may be some correlation between the growth of GNP and growth in your income, but the relationship is far from perfect.

How GNP Differs from Well-Being

GNP would fall if you took a year off from work for a world tour. You might gain subjectively, but the GNP accounts would not reflect your enjoyment of added travel and leisure. An important recent economic change that improves the quality of life is the increased leisure most of us enjoy. The GNP accounts ignore the value of leisure.

This accounting system also fails to deduct for many negative aspects of economic growth, particularly environmental degradation. Greater outlays on packaging for products boost measured GNP, but the accounting process fails to deduct the accompanying destruction of national forests. GNP does include the costs of removing litter and of increased medical care caused by pollution or auto accidents, but do injurious wrecks increase our welfare? Would we be better off if a nuclear meltdown necessitated a billion-dollar cleanup? Some people argue that we need an index that emphasizes economic well-being instead of economic production.

A Measure of Economic Welfare (MEW)

Work in this direction has been done by William Nordhaus and James Tobin. They attempted to adjust GNP to account for some of the deficiencies we have described. Their statistic is called a Measure of Economic Welfare.

Errors in International Comparisons of Per Capita GDP

Could anyone survive for a year on less than typical American families spend on Thanksgiving dinners? In the mid-1980s, Chinese per capita income was reported as below $50 annually. It seems unlikely that average Ethiopians, with per capita income of $150, were nearly three times more prosperous than the Chinese. Comparisons such as those displayed in Table 5 are too often presented uncritically.

Per capita GDP may provide grossly distorted snapshots of standards of living in different countries. We should recognize, first, that the underground economy and do-it-yourself production per capita tend to be negatively related to per capita GDP, being relatively less important in industrialized nations that rely heavily on specialization. Colombia's highly publicized underground economy, for example, is disregarded in computing Colombian GDP. Meals cooked from a family's garden or from foraging are largely ignored in GDP estimates for primitive economies. A discarded shirt has zero value until it is scavenged from a garbage dump in Calcutta. Although such salvage does not enter India's accounting GDP, value was produced, so it should be. Similarly, hovels newly constructed of crushed tin cans on the outskirts of Cairo are not treated as investment in Egypt's GDP accounts but should be.

Table 5 *International Per Capita GDPs*

Country	Per capita GDP, 1990*
Colombia	$ 1,130
Egypt	$ 700
Ethiopia	$ 150
India	$ 400
Japan	$15,500
Kenya	$ 360
Mexico	$ 2,400
Soviet Union	$ 2,500
Switzerland	$17,600
United States	$21,000

*Central Intelligence Agency, *The World Factbook 1992* and author updates.

Second, intentional misstatements of income and output are common. National incomes are probably understated in the United States and much of Western Europe because the data bases reflect legal tax avoidance or illegal evasion. On the other hand, dictators often inflate GDP to feed their egos. In Romania, for example, output was systematically overstated by followers of Nicolai Ceaucescu until he was deposed and executed in 1990. Contrary to the CIA's estimates, scholars have recently concluded that the per capita GDP of Russia does not exceed that in Mexico. The former USSR's data were highly exaggerated. Misrepresentation may also arise if statistics about impoverished nations are the basis for foreign aid. The leader of a less developed country may intentionally mislead aid providers in hopes of getting more aid.

Third, costs of living differ markedly. Hamburgers cost roughly $16 in Tokyo, and hotel rooms in Zurich are 600 percent more than comparable rooms in Lima. A related problem is that foreign GDP figures are converted into U.S. dollars at prevailing *exchange rates*—the dollar prices of foreign currencies. Using current rates to translate foreign GDP into dollars creates a ludicrous situation where a decline in the dollar in international currency markets causes our estimates of foreign GDPs to rise proportionally, while a rising dollar causes estimates of foreign GDPs to plummet.

Finally, income is only one dimension of the quality of life, which is also affected by such things as weather and scenery, political liberty, job opportunities, access to medical care and education, and personal security (e.g., low crime rates and freedom from conflicts such as war).

The message here is that international comparisons of per capita income should be greeted with more than a grain of salt. Nevertheless, the data leave little room for doubt that most people in Ethiopia or India endure lives of destitution relative to the prosperity enjoyed by most people living in advanced economies.

The **Measure of Economic Welfare (MEW)** *deducts items that do not contribute to economic welfare and adds items that do, but that are not now counted in GNP.*

Major items deducted from GNP include (*a*) spending that does not add to a better life – e.g.,

police protection, costs of commuting, and national defense – and (*b*) losses associated with pollution, urban congestion, and so on. The major additions are estimates for (*a*) values of goods that do not pass through the market and (*b*) increased leisure.

The crude MEW estimates done by Nordhaus

FIGURE 5 Percentage Rates of Change in Real U.S. GNP Per Capita, 1900–1990

Per capita GNP equals nominal GNP divided by population. These data must be divided by (1% of) the CPI to make the data comparable over time, a process described in Chapter 6. Panel A loosely reflects growth in the material welfare of Americans across this century, measured in 1990 dollars. Panel B shows that this growth has not been smooth.

Source: U.S. Dept. of Commerce, *Business Conditions Digest*, various issues, 1970–1990.

FOCUS 3

Comparing GNP and GDP

Gross National Product measures the values of goods produced by U.S. residents while GDP measures output produced within our borders. For several reasons, these differences are not particularly large for the United States. First, a relatively few proportion of our citizens work abroad. Second, the earnings from U.S. investments overseas are roughly the same as earnings of foreign corporations operating in the United States. Gross Domestic Product, however, is considered by most economists to be the best measure of what is happening with the U.S. economy. Figure 6 shows that GNP and GDP move in tandem, with less than 1 percent difference between the two being typical. This figure does show, however, that since 1982, GNP has been consistently below GDP reflecting an expansion of foreign firms' operations

Real GDP and GNP

GDP

GNP

Billions of 1987 Dollars

6000.00
5500.00
5000.00
4500.00
4000.00
3500.00
3000.00
2500.00
2000.00

0.00

'72   '76   '80   '84   '88   '92

FIGURE 6

in the U.S. relative to U.S. investments overseas.

For other countries, however, the distinction between GNP and GDP is important. For example, such countries as Pakistan have relatively large proportions of their citizens working abroad, yielding a lower GDP than their GNP.

Conversely, Canada, with significantly more foreign investment at home than abroad, enjoys a much larger GDP than its GNP figures would indicate. The trivial difference allows us to use GNP for which historical data is more available, through the rest of the book.

and Tobin suggest that our welfare has grown more slowly than has GNP. One important question society must answer is, "How much growth in GNP might we be willing to sacrifice to improve our quality of life (as measured by MEW growth)?" Even these MEW accounts leave many questions unanswered. For example, if water prices rise because of drought, should we rejoice because the value of water consumed as measured by our water bills has risen?

Despite the many difficulties associated with accurately measuring GNP and its components, it remains our best measure of economic growth and aggregate economic activity. Figure 5 traces changes in real per capita GNP over the years. In the discussions of macroeconomic theory and policy that follow, we will constantly refer to GNP (both real and nominal) and the rates of unemployment and inflation. While making these evaluations, however, you should keep in mind the limitations described in this chapter and the previous one.

Chapter Review: Key Points

1. *GNP* is the total market value of a nation's annual production. GNP measures estimate the economic performance of an economy and are important for government policy and business decisions.

2. The *expenditures* approach to GNP sums *consumption* spending (C), business *investment* spending (I), *government purchases* (G), and *net exports* (X − M):

    GNP = C + I + G + (X − M)

3. *Gross Private Domestic Investment (GPDI)* is the economic term for business spending. To arrive at net investment, we need to subtract depreciation from GPDI.

4. Government purchases (G) do not include *transfer* (welfare) *payments*, which are treated as flows of income from some households to others.

5. The *income* approach to GNP sums wages, interest, rent, and profits. We use the figures available, which are (*a*) wages and salaries, (*b*) proprietors' income, (*c*) corporate profits, (*d*) rental income, and (*e*) interest. The sum of these figures is *National Income (NI)*. Addition of *indirect business taxes*, which is not anyone's income, yields *Net National Product (NNP)*. The *capital consumption allowance (depreciation)* is the difference between GNP and NNP.

6. The *value-added* approach to GNP sums the sales of all firms and subtracts their purchases of intermediate products, which are goods bought by one firm from another for further processing. Failure to exclude purchases of intermediate goods from GNP figures would result in substantial *double counting* of production.

7. GNP figures should be used cautiously in any discussions of economic welfare. One problem is that they may be systematically biased and are often presented in an artificially precise fashion. Another problem is that they ignore most nonmarket production (e.g., housewives' services, do-it-yourself projects, and the like). GNP accounts include as production many disproducts (for instance, pollution abatement equipment is added to

GNP, while environmental decay is not subtracted).

8. A *Measure of Economic Welfare (MEW)*, which attempts to correct for some of these flaws in GNP accounts, shows much less rapid growth than GNP.

Key Concepts

Ensure that you can define these terms before proceeding.

Gross National Product (GNP)
consumption (C)
investment (I)
government purchases (G)
net exports (X − M)
National Income (NI)
depreciation

Net National Product (NNP)
Personal Income (PI)
Disposable Personal Income (DPI)
Measure of Economic Welfare (MEW)

Problems and Questions

1. Suppose a car dealer sells a new car in September 1992 for $10,400, but allows a trade-in of $3,800 for a car that turns out to be a clunker. After $600 worth of repairs, the clunker is sold for $2,900. The new car cost the dealer $9,000. How will each phase of these transactions affect the GNP accounts? What were the values added at each step?

Questions 2–4 use the data in this table.

	$ billions
Gross Private Domestic Investment	666.1
Exports	363.2
Personal Tax Payments	498.2
State and Local Government Purchases	467.7
Capital Consumption Allowance	441.4
Imports	451.0
Personal Consumption Expenditures	2,606.1
Federal Government Purchases	364.8
Personal Income	3,298.5

2. Calculate Gross National Product.

3. Calculate Net National Product.

4. Calculate Personal Saving.

Questions 5–10 use these National Income accounts for the mythical kingdom of Northpolia.

wages	800
consumption	900
proprietors' income	100
gross investment	150
corporate income	100
rental income	75
interest	75
government purchases	200
exports	100
imports	50
indirect business taxes	75
transfer payments	50
personal income taxes	100
corporate retained earnings	50
corporate income taxes	75

5. Calculate GNP.

6. Calculate National Income.

7. Calculate the capital consumption allowance.

8. Calculate Net National Product.

9. Calculate Personal Income.

10. Calculate Disposable Personal Income.

11. You own a company with annual sales of $500,000. Value added for your firm's production (your addition to GNP) is $250,000. Is your firm making a profit of $250,000? If not, how is the difference between your firm's sales and your firm's addition to GNP explained?

12. What would be the effect on GNP accounting if marijuana, prostitution, and gambling were legalized nationwide? What do you think would happen to economic well-being? Why?

13. If you start your own business and use $23,000 of your savings to buy used equipment from a dealer, is the $23,000 considered economic investment? Will any part of the $23,000 add to GNP? Explain.

14. Suppose that all homeowners in America decided to move into their next-door neighbor's house and pay that neighbor rent. What would happen to GNP? Would your answer be the same if GNP estimates did not include an estimate of the rental value of owner-occupied housing? How would it differ?

15. What is the effect of arson on estimates of GNP? What should it be?

16. Suppose one-fourth of all young women workers take a maternity leave and then, after their children are born, decide to stay home permanently. What will happen to our GNP accounts? As we defined GNP conceptually, what happens to actual GNP relative to measured GNP? Measured GNP relative to economic welfare?

17. Why is NNP a more appropriate measure of true economic productivity than GNP? As they are currently constructed, which do you think is the best measure of economic welfare on a per capita basis: (a) GNP, (b) NNP, (c) NI, (d) PI, (e) DPI, or (f) consumption? Why is this category preferable to the others?

18. National Income accounting values government services at the costs of the inputs government uses. Why does the government value its output in this manner? Do you feel that this understates or overstates the value of government? How would you measure the value of government services?

19. Should spending on education be viewed as consumption or investment expenditure? Why? What would happen to the National Income accounts if purchases of education, medical care, and dental care were counted as investment and not consumption?

20. The government has gone to great lengths to compile and distribute measurements of aggregate economic activity. Some critics would say, "This information is not all that useful, and collecting it is just a method to employ a sizeable portion of the federal bureaucracy." Your reaction?

PART 3

Keynesian Macroeconomics

Isaac Newton's theories of gravity and mechanics suggest that cosmic interactions in our universe follow a natural harmony. Adam Smith, in his *Wealth of Nations* (1776), extended Newton's view into the realm of economics with the idea that an "invisible hand" governs the marketplace. Smith's theory of markets led to *laissez-faire* policy prescriptions that were compatible with the hostility toward powerful government expressed in the American Declaration of Independence — which also appeared in 1776.

Several generations of economists expanded Smith's ideas about macroeconomics into *classical theory*, which we explore in the beginning of Chapter 8. The political climate and the "invisible hand" approach, which concludes that simple market economies quickly gravitate toward full employment, merged to shape an American economy that, with some exceptions, was dominated by a free-market perspective until the worldwide Great Depression of the 1930s. Between roughly 1790 and 1930, however, most economies in Europe and North America steadily became more industrialized, and they were increasingly dominated by giant firms. Conventional economic theory adapted relatively slowly to this evolution beyond reliance on agriculture and local forms of simple manufacturing.

Frequent booms and busts did not shake most economists' faith in laissez-faire policies until the 1930s depression launched the *Keynesian Revolution* in economic theory. Keynesian theory is examined in Chapters 8 and 9, and is blended with Keynesian policy in Chapter 10. This Keynesian approach to macroeconomics suggests that only proper manipulation of the government budget (taxing and spending) can ensure reasonable macroeconomic stability in a market economy.

In Part 4 of this book, we will explore the important role of money from a classical macroeconomic perspective. Then, in Part 5, we will combine Keynesian and classical analytics in a more sophisticated way to provide even better insights into macroeconomic problems and how they might be solved.

Classical Macroeconomics and Keynesian Aggregate Expenditures

Classical and Keynesian theories are at the core of the two major alternative approaches to modern macroeconomics. Classical economics focuses on how automatic adjustments in microeconomic markets ensure macroeconomic stability in the long run, pinpointing increases to Aggregate Supply as the key to resolving the problem of scarcity. Its conclusions tend to support laissez-faire government policies. Keynesian theory, on the other hand, suggests that disruptions to Aggregate Demand may frequently destabilize an economy for prolonged periods, and concludes that stimulative government policies are appropriate cures for excessive unemployment.

This chapter opens with an overview of classical reasoning. Then, in this and the next two chapters, we develop the Keynesian model one step at a time. In Chapter 9, we will explore interactions between Aggregate Expenditures and National Output and scrutinize macroeconomic adjustments toward equilibrium. Chapter 10 explores the role of government in stabilizing a market economy from the alternative perspectives of both Keynesian theory and the new classical macroeconomics. Understanding the anatomy of Aggregate Expenditures is a necessary first step, so this is our focus for much of this chapter.

Classical Theory

Classical economics is a synthesis of theories put forth by numerous individuals from Adam Smith's time (the late 1700s) to the early twentieth century. Central to classical theory is the idea that the economy will automatically adjust to a full employment equilibrium as long as prices, wages, and interest rates are flexible.

> **Classical economics** *concludes that Aggregate Supplies and Demands adjust naturally to offset pressures for long-term unemployment or substantial economic inefficiency.*

Thus, classical macroeconomics shows how the negative effects of the business cycle are automatically overcome by market forces.

Classical reasoning hinges on stabilizing mechanisms that resemble biological processes called *homeostasis*. For example, you begin to sweat if your temperature rises above 98.6°. Your body cools as your perspiration evaporates. Low temperatures cause shivering and your teeth to chatter; friction in your muscle tissues then generates heat, raising your temperature toward 98.6°. Just as homeostasis automatically restores health, classical economics suggests that an economy with flexible prices, wages, and interest rates automatically moves toward full employment and economic health. Behind the classical perception of a self-equilibrating economy is an idea known as Say's Law.

Say's Law

Jean Baptiste Say, a nineteenth-century French economist, believed that the very act of production creates an equivalent amount of demand.

> **Say's Law** asserts that "Supply creates its own demand."

This law pivots on the notion that people work, not for the sake of work itself, but instead, only to obtain income to spend on goods they want. People produce (*supply*) fish sticks or roller skates only so they can buy (*demand*) food, cars, and other goods to make life more enjoyable. Similarly, investors do not seek income per se. Rather, they seek what their income will buy. Thus, the act of producing requires resources to be hired and paid, which in turn leads to resource owners' incomes being spent on other goods.

Say conceded that there might be sporadic gluts of some goods, but reasoned that surpluses in any market must be offset by shortages in another; economy-wide gluts of most goods are impossible. Surpluses and shortages in specific markets are remedied because surpluses drive down both prices and production in the long run, while both rise to cure shortages. For example, a pinto bean surplus depresses bean prices which, in turn, will reduce bean production. Thus, automatic adjustments will quickly eliminate any surpluses in a market system.

The Challenge of Underconsumption

Challengers of Say's Law point out that people seldom spend all they earn, so saving might result in inadequate Aggregate Demand. If consumers do not spend all their income, some production may not be bought; firms' inventories will rise, causing disemployment when firms adjust to deficient demand. The classical rebuttal is that, in a pure market economy, all consumer saving is invested by business.

FIGURE 1 The Classical Capital Market

Classical economists argued that flexible interest rates would equate saving and investment in the capital market. Savers elect to postpone current consumption, and interest is their reward. A higher reward (higher interest) encourages more saving. The rate of return curve, on the other hand, represents the "marginal benefits" to investors as the level of annual investment rises. Business would demand more loans for investment purposes at lower interest rates. Thus, flexible interest rates equate saving and investment at $S_e = I_e$ when the interest rate is i_e.

Early classical reasoning asserted that people save only to facilitate higher future consumption. In a monetary economy, saving is translated into funds available for loans. Stocks and bonds are financial investments representing saving. According to classical reasoning, interest payments encourage consumers to forgo current consumption. Thus, the rate of saving is positively related to the interest rate, as shown in Figure 1.

The other side of the saving/investment market is business demands for loans for new capital. Lower interest rates stimulate more rapid investment in capital goods. This occurs because, after adjusting for risk, firms rank potential investment opportunities by rate of return—from those with the highest expected rates of return to those with the lowest. Individual firms then try to borrow funds to invest in activities for which the expected rate of return exceeds the interest they must pay. Thus, saving is positively related to interest rates, as shown in Figure 1, while investment is negatively related to interest rates.

Flexible Wages, Prices, and Interest Rates

Flexible interest rates tend to equalize the amounts of saving and investment. If interest rates were below i_e in Figure 1, there would be pressure for interest rates to rise as firms sought more financial capital for investment than savers willingly provided. Conversely, if interest rates were above i_e, firms would not be willing to borrow all the funds being offered by savers. Surpluses of saving would force some savers to lower their interest rates to borrowers. Competition would then force all other savers to lower their rates as well. It follows that interest rates respond to changes in the demands and supplies of loanable funds that facilitate investment; this balances aggregate saving with investment. Any deficiency in consumption demand caused by saving is matched in equilibrium by business demands for financial capital to invest.

Classical economists went a step farther, arguing that **flexible wages and prices** would ensure full employment even if interest rate adjustments in capital markets failed to do so. Wages and prices are like readings on an automatic thermostat. If saving exceeds investment, then Aggregate Supply exceeds Aggregate Demand. This deficiency of demand presses prices down when firms accumulate unwanted inventories, resulting in layoffs and causing temporary surpluses in labor markets. If wages and prices fall, the quantities of goods and labor demanded will rise, restoring the economy to full employment. On the other hand, any excess demands would cause the thermostat of price adjustments to generate wage hikes and price increases.

Notice that much of classical economics merely applies supply and demand analysis to macroeconomics. Suppose firms will hire only 80 million people at the $10 hourly wage shown in Figure 2, but 100 million people want jobs at $10 hourly. Will 20 million workers suffer prolonged unemployment? Classical reasoning answers "No" to this question, arguing that when this labor surplus lowers average wages to $8 per hour, all 90 million people willing to work for $8

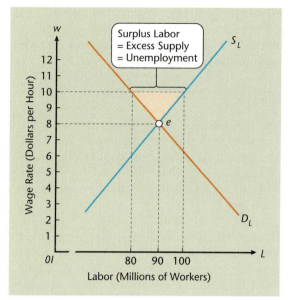

FIGURE 2 Unemployment: The Classical View

Unemployment occurs, according to classical reasoning, primarily because wages are too high. The economy will self-correct for this problem when workers bid wages down to get jobs. This is what has happened at point *e*. The 90 million people who are willing to work have found employment at an hourly wage of $8. This fails to occur only if unions or legal minimum wages prevent wages from falling. Without legal wage floors, most who are employed must be so voluntarily (according to classical reasoning). They could cure their own unemployment by accepting lower pay.

hourly will find jobs. What about the other 10 million? Unwilling to work at an $8 hourly wage, they would drop out of the work force.

Thus, flexible wages and prices are another safety valve in a market system. In the classical view, people without jobs are *voluntarily* unemployed, because they prefer leisure to working at equilibrium wages. Jobs are always available for people willing to work at sufficiently low wages. Thus, classical economists use intuition and logic to conclude that involuntary unemployment is impossible — joblessness is not a social problem; it is an individual choice.[1]

---

1. Recall from Chapter 1 that logical structure alone does not validate a model. A good model must explain real-world behavior. As you will see, the logical structure of the Keynesian model offers the possibility of excessive and prolonged unemployment.

Classical Theory and the Price Level Say's Law, coupled with flexible interest rates, prices, and wages would, according to classical theory, keep workers fully employed. Essentially, classical reasoning views the Aggregate Supply curve as vertical at full employment. Figure 3 illustrates this concept by its initial equilibrium at point *a*, with national output of Q_f and a price level of P_o.

Suppose private spending fell because of increased desires to save (the underconsumption problem mentioned earlier). This would cause Aggregate Demand to fall from AD_0 to AD_1. Excess supplies would result in layoffs, reduced output, and rising inventories (point *b*). According to classical economics, the economy would quickly move to point *c* after interest rates, prices, and wages fell, restoring full employment at a lower price level (P_1). Reversed pressures (Aggregate Demand rises to AD_2) would expand the economy along a path like *ade*, restoring full employment at Q_f with higher price level P_2. There might be short-run deviations from full

employment, but the economy would self-correct rapidly through price-level changes without government intervention, in conformity to the laissez-faire political atmosphere of earlier times.

In summary, classical economics depends on Say's Law and flexible interest rates, prices, and wages to ensure full employment. Classical analysis also teaches that the price level is directly related to Aggregate Demand, which in turn depends strictly on the money supply. Thus, a stable money supply is the key to solving price-level instability. Consequently, some fervent advocates of the laissez-faire policies emerging from classical analysis favor a gold standard. They believe that the supply of gold is inherently stable, so that policies requiring all money to be backed 100 percent by gold would stabilize Aggregate Spending, which would, in turn, preclude significant inflation or deflation.

The Great Depression: Classical Theory at Bay

Until the Great Depression, classical economists steadfastly believed that laissez-faire capitalism automatically gravitates toward full employment. Faith in classical theory began a sharp erosion on October 29, 1929, when the stock market crashed. Dana Thomas recalled that day, known since as "Black Friday," with the following story:

The newspapers recounted the plight of a jury that before the crash had been sworn in for the trial of a former State Banking Superintendent indicted on charges of bribery. Several jurors had heavy commitments in the stock market. They were under strict orders from the judge not to read newspapers or engage in any conversation with outsiders. Nevertheless, news of the debacle in Wall Street had leaked into them and they pleaded with court attendants to let them contact their brokers to find out how they stood. But there was nothing that could be done. One juror, while he sat in a sweat listening to courtroom testimony, lost $80,000.[2]

FIGURE 3 Aggregate Supply and Classical Theory

Unexpected expansions of Aggregate Demand (from AD_0 to AD_2) may cause a temporary boom (movement of the economy along a path like *ade*). Unexpected contractions of Aggregate Demand (from AD_0 to AD_1) might create a temporary recession (movement along a path like *abc*). According to classical reasoning, however, full employment is always quickly restored, and the price level also adjusts very rapidly.

2. Dana L. Thomas, *The Plungers and the Peacocks* (New York: Putnam, 1967), p. 211.

The ranks of the jobless grew from 3 percent to around 25 percent of the labor force between 1929 and 1933. While unemployment mounted, investment spending collapsed even though interest rates dropped to around 1.5 percent. Many people were willing to work for almost nothing; for them, the employment opportunities promised by classical theory seemed a mirage. The September 1932 issue of *Fortune* noted:

Dull mornings last winter the sheriff of Miami, Florida, used to fill a truck with homeless men and run them up to the county line. Where the sheriff of Fort Lauderdale used to meet them and load them into a second truck and run them up to his county line. Where the sheriff of Saint Lucie's would meet them and load them into a third truck and run them up to his county line. Where the sheriff of Brevard County would not meet them. And whence they would trickle back down the roads to Miami. To repeat.

The classical view that the people described in this passage were "voluntarily unemployed" seems callous and unrealistic. They were willing to work for considerably less than prevailing wages, but were unable to find jobs.

The paradox for classical theory presented by the Great Depression set the stage for the development of a theory to explain involuntary unemployment. Classical macroeconomics stressed the stability of a market system and had as its central goals (a) expansion of Aggregate Supply — our productive capacity — and (b) limiting growth of Aggregate Demand to keep inflation muzzled. According to Say's Law, *supply creates its own demand*, so classical theory suggested that severe unemployment would be rare, and certainly could not persist. Thus, most economists were baffled by the momentum and depth of the Great Depression. A reassessment of economic theory seemed in order.

The first major economist to challenge the classical stress on Aggregate Supply was John Maynard Keynes. (See his biography.) *The General Theory of Employment, Interest, and Money* (1936) turned Say's Law upside down. Keynesian theory assumes that "demand creates its own supply."

The Keynesian focus yields a model of *depression* with a punch line that contrasts sharply with the optimistic classical conclusion of full employment "in the long run." Keynesian analysis suggests that substantial unemployment may plague a market economy in a "short-run equilibrium" that may be so persistent that the long run seems almost irrelevant. To some degree, the widespread acceptance of Keynes's model in more prosperous times stems from its appealing policy prescriptions to remedy a depression — lower taxes and increased government spending.

The Keynesian Focus on Aggregate Demand

Keynes's major concern was ensuring that Aggregate Demand is adequate for full employment of all resources. Keynes and his early followers demoted expansion of productive capacity and maintenance of price-level stability to secondary goals, to be pursued only *after* an economy reaches full employment — where, as classical theory suggests, Aggregate Supply is vertical (see Panel A of Figure 4). Keynes argued that although classical theory might apply in a fully employed economy, Aggregate Demand alone determines output and employment in the midst of a depression because Aggregate Supply in this range would be relatively flat.

Keynes's reasons for ignoring the price level and focusing primarily on Aggregate Demand can be seen in Panel B of Figure 4, which shows real GNP and the price level during the Great Depression. Real output began to grow after the Depression bottomed out in 1933. This recovery occurred when Aggregate Demand grew without stimulating major hikes in the price level.

In essence, Keynes assumed that idle productive capacity during depressed times allows production and income to stretch to accommodate growth in Aggregate Demand without spawning much inflationary pressure, as reflected in Panel A of Figure 4. Real output grew by more than 60 percent during the seven years after the Depression reached its trough, while the price level rose less than 12 percent. Keynes's perception that

John Maynard Keynes (1883–1946)

Bernard Baruch once put an end to an economist's badgering with the question, "If you're so smart, why aren't you rich?" John Maynard Keynes would not have been daunted by such a question. A keen observer of economic and human affairs, Keynes amassed a private fortune by speculating in commodities, foreign currencies, and stock market securities. He was equally successful in the social, political, and academic arenas.

Keynes married a world-famous Russian ballerina and was a gay and shining light in the illustrious Bloomsbury group, England's foremost intellectual set. He served as a treasury official and major representative of the British government during important negotiations following both World Wars. Nevertheless, he will be remembered longest as a leading figure in economics. Only the works of Smith and Marx rival Keynesian theories and policies in their impact on economic thought and practice in the twentieth century.

Much of modern macroeconomics is based on Keynes's 1936 treatise, *The General Theory of Employment, Interest, and Money,* his reaction to contradictions between classical economic theory and the worldwide Great Depression. This work challenged the conventional view that *aggregate equilibrium* is synonymous with *full employment.* Keynes reconstructed economic theory to explain persistent and high unemployment throughout market-oriented economies. He concluded that, far from being inconsistent with aggregate equilibrium, unemployment might be a consequence of it.

In brief, Keynes argued that a capitalist economy might experience high unemployment as a semipermanent situation unless some external force were used to reduce it. For practical and political reasons, he thought that this external force must come from government and should take the form of large expenditures on public works projects capable of mobilizing idle labor. Therefore, Keynes turned away from the long tradition of laissez-faire economic thought, which held that any government intervention in the economy is misguided and harmful.

There is generally a long lag between ideas and actions. In the United States in the early 1960s, the Kennedy Administration ushered in our first explicit experiments with Keynesian economic policies. Keynesianism cut across party lines and continued to dominate economic policy until the election of Ronald Reagan. Two decades of activist Keynesian economic policies in this country yielded mixed results. Because the specter of deep depression largely gave way to persistent inflation in the 1960s and 1970s, Keynesian economics has been under fire from many quarters.

Former President Reagan's "supply-side" economic policies represented an attempt to turn back the Keynesian clock in favor of classical economic remedies. Many observers, however, attributed the strong recovery of 1983–1990 to powerful Keynesian policies—tax cuts, expanded government outlays, and huge deficits.

FIGURE 4 The Keynesian Focus on Aggregate Demand

Keynes believed that increased Aggregate Spending would stimulate hikes in employment and output in a depressed economy without raising the specter of inflation. This idea is illustrated in Panel A by a flat Aggregate Supply curve in the region where Aggregate Demand grows from AD_0 to AD_f. Panel B indicates that Keynes's predictions were borne out during the recovery from the trough of the Great Depression. The economy increased its real annual output by roughly $100 billion between 1933 and 1940 without significant increase in the price level. For this and other reasons, Keynes argued that Aggregate Demand alone determined the level of real output in a severely depressed economy.

Source: *Business Conditions Digest*, various issues, 1980–1990.

Aggregate Supply is effectively horizontal in a depression let him build a model focused on Aggregate Expenditures that ignores changes in the price level.

Keynesian Aggregate Expenditures

Certain standard macroeconomic terminology largely follows Keynes's lead.

Aggregate Expenditures (AE) — *also known as Aggregate Spending — is the total value of spending on domestic production annually. An* **Aggregate Expenditure curve** *is the relationship between total spending and national income.*

Spending generally rises when income grows, so there is a positive relationship between Aggregate Expenditures and income.

Components of Aggregate Spending You have learned that both Aggregate Demand and Gross National Product (GNP) consist of spending for consumer goods (C), capital investment by private firms (I), government purchases of goods and services (G), and net exports (X − M). These are also useful categories for examining the structure of Aggregate Expenditures. A glance at Figure 5 shows that consumption absorbs almost two-thirds of GNP, with private investment and government spending comprising most of the rest. Exports are part of Aggregate Expenditures, while imports add to the goods and services available; hence, imports contribute to Aggregate Supply. However, because Keynes viewed imports as replacing sales of domestic production, only the net influence of foreign trade (X − M) is considered in constructing Aggregate Expenditures.

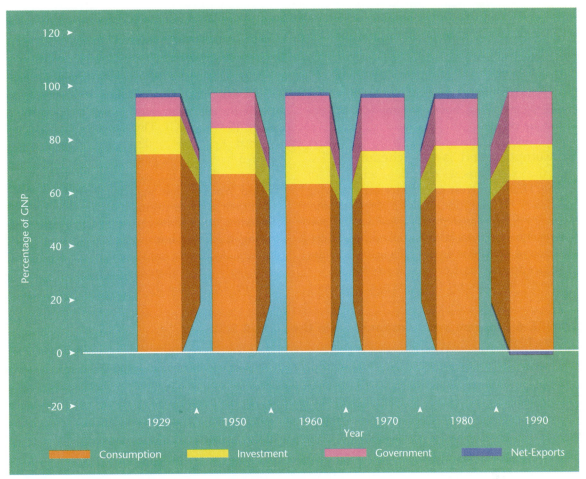

FIGURE 5 Components of Gross National Product

The four major components of GNP, from the vantage point of Aggregate Demand, are consumption, investment, net exports, and government spending. Consumer spending is rather stable at roughly two-thirds of the total. Investment and government spending constitute the bulk of the remainder. Net exports are a relatively minor proportion of the total.

Source: *Economic Report of the President,* 1991.

Consumption and Saving

What determines total consumer spending? You may be able to identify other things that influence your family's spending, but the single most important factor is probably your family's current income. In his *General Theory* (1936), John Maynard Keynes asserted:

The fundamental psychological law, upon which we are entitled to depend with great confidence both a

priori from our knowledge of human nature and from the detailed facts of experience is that men are disposed, as a rule and on the average, to increase their consumption as their income increases, but not by as much as the increase in their income. (p. 96)

This insight, which now seems obvious, drastically changed the thrust of economic reasoning. Classical economists had recognized that consumer spending is affected by income, but their belief that National Income automatically moves to a full employment level caused them to focus on Aggregate Supply and economic growth. Consequently, they were much more interested in how interest rates cause income to be split between consumption and saving than they were in questions about how consumption and income are related.

Consumption and Saving Schedules   Classical theory emphasizes interest as a reward for saving. Higher interest rates foster higher saving and lower consumption out of a given income. Keynes's *fundamental psychological law of consumption* barely hints at the totally different orientation of Keynesian analysis. Figure 6 provides evidence to support Keynes's observation.

The 45° line in Figure 6 reflects points mapped if consumption exactly equaled disposable income. (Any variable plotted against an equal variable is a 45° line.) If consumption points for all years were located on this reference line, then consumption would always equal disposable income. How can after-tax (disposable) income be used? By definition, anything not consumed is saved ($S = Y_d - C$). Thus, the 45° line may be labeled $Y_d = C + S$; disposable income is absorbed by what you consume and save.

Notice that saving was relatively high during World War II, while many families spent more than their incomes during the Great Depression. Spending more than your income is called **dissaving**; it requires borrowing or dipping into past savings. Aggregate consumption and saving absorb fairly stable shares of aggregate disposable income. Until recently, saving averaged roughly

FIGURE 6   Income and Consumption in the United States, 1929–1990

Keynes stressed the relationship between income and saving or consumption. The 45° line represents income plotted against itself. Since disposable income is either consumed or saved, the 45° line is labeled $Y_d = C + S$. The darkened area represents saving (or dissaving), and is measured as the distance between the year point and the 45° line. During the Great Depression, saving was negative (dissaving), while during World War II, saving was over 20 percent of disposable income.

Source: *Economic Reports of the President, 1980–1991.*

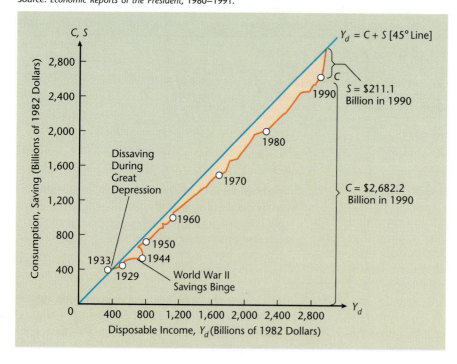

7 percent of disposable income except during World War II and the Great Depression. Even though saving slipped a bit in the past decade, consumption has consistently been the most stable component of Aggregate Expenditures.

Saving is not necessarily the amount of money put in a financial institution during some income period. Saving reflects unconsumed income, or changes in your wealth.

Saving *is the change in total wealth over some period of time.*

Your wealth is the **stock of savings** accumulated out of past saving periods. (Thus, saving is a flow variable.) But what if there is a loss of wealth?

Dissaving *occurs when people spend more on consumption than their annual income. It is financed by borrowing, or by spending out of past savings.*

Consumption occurs when goods are used up to satisfy our wants. Consumption falls into five main categories: food, housing, clothing, transportation, and medical expenses. Low-income families often dissave by spending more than their income on bare necessities. As gross incomes rise, growing shares of income are allocated to taxes, transportation and housing services, and various luxuries. Figure 6 indicates how consumption is related to aggregate disposable income.

Autonomous and Induced Consumption and Saving

Keynes asserted that as income grows, so does planned consumption — but by less than income. People must consume something to live, however, even if they have zero income. This part of consumption is independent of income.

Autonomous consumption (C_a) *is consumer spending that is unrelated to income.*

People tend to spend more on consumer goods if they receive more income.

Consumption that occurs because people have income to spend is **induced consumption.**

Thus, consumption includes both autonomous and induced elements. The bulk of consumption in a prosperous economy is induced; autonomous consumption accounts for most of consumption behavior only at very low levels of disposable income.

Consider Table 1. At zero income, autonomous consumption requires dissaving equal to spending, which is $2,000 in this example. Thus, autonomous saving equals minus $2,000. Where planned consumption exceeds low levels of disposable income, there is planned dissaving. In Table 1, dissaving occurs at all income levels below $10,000. Saving is zero at the *break-even point*, which occurs when both income and

Table 1 *Representative Annual Consumption and Saving Schedules*

(1) Annual Disposable Income	(2) Annual Planned Consumption	(3) Annual Planned Saving (1) − (2)	(4) Average Propensity to Consume (2)/(1)	(5) Average Propensity to Save (3)/(1)	(6) Marginal Propensity to Consume (Δ2)/(Δ1)	(7) Marginal Propensity to Save (Δ3)/(Δ1)
0	$ 2,000	$−2,000	—	—	—	—
$ 2,500	4,000	−1,500	1.60	−.60	.80	.20
5,000	6,000	−1,000	1.20	−.20	.80	.20
7,500	8,000	−500	1.07	−.07	.80	.20
10,000	10,000	0	1.00	0	.80	.20
12,500	12,000	500	.96	.04	.80	.20
15,000	14,000	1,000	.93	.07	.80	.20

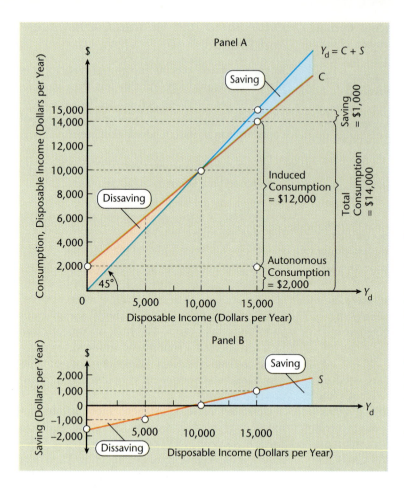

Panel A

$Y_d = C + S$

Saving

C

Saving = $1,000

Total Consumption = $14,000

Induced Consumption = $12,000

Dissaving

Autonomous Consumption = $2,000

45°

Consumption, Disposable Income (Dollars per Year)

Disposable Income (Dollars per Year)

Panel B

Saving

S

Dissaving

Saving (Dollars per Year)

Disposable Income (Dollars per Year)

FIGURE 7 Consumption and Saving Schedules

This figure depicts the consumption (C) and saving (S) schedules from Table 1. Consumption (column 2) is plotted against disposable income (column 1) in Panel A. Again, the 45° line represents $Y_d = C + S$. When disposable income is $10,000, saving is zero; saving is plotted on the horizontal axis in Panel B. Dissaving occurs at income levels below $10,000, as reflected by the red shading in both panels. (The vertical distance in red above a given income level equals dissaving for that income.) Above $10,000, saving is represented by the blue shading in both figures. (Saving equals the vertical distance in blue at each income exceeding $10,000 annually.)

planned consumption equal $10,000 in this example. Plans for saving are positive for income that exceeds $10,000.

Data from Table 1 are used to construct Figure 7. Autonomous consumption causes the intercept in Panel A to equal $2,000; induced consumption equals the vertical rise in consumption as income grows. The vertical distance between the 45° reference line (in blue) and the consumption line (red) is saving or dissaving. Panel B plots the amount of planned saving associated with the levels of planned consumption from Panel A. For example, when disposable income is $12,500, saving is $500.

Average Propensities to Consume and Save

Keynes asserted that consumption grows as income grows but by less than income rises. We

will now examine what happens to spending as income rises, both on average and at the margin. Remember that disposable income can be either consumed or saved. We need to develop these relationships further by examining the average and marginal propensities to consume and save.

The **average propensity to consume (*apc*) is** *the fraction of disposable income consumed.*

Arithmetically,

$$apc = \frac{\text{consumption}}{\text{disposable income}} = \frac{C}{Y_d}$$

Thus, your *apc* = 0.8 if you spend 80 percent of your income. In Table 1, the average propensity to consume is (*a*) more than 1 at income below $10,000, (*b*) exactly 1 at a $10,000 income, and (*c*) below 1 when income exceeds $10,000.

The **average propensity to save (*aps*)** *is the fraction of disposable income that is saved.*

Like the *apc*, it varies with the level of income. Because the *apc* falls as income grows,

$$aps = \frac{saving}{disposable\ income} = \frac{S}{Y_d}$$

the *aps* becomes larger as income grows.

The sum of the *apc* and the *aps* is one.[3] Thus, if you spend 80 percent of your income (*apc* = 0.8), then you save 20 percent (*aps* = 0.2). The national *apc* has varied only slightly over time, averaging approximately 93 percent. The *aps* has historically averaged roughly 6 to 7 percent of disposable income.

Marginal Propensities to Consume and Save

Average propensities to consume and save indicate the shares of total income spent and saved, but not how an *additional* dollar of disposable income will be divided between consumption and saving. It is easier for policymakers to affect disposable income a little (through, e.g., taxes) than to directly control total income. What you will do with a bit more or less income is crucial.

The **marginal propensity to consume (*mpc*)** *is the relative change in consumption induced by a small change in disposable income.*

Throughout this book, we will use Δ (the Greek letter delta) to represent a change in a variable. Arithmetically, the *mpc* is

$$mpc = \frac{change\ in\ planned\ consumption}{change\ in\ disposable\ income} = \frac{\Delta C}{\Delta Y_d}$$

The marginal propensity to consume in the example in Table 1 is 0.8. For every dollar increase (decrease) in disposable income, consumption

increases (decreases) by 80 cents ($0.80). For example, when disposable income rises from $7,500 to $10,000 (by $2,500), planned consumption rises from $8,000 to $10,000 (by $2,000). Thus, the marginal propensity to consume is: $2,000/$2,500 = 0.8.

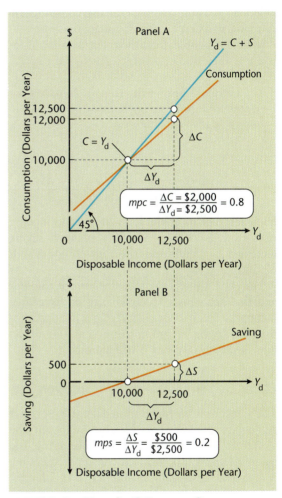

FIGURE 8   Marginal Propensity to Consume (*mpc*) and Marginal Propensity to Save (*mps*)

This figure depicts the marginal propensity to consume (*mpc*) and the marginal propensity to save (*mps*) and is based on the data in Table 1. The *mpc* is defined as the change in planned consumption associated with change in disposable income, and it equals the slope of the consumption schedule. If, for example, disposable income increases from $10,000 to $12,500, planned consumption rises from $10,000 to $12,000. Thus, the *mpc* equals $2,000/$2,500, or 0.8. Similarly, in Panel B, when disposable income increases from $10,000 to $12,500, planned saving increases by $500, and the *mps* equals 0.2 ($500/$2,500).

---

3. Since $C + S = Y_d$, we can divide both sides of this equation by Y_d and find that

    $$\frac{C}{Y_d} + \frac{S}{Y_d} = \frac{Y_d}{Y_d} = 1$$

    so the *apc* + *aps* = 1.

A geometric treatment of the *mpc* is shown in Panel A of Figure 8. Recall that slope is computed as *rise over run*. The change in planned consumption is measured by the vertical increase (*rise*) on the graph of consumption and is labeled ΔC. The change in disposable income is measured along the horizontal axis (*run*) and is labeled ΔY_d. Thus, the slope of the consumption function is $\Delta C/\Delta Y_d$, which equals the *mpc*.

What do people do with an extra dollar of income if they don't spend it? They save it.

The **marginal propensity to save (*mps*)** *is the relative change in saving induced by a small change in disposable income.*

Arithmetically,

$$mps = \frac{\text{change in planned saving}}{\text{change in disposable income}} = \frac{\Delta S}{\Delta Y_d}$$

For example, in Table 1, as disposable income rises from \$7,500 to \$10,000, planned saving increases by \$500 and the *mps* equals \$500/\$2,500, or 0.2.

You may already see that the sum of the *mpc* and the *mps* equals 1; any change in disposable income is divided between changes in consumption and saving.[4] A graphic representation of the *mps* is shown in Panel B of Figure 8.

Other Determinants of Consumption

The consumption function in Figure 8 portrays Aggregate Expenditures by consumers. In the simple Keynesian model we are developing, the sole determinant of induced consumer spending is aggregate disposable income (Y_d). In Chapter 5, we discussed five other categories of variables that largely determine autonomous consumption. These include (*a*) wealth and expectations

---

4. From $C + S = Y_d$, it follows that any change in disposable income (ΔY_d) must result in changes in consumption (ΔC) or changes in saving (ΔS). Thus, $\Delta C + \Delta S = \Delta Y_d$. Dividing both sides of this equation by ΔY_d yields

$$\frac{\Delta C}{\Delta Y_d} + \frac{\Delta S}{\Delta Y_d} = \frac{\Delta Y_d}{\Delta Y_d} = 1$$

so $mpc + mps = 1$.

about future income, (*b*) customary standards of living, (*c*) household sizes and age structures, (*d*) household balance sheets and stocks of consumer goods on hand, and (*e*) consumer expectations about the prices and availability of products. When any of these five influences change, autonomous consumption changes, which shifts the entire consumption/income relationship up or down. These shift variables tend to change fairly slowly, however, so the relationship between consumption and disposable income has been fairly stable historically.

Consumption spending accounts for about two-thirds of Aggregate Expenditures. Three other components must be added to consumption to reach Aggregate Expenditures: investment, government spending, and net exports. We turn now to a discussion of investment and its determinants. Then we briefly consider government spending and look at the foreign component of Aggregate Expenditures.

Investment

While consumption is the most stable component of GNP and Aggregate Expenditures, investment is relatively the least stable. According to Keynesian theory, the volatility of investment may be the root cause of most business cycles.

Types of Investment

Economic investment entails buying new physical capital (buildings, machinery, tools, equipment, inventories, and the like) that can be used in the future to produce and sell other goods and services. Some financial investments facilitate economic investment (for instance, purchases of newly issued stocks or bonds, which are just specialized instruments for saving), others do not (e.g., speculative purchases of land).

In Chapter 7, you learned that Gross Private Domestic Investment (GPDI) is an important component of GNP, and that economic investment can be classified into three basic groups: (*a*) new construction, which includes such things as office buildings, manufacturing plants, warehouses, hotels, retail stores, and private homes;

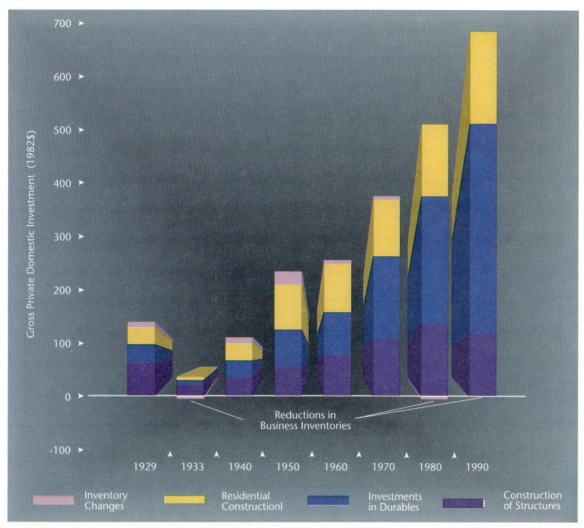

FIGURE 9   The Composition of Gross Private Domestic Investment

This figure details the composition of investment spending, the least stable component of GNP.

Source: *Economic Report of the President*, 1991.

(*b*) new machinery and equipment, including tools and office equipment and furnishings; and (*c*) inventory accumulation. The composition of investment is illustrated in Figure 9.

Planned business investment is often unstable because investors tend to develop similar expectations about future business conditions. Even conscious planning yields cyclical investment patterns for construction — residential and office buildings, manufacturing facilities, and such.

Planned investment in new machinery and equipment is also very sensitive to expected ups and downs in economic activity.

Investment or disinvestment in inventories is even more volatile because much of it is unplanned. Firms maintain inventories because they cannot accurately predict sales on a week-to-week, or even a year-to-year basis. A firm's merchandise could arrive almost simultaneously with customers if it could forecast sales precisely,

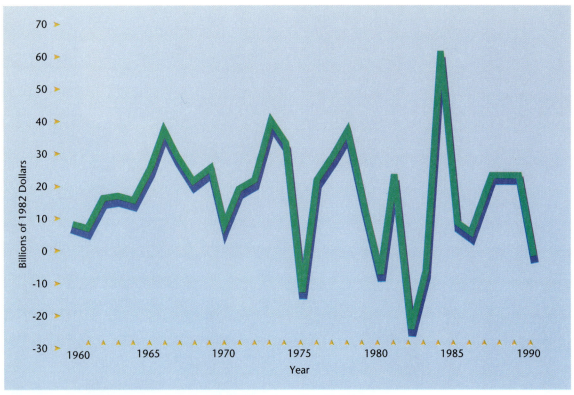

FIGURE 10   Changes in Business Inventories (1982 Dollars)

Inventory changes are by far the most volatile component of investment, which, in turn, is the most erratic part of GNP. Inventories decline sharply when business sales unexpectedly boom or when business firms become very pessimistic in forecasting future sales. Inventories mushroom when business firms anticipate sharp increases in sales or when customers unexpectedly quit buying.

Source: *Economic Report of the President*, 1991.

and inventory requirements would be minuscule. All firms try to time inventories by their sales forecasts, but customers often fail to buy according to these (sometimes intuitive) plans.

Failures of sales to go "according to plan" make inventory accumulation especially volatile, as shown in Figure 10. Firms unintentionally invest in new inventories if sales fall below business forecasts, but inventories shrink and there is unplanned disinvestment if sales are unexpectedly high. Inventories that unexpectedly dwindle signal firms to hire more resources and boost orders to suppliers, while unexpected inventory growth is a signal to lay off workers and slash orders. In the next chapter, you will see how these inventory adjustments set forces in motion to balance aggregate spending and output.

Expected Returns from Investment

We asserted in Chapter 5 that investments will be made if they are expected to generate rates of return exceeding the market rate of interest. Rates of return are compounded annually, much like interest rates paid on checking accounts.[5] We will discuss factors that influence expected returns from investment before delving into some of the intricacies of the costs of investment.

---

5. We defined the rate of return as the annual percentage of earnings from an investment after all opportunity costs. Expressed more analytically, the rate of return is the annual percentage by which assets will grow if the profits from an investment are continually reinvested.

Expectations about the Business Environment New capital goods are expected to generate extra output that, when sold, will yield extra revenue for the firm. Confidence that there will be demand for more output is necessary before firms will make new investments. When consumer spending is expected to grow and existing capital is already pressed to capacity, the stream of new investment will rise. Conversely, if consumer demands are expected to be weak, or if there is substantial excess capacity in existing production facilities, businesses will not invest very much.

A major problem for business investors is the long lag that is common between placing orders for new investment goods and actually achieving the greater capacity made possible by these investments. Time is required to acquire the appropriate building or to produce new equipment and to comply with laws and regulations that control new facilities. Another lag arises between production from the new capital and final sales of the output. These lags make it necessary to forecast consumer demand far into the future. The risks involved in long-range projections make firms leery of many investments.

Difficulties in predicting swings in a firm's sales are only one source of risk for investors. Expected changes in government policies may either encourage or squelch investment. For example, Atlantic City experienced a flurry of investment to prepare casinos and "tourist traps" when the New Jersey government was expected to legalize gambling. On the other hand, if policies restricting foreign trade were anticipated, firms that relied heavily on exports or imports might postpone investment plans indefinitely.

Changes in business expectations that affect investment may be contagious. If most other investors become bearish (pessimistic), might it be wise for you to reconsider your riskier ventures? If they become bullish (optimistic), might you be more willing to take a plunge? Investment may be volatile because expectations about business conditions tend to move in concert, but there are other explanations.

Technological Innovations Many firms and government agencies are extensively involved in research and development (R&D). Methods are developed to produce new or better goods, or to find less costly production methods for existing products. Investment to implement technological breakthroughs tends to be clustered over time, because new technologies often arrive erratically and in waves. Consequently, some economists attribute much of investment volatility to the bunching of new technologies. For example, the space program refined the computer, gave birth to solid-state electronics, and generated a host of other technological innovations.

Stocks of Capital Relative to Total Production Just as consumption is affected by the consumer durables households already own relative to their incomes, the stock of physical capital relative to GNP influences investment. Strong incentives for new capital investment emerge when near-peak levels of economic activity press against capital capacity. On the other hand, purchases of new capital will decline when economic activity drops and substantial amounts of capital become idle.

The Equilibrium Rate of Investment

Firms will buy machinery, construct buildings, or try to build inventories whenever they expect the gross returns on these investments to exceed their total opportunity costs. Let us see how expectations and costs interact to determine the level of investment.

Diminishing Returns to Investment Suppose most economic forecasts reflect substantial business optimism. Many potential investors probably know of a few investments that could be expected to generate healthy rates of return (r) of, say, 30 to 40 percent—a new hamburger franchise, an apartment complex, or a plant to manufacture solar cells might be examples. Once these investments were made, only less profitable investments would be available—a fried chicken outlet, a duplex, or a new laundromat might be expected to yield annual rates of return of 20 to 30 percent. After these investments were made, still less profitable investments would be the only options available—a

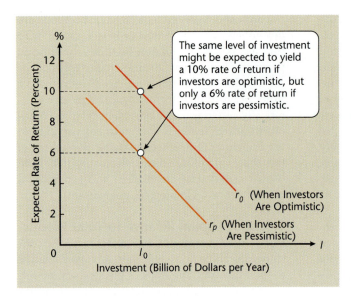

The same level of investment might be expected to yield a 10% rate of return if investors are optimistic, but only a 6% rate of return if investors are pessimistic.

r_o (When Investors Are Optimistic)

r_p (When Investors Are Pessimistic)

Investment (Billion of Dollars per Year)

FIGURE 11 The Negative Relationship Between Expected Rates of Return and the Level of Investment

For any given level of business optimism, a negative relationship exists between the quantity of investment and the rate of return. The most profitable investments will be made first, and, as more projects are undertaken, those with lower profit opportunities (lower rates of return) will be included. Furthermore, as the level of optimism or pessimism changes, the entire curve (relationship) will shift—e.g., from r_o, the expected rate of return curve when investors are optimistic, to r_p, the rate of return curve when they are pessimistic.

hot dog franchise, renovation of a seedy motel, or a used-book store might be anticipated to return 10 to 20 percent on investment.

We are now at rock bottom—a shovel-sharpening shop or greasy spoon franchise might generate near zero rates of return, plus or minus 10 percent. The point is, for a given mood among investors, the higher the level of investment in the economy, the lower the expected rate of return on additional investment. Changes in business expectations shift the investment demand schedule. Expected rate of return schedules when investors are optimistic and when they are pessimistic are shown in Figure 11.

Costs of Investment Investment decisions depend, in part, on costs for new capital. Rate of return schedules like those in Figure 11 rise (shift to the right) when the prices of equipment and other capital fall, and shrink (move leftward) when these costs rise. Spurred by prosperity, increases in the demand for new capital boost capital prices, dampening surges in investment. Conversely, economic downturns reduce the demand for new capital, and capital suppliers may accumulate inventories they view as excessive. Equipment prices fall as capital suppliers liquidate these inventories, slightly dampening drops in investment.

Taxes on investment income are another cost consideration. For example, higher corporate income taxes cause the (after-tax) rate of return curve to fall. Investment tax credits, on the other hand, may boost demand for investment goods.

Interest is among the most important costs from investors' perspectives. When interest rates rise, investors' opportunity costs rise. If investors have money, they might make loans instead of buying investment goods. If most investors borrow to invest, then a hike in the interest rate makes investment less attractive. Interest rates (i) and rates of return (r) are both expressed as annual percentages, making it possible to put both on the vertical axis of Figure 12. Changes in interest rates involve movements *along* rate of return curves, while other types of changes shift these curves.

Ignoring transaction costs and risk for simplicity's sake, investment will occur as long as the expected rate of return is at least as great as the interest rate. Here is an example to show why. If you can borrow money at 11 percent interest and expect an 11.5 percent rate of return from some investment, you probably will make the investment. If not, then someone else will go after this profit. It is just like trading 11 cents for 11.5 cents. How many times will you go for a deal like this? Infinitely repeating this process

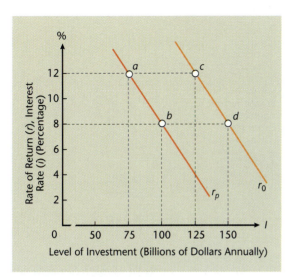

FIGURE 12   How Changes in Interest Rates and Expected Rates of Return Cause Changes in Investment

One important cost of investment is interest rates. If investors do not have money, they must borrow, and the level of interest, combined with the expected rate of return schedule, will determine the level of investment. Investors with adequate personal funds could simply make loans if their investment options were expected to yield rates of return that were exceeded by the interest rate. Thus, the interest rate represents the opportunity costs of investing a given amount of capital. If the expected rate of return curve is r_p and investment rates fall from 12 percent to 8 percent, investment rises from $75 billion to $100 billion. Similarly, if interest rates are stable at 8 percent and the expected return schedule shifts from r_p to r_o (reflecting increased investor optimism), investment rises from $100 billion to $150 billion.

would make you infinitely rich. Thus, any investment expected to yield a rate of return exceeding the interest rate will be profitable and will be undertaken. Those yielding returns lower than interest rates will not be profitable and will not be made. This is why investment will be $100 billion in Figure 12 if the interest rate is 8 percent and the expected rate of return is reflected in curve r_p.

In summary, the expected rate of return schedule rises (shifts right) when GNP grows and investors become optimistic, or when capital prices decline. Investor pessimism or higher capital prices shrink expected rates of return and

investment. For a given expected rate of return, higher interest rates discourage investment (this is a movement along a rate of return curve), but falling interest rates foster investment and economic growth. Interest rate changes induce movements along a rate of return curve.

Imperfect forecasts of future sales lead to unexpected changes in inventories. When these are coupled with the effects of herdlike changes in investors' expectations and wide swings in interest rates, no wonder investment is the most volatile component of GNP. The example in Figure 12 suggests that annual investment would grow from $75 billion (point a) to $100 billion (point b) if the interest rate fell from 12 to 8 percent when investors were initially pessimistic (movement along the r_p curve).

A similar decline in interest rates would boost investment from $125 billion to $150 billion annually if investors are more optimistic (along the r_0 curve from point c to point d). For every interest rate, shifts from optimistic to pessimistic outlooks (shifts in the curves), or vice versa, alter annual investment by $50 billion. Thus, in this example, swings in investors' moods and interest rates may mean that investment is doubled or halved. The real-world volatility of investment is probably attributable to changes both in expectations and in interest rates.

Investment and Aggregate Expenditures

We know that investment is affected by the level of National Income because the state of the economy significantly shapes investors' expectations. Business profits are bolstered by economic growth, which gives corporations greater opportunities to retain earnings for investment purposes. We will treat investment as autonomous, however, because we want the Keynesian model we are building here to be as simple as possible.

Autonomous investment *is independent of income in the simple Keynesian model.*

Figure 13 shows the level of autonomous investment (I_a) to be determined by expected rates

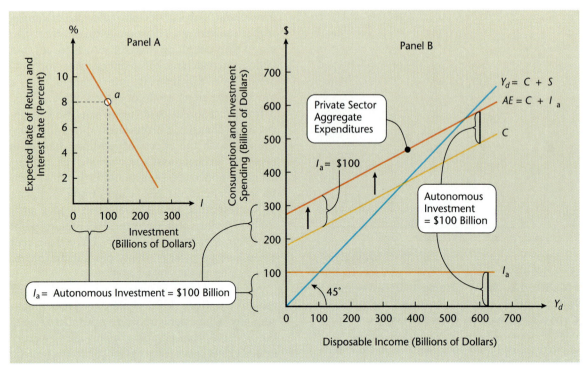

FIGURE 13   Aggregate Expenditures for the Private Sector (Households + Business)

In Panel A, the level of investment is determined by the intersection of the rate of return (r) curve and the level of interest rates (i). If the interest rate is 8 percent, autonomous investment (I_a) will be $100 billion (point a, Panel A). Adding this level of investment to the consumption line (C) in Panel B results in the Aggregate Expenditure curve labeled $AE = C + I_a$. Notice that the Aggregate Expenditure curve is equal to consumption plus investment ($AE = C + I_a$) when the economy consists only of households and businesses. Finally, note that the 45° reference line is equal to $Y_d = C + S$.

of return and the market rate of interest. It also shows how this externally determined level of investment affects Aggregate Expenditures. This investment is considered "external" because it is independent of income. In Panel A, an interest rate of 8 percent yields autonomous investment of $100 billion. In Panel B, the $100 billion of autonomous investment is added *vertically* to the consumption curve to obtain the private sector Aggregate Expenditures curve ($AE = C + I_a$).

Optimism joined with low interest rates creates high levels of autonomous investment. Pessimism or high interest rates cause autonomous investment to be very low. In fact, Keynesians believe that pessimism may so overwhelm even very low interest rates that investment will be trivial.

Government Purchases

Government purchases include highways, flood control projects, education, police and fire protection, school lunch programs, and Medicare payments. Cash transfer payments are only translated into Aggregate Expenditures when the recipients spend these funds on consumer goods, so these outlays are not included in government purchases. To help keep our analysis of Aggregate Expenditures simple, we will assume (artificially) that government purchases are independent of income.

Autonomous government purchases (G_a) *involve purchases of goods and resources, and are assumed independent of income.*

Although government purchases appear loosely related to National Income, they are affected even more by the state of international relations (e.g., military buildups or disarmament agreements). Moreover, most government outlays have considerable momentum regardless of the state of the economy. Expenditures for public health, highways, and education, for example, seem impervious to swings in the economy.

The Foreign Sector

Exports (X) reflect foreign demands that increase Aggregate Expenditures for American outputs. Imports (M) are goods produced by foreigners but available for use by American consumers, investors, or government. In fact, the accounting categories of consumption, investment, and government spending include goods produced abroad. Although imports add to the Aggregate Supply available to Americans, Keynesian analysis treats them as reducing Aggregate Expenditures on domestically produced goods, because imports presumably replace some purchases of domestic output. Consequently, the Keynesian convention is to look only at the net effect of the foreign sector on Aggregate Expenditures, so that $AE = C + I + G + (X - M)$.

Imports are clearly influenced by National Income. When times are prosperous domestically, we import more Volkswagens and Minolta cameras, and booming industrial production and vacations require more foreign oil. On the other hand, our exports depend primarily on economic conditions abroad, which may be in the doldrums even if the American economy is prosperous. International economic interdependence is, however, accurately characterized by a cliché that "When America sneezes, the rest of the world catches a cold." The net effect of international trade on Aggregate Expenditures, however, is relatively small. Exports and imports each *average* around 10 percent of GNP, so net exports $(X - M)$ are usually within plus or minus 2 percent of GNP.

Sophisticated Keynesian models explicitly consider interdependencies between nations. For the purposes of the Keynesian model of Aggregate Expenditures we are building here, however, we will treat net exports as independent of income.

Net exports $(X_a - M_a)$ *are treated as* **autonomous** *in the simple Keynesian model.*

Note that the classical emphasis on Aggregate Supply probably treats the importance of trade more realistically than does the simple Keynesian model, especially during reasonably prosperous times. International trade enhances the value of domestic output through specialization according to comparative advantage. In addition, trade (*a*) stimulates technological competition (e.g., the race with the Japanese to produce faster and more powerful computer chips), (*b*) improves competition in many industries (e.g., cars and textiles), (*c*) provides certain goods that otherwise might not be available (e.g., coffee and chrome), and (*d*) reduces production costs (e.g., Mexican *maquilladero* plants assemble Japanese TVs at low cost for distribution in the United States). Nevertheless, net exports are treated as independent of income in our simple Keynesian model.

Aggregate Expenditures

Consumers account for the bulk of Aggregate Expenditures for domestic output ($C = C_a + mpc \cdot Y$), but some output is bought by investors (I_a), some is purchased by government (G_a), and the rest is exported to foreigners ($X_a - M_a$). In the Keynesian model used in the next two chapters, we assume that income is the major influence on consumption, while private investment, net exports, and government spending are not affected by income.

Aggregate Expenditures (AE) are the sum of all these types of spending.

$$AE = C + I + G + (X - M)$$

Rearranging terms to reflect differences between the autonomous spending and the induced

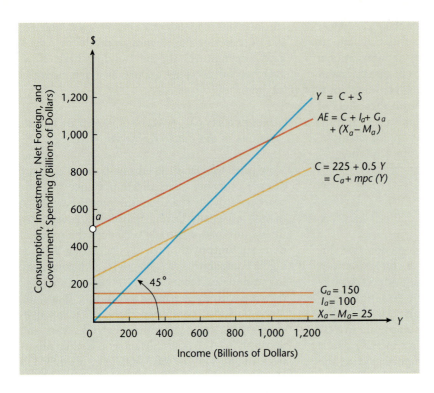

FIGURE 14 Aggregate Expenditures for the Entire Economy (Private + Public + Foreign Sectors)

The Aggregate Expenditure curve (*AE*) is the vertical summation of consumption (*C*), investment (*I*), government (*G*), and net foreign spending (*X* − *M*). Point *a* reflects the sum of autonomous spending [$A = C_a + I_a + G_a + (X_a - M_a)$], which is 500 in this example. Spending in excess of 500 (measured vertically) reflects induced consumption (*mpc* · *Y*), which equals 0.5*Y* in this figure. Thus, this $AE = A + 0.5 \cdot Y$.

spending (*mpc* · *Y*) components of *AE* yields[6]

$$AE = C_a + mpc \cdot Y + I_a + G_a + (X_a - M_a)$$

Suppose we assume that (*a*) autonomous investment (I_a) is $100 billion, (*b*) autonomous net exports ($X_a - M_a$) equal $25 billion, (*c*) autonomous government purchases (G_a) equal $150 billion, (*d*) autonomous consumption (C_a) is

$225 billion, and (*e*) the marginal propensity to consume (*mpc*) is 0.5. Figure 14 depicts the resulting relationship between National Income (*Y*) and Aggregate Expenditures. The autonomous components (*A*) of Aggregate Expenditures sum to $500 billion, which corresponds to point *a* in Figure 14. [$A = C_a + I_a + G_a + (X_a - M_a) = 500 billion.] We must also consider induced consumption, which equals the *mpc* times income, or 0.5 *Y*. Thus, total Aggregate Expenditures rises by one-half of any increase in income as income rises, and vice versa.

Note that (*a*) these categories of spending are all summed *vertically* to arrive at Aggregate Expenditures and (*b*) this Keynesian depression model assumes a fixed price level. In the next chapter, we will explore how equilibrium levels of Net National Product and National Income are determined by Aggregate Expenditures.

---

6. You soon will see that autonomous spending has the same effect on national income regardless of its source, so all types of autonomous spending (*A*) can be summed to simplify our analysis ($A = C_a + I_a + G_a + X_a - M_a$). The only type of spending affected by income is induced consumption (*mpc* · Y_d). Thus, in the simplest linear Keynesian models, Aggregate Expenditures equal autonomous spending (*A*) **plus** consumption that is induced (*mpc* · *Y*) by disposable income: $AE = A + mpc \cdot Y_d$.

Chapter Review: Key Points

1. *Classical theory* is a conglomeration of the thoughts of many economic thinkers dating back to Adam Smith.

2. Classical economists based their theory on *Say's Law: Supply creates its own demand.* Coupled with assumptions that wages, prices, and interest rates are all perfectly flexible, Say's Law quickly drives a market economy toward full employment. All unemployment is considered voluntary — simply a refusal to work at the equilibrium wage. The protracted unemployment of the early 1930s diluted acceptance of classical theory and led to the development of the radically different *Keynesian theory*.

3. Keynesian analysis focuses on Aggregate Demand. During the Great Depression, much of the economy's productive capacity was idle. During a slow recovery from 1933 to 1940, real output expanded by more than 60 percent with only slight increases in the price level. Keynesian economics assumes that Aggregate Supply is flat in a depressed economy so that the price level can be ignored; it is primarily concerned with maintaining Aggregate Demand consistent with full employment.

4. *Aggregate Expenditures* (AE) encompass total spending on domestic output during a year. Aggregate Expenditures has four components: (a) personal consumption expenditures, (b) Gross Private Domestic Investment, (c) government purchases of goods and services, and (d) net exports of goods and services. $AE = C + I + G + (X - M)$.

5. The single most important determinant of consumer spending is disposable income through its influence on *induced consumption*. Consumer spending is related directly to disposable income and is a stable component of Aggregate Expenditures. Other important determinants of consumption and saving include (a) wealth and expectations of future income, (b) customary living standards, (c) the sizes and age composition of typical households, (d) consumer goods on hand and household balance sheets, and (e) consumer expectations about prices and product availability. These determine the level of *autonomous consumption* (C_a).

6. The *average propensity to consume* (**apc**) is the share of total disposable income that is consumed (C/Y_d). The *average propensity to save* (**aps**) is the fraction of total disposable income saved (S/Y_d). Disposable income is either consumed or saved, so $apc + aps = 1$. Until recently, the average propensities to consume and to save were relatively constant over time — at roughly 93 percent and 7 percent, respectively. The *aps* has averaged only 4 to 5 percent over the past decade.

7. The *marginal propensity to consume* (**mpc**) is the change in planned consumption arising from a given small change in disposable income; it tells us how much of an additional dollar of income will be consumed. Similarly, the *marginal propensity to save* (**mps**) is how much of an additional dollar in income will be saved, so $mpc + mps = 1$.

8. Capital investment refers to purchases of new output that can be used in the future to produce other goods and services. The three major components of investment are (a) new business and residential structures, (b) machinery and equipment, and (c) inventory accumulation.

9. Investment is the least stable component of Aggregate Expenditures, fluctuating widely over the course of a business cycle. The most volatile component of investment is inventory accumulation.

10. The primary factors determining the quantity of investment are (a) expected returns from investment, (b) market interest rates, (c) expectations about the business environment, (d) rates of technological change and innovation, (e) the level of existing stocks of business capital relative to total production, and (f) the costs of capital goods. All else equal, changes in items (c) through (f) shift rate of return curves, while changes in interest rates cause movements along an expected rate of return curve. In simple Keynesian models, investment is treated as *autonomous* (I_a).

11. While government spending is probably influenced by changes in income, it is even more strongly affected by the state of inter-

national relations and domestic politics. Thus government spending as a component of Aggregate Expenditures is also treated as autonomous.

12. Exports and imports are reasonably balanced, so net exports $(X - M)$ make a comparatively small contribution to Aggregate Expenditures. Simple Keynesian models treat net exports as autonomous.

Key Concepts

Ensure that you can define these terms before proceeding.

classical economics
Say's Law
flexibility of wages, prices, and interest rates
Aggregate Expenditures $AE = C + I + G + (X - M)$
fundamental psychological law of consumption
dissaving
autonomous consumption (C_a)
induced consumption
average propensity to consume (apc)
average propensity to save (aps)
marginal propensity to consume (mpc)
marginal propensity to save (mps)
autonomous investment (I_a)
autonomous government purchases (G_a)
autonomous net exports $(X_a - M_a)$

Problems and Questions

1. Is it possible for the average propensity to consume to be 110 percent when the marginal propensity to save is 20 percent? If your answer is "No," explain why not. If your answer is "Yes," what are the corresponding values for the average propensity to save and for the marginal propensity to consume?

2. Are the classical writers correct in asserting that all unemployment is voluntary? Can you conceive of circumstances under which people willing to work for the wages paid other people with similar skills and experience would be involuntarily unemployed?

3. Complete this table.

Disposable Income	Planned Consumption
0	500
500	800
1,000	1,100
1,500	1,400
2,000	1,700
2,500	2,000

Planned Saving	aps	mpc	mps
___	___	___	___
___	___	___	___
___	___	___	___
___	___	___	___
___	___	___	___
___	___	___	___

4. Suppose that in the economy depicted in Figure 15, autonomous consumption = 2(autonomous investment) = (autonomous government purchases)/2, while exports = imports = 100. (a) What are the respective values for each autonomous component of Aggregate Spending? (b) What is autonomous saving? (c) What is the mpc? (d) What is the mps? (e) What is the break-even level

FIGURE 15

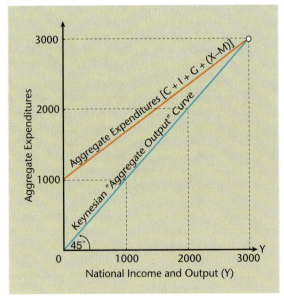

of income? (*f*) What is the *apc* at income = 200? At income = 1,000? (*g*) What are the corresponding values for the *aps*?

5. Construct a graph to show an Aggregate Expenditures curve based on the following relationships.

    Consumption = $500 + .6(Income)

    Autonomous government spending = $400

    Autonomous investment spending = $200

    Autonomous exports = $300

    Autonomous imports = $200

    Plot the new Aggregate Expenditures curve if the consumption relationship changes to Consumption = $800 + .75(Income).

6. Classical economics relies on "invisible hand" mechanisms to ensure full employment. (*a*) What adjustments in a capital market might help avoid the "underconsumption" problem? (*b*) What adjustments in output markets eliminate "gluts" of goods? (*c*) How do labor markets adjust to eliminate unemployment?

7. The vertical Aggregate Supply curve compatible with classical economics implies that Aggregate Demand only determines the price level. Keynesians insist that the Aggregate Supply curve is almost horizontal during a depression, so that changes in Aggregate Demand affect output and employment, but not the price level. What differences in assumptions about human behavior account for the different perspectives of classical economics and Keynesian economics?

8. Saving was negative for the economy as a whole during part of the Great Depression of the 1930s. How did this occur? What were the long-term effects of this negative rate of saving?

9. Do you think people's consumption depends most on their current income or on their expectations of income over the future? What does this imply about the stability of Keynes's *consumption function*? Why?

10. We are treating investment, government spending, and net exports as autonomous. To what extent do you think each of these spending categories is influenced by National Income? Why are we treating them as autonomous here if they are all influenced by income in fairly consistent ways?

Macroeconomic Equilibrium

Market forces yield an equilibrium where the quantity demanded of a specific good equals the quantity supplied at the current price. All forces are in balance, with no net pressures for prices, outputs, or purchases to change. The classical concept of macroeconomic equilibrium is similar. John Maynard Keynes and his followers, however, differ sharply with adherents of classical economic reasoning in their perceptions of exactly what constitutes equilibrium.

Classical macroeconomics concludes that laissez-faire policies will allow a market economy to hover around full employment in the long run, with automatic adjustments quickly overcoming any shocks to the economy. Confronted with the evidence of the Great Depression, Keynes countered that "in the long run, we are all dead," and dismissed the pressures that classical writers counted on to swiftly restore economies to full employment as either unbearably slow and weak or, worse, nonexistent. Keynes compared continuous economic changes to an ocean's waves — waiting for a long-run classical equilibrium is like waiting for the ocean to become flat. Consequently, Keynes focused on short-run problems, describing how the economy might become stuck in a short-run equilibrium with substantial idle capital and unemployed labor.

How plans for purchases by consumers, investors, government, and foreigners are summed to form an Aggregate Expenditures curve (sometimes called a *Keynesian cross*) was explored in Chapter 8. In this chapter, we inspect Keynes's view that a short-run macroeconomic equilibrium might persist at less than full employment. For now, we will focus exclusively on private sector activities. In the next chapter, government spending and taxes are brought into the picture so that we can examine what policymakers might do to correct for excessive inflation or unemployment.

Aggregate Expenditures and Equilibrium

We will assume initially that there are no taxes, depreciation, transfer payments, government expenditures, or undistributed corporate profits. This simplification blurs distinctions among GNP, NNP, and disposable income and permits us to use the term *income* (Y) to refer to all three. Net income and net output are also equal, because profit acts as a balancing item.

Labor is required to produce the output, which, if sold, translates into National Income and maintains employment. If output is unsalable at prices that cover costs, some workers will lose their jobs. Thus, when we say that National Income is rising, employment will also rise. Higher employment usually means lower unemployment, and vice versa; thus, growth in National Income or product tends to reduce unemployment, while downturns in National Income usually boost unemployment rates. Aggregate Spending interacts with National Output to yield a macroeconomic equilibrium.

National Output

Table 1 presents hypothetical data for income, employment, and output. The relationships among these aggregates illustrate how an economy approaches macroequilibrium. Column 1 shows the employment required to produce the levels of National Output (column 2) that producers are willing to offer at current prices if they are confident that it will be sold. You might think of the National Output schedule as reflecting a Keynesian Aggregate Supply curve because firms willingly produce whatever is demanded. For example, firms will employ 85 million workers and produce $2,750 billion in output and income *only* if they expect to be able to sell the output for $2,750 billion. Remember, *demand creates its own supply* in Keynesian analysis.

Aggregate Expenditures

You learned in Chapter 8 that planned Aggregate Expenditure is the sum of all plans for consumer spending, investment, government purchases, and net foreign spending. The basic Keynesian model we are building here ignores government and the foreign sector to simplify our analysis, so column 7 in Table 1 reflects Aggregate Expenditures (*AE*) as the sum of planned consumption (column 3) and planned investment (column 5). Thus, *AE* = C + I indicates planned levels of Aggregate Spending for each level of output and income.

Keynesian Equilibrium

National Output is graphed as a 45° ray from the origin in Figure 1, because, in Keynesian analysis, Aggregate Supply (output) adjusts passively to Aggregate Demand (expenditures).

> **Keynesian equilibrium** *requires Aggregate Output and Income (on the horizontal axis) to just equal planned Aggregate Expenditures (on the vertical axis).*

Keynesian macroeconomic equilibrium occurs when this Aggregate Expenditures curve intersects the 45° line. (Any variable plotted against

---

Table 1 *Levels of Income, Employment, and Output (Billions of Dollars)*

(1) Employment (Millions of Workers)	(2) National Output & Income	(3) Planned Consumption	(4) Planned Savings	(5) Planned Investment	(6) Unplanned Inventory Changes	(7) Aggregate Expenditures (AE) (Columns 3 + 5)	
70	$2,000	$2,100	$−100	$100	$−200	$2,200	Tendency for
75	2,250	2,300	−50	100	−150	2,400	income
80	2,500	2,500	0	100	−100	2,600	to
85	2,750	2,700	50	100	−50	2,800	rise
90	3,000	2,900	100	100	0	3,000	Equilibrium
95	3,250	3,100	150	100	+50	3,200	Tendency for
100	3,500	3,300	200	100	+100	3,400	income to
105	3,750	3,500	250	100	+150	3,600	fall

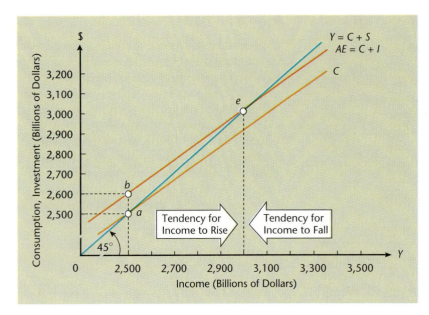

FIGURE 1
Consumption,
Investment, and
Income

Equilibrium income (point *e*) is found where National Output is just equal to Aggregate Expenditures. Whenever the system is not in equilibrium, pressures will exist to move the economy to an equilibrium income level of $3,000 billion. When income is below $3,000 billion, Aggregate Expenditures exceed National Output generating expansionary pressures in the form of declining inventories moving the economy upward to point *e*. When income exceeds $3,000 billion, pressures mount to move the economy back to equilibrium. (*Note:* This figure is based on the data in Table 1.)

an equal variable is on this 45° line.) Following convention, *Y* (on the horizontal axis) denotes real National Income and is measured against planned Aggregate Expenditures (on the vertical axis).

Classical economics suggests that any deviation from full employment represents disequilibrium that is, at most, a short-run phenomenon that will be quickly remedied by Say's Law and flexibility of interest rates, wages, and prices. The Keynesian perception of a short-run disequilibrium is very different.

Disequilibrium *occurs whenever plans for Aggregate Spending differ from Aggregate Income and Output.*

What pushes an economy back to equilibrium? Classical reasoning suggests that *supply creates its own demand* — Aggregate Spending automatically rises to accommodate the full employment level of output. Keynesians respond that *demand creates its own supply* — that supply passively adjusts to demand. In this context, *spending* and *demand* are synonymous. We will now scrutinize Keynesian adjustment processes: In situations of disequilibrium, National Output adjusts to the level of Aggregate Spending.

Eight possible levels of National Output and planned Aggregate Expenditures are listed in Table 1. What level of income and output will bring the economy into equilibrium? Consider for a moment employment of 75 million with National Output equal to $2,250 billion. Planned Aggregate Expenditures equal $2,400 billion and so exceed the $2,250 billion National Output. What adjustments will yield an equilibrium such that National Output equals Aggregate Spending?

In this situation, there will not be enough output to enable most firms to maintain sufficient inventories to meet the demands of their customers — consumers and other firms. When firms' inventories fall below desired levels, they respond by expanding employment and output. This causes income to grow. Suppose employment grows from 75 to 80 million. Even at employment of 80 million workers, the problem remains: Aggregate Expenditures — now $2,600 billion — still exceed National Output — now $2,500 billion. Employment, output, and income will continue to climb until 90 million people are working. Aggregate Expenditures and National Output both equal $3,000 billion at this employment level. Any further pressures to expand output are countered by offsetting pressures to contract output because firms are able to maintain the inventories needed to meet their customers', demands.

Pressures to move the economy to equilibrium are shown in Figure 1. For example, if National Output is only $2,500 billion (point *a*), then planned Aggregate Expenditure is $2,600 billion (point *b*). Excess Aggregate Spending ($100 billion = *b* − *a*) shrinks inventories and generates expansionary pressures that push the economy rightward from both *a* and *b* up the 45° reference line (National Output) to equilibrium at point *e* ($3,000 billion).

What happens if National Output exceeds planned *AE*? Suppose that most firms were overly optimistic in forecasting consumer and investor demands and produced $3,750 billion worth of goods and services. Firms would find their inventories of unsold goods swelling. Businesses cannot precisely regulate their inventories because customers may buy either more or less than firms expect. In this case, firms would reduce inventories and output by cutting back production, necessitating layoffs of employees. As output fell to point *e* in Figure 1, business inventories would shrink to the planned levels. This economy settles at an equilibrium income of $3,000 billion.

Both Table 1 and Figure 1 indicate that National Income will expand when output is less than $3,000 billion because spending exceeds production. When income or output exceeds $3,000 billion, income falls because production exceeds spending. Only when National Output is *exactly* $3,000 billion are all decision makers content to continue operating at existing levels of production, consumption, and investment. All forces are balanced, and there are no net pressures for the economy to shrink or grow from this short-run equilibrium.

Price vs. Quantity Adjustments

In individual markets, price adjustments are part of the cure for any disparities between the quantities of specific goods demanded and supplied. Price rises in individual markets if quantity demanded exceeds quantity supplied; if quantity supplied exceeds quantity demanded, price falls.

You may wonder why such price adjustments are absent in this example. The reason is that Keynesian analysis assumes that only *quantity adjustments* occur in situations of high unemployment and excess capacity — the Aggregate Supply curve is treated as horizontal.

The price level is constant because the simple Keynesian depression model assumes that capacity poses no problem. Expanding output in an economy with many idle workers does not require higher wage or price incentives. Classical analysis presumes severe capacity constraints, because the economy is thought to hover close to full employment. Thus, the classical Aggregate Supply curve is vertical, and a classical model would use *price-level adjustments* to resolve shifts of Aggregate Demand. This part of the book focuses on the Keynesian model, so detailed treatments of price movements are postponed until later chapters.

A Keynesian Saving = Investment Equilibrium

Investigating how investment and saving are related provides another view of how levels of National Income and Output are determined. Scrutiny of Table 1 and Figure 1 reveals that a stable equilibrium requires planned levels of saving and investment to be equal.

Actual and planned saving and investment are all equal (S = I) in a macroequilibrium.

Both households' plans for saving and firms' plans for investing must be realized, regardless of whether the model used is Keynesian or classical.

Planned Saving and Investment

Study columns 4 and 5 in Table 1, which are also graphed in Figure 2. In our simple Keynesian model, firms plan to invest $100 billion regardless of the level of income, while consumers' plans to save are tied to income. Suppose income were $3,500 billion. Consumers would try to save $200 billion (point *f* in Figure 2), but invest-

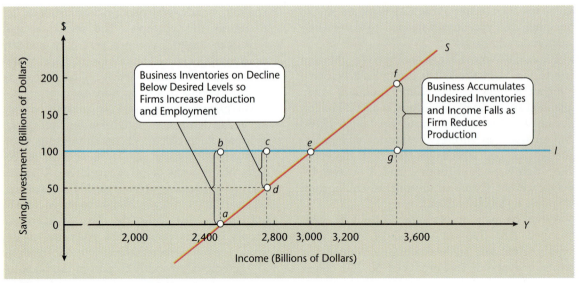

FIGURE 2　Saving and Investment Approach

Equilibrium in the economy is achieved when desired saving and desired investment are equal. If income falls below equilibrium (point *e* = $3,000 billion), business inventories decline below desired levels. When income is above equilibrium, business accumulates undesired inventories and, consequently, cuts production to bring inventories back in line. Only at equilibrium are desired saving and desired investment equal. (*Note:* Points *a*, *b*, and *e* correspond to points *a*, *b*, and *e* in Figure 1. This figure is also based on data in Table 1.)

ment plans are for only $100 billion (point *g* in Figure 2). What will be the result?

Saving is the act of not consuming. Because income saved is money not spent, saving is a withdrawal of funds from the system.

Withdrawals *occur when income is not spent on domestic output.*

In addition to saving, withdrawals include taxes (income paid to the government) and imports (most foreign income is spent in the recipients' own countries). Because spending is perceived to drive a capitalist system, withdrawals tend to suppress income generation in a Keynesian model.

Injections are the reverse of withdrawals; they reflect spending introduced into the economy.

Autonomous spending (regardless of source) represents an **injection** *into the Keynesian spending stream.*

We will discuss the effects of injections on National Income after we consider the consequences of such forms of withdrawals as household saving.

Withdrawal because of excess saving causes firms to accumulate unwanted inventories — output exceeds sales. (This discussion parallels our earlier description of adjustments to excess supply.) Firms will find total consumer and business spending (C + I) insufficient to clear new output from the market. Production and employment will fall, because firms do not desire these investments in inventory. Income drops as the economy moves back from points *f* and *g* toward equilibrium at point *e*, where planned saving and planned investment are equal. Planned and realized saving and investment are all equated, and income stops falling when the economy approaches equilibrium.

This adjustment process works in the opposite direction when National Output and Income are below the equilibrium level of $3,000 billion.

For example, when National Output is $2,750 billion, consumers desire to save $50 billion and consume $2,700 billion, while business plans to invest $100 billion; Aggregate Expenditures ($C + I$) are $2,800 billion. The $50 billion shortfall of goods required to satisfy consumer and investor demands causes inventories to shrink. Firms unintentionally disinvest in inventories, which fall by $50 billion in each period. Businesses will adjust by boosting production to raise inventories back to desired levels. Output and income rise to $3,000 billion (from c and d to point e in Figure 2) before planned inventories can be maintained; planned saving and investment are equal at $100 billion. Thus, equilibrium requires that planned saving equal planned investment ($S = I$).

Balancing Planned and Actual Saving and Investment

You can see that inventories are vital in movements from disequilibrium to equilibrium. Unintended inventory changes ensure that actual saving and investment are equal at all times. Firms use inventory changes as barometers. If inventories drop, there is an unintended disinvestment in inventories, and firms boost their production. If inventories unexpectedly rise, firms view this unplanned investment as a signal to cut production and employment. Thus, changes in inventories resolve any differences between planned saving and planned investment.

Fluctuating inventories provide signals to raise or lower output so that planned saving equals planned investment, but other mechanisms also aid in equilibration. Consumers sometimes are unable to buy all the goods they demand; people often wait in lines during shortages. Queues and shortages signal firms to expand their production facilities or, perhaps, to raise prices.

Keynesian models generally assume excess production capacity, so clearing the market takes the form of quantity adjustments — real National Income and employment adjust to eliminate disparities between Aggregate Spending and National Output. Classical reasoning assumes full employment, so all market-clearing adjustments take the form of wage and price changes. How

differing conditions may foster quantity adjustments instead of price adjustments is treated toward the end of this chapter.

In sum, only when planned investment exactly equals planned saving will the economy stay in equilibrium. When households' plans to save and firms' plans to invest are both realized, sales will just maintain equilibrium output, and there will be no net tendency for the economy to move.

The Multiplier Effect

If there were no investment in the simple example shown back in Figure 1, Aggregate Expenditures would consist only of consumption (C), and equilibrium income would be $2,500 billion (point a). When autonomous investment of $100 billion is injected, however, its effect is multiplied so that equilibrium income rises to $3,000 billion (point e). The total change in income that ultimately results is five times the initial increase in spending!

You may wonder why a relatively small injection of investment ($100 billion) so powerfully expands equilibrium income ($500 billion). The answer rests in a concept called the multiplier.

> The **multiplier effect** *occurs when one person's spending becomes someone else's income, and some of the second person's income is subsequently spent, becoming the income of a third person, and so on.*

But at what level of income does this multiple spending → income → spending cycle stop? The answer requires a bit of arithmetic.

> The **autonomous spending multiplier** *is the total change in income generated divided by the change in autonomous spending that triggered the spending → income → spending sequence.*

When the new autonomous spending is investment, this ratio is $\Delta Y / \Delta I$.

The example in Table 1 and Figures 1 and 2 is based on a marginal propensity to consume (*mpc*) of 0.8. Suppose we begin with zero investment. Table 1 suggests that equilibrium income will be $2,500 billion, because only at that level do planned saving and planned investment both equal zero. If firms decide to invest $100 billion on new capital goods, the workers and owners of firms producing capital goods receive $100 billion in additional income.

How will the workers and owners of firms who produce capital goods respond? Their *mpc* is 0.8 in their roles as consumers, so they can be expected to spend $80 billion of this new income on consumer goods and save $20 billion. When these producers spend the $80 billion, this sec-

ond round of spending adds $80 billion to Aggregate Expenditures; National Output must increase by $80 billion, which becomes new income to the firms providing these consumer goods and to their employees. In turn, they will spend 80 percent of the $80 billion, or $64 billion, and so on throughout the system.

This round-by-round spending is illustrated in Table 2 and Figure 3. The cumulative effect of new autonomous investment of $100 billion is also shown in Figure 4, which is based on the data from Table 1. As we noted earlier, the *mpc* is 0.8, so the *mps* is 0.2 and the multiplier in our example is 5. It is not a coincidence that the

FIGURE 3 The Multiplier Effect

The round-by-round cumulative spending effect is illustrated in this figure. An additional $100 billion in spending in Round 1 is multiplied throughout the economy and results in a total increase in income of $500 billion from an initial new injection of $100 billion.

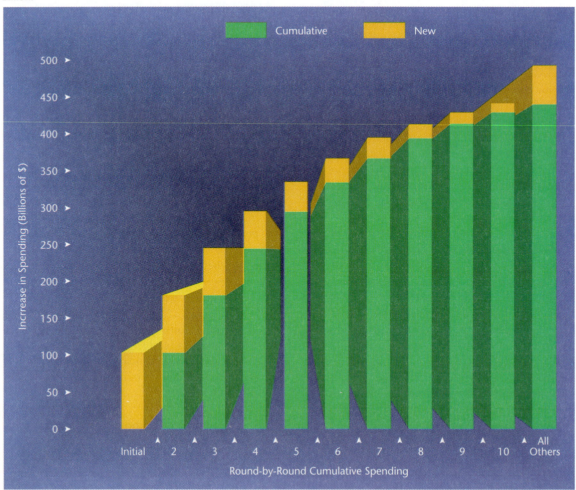

Table 2 *A Tabular Example of the Multiplier*

Round	Increases in Expenditures (Billions of Dollars)	Increases in Saving (Billions of Dollars)
Initial Increase	$100	
Round 2	80	$ 20
Round 3	64	16
Round 4	51	13
Round 5	41	10
Round 6	33	8
Round 7	26	7
Round 8	21	5
Round 9	17	4
Round 10	13	3
Sum of First 10 Rounds	$446	$ 86
Sum of All Other Rounds	54	14
Total Increase in Spending (Income)	$500	
Total Increase in Saving		$100

Note: Data in the table are from Table 1. The *mpc* is 0.8 and the *mps* is 0.2. Figures after Round 3 are rounded off to the nearest dollar.

multiplier is the reciprocal of the *mps*: $1/mps = 1/0.2 = 5$. In fact, any change in *injections* (e.g., either autonomous consumption or investment) divided by the marginal propensity to save yields the total multiplied effect on National Output and Income.

In our simplified model, the only withdrawal is saving, so the multiplier is $1/mps$. (A higher *mps* yields a faster rate of withdrawal and a smaller multiplier.) Alternatively, the multiplier is the change in income divided by the change in autonomous injections, so

$$\frac{\Delta Y}{\Delta I} = \frac{1}{mps}$$

The $mpc + mps = 1$, so the $mps = 1 - mpc$, and the multiplier may also be written as $1/(1 - mpc)$. If we consider withdrawals other than saving,

$$\begin{aligned}\text{autonomous spending multiplier} &= \frac{1}{\text{withdrawal fraction per spending round}} \\ &= \frac{1}{1 - \text{fraction respent}}\end{aligned}$$

and

$$\text{total changes in income} = \text{amount of injection} \times \text{multiplier}$$

FIGURE 4 The Total Effect of the Multiplier

The effect on total income from a spending injection is equal to the injection times the autonomous spending multiplier. When the *mpc* = 0.8, this multiplier is 5. This simple multiplier is $\Delta Y/\Delta I = 1/mps = 1/(1 - mpc)$. Therefore, an increase in investment (an injection) of $100 billion results in a total increase in income of $500 billion.

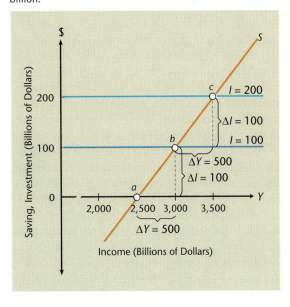

A mathematical derivation of this autonomous spending multiplier is provided in the optional material at the end of this chapter.

Our simplified model may seem to suggest an enormous multiplier effect – the marginal propensity to save is, historically, about 7 percent, which suggests a multiplier of between 14 and 15. However, the linkages between spending rounds are much looser in the real world than in this model. More sophisticated models consider other withdrawals of funds from the spending → income → spending sequence.

Withdrawals include taxes (roughly 30 percent) and other "leakages" such as imports – a case where the funds we spend go into the hands of foreign suppliers. Moreover, the full multiplier effect is felt only after all spending rounds have been completed. Realistically, only the first four or five rounds of spending will be completed in the year in which an injection occurs. For all these reasons and more, prudent statistical estimates of the value of the autonomous spending multiplier place its maximum effective value at around 2. The Depression is a prime case of the multiplier at work.

The Great Depression: The Multiplier in Action

Brother, can you spare a dime?

A Hit Song from the 1930s

No one alive in the 1930s escaped the effects of the Great Depression. The labor force was roughly at full employment in 1929; unemployment was only 3.2 percent. By 1933, unemployment had soared to 25 percent – one worker in four was unemployed. Soup kitchens could not feed all the hungry people, and windows along Wall Street became diving boards for those who chose suicide to avoid bankruptcy. A wave of failures threatened to collapse U.S. banks like a line of dominoes. Such programs as unemployment compensation and Social Security were not available to temporarily replace incomes. Economically, these were the hardest times this country has ever experienced.

Figure 5 illustrates the first four years of the Great Depression (1929–1933). This Keynesian portrayal of the Great Depression seems fairly simple and accurate by today's standards, but it was not understood at all during the early 1930s.

The actual data for the four components of Aggregate Expenditures (C, I, G, $X - M$) show that changes in net foreign spending and government purchases were quite small and largely offset each other during this period. Keynesians viewed the huge decline in Gross Private Domestic Investment (I in Figure 5) between 1929 and 1933 as the root cause of the collapse in Aggregate Spending – investment fell from $139.2 billion to only $22.7 billion. This $116.5 billion decline in investment spending was accompanied by a $211.1 billion drop in income (from $709.6 billion in 1929 to $498.5 billion in 1933). Remember that the multiplier is the change in income divided by the change in injections, which in this case is roughly $\Delta Y / \Delta I$. Thus, our highly simplified Keynesian model suggests a multiplier during the Great Depression of 1.81 ($-211.1 / -116.5 = 1.81$).

Government policies to combat instability have been refined considerably in the past half century. Most economists doubt that such a deep collapse will ever recur. How might government have prevented the Great Depression? In the next few chapters, we will examine tools the government can now use to combat both recessions and inflations.

The Paradox of Thrift

What happens if we as a society try to save more? Classical analysis suggests that saving promotes investment and growth, but a potential "paradox of thrift" may pose a problem.

Keynesian theory suggests that widespread attempts to save more may cause income to fall so much that actual saving shrinks, a problem known as the **paradox of thrift.**

Most of us consider thrift a virtue. Ben Franklin's adage, "A penny saved is a penny earned," haunts many of our psyches when we shop, and we think we might be better off if we saved more. The term *paradox* correctly reflects, how-

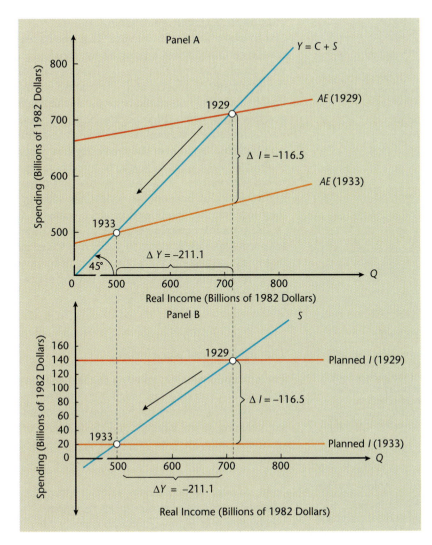

FIGURE 5 Saving, Investment, and Income During the Great Depression

These equilibrium points for the United States before and during the Great Depression illustrate the Keynesian explanation for such economic downturns. Investment spending fell by $4.75 billion from 1929 to 1933, causing a general collapse of spending. Keynes viewed this as the root cause of the Depression. (Data: *Economic Report of the President*, 1980–1991.)

ever, Keynesians' belief that Ben's adage is inappropriate for the general economy. Keynesian analysis indicates that if we *all* try to save more, we may *all* wind up worse off and actually save less.

Showing how the desire to save more may cause actual saving to fall requires a slight, but temporary, change in the assumptions used to build a simple Keynesian model. We have assumed that investment is autonomous, or unaffected by income. A more realistic assumption is that as income rises, firms become more optimistic about the profit prospects for new investment. Hence, for the moment we will assume that investment rises as income rises.

The paradox of thrift is illustrated in Figure 6, which shows households initially saving and firms initially investing $100 billion. National Income is $600 billion, with equilibrium at point *a* on curves S_0 and *I*. Suppose consumers decide to consume less (save more) at each income level, shifting the saving curve from S_0 to S_1. The average propensity to save (*aps*) rises, but the marginal propensity to save (*mps*) is constant at 20 percent. With their increased desires to save, people want to set aside $110 billion (point *c*) if National Income is $600 billion, and $50 billion (point *d*) if National Income is $300 billion. What happens as the economy adjusts to this increased desire to save?

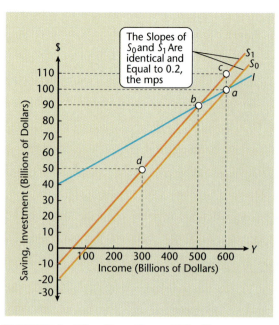

FIGURE 6   The Paradox of Thrift

When consumers attempt to save more (raise their *aps*), at every level of income the consumption curve (not shown in this figure) shifts down and the corresponding saving curve (S_0) shifts up to S_1. Unless there is some simultaneous increase in the investment schedule, income will fall from $600 billion to $500 billion (from point *a* to point *b*), and saving and investment will both fall from $100 billion to $90 billion.

Consumption falls when households try to save more. Firms will counter declining sales and rising inventories by cutting production, employment, and investment. Income and employment both fall, and the economy moves from the original equilibrium income and output of $600 billion (point *a*), to a new equilibrium position at $500 billion (point *b*). Notice that saving actually declines by $10 billion, to a level of $90 billion. Why? Because actual saving and investment and planned saving and investment all must be equal in equilibrium; at point *b*, consumers want to save $90 billion because income is $500 billion, and investors want to invest $90 billion at this new lower level of income.

But observe that consumption has fallen from $500 billion (600 − 100) to $410 billion (500 − 90). Thus, this Keynesian model suggests that increased desire to save may lead to cuts in actual

consumption, investment, saving, and income — and to lower standards of living. This line of reasoning certainly poses a paradox for those of us who think that more saving is always good for the economy. Unfortunately, increased saving may be a typical household response at the worst possible time, when the economy begins slipping into a recession. If families fear that breadwinners will lose their jobs, they may begin saving a little more each payday, trying to build nest eggs to cover expenses should income cease. If growing numbers of households adopt this strategy, they increase the likelihood of a recession.

The paradox of saving is not a problem in an economy operating close to capacity. Classical reasoning suggests that increased desire to save drives down interest rates, thus increasing investment and economic growth.

The Investment Accelerator

The multiplier process relies on the fact that any increase in autonomous spending creates income, which generates further consumer spending, creating more income, and so on. New investment may also be triggered by increased spending.

> An **investment accelerator** *exerts pressure for accelerated income growth when rising consumption and income stimulate new capital investment.*

New autonomous spending causes investment to accelerate, so that Aggregate Spending is both *multiplied* by induced consumption and *accelerated* by induced investment. A change in autonomous spending may therefore increase income by even more than is indicated by the multiplier process. (More sophisticated Keynesian models than any considered in this book explain how interactions between investment accelerators and multiplier processes may destabilize Aggregate Expenditures.) The effects on National Income of interactions between the multiplier and accelerator are traced in Figure 7.

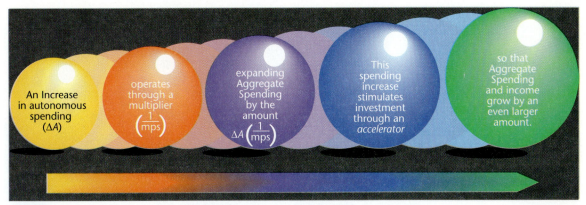

FIGURE 7 Integrating an Investment Accelerator into a Keynesian System

Investment is stimulated by a change in autonomous spending (ΔA) through the accelerator principle. This change in autonomous spending magnifies Aggregate Expenditures even more than is suggested by the multiplier process, but it also makes Aggregate Spending highly volatile.

Equilibrium Below Potential GNP

We now turn to the most important conclusion of Keynesian analysis. Keynes was the first major mainstream economist to argue (*a*) that "demand creates its own supply," and (*b*) that "sticky" adjustments of wages, prices, and interest rates could stall a market economy in a short-run equilibrium below full employment. Keynes's ideas departed sharply from those of classical economists, who counted on flexible prices, wages, and interest rates to restore the economy to full employment. The severity of the Great Depression indicated that "invisible hand" mechanisms might operate only slowly at times. High unemployment showed few signs of an automatic cure prior to World War II.

Potential GNP

Potential GNP and *full-employment* GNP (or income) are rough synonyms.

> **Potential GNP** *is an estimate of what the economy could produce at high rates of utilization of our available resources, especially full employment of labor.*

Estimates of potential GNP reflect trends in productivity, the size and composition of the labor force, and other influences on our capacity to produce. Estimates of the ratio of actual GNP to potential GNP for 1929–1990 are illustrated in Figure 8.

Potential GNP is not an absolute limit on productive capacity in the same way a production possibilities frontier is. For example, potential GNP might be exceeded through slavery, or if people who would not normally choose to work took temporary jobs to support a national defense effort (e.g., World War II), or if frictional unemployment artificially fell because many unemployed workers accepted jobs that, because of inflation, ultimately paid less than they expected. Ideally, potential GNP reflects only informed voluntary activity, a point addressed in more depth in Chapter 15.

The GNP Gap

Figure 8 illustrates that National Output can fall far below potential GNP.

> The **GNP gap** *is the difference between potential and actual GNP.*

In the simple Keynesian model described by

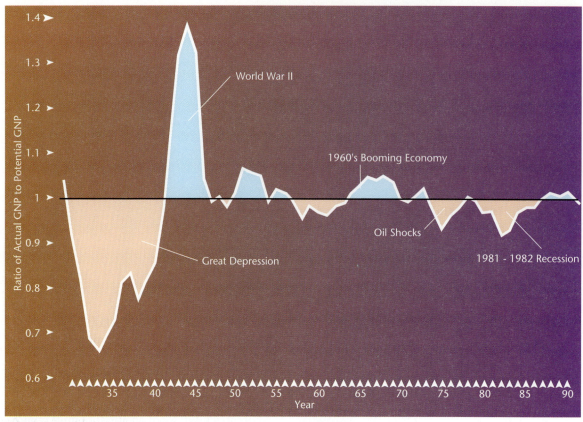

FIGURE 8 The Ratio of Actual GNP to Potential GNP, 1929–1990

Actual and potential GNP often diverge substantially. Since World War II, the differences between the two have been relatively minor. Nevertheless, recessions are costly in terms of lost output and income.

Sources: *Economic Report of the President,* 1991; Robert J. Gordon, *Macroeconomics* (New York: HarperCollins, 1990). Updated by authors.

Table 1 and graphed in Figure 9, equilibrium income is $3 trillion along expenditure curve AE_0. Suppose that potential GNP at full employment is $3.25 trillion, so that a *GNP gap* of $250 billion exists. Would market pressures quickly move the economy above its original equilibrium of $3 trillion? Keynesians believe the answer is *No.* How might this $250 billion GNP gap be filled to achieve equilibrium income and output of $3.25 trillion? The Keynesian answer is to increase Aggregate Spending from AE_0 to AE_1. How much of an increase in autonomous spending is required?

The Recessionary Gap

Given that the multiplier in our example is 5 $(1/0.2 = 1/mps)$, an increase in autonomous investment spending of $50 billion will result in increases in Aggregate Spending and output of $250 billion, filling the GNP gap and moving the economy to full employment.

*The **recessionary gap** measures the amount by which autonomous spending falls short of that needed to bring equilibrium income to full employment.*

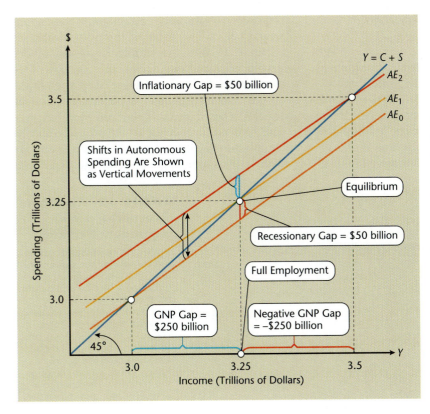

$45°$

FIGURE 9 Inflationary and Recessionary Gaps

With full employment income of $3.25 trillion and Aggregate Expenditures of AE_0, output will not automatically expand to reach full employment. Given that the multiplier in this example is 5, a $50 billion increase in autonomous spending will cause the economy to expand to full employment. This $50 billion deficiency in autonomous spending is referred to as the recessionary gap. Whenever autonomous spending exceeds that necessary to achieve a full employment level of Aggregate Spending, an inflationary gap exists. With Aggregate Spending of AE_2, the inflationary gap is $50 billion, and there is a (negative) GNP gap of $250 billion.

The recessionary gap is measured along the vertical axis in Figure 9. This means that the recessionary gap is defined by any shortfall in autonomous spending and *not* by the amount by which equilibrium income falls short of full employment income (measured along the horizontal axis).

GNP gap = recessionary gap × multiplier

Thus, any shortfall in equilibrium income is a GNP gap, which equals the recessionary gap times the autonomous spending multiplier.

The Inflationary Gap

An inflationary gap is the reverse of the recessionary gap.

*An **inflationary gap** is the amount by which autonomous spending exceeds that needed to achieve full employment equilibrium.*

Graphically, it is the vertical distance between AE_1 and AE_2 in Figure 9. The inflationary gap is $50 billion if Aggregate Spending is AE_2. This economy can only produce $3.25 trillion in output at full employment, so this additional demand will result in upward pressures on prices when potential buyers compete for this limited real output.

Keynesian Equilibrium and the Price Level

National Income (Y) is a monetary value and can be thought of as the product of the price level (P) and the level of real output (Q). Thus, $Y = PQ$, and as long as the price level is constant, National Income (Y) and real output (Q) are equivalent. Moreover, the Aggregate Expenditures curve (AE) and the Aggregate Demand curve (AD) will be positively related.

Aggregate Demand and Aggregate Expenditures

Keynesian theory views output decisions as based strictly on expected sales; prices are assumed fixed, so the Aggregate Expenditures curve is based on a constant price level. If the price level were to drop, however, autonomous spending would rise because consumers and investors would be able to buy more goods and resources. Naturally, autonomous spending would fall, all else equal, if the price level rose.

Figure 10 uses the simple Keynesian model developed earlier to derive an Aggregate Demand curve from three Aggregate Expenditure curves. Each Aggregate Expenditure curve in Panel A is based on a different price level. Aggregate Expenditures equal to $AE_{(P = 100)}$ result in equilibrium income of $3.25 trillion (point a) with a corresponding point on the Aggregate

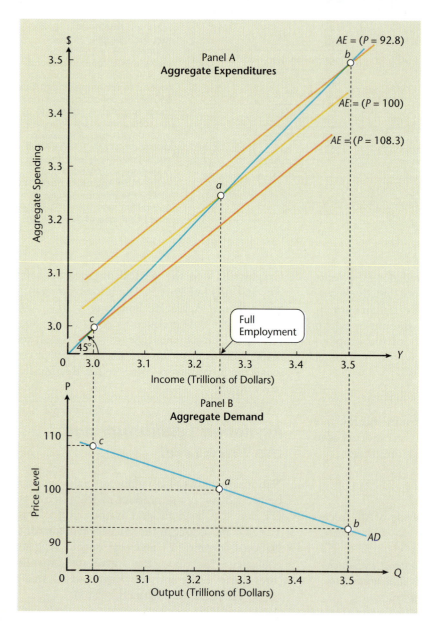

FIGURE 10 Aggregate Expenditures and Aggregate Demand

Aggregate Expenditures curves are constructed for a given price level and yield unique levels of equilibrium income and output for that price level. A rising price level would lead to declining Aggregate Expenditures ($AE_{(P = 108.3)}$ in Panel A) as consumers and business find their spending buys less (point c). Falling prices lead to the opposite (point b). This leads to a unique relationship, permitting us to derive the Aggregate Demand curve in Panel B.

Demand curve (point a). If prices fall, autonomous spending grows, resulting in a new equilibrium at $3.5 trillion (point b). Symmetrically, equilibrium income declines if the price level rises (point c). Connecting these points in Panel B yields an Aggregate Demand curve, so Aggregate Expenditures and the Aggregate Demand curve are closely related. Varying the price level in our simple Keynesian model allows derivation of a negatively sloped Aggregate Demand curve.

Shifts in Aggregate Demand Curves

We have seen that Aggregate Expenditures change when prices change, but spending can change for many other reasons. When the price level is constant and Aggregate Spending changes, the Aggregate Demand curve shifts, as illustrated in Figure 11. The Aggregate Demand curve AD_0 is associated with Aggregate Expenditures AE_0. Equilibrium income is $3 trillion at a

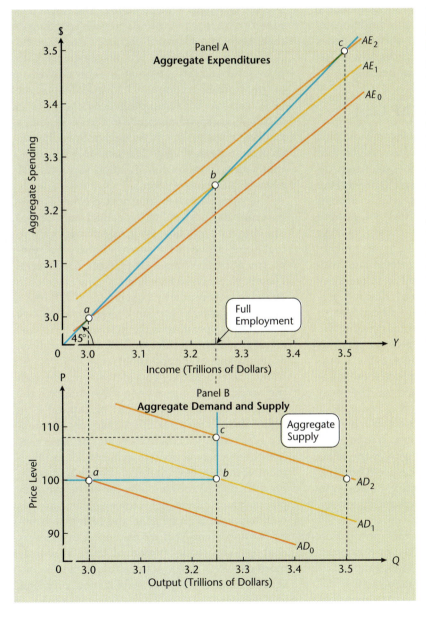

FIGURE 11   Shifting Aggregate Demand to Close GNP Gaps

Simple Keynesian theory operates as though "demand creates its own supply" because the price level is assumed fixed. As a result, the Aggregate Supply curve is horizontal until full employment is reached. Holding the price level constant and increasing Aggregate Expenditures from $AE_0 \rightarrow AE_1 \rightarrow AE_2$ (Panel A) results in horizontal shifts (increases) in Aggregate Demand curves from $AD_0 \rightarrow AD_1 \rightarrow AD_2$ (Panel B). If full-employment GNP is $3.25 trillion, closing the $250 billion GNP gap between points a and b (AD_0 to AD_1) requires additional autonomous spending of $50 billion. Conversely, when Aggregate Spending is AE_2, a $50 billion inflationary gap exists. Closing this gap will result in a rise in the price level of nearly 8 percent.

price level of 100 (point *a*). Improved business optimism, for example, could increase autonomous spending to AE_1, yielding a new equilibrium income of $3.25 trillion (point *b*). Thus, increased autonomous spending of $50 billion leads to additional income of $250 billion (the change in autonomous spending times the multiplier) at the existing price level ($P = 100$), and AD_1 is the new Aggregate Demand curve associated with this new level of Aggregate Spending, AE_1.

In summary, changes in autonomous spending shift the Aggregate Demand curve horizontally by the amount of autonomous spending times the multiplier. Now we will consider how recessionary and inflationary gaps can be closed.

Aggregate Demand and GNP Gaps

In our example (Figure 11), *real* income and output (Q) cannot exceed the $3.25 trillion full employment level (point *b*). If equilibrium income rises to $3.5 trillion ($AE_2$ in Figure 11), the price level must rise, because real output cannot exceed $3.25 trillion. Equilibration will require that $3.5 trillion = $P \times$ $3.25 trillion, so the price level must rise to 3.5/3.25, or roughly 1.077 (point *c*). (A price index would rise from 100 to 107.7.) Thus, this $50-billion inflationary gap will increase the price level by almost 8 percent. Preventing this inflationary adjustment to excessive Aggregate Spending entails cutting the autonomous spending of either consumers, investors, government, or foreigners. Some methods government might use to reduce these inflationary pressures are presented in the next chapter.

Keynesian analysis largely focuses on achieving full employment if the economy is operating below its potential; it generally ignores the inflation that might emerge from excessive Aggregate Demand. The price level is sensitive, however, to total spending by both consumers and investors, and vice versa. Let us see why.

Simple Keynesian theory views production decisions as being based strictly on expected sales; prices are assumed fixed. This is implicit in the idea that "demand creates its own supply." Thus, the Aggregate Supply curve compatible with Keynesian analysis of a recession is horizontal until a full employment level of output is reached. Then, paralleling a classical Aggregate Supply curve, the Aggregate Supply curve becomes vertical, as shown in Figure 11. Once the economy reaches full employment, growth in spending would result in pure price increases.

If Aggregate Demand is AD_0 in Figure 11, equilibrium output will be $3 trillion at a price level of 100 (point *a*). There is substantial excess capacity and unemployment in this equilibrium, and the GNP gap = $250 billion. The Keynesian prescription is to increase Aggregate Spending so that Aggregate Demand increases to AD_1, and the economy achieves full employment with price-level stability at point *b*. The growth in output from $3 trillion to $3.25 trillion to fill the GNP gap can be accomplished by increases in autonomous spending equal to the recessionary gap described earlier. If Aggregate Spending increases, more Aggregate Demand shifts to AD_2; the economy will suffer inflation as prices rise nearly 8 percent to point *c*.

The central topic in the next chapter is how government fiscal policy (spending and taxing) can eliminate inflationary or recessionary gaps so that GNP moves to a noninflationary full employment level. When Keynes wrote *The General Theory of Employment, Interest, and Money* in 1936, he was primarily concerned with filling a huge recessionary gap and suggested massive government spending as the best way to increase Aggregate Expenditures sufficiently to pull an economy out of a depression.

You have acquired considerable insight into the workings of our economy by studying the Keynesian model, but a word of caution is in order. Policies to shrink inflationary or recessionary gaps require accurate estimates of these gaps and then timely actions to achieve full employment with price-level stability. This is an incredibly difficult task, obscured by the crude oversimplification of our model. However, this analysis will help you to understand and formulate solutions to problems that we encounter in the next chapter. The model presented there is slightly more complex, making it possible for us to consider a broader range of stabilization problems and policies.

Chapter Review: Key Points

1. Keynesian theory suggests that erratic changes in *business investment spending* (especially inventories) play a major role in causing fluctuations in Aggregate Income and employment.

2. Equilibrium income and employment occur at the output level at which *Aggregate Spending equals National Output*; firms desire to produce and sell exactly the amounts consumers and investors want to purchase. Any deviation from equilibrium income sets forces in motion to drive the economy toward a new equilibrium.

3. When planned saving equals planned investment $(S = I)$, the economy will be in *equilibrium*. Actual saving and investment are equal at all times, because inventory adjustments and similar mechanisms ensure this balance.

4. When *autonomous spending* in the economy increases by \$1, income rises by an amount equal to the *autonomous spending multiplier* times the original \$1. The multiplier exists because the original \$1 in new spending becomes \$1 in new income, parts of which are then spent by successive consumers and businesses. The simple autonomous spending multiplier equals

$$\frac{\Delta Y}{\Delta A} = \frac{1}{mps} = \frac{1}{1 - mpc}$$

where A represents some form of autonomous spending. More generally, the multiplier equals 1/(withdrawal fraction per spending round).

5. Investment spending dropped precipitously during the 1929–1933 period. The effect of this decline was to reduce equilibrium income sharply, and it may have been a principal cause of the Great Depression.

6. The *paradox of thrift* appears to be an important challenge to our conventional wisdom. If more consumers decide to increase their saving, the result might be declining income, consumption, and saving.

7. *Potential GNP* is an estimate of the output the economy could produce at full employment. The *GNP gap* is the difference between potential and actual GNP.

8. The *recessionary gap* is the amount by which autonomous spending falls short of that necessary to achieve a full employment level of income; it is measured on the vertical axis. An *inflationary gap* is the amount by which autonomous spending exceeds what is necessary for a full employment equilibrium and is a measure of upward pressure on the price level.

9. Aggregate Expenditure curves are constructed for a given (fixed) price level. If the price level rises, Aggregate Expenditures fall, and vice versa. This leads to a unique relationship that allows us to derive an Aggregate Demand curve from specific levels of Aggregate Expenditures at various price levels.

10. If the price level is constant, higher autonomous spending increases Aggregate Demand by shifting the Aggregate Demand curve to the right, and vice versa.

11. Keynes thought that raising Aggregate Demand would boost output during a depression without raising the price level. Simple Keynesian theory suggests that the Aggregate Supply curve is horizontal up to the point of full employment. Once full-employment GNP is reached, classical reasoning reigns: The Aggregate Supply curve is vertical, and increases in Aggregate Demand cannot generate extra output. In a fully employed economy, additions to Aggregate Demand simply bid up prices and result in inflation.

Key Concepts

Ensure that you can define these terms before proceeding.

disequilibrium

saving = investment
  $(S = I)$

withdrawals

injections

multiplier effect

autonomous spending
  multiplier

paradox of thrift

potential GNP

GNP gap

recessionary gap

inflationary gap

Problems and Questions

1. A simple way to calculate an autonomous spending multiplier is to invert (turn upside down) the fraction representing the *mps*. For example, if *mps* = 1/6 (roughly .167), the multiplier equals 6. Compute the *mps* and the autonomous spending multiplier for the following values of the *mpc*: 1/2, 3/5, 2/3, 3/4, 4/5, 5/6, 6/7, 7/8, 8/9, and 9/10.

2. Use the consumption relationship from Table 3 to answer the following questions.

    a. If autonomous investment is $200, what is equilibrium income?

    b. Assume that full employment income is $4,000. What is the GNP gap?

    c. How much is the inflationary gap?

    d. What is the autonomous spending multiplier?

    e. If extreme pessimism caused investment spending to fall by $600, what would the equilibrium income be? What would the recessionary gap equal?

3. What alternatives are available to a retailer whose inventories are growing because sales are not as large as planned? Will the alternative retailers typically select be important in determining National Income? How? How will the strategies chosen by retailers with excess inventories vary over the business cycle? Why is this important?

4. Use the savings function in Figure 12 to answer the following questions.

    a. What does the marginal propensity to consume equal?

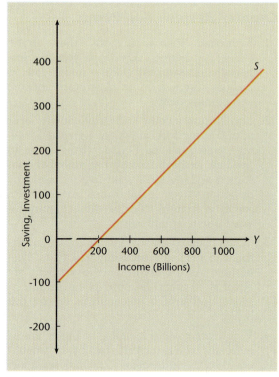

FIGURE 12

    b. What does the autonomous spending multiplier equal?

    c. If autonomous investment is $300 billion, what is equilibrium income?

    d. If full employment income is $600 billion and autonomous investment equals $300 billion, what does the GNP gap equal?

    e. Based on the information in question d, does a recessionary or inflationary gap exist?

    f. What does the recessionary/inflationary gap equal?

    g. Based on the information in question d, will there be upward pressure on prices? Why or why not?

5. What are the similarities and the differences between equilibrium for Aggregate Expenditure and National Output curves and equilibrium for Aggregate Demand and Supply when the price level is a consideration? How do these macroeconomic equilibria compare with the equilibria in markets for individual goods and services?

6. In the simple Keynesian model presented in

Table 3

National Output and Income	Planned Consumption
$ 0	$1,000
1,000	1,800
2,000	2,600
3,000	3,400
4,000	4,200
5,000	5,000
6,000	5,800
7,000	6,600

this chapter, the only forms of injection considered are autonomous investment and the only withdrawal is saving. What are other possible injections? Other withdrawals? How might exports and imports be incorporated to make this model a more complete picture of the way the world really works?

7. Do you think prices will fall in response to declines in Aggregate Demand, as classical economists suggest? Or will quantities decline, as Keynesians believe? What bearing does your answer have for designing policies to combat inflationary pressures? If the economy has considerable excess capacity, will expanding Aggregate Expenditures cause output to grow, or will the price level simply rise?

Optional Material: Autonomous Spending Multipliers

A more rigorous treatment of our hypothetical model will help you understand why income changes by some multiple of any change in autonomous spending. (We use delta (Δ) to signify change. Thus, ΔY is read "change in income.") How large will be the total change in income (ΔY) from a given change in, say, autonomous investment spending (ΔI)? This ratio ($\Delta Y/\Delta I$) is known as the **autonomous spending multiplier.**

We have assumed that consumption is related to income and that changes in income will cause consumption to change by a value equal to the *mpc* times the change in income. Since we know that

$$Y = C + I \qquad (1)$$

(output is either consumed or invested), then

$$\Delta Y = \Delta C + \Delta I \qquad (2)$$

(changes in output reflect changes in consumption and/or investment). We assume that consumption spending is related to income by the *mpc*, so

$$\Delta C = mpc \times \Delta Y \qquad (3)$$

(this is the change in induced consumption). The change in consumption is equal to the change in income times the proportion of the change you intend to spend.

Substituting Equation (2) into Equation (3) yields

$$\Delta Y = mpc\Delta Y + \Delta I \qquad (4)$$

Now we need to move all income (Y) terms to one side. This is accomplished by subtracting $mpc\Delta Y$ from each side of Equation (4), so

$$\Delta Y - mpc\Delta Y = \Delta I \qquad (5)$$

Factoring the ΔY terms on the left side of Equation (5) leaves

$$\Delta Y(1 - mpc) = \Delta I, \qquad (6)$$

and dividing both sides by $(1 - mpc)$ yields

$$\Delta Y = \Delta I \times \frac{1}{1 - mpc} \qquad (7)$$

The term $1/(1 - mpc)$ is the **autonomous spending multiplier**. Since $mpc + mps = 1$, $mps = 1 - mpc$. Another way to write the autonomous spending multiplier is $1/mps$.

We have used investment to show how hikes in autonomous spending yield increases in income via the multiplier. Mathematically identical effects occur if autonomous consumption, government spending, or exports are raised. Economists often use **A** to stand for all forms of autonomous spending when writing formulas for multipliers. Thus, the following are all equivalent ways to write the autonomous spending multiplier:

$$\frac{\Delta Y}{\Delta A} = \frac{1}{1 - mpc} = \frac{1}{mps} \qquad (8)$$

If the marginal propensity to consume is 0.8, the autonomous spending multiplier will be 5, because $[1/(1 - 0.8) = 1/0.2 = 5]$. Calculate multipliers for alternative values for *mpc* (e.g., 9/10, 6/7, 5/6, 4/5, 3/4, 2/3, and 3/5). Observe what happens to multipliers as *mpc* rises and *mps* falls. Naturally, reversed multiplier effects follow cuts in autonomous spending. Some multipliers that are appropriate for government purchases and taxes are treated in the optional material in the following chapter.

CHAPTER

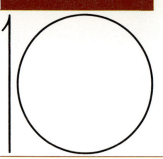

Government Taxing and Spending

Keynesian theory concludes that excessive unemployment may persist in a short-run macroeconomic equilibrium, but such stagnation is not inevitable. Appropriate fiscal policy is seen as a tool that can "fine-tune" Aggregate Expenditures to shield people from turbulent swings in their well-being.

> **Fiscal policy** *is the use of government spending and tax policies to stimulate or contract macroeconomic activity.*

Policymakers of the 1960s and 1970s relied heavily on Keynesian analysis to justify stimulative tax cuts and government spending programs.

Predictably, the Keynesian deemphasis of Aggregate Supply and the rejection of classical "laissez-faire" policies have not gone unchallenged. The *new classical macroeconomics* has rejuvenated classical analysis—in contrast to the "activist" role for government counseled by most Keynesians, it supports only a relatively passive governmental role in regulating Aggregate Demand. One line of attack on Keynesian policies arises from skepticism about the efficiency of big government and fear that government outlays may "crowd out" more valuable forms of private investment and consumption.

One wing of the "new classical" school, *supply-side economics*, is as much a political

agenda as it is a mode of economic analysis, and it was instrumental in engineering large tax cuts in the early 1980s. Supply-siders argued that high taxes may discourage productive effort so much that lower National Income would yield less tax revenue than if tax rates were lower.

Our initial task in this chapter is to add government activity to the simple Keynesian model of a private economy constructed in the previous chapter. Then we will examine how policymakers influenced by Keynesian models might adjust taxes and government spending to smooth cyclical swings in Aggregate Demand and, consequently, in output, income, and employment. Finally, we will examine some objections of new classical economists to this Keynesian approach, and the differences in policy recommendations that emerge from these competing schools of economic thought.

Fiscal Policy: The Demand Side

The Keynesian model of a private economy developed in the preceding chapter ignored government, a failure that we will now remedy.

> *The federal government operates a* **balanced budget** *when its tax revenues and outlays of funds are equal, a* **budget deficit** *when its*

outlays exceed revenues, and *a* **budget surplus** *if tax revenues exceed outlays.*

Changes in taxes and government outlays fall into two categories of policy: discretionary and automatic. We will initially consider how the federal government can use its discretion to enact new tax laws or to alter spending or transfer programs.

Discretionary fiscal policy *involves deliberate legislative changes in government outlays or taxes to alter Aggregate Demand (AD) and stabilize the economy.*

What is the Keynesian view of how fiscal policy affects planned Aggregate Expenditure? We begin by assuming, for simplicity, (*a*) that government spending (*G*) is autonomous and shifts neither the consumption nor investment schedules, (*b*) that investment (*I*) is also autonomous — at a constant level independent of income — and (*c*) that taxes (*T*) are also autonomous. These restrictive assumptions will be relaxed a bit after

you become more comfortable with our expanded model.

Discretionary Spending and Equilibrium

The numerical Keynesian model built in Chapter 9 is expanded to consider government in Table 1. These data are graphed in Figure 1. Without government, the private sector yields equilibrium spending and income of $3 trillion (point *a*). But this leaves a GNP gap of $250 billion if full employment income is $3.25 trillion. Keynesian analysis perceives any forces pushing the economy toward full employment as weak, so there is a recessionary gap of $50 billion that will not be remedied quickly through private action.

Note that, because the multiplier is 5, $50 billion in new autonomous spending will close the $250-billion GNP gap. One way to reach potential GNP would be to fill this recessionary gap through $50 billion in new government spending (column 8 in Table 1). When Aggregate Expenditure shifts from AE_0 to AE_1 in Figure 1 because government spending rises from zero to $50 bil-

Table 1 *Curing a Recessionary Gap with the Keynesian Remedy of Government Spending (Billions of Dollars)*

	Private Sector Only						Addition of Government Sector		
(1)	**(2)**	**(3)**	**(4)**	**(5)**	**(6)**	**(7)**	**(8)**	**(9)**	**(10)**
Employment (Millions)	**National Output**	**C**	**S**	**I**	**Aggregate Expenditures Without Government (AE_0)**	**Pressures on Income & Output**	**G**	**Aggregate Expenditures With Government (AE_1)**	**Pressures on Income & Output**
70	2,000	2,100	−100	100	2,200	Tendency	50	2,250	Tendency
75	2,250	2,300	−50	100	2,400	for	50	2,450	for
80	2,500	2,500	0	100	2,600	income to	50	2,650	income to
85	2,750	2,700	50	100	2,800	increase	50	2,850	increase
90	3,000	2,900	100	100	3,000	Equilibrium	50	3,050	
95	3,250	3,100	150	100	3,200		50	3,250	Full employment equilibrium
100	3,500	3,300	200	100	3,400	Tendency for income to decrease	50	3,450	Tendency for income to decrease
105	3,750	3,500	250	100	3,600		50	3,650	

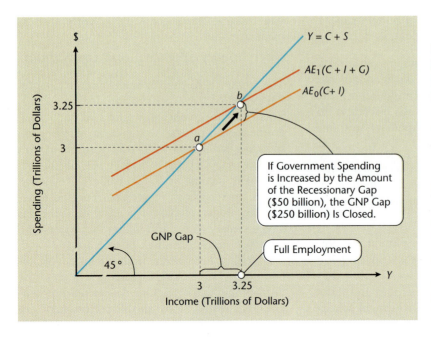

FIGURE 1 Using Fiscal Policy to Achieve Full-Employment Equilibrium Income

This figure graphically depicts the data in Table 1. Equilibrium without government spending is $3,000 billion (point *a*), and a GNP gap of $250 billion exists. The economy can be brought to full employment by government spending $50 billion. This increases Aggregate Spending from AE_0 ($C + I$) to AE_1 ($C + I + G$). The $50 billion in government spending is subject to the multiplier just as private autonomous spending is. Thus, the $50 billion times the multiplier (5 in this example) closes the GNP gap and moves the economy to full employment.

lion, equilibrium moves from point *a* to full employment at point *b*.

Also note that all autonomous spending, whether government or private, is "multiplied" in the same way. We originally described autonomous spending multipliers in terms of investment ($\Delta Y/\Delta I$), but all injections and withdrawals are subject to the multiplier principle. Government spending is merely a form of injection, so, dollar for dollar, it is as powerful as new investment in increasing Aggregate Expenditure. For example, a new federal contract generates new income for the contractors and their employees. Some of their new income is saved, but most will be spent. This spending in turn becomes new income for those from whom they buy, which is then spent or saved. And so on.[1]

The effect of a hike in government purchases can be described in a manner parallel to the planned saving = investment approach outlined in the previous chapter. Saving and taxes are both withdrawals, while investment and government purchases are both injections. *Planned injections must equal planned withdrawals at equilibrium.*[2]

Figure 2 illustrates the planned-injections-equal-planned-withdrawals approach, which parallels the savings-equals-investment approach we developed when only private spending was considered. Households would save $150 billion if income were $3.25 trillion. The introduction of $50 billion in new government spending boosts total injections ($I + G$) to $150 billion. Planned saving ($100 billion in planned withdrawals) at the initial equilibrium of $3 trillion is less than planned investment and government spending ($150 billion in planned injections), so output will rise until injections equal withdrawals. Equilibrium is reached only when output has risen to $3.25 trillion.

---

1. You may wonder how the government can spend more without raising taxes. One possibility is for the government to borrow the money by selling Treasury bonds. Alternatively, the budget deficit can be financed by printing more money. The ability to print money certainly distinguishes the federal government from the rest of us. (We address the specific mechanisms used by the Federal Reserve System (FED) in Chapter 12. The FED is the arm of government empowered to print and regulate money. The process of printing money to cover a deficit is a bit more complex than we suggest here.)

2. Algebraically, since $C + I + G = C + S + T = Y$ in equilibrium, then $I + G = S + T$ is an equilibrium condition.

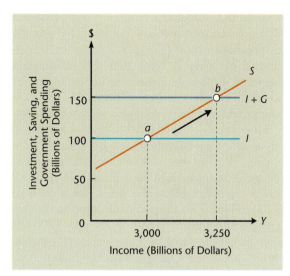

FIGURE 2 Injections-Equals-Withdrawals Approach to Equilibrium $(I = G = S + T)$

This figure examines the effect of an increase in government spending on equilibrium income using the injections-equals-withdrawals approach. Without government, the private economy will reach equilibrium at $3,000 billion (point a). Introducing $50 billion in government spending into the system increases income by $250 billion, so the economy moves to equilibrium at $3,250 (point b). Total injections $(I + G)$ are $150 billion and are equal to total withdrawals $(S + T)$ at the new equilibrium. Note that in this example, since $T = 0$, $S = I + G$.

Taxes and Equilibrium

We now know how raising government spending affects equilibrium. Introducing taxes (T) into our model will move us another step closer to reality. The autonomous tax multiplier can be expressed much like the autonomous expenditures multiplier.

> The **autonomous tax multiplier** *is the proportional change in income caused by a given change in autonomous taxes, and is written as* $\Delta Y / \Delta T$.

Taxes, like saving, are withdrawals that pull down spending and income. Thus, the autonomous tax multiplier is a *negative* number.

Suppose that people started spending their income almost as soon as they received it. Table 2 reflects this change in behavior by showing planned consumption (column 3) at $250 billion higher and planned saving at $250 billion lower (column 4) for each income level than in Table 1.

Private sector activity yields an equilibrium (where column 2 equals column 6) of $4.25 trillion in income, so Aggregate Spending is $1 tril-

Table 2 *Curing an Inflationary Gap with Taxes (Billions of Dollars)*

(1) Employment (Millions)	(2) National Output & Income (Y)	(3) C	(4) S	(5) I	(6) Spending Without Taxes (C + I)	(7) T	(8) Y_d	(9) C_t	(10) S_t	(11) Aggregate Spending $(C_t + I)$	(12) Net Pressure on Output
90	$3,000	3,150	−150	100	3,250	250	2,750	2,950	−200	3,050	Tendency for income to rise
95	3,250	3,350	−100	100	3,450	250	3,000	3,150	−150	3,250	0
100	3,500	3,550	−50	100	3,650	250	3,250	3,350	−100	3,450	Tendency for income to fall
105	3,750	3,750	0	100	3,850	250	3,500	3,550	−50	3,650	
110	4,000	3,950	50	100	4,050	250	3,750	3,750	0	3,850	
115	4,250*	4,150	100	100	4,250*	250	4,000	3,950	50	4,050	
120	4,500	4,350	150	100	4,450	250	4,250	4,150	100	4,250	

*Note: Equilibrium without taxes equals 4,250 $(Y = C + I = 4,150 + 100 = 4,250)$.

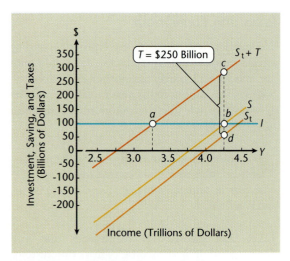

FIGURE 3 Eliminating Inflationary Pressure with Taxes (Injections = Withdrawals Approach)

This figure introduces taxes into the simple Keynesian model but ignores government spending in the interest of simplicity. The model assumes that taxes only affect spending behavior, not productive effort. Taxes reduce saving by the *mps* times autonomous taxes, or 0.2 ($250 billion), for a total reduction of $50 billion in autonomous saving. However, total net withdrawals increase by $200 billion at each income level: $\Delta S + \Delta T = -\$50$ billion + $250 billion. Thus, through the multiplier process, income is reduced from $4,250 billion to $3,250 billion, so inflationary pressure is diminished by tax withdrawals. The tax multiplier $\Delta Y / \Delta T$ is -4 in this case ($-\$1,000$ billion/$\$250$ billion $= -4$).

lion too high for price-level stability and the $3.25 trillion level of full employment output. This negative GNP gap of $1 trillion ($3.25 trillion − $4.25 trillion) combines with the autonomous spending multiplier of 5 (*mpc* = 0.8) to yield an inflationary gap of $200 billion, which means that autonomous spending is $200 billion too high. Alternatively, autonomous saving is $200 billion too low (distance *bc* in Figure 3). This model lacks government spending, so boosting tax withdrawals is the only way government can reduce Aggregate Expenditures.

Suppose autonomous taxes of $250 billion are now imposed (column 7). How will this $250 billion in taxes affect Aggregate Spending? Consumer decisions about spending depend on disposable income (Y_d) instead of Aggregate Income (Y) because households alone ultimately

bear all tax burdens. Subtracting taxes (column 7) from National Income (column 2) yields the disposable income ($Y - T = Y_d$) shown in column 8 of Table 2. Note that this relationship between disposable income and consumption is identical to the one between income and consumption from Table 1, when we ignored taxes.

How much of this $250 billion in taxes will come from consumption and how much from saving? With an *mpc* of 80 percent and an *mps* of 20 percent, consumption will initially fall 0.8 times the $250 billion in taxes, for a total of $200 billion. This shifts consumption in the Aggregate Expenditure schedule down by $200 billion for every level of gross (pretax) income, while the saving schedule falls $50 billion at all income levels.

The new saving curve S_t (saving after taxes are imposed) is exactly $50 billion lower (measured on the vertical axis) than the original saving curve S in Figure 3. (Remember, a drop in saving is shown as a shift of the saving curve to the right because consumers will now save less at each income level.) Let's look at this using the injections-equal-withdrawals approach.

Withdrawals in the form of after-tax saving are now shown as S_t. Taxes of $250 billion are also withdrawn from the economy. Consequently, total withdrawals = $S_t + T$. This combined withdrawal function is $S_t + T$ in Figure 3 and is exactly $250 billion above S_t (distance *cd* in Figure 3); thus, it is $200 billion above the original S curve for each income level.

On the other side of the ledger, business investment of $100 billion is still the only injection in this economy. Equilibrium requires total leakages (another term for withdrawals) to equal total injections, so $S_t + T = I$ (point *a* in Figure 3). Equilibrium National Income (determined now by Aggregate Spending of $C_t + I$, where C_t reflects after-tax consumption) falls from $4.25 trillion to $3.25 trillion. The autonomous tax multiplier ($\Delta Y / \Delta T_a$) equals $-\$1,000/\$250$, so it is -4. In this example, inflationary expectations cause saving to be $-\$150$ billion in equilibrium; therefore, taxes (withdrawals) of $250 billion just offset investment injections ($100 billion) and dissaving ($150 billion) to keep this economy at full employment without inflation.

Table 3 *Round-by-Round Effects of $100 Billion Increases in Spending, Taxing, and the Balanced Budget (Billions of Dollars)*

Effect	(1) $100 Billion Extra Government Purchases	(2) $100 Billion Extra Autono- mous Taxation	(3) $100 Billion Extra Taxes and Purchases
Round 1: initial effect of change on income	$100	0	$100
Round 2: induced spending	80	$ −80	0
Round 3: induced spending	64	−64	0
Round 4: through all subsequent rounds	256	−256	0
TOTAL CHANGE	$500	$−400	$100
MULTIPLIER (*mpc* = .8)	5	−4	1

Note: Each $1 increase in government purchases creates $1 in new income in Round 1, but each $1 in new taxes does not influence first-round income. In Round 2, each $1 in new government purchases has caused the person whose income was increased to spend $0.80, but this is offset by the reduced spending of $0.80 caused by each $1 in new taxes. Moreover, the effects of the new spending and taxing offset each other in all subsequent rounds. Thus, only Round 1 spending has any net effect on income, and the balanced-budget multiplier equals one.

The Tax Multiplier In our example, the autonomous spending multiplier ($\Delta Y/\Delta A$, where A = the sum of all forms of autonomous spending) is 5, because the marginal propensity to consume is .8. Our calculations indicate that the autonomous tax multiplier ($\Delta Y/\Delta T_a$) is −4 in this case. Notice the relationship: one minus the autonomous spending multiplier equals the tax multiplier

$$1 - (1/mps) = \Delta Y/\Delta T_a; \ 1 - 5 = -4$$

The *autonomous tax multiplier* is the negative value of one less than the spending multiplier.[3] An example of why this is so is shown in Table 3.

Table 3 traces the effects on spending of $100 billion increases in government purchases and taxes, both individually and together, through a few rounds of transactions, assuming that the *mpc* = 0.8. In column 1, 80 percent of each extra dollar of income is spent and becomes someone else's income. Thus, a new injection of $100 billion in government spending (Round 1) means

that $80 billion in consumer spending is induced in the second round. The people whose incomes rise by this $80 billion then spend $64 billion, which becomes other people's extra income. And so on. The autonomous spending multiplier is 5, indicated at the bottom of column 1.

The effect that new autonomous taxes of $100 billion have on spending and income is shown in column 2 of Table 3. Note that in Round 1; this tax has no effect on gross (pretax) incomes — the $100-billion tax hike may be viewed by taxpayers as a cut in disposable income, but it does not initially reduce production or National Income. It is only when this decline in disposable income is translated into lower spending that National Income is reduced. Thus, new government purchases have an initial effect on Aggregate Spending in Round 1; new taxes do not. Subsequent rounds cancel, so the autonomous tax multiplier is a negative value equal to one minus the spending multiplier.

The Balanced-Budget Multiplier You may have noticed something startling in Table 3. Expanding both government spending (column 1) and autonomous taxes (column 2) by $100 billion causes equilibrium income to rise, on balance, by exactly $100 billion (end of column 3). Thus, the *balanced-budget multiplier* in a simple

---

3. A more general form of this simple tax multiplier is −*mpc/mps*. We know that *mpc* + *mps* = 1. Substituting this into part of 1 − (1/*mps*), we get 1 − [(*mpc* + *mps*)/*mps*]. Factoring, we have 1 − [(*mpc*/*mps*) + (*mps*/*mps*)], which simplifies to 1 − (*mpc*/*mps*) − 1, which equals (−*mpc*/*mps*).

Keynesian model is exactly one.[4] The conclusion is that equal increases (*decreases*) in government spending and taxes will raise (*lower*) equilibrium National Income by an identical amount. Table 3 should help you discern the fiscal mechanisms at work when either spending or taxing is changed. The autonomous spending and tax multipliers and the balanced-budget multiplier are described in more detail in the optional material at the end of this chapter.

Let us summarize the discretionary fiscal policies Keynesians prescribe to remedy specific economic ills. Inflationary pressures can be relieved through tax hikes, cuts in government purchases, or both. Both tax increases and government spending cuts will drive the government budget toward surplus (or reduce deficits) during inflationary periods. If excessive unemployment is the major problem, then tax cuts or increases in governmental purchases will temporarily move the budget into a deficit (or reduce a surplus) and cause expansions of output, income, and employment.

Automatic Stabilizers

Keynesians view budget deficits as the right medicine to cure a recession and surpluses as remedies for inflation. Most politicians enjoy granting the tax cuts and new spending projects Keynesians prescribe for recession — such measures are popular with voters. But tax hikes and slashed budgets to fight inflation are universally unpopular. New laws to create surpluses during inflation, fortunately, are not always necessary. Certain features of our tax system and some government spending programs automatically push budgets toward surpluses during inflationary periods and into deficits during cyclical downturns.

Discretionary variations in spending and taxes require congressional action, but they are not the only fiscal instruments available to help us achieve full employment and price-level stability. Keynesians count on several built-in mechanisms to dampen swings in Aggregate Spending and economic activity. Until now, we have unrealistically assumed that neither taxes nor government spending depend on income. The fact that both are sensitive to changes in National Income lends an automatic resilience to the economy.

> **Automatic stabilizers** *are tax structures and government spending programs that cause budget deficits to grow automatically during recessions, or surpluses to grow during periods of rapid expansion.*

Automatic stabilizers are sometimes called *nondiscretionary* fiscal policy because no overt government action is required.

Automatic Tax Adjustments

Personal and corporate income taxes are both closely tied to income. When prosperity boosts National Income, federal revenues from progressive corporate and personal income taxes rise more than proportionally. Corporate profit is the most sensitive of all incomes to swings in economic activity. A 10 percent decline in National Income might totally wipe out corporate profit, while 10 percent growth may cause aggregate profit to double or even triple, as illustrated in Figure 4. Thus, tax revenue from corporate income is highly cyclical.

Progressive personal income tax rates are the main reason why tax collections rise or fall proportionally faster than income. This process acts as an automatic stabilizer during inflationary episodes because as income rises, tax collections rise even faster, increasing the rate of withdrawal from the economy and dampening inflationary growth of nominal income. This effect is now partially offset because Congress indexed personal income tax *rates* to inflation beginning in 1985.[5] When a recession begins, tax revenues tumble even faster than gross income falls, swelling budget deficits.

---

4. A bit of math shows why the balanced-budget multiplier in this simple Keynesian model equals one: The spending multiplier $(1/mps)$ plus the tax multiplier $(-mpc/mps)$ equals $(1 - mpc)/mps$. Because $1 - mpc = mps$, the ratio $(1 - mpc)/mps$ equals 1.

5. The Tax Reform of 1986 also reduced the progressivity of income tax rates. This "flattening" of tax rates slightly reduced the automatic stabilizer aspects of our tax structure.

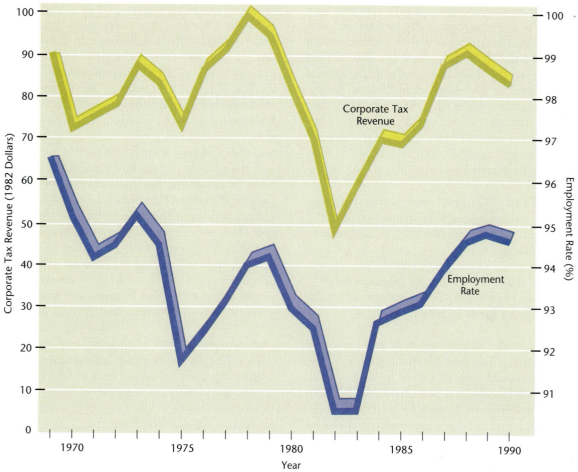

FIGURE 4   Corporate Tax Revenue and Employment

This figure illustrates the effect of automatic tax adjustments when unemployment increases or the economy enters a recession. A downturn in economic activity causes employment to fall, which causes corporate profits to decline (or their rates of growth to decline). As a result, corporate tax revenues decline substantially.

Source: *Economic Report of the President,* 1991.

Automatic Changes in Government Outlays

Transfer payments rise during recessions and bolster Aggregate Spending by keeping consumption up. More people are eligible for welfare payments during hard times. People retire earlier during recessions and later during booms. Consequently, Social Security payments help buffer the economy against both downturns and inflationary expansions. Unemployment compensation is another automatic stabilizer, because workers' incomes do not drop to zero when they are laid off. Consumption by unemployed workers' families would plummet during widespread layoffs without unemployment compensation, and economic downturns would be worse than they are. The Great Depression would probably have been much less severe had modern automatic stabilizers been in effect.

Falling tax collections and rising transfer payments during downturns help consumers maintain their customary spending levels. Facilitating the maintenance of consumption helps slow the momentum of declines in gross income. Just how powerful are our automatic stabilizers? Although inadequate to completely offset strong pressures for a recession, they do slow abrupt changes in the economy, giving policymakers more time to formulate discretionary policy. Some studies suggest that declines in income during recent recessions would have been from one-third to one-half more severe in the absence of automatic stabilizers. But automatic stabilizers may be a mixed blessing.

Fiscal Drag When potential income is growing rapidly, our built-in stabilizers may retard actual economic growth, a problem Keynesians refer to as fiscal drag.

> *Fiscal drag* occurs with any growth of GNP because rising income boosts tax revenue and may shrink needs for transfer programs.

Suppose all resources are fully employed and the budget is balanced. Technological advance, capital accumulation, and labor force growth all contribute to growth of potential GNP. Without bigger government outlays or lower tax rates, economic growth boosts tax revenues; a budget surplus may even emerge. This potential surplus hinders growth in disposable income and Aggregate Spending; withdrawals grow but injections do not. This may retard economic growth. Raising government spending or lowering tax rates may unshackle the economy. Both approaches are politically popular, so Congress quickly enacts Keynesian policies to counter potential recessions. A cynic has suggested that government deficits grow each year because of politicians' diligence in avoiding fiscal drag. Most of us can think of many areas where we would like more government spending, or where we would like our taxes cut.

Cyclical vs. Structural Deficits

To this point, we have treated budget surpluses or deficits as inconsequential in themselves, having importance only to the extent that they affect Aggregate Spending. A proposed constitutional amendment that the federal budget be balanced annually receives a lot of popular support, but embedded in this appealing notion are some serious pitfalls. Imbalance in the federal budget may be more a symptom of economic distress than a result of discretionary policy. As we just discussed, automatic stabilizers could create budgetary surpluses if unsustainable and inflationary growth mushroomed. Conversely, deficits swell during recessions because tax revenues fall and government outlays rise.

If the economy slides into a recession, should taxes be raised and government spending cut to balance the budget? If inflation looms, should we cut taxes or raise spending to balance the budget? The government deficit or surplus is affected by the level of GNP as well as by discretionary fiscal policy, so we cannot judge the appropriateness of policy merely by observing an actual deficit or surplus. Economists now differentiate between structural and cyclical deficits.

> A **structural deficit** is an estimate of the budget deficit (or surplus) that current tax and spending structures would have yielded if the economy were at full employment.

Structural deficits were termed "full-employment budget deficits (or surpluses)" in the 1960s. If the economy is well below full employment, estimating the structural deficit entails adding the extra tax revenues that would be collected if the economy moved to full employment and then subtracting the current outlays on unemployment benefits and other transfer payments caused by cyclical unemployment.

> A **cyclical deficit** occurs when falling income during a recession shrinks tax revenues and causes expanded transfer payments.

As economic conditions deteriorate, the cyclical budget deficit worsens and vice versa.

Government transfer payments can be treated as negative taxes (*negative* because the government pays people), which decline in importance as National Income rises. Figure 5 illustrates various possible relationships between **net taxes** (tax revenues minus transfer payments) and government purchases under three alternative tax structures. Notice that the tax functions are all

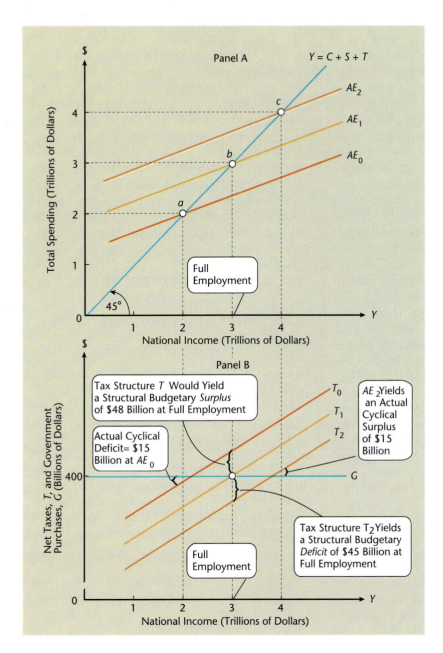

FIGURE 5 The Structural Deficit and the Cyclical Deficit

The structural deficit is the deficit that would exist at a full employment given the existing mix of government spending and tax rate structures. The cyclical deficit grows when economic circumstances prevent full employment. This figure illustrates the relationship between net taxes (taxes minus transfer payments) and government spending for three alternative tax structures. Tax structure T_0 is associated with Aggregate Expenditures AE_0, and a structural surplus prevents full employment, but at the equilibrium income of $2 trillion, the spending/tax structure results in a cyclical deficit of $15 billion. Budget–tax combinations T_2 and G are associated with Aggregate Spending of AE_2 and represent a considerably more expansionary budgetary mix. At full employment, this latter budget–tax mix would result in a structural deficit of $45 billion. Tax schedule T_1 is associated with Aggregate Expenditures AE_1 and yields a balanced budget at full employment, with a structural deficit of zero.

positively sloped; net taxes rise as income rises. We will assume that the noninflationary full employment level of income is $3 trillion and that government purchases of goods and services (G) are independent of income.

Very high tax rates may restrict Aggregate Spending to levels inadequate for full employment. This is the case with tax structure T_0 and Aggregate Expenditure AE_0, which together yield equilibrium at point *a* in Panel A of Figure

5. Because tax rates are high, the structural deficit is actually in surplus to the tune of $45 billion; however, the cyclical deficit at equilibrium ($2 trillion income) is $15 billion in this example. Thus, an excessive "structural surplus" can partially cause a cyclical deficit.

Contrast this with the budgetary mix of G and tax structure T_2. Simultaneous inflationary pressures and cyclical budgetary surpluses coexist if Aggregate Spending is AE_2 and the tax schedule is T_2; there is equilibrium at point c, with a realized budgetary surplus of $15 billion. This budget combination yields a structural deficit of $45 billion at full employment (ignoring inflationary pressure). This structural deficit is considerably more expansionary than that represented by G and T_0. Finally, a combination that yields a structurally balanced budget is represented by the tax schedule T_1, which yields Aggregate Expenditure AE_1. Cyclical deficits result below full employment, while surpluses are generated above full employment.

Suppose Aggregate Spending is excessive because of low tax rates. If the Aggregate Expenditure curve is AE_2 and the tax curve is T_2, there is a substantial cyclical budget surplus. If we follow a rule of perpetually balancing the budget, we would cut taxes and raise spending. This bad policy is certain to accelerate any inflationary tendencies. Fiscal policy of either raising tax rates or cutting spending can cure inflation by dampening Aggregate Spending while enlarging any current budget surplus.

During inflation, however, many voters react harshly to any proposal that "the cost of government, in addition to other prices, should be raised." On the other hand, the beneficiaries of public programs, including those whose livelihoods depend on government contracts, vigorously fight budget cuts because they perceive inflation as shrinking their real income. In fact, political opposition to spending cuts or tax hikes is now so intense that we need not worry about simultaneous inflation and actual surpluses.

The reverse situation is a budget structure yielding a structural surplus but a cyclical deficit, because tax rates are so high that the economy is stuck well below full employment; fiscal drag is quite powerful. Some analysts have suggested that the sluggish American economy of the late 1950s and the early 1980s suffered from this malady.

The critical point is that huge cyclical deficits do not imply a very expansionary tilt to fiscal policy, nor are large cyclical surpluses evidence of contractionary policies. The mounting federal deficits of the 1980s and 1990s were a mix of cyclical deficits, caused by high unemployment that subsided only slowly after peaking during the 1981–1983 recession, and huge structural deficits, instigated in part by large tax cuts and in part by the unrelenting growth of government outlays over the past decade. Recent estimates place the structural deficit at nearly two-thirds of the actual deficit and growing.[6]

In summary, the actual deficit is determined by the fiscal policy mix of the federal government and the state of the economy. Expansionary fiscal policy creates structural deficits, and depressed economic conditions create cyclical deficits.[7] Deficits may arise because high tax rates produce a sick economy. Congress can only set tax *rates;* it cannot dictate the resulting tax *revenues*.

Classical Economics and Fiscal Policy

Traditional classical economics leads to policies that (*a*) minimize government's economic role, and (*b*) balance the government budget. Requiring higher tax revenues to cover higher outlays is seen as a curb on politicians' impulses to spend. Keynesian analysis recognizes fiscal drag and the possibility that high tax rates may stifle an economy by reducing disposable income and spending. The "supply-side" branch of new classical economics points to another way high tax rates may be harmful.

The Laffer Curve

An advisor to an early Egyptian pharaoh is credited with observing that very high tax rates may result in severe disincentives against work effort and investment, causing actual tax revenues to

---

6. William Beeman, Jacob Dreyer, and Paul Van de Water, "Dimensions of the Deficit Problem," in Philip Cagan (ed.), *Essays in Contemporary Economic Problems, 1985: The Economy in Deficit* (Washington, D.C.: American Enterprise Institute, 1985).

7. The rising structural deficit of the 1970s and 1980s was not totally independent of changing economic conditions. Beeman et al. suggest that the reduced rate of productivity growth in the last two decades has added to rising structural deficits.

fall. Arthur Laffer, a celebrated supply-sider, explained this concept to a journalist after dinner at a Washington, D.C. restaurant, illustrating his point by sketching on a napkin what is now known as the Laffer curve.

> The **Laffer curve** *suggests that very low tax rates might be raised to generate higher tax revenues, but continually raising tax rates will eventually cause a heavily tax-burdened population to decide that the extra effort necessary to generate extra taxable income is not worth it, so tax revenue will fall.*

If Uncle Sam's bite is too fierce, many taxpayers will choose leisure over additional work and will consume immediately from income instead of saving and investing. Tax evasion may divert some productive activity into the underground economy. A modified Laffer curve is shown in Figure 6.

Supply-siders argue that high tax rates erode incentives to work and to invest, so that income shrinks as tax rates climb. This means that given tax revenues might be generated by both a high tax rate and a low one. In Figure 6, marginal tax rates (the percentage taxes paid on small amounts of extra income) that average either 15 percent or 75 percent yield tax revenues of $100 billion, while a marginal tax rate that averages X percent yields $200 billion to the tax collector. Any increase in marginal tax rates over X percent actually causes tax collections to fall.

What will people do if high marginal income tax rates reduce the advantages of working and of saving to invest? Economists of a classical bent, including supply-siders, typically treat saving and investing as almost synonymous. Keynes disagreed, arguing that in a modern monetary economy, savers and investors are very distinct groups with very different motives. Savers seek security, while investors bear risks and seek profits. As a result, saving may not necessarily be invested.

Potential workers may respond to high tax rates by engaging in many more nonmarket activities, such as do-it-yourself projects. Potential savers and investors will realize less interest income and profit if marginal tax rates are high;

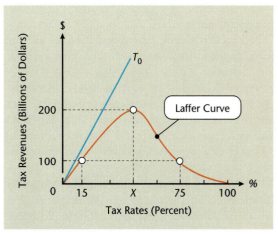

FIGURE 6   The Laffer Curve

If the tax base were unaffected by the tax rate, tax revenues would be exactly proportional to tax rates and could be graphed as a straight line, such as T_0. Declines in the tax base that result when people legally avoid taxed behavior or illegally evade taxes cause the base to erode, so tax revenues actually reach a peak and then decline.

therefore, they will consume more currently, forgoing future consumption. Evidence of this sort of behavior was provided when wealthy people in Britain went on shopping sprees in the 1970s, buying fur coats and Rolls-Royces. Investing was not worth while because of high inflation and high British tax rates on investment income. The British economy stagnated during the 1960s and 1970s, while areas of London where high society gathered abounded with conspicuous consumption of luxury goods.

Some economists believe the United States has been in the outer region of the Laffer curve and advocate reductions in taxes to eliminate major impediments to work effort and investment. They believe reduced tax rates will simultaneously stimulate economic growth and generate higher tax revenues. This idea picked up a lot of converts in the past two decades, including Ronald Reagan. Congress enacted a 5 percent tax cut in 1981, an additional 10 percent cut in 1982, and another 10 percent cut in 1983. Between 1980 and 1991, federal revenues rose over 115 percent, but government outlays grew 145 percent, resulting in record budget deficits. Massive deficits mounted, in part, because Congress and the Reagan and Bush Administrations were either unwilling or unable to reduce the growth of federal outlays.[8]

Notice that Keynesians may accept the general form of the Laffer curve while perceiving different behavior as its basic cause. New classical economists (including supply-siders) blame declines in tax revenues as tax rates rise on reduced incentives to supply goods and services. Keynesians perceive high tax rates and fiscal drag as smothering Aggregate Spending. Admitting that high tax rates also inhibit supply incentives, Keynesians still perceive most macroeconomic problems as originating from the demand side, while supply-siders see high-tax-rate disincentives as more powerful on the supply side.

Government Purchases and Transfers: A New Classical View

Keynesians view government purchases as direct sources of Aggregate Spending, and transfer payments as quickly translated by recipients into new consumer spending. Advocates of the new classical economics, especially supply-siders, sense that this focus on demand is shortsighted and worry about the incentive effects of government programs. Their reasoning goes like this: Modern government provides school lunch programs, public parks and highways, medical care for the poor and the aged, subsidized housing and transportation, and a host of other goods. There is less incentive to sacrifice our time by working and less net gain from investing if the government guarantees us a reasonably comfortable life by providing many necessities.

Transfer payments are viewed as a problem for two reasons. First, incentives to work and invest are reduced for those who work and invest, and who then pay taxes that government channels to welfare recipients. Second, those who receive transfer payments also suffer disincentives against work or saving. (Would you work as hard if you were forced to give your neighbors 20 percent of your income? Would your neighbors?) According to some new classical economists, extensive government purchases and transfer payments trap low-income individuals in a rut from which escape is almost impossible; they are discouraged from work effort and from trying to improve their economic status.

In conclusion, fiscal policy from the vantage point of new classical economics focuses on steady economic policies that permit markets to make long-run adjustments, and views high tax rates and massive government spending as embodying disincentives that dampen Aggregate Supply. Keynesians, in contrast, focus on curing short-run problems and see activist fiscal policy as being needed to augment Aggregate Demand. Specific differences between these schools of thought are summarized in Figure 7.

Fiscal Policy in Action

For almost half a century, changes in tax rates and spending by government have been viewed by Keynesians as cures for macroeconomic problems. The conventional wisdom before the Keynesian Revolution was that taxation and spending should be adjusted to balance the actual budget at all times. Then the economy would automatically adjust to a noninflationary full employment equilibrium. A problem with putting this idea into practice is that higher tax rates may yield lower tax revenues, and vice versa, because of the influence of tax rates on our major tax base — income. Failure to understand this led President Hoover and the Congress to raise tax rates in 1932, exacerbating the economic collapse of 1929–1933. The success of fiscal policy in the 1960s also hinged on this relationship between tax rates and tax revenues.

The Tax Increase of 1932

Keynesians and modern supply-siders agree that a fetish for balancing the budget was one reason why the economy, following what should have been a minor recession in 1929, continued tumbling downward until 1933. Their explanation

---

8. In *The Triumph of Politics: Why the Reagan Revolution Failed* (New York: Harper & Row, 1986), former Budget Director David Stockman documents political reluctance to slash any government spending programs. Even politicians who constantly attack ''big government'' appear to fear the backlash from voters whose pet programs are cut.

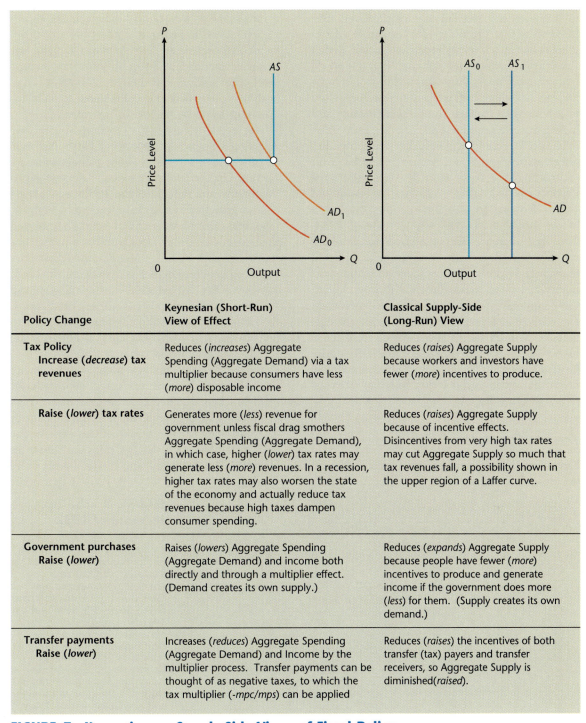

Policy Change	Keynesian (Short-Run) View of Effect	Classical Supply-Side (Long-Run) View
Tax Policy **Increase** (*decrease*) **tax revenues**	Reduces (*increases*) Aggregate Spending (Aggregate Demand) via a tax multiplier because consumers have less (*more*) disposable income	Reduces (*raises*) Aggregate Supply because workers and investors have fewer (*more*) incentives to produce.
Raise (*lower*) **tax rates**	Generates more (*less*) revenue for government unless fiscal drag smothers Aggregate Spending (Aggregate Demand), in which case, higher (*lower*) tax rates may generate less (*more*) revenues. In a recession, higher tax rates may also worsen the state of the economy and actually reduce tax revenues because high taxes dampen consumer spending.	Reduces (*raises*) Aggregate Supply because of incentive effects. Disincentives from very high tax rates may cut Aggregate Supply so much that tax revenues fall, a possibility shown in the upper region of a Laffer curve.
Government purchases **Raise** (*lower*)	Raises (*lowers*) Aggregate Spending (Aggregate Demand) and income both directly and through a multiplier effect. (Demand creates its own supply.)	Reduces (*expands*) Aggregate Supply because people have fewer (*more*) incentives to produce and generate income if the government does more (*less*) for them. (Supply creates its own demand.)
Transfer payments **Raise** (*lower*)	Increases (*reduces*) Aggregate Spending (Aggregate Demand) and Income by the multiplier process. Transfer payments can be thought of as negative taxes, to which the tax multiplier (-*mpc/mps*) can be applied	Reduces (*raises*) the incentives of both transfer (tax) payers and transfer receivers, so Aggregate Supply is diminished(*raised*).

FIGURE 7 Keynesian vs. Supply-Side Views of Fiscal Policy

for the intensity and duration of the Great Depression is that President Hoover and the Congress reacted to a minor recession-caused deficit (like the $15 billion for AE_0 and T_0 in Figure 5) by raising tax rates. This caused National Income and tax revenues to fall further, which resulted in attempts to balance the budget through still higher tax rates, and so on.

Figure 8 presents the actual relationships between expenditures and net tax revenues (after subtracting transfers) to real Gross National Product for 1929–1933. We have superimposed curves showing government spending and taxes before and after the tax rate increase of 1932. This tax increase was designed to generate roughly one-third more revenue in fiscal 1932 than in 1931. Policymakers failed to realize that higher tax rates could force GNP down. (Real GNP quickly fell by roughly 20 percent.) Keynesians interpret Figure 8 as evidence that massive withdrawals of funds arising from these higher tax rates led to much of the severity of the Great Depression. Some supply-siders see this as proof that, even in the 1930s, high tax rates stifled Aggregate Supply.

The Tax Cut of 1964–1965

Keynesians recommend tax rate cuts or increased government purchases when a recession causes even a slight cyclical budget deficit. In the example illustrated in Figure 5, cutting tax rates from T_0 to T_1 raises Aggregate Spending to AE_1, tax revenues increase to $400 billion at an income level of $3 trillion, and the federal budget is balanced. Notice that tax collections actually increase in response to cuts in tax rates.

The idea that cutting tax rates might stimulate Aggregate Spending and boost both National Income and tax revenues first gained wide acceptance in the 1960s. President Kennedy's economic advisors perceived the 1950s as a period of slow growth and stagnation caused by high tax rates that created severe fiscal drag. They argued that major cuts in tax rates would stimulate substantial growth, reduce unemployment and poverty, and generate higher tax revenues. In 1964, a massive tax cut enacted during the Johnson Administration supported these predictions. Keynesian (demand-side) reasoning was used to politically "sell" these tax cuts, although some supply-side arguments were also used.

The 1964–1965 tax law broadly reduced tax rates. Personal income tax rates were reduced from brackets of 18–91 percent to 14–70 percent. Taxes on corporate income were cut from 52 to 48 percent. The results of this experiment with broad-based cuts in tax rates are shown in Figure 9. The economy, and hence the tax base, expanded so rapidly that the 1964 deficit actu-

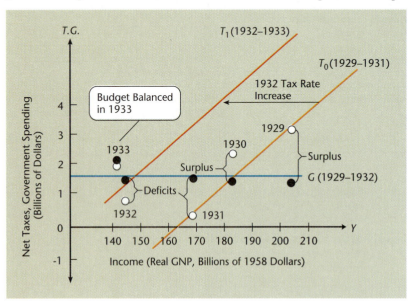

FIGURE 8 The Tax Increase of 1932

This figure (adjusted to 1982–84 dollars) uses Keynesian analysis to examine the effects of tax increases in 1932. Actual government purchases and net taxes (taxes minus transfers) are traced graphically from 1929 to 1933. A modest deficit in 1931 persuaded Congress and President Hoover to increase tax rates in 1932 in an attempt to balance the budget. Unfortunately, the result was a shift in the net tax function to the left and a reduction in equilibrium income. It was small comfort that by 1933 the budget was balanced. (*Note:* ● denotes government purchases of goods and services; ○ denotes taxes minus transfer payments.) Source: *Economic Report of the President*, 1980–1991.

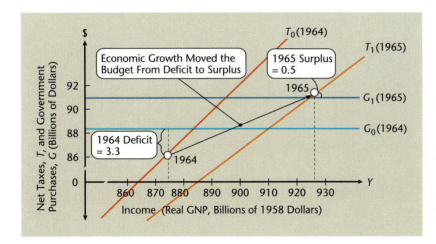

FIGURE 9 The 1964–1965 Tax Cut

In 1964–1965, tax rates were cut substantially, shifting the net tax schedule from T_0 to T_1. Income, employment, and tax revenues rose, converting a deficit in 1964 into a small surplus in 1965.

Source: *Economic Report of the President*, 1991.

ally gave way to a small surplus in 1965. Supply-siders naturally interpret this success as evidence that the economy was on the wrong side of the Laffer curve, and that tax revenue was stimulated as Aggregate Supply grew.

These examples provide evidence that putting fiscal policy to work is more complex than our simple theory suggests. Whether changes in tax rates will reduce budget deficits often depends on the state of the economy and the initial level of tax rates. The Kennedy-Johnson round of tax cuts suggests that if the economy is poised for growth, tax cuts may simultaneously stimulate growth and reduce deficits. Another possibility is that cuts in tax rates may stimulate economic growth, but budget deficits may skyrocket, as President Reagan discovered in the 1980s.

Budget Deficits in the 1980s and 1990s

The American economy followed a rocky path through the 1970s, with budget deficits at new record levels almost each year. (Our most recent budget surplus was experienced in fiscal year 1968–1969.) By the late 1970s, discomfort with the growth of federal spending had reached epidemic levels. President Reagan and the Congress tried numerous measures to reduce government's impact on the economy. It proved, however, far harder for Congress to restrain spending

growth than to restrain revenue growth.[9] The result has been annual deficits that have exploded from the $120 billion range in the early 1980s to over $350 billion by fiscal year 1991.

In the late 1970s, the supply-side wing of new classical macroeconomics gained the attention of several prominent politicians who blamed Keynesian fiscal policies for rising deficits, rapid inflation, and high unemployment. President Reagan sought, and the Congress passed, a 25 percent tax cut in 1981, phased in over three years. At the same time, eligibility for transfer payments was tightened, and nonmilitary government spending was slowed sharply. Advocates of these policies hoped to stimulate Aggregate Supply so much that inflation and unemployment would fall quickly. They also hoped that tax revenues would be so responsive to economic growth that budget deficits would abate.

This approach, illustrated in Figure 10, yielded income far below the optimistic predictions that had accompanied adoption of supply-side policies. Restrictive monetary policy during 1981–1983 began to reduce inflation sharply, but unemployment rose and the economy only slowly recovered from the severe Recession of 1981–1983. Annual federal budget deficits seemed

---

9. Robert Eisner and Paul J. Pieper, "A New View of the Federal Debt and Budget Deficits," *American Economic Review*, March 1984, pp. 11–29, and testimony before the Joint Economic Committee of Congress on January 16, 1986.

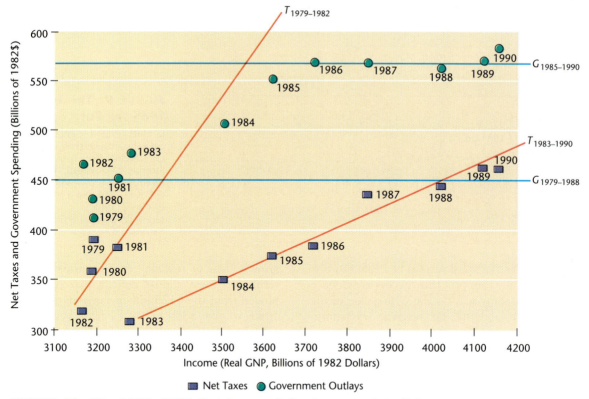

FIGURE 10 The 1981–1983 Tax Cuts and the Structural Deficit

Former President Reagan sought and received tax rate reductions between 1981 and 1983 that appear to have increased the structural deficit. Increased government spending, coupled with a flatter net tax function ($T_{1983-90}$), quickly yielded swollen deficits. Tax reform in 1986 flattened the progressivity of income taxes, but it was "revenue neutral" and so was not intended to cure persistent huge deficits, which are projected to continue through the 1990s. (*Note:* ● denotes government purchases with goods and services; ■ denotes taxes minus transfer payments.)

Source: *Economic Report of the President*, 1991.

stuck above the $200 billion mark. Figure 10 suggests that the 1981–1983 tax cuts increased the structural deficit by shifting the net tax function downward and to the right.

The Deficit Reduction Plan of 1990

Despite campaign promises of "No new tax," in 1990 President Bush succumbed to political pressure to raise taxes in an attempt to reduce federal budget deficits. The 1990 tax plan was designed to reduce cumulative federal deficits by $500 billion by 1995. Higher federal taxes were levied on income, gasoline, cigarettes, alcoholic beverages, luxury goods, and airline tickets. This 1990 attempt to raise tax revenues by increasing tax rates signified an abandonment of the

supply-side tax policies of the 1980s. Nevertheless, the federal deficit for 1991 rose to roughly $350 billion (in part because of military spending to remove Iraq from Kuwait) — about $1,400 in new federal debt for every American was piled up in just one year. And the 1992 deficit was projected to be even larger. Potential problems posed by huge deficits and growing national debt are treated in more depth in Chapter 14.

This chapter has examined government spending and tax policies from both Keynesian and classical (supply-side) perspectives. We have seen that government spending and tax policies can influence unemployment, inflation, and rates of economic growth. Our task in the next part of this book is to examine the macroeconomic role of monetary policy.

Chapter Review: Key Points

1. *Keynesian fiscal policy* is the use of federal spending and tax policies to stimulate or contract Aggregate Spending and economic activity to offset cyclical fluctuations. *Classical (supply-side) fiscal policies* rely on low tax rates and minimal government spending to allow Aggregate Supply to grow.

2. *Discretionary fiscal policy* consists of deliberate changes in federal government spending and taxation for stabilization purposes. Without congressional action, *automatic stabilizers* such as corporate and personal income taxes and various transfer programs cause changes in spending and taxation as economic conditions change.

3. Increases in *government spending* increase Aggregate Expenditure and National Income through the multiplier process in the same way as changes in investment or autonomous consumer spending.

4. Changes in *net tax revenues* (tax revenues minus transfer payments) affect Aggregate Spending differently than changes in government spending do. Changes in net taxes directly affect disposable income and, therefore, saving. These effects are transmitted into spending through the *autonomous tax multiplier* $[\Delta Y/\Delta T = 1 - (1/mps)]$, which is weaker than the spending multiplier.

5. In a Keynesian depression, the *balanced-budget multiplier* equals one, suggesting that equal increases (*decreases*) in government spending and taxes will increase (*decrease*) Aggregate Spending and equilibrium income by an equal amount. This result follows from the fact that the autonomous tax multiplier is one minus the autonomous spending multiplier.

6. *Automatic stabilizers* tend to cushion the economy. When income falls, automatic stabilizers keep the level of disposable income from falling as rapidly as income does. Our progressive income tax causes tax collections to fall proportionally faster when income is falling and to increase proportionally faster when income is rising.

7. Built-in stabilizers can pose the problem of *fiscal drag*. When potential income is rising, automatic stabilizers brake the economy and slow the rate of growth.

8. The *structural deficit* is an estimate of the deficit that would be generated at full employment under existing tax and expenditure structures. This is a way to estimate the expansionary or contractionary influence of any tax and expenditure mix.

9. The *cyclical deficit* is attributable to business conditions. As unemployment grows, the cyclical deficit grows, and vice versa.

10. The *Laffer curve* indicates that high tax rates may impose such large disincentives to productive effort that Aggregate Supply and tax revenues are both restricted.

Key Concepts

Ensure that you can define these terms before proceeding.

Keynesian fiscal policy

autonomous tax multiplier

balanced-budget multiplier

automatic stabilizers

fiscal drag

structural versus cyclical deficit

new classical economics

supply-side fiscal policy

Problems and Questions

We know that multipliers are difficult. We also know that economics students are often tested extensively on autonomous spending and tax multipliers and equilibrium income.

1. Calculate the autonomous spending multiplier, the autonomous tax multiplier, and the balanced-budget multiplier for values of the *mpc* equal to 1/2, 3/5, 2/3, 3/4, 4/5, 5/6, 6/7, 7/8, 8/9, and 9/10.

2. Compute National Income with these different values of multipliers when taxes equal $100 billion, government spending equals $200 billion, investment spending equals $150 billion, and autonomous consumption equals $400 billion. Now try other values for each of these autonomous components of Aggregate Spending. Work examples until you get these sorts of calculations down pat. Be sure you understand the meaning of these computations for determination of equilibrium National Income.

3. Do you think cuts in tax rates stimulate Aggregate Supply more than they do Aggregate Spending? Why or why not? Why is the answer to this question important in explaining what will happen to the price level?

4. Suppose that the most revenue that can be generated from taxes on income is $1 trillion. Draw a Laffer curve indicating the amounts of tax revenues that would be generated by marginal income tax rates of 0 percent, 100 percent, and the X percentage rate that you think would be most likely to generate the $1 trillion maximum. What tax rate did you select for X?

5–8. Suppose government spending is $1 trillion regardless of the state of the economy, that potential GNP is $8 trillion, and that net taxes are positively related to income.

5. Draw sets of functions for Aggregate Expenditures, government spending, and net taxes that yield cyclical deficits but structural surpluses.

6. Draw sets of functions for Aggregate Expenditures, government spending, and net taxes that yield structural deficits but cyclical surpluses.

7. Now draw a set of functions to portray the 1980s and 1990s, when the economy experienced both structural and cyclical deficits.

8. Show how a tax reform that reduced the progressivity of income tax rates might yield the same expected structural deficit as before the reform, and explain why this might make it more difficult to eliminate a persistent cyclical deficit.

9. Professional football teams sometimes trade their future draft choices for veteran players. In what sense is this like government financing current purchases through deficits? What are the crucial differences, if any, between the two situations in terms of future production?

10. Explain the sense in which federal taxes determine how much each of us will help control inflation. If you could print money, would you ever try to remove any from circulation as long as there were trees and green ink? Why? Then why does the federal government bother to collect taxes?

11. What are the similarities and differences between taxes and savings? Are these differences important for the purposes of determining National Income? Why or why not?

12. The Kemp-Roth Bill cut federal income tax rates by 25 percent in stages over the three years following its enactment in 1981. What happened to budget deficits over this period? By roughly what percentage would National Income need to have grown in order to have generated more revenues than would have occurred without the tax cut? Do you think it likely that National Income would ever grow at such a rate?

Optional Material: More Mathematics of Keynesian Multipliers

In our simple model of fiscal policy and equilibrium income, equal increases in government spending or cuts in taxes will have different effects on National Income and employment. Let us briefly review tax multipliers, balanced-budget multipliers, and autonomous spending multipliers. Then you will have a better perspective when you try to understand what the president and Congress are trying to do the next time a policy change is under consideration. You may benefit from trying to graph some of the discussion that follows.

The Autonomous Spending and Tax Multipliers

A recessionary gap can be erased (or an inflationary gap might be created) through increased autonomous spending. This will occur regardless of whether the increase comes from more government spending, expanded investment, higher autonomous consumption, or more autonomous exports. The autonomous spending multiplier applies to *all* new injections of spending — they are perfect substitutes for one another in their impacts on equilibrium income. Alternatively, tax cuts can be used to encourage economic growth. The autonomous tax multiplier equals one minus the autonomous spending multiplier. To see why, we will look at it algebraically.

Income is the sum of consumption, investment, government spending, and net exports: $Y = C + I + G + (X - M)$. We assume that taxes (T_a), investment (I_a), government purchases (G_a), net exports $(X_a - M_a)$, and part of consumption (C_a) are autonomous and that $mpc(Y - T_a)$ is induced consumption (the mpc is based on disposable income). Then

$$Y = C_a + mpc(Y - T_a) + I_a + G_a + (X_a - M_a)$$

We define total autonomous spending as $A = C_a + I_a + G_a + (X_a - M_a)$. This leaves $Y = A + mpc(Y - T_a)$ or $Y = A + mpcY - mpcT_a$. Subtracting $mpcY$ from both sides leaves $Y - mpcY = A - mpcT_a$. Simplifying by factoring Y out of the left side yields $Y(1 - mpc) = A - mpcT_a$. Dividing both sides by $1 - mpc$ gives the results we seek:

$$Y = A\left(\frac{1}{1 - mpc}\right) + T_a\left(\frac{-mpc}{1 - mpc}\right)$$

Translated into English, this equation means that aggregate income (Y) equals autonomous spending $[C_a = I_a + G_a + (X_a - M_a) = A]$ times the autonomous spending multiplier $[1/(1 - mpc)]$, plus the level of taxes (T_a) times the autonomous tax multiplier $[-mpc/(1 - mpc)]$. The autonomous tax multiplier $[-mpc/(1 - mpc)]$ can be rewritten $(-mpc/mps)$. Thus, if the spending multiplier is 5, the tax multiplier is -4; if the spending multiplier is 4, the tax multiplier is -3; and so on.

The Balanced-Budget Multiplier

All else equal, any changes in National Income can be traced to changes in autonomous spending or taxes:

$$\Delta Y = \Delta A\left(\frac{1}{1 - mpc}\right) + \Delta T_a\left(\frac{-mpc}{1 - mpc}\right)$$

If the mpc equals 0.8, the spending multiplier equals 5 and the tax multiplier equals -4. Thus, $\Delta Y = \Delta A(5) + \Delta T_a(-4)$. If government spending and taxes each rise by $20 billion, total income also increases by $20 billion: $20 billion $\times$ (5) plus $20 billion $\times$ (-4) equals $20 billion. We can generalize: Equal changes in autonomous government spending and taxes cause income to change in the same direction and by the same amount. The applicable multiplier is termed the *balanced-budget multiplier* and always equals one.

Why don't equal increases in government spending and taxes exactly offset each other? The change in income from such a policy results because the first-round effect of a $1 increase in government spending is to increase income by $1. The autonomous spending multiplier then applies. However, while the first-round effect of the $1 increase in taxes is to cut disposable income by $1, gross pretax income is not affected. Hence, the multiplier effect does not apply to income until the next round, when the taxpayers' spending falls by $1(0.8) = $0.80. This example suggests that if both government purchases and taxes are increased by $1, then, because the balanced-budget multiplier equals one, equilibrium income will rise by exactly $1. The balanced-budget multiplier equals one because it reflects the numerical sum of the autonomous spending and tax multipliers:

$$\frac{1}{1 - mpc} + \frac{-mpc}{1 - mpc} = \frac{1 - mpc}{1 - mpc} = 1$$

Much more realistic assumptions than the ones used in this chapter are the bases for the econometric models used to forecast national economic activity. For example, the effects of income on investment, government purchases, and taxes are recognized. Even though these forecasting models are much more complex than those we have considered, the approaches are similar. Assumptions are made about the behavior of various economic agents; these assumptions generate predictions regarding National Income.

PART 4

The Financial System

Modern macroeconomics has absorbed and extended insights from both Keynesian and classical economics, but some major issues remain unresolved. First and foremost is the question of how actively government should try to control business cycles. Most economists who favor a relatively passive macroeconomic role for government draw substantial inspiration from classical economics. In contrast, modern Keynesian economists endorse a broader and more "activist" role for government in countering business cycles.

A second, related issue centers on underpinnings for Aggregate Demand. Keynesians believe that income is the major influence on Aggregate Demand. New classical economists of all varieties—including supply-siders and modern monetarists—view the amount of money available as the major influence on Aggregate Demand.

You need to know more about monetary economics to appreciate the reasons behind areas of agreement and disagreement among Keynesians and the new classical economists. What money is, what services it performs, and how money is created are the questions addressed in Chapter 11. Then, Chapter 12 provides an overview of the Federal Reserve System and the tools it uses to regulate our financial system and to determine the money supply.

Chapter 13 looks at the demand for money and how the supply and demand for money jointly determine the price level, the rate of inflation, Aggregate Output, and the rate of interest. In addition to the nature and the burdens and benefits of budget deficits and public debt, Chapter 14 traces linkages between monetary policy and the federal budget, and addresses the international consequences of persistent budget deficits.

In the preceding part of this book, we discussed how government taxing and spending policies might interact with private spending (consumption, investment, and net exports) to alter Aggregate Demand and, ultimately, National Output. This part addresses money as a social convention, discusses the purposes of financial institutions, and explains how the government's monetary policies affect Aggregate Demand. In Part 5, we consider the underpinnings of Aggregate Supply in greater depth and, by melding Aggregate Demand and Aggregate Supply more completely, develop deeper insights into recent macroeconomic problems.

Money and Its Creation

The love of money as a possession — as distinguished from the love of money as a means to the enjoyment of the realities of life — will be recognized for what it is, a somewhat disgusting morbidity, one of those semi-criminal, semi-pathological propensities which one hands over with a shudder to the specialists in mental disease.

John Maynard Keynes

Any list of inventions that shaped the course of civilization would include the wedge, the wheel — and *money*. Suppose a cultural anthropologist from Venus visited Earth. Among the puzzles reported in Venusian scientific journals might be interpretations of why Earthlings work, invest, lie, cheat, steal, or commit murder for stones, beads, dirty pieces of paper, bits of metal, or bookkeeping entries in computers in buildings called "banks." The important roles played by money might seem an unsolvable mystery — unless Venus also had a monetary system. And, of course, it would.

Our first task in this chapter is to investigate why societies everywhere develop money as a mechanism to facilitate specialization and exchange. After we examine the economic functions performed by money, we survey different types of money and the components of the U.S.

money supply. Finally, we explore the processes of money creation and destruction.

Barter: Exchange Without Money

Some pundits have predicted a "cashless society" in which all transactions will be executed via computer. But can you imagine a moneyless society? Our ancestors used forms of money at least as early as the seventh century B.C., but we know that our earliest ancestors had no money. Only a few small tribes that were relatively isolated managed to enter the twentieth century without any form of monetary system.

If you lived in a society without money, you would be limited to producing or stealing everything you used — or you could engage in barter.

Barter *occurs when people directly exchange their goods for someone else's goods.*

One drawback of barter is that you must find someone who has what you want *and* who wants what you have before any exchange occurs. This requirement is called the *double coincidence of wants*. Even a double coincidence of wants, however, might not be enough for trade to occur. Even if you had a spare horse and wanted a loaf of bread, and met a baker with a lot of bread who wanted a horse, you still might not strike a bargain—making change without money is nearly impossible.

Acquiring information about potentially profitable bargains is enormously costly in a barter economy, so transactions are infrequent. As a result, most people tend to be largely self-sufficient producers/consumers. Few advantages of specialization of labor will be realized, which explains in part why standards of living tend to be low in moneyless economies. Small wonder that money is often rated with the wheel as an invention crucial to the development of the modern world.

What Is Money?

I measure everything I do by the size of a silver dollar. If it don't come up to that standard then I know it's no good.

Thomas A. Edison

What money is may seem obvious, but how would you respond if asked how much money you have? You could count only the cash in your purse or pocket. More likely, you would extend this to "money" you keep in checking accounts or savings accounts. You might include the total value of any U.S. Savings Bonds or corporate stocks or bonds you might own. But why stop there? Most of your possessions are worth money. How about the values of your other assets—a car, a house, clothes, books, a ping-pong table, or other things you own. Just how much money do you have? Ambiguities in this question arise from failure to differentiate between wealth and money. Your **wealth** is the difference between the value of your assets and the value of your liabilities. In addition to being an asset itself, money has the unique characteristic of being the unit by which other assets or liabilities are measured.

Functions of Money

Money performs certain functions in all but the most primitive societies. These functions provide a descriptive definition of money.

> **Money** is (a) *a medium of exchange*, (b) *a measure of value or standard unit of account*, (c) *a store of value*, and (d) *a standard of deferred payment*.

Memorizing this list might help you on an exam, but money will be more understandable if you consider what each part of this description implies. You may even be able to anticipate the operational definitions of money used by modern monetary analysts.

Medium of Exchange

Money makes the world go around.

Unknown

The necessity of a double coincidence of wants under barter is finessed by money.

> *Money is used as a* **medium of exchange** *when it is used to execute transactions.*

This is the most important and the most easily understood function of money. If you have assets for sale (for example, labor services), you normally expect to be paid in the form of cash or a check, although you may be willing to trade your assets for other assets. And when you want something, you generally expect to shell out cash or a check, although you may choose to use a credit card or take out a loan. *Credit* is simply an extension of money.

The prominent economist Robert Clower characterizes monetary economies as societies in which "money is traded for goods, and goods are traded for money, but goods are not traded for goods." His statement requires a slight disclaimer: Goods *seldom* trade for goods in a monetary economy—but barter organizations that spring up to avoid or evade taxes use bookkeeping "credits" that are actually a form of money.

A plumber who trades credits from working on a house for a pet pygmy pig is using these credits as money.

Measure of Value

Money is an elastic yardstick.

Unknown

If we did not have money to measure relative prices, the values of bearskin rugs might be stated in terms of bath brushes or Butterfingers, which in turn might be stated relative to shirts or shoelaces.

> Money performs as a **measure of value** or **standard unit of account** when it is used as a common denominator by which to state the relative prices of goods.

Use of money as a *standard unit of account* substantially reduces the information we need to make sound market decisions. Measuring the values of all goods in terms of all other goods would be tedious, involving enormous transaction costs, because the relative prices between goods increase faster than the number of goods considered.

For example, suppose apples (a) and burritos (b) are the only two goods in an economy. In this case, there is only one relative price to consider. If you know how many apples must be traded to get a burrito, you automatically know how many burritos must be traded for an apple. Introducing a third good, carrots (c), complicates things. You still need to know rates of exchange between apples and burritos, but it is now also necessary to know the price of carrots in terms of both burritos and apples. Three relative prices are now important: P_a/P_b, P_a/P_c, and P_b/P_c. Adding a fourth good, doughnuts (d), yields six relative prices. Focus 1 will help you grasp why the number of relative prices expands faster than the number of goods exchanged.

Money permits people in 100-good economies to worry about only 100 prices instead of 4,950. Thus, using money as a unit of account "greases the wheels" of exchange by reducing information costs. Small groups can reduce reliance on self-production because monetary exchange substantially boosts the value of total output as people are enabled to specialize in producing goods in which they have a comparative advantage.

Store of Value

Money . . . lulls our disquietude.

John Maynard Keynes

People hold money not only for transactions they anticipate, but also because money is normally a relatively riskless way of holding wealth.

> Money performs as a **store of value** when people prefer it as an asset because it is relatively less risky or because they view the transaction costs of conversion into other assets as too high.

You do not have to pay brokerage fees to hold money as an asset, but you would incur such costs if you held stocks, bonds, capital equipment, or real estate. The values of these other assets also tend to be much more volatile than the purchasing power of money in most economies. There is some risk, however, because money may lose its value during inflationary periods (but bonds, for example, do also).

Another way risk enters the picture emerges from *diversification*. The values of diverse assets are unlikely to be affected in the same ways by the same things. For example, if you own both a new-car dealership and a junkyard, a recession may kill new car sales while your junkyard does quite well. You learned earlier that the purchasing power of a dollar is $1/P$, where P is (1/100th of) the price level: Doubling the price level cuts the value of a dollar in half. Since World War II, inflation has steadily pushed up the price level. Even so, the old saying "Don't put all of your eggs in one basket" suggests that it can be wise for people to include some money in their portfolios of assets.

Prior to the Depression-era writings of John Maynard Keynes, orthodox economists rejected the notion that you might want money for other than reasonably immediate purchases. Since then, money has played an integral role in the

Relative Prices in a Four-Good Economy

In our four-good economy, each good is priced in terms of every other good. Follow the horizontal "Apples" column across the table until you hit the vertical "Burritos" column. That fraction, P_b/P_a, represents the price of burritos in terms of apples. We might find, for example, that it takes 4 apples to buy 1 burrito. Thus, the price of 1 apple is 1/4 burrito. Notice that the fractions P_a/P_a, P_b/P_b, P_c/P_c, and P_d/P_d are shaded. These elements are items priced in terms of themselves (1 apple/1 apple = 1) and thus can be ignored. Moreover, each price in the area below the shaded diagonal is the reciprocal of a price above this diagonal, so information is duplicated and the prices below this diagonal also can be ignored. The formula for

Good Used to Price	Good to Be Priced			
	Apples	**Burritos**	**Carrots**	**Doughnuts**
Apples	$\dfrac{P_a}{P_a} = 1$	$\dfrac{P_b}{P_a}$	$\dfrac{P_c}{P_a}$	$\dfrac{P_d}{P_a}$
Burritos	$\dfrac{P_a}{P_b}$	$\dfrac{P_b}{P_b} = 1$	$\dfrac{P_c}{P_b}$	$\dfrac{P_d}{P_b}$
Carrots	$\dfrac{P_a}{P_c}$	$\dfrac{P_b}{P_c}$	$\dfrac{P_c}{P_c} = 1$	$\dfrac{P_d}{P_c}$
Doughnuts	$\dfrac{P_a}{P_d}$	$\dfrac{P_b}{P_d}$	$\dfrac{P_c}{P_d}$	$\dfrac{P_d}{P_d} = 1$

determining the number of basic relative prices in an n-good economy (where n equals the number of goods) is $\{n(n-1)\}/2$, where n can be any number. For our example, the formula becomes $\{4(4-1)\}/2 = 6$ prices. For 100 goods, the number of relative prices jumps to 4,950. Imagine how complex pricing would be in a moneyless economy in which millions of different goods were traded.

development of modern "portfolio" theory, which is a vital part of modern financial analysis in American business.

Standard of Deferred Payment

Money is a contract with parties unknown for the future delivery of pleasures undecided upon.

David Bazelon, *The Paper Economy* (1965)

Money as a standard of deferred payment is implicit in the other three functions of money, but it is worth discussing to illustrate the relationship between time and money.

Money performs as a **standard of deferred payment** *by allowing intertemporal contracts.*

Money is a link between the past, present, and future.

Many forms of production require time for completion and would not be done without a contract specifying future monetary payments. Military or construction contracts are examples.

Repetitive exchanges are also conducted much more efficiently if only one contract is used for many present and future transactions. Labor contracts are examples. Still other deals are negotiated for immediate delivery of a good with delayed payment for the buyer's convenience. For example, you may be borrowing funds to finance your education. When you sign a credit contract, you agree to make later payment of the funds you borrow — plus interest. All these contracts are measured in money.

Liquidity and Money

One important aspect of any asset is its *liquidity*, which depends on the costs incurred in converting it into cash. Many people think that liquidity is defined only by the time required for conversion, but any asset can be converted into cash almost immediately. If you are willing to sell your stereo system for $10, I will buy it right now. *Time required to sell* and *certainty about price* are two crucial aspects of asset liquidity. Both time and certainty are inextricably tied together in transaction costs.

> **Liquidity** *is negatively related to the proportion of the transaction costs incurred in purchase or sale of an asset.*

One way to rank assets' liquidity is to estimate the percentage you would lose if you had to sell them immediately. Houses are relatively *illiquid* assets. You usually pay realtor fees and various other transaction costs when you sell one home and buy another. In contrast, most savings accounts are highly liquid. You can close one savings account at your bank and open another, losing almost no interest or principal in the process — just your time.

Types of Money

An incredible variety of items have served as money at various times and places, but all can be classified as either commodity money or fiat money.

> **Commodity money** *is valuable apart from what it will buy, but* **fiat money** *has value only because of its use as money.*

Use of fiat money is ultimately based on faith — faith in its purchasing power, in its general acceptability, and in the stability of the government that issues it.

Commodity Monies

Rubber balls were once used as money in the Amazon jungles. On the Pacific island of Yap, sculptured stones weighing up to three tons have served as money. From the beginning of the sixteenth century until late in the nineteenth, most American Plains Indians had no money as such, but measured their wealth in horses. Throughout Europe, Africa, and the Americas, beads, stone spearheads, and arrowheads were once used as money. Focus 2 describes one well-known transaction from American history.

What caused these forms of money to fall into disuse? Several characteristics are necessary for any commodity to be widely accepted as money over a long period:

1. Durability.
2. Divisibility.
3. Homogeneity (uniformity or standardization).
4. Portability (high value-to-weight and value-to-volume ratios).
5. Relative stability of supply.
6. Optimal scarcity.

These attributes are reasonably self-explanatory. Ice cream will not do for money — it is not durable (it melts). Diamonds are insufficiently homogeneous — there are fine diamonds, and then there are the "diamonds" some shifty-eyed rascal tries to sell you in a parking lot. Water and elephants are insufficiently portable, and elephants are indivisible. (If divided, they are not durable.) The wheat supply is too volatile — if the supply of money (wheat) grew too rapidly, money's value would plummet; a severe recession might follow a precipitous shrinkage of the

FOCUS 2

Wampum

You probably learned in a history course that the Manhattan Indians sold their island to the Dutch in the seventeenth century for $24 worth of beads, hatchets, knives, and firewater. History books generally give the impression that the Dutch took advantage of the unsophisticated Indians in this deal, although some estimates suggest that, at 6 percent interest, the $24 could now repurchase Manhattan.

Suppose that you were offered a box containing ten thousand $100 bills in exchange for everything you own (that's $1 million). You would probably count yourself very fortunate to be able to walk away from your house, car, stereo, and clothes with all that green stuff, even though you would be temporarily naked. However, if seventeenth-century Indians viewed the transaction, they would think you had been swindled.

The two situations are really very similar, because the Indians used strings of beads (wampum) for money and thought themselves rich because they had received so much money for a pitiful little island. In effect, the Dutch were counterfeiters; the Indians could not have predicted that Europeans would "counterfeit" so much wampum that it soon would become almost worthless as anything other than ornamentation. In effect, the Indians experienced hyperinflation in wampum.

wheat supply. Economic activity would be linked too tightly to good or bad harvests, which are often uncontrollable. *Optimal scarcity* means that any commodity used as money cannot be common. Sand, bricks, or two-by-fours are insufficiently scarce.

Historically, the only commodities that combine most of the desirable characteristics for use as money are rare metals, especially gold and silver. Standardization was achieved by making small ingots or coins of these precious metals and stamping "face values" on them. The earliest known metal coins date back to Imperial Rome in the sixth century B.C.

When the world relied almost exclusively on gold and silver coins for money, kings and queens often found royal treasuries inadequate for the palaces, ornate finery, and large armies and navies they thought due them. One common solu-

tion was to launch a war to secure foreign treasures. This solution was seldom successful. (War is a *negative-sum game*, which means that the total losses to all participants outweigh the gains to the "winners," if any.) An alternative for semi-impoverished (by their standards) heads of state was to *debase* the coinage so that profits from seignorage rose.

The profit government makes when it coins or prints currencies whose face values exceed their commodity values is known as **seignorage.**

Early government mints "stretched" relatively pure gold and silver coins by melting them down and then adding generous portions of nickel, copper, zinc, or lead before restamping coins. (Similar ideas have inspired people who put soybeans and sawdust into hamburgers.) One posi-

Gresham's Law

In the 1950s, it was very common to use silver coins minted 40 to 60 years earlier. What happened to all the gold and silver coins minted in the United States prior to 1964? Sir Thomas Gresham, a sixteenth-century financial adviser to Queen Elizabeth, may have had the answer. He observed that debased coins remained in circulation while relatively pure coins disappeared rapidly after debasement. This led him to state a famous economic doctrine that has stood the test of time: "*Bad money drives out good.*" This idea is known as **Gresham's Law**. People will spend coins that contain far less valuable metal than their face values and hoard (save) coins that contain metal worth close to or more than the coins' face values. This explains why almost all our current dimes, quarters, half dollars, and "silver" dollars are relatively recently minted cupronickel "sandwiches."

tive result from *debasement* of coinage is that it prevents private profits from melting coins down whenever face values are less than the value of the gold or silver contained in the coins. Focus 3 explores yet another consequence of debasement.

The inflationary pressure that may arise from debasement is a major reason many advocates of laissez-faire capitalism vehemently oppose government discretion in printing money. Some "gold bugs" favor a return to the gold standard because the amount of money in circulation would then be controlled by the forces of supply and demand. They are willing to accept the inefficiency of producing money through mining and then burying gold or silver in a place like Fort Knox; gold bugs view this costly process as worthwhile because it limits government's control over the money supply.

Paper money dates back to the Ming Dynasty in China (1368–1399). Until recently, many paper monies could have been classified as "pseudocommodity" money because governments would convert the paper money into spec-

ified amounts of gold or silver on demand. The United States was the last country in the world to abandon the gold and silver standards; it was not until 1933 that this country went off the gold standard domestically. From 1933 until 1974, foreign bankers and governments could proffer $35 in bills and get an ounce of gold from the United States Treasury, but it was illegal for American citizens to hold gold coins or ingots. American dollars were, however, redeemable for silver until the late 1960s.

Fiat Money

Some Americans still believe that currency is "backed by gold in Fort Knox."

Paper money and coins are collectively called **currency.**

Take a dollar bill from your purse or wallet. You will see "Federal Reserve Note" above George Washington's picture, but nowhere will you find any statement about the worth of the bill in gold or silver. Now look at any of your "silver" coins. These coins are "sandwiches" of cupronickel (not silver) around copper — the face value of the coin is about 15 to 40 times the total value of the metal. What makes this paper and these bits of metal valuable if they are not "backed" by gold or silver? One hint lies just to the left of George's picture: *THIS NOTE IS LEGAL TENDER FOR ALL DEBTS, PUBLIC AND PRIVATE.* The government declares that the pieces of paper printed by the Federal Reserve System and the bits of metal issued by the United States Mint are money by fiat. (*Fiat* can be interpreted to mean: "Because we command.")

Now that you know the secret that our money has no gold or silver backing, should your behavior change in any way? *No!* Even if you are convinced that the government perpetrates fraud in issuing coins and bills, you can buy just about anything for which you have the money, so you will continue to try to get money in the same ways as previously. The real foundation for fiat money is the *faith* we have that it can be used to buy goods and services. In other words, our money is "backed" by loaves of bread, Chevrolets, stereo systems, college educations, and also by government's ability and willingness to maintain money at a relatively stable value by controlling the money supply.

The major advantages of fiat money are that (*a*) its supply can be controlled fairly precisely by government; (*b*) it is much less costly to produce than commodity money, and, therefore, its use is comparatively efficient; and (*c*) if monetary policymakers do a good job, fiat money possesses all of the characteristics required of a good commodity money.

The Supply of Money

The purchasing power of money and the cost of credit (interest rates) are determined by supply and demand in much the same manner that prices are determined for such goods as concert tickets or fudge. In the remainder of this chapter, we describe the assets that make up the U.S. money supply and examine the role of financial institutions in determining the money supply. This sets the stage for analyzing how the demand and supply of money jointly determine the price level, the rate of inflation, and the rate of interest.

The functions of money provide us with a descriptive definition: Money is a medium of exchange, a measure of value, a store of value, and a standard of deferred payment. This provides a guide to operational definitions of money. Be aware, however, that just as no measure of unemployment conforms precisely to the economic concept of unemployment, no measure of the money supply is in perfect accord with the concept of money.

Narrowly Defined Money (M1)

Currency (paper, coins, and bills) is probably the most easily identified component of the money supply because (*a*) it may be used for virtually all transactions, (*b*) it is used to price goods and services, and (*c*) it counts as an asset. The only other assets that perform all monetary functions are demand deposits.

> **Demand deposits** *are funds in checking accounts in commercial banks, savings and loans, or credit unions.*

These funds are legally required to be available to depositors *on demand*. Together, currency and demand deposits (plus such minor accounts as travelers' checks) are the narrowly defined money supply known as M1:

M1 = currency + demand deposits in financial institutions

We do need to qualify this a bit. Only currency held by the nonbanking public is included in the money supply. We would be "double counting" if we included both the currency you deposit in your checking account and your demand deposits. We also ignore the deposits of the federal government because the government, via the Federal Reserve System, can print money at will. Moreover, because the federal government's spending is not constrained by the money it has in banks, inclusion of federal deposits would not aid us in predicting Aggregate Expenditures when using money supply data.

"But," you might object, "credit cards can be used to pay for just about everything. Aren't credit cards money? And how about my savings account?" Unfortunately, a credit card is simply an easy way to get into debt; a credit card is not a store of value, so credit cards are not money. Standard savings accounts are also not money because spending funds from a savings account first requires converting your savings account "money" into currency or a demand deposit. Just try to pay for your next meal out by presenting your savings passbook to a waiter — you will be washing dishes in no time!

Federal laws formerly prohibited banks from paying interest on checking accounts, but these laws were phased out in the 1980s. Savings-and-loan associations and credit unions now also offer checking account services where depositors receive interest on some checking accounts. These changes in legal constraints effectively make these thrift institutions into banks and some of their deposits into checking accounts. In most of the discussion in this book, we include all institutions performing the functions of banks when we say "banks" and consider all checkable accounts when we refer to "checks."

Only checking accounts and currency are assets that are both mediums of exchange and widely accepted as money. We admit that parking meters do not accept checks, that few cab drivers will change a $100 bill for a $3 fare, and that you cannot present 10 million loose pennies to a bank and expect them to settle a $100,000 mortgage. But checks and currency are assets that can be used for most transactions much more easily than can other assets.

Near-Money (M2, M3, and L)

Some economists do count certain highly liquid assets, such as savings accounts in commercial banks (*time deposits*), as parts of the money supply. The economists who use broader definitions of the money supply than M1 believe that people's spending levels are more predictable by monetary data if we include the liquid assets that

are highly interchangeable with currency and demand deposits.

One broader definition is **M2,** which adds such assets as noninstitutional money market funds and savings in commercial banks and thrift institutions to M1:

> **M2** = M1 + miscellaneous short-term time deposits
>
> = currency + demand deposits + small time deposits

Other monetary theorists expand the definition of money to M3, which includes such items as large time deposits and institutional money market mutual funds:

> **M3** = M2 + institutional money market mutual funds + large time deposits

There is one even broader official definition of the money supply, *L,* which adds such liquid assets as short-term government bonds and commercial paper to M3. Exactly which definition of the money supply is most useful depends on how it will be used. Throughout this book, when we say *money*, we mean *currency plus any funds available by writing checks (M1).* How various measures of the money supply have grown is shown in Figure 1.

All these measures of the money supply have grown substantially over the years, as have GNP and the cost of living (CPI). How should we interpret these positive correlations? Does monetary growth cause inflation? Does it cause GNP to grow, or does economic growth cause the money supply to expand? How does monetary growth affect the total output of goods, and vice versa? These questions are at the heart of a continuing controversy between monetarists and Keynesians, and they are examined in the next few chapters.

Banks and the Creation of Money

Where does money come from? We know that U.S. currency is printed by the Federal Reserve

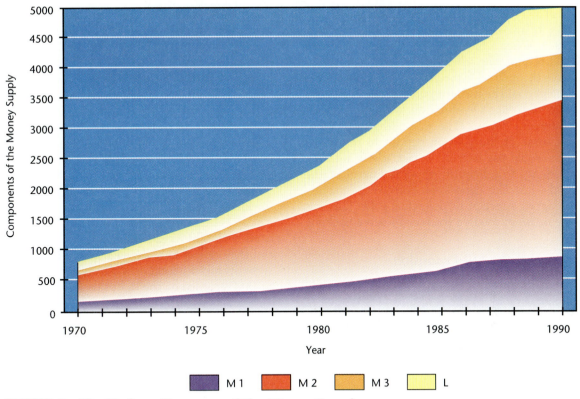

FIGURE 1 The Various Measures of the Money Supply
The money supply is composed of various aggregates, depending on how broadly you define it. M1 is the narrowest definition, while *L* is the most expansive.
Source: *Economic Report of the President,* 1991.

System (bills) or minted by the Treasury (coins). But demand deposits (checking accounts) are the largest component of our money supply. Currency is little more than convenience money—less than 30 percent of M1. How do demand deposits originate?

The Origin of Fractional Reserve Banking

Several centuries ago, money consisted primarily of gold coins. Wealthy people found the amounts of gold they accumulated quite heavy. (Gold is only semiportable.) An even bigger disadvantage of gold is that thieves love it; stolen gold pieces (or modern coins for that matter) are rarely identifiable. Looking around for safe places to store their gold, people in medieval Europe thought of goldsmiths. Goldsmiths made jewelry, gold statues, and other precious goods. They also generally had some excess space in their heavily guarded vaults.

Goldsmiths were generally willing to store other people's money for a small fee and issued receipts for the gold deposited with them. Buyers found it convenient to exchange these receipts instead of physically getting the gold, and sellers were happy to take these receipts because they knew they could redeem them for gold from the goldsmith whenever they wished. This was the beginning of checking accounts—the receipts issued by the goldsmiths were effectively demand deposits.

Goldsmiths observed that they stored nearly

all of a community's coins and that the amounts of gold in their vaults did not fluctuate very much. When a buyer paid for a purchase with a gold receipt, the seller was typically content to leave the gold with the goldsmith. After all, the receipt could be used for purchases just like gold. One depositor's withdrawal was just another customer's deposit. The goldsmiths began lending some of the gold on deposit to borrowers who would pay interest. In fact, it was not even necessary to relinquish physical control of the gold—just like depositors, borrowers generally preferred a receipt to the actual gold. This was the origin of modern fractional reserve banking.

Demand Deposit Expansion

Some people occasionally would physically withdraw gold, so the goldsmith was limited in the total amount of receipts he could write as loans. He would maintain reserves in the vault to meet withdrawals of deposits.

Banks keep **reserves** *on hand to meet withdrawals by depositors.*

Suppose a goldsmith observed that even though deposits and withdrawals were sporadic, the total amount of gold in the vault did not vary more than 10 percent a year. How much might the goldsmith be able to loan from a given amount of gold deposits?

To keep the analysis simple, we assume that the goldsmith is a monopolist who has the only local bank vault. (We will examine a multibank world in a bit.) The goldsmith prudently stops making loans when the value of receipts (demand deposits) issued is five times as large as the amount of gold on deposit. That is, the goldsmith keeps reserves equal to 20 percent of deposits; reserves are twice as much as the variations in current deposits (10 percent) that the goldsmith has observed, so this level is good insurance against a large number of people simultaneously wanting to withdraw gold.

Fractional reserve banking *legally permits financial institutions to hold less than 100 percent of their deposits as currency in their vaults.*

We also assume the goldsmith already has many deposits and loans outstanding prior to the transactions we will be considering and views himself as "fully loaned up" (reserves equal 20 percent of earlier deposits).[1] Finally, we initially assume that no one actually withdraws any gold during the period we are considering; receipts for gold are perfectly acceptable as money.

Suppose Allen, a gold miner, deposits $1,000 worth of newly mined gold into Goldsmith's bank. This deposit and issuance of a receipt are written in the bank's "T-account" statement shown in Table 1. These T-accounts represent partial balance sheets for the bank. The left-hand- and right-hand-side entries must be equal, and they reflect only the changes in the bank's accounts following the new $1,000 deposit. The $1,000 recorded on the right side (credit) represents a liability or debt of the bank—Goldsmith owes Allen $1,000 on demand. The left side (debit) shows an increase of $1,000 in the bank's reserves, which is Goldsmith's new asset.

When Bob, a local customer, wants to borrow money, Goldsmith is happy to accommodate him with as much as $800. How did we arrive at $800? Goldsmith calculates 20 percent times $1,000 equals $200, which is planned for reserves (RR). Actual reserves of $1,000 minus $200 in planned reserves equals $800 in excess reserves ($XR$) that are available for the loan. When Bob borrows the full $800, the bank deposits $800 to Bob's account, and the bank's accounts change as shown in the T-account of Table 2. When you borrow money from a bank, the standard practice is to credit your account instead of giving you cash. The bank's assets are increased by an $800 IOU from Bob; its new liability is Bob's demand deposit for $800.

Suppose Bob writes Carol a check for $800—he did intend to spend the money he borrowed. Table 3 shows the bank's view of this exchange. Bob's $800 demand deposit simply becomes Carol's demand deposit. In fact, because all de-

---

1. When we introduce the Federal Reserve System in the next chapter, you will learn that banks legally are required to keep certain proportions of deposits in reserves. The process of money creation is essentially the same analytically, regardless of whether banks plan to hold reserves in the interest of prudence or because the FED requires them to do so.

Table 1 *Initial Deposit of $1,000 in a New Account in Goldsmith's Bank*

Assets (Debits)	Liabilities (Credits)
+$1,000 Reserves (Gold) $200 Planned reserves (*RR*) $800 Excess reserves (*XR*)	+$1,000 (Demand Deposit—Allen)

Table 2 *First-Round Lending: Changes in Accounts in Goldsmith's Bank*

Assets (Debits)	Liabilities (Credits)
+$800 (IOU—Bob)	+$800 (Demand Deposit—Bob)

Table 3 *A Transaction Between Two Customers of Goldsmith's Bank*

Assets (Debits)	Liabilities (Credits)
(No change)	−$800 (Demand Deposit—Bob) +$800 (Demand Deposit—Carol)

Table 4 *Second-Round Lending: Changes in Accounts in Goldsmith's Bank*

Assets (Debits)	Liabilities (Credits)
+$640 (IOU—Deirdre)	+$640 (Demand Deposit—Deirdre)

posits stay in the bank, we can ignore further transactions between the bank's customers. Such transactions are irrelevant for the bank's asset/liability position and for the amount of money in circulation. Notice that the $1,000 in gold reserves now "backs" $1,800 in demand deposit money. This may sound like a magician's trick, but it is the way banks operate.

When Deirdre wants to borrow money, Goldsmith can still lend up to $640, because actual reserves of $\{\$1,000 - 0.20 \times (\$1,000 + \$800)\} = \$640$ (excess reserves available to lend her). Alternatively, 80 percent of Carol's deposit ($0.80 \times \$800$) is $640. Her IOU and the loan that is deposited to Deirdre's account are shown in the T-account in Table 4.

When Ed comes in to borrow money, Goldsmith offers a loan of as much as $512 because $\$1,000 - [0.20 \times (\$1,000 + \$800 + \$640)] = \$512$. Again, 80 percent of Deirdre's $640 deposit is $512 and is available to loan. Table 5 depicts this loan and demand deposit (*DD*).

At this point, the $1,000 the bank holds as reserves supports $2,952 in demand deposits ($\$1,000 + \$800 + \$640 + \$512$). How much longer can this process continue? The answer is that the bank can make more loans as long as 20 percent times all demand deposits is less than the $1,000 held in reserve. To spare you further agony, we have summarized all possible subsequent loans and demand deposits (*DD*) in Table 6.

Table 5 *Third-Round Lending: Changes in Accounts in Goldsmith's Bank*

Assets (Debits)	Liabilities (Credits)
+$512 (IOU—Ed)	+$512 (Demand Deposit—Ed)

Table 6 *All Remaining Rounds: Changes in Accounts in Goldsmith's Bank*

Assets (Debits)	Liabilities (Credits)
+$2,048 (IOU—All others)	+$2,048 (Demand Deposit—All others)

Table 7 *Summary of Transactions: Accounts in Goldsmith's Bank*

Entry (Assets) (Debits)	(Liabilities) (Credits)
1 +$1,000 Reserves	+$1,000 (Demand Deposit—Allen)
2 +800 (IOU—Bob)	+800 (Demand Deposit—Bob)
3 No change	−800 (Demand Deposit—Bob)
	+800 (Demand Deposit—Carol)
4 +640 (IOU—Deirdre)	+640 (Demand Deposit—Deirdre)
5 +512 (IOU—Ed)	+512 (Demand Deposit—Ed)
6 +2,048 (IOU—All others)	+2,048 (Demand Deposit—All others)
Total +$5,000 ($1,000 gold reserves) ($4,000 IOUs)	+$5,000 (Total new Demand Deposits)

How did we know how large this entry would be? We know the bank will continue to make loans until $0.20(DD) = \$1,000$. If both sides of this equation are multiplied by five, we get: $DD = 5(\$1,000) = \$5,000$. The $1,000 held in bank reserves will support up to $5,000 in DD, regardless of whether these DDs are based on loans or not. In fact, the original $1,000 in new money deposited by Allen allowed the creation of an additional $4,000 in demand deposits generated as loans. Table 7 summarizes all these transactions.

It is not absolutely necessary for Goldsmith, as a monopoly banker, to go through all these lending rounds. After experimenting a bit, he would learn that Allen's $1,000 deposit could be translated directly into a $4,000 loan to Bob. We have gone through each step of this *loan-money creation process* because of its relevance for a multiple-bank financial system.

The Potential Money Multiplier (m_p)

Notice that the multiplier by which the money supply is expanded (5) is the reciprocal of the percentage Goldsmith plans as reserves against demand deposits (1/5 or 0.20).

The **potential money multiplier** *($m_p = 1/rr$) indicates the total demand deposits that can be generated from a new deposit of $1 in a banking system that is "fully loaned up," if people keep all their currency in the bank (no one keeps any cash on hand).*

The arithmetic parallels that used to compute the autonomous spending multiplier. The autonomous spending multiplier is $1/mps$ (the marginal propensity to save), while the potential money multiplier is $1/rr$, where rr is the reserve ratio or percentage of demand deposits (*DD*) held as reserves.[2]

The Actual Money Multiplier (m_a)

Actually, banks are seldom fully loaned up, and most people do hold some currency for convenience in covering small transactions. These leakages from the deposit → loan → deposit stream hold the actual money multiplier far below its potential value. Let us see why.

Any reserves held by banks in excess of their planned (or legally required) amounts are available for loans. These funds, or *excess reserves* (*XR*), can be expressed as a proportion of a bank's total deposits: $XR/DD = xr$. Thus, the actual money multiplier (m_a) could be as high as $1/(rr + xr)$, but *only* if there are no other drains on the money multiplier. In reality, people keep some money as cash, and firms hold some currency. These currency drains from the banking system are a major reason the actual money multiplier never reaches its potential value. The Federal Reserve Bank of St. Louis estimates the historical average real money multiplier at 2.6.

This "real world" multiplier can be expressed through a complex formula that accounts for every form of withdrawal of cash from the banking system.[3] The critical thing for you to remember is that the actual money multiplier (m_a) never reaches its potential value ($1/rr = m_p > m_a$) because of these and other drains of cash.

---

2. If we denote total planned reserves as *RR*, the proof is simple: Because $rr \cdot DD = RR$, then $DD = (1/rr) \times (RR)$.

3. For example, an intermediate formula is $m_a = 1/(rr + xr + \text{other leakages})$, where other leakages include such things as cash held by the public or transfers of currency to foreign banks. Expanded algebraic versions of the actual money multiplier treat currency separately from funds used as reserves by various types of financial institutions, which are decomposed into different types of accounts.

The **actual money multiplier (m_a)** *expresses the relationship between the money supply and currency in circulation or in bank vaults.*

The simplest algebraic expression of the actual multiplier (m_a) is

$$m_a = MS/MB$$

where *MS* is the money supply and *MB* is the currency that legally can serve as reserves in banks. *MB* is known as the *monetary base*, or *high-powered money*; it is the base on which the money multiplier operates in the money creation process (much as autonomous spending is the base for total spending in the Keynesian model).

The **monetary base** *equals currency in the hands of the nonbanking public plus all bank reserves.*

Failure to distinguish the monetary base from the money supply is a common mistake among students. Notice that a specific relationship between the monetary base and the money supply is embedded in the preceding equation for the actual money multiplier:

$$MS = m_a \cdot MB$$

Thus, the money supply equals the actual money multiplier times the monetary base.

A Multibank Model   When a community has many banks, each bank expects most checks written by its customers to be deposited in the banks of the payees. Does this mean that the total amount of deposits in any single bank is likely to be highly volatile? Not really. Most banks find that even though their customers' individual accounts vary tremendously over the month, the average daily amount in a given account is fairly stable on a month-to-month basis over the year. This occurs because most people have reasonably stable patterns of income and spending and seldom let their accounts drop below some comfortable minimum value.

Flows of deposits among banks do not affect the total amounts of reserves in the banking system, but will cause individual banks to hold slightly higher percentages of excess reserves (*xr*) than would be held by a monopoly banker. This reduces the size of the real-world money multiplier. Other than this, the process of money creation follows the pattern outlined in the preceding section, which assumed a monopoly bank.

Let us look at an example in which IBM sells a $1 million computer system to an oil firm in Venezuela. The payment is from a Venezuelan bank, and so represents new money to the U.S. banking system. IBM deposits this $1 million in new money in the First National Bank, which enables First National to create $800,000 by giving USX (formerly U.S. Steel) a loan. The two entries in First National's accounts are shown in Table 8. USX took the loan to buy smelting equipment; it writes a check for $800,000 to American Smelting. But American Smelting banks with the PennState Bank. When PennState takes American Smelting's deposit of USX's check and demands $800,000 from First National, First National loses $800,000 in reserves and reduces USX's account by $800,000. This is shown as entry 2b in Table 8. Notice that First National still has USX's IOU for $800,000 plus $200,000 on reserve in the event that IBM wants to withdraw some money.

When American Smelting deposits USX's check and PennState collects the check from First National, PennState's accounts change per entry 1 in Table 9. PennState can loan $640,000 to Security Life Insurance if it regards anything greater than 20 percent as excessive reserves, shown as entry 2. (First National had to turn down Security Life's loan application — they had no excess reserves to spare.) If Security Life writes a check to Xerox, which banks with New York's City Bank, PennState loses $640,000 in reserves and Security Life's account falls to its original balance (entry 3). However, PennState still has $160,000 in reserves plus Security Life's IOU for $640,000.

City Bank's accounts now change as in entry 1 of Table 10. It can lend Sony $512,000 (neither First National nor PennState has excess reserves available). When Sony takes the loan, City Bank makes entry 2 in its books. The multiple expansion process can be continued from customer to customer as reserves flow between banks until an additional total of $4,000,000 in newly created money in the form of demand deposits is generated through loans. The money creation process for an entire banking system parallels that for a single monopoly bank.

You may have some nagging feeling that something is wrong because new money seems to have appeared out of thin air. If so, you are not alone in being a bit mystified by bankers' juggling acts. Still, the fractional reserve process of money creation is very old and is widely accepted as compatible with sound banking practices.

You may be concerned that there is not enough money in bank vaults to meet withdrawals of deposits. Suppose IBM tries to withdraw its $1,000,000 from First National. Will this system fall like a house of cards? One part of the answer is that we have only covered the changes in bank accounts as $1 million in new reserves was used to create an original demand deposit of $1 million and an additional $4 million in demand deposits based on loans. The reserves backing other deposits in First National are available to cover IBM's withdrawal. Another option is that First National might sell USX's $800,000 IOU to another bank. This is effectively what has happened if you have ever borrowed money from one lender for, say, a car, and then received a request that you pay a different lender. Your paper IOU was sold (or *factored*, as it is known in banking circles).

The "Money Destruction" Process

The reverse of the money creation process is *money destruction*. IBM can usually withdraw its $1,000,000 from First National without a problem because most banks hold adequate excess reserves. Suppose IBM withdraws its $1,000,000 and keeps it in the corporate vault. First National will feel uncomfortably short of reserves, to the tune of $800,000. Remember, First National was holding $200,000 in reserves against the $1,000,000 deposit, so it loses $800,000 in reserves that backed other accounts ($1,000,000 − $200,000 = $800,000).

When USX's $800,000 loan is due, First National will not renew the loan, nor will First National make new loans when USX repays its loan.

Table 8 *Transaction with Another Bank Account in First National Bank*

Entry (Assets)		(Liabilities)
1	+$1,000,000 Reserves	+$1,000,000 (Demand Deposit—IBM)
2a	+800,000 (IOU—USX)	+800,000 (Demand Deposit—USX)
2b	−800,000 Reserves	−800,000 (Demand Deposit—USX)
Reserve Position after Transaction		
(Assets)		(Liabilities)
$ 200,000 Reserves		$1,000,000 (Demand Deposit—IBM)
<u>800,000</u> Loan (IOU—USX)		<u> </u>
Total $1,000,000		$1,000,000 (Total Demand Deposits)

Table 9 *Second-Round Transactions Accounts in PennState National Bank*

Entry (Assets)		(Liabilities)
1	+$800,000 Reserves	+$800,000 (Demand Deposit—American Smelting)
2	+640,000 (IOU—Security Life)	+640,000 (Demand Deposit—Security Life)
3	−640,000 Reserves	−640,000 (Demand Deposit—Security Life)
Reserve Position after Transaction		
(Assets)		(Liabilities)
$160,000 Reserves (Cash)		$800,000 (Demand Deposit—American
<u>640,000</u> Loan (IOU—Security Life)		<u> </u> Smelting)
Total $800,000		$800,000 (Total Demand Deposits)

Table 10 *Third-Round Transactions Accounts in City Bank of New York*

Entry (Assets)		(Liabilities)
1	+$640,000 Reserves	+$640,000 (Demand Deposit—Xerox)
2	+512,000 (IOU—Sony)	+512,000 (Demand Deposit—Sony)
3	−512,000 Reserves	−512,000 (Demand Deposit—Sony)
Reserve Position after Transaction		
(Assets)		(Liabilities)
$128,000 Reserves (Cash)		$640,000 (Demand Deposit—Xerox)
<u>512,000</u> Loan (IOU—Sony)		<u> </u>
Total $640,000		$640,000 (Total Demand Deposits)

USX's repayment must come from existing bank reserves. Ultimately, PennState Bank will reduce outstanding loans by Security Life's $640,000, City Bank will reduce loans by Sony's $512,000, and so on. IBM's withdrawal of $1,000,000 from the banking system's reserves will cause a $4,000,000 drop in demand deposit money, originally created by expansionary lending. IBM's $1,000,000 demand deposit will also be lost, so demand deposits will drop by a total of $5,000,000. However, IBM will have $1,000,000 in currency, which was not included in the money supply while it was held as bank reserves. Thus, there is a net $4,000,000 reduction in the money supply caused by IBM's decision to hoard $1,000,000 in its own vault.

Banks holding 20 percent reserves should operate acceptably unless they rapidly lose 20 percent or more of their deposits. If this happens, are such banks insolvent? *No!* When only a few banks run short of reserves, other financial institutions will buy (at a discount) the IOUs from loans these banks have made. Alternatively, banks with inadequate reserves can usually borrow funds from institutions that have excess reserves available.

Banks lend and borrow from each other through a private banking network called the **federal-funds market.**

These interbank lending mechanisms normally enable banks that have inadequate reserves to replenish their reserves and honor all their demand deposit liabilities.

Unfortunately, there have been times when reserves in the financial system as a whole were inadequate, and there were a lot more loans for sale than there were buyers. The "runs on banks" and financial panics that resulted finally caused the Congress to establish a "banker's bank" (the Federal Reserve System, which is the subject of the next chapter) with the enactment of the Federal Reserve Act of 1913. Before we investigate government regulation of the banking system, we need to survey other types of financial institutions.

Financial Institutions

Major types of financial institutions include credit unions and savings-and-loan associations, which act as banks when they make loans based on accounts that are, effectively, demand deposits. Insurance companies and stock exchanges also facilitate efficient allocations of capital in a market economy. Important economic roles performed by financial institutions include (*a*) channeling funds from savers to investors, (*b*) providing secure places for savers to keep their deposits, and (*c*) facilitating flows and payments of funds—most payments are made through checking accounts.

Financial Intermediation

Channeling savings to investors is the single most important macroeconomic function of our financial system. Households allocate their after-tax incomes between consumption and saving. Rather than let your savings sit idle, you are probably willing to let other people use them if they pay you interest so that you ultimately receive more than they borrow. Financial institutions find borrowers willing to pay higher interest rates than must be paid to savers.

Differences between interest paid by borrowers and that paid to savers generate income to the owners of financial institutions. Imagine how chaotic it would be if all savers had to seek out their own borrowers, and vice versa. Transaction costs might be insurmountable. How could borrowers find savers willing to entrust them with loans? If you were a saver, how would you locate people who wanted to borrow? How would you screen loan applicants to ensure a high probability of repayment?

Financial institutions specialize in evaluating the "credit-worthiness" of loan applicants, and then they monitor borrowers. By "spreading the risk" of default across large numbers of loans, financial intermediaries are able to pay interest rates that will attract deposits from savers.

Financial intermediation *occurs when financial institutions make the savings of households* *whose incomes exceed their spending available to investors, or to other households that wish to spend more on consumer goods than their incomes allow.*

The Diversity of Financial Institutions

Different financial institutions use different methods to secure the savings of individuals, which then can be either loaned or invested directly. Since people have different ideas about the best way to save (or borrow) and firms differ in the types of debt they are willing to incur, it seems natural that various types of financial intermediaries have developed to meet these diverse needs. A second reason for the diversity of financial institutions is the mix of federal and state laws and regulation governing them. Because of major banking deregulations that began in 1980, many of these institutions are growing less distinct.

Commercial Banks "Full service" *commercial banks* provide more services to their depositors than simple maintenance of checking and savings accounts. Most banks offer a variety of personal and commercial loan services, issue bank credit cards such as MasterCard and Visa, and have trust departments available to administer wills and estates.

Thrift Institutions Savings-and-loan associations, mutual savings banks, and credit unions are all called *thrift institutions*. The major difference between thrift institutions and commercial banks *used to be* that commercial banks offered checking accounts while thrift institutions could not. However, a major revision of our banking laws in 1980 made it possible for thrift institutions to offer accounts that are almost identical to bank checking accounts.

Most of the loans made by savings-and-loan associations and mutual savings banks are used to finance housing, although S & Ls are broadening the types of loans they make. Membership in a credit union is normally limited to the employees of a particular firm or members of a particular labor union or profession, although in some rural areas a geographic boundary determines eligibility for membership. Credit unions offer their members loans for many consumer purchases, including housing.

Insurance Companies Many people will bet a small amount of money on the outcome of the flip of a coin. However, only a few high rollers are willing to bet thousands of dollars with no better than even odds of winning. Most of us want the probable outcome of risky activities to favor us substantially, or we just don't want to play. **Risk aversion** entails a willingness to pay to avoid risk. Most of us are willing to pay money to avoid some of the financial consequences of taking risks, so **insurance companies** can sell us a guarantee against risk for a fee that is large enough to cover their claims and operating costs and still permit a profit. No one can predict whose house will burn down next — yours or your neighbor's. Thus, all insurance policy buyers make small contributions toward a fund that can be used to compensate the person whose house goes up in flames.

Insurance companies can provide this service and expect to make profits as long as the fee (premium) is greater than the amount they might have to pay, multiplied by the probability of payment. Vast amounts of money are paid to insurance companies as premiums for life, auto, and health insurance, or as contributions to pension funds, many of which are administered by insurance companies. These funds are made available for loans to business firms or are invested directly by the insurance companies.

Securities Markets Brokers who buy and sell financial securities also provide financial intermediation.

> **Securities** *include paper assets such as stocks and bonds. A* **bond** *is simply an IOU issued by a corporation or government agency that pays interest to the lender. A* **share of stock** *is a claim to partial ownership of a corporation.*

Most corporations and government agencies do not solicit you directly for funds that you might be willing to lend. Instead, they typically

Table 11 *Financial Intermediaries*

	Commercial Banks	Thrift Institutions: Savings and Loans Mutual Savings Banks	Thrift Institutions: Credit Unions	Insurance Companies	Securities Markets
Primary sources of funds (liabilities)	Deposits Checking accounts Savings accounts	Deposits Shares (savings) Checking accounts Other	Deposits Shares Checking accounts	Insurance policies	Sales of stocks and bonds are accomplished primarily through stockbrokers and investment bankers who charge brokerage fees for getting savers (purchasers) together with business firms that do the direct economic investment with the funds made available
Primary uses of funds (assets)	Business loans Consumer loans Automobiles Home equity loans Furniture and appliances Education Personal	Home mortgages Home equity loans and improvements	Consumer loans Autos, etc.	Business loans Real estate Direct financial investment	
Notes	Banks "create" money by crediting your account when they extend a loan to you	Major function is to finance housing (not business construction)	Focus on consumer loans for members only	Insurance company premiums exceed their expected payouts; people buy insurance because they are risk averse	

leave this specialized sort of solicitation to brokers, who communicate offers to buy or sell securities through stock exchanges. Although the New York Stock Exchange (also known as *Wall Street*) is the best known, there are a number of lesser and regional stock exchanges.

Table 11 summarizes the different roles played by various financial intermediaries. Be aware, however, that differences among these institutions are increasingly blurred because of recent deregulation. The major financial regulator in the United States is our central bank, the Federal Reserve System, which is the topic of the next chapter.

Chapter Review: Key Points

1. *Barter* requires a *double coincidence of wants* — trade can only occur if each party has what the other wants and if divisibility poses no problems.

2. *Money* ensures this double coincidence of wants — the seller will accept money because of what it will buy, while the buyer is willing to exchange money (and, thus, all else it will buy) for the good or service in question.

3. Money facilitates specialization and exchange by decreasing transaction costs. The more sophisticated the financial system, the greater the level of production and consumption and the higher the standard of living.

4. Money is a *medium of exchange*. It is used for most transactions in monetary economies.

5. Money is a *measure of value*. Used as a standard unit of account, it is the common denominator for pricing goods and services.

6. Money is a *store of value*. It is among the most nominally secure of all assets people can use to hold their wealth.

7. Money is a *standard of deferred payment*. Serving as a link between the past, present, and future, it is used as a measure of *credit* to execute contracts calling for future payments.

8. *Liquidity* is negatively related to the transaction costs incurred in exchanges of assets. *Time, certainty regarding price*, and the *quality of information in a market* are all dimensions of liquidity. Assets are liquid if transaction costs are low, *illiquid* if transaction costs are high.

9. *Commodity monies* (precious metals, stones, or arrowheads) have values that are independent of what they will buy. *Fiat money* (paper currency) is valuable only because it is money; its use is based on *faith*.

10. The profit governments make from printing money or stamping coins is called *seignorage*.

11. According to Gresham's Law, "Bad money drives out good."

12. The very narrowly defined money supply (*M1*) is the total of (*a*) *currency* (coins and bills) in the hands of the nonbanking public plus (*b*) *demand deposits* (checking accounts of private individuals, firms, and nonfederal government units in financial institutions).

13. Some highly liquid assets are viewed as near-monies and are included in broader definitions of the money supply (*M2* and *M3*) by monetary analysts who believe the spending of the public can be predicted better if these assets are included. Examples of such highly liquid assets include short-term *time deposits* (savings accounts) or *certificates of deposit* (*CDs*). The assets included in "money supplies" defined more broadly than *M1* are judgmental, because these assets are not mediums of exchange.

14. Banks "*create*" money through loan-based expansions of demand deposits (checking account money). They make loans based on currency they hold as reserves, and these loans take the form of new demand deposit money.

15. Banks hold *reserves* that are far less than their deposit liabilities. The larger the proportion of deposits held as either excess or required reserves, the smaller are the money multiplier and resulting money supply, given some fixed total amount of reserves.

16. The *potential money multiplier* (m_p) equals $1/rr$, where rr is the banking system's planned or legally required reserves as a percentage of deposits. The *actual money multiplier* is much smaller because (*a*) households and firms hold currency that could be used as a base for the money creation process were this currency held in bank vaults as reserves against deposits, and (*b*) banks hold excess reserves to meet withdrawals of deposits.

17. The *actual money multiplier* (m_a) equals MS/MB, where MS is the money supply and MB is the *monetary base*, or high-powered money. Naturally, $MS = m_a MB$.

18. *Financial institutions* facilitate flows and payments of funds and provide secure places for savers' deposits. Their most important economic function is to channel funds from savers to financial investors and other borrowers through a process called *financial intermediation*. Commercial banks, savings-and-loan associations, mutual savings banks, credit unions, insurance companies, and stock exchanges are all financial intermediaries.

Key Concepts

Ensure that you can define these terms before proceeding.

barter	liquidity
money	commodity money
fiat money	reserves
seignorage	money creation process
M1, M2, M3, *L*	actual and potential
fractional reserve	money multipliers
banking	financial intermediation

Problems and Questions

1. Calculate potential money multipliers for reserve requirement ratios (rr) equal to: 1/10, 1/9, 1/8, 1/7, 1/6, 1/5, and 1/4.

2. How large is the potential money supply for each value you calculated in the preceding question if there is initially $1 million in bank reserves and $1 million in currency in circulation? What will be the actual money multiplier for each reserve requirement ratio in the preceding question if banks hold no excess reserves? If banks hold an extra 10 percent in reserve for each reserve requirement ratio listed in the preceding question?

3. How many relative prices are relevant for market decisions if 50 goods are traded in a society that does not use money? How many relative prices would people keep track of if money were introduced into this society?

4. If the Obsidian Bank receives a deposit of $50,000 and the required reserve ratio equals 0.25 for all banks, what is the maximum amount of money Obsidian can loan? What does the potential money multiplier equal? How much additional money could be created by the entire banking system from the $50,000 deposit?

5. Money is (a) a medium of exchange, (b) a unit of account or measure of value, (c) a store of value, and (d) a standard of deferred payment. There are items that perform some, but not all, of these functions. Which functions do credit cards (Visa, MasterCard, Discover) serve? Which are not served? How about savings deposits? Gold or silver? Stocks and bonds?

6. How important is the degree of liquidity in determining which assets qualify as money? List the following items according to their degree of liquidity, from least liquid to most liquid: (a) dollar bill, (b) U.S. government bond, (c) house, (d) car, (e) pedigreed dog, (f) television set, (g) savings account, and (h) human skills.

7. Explain how the introduction of money permits society to better realize the advantages of specialization of labor. Would you expect to find a sophisticated division of labor in a barter economy? Explain why the standards of living tend to be very low in moneyless economies.

8. Explain what is meant by the phrase "Money is a link between the past, present, and future." Can you explain how the use of money makes the economy operate more smoothly through time?

9. What financial barriers might confront people who live in different societies with different monetary systems and who wish to trade with one another? Would it be advantageous if the entire world used a common currency? What do you think are some of the reasons we do not have a world currency?

10. In 1933, Adolph Hitler decreed that the old German deutsche mark was worthless and could be exchanged at a fixed rate for new reichsmarks. The British redeemed their old currency in the late 1960s, replacing it with a "metric" style currency. What circumstances might make it appropriate to completely withdraw one currency from circulation and replace it with a new currency?

CHAPTER 12

The Federal Reserve System

Whoever controls the volume of money in any country is absolute master of all industry and commerce.

President James A. Garfield

Charges of fraud resounded when savings-and-loan institutions collapsed like toppled columns of dominoes during 1988–1991. This scandal is a symptom of the potential for abuse by the owners and managers of the institutions we entrust with our money. Thus, it is not surprising that financial institutions are regulated more tightly than any other U.S. industry except, perhaps, secret weapons research or atomic energy.

> *The* **Federal Reserve System (the FED)** *is the central bank of the United States, which regulates* (**a**) *banks and related financial institutions, and* (**b**) *the volume of money in circulation.*

The FED may be the most powerful and independent of all government agencies.[1] During hearings on the FED's policies, one senator com-

---

1. Former Representative Jack Kemp (R-NY), on being asked whether he would run for president in 1988, replied that he wanted to hold the most powerful position in the world: Chairman of the FED. He ran for president anyway, but was clobbered in the primaries by George Bush.

pared getting an answer out of the chairman of the FED's Board of Governors to "nailing a chocolate cream pie to a wall."

The structure of the FED and the tools it uses to control the money supply and shape financial conditions are examined in this chapter. We also survey different types of financial institutions, the major goals of the FED and other financial regulators, and the consequences of certain policies intended to alter economic activity.

The Purposes of Financial Regulations

The major macroeconomic purpose of a financial system is to channel saving to its most productive uses, but financial intermediation can be an unstable process. For example, waves of nervous depositors sometimes try to withdraw all their savings simultaneously — not always a possibility in a fractional reserve banking system. A related problem is that inept or dishonest officers of financial institutions may mismanage the savings with which they are entrusted. Thus, major goals for a government's central bank in regulating financial institutions include (*a*) protection of savers, (*b*) macroeconomic stability, and (*c*) promotion of efficiency.

Financial institutions are not lenders per se,

but merely act as intermediaries between savers and borrowers. In this context, **financial efficiency** means minimizing the costs of intermediation, or the bankers' "spread" — the differences between the costs of loans to borrowers and the interest incomes received by ultimate lenders. This is the financial equivalent of the principle that efficiency requires all services to be produced at the lowest possible opportunity cost. Unfortunately, protecting people's savings and ensuring economic stability can conflict with efficiency in financial intermediation.

Early Central Banks Many of this nation's founders feared that a central bank would concentrate economic and political power. Alexander Hamilton's persuasive skills were stretched to capacity to secure the establishment of the first Bank of the United States shortly after the U.S. Constitution was adopted. This central bank replaced a system in which the federal government, various states, and many private banks all issued different currencies. The phrase "Not worth a continental" crept into our language when currency issued by the Continental Congress became worthless. The dollar became a sound currency only after the Bank honored government debts incurred in fighting the Revolutionary War.

The Bank of the United States was privately owned and operated, but it was also the government's bank because it (*a*) stored tax revenues, (*b*) paid the government's obligations, and (*c*) arranged loans to and from the government. The Bank was unpopular with most Westerners and agricultural interests, who felt it served only the rich "Eastern Establishment." The death of Hamilton and ascendance of his political rival, Thomas Jefferson, led in 1811 to the end of our first experiment with central banking.

The Second Bank of the United States, chartered in 1816, was operated by Nicholas Biddle, a member of a prominent Philadelphia family. Despite some initial success, President Andrew Jackson vetoed the act to recharter it. In 1836, the original charter expired. Nicholas Biddle lost his power in a minor financial scandal, and the collapse of the Bank precipitated the financial crash of 1837. For the next 75 years, the American economy experienced substantial but erratic growth without a central bank.

The Federal Reserve System

The U.S. economy prospered even though it suffered financial crises roughly every 20 to 25 years from the American Revolution through the Great Depression. Most financial panics were followed by periods of stagnation. A wave of bank failures in 1906–1907 led to establishment of a third central bank, the Federal Reserve System, in 1913. Among the FED's major objectives is to act as a "lender of last resort." This means that the FED lends money to inherently sound banks so they can survive bank "runs," when financial panics cause armies of bank customers to demand withdrawals of their deposits.

The seven members of the FED's *Board of Governors* are appointed to staggered 14-year terms because Congress feared the instability of a highly politicized central bank. Each president and Congress has limited power over the FED because they appoint only one new member of the Board of Governors every other year. The majority of Board members traditionally have been bankers, causing some people to question how diligent they are as public "watchdogs." Recently, however, presidents have nominated increasing numbers of governors drawn from the general public, including more than a few economists.

The FED (in concert with the Comptroller of the Currency, the Federal Deposit Insurance Corporation, and various state government agencies) audits banks to guard against fraud, and enforces a maze of regulations. Among its other services to the banking community, the FED processes checks drawn on one bank and deposited elsewhere. The FED's key role, however, is to conduct monetary policy. Before we examine monetary policymaking, you need to know a bit more about the structure of the FED.

Federal Reserve Bank Districts

The 12 regional districts of the Federal Reserve System are depicted in Figure 1. Each district has a primary bank and one or more branch offices. If you check any bills you have on hand, you may find that many have travelled far from their points of issue.

Federal Reserve Banks and their branches do not serve the general public directly. They are "bankers' banks" that help member banks clear checks drawn on other banks, make loans to bankers, and otherwise facilitate efficiency in the financial sector of the economy. The FED operates under the fiction that it is a private organiza- tion "owned" by federally chartered private banks, but it is actually an arm of the government created by Congress. The FED's actions and decisions have the force of law, and any returns on investment greater than 6 percent annually must be paid to the U.S. Treasury.

Member Banks Roughly 14,000 privately owned banks now operate in the United States, of which fewer than 5,000 are national banks chartered by the Comptroller of the Currency;

FIGURE 1 Federal Reserve Branch Banks

The Federal Reserve System consists of 12 districts. Each district has a Federal Reserve Bank. Some of the larger districts also have Branch Banks. This figure depicts the locations of these primary and Branch Banks and outlines their boundaries.
Source: *Federal Reserve Bulletin.*

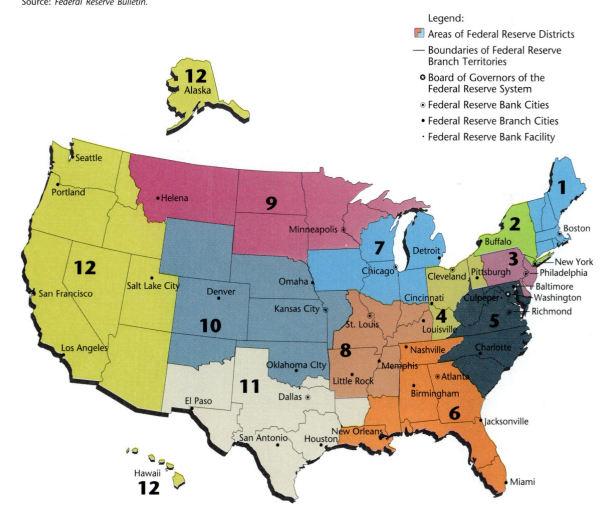

Legend:
- Areas of Federal Reserve Districts
— Boundaries of Federal Reserve Branch Territories
⊛ Board of Governors of the Federal Reserve System
⊙ Federal Reserve Bank Cities
• Federal Reserve Branch Cities
· Federal Reserve Bank Facility

9,000 or so are state banks chartered by state governments. *National banks* must be members of the Federal Reserve System; *state banks* may (upon approval) qualify as *member banks*. Over 70 percent of all deposits are in member banks, and the FED now sets legal reserve requirements on deposits in *all* financial institutions. Thus, the Federal Reserve System has considerable direct power over most of our financial system.

Organization of the FED

The Federal Reserve System's official structure is shown in Figure 2. The chairman of the Board of Governors is supposedly only a "first among equals." Like the chief justice of the Supreme Court, he nominally has only one vote in any decisions made. However, the chairman in fact has disproportionate power within the Board of Governors. Of course, the effectiveness of the chairman in controlling monetary policy depends on personality and on the dynamics of the relationships among the various governors.

Congress established the FED as a pseudo-private organization in an attempt to prevent political chicanery from distorting its regulatory and stabilization policies. As a "private" organization, FED member banks elect six of the nine directors of each District Bank; the other three are appointed by the Board of Governors. But real policymaking power is exercised by the *Federal Open Market Committee (FOMC)* — all seven members of the Board of Governors plus the president of the New York District Bank. Four other District Bank presidents rotate on the committee. The FOMC has enormous control over our entire financial system through its conduct of monetary policy. Committee members' terms of office and votes give the real clout within the FOMC to the Board of Governors,

FIGURE 2   The Formal Organization of the Federal Reserve System

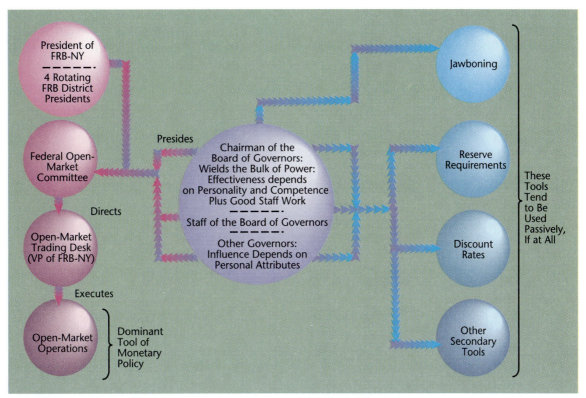

FIGURE 3   Real Policymaking Power in the Federal Reserve System

Real policymaking power seldom follows an institution's formal organization chart. The Federal Reserve System is no exception. This figure depicts the flow of real policymaking power within the FED.

especially the chairman. Figure 3 portrays the actual channels of power within the FED.

Economists focus on incentives. Should our central bank maximize profits? Should monetary policymakers be subjected to political pressures in our democracy? Before we tackle these problems, let us see why the answers to these questions are so important.

Tools of the FED

The Federal Reserve System's major tools to control the money supply and broad financial conditions are (*a*) reserve requirements, (*b*) open-market operations, and (*c*) discounting operations. Secondary tools of the FED include controls over stock market credit and "jawboning." Day in and day out, the FED actively uses open-market operations to implement its ever-

changing policies. Reserve requirements and discounting operations are important, though generally passive, instruments of monetary policy.

Reserve Requirements (rr)

Bank reserves can be kept in banks' vaults or on deposit at Federal Reserve banks.

> *The Federal Reserve System sets the **reserve-requirement ratio (rr)** – a legal floor on the percentage of a bank's deposits that must be held in reserves.*

Suppose the reserve-requirement ratio (*rr*) is 1/6 or 16.7 percent. For the actual money multiplier (m_a) to equal the potential money multiplier ($m_p = 1/rr = 6$), banks must be "fully loaned up" (no excess reserves), and no currency can be held outside the banking system. Only then are the actual (m_a) and potential (m_p) money multipliers equal.

Banks cannot survive for long if reserves sink to the legal minimum; they need excess reserves to accommodate any outflows of funds. Otherwise, they would be unable to meet any demands for withdrawals of deposits without being in trouble with the FED.

Legal reserves (LR) = required reserves $(rr \cdot DD)$ + excess reserves (XR)

Note that all reserves available to meet the FED's reserve requirements are *legal reserves*, which include both *excess reserves* and *required reserves*. The overall banking system usually operates with very few excess reserves, however, because banks lend and borrow money from each other daily through the privately operated *federal-funds market*.

Electronic Banking and "Real Money"

Electronic deposits of paychecks and payments of bills are increasingly common, and credit cards have replaced cash for many purchases. On average, people today handle much less cash relative to their income than was typical in earlier times. Most money is kept in banks. But do banks keep much "real money" in their vaults? If *real money* is interpreted as meaning bills and coins, the answer is "Not much." Banks keep enough currency on hand to meet their customers' demands for cash, and that is about it.

Typical banks now hold deposits of well over $20 million. Where do they store all this money? You learned in the previous chapter that banks in a fractional reserve system hold only about 15 to 30 percent of their deposits as reserves. However, a $20-million bank will not keep $3 to 6 million on hand in cash—keeping track of the inventory might be a problem, and there is no sense in tempting thieves. Consequently, banks keep most of their reserves on deposit with Federal Reserve Branch or District Banks.

Even these FED banks do not hold your bank's deposits in the form of cash, because literally tons of the green stuff would need to be warehoused. You have probably figured out that your bank account is simply a few electronic impulses stored in the bank's computer. The FED does the same thing with the reserves that banks keep on deposit at Branch or District Banks—it is all in the computer. Roughly two-thirds of the nation's money supply now exists only in computers.

Reserve Requirements and the Money Multiplier

One way the Federal Reserve System can vary the money supply is through changes in the reserve-requirement ratio (rr). If the FED *raises* the reserve-requirement ratio, then $1/rr$ falls. The smaller potential money multiplier (m_p) means the total reserves in the banking system will support only smaller potential totals of loan-based demand deposits. Conversely, a *decrease* in the reserve-requirement ratio enables banks to increase the money supply through expansion of demand-deposit-based loans.

Most banks try to hold roughly the same percentage of excess reserves against demand deposits no matter what happens to the reserve-requirement ratio because the percentage fluctuations of bank deposits depend on people's behavior rather than on the FED's reserve requirements. Notice that the reserve-requirement ratio does not influence the total amount of reserves in the banking system. Instead, it affects the m_p. Naturally, whenever the m_p changes, the actual money multiplier (m_a) moves in the same direction.

The amounts of excess reserves held by banks will depend on (*a*) the expected profitability of lending any excess reserves, and (*b*) the expected costs of acquiring reserves should borrowing be necessary to meet the FED's reserve requirements. In other words, the percentage of deposits held as excess reserves will be *negatively* related to the difference between the interest rates banks can charge borrowers and the interest rates banks themselves must pay to borrow reserves from other banks or the FED.

The reserve-requirement ratio (rr) is the FED's most powerful tool. Suppose that the rr were increased from 1/6 (16.7 percent) to 1/5 (20 percent)—a change of 3.3 percentage points. The potential money supply would fall by roughly 1/6 (m_p falls from 6 to 5). Curiously, this powerful tool is seldom used; reserve-requirement ratios have been changed only about two dozen times since the Great Depression. Why? The very power of changes in *rr* makes it difficult to predict the magnitude of their effect.

An analogy may help you understand why. Imagine that you were scheduled for brain surgery. Would you want the surgeon to use the most powerful tool available — a chainsaw? Or would you prefer that the surgery be done with more finesse, using a tool such as a scalpel? A second tool of the FED, open-market operations, is the best tool available for the conduct of monetary policy. It is the FED's scalpel.

Open-Market Operations (OMO)

The FED's most important tool, open-market operations, links monetary policy with the bonds issued by the U.S. Treasury to finance federal budget deficits.

> **Open-market operations (OMO)** *entail buying and selling securities issued by the U.S. Treasury and are used to increase or decrease the size of the monetary base.*

In the previous chapter we indicated that the monetary base (*MB*) is the total of currency held by the nonbanking public plus reserves held by banks: *MB* = currency + bank reserves. Thus, the monetary base is the foundation for our money supply because the money creation process builds from the reserves in the banking system.

The FED's Open Market Committee (FOMC) adjusts the size of the monetary base through *open-market* purchases or sales of U.S. Treasury securities. To increase the money supply by expanding the monetary base, the FOMC's "open-market desk" buys Treasury bonds — primarily from commercial banks, but also from private individuals or nonbank firms. If the FOMC sells bonds, the monetary base is reduced. Funds paid by the FED to nonbank sellers are invariably deposited in banks, however, so they end up as bank reserves. Similarly, private buyers of bonds withdraw funds from banks to pay for their purchases. Thus, regardless of with whom the FED deals, the effects on total bank reserves and the money supply are similar.

When the FED buys bonds, bank reserves are increased and the banking system will increase loan-based demand deposits in accord with the money creation process discussed previously. You may wonder where the FED gets the money to buy the bonds. The answer is that the FED can print new currency or it can simply credit the reserve accounts of the private banks via computer at one of the Federal Reserve District Banks.

"T-account" entries for a typical expansionary open-market transaction are shown in Table 1. When the FOMC buys $1,000 in Treasury bonds from Bank A, the Federal Reserve Bank increases reserves held for Bank A by $1,000; the FED's assets are debited by $1,000 in Treasury bonds. Bank A's assets change from $1,000 in Treasury bonds to $1,000 in new reserves. Bank A views the sale of the bond to the FED in the same way

Table 1 *T-Account Changes for a Typical Open-Market Transaction*

Federal Reserve Bank	
Assets	**Liabilities**
+$1,000 Treasury bonds	+$1,000 Reserves held for Bank A
Member Bank A	
Assets	**Liabilities**
−$1,000 Treasury bonds +$1,000 Loanable reserves	No change

FOCUS 1

The "Go-Around"

The time is early afternoon on a Wednesday in mid-June. The place is the trading room on the eighth floor of the Federal Reserve Bank of New York. The manager of the Open Market Account for Domestic Operations gathers with his trading room officers to reaffirm the judgment reached earlier to buy about $1¼ billion of Treasury bills. The banking system has a clear need for additional reserves to meet the increased public demand for currency and deposits expected as the end of the quarter and July 4 approach. The markets for bank reserves and Treasury securities are functioning normally with prices moving narrowly. After a brief debate, the manager gives approval for the operation.

The officer-in-charge at the FED's Trading Desk turns to the ten officers and securities traders who sit before telephone consoles linking them to three dozen primary dealers in U.S. government securities. "We're going to ask for offerings of all bills for regular delivery," she says. Each trader knows this means delivery and payment will take place the next day. Each picks up the vertical strips on which the offerings will be recorded for the four dealers he will call.

Bill, one of the group, presses a button on his telephone console, sounding a buzzer on the corresponding console of a government securities dealer.

"John," Bill says, "we are look-ing for offerings of bills for regular delivery."

John replies, "I'll be right back." He turns and yells, "The FED is in, asking for all bills for delivery tomorrow." Moments later, information screens around the country and abroad flash the news. Salespeople begin ringing their customers to see if they have bills they want to offer. Meanwhile, John checks with the trading manager of his firm to see how aggressive he should be in pricing the firm's own securities.

Twenty minutes later John rings back. "Bill, I can offer you $15 million of bills maturing August 9 at 9.20 percent, $40 million of September 13 bills at 9.42, $25 million of September

that it would the payback of a loan by a private borrower. Note, however, that this "payoff" creates new reserves for the banking system as a whole, while payment of a private loan does not. These new reserves can then be loaned to private borrowers, creating new demand deposit money via the expansionary money multiplier process.

If the FED wants to reduce the money supply, it sells bonds to commercial banks. This sops up excess reserves and may even threaten to cut into banks' required reserves. As banks attempt to rebuild their reserves to desired levels, they turn down applications for new loans or renewals of old loans, and the amount of loan-based demand deposits falls. The "money destruction" process that results from the FED's sale of Treasury bonds is exactly the opposite of the money creation process. If the positive numbers in Table 1 were negative, and vice versa, the table would illustrate a contractionary open-market operation.

You may wonder how the FED can persuade banks or private individuals to sell bonds when the FOMC conducts expansionary open-market operations. A bidding process is used; the sellers are those willing to offer desired amounts of

20s at 9.46 and another 25 at 9.44. I'll sell $75 million December 13s at 10.12 and another 100 at 10.09. I can offer $20 million of March 21s at 10.25 and 50 May 16s at 10.28. All for delivery tomorrow."

Bill reads back each of the offerings to double check, then says, "Can I have those firm?"

"Sure."

Within ten or fifteen minutes each trader has written the offerings obtained from his calls on preprinted strips. The officer-in-charge arrays the individual dealer strips on an inclined board placed atop a stand-up counter. A quick tally shows that dealers have offered $7.8 billion of bills for regular delivery—that is, on Thursday.

The officer and a colleague begin comparing rates across the different maturities, seeking those that are high in relation to adjoining issues. She circles any special bargains with a red pencil. With an eye on heavy existing holdings, she circles other propositions that offer yields on or above a yield curve she draws mentally through the more heavily offered issues. Her associate keeps a running total of the amounts being bought. When the desired volume has been circled and cross-checked, the individual strips are returned to the traders, who quickly ring up the dealers.

Bill says, "John, we'll take the $25 million of September 20s at 9.46, the 75 of December 13s at 10.12, and the 50 of May 16s at 10.28 for regular delivery. A total of $150 million. No thanks on the others."

Forty-five minutes after the initial entry, the follow-up calls have been completed. The Trading Desk has bought $1,304 million of Treasury bills. Only the paperwork remains. The traders write up tickets, which authorize the accounting section to instruct the Reserve Bank's Government Bond Department to receive and pay for the specific Treasury bills bought.

Source: Paul Meek, Open Market Operations *(New York: Federal Reserve Bank of New York, 1985). Reprinted by permission of the Federal Reserve Bank of New York.*

bonds at the lowest prices. No matter how high the prices are, the FED buys the bonds. When the FED wants to withdraw reserves from the banking system to reduce the money supply, it sells some of the Treasury bonds in its portfolio. As Focus 1 illustrates, the FED takes the highest bids for bonds it sells, no matter how low the bids are.

Actually, the open-market desk of the FOMC both buys and sells bonds every business day, primarily to adjust the maturity dates of the bonds it holds, but also, occasionally, to mask the direction of its policies.

1. If the FED buys more bonds than it sells, total bank reserves are increased and the money creation process leads monetary growth.

2. If the FED sells more bonds than it buys, reserves are reduced and the money destruction process causes the money supply to shrink.

Open-market operations ultimately affect the money supply *only* through changes in the amounts of reserves in the banking system, *not* through changes in the money multiplier. The maximum possible value of the multiplier (m_p) is determined by the reserve-requirement ratio (rr). The FED's discounting operations affect both the size of the monetary base (MB) and the value of the actual money multiplier (m_a).

Discounting Operations

When banks have insufficient reserves to meet the FED's reserve requirements or want to increase their reserves, they can borrow money from the *discount windows* of the FED's District or Branch Banks; the FED is a bankers' bank. Loans from the FED become a part of a bank's reserves and thus increase the monetary base.

The interest rate the FED charges bankers is called the **discount rate (d).**

Most bank borrowing from the FED is to cover temporary deficiencies. Whether banks will have deficient reserves, however, depends strongly on the discount rate. Whenever the discount rate (d) is substantially less than market interest rates (i), the monetary base grows—the FED extends credit (reserves) to banks, which allows bankers to expand their loans and demand deposits. When the discount rate the bank pays is below the interest rate it charges on loans, it is a bit like trading nickels for dimes.

On the other hand, if the discount rate is substantially above the market rate of interest, it penalizes bankers forced to borrow from the FED because of unforeseen withdrawals of deposits. Consequently, banks try to avoid any need to borrow by holding greater excess reserves. Thus the actual multiplier m_a shrinks as the difference between the discount rate and the market interest rate grows.

All else equal,

1. When the FED raises the discount rate, banks will borrow less, reducing total reserves or limiting their increase. Banks will also lend less, so excess reserves in individual banks grow while the actual money multiplier and money supply decline.
2. When the FED decreases the discount rate, banks increase their borrowing from the

FED and cut holdings of excess reserves; this increases the actual money multiplier and money supply.

The FED's Secondary Tools

Although the reserve-requirement ratio, open-market operations, and the discount rate are the major mechanisms at the FED's disposal, some other devices in the FED's toolbox help it control financial markets and economic activity:

1. The FED sets "margin requirements" to control stock-market credit.
2. The FED "jawbones," which means it rages at people or institutions who do things it does not like.

Until recently, the FED could also (*a*) regulate credit to consumers and business firms during wars or crises, and (*b*) set the maximum interest rates payable to depositors. Congress rescinded both these FED powers during a wave of deregulation in the 1980s.

Margin Requirements   Many people blamed overspeculation caused by *buying on margin* for the Stock Market Crash of 1929 and the Great Depression. In the 1920s, stock could be purchased with a down payment of as little as 10 percent.

The FED sets the **margin requirement** *(the percentage down payment required) for purchases of corporate financial securities.*

Some 1920s' investors used almost all their assets for down payments. Then, when stock prices fell, they were wiped out financially. In the aftermath of the Crash, the Federal Reserve System was granted power to determine *margin requirements*, which have hovered around 50 percent for the past three decades. Presumably, higher margin requirements squelch speculation and lower margin requirements stimulate speculation.

There is, however, little evidence that margin requirements significantly influence stock prices. Indeed, a powerful economic theory suggests that adjustments by prudent financial investors will offset any speculative bubble caused by stock buyers who become overly enthused by low margin requirements. Suppose financial investors expected a 10 percent return on stocks but a 12 percent return on equally risky real estate. Funds would flow into real estate from the stock market. The stock market would fall a bit, and real estate prices would rise until the returns were equalized at, say, 11 percent.

These sorts of adjustments will cure even minor overspeculation in stocks. If low margin requirements prompt speculation that boosts stock prices slightly, the expected returns (dividends, etc.) per dollar invested in stocks decline. This makes real estate or other investments comparatively more attractive to prudent investors, so money will flow from the stock market until the returns from all investments are equated. Overspeculation in stocks because of low margin requirements is eliminated automatically.

Jawboning Self-restraints on union wage increases or price increases by business are commonly advocated by presidents seeking to contain inflation.

> **Jawboning** *is oratory used by policymakers who want people or institutions to act against their individual interests (or to see their interests in a different light).*

The FED occasionally has tried to "jawbone" banks into expanding or contracting credit, but economists tend to be skeptical that appeals to public-spiritedness are effective. FED jawboning may have some effect, however, because it is backed up by the power to audit and otherwise harass banks. A major problem is that jawboning is less predictable than virtually any other tool. Consequently, few recent chairmen of the Federal Reserve System have tried to exhort bankers to do something other than maximize their profits.

Which Tools Are Used?

The Federal Reserve System strongly influences the money supply, but it lacks precise and direct control. We indicated previously that the money supply (MS) is the product of the money multiplier (m_a) and the monetary base (MB):

$$MS = m_a(MB)$$

The FED can use active changes in the discount rate, reserve-requirement ratios, or interest ceilings on deposits to try to manipulate the value of the actual money multiplier and thereby change the money supply. Alternatively, it can use open-market operations (and, to a lesser extent, discount operations) to vary the monetary base in attempts to alter the money supply. Table 2 summarizes how tools of the FED affect the money supply by altering the behavior of banks and the public.

If the FED does not independently determine the money supply, what other groups have influence, and how? The FED directly and tightly controls the monetary base through open-market operations. The public can affect the money multiplier through its holding of cash. As private stores of cash grow, currency available for bank reserves shrinks; the actual money multiplier and the money supply are reduced, because the money expansion process only applies to currency in bank vaults or reserves at the FED. Independent of FED policies, banks may unintentionally alter the actual money multiplier by varying their percentages of excess reserves: The greater the excess reserves held by banks, the smaller will be the actual money multiplier and the money supply.

If private activities can alter the actual money multiplier and thwart the desire of the FED to change the money supply, then which tools most effectively accomplish the FED's goals? Any versatile do-it-yourselfer accumulates some tools that rust because they are seldom, if ever, used. This analogy applies to changes in stock-market margin requirements and jawboning, which are used only rarely. Reserve-requirement ratios are seldom varied, and then only slightly. They are too powerful to be very useful.

In recent years, the discount rate has been pegged slightly above interest rates in the federal-funds market. This prompts banks to borrow from each other and discourages borrowing from the FED. The discount rate is typically

Table 2 *Fed Tools and Effects*

Tool Used	Potential Money Multiplier ($m_p = 1/rr$)	Excess Reserves Ratio ($xr = XR/DD$)	Actual Money Multiplier ($m_a = MS/MB$)	Monetary Base (MB)	Currency NBP*	Bank Reserves	Loans, Demand Deposits, and Money Supply (M1)
Reserve-requirement ratios (rr)							
Raise rr	Lower	No change	Lower	No change	No change	No change	Lower
Lower rr	Higher	No change	Higher	No change	No change	No change	Higher
Open-market operations (OMO)							
Buys bonds	No change	No change	No change	Higher	Higher	Higher	Higher
Sells bonds	No change	No change	No change	Lower	Lower	Lower	Lower
Discounting operations							
Lower rate	No change	Lower	Higher	Higher	Higher	Higher	Higher
Raise rate	No change	Higher	Lower	Lower	Lower	Lower	Lower
Jawboning	No change	Ambiguous		No change		Ambiguous	
Stock market margin requirements	Lower margin requirements presumably cause more stock market speculation while higher margin requirements presumably discourage speculation. There is, however, little statistical support for this proposition and a powerful theory to refute the idea.						

*Note: Unless interest rates paid on deposits change, households and firms are assumed to keep stable proportions of their money holdings in the forms of cash and demand deposits, respectively.

changed no more than three times a year to reflect changes in interest rates in the federal-funds market. Changes in the discount rate normally are not intended to affect the money supply directly, because the FED would like the actual money multiplier to be stable. Thus, discount rate changes are used primarily to keep the percentage of deposits held as excess reserves constant.

Open-market operations are the best tool to control the money supply. It took a long time for the FED to understand this, but open-market operations are now the FED's dominant actively used tool. Open-market operations directly alter the reserves in the banking system. In the long run, open-market operations have no effect on the money multiplier. Active changes in reserve-requirement ratios or the discount rate operate primarily through changes in the actual money multiplier. The results of policy-caused changes in the actual multiplier have been erratic and unsatisfactory when used.

Our Changing Financial Climate

Competition among bankers has historically been limited by a maze of state and federal laws. Rural banks once depended primarily on local customers and nearby farmers, while banks in big cities catered to their own neighborhoods. The expanding scope of interstate trade then generated pressure for legal reforms to allow banks to establish branches. Thus, banking is increasingly concentrated in the hands of bigger banks. However, pressure for financial reform continues to grow, largely because of growth in international competition.

The growth of international trade is apparent in our diets, the clothes we wear, and the cars we drive. Internationalization of financial markets is proceeding at an even faster pace. In 1970, the United States was headquarters for virtually all of the world's 10 largest banks. Today, the United States holds only 20 percent or so of the world's banking giants. In recent decades, international inflation, the dollar's decline from virtual dominance in world money markets, and a host of other factors have contributed to pressures for changes in the financial sector of our economy. Major deregulation occurred in 1980, but many reforms were phased in gradually.

Deregulation enabled many banks to become virtual "money supermarkets," but it also opened the doors for expanded lending activity by such firms as General Electric, Sears, Ford, and AT&T. Although the magnitude of financial intermediation continues to grow rapidly, banks' shares of total lending in the United States had fallen from roughly 40 percent in 1960 to under 30 percent by 1990. Parallel losses of competitive advantage were experienced by savings and loans and credit unions. Banks and similar institutions need flexibility to meet the financial needs of our changing economy, but, as Focus 2 indicates, the specific forms taken in some deregulation may have contributed to recent problems in the financial sector.

The FED's Independence Under Attack

The Great Depression of the 1930s obliterated faith in monetary policy. The Keynesian Revolution (from 1936 through the 1960s) convinced most economists that fiscal policy is the best way to stabilize the economy. In the 1970s, however, monetary policy made a strong comeback—few economists now believe that "money doesn't matter."

A gradual reaffirmation of the importance of monetary policy began in the 1950s. At that time, the FED's policy of slow monetary growth was widely attacked as hindering the economy from achieving its potential. In the early 1960s, William McChesney Martin, Jr., was the chairman of the Board of Governors. He was roundly condemned by Keynesians for following contractionary monetary policies that partially offset the expansionary fiscal policies adopted by Presidents Kennedy and Johnson. The failure of a 1968 tax surcharge to slow inflation was blamed by some on excessive monetary growth during 1968 and 1969. In the 1970s, "stop-and-go" monetary policies were partially blamed for stagflation and the reemergence of the business cycle. Then, in the early 1980s under the chairmanship of Paul Volcker, the FED's restrictive monetary policies were blamed for a severe slump in business activity. Most observers conceded, however, that these policies did dampen inflation and eventually reduced interest rates.

One consequence of the renewed recognition of the power of monetary policy is pressure for the FED to be "politically accountable." Many regulatory agencies are thought to be controlled by the industries they are supposed to oversee. The FED is often accused of being a captive of banking interests and of following monetary policies that benefit bankers without regard for the public interest.

Focus 3 provides insight into why the FED has been accused of following erratic policies that have fostered macroeconomic instability. A congressional resolution prescribes that the FED should limit monetary growth to a range of from 2 to 6 percent annually and should announce its targets for growth well in advance so that businesses and financial institutions can adjust. (This proposal is closely related to the argument that rules, not discretion, should determine the course of demand-management policies. Reasons for monetary growth rules are described in more detail in later chapters.)

The FED has mounted a multifaceted defense of its independence and discretion over policy. The fear of politicizing policy is a central issue. The FED argues that it should be free to follow what it perceives to be the best monetary policies possible, not policies based on political considerations.

FOCUS 2

The Savings-and-Loan Crisis

. . . the weak, meek and ignorant are always good targets.

> Lincoln S&L memo to bond salespeople

Half of the savings-and-loan associations (S&Ls) operating in 1980 had closed by 1991. Cleaning up the "S&L mess" will cost taxpayers between $200 billion and $400 billion, as reflected in Figure 4. Critics blamed rampant fraud and mismanagement for most of the calamity, although it was precipitated by a sequence of events.

Until the 1970s, S&Ls were generally controlled by conservative financial managers and were safe havens for savers who wanted slightly higher interest rates than those paid by banks. Regulations limited competition in two major ways. First, new banks and S&Ls could open only if the prospective founders convinced regulators that a commu-

nity had an unserved "need" for more financial services. Second, legal ceilings limited the interest rates that banks or S&Ls could pay depositors. The security of S&Ls was also enhanced by federal programs to encourage home ownership by families. For example, the Veterans Administration (VA) and Federal Home Administration (FHA) guaranteed repayments of most home loans.

Erratic inflation and interest rates in the late 1970s sowed the seeds for the current S&L mess. Most S&L assets (mortgages) were long term and at relatively low interest—20- to 40-year mortgages at 5 to 8 percent annually were common, but depositors could withdraw their savings with little prior notice. Rising interest rates on other financial assets caused enormous losses of deposits in S&Ls (a process termed *disintermediation*), but the S&Ls could not force

homeowners to pay off their mortgages before the payments were due. Figure 5 traces some macroeconomic shifts that contributed to this calamity.

Windfall gains for homeowners with low-interest mortgages were a disaster for S&Ls, which had to borrow at high interest rates (up to 14 percent annually) to cover withdrawals, while long-term S&L assets yielded only much lower interest rates. S&Ls suffered severe losses and capital-to-asset ratios (the ratio of stockholder capital in the S&L to total assets) plummeted.[*] Few

---

[*]J. A. Cacy, "Thrifts in the Troubled 1980s: In the Nation and the District," Economic Review, *Federal Reserve Bank of Kansas City, December 1989, pp. 3–23. Also see Frederick E. Balderston,* Thrifts in Crisis: Structural Transformation of the Saving and Loan Industry *(Cambridge, MA: Ballinger Publishing Company, 1985).*

FIGURE 4 Sources of Savings-and-Loan Losses

Cleanup costs for the S&L mess are equally divided between government administrative costs, real estate losses (overbuilding and benefits to low-interest mortgage holders), and mismanagement (fraud, S&L overcapacity, brokered deposits, and junk bond defaults).

Source: Paulette Thomas and Thomas E. Ricks, "Tracing the Billions: Just What Happened to All That Money Savings & Loans Lost?," *Wall Street Journal,* Nov. 5, 1990, p. 1.

Pie chart:
- Administrative 35.5%
- Real Estate 20%
- Homeowners 15%
- S & L Overcapacity 7.5%
- Fraud 10%
- Brokered Deposits 10%
- Junk Bonds 2%

FIGURE 5 Inflation and Interest Rates and Savings-and-Loan Closures

When interest rates jumped to 14 percent in the early 1980s, S&L institutions were caught in a funds squeeze—the cost of deposits rose (interest paid), but returns on the S&L's investment portfolios remained relatively constant (their portfolios consisted primarily of low-interest, fixed-rate real estate mortgages). Profits and capital ratios fell while closings rose. To increase their profits, those who survived this initial squeeze committed to more risky real estate and corporate bond investments. This strategy, combined with the nationwide real estate collapse (the result of declining inflation and the 1986 Tax Reform Act), caused savings-and-loan closures to soar in the late 1980s.

Sources: *Federal Reserve Bulletin* and *Economic Report of the President,* 1990, and Norman Strunk and Fred Case, *Where Deregulation Went Wrong,* U.S. League of Savings Institutions, 1988.

new mortgage loans were available, and mortgage interest rates soared.

This squeeze on home financing added to other pressures for financial reform, so the Depository Institutions Deregulation and Monetary Control Act of 1980 was enacted. It forced S&Ls to compete with banks and other financial institutions for deposits, permitted investments other than residential real estate, and raised the cap on insured deposits from $40,000 to $100,000 per account. Few S&Ls were equipped for a more competitive environment, however, and many quickly sank into deeper trouble. Just as sharks and pirates are attracted by a sinking ship, financial sharks quickly began circling potential S&L victims.

Many S&Ls began to underwrite more risky, but potentially more profitable investments that included commercial real estate (shopping malls, condominium developments, and office buildings), raw land, and junk bonds (risky, high-yielding bonds, often issued to finance highly speculative mergers). As interest rates dropped during the 1980s, S&L profits rose—the spread between cost of funds and returns on investments became positive, and the industry appeared to be weathering the storm. But the future for S&Ls suffered more reversals in 1986.

First, anti-inflationary monetary policies began to take effect, weakening real estate markets. Second, the Tax Reform Act of 1986 cut the highest tax brackets in half and slashed tax breaks from real estate holdings. These changes reduced the desirability of real estate as an investment. The result was a dumping of real estate which resulted in a nationwide average price decline of 20 to 40 percent.

Roughly three-fourths of S&L assets were in real estate mortgages at precollapse values, so S&L balance sheets nosedived as real estate foreclosures rose. By the late 1980s, S&L insolvencies skyrocketed, depleting funds in the Federal S&L Insurance Corporation (FSLIC). The FSLIC was intended to be self-financing, but political pressures forced Congress to finance the bailout, at an estimated cost of more than $200 billion. Congress established the Resolution Trust Corporation (RTC) to handle collapsing S&Ls.

The S&L house of cards was flattened by a multipronged attack. First, the restrictions imposed by the short-term liabilities (deposits) and long-term earning assets posed severe problems for most S&Ls. When short-term interest rates rose, the interest paid to savers was greater than the interest earned by S&Ls on past loans.

Second, the *moral hazard* situation inherent in the deposit insurance system accounted for a significant part of S&L losses. Depositors felt safe because of FSLIC insurance and cared little about whether an S&L was prudently managed. (People are less careful with assets if they are insured.) Deregulation attracted large numbers of "sharks" who aggressively made highly speculative loans with depositors' money.

Richard Breeden, chairman of the SEC, concluded that "The institutions that grew 2,000 percent or 3,000 percent weren't getting those funds because investors thought they were well-run businesses. Deposit insurance made those funds avail-

What incentives do the governors of the FED have to follow policies most beneficial for the economic well-being of the American people? The banks that "invest" in the FED are limited to a 6 percent rate of return, and there are no strong political checks on FED governors. The FED responds that its officers and administrators are public-spirited people who simply want the satisfaction of knowing that they are doing the best job they can for the American public. This answer is not very satisfying to economists, who believe that the most powerful of human motivations is self-interest. However, subjecting the FED to political pressure is not an especially able." Or as William Seidman, chairman of the FDIC and RTC has noted, "Thrifts were essentially printing money through deposit insurance." Deposit insurance was akin to an auto insurance fund where drunks, teenagers and Sunday drivers paid the same rate. Why would anyone but the accident-prone apply? Similarly, depositors had no incentive to put their money in well-run safe-havens — all were equally safe; only the interest rate mattered.

Third, Regulatory Accounting Procedures (RAP) contributed to the collapse. By requiring that asset values be maintained on the books at precollapse values (loan values), weak S&Ls had the incentive to sell off their best assets to show profits, leaving the worst assets on the books, thereby inflating their true condition. These accounting procedures partially explain why it took so long for the Federal auditors to discover the massive problems in the industry. At least one economist has called these accounting procedures Creative Regulatory Accounting Procedures, or CRAP.†

Fourth, the Tax Reform Act of 1986 and the disinflation of the mid-1980s combined to reduce the attractiveness of real estate as an investment. A flood of properties on the market depressed real estate prices — a catastrophe for S&Ls that had made speculative loans.

The S&L problem may take two decades to unravel. Understandably, a Congress operating on a 2- to 6-year election time-table wants to push the cost as far into the future as possible,

†See William Poole's comments in R. Dan Brumbaugh and Andrew S. Carron, "Thrift Industry Crisis: Causes and Solutions, Brookings Papers on Economic Activity, Vol. 2 (Washington, DC: The Brookings Institution, 1987), p. 383.

but this will increase both administrative and interest costs. In addition to the activities of the RTC, Congress is considering regulatory changes to ensure that taxpayers will not face a similar crisis in the future. Leading the list of reforms are such changes to FDIC and FSLIC insurance as reducing the amount covered in each account and limiting the number of accounts covered for large depositors.

As a result of the S&L bailout, the RTC has become the nation's largest "junk dealer" with a $4-billion (face value) portfolio in junk bonds currently worth less than 50 cents on the dollar. In the end, the true economic costs of the S&L crisis were the squandered scarce capital investments on overbuilt shopping centers, office space, and condominiums that now stand empty. Wiser use of our capital would have allowed more rapid economic growth over the past decade.

appealing alternative to relying on the FED management's interest in the public welfare. Will the role of the FED change? Should it? If so, how? Only time will tell.

In this chapter, we discussed the most regulated industry in America. These regulations stem from the Great Depression and a recognition that controlling monetary aggregates is necessary to control aggregate economic activity. The FED uses three main tools to alter the money supply: reserve requirements, open-market operations, and discounting operations. How monetary policy can be used to control inflation or avert a recession is the focal point of the next chapter.

FOCUS 3

Monetary Targets and Stop-and-Go FED Policies: 1976–1990

Abrupt changes in monetary policy can cause economic chaos. Monetary growth was erratic in the 1970s and 1980s. Indeed, many observers lay the full blame for a deep recession in 1981–1983 at the Federal Reserve's doorstep. Supply-side economists blamed restrictive monetary policies for keeping the full effect of President Reagan's tax cuts from taking effect in the early 1980s. Other critics perceive the FED as blameworthy for swings in the international value of the dollar during 1976–1990.

Uneven but growing inflation plagued the 1970s. One group of new classical economists, the monetarists, cited accelerating growth of the money supply as eroding the dollar's purchasing power. Keynesians tended to point to other causes, such as

OPEC's huge oil price hikes during 1974–1980.

Paul Volcker, then chair of the FED, believed that curbing the growth rate of the money supply was the key to halting inflation. Figure 6 indicates, however, that lowering the growth rate of the money supply to from 2 to 4 percent annually is a painful process if people expect more rapid growth. The drop in the rate of monetary growth during 1979–1980 was so abrupt that, although inflation decelerated, the economy went into a deep slump. Severe monetary restrictiveness was then temporarily abandoned to facilitate economic recovery. Between 1986 and 1991, however, the FED held monetary growth under a tight reign.

The economy has followed a jerky path since World War II.

Such disruptions as the Vietnam War, conflict in the Persian Gulf, and OPEC oil price hikes may be partial explanations, but most monetarists view attempts to fine-tune the economy as doomed to failure.

Attempts at monetary fine-tuning are illustrated in Figure 6. In 1979, the FED announced that it would target M1 and control its rate of growth. Since then, monetary growth and GNP growth continue to be on a roller coaster—up for a few quarters, and then down for the next few. The FED announces targets, but then adjusts them when economic conditions seem to warrant different targets.

Milton Friedman, a leading monetary economist, compares the FED to the farmer who used his barn door for target practice. "A visitor was astounded to find

Chapter Review: Key Points

1. Because fractional reserve banking makes it impossible for all banks to pay all demand deposits simultaneously, resolutions of monetary crises may require intervention by a *central bank,* or "bankers' bank."

2. The value of the potential money multiplier (m_p) is the reciprocal of the *reserve-require-ment ratio* ($1/rr$). Excess reserves in the financial system and cash holdings by the public are drains on the potential multiplier. The actual multiplier (m_a) is the amount of currency and bank reserves issued by the *Federal Reserve System* (the *FED*) (*MB*) divided into the money supply (*MS*): $m_a = MS/MB$.

FIGURE 6 Rate of Change in M1 and GNP (Current Dollars, Quarterly Percentage Change)

In 1979 the FED announced it would target and control the rate of growth of M1. Since then, both M1 and GNP have risen for a few quarters, then fallen the next few. Targeting M1 in the 1980s has proven so difficult for the FED that it recently broadened the targeted rate of growth for M1 to an annual rate anywhere between 3 and 8 percent.

that each of the numerous targets on the door had a bullet hole precisely in the center of the bull's-eye. He later discovered the secret of such remarkable accuracy. Unobserved, he saw the farmer first shoot at the door and then paint the target."*

*Milton Friedman, "The FED Hasn't Changed Its Ways," The Wall Street Journal, 20 Aug. 1985.

Friedman contends that the FED "simply repaints the target" to cover its discretionary policymaking.

3. The Federal Reserve System's most powerful but least used primary tool is its power to change reserve requirements (*rr*). Increases in *rr* reduce the money multiplier and money supply, and vice versa.

4. The most useful tool of the FED is *open-market operations* (OMO). After all adjustments, open-market operations affect the monetary base, not the money multiplier.

When the FED sells government bonds, bank reserves are reduced and the money supply declines. FED purchases of bonds increase bank reserves and the money supply.

5. The *discount rate* (*d*) is the interest rate the FED charges member banks. When the discount rate is low relative to market interest rates, banks hold few excess reserves and will borrow funds from the FED. Consequently,

the money supply increases. High discount rates relative to market interest rates cause banks to borrow less from the FED and provide incentives for larger holdings of excess reserves. The actual money multiplier and total bank reserves fall, and the money supply falls.

6. The FED's other tools include *margin requirements* to limit stock-market credit and *jawboning*.

Key Concepts

Ensure that you can define these terms before proceeding.

Federal Reserve System (FED)
Board of Governors
Federal Open Market Committee (FOMC)
reserve-requirement ratio (*rr*)

federal-funds market
open-market operations (OMO)
discount rate (*d*)
margin requirements
usury laws
credit rationing

Problems and Questions

1. What effect will a million-dollar bank robbery have on the M1 money supply? (Remember that M1 is cash in the public's hands plus demand deposits.)

2–3. Problems 2 and 3 are simple if you know that the potential money multiplier is most easily calculated by inverting (turning upside down) the fraction for the reserve-requirements ratio *rr*. For example, if *rr* = 1/10, this multiplier equals 10.

2. Compute the potential money multiplier for the following values of *rr*: 1/2, 2/5, 1/3, 1/4, 1/5, 1/6, 1/7, 1/8, 1/9, and 1/10.

3. Complete this table.

4. Until 1980, the reserve-requirement ratios for state-chartered banks were generally lower than the ratios required for national banks. How might this partially explain the growth in state banks relative to national banks during the preceding 60 years? What effects would this have on the FED's ability to control the money supply? On pressures for the FED to reduce reserve-requirement ratios for national banks? How might you test to see whether your answers to these questions are correct?

5. Banks have been forbidden to establish branches across state borders, and many states absolutely forbid branch banking. Bank "holding companies" have finessed those laws in some places, and there is now substantial political pressure to relax these laws. President Bush proposed legalizing nationwide interstate branch banking in 1991. What potential gains and losses do you perceive from allowing nationwide branch banking?

6. Should opening a financial institution be more complicated than starting a business as a florist? What special controls, if any, should the government exercise over financial institutions?

7. Given that most bank deposits are insured for up to $100,000 by the Federal Deposit Insurance Corporation (FDIC), do reserve requirements add to the safety of depositors? If not, what is the purpose of requiring banks to hold reserves?

8. Would it matter if the FED eliminated the discount rate entirely and abolished bank borrowing from the Federal Reserve? One of the original roles played by discounting operations was averting panics touched off by the withdrawal of currency from banks in response to the fear of bank insolvency. Is this role still valid today? What benefits are derived from current discounting operations?

Monetary Base	Reserve-Requirements Ratio (*rr*)	Potential Money Multiplier (*m_p*)	Potential Money Supply
a. $1 billion	1/6	_____	_____
b. $8 billion	_____	5	_____
c. _____	1/7	_____	$700 billion
d. _____	_____	6	$100 billion

CHAPTER

Monetary Theory and Policy

[The possession of money] in quantity can be a blessing to the virtuous individual, but a curse to masses afflicted by gluttony. Prudent coiners of a society's money gain for their country a stable prosperity, but profligate masters of money can visit ruin on their nation and all of its neighbors.

Attributed to Daniel Webster

Money is important to each of us. You would gain if the amount of money you have now were doubled. But how important is the total quantity of money in circulation? If everyone's money holdings doubled, would you benefit? Would the average person?

Controversy raged over questions like these even before the conquistadors shipped tons of stolen gold from the "New World" to sixteenth-century Spain, triggering a wave of inflation throughout Europe. The Depression-era work of John Maynard Keynes rekindled the fires surrounding these issues. They are still far from resolved.

Just as markets for goods are in equilibrium only if the quantities supplied and demanded are equal, the quantities of money supplied and demanded must be equal to balance financial markets. In this chapter, you will learn how monetary equilibrium helps stabilize national income, the price level, and the interest rate, and

how classical, Keynesian, and monetarist views of equilibration differ. Differences in adjustment processes determine whether monetary policy or fiscal policy is more potent, and whether government should actively try to dampen business cycles, or whether passive policies that rely heavily on market forces are more likely to achieve a prosperous stability.

The Demand for Money

I have all the money I need for the rest of my life — provided I die by 4 o'clock this afternoon.

Henny Youngman

As with "What is money?" the answer to "Do you have enough money?" seems obvious. Your behavior, however, indicates that at times you have too much money, so you spend it; at other times you try to acquire more money because you have too little. Ambiguity arises because people often use *money, income,* and *wealth* interchangeably. You might easily justify answering "No" if you were asked if you had enough income or wealth. But money is identical to neither income nor wealth — although it is related to both. Money is the device used to buy goods and by which we measure our incomes, wealth, and the prices we pay.

Most people spend in predictable ways and receive money at regular intervals. If you try to secure more money income by selling your time or goods, or by saving more money from your income, you have temporary shortages of money relative to your time or goods. But when you spend money, you see your purchases as more desirable than their monetary costs; relative to these goods, you have temporary surpluses of money.

Individual demands for money are fairly complex. It would be fruitless to break up our demand for cars into "vacation," "work," "commuter," or "shopping" motives. Some economists, however, find it useful to compartmentalize the reasons we hold money instead of consuming more or investing in other assets. The functions money performs were addressed previously: Money is a medium of exchange, a unit of account, a store of value, and a standard of deferred payment. One trivial way to explain your demand for money is to say that you desire money for the functions it performs. You can gain deeper insights into the way money works by looking at three basic motives for holding money.

Transactions Demands

Before the Great Depression, classical reasoning focused on spending plans as the sole rational motive for holding money. This is called the *transactions demand for money.*

> The **transactions demand for money** *arises because people anticipate spending it.*

This is usually the dominant reason for holding money. You can predict many if not most transactions fairly accurately. You know how much your monthly rent and car payment will be, and roughly how much you will spend on utilities, gasoline, and meals. You probably also have a good idea about how much money you will receive in the near future. Most workers receive their paychecks regularly — either daily, weekly,

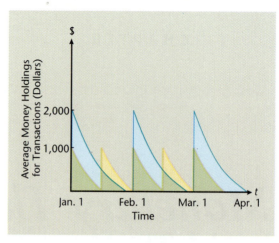

FIGURE 1   Transactions Balances

Transaction patterns with money cause most of us to have far less money on hand at the end of a pay period than at the beginning. Most people tend to pay their major bills as soon as they get paychecks, and their spending then shrinks to a relative trickle until the next payday. Consequently, people paid more often tend to hold less money than people with the same total income, but who must wait longer between paychecks. For example, a person whose paycheck is $1,000 twice a month will hold only half the average money balances held by someone paid $2,000 once each month.

biweekly, or monthly. Students may receive money monthly or once or twice a semester.

Predictable transactions flows of money to and from an individual paid $2,000 monthly are reflected in the blue line in Figure 1. The vertical rise of the area shaded in yellow shows money-holding patterns for someone with an identical $2,000 monthly income, but who is paid $1,000 at the middle and again at the end of each month. Notice that this person's average holdings of money are much lower than for the individual paid monthly. We have shown more rapid declines in money holdings right after a payday than toward the end of the pay period. You are typical if you write a lot of checks right after you get paid, and then find yourself almost broke before you are paid again.

Precautionary Demands

Even people who hold enough money to cover their planned spending feel uncomfortable with no extra money in reserve. There always seem to be little — and sometimes big — emergencies that require money. For example, you may have the hard luck of a flat tire or lost textbooks, or you may pleasantly discover that the "Blue Light Special" at a department store is a record you want. You hold precautionary balances to ensure that you will have money on hand to meet unexpected expenditures.

The **precautionary demand for money** *arises because people know that unanticipated spending is required at times.*

The major difference between the transactions and precautionary demands for money lies in the degree of predictability about future spending. Both motives, however, suggest that your average of money balances held will be positively related to your income — you probably hold more money now than when you were ten years old, and far less than you will hold when you put your student days behind you and find a good job. Figure 2 stacks the precautionary demand for money on top of the transactions demand to

FIGURE 2   Nominal Income, Precautionary Balances, and the Demand for Money

As people's incomes rise, the average amounts they will hold to meet both expected transactions and emergencies ("money for a rainy day") will rise. Transactions balances will vary over pay periods (as you saw in Figure 1) much more than precautionary balances will.

show how the total of these two demands is related to income. One of Keynes's innovations in monetary theory is the idea of the precautionary motive. While earlier classical writers ignored this motive in their writings on money, they would have had little difficulty accepting this idea because, like transactions balances, precautionary balances of money are closely related to income.

Asset Demands

Keynes's major innovation in monetary theory is the concept of an asset demand for money, an idea that clashes with early classical theory.

The **asset demand for money** *arises because people sometimes want to hold part of their wealth in the form of money.*

Early classical theorists argued that no one will hold money as an asset because they could earn interest on stocks or bonds if they made these financial investments instead. Keynesians argue that a desire to hold some wealth in the form of money originates from (*a*) expectations that the prices of stocks or bonds will fall in the near future, (*b*) reluctance to hold only assets that tend to swing widely in value, or (*c*) a belief that transaction costs are higher than any expected return from investments in stocks or bonds.

Speculative Balances   Suppose you intend to buy stocks, bonds, or real estate out of funds you have saved. If you expect the prices of these financial investments to fall in the near future, you will postpone their purchase until prices are down, holding money as an asset in the interim.

People hold **speculative money balances** *if they expect the prices of alternative assets to fall in the near future.*

Bond Prices and Interest Rates   Rising interest rates cause bond prices to fall and lower interest rates mean higher bond prices. Suppose you were offered a chance to buy a government bond that offered the following terms:

If it required a 10 percent return to persuade you to buy this bond, you would be willing to pay $1,000 for it, because 10 percent times $1,000 equals $100, which is the annual payment. If you required a 20 percent return on your financial investment, the bond would be worth only $500 to you {0.20($500) = $100}. Thus, higher interest rates imply lower bond prices (20 percent > 10 percent, and $500 < $1,000).

A general formula for this type of bond (called a *perpetuity*) is:

$$\text{present value} = \frac{\text{annual payment}}{\text{interest rate}}$$

Rising interest rates reduce bond prices, and falling interest rates drive bond prices up. If you and other potential bond buyers believe that interest rates will rise soon, you will speculate against bonds and hold money while waiting for bond prices to fall.

Risk Avoidance Keynes emphasized the speculative aspect of the asset demand for money. Other economists have developed other reasons why individuals may hold money as an asset. Assets that yield relatively high average rates of return tend to be relatively more risky. Most people are *risk averse*, so they buy various kinds of insurance. We invest only if the assets we buy with money are expected to yield returns that compensate us for our reduced liquidity *and* the increased risk of loss.

Magazine stories occasionally profile eccentrics who seemed destitute, but who left their heirs hoards of cash hidden in attics or closets. Many risk-averse people hold money because they view expected rates of return from other assets as too low to overcome the risks. Consider, for example, two financial investments: (*a*) holding $10,000 in cash, with a zero return, or (*b*) buying $10,000 worth of ZYX stock, which has a 96 percent probability of yielding a 6 percent rate of return, but a 4 percent chance of losing the $10,000. Buying ZYX stock is probabilistically more valuable than holding the cash (0.96 · $10,600 = $10,176 > $10,000), but many people would hold the cash in preference to bearing the 4 percent probability of losing the entire $10,000.

Transaction Costs Money is the most liquid of all assets. If you have so little wealth that transaction costs overshadow any potential gains, you will hold money instead of investing. For example, if you have only $50 to invest and expect a $50 share of stock to generate a $5 profit, it is better to hold money if the stockbroker's fee is more than $5.

All these reasons for people to hold money as an asset lead to the conclusion that their money holdings will be negatively related to the interest rate. Transactions demands are related to time, as suggested in Figure 1. But neither precautionary nor asset demands for money are systematically related to time. It is impossible to compartmentalize chunks of money precisely, but the transactions, precautionary, and asset motives are reasonable explanations for why most of us

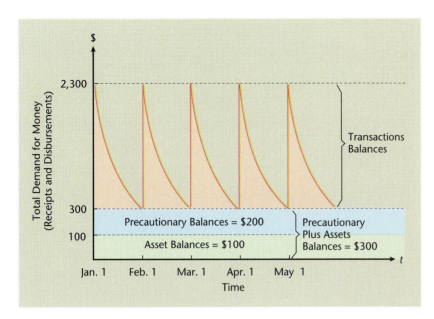

FIGURE 3   Typical Patterns of Money Holdings

Asset and precautionary balances vary little over time, but transactions balances swing widely over pay periods. Note that the transaction balances reach a peak of $2,000 in this figure, but they are vertically stacked atop asset and precautionary balances, so the total reaches as much as $2,300.

keep positive balances of money handy. Typical total money holdings for a person paid $2,000 once a month are depicted in Figure 3.

The Costs of Holding Money

As with other goods, the quantity of money demanded will depend on its opportunity cost. Most goods or resources can be bought with money, so it might seem difficult to specify the sacrifice associated with money holdings. These sacrifices, however, take the form of either interest forgone from income-earning assets not held (the Keynesian view) or forgone consumer goods and services (the classical view).

The Classical View   The amount of consumption you sacrifice by holding a dollar falls as the cost of living rises. For example, if the price of a candy bar rises from $0.50 to $1, then the candy you sacrifice to hold $1 drops from two bars to only one bar. You previously learned that comparing nominal values (e.g., dollars) requires deflating for inflation — dividing the nominal value by the price level. Thus, the real subjective value of a dollar in exchange for consumer goods from the vantage point of a typical consumer is roughly the reciprocal of the price level ($1/P). If the price level rises, you must hold more dol-

lars to consummate given amounts of "real" transactions. This implies a negative relationship between the quantity of money demanded and the reciprocal of the price level, as shown in Panel A of Figure 4. This cost of holding money is at the root of classical monetary theory.

But the relationship between the cost of living and the quantity of money demanded is not quite this simple. Suppose that we have experienced inflation for a substantial period of time and that you expect inflation to continue. Fearing the decline in value of money, you will want to *reduce* your dollar holdings and purchase more goods (because those dollars buy more today than you expect them to in the future). Consequently, new classical theory posits a negative relationship between the expected rate of inflation and the demand for money. We will explore this relationship more in a moment.

The Keynesian View   Keynesians perceive the interest rate as the cost of holding money, because they view stocks or bonds that pay interest as the closest alternatives to money as an asset. You receive no interest on cash holdings and relatively low interest rates on demand deposits. If interest rates are relatively high on nonmonetary assets, you are more likely to hold your wealth in stocks or bonds than if interest rates are low,

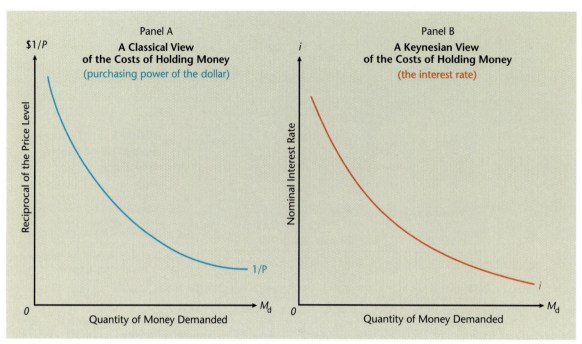

FIGURE 4   Classical vs. Keynesian Views of the Cost of Holding Money

Panel A illustrates that classical economics views the value of what you could purchase with a dollar (which equals $1/P$) as your sacrifice in holding a dollar. The Keynesian perspective that the true cost of holding money is the interest you sacrifice by not making a different investment is reflected in Panel B.

when money is a more attractive asset. This Keynesian emphasis on interest rates (reflected in Panel B of Figure 4) differs sharply from the classical view that the costs of holding money are the goods that might be enjoyed were the money spent.

Classical Monetary Theory

Before Adam Smith cleared the air with his *Wealth of Nations* in 1776, the economic policies of most European monarchs were grounded in *mercantilism*, a doctrine based on a misunderstanding of the difference between money and wealth. Gold and silver were thought to be real wealth, so England, Spain, and other European countries engaged in colonial expansion to find gold or silver and fought numerous wars in the process. The losers were invariably forced to pay

the winners out of their national treasuries. Aztec gold and Inca silver poured into Spain. Monarchs often debased national currencies to finance wars in the Old World and colonization of the New World.

Whether debasement or foreign conquest enriched the royal coffers, the amount of money in circulation grew. Several early economic thinkers noted that inflation always seemed to follow rapid monetary growth.

Quantity theories of money *indicate that the money supply is the primary determinant of nominal spending and, ultimately, the price level.*

Earlier quantity theories of money were formalized about a century ago by some British economists at Cambridge University and by Irving Fisher of Yale University. Fisher's analysis began with the equation of exchange.

The Equation of Exchange

Gross National Product can be written as PQ because GNP has price level (P) and real output (Q) components. But how is the money supply (M1) related to GNP? Economists approach this question by computing how many times, on average, money changes hands annually for purchases of final output. For example, GNP in 1991 was roughly $6 trillion and the money supply (M1) averaged about $865 billion (or $0.87 trillion), so the average dollar was used roughly seven times for purchases of output produced in 1991.

> *The average number of times a unit of money is used annually is called the* **income velocity (V)** *of money.*

Velocity is computed by dividing GNP by the money supply: $V = PQ/M$.

Multiplying both sides of $V = PQ/M$ by M yields $MV = PQ$, a result called *the equation of exchange*.

> *The* **equation of exchange** *is written* $(M \times V = P \times Q)$.

This equation is definitionally true given our computation of velocity[1] and is interpreted: The quantity of money times its velocity is equal to the price level times real output, which equals GNP. Note that this equation suggests that the *velocity* of money is just as important as the quantity of money in circulation.

A rough corollary is that *the percentage change in the money supply* plus *the percentage change in velocity* equals *the percentage change in the price level* plus *the percentage change in real output*[2]:

$$\frac{\Delta M}{M} + \frac{\Delta V}{V} = \frac{\Delta P}{P} + \frac{\Delta Q}{Q}$$

Focus on the right-hand side of this equation for a moment. Does it make sense that if the price of, say, tea bags rose 1 percent and you cut your purchases 2 percent, your spending on tea would fall 1 percent? Intuitively, the percentage change in price plus the percentage change in quantity equals the percentage change in spending. Now examine the equation once more. Suppose that output grew 3 percent, that velocity did not change, and that the money supply rose 7 percent. Average prices would rise 4 percent (7 percent + 0 percent = 4 percent + 3 percent). Learning these relationships will help you comprehend arguments between classical monetary theorists and their detractors.

The Crude Quantity Theory of Money

From certain assumptions about the variables in the equation of exchange (M, V, P, and Q), classical economists (including Fisher) conclude that, in equilibrium, the price level (P) is exactly proportional to the money supply (M). Let us see how they arrived at this conclusion.

Constancy of Velocity Classical economic reasoning views the income velocity (V) of money as determined solely by institutional factors, such as the organizational structure and efficiency of banking and credit, and by people's habitual patterns of spending money after receiving income. Velocity is thought to be constant, $(\overline{V})$, at least in the short run, because changes tend to occur slowly (a) in the technologies of financial institutions (the ways checks clear or loans are granted or repaid) and (b) in the inflows and outflows of individuals' money (frequencies of receipts of incomes and people's habits when spending their money).[3] Thus, we see a central assumption of the classical quantity theory: $\Delta V/V = 0$. Focus 1 reveals, however, that assuming constant velocity would be unrealistic for international monetary data in recent years. Nor would this assumption fit U.S. data

---

1. Irving Fisher, whose biography appears in Chapter 16, focused his version of the equation of exchange on total transactions (T) in an economy rather than real National Income (Q). Transactions differ from GNP because of sales of things not produced in the relevant year, such as used goods or land, and because of transactions involving intermediate goods, which would be double counted compared to the income version of the equation. Thus, Fisher's equation of exchange is $MV = PT$ rather than the $MV = PQ$ that we discuss later, and V stands for *transactions* velocity instead of income velocity.

2. For math purists only: This is roughly equivalent to taking the time derivative of this equation in its natural logs and ignoring the cross partials.

---

3. Bars over variables indicate constancy.

FOCUS 1

Velocity in the 1980s: The International Scene

The results postulated by monetarism and the quantity theory of money depend heavily on the relative constancy of velocity. If velocity is constant, then a more rapid rate of monetary growth would mean higher inflation. But what happens if the public desires more money as the FED expands the money supply? Income velocity falls and the inflationary effects forecasted by monetarists may not be forthcoming.

Velocity fell substantially in most Western countries during the first half of the 1980s, as shown in Figure 5. The inflationary effects of increased monetary growth were partially offset by declining velocity. High real interest rates attracted saving into interest-bearing accounts, and these accounts now constitute a large fraction of all monetary aggregates. The deregulation of financial markets in the 1980s generated dozens of new instru-

ments and virtually eliminated the boundaries between different types of financial institutions. Monetarists would argue that the early 1980s were unique and that once people have thoroughly adjusted to deregulation, velocity will regain its relative stability and the classical relationship between the rate of change of the money supply and inflation will resume.

FIGURE 5 The Velocity of Money, 1980—1990 (Selected Western Countries)

The velocity of money equals nominal GNP divided by the money supply. The measure of the money supply used for the United States is M3; for Britain, M3; for Japan, M2 + CDs; and for West Germany, Central Bank Money (CBM).

Source: *The Economist,* July 27, 1985. With updates by authors. Reprinted by permission of *The Economist.*

for different measures of the money supply—between 1970 and 1991, for example, velocity for M1 increased by roughly 40 percent, while velocity for M2 was relatively constant and velocity for M3 fell by roughly 15 percent.

But why does classical economics view velocity (V) as unaffected by the price level (P), the real level of output (Q), or the money supply (M)? The answer lies in why people demand money. Classical macroeconomic models assume that people want to hold money only to consummate transactions and that people's spendings are fixed proportions of their incomes. Our previous discussion of the transactions motive is basically classical. Since National Income is approximately GNP (or $P \times Q$), then the demand for money M_d (a transactions demand) can be written:

$$M_d = kPQ$$

where k is the constant proportion of income that would be held in monetary balances.[4] For example, if each family habitually held one-fifth of its average annual income of $10,000 in the form of money, then the average quantity of money each family would demand would be $M_d = 0.20(\$10,000) = \$2,000$. The quantity of money demanded in the entire economy would be $2,000 times the number of families.

Constancy of Real Output   Classical theory also assumes that real output (Q) does not depend on the other variables (M, V, and P) in the equation of exchange. Classical economists believe that the natural state of the economy is full employment, so real output is influenced solely by the state of technology and by the amounts of resources available. Full employment is ensured by Say's Law if prices, wages, and interest rates are perfectly flexible. Moreover, both the

amounts of resources available and the state of technology are thought to change slowly, if at all, in the short run. Thus, real output (Q) is assumed to be approximately constant and $\Delta Q/Q = 0$. This may seem like a very strong assertion, but the intuitive appeal of the idea that real output is independent of the quantity of money (M), its velocity (V), or the price level (P), is convincing both to classical monetary theorists and to the new classical economists who have updated the classical tradition.

The idea that the amount of paper currency or coins issued by the government has virtually no effect on the economy's productive capacity seems reasonable. Similarly, the velocity of money should not influence capacity. But what about the price level? After all, the law of supply suggests that the quantities of individual goods and services supplied will be greater the higher the market prices are. Shouldn't the nation's output increase if the price level rises? Classical economists say *No!* Here is why.

A Crude Monetary Theory of the Price Level

Suppose that your income and the values of all your assets exactly double. (That's the good news.) Suppose that the prices of everything you buy and all your debts also precisely double. (That's the bad news.) Should your behavior change in any way? Your intuition should suggest not. Using similar logic, classical economists conclude that, in the long run, neither real output nor any other aspect of "real" economic behavior is affected by changes in the price level. Economic behavior is shaped by relative prices, not the absolute price level.

Recall that the percentage changes in the money supply and velocity roughly equal the percentage changes in the levels of prices and real output. If velocity is constant and output is stable at a full employment level in the short run, then $\Delta V/V = \Delta Q/Q = 0$. Classical economists are left with a fixed relationship between the money supply (M) and the price level (P). In equilibrium, the rate of inflation is exactly the same as the percentage rate of growth in the money supply: $\Delta M/M = \Delta P/P$. Thus, any increase in the rate of monetary growth would not affect real output, just inflation.

---

4. We know that the equation of exchange relates the supply of money to National Income through velocity: $MV = PQ$. Let us divide both sides by V: $M = PQ/V$. Because the quantities of money supplied and demanded must be equal in equilibrium ($M = M_d$), k must be equal to $1/V$, both k and V being constants. As a result, classical monetarists discerned a fixed relationship between k (the proportion of annual income people want to hold as money) and V (the velocity of money).

The Classical View of Investment

Firms will buy machinery, construct buildings, or attempt to increase inventories whenever they expect the gross returns on these investments to exceed the total costs of acquiring them. Classical economists assume relatively stable and predictable economies, so they focus on the costs of acquiring investment goods; business investors' expectations of profits are assumed realized, and the costs of new capital goods are presumed stable.

Equilibrium investment occurs when the expected rate of return on investment equals the interest rate. Since the prices of capital equipment are fairly stable, any changes in the costs of acquiring capital are primarily the result of changes in interest rates. [Investors are effectively trading dimes for dollars as long as the cost of borrowing (the interest rate) is less than the return from investments made possible by borrowing.] Naturally, businesspeople will not make an investment unless they expect a return at least as high as they would receive if they simply lent their own money out at interest.

Classical writers believe that investment is very sensitive to the interest rate and that large swings in the level of investment occur because of minute changes in interest rates. The expected rate of return (r) curve in Figure 6 is relatively sensitive, or flat. In this example, a decline in interest of 1/2 percent (from 8 percent to 7.5 percent) will cause a 60 percent increase in investment [$(80 − 50)/50 = 30/50 = .60$]. Flexible interest rates and a highly sensitive investment (rate of return) schedule easily equate planned saving and investment, stabilizing the economy at full employment.

The Classical Monetary Transmission Mechanism

Monetarists view linkages between the money supply and National Income as not only strong, but direct. This **classical monetary transmission mechanism** (how money enters the economy) is shown in Figure 7. Panel A reflects the effects of monetary changes on nominal income, and Panel B translates these changes into effects on real output.

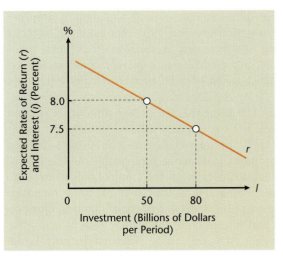

FIGURE 6   The Classical View of Investment

Classical economists view investment as very sensitive to even slight changes in interest rates and view expectations about the business environment as reasonably normal and normally realized.

Nominal income in Panel A is $4 trillion (point *a*) if the money supply is initially $2 trillion ($M_{s0}$). Note that $\overline{Q}_f$ is the full employment level of output and $M\overline{V} = PQ$, so $M = \overline{k}P\overline{Q}_f$, where $\overline{k} = 1/\overline{V}$. This figure initially assumes that $V = 2$ and, thus, that $k = 0.5$. This $4-trillion nominal income ($\overline{Y} = P_0\overline{Q}_f$) is equal to 4 trillion units of real output (point *a* in Panel B) at an average price level P_0 of 100 ($MV = PQ_f \rightarrow 2 \times 2 = 1 \times 4$). Money supply growth to $3 trillion ($M_{s1}$) boosts nominal income to $6 trillion (point *b* in Panel A). Output is fixed at full employment ($\overline{Q}_f$) and velocity is constant at 2, so introducing this extra money into the economy increases Aggregate Demand from AD_0 to AD_1, which pushes the price level to 150 (point *b* in Panel B where $M\overline{V} = P\overline{Q}_f \rightarrow 3 \times 2 = 1.5 \times 4$). Thus, in a classical world, monetary policy shifts Aggregate Demand up or down along a vertical Aggregate Supply curve with only price effects, not quantity effects.

Summary: The Crude Quantity Theory of Money   Summarizing the foundations of the early *crude quantity theory of money*, we know that the equation of exchange is a truism because

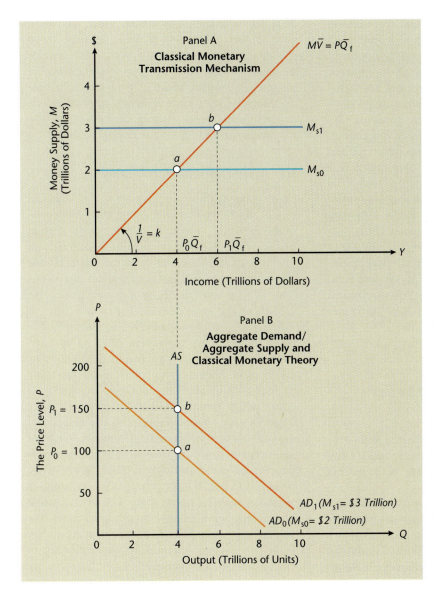

Panel A
Classical Monetary Transmission Mechanism

$M\bar{V} = P\bar{Q}_f$

M_{s1}

M_{s0}

$\frac{1}{V} = k$

$P_0\bar{Q}_f$ $P_1\bar{Q}_f$

Income (Trillions of Dollars)

Panel B
Aggregate Demand/ Aggregate Supply and Classical Monetary Theory

AS

$P_1 = 150$

$P_0 = 100$

$AD_1(M_{s1}= \$3\ Trillion)$

$AD_0(M_{s0}= \$2\ Trillion)$

Output (Trillions of Units)

FIGURE 7 The Classical Monetary Transmission Mechanism and the Price Level

Expanding the money supply from M_{s0} ($2 trillion) to M_{s1} ($3 trillion) causes Aggregate Spending to grow in Panel A so that nominal income ($P \times Q$) rises from $4 trillion to $6 trillion. Output is assumed to be at the full employment level of 4 trillion units in Panel B, however, so all of this growth is absorbed in price increases. When Aggregate Demand rises from AD_0 to AD_1 in Panel B, the price level inflates from its base of 100 to a new level of 150.

of the way velocity is computed: $MV \equiv PQ$. It follows that

$$\frac{\Delta M}{M} + \frac{\Delta V}{V} = \frac{\Delta P}{P} + \frac{\Delta Q}{Q}$$

If velocity is assumed constant (written $\bar{V}$) and real output is fixed at a full employment level (written $\bar{Q}_f$), then $\Delta V/V = 0$, and $\Delta Q/Q = 0$. Moreover, $\Delta M/M = \Delta P/P$. Any changes in the money supply will be reflected in proportional

changes in the price level. This is the major result of the crude quantity theory of money:

$$M\bar{V} = P\bar{Q}_f$$

Another conclusion is that real output (or any other "real" economic behavior) is unaffected in the long run by either the money supply or the price level. These early versions of the quantity theory of money are clearly misnamed—they should be called *monetary theories of the price level*.

Classical theorists concluded by saying "Money is a veil." By this they meant that money, inflation, or deflation may temporarily disguise the real world, but in the long run, money affects only the price level and has virtually no effect on such real variables as production, employment, labor force participation, unemployment, or relative prices. Even though classical theorists vehemently opposed large expansions of the money supply because of fear that inflation temporarily distorts behavior, it is probably fair to say that classical monetary theory leads to the conclusion that in the long run, "money does not matter." It does not affect production, consumption, investment, or any other "real" economic behavior. When we deal graphically with the demand and supply of money in later sections, we will resurrect these classical propositions to see how modern monetary theory treats them.

Keynesian Monetary Theory

The brunt of Keynes's attack on the classical quantity theory of money was directed at its conclusions that (*a*) velocity is constant, and (*b*) full employment is the natural state of a market economy.

Early classical economists believed that money balances are held only for transactions purposes and that the transactions anyone engages in are roughly proportional to that individual's nominal income. Thus, planned money balances were assumed roughly proportional to nominal income. "Why," they asked, "would people want to hold money unless they intend to spend it? Virtually any other asset yields a positive rate of return — and money holdings do not. No one holds more money than they need for transactions. They hold income-earning assets instead of money whenever possible." Keynes responded by adding the precautionary and asset (speculative) motives to the transactions motive for holding money.

Remember that people adjust their money balances until what they demand equals what they have. If you have more money than you

demand, you spend or invest more, reducing your money balances. If you demand more money than you presently hold, you acquire more by cutting back on your spending out of income, liquidating some of your assets, or selling more of your time. Keynes emphasized financial investments (stocks or bonds) as the major way to reduce one's money holdings.

The Asset Demand for Money

One major difference between the classical model and Keynes' model is that classical economists view the world as a reasonably certain place, while Keynesian reasoning emphasizes uncertainty and describes how our expectations about uncertain futures might affect the economy. Rising uncertainty is a major reason for growth of the asset demand for money.

Suppose you are working on an assembly line when the economy nose-dives. Many of your co-workers are laid off. You would probably start saving more because you could be the next one to find a "pink slip" in your pay envelope. As your savings mount, assets in the form of money balances grow. What happens to the velocity of money? *Velocity falls as saving increases.* Why not invest these funds in a stock or bond that pays interest or some positive rate of return? You must be kidding! The economy is in a tailspin — a recession may be under way. The crucial point here is that when people expect hard times, the velocity of money falls, as people convert money from transactions balances to precautionary or asset balances. Conversely, money balances are increasingly held for transactions purposes when prosperity seems just around the corner. This causes velocity to rise.

Let us see what all this means within the context of the equation of exchange. Because the percentage changes in the money supply plus velocity are equal to the percentage changes in the price level plus the real level of output, a 5 percent decline in velocity (money supply assumed constant) will cause nominal GNP to fall by 5 percent. If prices do not fall fairly rapidly, output and employment will decline by about 5 percent. (One economic law seems to be that *if circumstances change and prices do not adjust, quantities will.*) The economy may settle in equilibrium at less than full employment.

Keynes and his followers assumed that price adjustments are *sticky* (slow), especially on the down side, and that people's expectations are volatile. This implies that the velocity of money may vary considerably over time and that the real economy may adjust only slowly, if at all, to these variations.

The Liquidity Trap Classical economists viewed the interest rate as an incentive for saving — you are rewarded for postponing consumption. Keynes's rebuttal was that interest is a reward for sacrificing liquidity. According to Keynes, how much you save is determined by your income and will be affected very little by interest rates. However, interest rates are important in deciding the form your saving takes. You will hold money unless offered some incentive to hold a less-liquid asset. Interest is such an inducement. Higher interest rates will induce you to relinquish money and hold more of your wealth in the form of illiquid assets.

Keynes believed that very high interest rates cause people to hold little, if any, money in asset balances — the demand for money consists almost exclusively of transactions and precautionary balances. But low interest rates result in large asset balances of money. Just as we horizontally sum individual demands for goods to arrive at market demands, we can sum the transactions, precautionary, and asset demands for money to obtain the total demand for money. This demand curve for money is shown in Figure 8.

Note that at a very low interest rate, the demand for money becomes flat. This part of the demand curve for money is called the *liquidity trap*.

> A **liquidity trap** *occurs if people will absorb any extra money into idle balances — because they are extremely pessimistic or risk averse, they view transaction costs as prohibitive, or expect the prices of nonmonetary assets to fall in the near future.*

It implies that if the money supply grew (say, from M_{s0} to M_{s1}), any extra money you received

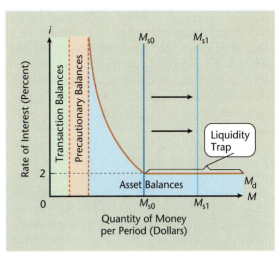

FIGURE 8   Liquidity Preference and the Demand for Money

The Keynesian total demand for money is the horizontal summation of transactions, precautionary, and asset demands for money. Keynesian theory predicts a liquidity trap at very low interest rates in which increases in the supply of money result in no extra spending and no declines in interest rates. Extra money is simply absorbed through hoarding into idle cash balances in a liquidity trap.

would not be spent, but hoarded — that is, absorbed into idle cash balances. Monetary growth would increase Aggregate Spending very little, if at all. Expectations about economic conditions might become so pessimistic that people would hoard every cent they could "for a rainy day," an instance of the liquidity trap. Alternatively, historically low interest rates might persuade nearly everyone that interest rates will soon rise. You would not want to hold bonds because rising interest rates would reduce bond prices and you would suffer a capital loss — you and many other investors would hold money while waiting for interest rates to rise and bond prices to fall.

Even though Keynes was writing during the Depression, he suggested that no economy had ever been in a perfect liquidity trap. At the trough of the Great Depression, however, the nominal interest rate hovered around 1.5 percent and we may have been in a "near" liquidity trap. Severe depressions may cause near-liquidity traps — because (*a*) banks pile up huge excess reserves when nominal interest rates are very low because the returns from lending are small, (*b*) bankers fear that all loans are very risky, even those that normally would pose no problem of repayment, and (*c*) private individuals hoard their own funds, fearing that bank failures are probable and that neither their job prospects nor investment opportunities are very bright.

Keynes rejected classical theory in his thinking about the demand for money, broadening the earlier perspective to consider precautionary and asset demands for money. Keynes thought that interest rates are determined solely by the demand and supply of money. His classical predecessors viewed interest rates as being determined in the market for capital goods. Thus, Keynesian and classical economists differ sharply in their perceptions of investment.

The Keynesian View of Investment

The capital stock consists of all improvements that make natural resources more productive than they are in their raw states — equipment, buildings, inventories, and so forth. Net economic investment is the growth of the capital stock during a given period. Classical and Keynesian theories differ about how variations in the money supply affect investment. Over a business cycle, investment fluctuates proportionally more than either consumption or government purchases. Inventory accumulation is especially unstable.

Keynesians focus on investors' volatile moods: Optimism and expectations of large returns generate high levels of investment, while pessimism stifles investment. Both Keynesian and classical writers agree that greater investment eventually leads to lower rates of return. Keynesian analysis takes the position that the interest rate, which is the major opportunity cost of investment, is only one aspect of investment planning and is not the overwhelming influence posited by classical economists. This perspective emphasizes changes in investors' expectations about future economic conditions as far more important in explaining changes in investment. Figure 9 shows why.

Suppose that the initial investment curve is r_0

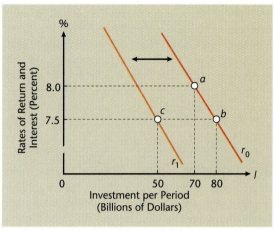

FIGURE 9   The Keynesian Explanation of Volatile Investment

Keynesians perceive investment as only mildly influenced by interest rates but very sensitive to even minor changes in business perceptions of the future of the economy. Pessimism causes investment to plummet, while optimism causes sudden, and perhaps unsustainable, surges in investment.

and that equilibrium investment is \$70 billion (point *a*) at an 8 percent interest rate. Note that the rate of return curves are relatively steep in this Keynesian view of the world. A drop in the interest rate to 7.5 percent moves the equilibrium from point *a* to point *b*, causing investment to grow only slightly, from \$70 billion to \$80 billion.

Now suppose that investors become skeptical about future economic conditions so that the expected rate of return schedule shifts leftward from r_0 to r_1. Equilibrium shifts from point *b* to point *c*, and investment falls sharply to \$50 billion. If investors' herdlike mentality (Keynes described them as possessed of "animal spirits") then caused them to begin bubbling with optimism, the schedule would shift rightward, moving equilibrium from *c* back to *b*, so that investment rises back to \$80 billion. Keynesians argue that investment is not very responsive to small changes in interest rates but investment demand responds strongly to changing expectations.

To summarize, both Keynesian and classical economists agree that equilibrium investment requires the expected rate of return on investment to equal the rate of interest. However,

Keynesians attribute cyclical swings of investment to changes in investors' expectations of future returns. They believe that investment is less influenced by changes in interest rates than it is by the unpredictable expectations of investors. Classical economists perceive investors' expectations about returns as quite stable and explain large variations in investment as responses to small changes in interest rates.

The Keynesian Monetary Transmission Mechanism

The demand and supply of money determine the nominal rate of interest in financial markets, as shown in Panel A of Figure 10. Keynesian theory suggests that during recessions, changes in the interest rate (Panel A) may cause small changes in the level of investment (Panel B), and thus in National Income (Panel C). However, the demand for money is thought to be fairly sensitive with respect to the interest rate, especially during economic downturns. Hence, interest rates may not decrease (*increase*) very much as the money supply is increased (*decreased*). Even if expansionary monetary policies do reduce interest rates a bit, Keynesians believe that investment is relatively insensitive to the interest rate, and so income is affected little, if at all, by monetary policies.

Keynesians argue that changes in the money supply do not affect consumer spending directly, but only indirectly through a

money → interest rate → investment → income

sequence. Even then, the effects of monetary policy are thought to be slight and erratic, because the linkages are perceived to be weak. This view of the chain of events emanating from a change in the money supply is called the **Keynesian monetary transmission mechanism.** If the money supply is increased from $400 billion to $500 billion (a 25 percent increase) in Panel A of Figure 10, the interest rate falls from 8 percent to 7 percent and investment grows slightly from $100 billion to $110 billion (a 10 percent increase). Total output grows via the multiplier effect from $2 trillion to $2.02 trillion (only a 1 percent increase). This suggests that monetary

policy will be weak compared to fiscal policy. Note that Panel D reflects the Keynesian view of a slack economy (Aggregate Supply is horizontal up to the full employment level of output); monetary expansion induces only quantity adjustments, and the price level is unaffected.

Keynesian Analyses of Depressions and Inflations

Classical and Keynesian predictions differ the most during a depression. New classical economists generally advocate laissez-faire policies because they believe that the natural long-run state of the economy is a full employment equilibrium. If pressed, however, most new classical economists would assert that expansionary monetary policies increase Aggregate Spending enough to rapidly boost the economy out of any persistent depression. Classical reasoning also suggests that restrictive monetary policies are the only lasting cure for inflation.

Most Keynesians agree that monetary restraint dampens inflationary pressures, but they disagree with the notion that monetary expansion will cure a depression. During a depression people are generally pessimistic, and interest rates tend to plummet. Consequently, Keynesians suggest that expansionary monetary policies will not bring the economy out of a recession, because any extra money people receive is seldom spent but is hoarded. This is another way of saying that the velocity of money falls to offset monetary growth. Keynesians compare money to a string — you can pull on it to restrain inflation, but trying to push the economy out of the doldrums through expansionary monetary policy is like "pushing on a string." Expansionary monetary policy is viewed as stringlike both because banks may not lend out their reserves if their view of the economic horizon is pessimistic and because people may simply hoard rather than spend most of any extra money that comes their way.

Early Keynesians recommended massive government spending and tax cuts to cure recessions. They emphasized fiscal policy because of a widespread (though mistaken) belief that central banks throughout the world attempted to push

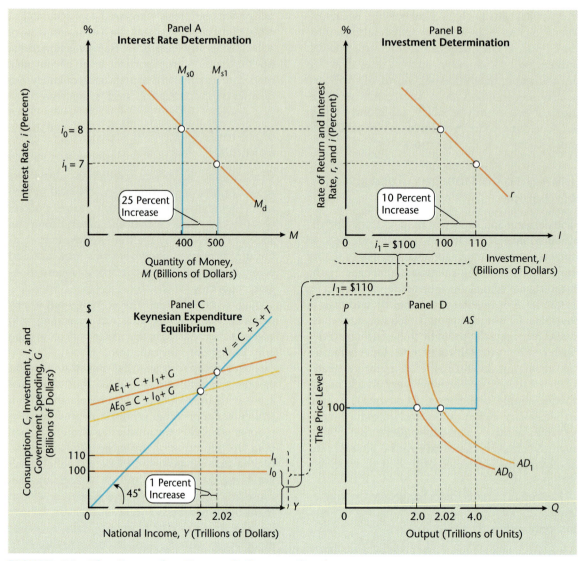

FIGURE 10   The Keynesian Transmission Mechanism: Money, Interest Rates, and National Income

According to Keynesians, expansionary monetary policy operates by reducing interest rates slightly (Panel A), which induces a small increase in investment (Panel B). Through the multiplier process, the new autonomous investment causes income to rise (Panel C). In Panel D, expansionary monetary policy increases Aggregate Demand from AD_0 to AD_1, boosting national output from 2 trillion to 2.02 trillion units. The increase in Aggregate Demand results in only minor changes in output and no changes in the price level. Thus, Keynesians view monetary policy as having only a minimal impact.

their respective nations out of the Depression with expansionary monetary policies. Only long after the Depression did researchers discover that although the U.S. monetary base rose slightly between 1929 and 1933, the money multiplier shrank and the money supply fell sharply. Remember that good information is costly; the economic data of the time were awful.

Modern Monetarism

The Keynesian Revolution stirred a counterrevolution by *modern monetarists*, who recognize some holes in older versions of classical theory but reject any need for massive government intervention to stabilize an economy. Their counterattack, led by Milton Friedman, began with a reformulation of the demand for money.

The Demand for Money Revisited

Modern monetarists concede that money might be demanded for reasons other than anticipated transactions, but they see no reason to compartmentalize the demand for money as Keynesians have. Instead, they have identified certain variables that influence the amounts of money demanded. Milton Friedman has arrived at the most widely accepted formulation of the *new quantity theory of money*. Friedman distinguishes the nominal money people hold from their "real" money holdings. *Real money* is the purchasing power of the money a person holds. It can be computed by dividing the face values of money assets by the price level (M/P). As the price level rises, the face amount of money needed to buy a particular bundle of goods rises proportionally.

Determinants of the Demand for Money

According to Friedman, the variables (besides the price level) that will be *positively* related to the quantity of money demanded are (a) people's total real wealth (including the value of their labor), (b) the interest rate, if any, paid on money holdings, and (c) the illiquidity of nonmonetary assets. He also identifies some variables as *negatively* related to the real (purchasing power) amounts of money people will hold: (a) the interest rate on bonds, (b) the rate of return on physical capital, and (c) the expected rate of inflation.

Wealth (or Permanent Income)   Classical economists (and Keynesians, to a lesser extent) relate the demand for money to current income. Friedman suggests that expected lifetime income better explains both consumption patterns and money holdings. Take two twenty-five-year-olds—one, a recent college graduate in accounting and the other, a manager of a convenience store. Each has a current annual income of $24,000. The consumption level of the young accountant is likely to be higher than that of the convenience store manager because higher expected lifetime income increases the prospects of borrowing money; thus, the accountant will hold more money for transactions purposes.

The Interest Rate on Money   You do not receive interest on cash you hold and only relatively low interest on your demand deposits. Banks do, however, offer free checking accounts and other incentives for depositors who keep certain minimum balances in their accounts. Most people would probably maintain higher checking account balances if the interest rates paid to depositors were increased.

The Illiquidity of Nonmonetary Assets Most college students are not poor, they are just broke. That is, they have highly marketable skills. Another way of saying this is that they have substantial wealth in the form of human capital but not many other assets. According to Friedman, if most of your assets are very illiquid, you will want higher money holdings than will people who have similar amounts of wealth but whose major assets are more liquid. His reasoning is that some liquidity is desired to meet emergencies, and people with large amounts of human capital may not be able to liquidate their major assets (themselves) very easily. Selling yourself into bondage or slavery is illegal, and marketing your skills takes time. Consequently, Friedman expects that you will probably hold more cash than similarly "wealthy" people who are not in college. (Our memory is that when we were students, we were flat broke most of the time.)

Interest Rates on Bonds and Rates of Return on Investment   The major alternatives to holding money are spending it on consumer goods *or* buying stocks, bonds, or capital goods. While modern monetarists emphasize the value

Milton Friedman (b. 1912)

Milton Friedman is among the most publicly visible of modern economists. He has won respect from both his followers and those economists who disagree strongly with his views. Few significant honors in economics have not come Friedman's way. He was president of the American Economic Association in 1967 and in 1976 received the Nobel Prize in economics. Looking very much like everyone's "favorite uncle," Friedman often disarms his adversaries with a wink and a gentle smile, but those who have argued with him find him a formidable debater. He is able to express complicated ideas in simple terms understandable by those untrained in formal economic theory. This makes him popular with the media and keeps Friedman in touch with a wide audience.

Friedman has been a vital force in attacking the orthodoxy of the "new" (Keynesian) economics. He has done this in a way that combines his argumentative talents with solid, empiri-

cal research and a desire not merely to tear down existing economic theory but to restructure it. Friedman's most notable research has involved monetary theory, but, as with all master economists, his thoughts have touched many areas of economics. In the monetary field, Friedman has reconstructed the quantity theory of money, reemphasized the importance and significance of monetary policy, questioned the Keynesian interpretation of the Great Depression, and developed his own prescriptions for preventing future economic catastrophe.

Friedman has also made major contributions in such areas as risk and insurance (answering why people simultaneously gamble and buy insurance) and has developed a theory of consumption based on wealth, as opposed to the Keynesian view that consumption depends only on current income.

Along the way, he has attempted to restate the classical liberal philosophy of Adam Smith in terms pertinent to the modern era. (Friedman's admiration of Adam Smith is virtually unbounded—he has a necktie patterned with cameos of Smith that he wears during public appearances.) Friedman has offered many ideas about replacing the influence of government with market solutions. For example, he argues that government could eliminate public schools and give

the parents of students vouchers (grants) so that all children could attend private schools tailored to their individual needs. He also argues that cash grants to poor people make more sense than such programs as food stamps because these grants would leave more choices in the hands of the poor as well as require fewer tax dollars.

Friedman's restatement of the quantity theory of money is important because it made the theory statistically testable, something the old theory was not. His restatement is essentially a theory of the demand for money, whereas the original version was a theory of the price level. Friedman's analyses of the statistical evidence indicate that the demand for money is stable over the long run and conclude that large changes in the supply of money cause undesirable fluctuations in employment and in the price level. His disenchantment with fiscal policy is due in large measure to the fact that government deficits are most often financed by inflationary expansions of the supply of money and credit. Finally, Friedman has been critical of the performance of the Board of Governors of the Federal Reserve System, because he sees the FED as either following the wrong policy (trying to control interest rates instead of the money supply) or yielding to political pressure rather than sound economic logic.

of consumption as the alternative cost of holding money $(1/P)$, they also recognize either direct investment or purchases of stocks or bonds as possibilities. If such activities are your best alternatives to holding money, then the prices you pay for holding money are the interest (i) that could be received from a bond or the rate of return (r) you might expect from buying stocks or investing directly in physical capital.

Friedman accepts a negative relationship between the interest rate or rate of return on capital and the quantity of money demanded, but, in support of earlier classical reasoning, his studies conclude that the demand for money is relatively insensitive to the interest rate. He absolutely rejects any hint that a liquidity trap has ever existed.

Expected Rates of Inflation The idea that gaining wealth requires you to "buy low and sell high" implies that if you expect inflation, then you should get rid of your money while it has a high value and buy durable assets instead. During inflation, money becomes a hot potato, because expectations of inflation cause people to reduce their money holdings. The greater the expected inflation, the more rapid the velocity of money.

The Stability of the Demand for Money

Modern monetarists are willing to accept the idea that the demand for money is influenced by variables other than income, but they view these relationships as very stable. Moreover, they believe that most variables that influence the demand for money are relatively constant because they are the outcomes of an inherently stable market system. Table 1 summarizes variables that influence the amounts of money people will want to hold. Monetarists believe that the bulk of any instability in a market economy arises because of erratic government policy — the Federal Reserve System is the main villain in their scenario. Before investigating why the FED is perceived as the culprit, we need to examine the modern monetarist monetary transmission mechanism.

Table 1 *Variables Affecting the Nominal Demand for Money*

Positively

1. Income
2. Wealth
3. Cost of living (CPI)
4. Uncertainty about future income and expenses
5. Expected hikes in interest rates
6. Expected declines in the prices of bonds, stocks, or real estate

Negatively

1. Interest rate (i)
2. Rate of return on capital (r)
3. Expected inflation
4. Frequency of receipt of income

The Modern Monetarist Monetary Transmission Mechanism

Modern monetarists, like their classical predecessors, believe that linkages between the money supply and nominal National Income are strong and direct. Monetarists perceive the demand for money as stable, so an expansion in the money supply is viewed as generating surpluses of money in the hands of consumers and investors. These surpluses of money, when spent, quickly increase Aggregate Demand.

Classical economics stresses Aggregate Supply, viewing Aggregate Demand as adjusting quickly and automatically when supply conditions change. (Supply creates its own demand.) Recognizing the importance of Aggregate Demand in the short run, because the economy may falter occasionally, most monetarists believe that growth of the money supply can boost spending and drive a slumping economy toward full employment. Much like classical theorists, modern monetarists perceive the market system as inherently stable and think that the economy will seldom deviate for long from full employment.

Modern monetarists consequently predict that, in the long run, growth in the money supply will be translated strictly into higher prices, even if monetary expansion occurs during a recession. Expansionary macroeconomic policies will, however, induce greater output more quickly in the midst of a recession. In other words, the Aggregate Supply curve described by Keynesians may accurately represent a recessionary economy, but only in the very short run. This view of the world is portrayed in Figure 11.

Suppose the money supply is initially at $400 billion and the price level is 100. The economy is temporarily producing at point a — which is half a trillion units of real GNP below capacity, because full employment income is 4 trillion units. If the money supply and Aggregate Demand were held constant, then prices and wages would eventually fall to a long-run equilibrium at point b. Full employment would be realized when the price level fell to 80. If the money supply were expanded to $500 billion, Aggregate Demand would grow and full employment output of 4 trillion units would be realized more rapidly (point c). However, the price level is higher in this long-run equilibrium, being maintained at 100.

Most modern monetarists oppose active monetary policy to combat recessions. They view long-run adjustments as fairly rapid, believing instead that deflation will quickly restore an economy to full employment. An even greater concern is their fear that discretionary monetary policy might "overshoot," causing recession to move into inflation. This is shown in Figure 11 by too rapid growth of Aggregate Demand when the money supply is increased to $600 billion. In this case, the consequence of policy to combat recession is a 20 percent increase in the price level (point d). According to this monetarist line of thinking, overly aggressive monetary expansion can eliminate recession and unemployment more quickly than "do-nothing" policies, but only at the risk of sparking inflation.

Summary: Classical, Keynesian, and Modern Monetary Theory

The monetary theories of classical economists, Keynesians, and modern monetarists are outlined in Figure 12. The major differences in these schools of thought are found in (a) the nature of the demand for money, (b) the nature of the investment relationship, (c) the monetary transmission mechanism, and (d) assumptions about the velocity of money.

Assumptions about the creation of money and, thus, the effectiveness of monetary policy are crucial differences between Keynesians and monetarists. Most monetarist models ignore the institutional mechanisms used to create money

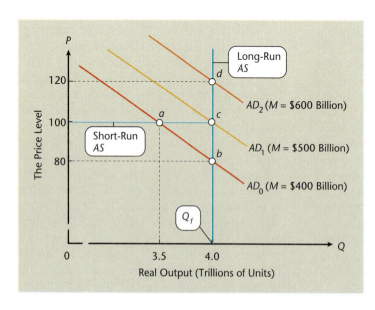

FIGURE 11   Modern Monetarist Views of the Short-Run and Long-Run Effects of Expansionary Monetary Policy

Modern monetarists recognize that variations in Aggregate Demand may entail short-term quantity adjustments so that recessions are possible. For example, movement from c to a would be a recessionary movement caused by falling Aggregate Demand. Monetarists perceive Aggregate Demand as proportional to the money supply but are extremely leery of short-term adjustments to the money supply as a means of correcting for recessions. In their view, the long-term effect of any increase in the money supply is a proportional movement of the price level, which raises the prospect of inflation.

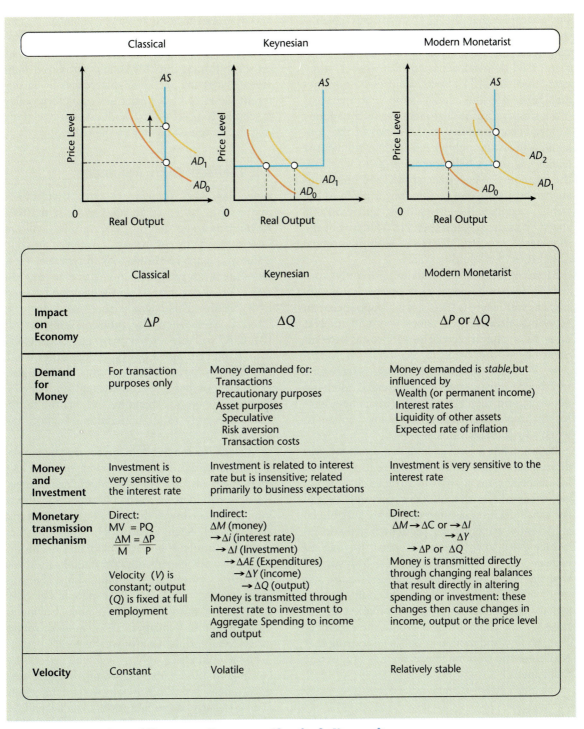

	Classical	Keynesian	Modern Monetarist
Impact on Economy	ΔP	ΔQ	ΔP or ΔQ
Demand for Money	For transaction purposes only	Money demanded for: Transactions Precautionary purposes Asset purposes Speculative Risk aversion Transaction costs	Money demanded is *stable*, but influenced by Wealth (or permanent income) Interest rates Liquidity of other assets Expected rate of inflation
Money and Investment	Investment is very sensitive to the interest rate	Investment is related to interest rate but is insensitive; related primarily to business expectations	Investment is very sensitive to the interest rate
Monetary transmission mechanism	Direct: $MV = PQ$ $\dfrac{\Delta M}{M} = \dfrac{\Delta P}{P}$ Velocity (V) is constant; output (Q) is fixed at full employment	Indirect: ΔM (money) $\rightarrow \Delta i$ (interest rate) $\rightarrow \Delta I$ (Investment) $\rightarrow \Delta AE$ (Expenditures) $\rightarrow \Delta Y$ (income) $\rightarrow \Delta Q$ (output) Money is transmitted through interest rate to investment to Aggregate Spending to income and output	Direct: $\Delta M \rightarrow \Delta C$ or $\rightarrow \Delta I$ $\rightarrow \Delta Y$ $\rightarrow \Delta P$ or ΔQ Money is transmitted directly through changing real balances that result directly in altering spending or investment: these changes then cause changes in income, output or the price level
Velocity	Constant	Volatile	Relatively stable

FIGURE 12 Major Differences Between Classical, Keynesian, and Modern Monetarist Monetary Theories

(for example, that the FED might buy government bonds from banks, thereby increasing excess reserves, which are multiplied into new loan-based demand deposits). Remember, however, that the FED directly controls the monetary base, not the money supply. Monetarists often simply assume that increases in the money supply become money in the hands of the consuming/investing public. A common monetarist analogy is that a helicopter dumps money into the economy. They then argue, not unreasonably, that if sufficient new money is given to the public, people will feel wealthier, quit worrying about "bad times," and spend it. This part of the monetarist scenario dispenses with theoretical difficulties like liquidity traps.

Modern Keynesians describe not only consumer/investor liquidity traps, but bank liquidity traps as well. Here is their story. Suppose that an economic downturn is under way and interest rates have plummeted. The FED buys government bonds from banks to counteract the recession. Will the banks' new excess reserves be translated into borrowing, increased demand deposits, and then spending? (This is necessary for the monetarist transmission mechanism to work.) Keynesians think not.

If you were a banker and the economy was depressed, would you want to reduce already low interest rates in order to attract new borrowers, many of whom look like deadbeats? Would the small declines in interest that are feasible be sufficiently attractive to prudent borrowers to induce them to apply for new loans? Keynesians answer "No" to both questions. They suggest that the banks will simply accumulate more and more vault cash if the FED tries to counter recessionary tendencies through open-market operations. This is just another aspect of the argument that money (and monetary policy) is a string that is useless for pushing the economy out of the doldrums.

Monetary Policy vs. Fiscal Policy

Classical economics and supply-side approaches lead to the conclusion that Aggregate Demand matters little, if at all, in the long run. Keynesians and monetarists alike, however, focus on Aggregate Demand. Modern monetarists and contemporary Keynesians clearly have different views on some things, but this should not cloud their areas of agreement. Their differences lie in different views of how important monetary policy is relative to fiscal policy, and not that one alone matters to the exclusion of the other.

The Ineffectiveness Argument

Keynesians and monetarists agree that money matters but differ as to *how much* it matters. Keynesians argue that monetary growth will not raise spending or cut interest rates very much in a slump. Figure 13 shows why. Keynesians view investment as relatively insensitive to interest rates, depending instead primarily upon business expectations. This suggests that slight drops in interest rates when the money supply grows (Panel A) will affect investment and output very little (Panel B). Fiscal policy, on the other hand, is extremely powerful in a slump. Adding government purchases to investment in Panel B boosts autonomous spending and, via the multiplier, massively raises national production and income.

Monetarists see the demand for money as relatively insensitive to interest rates but perceive investment as highly dependent on interest. Even a small increase in the money supply drives interest rates down sharply in the monetarist view (Panel A in Figure 14), which in turn strongly stimulates investment (Panel B). Monetarists also see expansionary monetary policy as bolstering consumer spending, both because extra money "burns holes" in people's pockets and because lower interest rates make buying on credit easier and cheaper. Thus, modern monetarists view money as a powerful tool.

Fiscal policy has only a negligible effect, according to monetarist reasoning, because new government spending does not raise injections $(I + G)$ nearly as much as does even a small decline in interest rates. Moreover, monetarists object that government spending may "crowd out" investment. Careful study of Figures 13 and 14 will enable you to understand the fundamental reasons why Keynesians advocate fiscal policy

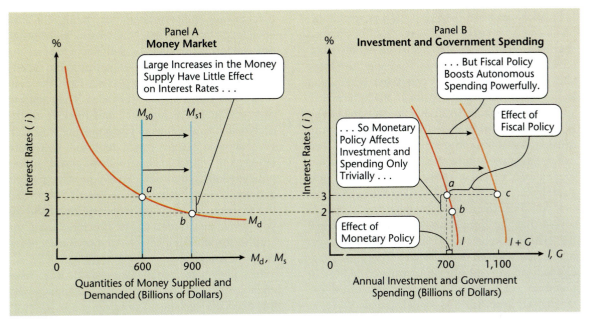

FIGURE 13 Monetary vs. Fiscal Policy: The Keynesian View

An expansion of the money supply from $600 to $900 billion reduces interest rates by only 1 percent in a Keynesian slump (Panel A). This small decline in interest rates only raises investment by $50 billion in Panel B because investment is insensitive to interest rates in the Keynesian view. Fiscal policy, on the other hand, is very effective in the Keynesian slump, because dollar for dollar it is just as powerful as new investment in inducing further income through the multiplier process. New government spending of $400 billion ($c - a$) in Panel B expands autonomous spending far more powerfully than does the 50 percent monetary growth depicted in Panel A.

to regulate Aggregate Spending, while monetarists prefer monetary policy.

Keynesians and modern monetarists agree that when an economy is at full employment, growth of Aggregate Demand results in a rising price level. Both would agree that, when an economy is in a severe slump, increases in Aggregate Demand will restore full employment. They would, however, disagree on the appropriate way to expand Aggregate Demand. Monetarists favor expansionary monetary policy to increase private consumption and investment, while Keynesians view that approach as ineffective because of widespread pessimism on the parts of workers, consumers, and business firms. Keynesians, therefore, favor expansionary fiscal policy.

We have examined the theoretical arguments that explain why Keynesians prefer fiscal policy and why monetarists prefer monetary policy to stabilize the economy. Just how convincing are these positions when applied to the art of policy-

-making? And how frequently should policy be changed?

Rules Versus Discretionary Policies

Most modern monetarists believe that designing discretionary monetary and fiscal policies to buffer business cycles is an impossible task. They favor doing away with all discretion in policy-making and adopting stable and permanent monetary and fiscal rules. These critics believe that the market system is inherently stable and that severe swings in business activity inevitably follow ill-advised discretionary policies. One mechanism to eliminate discretion in monetary policy-making is a monetary growth rule.

A **monetary growth rule** *would dictate that the money supply be increased at a rate compatible with historical growth of GNP, say 3 percent annually.*

Suppose you are driving a high-powered car on a fairly straight highway that is banked slightly along the edges to keep you on the road. Unfortunately, someone has blackened the front and side windows—you cannot see where you are or what lies ahead. To make matters worse, your gas pedal sticks at times, the steering wheel is loose, and your brakes alternate between pure mush and grabbing so sharply that you skid. You can vaguely see where you have been through a fogged-over rearview mirror. What is your best strategy?

If you press the gas pedal too hard, you may go so fast that the curbs at the edge of the road will fail to keep you on course. If you try to steer, you may guide yourself over the side. Your best strategy will be to carefully adjust the accelerator to maintain a slow but steady speed and let the car steer itself away from the road's edges.

The economists who blame cyclical swings on erratic monetary or fiscal policies perceive mac-roeconomic policymakers as being in our economy's "driver's seat." Attempts to fine-tune the economy through discretionary policies are viewed as the fumblings of people who barely deserve learners' permits playing with the controls of an Indianapolis 500 racer. They tend to oversteer and to jump back and forth from the accelerator to the brake. The resulting stop-and-go economic pattern might resemble your path when you were learning to drive—and, unlike policymakers, you knew what you were passing and could see what lay ahead. We also hope that the steering, braking, and acceleration of the car you drove responded more precisely than the cumbersome tools available to monetary and fiscal policymakers.

In addition to a monetary growth rule, most economists opposed to discretion in policymaking advocate certain fiscal rules:

1. Government spending should be set at the

FIGURE 14 Monetary vs. Fiscal Policy: The Monetarist View

Panel A illustrates the monetarist contention that a slight increase in the money supply (M_{s0} to M_{s1}) will reduce interest rates dramatically (from 10 to 5.5 percent) because the demand for money (M_d) is relatively insensitive to interest rate changes. Marked declines in interest rates resulting from the extra $100 billion in money cause investment to soar by $1.5 trillion (in Panel B), stimulating autonomous spending far more than even a massive dose ($400 billion) of new government spending.

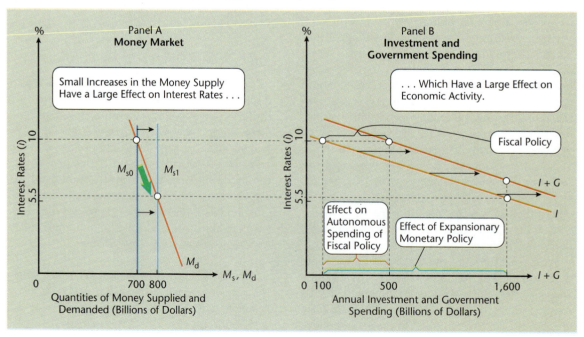

amounts of government goods and services that the public would demand if the economy were at full employment; no "make work" projects should be permitted.

2. Tax rates should then be structured so that the federal budget would be roughly in balance if the economy were at full employment.

Although monetarists perceive some problems emerging from improper spending and tax policies (e.g., Hoover's tax hike in 1930–1932, Johnson's simultaneous wars on poverty and in Vietnam, and the enormous budget deficits of the Reagan years), they cast central bankers (the FED) as the major villains in their explanations of cyclical chaos in market economies.

The Culpability of the FED

Modern monetarists view the market system as largely self-stabilizing and predictable; they perceive erratic government policies as the leading cause of business cycles. Monetarists believe that rapid inflation is explained by excessive monetary growth, which results in "too much money chasing too few goods." Alternatively, severe deflations, recessions, or depressions result when the money supply grows too slowly (or even falls), resulting in "too little money chasing too many goods." Government can prevent macroeconomic convulsions by simply holding the rate of growth of the money supply roughly in line with our (slow growing) capacity to produce.

Monetarists view income (or wealth) as the major determinant of the demand for money. Recall the equation of exchange: $MV = PQ$. If the money supply (M) grows at the same rate as our ability to produce (Q), and if velocity (V) is constant, then the price level (P) will be stable. Given that

$$\frac{\Delta M}{M} + \frac{\Delta V}{V} = \frac{\Delta P}{P} + \frac{\Delta Q}{Q}$$

then, if $\Delta M/M = \Delta Q/Q$, and if $\Delta V/V = 0$, it follows that $\Delta P/P = 0$.

This sounds fairly easy. Why has government not learned these simple monetary facts of life and followed policies to achieve a stable price level and facilitate smooth economic growth? The monetarist answer to this question is that no one is able to predict precisely what will happen to our productive capacity in the near future. Moreover, instituting policies and having them take effect requires time. (We discuss the problems posed by time lags in chapter 17.) Monetarists also believe that the FED tries too hard to control the economy. Finally, political considerations too often dominate sound policymaking. The solution, according to many monetarists, is to follow a rule of expanding the money supply at a fixed annual rate in the 2 to 4 percent range compatible with historical growth of our productive capacity. (Take a look at Focus 2.)

The Failure of Discretionary Fine-Tuning

Many economists view the Great Depression and the 1960s as evidence that only Keynesian engineering can keep the economy stable and ensure its prosperity. Discretionary changes in taxes and spending are the fiscal tools Keynesians recommend. Others argue that the FED can keep the economy on track by expanding or contracting the money supply as needed. Fiscal and monetary policies both have been frequently changed to try to fine-tune the economy so that Aggregate Demand and Aggregate Supply are balanced.

Tax rates were cut and the money supply was expanded to stimulate a previously sluggish economy during the early 1960s. Then, monetary restraint was applied in 1966 to curb mounting inflationary pressures. A temporary tax surcharge was imposed in 1969. The money supply grew rapidly in the early 1970s, screeched to a halt causing a short collapse in 1975–1976, accelerated from 1977 to 1979, and then slowed sharply in the early 1980s. Cuts in tax rates from 1981 to 1983 were coupled with a monetary slowdown to yield mixed results.

Keynes believed that central banks tried to follow expansionary policies but failed to cure the Great Depression. This is, in part, why Keynes and his followers sought to replace passive monetary policy with activist fiscal policies. Milton Friedman and other monetarists question the widely held belief that the Great Depression

Is Monetary Policy a String? The Recession of 1990–1992

Our deepest recession since the 1930s occurred during 1981–1983, and our longest, during 1990–1992. Predictably, critics blame the FED for this apparent lapse into relative instability. Digesting the FED's policies so that they can be understood in historical context requires time. Economists have reached consensus that FED "disinflation" strategies, adopted to squelch the "double-digit" inflation of the 1970s, propelled the downturn of 1981–1983. (No consensus exists, however, as to whether the benefits of slower inflation outweighed the losses of employment and output because of the recession.)

Discerning a pattern in the FED's policies during the early 1990s requires more detective work. Most non-Keynesian economists view low interest rates as critical for balanced investment and economic growth. Based on a blend of Keynesian and monetarist theories, the FED lowered its discount rate 23 times during 1989–1992. Federal deficits during the early 1990s were at record levels, so expanding the monetary base should have been easy: The FED could simply absorb (*monetize*) substantial chunks of new federal debt by buying Treasury bonds. Then, the expansion of available bank reserves would swell the money supply—after bankers made loans to investors.

But some major glitches marred this predicted chain of events. Since 1979, the FED has announced monetary growth

FIGURE 15

targets in the moderate range (2–6 percent), with precise targets depending on economic conditions. However, Figure 15 indicates that while unemployment rates hovered between 6 and 8 percent during the Recession of 1990–1992, the money supply (M2) fell below the FED's targeted growth rates.

This slow growth was a sharp departure from most economic recoveries since World War II, when the real (inflation-adjusted) money supply grew at an average annual rate of 7 percent. Among possible explanations for sluggish monetary growth:

1. The FED'S Open Market desk bought too few Treasury bonds so the monetary base expanded too slowly.

2. Despite increased bank reserves, banks, fearing widespread defaults, were reluctant to lend, and pessimistic investors were reluctant to borrow.

3. Foreign investors responded to lower U.S. interest rates by shifting funds to countries with higher interest rates, reducing the loanable funds in the U.S.

More detective work is needed to identify which factors account for this slow monetary growth. One thing, however, is certain. Voters often "throw the rascals out" in a stagnant economy. In 1992, more incumbent senators and members of congress retired or were defeated than in any other election in the preceding four decades.

During this "triple-dip" recession, Ross Perot, a billionaire entrepreneur, had more voter support for his brief run at the presidency than either the Democratic or Republican candidates. George Bush's "favorable ratings" dropped below 30 percent by August 1992, and Democrat Bill Clinton led Bush in most political popularity polls by a 2 to 1 margin.

occurred despite expansionary monetary policies. Collecting and reviewing monetary data for the United States for the past century, they discovered that the money supply fell considerably just before and during the Depression. Their interpretation is that the Federal Reserve System caused the Depression because (perhaps unwittingly) it followed contractionary policies.

In fact, most monetarists believe that the business cycle is largely a consequence of improper monetary policy — when the money supply grows too slowly, economic downturns and stagnation soon follow; when the money supply mushrooms, increases in the price level are inevitable. These difficulties are the major reasons for monetarists' advocacy of stable monetary growth rates. The crucial differences between fiscal and monetary policies according to the theories of Keynesians, monetarists, and new classical macroeconomists are summarized in Table 2.

The FED has meandered back and forth between the advice offered by Keynesians and that given by modern monetarists and others of a classical tilt. Recently, the FED has aimed at a range of monetary growth while also focusing on a new monetary indicator, P^* (pronounced P-star), which is discussed in Focus 3. This new indicator reflects an amalgam of competing theories.

We will look at various ways to finance government activity in the next chapter; monetary and fiscal policies are linked through the government budget equation. We will also examine the effects of the growth of government debt caused by persistent federal deficits. Then, in subsequent chapters, we will examine pressing macroeconomic issues from the perspectives of theorists who favor activist policies versus the perspectives of theorists who prefer more passive policies based closer to a laissez-faire philosophy.

Table 2 *Alternative Views of Monetary and Fiscal Policies*

Keynesians	New Classical Economics	
	Monetarists	**Supply-Siders**
1. Fiscal policy is very powerful.	1. Fiscal policy is relatively unimportant due to *crowding out*.	1. High tax rates and vast government spending both reduce the incentives for people to be productive.
2. Monetary policy is not very powerful or important during economic slumps.	2. Erratic monetary policy is the major cause of business cycles. Money is important at all times.	2. Erratic fiscal policy confuses investors and workers, reducing incentives for productivity. Erratic monetary policy diverts resources from production into hedges against inflation or deflation.
3. Monetary policy affects spending through changes in interest rates and investments.	3. Monetary policy affects spending in all markets simultaneously ($MV = PQ$).	3. Money is a veil.
4. Discretionary policies are necessary to offset the economy's inherent instability.	4. Smooth growth of the money supply is crucial. Rules should replace discretion in policy. Economy is inherently stable.	4. Steady monetary policy enhances the quality of information about economic decisions.
5. Velocity is erratic; it rises during inflation but falls sharply during recessions.	5. Velocity is relatively stable.	5. Velocity is stable if monetary policy is stable.
6. During deep depressions, fear causes velocity to plummet, resulting in *liquidity traps*.	6. Liquidity traps are highly implausible and have never actually occurred.	6. Liquidity traps are irrelevant to the real world.

FOCUS 3

P-Star: The Equation of Exchange in Action

The FED recently unveiled a new monetary indicator, P^* (pronounced P-star), which, since 1989, has been used to indicate potential inflation and to evaluate monetary policies aimed at price stabilization. P^* is a rearranged version of the equation of exchange, computed as:

$$P^* = (M2 \times V^*)/Q^*$$

where M2 is the measure of the money supply, V^* is an estimate of the long-run value of the velocity of M2, and Q^* is potential GNP.

FED studies suggest that the velocity of M2 is relatively stable, averaging 1.65. Potential GNP (Q^*) is estimated to have grown at an average annual rate of between 2.5 and 3.0 percent for several decades. Thus, P^* is an estimate of the long-run price level consistent with current levels of M2. When P^* exceeds the current price level, inflation should begin to rise shortly thereafter. Conversely, when P^* is below the current price level, inflation will likely fall in the near future. Given the lagged relationship between the current price level (P) and P^*, the FED can use P^* to determine whether to follow expansionary ($P^* > P$) monetary policy to achieve long-run price stability.

Like any innovation in policy-making, P^* is controversial. The use of P^* is justified by a mishmash of monetarist and Keynesian theories, and predictably, is under attack from both camps. The assumption that the velocity of M2 is stable is a monetarist proposition, while the idea that potential GNP can be estimated with reasonable precision is inherently a Keynesian notion. The idea that potential GNP grows at a relatively constant rate has also been challenged by critics. Despite these potential problems, P^* is new (introduced in 1989) and will undoubtedly be tested by the FED until its usefulness can be fully determined.

Chapter Review: Key Points

1. You increase your *spending* when you have "too much" money; your rate of *saving* increases when you have "too little" money.

2. People hold money for predictable spending (*transactions demands*) with a cushion for uncertain outlays or income receipts (*precautionary demands*). People also have *asset demands* for money because (a) money is relatively riskless, (b) transaction costs associated with less-liquid assets may exceed expected returns, or (c) people speculate by holding money when they expect the prices of alternative assets (e.g., stocks, bonds, or real estate) to fall.

3. According to classical monetary theory, the sole rational motive for holding money is *to consummate transactions*.

4. Interest rates and bond prices are *inversely related*. Bond prices fall if interest rates rise, and vice versa.

5. The costs of holding nominal amounts of money are (a) *the reciprocal of the price level* ($1/P$) if the choice is between saving money

or buying consumer goods, or (b) *the interest rate*, if money is viewed as an asset substitutable for some highly liquid income-generating asset, say a bond. *Inflation* also imposes costs on holdings of money.

6. The *income velocity* (V) of money equals GNP (PQ) divided by the money supply (M).

7. The *equation of exchange*, a truism, is written $MV = PQ$. Therefore, the percentage change in the money supply plus the percentage change in velocity roughly equals the percentage change in the price level plus the percentage change in real output:

$$\frac{\Delta M}{M} + \frac{\Delta V}{V} = \frac{\Delta P}{P} + \frac{\Delta Q}{Q}$$

8. Classical economics assumes that *velocity* (V) and *output* (Q) are reasonably constant and independent of the money supply (M) and the price level (P). Classical economists believe that changes in the money supply result in proportional changes in the price level and expressed this belief in early versions of the *quantity theory of money*. The quantity theory of money is more accurately a *monetary theory of the price level*.

9. Keynes's attack on the quantity theory disputes the assumptions that (a) the natural state of the economy is full employment, (b) the velocity of money is inherently stable, and (c) the only rational motive for holding money is for transactions purposes.

10. Modern monetarists perceive a direct link between the money supply and National Income. Because the demand for money is relatively stable, growth of the money supply puts excess money balances in the hands of consumers and investors who, in turn, spend this surplus money on goods and services. Monetary growth may expand output in the short run, but modern monetarists conclude that in the long run, higher prices will result.

11. The difficulties confronting monetary and fiscal policymakers have caused many economists to favor putting the economy on "automatic pilot." The advocates of replacing *discretionary policy* with *monetary growth rules* would replace the Federal Open Market Committee with a couple of reliable but unimaginative clerks. Their job would be to increase the money supply by a fixed small (3 percent?) increase annually, and the federal budget would be set to balance at full employment.

Key Concepts

Ensure that you can define these terms before proceeding.

transactions demands	$MV = PQ$
precautionary demands	income velocity (V)
asset demands	monetary transmission mechanisms
quantity theory of money	liquidity trap
equation of exchange	monetary growth rules

Problems and Questions

1. Suppose the money supply grows by 12 percent and real output grows by 3 percent, but the income velocity of money is constant. What happens to the price level?

2. If potential output grows by 2 percent while velocity falls by 3 percent, what rate of monetary growth should keep the price level stable?

3. If average prices are rising 20 percent annually while monetary growth is 12 percent in a stagnant economy, what is happening to velocity? Has anything like this occurred in the U.S. economy? When?

4. If both velocity and the price level fall by 8 percent while real output drops a startling 15 percent, what must be happening to the money supply? Has anything like this ever happened in the U.S. economy? When?

5. According to monetarists, expanding the money supply inevitably causes higher prices. In what ways do Keynesians disagree and why?

6. Do you think most people want to balance illiquid assets against highly liquid assets, such as money? Why? How does your line of reasoning lead to the demand for money? Does your answer suggest that the demand for money will be sensitive to interest rates?

To the cost of living? How, and why or why not?

7. Describe the differences between Keynesian and monetarist monetary transmission mechanisms. Why are these differences important? In what way does Keynesian fiscal policy short-circuit the difficulties they perceive in transforming new money into new spending?

8. If the economy took a tailspin into a depression, would you expect any (short-run) liquidity trap to emerge more from the banking sector or from the behavior of the nonbanking public?

9. According to Keynesians, interest is a reward for sacrificing liquidity. Classical and modern monetarists describe interest as a reward for postponing consumption or as a return on investment. Which of these explanations seems more plausible to you? Is either approach totally false?

10. As people expect more inflation, they may begin treating money as a "hot potato"; average money holdings may fall, with the result that velocity increases. On the other hand, increased inflation may generate more uncertainty, which may cause people to *increase* their money holdings. People who anticipate higher inflation and want to accumulate a given real amount of saving before retirement, but who are leery of most financial investments, may try to build their holdings of money. On average, do you think the inflation of the past 20 years has caused real money balances per capita to rise or fall? How would you test this hypothesis? To what extent can inflation be considered a tax on money balances?

11. Do you think the evidence better supports the Keynesian view that velocity is erratic or the monetarist position that velocity is stable? What economic forces are you aware of that may explain trends and fluctuations in velocity?

12. In late 1979, the Federal Reserve announced that it would focus its attention primarily on rates of monetary growth instead of interest rates. Although this action has often been urged by monetarists, the monetarist camp received the announcement with less than full enthusiasm. Many monetarists would like the FED to concentrate on the monetary

base, citing statistical studies that suggest a reasonably stable and predictable relationship between the base and GNP. The FED does not yet seem ready to adopt such a simple approach.

What is necessary for the monetary base and money supply to be tightly linked? Is it possible for the FED to maintain money supply or monetary base growth rate goals in the face of political pressures if interest rates rise to levels that are perceived to be too high? Can both targets (money supply growth rates and reasonable interest rates) be controlled simultaneously? How? Numerous economists are skeptical because the FED has made similar announcements in the past, but policies did not change. What makes a monetary growth approach so hard for the FED to implement?

13. Keynesian theory suggests that the relevant substitutes for money are securities, while monetarists argue for a broader range of substitutes that include consumer and investment goods. How important is this difference in explaining the impact of money on economic activity? Why?

14. Suppose a rule of 3-percent annual monetary growth were imposed. How long should policymakers doggedly follow such a policy if inflation soared to more than 20 percent or unemployment hovered around 15 percent?

15. Paul Volcker, then chair of the FED, testified before Congress in 1986 that NOW and other interest-bearing demand deposit accounts, disinflation, and falling interest rates have (at least in the short run) altered the basic relationship between the rate of change in M1 and inflation. Accordingly, given the greater uncertainty associated with the relationship between M1 and economic activity, the FED adopted a broader range for its M1 growth rate. Thus, if velocity continues to fall, M1 growth can be near the upper end of the target range and vice versa. Does Volcker's testimony of a wider M1 range confirm Milton Friedman's argument that the FED simply adjusts its target to cover its discretionary policymaking? What would be the effect on the economy of a fixed (3 percent) rule for M1 growth if velocity is falling?

Deficits and Public Debt

Unemployment and inflation are macroeconomic problems with obvious relevance to our lives, but few Americans can identify how federal budget deficits and an enormous public debt affect them personally. Nevertheless, many people are upset because our federal budget has been awash in red ink. Budget deficits during the Reagan and Bush years were greater than those piled up by all presidents from George Washington through Jimmy Carter, exceeding $300 billion in 1991 alone. Our national debt more than tripled during the 1980s and was approaching $4 trillion at the end of 1992.

> The federal **budget deficit** *is the annual difference between federal outlays and receipts* $(G - T)$. **National (public) debt** *results from cumulated federal deficits.*

Critics of astronomical deficits and soaring debt often argue that any organization that spends more than its receipts is doomed, asserting that government should be run "more like a business." The Gramm-Rudman-Hollings Deficit Reduction Act (1985) was intended to eliminate federal deficits by 1991. When the recession of 1990–1991 pushed this target beyond reach, eleventh-hour negotiations culminated in the 1990 Deficit Reduction Act. Under this most recent plan, deficit targets become more flexible,

but several broad categories of government spending were curtailed. Are huge budget deficits really cause for concern? Or are deficits and the debt just political issues used to bash incumbent officeholders around election time?

In this chapter, we will address a number of issues about deficits and the national debt: Are budget deficits, government spending, and the national debt out of control? How can the federal government finance deficits year after year for decades? What macroeconomic consequences follow binges of deficit spending? When, if ever, is a deficit desirable? Have linkages between budget deficits and deficits in our international trade caused us to sell U.S. resources to foreigners wholesale? Must future generations of Americans pay for our free-spending ways?

Recent Growth of Deficits and Debt

Every modern president has promised to balance the federal budget, but it has been in deficit 90 percent of the time since World War II. Figure 1 traces the history of federal budget deficits and total interest-bearing public debt for the past four decades. Our most recent budget surplus

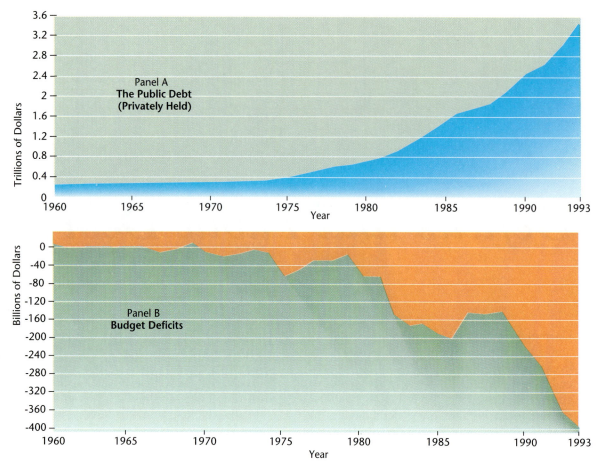

FIGURE 1   Budget Deficits and the Public Debt

Budget deficits from the 1950s through the 1970s were considered enormous at the time, but they have been swamped (even after adjustments for inflation) by the deficits since 1980. National debt more than tripled during the Reagan and Bush years of 1981 through 1990.

Source: *Economic Report of the President,* 1991.

occurred in 1969. Political battles over the budget have normally pivoted on spending priorities instead of balancing the budget. Whose programs will be sacrificed? For example, Presidents Ford and Reagan both sought to build up national defense and urged cuts in transfer programs to reduce deficits. Congress, however, resisted cuts in transfer payments. The result was that both defense and transfers grew, swelling both deficits and debt.

The rapid growth of public debt shown in Figure 1 concerns many people. Our analysis in earlier chapters, however, has suggested that during a recession, deficit spending may help stabilize the economy—Herbert Hoover's attempts to balance the budget deepened the Great Depression. We will now examine how deficits can be financed and the different budget constraints facing the private and public sectors.

Private vs. Public Finance

What mechanisms enable individuals and governments to run deficits? How can governments run persistent deficits? Many people draw an incorrect analogy between government finance and business or private household budgeting because they fail to understand the different spending constraints facing the private and the public sectors.

Private Budget Constraints

The availability of funds limits spending by households, proprietors, and partnerships. Funds are made available through (a) sales of current assets, (b) current income (including gifts or inheritance), and (c) potential borrowing against assets or expected future income. You know how tightly credit is rationed to fund private spending if you have ever exceeded your MasterCard credit limit. Even young people with great potential future income have problems borrowing. This is one reason the government guarantees most student loans. Big corporations tend to have fewer problems in securing funds.

Corporations The idea that corporations balance their budgets regularly is contrary to fact. Most corporate giants that survive have more debt outstanding with each passing decade. However, they also have more assets and income with each passing decade. Big corporations establish huge lines of credit with major financial intermediaries, but they also borrow by issuing bonds. Their bonds tend to be more salable than the IOUs of households, proprietorships, or partnerships, because most large corporations are superior credit risks. Corporations have an additional source of purchasing power available to neither households nor to noncorporate firms: They can sell stock to finance spending. The ability to sell bonds and to offer ownership shares (stock) makes corporations more flexible and powerful than other firms in securing funds to cover operating expenses or new investments in plant and equipment.

Local Government Budget Constraints

States, counties, cities, school districts, and other local government units face slightly different spending constraints. Like proprietorships or partnerships, they can finance current spending with revenues from selling goods and services or some of their assets. Like corporations, they may issue bonds to obtain purchasing power, but government does not sell ownership shares (stock).

Taxes Another major difference between private and government organizations is that government can enact *taxes* to finance its spending, which gives government tremendous power to use resources as it wishes.

Even the power to tax allows only limited command over resources. Excessive spending by the governments of New York City and Cleveland, for example, almost forced them into bankruptcy in the 1970s. Local governments sometimes default on their loans. Some hobbyists collect defunct municipal bonds the way others collect stamps. They have little hope that these bonds will ever be redeemed; rarity and appearance alone determine their values.

Regulation or Confiscation Government can also channel the allocation of resources through *regulation* or *confiscation*. For example, regulation now forces car owners to buy emission-controlling exhaust systems and limits firms' pollution levels. Through such regulations, the government buys a cleaner environment for all of us and makes us pay for it without explicit tax increases. You may think that direct confiscation is not used by governments in the United States. The right of eminent domain, however, can be and is used by all levels of government to secure land for such things as highway rights-of-way or areas for dams or parks. When the government exercises *eminent domain*, those who are forced to surrender their property are typically paid what the government views as a "fair market value." Although the military draft is not used at present, it is another example of government confiscating resources.

The Federal Budget Constraint

A national government has another major tool available: It can print additional *monetary base* to pay for its outlays. (Recall that the monetary base equals currency plus all reserves in the banking system.) In many countries, the central bank covers government outlays by issuing bonds, collecting taxes, or creating additional monetary base. In the United States, financing a deficit $(G - T)$ with monetary base is a more indirect process because, in an accounting sense, our Treasury "borrows" money from the FED, which actually creates the additional monetary base.

The Treasury first issues new bonds to cover a federal deficit. The FED then uses expansionary open-market operations to buy these bonds. This expands bank reserves, which are then transformed into new money through the money multiplier process. Bonds bought by the FED are considered, for accounting purposes, to be part of our national debt. It is nonsense, however, to suggest that our national debt is enlarged because one government agency (Treasury) owes another (the FED). Thus, in what follows, we ignore Treasury bonds held by the FED when we count the national debt.

In summary, government can secure resources to provide goods and services through (a) sales of current assets or outputs; (b) loans from U.S. citizens and firms, foreign citizens or governments, or commercial banks; (c) taxation; (d) confiscation; or (e) expansion of the monetary base (currency in circulation plus bank reserves).

Confiscation can be regarded as taxation in kind, so central government outlays are characterized by a government budget constraint.

The **government budget constraint** *identifies financing options open to the federal government:*

$G = T + \Delta B + \Delta MB$

where,

 G = total governmental outlays
 T = total governmental revenues from taxes, charges, and sales
 ΔB = change in the national debt
 ΔMB = change in the monetary base (currency in circulation plus bank reserves)

Consequently, the federal deficit can be expressed as $G - T = \Delta B + \Delta MB$.

If the federal government spends more than it collects $(G - T > 0)$, it must either borrow $(\Delta B > 0)$ or create (print) the monetary (base) difference $(\Delta MB > 0)$. The money expansion process applies to any increase in the monetary base, as described earlier. If the government collects more than it spends $(G - T < 0)$, it can either retire some existing debt $(\Delta B < 0)$ or retire some money it has previously created $(\Delta MB < 0)$. Budget deficits cause growth in the national debt or in the money supply, while government surpluses make it possible to pay off some of the national debt and/or remove some money from circulation. Borrowing money or selling current assets to secure purchasing power are common to both private and government decision makers. But private citizens cannot legally tax, confiscate, or create (print) more monetary base.

Are there limits to a government's command over resources? The ultimate limit is people's faith that government will survive, honor its contracts, and maintain reasonable stability in the value of the money it issues. The worthlessness of bonds issued by Russian czars, Chinese warlords, and other dictators overthrown by military coups or revolutions attests that this faith is not always justified. Fiscal mismanagement has been the problem as frequently as political oppression or widespread corruption.

Functional Finance vs. Balanced Budgets

Should the federal budget be balanced continuously or only over the business cycle? Or is balancing the budget irrelevant? Each of these positions finds some adherents among politicians, economists, and the public at large. We will examine the economic logic of these positions on balancing the budget or running deficits.

Balancing Budgets Annually

Many people who want less government also favor continually balancing the budget for political reasons. Their rationale is that more of a laissez-faire approach will unchain market forces and stimulate economic growth. This group sees government as so intrusive that many favor a constitutional amendment requiring an annually balanced budget. Their view is that a constitutional requirement to balance budgets would force Congress to limit its spending.

Even if you favor tighter limits on government, however, you should recognize that a balanced-budget amendment might open a Pandora's box. We could find ourselves faced with Herbert Hoover's dilemma — curing deficits may worsen unemployment. If GNP began falling, tax revenues would fall. At the same time, rising unemployment would mandate more outlays for such transfer payments as unemployment compensation.

Trying to cure massive current deficits might create chaos if we decided to mandate a balanced budget. Raising tax rates would shrink both Aggregate Supply and Aggregate Demand and could reduce tax revenues. Attempts to slash government spending might even cause GNP to fall so much that tax revenues would fall even more than the spending reduction, worsening any deficit. Few economists are convinced that fiscal policy has absolutely no effect on National Income, and even fewer advocate rigidly balanced budgets. Focus 1 describes a recent revival of an ancient argument that total government spending matters, but how the budget is financed is irrelevant.

Balanced Budgets Over the Business Cycle

A more sophisticated view admits that annually balanced budgets may foster instability. This proposal is to balance the budget *over the business cycle*. Its advocates realize that we should not raise taxes or cut spending to cover cyclical deficits caused by recessions, or liquidate inflation-caused surpluses through tax cuts or hikes in spending. This group contends that cyclical deficits should be offset by surpluses collected during prosperity. Thus, over a complete business cycle, there would be no net growth in national debt.

A major problem with this approach is that prosperity may not last long enough or be strong enough to permit the generation of surpluses sufficient to offset deficits, especially if recessions tend to be either extended or especially severe. Our economy might equilibrate around a

lower average level of income than might otherwise be sustainable.

Functional Finance

Most Keynesian economists favor "activist" fiscal policies. They argue that we need to balance the economy at full employment, and that balancing or not balancing the budget is irrelevant per se. In this view, injections (investment plus government spending plus exports) need to be set to equal withdrawals (saving plus taxes plus imports) at a high rate of capacity utilization. The mix that works best should be used; taxes and government outlays never need to balance precisely.[1]

> The **functional finance** approach to the government budget emphasizes that taxes are only one way to finance government outlays. How best to pay for government depends on which policies are least costly under existing economic conditions.

Taxation to cover new government spending is the least expansionary path and is most appropriate when the economy is close to full employment. If the Treasury borrows to cover a deficit, the people who buy government bonds may reduce their spending. Investors also tend to be squeezed, because Treasury bonds absorb private saving and drive up interest rates. Nevertheless, bond financing is usually considered more expansionary than taxation as a way to finance government outlays. The most expansionary method of all is creating more monetary base to cover a deficit.

In the 1980s, Bolivia financed about 15 percent of its government budget with taxes and 85 percent with new money. The result? Annual inflation exceeded 500 percent. Accelerating inflation caused the Bolivian economy to collapse until a severe austerity program finally slowed galloping inflation to a trot.

---

1. Abba P. Lerner, "Functional Finance and the Federal Debt," in Richard Fink and Jack High (eds.), *A Nation in Debt: Economists Debate the Federal Budget Deficit,* 1987.

FOCUS 1

Ricardian Equivalence

The debate about how to finance government dates back for centuries. The great classical economist David Ricardo analyzed public debt and deficits as if people regarded public debt as equivalent to private debt. The Ricardian equivalence theorem as he elaborated it stated:

When for the expenses of a year's war, twenty millions are raised by means of a loan, it is the twenty millions which are withdrawn from the productive capital of the nation . . . . Government might at once have required the twenty millions in the shape of taxes; in which case it would not have been necessary to raise annual taxes to the amount of a million. This, however, would not have changed the nature of the transaction. An individual instead of being called upon to pay £100 per annum, might have been obliged to pay £2000 once and for all.[*]

A modern economist, Robert

Barro,[†] has resurrected Ricardo's argument that loans (public debt) and taxes are equivalent. According to Barro, if government borrows more today (issues bonds), all taxpayers recognize that higher future taxes will be required to pay interest on the debt and eventually repay the debt, so our current saving rates should rise as we bank funds to pay these future tax bills.

Barro's version of Ricardian equivalence essentially treats the burden of paying for government spending as unaffected by the mode of finance—citizens adjust to taxes, public debt, or new monetary base as mechanisms that simply transfer parts of gross private saving to use by the public sector. Ultimately, nominal variables such as the price level or the monetary rate of saving or interest might be affected by how government budgets are financed, but real macroeconomic variables—employment, output, and Na-

tional Income—would be unaffected. Thus, we gain nothing by piling up public debt or issuing monetary base instead of financing government through taxes. We might as well balance the budget annually.

One important assumption of Barro's model is that taxpayers have an infinite time horizon because they are concerned about the effects of present debt on their children and future generations. This seems unlikely. Moreover, predictions based on Ricardian equivalence have not been borne out. The tax cuts and rising deficits of the early 1980s did not yield higher saving rates. In fact, saving rates fell. Rising saving during 1985–1990 might seem to support Barro, but his model is inconsistent with such lags. This recent rise in saving is, however, consistent with Keynesian theory (rising income during the 1983–1990 recovery stimulated saving) or with demographic changes (baby boomers are outgrowing the high consumption period of young family formation and are beginning to save for retirement).

[*]*David Ricardo, "Principles of Political Economy and Taxation,"* Works and Correspondence, Vol. 1, Cambridge, 1951 (reprint).

[†]*Robert Barro, "Are Government Bonds Net Wealth?,"* Journal of Political Economy, *December 1974.*

Crowding Out

What the government gives it must first take away.

John S. Coleman

Keynesians believe that increased government purchases can stimulate a depressed economy. New classical economists disagree, arguing that government spending tends to "crowd out" private economic activity. They point out that *gross private saving* (total output minus private consumption) is absorbed by government purchases regardless of whether government taxes (T), borrows (ΔB), or inflates the money supply (ΔMB). Nevertheless, how government is financed strongly affects the impact of government purchases. The FED is the government's banker and, with the Treasury, determines how deficits and surpluses are financed. This resolution is crucial in determining levels for prices, interest rates, trade balances, and National Income and Output.

Crowding out and paying for government are closely related.

> **Crowding out** *is the idea that increases in government purchases inevitably cause reductions in private consumption or investment.*[2]

Government outlays may crowd out private activities through (*a*) less leisure for workers, (*b*) reduced consumer purchasing power (caused by inflation or tax hikes), or (*c*) lower profits for investors (because of higher interest rates). Keep in mind, however, that it is possible that the goods government provides may be more valuable than the activity crowded out.

Government's Costs When Resources Are Idle

The alternatives individuals lose when government acquires more resources determine who really pays for government. Suppose that our economy is in a depression with massive unemployment of land, labor, and capital. Government might boost output by drafting (confiscating) idle resources, or it could secure money to pay for them through taxes, growth of the monetary base, or borrowing. If these resources would have been completely unproductive in the absence of government action, the opportunity costs of the extra output are zero; the additional government services would not cost anyone anything.

The production possibilities frontier in Figure 2 allows us to examine an increase in government spending and the resulting induced consumption. If many resources are idle and the economy is initially at point *a*, raising govern-

---

2. Early "crowding-out" hypotheses focused only on how government deficits drive interest rates up and, consequently, reduce investments. Our treatment follows a more recent convention that crowding out encompasses all reduction in private activities caused when government programs grow.

FIGURE 2 The Costs of Additional Government: Crowding Out

The general problem of government spending crowding out private activity is illustrated in this figure. Beginning from a point of considerable unemployment (*a*), government can increase spending from G_0 to G_1; new consumption equal to $C_1 - C_0$ will be induced through the multiplier. The opportunity costs of such increases are the value of the private uses to which the ΔG would have been put, including the leisure forgone by the newly employed. Once the economy has achieved full employment (point *c*), increased government spending to G_2 (point *d*) necessarily causes a reduction in private spending from C_1 to C_0. Critics of the growth of government relative to private activity view expanded government as an inefficient block to investment that would foster healthy long-run economic growth.

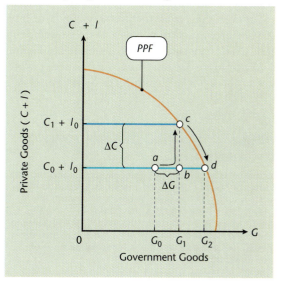

ment spending from G_0 to G_1 closes the recessionary gap in this idealized case. Consumption induced through the Keynesian multiplier process will drive total consumption from C_0 to C_1. This completes the closure of the GNP gap, so the path to full employment is $a \rightarrow b \rightarrow c$.

This seems to be an exception to the *TANSTAAFL* rule that "There ain't no such thing as a free lunch." It is not. Few resources are ever totally without valuable uses "in the absence of government action." For example, idle labor produces leisure; most of us prefer no work to work with no pay. To induce idle labor to work voluntarily, government must pay a wage that offsets the value of the leisure lost in producing the extra output; increases in employment come at the cost of forgone leisure.

Government might use simple confiscation to impose on the owners of idle resources the full cost of providing extra government goods; drafting unemployed labor for armies of conservation workers or highway repair crews would be examples. (Siberian salt mines developed under the Russian czars continue today in the Soviet Union.) If tax revenues are used to pay the owners of the newly employed resources, the burden falls largely on taxpayers. If government creates money to pay for these resources, then the higher incomes of the owners of previously idle resources may be partially offset by inflationary reductions in the purchasing power of other citizens.

Suppose the government issues bonds to buy the resources used to produce extra government goods. The consequences are illustrated in Figure 3. When more Treasury bonds are issued, raising the supply of bonds from S_0 to S_1 (in Panel A),

FIGURE 3 The Crowding-Out Effect: Investment

Increased sales of bonds by the government increase the supply of bonds in the bond market in Panel A from S_0 to S_1, resulting in the price of bonds falling and interest rates rising. As interest rates rise from i_0 to i_1 in Panel B, investment falls from I_0 to I_1, diminishing the increase in Aggregate Demand by $AD_2 - AD_1$ (Panel C). Thus, the growth in Aggregate Income is hindered because of crowding out.

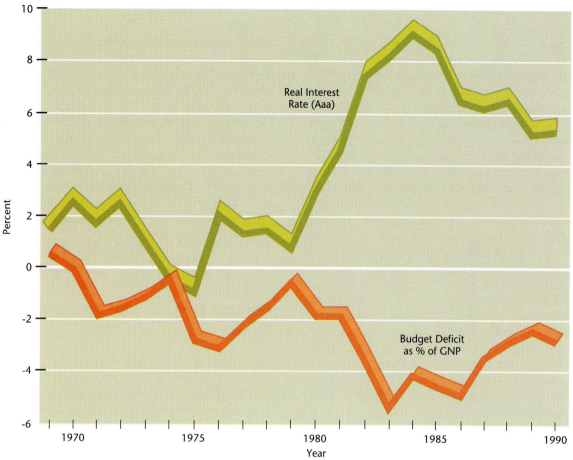

FIGURE 4   Budget Deficits (as a Percentage of GNP) and Real Interest Rates

When budget deficits (measured as negative numbers in this figure) have grown relative to our GNP, real interest rates (money rates of interest adjusted for inflation) have also tended to rise.

bond prices fall. The falling price of bonds causes interest rates to climb from i_0 to i_1 (from point a to point b in Panel B). Successful borrowers pay higher interest rates and some private investment is crowded out. This dampens the growth in Aggregate Demand, which rises only from AD_0 to AD_1 — not to AD_2 — in Panel C, as would occur without crowding out.

Borrowers and potential borrowers pay the short-run burden of more government spending when a budget deficit is financed by sales of new government bonds. Figure 4 illustrates how real interest rates jumped with the record deficits of the late 1970s and early 1980s and then fell when deficits declined temporarily in the late

1980s. In the longer run, consumers will pay higher prices because investment shrinks, adding less to the stock of capital. With less capital growth, real wages and output will not rise as fast.

When the economy is at less than full employment, the degree of crowding out depends in part on the interest sensitivity of demands for loans by investors and consumers. During severe recessions, induced Keynesian growth of income can overwhelm any losses in purchasing power caused by crowding out. Crowding out restricts the power of the Keynesian multiplier process to boost real income — especially in a fully employed economy.

Government's Costs During Full Employment

We have assumed that some resources were idle when government purchases grew. Expanded government spending is a standard Keynesian prescription when the economy is in a slump. Who pays for government growth if the economy is fully employed? Either private consumption, investment, or exports must fall if government purchases are raised when there is efficient and full employment of all resources. Refer back to Figure 2. If the economy were initially fully employed at point c, boosting government purchases from G_1 to G_2 would move the economy to point d and shrink the sum of private spending (consumption and investment) from $C_1 + I_0$ to $C_0 + I_0$.

Government causes crowding out through tax hikes, confiscation, inflation, or higher interest rates. Excessive reliance on any single mechanism may cause political turmoil and significantly reduce some resource owners' incentives to be productive; therefore, government commonly chooses a mix of these ways to cover new government spending.

For example, President Johnson realized that tax increases to pay for the war in Vietnam and the "War on Poverty" would encounter tremendous political resistance in the late 1960s. In spite of advice from his Council of Economic Advisors that tax increases were necessary to avoid inflationary pressures, President Johnson chose to run budgetary deficits. What choices were available? Because $G - T = \Delta B + \Delta MB$, the alternatives were either to borrow the money or print it.

The Treasury initially covered the deficits by issuing new bonds. A large proportion of the loanable funds available would have been absorbed if these bonds had been purchased solely by the public; interest rates would have soared, leaving little money available for private investment. The Federal Reserve Board elected to buy many of the new bonds issued by the Treasury. This expanded the monetary base and caused the money supply to rise, preventing the full brunt of financing the Vietnam War from falling exclusively on private investment. Inflation caused prices and nominal income to swell, so total tax revenues increased.

The overall result was that crowding out spread the costs of the War on Poverty and the Vietnam War across four groups: (*a*) investors, who paid higher interest rates; (*b*) consumers, who paid higher prices; (*c*) taxpayers, who paid higher taxes; and (*d*) Selective Service draftees — being drafted was a form of confiscation of labor to pay for the Vietnam War. This example correctly suggests that the mix of policies government uses to finance its spending has important implications for the distribution of income; each method of reducing private activity imposes burdens on different groups.

Federal Deficits and Foreign Trade

The government budget equation ($G - T = \Delta B + \Delta MB$) reveals that government deficits can be funded through expansionary open-market operations by the FED or by having the Treasury issue new bonds. If the FED does not monetize the deficit by buying Treasury bonds, national debt that is privately held by Americans or foreigners grows.

Government spending not covered by taxes ($G - T > 0$) represents production saved by households but unavailable for investment. This saving may be voluntary (private purchases of Treasury bonds) or involuntary (new money creates inflationary pressure that has been called "the cruelest tax"). This private but uninvested saving may be made available to government by domestic entities or by foreigners.

Trade Deficits

Foreigners make parts of their gross saving (production minus consumption) available by exporting more to us than we export to them; we experience a trade deficit in which imports exceed exports. To see how foreign trade and budget deficits are related, remember that in a macroeconomic equilibrium all injections

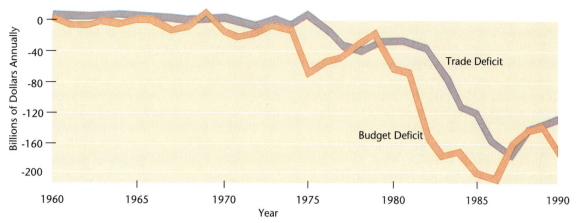

FIGURE 5   Budget Deficits and Trade Deficits

Large shares of the massive federal budget deficits of the past decade have been financed by foreigners who have used the dollars they have received from our trade deficits to buy U.S. government bonds, corporate securities, and real estate. Thus, U.S. trade deficits have paralleled our budget deficits.

$(G + I + X)$ must be balanced by total withdrawals $(S + T + M)$. Thus,

$$G + I + X = S + T + M$$

Rearranging terms to isolate the budget deficit yields

$$G - T = S - I + M - X$$

Thus, if we integrate the foreign sector into the government budget equation, it can be expressed as

$$G - T = (S - I) + (M - X) = \Delta B + \Delta MB$$

where S = domestic savings, I = domestic investment, M = imports, and X = exports.

Adding the international sector explicitly into the government budget constraint suggests that federal deficits must equal the domestic savings surplus (saving minus investment) plus the trade deficit (imports minus exports). For example, in 1980 the budget deficit was $61.3 billion, the savings surplus was $93.4 billion, and the United States ran a trade surplus of $32.1 billion $[61.3 = (93.4 + (-32.1)]$. By 1990, the budget deficit had grown to $161.3 billion and the domestic savings surplus had grown to $123.3 billion, balanced by a trade deficit of $38.0 billion $[(161.3 = (123.3) + (38.0)]$.

Thus, federal deficits can be financed by increasing domestic saving or by borrowing for-

eigners' savings. Alternatively, the deficit can be financed by a reduction in domestic investment or a reduction in our exports of goods and services. In effect, a trade deficit represents net funds that the United States borrows from abroad. Finally, note that for a given budget deficit, increased domestic investment (saving held constant) must ultimately be financed by a worsening trade deficit.

In summary, with aggregate levels of saving fixed, rising budget deficits will inevitably result in growing trade deficits or a reduction in domestic investment. Figure 5 illustrates what Gary Stern, President of the Federal Reserve Bank of Minneapolis, has called "the unpleasant arithmetic of budget and trade deficits."[3] As budget deficits mushroomed in the 1980s, trade deficits widened as well. The persistent budget deficits of the 1980s were paralleled by mounting trade deficits, which will probably not be resolved until our federal budget deficit shrinks.

Some people, alarmed by huge U.S. deficits in international trade, have proposed high tariff walls and restrictive import quotas. This might prevent a flood of imports from competing with U.S. output, but the expanded government bud-

---

3. Gary H. Stern, "The Unpleasant Arithmetic of Budget and Trade Deficits," Federal Reserve Bank of Minneapolis, *1986 Annual Report.*

get deficit $G - T = (S - I) + (M - X)$ reveals that protectionist policies would also shift the brunt of the budget deficit into greater crowding out of private investment. Thus, the only options to borrowing from abroad $(M - X)$ are (a) to cut government outlays, (b) to increase taxes, (c) to increase domestic saving rates, or (d) to suffer lower rates of domestic investment. The other options are so unlikely that the brunt of reduced loans from foreigners would be losses of capital accumulation in the United States. The Laffer curve (described earlier) depicts one possible constraint on government's ability to slash a budget deficit by raising taxes. Reducing the budget deficit through spending cuts is also very difficult because large parts of federal outlays are mandated by law.

The Public Debt

Prophets of doom who cite growth of public debt as a sign of impending collapse and urge government to operate more like a business just aren't paying attention. Although the federal debt is enormous and growing, private debt has grown even faster. Part of this is household debt, but most private debt is corporate. Although substantial corporate debt is accounted for by merger activity, successful corporations that are not involved in mergers also invariably owe more with each passing decade.

You may have heard someone say that the United States teeters on the verge of bankruptcy. Doomsayers fail to consider (a) the ability of government to tax and to create money to cover budget deficits or to pay off the national debt, (b) the basic differences between internal and external debts, and (c) the relative versus absolute size of the debt.

External vs. Internal Debt

The major difference between private and public debt is that all private debt is held externally — the borrowers owe other people — whereas public debt is primarily held internally — we owe most of our *national debt* to Americans. That is, we owe it to ourselves. (Do you own any U.S. Savings Bonds?)

External debt *is owed to outsiders;* **internal debt** *is owed to those who, at least in part, are obligated to pay the debt.*

Borrowing from internal sources does not change the total current amount that may be spent. When our government issues new bonds, the purchasing power temporarily surrendered by U.S. bond buyers just offsets the government's gain in purchasing power. People in the United States as a whole neither gain nor lose immediately through such transactions, although the uses of these funds may affect future American purchasing power. If borrowed funds are used for a government investment in, say, a hydroelectric dam, then real future income may be increased, because more and cheaper electricity may be available over the productive life of the facility.

On the other hand, if government borrows to pay for such current operating costs as police protection or transfer payments, and this diverts funds from private investments, then future purchasing power may fall. For example, if a war is financed by bonds, lower rates of domestic capital formation may hinder standards of living for generations. Just as borrowing funds internally does not change total current purchasing power, repayment of internal debt does not change total American purchasing power at the time of repayment. People who cash their bonds receive purchasing power exactly equal to the loss of

Table 1   *Percentage of the Public Debt Held by Foreigners*

Year	Percentage of Public Debt Owned by Foreigners
1939	.5
1946	.8
1965	5.2
1970	5.3
1975	11.5
1978	17.5
1980	16.3
1990	18.3

Sources: Board of Governors of the Federal Reserve System, *Federal Reserve Bulletin,* February 1991; and *Economic Report of the President,* 1991.

FIGURE 6 International Comparisons of Interest Rates, Deficits, and Inflation (1990)

Relative to many other countries, U.S. federal deficits as a percentage of Gross Domestic Product, the rate of domestic inflation, and real interest rates (monetary interest adjusted for inflation) were not out of line in 1990. Note, however, the consistently superior position of the Japanese economy.

purchasing power to taxpayers or the government sector.

When private households or firms borrow externally, they immediately gain the purchasing power that lenders temporarily sacrifice. Similarly, when the government sells bonds to foreign governments or investors, the United States as a whole temporarily gains purchasing power. But, unless the external lender permits repeated refinancing, external borrowing entails eventual repayment to the external sources of funds. If the borrowed funds were used for investment goods that were sufficiently productive to cover the principal borrowed plus interest charges, the borrowers still would be ahead after repayment. If, on the other hand, the loans were used to finance consumption, then repayment to external lenders could entail net losses of purchasing power. This case requires curtailing future consumption because higher consumption is enjoyed today.

Table 1 indicates that the proportion of the national debt held by foreigners grew markedly after 1970. Before 1975, foreign holdings of U.S. government debt were negligible. As real interest rates rose, foreigners bought greater quantities of our debt. When foreigners buy U.S. bonds, we experience gains in purchasing power. Future generations of Americans may lose purchasing power if foreigners decide to hold fewer U.S. bonds and redeem their bondholdings. Future generations also bear the burden of paying the interest on externally held debt.

Figure 6 illustrates how real interest rates, inflation, and deficits as a percent of Gross Domestic Product compare among developed nations. This figure indexes all countries to the United States (U.S. = 100). Big budget deficits are usually associated with high real rates of interest. The relatively high U.S. real interest rates partially explain why Japanese investors have been major buyers of U.S. government bonds, corporate bonds, companies, and real estate since the mid-1980s.

Interest on Public Debt

Until recently, national debt held by the public was declining as a proportion of GNP (see Figure 7). Beginning in the early 1970s, rising deficits

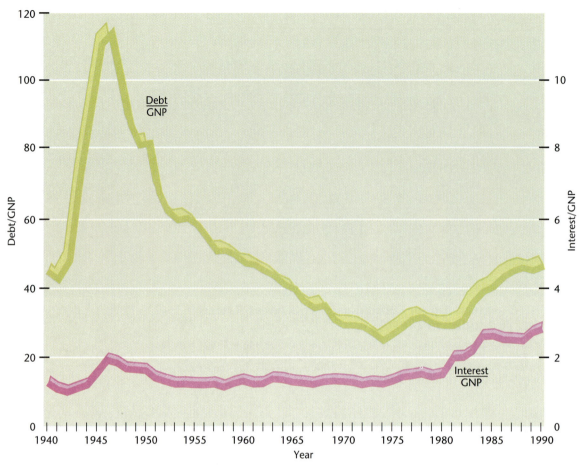

FIGURE 7 Federal Debt Held by the Public and Interest on the Debt as a Percentage of GNP

The public debt as a percentage of GNP declined until the mid-1970s. Right after World War II, the public debt exceeded GNP; today, the ratio is nearly 50 percent. When greater public debt has been financed, interest rates have risen. New debt and old debt that was rolled over have to be floated at these higher rates of interest. The result is that interest paid on public debt as a percentage of GNP rose during the early 1980s. Since the mid-1980s, however, interest rates have fallen, and as debt was refinanced, interest costs as a percentage of GNP leveled off. *Economic Report of the President,* 1991.

and relatively high interest rates caused total public debt and interest payments—as a percentage of GNP—to grow. Interest rates fell in 1986, slowing the upward trend in interest as a percentage of GNP as old debt was "rolled over" and new debt was financed at lower real rates.

Debt roll-over *occurs if, when a bond issue comes due, the debt is refinanced.*

Government and corporations typically go deeper and deeper into debt as time passes. (Most corporations also roll over their debts.)

However, investors who buy government bonds must have confidence in the stability and taxing power of the government.

Politically unstable countries find it difficult to borrow, because investors fear that the current government may fall or disavow the debt. New regimes commonly disavow the debt of overthrown governments, rendering it worthless. For example, owners of bonds issued by czarist Russia, post–World War I Germany, and many South American countries experienced this misfortune. The discounts at which the debts of some countries are sold are shown in Table 2.

Table 2 *Discount Debt*

Recent secondary market price quotes for debt of various countries, in cents on the dollar.

	Bid price May 1988	Bid price Sept. 1991
Argentina	28.0	40.3
Bolivia	10.5	11.0
Brazil	55.0	39.0
Chile	61.0	89.0
Mexico	53.5	59.6
Nicaragua	2.0	6.0
Nigeria	29.0	42.7
Peru	4.0	13.0
Philippines	50.0	57.3
Venezuela	55.0	67.3

Source: Reprinted by permission of Bear, Stearns & Co. Inc.

The amount of the discount is roughly proportional to the difficulties faced when one of these countries tries to borrow or to refinance (roll over) its debt. Debt can be floated almost perpetually, however, as long as the government of a country is reasonably stable and maintains its credit (pays its interest payments).

An often-ignored aspect of federal debt is that the FED acquires large chunks of national debt when it buys bonds during expansionary open-market operations. Other government agencies also buy bonds when they run surpluses. Accountants count these agencies' bondholdings as national debt, but this is a lot like saying that your right pocket owes your left pocket if you shift spare change from one pocket to another.

If taxes are raised to pay interest on federal debt, incentives to work and invest may wither. In 1990, the interest cost of the national debt was nearly $150 billion, or nearly 13 percent of all federal outlays. When the federal government finances a huge deficit by selling debt securities, real interest rates climb or remain high, and considerable private borrowing for investment may be crowded out. The exact effect will depend on the state of the economy and private saving rates. If the economy is especially sluggish, increased deficits may not crowd out investment. If saving rates rise, large deficits may not raise interest rates. However, in general, large deficits push up interest rates. The end result is that future generations may inherit a smaller capital stock and, hence, reduced production possibilities—one real burden of the public debt.

Burdens on Future Generations

Does national debt burden future generations? As we discussed previously, if newly incurred debt diverts funds from investment to satisfy present consumption, then future generations lose the investment income that might have been generated. But future generations do not lose because of national debt per se. Rather, they lose because the current generation opts for more consumption and less investment out of today's income.

Future generations may bear higher taxes to pay interest on the national debt. Of course, members of future generations also receive the interest payments as bondholders, so the burden nets out as long as the national debt is held internally—that is, as long as we owe it to ourselves. Future generations can lose, however, if foreigners decide to reduce their holdings of U.S. bonds. It is not obvious that they will, or that the national debt will ever be retired, or that it would be desirable for us to retire it.

Must the National Debt Be Repaid?

What would happen if we retired the national debt? Would the government be ruined? Suppose government raised income taxes enormously to repay the outstanding debt. People who hold the existing public debt tend to be individuals in high-income categories, so they would be paying a lot of the higher taxes and then would receive the payments—a transfer to themselves. Alternatively, the value of all Treasury bonds could be taxed 100 percent. Goodbye national debt. (This is not a likely option.)

Some critics of national debt policies argue that if the government can issue unlimited debt, it will continually overspend. These critics argue that Congress often mistreats the ability to issue debt and is unwilling to exercise fiscal restraint. Persistent increases in both government debt and

Is There a "Moral Dimension" to Debt and Deficits?

Outcries against large deficits and the growing national debt are frequently heard. Why would a society seemingly so united against deficits and an escalating public debt do so little to reverse the trend? As Nobel Prize winner James Buchanan has asked: Why do we choose to "eat up" our national capital through debt-financed current consumption?[*]

The answer may lie in research by Alex Cukierman and Allan Meltzer that analyzes the reasons for issuing public debt.[†] Their analysis is based on the simple but powerful premise that rising deficits and national debt in a democracy are the result of the desires of the majority. Given the inequality in the distribution of income and wealth in the United States, one legitimate role of government may be to redistribute income between generations.

Their analysis uses an intergen-erational model introduced by David Ricardo and recently refined by Robert Barro.[‡] The intergenerational model assumes that present taxpayers will leave bequests (money and property) to their future generations to enable them to pay the future taxes for today's debt. However, poor individuals are *bequest constrained*—they have no money or valuables to will to their offspring—and since some of their children will be wealthy, they can relax this constraint and increase consumption now by voting for deficits and higher public debt. Similarly, individuals with substantial wealth may gain as rising debt increases real interest rates and their return. In summary, the very poor, the very rich, and retired people tend to benefit from rising public debt that finances current consumption.

Alternatively, individuals with significant human wealth who are highly productive lose. Real wages decline as public debt and deficits crowd out investment and reduce the rate of growth of capital. A reduced future capital stock means that real wages do not rise as rapidly and productivity increases decline.

This analysis suggests that the growing national debt may simply reflect the will of the voting majority. All of the current uproar about the present generation burdening future generations may not only be true, but what the majority desires. James Buchanan attributes this change in attitude about deficits and debt to a marked change in moral norms that is a result of the Keynesian Revolution in macroeconomic policy. This moral dimension of fiscal policy, in Buchanan's opinion, argues forcefully for a constitutional amendment to balance the federal budget. In his view, this is the only way the current generation can be prevented from "eating up" the capital stock of future generations.

[*]James M. Buchanan, "The Moral Dimension of Debt Financing," Economic Inquiry, *January 1985.*
[†]Alex Cukierman and Allan H. Meltzer, "A Political Theory of Government Debt." A paper presented at the American Economic Association meetings, December 1987.

[‡]Robert Barro, "Are Government Bonds Net Wealth?," Journal of Political Economy, *December 1974. For an alternative point of view, see Olivier Blanchard, "Debt, Deficits and Finite Horizons," Journal of Political Economy, April 1985.*

spending tend to support their line of argument. It may be easier to increase the national debt (and the debt ceiling) than to say no to projects supported by powerful special-interest groups. Focus 2 suggests that a growing national debt may be the natural (but undesirable) result of democratic processes.

Some Benefits of Public Debt

National debt would not exist if it did not have a benefit side. (This is true even if the only benefit is that alternatives for financing federal deficits were worse.) Stabilization policy depends heavily on the ability of the federal government to deficit spend and pay for this spending with bonds. Annually balancing the budget could prove disastrous during recessionary periods. Additionally, the national debt provides a relatively risk-free asset (government bonds) for individuals who need to protect their financial capital. (Of course, there is the risk of inflation.) You should realize by now that manipulation of the public debt is crucial for the most effective instrument of monetary policy—open-market operations. The FED buys bonds from banks when it wants to expand the money supply and sells bonds to restrict the money supply.

One recent development is the potentially explosive growth of surpluses in the Social Security Trust Fund. These surpluses legally must be invested in federal debt and, as Focus 3 indicates, may make growth of our national debt a moot issue.

Remeasuring Public Debt and Budget Deficits

The deficit and debt statistics reported earlier in Figure 1 reflect a federal budget that began moving severely out of balance in the early 1970s. However, a growing number of economists are disputing these figures. They suggest that we would have been better off had we totally ignored these data instead of adopting incorrect policies based on these numbers.[4]

---

4. Robert Eisner, *How Real Is the Federal Deficit?* (New York: The Free Press, 1986).

Correcting alleged flaws in budget deficit and debt data requires (a) converting the nominal budget and the public debt to real values, (b) adjusting public debt for interest rate changes (converting the value of the debt from par value to market value), and (c) revising the budget so that reported values conform to generally accepted accounting principles.

For the same reasons that nominal GNP is adjusted for inflation to yield real GNP, the nominal budget deficit and public debt should be deflated to reflect changes in the price level. Real national debt remains constant if it doubles while the price level also doubles. In the same way that inflation wipes out the value of money, it also reduces the value of the national debt.

Similarly, if interest rates rise, all bond prices fall—and the national debt issued previously becomes less burdensome. The reported public debt is the par value of government bonds in the hands of the public or foreigners. Par value means that if a government bond was issued for $100,000 in 1970, the public debt grew by $100,000. Public debt statistics are not adjusted to reflect changing market values if interest rates later change so that the market value of this bond changes. The par value of a bond remains constant, but the market value of the debt changes as interest rates fluctuate. Consequently, to measure national debt accurately, published government statistics should be adjusted for changes in interest rates.

Finally, the government has a large stock of tangible assets, including land, buildings, and equipment. Annually adjusting our public debt data in the same way as corporations would to obtain net worth tells a different story. Figure 9 shows the budget deficit and public debt adjusted for inflation, its market values, and changing values of assets and liabilities since 1960. An interesting note is that there are years in which the government reported a deficit and this adjusted budget indicates a surplus.

The reported "official" deficit may provide misleading signals for macroeconomic policy. In years when policymakers think there is a deficit and the budget is really in surplus, contractionary measures to balance a budget would be counterproductive. Even after the adjustments are

Will Social Security Absorb Our National Debt?

The 1930s ushered in an era in which federal budget surpluses have been tiny, rare, and cumulatively swamped by deficits that have driven our national debt toward the stratosphere. Explosive growth of government debt has been dwarfed by growth of private debt, with U.S. saving rates being relatively low compared to many other industrialized countries.

In part, private saving rates were depressed by family formation among "baby-boomers," many of whom borrowed heavily to acquire the houses and other amenities that have become the norm for those who pursue the American Dream. By the 1980s, private domestic saving fell far short of the funds needed for adequate domestic investment and to finance record federal deficits. As we have indicated, the result was that U.S. federal deficits were covered by imports that allowed foreigners to invest heavily in the United States.

Many people are concerned that our deficits have effectively "sold our country to foreigners at cut-rate prices." Others worry that some future day of reckoning will usher in financial catastrophe and economic collapse. Are there natural economic limits to the size of our national debt? Do any natural forces exist to offset our national momentum toward infinite debt? One force

that soon may relieve swollen deficits and rising debt is projected growth of the Social Security Trust Fund.

The Social Security system ran large deficits from the 1970s into the early 1980s. Deficits during this era, when each retiree was supported by about four active workers, threatened to bankrupt the Social Security Trust Fund when post–World War II "baby-boomers" begin retiring in 2010. Demographers predicted that by 2030, each retiree would be backed up by only about two active workers. A "blue ribbon" panel was appointed to find a solution to this problem.

This panel based its recommendations on relatively pessimistic forecasts about unemployment rates and rates of economic growth; it wanted to ensure that another crisis would not arise from a temporary Band-Aid solution to the problem. The resulting 1983 reform of the Federal Insurance Contribution Act (FICA) more than doubled the FICA tax. Consequently, FICA revenues exceeded Social Security benefit payments by a healthy $140 billion in 1990, with even heftier surpluses on the horizon.

Social Security surpluses are legally required to be placed in "reserves" that are based on "investments" in long-term U.S. Treasury bonds. This seems, on

the surface, to be both prudent policy and a good way to ensure a healthy market for government securities. Figure 8 reflects Social Security Administration long-term forecasts of its expected outlays (benefit payments), income (FICA tax revenues), and reserves (holdings of U.S. Treasury bonds). The Social Security Trust Fund Reserve, based on expected cumulative surpluses, is anticipated to mount to roughly $12 *trillion* by 2030. A wave of "boomer" retirements should begin around 2008, however, and last until about 2030. Reserves will gradually be dissipated until, by 2050, they are completely exhausted.

The enormity of the financial flows into and out of the Social Security Trust Fund will require major macroeconomic adjustments based on careful planning. The $12 trillion in total reserves expected by 2030, for example, is about 10 times as large as the level of privately held federal debt in 1990.

One effect of the imminent surge of FICA revenues may be a powerful reversal of federal deficits and national debt. Every dollar of surplus in the Social Security system will slash the federal deficit by a dollar. If the Social Security system's surpluses are, as is expected, larger than the rest of the U.S. Treasury's deficits, then the federal government

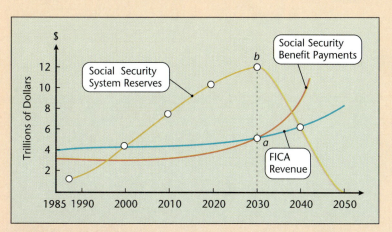

FIGURE 8   Long-Term Forecasts for Social Security Outlays, Income, and Reserves

Source: Social Security Administration estimates (1988), updated by authors. [*Note:* When FICA revenue exceeds benefit payments (up to point *a*), total FICA reserves grow (until point *b*). Thereafter, payments exceed revenue, so FICA reserves decline.]

will run a net surplus. Anticipated surpluses will undoubtedly absorb all outstanding national debt by the upcoming turn of the century.

In a sense, public saving (through the Social Security Administration) may become so enormous that real interest rates in private financial markets will plummet. This should facilitate both domestic investment by U.S. companies and substantial investment abroad. If these developments occur as expected, the United States, which moved from being the world's largest creditor nation in the 1980 to being its greatest debtor by 1986, could easily revert to being the world's largest supplier of investment funds.

The Social Security surpluses expected over the next 40 years are, in a sense, a nest egg that could, if invested properly, support our retirement system permanently. A major issue is: Into what should these funds be invested? Even if our national debt were to double by 1995, it would only amount to $2.5 trillion—and total reserve funds are expected to mount to $12 trillion. As you might expect, answers from all over the political spectrum have been offered to the question of how these retirement funds should be used.

Some critics argue that the expected Social Security surpluses justify huge current expenditures to fix our roads, enrich our educational system, or cure poverty everywhere. Others want to defend Social Security from any spending binge. Rep. Andrew Jacobs of the House So-

cial Security Subcommittee has characterized this task: "It'll be like walking through a bad neighborhood with a diamond ring."

Others assert that this public saving (Social Security) is just a distortive shift away from what should be decisions by private individuals. According to this line of reasoning, FICA taxes should be slashed so that private individuals could choose their own retirement plans. A variant of this approach would be to allow individuals to specify for themselves the types of investments into which their taxes would be placed. This approach has been described as "privatization."

The "baby-boomers" were a tidal wave that engulfed our educational system in the 1950s and 1960s and flooded the labor market in the 1970s and 1980s. The depressed saving rate of the 1970s and 1980s reflected their attempts to borrow huge amounts so that they could buy their way into the good life. It is predictable that the aging and then retirement of this bubble of humanity will have profound social and economic consequences. A burst of saving (albeit public saving) for retirement by this group will probably transform persistent federal deficits into surpluses, and national debt into national "credit." The precise ways in which this occurs will be determined by how macroeconomic policymakers choose to cope with the issues we have addressed in this chapter.

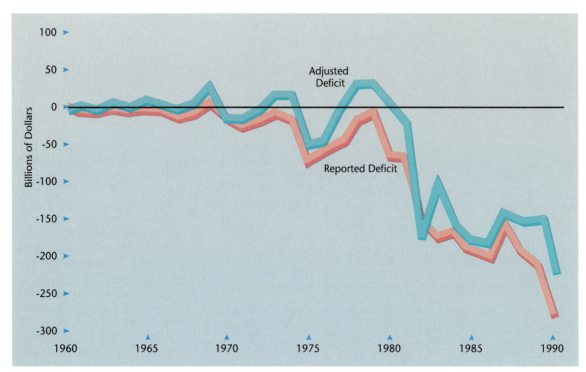

FIGURE 9   Reported and Adjusted Values of the Budget Deficit

Robert Eisner has dragged the antiquated accounting system used by the federal government for its budgeting into closer conformity with modern corporate accounting standards. His estimates suggest that recent federal deficits have not been as terrible as the official data indicate.

made, however, there is clearly a striking move toward a government in deficit in recent years.

International Comparisons of Debt

While U.S. policymakers struggle against budget deficits, how do our levels of debt and deficits compare to those of other industrialized countries? Until recently, national debt as a percentage of U.S. GNP was declining. Figure 10 shows budget deficits, gross public debt, and household savings rates as percentages of Gross Domestic Product (GDP) for 13 developed countries in 1990. (GDP excludes the foreign sector.) The lines across the figure are averages for these 13 countries. Most ran deficits and most had large public debts in proportion to their GDPs. The United States currently has an average deficit, a below average debt ratio, and a below average saving rate. U.S. debt and deficits are large absolutely, but don't appear disastrous relative to those in many other developed countries.

One area worthy of major concern is the net international investment position of the United States. Figure 11 traces our path as we deteriorated from the world's largest net international investor in 1981 to its biggest net debtor in 1990. This deterioration is partially explained by recent federal deficits, which have been financed in part by foreign investment in the United States.

The Ability to Control Government Spending

Virtually every president in the past 25 years has promised to curtail government spending, but all found that cutting the federal budget was an overwhelming task. Doing so quickly seems virtually impossible.

Relatively uncontrollable outlays *cannot be changed without changes in major federal laws. They are often beyond administrative control and involve contractual obligations of government.*

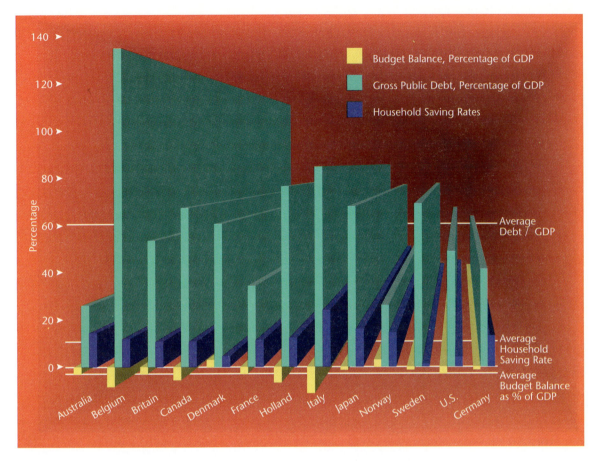

FIGURE 10   International Comparisons of Deficits, Debt, and Household Saving Rates (1990)

The U.S. budget deficit as a percentage of GDP was about average relative to international standards in 1990, and the U.S. public debt was relatively lower than in most countries, but Americans typically save smaller shares of their personal income than do average people elsewhere.

Many enormous items in the federal budget are continuing programs that Congress is legally obligated to fund. For example, Social Security payments are legally guaranteed to recipients, commitments for Medicare funding were made by the Congress years ago, and contracts for most transportation or defense systems take years to complete. Moreover, the government's legal obligations to provide public assistance, to operate the Post Office, to regulate pollution and industrial safety — the list seems to go on forever — are long-term commitments that simply cannot be abandoned during short periods of time. Estimates by the Conference Board, a research organization, indicate that roughly 60 percent of all outlays were relatively uncontrollable in the 1960s. That proportion has now grown to nearly 75 percent.

Panel A of Figure 12 shows the growth of real federal outlays and tax revenue. Despite wide political rhetoric in the 1980s about reducing the size of government, real outlays have grown steadily. Where has this growth in expenditures originated? Panel B shows the composition of federal expenditures. The major increases in spending shares since 1970 have been in interest on the public debt and transfer payments. Major declines as shares of total outlays have been in purchases of goods and services (both military and nonmilitary).

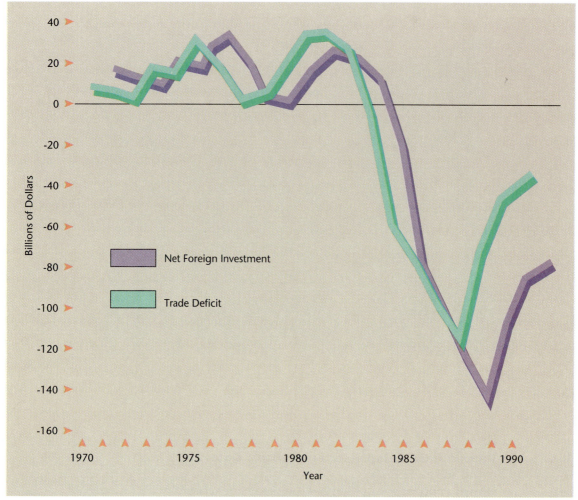

FIGURE 11 The Net International Investment Position of the United States

Between 1982 and 1990, the United States went from being the world's biggest creditor nation to being its biggest debtor, in large part because big chunks of persistent record federal deficits were financed by foreigners who bought U.S. Treasury bonds. That process seems to have reversed in the most recent past.

The Gramm-Rudman-Hollings Balanced-Budget Law

In 1985, Congress adopted a new strategy in an attempt to control soaring deficits: The Gramm-Rudman-Hollings Deficit Reduction Act set specific deficit reduction targets. If these targets were not met, "across-the-board" cuts in spending were mandated. In effect, Congress was like a dieter who puts a lock on the refrigerator and gives the key to someone else. Critics of Gramm-

Rudman charged that it made federal spending a captive of some deficit target instead of making the deficit the result of Congressionally determined spending. Many parts of the budget were excluded from the across-the-board cuts, however, including most in the categories labeled relatively uncontrollable. Cold comfort, indeed, for those who wanted to reduce the size of government!

Gramm-Rudman set limits to the size of the federal deficit beginning in 1986. In each of the

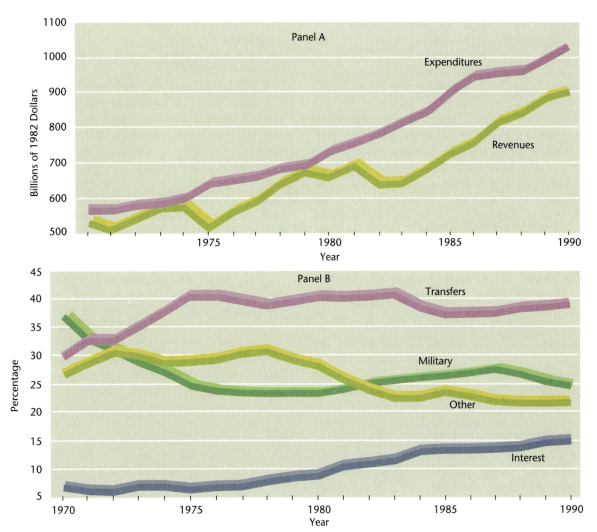

FIGURE 12   Real Federal Revenue and Outlays and the Composition of Federal Outlays

Deficits have been enormous and the national debt has grown rapidly in the past decade because federal expenditures have grown much faster than federal tax revenues (Panel A). Growing shares of government outlays are absorbed by transfer payments and interest rates on the national debt (Panel B), while the military budget, which had been declining relative to other types of spending from 1963 through 1977, recovered somewhat during the 1980s.

five fiscal years following 1986, the targeted federal deficit was to be reduced, until it reached zero in 1991. The law set up specific processes to enable agreement between Congress and the administration on a deficit reduction package. If Congress and the president were unable to reach agreement, then automatic selective spending cuts went into effect.

Despite the political fanfare and rhetoric that

accompanied Gramm-Rudman, the federal deficit did not reach zero by 1991. In fact, federal deficits grew. Gramm-Rudman's inability to achieve its stated target appears to have stemmed from the fact that projected deficits for each coming year understated the actual deficits that resulted. Congress also pushed up the deficit by adding funding to the budget after the October 15 automatic spending cuts.

The Deficit Reduction Law of 1990

Renewed attempts to reduce budget deficits culminated in the passage of the Deficit Reduction Law of 1990. The law mandates tax increases, spending cuts, and controlled federal spending to further reduce the federal deficit. Increased taxes on income, gasoline, liquor, cigarettes, and luxury goods (jewelry, furs, boats, etc.) are forecasted to raise $165 billion over a five-year period. Spending cuts are targeted for farm subsidies, student loans, and Medicare reimbursements to doctors and hospitals. Increased federal savings were also forecasted as arising from reduced military spending and lower interest payments on the public debt.

The 1990 Deficit Reduction Law also changed the focus of Gramm-Rudman. Previously, Gramm-Rudman set specific yearly deficit targets; under the new law the focus of Gramm-Rudman is to control federal spending as opposed to cutting the deficit. This means that the deficit is allowed to increase as long as the increase is not attributable to increased federal outlays.

Federal spending is now lumped into three broad categories (military, domestic, and international), which are subject to proportionate cuts to all programs within a category should spending on a particular category exceed the predetermined goal. For example, if the military exceeds its spending goal, all military programs will have their funding reduced by an equal amount to bring military spending back into line. It might appear that the government has effectively tied its hands behind its back, unable to allocate funds for emergencies, but this is not the case. Funding for the savings-and-loan bailout, Persian Gulf hostilities, and any emergencies fall outside of the spending targets. Uncle Sam has prohibited the right hand from writing checks over a certain amount, but the left hand can still sign at any time.

It is doubtful that the 1990 Deficit Reduction Law will achieve its stated goal. Tax revenues are likely to be less than forecasted as tax increases slow an already tepid economy from the demand and supply side. At the same time, federal spending does not appear to be under control when outside funding for contingencies and emergencies is included. Deficit reduction, like dieting, appears easier to formulate than to put into practice.

What can we conclude about the current state of deficits and the public debt in the United States? Clearly debt, no matter how measured, has been growing over the past decade. Any deficit must be financed with bonds or new monetary base and persistent deficits have predictable impacts on our international accounts.

To the extent that added debt is used for public investment, future generations may gain, but they will bear the burden if debt and deficits are used to finance consumption for the current generation. Large deficits and debts can increase real interest rates that may soak up additional government resources in the future. Reducing government spending appears quite difficult because so many federal outlays appear uncontrollable.

Finally, when we compare our national debt and deficits to other developed countries, the United States shows up rather well. All in all, the growing debt and continuing deficits in our country are a cause for concern and need to be addressed over the long haul, but they do not appear to be the crisis that so many politicians and pundits would have us believe.

Chapter Review: Key Points

1. The *budget deficit* equals annual government outlays minus receipts. The *public debt* is total federal indebtedness resulting from current and past deficits.

2. *Balancing the budget annually* might result in incorrect fiscal actions to combat either inflation or recession. Some have suggested balancing the budget *over the business cycle*. This would entail running deficits during recessions and surpluses over the boom. Unfortunately, business cycles are not symmetric, and the budget may not be easy to balance over

the cycle without hampering prosperity. Advocates of *functional finance* believe that the size of the public debt is unimportant. They suggest that we ignore the problem of balancing the budget and focus on balancing the economy instead.

3. The federal government can finance *public spending* by collecting taxes (T), creating additional monetary base (ΔMB), selling government securities (ΔB), or confiscation. All of these techniques are drains on *gross private saving* (production minus private consumption) that can crowd out private economic activities. The notion called *Ricardian equivalence* suggests that whether government spending is financed by taxes or borrowing is irrelevant.

4. The *crowding-out hypothesis* states that increases in government purchases inevitably reduce private consumption, investment, or leisure.

5. Federal deficits can be financed by increasing domestic saving, by securing the savings of foreigners, or by reducing domestic investment or exports. All else constant, a growing budget deficit will cause a growing trade deficit.

6. Some government spending (now estimated at three-fourths) is *uncontrollable*. These programs are long range or are committed by law each and every year. Reducing these outlays is virtually impossible.

7. A major difference between private and public debt is that *private debt* is entirely owned by persons *external* to the issuing institution, while the bulk of *public debt* is *internal*, being owed to ourselves. Private debt has grown faster than public debt since the early 1950s and is currently over twice as large.

8. The *real burden of the national debt* stems from the federal government "crowding out" private investment as it drives interest rates up when it competes with the private sector for loanable funds. As a result, future generations may inherit a smaller capital stock and a smaller production possibilities frontier.

9. Among the major benefits of the public debt are its use as a *stabilization instrument* and as a *risk-free asset* for savers.

Key Concepts

Ensure that you can define these terms before proceeding.

budget deficit
public debt
functional finance
government budget
  constraint
crowding out

relatively uncontrollable outlays
internal versus external debt
debt roll-over

Problems and Questions

1. What are the potential advantages and disadvantages of amending the Constitution to require that federal outlays and receipts be balanced each time the Earth circles the sun?

2. Explain the sense in which federal taxes determine how much each of us will help control inflation. If you could print money, would you ever try to remove any from circulation as long as there were trees and green ink? Why? Why does the federal government bother to collect taxes?

3. Fill in the blank so that it is compatible with the government budget constraint.

   a. $G = \$1,200$ billion, $T = \$975$ billion, $\Delta MB = \$0$, $\Delta B =$ _____

   b. $G = \$1,250$ billion, $T = \$1,025$ billion, $\Delta MB =$ _____, $\Delta B = \$150$ billion

   c. $G = \$1,300$ billion, $T = \$1,375$ billion, $\Delta MB = -\$25$ billion, $\Delta B =$ _____

   d. $G = \$1,350$ billion, $T = \$1,400$ billion, $\Delta MB =$ _____, $\Delta B = \$0$

   Which of these scenarios will result in a budget deficit? A surplus? In an increase in the public debt? In a reduction of public debt? In inflationary pressures if the economy is at full employment? In deflationary pressures if the economy is at full employment?

4. The Japanese government contends that persistent U.S. trade deficits with Japan reflect our persistent federal budget deficits, not Japanese trade policy. They argue that U.S. trade deficits will disappear as soon as we start balancing our federal budget. Is the Japanese argument essentially correct? Why?

5

Challenges to Macroeconomic Policymaking

Your new knowledge about how fiscal and monetary policies work should incite doubt that macroeconomic problems are easily resolved. (Even optimists believe that only careful blends of policy can "fine-tune" an economy.) This part of the book extends insights from Keynesian and new classical macroeconomic models into our Aggregate Demand/Aggregate Supply framework, which allows us to consider how varying circumstances may call for very different policies. Foundations for Aggregate Demand and Aggregate Supply curves are reviewed in Chapter 15. We then use these curves to interpret the prosperous 1960s, the "stagflation" of the 1970s, the erratic 1980s, and the recession that opened the 1990s.

Chapter 16 addresses a basic policy issue: Should government actively pursue full employment, price-level stability, and economic growth? Or should it rely on self-stabilizing market forces? On one side are "activists," who urge frequent adjustments to fiscal and monetary tools; on the other are policy "passivists," who believe the economy should be allowed to adjust to shocks based on more of a laissez-faire approach — relatively constant but sound macroeconomic policies.

We open Chapter 16 by describing how Aggregate Demand and Aggregate Supply may interact to yield a *Phillips curve*, a Keynesian notion that policymakers may face a trade-off between unemployment and inflation. New classical macroeconomics offers several challenges for this Keynesian theory, including (*a*) *natural rate theory*, which contends that, in the long run, discretionary policy cannot alter employment, real interest rates, or economic growth, (*b*) the theory of *rational expectations*, which implies that, even in the short run, private adjustments to discretionary policy may thwart its effectiveness, and (*c*) *real business cycle theory*, which suggests that even well-intended activist policies disrupt automatic market adjustments to Aggregate Supply shocks.

This debate about proper macroeconomic policy continues in Chapter 17. Opponents of activist policies cite imperfect information, improper timing, incorrect "doses" of policy, and political incumbents' desires for reelection as barriers that distort discretionary policymaking. At the other extreme are analysts who view markets as unstable and monetary and fiscal policies as insufficiently potent, by themselves, to push a market system toward macroeconomic stability and growth.

This part of the book concludes with Chapter 18, where we examine the challenge of achieving long-run economic growth and development, the hurdles confronted in countries plagued by inadequate natural resources, explosive population growth, and insufficient capital as people attempt to improve standards of living.

CHAPTER

Aggregate Demands and Aggregate Supplies

A major reason why conventional monetarist or Keynesian approaches offer few insights into why high rates of inflation and unemployment might occur simultaneously is that, from the 1940s into the 1970s, both schools of thought largely ignored shifts in Aggregate Supply. Monetarists used shifts in Aggregate Demand to explain price-level changes because, following the classical tradition, the Aggregate Supply curve was assumed to be vertical and stable. Keynesian theory also viewed Aggregate Supply as stable, but perceived it as horizontal during a recession. Thus, Keynesians focused on unstable Aggregate Demand as disrupting output and employment. The resulting debate over whether shifts in Aggregate Demand ultimately result in price-level adjustments (the monetarist/classical position) or adjustments to employment and the output level (the Keynesian position) caused most economists to neglect possible shocks to Aggregate Supply.

The world economy was bombarded by supply shocks during the 1970s, however, creating events that seemed enigmatic to most economists, whether monetarist or Keynesian. High unemployment and inflation first occurred simultaneously in 1974–1975, giving rise to the term "stagflation" – a contraction of stagnation and inflation.

Stagflation *is the simultaneous occurrence of high rates of inflation and unemployment.*

This malady proved persistent. Inflation and unemployment remained above historical norms for almost a decade. Attempts to knock down inflation from the double-digit range during 1979–1981 partially succeeded by 1982, but briefly drove civilian unemployment rates above 10 percent. Annual inflation dropped to less than 3 percent in the late 1980s, with unemployment rates gradually drifting below 6 percent. During 1990–1991, however, the rates of inflation and unemployment were both crawling upwards.

Double-digit inflation with high unemployment – or double-digit unemployment with rapid hikes in price levels – were once thought highly unlikely. Policymakers familiar with Keynesian theory believed that low unemployment rates might stimulate rapid inflation, and vice versa, but faith in government's ability to fine-tune Aggregate Demand to produce continuous growth and a reasonably stable price level was commonplace. During the 1970s, however, skepticism grew about government's ability to fine-tune the economy by manipulating Aggregate Demand. In the early 1980s, the Reagan administration turned its attention to expanding

Aggregate Supply, adopting policies that were moderated only slightly by the administration of George Bush.

The time paths of inflation, National Output and Income, and unemployment can be explained by relative shifts in Aggregate Demand and Aggregate Supply. In this chapter we will take a closer look at Aggregate Demand and Aggregate Supply, examining more completely how government policies can be used to shift these curves. Demand-side and supply-side inflation are then examined and put into a historical context.

The Aggregate Demand Curve

In Chapter 5, we introduced some reasons why Aggregate Expenditures on our domestic production tend to be sensitive to the price level.

> The **Aggregate Demand curve** *reflects a negative relationship between the price level* (P) *and the quantity demanded* (Q) *of National Output.*

We will take a moment to review why Aggregate Demand curves are negatively sloped.

Slope of the Aggregate Demand Curve

All else equal, planned spending on U.S. production falls when the domestic price level rises because:

1. Higher interest rates reduce planned investment, Aggregate Expenditures, and, ultimately, output (the *interest rate effect*).

2. The purchasing power of assets stated in money terms falls, causing declines in wealth, and, consequently, in spending (the *wealth effect*).

3. Consumers substitute goods produced elsewhere for American-made goods, while investors find that the profitability of foreign investment has increased relative to that for investment in the United States (the *foreign sector substitution effect*).

Each of these effects was introduced in Chapter 5. You now have a fuller background for understanding each mechanism. When the price level rises, all of these effects operate to reduce the Aggregate Expenditures schedule, which results in a leftwards movement along the Aggregate Demand curve. For simplicity, we will temporarily assume that all domestic prices — including wages and rents — increase by exactly the same proportion.

Interest Rate Effects A major reason for the negative slope of the Aggregate Demand curve is the effect that higher prices have on the chain reaction from interest rates to investment to Aggregate Spending and then to income and output. These adjustments closely parallel the Keynesian monetary transmission mechanism you saw earlier.

When prices rise, the real purchasing power of a fixed money supply (M/P) falls. Consider Figure 1. A rise in the price level from P_0 to P_1 has the following effect in Panel A: The nominal money supply is assumed constant at M_{s0}; so the real supply of money shifts from M_{s0}/P_0 to M_{s0}/P_1. Equilibrium interest rates rise from i_0 (point a) to i_1 (point b) as a result of the reduction in the real money supply. Rising interest rates result in equilibrium moving from point a to point b in Panel B; thus, planned investment falls from I_0 to I_1 because investment becomes more costly at higher rates of interest.

This reduction in planned investment shifts the Aggregate Expenditures schedule in Panel C from AE_0 to AE_1, resulting in a reduction in real National Income from Y_0 (point a) to Y_1 (point b). Finally, this reduced National Income at higher prices means real output must fall from Q_0 (point a) to Q_1 (point b), as shown in Panel D. Duplicating this same process for every possible price level results in the negatively sloped Aggregate Demand illustrated in Panel D. The higher interest rates that result from higher prices crowd out investment and, in addition, squeeze both consumer credit and government spending at the local and state levels (especially that which is bond financed). Thus, higher interest rates reduce all these sources of Aggregate Spending.

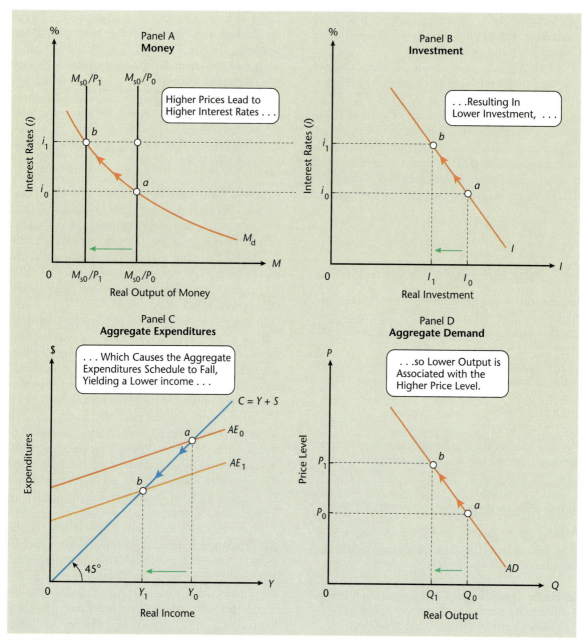

FIGURE 1 Interest Rates, Investment, and the Negatively Sloped Aggregate Demand Curve

A rising price level, all else equal, reduces the real supply of money (Panel A), which increases interest rates, reducing investment (Panel B) and Aggregate Expenditures and income (Panel C). Reduced income at higher prices means real output has fallen (Panel D). Repeating this process for all possible price levels produces a negatively sloped Aggregate Demand curve.

The Wealth Effect Suppose the price level were to fall sharply. To the extent that your wealth rises because of the increased purchasing power of your assets held as money, you can buy more goods and services, and so you will spend more. Conversely, even if your monetary income kept up with the price level during inflation, you would still lose to the extent that your wealth was stored as bonds, as cash, or in bank accounts, so you would reduce your spending.

Another adjustment occurs because most of us want to maintain fairly stable amounts of liquid assets relative to our income. Thus, even if your income rises at the same rate as the price level, you may temporarily reduce the proportion of income devoted to consumption so that the purchasing power of your liquid assets is restored through a short-term higher rate of saving. Because consumption declines as the price level climbs (due to the wealth effect), Aggregate Spending also falls in a manner similar to that described for interest rate/investment adjustments shown in Figure 1.

Foreign Sector Substitution We import goods when foreigners can produce them at lower cost and export goods when American production costs are lower than those in other countries. If the prices of U.S. goods rise, you will buy more imported goods than previously because they will be relatively cheaper. At the same time, foreign consumers will reduce their purchases of now higher-priced American goods. Thus, inflation causes imports to increase and exports to decrease, resulting in reduced Aggregate Expenditures and National Income and Output.

Increases in American prices are usually accompanied by higher U.S. costs of production. Higher wages and increased costs for land and machinery in the United States make it profitable for investors (both foreign and domestic) to reduce investment in the United States and substitute foreign investment, which reinforces the decline in Aggregate Spending as the price level rises from P_0 to P_1 in Figure 1.

To summarize, higher prices cause lower quantities of Aggregate Demand because (a) rising prices result in higher interest rates, which

reduce investment and purchases of consumer durables, (b) rising prices reduce the real value of assets stated in monetary terms, (c) imports grow and exports fall, and (d) domestic investment declines while foreign investment flourishes.

Shifts in Aggregate Demand

Any changes in planned Aggregate Expenditures (vertical shifts in Keynesian cross diagrams) are paralleled by shifts of the Aggregate Demand curve. Thus, spending plans ultimately determine the magnitude of Aggregate Demand. Movements of the Aggregate Demand curve are caused by changes in monetary or fiscal policies or by changes in planned consumption, investment, or foreign spending. How changes in the various influences that affect spending plans will shift the Aggregate Demand curve is summarized below Figure 2.[1]

How expanded spending plans shift Aggregate Demand to the right is shown in Panel B of Figure 2. Plans to spend more originate in tax cuts, increases in government purchases or transfer payments, or more optimistic expectations by consumers and investors. Expansionary monetary policies such as open-market purchases of bonds or reductions in either reserve requirements or the discount rate also cause growth of Aggregate Demand. Symmetrically, when the government pursues contractionary monetary or fiscal policies, the Aggregate Demand curve shifts to the left. This is shown as the movement from AD_0 to AD_1 in Panel A of Figure 2.

The Aggregate Supply Curve

Classical theory relies on supply and demand to keep a market economy close to full employment. Thus, it predicts a vertical long-run Aggregate Supply curve. Keynesian theory deals with a depressed economy — so many resources are idle that Aggregate Supply is horizontal. An interme-

---

1. This information expands the information from Figure 6 in Chapter 5 to indicate the probable effects of monetary and fiscal policies.

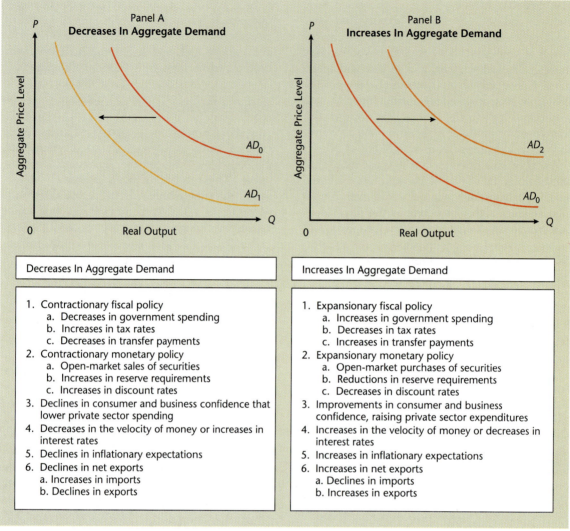

FIGURE 2 Events that Shift the Aggregate Demand Curve

diate position is that Aggregate Supply is positively sloped.

In the short run, the **Aggregate Supply curve** *reflects a positive relationship between the price level and the real quantity of National Output.*

This short-run positive relationship occurs primarily because production costs (e.g., wages) are "sticky" relative to output prices when demand changes. Growth of Aggregate Demand causes a movement up along the Aggregate Supply curve

in which prices rise more quickly than wages, so higher profit per unit induces more output. A drop in Aggregate Demand reverses this movement along the Aggregate Supply curve — prices fall more quickly than costs, so profits decline and firms reduce production.

Along the Aggregate Supply curve shown in Figure 3, if output is below Q_0 and much capacity is idle, then output can increase in the short run without significant hikes in the price level. But when the classical prediction of full employment is approached, even small increases in out-

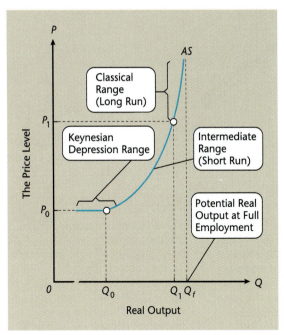

FIGURE 3 The Aggregate Supply Curve

The Aggregate Supply curve, like the market supply curve, is positively sloped. This suggests that increases in National Output normally entail increases in the price level.

put above Q_1 necessitate huge increases in the price level. Between output levels Q_0 and Q_1, moderate growth in output results in mild price hikes.

National Output and the Work Force

Increases in the total demand for labor generate pressure for higher employment and output levels and for hikes in wages and prices as well. Conversely, declines in the economy-wide demand for labor create pressure for lower employment, output, wages, and prices. There are, however, differences between short-run and long-run adjustments. Understanding Aggregate Supply requires an appreciation of these differences.

Labor Markets: The Short Run The Keynesian model emphasizes short-run adjustments. Suppose Aggregate Demand grew slightly during a severe depression like that of the 1930s. Keynes believed that widespread unemployment

permits firms to fill any vacant positions at the going wage, so the relevant part of the aggregate labor supply curve is assumed to be flat, while extensive idle capital prevents diminishing returns from posing a problem. Thus, if the demand for labor grows during a depression, employment and output rise, but wages and prices may not. Consequently, Keynesian analysis assumes a horizontal Aggregate Supply curve (see the Keynesian depression range in Figure 3). Remember that from Keynes' point of view, Say's Law was backwards and should have read "Demand creates its own supply."

Keynes' assumptions about depressed labor markets are drawn from the 1930s experience of a prolonged depression. Labor's supply curve normally has a positive slope because drawing more workers into the labor force requires higher wages; rising wages also enable unemployed workers to more rapidly find jobs they perceive as suitable. As firms pay higher wages to attract additional employees, wages rise for all workers. This results in a moderately positive slope in the Aggregate Supply curve, shown as the intermediate range in Figure 3.

Workers know that higher prices lower their real wages, but there is a time lag between a given inflationary reduction in real wages and labor's recognition of this loss. Workers may temporarily be fooled by hikes in money wages that are less than inflation, so more labor services may be offered, even though real wages decline. Firms hire more labor to produce more output if they perceive increased profit opportunities—output prices that rise faster than nominal wages. In the short run, workers fail to revise their expectations about changes in the price level and are fooled because they believe the original price level will prevail. Workers may suffer from inflation illusion in the very short run, but their misconceptions are unlikely to persist.

Labor Markets: The Longer Run The long-run orientation of classical reasoning represents the polar extreme from Keynesian analysis. New classical economics assumes that workers react to changes in real wages almost instantly, keeping the economy close to full employment. At the

Why Inflation Is More Likely to "Fool" John Smith than General Motors

A couple of reasons help explain why individual workers may be more easily fooled by inflation than are the firms that employ them. First, a major decision by a big firm may put millions of dollars on the line, while each worker has only his or her salary at risk. Thus, firms devote more resources to forecasts of inflation. Second, a firm only needs to estimate how much extra revenue will be generated if extra work-

ers are hired to know how much of a monetary wage (w) it can profitably afford to pay. This calculation requires only estimates of the worker's physical productivity and a forecast of the price (P_i) at which the firm will be able to sell its own product.

Thus, the real wage paid a worker from the vantage point of the firm is w/P_i. Workers, on the other hand, must have forecasts of all the prices of all goods they

expect to buy (e.g., the CPI) before they can estimate the purchasing power of their monetary wages. The real wage from the point of view of a typical worker equals $w/$CPI. Thus, firms may need less information about future prices (only P_i) to make profitable decisions than workers need (forecasts of most prices in the CPI) in order to make personally beneficial decisions.

very least, there can be no involuntary unemployment.

Workers try to base decisions about work on real wages, not on nominal money wages — what their earnings will buy, not the money itself. In the longer run, workers recognize that price hikes reduce their real wages (w/P) and react by reducing the real supply of labor. Suppose Aggregate Demand grows in an economy that is close to full employment. Higher money wages may temporarily lure more workers into the labor force if they expect the price level to remain constant. Once workers recognize that prices have risen, they demand commensurate raises. This yields a vertical long-run Aggregate Supply curve like the classical range shown in Figure 3.

In reality, workers do not react quickly to changes in real earnings. Focus 1 indicates that firms may have better access to information about inflation while needing less of it than

workers do to react to changes in the price level. Workers also respond relatively slowly because (*a*) most long-term union contracts set nominal wages for the lives of these agreements, (*b*) many nonunion wages are adjusted only at scheduled intervals, and (*c*) changing jobs often entails considerable "search time" and lost income.

Shifts in Aggregate Supply

The Aggregate Supply curve shifts when technology changes or when resource availability or costs change. Technological advances boost Aggregate Supply, while disruptions in resource markets, higher tax rates, or inefficient new government regulations are among negative shocks to Aggregate Supply.

Shocks Arising in the Labor Market Analysis of this type was at the heart of the 25 percent cut in tax rates during 1981–1983 and also was partially responsible for attempts to cut growth in government transfer payment programs. The Reagan administration hoped that revitalized incentives to produce would raise Aggregate Supply more than these tax cuts increased Aggregate Demand, so that substantial growth would defeat any emerging inflationary pressure.

A second type of labor market disturbance to Aggregate Supply would occur if the power of unions grew and organized labor commanded higher wages. Wage hikes raise production costs and push up prices, shrinking Aggregate Supply. Another problem area would be any rise in the inflation rate expected by labor. Inflationary expectations continuously shift the supply of labor curve leftward, as workers try to protect the real purchasing power of their earnings. Naturally, decreases in inflationary expectations or in union power will shift the labor supply and Aggregate Supply curves toward the right. Finally, people's choices about work versus leisure affect Aggregate Supply.

Incomes Policies Some analysts think that "incomes policies" may moderate inflationary expectations. The term **incomes policy** refers to measures intended to curb inflation without altering monetary or fiscal policies. These methods include jawboning, wage-and-price guidelines or controls, and *wage-price freezes* of the type imposed by President Nixon in 1971. The Nixon administration hoped the freeze would reduce the anticipated inflation rate and halt continuous shrinkage of Aggregate Supply. Ideally, it might have increased the supplies of labor and output, shown as the shift of the Aggregate Supply curve from AS_0 to AS_2 in Figure 4.

Unfortunately, incomes policies may perversely affect inflationary expectations and Aggregate Supply. If workers and firms share a belief that prices will soar as soon as controls are lifted, they may withhold production from the market now in hopes of realizing higher wages or prices later. For example, suppose you face the following choices: (*a*) You could work during a period when wages are frozen and save money to cover your college expenses, or (*b*) you could borrow to go to college during a freeze and then repay the loan from funds you earn after the lid is removed from wage hikes. You (and many other people) might delay working until after the freeze. Incomes policies also hinder necessary relative price adjustments; in a couple of chapters we detail how the resulting distortions in economic behavior retard Aggregate Supply.

Other Shocks Affecting Productive Capacity New regulations that hamper production shift the Aggregate Supply curve to the left (a movement from AS_0 to AS_1 in Figure 4), but elimination of inefficient regulation shifts the curve rightward. From the mid-1970s onward, a drive to deregulate much of our economy has been aimed at removing inefficiency and boosting Aggregate Supply. The supply-side policies of the Reagan administration featured deregulation and major cuts in corporate taxes, favorable tax treatments for savers, investment tax credits, and accelerated depreciation allowances. All these policies were intended to expand Aggregate Supply.

Technological advances expand Aggregate Supply, while external shocks that increase the cost of imports or resources cause Aggregate Supply to shrink. Drastic shocks to the U.S. economy occurred when OPEC coalesced in 1973 and world oil prices quadrupled shortly thereafter. Most industrialized countries endured painful leftward shifts in their Aggregate Supply curves. Rightward shifts occur when new resources are discovered. For example, Great Britain was aided by its North Sea oil finds, and the discoveries of huge pools of Mexican oil during the late 1970s helped Mexico. Gluts of oil on world markets and the relative instability of OPEC drove prices down; energy costs fell in the mid-1980s, boosting our Aggregate Supply to the right.

Influences that shift Aggregate Supply are listed in the chart below Figure 4. Be sure that you understand why each factor moves Aggregate Supply as it does. Understanding macroeconomic movements requires a good grasp of these concepts. We will now turn to the interesting problems of demand-side and supply-side inflation.

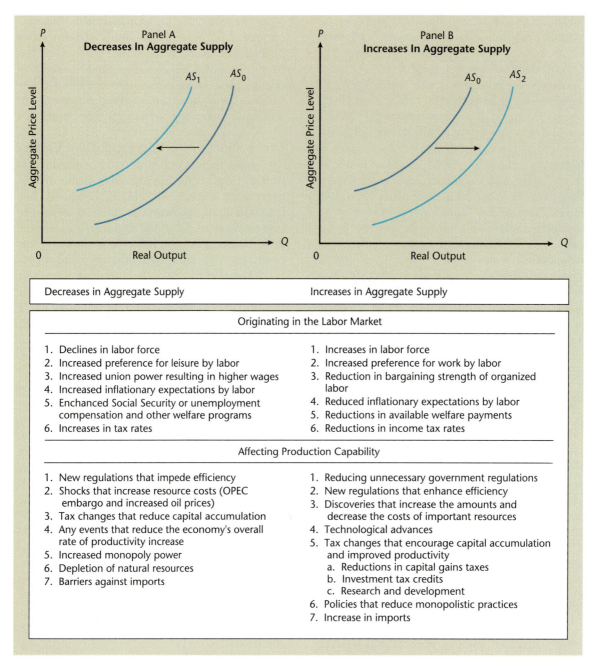

FIGURE 4   Events that Shift the Aggregate Supply Curve

The content of the figure is as follows:

Panel A
Decreases In Aggregate Supply
(Graph with axes: vertical *P* labeled "Aggregate Price Level", horizontal *Q* labeled "Real Output", showing curves AS_1 and AS_0 with leftward arrow)

Panel B
Increases In Aggregate Supply
(Graph with axes: vertical *P* labeled "Aggregate Price Level", horizontal *Q* labeled "Real Output", showing curves AS_0 and AS_2 with rightward arrow)

Decreases in Aggregate Supply	Increases in Aggregate Supply

Originating in the Labor Market

1. Declines in labor force	1. Increases in labor force
2. Increased preference for leisure by labor	2. Increased preference for work by labor
3. Increased union power resulting in higher wages	3. Reduction in bargaining strength of organized labor
4. Increased inflationary expectations by labor	4. Reduced inflationary expectations by labor
5. Enhanced Social Security or unemployment compensation and other welfare programs	5. Reductions in available welfare payments
6. Increases in tax rates	6. Reductions in income tax rates

Affecting Production Capability

1. New regulations that impede efficiency	1. Reducing unnecessary government regulations
2. Shocks that increase resource costs (OPEC embargo and increased oil prices)	2. New regulations that enhance efficiency
3. Tax changes that reduce capital accumulation	3. Discoveries that increase the amounts and decrease the costs of important resources
4. Any events that reduce the economy's overall rate of productivity increase	4. Technological advances
5. Increased monopoly power	5. Tax changes that encourage capital accumulation and improved productivity
6. Depletion of natural resources	a. Reductions in capital gains taxes
7. Barriers against imports	b. Investment tax credits
	c. Research and development
	6. Policies that reduce monopolistic practices
	7. Increase in imports

Demand-Side and Supply-Side Inflation

Equilibrium prices rise only if demands increase or supplies decrease. Inflation that originates on the *demand side* is referred to as "demand-pull inflation," while *supply-side* inflation is commonly termed "cost-push inflation."

You may have heard people complain, "If those #@*%! unions were less greedy and powerful, we would not suffer from inflation." Others blame all inflation on overly expansionary monetary policies. Still others cite government deficits as causing inflation: "Inflation would disappear if the federal budget ever balanced." Then there are those who blame wars or foreigners for our problems. What have been the basic sources of inflation in the last few decades? We will explore the expected equilibrium paths during both supply-side and demand-side inflation to begin to answer this complex question. Then we can compare these results with recent U.S. experience.

Demand-Side Inflation

Growth of Aggregate Demand in an economy operating below capacity causes employment, output, income, and, perhaps, the price level to grow. End of the Keynesian story. But suppose an economy is in a noninflationary equilibrium at full employment, such as that labeled point *a* in Figure 5: Full-employment GNP equals Q_f, and the price level is P_0. "Full employment" includes an allowance for frictional unemployment caused by flows of workers between jobs and in and out of the work force. Labor supplies reflect no expectations of inflation, which, along with other institutional characteristics and aggregate productive capacity, results in an Aggregate Supply curve of AS_0.

Now assume that Aggregate Demand rises from AD_0 to AD_1 because government spending grows, moving the economy toward a new short-run equilibrium at point *b*. Even an economy that started at full employment can expand if frictional unemployment falls and if business can be induced to employ the extra workers. If they can pass the costs of hiring these workers forward to consumers, firms will hire beyond the full employment point. The price level rises to P_1 with this swollen Aggregate Demand.

But what happens to workers' real wages? Money wages do not rise as quickly as prices rise, so real wages (w/P) fall. When labor eventually demands higher money wages to restore their purchasing power, the Aggregate Supply curve shifts leftward toward AS_1. Along the equilibrium path between points *b* and *c*, labor finds that although it receives higher money wages, these wages are partially eroded by continuing growth of the price level. How long will this process continue? Labor repeatedly reacts to price

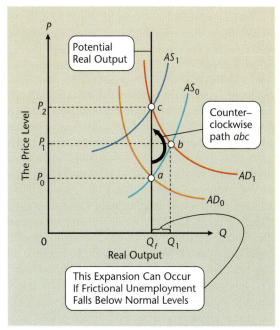

FIGURE 5 Demand-Side Inflation: The Counterclockwise Path

Frictional employment, a normal by-product of economic activity, is represented by the difference between Q_1, which assumes that everyone who wants to work is employed, and Q_f, which makes allowances for frictional unemployment. Frictional unemployment may artificially be reduced below normal levels $(Q_1 - Q_f)$ if expansions of Aggregate Demand temporarily fool some frictional unemployed workers into taking jobs that pay low real wages (movement from *a* to *b*). In the long run, however, workers will adjust their wage demands to reflect higher prices and unemployment will rise back to normal levels (movement from *b* to *c*).

Thus, if cyclical unemployment is negligible, expanding Aggregate Demand may temporarily reduce frictional unemployment, but this reduction is artificial, so the ultimate effect of expansionary policy is to increase the price level, and the economy follows the counterclockwise path shown in this figure.

hikes by demanding higher wages until equilibrium at point *c* is reached. At this point, real wages have regained their original values, the economy is back at full employment, and the aggregate price level equals P_2 — precisely labor's expectations about the price level.

Price-level increases initiated when the Aggregate Demand curve expands (shifts to the right) are called **demand-side** *(or demand-pull)* **inflation.**

Prices continue to rise when labor's inflationary expectations adjust and so might be thought of as supply-side inflation, but this is simply the second phase of a demand-side cycle — the original inflationary impetus came from increased demand. The forces that set this inflationary spiral in motion shift the Aggregate Demand curve to the right. Notice that as labor reacts to the inflationary spiral, the economy's equilibrium path runs from point *a* to *b* to *c*, following a *counterclockwise path*.

We indicated earlier that a Keynesian inflationary gap such as that reflected by $Q_1 - Q_f$ in Figure 5 creates inflationary pressure. In a sense, this is a "negative" GNP gap. *Overfull employment* can occur if frictional unemployment is artificially driven down by expansions of Aggregate Demand. Automatic pressures ultimately reduce output back to full employment levels. The economy shown in Figure 5 first moves from *a* to point *b*. Workers eventually realize that they have been fooled and the labor supply falls, returning the system to full employment at point *c* — but at a higher price level. Recall that (*a*) we initially assumed full employment, with allowances for normal frictional unemployment, and (*b*) if the economy is initially plagued by excess capacity, only the first phase of this cycle needs to occur — growing demand can yield much more output with only slightly higher prices.

Supply-Side Inflation

What happens if inflationary expectations do not drive workers' demands for higher wages? This could occur if unions became stronger, if new laws made it easier for labor to organize, or if hard bargaining by existing unions became the norm in key industries.

The effect of such actions by workers is shown in Figure 6. Demands for higher wages will shift Aggregate Supply to the left. Suppose the original equilibrium is at point *d*. As the Aggregate Supply curve shrinks from AS_0 to AS_1, equilibrium moves from point *d* to *e*. Firms will demand less labor, because higher wages can only partially be passed on to consumers in the form of higher prices. Unless something boosts Aggregate Demand, less real output is demanded at

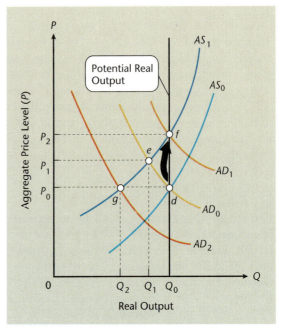

FIGURE 6   Supply-Side Inflation: The Clockwise Path

Shocks to the supply side cause prices to rise while output and employment fall (movement from point *d* to *e*). If policymakers follow expansionary policies to counter unemployment, prices will rise further (from point *e* to *f*). If, on the other hand, they fight inflation by reducing Aggregate Demand, the price level will return to the P_0 level, but output and employment will shrink dramatically (from point *e* to *g*).

the new price level P_1, and real output and employment are reduced to Q_1. For incumbent politicians, this is the worst of all worlds: rising prices and unemployment, and declining real incomes and output.

As the economy moves to point *e*, politicians may worry about voters' reactions to a recession. Why this can be a concern is indicated in Focus 2. Policymakers may also perceive a duty to maintain full employment under the Employment Act of 1946 and the Full-Employment and Balanced Growth Act of 1978 (the Humphrey-Hawkins Act). The movement from point *d* to point *e* portrays an economy moving into a recession, and political pressures will mount to launch expansionary policies. If, on the other hand, policymakers view inflation as an evil that must be tamed and try to restore the price level to P_0 by

Macroeconomics and Presidential Elections: *1929–1992*

Social commentators increasingly criticize political campaigns as resembling beauty contests— looks, personality, and images created by public relations specialists are viewed as dominating recent political contests. But there is growing evidence that macroeconomic circumstances have powerful effects on the outcomes of major elections.

Prosperity favors political incumbents and, apparently, the candidates of the party of the previous president. Ray Fair, a Yale economist, has developed a simple statistical equation based on three macroeconomic variables—unemployment, inflation, and growth of per capita real income—that "picked" the winner in all but two presidential elections held between 1948 and 1984 (and his equation predicted both of those elections to be close).

Republican President Hoover did not stand a chance of reelection in 1932; the Great Depression that began late in 1929 (the year he took office) continued to worsen until 1933. Democrat Franklin D. Roosevelt's reelection in 1936 occurred during recovery, as did his reelection in 1940—the economy had faltered again in 1937, recovering during 1938–1946. World War II yielded high levels of patriotic fervor and economic prosperity, ensuring Roosevelt's reelection for a fourth term in 1944. President Truman was reelected in November 1948—the month a business

cycle reached its peak. Republican Dwight Eisenhower (a popular hero from World War II) defied the odds in besting Adlai Stevenson in 1952 when the economy was expanding, but his victory in 1956 occurred in the middle of an economic recovery from a 1954 recession (the economy had weakened again in 1957).

Richard Nixon blamed a minor recession in 1960 for his narrow loss to Democrat John F. Kennedy. President Lyndon Johnson was reelected by a landslide in 1964, in the middle of the longest economic recovery since World War II. His vice president, Hubert Humphrey, lost a close election to Richard Nixon in 1968 even though the U.S. economy was relatively strong. Fair's equation picked Humphrey as the winner by a slim margin. (Humphrey's loss appears to have resulted primarily from dissension over the way Johnson conducted the unpopular Vietnam War.) Nixon was determined to win by a landslide in 1972; per capita income soared in that election year, and his wish (along with the wishes of most other incumbents) was granted.

President Ford (who succeeded Nixon after Nixon resigned because of the Watergate scandal) lost his 1976 bid for reelection to Jimmy Carter; the economy was still weak from the "energy crisis" and a severe recession in 1975. The economy

recovered somewhat during 1976–1978, but double-digit inflation and growing unemployment in 1979–1980 doomed President Carter to his loss to Ronald Reagan.

President Reagan's intention to stimulate rapid economic growth through incentive-based supply-side policies was frustrated when the FED followed disinflationary policies in the early 1980s; the period 1982–1983 was the deepest economic downturn that the United States had experienced since the Great Depression. However, a strong recovery that began late in 1983 swept Reagan into another four-year term.

This recovery continued through the 1988 election, which pitted George Bush against Michael Dukakis. Between 1983 and 1988, unemployment fell steadily, finally reaching a 5.5 percent rate—the lowest rate in nearly two decades. Inflation, which had been at double-digit rates in 1981, had stabilized by 1988 to a rate that most people perceived as tolerable, while moderate economic growth continued. Given this background, Bush's victory in the 1988 election was no surprise.

This analysis strongly suggests that George Bush was defeated by Bill Clinton in his reelection bid in 1992 because of the severity of the recession that began in 1990 and extended into late 1992.

decreasing Aggregate Demand to AD_2, the economy will move from point d to point g, further decreasing National Output and exacerbating unemployment.

Alternatives to achieving full employment by expanding Aggregate Demand would be policies to restore Aggregate Supply from AS_1 to AS_0. More output and employment would be generated at lower prices. This is a time-consuming process, so the federal government has historically tended to be demand-management oriented. President Reagan and his supporters were frustrated in the early 1980s because it became obvious that considerable time was required for supply-side policies to operate. Supply-side policies are aimed at increasing our productive capacity, a task not accomplished overnight. (Return to Figure 4 if you want to review policies that shift the Aggregate Supply curve to the right.)   In fact, many critics contend that sustained growth from 1983 to 1990 resulted primarily from growth of Aggregate Demand, which was stimulated by the enormous upward surge of budget deficits that began with major cuts in tax rates on income (both personal and corporate) during 1981–1983.[2]

Stimulating Aggregate Demand is a relatively quick and easy process; government cuts tax rates or boosts its outlays for goods and services or transfer payments, or the FED increases monetary growth. The government commonly counters shrinkage of Aggregate Supply by increasing Aggregate Demand, shown by a shift from AD_0 to AD_1 in Figure 6. With demand management, the economy will move along the equilibrium path described by the arrows from point e to f. Employment ultimately returns to a full employment level, but at a higher price level. Notice that the long-term equilibrium path for supply-side inflation is from point d to e to f, a *clockwise pattern*. Remember, a demand-side inflationary cycle follows a counterclockwise pattern.

Supply-side inflation *is initiated when the Aggregate Supply curve shifts to the left and the price level rises as output falls.*

A few qualifications should be noted at this point. First, shifts in the Aggregate Supply curve from AS_0 to AS_1 originate in a multitude of ways summarized previously under Figure 4. Second, the federal government need not increase government spending to shift the Aggregate Demand curve from AD_0 to AD_1. For example, monetary authorities might stimulate rapid monetary growth in attempts to push the economy out of a recession.

U.S. Inflation: Demand-Side or Supply-Side?[3]

You are now prepared to examine our recent experiences with inflation. We just showed that demand-side inflations cause an economy to equilibrate in a counterclockwise fashion, while supply-side inflations cause the economy to follow a clockwise pattern.

The inflations of the 1960s and 1970s are graphed in Figure 7. The most significant difference between this and previous graphs is that we have altered the axes slightly to accommodate the data. The GNP deflator (described in Chapter 6) is still measured on the vertical axes, but each period starts out at a base of 100. We also have converted the horizontal axis to real GNP divided by potential GNP to adjust for growth in our productive capacity. Potential GNP grows because of such things as technological advances, capital accumulation, or growth of the labor force.

The demand-pull inflation of the 1960s resulted primarily from increased government spending for domestic programs, the space program, the escalation of the Vietnam conflict, stimulation from the 1964 tax cut, and rising

---

2. Critics also point out that the highly publicized supply-side tax cuts of 1981 to 1983 were largely offset by a less publicized increase in Social Security taxes in 1982. According to supply-side logic, this huge increase in payroll taxes may have significantly harmed incentives for labor effort.

3. For an extended discussion of this issue, see Robert J. Gordon, *Macroeconomics*, 5/ed. (New York: HarperCollins, 1990), especially Part IV. Our discussion owes much to Gordon's pioneering efforts.

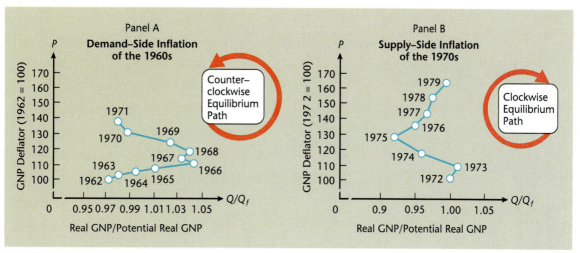

FIGURE 7   Supply-Side and Demand-Side Inflations in the United States, 1962–1979

When inflation originates from excessive growth in Aggregate Demand, the adjustment path follows a counterclockwise pattern, as was true of the 1960s. The clockwise pattern shows up for supply-side inflations, like that of the 1970s.

Source: *Economic Report of the President,* 1991.

monetary growth. As you can see in Panel A, the equilibrium process followed a counterclockwise path.

Contrast the 1960s inflation with that of the middle 1970s, which may have been triggered by rising prices for oil and other imported goods. A second major external shock was a worldwide agricultural drought, leading to price hikes in the United States as substantial domestic farm output found its way into the world market. The Arab oil embargo and ensuing OPEC price increases strengthened the inflationary pressures of this period. Many economists would include the 1971–1973 price controls as a shock to the supply side. Panel B of Figure 7 shows that the system equilibrated in a clockwise fashion, although price controls disguised inflationary pressure during 1971–1973. This figure indicates that inflation in the 1970s derived primarily from supply-side pressures.

Prosperity in the 1960s

The economy was recovering from a modest recession when John F. Kennedy took office in 1961. President Kennedy used small doses of fiscal spending to support expansion and, in 1962,

proposed cuts in tax rates to stimulate the economy and to reduce the government deficit as well. Appealing somewhat to "supply-side" arguments, he relied primarily on Keynesian multiplier analysis. Together, these approaches suggest that cuts in tax rates might increase both Aggregate Demand and Aggregate Supply (and, hence, GNP and income) sufficiently that tax revenues would actually rise rather than fall.

The 1960s were an era of fiscal stimulus unmarred by serious supply-side shocks. The path of the U.S. economy from 1961 to 1970 shown in Panel A of Figure 8 is based on actual data for real GNP and the GNP deflator.[4] Our model indicates that this path resulted from expansionary macroeconomic policies that accommodated the growth in potential GNP as baby-boomers began to enter the work force.

In Panel B of Figure 8, a set of curves representing Aggregate Demands and Supplies is superimposed over the equilibrium path shown in Panel A. The smooth rightward shifts in Aggregate Supply (Panel B) reflect regularity in the

---

4. This figure does not incorporate the adjustment of GNP by potential GNP, which was used to depict clockwise and counterclockwise patterns in Figure 7.

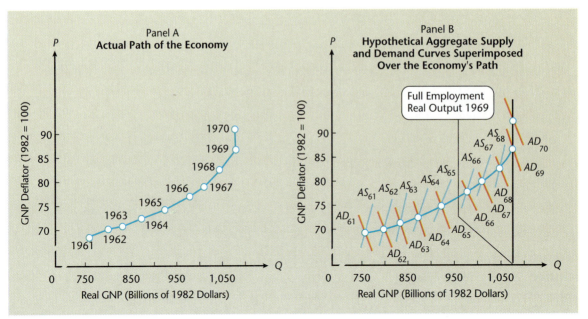

FIGURE 8 Prosperity of the 1960s

Aggregate Supply grew smoothly in the 1960s; Aggregate Demand grew even faster, but relatively smoothly as well, causing the price level to rise somewhat while unemployment rates fell a bit. Inflation was a minor but growing problem by the end of the decade. The Aggregate Supply and Aggregate Demand curves in Panel B are simply suggestive of the path of the economy; you should not infer that the economy was perpetually in equilibrium because symptoms of disequilibrium did occur from time to time.

Source: *Economic Report of the President,* 1991.

growth of potential output (full-employment real GNP) each year. The vertical portion of the curve represents potential GNP in 1969. This figure reveals that the slightly more rapid growth of Aggregate Demand than Aggregate Supply during 1960–1969 did not trigger much inflation. Generally, there is considerable excess productive capacity in the early stages of a recovery, which was the case between 1961 and 1964. As the economy recovered from the 1960 recession and approached full employment, further increases in demand brought forth ever greater increases in prices and smaller increases in output.

As the United States escalated its role in Vietnam and domestic spending accelerated, the economy experienced mild but increasing inflation. This can be seen in Panel A of Figure 8 by looking at the economy's path from 1966 to 1970. The events of 1969 and 1970 are espe-

cially interesting. The economy reached full employment and there was a slight surplus in the government budget for fiscal year 1969. Still, government continued to increase spending.

By 1971, the rate of inflation had become a matter of widespread concern, compounded because real output grew very little. Federal tax receipts fell 6 percent short of budget outlays, the prelude to a series of then record-breaking deficits — deficits that seem small by today's standards. As workers began to recognize erosion in the purchasing power of their wages, the shrinking supply phase of that demand-side cycle of inflation was activated. Rapid price increases unaccompanied by growth of real output between 1969 and 1970 prompted President Nixon to impose a wage-price freeze in August 1971, even though inflation had in fact begun to subside. The CPI grew at annual rates of 6.2 percent in 1969 and 5.2 percent in 1970, but inflation had fallen to 4.2 percent by the first half of 1971. As you will see, the freeze had only a temporary and artificial effect in holding down inflation, which seems to have been subsiding anyway.

Stagflation in the 1970s

Lingering effects of the demand-side inflation of the 1960s caused President Nixon and his advisors to fear that inflationary expectations would provide momentum for further inflation and lead to economic havoc. Although the Vietnam War was winding down, the war effort still absorbed hefty spending. Concern about the political repercussions of tax hikes necessitated federal deficits that further fueled inflation.

Under pressure from Congress and the general public, President Nixon took an unusual step for an avowed conservative: on August 15, 1971, he announced a 90-day wage-price freeze. Less stringent price controls were phased in when this freeze expired. As you can see in Panel A of Figure 9, these controls seemed partially effective in that nominal inflation abated during the 1971–1973 period. In reality, inflationary pressures continued to build throughout the period, only being disguised by price controls. Some people argue that the public anticipated substantial inflation when Nixon's temporary controls were scheduled to end, so controls may actually have increased inflationary momentum.

The economy suffered substantial stagflation (high rates of both inflation and unemployment) for the first time when price controls were re-

FIGURE 9 Stagflation of the 1970s and Early 1980s

The economy suffered from stagflation during 1973–1975, when the Aggregate Supply curve shifted to the left. The shift in the Aggregate Supply curve was due to (a) rising oil prices, (b) agricultural shortages, (c) a 20 percent depreciation of the dollar, which raised import prices, and (d) rising inflationary expectations.
Source: *Economic Report of the President*, 1991.

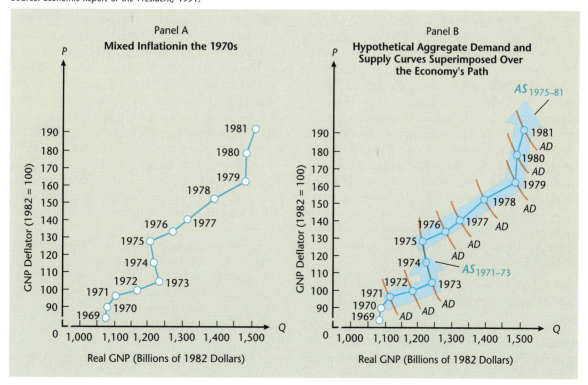

laxed between 1973 and 1975. The major reasons for this "stagflationary" downturn were supply shocks: the Arab oil embargo (followed quickly by a quadrupling of OPEC's price per barrel of oil), agricultural shortages, and depreciation of the dollar relative to most foreign currencies (which raised import prices). The U.S. economy went into a tailspin: Inflation exceeded 12 percent, and unemployment soared above 9 percent of the labor force during 1975. The economy followed a path of fairly steady recovery during 1975–1978. Inflation remained high but stayed below the double-digit range until 1979. Fiscal policy was aimed at continuing the recovery from supply shocks with the hope of avoiding a surge of inflation, although politicians spun a lot of rhetoric about balancing the budget.

In Panel B of Figure 9, an Aggregate Supply/Aggregate Demand model is superimposed over the actual data from Panel A to emphasize the most important trends. The period 1971–1973 was characterized by shifts in Aggregate Demand that moved the economy up along the supply curve labeled $AS_{1971-73}$. The shocks of 1973–1975 shrank Aggregate Supply, resulting in equilibration along the 1973–1975 demand curves. The stagflation of 1973–1975 might be traceable in part to the lifting of price controls. Both workers and businesses attempted to recoup their precontrol positions by boosting wages and prices. By late 1975, Aggregate Supply appears to have become relatively stable, and the economy resumed its equilibrating movement along the supply curve labeled $AS_{1975-81}$. Although the federal government used demand-management policies in trying to steer the economy to a smooth and steady recovery, policies to reduce unemployment toward the full employment level fostered the reemergence of inflationary pressures.

Disinflation and Recovery in the 1980s

Restrictive monetary policies intended to suppress an inflationary hangover from the 1970s pushed the economy into a severe slump during 1981–1983, but inflation continued at high rates. Interest rates skyrocketed in 1979 and again in 1981. Tighter monetary policies than had been followed in over a decade finally caused both inflation and interest rates to begin drifting down in 1982. One side effect, however, was that in 1983, unemployment rose to its highest rate since the Great Depression. Some economists viewed the 1981–1983 slump as the castor oil required to cure earlier policy excesses.

Panel A of Figure 10 uses our Aggregate Demand and Aggregate Supply framework to illustrate these general movements. Several years of growing demand and high inflation had boosted inflationary expectations, causing the Aggregate Supply curve to shrink. This is shown as the shift from AS_0 to AS_1. To slow this inflationary spiral, the FED tightened the screws during 1981 and 1982, shifting Aggregate Demand from AD_0 to AD_1. This dampened inflationary expectations and, coupled with tax cuts that kicked in during 1982 and 1983, helped stabilize the Aggregate Supply curve at AS_1. The resumption of mildly expansionary fiscal and monetary policies in 1983 allowed Aggregate Demand to drift back toward AD_0. The net result was disinflation and falling real output between points a and b (1980–1983) and then steady growth along AS_1 with significantly lower inflation (1983–1989).

The clockwise equilibration path is reflected in the actual equilibrium path for the economy illustrated in Panel B of Figure 10. The path of the economy between 1979 and 1983 indicates that Aggregate Supply continued to shrink and that tight monetary policies during this period decompressed inflation, but only by precipitating a severe recession. The growth in the economy between 1983 and 1989 points to an economy moving along a flatter and more stable Aggregate Supply curve.

Decompressing inflation was costly. In the early 1980s, the economy slipped below its earlier growth path. Cumulative losses of real income are estimated at roughly $3 trillion, due largely to policies intended to quell a resurgence of accelerating inflation.

Disinflation *is a significant reduction in the rate of inflation.*

FIGURE 10 Recovery in the 1980s and the Slump of 1990–1992

Panel A illustrates the disinflation process after the sustained buildup of an inflationary spiral. Leftward shifts of the Aggregate Supply curve (due to rising inflationary expectations) are combined with reduced Aggregate Demand to produce a recession and quell inflation. Disinflation occurs between points *a* and *b*. Once the inflationary psychology dissipates, rising Aggregate Demand allows growth without a resurgence of inflation. Panel B shows actual values for the economy during the 1980s. Note the economic slump (path *cde* in Panel A) that began in 1990 (1992 data in Panel B are preliminary). Source: *Economic Report of the President,* 1992.

Many people who had expected inflation to continue through the 1980s invested heavily in real estate and other inflation "hedges," so disinflation left them stuck paying high real rates of interest. When the real burdens of their mortgages were not eased by inflation as expected, many investors were clobbered by huge losses. Homes that had cost $75,000 in 1975 were typically over $100,000 by 1980. Disinflation burst the bubble of asset prices swollen by inflationary expectations. Real estate foreclosures reached record highs by the mid-1980s. A similar outcome befell farmers and the rural banks that supported them. Farmers who had borrowed to purchase high-priced land faced bankruptcy as both farm incomes and land values plummeted.

Firms had grown accustomed to price increases as cures for even major problems and workers had fully adjusted their expectations and wage demands to continue inflation. When disinflation smothered price hikes, firms were forced to find other ways to boost sales and profits. During disinflationary times, productivity growth and new products are keys to business success because prices cannot be raised. New products typically yield higher profits and facilitate growth. Another common solution of firms to the problems posed by disinflation is to cut labor costs. Disinflation causes firms to bargain harder, and workers, sensing reduced inflation, tend to be more receptive to lower wage increases.

Pressures to raise productivity during disinflation cause changes in firms' investment patterns. First, more investment is directed toward productivity-enhancing plant and equipment, and less is aimed at expanding capacity. Second, more investment is financed internally as firms attempt to limit their debt burdens. Finally, the acquisition binge that some firms undertake during inflationary periods is reversed when debt consolidation requires the selling off of subsidiaries.

The Slump of 1990–1991

During 1983–1990, the United States enjoyed its most sustained expansion since World War II, but the economy fell into a mild slump during 1990. A mild resurgence of inflation erupted in 1989, and the FED responded with restrictive policies. Then, in 1990, Congress tried to reduce the federal budget deficit through increases in excise taxes, and a 5 percent income tax surcharge (making the marginal income tax rate 33 percent) was levied on almost all families with annual incomes exceeding $50,000. The result of these attempts to curb budget deficits and dampen inflation can be seen in the slight economic downturn reflected in the data for 1990–1991 in Figure 10.

This chapter has illustrated how interpreting macroeconomic change is facilitated by the tools of Aggregate Demand and Aggregate Supply. Formulating appropriate policies to stimulate economic growth and counter inflation and unemployment is facilitated once we understand the effects of relative shifts in Aggregate Demand curves and Aggregate Supply curves. Nevertheless, proper policymaking remains a formidable challenge because the "experts" fall into several camps, and often disagree on (a) how to interpret the current position of the economy and (b) how particular policies are likely to operate. In the next two chapters, we will examine several of the dilemmas and limitations facing policymakers as they attempt to stabilize the economy.

Chapter Review: Key Points

1. *Stagflation*, a contraction of the terms *stagnation* and *inflation*, is the simultaneous occurrence of high rates of both unemployment and inflation.

2. Decreases in the Aggregate Supply curve cause *supply-side inflation* and declines in real incomes and output. Excessive increases in the Aggregate Demand curve cause *demand-side inflation*, which initially is accompanied by increased incomes and output.

3. If Aggregate Demand grows excessively in a fully employed economy, the first phase of the *demand-side cycle* entails rising prices, outputs, employment, and incomes. In the second phase, supply-side adjustments to the demand-originated disturbances cause prices to continue to rise, but total employment, production, and income fall. *Demand-side* inflation induces a *counterclockwise adjustment* path of inflation versus real output. If the economy starts at less than full employment, only the first phase necessarily occurs when Aggregate Demand is increased.

4. Supply-side inflation generates a *clockwise adjustment* pattern. During the first phase of a *supply-side* (cost-push) *cycle*, prices rise while real output and incomes fall. If the government attempts to correct for the resulting inflationary recession by increasing Aggregate Demand, the second phase occurs—prices continue to rise, but real output and income rise as well.

5. Mild but increasing demand-side inflation accompanied the prosperity of the 1960s. From the mid-1970s into the early 1980s, stagflation took over with a vengeance. Whether this stagflation was the supply-adjustment phase of the earlier demand-pull cycle or originated solely from supply-related shocks cannot be established conclusively. It seems likely, however, that even if the economy had been stable when the *supply shocks*

listed previously emerged, considerable supply-side inflation would have plagued the American economy from 1973 to 1980.

6. *Disinflation* is a significant reduction in the rate of inflation. Most people adjust their behavior if they expect inflation. Their expectations cause disinflation to entail losses in real income before it restores the economy to a relatively stable growth path. Thus, the 1981–1983 recession was especially severe.

Key Concepts

Ensure that you can define these terms before proceeding.

stagflation

Aggregate Demand curve

Aggregate Supply curve

demand-side (demand-pull) inflation

supply-side (cost-push) inflation

disinflation

Problems and Questions

Use up arrows (↑), down arrows (↓), zeros (0), or question marks (?) in the blanks to indicate how (*a*) Aggregate Demand and (*b*) Aggregate Supply will be shifted by the events described in questions 1–8, and how each will affect (*c*) National Income and Output, (*d*) employment, (*e*) unemployment rates, and (*f*) the price level. (*Note*: Aggregate Demand and Supply may both be affected in some cases, some reasonable arguments are debatable, and long-run consequences can differ from short-run effects.)

1. The FED increases sales of U.S. Treasury bonds to prevent a jump in energy prices from triggering excessive cost-push inflation.
   a. _____   b. _____
   c. _____   d. _____
   e. _____   f. _____

2. Voters blame incumbents for the Depression of 1995–1996. Federal income tax rates are cut by 10 percent just before the 1996 election.
   a. _____   b. _____
   c. _____   d. _____
   e. _____   f. _____

3. The Treaty of 1992 eliminates all barriers to free trade between Canada, the United States, and Mexico.
   a. _____   b. _____
   c. _____   d. _____
   e. _____   f. _____

4. An environmental protection law requires all U.S. firms to reduce their pollution per unit of output by 50 percent before the year 2000.
   a. _____   b. _____
   c. _____   d. _____
   e. _____   f. _____

5. Baby-boomers intent on maintaining standards of living when they retire double the percentages of disposable income they save.
   a. _____   b. _____
   c. _____   d. _____
   e. _____   f. _____

6. The federal budget is balanced by slashing defense spending by $300,000,000,000.
   a. _____   b. _____
   c. _____   d. _____
   e. _____   f. _____

7. The Japanese Parliament eliminates all tariffs and quotas on U.S. agricultural products.
   a. _____   b. _____
   c. _____   d. _____
   e. _____   f. _____

8. Congress relaxes our immigration laws to accommodate a new wave of political refugees.
   a. _____   b. _____
   c. _____   d. _____
   e. _____   f. _____

9. Draw a set of Aggregate Demand and Aggregate Supply curves and label them AD_0 and AS_0 respectively. Now illustrate the first step in demand-side inflation and label any new curves with a subscript 1. What might have caused this first step in demand-side inflation? (You should be able to list six broad possibilities.) Now illustrate the second step in demand-side inflation and label any new curves with the appropriate subscript. What causes this second step to take place? What path does demand-side inflation take?

CHAPTER

Active vs. Passive Policymaking

Demand-side and supply-side inflation are the two dominant types of hikes in the price level, but most inflationary episodes involve elements of both. Curing high unemployment by stimulating Aggregate Demand may set off inflation, but reducing inflation may yield rising unemployment. Political leaders face a policy dilemma because high rates of unemployment and inflation each create economic stress and are unpopular with voters.

Another dilemma is that most Keynesians advocate active policies to counter major macroeconomic shocks, while economists influenced by classical reasoning favor allowing markets to adjust to any shocks and view erratic government policies as causes, not cures, for instability. Should policymakers actively try to counter economic shocks, or should they rely on automatic market adjustments to stabilize the economy?

This chapter addresses trade-offs between inflation and unemployment, and explains why these trade-offs may "worsen" to yield stagflation. How output and inflation are related is a central issue. Aggregate Output is positively related to employment and tends to be negatively related to unemployment. Another issue addressed is why inflation and interest rates seem positively related. Finally, we introduce recent theories—*efficient markets*, *real business cycles*,

and *rational expectations*—which support the views of new classical macroeconomists that government should provide a stable environment of sound, but passive, policies within which the market system can adjust to any destabilizing shocks.

Trade-Offs Between Unemployment and Inflation

We all, or nearly all, consent,
when wages rise by ten percent,
it leaves the choice before the nation,
of unemployment or inflation.

Kenneth Boulding

Boosting Aggregate Demand raises real output and employment in an economy with idle productive capacity, but ever greater upward pressures on prices and wages emerge as excess capacity disappears. Output growth cannot be sustained in the long run once an economy reaches its capacity; further increases in Aggregate Demand only cause inflation. Our general Aggregate Demand/Aggregate Supply framework hints at a possible inverse relationship between unemployment and inflation. This chapter explores this trade-off in more detail.

More than three decades ago, A. W. Phillips compared plotted data for wage inflation and unemployment rates for the preceding century in Great Britain. Curves that seem to fit such data have become known as *Phillips curves*.

> The **Phillips curve** *portrays an inverse statistical relationship between the rate of inflation and the unemployment rate.*

Phillips's original work examined wage inflation, but subsequent researchers focused on trade-offs between unemployment and price inflation. For example, reducing inflation to zero might require an unemployment rate of 8 percent, while pressing unemployment below 5 percent might require 6 percent annual inflation.

Productivity and Inflation   A fairly tight relationship linking nominal wage inflation, price inflation, and productivity can be expressed as:

$$\dot{p} = \dot{w} - \lambda$$

where $\dot{p}$ is the percentage rate of inflation, $\dot{w}$ is the percentage change in wages, and λ is the percentage change in productivity.

For example, if typical workers can produce 5 percent more this year than last, then wages can rise by 5 percent before firms feel pressure to maintain profit margins by raising prices. This relationship is illustrated in Figure 1. An annual rate of productivity gain (λ) of 2 percent (based on rough historical averages) is assumed and is reflected by shifting the scale for price inflation ($\dot{p}$) down by 2 percent relative to wage inflation ($\dot{w}$). Thus, 4 percent wage hikes combined with 2 percent productivity gains only impose pressures for prices to rise by 2 percent. But if productivity gains for the economy are nil and workers successfully demand higher wages, the net result is likely to be price inflation.

The 1960s: An American Phillips Curve?

Figure 1 superimposes a Phillips curve over U.S. data for the 1960s. Because Aggregate Supply was thought relatively stable, the Phillips curve was also thought to be so; policymakers could adjust Aggregate Demand to achieve the least harmful combination of unemployment and in-

FIGURE 1   A Phillips Curve for the 1960s (U.S. Data)

Phillips curves indicate that if Aggregate Demand is high and rising steadily, there will be substantial inflation but little unemployment; consistently low Aggregate Demand will yield less inflation but greater problems of unemployment. Wages may rise faster than prices if productivity advances. We have assumed that productivity grew by 2 percent annually in calibrating the two vertical axes differently. Overall, the movement from 1959 to 1969 reflected the expansionary fiscal and monetary policies of this era.
Source: *Economic Report of the President,* 1991.

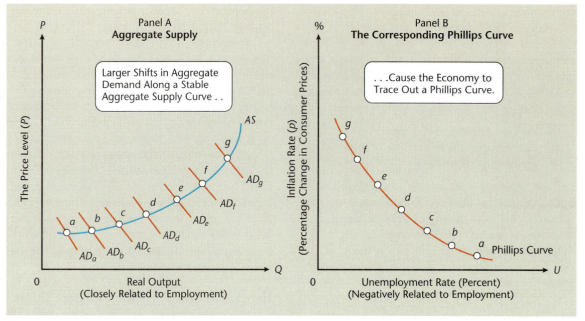

FIGURE 2 Aggregate Supply and the Phillips Curve

Ever larger sustained increases in Aggregate Demand in Panel A along a stable Aggregate Supply curve would trace out a series of equilibria like *a, b, . . . , g* in Panel A as employment and output increased. The unemployment rate would fall during these movements, but prices would rise, tracing a pattern roughly like *a, b, . . . , g* along the stable Phillips curve in Panel B.

flation. The dilemma seemed clear to Keynesians: If high inflation is associated with low unemployment (and vice versa), then the Phillips curve is a "menu" showing the trade-off facing policymakers who seek to minimize our economic woes.[1]

The Phillips curve shown in Figure 1 was thought roughly reflective of the trade-off confronting U.S. policymakers. At a target of zero price inflation, American workers would suffer roughly 6 to 8 percent unemployment. Unemployment rates as low as 3 to 4 percent were thought feasible only with inflation of 4 to 6 percent. Policymakers would have preferred less of each, but Phillips curve analysis suggested that this was impossible.

---

1. Recall (from Chapter 6) that the misery index is the sum of the rates of unemployment and inflation. Sluggish productivity growth, high interest rates that depress investment, or imbalances of international trade are among a variety of other difficulties that can also signal macroeconomic distress.

Shifts in Aggregate Demand: A Stable Trade-Off?

National Output and Income are closely related to employment. In turn, there is a close negative relationship between employment and unemployment: higher employment generally means lower unemployment, and vice versa. But changes in the size or composition of the labor force may obscure this relationship. For example, rapidly rising labor force participation rates may cause frictional unemployment to rise even if real output and employment grow.

An Aggregate Supply curve is a positive relationship between the level of output and the price level, while a typical Phillips curve depicts an inverse correlation between unemployment and inflation. Thus, Phillips curves roughly mirror Aggregate Supply curves, as shown in Figure 2. Points *a, b, . . . , g* in Panel A roughly correspond to points *a, b, . . . , g* in Panel B. Expanding Aggregate Demand from AD_a to AD_b in

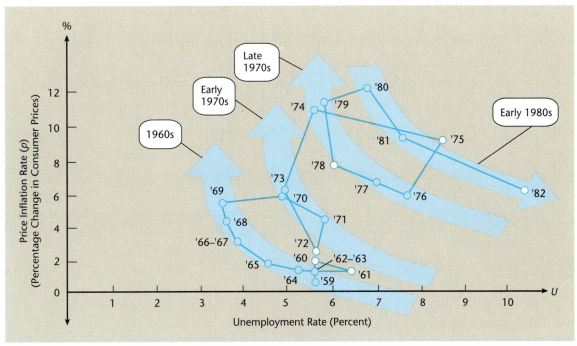

FIGURE 3   The Shifting Phillips Curve Relationship

Shifts of Aggregate Supply caused the Phillips trade-off to worsen between the 1960s and early 1970s, between the early and mid-1970s, and again between the late 1970s and early 1980s.

Source: *Economic Report of the President,* 1991.

Panel A moves the economy from point *a* to point *b* in Panel B. Keeping the economy at point *b* requires raising Aggregate Demand by the same proportion in each subsequent period. Similarly, expanding Aggregate Demand from AD_a to AD_c moves the economy to point *c* in Panel B; staying at point *c* would require continuous similar expansions of Aggregate Demand.[2] And so on, for points *d, e, f,* and *g*.

The 1970s: Stable Phillips Curves at Bay?

The notion that the Phillips curve was stable unraveled in the 1970s. Four Phillips curves are superimposed over 1970s data in Figure 3. It seemed that ever greater inflation had to be endured to keep unemployment rates in the 5 to 6

percent range. Why did the Phillips curve worsen (shift rightwards)?

Supply Shocks and Unstable Phillips Curves

Continually expanding the growth rate of Aggregate Demand while Aggregate Supply remains stable results in upward movements along a stable Phillips curve, as in Figure 2. The 1960s seemed to provide evidence of a roughly stable Phillips curve, but bouts of stagflation in the 1970s betrayed the naïveté of this view. Shocks to Aggregate Supply apparently worsened the short-run trade-off between unemployment and inflation, as shown in Figure 4. Suppose that Aggregate Supply begins to shrink, declining from AS_0 to AS_1 to AS_2, and so on, in Panel A. Output and employment fall while the price level rises (stagflation), so that policymakers are

---

2. Readers familiar with differential equations will recognize this discussion as a description of moving from static analysis of price-level changes to a more dynamic analysis of sustained inflation.

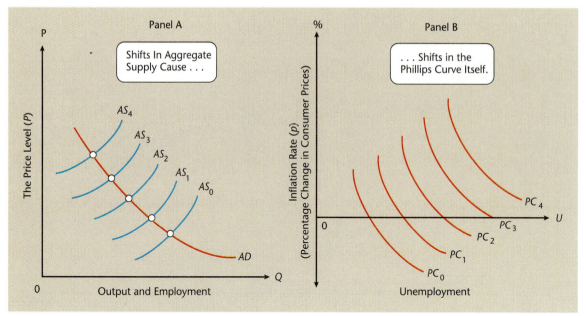

FIGURE 4   Shifting the Phillips Curve

Shifts in Aggregate Supply, as shown in Panel A, cause shifts in Phillips curves (*PC*), as shown in Panel B, and account for the stagflation of the 1970s and early 1980s.

presented with worse short-run options such as curves PC_0, PC_1, PC_2, and so on, in Panel B. As Phillips curves move to the right, achieving a given level of unemployment requires suffering more rapid inflation.

Since its inception, the Phillips curve has been in the eye of a stormy controversy about policy. Keynesians initially viewed Phillips's discovery of a negative statistical relationship between unemployment and inflation as confronting policymakers with a stable trade-off. Economists of a classical bent view the Phillips curve as a short-run artifact and argue that policymakers who try to swap inflation for lower unemployment will soon find the relationship a mirage. Their *natural rate* theories suggest that, in the long run, macroeconomic policies affect only the price level and not such "real" variables as unemployment or interest rates. We need to examine these alternative theories and explore differing interpretations of why Phillips curves may shift so that an economy experiences stagflation, as the United States did in the 1970s.

Keynesian Phillips Curves

Keynesian theorists initially explained the existence of the Phillips curve as caused by "bottlenecks" encountered as an economy moved ever closer to full employment. After it became apparent that any trade-off between unemployment and inflation might be unstable, modern Keynesian theorists developed a "structural-shock" theory to show why Phillips curves might shift. We explore both approaches in this section.

The Keynesian Structuralist Approach

The first Keynesian explanation for the Phillips curves—the *structuralist* approach—goes like this: As unemployment falls and full employment is approached, it becomes increasingly costly to produce extra output. One reason is that as more and more industries operate nearer their capacities, increasing numbers of firms encounter "bottlenecks" that boost costs, which are then passed on to consumers as higher prices.

Major structural bottlenecks occur in labor markets. Competition among firms for the best workers becomes increasingly vigorous as unemployment rates fall. Most of the best workers retain jobs even when unemployment is high. Workers remaining unemployed in prosperous times often lack the skills required for jobs during hard times; other workers' skills may have depreciated during extended periods of joblessness. Consequently, employers begin offering higher wages to "pirate" qualified workers away from other firms as unemployment rates fall. This competition drives up costs, prices, and so on.

Structural Shocks and Wage/Price Stickiness

Modern Keynesian explanations for Phillips curves' shapes hinge on two key ideas: (a) Shocks to market demands and supplies continually bombard all economies, and (b) wages and prices are assumed downwardly "sticky." That is, wages and prices rise more easily than they fall. At any moment in time the structure of demands — both private and public — is changing. These are shocks to the economy. As new products are developed or national priorities change, the demands for some goods rise while those for others fall.

Output growth in sectors where demand grows is limited in the short run by the capital and trained labor readily available. Thus, wage and price hikes are the primary adjustments to stronger demand. In sectors where demand shrinks, the norm is production cutbacks and layoffs — not price reductions. Workers accept wage cuts only reluctantly, so firms find it easier to cut wage costs through layoffs. Some temporary price cuts (e.g., automobile rebates) may be used to liquidate excess inventories, but these price cuts will be accompanied by declining output and rising unemployment.

Suppose that Aggregate Demand is stable while the structure of demand changes. Prices in growing sectors rise faster than outputs, but prices fall slowly if at all in declining sectors, while outputs plummet. The net result is a higher price level, more unemployment, and less total output.

Structural shocks *cause Aggregate Supply to fall temporarily because of friction encountered in moving resources from declining to growing sectors.*

How this Keynesian analysis is consistent with Phillips curves is shown in Figure 5.

At our initial equilibrium at both points a, the price level is stable at 100. Assume that Aggregate Demand remains constant at AD_0 but that its structure changes, dislocating labor and other resources so that Aggregate Supply shrinks from AS_0 to AS_1. Equilibrium moves from point a to point b. Given the downward wage-price stickiness in declining markets, structural changes cause the price level to rise. Again, if policymakers desire to maintain output at Q_f and unemployment at U_f, expansionary policies are necessary so that Aggregate Demand grows from AD_0 to AD_2. These expansionary policies will move the economy from point b to point c in both panels of Figure 5. Thus, adopting policies to maintain unemployment at U_f will result in an annual inflation rate of 3 percent if structural changes of the same magnitudes and frequencies continually recur.

This result suggests that our economy has a "natural" *inflationary bias* caused by continuous changes in the structure of economic activity. If policymakers chose to suppress this natural inflation, they might reduce Aggregate Demand to AD_1 (point d in Panel A), but unemployment would then rise to U_1 in Panel B. Thus, policymakers can reduce either the unemployment or the inflation caused by structural changes in economic activity, but not both. Less inflation means more unemployment, and vice versa.

The Keynesian structuralist and "shock" theories explain the existence of Phillips curves, but we need to probe a bit deeper to see how these approaches illuminate the rocky path of our economy over the past two decades.

A Keynesian Theory of Stagflation

Classical theory emphasizes the inherent stability of the market system, stressing erratic government policy as the major source of shocks to the economy. Modern Keynesians consider other disruptions as important in destabilizing Aggre-

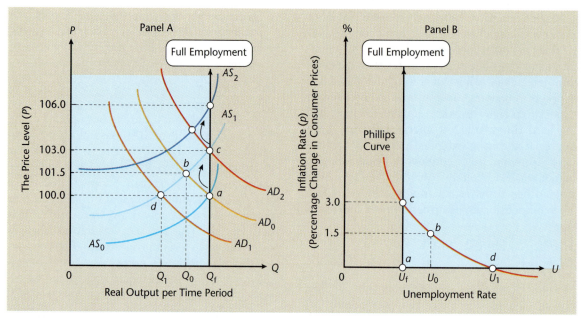

FIGURE 5 Full Employment Output, Shocks, and the Rate of Inflation: The Modern Keynesian Approach

A modern Keynesian approach suggests that recurring shocks to individual markets may create excessive unemployment that can only be overcome by expansionary policies, lending a natural bias for inflation to the economy. This theory is elaborated in James Tobin, "Inflation and Unemployment," *The American Economic Review*, 62, No. 1 (March 1972), pp. 1–18.

gate Supplies and Phillips curves during the 1970s. Keynesians classify shocks to Aggregate Supply under five broad headings: (*a*) inflationary expectations, (*b*) external shocks, (*c*) labor market disturbances, (*d*) structural changes in product markets, and (*e*) disruptions emerging in the public sector. Let us examine each, remembering that Aggregate Supply and the Phillips relationship can shift in either direction.

Adaptive Inflationary Expectations   Any event that shifts Aggregate Supply to the left causes supply-side inflation and worsens the trade-off between unemployment and inflation. Keynesians recognize that inflationary expectations can shift Aggregate Supply negatively. (In fact, A. W. Phillips' 1958 analysis of historical trade-offs between unemployment and inflation included statistical adjustments for past inflation and several other factors that he viewed as explaining placement of the curve.) The theory of *adaptive expectations* suggests that recent infla-

tion is the major determinant of expectations about future inflation.

> *The theory of* **adaptive expectations** *suggests that expectations about future inflation are typically a weighted average of past rates of inflation.*

Suppose, for example, that people expected inflation during the next year to equal (1) half the inflation of the past year, plus (2) one-third of the inflation experienced a year ago, plus (3) one-sixth of the inflation from two years back. If inflation was 14 percent in the past 12 months, 9 percent for the year earlier, and 18 percent three years ago, then, because 14/2 + 9/3 + 18/6 = 13, people would expect roughly 13 percent inflation in the coming year. Although different people might assign different weights to different years, this approach suggests that the more severe the recent history of inflation, the faster Aggregate Supply will recede to the left and the worse will be the position of the current Phillips curve.

Shocks to the System   During 1974–1981, recurrent oil price hikes boosted firms' energy costs, reducing Aggregate Supply and eroding the Phillips curve. This is shown in Figure 5. Wars and bad weather or other natural disasters will have similar effects. On the other hand, discoveries of new resources, technological advances, prolonged periods of economic stability, or reductions in international tensions may improve the Phillips trade-off.

Labor Market Changes   Incentive structures that affect work effort also help explain the Phillips curve's location. Unemployment compensation, for example, affects many workers' labor-leisure choices. Raising unemployment compensation payments will encourage greater unemployment, intensifying inflationary pressure. Unemployment compensation apparently (a) encourages temporary layoffs by firms because it eases hardships on firms' workers when orders for output drop, and (b) extends the average duration of unemployment. Social Security currently encourages early retirement. Increased payments under most welfare programs may also worsen the trade-off between unemployment and inflation.

Some recent reforms are intended to reverse these negative effects. For example, welfare recipients who work can use subsidized day-care facilities for their children, the government now supports job training for the "hard-core" unemployed, and the penalties exacted from Social Security recipients who earn income have been reduced. All these reforms may reduce the severity of the inflation/unemployment trade-off by increasing work effort and Aggregate Supply. Policies to enhance job mobility and match idle workers and job openings will also improve the Phillips trade-off, as will programs to reduce discrimination so that productivity becomes the primary criterion for employment.

Demographic changes also affect the relationship between inflation and unemployment. The post–World War II baby boom provided a growing pool of labor in the 1960s. But younger workers tend to bounce from job to job and are unemployed more often, worsening the Phillips relationship. As this group becomes older, the changing age structure of the population should reduce the severity of this trade-off. Women's labor force participation rates grew markedly from the late 1950s onward. Even though this influx of labor bolstered Aggregate Supply, it also seems to have worsened the Phillips curve because women's unemployment rates are typically higher than those of males.

Collective bargaining may also affect the Phillips curve. If growth of unions' power enables them to obtain contracts with inflationary wage hikes, or if strike activities intensify, the trade-off between inflation and unemployment will deteriorate.

Structural Changes in Product Markets
One explanation for the shape and existence of Phillips curves is drawn from continuous changes in the structure of demands for goods, combined with wage and price stickiness and a policy of trying to maintain full employment. The menu of choices between unemployment and inflation worsens if external shocks become stronger or if structural changes occur more rapidly. If consumer tastes and preferences or investors' perceptions of the economic outlook change markedly, the structure of output may also change drastically. Of course, this trade-off is more favorable the slower or less extreme these changes are during a given interval.

Changes in laws governing foreign trade become more important as our economy becomes more internationally oriented. Hikes in tariffs or cuts in import quotas raise the prices of imported goods and can certainly worsen the dilemma posed by the Phillips curve. Competition is also reduced. Similarly, growth of domestic monopoly power and the resulting drives for greater profits will worsen the inflation/unemployment trade-off.

Public Sector Changes   Just as disruptions to the structure of private demands can shift the Phillips curve, so can changes in the composition of public sector demands for goods and resources. Changes in tax structures, subsidies, and transfer payments also influence the trade-off. Major revisions of such regulations as those policed by the Occupational Safety and Health Administration (OSHA), minimum-wage laws, environmental protection regulations, leasing policies for mineral exploration on public lands, or changes in property rights structures may all shift the Phillips curve relationship. The direction of the shift depends on whether a particular regulatory change enhances or encumbers economic efficiency.

For modern Keynesians, an explanation for the stagflation of the 1970s goes something like this: Rising inflationary expectations and disruptions associated with the Vietnam War caused the first shift in the Phillips curve in the early 1970s. The increase in world oil prices in 1974 caused the second shift. More oil price hikes in 1979 and 1981, coupled with worldwide crop failures, caused further shifts of the Phillips curve in the early 1980s. And relative cessation of shocks to the economy in the mid-1980s ultimately improved the Phillips curve trade-off.

The New Classical "Natural Rate" Theory

New classical economists predictably disagree with this Keynesian interpretation of recent economic history. A strand of this new classical perspective known as **natural rate theory** centers on the idea that macroeconomic policy will not ultimately affect any "real" variable. Thus, these theorists perceive no permanent connection between unemployment and inflation. They reason that money is a veil in the long run and that nominal things, such as the price level, are determined by the money supply but will be unrelated to any aspect of real behavior, such as unemployment or relative prices. Natural rate theory concludes that a negatively sloped Phillips curve is transitory, and that Aggregate Supply will shift persistently only because of changing inflationary expectations.

The Natural Rate of Unemployment

Would it be good if unemployment were always exactly zero? "Yes, of course" seems an easy answer. But keeping the unemployment rate at zero would require people who were unhappy with their jobs to stay in them until they found new ones — or else they would be unemployed. Moreover, there would be pressures on firms to immediately hire anyone who applied for work. And if you were not in the labor force and then decided to look for a job, you would be forced to take the first job offered — otherwise you would be unemployed. Zero unemployment is not as attractive a goal as it sounds.

Natural rate theorists view nearly all unemployment as voluntary, the sole exception being unskilled people who are unemployed because minimum-wage laws prevent employers from hiring these workers at the low wages commensurate with their productivity. Natural rate theorists view all other unemployment as the result of friction — it takes people time to find what they regard as suitable employment, and while they are looking for work, they are unemployed by choice. Individuals can presumably get jobs almost instantly if they are willing to take the wage they are worth to the first employer willing to hire them. Frictional unemployment can be viewed as a cost of investment in labor market information and mobility. Table 1 presents estimates of the natural rate of frictional unemployment for several developed economies.

According to natural rate theory, expansionary

Table 1 *Unemployment (Frictional) Rates Required to Keep Inflation Stable (%)*

The rate of unemployment required to keep inflation in check moved up sharply throughout much of the industrialized world after 1970. Whether this reflected higher inflationary expectations or structural changes that boosted frictional unemployment is debatable.

	1971–1975	1981–1983
United States	6	6½
Japan	1	2
West Germany	1½	8
France	3½	8
Britain	4	9
Italy	7	6½
Canada	7	7½
Holland	4	10½

Sources: OECD, Layard and Nickell, 1984, from *The Economist*, 14 May 1988, p. 69. Reprinted by permission.

macroeconomic policy reduces frictional unemployment only because workers are fooled by unanticipated inflation into thinking that the higher wages offered by employers represent real increases in the purchasing power of their earnings. Anyone who is unemployed can get a seemingly "suitable" high-paying job quickly during expansionary periods, when the pool of frictionally unemployed workers is small. In the natural rate view, these artificial declines in frictional unemployment reflect cyclical overemployment that is a consequence of inadequate investment in labor market information. But why do employers offer higher wages when expansionary policies are followed? Expansionary policies cause business firms to forecast booming sales that will enable them to raise the prices of their products. After workers recognize that their wages do not buy as much as expected because prices are also rising, many will become dissatisfied and quit to look for more lucrative work.

The eventual result is that frictional unemployment will rise back to its "natural rate" when workers cease being fooled. The natural rate of unemployment is the rate that exists before expansionary policy is initiated; it is achieved when all transactors have accurate expectations about inflation. If expansionary policies are continued, workers will learn to expect inflation and will demand wages that rise continuously to compensate for inflation. This means that Aggregate Supply will shrink continuously.

Wage Adjustments to Inflation

Consider Figure 6. A starting point for the natural rate explanation for Phillips curves is to assume a macroeconomic equilibrium with no inflation at points a in both panels. The price index is 100 (point a in Panel A), and unemployment is at a level compatible with potential real output (point a in Panel B). Inflation is initially zero, and the natural rate of unemployment, U_n, is between 5 and 7 percent. The shaded parts of

FIGURE 6 Equilibrium Output and the Rate of Inflation (Natural Rate Approach)

"Natural rate" theory suggests that attempts to maintain unemployment below its normal, frictional rate require continuous expansions of Aggregate Demand, raising the possibility of accelerating inflation.

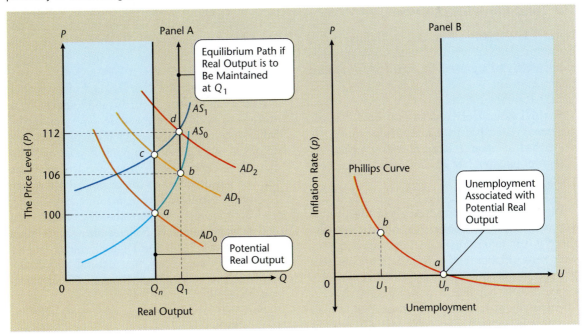

Figure 6 represent output and unemployment below and above the natural rate respectively.

Now assume that overly expansionary monetary policy drives Aggregate Demand up to AD_1. Real output will rise to Q_1 (point b), but the adjustment process entails 6 percent inflation, and the price level rises from 100 to 106. We suggested earlier that this equilibrium cannot be sustained for long. Workers will find their real wages falling, triggering attempts to catch up. As they do so, the Aggregate Supply curve shrinks to AS_1 and the economy moves toward point c in Panel A. If policymakers try to maintain output at Q_1 and unemployment at U_1 by shifting Aggregate Demand to AD_2, another inflationary round equal to roughly 6 percent is unleashed as the economy moves to equilibrium at point d in Panel A. The equilibrium path for the economy is denoted by the arrow: Policymakers must continually create 6 percent inflation to maintain unemployment at U_1.

Our model to this point naïvely supposes that workers always expect inflation to be zero, only seeking wage adjustments after the price level has risen. Policymakers are confronted with additional problems if workers begin to anticipate inflation.

The Long-Run Phillips Curve

Natural rate theory suggests that Phillips curves do not present policymakers with stable frontiers along which inflation can be "traded off" against unemployment.

> **Natural rate theory** *implies that each Phillips curve is associated with a particular rate of expected inflation. If workers foresee higher rates of inflation, the Phillips curve worsens by shifting outward.*

Panel A of Figure 7 illustrates how this occurs. Suppose that the economy is at point a initially; there is frictional unemployment equal to U_n, with zero inflation and zero inflation expected; $E(\dot{p})$ indicates the inflation rate that workers expect. What happens if policymakers view an unemployment rate of U_n as unacceptably high and follow expansionary policies? Growth of

Aggregate Demand yields increased sales, so firms offer higher wages to attract new workers to accommodate the higher demands for their products. Workers who are frictionally unemployed will have little difficulty finding what they perceive as good, high-paying jobs. Thus, expansionary policies push the economy along the $E(\dot{p}) = 0$ Phillips curve from point a toward point b.

The fly in this ointment is that higher demands for goods are seen as opportunities to raise prices. As workers learn to expect 5 percent price hikes, the Phillips curve shifts rightward and the economy moves to point c at the old natural rate of unemployment U_n. This occurs because workers will demand wage increases of 10 percent — 5 percent to cover past inflation plus 5 percent for expected inflation. But firms forecast only 5 percent growth in nominal demands for their outputs and will refuse to meet workers' demands for 10 percent wage hikes. Frictional unemployment rises as workers hit the pavement looking for better jobs.

If policymakers again view unemployment (U_n) as unacceptably high, they might follow even more expansionary policies. If so, the economy initially will move from point c to d, but then ultimately to e as workers again cease being fooled. All that policymakers will have achieved is 10 percent inflation with no long-term reduction in unemployment. If policymakers were undaunted by their failures, they might even proceed to f.

If they had learned their lesson, however, they would find moving directly and quickly back from e to a almost impossible. The buildup of inflationary momentum may force policymakers to engineer a recession to point g to dampen inflationary expectations. An extended recession may be required before the economy will return to point a. Similar adjustments may explain why a severe recession occurred in 1981–1983 when deflationary monetary policies brought inflation under control. Panel B of Figure 7 shows data for 1960–1990, suggesting that natural rate theory explains the experience of recent decades reasonably well.

Pure natural rate theorists view rising expectations of inflation as the only explanation for any

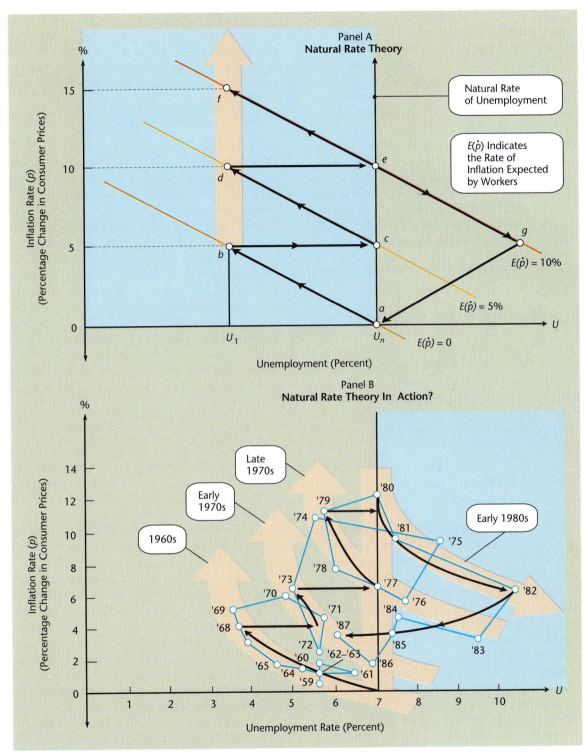

FIGURE 7   Natural Rate Theory and the Shifting Phillips Curve

Natural rate theory suggests that unemployment will be less than the natural rate (U_n) only if workers expect less inflation than occurs and that it will be more than the natural rate if workers expect more inflation than results from macroeconomic policy. In the long run, workers will adjust perfectly to any changes in price levels so that normal, frictional unemployment will be maintained, which is totally independent of the price level or inflation.

Source: *Economic Report of the President,* 1991.

worsening of any short-term relationship between inflation and unemployment. There is a family of short-run Phillips curves; each depends on different expectations of inflation by labor. Unemployment will gravitate back to its natural rate in the long run. Thus, there is no long-run trade-off between inflation and unemployment. In Figure 7, the long-run Phillips "curve" is the vertical path *ace*. According to natural rate analysis, if policymakers attempt to maintain unemployment below the natural rate, the short-run Phillips curve trade-off worsens. Accelerating bouts of inflation (up the vertical arrow in Panel A) are inevitable until policymakers accept the futility of trying to hold unemployment below its natural rate.

The Natural Rate of Interest

Natural rate theory also views attempts to achieve lower interest rates than are consistent with people's individual decisions as ultimately self-defeating. We will now examine why the natural real rate of interest hypothesis identifies the interest rate as an inappropriate target for monetary authorities.

The Natural "Real" Rate of Interest Hypothesis

Just as there are any number of wage rates or prices in the economy, there are also any number of interest rates. The interest rates paid by borrowers to lenders reflect, among other considerations, risk, length of time to maturity of the note or bond, the availability of credit, and legal constraints. For simplicity, however, we will assume that there is only one interest rate for borrowing.

When people discuss "the" interest rate, they usually mean the average annual percentage monetary premium paid for the use of money. Economists refer to this percentage monetary premium as the nominal rate of interest.

*The **real rate of interest** is the annual percentage of purchasing power paid by a borrower to a lender for the use of money.*

Estimating the realized real rate of interest (r) is simple — the nominal interest rate (i) minus the percentage rate of inflation ($\dot{p}$) yields the percentage purchasing power premium, or real interest rate (r), paid over the life of a note or bond:

$$r = i - \dot{p} \quad \text{(real interest rate)}$$

For example, if the nominal interest rate is 12 percent and the price level rises 15 percent annually, the real rate of interest is roughly -3 percent, so lenders lose 3 percent of purchasing power each year.

Workers bargain for higher nominal wages in order to protect their real wages when they anticipate inflation. Naturally, people whose incomes are based on interest will react similarly. The natural real rate of interest hypothesis suggests that borrowers and lenders adjust nominal interest to expected inflation $E(\dot{p})$, so that borrowers' willingness to pay purchasing power premiums (desired real interest, r_d) exactly equals the purchasing power premiums lenders require for the use of money. Thus, when a note or bond is issued:

$$i = rd + E(\dot{p}) \quad \text{(nominal cost of borrowing)}$$

If inflation is expected, lenders try to charge higher interest to ensure that they will not lose purchasing power, but why will borrowers be willing to pay such "high" interest rates? To understand this essential point, consider the housing market during the late 1970s, during which housing prices increased by from 10 to 30 percent annually in some regions.

Suppose that you expect housing prices in your area to increase by 15 percent annually. To keep it simple, we will assume that you can borrow money at a nominal interest rate of 10 percent. If you are able to repay the loan with dollars that have depreciated in value by 15 percent annually, this situation is similar to being paid 5 percent of the price of your house annually to live in your own home. Negative real rent sounds pretty good to most of us, which explains, in part, the 1970s boom in housing prices.

The **natural real interest rate hypothesis** suggests that the desired real rate of interest (r_d) reflects (*a*) the real (purchasing power) premium necessary to induce savers to delay gratification (most people value having goods today more than having goods tomorrow), (b) the premiums necessary to induce people to hold their wealth in less liquid forms, and (c) the expected productivity of capital, which yields extra goods in the future. The real interest rate is the percentage of extra goods that can be enjoyed if consumption is delayed so that extra capital is available for production.

Keynes and Fisher Effects

According to the natural real interest rate hypothesis, expansionary monetary policy might temporarily reduce nominal interest rates, but in the long run, overly expansionary policies cause nominal interest rates to climb, not fall. Figure 8 shows why by relating the supply and demand for loanable funds to nominal interest rates. The supply and demand for loanable funds is linked closely to the supply and demand for money discussed earlier. Changes in real interest rates will cause these supplies and demands to shift.

Suppose that monetary policymakers view the nominal interest rate of 6 percent (given by the intersection of D_0 and S_0 at point a) as too high — they perceive it as inhibiting investment and spending. If they follow expansionary open-market operations, the supply of loanable funds initially rises to S_1 and the nominal interest rate falls to 4 percent (point b). This temporary decline in nominal interest rates caused by expansionary policies will result in even larger declines in real interest rates because natural rate theory predicts that overly expansionary policies cause inflation.

*The **Keynes effect** predicts declines in interest rates following expansionary monetary policy, and vice versa.*

If expansionary policies cause the price level to rise by 4 percent annually, the real rate of interest is zero ($r = i - \dot{p} = 4\% - 4\% = 0\%$). Borrowers eventually will increase their real demands for funds to, say, D_1 because borrowing seems so cheap; they repay these loans in depreciated dollars. Lenders will reduce supplies to S_2 because

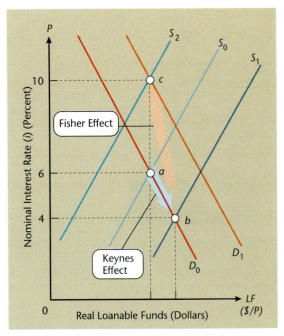

FIGURE 8 Keynes and Fisher Effects in the Market for Real Loanable Funds

The natural rate of real interest theory suggests that an expansion of the money supply may temporarily increase the supply of loanable funds and drive nominal interest rates down via the Keynes effect, but if inflation results and comes to be expected, the Fisher effect may cause nominal interest rates to rise above the inflation level. These effects operate in exactly opposite directions when contractionary policies are followed. The lesson here (paralleling that for the natural rate of unemployment) is that policymakers' attempts to artificially reduce interest rates are ultimately doomed to failure.

they gained no real purchasing power at a real interest rate of zero. In the long run, the nominal interest rate will rise to 10 percent (point c in Figure 8). These types of adjustments were addressed systematically by Irving Fisher, the first prominent American monetary theorist (see his biography).

*The **Fisher effect** predicts upward adjustments in nominal interest rates as borrowers and lenders compensate for expected inflation, and downward shifts if deflation is expected.*

Contractionary monetary policies tend to reduce the availability of credit in the short run;

Irving Fisher

Irving Fisher was the premier American economic theorist of the early twentieth century. His best-known works address monetary economics and theories of capital and interest. He was also a pioneer in the explicit use of mathematics as a major tool of economic theory and cofounded the Econometric Society. Though Fisher was a theoretical economist, his objective was not only to develop theories with great explanatory power, but to develop them in operational terms—he tried to base his theories on measurable variables that permitted his hypotheses to be tested.

Let us look at Fisher's equation of exchange as an example of his work. He stated that $MV + M'V' = PT$, where M is the quantity of currency, V the velocity of currency as it circulates, M' represents the quantity of demand deposit dollars times V', the ve-locity of demand deposits, P is the price level, and T the number of transactions in the economy. Modern quantity theorists have reduced this equation to $MV = PT$ by adding together the two forms of money. In this equation M, P, and T are directly observable and measurable. Hence the equation can be solved for V. (Most quantity theorists now use the $MV = PQ$ formula discussed earlier.) The equation of exchange plays a very important role in current macroeconomic theory and policy disputes.

Fisher was impressed by the power of money and strongly advocated policies of monetary stability, an important theme in two of his major works, *The Purchasing Power of Money* and *The Theory of Interest*. In the latter Fisher also distinguished between the real rate of interest and the nominal rate of interest. The nominal rate consists of the real rate, based on the real productivity of new capital investments, plus a premium for anticipated inflation on the part of lenders. The nominal rate, then, is the stated or contractual rate of interest observed in the market. The premium for expected inflation generates the Fisher effect: $i = r + E(\dot{p})$.

In addition to teaching and research, Fisher was a successful inventor who patented scores of devices. Among other items, he invented a folding chair and the Rolodex (wheels used in most offices today to hold business cards and addresses). Income from his inventions enabled him to invest. He was very interested in public health issues and put time and money into the temperance movement. He also invested heavily in health food companies.

Few of the reform movements Fisher supported ultimately achieved their goals. For example, the constitutional amendment that prohibited alcoholic beverages was repealed after it ushered in an era of lawlessness. Some health food firms he invested in—Kellogg's and Post—now produce such sugary cereals as Coco-Puffs and Sugar Pops, which says something about where the profit motive can lead even the most well-intentioned of reforms. Nevertheless, Fisher was an active participant in the social and economic debates of his time. His life was one of accomplished scholarship and useful invention. Fisher's ideas live on. Growing numbers of modern economists now echo his call for monetary stability.

thus, in such cases the Keynes effect drives nominal interest rates up. After borrowers and lenders have learned to expect the deflationary pressures resulting from contractionary policies, however, the Fisher effect brings nominal inter-est rates down. Focus 1 provides an example of both Keynes and Fisher effects in recent years.

Overall, natural rate analysis suggests that discretionary macroeconomic policies are futile in the long run; they cannot permanently reduce

FOCUS 1

Keynes and Fisher Effects in Action—1978–1982

FIGURE 9   The Keynes and Fisher Effects in Action

Expansionary money policies in 1978 drove real interest rates down via the Keynes effect as inflation exceeded nominal interest in 1979. Nominal interest rates rose to compensate for unexpected inflation in 1980–1981, even though inflation was falling; this was the Fisher effect in action.

Sources: *Moody's Bond Record* and *Business Conditions Digest.*

The Federal Reserve eased monetary policy in 1978, reducing real rates of interest (the Keynes effect). During most of 1978–1980, real rates of interest were actually negative or nearly zero. By 1981, real and nominal interest rates began to soar as financial markets adjusted to higher expected inflation (the Fisher effect). Figure 9 illustrates the Keynes and Fisher effects as they occurred during 1978–1982.

either real interest rates or unemployment below their natural rates. The advocates of a *fixed monetary growth* rule believe that discretionary policies work temporarily only if people suffer from *money illusion*. Even temporary reductions of interest and unemployment are harmful because they are achieved only by thwarting people's desires; everyone eventually compensates for having been fooled by policymakers. But can policymakers consistently fool people? A recent theory answers *No*.

New Classical Macroeconomics

You can fool some of the people all of the time,
and all of the people some of the time, but you
can't fool all of the people all of the time.

Abe Lincoln

You can fool some of the people all of the time,
and all of the people some of the time, and them's
pretty good odds.

Motto of Brett Maverick (a gambler played by
James Garner in a TV western)

Another challenge to demand-management policies has been issued by new classical macroeconomists who doubt that activist macroeconomic
policies will work consistently, if at all. Their
predictions are based on theories about competitive markets.

Competitive Markets

The theory of competitive markets is predicated
on a number of assumptions. The most important of these for analyzing macroeconomic policy
are:

1. All economic behavior is based on perfect
   information among market participants.

2. Transportation costs are zero, so all goods
   and resources can move freely and instantaneously between markets.

3. Buyers try to maximize their satisfactions;
   sellers, their profits; and workers, their net
   well-being.

4. All prices are perfectly flexible.

A perfectly competitive economy will operate
efficiently at all times, because any profit opportunities or opportunities for workers or consumers to improve their welfare will be exploited
instantly. The problem posed for activist policymaking is that fiscal and monetary policies based
on Keynesian analysis only work if the economy
is inefficiently operating inside its production
possibilities frontier. If the economy is efficient
and at its capacity, policy generates only price
adjustments (inflation or deflation), not quantity
adjustments (e.g., changes in output and employment).

Equally critical is the fact that fiscal and monetary policies will have different effects in the
short run than in the long run only if people are
ignorant either about the thrust of policies or
their long-run effects. We discussed in the previous section how expansionary or contractionary
policies might have different effects in the short
run than in the long run. Let us see why perfectly
efficient competitive markets might cause long-
run adjustments to occur instantly when demand-management policies are used.

Efficient Markets

Efficient markets theories suggest that activist
policymakers try to fool people in the fashion of
riverboat gamblers, but these policies do not
work—Lincoln was a better observer of human
nature than was the scriptwriter who authored
Maverick's famous line. In fact, these modern
classically oriented theorists go beyond Lincoln,
asserting that you can't fool all of the people *any*
of the time because markets operate efficiently if
substantial information about profit opportunities is widely available.

> The **efficient markets** *theory assumes vigorous
> competition for any ideas or information that
> might prove profitable. Competition causes any
> predictable abnormal gain from an investment
> to be exploited almost instantly.*

Profits that might reasonably be expected from
some activity will draw alert profit-seekers the
way garbage trucks draw flies. Thus, easily anticipated economic profits will evaporate because
of competition. When an attractive investment
becomes public knowledge, the cost of investing
will be bid up so that only normal returns can be
realized. Only above-normal profits that reasonable people would not anticipate remain as possibilities. Thus, extraordinarily high returns from
an investment are largely a matter of luck.

Rational Expectations

A close relative of efficient markets theory is the
theory of rational expectations. If people's expectations are formed rationally, they will learn
to identify the variables that shape the circumstances affecting their lives.

*The theory of **rational expectations** suggests that after policymakers pursue either expansionary or contractionary policies a few times, people learn how to predict both changes in policies and the policies themselves. Consumers and investors will then behave in ways that prevent predictable policies from having any real effect.*

Accordingly, adherents of the rational expectations approach believe that policy goals cannot be achieved, even in the short run, unless the effects of demand-management policies come as complete surprises to the public. Rational expectations theorists believe that predictable policies cannot consistently fool the public. This is a modern extension of the idea that inflation illusion is never permanent.

Natural rate theory is an important cornerstone for rational expectations theory. The concepts of natural rates of interest and unemployment are starting points in exploring the view that demand-management policy is impotent even in the short run.

Consider Figure 10. Suppose a heavy short-run dose of expansionary monetary policy shifts Aggregate Demand from AD_0 to AD_1, boosting prices and real output to P_1 and Q_1 respectively (point *b*). This drives down unemployment rates and both nominal and real interest rates. When people eventually begin to anticipate inflation, then output, unemployment, and the real interest rate return to their original values while prices and nominal interest rates rise (point *c*). After this cycle occurs once or twice, most people learn to anticipate it and try to take advantage of their ability to "predict the future."

Suppose you are one of those who have observed this cycle and begin following the FED's policies closely. If increases in the prices of bonds and declines in interest rates invariably follow expansionary monetary policies within a few weeks, then you should make some money if you buy bonds the instant that monetary expansion begins. Since you will be holding bonds when interest rates fall, the increase in bond prices should profit you immensely. (Recall the inverse relationship between bond prices and interest rates.) As you and other "money-watchers" try to put this strategy into practice, the demand for

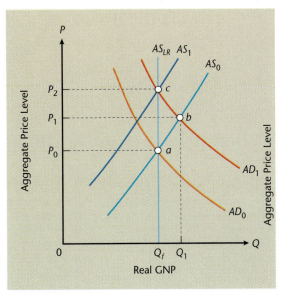

FIGURE 10 Rational Expectations and Equilibrium Output and the Price Level

Expansionary monetary or fiscal policy shifts the Aggregate Demand curve from AD_0 to AD_1. As both output and the price level rise, people begin to anticipate inflation and take steps to counter the effects of inflation and federal policymaking. Simple natural rate theory would predict a path for the economy of $a \rightarrow b \rightarrow c$, while rational expectation theorists would expect the economy to move directly from $a \rightarrow c$ as individuals instantly take countermeasures to expansionary policies.

bonds, and hence, their prices, would begin to rise just as soon as expansionary monetary policies are adopted. The short-run lag between expansionary policies and the declining interest rate will collapse to zero—the adjustment becomes instantaneous. In Figure 10, as individuals anticipate the effects of policy, the economy will move directly from point *a* to point *c* and Aggregate Output will not change.

This is not, however, the end of the story. In the long run, nominal interest rates presumably rise to reflect inflationary expectations. Therefore, you and all the other "FED watchers" will want to sell all your bonds before interest rates increase. Because the short run is now extremely short, the time to sell bonds is the instant you discern an expansionary policy. Because you will only be one among many unloading bonds when

FOCUS 2

Rational Expectations and Hyperinflation

[Rational expectationists] are optimistic that inflation can be wiped out with little pain if only the government makes credible its determination to do so.

Paul Samuelson

Hyperinflation—inflation of at least 50 percent per month—tends to cause monetary systems to collapse, so barter takes over. Most modern analyses of inflationary spirals suggest that halting inflation requires protracted high unemployment; presumably, the more rapid the inflation, the more severe the adjustment process. Surprisingly, several hyperinflations have been stopped almost overnight with minimal increased unemployment.

Figure 11 provides data for major hyperinflations in Austria, Hungary, Poland, and Germany right after World War I. In each country, the abruptness of the halt in inflation was as spectacular as the rise itself. How did policymakers gain control of their monetary systems to end hyperinflation? The answer lies in

the events preceding the hyperinflations and the actions taken to end them. Paul Samuelson's observation (above) provides a clue to the solution, but first let's examine the causes.

In commenting on inflationary finance, John Maynard Keynes noted:

It is common to speak as though, when a government pays its way by inflation, the people of the country avoid taxation. We have seen this is not so. What is raised by printing notes is just as much taken from the public as is beer-duty or an income-tax. What a government spends the public pays for. There is no such thing as an uncovered deficit. But in some countries it seems possible to please and content the public, for a time at least, by giving them, in return for the taxes they pay, finely engraved acknowledgments on water-marked paper. The income tax receipts which we in England receive from the surveyor, we throw into the wastepaper basket; in Germany they call them bank-notes and put them into their pocketbooks; in France they are

termed Rentes and are locked up in the family safe.[*]

After World War I, Austria, Germany, Hungary, and Poland all faced severe hardships and financed massive budget deficits by printing fiat money; all except Poland owed sizable war reparations. Their currencies depreciated at alarming rates, and inflation had a momentum that appeared unstoppable. But in Thomas Sargent's view,

. . . inflation only seems to have a momentum of its own; it is actually the long-term government policy of persistently running large deficits and creating money at high rates that imparts the momentum to the inflation rate.[†]

[*]John Maynard Keynes, Monetary Reform (New York: Harcourt Brace Jovanovich, 1924), pp. 68–69.
[†]Thomas J. Sargent, Rational Expectations and Inflation (New York: Harper & Row, 1986). This book discusses how these four and several modern hyperinflations were ended.

the money supply increases, the almost immediate result of an expansionary monetary policy will be to drive bond prices down and interest rates up in anticipation of inflation. But the story goes on.

If you expect inflation, you (and just about everyone else who is paying attention) will want to spend your money on goods and services while they are still cheap. (Remember, *buy low.*) If you manage a firm, you will immediately raise prices

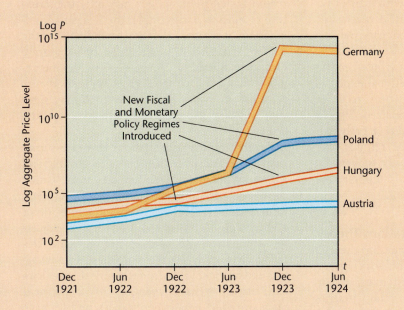

Log *P*

10^15

Log Aggregate Price Level

New Fiscal
and Monetary
Policy Regimes
Introduced

10^10

10^5

10^2

Germany

Poland

Hungary

Austria

t

Dec
1921

Jun
1922

Dec
1922

Jun
1923

Dec
1923

Jun
1924

**FIGURE 11   The Ends of
Four Major Hyperinflations**
Source: Thomas J. Sargent, *Rational
Expectations and Inflation* (New York: Harper
& Row, 1986).

One rational expectations perspective is that stopping inflation, especially hyperinflation, requires more than just temporary adjustments in monetary and fiscal policy; the entire policy regime must be altered. Government finance must change in a *credible* way so that the public *believes* that government is committed to eliminating the abuses that caused hyperinflation. Such measures ended hyperinflation in all four countries.

First, all four governments created independent central banks that were prohibited from issuing unsecured credit. Second, all four committed to relatively balanced budgets and agreed to cover government debt strictly through bond financing. Finally, the debtor countries renegotiated war reparations. Thus, by altering the "rules of the game," these governments literally stopped hyperinflation in its tracks.

Argentina recently went through a similar experience. Throughout the 1970s and early 1980s, inflation in Argentina rose until it exceeded 500 percent per year. In 1985, a new government instituted austerity measures, a new currency, and the will to stop hyperinflation. By early 1986, relative normalcy had returned to Argentina. It appears that policies that worked after World War I in Europe continue to work today.

when monetary expansion begins; higher prices might help you build inventories that will be worth more money if you just wait a bit before you sell. Thus, inflationary policies will cause almost immediate increases in nominal demands

for goods and reductions in their nominal supplies.

If you are unemployed, your inflationary expectations will adjust quickly to expansionary policies and you will be unwilling to accept a job at lower real wages. Therefore, unemployment will not fall below the natural rate as a consequence of expansionary policy. The end of this rational expectations story is that unless the government disguises its policies, an expansionary policy will almost instantly drive up the price level and nominal interest rates, with little or no effect on employment and output. A reversal of this story can be told for contractionary policies (see Focus 2).

Note that one essential difference between the simple natural rate theory and rational expectations theory is the speed with which accurate expectations are assumed to be realized. Simple natural rate analysis would predict a path like $a \rightarrow b \rightarrow c$ in Figure 11, while rational expectationists would expect a direct movement from point a to point c, with no temporary increases in output and employment.

Limitations of Rational Expectations Theory

Just how realistic is rational expectations theory? You and most of the population may ignore monetary and fiscal policies, but many major economic institutions carefully study government policies in the hopes of predicting future economic activity so they can get the jump on their competition or buffer themselves from hardship. Examples include banks, major corporations, unions, trade groups, and foreign governments. These groups do have substantial resources that can be shifted rapidly whenever the direction of policy seems likely to change. For example, price hikes are common adjustments whenever the imposition of wage and price controls appears imminent.

Other factors, however, may limit the potential impact of rational expectations adjustments. First, rational expectations analysis assumes that people are able to accurately forecast government policymaking when it often seems the government is unable to do this itself. Information about government policies is unavoidably expensive and imprecise. As a result, many people remain "rationally ignorant." Critics contend that, in the short run at least, government policy may push employment, prices, and interest rates away from their natural levels.

Second, this theory assumes that many people

understand how the economy will adjust to particular policies. Economic forecasters who have studied the economy for years often disagree on the paths of economic adjustment. The idea that anyone can systematically forecast the effects of policy with precision is extremely dubious. One reason is that public policy may alter the structure of output. For example, the Reagan administration increased defense spending in the 1980s, changing the structure of Aggregate Output. Similarly, expansionary monetary policy may reduce interest rates in the short run, resulting in rising investment that may alter the long-run production possibilities for the economy.

Finally, rational expectations theory assumes that wages and prices are perfectly flexible and adjust instantaneously to market forces. Union contracts, certain laws and regulations, long-term business contracts, and numerous other obstacles all keep wages and prices from adjusting immediately to changes in Aggregate Demand and Supply. It takes time for private investors and households to (a) recognize that policies and situations have changed, (b) implement plans to reflect new circumstances, and (c) have their new plans take affect. Government policymakers face parallel recognition, administrative, and impact lags. (These policy lags are discussed in more depth in the next chapter.) All of these reasons cause critics of this version of new classical macroeconomics to believe that short-run macroeconomic movements can be controlled by appropriate policies.

Real Business Cycles

Most economists, whether Keynesian or classically oriented, traditionally perceived business cycles as temporary departures from some long-run trend of economic growth. For more than 60 years, these deviations were viewed as resulting primarily from erratic changes in Aggregate Demand. This focus on Aggregate Demand helps explain why Keynesians typically argue that fiscal policy should be used to dampen business cycles, while modern monetarists and rational expectationists favor a stable monetary growth rule, viewing fiscal policy as counterproductive and/or ineffective.

Concentration on Aggregate Demand is viewed as misdirected by **real business cycle** analysts. This group, a subset of new classical macroeconomists, disputes the assumed temporary nature of business cycle effects and differs with the traditional view that changes in Aggregate Demand are responsible for changes in economic activity. Real business cycle analysts contend that most fluctuations in real GNP are permanent — not temporary. These economists also contend that shocks to Aggregate Supply are the principal causes of business cycles.

Shocks to the system, according to the theory of real business cycles, are often random and include such events as the introduction of new production techniques (e.g., Henry Ford's assembly line or the Japanese "team" concept), introduction of new products (the steam engine, lasers, and microchips), changes in climatic conditions (freezes, floods, or droughts), new discoveries of basic resources (oil fields in Mexico, Alaska, and the North Sea), price shocks for important raw materials (oil price hikes in the 1970s), or widespread changes in life-styles.

For example, consider the negative shock shown in Figure 12. Assume that the shock (e.g., an oil price increase) reduces the economy's productive capacity, thereby reducing labor's productivity. This reduces the demand for labor so less labor is hired, reducing employment and output. Graphically, the Aggregate Supply curve shifts leftward from AS_0 to AS_1, and real GNP falls from Q_0 to Q_1. Notice that this shift is permanent unless something pushes Aggregate Supply back to AS_0.

The policy conclusions of this analysis echo those generated by other new macroeconomic models: Government should follow passive policies. If government actively responds to a supply shock with expansionary policies, the end result will merely be increases in the price level. If contractionary policies are pursued in hopes of suppressing cost-push inflationary pressure, the result will be a longer recession than would occur if government policy had remained passive.

Most economists largely reject the real busi-

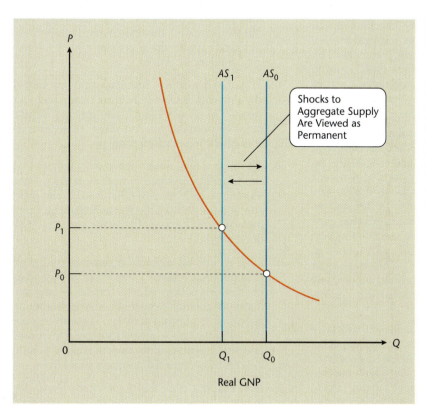

FIGURE 12 Real Business Cycles

Real business cycle theorists argue that shocks to Aggregate Supply permanently change economic activity. A negative shock (oil price increase) would cause Aggregate Supply to shift from AS_0 to AS_1, lowering employment and output. Changes in technology, productive capacity, and life-styles are the main instigators of business cycles according to real business cycle analysts.

ness cycle model for several reasons. First, its advocates have had difficulty in showing that periodic supply shocks have been sufficiently strong to explain cycles that have averaged roughly four years in duration. Second, proponents of real business cycle theory have been unable to connect particular technological events (or shocks) to subsequent business cycles (the lone exception is the 1973–1974 oil price shock). Finally, this theory suggests that negative Aggregate Supply shocks reduce productivity and the demand for labor, thereby reducing real wages. The empirical record of business cycles and wages does not support this chain of events. Nevertheless, this theory has sharpened our focus on the distinction and links between short-term business fluctuations and long-term economic growth.

All the different strands of the new classical macroeconomics are critical of activist macro policy. To this point in the book, we have addressed monetary and fiscal policy instruments and a few of their limitations. In the next chapter, we tackle other objections to discretionary macroeconomic policies and introduce some alternative approaches to policy.

Chapter Review: Key Points

1. The *Phillips curve* depicts a trade-off for policymakers between unemployment and inflation. Lower unemployment rates presumably might be purchased through higher inflation or vice versa; it is up to policymakers to choose the least harmful mix of evils. The Phillips curve appeared to be relatively stable through the 1960s, but it shifted sharply in the 1970s and early 1980s so that much higher rates of unemployment appeared necessary to dampen inflationary pressures. The reasons for the instability of the Phillips curve are the subject of a continuing debate within the economics profession.

2. Modern Keynesian analysis suggests that several factors in addition to inflationary expectations can cause stagflation and instability in the Phillips curve. Wages and prices are assumed "sticky," especially in a downward direction. Unexpected shocks to the supply side, rapid structural changes in demand or output, changes in labor institutions that generate disincentives for work, and changes in public regulatory policies all are capable of shifting the Phillips curve. The Keynesian *structuralist* approach emphasizes production "bottlenecks" as foundations for the Phillips curve.

3. The *natural rate theory* of the instability in the Phillips trade-off focuses on worker expectations of inflation. As labor begins to anticipate inflation, greater increases in wages are required for a given level of real output. Thus, accelerating inflation is required if policymakers desire to hold unemployment below its "natural rate," but even this policy will not work forever.

4. If interest rate targets or unemployment rate objectives are set below their "natural rates," expansionary policies may ultimately cause *nominal interest rates* to rise, not fall. *Natural rate* theorists believe that only temporary reductions in interest rates or unemployment can be obtained through expansionary policies, and even in the short run, only by "fooling" lenders or workers.

5. The *Keynes effect* predicts that monetary growth will decrease interest rates, and vice versa. The *Fisher effect* is the upward adjustment of nominal interest rates when transactors begin expecting inflation.

6. The *new classical macroeconomics* is based on the model of perfect competition, or *efficient markets*, which suggests that even in the short run, macro policy only works when the economy is operating inefficiently and that this does not occur.

7. The theory of *rational expectations* suggests that people eventually figure out how a given change in policy affects the economy and learn to predict how policymakers react to swings in economic activity. Thereafter, people will focus on what policymakers are doing and make adjustments that prevent the policies from accomplishing their objectives.

8. *Real business cycle theory* views shocks to Aggregate Supply as permanent and suggests that attempts by macroeconomic policymak-

ers to "fine-tune" the economy are either self-defeating or harmful.

Key Concepts

Ensure that you can define these terms before proceeding.

Phillips curves
structural shocks
adaptive expectations
natural rate theory
real rate of interest

Keynes effect
Fisher effect
efficient markets
rational expectations
real business cycles

Problems and Questions

1. What is the realized real rate of interest in the following situations?

   a. $i = 8\%$, $\dot{p} = 8\%$.

   b. $i = 12\%$, $\dot{p} = 15\%$.

   c. $i = 2\%$, $\dot{p} = -10\%$.

2. After full adjustment for the Fisher effect, what will be the nominal interest rate in the following situations?

   a. $r_d = 8\%$, $E(\dot{p}) = 8\%$.

   b. $r_d = 5\%$, $E(\dot{p}) = -3\%$.

   c. $r_d = 6\%$, $E(\dot{p}) = 18\%$.

3. Suppose people form their expectations about inflation adaptively, with half of their expectations being based on the preceding year, one-fourth being based on inflation the year before that, one-eighth of total expectations being based on inflation two years earlier, and one-eighth being based on inflation three years earlier. Based on the following hypothetical data, at the beginning of each year, roughly what rate of inflation would people expect for 1995? For 1996? For 1997? What would be the nominal rate of interest if the desired real rate of interest were 6 percent throughout this period? What would be the realized rate of interest during each year from 1995 through 1997?

   a. 1990   5% inflation

   b. 1991   6% inflation

   c. 1992   3% inflation

   d. 1993   7% inflation

   e. 1994   8% inflation

   f. 1995   3% inflation

   g. 1996   5% inflation

   h. 1997   4% inflation

4. If indexation is used for such retirement programs as Social Security, should pensions be adjusted using average changes in take-home salaries so that retirees share in the gains and losses of workers, or should cost-of-living adjustments be used to ensure pensioners a constant purchasing power income? What are the advantages and disadvantages of each approach?

5. Keynes argued during the Great Depression that the way to put unemployed workers back on payrolls and get machinery humming again was to increase the demand for goods and services by putting more money in people's pockets. His main argument concerned insufficient demand. If Aggregate Demand were increased, the economy would climb out of any recession or depression. Many economists believe that the Keynesian method for resolving the problems of recession may not produce the desired results in an era of stagflation. Why do most economists now believe that Keynesian demand management is effective only for problems like those of a depression era and cannot remedy the multitude of problems facing the economy today?

6. Some economists argue that the Smoot-Hawley tariffs enacted in 1930 were a major cause of the collapse in the stock market and the resulting Great Depression. Rational expectations analysis suggests that the impact of future events will be rapidly capitalized into stock prices. One political sage recently suggested that the Gramm-Rudman Act pointed to a new fiscal policy regime, accounting for the stock market's record performance in 1985–1987. What argument could you make that passage of Gramm-Rudman would be beneficial for the stock market? Are there other factors that might account for the stock market's sustained rise in 1985–1987?

Limitations of Stabilization Policy

Whether active or passive policymaking is more likely to moderate business cycles splits economists into two basic camps: Keynesians, who favor active countercyclical policy, and those who, based on classical reasoning, oppose activist policies. If policies operate in predictable ways, as most Keynesians believe, then macroeconomic stabilization is reasonably straightforward: Ascertain any trade-offs between price-level stability, employment, and economic growth so that goals can be set realistically, and then translate these goals into appropriate fiscal and monetary policies. Hard choices about goals may be necessary, but failures to achieve reasonable macrostability can be blamed on policymakers who are just "too dumb" to apply a few simple economic principles.

Adam Smith's preferred blend of laissez-faire government policies and "invisible hand" market solutions is mirrored in several modern schools of thought, including the *Austrian* school, a group of thinkers typified by Ludwig von Mises and Friedrich Hayek. (See their biography.) These groups contend that discretionary policy is more often a cause than a cure for macroeconomic problems. Various (and sometimes contradictory) reasons are offered for opposing discretionary policymaking. Some critics view activist policies as extremely harmful; others view them as largely useless minor irritants.

Many modern monetarists, for example, cite potentially erratic and damaging effects from activist policies as reasons for favoring a stable monetary growth rule. Most new classical macroeconomics, on the other hand, perceive that the reactions to policy by private individuals and firms may stifle the seemingly desirable effects of some countercyclical measures, so activist policies are seen as largely futile.

In this chapter, you will learn more about obstacles that make it difficult to properly design and implement discretionary countercyclical policies. Frankly, macroeconomic policymaking is as much an art as it is a science. Common difficulties facing policymakers include problems of timing and imperfect information, imperfect monetary and fiscal policymaking institutions, and imperfect politicians who adopt specific policies to maximize their prospects for reelection. These problems severely limit discretionary policymaking and stand as arguments for following macropolicy rules.

Lags, Doses, and Stabilization

Stabilization policy suffers from fits and starts because of lags in recognition, administration, and impact. Suppose that discretionary monetary and fiscal policies are equally powerful and

Ludwig von Mises (1881–1973) and Friedrich A. Hayek (1899–1992)

Ludwig von Mises was born in Austria and taught at the University of Vienna before fleeing to America to escape Hitler's invasion. As a youth he was fond of tennis, but when someone remarked that he was not very good at it, he replied: "The fate of the ball does not interest me very much." What did interest him was human reasoning's potential. Von Mises chose not to limit himself to a narrowly defined economics. He attempted, instead, to survey the whole range of human action. Von Mises's system of thought focused on the supremacy of the individual as a purposeful decision maker, constantly adjusting price, production, and consumption in order to live better and enjoy maximum personal freedom. In a free marketplace, *economic calculation* provides prices and profits as signals that motivate business to adjust production to the demands of consumers. But in a government-directed economy, agencies have no economic measure comparable to profits by which their operations can be evaluated.

Von Mises also rejected the Keynesian idea that a nation can solve the problems of inflation and unemployment by *countercyclical* fiscal policy. Such an idea ignores the fact that politicians have a strong propensity to spend in good times as well as bad. Von Mises added the conviction that government managers are always fumbling in the dark because they cannot possibly know all the data needed to make "correct" macroeconomic adjustments. He concluded that the likely outcome of *budget management* is inflation, followed by price controls and, ultimately, stagnation.

Friedrich Hayek was one among a number of Von Mises's brilliant disciples who later achieved prominence. This elder statesman of the *Austrian* school of economics became a Nobel Laureate in 1974. While Keynes advocated a very active role for government in controlling the economy, Hayek argued that the extension of government control is the enemy of freedom. He denounced a growing government role as "the road to serfdom."

Hayek decried constructivism more than anything else, calling it "the pretense of knowledge" and "the illusion of human omnipotence." **Constructivism** is the idea that enlightened leaders can remake society in the current fashionable image. Hayek believed that culture and civilization are not consequences of deliberate human design but are instead the products of the survival of society's successful groups. Hence, civilization depends on rules of behavior, not on goals. A couple of examples of con-structivism in action follow. In the early 1980s Iran's theocratic dictator, the Ayatollah Khomeini, wanted his people to be more zealous in following the precepts of Islam. His regime killed thousands in order to reconstruct society to his design. Hitler, too, was a constructivist, as was Stalin.

Hayek viewed Keynesianism is a much less virulent strain of the constructivism disease. Keynes's message is very seductive: Through simple manipulation of total spending, a government can control the twin problems of unemployment and unstable prices. Keynes's comforting message has not been lost on many politicians, who no longer consider themselves to be helpless before the convulsions of a business cycle or limited in what they can deliver voters. Keynesian policy analysis looks like an instruction manual for running the economy as a well-oiled machine.

The trouble, said Hayek, is that the economy is an organism, not a machine. Individual behavior and economic interactions are so complex that they cannot be manipulated in the ways many modern macroeconomists suppose. In vain attempts to maintain very low unemployment, government may feel compelled to spend faster and faster, so that prices wind up rising faster and faster as well. This kind of artificial stimulant, according to Hayek, distorts the price signals that indicate genuine scarcities in the marketplace when intervention is absent.

have equally harmful side effects. Because of the different timing lags that characterize them, there is still a question of whether monetary or fiscal policy is preferable.

Recognition Lags

Our perceptions of the present arc clouded, and our predictions about the future emerge only from more or less educated guesswork.

The time required for policymakers to realize that macroeconomic conditions have changed is the **recognition lag**.

Monetary and fiscal policymakers are equally affected. It takes time and effort to gather, compile, process, and interpret economic data so that we have some feel for macroeconomic trends. Even then, the data may be sketchy, contradictory, or misleading. Of course, if 25 percent of the work force were laid off tomorrow, policymakers would know by next weekend that we (and they) were in deep trouble. But our economy moves sluggishly, making it difficult for policymakers to determine exactly how hard and in which direction they should be steering.

Administrative Lags

After a macroeconomic change is identified, it still takes time to institute proper countercyclical policies.

The time required to implement new policies is called the **administrative lag**.

If recession seems to be on the horizon, monetary policymakers could print money and buy bonds (open-market operations), or they might lower the discount rate or reserve requirements. Reversed measures would be appropriate if inflationary pressures were picking up steam. Changes in monetary policy can be implemented quickly by the FED's Open Market Committee. Consequently, administrative lags pose only trivial problems for monetary policymaking.

Fiscal policymaking, however, does encounter major administrative lags, because discretionary changes in taxation or government outlays require legal changes. New legislation can take years to process, so minor crises may become catastrophic before (*a*) new laws are drafted, (*b*) congressional committees finish wrestling with questions about whose taxes to cut or raise or whose pork-barrel legislation to pass or kill, (*c*) both the House and Senate pass some compromise bill, (*d*) the president signs the bill, and, finally, (*e*) any legal challenges clear the courts.

This long administrative lag for fiscal policy might suggest a strong preference for monetary policy, which exhibits only short administrative lags. Some advocates of fiscal policy, however, suggest that this lag could be finessed if the president were granted discretionary power to raise or lower tax rates within narrow limits—say, 10 percent. Alternatively, the president might be given the discretion to impound funds for certain public works projects to fight inflation, or to authorize preselected projects if recession threatens. One major hurdle for this proposal is the reluctance of Congress and the voters to grant any president this much new power.

Impact Lags

It also takes time for any change in policy to affect the economy.

The time required for new policies to affect the economy is the **impact lag.**

Our $7 trillion economy can develop a lot of momentum—changing its direction through fiscal and monetary policies might be compared to using a rowboat oar to steer an ocean liner against a strong tide.

Even after legislation is passed, changes in most government outlays have long impact lags, because it takes time for old government contracts to lapse or for new contracts to be awarded and then begun. The personal income tax system, however, is the major fiscal policy tool for altering consumer spending via the multiplier process. Consumers quickly learn about changing tax rates, because their paychecks almost immediately reflect higher or lower withholdings. People rapidly translate tax cuts that increase their take-home pay into new cars, video cassette recorders, clothes, or more frequent chocolate chip ice cream cones. Adjusting to tax increases may be painful, but most consumers do so fairly rapidly because they must. The impact lag for fiscal policy may be long for changes in government purchases, but it is comparatively short when tax rates are changed.

In contrast, monetary impact lags may be relatively long and variable. When expansionary open-market operations are used, banks' excess reserves quickly grow. But bankers may ''hoard'' these funds if their confidence is down so that the lending → spending → lending sequence is squelched. Nevertheless, the loanable funds available generally rise and interest rates drop. While consumers may view this as an inducement to buy more durable goods, a decline in interest rates does not generally have nearly as large or immediate an effect on consumer spending as does a healthy cut in tax rates.

Lower interest rates will boost business investment, but investors may take time to respond. Decisions about new capacity involve extensive deliberations in the big firms that do the bulk of investment in our economy. Corporate planning is so complex that most major investments require heavy commitments of funds years before additional capacity comes on line. This extended investment process is countercyclical in itself because changes in economic activity may have little effect on these decisions in the short run. The impact of monetary expansion on consumption and investment spending is positive, but it may be both slow and erratic. While estimates of the effect of monetary policy on spending place the beginnings of the new spending at as soon as two or three months, the full effects of monetary expansion or contraction appear to take up to seven years.

Discretionary monetary policy is like an automatic baseball pitching machine that randomly selects its pitches. The first pitch a batter faces may take five minutes to float over home plate belt-high, while the second pitch whistles by low and outside. (If all pitches were identical, batters' problems would be over.) Just as the batter tires of waiting for the third pitch and starts across home plate for the dugout, the ball sud-

denly arrives. This analogy suggests that a variable lag is just as dangerous as a long lag. Baseball pitchers vary their speed or placement on purpose to frustrate batters. The variable impact lags of discretionary monetary policy are unintentional, but they similarly frustrate decision making in the private sector.

Thus, although fiscal policy exhibits a longer administrative lag than monetary policy does, this may be offset by the shorter impact lag and more certain outcome of revisions in tax rates. According to critics of discretionary fiscal policy, prolonged discussions of the need for tax reform or higher tax rates to eliminate ballooning deficits have introduced greater uncertainty for investment decision making. And the long and variable impact lag of monetary policy is a major shortcoming of discretionary policy in the eyes of proponents of monetary growth rules. Table 1 summarizes lags, effects, and major uses of several specific fiscal policies and the three main monetary policies. The table provides a glimpse of the complexity involved in choosing a policy mix.

Destabilizing Effects of Policy Lags

Critics of discretionary policies contend that recognition, administrative, and impact lags make fine-tuned macro policies an oxymoron. Suppose that the economy is self-stabilizing but that it does have a natural cyclical pattern as shown in Figure 1. The story of the effect of these lags may go like this.

Suppose the economy begins to heat up at the beginning of 1994. Policymakers recognize the emergence of inflationary pressures by the end of the first quarter of 1994 and implement contractionary policies by midyear. The braking effect of the engineered reduction in Aggregate Demand begins just as the economy would have begun to cool down by itself (point *b*). The effect of this seemingly correct policy is to cause a deeper recession than would have occurred normally in the latter half of 1995 (point *c*). Lags lead to a timing problem, making the cycle more severe.

The recognition, administrative, and impact lags consume nine months before proper expansionary policies to counteract this recession are

Table 1 *A Summary of Appropriate Lags, Timing of Major Effects, and Uses of Selected Specific Fiscal and Monetary Policy*

Policy	Administrative Lag	Impact Lag	Major Effects: Short Run vs. Long Run	Major Use
Fiscal Policies				
Change in taxes	L*	S	LR	Stimulate or curb private spending
Change in investment tax credits	L	L	LR	Stimulate investment, capital formation, and economic growth
Change in government purchases	L	L	SR	Countercyclical fiscal policy, pork barrel, etc.
Change in regulations	L	S	LR	Increase regulation to curb abuses and "cutthroat" competition; reduce regulations to improve efficiency in the market
Change in composition of government purchases	L	S	LR	Change the distribution of government spending — guns versus butter
Monetary Policies				
Change in discount rate	S	L	SR	Encourage or discourage borrowing (signals to market)
Change in reserve requirements	S	L	LR	Change the potential money multiplier
Open-market operations	S	L	SR	Week-to-week control of the money supply and interest rates

*The recognition lag is equal for both types of policymaking. The letter L stands for a relatively long lag, while S means that the lag is relatively short. The major effects of policies occur roughly in the short run, SR (1–3 years), or they occur in the long run, LR (4 years and over).

felt in the economy — again, just as self-correction mechanisms would have brought the economy out of the recession. Mistiming means that expansionary policies are too powerful and that the inflationary pressure of mid-1996 is accelerated (point *d*). And so on.

Figure 1 portrays the worsening of a business cycle by correct, but poorly timed, policies. This example suggests that active countercyclical policy may be self-defeating, actually making the business cycle worse than it would be with a fixed monetary growth rule and fixed tax and government outlay structures. For instance, you can stabilize "waves" in a water bed if you push

down on a wave at just the right time and with just the right pressure, but if your timing or pressure is off, you may synchronize with the waves and amplify them substantially. In a similar fashion, mistimed or incorrect policies may create chaos out of minor economic fluctuations.

Overdosing or Undermedicating a Sick Economy

Inflationary and recessionary gaps are, respectively, the decreases or increases in autonomous spending needed to decompress inflationary pressure or to push the economy out of a reces-

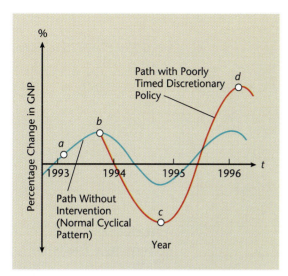

FIGURE 1   The Business Cycle with Poorly Timed Policies

You can stabilize "waves" in an unbaffled water bed by pushing down on waves at just the right time and with just the right pressure, but if your timing or pressure is off, the waves may be amplified. Similarly, incorrect policies may make business cycles more severe. If new classical macroeconomists are correct, business cycles self-correct quickly without discretionary changes in monetary or fiscal policy. Fluctuations may pose problems for proper timing of macroeconomic policy because of lags in (*a*) recognition, (*b*) administration, and (*c*) impact. It is even more possible that macroeconomic self-corrections may begin before all these lags have elapsed.

sion by filling the GNP gap. Unfortunately, these gaps cannot be measured precisely — because we never know the exact limits of our productive capacity, nor do we know in advance the precise sizes of autonomous spending or tax multipliers. Monetary policymakers are plagued with similar ignorance about capacity, and the values of either the money multiplier or its velocity may vary. [Recall that velocity (V) helps us measure how a stock of money is translated into spending: $V = PQ/M$.] Another problem for monetary authorities is that the growth rates of M1, M2, and M3 may vary substantially. Which of these should policymakers try to control? Of course, this is also a hurdle for establishing a monetary growth rule.

These difficulties make it nearly impossible for policymakers to know how much stimulus to inject or withdraw. At times, as with Franklin Roosevelt's first two administrations during the

Great Depression (1933–1939), discretionary policies may be "too little, too late." In the eyes of critics who advocate putting the economy on automatic pilot, policymakers more commonly administer too much medicine. Lags in discretionary policies make it easy to overdose the economy with stimulants so that recessions lead into periods of hyperactivity and inflation. The American economy began to exhibit these symptoms in 1968 under President Johnson.

Alternatively, excessive doses of sedatives may cause an overstimulated economy to crash into a deep depression. Opponents of fine-tuning cite the economic nosedives of 1974–1975 and 1981–1983 as evidence of the harm done by abrupt reductions in monetary growth after extended inflationary growth. In situations where occasional aspirin would cure our economic headaches, the FED may administer uppers and downers in a cyclical fashion. The result is that the economy follows a snakelike stop-go path, with demand-side inflationary cycles causing supply-side cycles, causing demand-side cycles, and so on, as shown in Figure 2.

Insulation Against Monetary Policymaking

Some modern Keynesians, most notably Hyman Minsky, also refute the idea that countercyclical monetary policy can be consistently effective. Their objection is based on a belief that technological changes in financial institutions are induced by *tight money* or *easy money* policies.

> **Financial insulation** *occurs when organizations develop new technologies that allow them to use money more efficiently so that more transactions can be supported from a given amount of monetary base.*

Among other effects, financial insulation tends to raise the income velocity of money (V). Here is one example of ways the financial system adjusts to tight money policies and, in the process, reduces the power of the FED's monetary tools.

Suppose monetary authorities try to combat

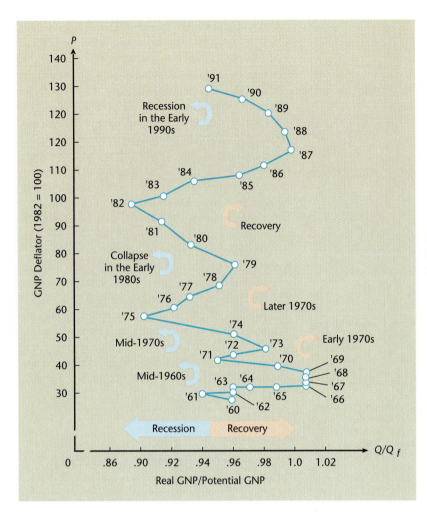

FIGURE 2 The Economy's Snakelike Path

A natural rate of unemployment of roughly 6 percent is assumed in this figure. Critics of discretionary policies attribute booms (rightward movements) and busts (leftward movements) of the economy both to mistimed policies and to policymakers' tendencies to administer overdoses. Keynesians argue that the economy would be far less erratic if policy were fine-tuned to cure our economic woes.

Sources: *Economic Report of the President*, 1991, and Frank deLeeuw and Thomas Holloway, "Cyclical Adjustment of the Federal Budget and the Federal Debt," *Survey of Current Business*, December 1983.

inflationary pressures with contractionary policies. Excess reserves throughout the banking system fall, and credit availability throughout the economy is diminished. Especially when interest rates are high, any single bank's profits are enhanced if it finds new ways to support more loans from given total reserves.

In the 1960s, bank officials found that they could conserve on reserves by pooling their excess reserves. If one bank needed funds temporarily to meet its reserve requirements, it would borrow some of the excess reserves of another bank at a lower interest rate than the FED charged at the discount window. The *federal-funds market* (a market for excess reserves) that grew out of this effort is now available to bankers across the country. Because of this financial insulation, banks can literally lend or borrow millions

of dollars for as little as one or two days at comparatively low interest rates.

Many institutions learn how to shield themselves from tight credit conditions. For example, high interest rates cause many firms to delay payments to suppliers while trying to push their own customers to make payments faster. Financial intermediaries, major corporations, accountants, and stockbrokers, among others, develop new techniques for minimizing money balances when a credit crunch hits. This is a "creative response" of the financial system. Discoveries of ways to dampen the effects of contractionary policy increase both velocity and the money multiplier and reduce the power of the FED. As Focus 1 illustrates, the FED's tools do not work as well when banks take steps to insulate themselves from the effects of FED policies.

FOCUS 1

Money, Prices, and Financial Insulation

Figure 3 illustrates how financial institutions may adjust to counter monetary policy. The growth rates of M1 (lagged eight quarters), real GNP, and the GNP deflator are graphed. Both real GNP and the GNP deflator track M1 growth during the 1970s. Beginning in 1982, price changes and M1 growth uncharacteristically diverged while real GNP continued on track. More recently, high rates of money growth have not translated into price increases because velocity has fallen. Many factors may account for velocity's decline, including financial inventiveness, monetary deregulation, disinflation, and declining interest rates.[*] One fact stands out: Basic departures from past relationships make implementing monetary policy more difficult.

[*]*For a detailed discussion of these issues, see J. A. Cacy, "Recent M1 Growth and Its Implications," Economic Review, Federal Reserve Bank of Kansas City, December 1985, pp. 18–23.*

FIGURE 3   Growth Rates of M1 (Lagged Eight Quarters), GNP Deflator, and Real GNP

Real GNP and the GNP deflator generally tracked the rate of growth of M1 until the 1980s. During the 1980s, the velocity of money fell due to financial inventiveness, monetary deregulation, disinflation, and declining interest rates.

Source: *Economic Report of the President*, 1991.

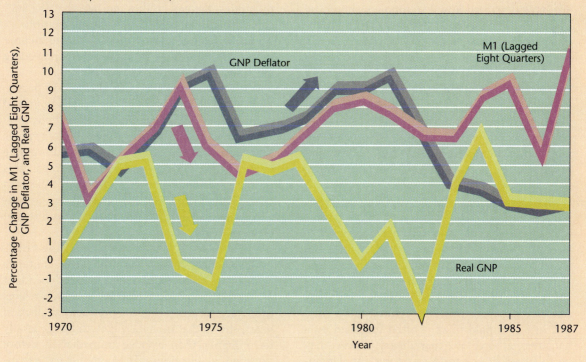

Discretionary monetary policy can be compared to a pesticide, with firms being a variety of insects. Just as initial doses of a new pesticide wipe out a lot of bugs, contractionary monetary policies may reduce the availability of credit, causing marginal firms to succumb. And just as the insects that survive repeated doses of the pesticide become immune to it after a few generations, the firms that have learned to adjust to credit crunches become immune to contractionary monetary policies. Moreover, these surviving firms have a profitable advantage: Many competitors will have collapsed during periods of tight money. Thus, adjustments by financial institutions to FED policies further limit the power of discretionary monetary policies.

Political Dimensions of Macropolicy

Every recovery is hailed by an incumbent president as the result of his own wise policies, while every recession is condemned by him as the result of the mistaken policies of his predecessor.

Gardner Ackley

We have described how macropolicy should be conducted if policymakers, for all their limitations, were selfless people interested only in the welfare of the entire populace. But macroeconomic policymakers are either politicians or their appointees. Might policies be affected by political goals? Both Keynesian and monetarist theories suggest that, in the short run, expansionary policies can move the economy toward full employment, while policymakers can use contractionary policies to combat inflationary pressures.

Political Business Cycles

Macropolicy has occasionally been compared to alcohol. Alcohol can be medicinal; a little can loosen you up and allow you to have more fun. At least in the short run, expansionary policies stimulate employment, investment, and new sales for business firms. Everything looks rosy. But just as a mild buzz is often followed by a hangover, a binge of expansionary policies may be followed by a period of drying out. Unemployment and inflation soar, and business activity slumps.

The idea that political tactics cause economic instability is reasonably straightforward. Incumbent politicians seeking reelection may hope for spillovers into the ballot box from short-lived pre-election upswings that follow tax cuts and a shot of new government spending. If monetary authorities are in cahoots with incumbents, they can help out with a chaser of expansionary monetary policy. Incumbents do well in elections during prosperity, but are turned out of office in droves when the economy sours. After the election, inflation emerging from politically motivated expansionary policies can be dealt with by a strong dose of tax hikes, cuts in government pork-barrel projects, and monetary restraint. Thus, democracies may be plagued by political business cycles.

Political business cycles *may occur if incumbent policymakers try to manipulate macroeconomic policies to enhance their reelection prospects.*

Politicians who adopt policies to influence voting patterns obviously hope that voters have short memories. Several studies indicate that the success of incumbents seeking to retain their offices is closely related to how fast disposable income grows during the year immediately preceding elections.

With these incentives for politicians to pursue policies leading to booms prior to elections and then to slowdowns immediately after the voting, what does the U.S. record show? Table 2 shows that between 1953 and 1990, our real disposable income typically grew at higher average rates during election years than during off-election years. The relationship is not perfect, but disposable income generally grew faster in presidential election years.

We already dealt with the issue of the FED's independence. Recall that the FED contends that it can do a better job if it is independent from political pressures. Figure 4, which relates monetary growth to recent presidential election years, shows that monetary growth has generally been higher than average immediately before presidential elections. These monetary expan-

Table 2 *Annual Percentage Change in Real Disposable Personal Income*

President(s)	Election Years	Off-Election Years
Eisenhower (1953–56)	2.7	1.0
Eisenhower (1957–60)	5.9	1.1
Kennedy/Johnson (1961–64)	4.1	4.2
Johnson (1965–68)	3.3	4.9
Nixon (1969–72)	4.1	4.0
Nixon/Ford (1973–76)	3.7	−.08
Carter (1977–80)	2.0	4.4
Reagan (1981–84)	3.1	.08
Reagan (1985–88)	7.3	2.1
Bush (1989–90)	—	2.0
Average	4.0	2.5

Source: *Economic Report of the President,* 1991.

sions yielded mixed results, however — the incumbent party's candidate lost four of the eight presidential elections during 1960–1988.

Political business cycles are not unique to the United States. Among the more striking foreign examples is the case of Israel. There were six major elections during the period 1952–1973. In every instance, the period immediately preceding an Israeli election was more prosperous than the period immediately after the election. After reviewing 1961–1972 data for 90 elections in 27 countries, an American political scientist found that for 19 of the 27 countries, "real disposable income accelerated in 77 percent of election years compared with 46 percent of years without election."[1]

In 1943, Michael Kalecki, a Polish economist, suggested that after World War II, cycles caused by business instability would be supplanted by political business cycles in modern democracies. The evidence seems to support his contention that when politicians have a working knowledge of fiscal and monetary tools, they try to use these tools for their own ends.

1. E. Tufte, *Political Control of the Economy* (Princeton, NJ: Princeton Univ. Press, 1978), p. 11.

FIGURE 4   Elections and Monetary Growth

In the past two decades, monetary growth has been higher than average immediately before presidential elections. (*Note:* The incumbent party and its candidate are shown for election years.)

Source: *Economic Report of the President,* 1991.

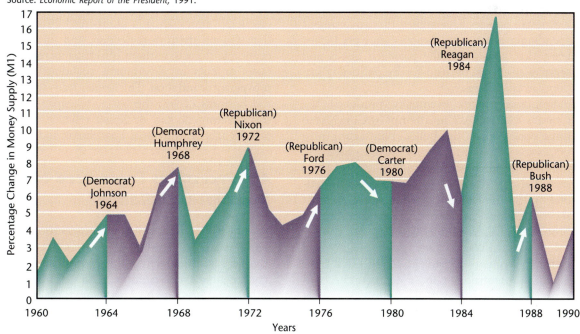

Has Keynesian Theory Induced Government Growth?

A final criticism of activist policies is that as politicians use these tools, the government sector will grow larger relative to the private sector. Opponents of large government have lost most battles in the past 50 years; government's role has expanded in most of the world's economies. Many of these critics identify Keynesian fiscal policy as the culprit.

Keynesian theory originated amid attempts to end a massive worldwide depression caused by inadequate demand during the 1930s. The Keynesian prescription? Spend your way into prosperity; ignore budget deficits and fight unemployment by boosting government spending and cutting taxes. Although largely ignored, the Keynesian cure for inflation is a healthy budget surplus. Nevertheless, as we indicated in our chapter on "Deficits and Debt," greater total deficits were sustained during the inflationary period from 1970 to 1980 than in the previous 200 years. And the deficits of the 1980s then tripled the size of our national debt.

Many conservative politicians and economists continued into the 1960s to preach the old-time religion of cyclically balanced budgets, but the Keynesian approach gained increasing acceptance from 1936 into the 1970s. Critics of Keynesian policies have argued that government spending inevitably mushrooms once politicians learn that governmentally provided goods and services need not be paid for by politically unpopular tax increases.

Immense deficits eventually produced the Gramm-Rudman Act, an attempt by Congress to force itself to bite the bullet. Eliminating programs and cutting budgets has proven a hard task for both the administration and Congress. Critics see a national debt exceeding $3 trillion, a federal budget exceeding $1 trillion, and persistent record deficits as evidence that Keynesian theory promotes governmental growth.

Since World War II, government spending and transfer payments as percentages of GNP have grown substantially in most democratic countries. This growth may be the result of the respectability of Keynesian policies. Until recently, deficits were not viewed with much alarm, even during inflationary periods. To the extent that deficits cause inflation, inflation should be viewed as a hidden tax. But if poorly informed voters blame government-generated inflation on unions or businesses, then politicians are encouraged to hand out "free lunches" — popular new government programs without unpopular tax hikes. Many voters are very aware of the direct benefits of deficit-financed special-interest spending but fail to recognize the inflation indirectly caused by such deficits.

During depressions, the deficits caused by higher government spending and lower taxes have beneficial effects — output and employment grow — but government also grows. Government outlays are seldom cut during inflationary periods, and proposals to raise taxes are political suicide. Few politicians are willing to be accused of "raising the price of government" by raising tax rates. The net result is that government grows during economic downturns but does not shrink during inflationary periods, as proper fiscal policy would dictate. According to critics of Keynesian policies, this occurs because the inflationary effects of high and rising government spending are disguised.

In summary, macroeconomic policies may be misused by politicians who cut taxes and increase government spending: (a) shortly before elections, anticipating a short-lived prosperity that will aid them in reelection; and (b) during economic slumps, without offsetting increases in taxes or cuts in government spending during prosperity or inflation. The former leads to political business cycles; the latter, to expansion of the government and declining reliance on the private acts of individual households and firms.

Are Recessions Engineered to Decompress Inflation?

The argument that political considerations upwardly bias the growth of government might suggest that incumbent politicians will do almost anything to avoid a recession. At times, however, inflationary pressure may overwhelm politicians' preferences.

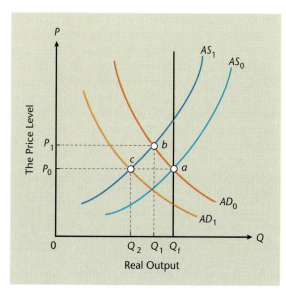

FIGURE 5 Dampening Supply-Side Inflation with Contractionary Demand-Management Policies

Dampening supply-side inflation with contractionary demand-management policies may diffuse inflationary pressures, but it is likely to generate a severe recession. If the Aggregate Supply curve shifts from AS_0 to AS_1, output falls to Q_1 but prices rise to P_1. If Aggregate Demand is reduced to AD_1, inflation is halted, but the economy suffers a serious recession.

Curbing Aggregate Demand can lessen inflation. A mild recession might defuse inflationary pressure caused by excessive demand, but severe depressions may emerge if contractionary demand-management policies are used to combat severe supply-side inflation. If, as Figure 5 illustrates, Aggregate Supply is shifting leftward from AS_0 to AS_1, equilibrium output will fall to Q_1. But if contractionary demand-management policies are used to keep prices stable, a severe recession (or worse) will result as output falls to Q_2. Mild supply-side inflations already bear the seeds of recession.

Recessions to Discipline Labor

Labor markets tighten during economic booms caused by excessive demand, so firms must hustle to fill their labor needs. Wages begin to rise, flattening profits. Hence, prices are pushed up because many firms seem to mark up costs by a fixed percentage to set their prices, a method known as *cost-plus* (or *mark-up*) *pricing.* Labor unions become more militant, strikes for higher pay and benefits proliferate, and labor productivity falls as more workers with lower skill levels find jobs during prosperity. Labor cost per unit of output rises as this occurs, intensifying upward pressures on prices.

Some observers argue that extended prosperity may necessitate a recession to dampen inflationary expectations and "discipline labor" so that workers will work harder and accept less. Only a bout of high unemployment will bring workers' expectations about wages, fringe benefits, and other job conditions into line with the real value of their production and firms' desires for higher profits. This is a minority view, unpalatable to most economists and policymakers, but the idea contains some kernels of truth.

Among the major benefits of recessions are the opportunities afforded firms to clear the shelves of "deadwood" and to boost labor productivity. Workers know that finding other jobs is more difficult during recessions and that substantial disposable income may be lost if they quit their present jobs. Therefore, they work harder and complain less. The natural long-run result of a recession is that profits rise and owners and managers of firms are again happy. The recurrence of this process led one radical economist, David Gordon, to entitle an article, "Recession Is Capitalism as Usual."

Policymakers' Abhorrence of Recessions

Engineering a recession to defuse inflation reflects desperation by nervous policymakers. Excessive unemployment makes voters irate and can lead to changes of the guard at the White House and in Congress. Business downturns create pressures for expansionary policies that may rekindle inflationary pressures. Some radical economists view recession as capitalism's way of restoring labor market equilibrium, but policies that predictably result in recessions are pursued only reluctantly. To some degree, however, the slumps of 1969–1970, 1973–1975, and 1981–1983 all resulted from such policies.

Incomes Policies to Combat Inflation

Monetary and fiscal policies have been our government's favorite macroeconomic tools, followed closely by more direct forms of economic regulation.

Incomes policies *include such strategies as wage and price controls, wage and price guideposts or guidelines, and presidential jawboning.*

Seven of the ten presidents following Herbert Hoover used some form of *incomes policy*. Wartime wage and price controls were abandoned at the end of World War II. For roughly five years, there were no explicit controls, but the onset of the Korean War prompted Truman to reinstate some curbs. Both sets of wartime restraints were mandatory, having the force of law. The Eisenhower era, from 1953 to 1961, was free of controls.

Guideposts were introduced under President Kennedy in 1962 and stiffened by President Johnson, who accompanied these efforts with considerable jawboning. These voluntary guideposts lost their bite as inflationary pressures mounted in the late 1960s, when both domestic spending and outlays for the Vietnam conflict escalated. President Nixon instituted full-fledged price controls, beginning with a 90-day price freeze in August 1971. In 1979, President Carter resorted to jawboning (with threatened losses of government contracts) to make his "voluntary" wage and price guidelines more effective.

Incomes policies are designed to reduce inflationary pressures without actually changing government spending, taxing, or monetary policy. If successful, both unemployment and inflation will be less severe. A wage and price freeze is the most restrictive form of incomes policy, followed by wage and price controls, guidelines and guideposts, and, finally, jawboning.

Evaluation of Incomes Policies

Incomes policies, like many other government policies, have both friends and foes. Supporters of wage-price policies point principally to their impression that market shares in many important markets in the United States are so concentrated that pricing decisions made within these "monopolistic" industries are not in the public interest. Properly administered controls presumably will make the behavior of these firms more compatible with the interests of society. Monopolistic attempts to expand profits are thought to cause price hikes that translate into supply-side inflation.

Unions or firms that dominate a market may unilaterally raise prices, fueling inflationary pressures. Many primary product industries (steel, oil, and lumber, among others) exhibit these characteristics, so their price increases tend to ripple through the economy. Proponents also argue that when the principal underlying cause of continuing inflation is the inflationary expectations of workers and firms, controls can simultaneously reduce these expectations and reduce the basic rate of inflation.

Opponents cite the results of the 1971–1973 wage and price controls as strong evidence that controls do not work. The evidence is diagrammed in Figure 6. The rate of inflation was actually declining just prior to President Nixon's announcement of a wage/price freeze in 1971. Throughout the freeze and during Phase II, when wage and price increases were strictly controlled, the inflation rate began soaring. Inflation continued even after controls were lifted in 1973 and it took a severe recession in 1975–1976 to temporarily slow the inflationary spiral. Figure 6 also shows that President Carter's guidelines had little effect on inflation in the late 1970s.

Critics have pointed to this evidence to counter the view that controls reduce the inflationary expectations of workers and businesses. These opponents contend that controls actually create the worst kind of expectation—the expectation that when the controls are lifted, prices will rise more rapidly than before the restraints were instituted.

Further, critics maintain that artificial wage and price restraints warp market signals and lead to widespread shortages. Long-term controls breed corruption in government as bribery for the right to raise prices becomes common. Black markets emerge when people seek shortcuts around shortages. Distortions are greater the

FIGURE 6 Inflation During the 1971–1981 Wage-Price Controls/Guidelines

Inflation actually increased during President Nixon's four phases of wage and price controls, and intensified, erratically, throughout the 1970s.

Source: *Business Conditions Digest,* January 1986.

tighter controls are or the longer they are in effect. Price signals to reallocate production from less desired to more desired items get lost in the shuffle because they are masked by controls. These problems might be handled by granting exceptions to the controls, but each exception precipitates numerous applications for other exceptions. The complexity of regulations and monitoring tends to escalate, and eventually the economy may be strangled by terminal red tape.

Guideline or guidepost policies unbacked by any legal muscle rely on appeals to patriotism. The battle is already lost if unions and managements of vital industries do not respond to the call. Most presidents have recognized this fact and have coupled voluntary controls with moral suasion or jawboning. Business and labor leaders are invited to the White House for little chats about antitrust investigations, public admonition, or various forms of regulatory harassment.

Such confrontations with business and labor seldom achieve more than surface compliance and public relations rhetoric. Firms commonly learn to announce even higher price hikes than they desire so that, when faced with political heat, they can roll back the prices a bit. In this way, business leaders and politicians can each claim victory.

A crucial question about incomes policies is whether such schemes, without appropriately restrictive monetary and fiscal policies, would actually solve the inflationary dilemma. An incomes policy could be seen as a panacea by policymakers, who might then feel free to follow expansionary monetary or fiscal policy if that suited their whims. Incomes policies are, at best, temporarily effective when expansionary monetary and fiscal policies are pursued; incomes policies will fail to hold the economy together for any longer than the very short run.

A Brief Evaluation of Policy Rules vs. Discretion

Many of the ideas in this chapter address the shortcomings of discretionary policy. Advocates of stable macroeconomic policy rules continue to mount powerful and often persuasive arguments that discretionary policies do not work as intended. But their assertions are at times contradictory. Can discretionary policies be perverse because of inefficiencies caused by lags, incorrect doses, improper targets, or venal politicians, and simultaneously impotent because markets operate efficiently or because of rational expectations? In combination, these arguments are logically inconsistent.

Advocates of discretionary policies also offer persuasive arguments, many of which were presented in Chapters 9 through 14. At times, discretionary policies have performed as advertised. The economic boom following the 1964 tax cut is one example of successful discretionary policy. On the other hand, the abysmal policy failures during the 1970s are testimony to the folly of fighting supply-side disturbances with demand-management techniques.

Whether discretionary policies or rules work better depends in part on the circumstances and on the people who control policies. However, the central questions remain: (*a*) Is the economy inherently stable, or is the market system unstable? (*b*) Can changes in spending, taxes, and monetary policies lend greater stability to a market economy, or are erratic government policies major sources of business cycles and instability? These questions cannot be answered definitively.

Just as generals are sometimes accused of always fighting the last war, economic policymakers in the 1970s used the demand-management tools that were developed to solve the demand-side problems of earlier decades. Table 3 summarizes various theories about demand-management policies and should help in organizing your thoughts about these issues.

Many economists view as increasingly moot all debates about whether management of Aggregate Demand is more or less important than policies to stimulate Aggregate Supply. Their perspective, outlined in Focus 2, is that spillovers from the increasing globalization of international markets swamp the macroeconomic policies of any single country in determining that country's prospects for prosperity or stagnation.

Although the supply-side policies of the 1980s yielded mixed results, healthy economic growth depends primarily on growth of Aggregate Supply, which expands a society's production possibilities frontier. Demand-side policy plays a less important role in economic growth and development. The next chapter focuses on aspects of Aggregate Supply that enhance economic growth and development.

Chapter Review: Key Points

1. Macroeconomic policymaking is at least as much an art as it is a science. A multitude of problems preclude perfect analysis and policy.

2. A *recognition lag* occurs because it takes time to get even a modestly accurate picture of changes in the state of the economy. An *administrative* (implementation) *lag* exists because it takes time to get the tax and monetary machinery in gear even when policymakers' plans are made. An *impact lag* confounds the proper timing of policy; the economy budges only stubbornly to the prods of the policymakers' tools. These lags, which may be long and variable, may cause discretionary policy to be more destabilizing than stabilizing.

3. Lack of precise knowledge about recessionary gaps, inflationary gaps, and GNP gaps, as well as uncertainty about multipliers and velocity, means that estimating the correct doses of monetary and fiscal medicine is extremely difficult.

4. Some modern Keynesians challenge the long-term effectiveness of monetary policy, arguing that adjustments in financial technologies will ultimately *insulate financial institutions* and make monetary tools inoperative.

Table 3 *A Summary of Theories about Demand-Management Policies*

	Critical Assumptions	Discretionary Monetary Policy	Discretionary Fiscal Policy	Monetary Growth Rules
Classical (Pre-Keynesian) (Policy is useless.)	Flexible wages, prices, and interest rates ensure full employment. *Supply creates its own demand.*	Only the price level is affected, and then in precise proportion to the money supply.	Irrelevant except to the extent that the size of government relative to the private sector is changed.	Might prevent price-level declines in a growing economy, but largely irrelevant. Money is a veil, not affecting real variables.
Keynesian (Policy works.)	Wages and prices are downwardly sticky but upwardly flexible. Interest rates will not fall below the level of interest of the liquidity trap. *Demand creates its own supply.*	Ineffectual in a liquidity trap. Only Influences Aggregate Demand through any decreases in interest rates causing increases in autonomous investment, which expands demand through the multiplier process.	Immediately increases Aggregate Demand via the multiplier process.	Irrelevant except to the extent that the interest rate is affected, and hence investment and Aggregate Demand are also affected.
Post-Keynesian monetarists (Policy works, but is probably harmful.)	Keynesian analysis may be correct for the very short run in its Aggregate Demand orientation, but classical assumptions are correct for the long run. Velocity and the demand for money are stable.	Nominal GNP will be proportional to the money supply. Discretionary policy causes business cycles. The Depression was a consequence of contractionary policies; inflation is the result of overly expansionary policies.	Affects the size of government relative to the private sector and may pose problems because of political pressures to print money to cover government deficits. Otherwise, irrelevant for macroeconomics, although crowding out may be a severe problem if government spending grows. Modern supply-siders also argue that potential GNP is shrunk because of disincentives when tax rates are high.	Permits the private sector to anticipate policy and facilitates noninflationary growth without raising the possibility of contractionary policies causing severe recessions.

A monetary growth rule will eliminate swings in real output because of changes in policies. Prices will rise only slightly if economic growth falls below monetary growth, and prices will fall if economic growth exceeds monetary growth. |
| **Natural rate theory (Policy is only temporarily effective, but it is also harmful.)** | There are "natural" rates of frictional unemployment and natural real rates of interest. Differences between natural rates and actual rates occur only when people inaccurately forecast changes in price levels. | Unemployment and real interest rates will decline below their natural rates only if people are fooled by overly expansionary policies. This can happen only in the short run; in the long run, everyone catches on. | | |
| **New classical macroeconomics (Policy does not work.)** | Markets are efficient. Rational expectations theory suggests that inflationary expectations will reflect predictable changes in policies quickly. | People will not be fooled by predictable policies, even in the short run, so expansionary policies will be immediately translated into higher prices and higher nominal interest rates. | | |

FOCUS 2

Internationalization and Macroeconomic Policy

Year after year, international trade accounts for growing shares of GNP in most countries throughout the world. Even the rapid growth of trade, however, seems slow when compared with growth rates for flows of funds between countries. International flows of funds were roughly six times greater than international flows of goods and services during the late 1980s, and this ratio appears to be accelerating into the 1990s.

Only small shares of these flows of financial capital between countries are used to pay for imbalances of international trade. Instead, they reflect the internationalization of markets for capital, which flows toward investments that are expected to be the most profitable without regard for national borders. A deposit in a new bank account in Delaware, for example, may be transformed into investment in new manufacturing facilities in Bangladesh or Poland within a few days. Symmetrically, a transnational corporation headquartered in Australia but seeking funds to finance the hostile takeover of a silicon-chip manufacturer in Hong Kong may find

that a broker in Berlin can offer funds at the lowest rate of interest.

The increasing mobility of financial (and ultimately, economic) capital improves the efficiency of economic activity throughout the world. An important side effect is that this mobility reduces the power of domestic monetary and fiscal policymakers everywhere to execute macroeconomic policies that are independent of global developments.

Suppose, for example, that the FED were concerned about inflation. If the FED tried to tighten U.S. credit markets by selling U.S. Treasury bonds through open-market operations, this might temporarily exert upward pressures on domestic interest rates. However, the higher U.S. interest rates would quickly attract, say, Japanese savers, who might buy more U.S. Treasury bonds in hopes that interest rates in the United States will soon fall. The net result is that the FED's contractionary policies could be largely offset by inflows of foreign financial capital. Similarly, expansionary open-market operations (purchases of U.S.

bonds) might be defeated because of outflows of financial capital from the United States.

Fiscal policy has also been weakened by the globalization of markets. Suppose a tax cut was initiated to stimulate the economy. The resulting increase in our National Income would be diminished because our higher income would cause us to import more, so that some of the expansionary impetus would be experienced in countries from which we import. Regional economic integration (e.g., the European Community, or agreements between the U.S., Canada, and Mexico) further dilutes the independent power of a country's monetary and fiscal policymakers, because prosperity or stagnation is diffused through the economies of the country's trading partners.

The internationalization of financial markets ultimately diminishes the power of discretionary policy. Advocates of passive economic policies cite the increasing futility of discretionary policy as one more reason why permanent policies should be established that allow markets to adjust to any economic shocks.

5. Incumbents' prospects for return to office improve as per capita disposable income grows immediately prior to elections. There is some evidence that policymakers try to manipulate Aggregate Demand to enhance their positions in the eyes of voters, which induces *political business cycles*.

6. Some critics of Keynesian fiscal policies also suggest that the government grows relative to the private sector because policymakers increase spending and cut taxes during downturns, but neither cut spending nor restore taxes during periods of prosperity or inflation.

7. *Intentional recessions* can decompress accumulated inflationary pressures and inflationary expectations. However, recessions tend to be very hard on political incumbents, so many politicians favor incomes policies of various sorts.

8. *Incomes policies* (mandatory wage-price freezes or controls, voluntary guidelines, or "jawboning") muzzle the effectiveness of the price system, creating shortages and widespread misallocations of resources.

9. The more involved a country is in international trade and finance, the less will be the impact of any given monetary or fiscal policy because the effects are diffused by foreign markets.

Key Concepts

Ensure that you can define these terms before proceeding.

recognition lag	financial insulation
administrative lag	political business cycles
impact lag	incomes policies

Problems and Questions

1. Evaluate the proposal of granting the president discretionary power to raise or lower taxes 10 percent in order to overcome the administration lag that plagues fiscal policy. If there are substantial differences between this proposal and the power the FED now has over the money supply, what are they? If such a presidential power were enacted, would the president or the FED have more discretionary power to control economic activity? Why?

2. If you were the president and were intent on having "four more years," what actions would you take to ensure a booming economic climate around election time? What might be the longer-term consequences of your policies?

3. Some economists argue that the Smoot-Hawley tariffs enacted in 1930 were a major cause of the collapse in the stock market and the resulting Great Depression. Rational expectations analysis suggests that the impact of future events will be rapidly capitalized into stock prices. One political sage recently suggested that the Gramm-Rudman Act pointed to a new fiscal policy regime, accounting for the stock market's record performance in 1985–1986. What argument could you make that passage of Gramm-Rudman would be beneficial for the stock market? Are there other factors that might account for the stock market's sustained rise in 1985–1986?

4. Interest rates skyrocketed in late 1979, with the prime rate exceeding 20 percent, but they then plummeted even more rapidly than they had risen. Interest rates then soared again in 1981 but dropped afterward. From today's perspective, which parts of these violent fluctuations represented the Keynes effect, and which parts the Fisher effect?

Economic Growth and Development

Economic growth is a major goal all over the world, in part because most people expect higher standards of living than their parents enjoyed and hope for even greater prosperity for their children. Before the Industrial Revolution, however, each generation lived much like their immediate ancestors. Identifying changes in the human condition that facilitate growth and development has challenged economists and social philosophers for centuries.

Americans gain from healthy economic growth abroad because trade now links people everywhere. For example, when the United States rebounds from a recession, the world economy tends to recover as well. Sluggish foreign economies, however, weaken demands for our exports. Prosperity abroad generates another benefit: Flourishing nations are less likely to engage in military adventures—they have too much to lose, and there is increasing recognition that military conflict tends to impose losses on all combatants.

From the 1920s into the 1960s, communist countries and countries based primarily on the market system competed intensely to see which would grow faster. The ongoing collapse of communist economies attests to the relative power of the market system as an engine for economic progress. Historically, economic growth (at least

our own) was regarded as unambiguously good. More recently, mounting concern about the environment and recognition that the world's resources are finite have caused many to ask, "Economic growth for what?"

Economic Growth

Most of us applaud economic development that enriches the quality of our lives, but is all economic growth necessarily good? If a population explosion increased the size of the work force and caused growth in our GNP, it might simultaneously reduce our average standard of living. Do we want maximum income? Maximum income per capita? And what about pollution and other economic bads that often accompany economic growth?

Connections Between Growth and Development

How are economic growth and development related? People become bigger as they emerge from the shelter of the womb and proceed through infancy and childhood into adulthood. But infants differ from adults both quantitatively

Growth and the Rule of 72

Many people are bewildered by all the concern over whether the economy grows at rates of 2 percent, 3 percent, 4 percent, or whatever the small number happens to be. U.S. policymakers and economists concern themselves with these small numbers because each 1 percent of growth represents extra production of roughly $50 billion worth of 1989 output—hardly small change. Because continuous growth is compounded over the years, a 1 percent difference in the annual growth rate would mean a total difference of approximately $500 billion in production between 1993 and 2000.

Growth is a cumulative process analogous to compound interest. If you are paid 10 percent interest on $100 compounded annually, then at the end of the first year your $100 stake is worth $110. At the end of two years you have interest on both the principal plus the accumulated interest, so your original $100 is now $121: [(1.10 × ($100 + $10) = $121]. And so on. Compounding calculations can be simplified by using the Rule of 72.

The **Rule of 72** *is a "rule of thumb" whereby the time required for any variable to double*

is calculated by dividing its percentage rate of growth into 72.

This rule works because growth or decline is compounded. Thus, if the annual interest rate is 10 percent, financial investments will double in about 7.2 years, not 10 years. A country's population will double in 36 years if population growth is 2 percent annually, but it will require only 18 years to double at a 4 percent annual rate of increase.

and qualitatively. Similarly, economies tend to mature as they grow and vice versa. Economic growth has only a *quantitative* dimension, while economic development refers to *qualitative* advances.

Economic growth *enables more goods to be produced;* **economic development** *entails improvements in the quality of life, in the qualities of goods available, or in how production is organized.*

Describing economic progress requires both concepts. Focus 1 discusses the Rule of 72, which is a handy technique for calculating economic growth and other quantitative variables.

Aggregate Demand, Aggregate Supply, and Economic Growth

What causes increases in potential Gross National Product? Before we confront the problem of growth in real per capita income or GNP, we need to explore the circumstances and events that cause potential real income itself to grow. The macroeconomic theory covered previously suggests that increases in Aggregate Demand during economic slumps can boost GNP toward full employment levels of output. While management of Aggregate Demand through monetary and fiscal policies may cause GNP to increase, this is not what we mean here by economic growth. Management of Aggregate

Demand is basically a short-term concept. Modifying dosages of Aggregate Demand is similar to administering food and medicine to a malnourished child.

Growth and development as an area of study focuses on enlarging potential real GNP. This is a long-run concept, so we ignore demand to look at expanding the limits of Aggregate Supply. Just as the malnourished child whom we have fed and medicated may remain developmentally impaired, so, too, proper Aggregate Demand policies do not ensure that a disabled economy will exhibit healthy economic growth. In this chapter, we will assume that monetary and fiscal policies are used to ensure that Aggregate Demand accommodates economic growth. Potential Aggregate Supply depends on the state of technology and the qualities and quantities of resources available for productive activities during some time period. All labor is not identical, nor are other resources—land, capital, or entrepreneurship—homogeneous.

How does growth in potential real GNP occur? Potential output rises through technological advances, increases in the amounts of land available, new discoveries of resources, capital accumulation, or through increases in the size or quality of the labor force. Although the land available to a given populace might be expanded by space exploration or imperialism, these strategies are so risky and expensive that in the long run, they are more likely to fail than to succeed. Growth, however, may be stimulated by a more efficient use of existing land or land reclamation. New discoveries of resources are so sporadic that we cannot rely on them. This reduces the feasible sources of economic growth to (*a*) increases in population and the labor force, (*b*) capital accumulation, or (*c*) technological advances. Let us examine aspects of each of these sources of growth.

Population and Labor Force Changes

Population growth per se may not yield economic growth. More people mean nothing for production unless the labor force grows, and the labor force drawn from a given population can

vary. We will treat this relationship first and then describe the interactions between population and National Income.

Population and the Work Force Population growth expands the size of the potential work force. All else being equal, if the work force increases proportionally as population grows, per capita GNP will decline. Why? Additional labor reduces the capital and land per worker, so labor productivity and per capita GNP will decline. This is one more example of the law of diminishing returns rearing its ugly head.

Consider Figure 1. Suppose that with 100 workers, 100 machines, and 1,000 acres of land we can produce 100 computers, 100 units of food, or any other combination on the production possibilities frontier labeled PPF_1. We assume that the use of labor is relatively more intensive in computer production, while capital and land are most intensively used in agriculture. If all these resources were exactly doubled, we would expect potential output to double. Feasi-

FIGURE 1 Increasing Population and Diminishing Returns

Unless all resources increase by the same proportion, the production possibilities frontier will expand unevenly and less than proportionally. This unevenness means that population growth will tend to push standards of living down.

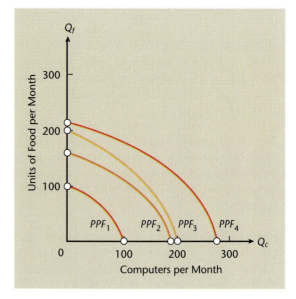

ble outputs are shown as the combinations along PPF_3, which is a radial expansion of (that is, it approximately parallels) PPF_1.

Now suppose we held capital at 100 machines and land at 1,000 acres, and doubled labor alone to 200 workers. The production possibilities frontier expands from PPF_1 to PPF_2: Maximum food output only grows to 160 units, and only 190 computers can be produced. The *PPF* does not expand to PPF_3 as labor doubles because we have not doubled land and capital inputs. Similarly, if labor were quadrupled to 400 units, diminishing returns would prevent the potential outputs of computers or food from also quadrupling. Using 400 workers, 100 machines, and 1,000 acres of land yields PPF_4, with maximums of only 205 units of food or 275 computers per month.

In a densely populated country such as India, needs for more housing, roads, and schools could cause standards of living to fall even if the labor force grew faster than population. Extra workers add to total output in all but the most heavily populated regions, however, so per capita GNP normally rises when the ratio of the work force to a given population increases.

The labor force as a percentage of the population is known as the *labor force participation rate*. Labor force participation rates are also calculated for such subpopulations as working women between the ages of 25 and 35 as a percentage of all women in that age group. Just what determines labor force participation rates? Certainly social customs and mores play a role. For example, the "Protestant work ethic" creates certain expectations, so roughly 80 percent of all American males between the ages of 25 and 55 are in the work force. Wage rates are also clearly important. High wage rates raise the cost of not working and encourage labor force participation.

Another important determinant of the work force relative to population is the rate of population growth. Variations in population growth rates may cause a society to have high proportions of young and dependent members during one decade and large numbers of old and dependent members six or seven decades later. Of course, this is only one of many possibilities.

Suppose birth rates have been declining for

some time. Labor force participation rates will first rise as the number of children in the population falls and more women are free to enter the labor force if custom permits. Then the work force will gradually decline relative to population as fewer young people enter the work force and the number of retirees rises relative to population. Finally, labor force participation will stabilize. Can you outline some of the short- and long-term economic effects of the post–World War II "baby boom"? Couple the high birth rates of the late 1940s and 1950s with the recent declines in birth rates and the gradually lengthening life span in the United States. What will happen to the number of dependents per worker over time? What are the implications for our Social Security system? For the health-care industry? Other groups?

Population Growth and Subsistence

In Chapter 5, we indicated that many early economists viewed unrelenting population growth as irresistibly depressing our existence down toward a subsistence level. Technological advances or extended periods of favorable weather for agriculture would simply result in higher wages, then population growth, and, ultimately, the misery of an even larger number of people. In the oft-quoted words of the Reverend Thomas Malthus, written in 1798:

I think I may fairly make two postulata. First, that food is necessary to the existence of man. Secondly, that the passion between the sexes is necessary, and will remain nearly in its present state . . . .

These two laws ever since we have had any knowledge of mankind, appear to have been fixed laws of our nature . . . . Assuming, then my postulata as granted, I say that the power of population is indefinitely greater than the power in the earth to produce subsistence for man . . . . Population, when unchecked, increases in a geometrical ratio.

Subsistence only increases in an arithmetical ratio. A slight acquaintance with numbers will show the immensity of the first power in comparison of the second.[1]

Reverend Malthus meant that food output might grow in a sequence like 1, 2, 3, 4, 5, 6, ... But if there were enough food, space, and other necessities, then human population would grow in a sequence like 1, 2, 4, 8, 16, 32, . . . (much like rabbits). Population would be kept in check, however, by disease, starvation, or war, to grow only at the same pace as food: 1, 2, 3, 4, ... This theory may draw a grim picture of how human population is naturally regulated, but such a fate seemed inevitable to Malthus.

A corollary of this theory is that population will be constantly pressing on the means of subsistence. The theory provides for a number of limits that Malthus classified as either positive (things that increase deaths) or preventive (things that reduce births). Each possible limit to population was seen as being derived from limited food supply; starvation constitutes the ultimate check in Malthus's theory. In this way, Malthus introduced the notion of a physiological "standard of living" that regulates population.

The second edition of Malthus's *Essay on the Principle of Population* (1st ed., 1798) allowed habits to influence the minimal standard of living — a notion designed to explain the fact that laboring classes in several countries during Malthus's era lived at levels considerably above subsistence. Malthus nevertheless felt that almost insurmountable difficulties block permanent improvement of the condition of the working classes. His theory states that changes in economic conditions ultimately yield no change in the average quality of life, only a decrease or increase of people living at this constant standard. Malthus preached that only through sexual continence could we avoid his grim predictions, but he was so pessimistic about the prospects for worldwide chastity that, to him, a razor's-edge existence for the bulk of humanity seemed inevitable.

Malthusian population theory, influential and popular throughout much of the nineteenth century, lost favor rapidly once scholars recognized that Malthus had underestimated the rate of technical change. Modern critics of Malthus's theory point out that humans, unlike rabbits, possess the ability to innovate and alter the carrying capacity of their environment. The most pertinent technological advances include several efficient birth control techniques and machinery and knowledge that have allowed food supplies to grow rapidly during the past century.

Prophets of doom and eternal optimists seem to share an inability to predict future directions for specific technological advances. For example, someone in the late 1800s might have predicted that the United States would "never sustain 250 million people because there wouldn't be enough land to pasture each person's horse." Our imaginations tend to be limited to the here and now, prisoners of current technologies. Thus far, optimists who believe that technological advances will permit adequate food, clothing, and shelter for the steadily increasing world population have been correct. There is little evidence of any increase in the proportion of the world's population living a razor's-edge existence.

Nevertheless, exploding populations in many underdeveloped countries have recently reawakened interest in Malthus's ideas. Many emerging countries have the worst of both worlds: the high birth rates of a typical agrarian economy and the low death rates of an industrialized economy. Barring major progress in the near future, these countries may face the unsavory choice of limiting the sizes of families — in opposition to widespread social values and religious beliefs — or the Malthusian checks of famine and disease that stem from limited food supply.

It is unclear whether overpopulation causes underdevelopment or whether economic development will cure overpopulation. In most advanced societies, children seem to be regarded as "inferior goods." That is, as per capita income rises, there is a tendency to substitute a higher standard of living and more leisure for more children, despite the fact that more children can be afforded at the higher income levels.

---

1. Rev. Thomas Malthus, *Essay on the Principle of Population*, 1/ed. (London: 1798), privately published.

Table 1 *Percentage Annual Population Growth for Selected Countries (Average Rates for 1980–1990)*

Developed Countries		Less Developed Countries	
Country	**Percent**	**Country**	**Percent**
Austria	0.0	Algeria	3.0
Belgium	0.0	Bangladesh	2.8
Canada	1.0	Brazil	2.5
Czechoslovakia	0.3	China	1.3
France	0.5	Ecuador	2.9
Germany	−.1	Ghana	3.6
Italy	0.2	Honduras	3.5
Japan	0.6	India	2.1
Norway	0.3	Iran	3.6
Sweden	0.1	Jordan	3.5
U.S.A.	1.0	Mexico	2.2
USSR	0.9	Pakistan	2.9
		Uganda	3.1
		Zambia	3.7
Average	0.3		2.9

Source: U.S. Department of Commerce, Bureau of the Census, *Statistical Abstract of the United States,* 1990.

The idea that equilibrium occurs at subsistence levels of income may seem naïve to people in advanced nations. The widespread misery and hardship experienced throughout much of Africa, Asia, and South America, however, at least partially confirm long-term economic forecasts made more than 180 years ago by Malthus and his cohorts. How have the people of Western Europe, Japan, and North America escaped this fate? Their production and incomes have grown faster than their populations, which in some nations have recently seemed at a standstill. In fact, as Table 1 indicates, population in many developed countries tends to be relatively stable or even declining, while primitive and less developed nations continue to experience explosive population growth.

But why has population growth in highly developed societies not responded to economic growth, driving per capita income down to subsistence levels? A partial answer to this question lies in the recent availability of low-cost, effective birth control devices—a development that Malthus would have regarded as immoral. More critically, rapid technological advances and the accumulation of both physical and human capital have caused income in developed nations to grow more rapidly than population. Hence, although war has been all too common, we have not had to endure the starvation and plagues that Malthus viewed as the other natural checks on population.

Saving, Investment, and Capital Formation

Potential real output will grow with increases in the labor force, but per capita income will grow only when the quality and/or quantities of the resources we work with expand. Let us take a bird's-eye view at how the capital stock grows so that you can appreciate the difficulty of traveling this route to the good life.

Recall that investment is a major component of GNP and that production and income (and, consequently, saving and investment) are flow variables. How is the flow of investment translated into a newer and bigger capital stock (K)?

Well, gross investment minus depreciation is net investment (I), which equals net *capital accumulation* during a given time period (t). That is, $\Delta K/\Delta t = I$. Omitting both government and the foreign sector for now, investment during any period will equal saving: $C + S = C + I$.

Thus, $S = I$. This familiar equation reveals that rates of saving must be high to achieve the high levels of investment necessary for rapid capital formation. Figure 2 indicates that if we choose to consume much and invest little of our National Income (point *a* on PPF_{1992}), economic growth will proceed slowly. On the other hand, if our society chooses to sacrifice substantial potential consumption (point *b*), we will be able to produce and consume at higher levels in the future because of the extra capital accumulation that lower current consumption permits.

The share of National Output devoted to capital goods instead of consumer goods may reflect individual decisions alone, or it may result from collective choice through government. When this decision is left to individuals, there is *voluntary saving*. When governments follow policies that force consumption down to allow capital accumulation, we describe the process as *involuntary saving*.

Voluntary Saving

The act of saving can be viewed as a decision to delay consumption. Just what factors influence the choice between consuming now and postponing consumption so that we can enjoy more later? Although there are a number of considerations, two important influences on individuals' consumption/saving choices are the interest rates paid to savers and the level of income. A third significant influence may be the distribution of income.

Interest Rates The Keynesian Revolution ushered in a de-emphasis on the importance of interest rates in determining rates of saving, suggesting that income is the major determinant of the level of saving. There has been a recent resurgence in the classical belief that the interest rate paid savers is critical in determining the saving/investment decision. The argument runs along the following lines.

An increase in the interest rate received by savers (who are the ultimate lenders) raises the relative price of consumption today versus consumption tomorrow. Thus, higher interest rates cause people to postpone consumption. Increases in interest rates will also discourage people who are marginal borrowers and who would use their borrowings for consumer purchases. This means that the quantity of funds supplied to investors will grow as interest rates rise, facilitating investment.

Must higher interest rates paid to savers discourage investment? Not necessarily. After-tax interest income is the concern of savers, and high after-tax rates of return are the goals of investors. A variety of government policies can be manipulated so that the net interest rates received by savers rise, while the interest costs of investors fall. For example, President Bush proposed restoring especially low tax rates for investment incomes (capital gains) and expanding eligibility

FIGURE 2   The Effects of Consumption/Savings Choices on Economic Growth

Societies that invest more by consuming less will experience greater economic growth and will expand potential consumption in the future. High rates of investment require high rates of saving.

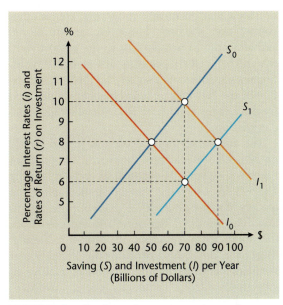

FIGURE 3 Saving, Investment, and Interest Rates

Saving can be encouraged by raising the after-tax interest rates paid to savers; some supply-side policies will also encourage investment because the net interest costs to investors fall, while after-tax rates of return on investment are increased.

for tax-exempt *Individual Retirement Accounts* (*IRAs*) to more savers.

Suppose that in Figure 3, the initial equilibrium between investment (curve I_0) and saving (S_0) resulted in savers receiving and investors paying a taxable 8 percent interest rate on $50 billion in loanable funds. The Bush plan of tax breaks for both savers and investors could increase the demand for investment goods to I_1, while simultaneously increasing saving from S_0 to S_1 — if savers view an untaxed 6 percent interest rate (on S_1) as equal to a taxed interest rate of 10 percent (on S_0). After interest is exempted from taxes and taxes on capital gains are slashed, investors have $90 billion available to invest at an annual interest cost to them of 8 percent.

Other policies to simultaneously increase after-tax interest payments to savers and after-tax rates of return to investors include general reductions in marginal tax rates, rapid depreciation allowances, or investment tax credits. Direct government subsidies to investors would also automatically reward savers as the demand for

investment grew. Taxes on consumption rather than income would stimulate saving and facilitate investment; saving would be deducted from taxable income if this proposal were enacted.

This line of attack is increasingly popular. For example, after suffering a serious recession in 1985, Singapore's Economic Committee adopted a strong supply-side approach to revive Singapore's sagging economic growth rate, including (*a*) sharply reduced corporate and personal income tax rates, (*b*) tax breaks for firms engaged in research and development, (*c*) cuts in compulsory pension fund payments (similar to our Social Security taxes), and (*d*) pressure on Singapore's government to stabilize laws and regulations and reduce the uncertainty encountered in business planning. Singapore's rate of growth did recover somewhat during 1985–1990. These are only a few examples of the supply-side policies that many analysts see as the road to economic growth.

Income In a Keynesian model, income (*Y*) largely determines saving (*S*). The relationship between the average propensity to save (*S/Y*) and income is important in understanding barriers that limit economic growth in impoverished countries. If you are poor, you face the hard alternatives of consuming at low levels forever or reducing already low levels of consumption now to finance investments that might pay off in the future. You faced a similar choice when you decided to invest in your education; you probably could be consuming more if you were not in school. Hardships encountered in this saving/consumption decision are less of a burden for wealthy people or wealthy countries. Widespread poverty, on the other hand, inhibits saving and capital accumulation.

Inequality Impoverished countries tend to have less-equal income distributions than highly developed nations. One way to accumulate capital is to rely on high saving rates by the wealthy and to hope that current deprivation of the masses will pay off in higher incomes for future generations. This idea is called the *trickle-down theory*. The wealthy may not save in ways that foster domestic growth, however; instead, they might buy foreign stocks or bonds or consume imported luxury goods. Foes of income redistribution programs often assert that saving and investment will fall if money is transferred from the rich to the poor. They argue that recent declines in American saving relative to GNP are consequences of rapid expansion of social programs.

Involuntary Saving

Governments do have some alternatives to voluntary saving if, for whatever reasons, they view voluntary saving and capital accumulation as inadequate for the desired growth rate. The trick is to divert relatively more of total output into the production of new capital goods by forcing consumption down.

Central Planning and Confiscation Government sets wages and prices in a centrally planned economy. Under Soviet five-year plans initiated in 1929 and still used today, wages were held low relative to individual output, while prices for most consumer goods were kept artificially high. Holding consumption far below production forced people to "save." This forced saving enabled the Soviet economy to grow, and the USSR rapidly attained the status of a world power. The costs of this forced growth were declines in already low standards of living.

The Marxist term *surplus value* refers to gaps between what people are paid and the average value of their total output. Marxists contend that capitalists exploit workers by seizing surplus values. It is ironic that Marxist societies are historically among the most exploitative. Although Stalin was succeeded by Khrushchev, Brezhnev, and now Gorbachev — each seemingly more moderate than his predecessor — the USSR has only gradually reduced its "expropriation" of surplus value. This "expropriation strategy" was intended to generate rapid economic growth, but we now know that economic growth in the USSR was much slower than it was in many countries that relied more heavily on private decisions about saving and investment.

This sort of exploitation is just one way a government can confiscate resources to use for capital accumulation and economic growth. Revolu-

tionary "land reform" programs are another confiscation method: Large estates are seized and allocated to peasants, or to the government, which then selects peasants as tenants. Revolutionary governments also rely on direct confiscation of the factories or financial assets of deposed wealthy elites as sources for "social" capital accumulation.

The apparently rapid evolution (based largely on bloated statistics) of the Soviet Union from "sleeping giant" to industrial power during 1930–1970 seemed a model of success for the leaders of many underdeveloped countries to follow. The result? Their countries suffered from the inefficiency inherent in central planning. Moreover, downward revisions of official Soviet statistics paint an increasingly bleak picture of growth since 1970. To remedy recent slowdowns in the USSR, President Gorbachev's new economic policy (*perestroika*) calls for heavier reliance on market forces. The transition costs of this change in orientation have included sharply reduced forced rates of saving, high rates of unemployment, and a broad collapse of Soviet productivity. Although the forced saving of the USSR had mixed results, other ways to force higher saving exist in democratic, market-oriented economies: inflation and taxation.

Inflation A government can issue contracts for schools, highways, or industrial facilities and then pay the contractors with freshly printed money. If the economy is initially at full employment, inflation will crowd out private consumption. This has been a very popular form of forced saving in a number of countries, most notably in South America. For example, from the 1950s through the 1970s, Brazil experienced high rates of real economic growth despite high inflation. The Brazilian economy faltered, however, in the 1980s — in part because its enormous foreign debt was stated in terms of foreign, not Brazilian, currency. A new government's attempts to halt the momentum of past inflationary policies had resulted in a relatively severe recession during 1990–1991.

Taxation High rates of taxation may also be used to reduce private purchasing power and consumption and to increase rates of government investment. But there is a danger that very high tax rates may result in such severe disincentives for work effort and private investment that GNP falls so much that tax revenues shrink.

Capital Widening and Deepening

The rate at which the capital stock grows is crucial for economic growth and determines the relative capital/labor mix in the economy.

Capital widening *occurs if the capital stock grows, but only at or below the percentage growth rate of the labor force.*

Let us assume that the labor force is a fixed percentage of population. Capital widening (even if population and capital grow at identical rates) will not even stabilize per capita GNP, because the increased doses of capital and labor relative to land result in diminishing returns. Because land resources cannot grow, it is likely that even if the growth of the capital stock does keep pace with population, standards of living will fall.

Capital deepening *occurs when the capital stock grows faster than population.*

The cumulative effect of high rates of saving and investment (capital deepening) over an extended period is a higher ratio of capital to labor (the K/L ratio). This tends to raise labor productivity and yield higher levels of real per capita income. However, the fixity of land yields diminishing returns in the enhanced labor productivity that occurs as the capital stock grows. Thus, the higher a country's capital-to-labor ratio, the harder it is to use new capital formation as a source of additional economic growth.

Recently, the growth rates of the "four tigers" — South Korea, Taiwan, Hong Kong, and Singapore — slowed down. Earlier double-digit real growth was based on the simple formula of labor intensive exports. But wage rates rose faster than productivity as these economies grew. Slower growth in the 1980s caused policymakers in all four countries to try to expand their capital-to-labor ratios by channeling investment into capital intensive, high-tech industries.

South Korea and Singapore have tried tax breaks, credits for private groups, government public works projects, and higher wage floors to discourage labor intensive investment. The results have been disappointing. Capital deepening has not produced growth rates that exceed those in Hong Kong and Taiwan, whose governments decided to do nothing to make one industry more attractive than another.

The preceding analysis suggests that even though rich countries with high capital to labor ratios may find it easier than poor countries to finance capital accumulation through saving, capital deepening is less likely to foster growth in rich countries than in poor ones. It is crucial, however, that saving be channeled to the most productive investments — a task that seems to be done better by unregulated financial markets than by government planners. Nevertheless, many analysts who recognize that U.S. growth rates may have been lower than those experienced in parts of Western Europe and along the Pacific rim (Taiwan, South Korea, Singapore, Hong Kong, Japan, and parts of China) predict that growth rates elsewhere in the world will slow down as other countries attain our levels of per capita GNP.

Saving to facilitate capital formation can be voluntary, or governments can use various tactics to compel greater saving. Voluntary saving is encouraged by attractive interest rates and high per capita income. Centrally planned economies can force consumption below production, thus creating forced savings. Several Far Eastern countries have recently discovered that as a country's capital-to-labor ratio grows, the generation of further growth through capital deepening faces diminishing returns.

Finally, critics of the traditional capital formation → development sequence point out that added capital may not help for several reasons. First, housing construction typically absorbs a sizable chunk of total investment (roughly 30 percent in the U.S. from 1980 to 1990). This spending, critics argue, should be classified as spending on consumer durables. Second, much investment is often public investment for social/political reasons, and rates of return may be quite low. Investment that yields excess capacity and underutilization of plants and equipment is especially useless. For example, the British steel industry spent huge sums on plant modernization in the 1970s. But their new plants were consistently underutilized and therefore added little to National Income. (After Prime Minister Thatcher sold these plants to private owners in the 1980s, the British steel industry recovered somewhat.) These critics argue that real long-term economic growth is the result of technological advances, changes in habits, and advances in education. We will now examine one widely accepted ingredient of growth—technological change.

Technological Advances

Given amounts of resources, if used efficiently, will produce specific levels of output over a stated time interval. At a later time it may be possible to produce more output with the same resources. This is not magic.

> **Technological change** *is the process that permits us to produce more from a given resource bundle, or the same output with fewer resources.*

Subcategories of technological change include (*a*) greater efficiency in market processes, (*b*) improved knowledge about how to combine resources, (*c*) totally new production processes, (*d*) improvements in the qualities of human and nonhuman resources, and (*e*) new inventions and innovations. The idea of "progress" is inextricably bound up in the process of technological change.

Technological change can be viewed in two ways. In one sense it is embodied in new forms of capital; in another, technical changes or innovations encourage substantial investment and thus increase the capital stock. The emergence of money, electricity, automobiles, supermarkets, and computer chips are examples. Joseph Schumpeter saw major technological breakthroughs as avenues for increased profits for capitalists and as the major source of progress for society.

Technological change can be stimulated by research and development. Innovative entrepreneurs such as Thomas Edison, Alexander Gra-

ham Bell, and Henry Ford were responsible for much of the early technological progress in the United States. Government can foster technological advances by directly funding research and development projects or through tax incentives to innovators. Less developed countries may stimulate growth and progress by importing new technologies. Another possibility is to import capital goods from more advanced countries. A slightly different method of securing technology is followed by countries that send some of their most promising young people to more advanced countries to study at colleges and universities. This is one popular way to build the foundations for economic growth.

Social Foundations: The Infrastructure

The path to economic growth in some societies rests on rich lodes of natural resources. The world beats paths to the doors of oil-rich sheikdoms and mineral-rich feudal societies, strewing money left and right that can be used as developmental "seed" money. Other primitive economies have tougher rows to hoe—they must build the foundations of economic development carefully.

> *The* **social overhead capital** *or* **infrastructure** *of a country includes institutions such as a well-organized financial system, efficient communication and transportation networks, and a well-educated and disciplined work force.*

Any smooth-running economy needs a well-organized and sophisticated financial system. Without such a system, existing firms and industries must rely on internally generated funds (retained earnings) or on foreign sources to finance capital expansion. The same is true for other types of social overhead capital like communication and transportation networks. Methods for selling their products nationwide or worldwide are needed because, over some range of output, average production costs fall as output increases for virtually all production processes. Well-developed communication and transport systems aid firms in exploiting these declining costs.

Finally, no country grows very rapidly or experiences industrialization without a capable labor force. This includes not only a well-educated population but a healthy one as well. Thus, a nation must set high priorities in the areas of health and education if its economy is to sustain a high level of growth. Edward S. Denison, an expert in this area, attributes nearly 20 percent of U.S. growth between 1929 and 1982 to improved education.[2]

Development and the Unfolding of History

Many historians and social philosophers have attempted to chart the progress of civilizations in broader terms than we have been discussing. Economic events often play central roles on the stage of history. Are there long-term patterns of growth and development common to the economic advances of all societies? Many observers believe so. Does growth ultimately bring stagnation? Most of us hope not, but some students of civilization believe it does.

Economic Development According to Marx

One of the most influential thinkers of the last century was Karl Marx, who suggested an unabated course of progress and development. (Optimists about the prospects for humankind are increasingly convinced that he was wrong about the specifics.) Marx's prognosis was that every society goes through six major stages of history, culminating in an ideal state.

1. *Prehistory.* Prior to the dawn of civilization, humankind consisted largely of self-sufficient but nomadic hunters/scavengers/foragers. Gradually, these random groups evolved into

2. *Primitive culture.* Extended families and tribes emerged during this period. Agriculture began to bind small groups to specific

territories, but animal herding and hunting continued to be important. As claims to exclusive territories became more extensive, some families were more successful than others in establishing their rights to land, resulting in a system known as

3. *Feudalism.* The offspring of successful warlords became wealthy landholders, who were titled but most of whom owed their ability to protect their turf to a king. Kings typically extracted "protection" tributes from lesser royalty; however, the actual production on the manors held by the minor lords was done by peasants, who owned no land and paid a share of their crops to the titled landowners. (The sharecropping system continues to this day in many regions.) This chain of exploitation governed the social and economic behavior of all members of society from the highest-born prince to the humblest peasant. Industrialization and the gradual evolution of shopkeepers into powerful merchants slowly eroded the powers of feudal royalty, although some merchants and feudal lords became industrial magnates during the transition to

4. *Capitalism.* The Industrial Revolution and growth in commerce were facilitated by urbanization. Dispossessed peasants streamed into the cities. They owned no resources except their own labor, because their income was held at subsistence levels. According to Marx, capitalists accumulated enormous wealth during this period through the expropriation of a *surplus value* equal to the difference between the total value of production and the subsistence wages paid to workers. In Marxist jargon, all rents, interest payments, and profits are surplus values. Marx predicted that ever-growing disparities between the wealth of capitalists and the impoverishment of labor would generate class conflict and the triumph of a workers' revolution. The successful revolution would lead to a transition period called the

5. *Dictatorship of the proletariat.* During this period, all basic industries and productive resources would be *nationalized*, which means that revolutionary governments would seize them from capitalists and hold

2. Edward F. Denison, *Trends in American Economic Growth, 1929–1982* (Washington, D.C.: The Brookings Institution, 1985), p. 30.

them in trust for the workers, or *proletariat*. Each worker would receive compensation only for his or her own production to ensure an absence of capitalistic exploitation. There would be a highly progressive income tax and a confiscatory inheritance tax. Gradually, all material wants would be satisfied, and the need for government would fade—leading to the ultimate state of

6. *Communism or socialism*. In this highest stage of economic development, basic human needs and wants would be met according to the Marxist principle, "From each according to his ability to produce, to each according to need." And everyone would live happily ever after.

Turmoil and the overthrow of Marxist dictators in Eastern Europe, and the increasing adoption of market-based development strategies in countries still led by avowed Marxists, indicate that Marx's theories, however plausible in the minds of many people, simply did not work.

Stages of Economic Growth

There have been many non-Marxist theories of the stages of economic development. Among the most noteworthy is one offered by Walt W. Rostow, who is concerned with transitions from a primitive economy to a fully developed and mature industrial economy. Rostow identified certain stages on the path of growth and development to economic maturity:

1. *Traditional society*. Traditional societies are based on agrarian economies that employ primitive technology.

2. *Preconditions for growth*. The traditional economy begins to change, with rapid increases in agricultural productivity. Growing agricultural surpluses free workers for industry and allow investment in capital goods. At this point, entrepreneurship begins to blossom.

3. *Take-off*. High saving rates during this period permit rapid expansion of productive capacity.

4. *Drive to maturity*. Output and income from industrialization grow rapidly.

5. *High mass consumption*. During this stage, services become very important, and consumer goods are for all members of society.

Marxist and non-Marxist models are similarly abstract in failing to provide clear guidelines for initiating and then sustaining economic development. Many less developed countries seem caught in an almost insurmountable maze of problems.

Problems of Developing Nations

Underdeveloped countries often seem caught in what has been called the *trap of underdevelopment*. For these countries, the prospects for curing poverty appear dismal, with most families living on the razor's edge of subsistence. The trap of underdevelopment is illustrated in Figure 4.

The Trap of Underdevelopment

Less developed countries typically experience high rates of population growth that result in low per capita incomes. Meager incomes leave families so little extra that saving per worker is very low, resulting in low national capital-to-labor ratios. Further, low-income families spend most of their earnings on rather primitive products. Finally, low saving rates and little capital per worker cause productivity to be stagnant. This again translates into poor wages and, thus, low per capita income. No matter where you begin in Figure 4, the story is the same. How do countries escape from this vicious circle of poverty?

Breaking the Bonds of Underdevelopment

Impediments to development include (*a*) explosive population growth and lack of education and job skills, (*b*) little capital per worker, (*c*) primitive technology, (*d*) cultural norms that are hostile to commercial ventures, (*e*) few domestic natural resources, and (*f*) unstable political systems. How can countries suffering from such barriers break the bonds of underdevelopment?

Economic development does not happen over-

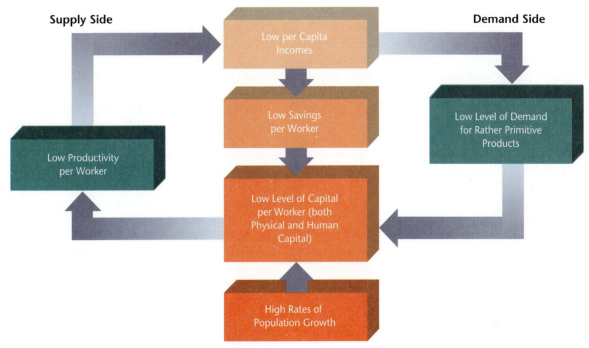

Supply Side

Demand Side

Low per Capita Incomes

Low Savings per Worker

Low Level of Demand for Rather Primitive Products

Low Productivity per Worker

Low Level of Capital per Worker (both Physical and Human Capital)

High Rates of Population Growth

FIGURE 4 The Trap of Underdevelopment

In many less developed countries, high rates of population growth lead to little physical or human capital per worker, which results in low productivity and income, which leads to low levels of saving and Aggregate Demand. This in turn leads to little capital per worker, and so on. Such a cycle makes it extremely difficult for primitive economies to escape the trap of underdevelopment and achieve economic growth.

night, but less developed countries (LDCs) can do several things to facilitate development. They can eliminate and streamline government impediments to business activity, encourage the adoption of modern agricultural technology, improve the country's infrastructure so that the labor force can use modern agricultural and industrial technologies efficiently, and institute policies to reduce population growth and increase saving.

This is a tall order for any country. Consider the task of reducing population growth. "Free" birth control programs are barely more successful than exhorting people to abstain from sex. Many people in underdeveloped lands view children as old-age insurance and measure their own success by how many of their children attain adulthood. Better medical care or increases in National Income are quickly translated into population growth. One example is the recent population explosion in Mexico following major discoveries of oil and other natural resources. Some

countries consider population growth to be such a desperate problem that they have resorted to involuntary programs. Indira Gandhi's government in India lost power for a period in the 1970s when her oldest son, Sanjay, directed the army to grab men off the streets in rural areas and sterilize them. In 1981, China passed laws limiting rural couples to two children, while urban couples were prohibited from having more than one child. Press releases periodically reveal that thousands of infant girls have been killed by Chinese parents who want male children. This is further evidence that government policies may have unforeseen and undesirable (or even tragic) side effects, and that devising policies to accomplish growth and development may be an overwhelming task.

The effect of policies that overcome the bonds of underdevelopment is diagramed in Figure 5. Reducing population growth, increasing capital per worker, and implementing improved technology produce self-reinforcing benefits.

As per capita incomes rise, saving per worker and consumer demands for new and improved products also rise. As more capital per worker is acquired, worker productivity will rise, resulting in greater wages and income. The circle begins again, this time for the better. It is generally very difficult, however, for any country to begin the development process on its own. Start-up capital often comes from foreign, more highly developed countries.

Is There Really a Trap of Underdevelopment?

The vicious circle of underdevelopment suggests that breaking the bonds of poverty requires domestic sacrifices supplemented by aid from abroad. Growth may depend on the rate of capital formation (investment), which in turn is a function of saving, which is determined by income. Low income levels prevent the saving necessary for sufficient investment to fuel economic growth.

Critics of the trap of underdevelopment thesis point out that it is refuted by the very existence of developed countries. These countries all started out poor with low levels of capital; if the vicious circle of poverty thesis were true, developed countries would not exist today.

For example, in the early 1800s Hong Kong was a barren rock; by 1900 it was a substantial port. Hong Kong has little land and may be the most densely populated country on Earth. It has few natural resources and must import most of its raw materials. Today, Hong Kong is a major manufacturing, trading, and banking center. In fact, the Hong Kong experience is so successful that India is in the process of turning its Andaman Islands in the Bay of Bengal into a free port and huge export processing zone. Critics ask, "How can all of this be true if the trap of underdevelopment thesis is true?"

Critics of this thesis further argue that development is based on factors other than natural resources, capital accumulation, and reduced population growth. They argue that successful development hinges on such factors as human

FIGURE 5   Breaking the Bonds of Underdevelopment

Facilitating advancement in developing nations may require reducing population growth, improving technology, and increasing the saving rate—all very difficult tasks.

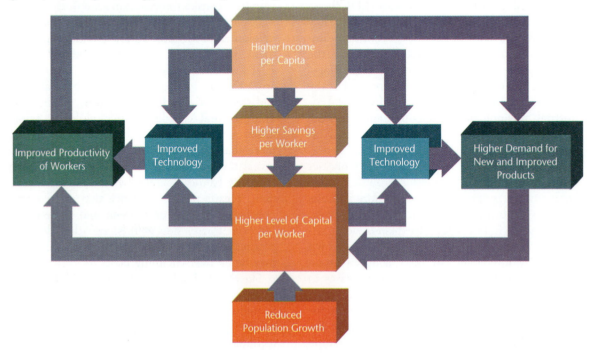

aptitudes and attitudes, social and political institutions, external contacts, market opportunities, and natural resources (to a lesser extent). Development is not just a matter of capital accumulation and saving, it is vitally related to individual entrepreneurs being able to perceive opportunities and then take advantage of them. Growth is, of course, conditioned by the opportunities offered by the environment – natural resources and social institutions – but the pace and pattern of growth will depend on the quality of an economy's entrepreneurial talent.

These critics point to Hong Kong, Taiwan, and Singapore as counterexamples to the traditional capital accumulation theory of growth and development. Only when free trade and unrestricted entrepreneurial activity are available as springboards to economic growth will injections of foreign capital be helpful because as P. T. Bauer has noted, "A society which cannot develop without external gifts is altogether unlikely to do so with them."

How Developed Countries Can Aid Less Developed Nations

The case for foreign aid is regarded as axiomatic, so that either progress or lack of progress can be used to argue for more aid. Progress is evidence of success, and lack of progress is evidence that more must be done.

P. T. Bauer

Many people perceive the most pressing needs of developing nations to be enormous injections of capital, introduction of new technology, and substantial education and job training programs. Developed nations are often in a good position to provide physical capital because many have an abundance and their investors are looking for profitable places to invest. Similarly, the educational systems of developed countries can train technically qualified people for developing industries. Moreover, industrialized countries can provide technology to raise the productivity of workers in less developed countries.

The Role of International Credit

International capital flows permit countries with more attractive investment opportunities than their domestic savings can finance to obtain resources from countries with excess saving. Countries experiencing temporary economic problems might borrow from world capital markets rather than suffer sharp contractionary policies that restrict consumption and investment. Countries such as Hong Kong, Taiwan, Malaysia, and Israel, to name a few, have benefited from foreign capital infusions. From World War II until the 1980s, the United States was a net supplier of capital to the rest of the world, primarily through direct investment by private firms in foreign countries. Before World War I, the United States financed domestic investments with loans from Great Britain and other European countries.

During the 1980s, enormous U.S. federal budget deficits were financed by balance of trade deficits. This net inflow to the United States drains funds that might have financed development in less developed countries. Although the 1990 federal deficit soared to an all-time high, exceeding $300 billion, swelling Social Security revenues should soon reverse the U.S. demand for foreign capital. (The U.S. balance of trade deficit declined during 1987–1990.) In general, however, international capital flows move into countries with good growth and profit opportunities.

New capital may also be provided in the form of foreign aid – either grants or loans. The United States has provided billions of dollars in aid each year, administered through the Agency for International Development (AID). Another source of funds for less developed countries is the World Bank, funded by highly developed member nations, which arranges huge loans for social investments such as dams, education, communications, and transportation systems. Most investment flows between countries, however, are private and are channeled through multinational corporations. These companies must perceive substantial potential profits before they invest, and seek opportunities where there are abundant natural resources, a ready (and cheap) labor force, and a favorable political climate.

One problem that arises when development is financed by long-term loans from more mature economies is that, to maintain an acceptable credit rating, a less developed country must make regular payments. A worldwide recession such as the 1981–1983 slump reveals how much financial juggling this can entail. Hundreds of billions of dollars in development loans were due for repayment to major American banks. These banks had primarily loaned out the deposits of OPEC countries, and many of the OPEC countries wanted to withdraw funds because of declining oil revenues. The worldwide recession, high nominal and real interest rates, the strengthening of the U.S. dollar until 1985, and the fall in the prices of many commodities exported by developing countries put incredible strains on debtor countries' ability to service their external debts. Some analysts warned that the entire international financial system teetered on the brink of collapse. However, refinancing (or rescheduling) of the debt payments, collapsing oil prices, and the sustained economic recovery of the 1980s reduced the financial pressures on many developing nations that do not rely primarily on oil revenues.

The world's industrialized nations are not totally philanthropic in contributing to the growth and development of less developed countries. Facing diminishing returns to more capital within their own borders, these countries seek outlets for their internally generated technological advances and capital growth, sources of raw materials and cheap labor, and markets for their finished products. Viewing our world as a self-enclosed "Spaceship Earth" emphasizes the international scope of our interdependencies. As the entire world matures economically, disparities in living standards between countries should decrease. Many have argued that developed countries have a moral responsibility to aid less developed countries in their search for the good life. For whatever reason, most observers believe that the fortunes of the developed nations and their less developed neighbors are inextricably intertwined.

Chapter Review: Key Points

1. *Economic growth* refers to quantitative changes in the capacity to produce goods and services in a country. It occurs through expanding capital or labor resources, discoveries of new sources of raw materials, or development of more productive technologies. *Economic development* refers to improving the qualitative aspects of economic growth, including changes in the quality of life.

2. The *Rule of 72* is a rule of thumb for estimating how long it takes for a variable to double in value given some percentage growth rate. Simply divide 72 by the growth rate. For example, if growth in GNP is occurring at 6 percent per year, GNP will double in approximately 12 years (72/6 = 12).

3. *Diminishing returns* because of the fixity of land cause output to grow more slowly, even if labor and capital increase in fixed proportions.

4. Reverend Thomas Malthus and other nineteenth-century economists were convinced that population growth is almost uncontrollable, and theorized that equilibrium is attained only when bare subsistence is common to all.

5. *Population growth* tends to slow as a country develops. The least developed countries of the world tend to have the highest rates of population growth.

6. *Capital formation* requires high saving rates. If *voluntary saving* is used to finance development, greater incomes, higher interest rates paid to savers, and (perhaps) less equal income distributions will lead to higher rates of investment. *Involuntary saving* may be used to free investment resources through confiscation, taxation, or inflation.

7. *Capital widening* occurs when the capital stock and labor force grow at the same rates. *Capital deepening* requires the capital stock to grow faster than the labor force.

8. *Technological advances* occur when given amounts of resources acquire greater productive capacity.

9. Rapid development requires a strong *social infrastructure* — education, communications, transportation, and other networks that facilitate production.

Key Concepts

Ensure that you can define these terms before proceeding.

economic growth
economic development
Rule of 72
capital widening

capital deepening
voluntary saving
involuntary saving
infrastructure

Problems and Questions

1. How long will it take the following variables to double?

   a. Your savings account, if the bank pays annual interest of 4 percent?

   b. GNP, if economic growth proceeds at 2 percent annually?

   c. Housing prices, if they grow by 6 percent annually?

   d. Population, if the annual population growth rate is 1.5 percent?

2. How long will it take for the value of money to fall by one-half if the annual inflation rate is

   a. 2 percent?

   b. 12 percent?

   c. 24 percent?

3. How long will it take for the CPI to move from 100 to 400 if inflation is 1 percent annually?

4. By what total percent will population increase in the course of a century at a 3 percent annual growth rate.

5. Despite relatively low saving rates in the United States, we have typically grown faster than have many countries with higher rates of saving (e.g., England). What does this say about the importance of the structure of investment relative to its level?

6. If all taxes on saving were eliminated, the average saver's return would be increased by roughly 30 percent. Increased incentives to save would add $30 to $40 billion to annual savings. Would such a policy increase productivity? Long-term growth? The real earnings of workers? Would it reduce inflation? Reduce unemployment? Would different groups gain in the short run than in the long run? Is such a policy politically feasible?

7. If you were the leader of an impoverished and densely populated country, what policies might you adopt to foster economic growth and development? To what extent would you encourage private entrepreneurs and for which kinds of projects? What role should your government play in developing social infrastructure?

8. How do people in wealthy countries gain through foreign aid to impoverished countries? Do you think the costs to us exceed the benefits? Should foreign aid programs be shrunk or expanded? Why?

9. Why do many highly trained people from developing nations seek employment in advanced countries? Why are these highly educated people apparently more productive and highly paid in these advanced countries than they are in their home countries?

10. P. T. Bauer, a critic of foreign aid, has argued that "development depends on personal and social factors, not on handouts." He further asserts that "foreign aid means at most some capital is cheaper than if it had been raised independently at market rates." His argument refutes the notion that foreign aid is indispensable for progress. Do you agree with him? Why or why not?

11. Is foreign aid nothing more than a conscience-appeasing payment from rich to poor nations? Is there something wrong with developed countries seeking greater economic growth even if it means that the gap between rich and poor nations may grow wider? Would we in the United States accept greater unemployment for the long run if it meant a greater rate of growth for some developing countries? Are development questions really questions of income distribution on an international scale?

PART

6

Core Concepts of Microeconomics

We concentrate on decisions in households and business firms for the next eight chapters and then introduce the micro role of government. You now know how useful supply and demand are in analyzing problems ranging from yam prices to fuel shortages. Until now, we have relied heavily on your intuition to explain the slopes of supply and demand curves. This part of the book allows you to explore in depth just why supply curves slope upward, while demand curves slope down.

Chapter 19 introduces *elasticity*, which allows a more precise use of supply and demand analysis to predict how market prices and quantities change. In Chapter 20, we analyze *consumer choice* and develop the underpinnings of consumer demand curves. Chapter 21 explores the nature of *business firms*. Finally, Chapter 22 delves into *production*—how inputs are transformed into outputs, and how technology shapes a firm's *production costs*. You need to understand these foundations for firms' decisions in Part 7; firms decide which goods to produce and what prices to charge by weighing consumer demands against production costs.

EQUAL MARGINAL ADVANTAGE Individuals try to maximize their satisfaction, and firms try to maximize their profits. These types of *optimization* require minimizing costs incurred in accomplishing any given task. The following concept governs all optimization processes: The *law of equal marginal advantage* requires equivalent goods or similar resources to be allocated in equally advantageous ways at the margin. Failure to conform to this principle is inefficient. For example, if the last dollar you spend on rhubarb fails to yield the added pleasure you would receive were it spent on an extra sundae, you will gain by spending less on rhubarb and more on sundaes.

People change patterns of consumption or production whenever resources (in this example, the command over resources represented by your last few dollars) are inefficiently allocated. Thus, you would gain by eating an extra sundae and a bit less okra, and probably make these sorts of adjustments with very little conscious thought. You settle into a stable consumption pattern only when the last cent spent on any good yields satisfaction equal to that gained from the last cent spent on any other good.

Similar *marginal adjustments* span all economic decision making. Suppose you and your identical twin are equally strong, experienced, and intelligent. If your twin produces $64 worth of mowed lawns in 8 hours, while you generate only $48 worth of cleaned windows, you should shift into mowing lawns so that your labor resources are allocated equally advantageously, at $8 instead of $6 per hour. Whenever equivalent resources are not used to equal advantage, there is economic inefficiency.

Elasticity

Firms know they will sell less output if they raise prices because buyers' demand curves slope downward, but how much less? Buyers who offer higher prices expect more to be available because supply curves are positively sloped, but how much more? *Elasticity*, a tool that addresses questions of this type, can help guide decisions. Predictions about the costs and benefits of alternatives are necessary before people can make informed choices.

Elasticity and Responsiveness

The concept of elasticity provides a systematic way to estimate how one variable responds to changes in some other variable, and has applications throughout the sciences.

> **Elasticity** *measures the proportional responsiveness of one variable with respect to changes in another.*

If X influences Y, then the elasticity of Y with respect to X equals:

$$\frac{\Delta Y}{Y} \bigg/ \frac{\Delta X}{X}$$

Elasticity helps us predict changes in a firm's revenues if prices change, but other uses abound.

For example, firms substitute capital for labor if capital costs fall relative to wages. How much substitution occurs as resource prices change? Experience shapes our expectations, but how is past inflation translated into people's inflationary expectations? Understanding how to calculate elasticity for these examples is unimportant for now, but remember that elasticity is useful whenever variables are systematically related.

Suppose you are the chief executive officer (CEO) of United Bullmoose Enterprises (UBE) and are irritated because profit is less than you think possible. UBE's chief economist assures you that all demand curves are negatively sloped, so if you raise the price of plastic mooseheads (UBE's big novelty seller), annual sales will slip below the million you currently sell. Total production costs will fall, but will sales revenues rise? . . . fall? . . . remain constant? Suppose producing each moosehead costs $10. Raising the price from $20 to $25 might be disastrous if you lost half your customers, but if only 50,000 of UBE's million annual moosehead sales were lost, profits would rise by $4.25 million. (Why?)[1] How should UBE deal with this dilemma?

---

1. After the price hike, sales revenue ($P \times Q$) is equal to 950,000 × $25 = $23,750,000 while costs are $9,500,00 (950,000 × $10). This yields profit of $14,250,000. The original profit was $10,000,000 [(1,000,000 × $20) − (1,000,000 × $10)].

The Price Elasticity of Demand

The problem you are wrestling with is the price elasticity of the demand for mooseheads.

> **Price elasticity of demand** *is a measure of the proportional (**a**) decline in units purchased when price is increased by a given small proportion, or (**b**) the increase in purchases when the price is reduced by a given small proportion.*

If both changes are quite small, this roughly equals the percentage change in quantity divided by the percentage change in price. Price elasticity can be written:

$$e_p = \frac{\text{Change in } Q}{Q} \bigg/ \frac{\text{Change in } P}{P}$$

$$= \frac{\Delta Q}{Q} \bigg/ \frac{\Delta P}{P}$$

$$\cong \frac{\text{Percentage change in } Q}{\text{Percentage change in } P}$$

$$= \frac{\%\Delta Q}{\%\Delta P}$$

Such calculations always yield negative numbers because if price is increased, quantity demanded falls, and vice versa. To simplify things, economists conventionally use the *absolute value* of price elasticity, eliminating the need to deal with negative numbers.

The Problem of Bases

Suppose the price of plastic mooseheads is cut from $20 to $12, and annual sales surge from 1 million units to 5 million. Price elasticity (e_p) is 10 using the percentage formula:

$$e_p \cong \frac{\%\Delta Q}{\%\Delta P} = \frac{5 - 1/1}{12 - 20/20} = \frac{400\%}{-40\%}$$

$$= -10 \quad \text{(Absolute value = 10)}$$

Watch what happens if we turn this example around. Sales shrink from 5 million to 1 million mooseheads if prices rise from $12 to $20, and the percentage formula yields:

$$e_p \cong \frac{\%\Delta Q}{\%\Delta P} = \frac{1 - 5}{5} \bigg/ \frac{20 - 12}{12} = \frac{-80\%}{66.7\%}$$

$$= -1.2 \quad \text{(Absolute value = 1.2)}$$

Divergent elasticity estimates in this example (10 if price is cut, 1.2 if price is raised) demonstrate that calculations using the percentage formula depend on whether prices rise or fall.[2] We need to discuss this inconsistency before we provide a cure for it.

The basic problem results from a standard practice in math courses of using initial values as bases to calculate percentage changes. Percentage changes computed this way may create substantial ambiguity. For example, suppose the annual profit of a subsidiary, United Bullmoose Oil, climbs from $200 million to $1 billion. The media report the 400 percent jump and imply that UBE's profits are somehow responsible for inflation. The next year, profit drops to $150 million, and the media dutifully report an 85 percent decline. Readers are likely to think that UBE is still way ahead because a 400 percent gain seems to overpower an 85 percent decline, but it does not . . . $200M → $1,000M → $150M. UBE had one very good year, but its profit is now less than it was initially.

Using Midpoints as Bases Elasticity estimates computed by standard percentage changes may be only trivially inconsistent if prices and quantities change very little, but inconsistency poses major problems when prices or quantities change drastically. Such problems with percentages as normally computed have led economists to compute elasticity using as bases the *midpoints* of changes in prices and quantities:

$$e_p = \frac{Q_n - Q_o}{(Q_n + Q_o)/2} \bigg/ \frac{P_n - P_o}{(P_n + P_o)/2}$$

The subscript o refers to the original price and quantity, and the subscript n refers to the new price and quantity.[3] Naturally, the 2s in both denominators can be canceled out, but we use

---

2. The percentage change formula that uses original values for bases yields "point elasticity" estimates. Our midpoint-based calculations are referred to as estimates of **arc elasticity**.

3. The formula for elasticity can be manipulated in ways that some students find easier to calculate. One example is:

$$e_p = \frac{\text{Change in } Q}{\text{Change in } P} \times \frac{\text{Sum of } P}{\text{Sum of } Q}$$

them here to provide consistency and to remind you that we are using midpoints.

Returning to our example of prices of $12 and $20 for plastic mooseheads generating sales of 5 million and 1 million units, respectively, we now get the same elasticity estimate, 2.67, regardless of whether the price is raised or lowered:

$$e_p = \frac{1-5}{(1+5)/2} \Big/ \frac{20-12}{(20+12)/2}$$

$$= \frac{-(4/3)}{8/16} = -2.67$$

and

$$e_p = \frac{5-1}{(1+5)/2} \Big/ \frac{12-20}{(20+12)/2}$$

$$= \frac{4/3}{-(8/16)} = -2.67$$

(*Note:* Both absolute values = 2.67.) These elasticity coefficients suggest that for each 1 percent change in price, the quantity demanded changes by roughly 2.67 percent. Thus, using *midpoint bases* to calculate price elasticity clears up ambiguities created by using standard percentages.

Ranges of Elasticity

Price elasticity of demand is a measure of the relative responsiveness of quantity demanded to given small changes in price.

Demand is **relatively price inelastic** *if the elasticity coefficient (e_p) is less than 1.0.*

Price changes are proportionally greater than the resulting quantity changes for goods with inelastic demands. Inelastically demanded goods include what people tend to consider "necessities"—the amounts you demand are somewhat immune to price changes, so the share of your income absorbed by such items grows if prices rise or shrinks if prices fall. For example, if the price of dog food doubled, would people put their pets on half rations? No. Most people view their pets and, consequently, pet food as one item that is relatively insensitive to price changes. (But in the longer run, they might switch to cats or smaller dogs.)

FIGURE 1   Demand Curves with Different Elasticities

Slope is, at best, only a crude indicator of elasticity. As you will see in a few pages, all negatively sloped linear demand curves have elasticities that range from 0 to infinity. In this figure, the D_1 demand curve is more elastic at every given quantity than is the D_0 demand curve.

Demand curve D_0 in Figure 1 is *relatively inelastic* at a price of $2. When price rises from $2 to $2.50, quantity demanded only falls from 100 to 98—not much of a change ($e_p = 1/11$, or roughly 0.09). Compare this to demand curve D_1 in the same figure, where a change in price from $2 to $2.50 results in quantity demanded falling from 100 to 40. Quantity demanded is very responsive to a change in price ($e_p = 27/7$, or roughly 3.833). Thus, D_1 depicts a product with a *relatively elastic* demand at a price of $2.

Demand is **relatively price elastic** *if the absolute value of the elasticity coefficient exceeds 1.0.*

Many consumers are willing to forgo elastically demanded goods if their prices rise significantly, a sign that a product may have numerous close substitutes. Goods that exhibit relatively elastic demand curves include Saabs, Häagen-Dazs ice cream, Wendy's hamburgers, and Salem cigarettes. Note that total cigarette consumption is probably very unresponsive to price changes, while the demand for a specific brand is likely to be extremely sensitive to price changes because numerous substitutes are available.

Slope and Elasticity

Slope as an indicator of how one variable responds to changes in another suffers from a major disadvantage — units of measurement affect slope. For example, a demand curve for which coffee prices are stated in dollars will have 1/100th the slope of the same demand curve if prices were stated in pennies. And that same demand curve would have 1/2,000th as much slope if quantity were measured in tons of coffee instead of pounds.

The superiority of elasticity as an indicator of relative responsiveness is that only proportions matter; elasticity is *dimensionless*, which means that units of measure do not bias results. The price elasticity of the demand for coffee is the same regardless of whether prices are stated in cents, dollars, or cruzados (a Brazilian denomination), nor is it affected by whether weight is stated in pounds, tons, or kilograms. Thus, slope is, at best, only a crude indicator of elasticity.

Elasticity and Total Revenue

Price elasticities of demand are guides to what will happen to *total revenue* (the dollar sales of firms) if prices change slightly. The total revenue of a firm equals the price charged times the quantity sold ($TR = P \times Q$). For example, a hamburger stand will generate $1 million in total revenue if it sells a million burgers at $1 apiece (or one burger at $1 million). Naturally, firms' total revenues equal total spending by consumers.

When quantity rises because prices fall, offsetting effects make the direction of change in total revenue ($TR = P \times Q$) uncertain. If we know, however, that demand is inelastic, then when prices fall, the increase in quantity will be relatively less than the decrease in price, and total revenue will fall. Conversely, if demand is elastic and prices fall, then revenue rises because quantity grows relatively far more than price falls. The opposite story holds when prices rise. Inelastic demands mean that quantities decrease little relative to the increase in price, so total revenue

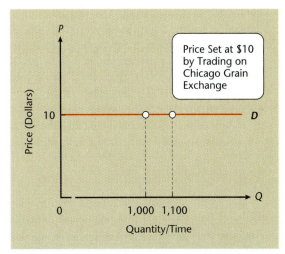

FIGURE 2 A Demand Curve Confronting an Individual Soybean Farmer (Perfectly Elastic Demand)

A demand curve that is horizontal has infinite price elasticity ($e_p = \infty$). Because total revenue equals $P \times Q$, and the price does not change with output, total revenue is exactly proportional to output.

rises. Elastic demands, on the other hand, yield declines in quantity that are large relative to any price hike. Let's look at two extreme cases to illustrate how total revenue and price elasticity are related.

Elastic Demands Firms producing outputs with perfect substitutes in buyers' eyes confront horizontal demand curves, as illustrated in Figure 2. Attempts to raise the price even slightly above the market price will switch all potential buyers to substitutes.

Perfectly elastic *demand curves have price elasticities of infinity and are horizontal.*[4]

For example, one soybean farmer's crop is the same as another's. Because even the largest soybean farmers produce only a small part of total world supplies, no single farm's output has a distinguishable impact on world soybean prices.

---

4. For those who are mathematically inclined: As the slope of the demand curve approaches zero, the elasticity of demand approaches infinity.

This means that any attempt by the farmer represented in Figure 2 to price soybeans above $10 per bushel will generate zero sales. The farmer can sell all the farm can produce at $10, and so would never charge less than $10. Since price will not vary from $10 per bushel, the farm's *total revenue will be exactly proportional to its output*. If the farm initially produces 1,000 bushels of soybeans annually and then expands output by 10 percent to 1,100 bushels, revenue also increases by 10 percent, rising from $10,000 to $11,000.

If demand is relatively elastic, then price changes trigger proportionally larger adjustments in quantity. Consequently, if $1 < e_p < \infty$, then total revenue will fall when prices are raised, but revenue will grow if prices drop.

Inelastic Demands The other extreme case would occur if a demand curve were vertical, as in Figure 3.

Perfectly inelastic *demand curves would have zero elasticity and be vertical.*

FIGURE 3 A Hypothetical Perfectly Inelastic Demand

Vertical demand curves have price elasticity of zero ($e_p = 0$). Although such perfectly inelastic demand curves are impossible, this figure shows that total revenue will be exactly proportional to price. This example is useful because it represents the opposite end of the spectrum from the perfectly elastic demand shown in the previous figure.

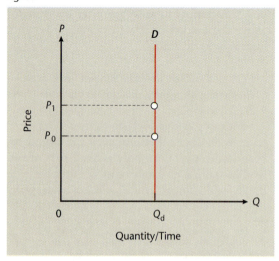

If such cases ever existed, the firm's *total revenue would be exactly proportional to the price* charged.

Perfectly inelastic demand curves are nonsensical; one is shown here only to help you understand elasticity. Zero price elasticity implies not only a total lack of substitutes for the good, but also that consumers could and would pay any price to receive a specific quantity of it. A profit-maximizing manager of a firm faced with a perfectly inelastic demand would charge an infinitely high price for the product. Any such good would be essential for life, but our limited budgets would make it impossible to afford.

You might think that the prices of insulin for diabetics or dialysis for people with defective kidneys would not affect the quantities demanded by patients who needed them. The cruel facts are that if the prices of these medical necessities were raised, more diabetics would try to control their disease with diet therapy. If prices were raised sufficiently, poorer patients would die and the quantities of insulin or dialysis demanded would fall. Every year millions of people die because they cannot afford expensive specialized medical treatment.

If demand is relatively inelastic, then price changes trigger proportionally smaller adjustments in quantity. Consequently, if $0 < e_p < 1$, then total revenue will fall when prices fall, but it will rise if the price is increased.

Unitary Demands An interesting intermediate case occurs when total spending on a good does not vary with the price charged. An example was provided by a farmer who observed that revenues from peach sales were about the same regardless of whether blight wiped out most of a peach crop or there was a bumper harvest. If 1 percent declines in peach harvests boost peach prices 1 percent, total spending on peaches is virtually unchanged and the price elasticity of demand equals one.

A **unitarily elastic** *demand curve occurs when the elasticity coefficient equals one, so total revenue from the good is unaffected by price.*

Spending on a good for which demand is unitarily elastic does not vary with the price charged.

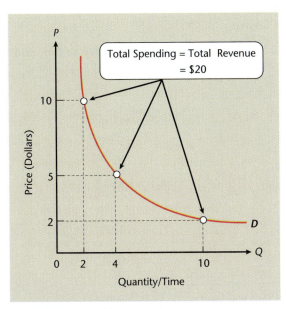

Total Spending = Total Revenue = $20

FIGURE 4 A Demand Curve with Unitary Elasticity

Total revenue ($P \times Q$) is unaffected by changes in price and quantity if demand is unitarily elastic. Unitary elastic demand curves ($e_p = 1$) are rectangular hyperbolas, which have the characteristic that all rectangles drawn from the curve to the axes have exactly the same geometric area ($P \times Q$). You will see more rectangular hyperbolas as we proceed further in economics.

Examples of unitarily elastic demands occur when a person budgets a certain amount of money for, say, meat or magazines, and will not deviate from that figure regardless of price. A representative unitary elastic demand curve is shown in Figure 4.

If the price elasticity of demand for a product is greater than zero but less than one, the de-

mand curve is *relatively inelastic*. Economists sometimes shorten this to *inelastic*. If the price elasticity is greater than one but less than infinity, the demand for the product is *relatively elastic*, or *elastic*.

Price elasticities of demand are obviously important to firms because they indicate what will happen to sales revenues when prices are raised or lowered. Price elasticities of demand are also important to consumers because they reflect how desperately buyers want particular goods and how the composition of consumer budgets will change as relative prices change. Table 1 summarizes how the firm's total revenue (and consumers' total spending) for a good changes as prices change.

Determinants of Elasticity of Demand

Demand curves rarely have constant elasticities along the full range of possible prices and quantities, but Table 2 presents some estimates of price elasticities of demand for several goods within the price ranges you would roughly expect each to have. Major determinants of elasticities of demand include:

1. the number and quality of substitutes for a good,

2. the proportion an item absorbs as a share of typical budgets, and

3. the length of time considered.

The number of substitutes available is the dominant influence on price elasticities of demand. Rising prices drive consumers toward sub-

---

Table 1 *Price Changes, Elasticities, and Total Revenues/Expenditures*

	How Total Revenues Change	
Price Elasticity of Demand	**Price Increases**	**Price Decreases**
Perfectly Inelastic $e_p = 0$	*TR* increases	*TR* decreases
Relatively Inelastic $0 < e < 1$	*TR* increases	*TR* decreases
Unitarily Elastic $e = 1$	No change in *TR*	No change in *TR*
Relatively Elastic $\infty > e > 1$	*TR* decreases	*TR* increases
Perfectly Elastic $e = \infty$	*TR* falls to zero	*TR* decreases

Table 2 *Price Elasticities of Demand for Selected Goods and Services*

Good or Service	Price Elasticity of Demand
Marijuana	1.51
Automobiles	1.35
Beer	1.13
Housing	1.00
Alcohol	0.92
Tobacco	0.33
Major League Baseball	0.23
Hospital and physician services	0.05 to 0.15
Gasoline (transportation only)	
short run	0.1 to 0.3
long run	1.50
Electricity	
long-run residential and commercial usage	0.88
short-run residential	0.13

Sources: Marijuana—T. C. Misket and F. Vakil, "Some Estimates of Price and Expenditure Elasticities among UCLA Students," *Review of Economics and Statistics*, November 1972. Automobiles—Gregory C. Chow, *Demand for Automobiles in the United States* (Amsterdam: North-Holland Publishing Company, 1957). Beer—T. F. Hogarty and K. G. Elzinga, "The Demand for Beer," *The Review of Economics and Statistics*, May 1972. Housing—Richard F. Muth, "The Demand for Non-Farm Housing," *The Demand for Durable Goods*, Arnold C. Harberger, ed. (Chicago: University of Chicago Press, 1960). Alcohol—H. S. Houthakker and Lester D. Taylor, *Consumer Demand in the United States*, 2/e (Cambridge: Harvard University Press, 1970). Hospital and physician services—Joseph P. Newhouse and Charles E. Phelps, "New Estimates of Price and Income Elasticities of Medical Care Services," *The Role of Health Insurance in the Health Services Sector*, Richard N. Rosett, ed. (New York: National Bureau of Economic Research, 1976). Gasoline and electricity—J. M. Griffin, *Energy Conservation in the OECD, 1980–2000* (Cambridge, MA: Ballinger, 1979). Tobacco—B. Gordon Watkins III, "The Tobacco Program: An Econometric Analysis of Its Benefits to Farmers," *The American Economist*, 1990. Baseball—Bruce R. Domazlicky and Peter M. Kerr, "Baseball Attendance and the Designated Hitter," *The American Economist*, 1990.

stitutes; falling prices are incentives to find more uses for a good. For example, the demand for Campbell's pork and beans is very price elastic because slight price hikes will switch consumers to other brands, and slight price cuts will raise Campbell's sales at the expense of competing brands. On the other hand, the demand for local telephone services is relatively inelastic because few substitutes are available.

Transaction costs are a major reason that importance in your budget is positively related to the price elasticity of demand. Price changes for items absorbing little of your income may go unnoticed (maraschino cherries, for example), but you will probably adjust quickly to changes in the prices of more important items (e.g., clothes or gasoline). Another important determinant of price elasticity is the period allowed for adjustments to price changes. Elasticity generally rises as longer intervals are considered, because as time elapses, more substitutes become feasible. Elasticities are measured for a specified period for this reason. For example, Table 2 indicates that the demand for gasoline is relatively inelastic in the short run, but relatively elastic in the long run. Increases in gasoline prices eventually induce some people to buy smaller cars, get more frequent tune-ups, use mass transit, or relocate closer to their schools or jobs.

A firm facing a demand curve with price elasticity of one or less always finds it profitable to raise the product's price because revenue will rise, and as output and units sold fall, total production costs will decline. (Profit must increase if revenues grow and total costs fall.) As the price is increased, growing numbers of consumers will buy substitutes for the good; those who cannot substitute ultimately will be forced to do without.

Elasticity Along a Demand Curve

Constant elasticities of demand are rare. You might think the linear demand curve in Panel A of Figure 5 would have a constant price elasticity. Not so. The rectangle drawn at point *a* represents the highest revenue available on this demand curve — $P \times Q$ is maximized. Any price deviation from $10 lowers revenue, as shown in Panel B and its table. This demand curve is price elastic above point *a*, because price hikes reduce revenue: e_p exceeds one. Symmetrically, price cuts below $10 shrink revenue, so below point *a* the demand curve is price inelastic: e_p is less than one. At point *a*, demand is unitarily elastic: e_p equals one. The conclusion is that price elasticities of demand tend to rise as higher and higher prices are charged.

FIGURE 5   Varying Price Elasticities along a Linear Demand Curve

A negatively sloped linear demand curve has price elasticities ranging from 0 to infinity. At low prices, demand is relatively price inelastic, which means that price hikes generate rising revenues. At high prices, price hikes cause declining revenues, because demand is relatively price elastic.

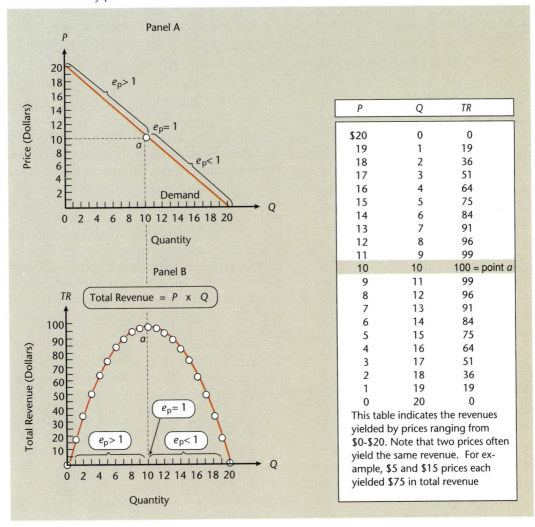

P	Q	TR
$20	0	0
19	1	19
18	2	36
17	3	51
16	4	64
15	5	75
14	6	84
13	7	91
12	8	96
11	9	99
10	10	100 = point *a*
9	11	99
8	12	96
7	13	91
6	14	84
5	15	75
4	16	64
3	17	51
2	18	36
1	19	19
0	20	0

This table indicates the revenues yielded by prices ranging from $0-$20. Note that two prices often yield the same revenue. For example, $5 and $15 prices each yielded $75 in total revenue

Table 3 *Income Elasticities of Demand for Selected Goods and Services*

Good or Service	Income Elasticity of Demand
Automobiles	3.00
Housing	1.15
Beer	0.93
Charitable donations (households)	0.70
Corporate contributions	0.85
Major League Baseball	1.30
Hospital and physician services	0.09

Sources: Automobiles — Gregory C. Chow, *Demand for Automobiles in the United States* (Amsterdam: North-Holland Publishing Company, 1957). Housing — Richard F. Muth, *Cities and Housing: The Spatial Pattern of Urban Residential Land Use* (Chicago: The University of Chicago Press, 1969). Beer — T. F. Hogarty and K. G. Elzinga, ''The Demand for Beer,'' *Review of Economics and Statistics*, May 1972. Charitable donations — M. Feldstein and A. Taylor, ''The Income Tax and Charitable Contributions,'' *Econometrica*, November 1976. Hospital and physician services — Joseph P. Newhouse and Charles E. Phelps, ''New Estimates of Price and Income Elasticities of Medical Care Services,'' *The Role of Health Insurance in the Health Services Sector*, Richard N. Rosett, ed. (New York: National Bureau of Economic Research, 1976). Corporate contributions — Peter Navarro, ''The Income Elasticity of Corporate Contributions,'' *Quarterly Review of Economics and Business*, Winter 1988. Baseball — Bruce R. Domazlicky and Peter M. Kerr, ''Baseball Attendance and the Designated Hitter,'' *The American Economist*, 1990.

Other Elasticities of Demand

Before addressing such issues as how elasticities determine who bears the burdens of taxes, we will look at other major types of elasticities.

Income Elasticity of Demand   Rich people do not just buy more goods; the things they buy also differ from the purchases of poor people.

*The **income elasticity** of demand for a good measures the proportional change in the amount demanded resulting from a given small proportional change in income.*

You might think of income elasticity as the ratio of percentage changes in the amount of a good demanded relative to income, but, for reasons that parallel the rationale for midpoint-based computation of price elasticities, we actually compute income elasticity as:

$$e_y = \frac{Q_n - Q_o}{(Q_n + Q_o)/2} \bigg/ \frac{Y_n - Y_o}{(Y_n + Y_o)/2}$$

Again, subscript n refers to new values while subscript o represents old values, and both 2s

could be dropped from the denominators without affecting this calculation.

Such luxuries as scuba lessons or limousines are highly *income elastic* because each 1 percent rise in income increases the amounts sold by over 1 percent. If income grows 1 percent and the amount of a good sold rises slightly, but by less than 1 percent, demand is *income inelastic*. Rising incomes stimulate purchases of all **normal goods** (income elasticities are positive).[5] Purchases of **inferior goods** decline as income rises, and their income elasticities are negative. Lard, pinto beans, and used tires are examples. Income elasticities of demand for some broad product categories are displayed in Table 3.

Business decisions often pivot on forecasts and income elasticities. How might a recession affect sales, for example? Income elasticities are critical

---

5.   Sometimes data for the prices or quantities of goods are not available, but sales data ($P \times Q$) are. In such cases, economists approximate income elasticities by:

Percentage change in expenditures
Percentage change in income

If the result exceeds (*is less than*) one, demand is presumed to be income elastic (*inelastic*).

for planning in such industries as oil and gasoline, used auto parts, specialty foods, and retailing. Would the operator of a travel agency be exuberant about forecasts of an economic boom, and depressed if a recession hit? Clearly yes, if the demand for travel is income elastic. Income elasticity estimates help firms plan production, employment, and investment.

Cross Elasticity of Demand   Cross elasticities of demand are also important information about consumer behavior.

The **cross elasticity of demand** *estimates the proportional changes in units sold when the prices of related goods are changed slightly.*

Formally, cross elasticity is calculated by:

$$e_{xy} = \frac{Q_{xn} - Q_{xo}}{(Q_{xn} + Q_{xo})/2} \bigg/ \frac{P_{yn} - P_{yo}}{(P_{yn} + P_{yo})/2}$$

where Q_{xo} (old) and Q_{xn} (new) are good x purchases before and after price changes for good y (P_{yo} and P_{yn}, respectively). Again, the 2s could be dropped from the equation.

Consider the sales of American cars (Brand X) after U.S. import restrictions in the early 1980s drove up the prices of Japanese cars (Brand Y). All else constant, we would expect American car sales to grow when imported cars became higher priced. Thus, we would expect a positive relationship between the prices of imported cars and the quantities of American cars sold domestically; the price cross elasticity of demand (e_{xy}) should be positive. When price cross elasticities of demand are *positive*, the items in question are **substitute goods**. Other sets of substitutes are artificial turf and natural grass, golf clubs and tennis racquets, and vans and travel trailers. In fact, broad competition for consumers' dollars causes most goods to be at least weak substitutes for each other.

Sets of goods for which cross elasticity of demand is *negative* are **complementary goods**. For example, as prices for calculators and electronic toys have fallen, the demand for alkaline batteries has jumped markedly. Other examples of complementary goods include ham and eggs, cameras and film, suits and ties, and pretzels and beer.

The Price Elasticity of Supply

Price elasticities of supply are typically positive because supply curves slope up.

The **price elasticity of supply** *measures the relative responsiveness of quantity supplied to changes in price.*[6]

The formula for this elasticity is the same as for computing price elasticities of demand:

$$e_s = \frac{Q_n - Q_o}{(Q_n + Q_o)/2} \bigg/ \frac{P_n - P_o}{(P_n + P_o)/2}$$

If extending the supply curve of a good would result in an intersection with the vertical (price) axis, the amount of the good supplied is highly responsive to its price. In a case such as S_2 in Figure 6, the elasticity of supply exceeds one and the supply curve is **relatively elastic**. If a supply curve is horizontal, such as S_∞ in Figure 6, then the elasticity of supply is infinity and supply is **perfectly price elastic**. Buyers can demand any amounts of these goods without affecting the price at all. Examples of goods having perfectly elastic supplies include such things as a family's groceries — no matter how many cans of tuna your family personally consumes, your purchases will not affect the price you pay. Thus, the supply of tuna to you is perfectly elastic, even though the market supply of tuna is positively sloped. Similarly, any small bakery that buys flour in bulk is faced with a perfectly elastic supply of flour. In these and similar cases, individual demands determine the amounts people buy, but not the prices they pay.

If extending the supply curve would result in intersection with the quantity axis, the amount of a good supplied is comparatively unresponsive

---

6. Note for the mathematically adept: As the slope of a supply curve approaches zero, the elasticity of supply approaches infinity.

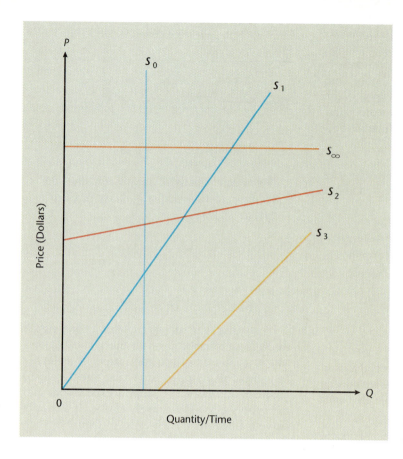

FIGURE 6 Ranges of Elasticity in Supply Curves

Supply curves that intersect the price axis (S_2) are *relatively elastic* ($e_s > 1$). Horizontal supply curves (S_∞) are *perfectly price elastic* ($e_s = \infty$). In such cases total revenues or spending will be exactly proportional to the quantity demanded. If the amount supplied is comparatively unresponsive to price (S_3), supply is *relatively inelastic* and, if extended, intersects the quantity axis. A vertical supply curve (S_0) is *perfectly price inelastic* ($e_s = 0$) and intersects the quantity axis. Although rare, such supplies do exist. Land sites are an example. In such cases, total spending (revenue) is exactly proportional to price. All supply curves that are straight lines from the origin (S_1) are *unitarily elastic* ($e_s = 1$).

to its price. A supply curve such as S_3 in Figure 6 is **relatively inelastic**. In the extreme situation where the quantity supplied is totally unresponsive to price, the supply curve is vertical (S_0 in Figure 6) and the price elasticity of supply is zero ($e_s = 0$). Examples of these **perfectly inelastic** supplies include land (the fixed amount available is unaffected by price) and other highly specialized items or resources—Rembrandt paintings, Stradivarius violins, and the comedy of Eddie Murphy are each unique. When supplies are fixed, demand alone determines a good's price or person's wage, but the quantity exchanged is not related to the price paid.

You may have noticed that perfectly inelastic supplies look just like perfectly inelastic demands and that perfectly elastic demands and supplies also appear to be identical. How about **unitarily elastic** supply curves ($e_s = 1$)? Do they resemble unitarily elastic demand curves? Not at all. For e_s to equal one, the quantity supplied

must change in fixed proportion with price. All supply curves that are straight lines through the origin have this characteristic (supply curve S_1 in Figure 6).

Elasticities and Time

Consumers demand certain numbers of shrimp dinners, surfboards, and bottles of perfume weekly, larger amounts monthly, and still larger amounts annually. A Domino's that sells 891 pizzas on an average day is probably much more profitable than one selling 891 weekly. These examples illustrate that demands and supplies are *flows*; consumer purchases or sales by firms mean little unless time intervals are specified.

Another effect of time is that quantities demanded respond more to price changes as time passes because more adjustments become feasible. Thus, the price elasticity of demand is positively related to the time interval considered. For example, a gasoline price hike might reduce purchases only trivially in the *very short run* (say, a week or two), and only slightly more in the *short run* (say, 6 months to a year). People will gradually modify their driving habits to save gas and thus, will demand a little less. Car pooling is one possibility. But in the *longer run* (say, 2 to 5 years), gas price hikes induce people to buy smaller cars, get tune-ups more regularly, or rely more on mass transit. Some may even move closer to work, shopping, and so on. Longer periods allow consumers to adjust gas consumption more in response to any given price change.

Another interesting influence of time on demand is that some goods require substantial time for consumption. Time limits your enjoyment of food. (Your stomach does not have unlimited capacity — eating one burger a week is possible, averaging one per minute is not.) You can only wear one hat at a time. Vacations are expensive not only because of the money you spend but also because of income sacrificed when you do not work. Airline tickets typically have higher monetary prices than touring by car, but air travel is increasingly popular because of the time it saves.

Time spans also influence supply. Longer periods obviously enable firms to make more of a good available. Less obviously, supplies respond more strongly to price changes as time elapses because the ranges of feasible adjustment grow. For example, if eggplant prices rise, vegetable growers can increase their crops very little in only a month or two. A year or so, however, enables a farmer to acquire more seed and plow and fertilize more acreage. Thus, the price elasticity of supply is also positively related to the time interval considered. (In fact, all economic elasticities tend to be positively related to time.) Figure 7 summarizes these effects of time on supply and demand.

FIGURE 7 Time and Elasticity

The longer the time interval considered, the more price elastic (responsive) will be the quantity demanded or quantity supplied to any changes in the price of the product. The more time consumers have to make adjustments to higher prices, the less they will demand. Similarly, the longer firms have to adjust supplies, the more price elastic supplies are in response to price changes.

Elasticity and Tax Burdens

Tax reform is among the most pressing domestic issues facing the United States. The phrase *tax reform* is just empty rhetoric unless we know who bears the burden of various taxes. Elasticity plays a major role in answering the question of who bears the tax burden.

Tax Incidence

The *legal incidence* of a tax falls on the individual or firm responsible for writing the check for taxes to government.

> The **economic incidence** of taxation (or **tax burden**) *falls on the person who suffers reduced purchasing power because of the tax.*

Tax burdens can be avoided by the party bearing the legal incidence through *tax shifting.* A tax passed on to the consumer in the form of higher prices is **forward-shifted**. Taxes are **backward-shifted** if tax burdens are transferred to workers in the form of lower take-home wages, or to other resource suppliers in the form of lower factor payments.

Taxing a good drives a *wedge* between the price paid by buyers and the price received by sellers. Taxes tend to be shared between buyers and sellers. Supply and demand analysis allows us to see how taxes are shared.

Equilibrium in Figure 8 occurs at point *e* without taxes, and 16 million video cassettes are sold monthly for $7 each. Suppose a $2 tax per cassette drives a $2 wedge between the price the buyer pays and the price the seller receives. Graphically, the market demand curve from sellers' perspectives shifts vertically downwards by $2 to D_1 (distance *ca*) while the supply of cassettes falls to S_1 from the vantage points of buyers. (Although this supply curve "rises" vertically by $2 (distance *ca*) at each quantity, recall that shifts toward the price axis reflect declines in both supply and demand curves.)

At the new equilibrium, the quantities supplied and demanded must be equal, but the demand price and the supply price differ by the $2 tax. One easy way to identify this new equi-

librium is to slide a $2 tax wedge in from the left of the original curves (D_0 and S_0) until the vertical distance between them (*ac*) just equals the tax. Thus, at the new equilibrium, buyers pay $8 for each of 12 million video cassettes per month, while, net of the $2 tax, suppliers receive $6 per cassette.

The intersection of taxed supplies and demands helps to identify the proportions of taxes borne by buyers and sellers respectively. In this simple case, each side bears $1 of the tax, but different elasticities and slopes for the supply and demand curves will yield different proportional burdens. Note that the tax reduces incentives to produce video cassettes, as well as incentives to buy them. This may create inefficiency and is one reason economists refer to tax wedges as creating *disincentive effects.*

A critical point is that, after adjusting for taxes, the quantity demanded at the total price paid by the buyer must equal the quantity supplied at the net price received by the seller—neither excess demands (*shortages*) nor excess supplies (*surpluses*) can exist. Considering extreme elasticities helps us develop general principles about tax burdens.

Inelastic Supply The supply of land is perfectly inelastic. Rental prices paid for land reflect demands for land, and renters do not care whether their rent is kept by the landlord or split between an owner and Uncle Sam. Figure 9 illustrates the effects of taxes on the demand and supply of land. The annual rental value of the land is $100 per acre when demand is D_0 and supply is S_0. (If landowners do not rent their land out, we might treat them as their own tenants; the opportunity cost of not renting is $100 per acre per year.)

Suppose that a 50 percent tax on land rents were imposed. If landlords tried to recoup the $50-per-acre tax by raising rents to above $100, there would be a surplus of rentable land. As landlords with vacant land tried to attract renters, the gross rental price of land would fall back to $100. The owners cannot avoid the $50 tax burden per acre by selling, because any buyer would base the value of land on the $50 net rent per acre it yields, not the initial $100. From the

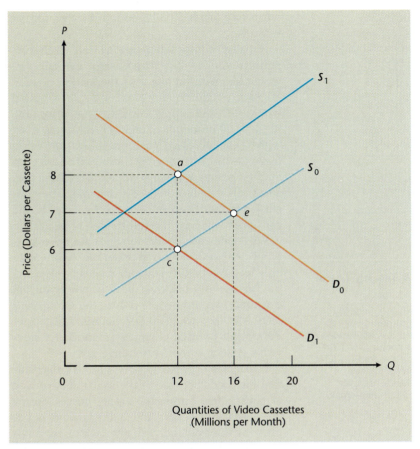

P

Price (Dollars per Cassette)

S_1

S_0

a

D_0

D_1

8

7

6

e

c

0   12   16   20   Q

Quantities of Video Cassettes
(Millions per Month)

FIGURE 8   The Incidence of Taxation

Regardless of the legal incidence, the burdens of taxes are normally shared by buyers and sellers. A $2 tax shrinks demand from the seller's perspective (from D_0 to D_1), but does not affect demand from the consumer's perspective. Rather, the consumer perceives supply as shrinking from S_0 to S_1 because of the $2 tax, while the sellers view their supply as unchanged. In this example, the tax burden is split evenly between buyers and sellers, but the tax may be quite unevenly split in other situations.

standpoint of landowners, the demand for land has fallen to D_1. Thus, land prices would be halved because of the 50 percent land rent tax; landowners bear both the legal and the economic incidence of the land tax because the supply of land is perfectly inelastic.[7]

Inelastic Demand   The demand for common table salt is among the least price elastic of all

regular household purchases. Recognizing the inelasticity of this demand, the early Romans enacted a tax on salt to ensure that the tax burden fell on the consumer. Let us see why you as a consumer would bear nearly the full burden of a salt tax. Suppose your annual demand for salt is shown in Figure 10. Because spending on salt absorbs so little of your budget and because of an absence of substitutes, even a 300 or 400 percent increase in its price probably would not noticeably affect the amount you use on your eggs or the rest of your food. You will consume roughly four pounds of salt annually, whether

---

7. An issue addressed later in this book is the "single tax movement," whose advocates like the idea that landowners fully bear any tax on land.

FIGURE 9   The Burden of a Tax on Land (Inelastic Supply)

The full burden of a tax on anything that is perfectly inelastically supplied is borne by the current owner or seller. Attempts to forward-shift such taxes cause excess supplies and downward pressures on prices. *(Note: The shift of the demand curve from D_0 to D_1 represents only the part of the demand curve that affects the net incomes of land owners. The full demands of buyers continue to be reflected by D_0, but half of the demand is absorbed as government revenue.)*

FIGURE 10   The Burden of a Tax on Salt (Inelastic Demand)

If demand were ever perfectly inelastic (and it cannot be), the full burden of the tax would be borne by the consumer.

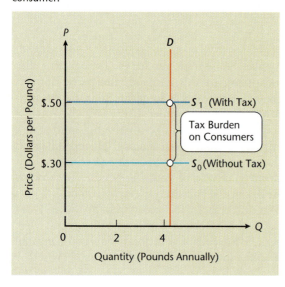

salt is free, costs $0.30 a pound, $1 a pound, or whatever.

Initially, competition among salt producers permits you to buy almost any amount you would like without affecting the market price of $0.30 a pound. A new tax of $0.20 a pound would shift the supply curve to S_1 as firms now need $0.20 more per pound to break even. Even with these increased costs, suppliers can easily forward-shift the tax by raising the price to $0.50 a pound, a price at which there is neither an excess supply nor excess demand. The conclusion is that if demand is perfectly inelastic, the consumer will bear the full burden of any taxes.

We stated earlier that demands are never perfectly inelastic. This salt example is intended only to show that if demand were very inelastic, the burden of a tax would fall primarily on the consumer. Would people reduce the salt in their diets if it rose to $100 per pound? Of course. Would salt be used on snowy roads or icy sidewalks at such prices? Of course not.

Elasticities of demand reflect buyers' desperation for goods because of the availability or lack of substitutes. Similarly, supply curves mirror the urgency of sellers' needs for customers because of the availability or the lack of good options for their resources. The more desperate buyers or sellers are, the less elastic are their respective demands or supplies, and the more difficult it is for them to alter their behavior to avoid a tax. This makes it easier to stick them with the burdens of taxes.

Our analyses of land and salt show why governments are fond of taxes on inelastically demanded goods (tobacco) or inelastically supplied resources: such taxes maximize government revenue. The story changes when elastic demands or supplies are taxed.

Elastic Demand   Arizona mines dominate U.S. copper production. Suppose Californians buy huge amounts of copper at a world price of $900 per ton after delivery costs, and that low transportation costs to California generate exceptional profits for Arizona mines. This would cause Arizonans to rely on the California market, so their supply of copper to California would slope upward (be less than perfectly elastic) as shown in Figure 11.

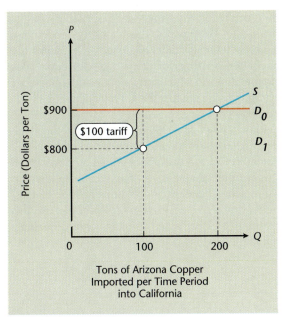

FIGURE 11 **The Burden of a Hypothetical California Tariff on Arizona Copper (Elastic Demand)**

If demand is perfectly elastic ($e_p = \infty$), the seller bears the full burden of any tax.

If individual Californians are indifferent between Arizona copper and that produced in, say, Chile, then the demand of Californians for Arizona copper is perfectly elastic at a price of $900 per ton, as shown in Figure 11. Now suppose the California Legislature imposes a special $100 "state tariff" only on Arizona copper. Californians can readily buy foreign copper at $900 per ton, so the Californian demand curve facing Arizona mines falls from D_0 to D_1. Arizona miners wind up with net prices of $800 per ton. In this case, the tariff is completely backward-shifted to Arizona copper mines' resource suppliers, whose wages, profits, rents, or receipts of interest must absorb this tax. Whenever demand for a good is perfectly elastic, suppliers bear the full burdens of any taxes.

Trade wars were precipitated by high state tariffs when states attempted to export their taxes to other states' citizens immediately after the American Revolution. This prompted authors of the U.S. Constitution to include a "commerce clause," which reserves to the federal govern-ment the right to regulate interstate commerce. Consequently, the ability of individual states to export taxes is now quite limited.

Elastic Supply The long-run supply curve of the aluminum industry is thought to be roughly perfectly elastic because average production costs are constant, no matter how much or how little aluminum is produced. Many materials are substitutes for aluminum in some uses, but none are close substitutes in all uses. Thus, Figure 12 shows a perfectly elastic supply of aluminum and a less elastic demand for it.

Without taxation, 140 million tons of aluminum will be sold annually for $500 a ton. Suppose that a tax of $100 a ton were levied on aluminum producers. Supply shifts from S_0 to S_1, because the producers would be unable to cover production costs unless they received at least $600 per ton from consumers, who cut back purchases to 120 million tons annually at this higher price. (As an exercise, compute the price elasticity of demand.) Notice that at $600 a ton, there are neither excess supplies nor excess demands. Production and consumption are both 120 million tons annually. The conclusion is that taxes will be 100 percent forward-shifted if supplies are perfectly elastic.

FIGURE 12 **The Burden of a Tax on Aluminum (Elastic Supply)**

If supply is perfectly elastic ($e_s = \infty$), consumers pay 100 percent of any taxes in the form of higher prices.

Summary: Taxes and Elasticity

Taxes will be 100 percent forward-shifted (borne by consumers) if either (a) demand is perfectly inelastic (salt), or (b) supply is perfectly elastic (aluminum). Taxes will be backward-shifted completely (borne by suppliers) if either (a) supply is perfectly inelastic (land), or (b) demand is perfectly elastic (copper). You may believe that these extreme cases of elasticities are rare in the "real world." Four chapters hence, you will learn that competition makes perfectly elastic supplies and demands reasonably common.

Few products have demands and supplies that are either perfectly inelastic or perfectly elastic,

but our results do suggest a workable general principle: The greater the elasticity of demand relative to the elasticity of supply, the greater the backward-shifting of any tax burden. The smaller the ratio (*elasticity of demand*)/(*elasticity of supply*), the greater the forward-shifting of the tax burden.

Elasticity is vital for understanding the decisions of consumers and suppliers, and you will encounter numerous applications of elasticity in the coming chapters. If you feel befuddled at times when you encounter applications of elasticity, don't give up in despair. Refer back to this material to clarify terminology and then keep plugging forward.

Chapter Review: Key Points

1. The *price elasticity of demand* is a measure of the responsiveness of the amount demanded to small price changes and is defined as:

$$e_p = \frac{\text{Relative change in quantity demanded}}{\text{Relative change in price}}$$

$$\cong \frac{\%\Delta Q}{\%\Delta P}$$

2. Problems result when calculating elasticity if initial prices and quantities are used as bases, so economists typically use *midpoint bases*. The price elasticity of demand is negative but, for convenience, we use absolute values to avoid the negative sign.

3. If price elasticity is less than one, then demand is relatively unresponsive to changes in price and is said to be *inelastic*. If elasticity is greater than one, the demand is very responsive to price changes and is *elastic*. Demand is *unitarily elastic* if the elasticity coefficient equals one.

4. Elasticity, price changes, and total revenues (expenditures) are related in the following manner: If demand is inelastic (*elastic*) and price increases (*falls*), total revenue will rise. If demand is elastic (*inelastic*) and price rises (*falls*), total revenue (expenditures) will fall. If demand is unitarily elastic ($e_p = 1$), total revenue will be unaffected by price changes.

5. The number and quality of substitutes, the proportion of the total budget spent, and the length of time considered are three important determinants of the elasticity of demand. Demand is more elastic the more substitutes are available, the more of the budget the item consumes, and the longer the time frame considered.

6. Along any negatively sloped linear demand curve, parts of the curve will be elastic, unitarily elastic, and finally, inelastic. The price elasticity of demand rises as the price rises.

7. Income elasticity of demand is the proportional change in the amount of a good demanded divided by a given proportionate change in income. Normal goods have income elasticities above zero, while inferior goods have negative income elasticities.

8. Cross elasticity of demand measures the responsiveness of the quantity demanded of one good to price changes in a related good. That is, price cross elasticity is the proportional change in the quantity of good *X* (Chevrolets) divided by a given proportional change in the price of good *Y* (Fords). If the cross elasticity of demand is positive (*negative*), the goods are substitutes (*complements*).

9. The *price elasticity of supply* measures the responsiveness of suppliers to changes in

prices, and its definition parallels that for the price elasticity of demand: the proportional change in the amount supplied divided by a given proportional change in price. The price elasticity of supply is typically positive, reflecting the positive slope of the supply curve.

10. All economic elasticities tend to increase as the time interval considered becomes longer. Thus, long run supplies and demands are more price elastic (and flatter) than short run supplies and demands.

11. The individual who actually loses purchasing power because of a tax is said to bear the tax's *economic incidence (tax burden)*. This may be quite different from the individual who is legally responsible for the tax, who bears its *legal incidence*. When these individuals differ, the tax has been shifted. A tax can be *forward-shifted* (to consumers) or *backward-shifted* (to labor or other resource owners).

12. If demand is perfectly inelastic or supply is perfectly elastic, a tax will be completely forward-shifted. If supply is perfectly inelastic or demand is perfectly elastic, the tax will be completely backward-shifted.

Key Concepts

Ensure that you can define these terms before proceeding.

price elasticity of demand
inelastic demand
elastic demand
unitary elasticity
income elasticity of demand
cross elasticity of demand
price elasticity of supply
tax incidence

Problems and Questions

1. The Jukes family buys 360 lollipops annually at $0.20 each, but would consume 480 per year if the price dropped to $0.16. Their price elasticity of demand is _____.

2. The U.S. Air Force purchased 170 ashtrays for their latest jets when the price was $875 each, but ordered only 130 when the defense contractor raised the price to $1,125. The Air Force's price elasticity of demand for ashtrays is _____.

3. If American drivers burned 185 million gallons of gasoline on average when the price was $1.15 per gallon, but cut back to 155 million gallons weekly when the pump price rose to $1.35 per gallon, the price elasticity of the U.S. demand for gas equals _____.

4. If a $5.98 sale on regular $8.99 cassettes raises a store's sales from 600 to 6,000 per week, the price elasticity of the demand faced by the store is roughly _____.

5. If national income booms from $4.0 trillion to $4.4 trillion and macadamia nut sales jump from 3 to 5 million pounds annually, their income elasticity of demand is _____.

6. If each 1 percent hike in the price of mousetraps reduces sales of cheese by 2 percent, the price cross elasticity of demand for these complementary goods is roughly _____.

7. When the Kallikak family can sell Shar-Pei puppies for $1,800 each, they offer 60 to the market annually, but when the price falls to $600 apiece, the family is willing to sell only 12 each year. The price elasticity of their supply is _____.

8. When the temperature drops from 34°F to 18°F, average attendance at Cincinnati Bengal football games dips from 56,000 fans down to 28,000 diehards. During cold spells, the temperature elasticity of the demand for Bengal tickets is _____.

9. When 200,000 gallons of water are applied per acre, 4 tons of jelly beans are harvested from each acre annually, but cutting back to 140,000 gallons reduces the crop per acre to 2 tons annually. The water elasticity of jelly bean production is _____.

10. If doubling your consumption of pasta to 6 pounds per week balloons your weight from a svelte 125 to a rotund 175 pounds, your pasta elasticity of blubber is _____.

11. Prices for precious metals are set on worldwide commodity exchanges and are influ-

enced by the values of major currencies, investors' inflationary expectations, and the state of international relations. These price changes clearly affect the quantities of gold and silver ingots sold, as well as the amounts of jewelry sold. Gold is also used extensively by dentists for bridges, inlays, and crowns. The *Wall Street Journal* reported that when gold prices jumped from $415 to $875 per ounce in the late 1970s, gold consumption by dentists fell from 706,000 ounces to 341,000. Compute the price elasticity of demand for gold as used by dentists for bridges, inlays, and crowns.

12. Suppose you calculate that the price elasticity of demand for your firm's product is 0.7. Your firm's policies should be changed immediately to increase profits. What policies should be changed? How do you know this?

13. When you calculate cross elasticity of demand, what are you trying to determine? What does a negative coefficient signify? A positive coefficient?

14. Suppose you calculate the income elasticity of demand for your firm's product, and the coefficient equals 0.45. What type of good does your firm sell? If the coefficient is −0.35 instead, what type of good is your firm selling? Why might your firm want to know the income elasticity of demand for its outputs?

15. Distinguish between the legal and economic incidence of taxation. Who bears the burden of a tax if it is forward-shifted? . . . if it is backward-shifted? Graphically illustrate two examples of a forward-shifted tax, and two examples of a backward-shifted tax.

16. Some sports fans support the home team regardless of how well the team does; others only buy tickets if the team is a winner. Demand grows as a team's record improves. Would you expect the price elasticity of demand to rise or fall as a result of a winning season? That is, would you expect season-ticket prices to rise more than proportionally relative to other tickets as a team's record improved, or less than proportionally? Is the elasticity of supply of tickets to sporting events zero, or is it positive over the long run? Why?

17. Prices for small, gas-efficient imported cars

rose even faster than the prices of American gas hogs during the 1970s, but these imports cornered a growing share of the American market. Rising gas prices were a key to this puzzle. What does this suggest about how demands for gasoline, imported cars, and full-sized Detroit products are related? Analyze pairs as complements or substitutes for all possible pairs.

18. After the price of oil began to rise in the early 1970s, revenues from oil exported by members of the Organization of Petroleum Exporting Countries (OPEC) rose each year until 1981. What does this suggest about the short-run price elasticity of the international demand for oil? Even though oil prices rose, worldwide consumption of oil also rose. What does this suggest about the income elasticity of the demand for oil?

19. From the perspective of the OPEC countries, what would happen to the elasticity of demand for oil if all countries that import oil imposed sliding tariffs just equal to any future increases in OPEC's oil prices? Why would OPEC be less prone to raise oil prices?

20. Suppose you are the State Tax Commissioner, and your state legislature decides to raise $120 million in annual tax revenues by imposing a $1 tax per case of beer. They have looked at the figures, and 10 million cases of beer are sold monthly at $3 per case in your state. If you were called to testify before the Legislative Tax Committee, what would you have to say about their prospects for $120 million in new revenues? Suppose your estimate of the price elasticity of the demand for beer equals one. How high would the tax need to be to yield the desired revenues?

21. Use numerical examples to prove the text's assertion that a demand curve for which prices are stated in dollars has 1/100th the slope of the same demand curve if price is stated in cents, and that stating quantity in tons yields a measure of slope that is 1/2,000th as great when using the same demand curve but measuring quantity in pounds.

22. The British *Globe and Mail* reported that in 1981, England drastically increased taxes on cigarettes:

In an austere March budget, the conservative Government slapped an extra 30 cents on the tax for a pack of 20. It followed with another increase in July, sending the tax up 30 percent [44 cents total increase in taxes] in six months and the average price of a pack to the equivalent of about $2.50.

Taxes grew to absorb roughly 75 percent of the total price of a pack of cigarettes; one industry expert estimated that cigarette sales would decline to 107 billion from the 121.5 billion sold in 1980.

a. Use the expert's forecast of industry sales to compute the price elasticity of demand for cigarettes. Is the demand for cigarettes relatively elastic or relatively inelastic? Does your answer conform to your intuition about the nature of the demand for cigarettes?

b. How much added tax revenue could the British government expect to collect? How much sales revenue (after taxes) could the tobacco companies expect to lose?

c. Approximately how much would the tobacco companies have had to increase prices to keep their after-tax revenues from falling?

CHAPTER

Consumer Choice

Economics relies on some concepts of human behavior that are closely akin to psychology in explaining consumers' choices as they try to maximize their satisfactions, either individually or as family units. Scarcity forces people to choose. In this chapter, we consider how individuals choose rationally in attempts to maximize their satisfaction or economic welfare. You will see that marginal analysis provides a logical view of consumer choices, which sometimes superficially seem dominated by fads or whims.[1] The consumer behavior we describe is also vital information for making business decisions, as you will discover while studying the next few chapters.

Our major goal in this chapter is to explore some foundations of consumer behavior. What lies behind demand curves, and why do they slope downward? We begin by categorizing things that satisfy or displease people and distinguishing between commodities and services. Our focus then turns to utility analysis, which offers a psychological interpretation of consumer behavior. How substitution and income effects translate into total price effects along a demand curve

is also explored. Then we address the issue of consumer sovereignty versus consumer regulation. Optional material on indifference analysis concludes the chapter. All these concepts should provide many insights into your own behavior and the behavior of others in their everyday living and consuming.

Commodities and Flows of Services

A **good** is anything that adds to our enjoyment of life; a **bad** detracts from our happiness. *Consumer goods* directly enhance satisfaction and include most ordinary objects of everyday use: food, clothing, cars, and so on. *Capital goods* include machines and other produced resources that benefit us less directly by generating consumer goods. Distinguishing these types of goods may require looking at use. For example, identical cars are consumer goods when used by households, but capital goods if used by firms. Huge surpluses may convert goods into bads—many home gardeners are inundated with more zucchini than they or their neighbors can eat, and much of it winds up in the trash.

Commodities are produced goods that can be owned—cowboy boots and garden hoses are

---

1. The introduction to marginal analysis (from Chapter 3) was expanded slightly in the opener to this part of the book. If you are unfamiliar with the Law of Equal Marginal Advantage, please read our part opener before continuing.

examples. We can hire and enjoy **services** without necessarily buying the items or agents that produce them: Tuition gives you access to classes, but you own neither your desk nor your instructor. Other services include medical care and TV broadcasts.

It is important to note, however, that all goods are ultimately reducible to services. For example, different foods service various parts of our bodies. Bicycles transport us. Houses protect us from foul weather, and clothes warm and adorn us. Machines transform materials to create commodities that are enjoyed when they generate services. In fact, virtually every economic activity has value only to the extent that it generates useful services. Capital goods, land, and commodities simply embody streams of services.

Market systems allow ownership of most service-producing goods, but the government prohibits owning slaves, nuclear weapons, or certain illegal substances. Development of a consumer theory to explain how individuals select among service-producing goods begins with a look at the concept of utility.

Utility

Nineteenth-century economists were fascinated by utilitarianism, a school of thought founded by Jeremy Bentham, an eccentric English philosopher.

> **Utilitarianism** *is the idea that the pleasure or pain from any activity respectively adds or detracts from a person's* **utility,** *or satisfaction.*

Utilitarians proposed numerous social reforms in hopes of achieving their central goal, *the greatest happiness for the greatest number*. Utilitarians assumed that individual pleasure can be measured and then summed, each person being weighted equally, to calculate aggregate social welfare.

Imagine that people were born with forehead gauges that recorded satisfaction in *utils*, an imaginary measurement, much as your electric meter measures kilowatts. Over lunch your head registers: 1 burger = 73 utils; 17 french fries = 31 utils; a small cola = 24 utils . . . net gain =

125 utils. Measuring the subjective value of national income would be a snap; simply sum everyone's gains in total utility. A utilitarian goal would boil economic policy down to doing whatever was necessary to maximize the utility score.

The appealing goal of achieving the "greatest happiness for the greatest number" remains a basis for policies advocated by many politicians and economists, but raises some acute normative issues. The author Dostoevski confounded utilitarians with his anguished question: "What if eternal happiness for the rest of humanity could be bought with the death by torture of an innocent babe?" Policies that *unambiguously* maximize social utility in an ethical manner could not be devised even if "utilometers" existed.

Modern economics rejects direct utility measures because: (*a*) most of us cannot specify our preferences more precisely than by a rank order (first, second, and so on) of possible bundles of goods, and (*b*) satisfaction is not scientifically comparable between individuals. There is no way to ascertain exactly how much anyone likes candy (or anything else) relative to someone else's enjoyment of candy. This led economists to develop *indifference analysis*, a more scientific technique explored at the end of the chapter. Even so, utility analysis offers rich insights into human behavior. Although subjective gains from a dollar's worth of goods may vary considerably among individuals, the following section shows how we can approximate the relative satisfactions from various goods to a given individual by looking at utility in monetary terms.

Total and Marginal Utility

Suppose you enjoy quenching your thirst on hot days with fresh lemonade; artificial or frozen will not do. If we measure utility in dollar terms, then MU_L is roughly the amount you would willingly pay for an extra lemonade. After three sets of tennis on a 90-degree afternoon, you stroll into your town's only air-conditioned lemonade stand, where the server, an old friend, informs you that icy, fresh lemonade is now $1 per glass. Your throat parched, you decide that one glass is barely worth $1. As you finish it and rise to

Jeremy Bentham (1748–1832)

Jeremy Bentham—lawyer, philosopher, and social reformer—was hardly an economist, although his influence on subsequent economic thought was immense. He admired the ideas of Adam Smith but rejected Smith's view that people's interests are smoothly reconciled through the *invisible hand* of competitive markets. Bentham focused on conflicts between private and public interests, especially as manifested in illegal activities. He saw Smith's "harmony of interests" as desirable, but not as a natural consequence of human behavior. Thus, Bentham devoted his long life to designing institutions that would facilitate the harmony of interests Smith took for granted.

Bentham tried to integrate law, economics, politics, and education into a unified science of behavior. His theory identified pleasure and pain as the forces controlling human actions. The goal of Bentham's hedonistic philosophy was the attainment of "the greatest good," or *maximum utility*.

Bentham's most conspicuous successes were in law and judicial procedure. He applied the principles of utility and "felicific calculation" to crime and punishment, suggesting that the evil of a crime is proportionate to the number of people it harms. It follows, therefore, that punishment of crimes should not be based on mere motive, but on the amount of social pain caused by a felony. Properly speaking, Bentham viewed law and law enforcement from the economic perspective of incentives. He theorized that stiffer punishments would raise the "cost" of crime, compelling self-interested individuals to commit fewer misdeeds, and the public interest would be served.

Bentham was notably eccentric. His pet pig roamed freely through his mansion, and he once petitioned the London City Council for permission to line his driveway with mummified human cadavers, which he thought "far more aesthetic than flowers." At the age of 32, Bentham immodestly "dreamt the other night that I was a founder of a sect; of course a personage of great sanctity and impor-

tance. It was the sect of the utilitarians."

Despite his eccentricities, Bentham's dream proved prophetic. His ideas attracted a loyal group of disciples (including the philosophers James Mill and his son, John Stuart Mill), and his proposals for social reforms were widely translated into action. Benthamite principles were among the intellectual wellsprings of many nineteenth-century social reforms. Possibly the secret of Bentham's success is that he instilled in his disciples not only specific ideals but also concrete plans to achieve them.

Bentham also dreamed of immortality. His sizable estate was left to the University of London on the condition that his body be embalmed in a certain way, stuffed and dressed in his own suit of clothes, and that it attend all meetings of the University's trustees. In this way, Bentham hoped to be "present" whenever utilitarian principles were discussed at "his" university. Bentham's wishes were carried out. (Minutes of all trustees' meetings record him as "present but not voting.") Over 160 years later, the dauntless utilitarian still resides in his glass closet in a corridor at University College, the University of London.

---

leave, the ade-tender offers you a break: a second lemonade for only $0.85. "All right," you say, "just one more." After gulping it down, you are already off your stool when the ade-tender asks, "How about another for $0.60?" Sitting back down, you put money on the counter. After your third lemonade, she asks, "How about a fourth

at the old price of $0.50?" Somewhat befuddled, you nod your head. The four lemonades have cost you $2.95 ($1.00 + $0.85 + $0.60 + $0.50), and your total utility is shown in Panel A of Figure 1. Notice that total utility is rising as you drink these additional lemonades.

After the fourth glass, you are ready to face

Total Utility from Lemonade Estimated in Dollars

$1.00 + .85 = 1.85
$1.00 + .85 + .60 = $2.45
$1.00 + .85 + .60 + .50 = $2.95
$1.00 + .85 + .60 + .50 + .25 = $3.20
$1.00 + .85 + .60 + .50 + .25 = $3.20
$1.00 + .85 + .60 + .50 + .25 - .50 = $2.70
$1.00 + .85 + .60 + .50 + .25 - .50 - 1.00 = $1.70

Panel A
Total Utility of Lemonade

$U

The Dollar Value You Place on Drinking Various Amounts of Lemonade

$3.20
$2.95 $3.20
$2.45 $2.70
$1.85 $1.70
$1.00

Quantity of Glasses of Lemonade per Hot Afternoon

$\frac{\Delta \$U}{\Delta q}$

Panel B
Diminishing Marginal Utility of Lemonade

The Dollar Value You Place on Drinking More Lemonade ($\Delta \$U / \Delta q$)

$1.00
$ .85
$ .60
$ .50
$ .25
0

Quantity of Glasses of Lemonade per Hot Afternoon

FIGURE 1 Total and Marginal Utility of Lemonade

The total value you place on consuming a good initially increases but at a decreasing rate (from 0 to 6 lemonades in Panel A), so its marginal utility is positive but diminishing (Panel B). You may eventually reach a point of satiation where the total satisfaction from consuming a good is maximized (6 lemonades in Panel A). At this point the marginal utility of the good is zero (6 lemonades in Panel B); thereafter, marginal utility is negative, as the good becomes, in a sense, a bad (more than 6 lemonades in Panel B).

the heat outside but the ade-tender offers you still another glass, this one for only $0.25. You cannot pass up the bargain. Then she invites you to "Have a sixth lemonade on the house." It is 90° in the shade, so you assent. Feeling a bit waterlogged, you turn down the offer of a seventh, even though it is free. "Tell you what," she says, "will you drink it if I pay you $0.50?" Being an impoverished student, you agree. You also drink an eighth, for which you are paid $1. Ultimately, however, you approach your capacity. You offer to drink the ninth for the $3 she offers, but only if you can wait a half hour. Since "It's now or never," you decide to pass. (You would drink the ninth for $25, but she will not offer that much.)

Marginal utilities from different goods reflect our subjective preferences.

> **Marginal utility (MU)** *is the gain in satisfaction derived through the consumption of one additional unit of a good.*

Panel B of Figure 1 shows how the marginal utilities in dollars are related to your total satisfaction from lemonade (Panel A). The points on both curves are connected as if the server had offered these deals by sips rather than glassfuls. Study the relationship between total utility and marginal utility. The accumulated area under the marginal utility curve (note the expanded vertical axis) equals the height of the total utility curve. That is, total utility is the sum of the marginal utilities for each lemonade you drank.

The Law of Diminishing Marginal Utility

The declining marginal utility from lemonade as you drink more and more during a given time interval occurs with virtually all goods and all people. Observing that similar reactions were common, classical economists generalized this behavior into:

The law of diminishing marginal utility: *The marginal utility from consuming equal units of a good eventually declines as the amount consumed increases.*

The word "eventually" is important. Horror movie fanciers might enjoy their first movie this week immensely, and their second film even more. But they almost certainly will not enjoy their sixteenth movie of the week as much as their third. Benjamin Franklin's observation in *Poor Richard's Almanac*, "Fish and visitors stink in three days," says far more about the diminishing marginal utility of visitors than about the deterioration of fish.

Consumer Equilibrium and Demand

Notice that the marginal utility curve in Panel B of Figure 1 contains all the data needed for a demand curve for lemonade: *Consumers buy an extra unit of a good only if its expected marginal utility is not exceeded by its price.* According to this demand curve, you buy only one lemonade at $1, two at $0.85, three at $0.60, four at $0.50, five at $0.25, and drink six only if they are free. This example illustrates how early economists explained negative slopes of demand curves by the law of diminishing marginal utility.

Maximizing Utility

We asserted that relative satisfactions from goods can be approximated by looking at utility in terms of money. We cannot scientifically ascertain whether one person gains more than someone else from an extra dollar of income or extra syrup on a waffle. We may be fairly sure, however, that the personal marginal utilities of each person from particular goods are roughly proportional to the goods' prices, because people adjust their spending patterns whenever relative prices and marginal utilities are not in balance.

Suppose that you allocate $7 from your weekly budget for ice cream, your favorite snack. Table 1 lists your total and marginal utilities from macadamia nut crunch and chocolate ice cream cones. How many of each will you buy at $1 apiece to maximize your satisfaction? Eating three chocolate and four "crunch" cones maximizes your total satisfaction at 30 utils per week. No other $7 combination yields more utility.

Let's see how this purchasing pattern develops. Table 1 shows that your first macadamia nut cone generates 6 utils. What flavor would you buy second? Each cone is $1, and either a second macadamia or a first chocolate cone would yield extra satisfaction of 5 utils. You are indifferent. Suppose you bought the chocolate cone, so that your choice for the third day would be macadamia nut. You will ultimately spend the $7 on four macadamia nut and three chocolate cones per week. Notice that the decision for each purchase hinges on the flavor with the greatest marginal utility per dollar spent.

Balancing Marginal Utilities

The *law of equal marginal advantage* (introduced in the opener to this part) indicates that decision makers allocate equivalent goods or resources (including units of purchasing power) in ways that are equally advantageous to them at the margin. Any other pattern is inefficient. Applying the law of equal marginal advantage to consumer behavior yields:

The **principle of equal marginal utilities per dollar:** *A consumer maximizes utility when the last cent spent on any good generates the same satisfaction as the last cent spent on every other good.*

The term "dollar" is used as an arbitrary small denomination of money. In fact, your purchasing pattern becomes stable only when the last *cent* spent on ice cream yields the same satisfaction as the last *cent* spent on lemonade, clothes, books, or housing. The price hike for macadamia nut

Table 1 *Total and Marginal Utilities for Ice Cream Cones*

	Macadamia Nut Crunch				Chocolate		
Quantity	Total Utility	Marginal Utility	$\dfrac{MU}{P_{S2}}$	Quantity	Total Utility	Marginal Utility	$\dfrac{MU}{P_{S1}}$
1	6	6	3.0	1	5	5	5.0
2	11	5	2.5	2	9	4	4.0
3	15	4	<u>2.0</u>	3	12	3	3.0
4	18	3	1.5	4	14	2	<u>2.0</u>
5	20	2	1.0	5	15	1	1.0
6	21	1	0.5	6	15	0	0
7	21	0	0	7	14	−1	

The price hike for macadamia nut crunch reduces its marginal utility per dollar (*MU/P*), so you substitute away from macadamia towards plain chocolate.

crunch reduces its marginal utility per dollar (*MU/P*), so you substitute away from macadamia towards plain chocolate.

Satisfaction from the last spending on a good is calculated by dividing its marginal utility by its price. For example, if the last video tape you rented was $2 and its marginal utility was 6, then $MU_{vt}/P_{vt} = 6/2 = 3$, and the marginal utility per dollar of the last tape you rented was 3. Individuals are in equilibrium when:

$$\frac{MU_a}{P_a} = \frac{MU_b}{P_b} = \cdots = \frac{MU_z}{P_z}$$

where $a, b, \ldots, z$ are the various goods purchased. In our ice cream cone example, the marginal utilities per dollar equaled three for both macadamia nut crunch and chocolate cones. A little introspection should confirm that your own spending pattern conforms to this aspect of the law of equal marginal advantage.

A corollary of the principle of equal marginal utilities per dollar is that consumer equilibrium requires that *marginal benefits from every good are proportional to their relative market prices*. Market prices and the subjective demand prices discussed in Chapter 1 are different ways of viewing opportunity costs. Demand prices can be thought of as the ratios of the marginal utilities of various goods. Only if market prices and demand prices are in accord will you buy. In equi-

librium, these subjective price ratios must equal the relative market prices for all the goods you choose to purchase. That is, $MU_a/MU_b = P_a/P_b$ for any two goods we choose to label *a* and *b*, respectively.[2]

Price Adjustments and Marginal Utility

Let's use this format to describe how quantities demanded adjust as relative prices change. First, consider what would happen to your equilibrium purchases of ice cream cones (from Table 1) if a worldwide macadamia nut crop failure boosted the price of macadamia nut crunch to $2 per cone. The purchasing power of the $7 weekly you budget for ice cream is no longer adequate; suppose that your spending on ice cream rises to $10 weekly in the new equilibrium. You now buy only three macadamia nut crunch cones, but your consumption of chocolate cones rises to four per week. Marginal utilities per dollar now equal 2. Adjusting your spending pattern to various possible prices for macadamia nut ice cream traces out the demand curve shown in Figure 2.

---

2. This statement is compatible with the principle of equal marginal utilities per dollar because in equilibrium, $MU_a/P_a = MU_b/P_b$; if each side of the equation is multiplied by P_a/MU_b and then simplified, the result is that $MU_a/MU_b = P_a/P_b$.

FIGURE 2 The Demand for Macadamia Nut Ice Cream

When the price of macadamia nut ice cream cones rises from $1 to $2, the equilibrium quantity falls from 4 to 3 cones per week (based on the data in Table 1). As an exercise, calculate the price elasticity of demand for these cones for this price change.

To summarize, the higher-priced goods you buy uniformly generate more marginal utility than your lower-priced purchases: The more you pay for a good, the more it is worth to you at the margin. Ultimately, the last dollar you spend on any good, including cash holdings, yields the same satisfaction as the last dollar spent on any other good.

Effects of Price Changes

You will buy less of any good that rises in price, substituting for it goods that decline in relative price. Another effect when the price of a good rises is that the purchasing power of your income shrinks. This drop in purchasing power reduces your total ability to buy consumer goods and services. How purchasing patterns respond when the prices of goods change can be decomposed into substitution effects and income effects.

Substitution Effects Substitution is the primary cause of negative slopes along demand curves.

*The **substitution effect** is that portion of the change in quantity demanded due solely to a change in relative prices.*[3]

Most goods have numerous possible uses. When the price of a good is reduced, it will be advantageous to devote the good to more of these uses.

For example, buses now provide low-priced transportation for many of us. Rides would be economical for far more people if fares were $0, and the homeless might sleep on warm buses instead of in cold alleys or under bridges. A $15 bus fare would induce most of us to walk, drive cars, or hire taxis. When ballpoint pens were introduced in the 1940s, they were refillable, cost about $25 each, and were a status symbol for business executives. They currently cost about a quarter, are used by almost everyone, and are discarded when the ink runs dry. Expensive ink pens are a rarity, and pencils are less commonly used than they would be if ballpoints still cost $25.

These examples suggest that we substitute some uses of some goods for similar uses of related goods as relative prices change. The critical point is that it is always advantageous to substitute away from goods that become relatively more costly and to expand uses for goods that become cheaper. Substitution effects underpin the law of demand: *quantity demanded falls as price increases, and vice versa.*

The substitution effect is the change in purchasing patterns caused by changes in relative prices alone, artificially assuming constancy in total purchasing power. But rising prices, for example, will reduce the purchasing power of your income. We need to deal separately with how such changes in real income alter purchasing patterns.

---

3. Mathematically, the substitution effect of a change in the price of a good is always negative. This means that an increase in the price ($\Delta P > 0$) of some good (coffee, for example) will result in a substitution effect (toward tea?) that decreases the amount of coffee consumed ($\Delta Q < 0$). Thus, $\Delta Q / \Delta P$ is negative. Conversely, the substitution effect means that a decrease ($\Delta P < 0$) in the relative price of a good (say, ham) will cause increases ($\Delta Q > 0$) in the quantity consumed (and substitution away from beef). Again, $\Delta Q / \Delta P$ is negative.

Income Effects The purchasing power of your dollars falls if prices rise, but a dollar buys more consumer goods if prices fall.

Income effects *are adjustments people make because the purchasing power of a given income is altered when prices change.*[4]

Suppose that a $400 tuition per semester hour absorbs so much of your budget that you initially only take classes part time. If stellar performance elicited a 90 percent scholarship, you could afford everything you bought previously and might simply pocket the $360 per hour your scholarship now covers. Instead, you would probably enroll in more courses, in part because of substitution in response to this drop in the relative cost of tuition, but also because of the now greater purchasing power of your income. This income effect would allow enrollment in even more courses, or you might buy more books, a better calculator, nicer clothes, tastier food, or more frequent concert tickets.

A slightly different type of income effect (only recently explored by economists) occurs when your money income is affected by price changes. If growth of demand increases prices, some seller's income must increase. Suppose you are the resident owner-manager of an apartment building. If rents in your area rise, opportunity costs rise for living in your own apartment instead of renting it out, but you now have more wealth and income because of the higher rents you can

charge. You might move into a smaller apartment because of the substitution effect, but if you are typical, you will opt for more luxurious accommodations. This type of income effect explains why some wildcat drillers who strike oil drive bigger gas guzzlers longer distances when oil prices rise.

Consumer Surplus

We can look at an individual's demand curve for a specific good from two different perspectives:

1. Most of the time we see demand curves as answers to the question, "How much will be bought at each possible price?" The quantity demanded depends on the price.

2. Alternatively, we might view demand curves as graphing answers to the question, "If people have certain amounts of good X, what is the most they would be willing to pay for an extra unit of X?"

This second perspective views price as depending on quantity. Both approaches yield the same demand curves.

The view that a good's marginal value depends on the amount available is a key to specifying in monetary terms the satisfaction gained from being able to buy at a single market price. Using our original lemonade example (see Figure 3), you paid $2.95 total for the first four glasses, but only $0.50 for the fourth (last) glass. But if lemonade sold for a flat price of $0.50 per glass, you would spend $2 to drink four lemonades, thereby gaining $0.95 worth of utility. This gain represents consumer surplus.

Consumer surplus *is the difference between the amounts people would willingly pay for various amounts of specific goods and the amounts they do pay at market prices.*

This is roughly the area below the demand curve but above the price line, assuming that income effects are trivial.

Even though consumer surplus cannot be measured quantitatively, this concept permits

---

4. The income effect may be negative, positive, or zero. All else being equal, when the price of a good rises, your purchasing power falls. For normal goods, the income effect (ΔY) is positive. For example, a decrease in the price of gasoline (G) increases the purchasing power of your income ($\Delta Y > 0$). This alone results in higher levels of gas purchases ($\Delta G > 0$). Thus $\Delta G / \Delta Y$ is positive. However, the income effect is negative for inferior goods such as lard, potatoes, lye soap, or black-eyed peas. For example, if your diet largely consists of potatoes because you are poor and they are cheap, your purchasing power increases if the price of potatoes falls ($\Delta Y > 0$) and you can afford to buy tastier foods to secure your caloric needs. Even though you may buy more potatoes because of the substitution effect, the independent effect of your higher real income is to reduce potato consumption ($\Delta Potato < 0$), so $\Delta Potatoes / \Delta Y$ is negative.

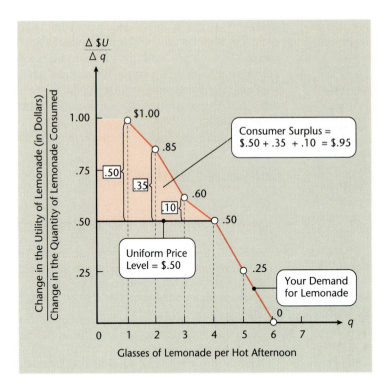

FIGURE 3 Consumer Surplus and the Demand for Lemonade

Consumer surplus is the area below the demand curve but above the uniform price level. It is the difference between the maximum total amount you would pay to consume a certain quantity of a good as opposed to having none and the amount you do pay because you face a uniform price for the good. Consumer surplus analysis assumes that income effects are absent. (*Note:* This figure is based on Figure 1 in this chapter.)

qualitative assessments of such things as the efficiency of some of the government policies addressed in a later chapter.

The Paradox of Value

Two hundred years ago, economists were stumped by an apparent paradox.

*The **paradox of value** addresses why absolute necessities such as water are valued (priced) so cheaply, while frivolities like diamonds are highly valued and command outrageous prices.*

Questions about the paradox of value were used to stump Ph.D. candidates in economics for generations. This paradox arises from difficulties in distinguishing between total utility and marginal utility.

Suppose that Panel A in Figure 4 depicts your family's demand for water. If you are typical, water is so cheap that you treat drinking water as if it were free: You drink water until an extra glass would actually detract from your well-being—the marginal utility is zero. However,

because you know that your water bill (which averages $20 monthly) reflects total use, you are probably somewhat careful about watering your lawn, washing your car, letting leaky faucets drip, running bath water, and so on.

But suppose you were offered an all-or-nothing choice: 100 gallons of water for $500 monthly or no water at all. (Many American families use 100,000 gallons or more a month.) If you could afford it, you would willingly pay at least $500 per month for water, limiting its use to drinking, preparing food, and sponge baths. Your lawn and plants would die, your car would go dirty, and washing machines and flush toilets would be forgotten luxuries. (Do you think this might explain why prospectors smell ripe after a few days of roaming the desert?) If you had to, you would pay considerably more for the 10,000 gallons of water you use each month than the $20 or so you do pay, so water yields an enormous consumer surplus.

The total utility of water is substantially higher than its marginal utility and price, while the total utility of diamonds is close to their marginal utility and price. We have shaded the areas representing consumer surpluses in Figure 4. This analysis should help you understand why diamonds, which are not nearly as necessary to life as water is, are valued and priced much higher than water. The total utility, marginal utility, and price of diamonds are nearly identical for those of us who own, at most, a few of the baubles.

Information and Rational Choice

Some critics doubt that people are as rational as economic theory presumes. If you asked typical shoppers in a grocery store if their buying patterns caused their marginal utilities for various goods to be in fixed proportions to the prices of these goods, they would think you were off your rocker. Suppose instead that you asked them why they do not buy more (or fewer) of particular goods than they do, or why they reject other items. They would probably begin talking about some things being "good buys," while referring to others as "too high" or "not worth it to me."

Most people seem to behave as economic models of demand suggest, even if they find incomprehensible the economic jargon used to describe their behavior. There is, however, far from unanimity that people really act in very rational or calculating ways. Take a moment to read the biographical sketch of Thorstein Veblen, a founder of the institutionalist school of thought, which largely rejects the kind of reasoning we have described. One reason for skepticism is that many goods are much more complex than the simple abstractions considered by much of economic theory.

Goods as Bundles of Attributes

Consumer theory has been expanded recently to consider every good as embodying a variety of utility-relevant characteristics, or *attributes*. Cig-

FIGURE 4   The Paradox of Value

Water generates substantial total utility and consumer surplus because of its low price, while diamonds have a very high price and generate far less total utility and consumer surplus. Marginal utility, not total utility, determines market prices and value.

Thorstein B. Veblen (1857–1929)

The economic characterization of human behavior as the rational calculation of benefits and costs seemed ludicrous to Thorstein Veblen, one of the great iconoclasts and tragicomic figures of economics. Veblen was trained in philosophy but concentrated on economics because of what he perceived as deficiencies in economic analysis.

A first-generation American of Norwegian stock, Veblen viewed capitalism and the American scene as if he were a newcomer to the planet. He found the institutions and behavior of Americans more than a bit strange—"exotic" and "bizarre" are probably more appropriate terms. His intellectual work consists primarily of "cultural analysis," the

high-water mark of which is pungent criticism. A good example of his satire is contained in this attack on the marginal utility principle:

The hedonistic conception of man is that of a lightning calculator of pleasures and pains, who oscillates like a homogeneous globule of desire . . . under the impulse of stimuli that shift him about the area but leave him intact. . . . He is an isolated, definitive human datum, in stable equilibrium except for the buffets of the impinging forces that displace him in one direction or another. . . . When the force of the impact is spent, he comes to rest, a self-contained globule of desire as before.

Veblen believed that human behavior is best analyzed as interactions of instincts and habits and that many social processes can be interpreted as results of cultural lags. In his doctrine of *conspicuous consumption* (status competition), Veblen explained how the desire to "keep up with the Joneses" motivates people to buy goods in a way that is culturally determined, not price

determined. In a more general sense, Veblen insisted on studying the origin and nature of economic institutions. He was especially critical of the *leisure class* and businessmen, whom he viewed as parasites. He argued that conventional economics fails to consider social and economic institutions, artificially reducing human nature to a matter of rational calculation.

As eccentric as Bentham, Veblen washed his dishes in a rain barrel and seldom bathed. Though grubby and quite homely, he lost several academic positions because he was a promiscuous and indiscreet womanizer, and he was still an assistant professor when he died at age 72.

Veblen's criticisms of economic theory were largely based on antirationalist premises and were certainly not the first of their kind. However, Veblen's savage humor and great erudition made him a formidable critic of the business system. He originated a distinctively American line of inquiry into economics, *institutionalism*, which continues to find proponents to this day.

---

arettes provide oral gratification and give smokers "something to do with my hands"; they are also carcinogenic, stimulate hostility from non-smokers, and waste time. Similarly, Sugar Smacks have a certain texture and taste and loads of calories. Rice and potatoes have very similar attributes and are thus substitutes; each is also quite complementary with steak.

The complex mixes of attributes embodied in most goods complicate many decisions. For example, even doctors and pharmacists may be

unaware of drug interactions that can leave tragedy in their wake. Nevertheless, we all must make decisions in an imperfect world rife with uncertainty.

Uncertainty and Imperfect Information

You can never be 100 percent certain of the attributes of a specific unit of any good, no matter how familiar. You may buy a moldy loaf of your favorite bread or be injured by an exploding cigarette lighter. There is even less certainty about unfamiliar goods that are bought only once or twice in a lifetime. No one who undergoes surgery can ever be certain in advance about the outcome of an operation. Nor, for that matter, can any surgeon. Uncertainty exists because we have only imperfect information about the present and no crystal ball to predict the future.

Information is costly. Acquiring full information might be incredibly expensive, and the value of some information may be trivial. The result is that decisions are made in an environment of rational ignorance.

> **Rational ignorance** *occurs because people seek information only as long as their expected benefit exceeds their expected cost. Thus, consumers choose to be rationally ignorant of much information.*

For example, most goods are available at a wide range of monetary prices, and most people pay more than the lowest monetary prices at a given time. But searching until you were sure you were paying the least possible for a good would probably absorb time and effort worth more than any resulting monetary saving. Similarly, you might spend a lifetime trying to identify the perfect spouse for you from the population of single people. The costliness of search, however, probably accounts for findings that propinquity (geography) is a major determinant of whom one marries. Broadening the options available in any decision-making situation can be costly and pose unforeseen problems.

Bewildering Arrays of Choices

Thousands of products fade into oblivion each year, but even more thousands are launched in the marketplace. Ever-widening ranges of choice become available as firms attempt to attract huge customer bases to their product lines. This is often held up as a major advantage of market systems: Even eccentric tastes and preferences may be accommodated when almost innumerable different goods are available. Typical grocery stores now carry over 15,000 different items; together, the stores in a large shopping mall often offer five times as many.

One result of having many choices and constant flux in markets is that the additional information required for wise consumer decisions is costly.[5] Firms constantly modify products in hopes of getting noncustomers to sample their goods: "Try our new, improved _____." You might be irritated if you searched high and low for a familiar red box of your favorite cereal, concluded that the store was out, and then, on a later shopping trip, discovered that the maker had switched to a blue box.

Even more confusion arises when choices are wider. A few happily married couples may swear that they are perfectly matched, but most singles who want to marry agonize over ever finding "Mr./Ms. Right." A gourmet may dither for hours over a lengthy menu at a posh restaurant. Some people spend days trying to find the perfect gift for a friend or the perfect suit for a job interview. Selecting goods would be simpler if fewer options were available. You may know people who would have few problems in finding a TV program to watch if fewer channels were available, but who cannot stop pushing the changer when a cable system offers 50 or 60 choices?

Soviet émigrés to the United States often remark that the biggest culture shock is choosing from the millions of options our society offers. Might some people who dislike decision making feel more comfortable in more regimented societies? For example, the arranged marriages common in traditional societies might reduce the anxiety many people experience when less rigid mating rituals prevail. Career choices might be far less traumatic for some people if they were simply assigned jobs. Social institutions exist, however, that lessen the need to choose. Private schools that require uniforms eliminate concerns about what a child will wear. A military career limits the scope of individual choice. At the extreme, few choices are required of prison inmates. Indeed, some convicts become so "institutionalized" that they cannot bear life outside prison walls.

---

5. Product differentiation may also drive up production costs, and hence, market prices—a process we describe later in this book.

Rational Ignorance and Artificial Intelligence[*]

Research into **artificial intelligence (AI)** has traditionally relied on pure logic to create computer programs intended to mimic the thinking of rational people. After two decades of research, researchers are beginning to conclude that "being logical and behaving rationally are not necessarily the same thing."

Logical thinking generally means that absolutely sound inferences require consistency with precisely specified sets of assumptions. Unfortunately, according to MIT's Jon Doyle, "any set of beliefs and any sound inference is as good as any other. Logicism ignores the purpose of reasoning and the value of beliefs and reasoning to the reasoner."

To avoid this conundrum, Professor Doyle argues that economic notions of consumer rationality and choice offer a set of tools that may help AI researchers design machines that are as rational as humans. As this chapter illustrates, the economic concept of consumer rationality involves:

1. Consumer preferences.

2. Limited resources that entail costs—accomplishing any objective involves expenditures of time, money, and effort.

3. Maximization of some goal, generally utility.

Dr. Doyle notes that economic analysis "provide(s) the proper framework for addressing the problem of how one should think, given that thinking requires effort and that success is uncertain." Computers, like people, must make trade-offs. For example, examining all possible moves in a chess game may be possible, depending on how long you are willing to wait for an answer, but inefficient. People inherently seem to know that learning involves something other than memorization. Indiscriminant memorization simply leads to "memory clogging" for both people and computers (although a few people may have photographic memories, a mixed blessing. Do you recall Raymond in the movie *Rain Man*?).

In the future, rational learning and artificial intelligence should combine to better equip computers (which have only limited storage capacity) so that they can discern what information is important, and what to ignore. Future computers ideally will mimic people's thinking processes in sensing when it is wise to be rationally ignorant.

[*]*Sources: Jon Doyle, "Rationality and Its Role in Reasoning," Proceedings of the Eighth National Conference on Artificial Intelligence, AAAI Press, 1990, pp. 1093–1100, and "When Logic Is Not Enough," The Economist, Aug. 25, 1990, pp. 69–70.*

Most of us, however, enjoy the wide range of options in a market system, and view the cars, houses, or clothes we purchase as expressions of our individuality. We are accustomed to the inconvenience and confusion of shopping or sorting out the activities we want to do. We almost intuitively develop techniques to make reasonable judgments in an environment of rational ignorance. Focus 1 addresses the issue of whether economic assumptions about how people process information are reasonable.

An even greater problem for any type of decision making is that *rational ignorance* may yield decisions that seem wrong in retrospect. People try to maximize their satisfaction by balancing *expected* marginal benefits (e.g., marginal utilities or marginal revenues) against *expected* marginal costs. Some expectations may prove too pessimistic; a dreaded blind date may turn out to be the person you've dreamed about. If people form their expectations reasonably, however, the probability of a pleasant surprise should, on average, be balanced by the probability of a disappointing outcome. This partially explains hangovers, high divorce rates, food poisoning, the spread of AIDS and other venereal diseases, fatal accidents, and why some people suffering serious illness may be stuck with incompetent quacks and die for lack of information about specialists who might have cured their disease.[6]

Quality and Prices

Why does anyone ever leave a tip after eating at a restaurant? Why, when shopping may entail driving longer distances, do so many people buy at high-priced stores — even if the same brands and items are available at discount stores closer to the customers' homes? And why would any firm ever pay any employee more than the most that worker could earn in another job? These three examples superficially seem to contradict the economic assumption that, after adjusting for transaction costs, people always try to pay the lowest possible prices for any good or resource. Habit plays a role in some cases, but desires for superior service and attempts to avoid unpleasant surprises are also important.

That the price people are willing to pay is positively related to the perceived quality of a good or resource is not a secret. Plump red tomatoes sell for higher prices than mushy ones. Renting a room in Aspen during peak ski season costs more than renting that same room in July. Skilled people who work hard, cooperate with managers and other employees, and are polite to customers are usually paid more than chronic complainers or those who prefer philosophical reflection to a solid day's work. But quality differentials in such

cases are not a key to answering our questions about tips and premium prices or wages.

Economists analyzing close substitutes that differ primarily in quality usually treat the markets as related, but separate. For example, race horses and nags are assumed to be sold in separate markets. A subtle point is that people will pay higher prices as implicit "insurance policies" intended to ensure quality and avoid mistakes caused by uncertainty and imperfect information. This inverts the notion that higher quality induces higher prices. Instead, the idea is that higher prices induce higher quality — sellers who receive "bribes" in the form of premium prices are expected to alter their behavior in ways that satisfy the buyer. This is different from paying a higher price for existing quality.

Thus, the prospect of a tip presumably secures faster service at a restaurant, especially one where you are a regular customer. Premium prices at swanky stores presumably secure better service and easier refund policies when dresses or sets of tires prove unsatisfactory. And workers are expected to be more diligent so that they can continue to draw premium wages instead of looking for other jobs.

In many instances, prices exceeding the minimums necessary reflect attempts to ensure that suppliers help buyers avoid mistakes in contending with uncertainty and imperfect information. There are circumstances, however, when society skews market outcomes; buyers are protected from the consequences of their own decisions.

Caveat Emptor, Caveat Venditor, *and* Government Edict

Can consumers make appropriate choices for themselves? *Caveat emptor* ("let the buyer beware") is an ancient legal doctrine that buyers are the best judges of whether they receive full value and so should bear the consequences of their own decisions. But the doctrine of *caveat venditor* ("let the seller beware") also has a long history, reflected in prohibitions against fraud and in imposing legal liability on sellers for damages if unknown dangers lurk in a product. Society increasingly holds firms responsible for product safety and reliability. Naturally, these

---

6. Some of these examples are drawn from Gary Galles' "The Best Choice May Be the Wrong One," in *Great Ideas for Teaching Economics*, 5/ed., edited by Ralph T. Byrns and Gerald W. Stone (New York: Harper-Collins, 1992).

regulatory costs are passed forward as higher prices, forcing us to buy "built-in" insurance policies on some goods we purchase.

The strongest trend, however, is toward government edicts that either prohibit or mandate certain activities. A century ago, one could legally purchase any available drug. Today, many drugs are absolutely banned (LSD and heroin are examples); others require doctors' prescriptions. And producing automobiles without a laundry list of safety equipment is forbidden (never mind that most car passengers fail to buckle up).

Cyclamate (an artificial sweetener) was withdrawn from the market in the late 1960s. This may have caused some folks to die of "fat attacks" until NutraSweet appeared in 1983. During this interval, the incidence of heart disease may have been inflated because heavy people could not choose to trade the risk of heart attack from obesity for the risk of cancer associated with certain diet foods. This list could be extended substantially.

We know that people's ideas cannot be pigeonholed precisely, but those who favor market solutions over government regulation tend to have faith in people's abilities to choose for themselves. They reason that if consumers lack information, government can either provide the information or leave it to organizations such as Consumers Union. On the other side of the fence sit those who distrust the market system and have little faith in the ability of the average person to choose.

The positions you take on such issues depend on whether you view individuals themselves or government experts to be better judges of a person's well-being. Both groups will suffer from uncertainty and rational ignorance. Should using seat belts be mandatory? Should AIDS patients be denied access to potentially beneficial drugs until the Food and Drug Administration has approved them? Should hang gliding be prohibited? If you are certain to die of cancer if you drink a case of artificially sweetened cola every day for 127 years and you want to do it anyway, should the government let you? These and similar questions about the role of government regulation are addressed in a later chapter.

Some consumer issues and the basis of demand theory have been our focus in this chapter; in the next, you will study firms' goals and objectives, and then, firms' production and costs. These foundations of demand and supply will be blended in the next part of this book to explain pricing and output decisions by firms under a variety of market situations.

Chapter Review: Key Points

1. *Utilitarianism* proposes that the best society is the one that provides the greatest happiness for the greatest number of people.

2. *Marginal utility* is the extra satisfaction gained from consuming a bit more of a good. The *law of diminishing marginal utility* states: The marginal utility of any good eventually declines as the amount consumed increases.

3. Measured in dollars, the declining portion of a marginal utility curve translates into a demand curve.

4. Maximum consumer satisfaction (*consumer equilibrium*) requires that the last cent spent on any good yield the same gain in satisfaction as the last cent spent on any other good:

$MU_a/P_a = MU_b/P_b = \cdots = MU_z/P_z$. This application of the *law of equal marginal advantage* is known as the *principle of equal marginal utilities per dollar*.

5. *Substitution effects* are changes in consumer purchasing patterns that emerge if relative prices change, artificially assuming that the purchasing power of income is constant.

6. *Income effects* are changes in buying patterns that occur solely because the purchasing power of one's monetary income changes when the prices of individual goods rise or fall.

7. *Consumer surplus* is the area above the price line and below the demand curve. It is a con-

sumer's gain from buying at a uniform price instead of paying prices equal to the marginal utility of each unit.

8. The *paradox of value* is resolved by recognizing that necessities may yield more total utility than luxuries, but that people adjust their purchases so that prices reflect marginal utility.

9. We are seldom certain about the *attributes* of any unit of a good. Information is costly and its marginal benefits may be trivial. Thus, our decisions are based on less than full information; we are *rationally ignorant* because we pursue information only as long as its expected benefit exceeds its expected cost.

10. Market prices commonly are positively related to quality, but higher prices than necessary often reflect attempts to alter suppliers' behavior so that higher quality is delivered to buyers. These "bribes" are intended to help us avoid unpleasant surprises arising from making decisions in an imperfect world.

11. There is an increasing tendency toward government edict as a means of overcoming transaction costs or solving the problems of rational ignorance and uncertainty. This is controversial, as critics ask: Do government experts know better than you do what things are good for you and what things will harm you?

Key Terms

Ensure that you can define these terms before proceeding.

utilitarianism
marginal utility
law of diminishing
  marginal utility
consumer equilibrium
law of equal marginal
  advantage
principle of equal
  marginal utilities
  per dollar

substitution effect
income effect
consumer surplus
paradox of value
rational ignorance
caveat emptor
caveat venditor

Problems and Questions

1. What concept in this chapter helps explain why a joke is seldom as funny the second or third time you hear it?

Table 2 illustrates Mabel's total utilities per week from apple pies and detective novels.

2. Fill in the columns with Mabel's marginal utilities from these goods.

3. Does Mabel's response to both goods obey the law of diminishing marginal utility? Why or why not?

4. Plot Mabel's total and marginal utilities from both goods on a sheet of graph paper.

Table 2 *Mabel's Utilities from Pies and Novels*

Apple Pies	Total Utility	Marginal Utility	Detective Novels	Total Utility	Marginal Utility
0	0	_____	0	0	_____
1	200	_____	1	250	_____
2	290	_____	2	295	_____
3	370	_____	3	335	_____
4	440	_____	4	370	_____
5	500	_____	5	400	_____
6	550	_____	6	425	_____
7	590	_____	7	445	_____
8	620	_____	8	460	_____
9	640	_____	9	470	_____
10	650	_____	10	475	_____

5. Suppose Mabel has $36.00 to spend on apple pies and detective novels; each pie is $6.00 and each novel is $3.00. How much of each will Mabel purchase in equilibrium?

6. Could Mabel increase her total utility by choosing a combination of apple pies and detective novels that differs from the equilibrium solution you just calculated? If so, what combination of goods should she pick to maximize her total utility?

7. Suppose the prices of pies and novels both drop to $1 because of a bumper crop of green apples and the advent of a cheap printing process, while at the same time, Mabel's budget shrinks to $10. How much of both goods will she purchase in equilibrium?

Mabel's demand for apple pies is listed in Table 3.

8. Compute Mabel's consumer surplus from pies if the price is $3.00 apiece.

9. What happens to Mabel's consumer surplus if the pie supply is perfectly elastic at $3.00 per pie and the government levies a tax of $3.00 per pie?

10. Would the substitution effect or the income effect be more useful in explaining why many students flock out of classes taught by professors who have reputations for being hard into courses taught by instructors who have reputations for easy grading?

11. Leisure is a good. When wages increase, the cost of leisure rises because you sacrifice more if you don't work. Thus, the substitution effect of a wage hike reduces leisure. How does the income effect of an increased wage rate affect decisions about work if leisure is an inferior good? . . . if it is a normal good? . . . if it is a luxury good?

Table 3 *Mabel's Demand for Apple Pies*

Quantity	Price ($)
1	10.00
2	8.00
3	6.00
4	3.00
5	2.00

12. Why do marginal utilities diminish more rapidly as consumption of a good is increased during short periods (a day) as opposed to longer periods (a year)?

13. The law of equal marginal utilities per dollar suggests that the last cent spent on any good yields the same gain in satisfaction as the last cent spent on any other good. Do your spending patterns conform to this idea? Are there ever barriers that prevent people from achieving this equilibrium for consumption?

14. Some reliable companies state that their policy is "Satisfaction guaranteed or your money will be cheerfully refunded." Are there some goods for which such guarantees by retailers do not alleviate a need for government regulation? If so, what are they?

15. What attributes distinguish goods whose regulation we can leave to the marketplace from those for which government regulation of consumer purchases seems appropriate? What criteria might be appropriate to differentiate between people who should be allowed to make their own choices from people who "need to be looked after"? Society does allow some people to make some choices denied to others. Can you name some instances?

Optional Material: Indifference Curve Analysis

The impossibility of measuring utility by more objective units than in imaginary "utils" vexed economists until early in this century. Economists developed a new approach, *indifference analysis*, which finally allowed them to sidestep this difficulty. This modern approach to consumer choice begins with a look at individual budget constraints.

Budget Lines

Just as production possibilities frontiers limit society's ability to produce and consume, each individual family is constrained by its income in choosing among consumption alternatives. A consumer's budget line is usually straight because the purchasing pattern a family chooses seldom affects market prices.

Budget lines *depict the choices available to consumers who face constant prices and who have given levels of income.*

Figure 5 shows budget lines for two levels of income using the assumption that asparagus (A) and a proxy for all other goods, called shmoo, (B) each cost $1 per pound. Any point in the AB space represents a specific combination of asparagus and shmoos—and would require a certain level of income.

FIGURE 5 Typical Budget Lines for Two Levels of Income

Budget lines depict the maximum possible combinations of goods available to consumers with given incomes and faced with specific prices. The slopes of budget lines reflect the relative prices of goods, and higher incomes yield higher budget lines. The budget line facing a consumer is analogous to the production possibilities frontier facing society.

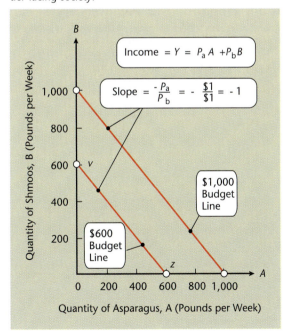

Quantity of Asparagus, A (Pounds per Week)

We can write the family's budget constraint as equal to:

$$Y = P_a A + P_b B$$

All family income (Y) is spent on either asparagus (A) or shmoos (B). Because income is limited, asparagus can be traded for shmoos as long as the family stays within its income constraint. Subtracting $P_a A$ from each side yields:

$$P_b B = Y - P_a A$$

Finally, we can solve for the amounts of B, given certain purchases of A, if we divide this equation by P_b:

$$B = \frac{Y}{P_b} - \frac{P_a}{P_b} A$$

This equation defines the budget constraint for the family in Figure 5.

Because both asparagus and shmoos cost $1 per pound ($P_a = P_b$), point v represents the situation where the family has $600 per week, all of which is spent on shmoos. Note that $Y/P_b = \$600/\$1 = 600$ pounds of shmoos. Point z represents just the opposite: All income is spent on asparagus, nothing is spent on shmoos.

The slope of the budget line equals $-P_a/P_b$ and is equal to -1, because shmoos and asparagus are priced identically. Thus, as income changes, the family's budget line moves in or out, but as long as the ratio of the two prices remains the same, the slope of the budget constraint will not change.

The budget line pivots if asparagus prices double to $2 a pound. A consumer with a $600 weekly income could now buy a maximum of only 300 pounds of asparagus, but could still buy as much as 600 pounds of shmoo. Alternatively, if the price of asparagus fell to 50 cents a pound, up to 1,200 pounds of asparagus might be purchased from a $600 income. Budget lines reflecting various possible prices for asparagus, with the price of shmoos still at $1 a pound and with a $600 weekly budget, are shown in Figure 6.

Indifference Curves

Consider two arbitrarily selected combinations of shmoos and asparagus, shown as bundle x and bundle y in Figure 7. Indifference analysis assumes that you always prefer more of each good to less, and that you either: (*a*) prefer bundle x to

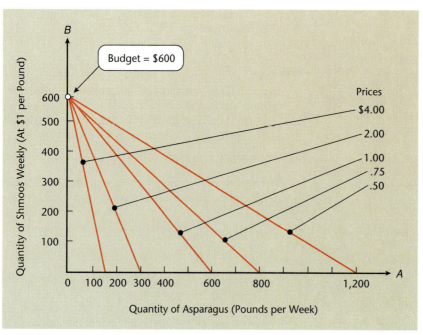

FIGURE 6   Budget Lines for $600 Income with Various Prices for Good A

All else being equal, as the price of asparagus falls, the budget line expands and becomes less and less steep. This reflects the declining price of asparagus relative to its alternatives. Alternatively, as the price of asparagus rises, less and less can be purchased if the entire budget is spent on asparagus.

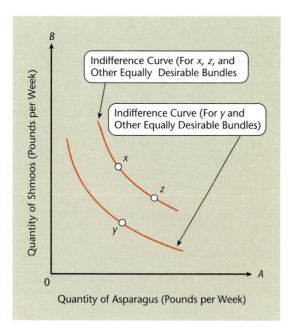

FIGURE 7   Typical Indifference Curves

Indifference curves reflect consumer tastes and preferences and connect combinations of goods that are equally desirable to a given consumer.

y, (*b*) prefer *y* to *x*, or (*c*) are indifferent between bundle *x* and bundle *y*.[7] Clearly you prefer *x* to *y* because *x* has the same amount of asparagus but more shmoos. Now let us create a new bundle *z* by adding small amounts of asparagus or shmoo or both to combination *y* until you are indifferent between *x* and the new bundle *z*. These bundles are shown in Figure 7.

We have connected the points representing the combinations where you are indifferent between *x*, *z*, and similarly desirable bundles.

> **Indifference curves** *reflect a consumer's preferences and connect all bundles of goods between which the consumer is indifferent.*

Indifference curves have the following properties:

1. Every possible combination of goods is on some indifference curve.

2. Indifference curves are negatively sloped because you will have to get more of one good in order to maintain your level of satisfaction when you give up some of the other good.

3. Indifference curves that are further from the origin are preferable because they represent larger bundles of goods.

4. Indifference curves never intersect.

5. The slope of an indifference curve reflects the *relative* subjective prices (marginal utilities) of the goods, $-MU_a/MU_b$.

6. Indifference curves are convex (bowed in toward the origin).

The first five of these properties should be fairly obvious. The sixth is predicated on diminishing *relative* marginal utilities. In this context, this means that *consumers prefer variety to monotony.*

---

7. Steven Plaut argues that the assumptions of indifference analysis are so unrestrictive that his cat is a rational consumer. Tuli chooses between bundles (tuna, milk, dry food) in an orderly way and suffers from diminishing marginal utility. See his "Illustrating the Rationality Assumption," in *Great Ideas for Teaching Economics*, 5/ed., edited by Ralph T. Byrns and G. W. Stone (New York: HarperCollins, 1992).

The following example asks you to use your intuition to show why.

Suppose that steak is your favorite meat and that you almost despise chicken. What would happen if your meat intake were restricted to steak for a solid year? We would bet that you would sacrifice a few steaks for a box of fried chicken. The more you have of a single thing, the more you are willing to give some of it up to have a given larger amount of something else. This preference for variety over sameness causes indifference curves to be bowed toward the origin (convex).

Consumer Equilibrium

Figure 8 shows a $600 weekly budget line when prices for shmoos and asparagus both equal $1 a pound, and various indifference curves for one consumer. Indifference curve I_2 reflects the highest level of satisfaction this consumer can attain, given her income level. Any other indifference curve that is on or below the budget line (for instance, I_0 or I_1) represents less satisfaction than I_2. Indifference curves such as I_3 would be preferable to I_2 but are not feasible because they lie beyond the consumer's budgetary constraint.

Indifference curve I_2 is tangent to the budget line at point *z*. The amounts of asparagus and shmoos associated with point *z* (A_0 and B_0) represent this consumer's best choices for consumption, given current prices and income. Notice that at point *z* the slopes of the budget line and indifference curve I_2 are equal. This means that relative market prices (the slope of the budget line) equal relative marginal utilities (the slope of the indifference curve).

Thus the slope of indifference curve I_2 at point *z* is $(-MU_a)/MU_b$ and the slope of the budget line at point *z* is $(-P_a)/P_b$. Because both are equal at point *z*,

$$\frac{-MU_a}{MU_b} = \frac{-P_a}{P_b}$$

or

$$\frac{MU_a}{P_a} = \frac{MU_b}{P_b}$$

Notice that indifference curve analysis yields the same condition for *consumer equilibrium* as the principle of *equal marginal utilities per dollar*, but

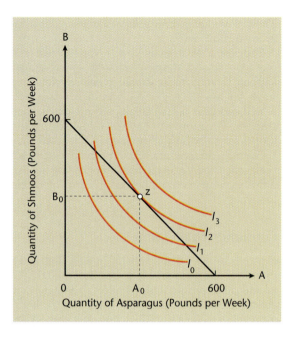

FIGURE 8 A Consumer's Equilibrium

Consumer satisfaction is maximized by purchasing the bundle of goods where the highest indifference curve is just tangent to the budget line. Any other affordable bundle is less satisfying; any more desirable bundle (than *z*, in this case) cannot be afforded.

we do not have to assume that consumers have "utilometers" and accurately measure utility for each product.

Deriving Individual Demand Curves

We will keep this person's income at $600 weekly and look at changes in the consumer's equilibrium as the price of asparagus varies. This permits us to extract the information necessary to graph a demand curve for asparagus.

Panel A of Figure 9 superimposes a set of indifference curves on the budget lines from Figure 6 for a person with $600 weekly income who faces various possible monetary prices for asparagus. We have connected the equilibria for these different prices of asparagus with a **price–consumption curve**. Each point on this curve represents a different price for asparagus on its corresponding $600 budget line. At these points of tangency, indifference curves reflect consumer preferences and budget lines reflect income constraints. Each tangency point represents maximum satisfaction given the constraints of this consumer's income and the relative market prices of the two goods. We can find the quantity of asparagus associated with each price

by dropping a line from the price–consumption line to the horizontal (asparagus) axis. Voila! We have the information needed to build a demand schedule and draw a demand curve, as in Panel B of Figure 9. Points *a* through *e* in the two panels correspond.

Income and Substitution Effects

You will substitute a good that falls in price for goods that rise in relative price. Additionally, when a good falls in price, the purchasing power of your income grows. These separate substitution effects and income effects can be analytically decomposed with indifference analysis.

In Figure 10, we initially assume that the price of asparagus is $2 per pound and our consumer is in equilibrium buying 100 pounds per week (point *a*). If the price of asparagus falls to $1 per pound, the new equilibrium is 280 pounds per week (point *b*). To decompose this total change into both income and substitution effects, we ask the question: How much would she have purchased if the price fell but real income (satisfaction) remained constant? The relevant budget line is tangent to indifference curve I_0 at point *c*. This budget constraint reflects the change in rel-

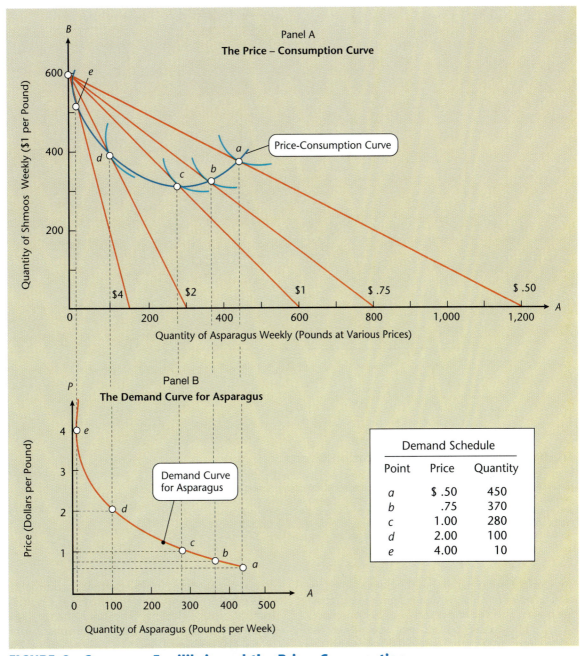

FIGURE 9 **Consumer Equilibria and the Price–Consumption Curve**

The *price–consumption curve* is traced out by the successive tangencies between indifference curves and the budget lines representing alternative prices for asparagus. In Panel A, points *a* through *e* show declining consumption of asparagus as its price rises. Points *a* through *e* from the price–consumption curve in Panel A translate into points *a* through *e* on the demand curve in Panel B.

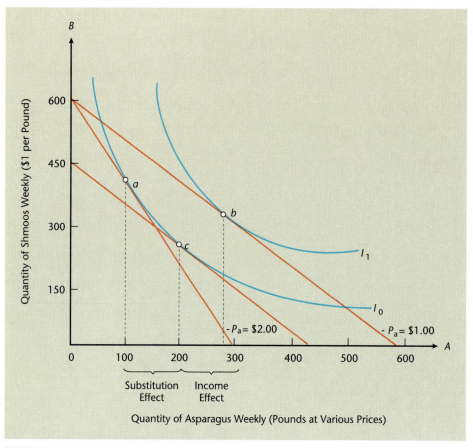

FIGURE 10 Income and Substitution Effects

With asparagus prices at $2 per pound, the initial equilibrium is point a, 100 pounds per week. With a reduction in price to $1 a pound, total consumption rises to 280 pounds per week. This total change can be decomposed into two components: income and substitution effects. The substitution effect is found by holding purchasing power (satisfaction) constant (point a to point c). The income effect is the difference in consumption associated with changes in income (point c to point b).

ative prices and is parallel to the budget line tangent to point b. Thus, with no change in purchasing power, this consumer increases her purchases of asparagus to 200 pounds per week when the price drops to $1 per pound (the substitution effect equals 100 pounds). The remaining in-

crease in consumption (80 pounds) is due to increased purchasing power (income) resulting from the price decline. The total change (180 pounds) thus equals the sum of the substitution effect (100 pounds) and the income effect (80 pounds).

Theory of the Firm

The business of America is business.

Calvin Coolidge

Home-cooked meals and public education are types of production, but the great bulk of production occurs in private firms — not households or government. Almost every building on a busy street houses a firm — from bakeries to car dealerships to insurance agencies and on and on. Firms are everywhere, sprouting like mushrooms even in nations that were, until recently, extremely hostile to private enterprise. Why does private business increasingly dominate production? Productive efficiency is the major reason.

Firms' roles as centers for production and as channels for the distribution of goods were introduced in Part 1. This chapter provides an overview of the international business environment, starting with an exploration of what production means to consumers, and some important aspects of the production process. We then examine reasons for firms to exist. Individuals and families don't personally produce all the goods they want, because such "self-sufficiency" would be incredibly inefficient. Firms coordinate team production to (a) reduce transaction costs and (b) exploit economies of scale. We also address the role of the entrepreneur and discuss the principal/agent problem, which arises when

monitoring behavior is costly and individuals don't share the goals of their employers.

Surveys of legal forms of business organizations and an explanation of how firms are financed lead to an examination of business goals — accounting measures of profit and the economic definition of profit seldom conform. This raises the question: Is the standard assumption that firms try to maximize economic profit consistent with the differing goals of decision makers within many firms? This chapter concludes by addressing criticisms of giant modern corporations and providing some evidence about the changing nature of business competition.

The International Scope of Business

Households and government generate some goods, but production — from prescription medicines to hot tubs to hot pizza delivered to your door — is concentrated in firms. Painting contractors, the Denver Broncos, and Honda are all business firms.

Firms *are specialized organizations that buy resources from households to allow the production and sale of goods or services.*

Firms range in size from an itinerant fruit vendor who ekes out a meager living by selling apples out of the back of a pickup to such multinational corporations as IBM, with billions of dollars in annual sales being generated by tens of thousands of employees operating out of hundreds of manufacturing facilities and offices spread around the globe.

Activities once operated by government are increasingly being "privatized" throughout the world. By 1991, for example, 6,000 retail shops formerly controlled by the Czechoslovakian government had been sold to private owners, and stock exchanges were being established in Leningrad, Moscow, and several other major cities in Eastern Europe. Western Europe, Mexico, and many South American countries are also experimenting with privatization. In the United States, privatization includes a trend towards local government contracts with private firms to operate municipal hospitals, garbage collection, or bus systems.

More than 80 percent of U.S. national output flows through firms, which also account for 75 percent of all employment. (Government accounts for most of the rest.) Any firm, regardless of its size, relies on production of goods and services that can be sold.

Figure 1 shows that privatization is not limited to countries that are in the process of abandoning centralized socialism. Throughout Western Europe and the Americas, the scope of government production and its direct control of output is giving way to production by private firms.

Production

Things that enter a production process are known as **inputs;** the transformed materials are **outputs.** Inputs include machine or labor hours, physical space (e.g., acres used yearly), raw materials, and partially processed (*intermediate*) products bought from other firms. A firm's output may be purchased by consumers, other firms, or government.

Natural forces or accidents may make things more valuable for human use. For example, geothermal heat and pressure convert coal into diamonds, and the life processes of generations of flora and fauna make soil more fertile. Relying exclusively on nature or luck would, however, sustain only a minuscule human population, most of whom would live a razor's edge existence. People's productive activities also enhance value.

> **Production** *occurs when goods are transformed to make them more valuable in* **form, place, possession,** *or* **time,** *and involves using knowledge to apply energy to transform materials.*

"More valuable," means that the goods ultimately generate greater consumer utility.

Altering *form* entails reshaping materials; crude oil is less valuable than gasoline. Augmenting *place* utilities requires movement; a lobster is worth more in a restaurant's glass tank than in the ocean. *Possession* utilities arise by shifting ownership from people who value goods less to people who value them more; realtors match home buyers who are moving into an area with sellers who are moving out. *Time* utilities are created when goods are made available when they are wanted most; speculators buy newly harvested wheat and store it to sell when wheat output is nil. Firms make goods more valuable in form, place, or time, or they transfer ownership to people who value them more highly.

The Short Run and the Long Run People often talk about short run versus long run consequences of events. For example, in the short run, winning a pie-eating contest may give you a bellyache. Repeatedly win pie-eating tournaments and, in the long run, you'll be able to get a job in a sideshow as Fatty _____ (fill in your last name). Short and long runs in economics (and pie-eating contests) refer to the completeness of adjustment rather than to time periods per se.

Relatively fewer options are available to firms in the short run.

> The **short run** *is a period during which the amount of at least one resource is fixed and firms can neither enter nor exit a market.*

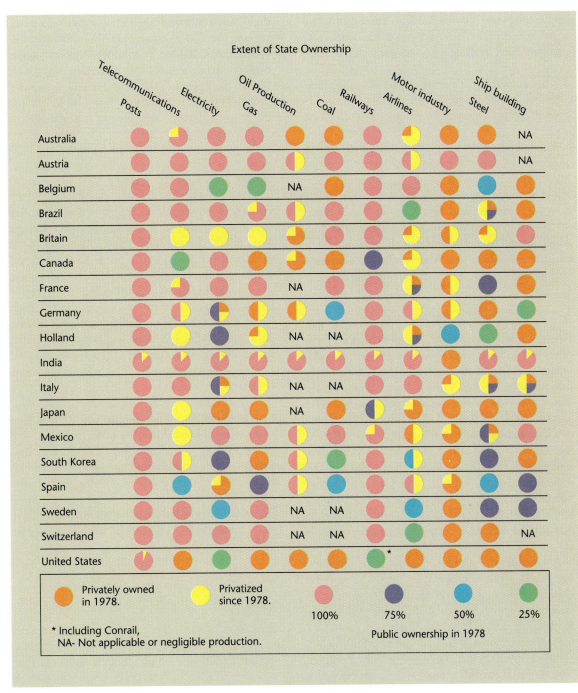

Extent of State Ownership

	Posts	Telecommunications	Electricity	Oil Production / Gas	Coal	Railways	Airlines	Motor industry	Steel	Ship building
Australia										NA
Austria										NA
Belgium				NA						
Brazil										
Britain										
Canada										
France				NA						
Germany										
Holland				NA	NA					
India										
Italy				NA	NA					
Japan				NA						
Mexico										
South Korea										
Spain										
Sweden				NA	NA					
Switzerland				NA	NA					NA
United States							*			

Privately owned in 1978. (orange)
Privatized since 1978. (yellow)

100% (pink) 75% (purple) 50% (blue) 25% (green)

Public ownership in 1978

* Including Conrail,
NA- Not applicable or negligible production.

FIGURE 1 Public Ownership and Surge of Privatization

In the past 15 years, a global quest for efficiency has resulted in the privatizing of thousands of financial and manufacturing operations, including many in these industries which are traditional targets for public ownership.

Sources: Originally appeared in *The Economist,* December 30, 1978. Author updates are based on data from 19 magazine/newspaper articles, and four books.

In the long run, however, a firm can completely adjust the amounts of all resources and can either enter or leave industries.

*The **long run** is a period of sufficient duration for all feasible resource adjustments to any event to be completed.*

The specific time intervals required for different firms to achieve long run adjustment differ markedly. Some firms could liquidate all their assets in days; others may require years. Children's lemonade stands shut down when it rains, but building a nuclear power plant can take decades. Capital requirements and the extent of regulation are only two of many influences on how long it can take to enter or exit an industry.

The Anatomy of Business

Firms operate one or more **plants**, which are production facilities ranging in size from the case a tattoo artist uses to carry ink and needles to a million acres of ranch land. Firms that operate more than one plant are *multiplant* firms. The Safeway grocery chain is an example. Most firms produce several types of goods and so are *diversified*; giant multiproduct firms are termed **conglomerates**. Conglomerates operate plants in several industries. For example, General Motors produces cars, trucks, and military electronics and hardware, and it is also heavily involved in consumer loans. In fact, most large corporations are conglomerates.

An **industry** is composed of all firms competing in a market: for example, tires, tobacco, or clothing. **Horizontally integrated** firms operate at a number of sites, each doing essentially the same thing. Thus, Toyota produces the same cars in Japan and California, and McDonald's "golden arches" grace the scenery from Berlin to Singapore. It might seem easy to identify the firms that make up an industry, but consider motor vehicles. Are limousines and golf carts reasonable substitutes? Should trucks and vans be included? . . . motorcycles? Is lumping all these goods in a single industry appropriate?

Another problem in identifying an industry is that conglomerates are often major players in several industries. Even nonconglomerates may operate at different production levels in an industry; these firms are **vertically integrated**. Most steel producers are vertically integrated, operating mines, smelting plants, mills for producing rolled steel, and fabrication plants.

Why Do Firms Exist?

No single household could produce even a respectable fraction of the array of goods most consumers take for granted — from brass beds to yogurt to films and TV programs to world tours. Businesses have huge comparative advantages over households in coordinating resources to generate vast amounts of output at low costs. Thus, firms exist because they are efficient. But firms can produce existing goods more efficiently or innovate new goods only if entrepreneurs recognize opportunities in the marketplace and then act.

Entrepreneurs The unique role that defines *entrepreneurs* is establishment of a firm that, with luck, generates profit; other qualities entrepreneurs seem to share are explored in Focus 1. Entrepreneurs prosper by establishing firms that efficiently coordinate specialized resources. To succeed, a firm's production teams must (*a*) reduce transaction costs, and (*b*) exploit economies of scale.

Team Production and Economies of Scale

Specialization and the division of labor are at the heart of modern production. People once relied almost exclusively on production within families or clans. Today, a few types of production remain relatively solitary pursuits, such as writing novels or customizing computer software, and relatively few resources are required to successfully operate such small organizations as magazine stands or mortuaries. But only huge organizations can efficiently produce and market steel,

So You Want to Be an Entrepreneur . . . ?

Work provides many people with the primary meaning for their lives. Surveys indicate that most students want interesting, secure, and remunerative careers. Many also seek jobs that reward hard work with rapid advancement or that contribute to social well-being. Finding "the right job" may entail a little job hopping, but most people spend most of their working lives employed by one large firm. With luck, it has a good pension plan.

Successful entrepreneurs, however, often march to the beat of their own drummers. Many seemed misfits early in their careers, losing a series of jobs because they were not team players. Most equated compromise with losing and would do almost anything to get their own way. People afflicted with personalities that conflict with large organizations often express desires to "be my own boss," but few who go off on their own enjoy much success. Indeed, most who eventually succeed do so only after a series of failures. Overstating how devastating bankruptcy can be is difficult, especially for entrepreneurs who stake their dreams on the success or failure of an enterprise.

Several characteristics seem to separate highly successful entrepreneurs from most small proprietors or heads of giant corporations:

1. *Vision and timing.* Entrepreneurs see opportunities where others see only problems. Being in the right place at the right time is often a key. Different people interpret the same complex facts differently. Successful entrepreneurs tend to organize information so that solutions seem obvious. Their solutions may improve quality in existing goods, cut production costs, or they may develop new products and introduce them to the marketplace.

2. *Conviction and action.* Entrepreneurs act when they perceive a problem. Other people may see solutions, but fear of losing regular paychecks prevents them from pursuing their ideas. Entrepreneurs tend to have powerful egos; they want to leave their marks on the world.

3. *Bearing of risk and uncertainty.* Successful entrepreneurs typically have such faith in their plans that they are willing to risk all their time and capital (and, where possible, other people's time and capital), rejecting the financial security most people seek.

4. *Workaholism.* Most people want high income from a job that allows leisure every evening and on weekends and regular vacations. A 40-hour, 9-to-5 job is not a goal of most successful entrepreneurs, some of whom put in 100+ hours per week for decades.

G. L. S. Shackle, a famous economist, describes enterprise as "action in pursuit of the imagined, deemed possible."[*] Entrepreneurs imagine alternative uses of resources, and by organizing resources to match their visions, they alter the course of history. If this brief discussion has not squelched any desire you might have to be an entrepreneur, then you need to watch for opportunities to provide things that people want, be willing to absorb risk, and work extraordinarily hard. Then pray for luck.

---

[*]Robert F. Hebert and Albert N. Link, The Entrepreneur, "Forward" by G. L. S. Shackle (New York: Praeger, 1982).

gasoline, or oil tankers. Specialized technology often requires teamwork by thousands of workers using billions of dollars' worth of economic capital.

> **Economies of scale** *in production occur when average costs decline in the long run as a firm expands its productive capacity.*

When production processes use vast amounts of capital and armies of employees, the *managerial coordination* of production teams becomes as specialized a function as engineering or piloting a jumbo jet, but planning and coordination go on regardless of the scale of production. Production can be coordinated by professional managers (who are employees of corporations or government agencies), or by entrepreneurs.

Reducing Transaction Costs

Transaction costs shrink consumers' purchasing power and resource suppliers' incomes. Enormous transaction costs would be incurred in trying to coordinate a formal dinner by hiring resources instead of buying products from specialized firms — information, mobility, and negotiation processes are far from instantaneous, perfect, and costless. Imagine how difficult it would be to operate a grocery store, build a home, or make all the parts and then assemble a car if all workers were independent subcontractors rather than employees.

You learned in Chapter 4 that intermediaries reduce transaction costs. Virtually all firms are intermediaries, in the sense that the materials they process to make more valuable are secured from other firms. For example, a chicken ranch that sells eggs to the supermarket where you buy groceries can be viewed as merely altering the form of the chicken feed it bought from a supplier. Thus, chicken ranches are intermediaries that, like all firms, could not survive without reducing transaction costs for their customers.

Shopping malls are in the business of renting space to retail firms. This reduces transaction costs for both retailers and consumers. Malls help slash transaction costs by bringing together large numbers of similar outlets that allow shop-

pers to see what is available without traveling extensively between stores, and to compare prices and quality. The variety of goods available in modern supermarkets provides another example of how a firm can "cluster" goods to minimize the transaction costs of customers.

One hurdle to efficient production is that a firm's goals may not be well served by the resource suppliers whose productive activities require coordination. Such conflicts are important determinants of the best legal form for a business. Therefore, we will explore sources of conflict a bit before dealing with alternative legal forms of business.

The Principal/Agent Problem

Cooking requires neither assent nor compliance from the food you buy. Firms, on the other hand, face major obstacles when coordinating the productive efforts of groups of employees with disparate goals and objectives. Specialization and the complexity of everyday life lead to countless situations where one party, a principal, contracts with another, an agent, in expectation that the agent will serve the principal's interest.

> A **principal** *is a party that contractually engages an* **agent** *who agrees to represent the principal's interests for certain purposes.*

Large firms operate primarily through agents, which include most of their employees. Pay incentives are one aspect of contracts by which people try to alter the behavior of others. Some contracts between principals and agents are verbal and informal. You are a principal, for example, if a friend agrees to fill your gas tank if she can "keep the change" from the $20 you hand her. Her agreement makes her your agent.

> The **principal/agent problem** *arises when the agent pursues personal goals that conflict with the principal's contractual rights.*

Your friend, for example, might keep more "change" from the $20 by not completely filling your tank, or she might buy cheap gas after you specified premium unleaded.

Table 1 *Sales, Employment, and Profits in U.S. Business Firms (1986)*

Form of Business	Numbers of Firms (thousands)		Total Sales (billions)		Profits (billions)	
	Number	Percent	Dollars	Percent	Dollars	Percent
Proprietorships	12,394	70.7	559.4	6.1	90.4	26.3
Partnerships	1,703	9.7	378.7	4.1	−17.4	−5.0
Corporations	3,429	19.6	8,281.9	89.8	269.6	78.7
TOTALS	17,526	100.0	9,220.0	100.0	342.6	100.0

Source: Statistical Abstract, 1990.

Conflicts between the legal rights of a firm (the principal) and the goals of its employees (one group of its agents) can cause inefficiency. A firm's costs will be inefficiently high if, for example, it hires a purchasing agent who solicits bribes from suppliers who then sell intermediate goods to the firm at inflated prices.

Just as most people would rather get goods free than pay for them, many workers want to minimize their effort but still be paid. The principal/agent problem of *shirking* occurs when workers fail to perform properly.[1] Shirking occurs, for example, if a security guard naps during a night shift, or when a professional athlete with a guaranteed contract reports to training camp flabby and poorly conditioned. Shirking also occurs if, say, a raw materials supplier tries to charge for more than it delivers. Consequently, monitoring resource suppliers' performance is a major task in coordinating production. Before we examine other aspects of the principal/agent problem, we need to look at the advantages and disadvantages of different possible legal forms of business that entrepreneurs must weigh before establishing firms, or when the nature of their operations changes.

Legal Forms of Business

Businesses are operated as sole proprietorships, partnerships, or corporations. Table 1 indicates that roughly 70 percent of all U.S. firms are pro-

prietorships, but they account for only 6 percent of total sales in the United States. At the other extreme, only one firm in five is incorporated, but corporations generate 90 percent of all revenues. The message seems to be that a first step toward success is to incorporate. Then why do 10 million or so sole proprietorships exist? The answer comes from an examination of the strengths and weaknesses of each type of organization.

Sole Proprietorships

Establishing a sole proprietorship requires little more than declaring, "I am in business."

A **sole proprietorship** *is a firm owned and operated by one individual.*

Major advantages are a proprietorship's relative (*a*) ease of organization, (*b*) flexibility, (*c*) control by the owner, and (*d*) freedom from government regulation.

Sole proprietors, however, suffer from some major drawbacks. Size is limited by the proprietor's initial wealth and credit standing and by business profits over time. Capital accumulation tends to be a slow process. Proprietors normally perform most management functions, and such firms lack permanence—they cannot outlive their owners. The greatest disadvantage, however, is a proprietor's unlimited liability.

Liability *refers to legal obligations to pay for debts or damages.*

Nearly all a proprietor owns, including personal assets (e.g., savings and cars), may be sold to pay

---

1. An employee/employer relationship can avoid possible principal/agent problems if a firm's owner closely and directly supervises the employee.

a firm's debts if it fails or is held liable for damages in a lawsuit. More is at risk than an owner's investment, although insurance can guard against some legal hazards.

Partnerships

Pooled resources in a partnership can expand the resource base that limits proprietorships.

> **Partnerships** *are extensions of proprietorships; two or more people combine their resources to form a business.*

Partnerships are easy to establish, relatively simple to control, allow some specialized management, and are subject to relatively few regulations. Many doctors, for example, operate as partnerships. This permits them to share office expenses and reduces the need for every doctor to be "on-call" to patients 24 hours a day and 7 days a week.

A type of principal/agent problem arises because each partner incurs unlimited personal liability for a firm's debts. A partner is automatically your agent, so dishonest or incompetent partners can cost you all your possessions. Shared ownership also creates discord about policies, decreasing personal control—a vital issue for many entrepreneurs. Other drawbacks are that resources for growth tend to remain quite limited, and partnerships automatically dissolve upon the withdrawal or death of any partner.

Corporations

The loss of entrepreneurial control that occurs when a sole proprietor takes on a partner escalates tremendously when even more people (e.g., stockholders, professional managers, and government) come into the picture because an entrepreneur decides to incorporate. Incorporating a firm requires submitting a *charter* to a state government outlining the intended line of business and specifying how the firm will be financed and governed.

> **Corporations** *are firms sanctioned by state laws and are considered legal persons separate and distinct from their owners.*

Once corporations are formed, numerous special taxes and regulations hinder their operations.

Then why are firms ever incorporated? A major reason is that corporations excel at raising financial capital because they can sell **common stocks** (ownership shares) and **bonds** (corporate IOUs). Combined with undistributed profits, these funds facilitate acquisition of economic capital. A second corporate advantage is the *limited liability* of stockholders, which means that owners of a corporation cannot lose more than they paid for stock. Their other assets are not directly jeopardized if the firm fails.

Other advantages include potential stability and permanence; corporations do not shut down when a stockholder dies. A final advantage is that large corporations can hire highly specialized management. In fact, large corporations are often controlled by their top managers because stock is so widely spread that individual stockholders have little influence on business policies. This type of principal/agent problem yields potential gains for corporate managers, but poses major disadvantages for stockholders.

Other negative aspects of incorporation are special corporate taxes and regulations. The divorce of ownership from managerial control opens up opportunities for fraud (a principal/agent problem), so strict accounting and reporting requirements govern corporate life and add to business costs. Because corporations are viewed as fruitful sources of tax revenue, corporate income is subject to *double taxation*: Corporations pay taxes on their incomes and then, after some after-tax income is distributed to stockholders, these *dividends* are taxed again at the individual's personal income tax rate. Table 2 summarizes the attributes of the three major forms of business organization.

Other Forms of Enterprise

Proprietorships, partnerships, and corporations dominate production, but other types of organizations exist. **Producer cooperatives** share profits from marketing such things as handicrafts or farm outputs. **Consumer cooperatives** share savings achieved by buying in quantity. Cooperatives are flourishing in China and the USSR,

Table 2 *Summary of Legal Forms of Business Organization*

Form of Business	Advantages	Disadvantages
Sole Proprietorship	1. Easy to organize. 2. Simple to control. 3. Freedom of operation. 4. Not subject to much government regulation.	1. Difficult to acquire funds (capital) for expansion. 2. Firm lacks permanence. 3. Unlimited liability. 4. Owner must perform all management functions.
Partnership	1. Easy to organize. 2. Greater specialization of management is possible. 3. Securing financial resources easier than in sole proprietorship (pooling of funds). 4. Subject to limited regulation.	1. Division of ownership may lead to disagreements. 2. Death or withdrawal of one partner automatically ends the organization. 3. Subject to unlimited liability. 4. Financial resources are typically quite limited.
Corporation	1. Capability of raising large amounts of capital through sale of stocks and bonds (but bank loans dominate financing). 2. Limited liability of stockholders. 3. Stability and permanence: is a legal entity (person) all its own. 4. Employment of specialized management personnel.	1. Subject to considerable government regulation. 2. Taxes and organizing costs for corporations are heavy burdens. 3. Double taxation of corporate income and dividends. 4. Separation of ownership and control (principal/agent problems).

primarily because many Chinese and Soviet citizens, while recognizing the shortcomings of state enterprises, don't yet feel ready to launch purely private business firms. Cooperatives may be an intermediate step on the road towards capitalism.

Nonprofit corporations operate most hospitals, private schools, public radio and TV stations, and charities. Standard corporations are run for profit — a purpose inconsistent with the goals of most people who operate charities. **Closely held corporations** and **limited partnerships** are intended to secure tax advantages and limited liability for family-owned businesses or partnerships. Many doctors, dentists, and lawyers who would normally be considered as sole proprietors operate as **personal corporations**. Still other minor organizational forms abound, varying in their specifics by the state laws governing them. Determining how a firm will be legally organized is only one step for an entrepre-

neur. Securing business funding is another hurdle in establishing a firm.

Financing Business Operations

Production is necessary before goods can be sold to generate revenue. The lag between incurring production costs and receiving revenue means that some great ideas for a business are never put into action. Few families have sufficient wealth to launch fledgling enterprises on even a moderate scale without some external financing. Economic growth in a healthy economy requires financial intermediation.

Financial intermediaries *channel people's saving to investors in economic capital.*

Financial intermediaries include commercial banks, insurance companies, and stockbrokers.

This process of moving private saving through markets for financial capital to investors in economic capital is shown in a circular flow model in Figure 2, which clearly illustrates that the ultimate capital suppliers in our economy are savers.

The relatively small amounts individual families save preclude devoting sufficient resources to secure information to ensure wise investment decisions. High transaction costs are incurred in identifying which financial investments are likely to be reasonably secure and capable of generating solid returns to savers. Consequently, although owners of noncorporate firms often sink all their savings into their firms, only a minority of other families buy stocks and bonds directly.

Most families' saving takes the form of deposits in financial institutions—banks, mutual funds, or other firms that specialize in trimming transaction costs and exploiting economies of scale while executing ironclad financial contracts

and processing financial information. Thus, external financing for business operations flows primarily through huge financial intermediaries.

Self-Financing and Retained Earnings

We have indicated that the initial size of a sole proprietorship or partnership is limited by the personal credit ratings and resources of the owners. Many small corporations are similarly limited to the resources of those who start them. Most proprietorships or partnerships that succeed build up slowly because growth depends on income from the business. Corporate growth may also be financed by *retained earnings* — income that is not distributed as dividends to stockholders. Unless an established and prosperous firm aggressively tries to absorb substantial numbers of other firms through merger, much of its growth tends to be internally financed.

FIGURE 2 Financial Intermediation in a Circular Flow Model

Household saving is channeled to investors in economic capital through financial intermediaries. More direct forms of investment are precluded for most families by high transaction costs, which include such costs as stockbrokers' fees and the costs of negotiating contracts.

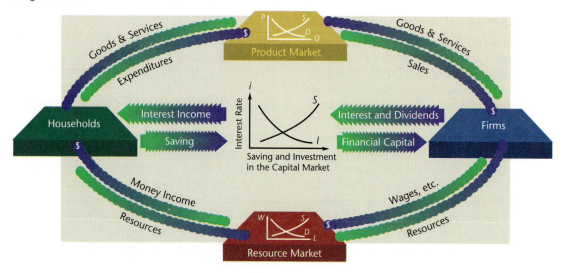

The prospect that internal financing may be adequate for growth at some distant future time is cold comfort for aggressive entrepreneurs in the throes of launching an enterprise. Some small firms are able to grow rapidly by preparing persuasive business plans that improve access to financial capital. The right to issue stocks and bonds facilitates this access if a firm is incorporated.

Common Stock

Issuing common stock is one way corporations may secure financing for economic capital.

> **Common stock** *provides holders with shares of ownership in a corporation.*

The shares of corporate profits distributed to stockholders are called **dividends;** stockholders may also realize **capital gains** if the market values of their stocks rise.

The *initial offering* of a stock raises funds for business firms, but most stock transactions occur in the **secondary market,** in which stockholders rather than firms transfer stocks to other financial investors. Although the total value of common stock in nonfinancial corporations was about $5 trillion at the end of 1990, less than 0.2 percent of this value was for stock in companies in business less than five years. Thus, few new corporations secure much financing by selling stock. A major reason is that financial investors try to minimize risk — the probability that a randomly selected new firm will fail in its first year is about 50/50. The concerns of financial investors about the principal/agent problem are another reason why stocks generate so few funds for new firms. Savers know that small stockholders (principals) have much less control than a firm's officers (agents) have. But those who establish and control a new corporation have less incentive to perform diligently than they would if they owned the corporation outright. Savers tend to opt for more security and lower returns than they are likely to get from stock ownership; the prospects of high returns from new stocks are very speculative.

Corporate Bonds

Bonds (corporate IOUs) are assets for their holders but liabilities for the corporations that issue them. Bonds are also transacted primarily in secondary markets. Only the initial sale of a bond generates funds for the firm that issues it. A higher price for a bond means that the firm issuing it pays a lower interest rate to borrow funds, and vice versa.

The principal/agent problem is less onerous for bondholders because they have legal rights to receive interest payments as long as the firm operates. High probabilities of default (nonpayment) by start-up companies, however, leave only large, well-established corporations with much access to funding through bond sales. In fact, only about 15 percent of new stocks or bonds from nonfinancial U.S. corporations are sold to families.[2] (Even smaller proportions are sold directly to households in other countries.)

Loans from Financial Intermediaries

Most people keep the bulk of their savings in commercial banks, which dominate financial intermediation processes in the United States. Although *venture capital* firms do specialize in funding new firms that develop promising business plans, most loans are made to huge, well-established firms. Even financial specialists tend to be amazed when they actually look at the numbers and discover that highly publicized sales of stocks and bonds account for only 1/25th as much of the recent financing of corporate activities as bank loans, which receive relatively little attention.[3]

You now have some notions about how firms are legally organized and financed and why society relies primarily on firms for production. We need to address the other side of explanations for the existence of firms — their purposes from the vantage points of those who own and operate them.

---

2. Frederic S. Mishkin, *The Economics of Money, Banking, and Financial Markets*, 3/ed. (New York: Harper-Collins, 1992).
3. *Ibid.*

The Goals of Business

Adam Smith's 1776 assertion that people pursue their own interests translates, for the purposes of consumer theory, into the idea that people try to maximize their utility, or satisfaction. People in business want to generate income for themselves, and most also want to produce goods and services of which they can be proud. But maximizing utility may be inconsistent with maximizing tangible income (the power to purchase goods). For example, most people could increase tangible income by working two jobs, or by enduring worse job conditions. Instead, most ultimately prefer more leisure and more enjoyable work to higher tangible income. In this section, after exploring the meaning of "economic profit," we address whether maximizing a firm's profit is consistent with maximizing the personal satisfactions of professional managers and other key employees.

Profit Maximization

Such slogans as "buy low, sell high" or "never give a sucker an even break" echo people's expectations that firms try to maximize their profits. **Profit maximization** is the standard economic assumption used to analyze the behavior of firms.

> **Profit** *is a firm's total revenue minus its total cost;* **loss** *is a parallel concept that occurs when revenue fails to cover costs. The two concepts differ only by sign.*

Economists and bookkeepers define profits and losses similarly, but economic profits and accounting profits often differ. Different definitions of costs explain this inconsistency.

Economic versus Accounting Costs You know that the value of the best alternative forgone is the economic cost of anything from lard to romance. Bookkeeping tends to focus on monetary costs. One way to break down economic costs of production is to view them as either explicit or implicit costs.

> **Explicit costs** *require outlays of money.*

For example, wages paid employees, rent payments, and utility bills are all explicit costs.

> **Implicit costs** *are the opportunity costs of resources the firm's owner makes available for production with no direct cash outlays.*

Examples include the value of an entrepreneur's labor and the interest that could be earned were the owners' assets (including the values of stock in corporations) not tied up in the business. Both implicit and explicit costs bear heavily on rational business decisions.

> *Economic costs of production include both* **explicit** *and* **implicit** *costs.*

Bookkeeping is a mechanical exercise focused only on explicit costs; it primarily records flows of funds and provides a base for computing taxes. Accounting requires evaluation of data for decision making — a purpose not well served by some standard bookkeeping practices for *cost accounting* or *tax accounting*. Fortunately, standards for *managerial accounting* increasingly conform to the economic view of cost. Let us look at some problems that emerge when implicit costs are ignored.

Profit Economists include explicit and implicit costs when they think of *total* (opportunity) *cost,* while bookkeepers commonly fail to include in total cost many implicit costs incurred by the owners of a firm.

> **Economic profit** *occurs only when a firm's revenue exceeds all production costs.*

Here is an example of how economic profits and accounting profits differ. Imagine that two years after receiving your college degree your annual salary as an assistant store manager is $28,000, you own a building that rents for $10,000 yearly, and your financial assets generate $3,000 per year in interest. On New Year's Day, after deciding to be your own boss, you quit your job, evict your tenants, and use your financial assets to establish a health food restaurant and pogo-stick shop.

At the end of the year, your books tell the following story:

Sales of food	$ 18,000	
Sales of pogo sticks	112,000	
TOTAL SALES REVENUE		$130,000
Cost of food	$ 23,000	
Cost of pogo sticks	62,000	
Employees' wages	20,000	
Utilities	5,000	
Taxes	5,000	
Advertising expenses	10,000	
TOTAL (Explicit) COSTS		
(subtract from revenue)		**−$125,000**

"Congratulations," your bookkeeper pipes up, "you made a

NET (accounting) PROFIT OF $5,000!"

"Hold it just a moment," you say, "I have studied economics. You forgot to subtract my *implicit costs*. Being in this business caused me to lose as income:

Salary	$−28,000	
Rent	−10,000	
Interest	−3,000	
TOTAL IMPLICIT COSTS		**$−41,000**

"Therefore, I've had an economic profit that's negative, a LOSS of $−36,000

You should be able to recognize that this harebrained business is a loser!"

If, however, you enjoy operating the restaurant and pogo-stick shop more than your best alternative (assistant store manager), your higher job satisfaction is called "psychic income." **Psychic income** is an implicit revenue that refers to nonmonetary satisfaction gained from an activity. Bookkeeping profit typically overstates economic profit because bookkeepers fail to subtract implicit costs, which tend to be significant, while implicit benefits are usually small.

The explicit cost data used to compute accounting profit for tax purposes are more accessible than the additional implicit cost data needed to estimate economic profits or losses. Thus, taxes and national income accounts are based on accounting data. Business decisions tend to be rational, however, and so are most frequently based on expected economic costs and profits.

Good accountants recognize that conventional bookkeeping costs and profits are inadequate; after calculating taxable profits, they subtract estimates of implicit costs from bookkeeping profit. This type of managerial accounting provides a better picture of a firm's track record. Many firms experience positive accounting profits but economic losses; they fail even though bookkeepers view them as "profitable."

Normal Profits as Production Costs One lesson is that "normal" profit should be considered a production cost. If a firm's accounting profit is less than that normally received by firms with comparable levels of investment and risks, in the long run its owners will move their resources into ventures where at least normal profits are expected. Chronic subnormal accounting profits ultimately force a firm to adapt or fail.

Economic profits and losses will be zero in the long run in competitive markets because profits attract new sellers like picnics attract ants; persistent losses (negative profits) drive firms from the market. Economic profits or losses persist only when entry and exit from an industry are constrained. Profits spur competition and growth of market supply, while losses signal that society wants resources shifted elsewhere. Not all markets, however, are highly competitive. Principal/agent conflicts suggest that top managers may have objectives other than maximizing profits for stockholders.

Separation of Ownership and Control

Maximizing a sole proprietor's utility is equivalent to maximizing his or her economic profit — but only after weighing all psychic benefits and costs, including losses of leisure. Do corporate managers necessarily try to maximize stockholders' profits? Executives are, after all, people who can be expected to maximize their own interests. Principal/agent problems may arise when maximizing a firm's profit conflicts with the self-interests of business decision makers. For example, the desires of business executives for such things as plusher offices, longer vacations, first-class travel, sycophantic subordinates, or higher personal salaries clearly raise costs and shrink profits.

Some economists contend that unless most stockholders become restless, managers pursue goals other than maximum profits. Bookkeeping practices that are not identical between firms sometimes obscure comparisons. What evidence can managers offer that stockholders' gains are being maximized? Stock prices reflect expectations about a firm's profits. But accounting profits in *annual reports* (corporate documents that legally must be published each year) seldom conform closely to a firm's economic profits.

Just as taxpayers try to maximize take-home pay by taking every possible deduction to minimize taxable income, some bookkeeping practices reduce accounting profit while increasing after-tax economic profits. For example, if an accountant uses a schedule established by the Internal Revenue Service that sets depreciation allowances (a tax-deductible cost) in excess of actual depreciation, a firm's taxes on income are reduced, which increases its economic profit. But the lower taxable income is reported in the firm's annual report, which may alarm stockholders. If the "bottom line" on annual reports is sometimes misleading, how can chief executive officers (CEOs) signal their competence to stockholders?

Other Possible Goals of a Firm   Executives' career ambitions and desires for job security sometimes conflict with maximizing corporate profit. Some analysts contend that firms try to *maximize sales revenues* (the "top line" in annual reports), hoping that growth of sales revenues will be interpreted as success by the stock market. Others argue that, after ensuring satisfactory profits that keep stockholders at bay, top managers try to follow *socially responsible* policies. Their contention, based on psychological theories, is that few people work for money alone; most of us want to feel that our contribution to society's welfare is positive. In several books, economist John Kenneth Galbraith takes a different tack, arguing that top managers attempt to

secure high incomes and job security for members of their own social class — other administrators and professional employees whom he characterizes as the *technostructure*.

Natural Selection

Few economists find these alternative views persuasive because competition for lucrative managerial slots pressures top managers to try to maximize profits. Most economists also reject the idea that accounting information systematically misleads stockholders. Some people might be fooled, but the enormous profits at stake cause experts to scrutinize annual reports so that corporate information is efficiently processed. Most economists contend that competitive pressures compel firms to efficiently maximize their profits.

> **Natural selection theory** *suggests that managers' failures to maximize profits cause* (a) *the firm's collapse, or* (b) *ouster of its managers, or* (c) *takeovers by outsiders.*

Nevertheless, mistakes are fairly common. Many executives survive despite gaffes that cost their firms enormous profits. *Errors of commission* occur when managers pursue policies that result in losses. For example, critics charge that Ross Johnson, the CEO of RJR Nabisco (the result of the largest merger in history), wasted tremendous amounts of funds on his personal comfort during 1988 and 1989, and generally mismanaged the firm's assets. Another error of commission was the launching of Ford's Edsel automobile in the middle of a recession, a decision that doomed the company to lose millions.

Errors of omission, on the other hand, occur when managers forgo options that would generate solid profits. For example, dozens of publishers turned down the opportunity to publish *In Search of Excellence*, by Tom Peters and Robert H. Waterman, Jr. The book ultimately sold millions of copies and reaped hundreds of thousands of dollars for the authors.

A key to success as an executive is to be *relatively* more efficient (or less inefficient) than your competitors. Bankruptcy of the firm or stockholder revolts occasionally dislodge top managers who consistently fail to maximize their firm's profits, but the most powerful pressures for efficiency in corporate giants probably emerge from the market for corporate control. A firm that does not perform at least as well as average at maximizing profit will have assets that are worth more than the total value of the corporation's stock. Such firms are natural targets for hostile takeovers — the acquisition of one firm by a group of owners and managers who think they can do a better job. We will deal with recent "merger mania" among corporate giants after you have learned more about business activities and market structures.

Criticisms of the Corporate Culture

Marxists and some other opponents of capitalism advocate revolutionary change as the only way to stop corporate giants from monopolizing economic activity and exploiting workers and consumers. John Kenneth Galbraith is among less radical critics who reject economic theories that stress competitive markets and the goal of profit maximization. In *The New Industrial State*, Galbraith argued that giant corporations:

1. Dominate economic activity because small competitive firms cannot afford the modern technologies required for efficient production.

2. Are controlled by corporate managers who seek maximum power and pay for themselves instead of maximum profits for stockholders.

3. Tend to corrupt government policies to help consolidate managerial power and achieve managers' goals rather than the public interest.

4. Use extensive advertising to avoid meaningful competition.

What evidence supports Galbraith's claims? First, corporations do account for five-sixths of U.S. business revenues and control large shares of our national resources. The top 2,000 manufacturing corporations have assets exceeding $10 million each, and the largest 200 control roughly 60 percent of all manufacturing assets. There is an erratic long-term trend towards even greater concentration in the ownership of total manufacturing assets, which contributes to corporate "giantism." Some giant firms substantially exceed the sizes of the governments of medium sized countries, as shown in Figure 3. According to Galbraith, our only hope for a just society is for modern corporate managers to become more *socially responsible*, but he is pessimistic about the prospects for such changes of heart.

Are Corporate Giants Immune from Market Pressures?

A competitive market system rewards those who serve consumers and society, while forcing inefficient firms to adapt or exit the market. Many firms vie for consumers' patronage in competitive markets. Will society derive the same benefits if a few firms dominate a market? Most people think not. Modern economic life often seems far removed from competitive models of the economy. There is, however, evidence that markets serve consumers reasonably well and that size alone does not insulate firms from competitive pressures. Giants compete with giants.

Such once dominant retailers as Sears, Montgomery Ward, and J. C. Penney have lost ground to firms like Walmart, Venture, and Target, while Woolco and other giants have collapsed. After Ford Motor Company lost millions of dollars when it launched the ill-fated Edsel in the 1950s, it more than recouped these losses when it developed the Mustang, a car that passed the test of the marketplace. A shaky economy and competition from foreign automakers imposed billions of dollars in losses on U.S. automakers in the late 1970s, and Chrysler teetered on the brink of bankruptcy. U.S. automakers recovered only when they marketed more fuel efficient and reliable cars. And what happened to the giant railroads of a century ago? Most disappeared or were absorbed into Amtrak, a government-subsidized money loser.

Interindustry competition has become increasingly important. Xerox once had a near monopoly on copying equipment, but now competes with IBM and a host of Japanese firms. IBM had

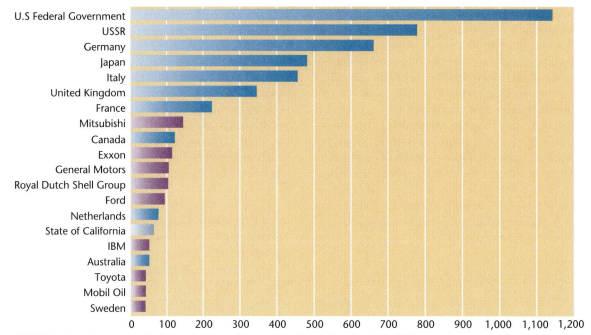

U.S Federal Government		1,150
USSR		770
Germany		650
Japan		480
Italy		450
United Kingdom		340
France		220
Mitsubishi		140
Canada		115
Exxon		110
General Motors		100
Royal Dutch Shell Group		100
Ford		90
Netherlands		75
State of California		60
IBM		50
Australia		50
Toyota		40
Mobil Oil		40
Sweden		35

FIGURE 3 Twenty of the Largest Organizations in the World, by Annual Receipts or Expenditures, Billions of Dollars, 1986–1987

The 20 largest organizations are not all governments. Nearly half, in fact, are private organizations—oil companies being the most numerous. (*Note:* Some giants may not be represented because reasonable estimates are not available.)
Source: CIA, *The World Factbook 1990; Business Week,* July 15, 1991.

a strangle-hold on computers in the 1960s, but now must compete with Apple, Radio Shack, Control Data, Wang, NCR, DEC, Xerox, Compaq, AT&T, and hundreds of small electronics firms.

Giants often emerge from nowhere when entrepreneurs perceive a void in the marketplace. Steve Jobs, a 17-year-old high school student, and Steve Wozniak, a 22-year-old college dropout, launched Apple Computers from a garage in 1978 for under $500, creating a billion-dollar firm within 4 years after they marketed the first low-cost personal computer. It is hard to overstate how risky business can be. A boom in personal computer sales and software in the early 1980s made overnight millionaires of hundreds of young workaholics in the "Silicon Valley," an area just south of San Francisco. Gluts on the market quickly appeared, however, and hundreds of computer firms collapsed during 1984 to 1986.

Examples of dynamic competition are almost innumerable. Some firms that have, relatively, lost or gained a lot in the past few years are listed in Table 3, which indicates how the corporate pecking order changes over time.

The key point is that high profits attract aggressive competition, both foreign and domestic, so consumers' needs are met in a reasonably efficient fashion. Many people remain unhappy with market outcomes, however, and increasingly turn to government to resolve economic problems. Income distributions that result from the market system are widely perceived as unfair. And what about national defense, or such problems as pollution and excessive unemployment? We explore these and similar questions later in the book when we examine areas in which government plays an active role in our society.

Underpinnings for consumer demands were discussed in the previous chapter, but supply has been addressed only intuitively. In the next chapter, we explore how production relation-

Table 3 *Turnover among the Top 10 and Top 50 U.S. Corporations, 1981–1991*

Entered the Top 10		Left the Top 10	
Philip Morris†		Standard Oil of Indiana*	
DuPont†		Gulf*	

Entered the Top 50		Left the Top 50	
Pepsico	McDonnell Douglas	Gulf Oil*	International Telephone
Conagra†	Hewlett-Packard	Conoco*	& Telegraph
Digital Equipment	Minnesota Mining and	Standard Oil of Ohio	Western Electric
International Paper	Manufacturing	Union Carbide	Getty Oil*
Allied-Signal	Georgia Pacific	Beatrice Foods*	Dart & Kraft*
Johnson & Johnson	Sara Lee†	Ashland Oil*	Marathon Oil*
Aluminum Company	Motorola	LTV	RCA*
of America	Anheiser Busch	City Service	Amerada Hess*
Bristol Meyers Squibb†	Coca Cola	Monsanto	Bethlehem Steel
General Dynamics	Unisys†	Esmark	International Harvester
Lockheed			

*Acquired or taken over by other firms during the 1980s.
†Substantial growth through mergers or acquisitions.
Source: *Fortune*, May 4, 1981 and April 22, 1991.

ships link inputs and outputs to determine costs and shape managerial decisions about how much to produce and which technology to use. Then, in the next few chapters, we investigate how competition for consumers' dollars differs in intensity across industries and interacts with production costs to determine prices, output, and consumer purchases.

Chapter Review: Key Points

1. Firms exist primarily to coordinate production teams that will (*a*) reduce transaction costs, and (*b*) exploit economies of scale. *Economies of scale* exist when average production costs decline as the level of output rises.

2. A *principal* is a party with contractual rights for performance of certain tasks by an *agent*. The *principal/agent problem* arises when the principal cannot adequately monitor the behavior of the agent, and the personal motives of the agent conflict with the objectives of the principal.

3. Four out of five firms are either *sole proprietorships* or *partnerships*, but *corporations* account for more than 90 percent of all goods and services sold and receive roughly two-thirds of all profits in the United States. Compared to corporations, however, sole proprietorships and partnerships are more easily formed and less subject to government regulation. The major advantages of corporations are the *limited liabilities* of stockholders and better access to markets for financial capital.

4. Financial intermediaries channel households' saving into the hands of investors in economic capital, and include such organizations as banks, mutual funds, insurance companies, and stockbrokers. Banks are the most important intermediaries, accounting for the bulk of the financing of business organizations.

5. Production increases the value of goods in their *form*, *place*, *possession*, or *time*.

6. The *short run* is a period in which at least one resource and one cost are fixed. In the *long run* all resources can be varied, but technology is assumed constant. These periods, therefore, are not defined by time, but rather by the nature of the adjustment process. Firms can enter or leave an industry in the long run because all resources are variable.

7. Economic costs include both explicit and implicit costs. *Explicit costs* involve outlays of money for goods or resources. *Implicit costs* are the opportunity costs of resources provided by a firm's owner. Payments for rent, electricity, and wages are explicit costs, while the values of the owner's labor and capital are implicit costs.

8. Bookkeeping rarely considers implicit costs, while both implicit and explicit costs are included in economic costs. Consequently, *accounting profits* often overstate the economic profitability of an enterprise because the opportunity costs of owner-provided resources are ignored. Normal accounting profits are an economic cost of production.

9. An erratic trend towards increased concentration of economic power in America has continued for more than a century — well over half of all manufacturing assets are held by the 200 largest corporations in the United States.

10. Corporate goals of making profits are under attack by people who believe "the new industrial state" is too powerful, both politically and economically. These critics argue that big business should be "socially responsible."

11. Even though control of much of modern economic life is concentrated in the hands of those who control giant corporations, changing market shares and the growth of various imports are evidence that the processes of competition are still reasonably vigorous.

Key Concepts

Ensure that you can define these terms before proceeding.

team production
economies of scale
the principal/agent problem
sole proprietors
partnerships
corporations
unlimited vs. limited liability
accounting vs. economic profit
separation of ownership from control
financial intermediaries
natural selection theory

Problems and Questions

1. How might a principal/agent problem arise in each of the following cases where you can identify a principal and an agent? (Be sure that a contract exists before answering.)

   a. A corporate giant hires a new chief executive officer.

   b. You buy 90 percent of the stock in a small company that your best friend is starting; she will manage the day-to-day operations.

   c. You consign an old junker to a used car dealer to sell for you.

   d. A parent tells a child to do a chore.

   e. A purchasing specialist contracts for paper to print this text for the publisher.

2. Which of the following would be more likely to be reflected in explicit costs, and which would be more likely to be implicit costs? Why?

   a. The time and effort of the president of a corporation.

   b. Interest on funds placed in corporate bonds.

   c. The time and effort of an entrepreneur.

   d. Interest that funds placed in corporate stocks could earn.

3. Which of the following would entail implicit costs for your firm, which sews tents under a contract with the Department of Defense, and which would involve explicit costs?

   a. The value of your own time and effort.

   b. Canvas, thread, and olive-drab die.

   c. Sewing machines.

   d. The use of your savings to fund daily operations.

   e. Your home office.

4. What differentiates production accomplished efficiently within a household from that which requires a firm for efficient production?

5. What distinguishes the short run from the long run? Can these periods be broken down into discrete periods of time? Why?

6. What types of implicit costs will tend to be relatively more important as a percentage of total costs for a small proprietorship than for a typical giant corporation? What implicit costs do you think might be relatively more important for the corporation? Overall, for which type of organization do you think implicit costs would be relatively more significant?

7. List five examples of the types of transaction costs that prevent most savers from investing directly in stocks and bonds.

8. Corporations have traditionally been private institutions that generate profits, create jobs, and accumulate capital — pursuits that Milton Friedman, Nobel Prize winner in economics, thinks they should continue to concentrate upon to promote economic efficiency. Friedman feels that corporations should ignore the "social responsibility" that critics of corporate policies would foist upon them because he sees the job of promoting social goals as belonging to government, not corporate management. These critics, however, want to make corporations accountable to the American public. How might corporations be forced to develop "social consciences"? Would profits and stock prices be lower? Who would bear the burden of the changes critics have advocated? Would society benefit? What are the arguments for and against these proposals to make corporations quasi-public institutions?

9. Some observers of the American business scene think that market power is so common that most giant firms do not maximize profits — they seek only satisfactory profits. Once these have been secured, management tries to maximize sales or growth, or to ensure comfortable, plush personal lives for management personnel. Pursuing the soft life is easy to understand, but how would modern corporate managers gain by maximizing growth or total sales? Do you think these commentators are right?

10. Suppose you were the chief executive officer of a major corporation. Would your primary goal be to maximize profits for stockholders or to maximize your own subjective income via a high salary, friendly subordinates, plush offices, private airplanes, and other "perks"? What does your answer suggest about the compatibility of maximum corporate profits and the separation of ownership from control? What does this imply for economic efficiency?

CHAPTER 22

Production and Costs

In this chapter, we explore how production links inputs and outputs to determine costs and shape managerial decisions about how much to produce and which technology to use. Our descriptions of production and cost may often make it seem as though business decisions are as mechanical as following a recipe — hire a few workers, buy machinery and raw materials, then heat iron ore to 3,000°F. "Voila! Steel!" But the world of business is never so simple. Entrepreneurs and managers often face enormous uncertainty while making decisions that can put millions of dollars at risk. Anyone who has implemented a new technology or written a computer program knows from experience that everything new takes twice as long as planned (no matter how conservative the plan) and that countless bugs, glitches, and bad breaks will be encountered along the way.

The idealized relationships presented in this chapter characterize production processes that use mature technologies, but these concepts may seem very abstract at times because we often ignore specifics to highlight more important relationships. Nevertheless, you need a starting point to understand the complexities of everyday business decision making. Production and costs are detailed in this chapter. We begin by surveying economic facets of typical production processes.

This leads to a discussion of various production costs in both the short run and the long run and, finally, to a brief overview of the mysteries of technological change.

Production Functions

A firm can vary all productive resources in the long run, but at least one resource is fixed in the short run. Long-run linkages between inputs and outputs are formalized in production functions.

> **Production functions** *summarize relationships between combinations of inputs and the maximum outputs that each combination can produce.*

Output = f(inputs) is an example of a production function, and is read as "output is a function *f* of inputs." The function *f* summarizes how current technology translates various combinations of inputs into specific amounts of output. In this context, technology encompasses current knowledge about production techniques, as well as such things as government regulations, weather, and the laws of physics and chemistry.

Production functions are commonly written $q = f(K, L)$ where q equals output, K equals capital services, and L equals labor services used per production period. (For simplicity, land and entrepreneurship are ignored for now.) Suppose that production engineers indicate that 1,000 swimsuits can be sewn daily using 600 machine hours (75 sewing machines per 8-hour shift) and 800 labor hours (100 workers each 8-hour shift). The function f summarizes a production relationship of this type. Technological advances boosting productivity 50 percent would require switching from the f production function to, say, g. Now, $q = g(K, L)$, and 600 machine hours plus 800 labor hours yield 1,500 swimsuits. Complete production functions identify output possibilities in the long run, when a firm can vary all resources, but in the short run, at least one resource is fixed.

Production in the Short Run

Imagine that 5 years after you finish your degree you are in the sand-and-gravel business. Most firms can vary labor more easily than any other basic resource. Thus, to keep things simple for now, suppose that you control the amount of labor hired in the short run, while all other resources are constant because you have long-term leases on fixed amounts of capital equipment (trucks and bulldozers) and land.

If no one works in your business, production and revenue obviously will both be zero. Working alone, you might excavate and sell 10 tons of earth material daily. Suppose that you hire an assistant and find that output expands to 22 tons daily. Production more than doubled while labor inputs only doubled. Does this mean your assistant is the better worker? Not at all. Working alone, you must run the truck, handle all marketing, operate the bulldozer, keep the books—the list goes on and on. The cliché "Chief Cook and Bottlewasher" fits too closely for comfort. After hiring an assistant, you can drive the truck while your helper excavates, keep the books while your employee runs the bulldozer, and so on.

You are able to produce much more as a team than as separate individuals because of gains from the *division of labor*. As you hire even more workers, you might find that specialization en-ables output to continue to rise more than proportionally for the first few extra workers. Eventually, however, the gains from specialization will be overwhelmed as the law of diminishing marginal returns comes into play, and each extra worker adds less than the preceding worker did to total production.

Marginal and Average Physical Products of Labor

Suppose that your work force is becoming so specialized that you decide to apply some concepts you learned in college. The total product curve in columns 1 and 2 of Table 1 relates production and various levels of labor inputs, holding other resources constant.[1]

If you know total output for each level of labor hired (columns 1 and 2), output per worker is calculated by dividing total output (q) by labor (L).

> The **average physical product of labor** (APP_L) *equals total output divided by labor* (q/L).

These figures are entered in column 3 of the table. You will also want to know how much each extra worker adds to total output.

> The **marginal physical product of labor** (MPP_L) *is the additional output produced by an additional unit of labor—computed by dividing the change in total output (Δq) by the change in labor (ΔL):* $\Delta q/\Delta L$.

Hiring decisions intended to maximize profit hinge on labor's marginal physical product. Extra workers will not be hired unless the extra revenue from their marginal physical products would exceed the extra costs of hiring them. Only

---

1. Note that total product curves and production functions are not the same things. A production function allows all inputs to vary, while the total product curve assumes that only one input changes. We are using labor as the variable input, but had we held labor constant and varied capital (or land), the analysis would be quite similar, although the specific curves would differ.

Table 1 *Total Output and the Average and Marginal Physical Products of Labor (Sand and Gravel Operation)*

(1) Workers per 8-hr. Shift (L)	(2) Tons of Sand and Gravel Removed Daily (q)	(3) Average Physical Product of Labor (q/L)	(4) Marginal Physical Product of Labor (Δq/ΔL)
0	0	0	0
1	10	10.00	10
2	22	11.00	12
3	36	12.00	14
4	52	13.00	16
5	70	14.00	18
6	86	14.33	16
7	100	14.28	14
8	112	14.00	12
9	122	13.55	10
10	130	13.00	8
11	137	12.45	7
12	143	11.92	6
13	148	11.38	5
14	152	10.85	4
15	155	10.33	3
16	157	9.81	2
17	158	9.29	1
18	158	8.78	0
19	157	8.26	−1

workers generating at least as much revenue as it costs to hire them will be employed, a decision we detail in a coming chapter. In most cases, each worker's productivity (the MPP_L) will be higher as the amounts of other resources used rise — a worker operating a bulldozer on a dry river bed will produce more sand and gravel than a shovel wielder digging on a city lot.

The MPP_L is calculated by looking at small changes in labor hired and the resulting changes in output. With large numbers of workers (as at a steel mill), a given change in the amount of labor (ΔL) is divided into the resulting change in output (Δq) to approximate the MPP_L. One worker $= \Delta L$ for a small firm like your operation. Labor's marginal physical products ($\Delta q/\Delta L$) for your firm are listed in column 4 of Table 1.

The **total product curve** graphed in Panel A of Figure 1 (from columns 1 and 2 of Table 1) for your sand-and-gravel operation relates produc-

tion and various levels of labor inputs, holding other resources constant. Panel B shows the corresponding marginal and average physical products of labor.

The Short Run Law of Diminishing Marginal Returns

A problem of congestion emerges as your organization grows. Your dump trucks' passenger compartments become crowded and more time is wasted at the excavation site waiting to load trucks that arrived earlier. A second challenge emerges from coordinating increased work effort — ensuring that the left hand knows what the right hand is doing, limiting coffee breaks to 15 minutes, and so on. Table 1 and Figure 1 indicate that congestion and loss of coordination eventually become so severe that the seventeenth worker adds only one ton of material per day, the

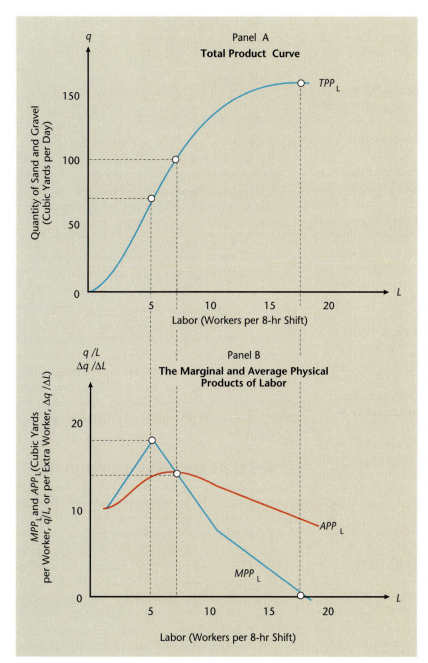

FIGURE 1 The Total, Marginal, and Average Physical Products of Labor (Sand-and-Gravel Example)

As more and more labor is employed, total output (Panel A) initially rises at an increasing rate because of gains from specialization. In this range, the marginal and average physical products of labor both grow (Panel B). As congestion begins to emerge, total output continues to grow, but at a falling rate. In this range, average physical product continues to climb, but marginal productivity diminishes. Once marginal physical product falls below average physical product, average physical product begins to fall. However, total output continues to rise until the marginal physical product is zero. This occurs when congestion or other problems are so severe that further labor inputs cause output to fall.

eighteenth's contribution is nil, and hiring the nineteenth worker actually yields a drop in output.

The decline in extra output as extra workers are employed might seem a consequence of hiring better workers first and then hiring mediocre or inferior workers. This is unnecessary to explain diminishing marginal returns. In fact, we might assume that all workers were clones from a robot factory. Every worker is then the last or marginal worker, because if you fired any one of them, you would have one less employee. Declining amounts of capital, land, and supervision per worker cause marginal physical products to diminish as the number of workers grows, and this occurs regardless of the qualities of the individual workers.

The **law of diminishing marginal returns:** *When equal increases of variable resources are successively added to some fixed resource, marginal physical products eventually decline.*

The fixity of at least one resource in the short run makes diminishing marginal returns unavoidable: Not all resources can be varied proportionally, so capital and land per worker fall as more workers are hired, inevitably leading to diminishing additions of output as extra labor is hired. This basic economic law is without exception. Were it not for diminishing returns, enough food might be grown in a flower pot to feed the world.

Table 1 and Figure 1 reflect the outputs produced if various numbers of workers put in 8-hour days. Gains from specialization enable each of the first five workers to add more than the preceding worker to total output, but the forces that compel marginal productivity to diminish overwhelm any gains from further specialization for the sixth and subsequent workers. While total output continues to increase, it increases at a declining rate, until the eighteenth worker adds nothing to total output.

Short Run Production Costs

Production is tightly linked to the costs that shape business decisions. Now that we have studied production, we turn to the process that translates the total, average, and marginal physical products of labor into production costs. Production costs are divided into *fixed costs* and *variable costs*. All production costs fall within these two categories, so total costs (*TC*) equal total fixed costs (*TFC*) plus total variable costs (*TVC*), or

$$TC = TFC + TVC$$

Businesspeople commonly refer to fixed costs as *overhead*, while variable costs are often called *direct costs* or *operating costs*.

Fixed Costs

History is bunk.   Sunk costs are sunk.
   Henry Ford   Anonymous

At least one resource is fixed in the short run, which implies that some short run costs are also fixed. These **fixed costs** were incurred previously, so they are also known as *historical* or *sunk costs*.

Fixed costs *are the sum of all short-run costs that are not related to the level of output.*

For your sand-and-gravel operation, fixed costs would include such things as business licenses, the value of your time, rent you are obligated by a lease to pay, principal and interest on leases for trucks or other equipment, utility hookup charges, and franchise fees. You might be required to make payments during each period, but fixed costs are unaffected by your firm's output.

Fixed Costs and Decision Making   Suppose you bought a deluxe mountain bike and were dismayed when its price was slashed 2 weeks later. Then a broken leg persuaded you to sell the bicycle to cover the unexpected medical bills. *Least* relevant to the price you should charge would be: (*a*) the price you paid, (*b*) the current sales price, (*c*) storage costs, (*d*) expected enjoyment from riding after you get out of your cast, or (*e*) the current prices of similar used bikes?

If you chose answer (*a*) to this question, you intuitively understand the irrelevancy of fixed cost for rational decision making, a point illustrated in Focus 1. Many people are astounded when told that fixed costs have no bearing on rational decisions about how much to produce, how much to charge for your output, and so on.

Fixed costs are meaningful only to the extent that, like history or archaeology, we can learn from them. Since they are fixed, there is a sense in which no alternative exists, so the *opportunity*

Sunk Costs in Stud Poker

In the following example, intended to help you see why fixed costs are irrelevant, all you need to know about stud poker is that any hand with four similar cards (four 7s) beats any hand with three identical cards (three queens and two 10s, for example).

Suppose that a notoriously poor player is dealing five-card stud, and deals four players plus himself one card each in the hole (face down), then one card each face up. Both you and the player to your left have aces showing. With *? A*, she bets $10,000 (we might as well fantasize a bit). You peek at your hole card and discover that you have a second ace—*A A*—so you call. The dealer, showing *? 3* is the only other player who calls. (We told you he was a bad player.) The dealer rolls the player on your left a seven—*? A 7*, you another ace—*A A A*, and himself another three—*? 3 3*. Having three aces yourself, you hope the dealer has three 3s and you bet $25,000. The dealer calls, but the other player folds her hand. You are then dealt a king—*A A A K*, and the dealer rolls a third three for himself—*? 3 3 3*. Afraid that the dealer (a wild man) has four 3s, you reluctantly call his $50,000 bet. Now the dealer deals you a second king. You have *A A A K K*—a full house with aces up! He blithely rolls another 3, so he is sitting with *? 3 3 3 3*. (The lunatic probably has something like a 6 in the hole.) He bets a dime. *The Big Question*: Should you call the bet? *The Answer*: If you are rational, absolutely NOT. No matter what the dealer has in the hole, you lose, because a hand with four of a kind beats a full house. Why should you lose another dime? The $85,000 you put in the pot is no longer yours. It is a sunk cost and, so, is irrelevant to your rational decision.

---

costs of fixed resources are zero, at least in the short run. Therefore, only opportunity costs should affect production decisions — costs that vary with output because alternatives are forgone while incurring these costs.

Variable Costs

Such expenses as labor costs, gasoline, truck maintenance, and office supplies will be positively related to the amount of business your sand-and-gravel operation does.

> **Variable costs** *are costs incurred when a firm produces, and vary with the level of production.*

Any costs incurred only when a firm produces are variable costs. Consider the data for your business in Table 2 and Figure 2. Labor is the only variable resource in the short run, and we will assume that the supply of workers is perfectly elastic at $50 each per 8-hour shift. All other resources and costs are assumed constant, and total fixed cost is assumed to be $100 per day.

The total physical product curve (*TPP*) in Figure 1 shows the amounts of labor (*L*) required to produce varying levels of output. When we multiply the horizontal (labor) axis of Figure 1 by the wage rate (*w*), it becomes the total wage bill ($w \times L$) incurred for each level of labor you might hire. (Basic relationships are unchanged

Table 2 *Total Output, Total Costs, and Fixed and Variable Costs (Sand and Gravel Example)*

(1) Workers per 8-hr. Shift (L)	(2) Tons of Sand & Gravel Removed Daily (q)	(3) Wages per Worker (8 hrs. Daily) (w)	(4) Total Variable Cost (w × L) (TVC)	(5) Total Fixed Cost (TFC)	(6) Total Costs (TVC + TFC = TC)
0	0	$50	0	$100	$ 100
1	10	50	$ 50	100	150
2	22	50	100	100	200
3	36	50	150	100	250
4	52	50	200	100	300
5	70	50	250	100	350
6	86	50	300	100	400
7	100	50	350	100	450
8	112	50	400	100	500
9	122	50	450	100	550
10	130	50	500	100	600
11	137	50	550	100	650
12	143	50	600	100	700
13	148	50	650	100	750
14	152	50	700	100	800
15	155	50	750	100	850
16	157	50	800	100	900
17	158	50	850	100	950
18	158	50	900	100	1,000
19	157	50	950	100	1,050

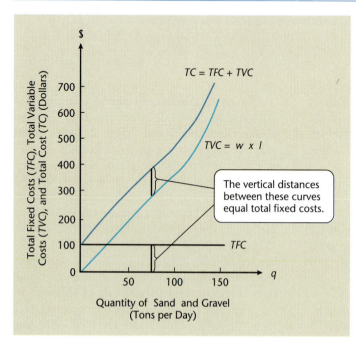

The vertical distances between these curves equal total fixed costs.

Quantity of Sand and Gravel (Tons per Day)

FIGURE 2 Total Costs, Total Fixed Costs, and Total Variable Costs (Sand-and-Gravel Example)

Total cost (TC) and total variable cost (TVC) curves are "parallel" because their difference is total fixed cost (TFC), which is constant, no matter how much or how little is produced. Both TC and TVC rise slowly at first, because total product (from Figure 1) initially increases at an increasing rate. Then, as total product continues to rise, but at a decreasing rate, TC and TVC rise at increasing rates.

when any function is multiplied by a constant.) Wages are the only variable costs of production, so this wage bill equals total variable cost (TVC — column 4 in Table 2). Thus, the relationship between the quantity of output and total variable costs is the TVC curve in Figure 2.

When total fixed costs (TFC) are added vertically to the TVC (wage bill) curve, we have a picture of how your total costs (TC) vary with output. Total fixed costs are unaffected by production (a constant $100). We need to explore costs a bit more, however, before we launch into decision making.

Note that Figure 2 turned sideways roughly "mirrors" Panel A in Figure 1. Variable costs reflect wages to labor, and labor employed determines the amount of output, so there is a natural, tight link between total cost, production, and the amount of labor hired. Now we will explore other costs that are closely related to labor's average and marginal products.

Average Costs

Some definitions will enable us to examine costs more completely. *Average total cost* (ATC) is total cost incurred per unit of output, and is sometimes termed *unit cost*, or simplified to *average cost*.

> **Average costs** *equal total costs divided by output* (TC/q).

Total costs are composed of fixed and variable costs, so average total cost (ATC) equals average fixed cost (AFC) plus average variable cost (AVC).[2] After the cost data for excavating various amounts of earth have been collected, computing each type of average cost only requires dividing each by the output level.

---

2. Proof: Dividing both sides of $TC = TFC + TVC$ by output (q) yields

$$\frac{TC}{q} = \frac{TFC}{q} + \frac{TVC}{q}$$

and thus, $ATC = AFC + AVC$.

> **Average fixed cost** (AFC) *is the fixed cost per unit of output, or* (TFC/q).

> **Average variable cost** (AVC) *is the variable cost per unit, or* (TVC/q).

Table 3 lists these costs for your sand-and-gravel operation. Let's explore all these averages in more detail to see how they are typically related to production.

Average Fixed Costs   Just because total fixed costs do not vary with output does not make an AFC curve horizontal. $AFC = TFC/q$, where TFC is constant. Figure 3 shows how the AFC is related to the output of your operation, calculated in column 6 of Table 3. Total fixed costs are constant, so, as output increases, fixed costs per unit of output decline — a process that many managers describe as "spreading overhead" through high volume.[3]

Average Variable Costs   Managers can control variable costs by changing the level of output. As output grows, the AVC initially tends to fall. But eventually, diminishing marginal returns will drive up average variable costs. Seeing why this occurs requires understanding a bit about marginal cost, which is the most important cost concept of all for business decision making.

Marginal Costs

The extra production costs incurred are vital for decisions about changing output levels.

> **Marginal cost** (MC) *is the change in total cost associated with producing an additional unit of output.*

---

3. Notice that if we arbitrarily select any two points on the AFC curve (say, a and b), the rectangles formed by dropping horizontal and vertical lines to the axes have identical areas ($100). (Since $AFC = TFC/q$, multiplication of AFC by q yields TFC: $TFC/q \times q = TFC$, which is constant.) Thus, the AFC curve is a rectangular hyperbola. Recall that unitary elastic demand curves are also rectangular hyperbolas.

Table 3 *Average Total Costs, Average Fixed Costs, Average Variable Costs, and Marginal Cost*

(1) Workers per 8-hr. Shift (L)	(2) Tons of Sand and Gravel Removed Daily (q)	(3) Total Variable Cost (w × L) (TVC)	(4) Total Fixed Cost (TFC)	(5) Average Variable Cost (3)/(2) (AVC)	(6) Average Fixed Cost (4)/(2) (AFC)	(7) Average Total Cost (5) + (6) (ATC)	(8) Marginal Cost (Δ3)/(Δ2) (MC)
0	0	0	$100	—	—	—	—
1	10	$ 50	100	$5.00	$10.00	$15.00	$ 5.00
2	22	100	100	4.54	4.55	9.09	4.17
3	36	150	100	4.17	2.78	6.95	3.57
4	52	200	100	3.85	1.92	5.77	3.13
5	70	250	100	3.57	1.43	5.00	2.78
6	86	300	100	3.49	1.16	4.65	3.13
7	100	350	100	3.50	1.00	4.50	3.57
8	112	400	100	3.57	0.89	4.46	4.17
9	122	450	100	3.69	0.82	4.51	5.00
10	130	500	100	3.85	0.77	4.62	6.25
11	137	550	100	4.01	0.73	4.74	7.14
12	143	600	100	4.20	0.70	4.90	8.33
13	148	650	100	4.39	0.68	5.07	10.00
14	152	700	100	4.60	0.66	5.26	12.50
15	155	750	100	4.84	0.65	5.49	16.67
16	157	800	100	5.10	0.64	5.74	25.00
17	158	850	100	5.38	0.63	6.01	50.00
18	158	900	100	5.69	0.63	6.32	—
19	157	950	100	6.05	0.64	6.69	—

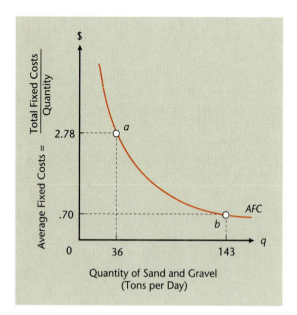

FIGURE 3 Average Fixed Costs

Since total fixed costs (*TFC*) do not vary with output (*q*), increases in output cause average fixed costs (*AFC* = *TFC/q*) to decline. Businesspeople refer to this as "spreading their overhead."

Since $TC = TFC + TVC$, any change in total cost reflects changes in variable costs; fixed cost does not depend on the output level.[4] Thus, producing an extra unit of output incurs marginal cost that equals either (a) the change in the total cost, or (b) the change in the total variable cost. Marginal cost for your firm is listed in column 8 of Table 3.

Figure 4 shows how average variable cost (AVC) and marginal cost (MC) change as you process various amounts of earth. Why are these curves U-shaped? Recall that the marginal physical product of labor (MPP_L) initially rose as you hired more labor but then fell when diminishing marginal returns were encountered. This means that the labor costs of additional output (its MC, in this case) initially decline, but diminishing returns ultimately cause marginal costs to rise as more workers produce higher outputs. Similarly, the average physical product of labor (APP_L) initially rose, but then declined as more workers were employed, causing the U shape of average variable cost curves. These relationships between production levels and costs will be detailed in a moment.

Graphically Summing Average Costs In Figure 5 we tack an average fixed cost (AFC) curve onto a graph with typical U-shaped marginal cost (MC) and average variable cost (AVC) curves. Summing vertically the AVC and AFC associated with each output level yields the average total cost (ATC) curve shown. Notice that as output increases, differences between the AVC and ATC curves shrink. The ATC and AVC converge, because their vertical differences equal AFC, which falls as output rises. We now take a quick look at how costs relate to production.

---

4. Proof: Dividing $\Delta TC = \Delta TFC + \Delta TVC$ by a small change in output (Δq) reveals that

$$MC = \frac{\Delta TC}{\Delta q} = \frac{\Delta TFC}{\Delta q} + \frac{\Delta TVC}{\Delta q}$$

But output does not affect fixed costs, so $\Delta TFC/\Delta q = 0$ and

$$MC = \frac{\Delta TC}{\Delta q} = \frac{\Delta TVC}{\Delta q}$$

FIGURE 4 Marginal Cost and Average Variable Cost

The average variable cost (AVC) curve falls when marginal cost (MC) is below it, and rises when MC exceeds AVC. Average variable cost is at its minimum when $AVC = MC$. Both curves are U-shaped because, initially, gains from specialization push AVC and MC down. But eventually, as output is expanded, diminishing returns are encountered and the MC and AVC both rise.

Relating Costs to Production

It is no coincidence that total physical product and total costs are closely related, and that Panel A of Figure 1 is "mirrored" in Figure 2. In a similar fashion, average variable costs "mirror" average physical product, and marginal costs "mirror" marginal physical product. Let's see why.

Suppose, for a moment, that you start a second operation with no fixed costs and hire one worker for $10 per hour to convert trash into trinkets sold at tourist traps. (Labor is your only expense because trash is free.) If this worker converts trash into two trinkets per hour, average variable cost is $5 per trinket. ($10 wage/2 trinkets = $5 per trinket.) Thus, average physical product is related to average variable cost by the formula $AVC = w/APP_L$ when labor is the

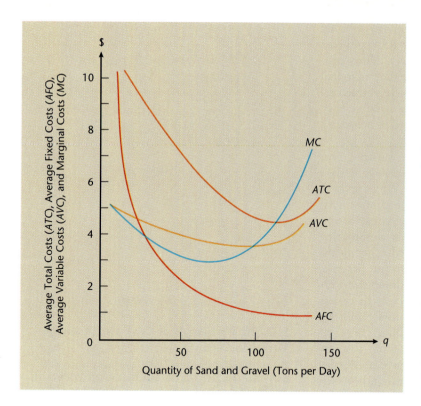

FIGURE 5 **Short Run Costs of Production**

As long as marginal cost (*MC*) is below average total cost (*ATC*) or average variable cost (*AVC*), then *ATC* and *AVC*, respectively, will fall when output is increased. When *MC* exceeds *AVC* or *ATC*, then *AVC* and *ATC* will rise as output expands. The *ATC* and *AVC* curves are generally U-shaped. Gains from specialization eventually are overcome by diminishing returns, so the *ATC*, *AVC*, and *MC* curves are all U-shaped. Higher output levels spread a firm's overhead, so the *AFC* curve declines continuously. Notice that the *MC* curve intersects the *AVC* and *ATC* curves at their minimum values (points *a* and *b*).

only variable cost.[5] If a second $10-per-hour worker increased total hourly output to 3 trinkets, that worker's marginal product is 1 trinket, but it raised labor costs by $10. Thus, its marginal cost is $10 and, when wages are the only variable cost, marginal physical product is related to marginal cost by $MC = w/MPP_L$.[6]

Let's return to the sand-and-gravel operation. Table 4 replicates labor's total, average, and marginal physical products from Table 1. Average variable costs (w/APP_L) and marginal costs (w/MPP_L) based on these data are reported in col-

---

5. To derive this relationship a little more formally, recall the simplifying assumption for your sand-and-gravel firm that all nonlabor resources were fixed. Therefore, total variable cost (*TVC*) equals the wage bill ($w \times L$), and average variable costs ($AVC = TVC/q$) equal wL/q. Since the average physical product of labor (APP_L) is q/L, if we invert APP_L (it is then $1/(q/L) = L/q$) and multiply by the wage (a constant, w), we have calculated the average variable costs of production ($w/(q/L) = w/APP_L$). Algebraically,

$$AVC = \frac{TVC}{q} = \frac{wL}{q}$$

$$= w\left(\frac{L}{q}\right) = w\left(\frac{1}{APP_L}\right)$$

$$= \frac{w}{APP_L}$$

6. Only labor costs change as your sand-and-gravel operation processes more tons of earth, so marginal costs ($MC = \Delta TC/\Delta q$) are simply the changes in the total wage bill associated with higher production:

$$MC = \Delta(wL)/\Delta q.$$

The wage rate is constant, so

$$MC = \Delta(wL)/\Delta q = w\Delta L/\Delta q.$$

Since the marginal physical product of labor (MPP_L) equals $\Delta Q/\Delta L$, we can invert the MPP_L, multiply by w, and arrive at the marginal cost of production. Again the algebraic sequence is

$$MC = \frac{\Delta TVC}{\Delta q} = \frac{\Delta(wL)}{\Delta q} = w\left(\frac{\Delta L}{\Delta q}\right) = w\left(\frac{1}{MPP_L}\right) = \frac{w}{MPP_L}$$

Table 4 *Relating Production and Costs (Sand-and-Gravel Example)*

(1) L	(2) Q	(3) (q/L) APP	(4) (Δq/ΔL) MPP	(5) w	(6) (w/APP) AVC	(7) (w/MPP) MC	(8) AFC	(9) ATC
0	0	—	—	$50	—	—	—	—
1	10	10.00	10	50	$5.00	$ 5.00	$10.00	$15.00
2	22	11.00	12	50	4.54	4.17	4.55	9.09
3	36	12.00	14	50	4.17	3.57	2.78	6.95
4	52	13.00	16	50	3.85	3.13	1.92	5.77
5	70	14.00	18	50	3.57	2.78	1.43	5.00
6	86	14.33	16	50	3.49	3.13	1.16	4.65
7	100	14.28	14	50	3.50	3.57	1.00	4.50
8	112	14.00	12	50	3.57	4.17	0.89	4.46
9	122	13.55	10	50	3.69	5.00	0.82	4.51
10	130	13.00	8	50	3.85	6.25	0.77	4.62
11	137	12.45	7	50	4.01	7.14	0.73	4.74
12	143	11.92	6	50	4.20	8.33	0.70	4.90
13	148	11.38	5	50	4.39	10.00	0.68	5.07
14	152	10.85	4	50	4.60	12.50	0.66	5.26
15	155	10.33	3	50	4.84	16.67	0.65	5.49
16	157	9.81	2	50	5.10	25.00	0.64	5.74
17	158	9.29	1	50	5.38	50.00	0.63	6.01

umns 6 and 7, respectively, and average fixed costs (column 8) are computed by dividing fixed costs by output levels. Summing *AFC* and *AVC* then yields the *ATC* of production (column 9).

Average Product and Average Variable Cost

Figure 6 shows that when six workers are on the job (points *b*), average product is at its maximum (14.33 tons) and average variable cost is at its minimum value ($3.49). Workers receive a constant wage, so we can calculate labor costs when *AVC* (which is wL/q) is at its lowest. Symmetrically, from this wage bill, you can infer the hiring of labor when average variable cost is minimized. This result can also be seen in Table 4.

Let us get away from technical descriptions for a moment and look at the intuitive result of this analysis. If the amount produced per worker (APP_L) is at its highest value (point *b* in Panel A), then the amount spent on labor per unit of output (*AVC*) logically must be at its lowest value (point *b* in Panel B).

Marginal Product and Marginal Cost

Labor's marginal physical product at your sand and gravel firm is drawn in Panel A of Figure 6; the corresponding marginal cost curve is in Panel B. These curves parallel the data in Table 4, and thus are reflections of each other. Marginal product is maximized (18 tons daily) and marginal cost is minimized ($2.78) if five workers are hired. Clearly, if the last worker hired produced the most (maximum MPP_L at point *a* in Panel A), then the last few tons of gravel processed cost the least (minimum *MC* at point *a* in Panel B).

The relationship between production and costs is critical for the supply decisions of firms. Of course, production costs are only one dimension of a firm's decision matrix. The other side is demand. In the next few chapters, demand-originated constraints on firms facing various degrees of competition will be dealt with at length.

To simplify the analysis of short-run production and costs, only labor has been allowed to

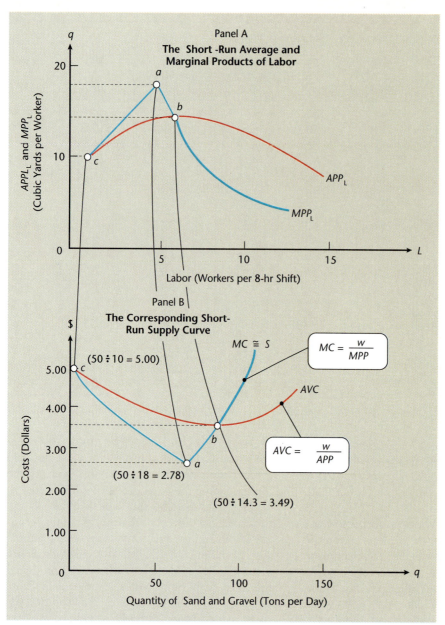

FIGURE 6   The Relationships Between APP_L, MPP_L, AVC, and MC

For simplicity we assume that only labor (L) can be varied in the short run. Thus, all marginal costs and variable costs are associated with the wage bill (wL). When the marginal physical product of labor (MPP_L) is at its maximum (point a in Panel A), the last worker hired added the most output, so the marginal cost (MC) of the last unit produced is at its minimum (point a in Panel B). Similarly, when the average physical product of labor (APP_L) is at its maximum (point b in Panel A), the average amount of labor used (and hence, the average amount of wage cost) per unit of output is at a minimum, so average variable cost (AVC) is also at its minimum (point b in Panel B).

vary, but our results would be qualitatively similar if we allowed all resources but one to vary. The approach to long-run production costs is slightly different because all of a firm's resources are variable. Technology is assumed constant in the long run, however, in part because most resources may be varied more quickly than technology is likely to change, and in part because technological changes tend to be somewhat unpredictable — a topic we will deal with later in this chapter.

Costs in the Long Run

The long run allows a firm to completely adjust all resources and costs. Fixed costs eventually become variable because no resource is fixed in the long run. Just when do fixed costs become variable? In the long run, you might sell previously fixed resources to other firms and rid yourself of obligations to meet fixed payments. The original obligation, however, remains a sunk cost — you cannot change history. Alternatively, you might obligate your firm to pay for more machinery, another short-run fixed cost. Until your name is on the dotted line for a new building or machine or to renew a franchise or lease, these expenses are variable costs. Then they become fixed costs, but only for the short run.

In the long run, a firm may enter or leave an industry and either expand or contract the scope of any operation. More land, buildings, or new machinery can be acquired. Alternatively, property holdings can be reduced through sale or by allowing leases to lapse; old equipment can either be sold or depreciated and scrapped.

Least Cost Production

Profit-maximizing managers can alter their resource mix in the long run to achieve productive efficiency so that production costs for any given amount of output are minimized. Equivalently, they try to maximize the output produced for a given total cost. Efficiency requires conformity with the law of equal marginal advantage, which,

applied to consumer behavior, yields the principle of equal marginal utilities per dollar (described in the preceding chapter). This law applies in a parallel way to production.

> The **principle of equal marginal productivities per dollar:** *Marginal physical products of resources must be proportional to their prices.*

This application of the law of equal advantage to production means that

$$\frac{MPP_L}{w} = \frac{MPP_K}{i} = \frac{MPP_N}{r} = \cdots$$

where MPP_K equals the marginal physical product of capital, MPP_N equals the marginal physical product of land, i equals the interest rate, and r equals the rent rate for land. To see why this equation works, suppose that the last $1 paid in wages generated 1 ton of sand while the last $1 you spent on capital yielded 2 tons of sand. You would gain an extra ton of sand to sell if you shifted $1 away from labor towards capital.

Similar gains of output (or reductions in cost) are possible any time the marginal productivities of resources are not proportional to resource prices.

> **Least cost production** *in the long run entails adjustments until this principle of equal marginal productivities per dollar is met.*

This principle suggests that relatively higher wages will induce a firm to *substitute* capital for labor. This has occurred in the auto industry in recent years as high labor costs have caused an army of industrial robots to invade the assembly line. Symmetrically, higher capital costs induce substitution toward labor. When interest rates are high, investment in new capital falls, and labor is substituted for capital.

You should not get the impression, however, that resources are only substitutes for one another. Resources may also be *complements* in production. Labor productivity, for example, tends to be positively related to the capital and land with which labor has to work. Increases in non-labor resources tend to raise labor's total, average, and marginal physical products. The close short run relationships between production and costs (total, average, and marginal products and costs) suggest that in the long run, average and marginal costs will be influenced by all the resources used.

Long Run Average Costs

Plants of different sizes can be built in the long run, so a unique set of short run cost curves exists for each possible plant size. Possible changes in the short run marginal costs and average total costs of a garment manufacturer with (a) 100, (b) 200, or (c) 300 sewing machines are highlighted in Figure 7. Under these short run cost curves, we have placed an *envelope curve*, which reflects the plant sizes associated with the average costs of producing each level of output. This envelope is the long run average cost (*LRAC*) curve for the firm.

A **long run average total cost (LRATC)** curve reflects the plant size that allows the *minimum possible short run average costs to produce each possible level of output.*

Notice that this envelope curve is *not* tangent to the minimum point on each *SRATC* curve. Only a plant in which 200 machines are used to produce 4,000 garments per day (point *a*) yields the absolute minimum long run average cost of production. At this point, the envelope curve is tangent to the minimum point of the *SRATC* curve. To the left of this point all short run cost curves are tangent to the *LRATC* curve on the left side of their respective minimums. To the right of point *a*, tangencies with the envelope curve are at the right sides of the short run curves.

Economies and Diseconomies of Scale

Notice that the long run average cost (*LRAC*) curve in Figure 7 falls as output rises and then increases as output rises further.

Economies of scale *exist when long run average costs decline as output rises, and larger firms will be more efficient than smaller firms.*

FIGURE 7 The Long-Run Average Cost Curve

Short-run costs depend on the fixed amounts of capital and land used in concert with labor, which, for convenience, we assume is the only variable resource. The long run average total cost (*LRATC*) curve is an *envelope* of short-run average total cost (*SRATC*) curves. Economies of scale occur if expanding land and capital reduce average costs. Diseconomies of scale are present when average costs rise as capacity grows.

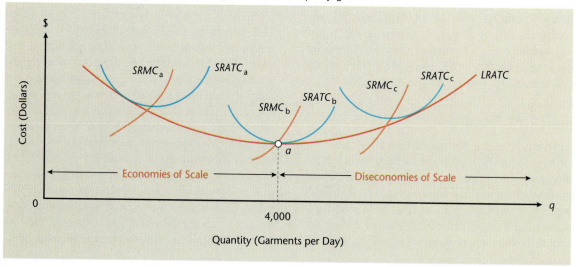

Diseconomies of scale *occur in the range where long run average costs rise with increases in output.*

When diseconomies are encountered, reducing the scale of operations is efficient because it allows production at lower average costs.

It might seem that if all resources were expanded by some fixed proportion, output must expand by that same proportion. Gains from specialization, however, may expand output more than proportionally as the scale of operation grows from some small level. These advantages give rise to economies of scale, causing average production costs to fall.

On the other end of the spectrum, diseconomies of scale emerge because of the application for the long run of the law of diminishing returns. The firm can decide how much capital, land, or labor to use, but diminishing returns remain pervasive, even in the long run, because it is impossible for a firm to vary all technological influences on production proportionally and simultaneously. For example, even in the long run, powerful firms cannot precisely tailor laws or regulations that influence production costs to suit themselves. Moreover, such influences on production as weather and gravity and the laws of physics and chemistry are totally beyond our control, and technology is assumed constant in the long run.

The eminent economist Kenneth Boulding offers the following example of diseconomies of scale to drive home the problem of long run diminishing returns. Imagine that the Empire State Building shrinks until a high-jumping flea could hop it. Now, increase the heights of both the flea and the Empire State Building proportionally until this skyscraper is back to normal size. The flea would be bigger and heavier than an elephant. Can you imagine what strength would be required for it to make this leap now? Move over, Clark Kent.

One reason giant firms encounter diseconomies of scale is that managerial control decays as layers are added to any hierarchy. The information that must be digested and acted on snowballs, so coordinating the activities of ever larger groups becomes an ever more formidable task.

Another problem is that vertical hierarchies require decision making at many different levels. The principal/agent problem becomes pervasive because monitoring performance is increasingly difficult; not all these decision makers will focus on doing everything with maximum efficiency to realize maximum profits. Organizations may become so large and clumsy that, like dinosaurs, extinction is a real possibility.

Measuring Long Run Average Costs

Any firm that fails to exploit economies of scale will have higher average costs than those of competing firms that do; firms that are too small for efficient operation must either grow or fail. Many people think that bigger firms can almost always produce at lower costs than smaller firms. While it is true that a firm must be large enough to exploit all feasible economies of scale, bigger plants may encounter diseconomies of scale and be forced to reduce the scope of their operations or sink.

Studies of Portugal's decline as a world power from 1400 to 1600 indicate that its wooden sailing ships were too large for then-current technology. A large part of the Portuguese fleet sank in bad weather, in part because of huge cargos. The U.K./French *Concorde* passenger jets suffered such great cost disadvantages that their government sponsors took financial nosedives. How large is the optimal convenience store or gas station? How about atomic power plants or oil refineries? In the 1930s, the world's largest auto assembly plant was Ford's River Rouge plant. It was never fully utilized, and today much of it has been torn down. It was simply too large to be efficient.

The ranges where economies or diseconomies of scale are actually encountered vary substantially among industries. Engineering estimates and the few statistical studies of cost functions that are available indicate that there typically are substantial ranges of output for which average costs are roughly constant, as depicted in the middle of the *LRATC* curve in Figure 8.

An idea known as the *survival principle* suggests that clustering within an industry of firms or plants of a particular size is conclusive evidence about the efficient scale of operations. Some economists have tried to apply this principle to specific industries as a way of measuring the minimum points of long run average cost curves. Critics, however, argue that survival depends on a multitude of factors (luck, monopoly power, business acumen, growth or decline of an industry, and so on) and thus, that some inefficient firms may survive, while some efficient firms fail.

Minimum efficient scale (MES) *plants are the smallest that will produce output at minimum average total cost.*

Minimum efficient scale (point *a* at the beginning of the flat portion in Figure 8) has been estimated for various industries using accounting data, engineering estimates, and the survival technique. Typically, *MES* is reported as a percent of the total market. Figure 9 presents some estimates of *MES* for selected industries here and abroad. Measuring long run cost curves is unavoidably imprecise, but the concept is still useful in analyzing industry adjustments to changes in demands, resource prices, or other events.

In summary, economies of scale encourage size. If the minimum efficient scale of production in an industry requires huge firms, then fewer firms will inhabit that industry. (This raises questions about government policies to control excessive market power — issues that are addressed in later chapters.) On the other hand, significant diseconomies of scale tend to reward compact firms so that many competitors inhabit an industry.

FIGURE 8   Typical "Real World" Average Cost Curves

Although long-run average cost curves are normally U-shaped, there is typically a large range of production where average costs are constant and there are neither economies nor diseconomies of scale.

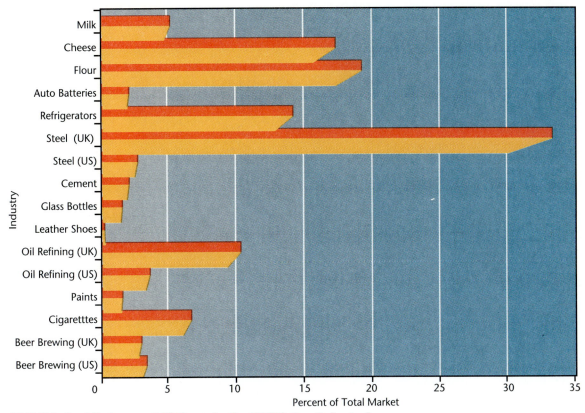

FIGURE 9   Minimum Efficient Scale (MES) for Selected Industries 1974–1990

The minimum efficient scale (*MES*) is the smallest size plant (point *a* in Figure 7) that has long-run average total cost near its minimum. *MES* is usually reported as a percent of total industry output and is used as an explanation of industrial concentration. The larger MES is, the fewer efficient firms a market can support.

Sources: F. M. Scherer and D. Ross, *Industrial Market Structure and Economic Performance* (Princeton, N.J.: Houghton Mifflin), 1990; Dennis Carlton and Jeffrey Perloff, *Modern Industrial Organization* (New York: HarperCollins), 1990; William S. Comanor and Thomas A. Wilson, *Advertising and Market Power* (Cambridge, Mass.: Harvard University Press), 1974; Stephen Davies, "Minimum Efficient Size and Seller Concentration: An Empirical Problem," *The Journal of Industrial Economics*, March 1980, pp. 287–297; Gary L. Shoesmith, "Economies of Scale and Scope in Petroleum Refining," *Applied Economics*, 1988, pp. 1643–1652; and Craig MacPhee, "The Economies of Scale Revisited: Comparing Census Costs, Engineering Estimates, and the Survivor Technique," *Quarterly Journal of Business & Economics*, Spring 1990, pp. 43–67.

Firms and industries grow in response to widespread perceptions of profit opportunities, or wither when economic losses are expected to persist. Long run adjustments allow firms to enter an industry and grow infinitely, or to shrink to zero and leave an industry; a firm can perfectly adjust its size by purchasing more or fewer resources, but, by assumption, we hold technology constant. We need to consider the possibil-

ity, however, that research and development may respond strongly to profit opportunities.

Technological Change

Much human progress arises from incremental improvements in the methods available to satisfy our wants.

Table 5 *Contributions to the Growth Rate of Potential National Income (1929–1982)*

Growth rate (national income)			3.20
Factor inputs (total)		2.03	
Labor	1.49		
Capital	0.54		
Productivity (output/unit of input)		1.17	
Technological change	0.68		
Reallocation of labor from farming	0.25		
Economies of scale from growth of national and international markets	0.27		
Miscellaneous factors	−0.03		

Source: From "Contributions to 1929–82 Growth Rates," *Trends in American Economic Growth, 1929–82,* by Edward F. Denison. Copyright © 1985 The Brookings Institution. Reprinted by permission.

Technological change *increases output from a given set of resources, or allows distribution of previously unknown goods.*

Technological change takes two basic forms: (*a*) improvements to nonhuman resources or (*b*) new knowledge about how to combine resources. New capital equipment that cuts production costs or a new strain of seed that boosts crop yields are examples of technological advances in nonhuman resources. New plowing methods that conserve topsoil or medical procedures that reduce a transplant patient's recovery time would be examples of new knowledge that represents technological progress.

Major technological breakthroughs tend to arrive in waves that influence numerous industries or forms of production. Predicting the direction of such sweeping technological advances is impossible. In a few instances, however, profit incentives within a specific industry cause the direction of technological change to be reasonably predictable.

Consider, for example, adjustments to higher energy costs. Most industries had adapted to low-cost, abundant energy sources during the period 1900 to 1973. Oil drove much of our technology. Then oil prices quadrupled between 1974 and 1975. Car buyers' demands for more mileage were echoed in many industries when firms scuffled to find energy-efficient technologies. New types of insulation were developed, as were production processes that recycled heat or used less of it.

Profit opportunities may induce new technologies that change outputs and production techniques or improve resources, and ultimately drive down costs. Some technological changes occur as quickly as a creative mind can solve a new problem. At other times, refining a technology is never-ending. It is also uncertain whether giant or small enterprises are systematically favored by technological advance. Some new technologies enhance economies of scale; others work best when an operation is small. We can be sure, however, that technological advances make options available that reduce average production costs.

Table 5 summarizes estimates of the sources of long term U.S. economic growth. These estimates illustrate the impact of technological change on economic growth and productivity. Second only to growth in the labor force, technological change has accounted for over 20 percent of long-term economic growth and over half of our productivity gains during the last half century.

Predicting the precise duration and effect of technological change is impossible, so we usually consider only the long-run adjustments of entry and exit into an industry, or the shrinkage or growth of a firm. We will examine economic responses to changing circumstances in the next few chapters.

Chapter Review: Key Points

1. A *production function* expresses a relationship between inputs and output. Production transforms goods to make them more valuable in form, place, time, or possession. A *total product curve* shows how output is affected as the amount of only one input changes.

2. The *short run* is a period in which at least one resource and one cost are fixed. In the *long run* all resources can be varied, but technology is assumed constant. These periods, therefore, are not defined by time, but rather by the nature of the adjustment process.

3. The *average physical product of labor* (APP_L) equals q/L. The *marginal physical product of labor* (MPP_L) equals $\Delta q/\Delta L$, and is the output generated by an additional unit of labor.

4. According to the *law of marginal returns*, when increasing amounts of a variable resource are applied to a fixed resource, although the marginal physical product of the variable factor may initially rise, beyond some point its marginal product inevitably falls.

5. A firm's total costs can be separated into *fixed* (or *overhead*) *costs* and *variable* (or *operating*) *costs*. Fixed costs do not vary with output and do not alter rational decisions. Leases, utility hookup charges, opportunity costs of an owner's resources, and other overhead expenses are fixed costs in the short run. Wages paid employees, bills for raw materials, and other costs that change when output is changed are variable costs.

6. When total fixed costs and total variable costs are each divided by output, *average fixed costs* (*AFC*) and *average variable costs* (*AVC*) are obtained, respectively. Summing the two yields *average total cost* (*ATC*). *Marginal cost* (*MC*) is defined as the additional cost of producing one more unit of a good and equals $\Delta TC/\Delta q$.

7. Firms can enter or leave an industry in the long run because all resources are variable. The *long-run average total cost* (*LRATC*) *curve* is an *envelope curve* under all short-run average cost curves (different-sized plants). It shows the minimum long run average costs for each output level. Long run average cost curves typically have *economies of scale* (*LRATC* falling) over some portion of the

curve, but eventually exhibit *diseconomies of scale* (*LRATC* rising).

8. Measuring long run costs is a complex problem. One method is to examine the size (and cost structure) of firms that have been successful and have "survived" in an industry over a long period of time. Other methods include using both accounting and engineering data to estimate the *LRATC* curve. Economists have estimated *minimum efficient scale* (*MES*), the smallest plant that can be operated at minimum *LRATC*. *MES* is typically reported as a percent of industry output.

9. *Technological progress* increases output from given resources. New technology resides in new knowledge or improved nonhuman resources, and results in new products or lower costs. Technological improvements account for much of our long-term economic growth and rising productivity.

Key Concepts

Ensure that you can define these terms before proceeding.

production functions	variable costs
average physical product of labor	average costs
	marginal cost
marginal physical product of labor	least cost production
law of diminishing marginal returns	economies of scale
	minimum efficient scale (*MES*)
fixed costs	technological change

Problems and Questions

1. Which of the following tend to be fixed costs, and which are probably variable costs? Why does the time period considered matter for each case?

   a. Silk purchased by a Parisian "haute couture" dress designer.

   b. The guaranteed salary of NBA all-star Michael Jordan.

   c. A $1,000,000 contract signed by a specu-

Table 6 *Labor Requirements for a Microcomputer Firm*

Labor	Output	APP_L	MPP_L	AVC	MC
0	0	—	—	—	—
1	30	—	—	—	—
2	70	—	—	—	—
3	120	—	—	—	—
4	200	—	—	—	—
5	260	—	—	—	—
6	300	—	—	—	—
7	335	—	—	—	—
8	350	—	—	—	—

lator who buys a building after foreclosure by the bankruptcy referee of a savings-and-loan institution.

d. A magazine subscription for a doctor's office.

e. Student loans taken out to pay a student's tuition.

f. Payments to migrant workers for harvesting ripe plums.

2–5. Your microcomputer firm's labor requirements for various levels of output per year are described in Table 6.

2. Fill in the columns for APP_L and MPP_L.

3. Use graph paper to plot curves for the total, average, and marginal physical products of labor.

4. Assume that wages are the only variable costs, and that each employee is paid $10,000 annually. Fill in Table 6 for average variable costs (AVC) for each level of labor. (*Note:* Average variable costs are measured per unit of output.) Now compute marginal costs for each level of labor employed.

5. What happens to average and marginal costs as production is expanded?

6. Describe the forces that, as more and more labor is hired, cause output to rise at an increasing rate, and then at a decreasing rate, and that may ultimately cause output to fall as more labor is employed. How do these forces affect marginal and average costs in a similarly systematic fashion? Why? Can you

think of any production processes that would not operate in accord with these general principles? What are they?

7–9. A weekly total product schedule for your car wash is listed in Table 7. Plant and overhead (fixed) costs are $2,000 and the weekly wage is $300.

7. Complete Table 7.

8. Does Table 7 describe the short run or long run? Why?

9. If fixed costs rise to $4,000 per week, does the output where *ATC* is the lowest rise or fall?

10. Suppose that you offered to buy pizza and cold drinks to bribe your friends to help you move into a new apartment and were deluged with offers of help. What problems would you encounter if too few actually showed up? How would this affect your "average cost" per box or stick of furniture moved? What are some possible "fixed factors" that would decrease the efficiency of your move and drive up its cost if too many helpers volunteered? How would this raise the cost of your move? How many big strong friends do you think would be the ideal number to accomplish this task?

11–13. Use Figure 10, which illustrates costs per barrel of crude oil daily at a Nigerian oil field.

11. Compute total costs (TC) when 40,000 and 80,000 barrels are produced.

Table 7 *Car Wash Total Product Schedule*

Labor	Output	TVC	TC	AFC	AVC	ATC	MC
0	0	—	—	—	—	—	—
1	82	—	—	—	—	—	—
2	230	—	—	—	—	—	—
3	450	—	—	—	—	—	—
4	700	—	—	—	—	—	—
5	900	—	—	—	—	—	—
6	1,050	—	—	—	—	—	—
7	1,130	—	—	—	—	—	—
8	1,180	—	—	—	—	—	—
9	1,185	—	—	—	—	—	—

FIGURE 10 Solving for Total Costs, Total Fixed Costs, and Total Variable Costs

12. Compute total fixed costs (*TFC*).

13. Compute total variable costs (*TVC*) when 40,000 and 60,000 barrels are produced.

14–17. Table 8 illustrates four short-run average cost schedules (curves) for leather purses produced in Guatemala.

14. Use graph paper to plot all four short run average cost curves and plot the envelope long run average cost curve.

15. Long run minimum costs are reached at what level of output?

16. If the Guatemalan government limited output to 5,000 purses per month, which plant size would you build?

17. Does the envelope curve touch each short run average cost curve at its minimum point? Why or why not?

18. The average productivity of labor rises as long as labor's marginal productivity exceeds the average. We call this range of production Zone 1. Do you think firms would knowingly choose to operate in Zone 1, where hiring additional workers raises average productivity? Why or why not? Would firms ever operate in Zone 2, the range of output where the marginal returns from labor were positive but diminishing? Would they operate in Zone 3, where the marginal physical productivity of labor is negative? In what zone will firms operate? (A colleague once described another professor as a "Zone 3 personality." What do you suppose was meant by this remark? Have you ever worked with such a person?) Draw a typical total product curve and include average and marginal physical products. Identify these production zones. *(Note:* Firms always try to operate in one of these zones, but most firms will close down rather than operate in the other two.)

19. Why does marginal cost decline if output increases at an increasing rate when additional workers are hired? Why does average variable cost decline as long as the marginal physical product of labor is greater than the average physical product of labor?

20. Can you construct a total product curve for "knowledge of economics," with your study time as the variable (labor) input? How might this curve shift with variations in time with tutors, reference books, reading the *Wall Street Journal*, studying only when you are too tired to party, and so on? At what point would the law of diminishing marginal returns come into play? Should you cease studying at the onset of diminishing returns? You may have heard people suggest that "when you reach the point of diminishing

Table 8 *Four Short-Run Average Cost Schedules*

q(000)	SRAC_A	SRAC_B	SRAC_C	SRAC_D
1	7.50	—	—	—
2	5.40	6.00	—	—
3	5.00	4.50	5.50	—
4	5.30	4.30	4.30	—
5	6.00	4.75	3.85	4.50
6	—	5.70	3.50	4.10
7	—	—	4.00	3.80
8	—	—	4.80	4.00
9	—	—	6.00	4.75
10	—	—	—	6.00

returns, it's time to quit." Are they using this term correctly?

21. What are the similarities and differences between the ways in which the general law of diminishing returns (described in Chapter 2) applies to consumption and to production?

Optional Material: Isoquants and Production

How the resource mix is varied in the long run to maximize a firm's profit was touched on in our discussion of the principle of equal marginal productivities per dollar. Now we will address these long-run adjustments using slightly more sophisticated tools.

Isoquants

Producing any given amount of output can be accomplished with numerous combinations of inputs. For example, suppose you own a firm that packages and sells "Birdhouse" gourd seeds to home gardeners who grow houses for their feathered friends. You estimate that you can wholesale 10,000 cases of packaged seeds at $2 per case over the course of a season. Five of the many different possible combinations of capital (machines) and labor (workers) that will accomplish the job are listed in Table 9. These combinations run the gamut from a few machines with many workers hand-counting and stuffing the packages to production processes using numerous automated machines and very few workers to load seeds and watch the machines work. As you might expect, the process you would eventually gravitate to will be the one with the lowest cost. The last column of Table 9 depicts the total costs of packaging 10,000 cases of seeds if labor and capital each cost $1,000 per unit. To minimize the costs of producing 10,000 packages, you would employ three machines and three workers. The information in Table 9 is graphed in Figure 11; a smoothly curved line connects the five combinations from Table 9. This curve represents all possible mixtures of labor and capital that can produce 10,000 cases, and is referred to as an **isoquant**.

Isoquants are similar to the consumer indifference curves discussed in the optional material at the end of an earlier chapter, but with one major difference. Isoquants show constant levels of output, which is measurable; indifference curves show constant levels of satisfaction, which cannot be measured with precision. Just as the slope of an indifference curve reflects the relative subjective desirability of the two goods considered $(-MU_a/MU_b)$, isoquants reflect the relative marginal productivities of the two resources $(-MPP_L/MPP_K)$. We will develop this point more in a moment.

Table 9 *The Various Combinations of Labor and Capital that Will Package 10,000 Cases of "Birdhouse" Gourd Seeds*

Point	Units of Capital (K)	Units of Labor (L)	Output: Cases of Gourd Seeds (q)	Total Cost if w = $1,000, r = $1,000 (TC)
a	1	9	10,000	$10,000
b	2	5	10,000	7,000
c	3	3	10,000	6,000
d	5	2	10,000	7,000
e	9	1	10,000	10,000

Isocost Curves

Superimposed on the isoquant for 10,000 cases of seeds in Figure 11 is a set of isocost curves. **Isocosts** represent different levels of expenditures by your firm for various combinations of labor and capital when the price of labor is $1,000 per unit and the price of capital is $1,000 per unit. These isocosts are close relatives of the consumer budget lines described in the optional material in an earlier chapter.

Just as the slope of the budget line reflects the prices of the two goods considered $(-P_a/P_b)$, the slopes of isocosts reflect the prices of the resources considered $(-w/r$, where w is the wage rate and r is the unit cost of capital). Notice that production process a $(L = 9, K = 1)$ yields total costs of $10,000, which lies on the $TC = \$10,000$ isocost curve. As Figure 11 illustrates, 10,000 cases of seeds can be packaged at a minimum cost of $6,000 using three workers

and three machines (point c). Graphically, costs are minimized for a given level of output where the isocost curve is just tangent to the isoquant, for an output level of 10,000 packages. At this point, $MPP_L/MPP_K = w/r$.

This is similar to the tangency between consumer indifference curves and budget lines in which maximum satisfaction is attained for a given budget. Recall (from the preceding chapter) that this point conformed to the principle of equal marginal utilities per dollar: $MU_a/P_a = MU_b/P_b$ or $MU_a/MU_b = P_a/P_b$. Thus, in accord with the principle of equal marginal productivities per dollar, our result that $MPP_L/w = MPP_K/r$ or $MPP_L/MPP_K = w/r$ means that minimizing costs requires the marginal payments to resource owners to be in accord with the resource's contribution to production.

One final note: Just as there are numerous isocost curves that represent different levels of cost, there are also numerous isoquants for pro-

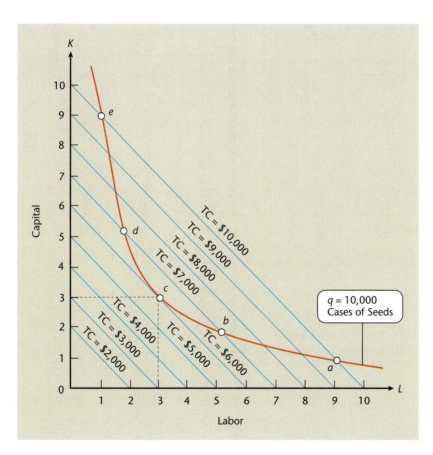

FIGURE 11   Isoquant (Equal Output) Curve for Birdhouse Gourd Seeds

An *isoquant* shows the various combinations of resources that will produce a specific level of output. The isocost curves (designated $TC = \$2,000$ to $TC = \$10,000$) are analogous to consumer budget constraints and represent the feasible mix of inputs given a specific amount of spending available to the firm.

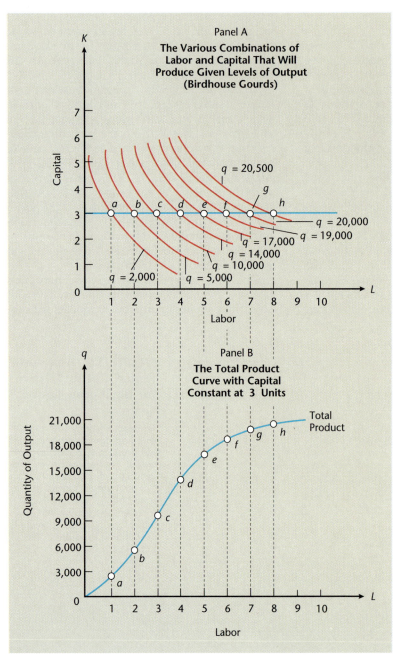

FIGURE 12 Diminishing Returns and Isoquants

If capital is held constant at 3 units (denoted by the horizontal line in Panel A), as the firm employs more and more labor, its output is subject to diminishing marginal returns.

duction levels other than 10,000 packages. We have simplified the analysis by assuming that you expected 10,000 packages of seeds per season to be the most profitable level of output.

Substituting One Resource for Another

Let us take a moment to examine what happens to the marginal products of labor and capital relative to each other when we substitute labor for capital or vice versa. When we change from production process c to production process b (move from point c to point b in Figure 11), we "give up" one unit of capital; to keep production constant, we must hire two units of labor, which suggests that the third machine does the work of two workers. When we move from point b to point a (giving up another machine), how many workers must be hired to keep production constant? The answer is four, suggesting that the productivity of four workers is required to replace that lost from the second machine. As we substitute more and more labor for capital (move down and to the right on the isoquant in Figure 11), ever-increasing amounts of labor are necessary to keep production constant. Alternatively, the marginal product of labor declines relative to

that of capital. The opposite is true when capital is substituted for labor (movements to the left on the isoquant). Thus, the law of diminishing marginal productivity is reflected in the shapes of isoquants, which are convex (bowed in) from the origin.

Diminishing Marginal Product

The analysis in this chapter assumes that the typical production process eventually is subject to diminishing returns to the variable input. The same principle applies to production analysis using isoquants. Figure 12 illustrates the diminishing marginal physical product of labor when the amounts of other resources are held constant. In Panel A of Figure 12, capital is held constant at 3 units. Points a through h represent the amounts of labor needed to produce output levels ranging from 2,000 to 20,500 units. In Panel B, the total product curve is derived from Panel A when capital is fixed at 3 units, and shows diminishing returns to labor. As we add more and more labor to a fixed stock of capital, the increased output from hiring additional labor eventually falls.

Product Markets

Vigorous competition is the norm for most landscapers, retailers, and homebuilders. Other firms only broadly compete for customers: your local phone company may vie with book stores or travel agents for shares of your budget. Some firms specialize in such standard goods as lumber; others focus on such unique goods as organ transplants. A tiny town may support only one gas station, while high capital costs create monopolies in bigger markets: one giant firm, COMSAT, operates most communications satellites. Our economy encompasses many types of competition. The purpose of Part 7 is to help you explore the many forms and consequences of competition among business firms.

The range of market structures shown in the figure below indicates that several factors shape the extent of competition in an industry. We analyze pure competition in Chapter 23. In Chapter 24, problems caused by monopolies are contrasted with the results of pure competition. Having discussed these extremes, we then survey the intermediate situations of monopolistic competition and oligopoly in Chapter 25. In Chapter 26, we introduce modern theories of strategic behavior — how interdependent decisions are shaped in this middle ground between monopoly and pure competition. Part 7 concludes with discussions of antitrust policies in Chapter 27. Government antitrust actions and regulations are attempts to direct market allocations of resources and incomes in ways thought to be more economically efficient or socially preferable.

Monopoly	Oligopoly	Monopolistic Competition	Pure Competition
1. One-Firm industry	1. Few firms	1. Numerous potential firms and buyers	1. Numerous potential firms and buyers
2. No close substitutes for products	2. Decision making is mutually interdependent	2. Differentiated products	2. Similar products
3. Substantial and effective barriers to entry	3. Major barriers to entry	3. No entry or exit barriers	3. No entry or exit barriers
4. Potential longrun profit	4. Potential longrun profit	4. No profit in longrun	4. No profit in longrun
5. Substantial market power and control over price	5. Shared market power and control over price	5. Diffused market power and little control over price	5. No market power, and no control over price

Highly Concentrated Markets

Competition Markets with Low Concentration

CHAPTER

The Competitive Ideal

High school students taking SATs recognize that their real competition for college scholarships and admissions is all the high school students taking SATs all across the country; competition from their immediate circle of acquaintances is almost irrelevant. Similarly, most farmers do not consciously compete with nearby farms, because they recognize that each is so small relative to the world market that no individual farm produces enough to affect prices for agricultural outputs. Impersonal competition that is fierce but diffused is the focus of this chapter; we will delay treatments of conscious and concentrated rivalry among corporate giants until our chapters on "Monopolistic Competition and Oligopoly" and "Strategic Behavior."

The model of pure competition presented here focuses on an idealized market structure containing so many small competitors that any single firm's behavior is irrelevant to its competitors. Firms lack any discretion about pricing in this competitive climate and must be efficient merely to survive. The chapter opens with requirements for a purely competitive market structure. Short-run pricing and output decisions are then explored, followed by a look at the importance of competitive entry and exit. These results are evaluated and set a bench mark for efficiency that will be used to evaluate other markets.

The World of Pure Competition[1]

The consequences of competition for the pricing and output decisions of firms are most easily established in the model of **pure competition,** which requires that:

1. Potential buyers and sellers are numerous and each is so small relative to the market that individual decisions about purchases or output do not noticeably affect market demand or supply, nor, consequently, do individual decisions affect the market price.

2. Firms in the industry produce a *homogeneous* (standardized) good.

3. Barriers to entry or exit are insignificant in the long run; new firms can enter the industry if doing so appears profitable, or exit if they anticipate losses.

Generic office supplies, most agricultural products, and a few other relatively homogeneous goods are produced in highly competitive mar-

---

1. A theory called perfect competition is more restrictive than the theory of pure competition. It adds perfect (costless and instantaneous) information about goods and resources and perfect (costless) mobility of resources and goods in the long run to the assumptions that underpin the purely competitive model. Nevertheless, the basic conclusions of these models are quite similar.

kets. Each buyer or seller is too insignificant to single-handedly affect the total demand or supply of the good, leaving competitive buyers and sellers as *quantity adjusting* price takers; they have no choice but to accept the price set in the market.

> **Price takers:** *Buyers or sellers who are so small relative to a market that the effects of their transactions are inconsequential for market prices.*

Thus, individual competitive buyers view the supply curves facing them as perfectly elastic (horizontal) at the current market price. Similarly, competitive sellers perceive the demand curves they face as horizontal at the market price.

Competition vs. Rivalry

Competition usually connotes rivalry. We all grow up competing for grades, merit badges, positions on teams, and dates. Iowa farmers broadly compete with other farmers from all around the globe. How are prices set for their corn, wheat, or pigs? Do farmers argue that their products are superior and so should command a premium price? Clearly not. Nor do they offer coupons or "instant winner bingo" to compete for buyers.

Competitive price setting occurs for basic farm products (from eggs to sugar to orange juice concentrate), raw materials (coal or crude oil), primary products (steel or lumber), and precious metals (gold or silver) roughly 240 business days each year at commodity exchanges in major cities around the globe.[2] Market prices are set for hundreds of commodities in an auction environment by the bids and offers of thousands of buyers and sellers or their broker representatives.

Commodity exchanges seem chaotic to visitors. Commodities are traded in a climate approaching pure competition, primarily by "public outcry." Wild-eyed traders angle various numbers of fingers overhead and scream bids and offers on a huge crowded "trading floor." The

---

2. Chicago's Board of Trade is the world's biggest commodity exchange.

din rivals that during the opening kickoff at the Super Bowl. No single buyer or seller can sway prices as bids and offers are accepted or rejected. A trader may buy cotton for a Tokyo customer one minute and sell Georgia peanuts the next, but most traders are narrowly specialized. Small farmers often sell their entire crop at the going market price in a single transaction. Farmers are examples of price takers.

If you struck gold at your sand-and-gravel site, you could sell all the gold you mined at the going market price, as shown in Figure 1. The demand curve facing each purely competitive mine is a horizontal line (d) at the market price (P_e). Trying to charge a price above P_e would result in no sales, while cutting price below P_e would not increase the ability to sell gold—all your output can be sold at the going price. Thus, competitive firms decide what amounts of output to produce and sell at current prices. Even firms mining hundreds of claims using millions of dollars worth of equipment can sell gold only at the going price. This is why competitive firms, including farmers, are price takers.

Purely competitive firms compete in one dimension—technically efficient production. They try to minimize costs while producing the level of output that maximizes their profit. We will present some recipes that a firm must follow in choosing the output that maximizes profit, but be aware that this also requires decisions about which resources and technologies to use. Real-world decisions usually involve coping with less precise information than we assume the firm has while building the purely competitive model.

Rivalry The stress on quantity decisions by pure competitors contrasts sharply with competition among carmakers, for example. It is difficult and costly for a new firm to enter the auto market. Cars are not standardized, and the pricing and output decisions of any of the big three U.S. automakers or their foreign counterparts clearly affect the sales of other producers. Advertising, styling, and aggressive marketing are as important as pricing strategy. These firms are rivals, but unlike purely competitive firms, they do not compete solely on the basis of efficient production of output at a market determined price.

FIGURE 1   Demand Curves for a Competitive Firm and a Competitive Industry

Although the market demand for gold is far from elastic, the demand curve facing an individual miner is perfectly elastic (horizontal). Competition forces small firms producing undifferentiated products to be price takers.

Freedom of entry and exit is probably the vital ingredient in maintaining competition over time.

Freedom of entry and exit: *In the long run, firms can enter an industry with no cost disadvantages relative to established firms, and old firms can costlessly transfer resources to other industries.*

Entry and exit is relatively unfettered in many types of agriculture. Existing farms responded quickly to unusual profits in 1973–1974 by expanding, and new farmers entered agricultural markets, causing gluts of many farm products. Then farm prices plummeted and entry faded. During 1977–1985, many farmers were hounded by the prospect of financial catastrophe. By 1990, agricultural markets had rebounded strongly, and many farmers who were close to going under in the mid-1980s began to prosper.

Few industries match all the assumptions of pure competition. But remember that a model should be no more complex than is required for the purpose at hand. (Models are judged by predictive accuracy and not by realism of assumptions.) Pure competition may be uncommon, but vigorous growth of international trade has made many markets much more competitive in recent years.

Pure competition tends to be more efficient than other market structures and has become a normative yardstick used to judge other market structures. More important, many results from simple competitive models apply in markets that deviate from pure competition. For example, the competitive model underpins supply and demand analysis, which enables us to predict qualitatively the effects of certain events on prices and outputs. Understanding competitive reactions to changed circumstances allows the use of supply and demand to explain everyday changes in prices and outputs. Not surprisingly, ranges of potential adjustment differ markedly when we consider different time frames.

Supply Responses and Time

All decision makers gain flexibility as the time horizon expands. Industry responses to shifts in demand depend in part on how long firms have to adjust. Alfred Marshall, an eminent British economist, designed a conceptual way for economists to treat time systematically. Responses are classified as occurring in the **market** (immediate) **period**, the *short run* (**SR**), or the *long run* (**LR**). The more time an industry has to adapt to changes in demands, the greater the impact on quantities and the smaller the effect on prices. Thus, the market elasticity of supply is positively related to the time allowed for an industry to adjust. In the market period, supply is perfectly inelastic because we assume, for simplicity, that neither resources nor inventories can be adjusted. Supplies are somewhat elastic in the short run and even more elastic in the long run.

This relationship is shown in Figure 2. Suppose the original demand for gold is D_0, where price is $600 and quantity sold is Q_0. If demand rises to D_1, gold would rise to $850 per ounce during the market period to reflect mining firms' temporary inability to boost output. If the higher demand persists, mines might boost output by paying overtime wages, hiring new workers, or through other short-run devices. This rise in quantity supplied by existing firms yields a short run price of $725, which is below the price of $850 per ounce immediately after demand rose to D_1. But prospectors will ultimately find more gold; as owners of new mines respond to higher profits, supplies will rise further, reducing the long-run equilibrium price to $650.

The range of potential adjustments in an industry expands when firms have more time to adapt. In the long run, quantities adjust more and price changes adjust less for a given change in demand than in the market period or the short run. Firms cannot modify output in a single market period to minimize losses or to exploit new profit opportunities when demands change.

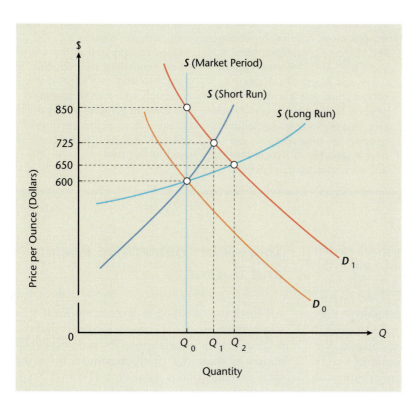

FIGURE 2 Industry Supply Response and the Market Period

Production is fixed and supply is nearly perfectly inelastic in the market period. (For convenience, we ignore possible variations in inventories.) In the short run, existing firms can vary their outputs so the industry supply curve is more elastic. In the long run, supply is much more elastic, because firms either enter or leave the industry in response to profit signals.

Alfred Marshall (1842–1924)

Few economists extend knowledge in any but their narrow areas of specialization. A handful of master economists, however, have broadly expanded the frontiers of economic analysis. Their names and ideas are scattered across these pages. Adam Smith, David Ricardo, John Maynard Keynes, Karl Marx, and, in our own time, Paul Samuelson, have covered the gamut of economic theory. Alfred Marshall belongs in this elite group.

Born in a middle-class London suburb, Marshall was destined for the ministry, according to his stern, evangelical father. An independent sort, Marshall declined a classics scholarship at Oxford, and instead studied math at Cambridge. His exposure to philosophy led to Marshall's lifelong concern with poverty and other social problems that plagued industrial England. This concern led him to study economics, in which he excelled. Marshall's most famous student, John Maynard Keynes, referred to Marshall as the greatest economist of the nineteenth century.

Marshall was a careful writer who tried to avoid controversy. Many ideas that eventually appeared in his *Principles of Economics* (1890) were developed much earlier, but Marshall's patience and diligence paid huge and lasting dividends. Despite the many changes in economics since his death, large parts of economic theory remain distinctly Marshallian. His major contributions include the concepts of both short and long run *competitive equilibria, price elasticity of demand, internal* and *external economies of scale, increasing* and *decreasing cost industries, quasi-rent,* and *consumer surplus.*

Perhaps Marshall's greatest contribution was the way he worked time into economic analysis, bequeathing to subsequent generations of economists not only a valuable analytical tool, but also rules for its effective use. Marshall handled continuous economic change by invoking conditional clauses that he grouped under the term *ceteris paribus. Ceteris paribus* allows analysts to study the issue at hand narrowly and precisely by temporarily ignoring other sources of disturbance. This step-by-step approach facilitates treatment of broader issues that contain the narrow one; each bit of new knowledge allows more and more restrictions to be relaxed.

This method is illustrated in Marshall's treatment of demand, in which the number of consumers, their tastes, expectations, and money incomes, and the prices of other goods are all assumed constant when studying how equilibrium price and quantity are determined. As things change over time, however, each restrictive assumption may be relaxed in turn so that the analysis proceeds to a new equilibrium. Marshall also applied this approach with fruitful results to the theories of value and production. In so doing, he developed an analytical technique used to this day.

Firms can only partially adjust in the short run, because at least one resource is fixed. Only in the long run are all resources variable so that firms can enter or leave markets as their owners choose. Given sufficient time, technology may even improve as miners seek new ways to exploit the higher market demand and price of gold. We will now study the short-run decisions of purely competitive firms before turning our attention to the long run.

Short-Run Competitive Pricing and Output

All firms are assumed to maximize profit (the excess of revenues over costs), a process that can be described in several ways. The simplest explanation of short run profit maximization is the total revenue minus total cost ($TR - TC$) approach.

Table 1 *Cost Data for a Competitive Gold Miner*

(1) Weekly Output in Ounces (*q*)	(2) Price per Ounce (*P*)	(3) Weekly Total Revenue (*TR*)	(4) Weekly Total Cost (*TC*)	(5) Weekly Profit (3) − (4) (*π*)
0	$600	0	$ 570	$ −570
1	600	$ 600	810	−210
2	600	1,200	1,000	200
3	600	1,800	1,240	560
4	600	2,400	1,530	870
5	600	3,000	1,920	1,080
6	600	3,600	2,410	1,190
7	600	4,200	3,000	1,200
8	600	4,800	3,690	1,110
9	600	5,400	4,480	920
10	600	6,000	5,370	630
11	600	6,600	6,360	240
12	600	7,200	7,450	−250

Total Revenue – Total Cost Approach

A purely competitive firm is a price taker, so how much to produce (quantity adjustment) is its major decision.[3] Will producing and selling as much as possible maximize profits? The example outlined in Table 1 leads us to the answer. Suppose you can mine weekly gold output levels ranging from nothing to twelve ounces and that the market dictates a price of $600 per ounce. Whether you sell one ounce of gold or twelve, each ounce sells for $600 this week. The total revenue curve in Panel A of Figure 3 shows how revenue grows as output rises; its slope is constant at $600 per ounce of gold. If fixed costs are $570 weekly, the production costs associated with each level of output are shown in column 4 of Table 1 and graphed in Panel A as *TC*.

Subtracting total costs from total revenue is a straightforward way to calculate profit. You can mine the amount where this difference – profit (*π*) – is the largest. Look at column 5 in Table 1; producing seven ounces of gold yields maximum

profit – $1,200. In Panel A of Figure 3, profit is maximized where the vertical distance between total revenue and total costs is greatest; in Panel B, profit is maximized where the vertical distance between the profit curve and the horizontal axis is greatest. The profit maximizing output in this example occurs at seven ounces.

The chief lesson is that there are at least two sides to profit maximization, regardless of market structure. First consider the demand side (total revenue and price), then the supply side (production costs). Each must be taken into account to arrive at appropriate output and/or pricing decisions.

Notice also that two break-even levels of output are shown in Panel A of Figure 3.

> **Break-even points** *occur where total revenue = total cost; economic profit is zero.*

These points are critical for decisions about entering risky lines of business. You would naturally like any risky activity to potentially break even at low levels of output and sales.

The total revenue minus total cost approach is easily understood. A more fruitful approach for operational decisions, however, is the *marginal*

---

3. There are choices about what technology to use, what kind and how much labor to employ, and so on. For simplicity, we lump all these as parts of the output decision, postponing our study of resource markets until later chapters.

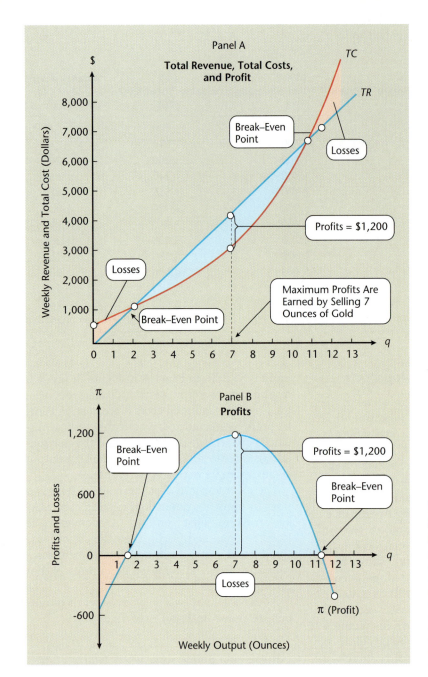

Panel A

Total Revenue, Total Costs, and Profit

Break–Even Point

Losses

Profits = $1,200

Losses

Break–Even Point

Maximum Profits Are Earned by Selling 7 Ounces of Gold

TC

TR

$

8,000

7,000

6,000

5,000

4,000

3,000

2,000

1,000

Weekly Revenue and Total Cost (Dollars)

0 1 2 3 4 5 6 7 8 9 10 11 12 13 *q*

Panel B

Profits

π

1,200

600

0

-600

Profits and Losses

Break–Even Point

Profits = $1,200

Break–Even Point

Losses

π (Profit)

1 2 3 4 5 6 7 8 9 10 11 12 13 *q*

Weekly Output (Ounces)

FIGURE 3 *TR − TC* Approach to Finding Maximum Profits

For a competitor who is a price taker, total revenue (*TR* = *PQ*) is exactly proportional to output. Diminishing returns imply that total costs (*TC*) rise at an increasing rate as output expands. Profit maximization entails producing where the difference between total revenue and total cost is the greatest (π = *TR* − *TC*).

cost equals marginal revenue (*MC* = *MR*) approach. The total revenue minus total cost (*TR* − *TC* = π) and marginal revenue equals marginal cost (*MR* = *MC*) approaches yield mathematically equivalent results, but arrive at profit maximization by different routes and provide different insights.

Marginal Revenue = Marginal Cost Approach

You studied marginal cost in the preceding chapter. We need to analyze marginal revenue before discussing how firms link these concepts to set output at its most profitable level.

Marginal Revenue Marginal cost is the increase in total cost incurred by producing one more unit of output.

Marginal revenue *is the increase in total revenue from selling one more unit.*

For a purely competitive firm, marginal revenue equals price ($MR = P$). Consider your gold mine. The price of gold is set in the international commodity market for precious metals centered in New York, London, and Zurich, so mining firms are price takers. If the going rate for gold is $600 per ounce, a firm's marginal revenue is $600 per ounce sold, regardless of how many ounces individual firms sell. Remember that each gold mine is too insignificant to affect the total market price or output. Return for a moment to Figure 1. Each mine operator views the demand curves faced as horizontal at the $600 price. Each firm's perception of demand curves as perfectly elastic means that each mine operator expects total revenues to be exactly proportional to output, because price is fixed and total revenue equals price times quantity. Thus, because the price is unaffected by the amounts sold by any firm, each ounce of gold is expected to generate marginal revenue equal to $600.

Review the data in Table 1. Column 2 reveals the market price to be $600 per ounce. Marginal revenue is the change in total revenue from the sale of one more unit, so as we go from five ounces to six ounces of gold sold, total revenue jumps from $3,000 to $3,600 weekly for a net change of $600. *Marginal revenue equals the price ($MR = P$) of the commodity in competitive markets.* Our next order of business is determining how competitive firms use this price and cost information to maximize profits.

Profit Maximization Suppose you have information about the marginal cost and the price of each unit of output. How much should be produced and sold? One rule of thumb for any firm (regardless of industry structure) might be: Make any small adjustment (including the production of an additional unit of output) that brings in at least as much in revenues as it absorbs in costs. This translates into economic jargon as the:

Marginal revenue = marginal cost rule: *All profit-maximizing firms produce and sell an extra unit of output only if marginal revenue is at least as great as marginal cost.*

Your revenue from selling one more unit of gold (from Table 2) is graphed in Figure 4 as the demand curve *d* ($P = MR = \$600$). Marginal cost from your cost data (column 7 in Table 2) is graphed as the *MC* curve in Figure 4. Consider what happens when you produce and sell the seventh ounce of gold. The extra revenue to your firm is $600, but the seventh ounce of gold only costs $590 to produce. Thus, extra profit from the sale of this seventh unit is $10. In fact, you will increase total profit by the shaded triangle below the demand curve as you increase output from six to seven ounces.

What would happen to profit if you produced the eighth ounce? You would receive only $600 for it, but its production costs would be $690. You will lose $90 on the eighth ounce if you produce and sell it. Your profit will fall by the area of the shaded triangle above the demand curve as output rises from seven to eight ounces. Conclusion? Price and marginal revenue are identical in pure competition, so a profit-maximizing competitive firm produces until marginal cost equals price: $P = MR = MC$ for maximum profits, which in this example occurs at seven ounces. This analysis leads to a profit maximization rule that holds for firms ranging from pure competition to pure monopoly: *All profit-maximizing firms produce and sell until marginal cost just equals the marginal revenue ($MR = MC$) derived from the sale of the good.*

Marginal revenue and marginal cost data for your gold mine (from Table 2) are graphed in Figure 5, along with average total cost. The marginal revenue equals marginal cost approach reveals that seven ounces is still the profit-maximizing output level (point *e*). The $TR - TC$ approach provides one way to compute total profit. Total revenue equals price times quantity; for seven ounces of gold at $600 per ounce, this is $4,200. Geometrically, this is the area *0dec* in Figure 5. But how much is total cost? Since average total cost for seven ounces is $428.58 for each ounce (point *a*), the total cost for all seven

Table 2 *Cost Data for Your Competitive Gold Mine*

(1) Weekly Output in Ounces (q)	(2) Total Fixed Cost (TFC)	(3) Total Variable Cost (TVC)	(4) Total Cost (TFC + TVC) (TC)	(5) Average Variable Cost (TVC/Q) (AVC)	(6) Average Total Cost (TC/Q) (ATC)	(7) Marginal Cost (ΔTC/ΔQ) (MC)	(8) Price Equals Marginal Revenue (P = MR)	(9) Total Revenue (TR = PQ)	(10) Profit (π)
0	$570	0	$ 570	0	—	—	$600	0	$−570
1	570	$ 240	810	$240.00	$810.00	$ 240	600	$ 600	−210
2	570	430	1,000	215.00	500.00	190	600	1,200	200
3	570	670	1,240	223.33	413.33	240	600	1,800	560
4	570	960	1,530	240.00	382.50	290	600	2,400	870
5	570	1,350	1,920	270.00	380.00	390	600	3,000	1,080
6	570	1,840	2,410	306.67	401.67	490	600	3,600	1,190
7	570	2,430	3,000	347.14	428.58	590	600	4,200	1,200
8	570	3,120	3,690	390.00	461.25	690	600	4,800	1,110
9	570	3,910	4,480	434.44	497.78	790	600	5,400	920
10	570	4,800	5,370	480.00	537.00	890	600	6,000	630
11	570	5,790	6,360	526.33	578.19	990	600	6,600	240
12	570	6,880	7,450	573.33	620.83	1,090	600	7,200	−250

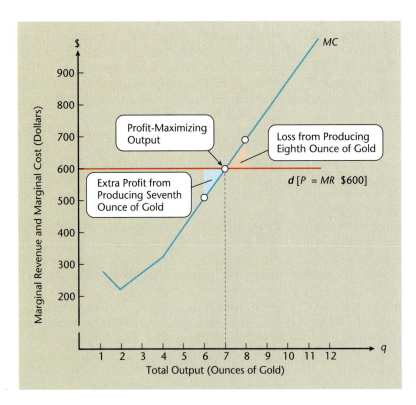

FIGURE 4 $MR = MC$ Approach to Finding Maximum Profits

Whenever marginal revenue (*MR*) exceeds marginal cost (*MC*), a firm can increase its total profit by expanding output. (Recall that marginal revenue and price are identical for price-taker firms.) If marginal cost exceeds marginal revenue, then the firm is losing money on the last few units produced, and will gain by reducing output. Thus, maximum profits require that $MR = MC$.

Source: Tables 1 and 2.

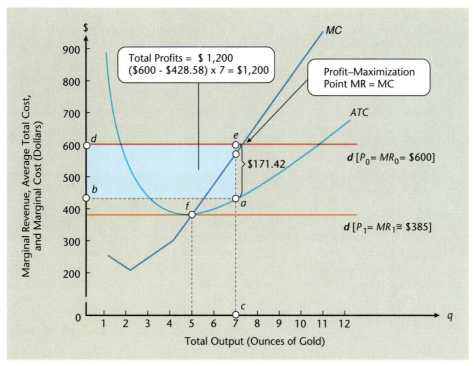

FIGURE 5 Measuring Short-Run Profits

Profit per unit is the difference between price and average total cost, which equals *ae* for seven ounces of gold. Profit per unit (*ae*) times number of units (*ab*) yields total profit to the firm (*bdea*). Firms maximize total profit, however—not profit per unit. Maximum total profits occur where $MC = MR$.

Source: Tables 1 and 2.

ounces is $3,000 ($428.58 × 7 = $3,000). The area *0bac* geometrically represents total cost (average cost times quantity). Thus, total weekly profit is $1,200 ($4,200 − $3,000), which is the shaded area *bdea* in Figure 5.

An alternative way to compute total profit is to multiply average profit per unit times output. Price minus average total cost ($P − ATC$) equals average profit per unit, so average profit per unit when seven ounces are produced is the distance *ae* in Figure 5, which is $171.42 ($600 − $428.58). Thus, total weekly profit is still $1,200 ($171.42 × 7 — the shaded area *bdea*, which also equals $TR − TC$). Whether we maximize total revenue minus total cost or use the marginal revenue equals marginal cost approach, the mathematical solution is the same for the firm's profit-maximizing decision.

Figure 5 also shows what happens if the price

of gold falls sharply. At roughly $385 per ounce, marginal revenue equals marginal cost at point *f*, or an output level of roughly five ounces. Average total cost, however, is in the $380 range, so the firm barely breaks even at a $385 price per ounce of gold. The lowest break-even price in a competitive industry occurs when the demand curve facing each individual firm (the price line) is tangent to the minimum point of the firm's average total cost curve. Typical firms will neither incur economic losses nor enjoy economic profits at such a price, so there will be no net tendency for the industry to shrink or grow because of entry and exit. In a moment you will see that this break-even situation characterizes firms in purely competitive industries in long-run equilibrium.

Measuring profits may seem a precise process, but decisions must be made even though managers never perfectly predict the profit yielded by any decision. What matters is the direction of change – will profit rise or fall if a firm adopts a certain policy? Expected marginal benefits and costs are crucial for all types of decisions. For example, when public policy decisions are made about tax structures, incentive systems, or various regulations, the same kinds of questions arise: If a specific policy were altered, in what direction would social welfare, net consumer satisfaction, or business profits change? If decision makers know this, they can adjust towards optimal policies.

Loss Minimization and Plant Shutdown

Alas, business is not always profitable. One of two choices must be made if sales revenues cannot cover costs. The firm will experience losses if

it elects to produce and sell output. If the firm shuts the plant down, however, it will incur losses equal to fixed costs. Which decision will yield the smaller loss?

Suppose the demand for gold collapses, dropping its price to $300 per ounce, as reflected in Figure 6. Should you mine any gold? Our rule that a firm maximizes profit or minimizes losses by equating marginal revenue and marginal cost seems to indicate that optimal weekly output in this instance is four ounces (point a). At this level of output, total revenue ($1,200) fails to cover total costs ($1,530), yielding a loss ($330 weekly). The result is the same if we apply an average revenue minus average cost approach to this situation. In Figure 6, average revenue (price) is $300 and average cost is $382.50. Thus, the average loss per unit of output of

FIGURE 6   Loss Minimization in the Short Run

Minimizing losses need not mean shutting down; a firm would still have incurred its fixed costs. A firm should operate as long as price at least covers average variable costs, because some of this surplus can be applied to fixed costs. In this way, a firm minimizes its losses. [*Note:* Profit is total revenue minus total cost; therefore, loss can be calculated as total cost minus total revenue, or loss = $q \times (ATC - P)$.]

FIGURE 7 Short-Run Shutdown Point

The short-run *shutdown point* is at a price of $215 per ounce and an output of two ounces per week. At any price below $215, the firm's losses would be larger if it continued to produce. At prices below $215, variable costs of production will not be covered. Thus, at prices below $215, the firm will close its doors to minimize losses.

Source: Tables 1 and 2.

$82.50 times four ounces yields a total loss of $330 (the colored area *efca* in Figure 6).

Suppose you closed the mine to avoid selling gold below its average total cost. Losses would equal fixed costs, or $570 in our example. Remember that fixed costs are incurred whether or not any output is produced. These include such expenses as rent payments, utility charges (for minimum service), administrative overhead, and insurance. Fixed (sunk) costs are not current opportunity costs because they cannot be avoided; the alternatives they once represented were lost in the past. Thus, exiting this competitive industry is virtually costless in the long run.

Variable costs are a firm's opportunity costs of production. Average variable costs of $240 (point *b* in Figure 6) are incurred in wages, mate-

rials, and other expenses when four ounces of gold are mined. Consequently, average variable costs will be covered as long as the mine can sell gold for more than $240 per ounce. As the mine operator, you could allocate the difference between price ($300) and average variable costs ($240) to a fund to cover fixed costs. Even if all fixed costs are not covered, at least some can be — a loss of $330 is better than a loss equal to fixed costs of $570. Note that the critical costs to cover are variable costs, not fixed costs. As the saying goes, sunk costs are *sunk*.

When will it pay the firm to shut down? The answer is that a firm will be ahead by closing its doors if the price of a good fails to cover its average variable costs. This is shown in Figure 7. You should close the mine if the price of gold falls below \$215 per ounce, which is the minimum value of the average variable cost curve. At a price of \$215, the mine just recoups its variable costs from the sale of two ounces of gold weekly because variable costs are \$215 per unit for labor, materials, and so forth. Consequently, total losses are \$570 whether or not two ounces of gold are produced and then sold for \$215; nothing is contributed to fixed costs from the production and sale of these units.

What happens if gold falls below \$215 per ounce — to, say, \$200? If the mine produced two ounces of gold, in addition to \$570 in fixed costs, you will lose at least \$15 more per ounce, yielding total losses of \$600 [\$570 + (\$15 × 2)]. Operating at all would not minimize your losses. If the price falls below \$215, temporarily abandon the mine. Thus, a \$215 price corresponds to the mine's *shutdown point*. It is the lowest price that will induce you to operate, and you will try never to mine less than two ounces of gold.

> **Shutdown point:** *Profit-maximizing (and loss-minimizing) firms shut down when the market price falls below the minimum point of the average variable cost curve.*

Take a moment to compare Figures 5, 6, and 7. Note that, regardless of market structure, profit can be realized if the demand curve facing a firm intersects its *ATC* curve. Unfortunately, short-run losses are inevitable if the firm's *ATC* curve lies above the demand curve at all output levels. In a moment, you will see that if the demand curve is exactly tangent to the *ATC* curve, the best the firm can do is break even.

In summary, the first question every profit-maximizing firm confronts, regardless of market structure, is whether to operate in a market. If the demand curve it faces has any segment that is above its average variable cost curve (which, among other costs, must reflect the values foregone from alternative types of production), then it will operate in that market. If operation in a market is profit-maximizing (or loss minimizing) then a second question addresses how much to produce; the answer is that profit is maximized when marginal cost equals marginal revenue.

Short-Run Supply Curves of Purely Competitive Firms

You may have deduced that a competitive firm's marginal cost curve is also its short-run supply curve as long as price exceeds the minimum point of the average variable cost curve. These points on a marginal cost curve reflect the profit-maximizing outputs corresponding to various market prices for the good. If price falls below minimum average variable costs (*AVC*), marginal costs and marginal revenue become irrelevant; the firm's best move is to close its plant and suffer losses equal to fixed costs. However, whenever the price exceeds the shutdown point (the minimum *AVC*), the firm minimizes losses or maximizes profit by supplying the amount of output where $P = MR = MC$. This is a firm's short-run supply response.

> A pure competitor's **short-run supply curve:** *The segment of the marginal cost curve that lies above the minimum point of the firm's average variable cost curve.*

This is shown in Figure 8. When price and marginal revenue equal P_0, the firm supplies only q_0. As the price rises, the firm increases the amount it supplies to maximize profit or minimize loss by equating that price with marginal costs, so if price increases to P_1 or P_2, the firm will supply q_1 or q_2, respectively. Now let us see how individual firm's supply curves are combined to form an industry supply curve.

The Short-Run Industry Supply Curve

A purely competitive industry contains numerous firms, so there is a predictably tight relationship between the industry supply curve and firm supply curves. Consider, for simplicity, an industry comprised of two firms with individual supply curves as shown in Panel A of Figure 9. When the market price is \$1, the first firm is willing to supply 10 units and the second firm is willing to supply 30 units. Together, they supply 40 units at the \$1 price, as plotted in Panel B. Recall from Chapter 3 that this process is called *horizontal summation*.

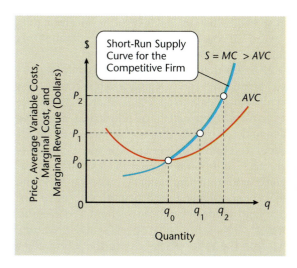

FIGURE 8   The Firm's Short-Run Supply Curve

A competitive firm's short-run supply curve is its marginal cost curve, as long as the point where the price equals marginal cost occurs above the minimum of the average variable cost curve ($P = MC > AVC$). If price cannot cover average variable cost, then the firm will shut down ($q = 0$).

*The **short-run industry supply curve:** The horizontal sum of the supply curves of all firms in a purely competitive industry.*

We simply add the quantities produced by each firm at each possible price to arrive at the industry short-run supply curve. You can verify this graphically by adding together the quantities

that each firm will turn out at various prices, and you will see that these total quantities supplied conform to those plotted in Panel B.

We have now related individual and market supplies. The output decisions of individual firms sum to determine the market supply schedule. This market supply, in concert with consumers' demands for a good, determines the

FIGURE 9   The Industry Supply Curve

The industry supply curve (Panel B) is the horizontal summation of the supply curves of individual firms (Panel A).

market clearing price. An industry is in equilibrium when firms supply all they are willing to at the going price and consumers can buy all they desire at that price. All firms maximize profit by producing where $MR = MC$. Firms minimize losses by shutting down if price falls below AVC.

Are markets stuck in a short-run equilibrium? What role does profit play in the longer run? What happens if new firms enter an industry? If technological breakthroughs substantially reduce production costs? These and other issues are examined in the next section as we step from short-run to long-run adjustments in purely competitive industries.

Long-Run Adjustments in Competitive Industries

The number of firms in any industry is fixed in the short run, but in the long run, the most important characteristic of competition is freedom of entry and exit. The number of firms in an industry may rise with entry, or fall as existing firms fail or move into different product lines. Economic profit attracts new firms to an industry, while economic losses signal owners to liquidate existing firms or to look for new product lines. Entry into prospering industries and exit from those that are faltering are basic to the smooth operation of a market economy and to accommodating consumers' priorities.

Economic Profits as Market Signals

Economic profits are a surplus after all implicit and explicit costs of production are subtracted from total revenue. Thus, average total costs include allowances for the opportunity costs of the entrepreneurial talents and capital a firm uses, among other things. Normal economic returns to these resources must be earned. Economic losses cause a firm's owners to move their resources into other activities. On the other hand, if revenues exceed all costs, a firm may try to expand in an attempt to capture as much economic profit

as possible. In a sense, however, profit ultimately "self-destructs" by attracting new competitors into the industry.

Suppose that markets for statues and for potted plants are both in equilibrium and that both are homogeneous products. Economic profits are zero for all firms in both industries. Then the demand for indoor plants plummets as interior decorators unite to convince people that plants are passé and that no corner in any room is complete without an imitation Greek statue. Statue makers are deluged with new orders, while florists and garden shops throughout the country watch their sales wilt. Specials and discounts become the order of the day in the house plant industry, and short-run economic losses occur as prices, outputs, and total revenues decline. On the other hand, the prices and outputs of statuary soar and economic profits are widespread in the short run.

In the long run, resources migrate from the houseplant industry. New investment declines, and florists train for other work as flower shops fold. Investment gravitates into statuary making as new firms flock to the industry in search of profits, and more workers become statue makers. Thus, over the long run, competition eliminates both economic losses in the plant industry and economic profits in statuary; plant prices recover from their depressed state, and statue prices fall from their short-run peaks. At the final equilibrium along the long-run supply curves for each industry, firms realize only normal (zero) economic profits, but all opportunity costs are covered by revenues.

Let us discuss market adjustments in more detail. The long run allows all resources (including capital) to enter or leave an industry. New firms move into growing industries, while existing firms wither or die in declining industries. Thus, we expect resources to flow from less profitable towards more profitable industries. Entry and exit from highly competitive industries can be accomplished with ease. Many "hit-and-run" competitors jump into profitable markets and leave as soon as other markets appear more profitable. This hit-and-run pattern is socially beneficial, because it ensures that even erratic consumer demands are accommodated quickly.

The Process of Competition

Social gains from competition depend heavily on freedom to enter or exit markets as firms seek profit or try to avoid loss. If typical firms make *zero economic profits*, then (all else equal) there will be no long-run changes in the number of firms in the industry, the amount of output supplied, or the price of the good. Recall that normal returns to capital owners and entrepreneurial talent are economic costs. Zero economic profits mean that all costs are covered; that is, the firm's resources cannot be used more advantageously elsewhere.

> **Zero economic profit:** *A long-run equilibrium condition for firms in a competitive industry. The output, price, and number of firms in the industry will all be stable.*

To summarize, in a long-run equilibrium, no firm will want to:

1. change its output, because price equals marginal cost ($P = MC$).
2. change its plant size, because short-run average total cost equals long-run average total cost ($SRATC = LRATC$).
3. enter or leave the industry, because price equals long run average total cost ($P = LRATC$).

But if most firms in an industry experience economic profits, competitive pressures tend to eliminate these profits over time, because prices will fall or costs will increase. Conversely, economic losses tend to cause prices to climb or costs to decline or both.

Price Changes Eliminate Economic Profits or Losses

If firms in an industry earn positive economic profits, existing firms try to capture greater profits by expanding capacity and output. Entrepreneurs outside the industry also have incentives to enter these markets in the long run. Both types of adjustments increase an industry's output, reducing prices because consumers will increase their purchases only if prices decline.

On the other hand, if most firms in an industry experience economic losses, then some will cut their production and, in the long run, the firms with the highest opportunity costs (best alternative uses of their resources) will leave the industry. Thus, the long-run effects of economic losses are that the industry's supply will decline and prices will rise.

How Profits or Losses Affect Costs

Competition will grow for the resources used by a profitable industry. If supplies are perfectly elastic for all resources used by an industry, production can expand without driving up average production costs. Resource costs will rise as production in an industry rises, however, to the extent that some resources are especially suited for certain industries and not others. For example, what do you think happens to the costs of acquiring oil drilling rights as the price of oil balloons? What happens to the prices of agricultural land when food prices soar? Costs rise to reduce profits in both cases.

Another example of how rising costs eliminate profits: If your firm enjoyed extremely high profits because it hired an exceptionally efficient management team, might some competitor try to hire members of this team? What would happen to their salaries?

The market forces that cause costs to rise in an industry in which most firms make economic profits also cause costs to fall in instances where most firms incur losses. Both average costs and marginal costs rise in profitable industries and shrink when economic losses are the norm. To simplify the analysis in the following discussion, we focus only on price (not cost) adjustments. Remember, however, that changes in either prices or costs will eliminate economic profits or losses in competitive markets in the long run. Moreover, we assume in the following discussion that prices adjust smoothly toward long-run equilibrium. You should recognize that some firms may overreact in unison to economic profits or losses, so that prices may swing somewhat before ultimately converging on their equilibrium values.

Long-Run Equilibrium in a Competitive Industry

Firms operate close to capacity in highly profitable industries, but if business conditions go sour, they slash production. Consider the industry shown in Figure 10. This industry is in the short-run equilibrium described in Panel A before the entry of new firms. Industry demand and supply are D_0 and S_0, respectively, and industry output equals Q_0; each firm produces an output of q_0, where $P = MR = MC$. Typical firms in this industry make short-run economic profits equal to the darkened area, causing firms to willingly incur higher than minimal per unit costs as they produce extra output to exploit profit opportunities.

Pure competition allows easy entry, so this is a short-run situation, because external entrepreneurs will seek shares of these profits. New firms will swell industry supply to S_1, with a higher output Q_1 and a lower equilibrium price, P_1. But observe what happens to each individual firm. As prices decline, each firm adjusts to a new profit-maximization output (q_1), which is less than the original level (q_0). Our industry consequently now contains more firms, but the absence of profit leaves each producing less than before.

What happened to profit? Each firm previously in the industry was earning positive profits. Entry reduces prices and the amounts that each firm produces. Economic profits shrink to "normal" levels (zero economic profits) because the price falls to the minimum of long-run average total costs (LRATC). Remember that the resources a firm's owners provide have opportunity costs that are included in average total costs. Accounting profits are not zero in the industry; they are simply at normal levels—just high enough so that the owners earn as much in this industry as in their next best option.

You may wonder whether symmetric exit adjustments occur in unprofitable situations. Such adjustments are illustrated in Panel B of Figure 10, which shows individual firms initially encountering short-run losses. Price is originally at P_0, which is below average total cost (ATC_0) but above average variable costs (not shown in the figure) because firms are continuing to operate. Losses are equal to the darkened area. The least efficient firms incur the largest losses and will fold or move into a different activity. Industry supply will shrink as these firms leave the industry, so the price will rise and losses will be eliminated. Profits might temporarily reappear if enough firms leave, curtailing the exodus of firms. Ultimately, however, price rises to P_1 and profits return to "normal" levels. Notice that this is just the opposite of the adjustment process described in the profitable situation just considered. Industry output falls, but individual firm's output grows as the price recovers to normal levels when some firms exit the industry.

At the ends of periods with economic losses or profits, why does profit settle at "normal" levels (zero economic profits)? A moment's reflection should provide the answer. Competitive theory presumes that entry and exit are virtually costless, so the logical stopping point occurs when each firm in the industry earns only normal profits. All opportunity costs are covered, so the owners of existing firms know of no opportunities for their resources that are more profitable. Nor do entrepreneurs outside the industry perceive profit opportunities in the industry. Only then will there be no net incentives for firms to enter or leave the industry.

Another important result of long-run competitive adjustments is that all firms in the industry are forced to adopt the most efficient technology available. This is shown in Figure 11. Long-run pressures will force the price of the product to P_{LR} because competition forces each firm to the lowest point on the LRATC curve. Any firm not adopting the technology and amounts of capital that yield the lowest minimum short-run average total cost (SRATC) curve will earn less than normal profits and will founder in the long run. No firm stays in any industry if it suffers sustained economic losses. Since $P = MC = ATC$ in the long run, the ultimate equilibrium point is the lowest point on the LRATC curve, which is also the lowest point on the relevant SRATC curve.

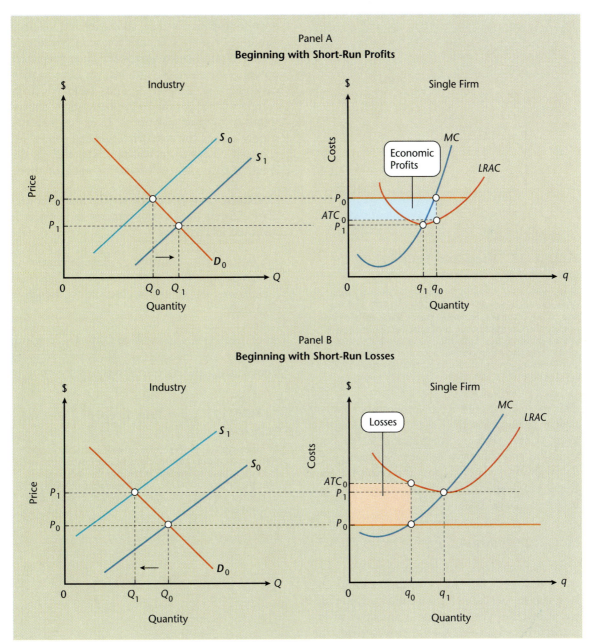

Panel A
Beginning with Short-Run Profits

Panel B
Beginning with Short-Run Losses

FIGURE 10   Entry and Exit and Long-Run Price, Output, and Profit

Firms in industries where economic profits are realized will produce where $P = MC$ and output is greater than that associated with minimum average cost. However, the entry of new competitors will cause industry supply to grow and price to fall. As this occurs, existing firms reduce output until $P = MC = LRAC$. LRAC is at its minimum, and there are no economic profits when competitive firms are in long-run equilibrium.

If most firms in an industry suffer economic losses, they will restrict production below the minimum point of their LRAC curves. As some firms leave the industry, the market supply falls and price increases. As the price rises, existing firms will expand their production to the level of output where long-run average cost is minimized. At this point, $P = MC = LRAC$, and neither economic profits nor economic losses are experienced.

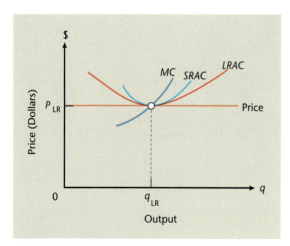

FIGURE 11 Long-Run Equilibrium for the Competitive Firm

In the long run, a firm in a competitive industry will produce where $P = MR = MC = SRAC = LRAC$, and the size of the plant will minimize the average costs of production. Neither economic profits nor economic losses will be realized; the firm's total revenues will just cover all its costs, including normal accounting profits to compensate owners for the resources they provide.

This means that outputs in competitive markets will be produced at the lowest possible long-run average cost. Hence, competition yields both technical and allocative economic efficiency. As you will see in a later section, this result has profound implications for maintaining competition in a free market economy.

Long-Run Industry Supply Curves

Now that you have some ideas about competitive adjustment processes, we can examine the long-run supply curve for the competitive industry as a whole. The horizontal summation of existing firms' short-run supply curves yields the short-run industry supply curve. The **long-run industry supply curve** reflects the effects on output as entry and exit occur in response to changes in demand. The industry is in long-run equilibrium only after all desired entries and exits have occurred so that active firms realize only normal profits.

Changing demands, technologies, and products cause erratic swings in many industries. The economy continually gropes toward equilibrium, but full equilibrium may never be attained in

most industries. Even so, short-run and long-run equilibria remain valuable concepts because of their analytical convenience and their predictive power. Without these notions, we have analytical mush—no reference points from which to compare other periods or to predict the eventual trends of outputs and prices. Long-run industry supply curves can take three general forms: (*a*) constant costs, (*b*) increasing costs, and (*c*) decreasing costs. We will examine each of these.

Constant Cost Industries The long-run supply (*LRS*) curve of a constant cost industry is illustrated in Figure 12.

> **Constant cost industry:** *Average production costs are unaffected if the market demand shifts and the number of firms in the industry changes.*

As demand grows from D_0 to D_1 to D_2, long-run responses are increases in short-run supplies from S_0 to S_1 and S_2, respectively, as the number

FIGURE 12 Long-Run Supply (Constant Cost Industry)

An industry's long-run supply curve is perfectly elastic (horizontal) if the resource costs of individual firms are unaffected by the number of firms in the industry. Industries that use only small percentages of highly specialized resources in an economy will operate under constant costs.

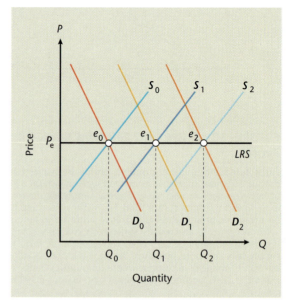

of firms in the industry grows proportionally with demand. As entry occurs, long-run average costs are the same for new entrants as they are for established firms. All cost curves for individual firms are identical: The number of firms in the industry adjusts proportionally as demand changes. Thus, the long-run supply curve for a constant cost industry is perfectly elastic. An industry can expand with constant equilibrium price and costs only if technology and the costs of the resources it uses are not affected.[4]

Increasing Cost Industries Industries deviate from the constant cost model for several reasons. The requirement that input prices not rise as an industry's output rises is especially difficult for industries that rely on limited supplies of specialized resources; larger amounts of these resources can be made available only at ever higher costs. This characterizes increasing cost industries.

> **Increasing cost industry:** *Cases where average production costs rise as market demand and the number of firms in the industry grow.*

In an increasing cost industry, growth of market demand pulls up resource costs, and the average total cost and marginal cost curves for each firm in the industry rise. Thus, demand growth shifts up the long-run break-even points for each firm as minimal long-run average costs rise, as shown in Figure 13.

If industry demand grows from D_0 to D_1, the industry expands as new firms enter. Competition for resources drives the short-run supply curve to S_1 and the equilibrium price to P_1. Rising equilibrium costs and prices yield a positively sloped long-run supply (*LRS*) curve. Higher prices to cover the higher resource costs allow provision of greater quantities to the market. Moreover, these higher costs will cause fewer firms to enter the industry than would enter constant cost industries experiencing similar growth of demand.

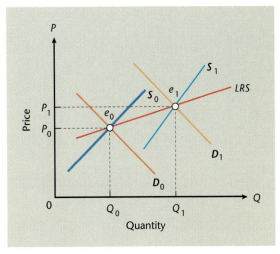

FIGURE 13 Long-Run Supply for an Increasing Cost Industry

The long-run supply curve of an increasing cost industry will be positively sloped because the prices of the specialized resources it uses will rise as industry output expands. This effect will be stronger the larger the industry is relative to national output and the more specialized resources are. This effect is common and yields production possibilities frontiers that are "bowed out" from below, as described in Chapter 2.

Regardless of the extent of competition, most industries are characterized by increasing costs in the long run. For example, our domestic oil industry faces increasing costs in attempts to boost petroleum production. Most readily accessible crude oil has been depleted. Higher oil prices induce landowners to charge more for drilling rights. Future oil supplies will be drawn from deeper wells or high-cost locations (offshore drilling or Alaska). Alternatively, Americans may try other energy sources, most of which are much more costly than oil.

Decreasing Cost Industries One industry's growth may stimulate efficiencies in complementary industries. For example, mass production in the auto industry early in this century stimulated a flock of support industries — tires, batteries, gasoline and oil, and so on. As these support industries grew and implemented new technology, their average cost curves shifted downwards, supplying intermediate products to the auto industry at lower prices. Car prices dropped.

4. Were all industries subject to constant cost, the production possibilities frontier would be a straight line. You might review the material in Chapter 2 if you are unsure why this is true.

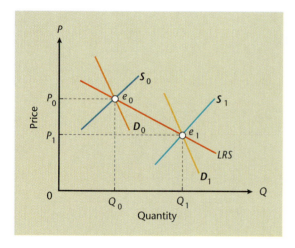

FIGURE 14 Long-Run Supply for a Decreasing Cost Industry

Decreasing cost industries generate negatively sloped long-run supply curves, and are extremely uncommon, because such decreasing costs rely on substantial economies of scale or on positive externalities within the industry or in support industries that supply with intermediate goods. In fact, many economists argue that this is only a theoretical possibility, never encountered in the actual world of production. The concepts of constant, increasing, or decreasing costs apply only for the long run. Decreasing cost industries do not seem so implausible, however, if we consider the possibility of technological advances.

Decreasing cost industry: *Cases where average production costs fall as market demand and the number of firms in the industry grow.*

Thus, in a decreasing cost industry, growing demand yields lower equilibrium prices as an industry's output expands, as shown in Figure 14.

In rare circumstances, a few industries might experience decreasing costs, but most industries eventually encounter increasing costs, so growing demand yields higher prices in the long run. The possibility that technological advances may be spurred by the search for profits, however, means that some industries may experience decreasing costs in the "super" long run. This seems to be true of many high-tech products today.

Evaluating Competitive Markets

Some important points in this chapter are useful in evaluating competition:

1. Pure competition is characterized by freedom of entry and exit by firms that are *price takers* and *quantity adjusters*.

2. A purely competitive firm maximizes profit or minimizes loss by producing the level of output that equates price and marginal cost ($P = MR = MC$).

3. In the long run, pure competitors use the most efficient technology available, and $LRMC = P$.[5] This will also be the minimum point on the $LRATC$ curve, because the long-run dynamics of entry and exit drive economic profits to zero regardless of whether the industry is characterized by constant, increasing, or decreasing costs.

In the long run

$$P = MR = SRMC = SRATC = LRMC = LRATC$$

and profits will be at "normal" levels — zero.

Economic Efficiency

In a purely competitive market, firms employ resources until the marginal cost of the last unit of a good equals its price. In the absence of external costs (e.g., pollution) or external benefits (e.g., education, inoculations), the opportunity cost to society of these resources equals the marginal cost of the resources to producers. If there are no externalities (discussed in depth in a later chapter), these resource costs equal their **marginal social costs (MSC)** — the value to society of the resources used to produce one more unit of a good. Competition through freedom of entry and exit ensures that this is at the lowest possible

---

5. Technical differences between short-run and long-run marginal costs are not considered here. Courses in intermediate microeconomics deal with these differences.

average cost and that there is no waste in production. A purely competitive economy is an efficient economy, both allocatively and technically. One aspect of economic efficiency is that all goods must be produced at their lowest possible opportunity cost (technical efficiency). Competition meets this requirement by ensuring production at minimal *LRATC*. Allocative efficiency requires the mix of goods produced to match consumer preferences. Here again, competition meets the criterion because consumers get the products they want at the least opportunity cost.

Social Welfare

Positive economic analysis cannot directly address the fairest way to divide the pie. If we assume, however, that the proper distribution of income is a normative problem best settled in the political arena and that the resulting political outcome is viewed as acceptable, then the competitive market system is not only efficient; it also maximizes social welfare. Here is why.

Your demand curve for any good is based on the marginal benefits (utility) that you would receive from consuming various possible amounts of the good, as we discussed in our "Consumer Choice" chapter. Our assumptions imply that the marginal utility you receive from consuming is also the marginal benefit society receives. That is, your gain is also society's gain

because you are a member of society. When we sum all consumer demands, we derive the market demand curve for an industry's product, which is also the *marginal social benefit (MSB)* to all of society from having a bit more of the good.

With consumer benefits and producer costs in mind, we can refer to the industry supply and demand curves, respectively, as the marginal social cost (*MSC*) and marginal social benefit (*MSB*) curves. When a purely competitive industry is in long-run equilibrium, *marginal social cost equals marginal social benefit (MSC = MSB)*: The industry is producing where the marginal social benefit from the last unit produced is just equal to the marginal social cost of the resources needed to produce that unit of product. This concept is illustrated in Figure 15.

The $MSB = MSC$ condition is optimal from society's point of view. Since the opportunity costs of resources represent alternatives for all of society, we want our resources to be used as efficiently as possible. If production were inefficient, then it would be possible for some people to gain without imposing losses on others.

Consider output level Q_0 in Figure 15. The social benefit from a bit more output than Q_0 is P_0, which greatly exceeds the cost (P_1) of the resources required to produce a little more of the good, so society as a whole could gain if more resources were used to produce more of this good. And in a competitive industry, they will

FIGURE 15 Economic Efficiency and Competition

If there are no externalities in production or consumption, then purely competitive markets generate efficient solutions. If, in addition, the distribution of income is deemed equitable, the competitive market equilibrium maximizes social welfare.

be. If Q_0 were initially produced and sold at price P_0, existing firms in a competitive industry would enjoy economic profit. This would cause the industry to grow until equilibrium output Q_e is reached at a price and (average and marginal) production cost of P_e. The adjustment process is just reversed if industry output exceeds Q_e. Competitive markets tend to squeeze the last bit of gain possible from the resources available.

Decentralized Decisions and Freedom

The ideas of Adam Smith and other early advocates of capitalism were forged during a period of revolt against the dictates of monarchs of their era. Isaac Newton had observed movements of the planets and stars and concluded that natural forces generate a stable and orderly universe. Smith perceived that the invisible hand of the marketplace had similarly beneficial effects and that the iron fist of government was exercised far too often.

Leon Walras elaborated with mathematical precision Smith's ideas about how people's wants are accommodated in a competitive market system, and Vilfredo Pareto developed a concept of economic welfare that still dominates economic analysis. Pareto also proved that a purely competitive equilibrium is efficient, and that other equilibria fail to maximize social welfare.

Most advocates of the market system point to the economic efficiency of competition as its major virtue, but prize even more the absence of any need for a central economic authority. In a truly competitive market system, each household and firm make decisions that, in large measure, affect only themselves. This diffusion of market power means that individuals cannot be controlled by other individuals. According to proponents of relying on the marketplace rather than government, this diffusion of coercive power allows the maximum possible personal freedom for everyone.

Efficiency and the absence of centralized coercion are major reasons why a purely competitive market is the ideal against which we measure industrial performance. From society's point of view, it might seem desirable that all industries be competitive so that Adam Smith's invisible hand would yield the results we have described. Competition and access to markets may, however, be very limited if technology dictates that large firms, relative to market demand, will be most efficient.

Some economists who believe strongly in competition as an effective and desirable allocative mechanism are convinced that the model of pure competition grossly *under*states the virtues of the market system. Their views are sketched in Focus 1.

Some Shortcomings of Market Economies

Many industries are far from competitive — in some, competition may be impractical. For example, competition among electric utilities would probably create inefficiencies because of the type of technology used. (People don't want multiple electric lines down their streets.) In other cases, lack of competition is a consequence of illegal collusion or government policies to protect other goals (patents, medical licensing to protect the public health, and so on).

Even if the economy were quite competitive, there might still be problems of fraud, inequity in the distributions of income and wealth, or externalities that the market would not resolve in ways society deems appropriate. Moreover, certain goods will not be provided optimally by a private market system. Atomic bombs, police services, and legal decisions are examples of items no society would want sold to the highest bidder.

Some economists also argue that research and development require bigness; such efforts might be less than optimal if left to small, competitive firms. Finally, there are questions about what social restrictions, if any, should be imposed on trade between people in different countries. The tools you have learned to use in the last few chapters will help clarify the remainder of this book as we examine the outcome of private market behavior and assess corrective government policies for these problems.

Leon Walras (1834–1910) and Vilfredo Pareto (1848–1923)

Leon Walras has been described as an architect rather than a builder of economics, meaning that he designed a general system of analytical principles rather than laying in the bricks and mortar of economic theory. Walras tackled the complex problem of the interdependence of all sectors of the economy and represented this complexity in a system of simultaneous equations.

This great architect of economics was descended from a Dutch journeyman tailor who migrated to the south of France in 1749. His father was a classmate of Cournot (discussed in the next chapter) in Paris and, like Cournot, was a school administrator. The young Walras learned from Cournot the meaning of functional relations between variables. However, concerns about the limits of Cournot's demand curve for a single good led Walras to seek a wider framework within which to express the demand for a good as a function not only of its own price, but of a host of prices of related goods. This was the point of departure for his *general equilibrium model* of an economy.

Most economic writers before Walras followed the lead of Alfred Marshall and employed a convention in dealing with particular markets called *partial equilibrium analysis*. This still common and useful convention calls for ignoring some determinants of demand and supply in order to concentrate on the more direct causes of equilibrium price and quantity. Walras departed from this practice by insisting on recognizing the interdependencies that exist between markets because the process of price determination necessarily occurs in all markets simultaneously. To isolate one market for study without regard to the others was no more appropriate, in Walras's view, than studying the position of the earth in the solar system without regard to other planets. His *architectonics* consequently was an elaborate but highly abstract system of mathematical equations that painstakingly detailed the economic conditions for simultaneous equilibrium in every economic market. Walras's general equilibrium approach to economics did not win favor with the reigning academic hierarchy in France, forcing him to take a teaching position in Switzerland at the University of Lausanne, where he labored until he was replaced in 1893 by Vilfredo Pareto.

Pareto, born of a Genovese father and French mother, was trained as an engineer. At 45, he accepted the chair at Lausanne. Pareto's system of thought and his vision of social processes differed from Walras's, but Pareto cast his pure theory of economics in much the same mold, extending and refining Walras's general equilibrium system. Moreover, Pareto did what Walras had not been able to do: He founded a full-blown school of thought. His disciples cooperated in theoretical research, cultivated personal contacts, and defended one another in controversy. The school, reflecting Pareto's own heritage, was primarily Italian.

Two of Pareto's contributions to economics are especially noteworthy. First, he identified a situation of maximum efficiency for a society as one in which it is impossible to increase the happiness of one individual without decreasing that of someone else. Today, all the conditions specifying economic efficiency are referred to as "Pareto optimal." Second, Pareto proved that a state of maximum efficiency and social welfare is identical with equilibrium under pure competition. This led him to conclude that the problems in reaching a position of maximum efficiency, as well as their solutions, were the same for a collectivist economy as for an economy founded on private property.

Pareto's work spilled over into the field of sociology. His chief objective was to develop general equilibrium models covering the whole spectrum of social phenomena. Both he and Walras were aware that their equations could not be solved due to the lack of data and the large number of variables involved. Nevertheless, their's was a great achievement from the standpoint of logical clarity, and the impact of their thoughts on modern economic theory ranks them both among the dozen most influential economists of all time.

Dynamic Entrepreneurs vs. Pure Competition

The model of pure competition is largely rejected by the *Austrian* school of thought. ("Austrian" refers to the national origin of this school's founders, but its ideas now have advocates around the globe.) Here is an Austrian perspective on competition:

How firms using the same technology adjust output of a homogeneous good is described accurately by models of pure competition, but this is a trivial aspect of real competition. Traditional analyses fail to address a major source of disequilibrium—the entrepreneur. What matters is how competition affects human progress. Why are the foods we eat more varied than those available in an earlier era? Why don't hand-cranked autos still clog our highways? The answer to these and thousands of similar questions, according to Austrians, is that entrepreneurial innovations are the competitive mechanisms that drive the growth and decline of industries and civilizations.

Entrepreneurs innovate new technologies that create better and cheaper products and force older firms to adapt or perish. The key to entrepreneurial success is finding creative ways to serve human wants by implementing new technologies or marketing new goods better, faster, and at less cost. This can mean producing existing goods at lower costs or enhancing their quality, or it may mean creating markets for entirely new goods.

The U.S. Post Office, for example, was an uncontested government monopoly until United Parcel Service was launched by entrepreneurs who thought that people would pay handsomely to have packages delivered faster and more conveniently. UPS prospered when shippers found it faster and more cost efficient to have packages delivered by this private firm. Then the founder of Federal Express put competitive heat on both UPS and the Post Office after he successfully tested the market demand for overnight delivery.

This dynamic form of competition creates new industries and destabilizes old ones. Thus, competition as a source of disequilibrium is more important in the Austrian view than the equilibrating entry and exit of firms conventional theory stresses. Austrians share conventional notions about pressures for competitors to adopt cost-saving technology or to mimic successful product lines. Extending our previous example, the overnight delivery market created by Federal Express has been invaded by UPS, the Postal Service, Flying Tiger, Emery, ... Conventional theory stresses the effects of this second wave of competition; the Aus-trian school emphasizes the initial entry by Federal Express.

Austrian economists offer countless examples of competition as a robust process, not as a stagnant set of equilibrium conditions specified by models of perfect competition: Gutenberg destroyed handwritten book publishing with his movable type; Thomas Edison's electric light changed our way of life; Henry Ford's assembly line made cars available for the masses. More recently, two kids working out of a garage launched Apple Computer and marketed the first personal computers. The original designers of computerized spreadsheets have changed the way accountants work. Members of the Austrian school stress the dynamic competition among entrepreneurs rather than the imitative behavior of firms now scrutinized in the model of pure competition.

Austrians also charge that "pure competition" assumes large numbers of similar firms to be vital for vigorous competition. The stress on numerous competitors is blamed for bizarre antitrust laws and business regulations that strangle much truly competitive behavior among entrepreneurs. The number of competitors is far less important, in this view, than the qualities of goods and the rate of technological advance in an industry.

Chapter Review: Key Points

1. Freedom of *entry and exit* is the hallmark of competition. A *purely competitive* market is comprised of numerous potential buyers and sellers of a homogeneous product, none of whom controls its price. All buyers and sellers are sufficiently small relative to the market that none is a *price maker*.

2. A competitive buyer faces a perfectly elastic supply curve, while competitive sellers face perfectly elastic demand curves. In competition, all are *price takers* or *quantity adjusters*.

3. We assume that no firm can adjust output in the *market period*, so total supply is perfectly inelastic. In the *short run* (SR), existing firms in an industry can vary output, but at least one productive factor is fixed, and entry and exit cannot occur. Total supply is at least somewhat elastic. Supply is much more elastic in the *long run* (LR), because all factors of production are variable and firms may enter or leave the industry.

4. A competitive firm maximizes profits by producing output up to the point where *total revenues minus total costs* (TR − TC) is maximized, which also occurs when *marginal revenue equals marginal cost* (MR = MC). Price must be greater than the minimum of the average variable cost curve, however, which is the *shutdown point*. Because competitive firms face perfectly elastic demands, price and marginal revenue are identical. *Break-even points* are the quantities at which total revenue and total cost are equal.

5. A *competitive firm's short-run supply curve* is its marginal cost curve above the minimum of its average variable costs. Horizontally summing the marginal costs from existing firms yields the *short-run industry supply curve*.

6. Competition erases *economic profits* through entry of new firms in the long run, and economic losses are eradicated by exit from the industry. Thus, competitive firms receive exactly enough revenue over the long run to pay the opportunity costs of resources used and realize only *zero economic profit*.

7. Short-run economic profits are ultimately eliminated, because output will be ex- panded by new firms in a competitive industry, or increased competition for profitable inputs will drive up resource costs. The long-run adjustments that eliminate short-run losses follow precisely reversed patterns.

8. In the long run, firms are forced by competitive pressures to adopt the most efficient (least costly) plant size and technologies. They operate at output levels where

$$P = MR = SRATC = SRMC = LRATC = LRMC$$

9. *For constant cost industries*, the minimum *LRATC* for firms is the same no matter how many firms are in the industry. Costs increase for each firm as firms enter increasing cost industries and decrease for decreasing cost industries. Thus, the *long-run industry supply curve* is positively sloped for *increasing cost industries*, horizontal for *constant cost industries*, and negatively sloped for *decreasing cost industries*.

10. A purely competitive market is efficient in the sense that goods desired by consumers (society) are produced at the lowest possible opportunity cost. Every feasible bit of net gain is squeezed from the resources available; *marginal social benefits* and *marginal social costs* are equated by competitive forces of supply and demand (MSB = MSC), assuming the absence of externalities. This will be socially optimal and maximize social welfare if the distribution of income is deemed appropriate. A market system does not require that decision-making power be vested in a central authority. This permits substantial personal freedom and the absence of coercion.

Key Concepts

Ensure that you can define these terms before proceeding.

price takers
entry and exit
profit maximization
total revenue minus
  total cost (TR − TC)

marginal revenue
  equals marginal cost
  (MR = MC)
shutdown point

firm and industry
short-run supply
curves

zero economic profits

increasing cost and
decreasing cost
industries

marginal social
benefit equals
marginal social
cost (*MSB = MSC*)

Problems and Questions

1. What three basic assumptions underlie pure competition? Why are these assumptions necessary and how do they ensure pure competition?

2. What are the three time periods into which supply responses fall? How does the elasticity of supply change with each period? Why?

3. What price must a firm receive to earn positive economic profits? To earn zero economic profits? To incur economic losses yet still operate? To shut down its operation?

4. Given all the pertinent cost information on a firm, how can you determine the firm's short-run supply curve? Why is this the firm's short-run supply curve?

5. How would you derive an industry supply curve if you only had cost information on the individual firms within the industry?

6. In pure competition, why does $P = MR = AR = D$?

7. Suppose your firm has a contract requiring delivery of 1,000 video cameras for $1,000 each, and your average total cost is $800. Why would it be an error to fill a special rush order for one more at a price of $1,500 if producing the extra camera would boost your average total cost to $801? How much would your profit fall if you filled this special order?

8. Cost and output data for a purely competitive firm are provided in the table below. Assume that fixed costs equal $40 and that the market price facing the firm is $30 per unit.

Quantity	1	2	3	4	5	6	7	8
TVC		30	55	75	90	110	135	165	200

What is the profit-maximizing rate of output? What does maximum profit equal? At what price will the firm close its doors?

9. Are there any differences between the pure competition described in this chapter and the *cutthroat* competition despised by many business executives?

10. The stock market is viewed by some critics of capitalism as the epitome of monopoly or market power. Are most people who buy or sell stock price makers or price takers? Do you think stock and commodity markets basically meet the requirements for purely competitive markets? Why or why not?

11. Some women now use tattoos to give the effect of permanent cosmetic eye shadow. The current industry demand (D_0) and supply (S_0) and representative individual firm demand and cost curves for "eye tattoos" are illustrated in Figure 16, which also shows another potential market supply curve (S_1). How many firms comprise the industry in the short run? How many firms will be in the industry in the long run? What will ultimately happen to the price of eye tattoos?

12. Is a big city economy more competitive than one in a small town? How? Do you think your grocer has monopoly or market power? How much? Can you cite recent market entry and exit among firms located within 5 miles of your home? What industries have been involved? Do you know of any giant firms that have emerged, almost from oblivion, in the past 5 years? Any that have failed? Is our economy basically competitive or noncompetitive?

13–15. Figure 17 illustrates the costs facing a firm in the robotic dog (K-9) industry.

13. If the market price for robotic dogs is $30, what is this firm's total revenue? Total costs? What is economic profit/loss equal to? If this firm is typical of others in the industry, what would you expect to happen in the long run?

14. If the market price for robotic dogs drops to $18, what is this firm's total revenue? Total costs? How much is economic profit or loss? If this firm is typical of others in the industry what would you expect to happen in the long run?

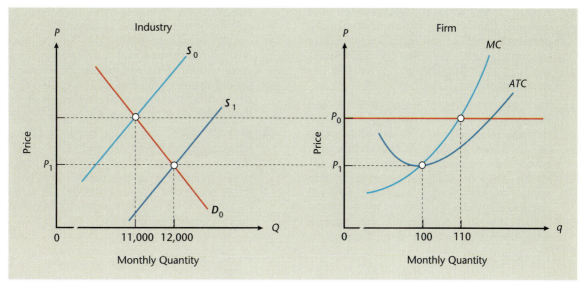

FIGURE 16 The Market for Eye Tatoos

15. What are total fixed costs (TFC) for this firm? If the market price is $25, what quantity will the firm produce to maximize their profits? Is the firm covering its implicit costs if the market price is $25? What will happen in the long run to this typical firm?

16. Would you expect someone who selected stocks by throwing darts at stock market reports in the *Wall Street Journal* to experience systematically different economic profits than an expert financial analyst who spent hours every day studying the stock market? If not, what might explain systematically different rates of return reported by their bookkeepers?

FIGURE 17 The Market for Robotic (K-9) Dogs

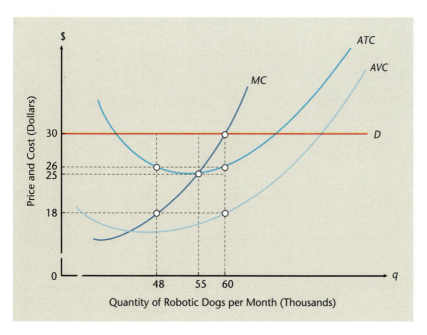

17. A *Wall Street Journal* editorialist noted, "As everyone knows, competition is vital to the preservation of a healthy, efficient market economy. But competition sometimes seems to have few friends." What did this writer mean?

18. State governments in Maine, Hawaii, and Wisconsin have passed laws regulating plant closings. Most require a 90-day prenotification, and some specify exit fees and the severance pay required for each worker displaced. Proponents of these laws argue that limits on plant closings minimize regional disruption. Notification allows workers time to find alternative employment and communities time to attract new firms. Opponents charge that such limits make it more difficult for firms to respond to changing market conditions. These limits, they argue, seriously diminish the social benefits of vigorous competition. Do you think government should protect jobs and local income security with restrictions on plant closings or relocations? Why or why not?

19. In 1978–1979, the Hunt brothers (Texas billionaires) allegedly attempted to corner the silver market. What happened to the price of silver during this period? Was their effort successful? What obstacles are faced by anyone who tries to monopolize a previously competitive industry?

24

Monopoly

Different people view monopoly very differently. To some, it evokes memories of a game involving Boardwalk, Park Place, and the B&O Railroad, in which the ultimate winner has all the property and money. Some firms see a monopoly position as desirable and try to eliminate all their competitors. Monopoly power sometimes seems sinister. Some people blame such evils as inflation and poverty on concentrated economic power. Orthodox Marxists perceive monopoly capitalism as a natural extension of a market system, and as the final stage before capitalism succumbs to a communist revolution.

This chapter focuses on the theory of pure, unregulated monopoly, even though very few pure monopolies exist, and most of these are regulated by government agencies. Just as we set 0° Celsius and 100° Celsius as bench marks from which to measure temperature, pure monopoly and pure competition (from the previous chapter) set relative bench marks for assessing economic performance. Comparisons of monopoly and competitive models point out major differences between the pricing and output decisions of firms having considerable market power and those of firms without such power.

The first systematic analysis of monopoly was pursued more than a century ago by a French economist, Antoine Augustin Cournot. One central concern of Cournot, and of economists today, is the inefficiency that may result from monopoly. This inefficiency provides a rationale for regulation to control economic concentration. We also discuss price discrimination, which requires firms to have control over prices, and barriers to entry — obstacles that prevent potential competitors from entering an industry.

Monopoly Markets

Monopolies raise the specter of concentrated power, economic inefficiency, and an inequitable income distribution. But what exactly is a monopoly?

> **Monopoly:** *A firm that is the lone producer of a good for which there are no close substitutes.*

Public utilities are probably the purest forms of monopoly in the United States, but even they face some competition. A local electric power company "competes" with solar cells or petroleum-based electric-generating systems, but these options to conventional electricity are insufficiently close to threaten power companies' retention of customers.

Antoine Augustin Cournot (1801–1877)

The life of Antoine Augustin Cournot was testimony to Andrew Carnegie's assertion, "It does not pay to pioneer." The value of Cournot's work was recognized only after his death. His life was characterized by anonymity and tragedy. This genius of economics and philosophy was born into a family of French farmers who had tilled the same lands for almost 300 years. He spent most of his life as a school superintendent, and even that job was secured only through the influence of his friend Poisson, the famous French physicist and statistician. Cournot is remembered best in his homeland as a philosopher; in the English-speaking world he is hailed as a brilliant pioneer in economics.

Only Cournot's first and most influential book was ever translated into English. It fairly bristles with originality: Cournot formally introduced demand and supply curves; he derived, mathematically, the marginal revenue equals marginal cost rule for profit maximization; and he also specified equilibrium conditions for monopolists, interdependent oligopolists, and firms operating under perfect competition.

Cournot's analysis of monopolistic profit maximization contains the kernel of his theory of the firm. As an example, Cournot considered a monopolist who could *costlessly* supply water from a mineral spring with uniquely healthful qualities. Sale of a single liter of water might bring an extremely high price, but Cournot demonstrated that a monopoly will not charge the highest price the market will bear. Rather, it will adjust its price to maximize total receipts; because costs are zero, this is equivalent to maximizing profit.

Cournot demonstrated that this is accomplished when marginal revenue (derived from the demand curve) equals marginal cost ($MR = MC$). Cournot's procedure seems commonplace today, but before 1838 there was no formal theory of profit maximization. Virtually every fundamental axiom in the economic theory of the firm stems from Cournot's trailblazing analysis.

Cournot's demeanor was solitary and melancholy, traits that intruded into his writing. His austere books are crowded with facts and rigorous mathematical proofs. He confessed to a fellow French economist that he was unpopular with his publishers because none of his books sold enough to be profitable until years after their first appearance.

Cournot's work was hampered by other economists' discomfort with mathematics and because his most productive years were absorbed by his duties as a school administrator. In addition, gradual deterioration of his eyesight impaired the accuracy of his mathematical notation. For their part, the prejudice and shortsightedness of his contemporaries blinded them to his advances in economic theory, which were hardly recognized at all until more than two decades after his death. Today, his contributions are increasingly recognized for inspiring mathematical game theory (discussed two chapters hence), which many economists view as the most promising approach for describing strategic interactions between firms.

Professional baseball, the National Football League, and the National Basketball Association operate somewhat like shared monopolies, with team owners jointly setting policies to govern such things as limits on player compensation. But even these organizations must compete for fans with college and high school teams. Internationally, the DeBeers group of South Africa has controlled roughly 90 percent of world diamond output for almost a century. When the Soviet Union's recent push in international markets threatened DeBeers' monopoly power as a supplier of gem quality stones, the USSR and DeBeers reached an agreement that effectively maintained DeBeers' market power.

The definition of monopoly raises several issues. How does a firm become a monopoly? Monopolies in some goods may enrich firms' owners at the expense of the rest of society, but does a monopoly position guarantee riches? How does a monopoly prevent entry into an industry by other firms? How narrowly are *close substitutes* defined?

You know of many goods for which there is only one producer/seller, but these firms are not necessarily monopolists. For example, Harper-Collins has an exclusive right to publish this text. Is our publisher a monopolist? No, because there are several close, albeit imperfect, substitutes for this text. Not only is a monopolist the only seller of a given product, but the good itself must lack close substitutes.

Consider the market for cameras producing instant snapshots. Polaroid is now the only producer of cameras that provide finished pictures in 60 seconds or less. Are regular cameras really close substitutes for instant picture cameras? Should the appropriate market for ascertaining whether Polaroid has a monopoly be the market for the "instant picture" camera rather than for cameras as a whole? When you consider the closeness of substitutes, our publisher's exclusive right to sell this book is clearly inferior to Polaroid's monopoly on instant cameras.

Monopoly Pricing and Output

Recall that a purely competitive firm faces a horizontal demand curve and can sell all it produces at the going market price. Therefore, a competitive firm's marginal revenue (its revenue from selling an extra unit of output) equals the market price. Pure competitors are price takers and can only select the *quantities* they will produce and sell.

Many firms that supply goods with close but imperfect substitutes are not true monopolists, but they possess *market power* because they have some discretion about pricing. Any firm with market power is a price maker.

> **Market power:** *A firm's ability to alter the price of its output because of inadequate competition or a lack of perfect substitutes for its products.*

Because it is the sole source of a good without close substitutes, a pure monopolist faces the entire market demand curve. Complete control of the supply side allows it to select a *price and output combination* from the market demand curve. Each feasible price generates a maximum amount the monopolist can sell. Alternatively, a monopolist might choose an output level and then charge the maximum price that causes that quantity to be sold. This discretion over price distinguishes monopolistic pricing from that established in purely competitive markets, where each firm can only choose the quantity it will sell. What price maximizes monopoly profits? Is it the price the most desperate buyer is willing to pay? That which maximizes total revenue? Or that which maximizes the output sold? None of these answers is correct. Then what price will a monopolist charge?

Market Power and Demand

The demand curve facing a monopolized industry slopes down; prices will be inversely related to quantity demanded. Any firm with market power must lower its price to sell more if it can charge only one price at a time. The differences between the marginal revenues for pure competitors and for firms with market power are illustrated in Figure 1.

Whenever a firm has market power, selling extra output requires lowering the price, because consumers are unwilling to purchase additional units at the previous price. Most monopolists can sell extra output only by cutting its price for all units sold. For example, if Polaroid wanted to sell more cameras next year, it could not just lower the price for the few extra customers who required discounts to buy over the next year; Polaroid would be forced to lower the price of its camera to virtually all customers. Thus, marginal revenue will equal the price a monopolist receives from selling an extra unit minus the revenue lost because prices must be reduced on all other units sold.

The demand curve D facing the monopolist in Panel B of Figure 1 is based on the data in the figure. The market demand curve is D because the monopolist controls the industry. Total revenue (TR) equals price per unit (P) times the amount sold (Q) and is listed in column 3. If the firm set its price at $9, 3 million units would be

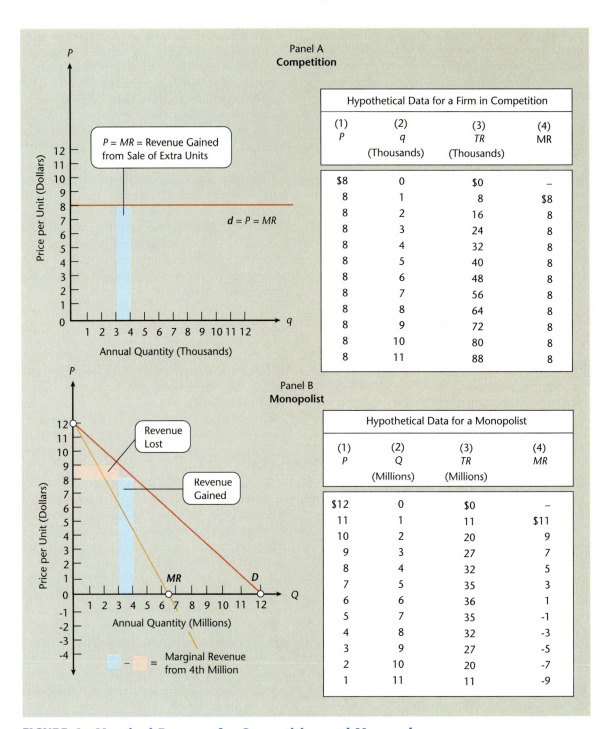

FIGURE 1 Marginal Revenue for Competition and Monopoly

The revenue gained by a purely competitive firm when it sells an additional unit of output equals the price of the output (MR = P), because demand for the firm's product is perfectly elastic (Panel A). A firm with market power must reduce price in order to sell extra output, so marginal revenue is always less than price (P > MR). In Panel B, a monopolist can sell 3 million units at $9 each ($27 million) or 4 million units at $8 each ($32 million). Thus, the fourth million only adds $5 per unit, on the average, in revenue ($32 million − $27 million = $5 million).

sold annually and total revenue would be $27 million. The firm would sell 4 million by lowering its price to $8, and annual total revenue would rise from $27 million to $32 million — for an extra $5 million. Why would total revenue fail to rise by $8 million, the full price of the million units sold? The answer is that the firm received $8 for each of the extra 1 million units sold, but it lost $1 per unit on the first 3 million units sold, resulting in an average increase in total revenue of only $5 for each of the last million units sold (8 − 3 = 5).

Marginal revenues are listed in column 4 of Figure 1. Marginal revenue equals $\Delta TR/\Delta Q$ and is labeled *MR*. Notice that when quantity sold exceeds 6 million units and price is reduced below $6, marginal revenue is actually negative. This means that total revenue falls when extra units are sold and the price is lowered.

Revenue and Elasticity   Recall (from our "Elasticity" chapter) that there are close relationships between elasticity, price, and total revenue. For example, if expanding output requires such large price cuts that total revenue falls, the demand curve is price inelastic and marginal revenue is negative. How demand, marginal revenue, price, total revenue, and price elasticity are related is graphed in Figure 2, which reflects the data used in Panel B of Figure 1.

When quantity is less than 6 million units and the price exceeds $6, demand is price elastic and the price cuts required to sell more output are proportionately less than the increases in output. Thus, when output expands and prices are lowered, total revenue rises, so demand is elastic, because marginal revenue is positive at prices above $6. Conversely, total revenues fall as the price is reduced below $6, and demand is inelastic; the inelastic range of a demand curve is associated with negative marginal revenue. If small price changes do not alter total revenue, marginal revenue is zero, and demand is in a unitary elastic range. Let's see how marginal revenue affects the short-run price/quantity combination a profit-maximizing monopolist selects from the demand curve.

Profit-Maximizing Price and Output   A monopolist (or any profit-maximizing firm) produces and sells extra output as long as each extra unit adds to total revenue at least as much as it adds to total cost; i.e., the firm will continue to produce and sell as long as marginal revenue is greater than or equal to marginal cost ($MR \geq MC$).

Table 1   *Profit Maximization and the Monopolist*

Revenue Data				Cost and Profit Data			
Q (Millions)	P	TR (Millions)	MR	TC (Millions)	ATC	MC ($\Delta TC/\Delta Q$)	Profit (Millions)
0	$12	0	—	$ 8.0	—	—	$−8.0
1	11	$11	$11	12.5	$12.50	$ 4.50	−1.5
2	10	20	9	16.0	8.00	3.50	4.0
3	9	27	7	19.5	6.50	3.50	7.5
4	8	32	5	24.0	6.00	4.50	8.0
5	7	35	3	29.5	5.90	5.50	5.5
6	6	36	1	36.0	6.00	6.50	0
7	5	35	−1	43.5	6.21	7.50	−8.5
8	4	32	−3	52.0	6.50	8.50	−20.0
9	3	27	−5	61.5	6.83	9.50	−34.5
10	2	20	−7	72.0	7.20	10.50	−52.0
11	1	11	−9	83.5	7.59	11.50	−72.5
12	0	0	−11	96.0	8.00	12.50	−96.0

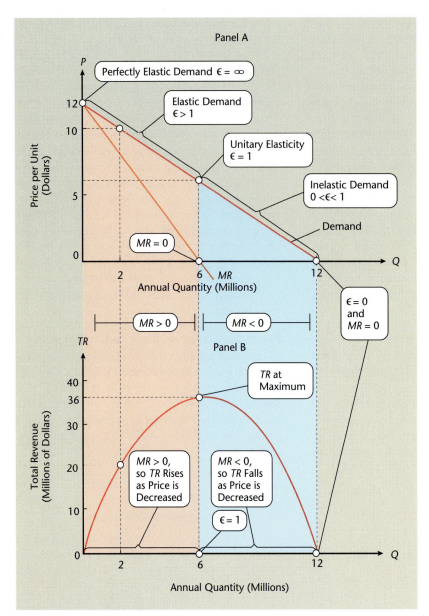

FIGURE 2   Relationship Between Demand, Marginal Revenue, Total Revenue, and Elasticity (e_p)

Total revenue rises as prices are cut in the price elastic range along a demand curve, so marginal revenue is positive. Marginal revenue becomes negative because total revenue declines with price cuts in the inelastic range. Marginal revenue lies below the demand curve facing a firm with market power because selling extra output requires price cuts.

The revenue data in our previous example are augmented in Figure 3 by cost data in Table 1. This firm will produce and sell 4 million units at a price of $8 each, receiving total revenues of $32 million. Average total costs are $6 per unit, so $24 million is absorbed in total costs, leaving a total profit of $8 million. In Figure 3, total profit is the shaded rectangle *bcde* and equals price ($8) minus average total cost ($6) times the number of units sold (4 million), for total profits of $8 million.

Why does the firm sell 4 million units? Why not 3 million or 5 million? Profit maximization requires any firm to produce and sell an extra

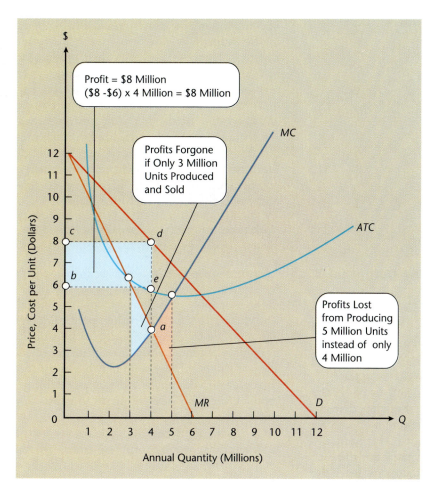

Profit = $8 Million
($8 -$6) x 4 Million = $8 Million

Profits Forgone if Only 3 Million Units Produced and Sold

Profits Lost from Producing 5 Million Units instead of only 4 Million

FIGURE 3 Profit Maximization and the Monopolist

Profit can be computed as the quantity produced and sold times price minus average total cost $[\pi = q(P - ATC)]$. Maximum profits are realized when marginal revenue equals marginal cost ($MR = MC$). Profits equal $8 million when $MR = MC$ at 4 million units of output (area $bcde$).

unit any time the funds brought in from an extra sale (*MR*) at least covers its cost (*MC*). If only 3 million units were sold, this monopolist would forgo profits of $500,000 (column 8 in the table: $8M − $7.5M = $500,000). If marginal costs exceed marginal revenues, a firm will lose by producing extra output. If 5 million units were sold, the last million would add costs that exceeded extra revenues by $2.5 million. As is always the case, the rule for profit maximization is that the firm should produce output up to the point where $MR = MC$.

Loss-Minimizing Price and Output A common myth is that monopoly is always profitable. Monopolists can control the prices they charge for their products, so it seems natural that they will earn economic profits. Figure 4 depicts an

instance where a monopolist would suffer losses if the good were produced. For example, surveys indicate that many people would like a trip on a space shuttle. Even for a monopolist, the current costs of such tours remain prohibitive relative to current demand. In the near future, however, such tours may become possible.

There are literally thousands of patented products for which demand is insufficient to justify production. The cost structures for these products are so high that no feasible price/output combination would allow a monopolist to make normal profits. For example, you probably could not profit from monopolies on disposable razor blade resharpeners, machines to reweave "runs" in pantyhose, or winders for string collectors. Demands would be trivial relative to costs. To protect against this problem, a shop in Toronto

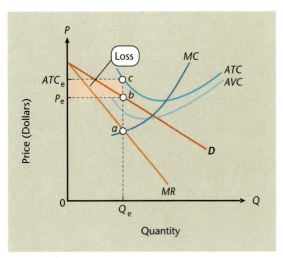

FIGURE 4 Loss-Minimizing Output for a Monopolist

The $MR = MC$ rule minimizes the losses of any firm, including a monopoly, as long as variable costs are covered by revenues.

called "The New Product Store" exhibits and test markets inventors' gimmicks for a fee.

Even if a monopolized good initially passes the market test, rising costs or shrinking demand may cause failure. In the short run, if P_e is above average variable costs, a firm would continue to produce despite losses. But what about the long run? This monopolist has two options: leave the industry and put its capital to more profitable use, or try to bolster demand sufficiently to lift its operations into the black, perhaps through aggressive marketing. No firm will tolerate persistent losses; in the long run, any firm will move its resources into more lucrative lines of business.

A Long Run for Monopolists? In competition, any short-run economic profits are eliminated when other firms enter the industry. Whether this is true of an industry controlled by one firm depends on how hard it is to prevent new firms from entering the market to exploit profit opportunities. If new competitors can be prevented from entering the industry, the monopolist may adjust its productive capacity along its long-run average cost curve to most profitably accommodate permanent changes in demand, as shown in Panel A of Figure 5.

Alternatively, protection from the discipline of competition may allow a monopoly to operate inefficiently. Why not hire your relatives and friends at higher salaries than their productivity justifies if a monopoly position ensures you a high income anyway? Why bother to work hard or to control costs? And why worry about quality and consumer satisfaction? Any customers who are going to buy the monopolized product must buy from your firm. If a monopolist chooses "the good life," X-inefficiency may absorb much of potential monopoly profit by driving up fixed costs, as is shown in Panel B of Figure 5.

Excessive costs incurred because a firm is not hard pressed by competitors is **X-inefficiency.**

Some monopolies also engage in *rent seeking* by strategically incurring expenses to defend their monopoly positions. Examples include wasteful outlays for advertising, political lobbying, unnecessary excess capacity, or litigation to intimidate potential entrants—a threatened suit alleging patent infringement may bar entry of an entrepreneur with a new twist on an established product, but who lacks resources to fight a lawsuit.

Of course, inefficient monopolies are natural targets for takeover by corporate raiders who intend to manage the firm more efficiently, allowing the previous owners to loaf on the beach. These two prospects—long-term economic profits or a rich comfortable life—are good reasons for a monopolist to fear market entry by new competitors.

Barriers to Entry

Maintaining a profitable monopoly requires keeping other firms out of the industry.

Barriers to entry: *Obstacles that make it less profitable or more difficult for new firms to enter an industry.*

Some barriers to entry arise from government regulations, others result from the strategies of existing firms, and still others are technological or "natural." A monopolized industry is not a requirement; entry barriers exist in a broad range of market structures.

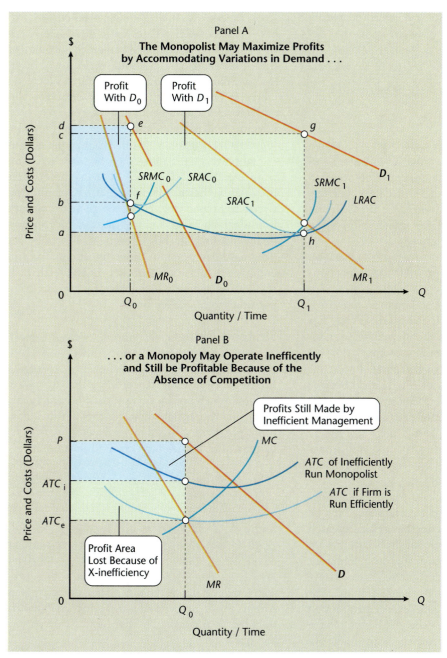

Panel A

The Monopolist May Maximize Profits by Accommodating Variations in Demand . . .

Profit With D_0

Profit With D_1

$SRMC_0$ $SRAC_0$

$SRMC_1$

$SRAC_1$ $LRAC$

MR_0

D_0

MR_1

D_1

Price and Costs (Dollars)

Quantity / Time

Panel B

. . . or a Monopoly May Operate Inefficiently and Still be Profitable Because of the Absence of Competition

Profits Still Made by Inefficient Management

MC

ATC of Inefficiently Run Monopolist

ATC if Firm is Run Efficiently

ATC_i

ATC_e

Profit Area Lost Because of X-inefficiency

MR

D

Price and Costs (Dollars)

Quantity / Time

FIGURE 5   Long-Run Adjustments by Monopoly Firms

If demand were D_0 in Panel A, a profit-maximizing monopoly firm would have a small plant, charge a high price, and earn profits equal to area *bdef*. If demand grew to D_1, the monopolist would expand its production facilities and realize greater profits, equal to area *acgh*. Thus, in the long run, a monopolist may accommodate variations in demand through growth or contraction. However, a monopoly whose management was not threatened by competition might make the long-run adjustment of operating inefficiently, as long as it realized satisfactory profits. Panel B assumes that such sloppy management is a fixed cost. This higher cost is an example of *X-inefficiency*. (Of course, in the long run, even sloppy managers die.)

Regulatory Barriers Some barriers erected by regulations are largely beyond the control of existing firms.

Regulatory barriers *to entry are erected by government policies.*

For example, compulsory auto safety standards increase per-unit costs, posing obstacles for potential entrants to the car market who want to produce cheap cars. Other regulatory barriers are strongly supported by existing firms in the industry and may result from intensive lobbying by these special interest groups.

Legal barriers include government bans on competition. Laws that prohibit most competition for profitable first-class mail carrying are strongly supported by postal unions and firms with contracts with the U.S. Postal Service. For example, its competitors cannot deliver to mailboxes. Without this constraint, competition for first-class mail delivery might parallel that for parcel-post deliveries from United Parcel Service and other package handlers. But even these statutes fail to discourage some entrepreneurs. Several delivery firms now hang "mail" in plastic bags on the doorknobs of recipients, and Emery and Federal Express offer one-day hand delivery between many major cities.

Regulatory barriers include patents and copyrights. Patent and copyright monopolies may be justified as incentives for technological research and development and for cultural enrichment. Many inventors count on profits from a patent monopoly to justify risky inventive efforts. However, patents and copyrights are licenses for monopoly; patents bar competitive production for 17 years, and may be renewed. Patents have provided the Polaroid Company with a monopoly in the market for "instant picture" cameras. In 1986, Polaroid was awarded hundreds of millions of dollars in a suit because Kodak had infringed on Polaroid's patents. More often, however, the "pirating" of patented or copyrighted products is conducted secretly, as discussed in Focus 1.

Government licensing restrictions ostensibly protect consumers from fraud or shoddy practices, but may actually be disguised entry barriers. For example, giving a friend advice about how to beat a traffic ticket might get you cited for "practicing law without a license." Some doctors recently advocated making it illegal for clerks in jewelry stores to pierce ears. Doctors and lawyers respectively may argue that such laws protect patients and clients, but they also help ensure customers for licensed professionals.

Elaborate regulations often bar smaller firms from competing effectively. For example, there is evidence that the Food and Drug Administration's tightened regulation of pharmaceuticals following the Thalidomide disaster of 1962 reduced research and development efforts by big drug companies, and drove most small firms completely out of that market. Even worthwhile regulations generate social costs by limiting competition from smaller firms.

Strategic Barriers Monopolists are ingenious in trying to keep competitors out of a market. For example, a monopolist might try to corner the market for a natural resource that was a key ingredient in a production process, hoping to stymie all potential competitors. But non-monopolists are also adept at developing policies to make life harder for potential entrants.

Strategic barriers *to entry result from policies of existing firms in an industry.*

Some strategic barriers are legally permissible (e.g., annual style changes or extensive national advertising), but others violate U.S. antitrust laws (e.g., establishing exclusive marketing territories or pooling patents may bar entry by new firms). Strategic behavior and antitrust laws are detailed in the last two chapters of this part of the book.

Natural Barriers Barriers may also emerge from the cost structures inherent in some types of production.

Natural barriers *to entry arise when economies of scale are substantial relative to market demand and severely limit the number of firms in an industry.*

Patents, Trademarks, Copyrights, and Counterfeit Goods

Monopoly rights for inventors are reserved by patents, business identities are guarded by trademarks, and intellectual properties such as music, films, and writing are protected by copyright laws.

Inventions like the telephone and the electric light have revolutionized our lives and enriched their inventors. Public and private research and development in the United States employed over a million scientists and engineers in 1990, and outlays exceeded $130 billion. Research funding is pouring into faster computer microchips and a rich array of sophisticated consumer goods, production technologies, and military hardware. The U.S. Patent Office recently began granting patents for new gene splicing techniques that have yielded new agricultural products, pharmaceuticals, and strains of laboratory mice.

Trademarks also generate market power. More than politeness causes your order for a "coke" in a restaurant to prompt the question, "Is Pepsi OK?" The Coca Cola Company fears that its trademarked label will go the way of "kleenex," "xerox," and "aspirin," which were all protected brand names at one time.

Any trademark that becomes widely used to refer to a product generically may lose its legal exclusivity. Consequently, Coca Cola prosecutes those who misuse its brand name. Fortunes are often spent to imprint a brand name in the public's consciousness, and then to protect a product's image—such firms as Gucci, Cartier, and Chanel each spend over $1 million a year on brand-name security alone.

In addition to books, recordings, and computer software, copyrights protect product designs (e.g., Teenage Mutant Ninja Turtles and "Slap" bracelets). Software developers have formed an organization to fight unauthorized duplication, and record producers use ASCAP and BMI to pressure businesses to license music for commercial purposes. ASCAP and BMI employ agents to see if businesses play background music to entertain customers. If, for example, a restaurant plays tapes to create an atmosphere for diners, the owner is asked to purchase a license to play the music. A lawsuit immediately follows any refusal. The law is clear—playing music for commercial purposes without a license is illegal. ASCAP and BMI

prorate their revenue to the music's copyright holders.

Today, counterfeit goods are threatening this legal protection of market power. "Pirated" copies of recordings rob musicians of millions in royalties annually. Most imitations of patented goods are inferior in quality. Dangerously brittle "high-strength" fasteners and other bogus parts have appeared in civilian and military planes. In 1990, the Justice Department seized over 18 tons of counterfeit auto parts. The U.S. Department of Commerce estimates that almost a million jobs are lost to product *knock-offs*—the industry's term for counterfeited goods.

It is interesting that both sides abhor publicity about this problem. Counterfeiters count on secrecy so they can sell knock-offs; legitimate firms are reluctant to admit that their product line has been reproduced. Publicity may encourage further copying, or consumers may become wary of the brand names being copied. In any event, counterfeiting increasingly erodes the market power derived from patents, trademarks, and copyrights.

That is, minimum efficient scales of production (*MES*s) are huge. Allocative efficiency requires one firm to fully service the market in extreme cases where the *MES* is 100 percent.

A **natural monopoly** *emerges if economies of scale permit only one firm to achieve the lowest possible average cost while serving a specific market.*

For example, a single natural gas company can efficiently service a given area. If 20 gas companies serviced your neighborhood and consumers did not collude to use gas from only one company, how often would the roads be torn up to install new pipe lines? How many pipes would run down every alley? How many firms might you need to contact before planting a tree? Installing a storm sewer system would be a nightmare.

Figure 6 illustrates how a *natural monopoly* arises from a production process with a high *MES*. An unregulated monopoly could charge P_3 for Q_2 amount of output, reaping profits equal to the shaded area. This production process is characterized by high fixed costs and relatively low variable costs. Economies of scale are tremendous because average costs decline when overhead costs are spread across large amounts of output.

Why does competition degenerate to monopoly in such markets? Suppose four firms were breaking even by producing Q_0 at price P_3, where $Q_0 = Q_2/4$. Each would try to wrest customers from competitors because the marginal revenue from servicing new buyers would exceed marginal cost. But as industry output grows, the price falls faster than average costs fall. Suppose, for example, that each firm doubled output. Price will be P_0 at industry output Q_3. If all firms are the same size (Q_1), average total cost will be P_2, and every firm will lose $P_2 - P_0$ per unit. Three firms must eventually exit this market, leaving the fourth to collect the full monopoly profit (the shaded area in Figure 6).

Such natural monopolies as utility companies are regulated in attempts to transfer benefits from economies of scale to consumers. Unregulated natural monopolies could reap immense profits and, as you will see in a moment, tend to be allocatively inefficient. In our "Antitrust" chapter, we consider illegal barriers to competition from artificial attempts to monopolize; we investigate potential regulatory benefits when technology makes monopoly a natural outcome of the market in our chapter on "Regulation."

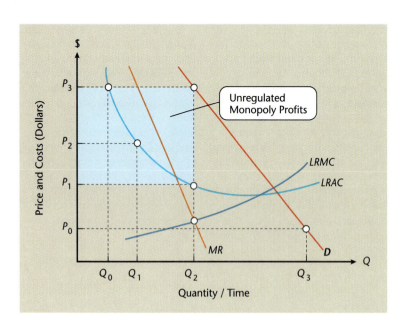

FIGURE 6   A Natural Monopoly Market

Competitive processes in markets where economies of scale cause average costs to decline across the full range of market demand will ultimately evolve into a natural monopoly. Economies of scale are so significant that local natural monopolies are almost inevitable for electricity, natural gas, water and sewer facilities, and telephone service.

Price Discrimination

Market power implies some control over price. We have shown how a monopoly that charges only one price maximizes profit. If a monopolist can separate buyers into submarkets and has control over price, different groups can be charged different prices.

> Price discrimination *occurs when a good is sold at different prices that do not reflect differences in production costs.*

We previously defined consumer surplus as the difference between the amounts people would willingly pay for various amounts of specific goods and the amounts they do pay at market prices. Price discrimination allows some of the monetary value of consumer surplus to be transferred from consumers to the producer.

Have you sat next to people who paid less than you did for tickets to see a film? Theaters often have different prices for children, students, adults, and senior citizens. Does it cost a theater more to seat a 32-year-old at a given show than to seat a senior citizen? Clearly not. Doctors often argue that they render charity by charging their richer patients more than their poorer patients pay for the same service. (Might they charge whatever the market will bear in both cases?) Airline ticket prices vary widely for roughly the same service (depending on early reservations and special promotions). And the family in front of you in a grocery checkout line may pay much less for the same food than you do if it uses coupons and you don't. These are all examples of price discrimination.

Why do firms charge different customers different prices? Is price discrimination socially beneficial or harmful? And what conditions make price discrimination possible?

Requirements for Price Discrimination

Price discrimination requires a firm to have market power. The firm need not be a monopoly. Any seller that is a price maker rather than a price taker possesses market power. This occurs whenever the demand curve facing an enterprise

has negative slope. In this sense, your local florist has market power even if it is not a monopolist.[1]

A second requirement for price discrimination is that buyers with different demand elasticities be separable into submarkets. Different demand elasticities may arise from disparities of incomes, preferences, locations, and so on. Once groups of customers are separated, a firm must be able to prevent *arbitrage* — buyers who pay a lower price must be deterred from selling to people charged a higher price. Price discrimination abounds in medical treatment because arbitrage is impossible. One patient cannot sell another a liver transplant or an inoculation against mumps. Focus 2 reports an interesting example of arbitrage. Price discrimination schemes fail when arbitrage cannot be prevented.

In summary, price discrimination raises the prices some groups pay, while it reduces prices for other groups. (Without price discrimination, both groups would pay a common price somewhere in the middle.) Price discrimination requires a firm to have market power and it must be able to (*a*) separate groups into submarkets with different price elasticities of demand, and (*b*) prevent low-price users from selling to high-price users. We will now look at how two types of price discrimination affect monopoly profits.

Profits from Price Discrimination

Different customers are charged different prices only if this increases a firm's profits. In the extreme case, a firm practicing **perfect price discrimination** extracts from all consumers their demand prices for every unit of a good it sells. These demand prices are the maximum payments each individual would willingly make rather than do without.

This case is illustrated in Figure 7, where we consider a monopolist marketing a cure for bald-

---

1. Pure competitors cannot charge different prices for a homogeneous product because the demand curves they confront are horizontal. If one pure competitor raised its price, all customers would simply go elsewhere and their business would be lost to the firm. A competitive firm could (if it were altruistic) sell its product at below the prevailing market price to a given group, but it would lose some of its normal profits in the process.

Arbitrage and Price Discrimination

In *Cartels in Action* (New York: Twentieth Century Fund, 1946, pp. 402–404), George Stocking and Myron Watkins reported a classic case of arbitrage:

Rohm & Haas of Philadelphia and DuPont [were] the only American producers of methyl-methacrylate plastics. They marketed methyl-methacrylate, in the form of molding powders, for a variety of industrial uses at $0.85 a pound. To licensed dental laboratories they supplied, at more than $22 a pound, prepared mixtures consisting of methyl-methacrylate powder (polymer) and liquid (monomer), both essential to the manufacture of dentures. At the same time they refused to sell the monomer in any other form to any other buyer. In this way they apparently planned to force the dental trade to rely exclusively upon them for supplies. The enormous price spread attracted "bootleggers" who found that they could "crack" the commercial powders back to the liquid, and sell the polymer and monomer together at a profit to the dental trade. To combat this practice, at the suggestion of a licensee, Rohm & Haas considered adulterating the cheap commercial powders so that, for use in dentures, they would come under the ban of the Food and Drug Administration. The licensee suggested that:

A millionth of one percent of arsenic or lead might cause them to confiscate every bootleg unit in the country. There ought to be a trace of something that would make them rear up.

Although Rohm & Haas thought this was a "very fine" suggestion, there is no evidence that they put it into effect.

Reprinted by permission.

---

ness. To keep the graph simple, we assume that fixed costs are zero while marginal costs are constant at $200 per bottle.[2] If it set a single profit-maximizing price, this monopolist would charge $500 per bottle of tonic and sell 6,000 units. Total profit would be $1,800,000 [($500 − $200) × 6,000 = $1,800,000]. But this firm can profit from price discrimination. For the firm to fully extract its customers' consumer surpluses, it must sell the first few bottles for between $800 and $799, the next few for between $799 and $798, and so on, until the last bottle is sold for only a fraction over $200.

Perfect price discrimination allows this firm to appropriate all consumer surplus above a price of $200. This form of price discrimination allows the tonic bottler to boost profit from the $1,800,000 (the rectangular area) associated with normal monopoly pricing to $3,600,000 (the area of the entire shaded triangle above marginal costs).[3] Perfect price discrimination would enable a monopolist to charge everything the market will bear. But no firm can determine the precise maximum that each individual is willing to pay for each unit of a good. At best, a firm might segment the public into a few distinct

---

2. Note that whenever marginal costs are constant, they also equal average variable costs. If fixed costs are zero, then $MC = AVC = ATC$.

3. Notice that the area of the two triangles equals the area of the rectangle. Thus, profit doubles from $1.8 million to $3.6 million.

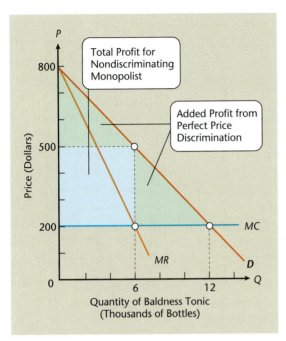

FIGURE 7 Monopoly Profits and Perfect Price Discrimination

Perfect price discrimination allows this patent medicine monopolist to charge everything consumers will pay to have hair rather than do without it. All potential consumer surpluses are converted into revenues for the perfectly price discriminating firm.

groups for whom arbitrage is impossible and whose elasticities of demand differ.

How even imperfect market segmentation can be profitable is shown in Figure 8, which illustrates demands for two groups of consumers. Fixed costs are zero and marginal cost is a constant $2. This firm charges $5 per unit in Market A, and profit is $18,000; the lower price ($3.75) in Market B yields a profit of $12,250. Total profit is $30,250. If this firm charged a single monopoly price, it would sell 13,000 units at $4.25 and make a total profit of $29,250. Price discrimination generates $1,000 per month more than regular monopoly profits.

This second form of price discrimination includes grocery coupons, frequent flyer bonuses, and student or senior citizen discounts for bus rides or films. Other types of price discrimination are more subtle. Residential phone lines cost less than business lines and long-distance rates historically generated higher profit rates than did local services. These gaps greatly exceeded cost differentials prior to reorganization of the Bell system in 1983.

We need to point out why some apparent price discrimination is illusory. It may seem price discriminatory that parking lots charge lower monthly rates than weekly rates, which are lower than daily, which, in turn, are lower than hourly rates. But wage costs for parking attendants fall as parking moves from short term to long term. Similarly, quantity discounts to major buyers of goods commonly reflect lower transaction costs. Lower rates for weekend parking or off-peak long-distance calls also reflect lower opportunity costs, and not mere differences in the desperation of buyers. Weekend parking or off-peak-hour phone calls are not the same goods as spaces or calls during busier hours. Price discrimination is not present when differences in opportunity costs are reflected in the prices of similar goods.

Competitive vs. Monopolized Markets

We showed in the previous chapter that pure competition yields efficient prices and outputs. Prices are higher when firms exercise market power, and output is less than would be produced were the industry competitive. Is the exercise of market power, therefore, allocatively inefficient? The answer is almost invariably "Yes." Market power may also cause what many people perceive as inequity in the distribution of income.

Differences in Prices and Outputs

A purely competitive equilibrium is shown in Panel A of Figure 9. At point a, industry output equals Q_c and price equals P_c. A competitive market supply curve is the sum of the marginal cost curves (above AVCs) of all firms in an in-

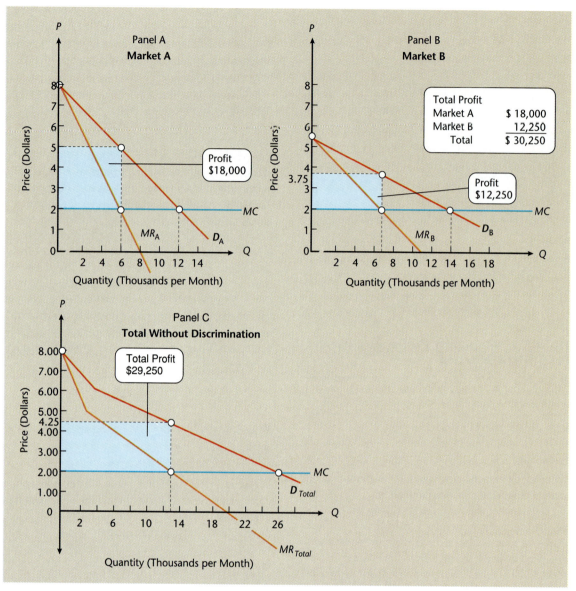

FIGURE 8   Group Price Discrimination and Firm Profitability

A firm can realize greater profits if it can charge higher prices to desperate buyers and lower prices to buyers who have more options available. (The more desperate you are for a product, the less elastic is your demand.) This type of price discrimination can occur only if the firm can prevent arbitrage, whereby someone buys at the low price and sells at the high price, making profits risklessly in the process.

dustry. Contrast these results with those for an unregulated, nondiscriminating monopolist, described in Panel B of the figure. Industry demand for the good is identical, and the monopolist's marginal cost curve is assumed to be the same as

that which collectively characterizes firms in the competitive industry. Equilibrium price and output will be P_m and Q_m, respectively. This higher price when market power exists often prompts complaints about "price gouging" from buyers;

FIGURE 9 Competition vs. Nondiscriminating Monopoly

Economic efficiency requires that marginal social benefit equal marginal social cost (MSB = MSC). This condition is met in competitive markets where supply equals demand (Panel A). Because price is greater than marginal cost in equilibrium for a nondiscriminating monopoly (Panel B), some could gain without losses to anyone if output were increased, as long as the monopolist's additional costs were covered.

the monopoly price is higher while the output is lower than for a competitive industry.

Note that in Panel B, the monopolist's marginal cost curve is not the market supply curve. Price is not a given for firms with market power. Since a monopolist can select a price that maximizes profit, its marginal cost curve is not a supply curve. We have denoted this as $MSC \neq S$. In fact, the quantities supplied by any firm with market power cannot be ascertained from price alone; such firms first want to know how desperate buyers are (How elastic are their demand curves?) before selecting both price and production. There is no supply curve per se.

The Inefficiency of Monopoly

In the preceding chapter, we showed that the demand curve for any industry's good is roughly society's marginal benefit curve for that good. Thus, the marginal social benefit of the good is

roughly its price ($P \cong MSB$). Pure competition forces each manufacturer to use the least costly production technology, so the marginal social costs of production are reflected in competitive supplies. This is shown in the competitive panel of Figure 9 with the notation that *marginal social cost* approximates supply ($MSC \cong S$). The purely competitive market equilibrium at point *a* equates society's marginal (opportunity) cost of producing this good with the marginal benefits as $MSB \cong P = MC \cong MSC$. Maximum benefits from available resources are realized only if the price equals the cost for the last unit produced and sold ($P = MC$). This is the reason purely competitive markets set standards for efficiency by which all other market structures are judged.

At the equilibrium for a nondiscriminating monopoly, price (marginal social benefit) exceeds marginal social cost; society would gain more from extra units of the good than their extra output costs. That is, $P > MSC$. This might seem desirable at first glance — Doesn't society get more from the marginal unit than it sacrifices? — but this is actually undesirable. Society would like more of its resources devoted to production of any good for which marginal benefits exceed marginal costs. Resources are not allocated efficiently because monopolists produce too little and charge too much. The potential gains to consumers from extra production exceed its production costs, so the allocative inefficiency of monopoly causes losses of social welfare equal to area abc in Panel B.[4]

Price Discrimination and Efficiency

Surprisingly, price discrimination may overcome inefficiencies associated with unregulated monopoly power. Recall from Figure 7 that a nondiscriminating monopolist selling cures for baldness would charge $500 per bottle, generating $1.8 million in profits. We saw that perfect price discrimination boosted profit to $3.6 million, but the $200 price charged for the last bottle would be identical to the constant unit price that would emerge if this market were purely competitive. In addition, the marginal social costs and benefits will both equal the price of that last unit. Thus, price discrimination can lead to the economic efficiency associated with pure competition. Price discrimination, however, is typically far from perfect (even at the margin). Moreover, under pure competition, most of the net social benefits of the marketplace are consumer surpluses, but these benefits are appropriated by owners of firms with market power if they can price discriminate.

---

4. This "excess burden" of monopoly is sometimes referred to as a welfare loss triangle.

Monopoly and Inequity

Charging prices far in excess of opportunity costs delights monopolists. Most of us, however, view monopoly pricing as a way to gouge the public to provide high incomes for a few people. Huge incomes are obtained at the expense of the general public because (a) inefficiencies from nondiscriminating monopoly behavior restrict real national income from reaching its potential, and (b) the purchasing power of nonmonopoly incomes is eroded. The total value of the national pie withers so that nondiscriminating monopolists can have more pie. Price discrimination may overcome some inefficiency, but the income distribution tends to be made even less equal, and perhaps less equitable.

In summary, an unregulated exercise of market power causes economic inefficiency ($P > MC$), which implies that national income will be below its potential. The lack of competitive pressure may permit some monopolists to operate in a slack and wasteful fashion, worsening the problem. Moreover, market power may pose problems of inequity in the distribution of income.

Ideally, all industries would be competitive. Unfortunately, this is impossible because certain technologies embody enormous economies of scale and lead to natural monopolies, or certain firms are able to erect significant barriers to entry.

Natural monopolies are typically regulated in an attempt to ensure optimal and efficient operation. The government uses antitrust laws to try to make other industries behave as if they were competitive, or it may split some industries into smaller firms to ensure competition. In the next chapter we examine monopolistic competition and oligopoly — the part of the spectrum between monopoly and competition.

Chapter Review: Key Points

1. An unregulated *monopoly* controls the output and price of a good for which there are no close substitutes.

2. Few monopolies are unregulated, but all firms with any ability to control prices have *market power*. Models of pure monopoly provide insights into the behavior of the many firms with this power.

3. *Barriers to entry* help firms maintain market power. *Regulatory barriers* are established by

government policies and include such things as patents or licenses. *Strategic barriers* include excessive model changes or advertising. *Natural barriers* result from extreme economies of scale, where average costs decline over a large range of output relative to market demand. A *natural monopoly* occurs if one firm can achieve the minimum efficient scale (*MES*) of production only when producing for the entire market.

4. A nondiscriminating monopolist's *marginal revenue* is less than its price. Marginal revenue equals the price the monopolist receives from the sale of the additional unit minus the revenue lost because prices must be reduced on all other units sold. Market power causes the marginal revenue curve to lie below the demand curve.

5. The demand for a good is elastic when output is below the quantity where marginal revenue is zero. Demand is unitarily elastic when marginal revenue is zero. Demand is inelastic for outputs above the point where marginal revenue is zero.

6. A monopolist maximizes profit (or minimizes loss) by selling that output where marginal revenue equals marginal cost. The price charged corresponds to the maximum price from the demand curve at this *MR = MC* output level.

7. Monopolists' profit-maximizing (or loss-minimizing) output levels do not normally occur at the minimum points on average total cost curves. Equilibrium output levels can be less or more than that which minimizes average total cost.

8. If a monopolist is able to maintain its monopoly position in the long run, then pricing, output, and economic profit will reflect variations in demand. A monopolist may also choose inefficient, but comfortable, policies, a problem known as *X-inefficiency*.

9. *Price discrimination* entails sales of essentially the same good at different prices when these differences are not justified by variations in costs. Price discrimination occurs in airline fares, theater ticket prices, charges for medical and dental services, and many other areas.

10. Effective price discrimination requires a firm to have some market power and the ability to separate customers into groups with different price elasticities of demand. It must also prevent *arbitrage* — the selling of the good to high-price customers by low-price customers.

11. Price discrimination boosts a firm's total profit. *Perfect* price discrimination allows a firm to reap as profit all the consumer surplus that could be derived from the product.

12. A nondiscriminating monopoly is less allocatively efficient from society's point of view than are competitive industries. A monopolist typically produces less than would be produced if the industry were purely competitive, and sells at a higher price. Price discrimination may reduce this inefficiency, but it intensifies issues of inequity in the distribution of income.

Key Concepts

Ensure that you can define these terms before proceeding.

monopoly

market power

X-inefficiency

barrier to entry

regulatory barriers

strategic barriers

natural barriers

natural monopoly

price discrimination

monopolistic inefficiency

Problems and Questions

1. Rank these firms according to the extent of their market power (control over price).

   a. A grocery store in the suburbs of Atlanta, GA.

   b. The daily newspaper in Peoria, IL.

   c. A public golf course in Phoenix, AZ.

   d. Pacific Gas and Electricity in Seattle.

   e. The biggest wheat farm in the United States.

   f. A New York taxicab owner.

2. How is the price elasticity of the demand a firm faces related to the extent of its market power?

3. Why is it easier for a surgeon to price discriminate than it is for a company that makes patent medicines?

4. Give two examples each of the three basic types of entry barriers.

5. How do theaters gain by offering discounts to students and senior citizens? How are the price elasticities of demand for theater tickets different for typical students and seniors than for other population groups?

6–9. Use Figure 10 to answer the following questions.

6. How much will this firm produce to maximize profits? What price will it charge at this level of output?

7. Is this firm earning economic profits or losses? How much are these profits/losses? Will this firm still be in business in the long run?

8. What portion of this firm's demand curve is elastic? Inelastic? How did you figure this out?

9. Is this firm operating efficiently from society's viewpoint? If not, what does the inefficiency cost society?

10. If one person recognizes that s/he is the sole supplier of affection to another, can the first person act like a monopolist to extract payoffs from the second person? Ignoring monetary transactions, what kinds of payments can be extracted? Is this behavior common?

11. What, if anything, limits the power of the following suppliers to price discriminate? Do typical members of any of these groups attempt perfect price discrimination? Rank these groups according to how much price discrimination you think they typically exercise.

   a. The only bank in a small farming community.
   b. A car dealer.
   c. A grocery store.
   d. A sole supplier of affection to someone who is head-over-heels in love.
   e. A private college with a large endowment fund for scholarships.

12. Price discrimination occurs when the price differentials charged for a good do not reflect differences in cost. Suppose that there

FIGURE 10 The Monopoly for Dehydrated Water

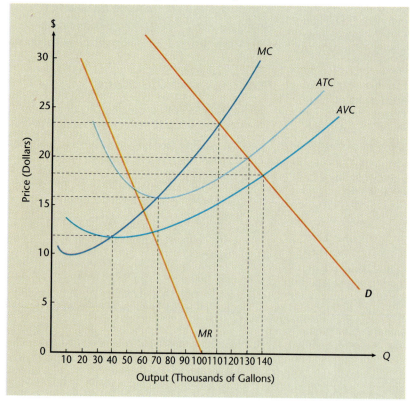

Table 2

Output	1	2	3	4	5	6	7	8	9	10
Price	100	90	80	75	70	65	60	50	40	30
TVC	100	175	225	265	300	330	365	410	475	575

are substantial differences in costs in serving different customers, but a uniform price is charged. In what sense is this also price discrimination?

13. Table 2 lists a demand schedule and total variable costs for a monopolist. Assume that fixed costs equal 30. Graph the demand, marginal revenue, average total cost, and marginal cost curves. What is the profit-maximizing output for this nondiscriminating monopolist? What will be the profit-maximizing rate of output if the monopolist can perfectly price discriminate? What is the profit differential between the two?

14. Government has a legal monopoly on most forms of violence outside of athletics. National defense, police services, prisons, and the like are all inherently violent. Do you think violence is lower because of government's monopoly power? Would a society without government be less violent, as anarchist philosophers suggest? Can you apply the analysis of this chapter to this question?

15. College students in some areas have access to only one institution. In other locations, numerous private or public colleges and universities are available. Since higher education is generally nonprofit, how do these institutions exercise their differing levels of market power? How might you expect treatment of students to differ between private and tax-supported schools?

16. Most industries are comprised of more than one firm. How would you apply monopoly theory to markets where individual firms have market power, but are not pure monopolists?

17–19. Suppose that materials and labor to duplicate audio tapes absorb marginal cost and average total cost at a constant $2, and that fans will buy 1,000,000 recordings by the hot music group *Chipped Beef on Toast* at $10 per tape. The producer's only other costs are the group's 20% royalties on total sales revenue. Suppose further that each 1 cent cut in price boosts sales by 5,000 tapes (e.g., $9 yields 1,500,000 sales, $8 yields 2,000,000 sales, and so on).

17. How many tapes will the company want to produce and sell? How much profit would the firm realize? Is demand elastic or inelastic at this price? How much will the group realize in royalties?

18. *Chipped Beef* will predictably argue that this price is excessive. What price and quantity would the group want the publisher to charge? How much profit would the firm receive? What is the price elasticity of demand at this point? How much extra income would *Chipped Beef* realize if it could dictate the price the company charged?

19. Now suppose royalties are a flat $1 per tape, with the proviso that the group's royalties cannot exceed the company's total revenue. What price will the firm charge, and for what quantity? How much profit would the firm receive? What is the price elasticity of demand at this point? What price would *Chipped Beef* want charged for its tapes? If the firm agreed, how many tapes would it sell? How much profit (or loss) would the firm realize? What is the price elasticity of demand at this point?

CHAPTER 25

Monopolistic Competition and Oligopoly

Competition throughout the world economy is being invigorated by international trade. IBM, Cray, and Compaq, for example, now face rivalry from European and Japanese computer manufacturers. At the same time, concerns about concentrated economic power were heightened by a wave of enormous mergers that swept through U.S. industry in the 1980s. Of the largest mergers of all time, 90 percent have occurred since 1979.

The bulk of our output now flows through the largest 200 American firms, which control roughly two-thirds of U.S. manufacturing assets, as indicated in Figure 1. These giants are in industries that lie between the extremes of pure competition and pure monopoly. None is a price taker; all have substantial market power.

Oligopoly Most major industries are dominated by a few huge *oligopolistic* firms, which individually lack the control possessed by unregulated monopolists — they must consider other firms' reactions in setting prices, production, and marketing strategy.

> **Oligopolies** *are industries dominated by a few firms whose decisions are strategically linked; barriers to entry tend to be significant.*

Models of pure competition and monopoly provide insights into oligopolistic behavior, but neither pure competitors nor monopolists base their decisions on the expected reactions of other firms. Thus, theories of oligopoly cannot just blend theories of competition and monopoly.

Oligopoly models must account for interdependence in decision making. That is, each individual firm must weigh the potential reaction of rivals when it chooses a business strategy. Theories of oligopoly abound because the dynamics of interdependence differ markedly from one industry to another. Just as proper play in poker depends as much on your opponents' characteristics as it does on the cards you are dealt, oligopolists' strategies depend on their individual positions relative to those of current competitors and potential rivals who might enter their industry. Consequently, no single model is sufficiently general to cover all oligopoly markets. In this chapter, we present some representative models that attempt to explain oligopolistic pricing and output.

Monopolistic Competition Oligopoly is closer to monopoly than to pure competition. Ease of entry and exit in monopolistically com-

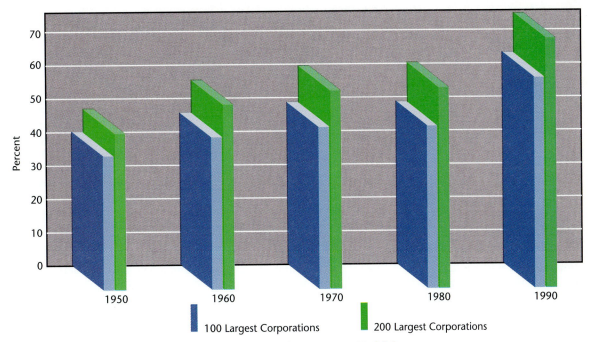

FIGURE 1 Proportion of U.S. Manufacturing Assets Held by the 100 and 200 Largest Corporations, 1950–1990

The share of manufacturing assets controlled by the 100 and 200 largest U.S. firms has been growing for more than a century. These figures suggest that economic power is increasingly being consolidated, but these data do not necessarily imply that specific industries are becoming more concentrated. In fact, most industries now have larger numbers of competitors than there were in earlier decades.

Source: *Statistical Abstract*, 1991.

petitive markets forces firms into a slightly more competitive mode.

> **Monopolistic competition** *requires easy entry and exit into industries in which many potential suppliers compete vigorously with makers of close, but not perfect, substitutes for their "brand-name" products.*

Monopolistic competitors do not base decisions on the anticipated individual reactions of their many competitors, so they are not mutually interdependent in the way oligopolists are. Product differentiation (e.g., packaging, advertising, or styling), however, gives them some control over prices.

The continuum from pure competition to monopolistic competition through oligopoly to pure monopoly is not smooth. Ascertaining where an industry fits is seldom easy and may change over time. For example, 40 years ago au-

tomaking was clearly an oligopoly; General Motors, Ford, and Chrysler sold roughly 95 percent of all cars in the United States. Rambler, Jeep, Hudson, Studebaker, and Packard sold the other five percent, but these firms have died or been absorbed into the "Big 3." However, competition from BMW, Fiat, Honda, Hyundai, Nissan, Toyota, Volkswagen, and other foreign carmakers has moved this industry toward a monopolistically competitive mode.

Most firms are clearly neither pure competitors nor pure monopolists, but few models of firm behavior occupied this vast middle ground until the 1930s, when the works of Joan Robinson and E. H. Chamberlin made most earlier models seem naive.[1] Indeed, many economists

---

1. A century earlier, A. A. Cournot (his biography is in the previous chapter) blazed a path for theories of strategic interactions among firms, but his work was written in French and was largely ignored by English-speaking economists before the 1930s.

E. H. Chamberlin (1899–1967) and Joan Robinson (1903–1983)

Until Edward Hastings Chamberlin attempted to fuse the theories of monopoly and competition, the case of many sellers offering differentiated products had been overlooked. Earlier mainstream economists concentrated on the theory of pure competition, which assumes many sellers of homogeneous products. Chamberlin instead saw close competitors in nearly every market trying to gain market power by differentiating their products. For example, firms often allege the superiority of their products over others.

Born in La Conner, Washington, Chamberlin revised his Harvard Ph.D. dissertation and published *The Theory of Monopolistic Competition* in 1933. His was among the few dissertations to ever profoundly alter economic theory. The central feature of his analysis is that it portrays the demand curves facing firms with differentiated products as being negatively sloped.

In other words, firms that compete on the basis of product differences could raise prices without losing all their customers, but they would sell less output. This fact mirrors elements of monopoly. However, competition tends to lower this negatively sloped demand curve to a point of tangency with the firm's average total cost curve, so that no monopoly profits are realized in the long run. Chamberlin's theory combined with Joan Robinson's ideas to spark numerous studies of industrial markets in the 1940s and 1950s.

I don't know much math, so I have to think.

Joan Robinson

The iconoclastic British economist Joan Robinson was a combatant in virtually every major controversy in economic theory and policy between 1930 and 1983. However, her foes joined her friends in admiring the innovative quality of her ideas and research. She married E. A. G. Robinson (another distinguished British economist) after completing her formal studies in economics, and was among the small group of Cambridge University economists who aided John Maynard Keynes in launching the Keynesian Revolution.

An avowed radical and Marxist, her writings blended the insights of Keynes, Marx, and neoclassical reasoning in a manner uniquely her own. Robinson's work bridged capital theory, the theories of value and distribution, macroeconomics, and the economics of policy making, but her most noteworthy contributions were in the area of imperfect competition. At almost exactly the same time that Chamberlin issued his theory of monopolistic competition from Cambridge, Massachusetts, Joan Robinson launched a parallel theory from Cambridge, England in *The Economics of Imperfect Competition*.

Robinson's "imperfect competition," however, stresses oligopolistic interdependence and views competition and monopoly as mutually exclusive, while Chamberlin identified modern business as a blending of the two. Robinson refined the theory of price discrimination, introduced the concept of *monopsony power* (that is, the ability of powerful buyers to control prices), and separated average revenue (demand) and marginal revenue curves. These analytical feats have provided useful insights into numerous market situations. In Robinson's phrase, she and Chamberlin introduced a "box of tools" sharper and more generally applicable than those that preceded their works.

argue that this area remains analytically fuzzy and insist that we need general models about how firms that lack total monopoly power select their outputs and prices.

Which theory of market structure best fits a particular industry may be difficult to determine, but each model can be useful in analyzing some policies of specific firms. Economists have never claimed that one or two simple models explain all business decisions. Your study of this chapter should, however, provide insights into how business operates between the polar extremes of pure competition and unregulated monopoly.

Product Differentiation

The model of pure competition assumes that numerous firms produce identical products. Farming and a few other industries may produce homogeneous products, but the outputs of most firms are differentiated.

> **Product differentiation** *is the process of altering goods that serve a similar purpose so that they differ in a minor (either real or imagined) way.*

Some firms differentiate within their product lines, e.g., GM produces Chevrolet, Buick, Pontiac, Oldsmobile, and Cadillac cars. Others concentrate on differentiating their products from those of competitors — ABC, CBS, NBC, and the Fox Network compete for advertisers' dollars by broadcasting slightly differentiated sit-coms, sporting events, and news programs, while the Cable News Network (CNN) offers continuous news coverage, ESPN specializes in sports, and MTV and VH-1 offer music videos.

Product differentiation can provide society with a beneficial mix of goods and may signal competition in process. Homogeneity, on the other hand, may result from orders by some central authority. For example, covered wagons in Western movies are all quite similar because the film industry created an image and has them built to order. Few pioneers loaded their belongings into picturesque prairie schooners while migrating to the Old West. They rode, instead, in the motley assortment of wagons then available; two men reportedly moved their gear from St. Louis to Denver in a wheelbarrow in 1867.

Nevertheless, many firms accentuate product differences to try to make us value their products more than those from rival firms. Restaurants, for example, may offer home delivery while specializing in French, Italian, Thai, Vietnamese, or Chinese cuisine. Customer service, especially that which saves time for consumers, is a growing arena for competition through differentiation. Video rentals are available from specialists (e.g., Blockbuster Video), or from firms ranging from grocery stores to coin-operated laundries. One enterprising Seattle dentist combines a coffee bar, his dental office, and a masseuse. Patients sip coffee before an appointment, and then have their feet massaged while their teeth are being filled.

You may think that gasoline is gasoline, but big oil companies expect promotion and advertising to alter customers' perceptions. Are Tide, All, Cheer, and Dash meaningfully different? Soap makers spend millions to persuade us that they are. Ford, GM, Chrysler, and numerous foreign producers all sell autos that provide the same basic transportation services. Despite their many similarities, most of us prefer certain cars based on advertising, styling, the frequency of repair, or our past experience.

Advertising

Some critics believe that marketing puffery persuades consumers to buy useless items or creates an image that a particular brand product is unique when it actually has many close substitutes. Can you remember the worst advertisement you ever saw or heard? If so, the advertiser partially accomplished its goal by making an unforgettable impression.[2] Different types of ads usually target different groups of consumers. An ad you view as obnoxious may be thought amusing or informative by most members of a targeted group.

Informative advertising helps consumers make more satisfactory choices.

> **Informative advertising** *conserves resources and enhances economic efficiency because it reduces transaction costs.*

---

2. This point is made by Robert M. Kenney, "Emphasizing the Effect of Advertising on Consumer Choice," in *Great Ideas for Teaching Economics*, 5/ed., edited by R. T. Byrns and G. W. Stone (New York: HarperCollins, 1992).

Examples include information about prices, availability, and meaningful differences between goods.

> **Persuasive advertising** *uses slogans and imagery to stimulate psychological impulses to buy.*

Beer commercials, for example, feature groups of people enjoying good times but convey little real information. Commercials that dwell on images while saying little about price or real features are usually intended to sell a product that lacks substantive differences.

Product differences can be real or illusory. Differentiation only requires that consumers perceive differences. An example of a differentiated product that is physically homogeneous is liquid bleach. All standard liquid bleach is chemically identical, but most people buy such advertised brands as Clorox instead of cheaper generic substitutes. Why? Because marketing programs create imaginary differences among brands.

Meaningless differences are also found in aspirin-based pain relievers that ads claim contain "the ingredient that doctors recommend most." We seldom hear that the ingredient is aspirin, and that generic brands are as potent as Bayer. Some folks seem convinced that "the more you pay, the more it's worth." Of course, product differentiation may also be real. Some goods truly are superior.

How firms gain from marketing differentiated products is obvious. Purely competitive firms are price takers that sell identical products. Firms try to use product differentiation to boost the demands for their goods and shrink their price elasticities. Successful differentiation provides a firm with market power; they become price makers. This enables the firm to sell more product even if it raises the price.

In Figure 2, we show that product differentiation gives firms some control over price. Without this control, firms can only adjust output levels to maximize profits — the demand curve facing a pure competitor is perfectly elastic. Successful product differentiation expands the demand curve and makes it less elastic. One important result is that each marginal revenue curve now lies below the demand curve facing the firm,

FIGURE 2   Production Differentiation and Firm Demand

There are numerous perfect substitutes for the output of competitive firms, so demand is perfectly elastic. The absence of perfect substitutes makes the demand for the output of a monopolistically competitive firm less than perfectly elastic. Even this small amount of market power pushes the marginal revenue curve for a monopolistic competitor below the price for its output. The fewness of competitors similarly causes oligopolists to possess market power, so the demand curve exceeds the marginal revenue curve.

much like that for the monopolist described in the previous chapter. Consequently, product differentiation causes prices to vary considerably among goods that are close substitutes.

Demands facing oligopolists or monopolistic competitors are more elastic than the industry (monopoly) demand because there are substitutes for each firm's products. Still, these firms can hike prices and not lose all their customers. Some of us will continue to eat Wheaties even if the price rises a bit, but if General Mills were to boost the price too much relative to other cereal prices, our breakfast habits would change to reflect our fading loyalty.

Monopolistic Competition

Monopolistic competition resembles pure competition in allowing easy entry or exit, but differs because each firm produces a differentiated good. Monopolistically competitive industries have:

1. Large numbers of potential suppliers.

2. Slightly differentiated products from each firm (and, sometimes, from within a firm).

3. Relative ease of entry or exit in the long run.

4. Each firm has some control over price.

Successful product differentiation creates market power by increasing the magnitude of the demand curve the firm faces and decreasing its price elasticity; this can allow a monopolistic competitor to act a little like a monopolist. But like pure competitors, monopolistic competitors earn only normal profit in the long run because entry by potential competitors is easy.

Short-Run Pricing and Output

A monopolistic competitor's profit-maximizing short-run price and output combination is shown at point a in Figure 3; output q_0 is sold at price P_0. Regardless of market structure, all firms maximize profit by producing where marginal revenue equals marginal cost. In the short run, this successful firm's economic profit equals the shaded area.

Monopolistic competitors may suffer short-run losses; profits would be impossible if a firm's average cost curve were always above the demand curve. Like all firms, a monopolistic competitor would minimize losses by selling that output where marginal revenue equals marginal cost, as long as the price it could set (average revenue) exceeded average variable costs.

Long-Run Adjustments

Monopolistic competitors differentiate products to exploit short-run profit opportunities, and would like their profits to persist. Their hopes are usually frustrated because typical monopolistic competitors earn only normal profits in the long run; the long-run industry adjustments parallel those for pure competition. Entry of new firms seeking profits cannot be prevented, which may increase production costs. Profits are also dissipated because prices fall when new competitors expand output and take customers from existing firms.

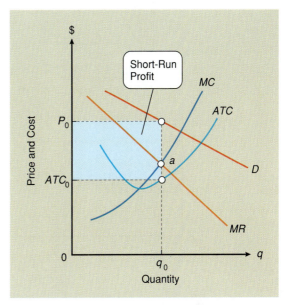

FIGURE 3 Short-Run Profitable Equilibrium for a Monopolistic Competitor

The $MR = MC$ cost rule for maximum profits applies to all firms, including those in monopolistically competitive industries, but the firms can make economic profits in the short run.

This shrinks the demand for a successful firm's products. When new firms enter the market, the demand curves of established firms shift leftward and become more elastic, ultimately leaving all firms in an equilibrium of the sort shown in Figure 4. Marginal revenue equals marginal cost at point a, and the long-run average total cost (*LRATC*) curve is just tangent to the demand curve at point b. This tangency allows the firm to sell its output at a price just equal to average cost ($P_e = ATC_e$), yielding only normal profits in the long run. Product differentiation causes the prices of comparable goods to vary in monopolistic competition, but only within a narrow range.

Resource Allocation and Efficiency

Pure competition is allocatively efficient because marginal social benefit equals marginal social cost ($P = MSC$), and is productively efficient because average costs are minimized. In Figure 4, demand would be d_c for a pure competitor; the

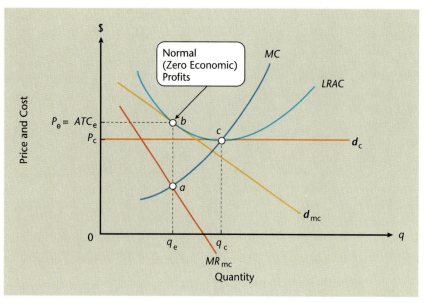

FIGURE 4 Monopolistic Competition: Long-Run Equilibrium and Efficiency

In the long run, entry and exit from the industry will prevent the monopolistically competitive firm from experiencing either economic profits or losses. Economic profits would be possible if the demand curve exceeded average costs over any range of output; economic losses would be unavoidable if the average cost was above demand at all output levels. Thus, competition yields an equilibrium where demand is just tangent to the long-run average total cost curve and the price equals long-run average total cost ($P = LRATC$). For pure competitors in the long run, $P = MR = MC = $ min $LRATC$, so there is economic efficiency. The long-run equilibrium for the monopolistically competitive firm is such that $P > MR$ and $MR = MC$. Even though $P = AC$, $P > MC$ suggests that there is allocative inefficiency. Moreover, average costs are not minimized, so there is productive inefficiency.

equilibrium at point c entails more production which is sold at a lower price ($P_c = $ min $LRATC = MC$). Note that, even though both pure and monopolistic competitors only realize normal profit in the long run, the monopolistically competitive price is higher (P_e), and each firm sells less (q_e).

Failure of monopolistic competitors to produce the output that minimizes average total costs is known as the **excess capacity theorem.**

This analysis suggests that monopolistic competition is both allocatively and productively inefficient. Product differentiation often entails little real value. *Allocative inefficiency* (failure to produce the mix of goods consumers want most) is present if price exceeds marginal social costs ($P > MSC$). Persuasive advertising is frequently

the culprit. Compare the equilibrium for pure competition with that for monopolistic competition in Figure 4, in which we assume that advertising instills "brand loyalty" in consumers by incorrectly persuading them that physically identical goods differ.

Even though monopolistic competitors reap only normal long-run profits, monopolistic competition creates *productive inefficiency* — costs are not minimized. A pure competitor would produce for P_c per unit; advertising and other costs of artificial differentiation drive up a monopolistic competitor's minimum to P_e, which is above the minimum average total cost in Figure 4. Monopolistic competition causes resource misallocation because costs, and thus prices, are higher and each firm's output is less. (This equilibrium resembles unregulated monopoly, but inefficiency is less severe.)

Some economists contend that any minor inefficiency is more than offset by the greater range of choices available. If you view product diversity as worthless and are unwilling to suffer from this type of inefficiency, a solution is to buy only generic goods. Alternatively, government could forbid firms to deviate from government specifications. You could buy any color Model T Ford you wanted — as long as it was black.

Is product differentiation desirable because consumers gain a greater range of choice, or is most differentiation an artificial and worthless consequence of misleading advertising? Your answer to this question, which may easily vary from one industry to the next, indicates whether or not you think monopolistic competition provides an offset to its allocative and productive inefficiency.

Oligopoly

Less competitive than monopolistic competition, oligopolies lie closer to monopolies in the spectrum of market structures. A few interdependent firms dominate a market.

Industries are **pure oligopolies** *if firms produce homogeneous outputs.*

The steel and aluminum industries are examples.

Industries are **impure oligopolies** *if firms' outputs are slightly differentiated.*

Tire makers, tobacco firms, and oil companies are impure oligopolists.

A market shared by two firms is certainly an oligopoly, but would 10 or 20 sellers still be considered few? The answer is not clear-cut. What matters is whether a handful of large *interdependent* firms consciously dominate an industry. If firms' decisions anticipate rivals' strategies, the industry is concentrated and oligopolistic.

Conscious interdependence *exists when firms consider their rivals' reactions while adjusting prices, outputs, or product lines.*

Oligopoly markets are dominated by so few firms that each is aware of its rivals' marketing strategies.

Dominance by a Few Firms

Measures of *concentration* are often used to identify oligopolistic industries.

Concentration ratios *are the percentages of domestic sales by the largest four (or eight) domestic companies in an industry.*

Figure 5 provides examples of relatively concentrated industries — automobiles, tires, aircraft, and cigarettes seem highly concentrated. In the aircraft industry, for example, the four largest domestic firms generate 66 percent of total industry sales; the eight top domestic firms account for 86 percent of the industry.

Be wary, however, of relying on concentration ratios alone to identify market power. Stable concentration ratios do not necessarily indicate a lack of competition. First, these ratios consider only U.S. sales by U.S. firms. Imports may offer robust competition. Second, markets containing few firms may be contestable if entry is relatively easy. The international automobile market is an example of an increasingly competitive and contestable industry. Concentration ratios, however, ignore the recent wave of foreign entrants into this market. Nevertheless, industries toward the right in Figure 5 appear to be among the more oligopolistic in the United States.

The Origins of Oligopoly

Some oligopolies started as monopolies, gradually becoming oligopolistic after new firms struggled to become established. Others emerged out of a competitive environment after big firms vanquished or absorbed their rivals. The major causes of oligopoly are mergers and barriers to entry.

Economies of Scale Technical efficiency sometimes requires enormous plants and massive equipment, which can act as major barriers to entry. Economies of scale cause an industry to gravitate into a natural monopoly when only a

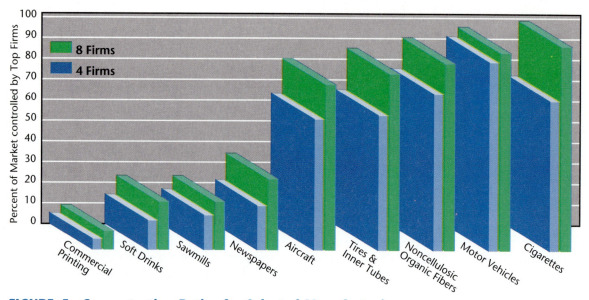

FIGURE 5   Concentration Ratios for Selected Manufacturing Industries, 1987

The shares of sales by the largest four and largest eight firms in an industry indicate little concentration in those industries toward the left side of this figure (e.g., commercial printing, soft drinks) but substantial concentration in those toward the right side (motor vehicles, cigarettes). These numbers must be taken with a grain of salt, however, because only the sales of domestic firms are considered. For example, inclusion of imports would cause a much lower concentration ratio for the automobile industry.

Source: *Statistical Abstract of the United States 1991*.

single firm of considerable size relative to market demand is able to produce at a low cost. An industry tends toward the oligopoly mold if economies of scale are less formidable.

Joe Bain, a pioneer in the study of industrial organization, concluded that the minimum efficient scale of production (*MES*) for copper, typewriters, and tractors required each plant to supply more than 10 percent of these markets. Ten or fewer firms might be expected in these industries. While Bain's study focused on manufacturing economies of scale, in some industries (automobiles, for example), marketing economies of scale may govern the sizes of firms. Bain concluded, however, that overall concentration in American industry was not generally justified by economies of scale.

Studies of efficient plant sizes are important, but technology may change so rapidly that some industry studies are obsolete shortly after they are written. For example, Bain's typewriter study

is now moot because printers hooked up to personal computers have replaced typewriters in most offices.

An offshoot of technological advance in the last century was pressure for ever larger plants (e.g., steel, railroads). Substantial entry barriers may exist if new technology (e.g., robotics) mandates huge operations. Existing firms with established product lines may be able to activate new technologies so rapidly that new firms cannot get a toehold in the industry. It is possible, however, for large amounts of old capital to be an anchor that keeps established firms from keeping pace with upstarts that adopt the latest technology. For example, U.S. steelmakers have had problems in recent decades because most American steel plants are ancient, while their competitors in Japan, Korea, and Germany operate modern equipment in newer facilities.

Recent technological advances have probably been relatively less favorable to huge firms than to smaller ones. For example, cable TV has diluted the oligopolistic power of major networks (ABC, CBS, and NBC), and recent entries in computers have gained on established giants like IBM. Some disadvantages of large firms may have been partially offset by computerization and improved communications, but recent U.S. employment growth has been most rapid among small firms in new industries (see Figure 6). Increasing numbers of people now work at home, being linked to their employers primarily through computer modems, FAX machines, and telephone calls. This trend probably favors small operations over large ones.

Strategic Barriers Strategic barriers may also impede entry into a profitable oligopoly. For example, firms may pool research and development efforts while excluding outsiders, or frequently change models, or conduct excessive advertising. Product differentiation is often a major entry barrier. Extravagant marketing may intimidate potential entrants with tight budgets; trying to combat established competitors' marketing outlays raises the minimum efficient scale of production for new entrants. Alternatively, an oligopoly may market numerous versions of a basic good (e.g., cereals, cigarettes, or over-the-counter drugs) or offer retailers huge discounts for preferential shelf space (Coke and Pepsi), leaving little space in retail outlets for potential rivals.

Regulatory Barriers Another strategy to bar entry occurs when mature industries and their unions lobby to erect legal import quotas and tariff walls against foreign competition. Textiles, apparel, automobiles, and steel are all industries with protection from foreign competition.

Industries often succeed in having laws tailored as hidden entry barriers. This is an international game. For example, mandatory safety

FIGURE 6 Employment by Size of Employer

Employment growth during the 1980s was higher in smaller firms. During the last decade, employment increased by roughly 45 percent in firms with less than 500 employees, and by only 17 percent in firms with greater than 500 employees.

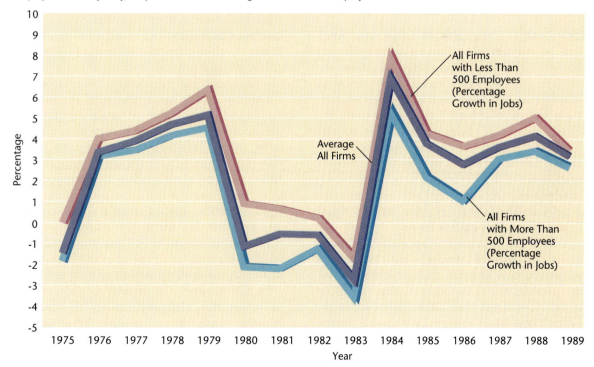

standards make it more costly to ship vehicles between countries. Curiously, some Japanese cars cannot be imported into the United States for reasons of safety, while most American autos must be retooled before export to meet Japanese safety standards. Sort of makes you wonder, doesn't it?

Merger Oligopolies also arise through **merger** — the absorption of one firm by another. The record rates of mergers in the 1980s are discussed in Focus 1. Merger may be a less rocky path for growth than using retained earnings, sales of new stock, or borrowing. A merger that has the added benefit of eliminating a direct competitor is called a **horizontal merger.**

Recent *takeovers* by corporate raiders illustrate two aspects of mergers. Top managers of takeover targets fear for their own job security and for the jobs of other employees. Communities often become embroiled in battles when a target firm provides a town's economic lifeblood. Laws making it harder for firms to close plants and aimed at inhibiting corporate takeovers have recently begun to appear on the landscape.

Conscious Interdependence

When entry is restricted and a few firms dominate an industry, each firm recognizes that any action it takes will be countered by others. For example, Chrysler's extended warranties were quickly matched by all carmakers. Then Chrysler equipped all its cars with air bags in 1989, and other automakers briskly followed suit. Any hit TV show or software program quickly spawns clones. Just as musicians mimic other successful musicians (Will Julio Iglesias soon record a rap album?), any successful competitive technique is rapidly imitated by other firms as they try to expand their own market shares.

Consciousness of rivals' expected reactions to policy changes arises primarily from the fewness of firms in an oligopoly. Success often depends on assessing rivals' responses. Failure to predict rivals' reactions may result in bad news on the bottom line of an oligopolist's annual report. Pressures for predictability often lead oligopolists to cooperate; this cooperation is generally not in the interest of society as a whole. You will see that a stable oligopolistic equilibrium presents a surface appearance quite similar to that of pure or monopolistic competition in the long run; prices are stable and there is no net entry or exit in the industry. This requires each oligopolist to behave predictably so that rivals know what to expect from each other.

Oligopolistic Decision Making

Interactions in extended families (parents, grandparents, aunts, uncles, siblings, cousins, in-laws, etc.) range from cooperation to violence, reflecting the vagaries of the personalities involved and coalitions among family members. Similar interdependence complicates analysis of oligopolies because how firms interact depends on cost structures, the number of competitors, the nature of outputs, and the personalities and perceptions of top managers.

Different models can be used to describe patterns of cooperation and rivalry when a few firms dominate an industry. If firms compete aggressively, their pricing and output may mimic that for competitive firms so that profits are negligible. Consequently, oligopolists often try to cooperate by boosting prices and limiting outputs; this benefits firms at the expense of the general public. Such oligopolistic scheming is generally either *collusive* (formal conspiracies) or *noncollusive* (informal, but consciously cooperative).

One obvious collusive strategy is for oligopolists to try to unite and share both the market and monopoly profits. This is known as forming a *cartel*. Noncollusive pricing may emerge naturally if each firm acts cooperatively because each realizes that others will offset any strategy aimed at enlarging market share and profit. One noncollusive model applies when a dominant firm sets policies that other firms follow without overt agreement. Most of these *price leadership* models leave pricing decisions to the largest firm or to the one with the lowest cost structure.

In this chapter, we investigate only two of many possible oligopoly models. The kinked demand model is noncollusive, while cartels depend on collusion. More complex oligopolistic interactions are described in our next chapter, "Strategic Behavior."

FOCUS 1

The International Market for Corporate Control

The market for corporate control is increasingly global. American firms have owned foreign subsidiaries worth billions of dollars for decades, but during the 1980s, this trend reversed when foreign firms swallowed scores of major U.S. firms in publishing and entertainment, banking, electronics, and resorts. More than 90 percent of the largest U.S. mergers and acquisitions of all time have transpired since 1980, with the total value of the firms absorbed averaging roughly $200 billion annually.

A **merger** involves combining two firms into a larger corporation; an **acquisition** is the purchase of one corporation by another or by a group of investors.

Some mergers are accomplished with the cooperation of the owners and managers of both firms. Others result from changing balances of power among stock owners.

A **takeover** is an acquisition opposed by the current management because it will be replaced.

Supporters of **corporate raiding** (taking over the management of an undervalued corporation by using creative financial techniques to buy a controlling interest in the firm's stock) argue that raiding is simply the process

of competition at work. Opponents charge that takeovers increase concentration and reward managers who focus on short-term performance at the expense of long-term growth.

This merger wave prompted new jargon in the world of corporate finance. Corporate raiding (or "leveraged takeover") follows a formula: A raider sets up a new corporation on paper. Investment bankers package a block of **junk bonds** (risky bonds with low credit ratings) to be issued by the paper corporation once the raider gains control through a stock **tender offer** (an offer to buy a given percent of stock in the target company for a premium price).

The investment bankers then obtain advance commitments from investors (pension funds and other institutional investors) to buy the junk bonds. Once in control, raiders raise cash by selling off pieces of the acquired company. In the words of one investment banker, "We take a minnow, identify a whale, then look to its assets to finance the transaction." Small companies have acquired much larger corporations through this technique. Attractive "whales" (or *cash cows*) are firms that generate massive cash flows, but whose stocks are undervalued by the market. Inept current managers

are commonly identified as the reasons for this undervaluation of stock.

Opposition by the target management is more likely when incumbent management owns less stock. As management's stock holdings rise, the average potential wealth gain to managers increases and is reflected in a greater likelihood of a friendly response, as reflected in Figure 7, which summarizes a study of 429 tender offers.

From the 1970s through 1989, the number of mergers and acquisitions was relatively stable, but an upward trend in their value indicates that giant firms were increasingly "in play," as shown in Figure 8.* Fortunes were made by some specialists in helping raiders identify and capture vulnerable targets. For example, Michael Milken, head of Mergers and Acquisitions for Bear, Stearns (a major brokerage), earned $550 million in commissions in 1987—an all-time record income for any employee.

By the end of 1990, however, two factors combined to squelch most merger activity. The first was a recession that began in 1990. Economic downturns

*"The Market for Corporate Control," Economic Report of the President *1985, Chapter 6.*

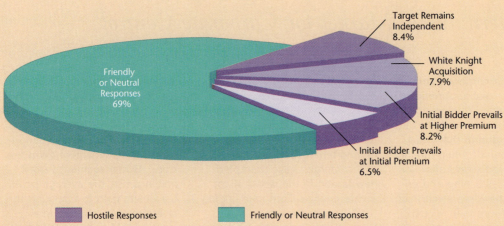

Target Remains
Independent
8.4%

White Knight
Acquisition
7.9%

Initial Bidder Prevails
at Higher Premium
8.2%

Initial Bidder Prevails
at Initial Premium
6.5%

Friendly
or Neutral
Responses
69%

■ Hostile Responses   ■ Friendly or Neutral Responses

FIGURE 7   Target Management Responses to and Outcomes of Takeover Attempts, 1978–1983

Source: *Economic Report of the President 1985*. Based on 429 tender offers compiled by W. T. Grimm and Company. Reprinted by permission of W. T. Grimm and Company.

erode the profit opportunities that are available from mergers during more prosperous periods. The second was the prosecution of a number of Wall Streeters, including Michael Milken, for misuse of inside information. Many of the brokerage firms that had specialized in mergers and acquisitions were forced to lay off thousands of their employees during 1990 and 1991. Whether mergers resume their rapid pace will depend on how quickly this recession turns around and on future public policies towards corporate restructuring.

Public policy toward the activity of raiders ideally depends on whether takeovers benefit the economy. Supporters of takeover activity point to several sources

of gain from mergers and acquisitions: (*a*) Firms in related industries can gain production and distribution economies, (*b*) transfers of technology are facilitated, (*c*) larger companies may produce at lower per-unit costs because of economies of scale, (*d*) national income increases when assets are shifted to higher valued uses, and (*e*) management is improved. The Council of Economic Advisors concluded that "The evidence is strong that takeovers generate aggregate net benefits to the economy."†

Opponents of hostile corporate takeovers argue that corporate

†*W. T. Grimm and Co.,* cited in Economic Report of the President *1985, Chapter 6.*

managers are responsible not only to stockholders but also to other *stakeholders* — including employees, customers, suppliers, and the communities in which the corporation operates. The most vocal opposition is registered by those whose managerial positions are threatened, who commonly try to mask their self-interest by appealing to the idea that social welfare should be a major consideration of American corporations.

Most economists view takeovers as a part of what Joseph Schumpeter labeled capitalism's process of creative destruction. Firms headed by inefficient managers are the ones most commonly targeted for takeovers. The absorbed companies usually

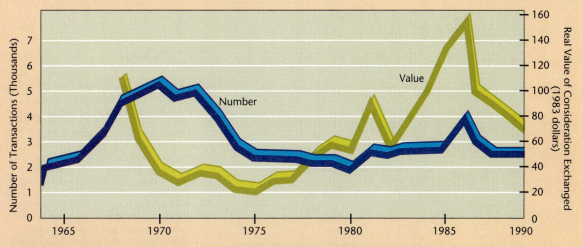

FIGURE 8 Trends in Mergers and Acquisition Activity

Source: *Economic Report of the President 1985*. Earlier data reprinted by permission of W. T. Grimm and Company. The data measure only publicly announced transactions that exceeded $500,000 and which entailed transfers of 10 percent or more of a company's assets or equity. Data for 1986–1990 from *Mergers and Acquisitions*, April, 1991.

grow more profitable when new managers restructure them. This often involves closing unprofitable subsidiaries of overly diversified conglomerates, or selling the subsidiaries if more specialized management can run them better. Some people, however, view laws that permit the breakup of established firms as counterproductive.

Such movies as *Wall Street* and *Pretty Woman* have popularized the idea that takeover artists invariably buy and then dismember firms with assets that have market values in excess of the value of the stock. Firms have, in a sense, become products that are bought and sold by other firms.

Real estate experts know that to sell your house, such cosmetic details as how nicely it is painted or the condition of the flowers in your garden are often more important for its marketability and price than are such fundamental things as how adequately your attic is insulated. Similarly, a glossy paint job and an excellent stereo may cause potential buyers of a used car to overlook a motor that burns a quart of oil every 100 miles. Applying a similar logic to the subsidiaries of firms that intend to sell them means that the actions of such subsidiaries may not conform to the predictions of profit-maximizing models. For example, a firm might be able to boost a

subsidiary's sale price if it neglects costly but desirable research and development (which takes a long time to pay off), and concentrates on shoddy sales practices that boost short-term revenues but alienate customers over the long haul.

Some mergers and acquisitions may operate against the interests of the broader society, but many mergers replace incompetent managers or, by shutting down failing firms in declining industries, help to make the United States more able to compete with aggressive foreign firms who are putting a premium on securing profits through international trade.

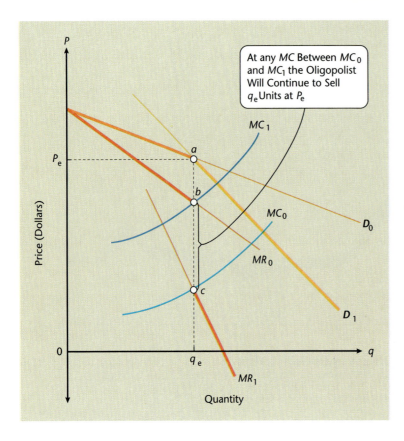

At any MC Between MC_0 and MC_1 the Oligopolist Will Continue to Sell q_e Units at P_e

FIGURE 9   Price Stability and Cost Changes under Kinked Demand Oligopoly

If an oligopolist's competitors are likely to match any price reductions but ignore price increases, then the demand facing each firm is comparatively inelastic with respect to price cuts but is highly elastic in response to price hikes. Only the thicker portions of the demand and marginal revenue curves shown are relevant for such firms. Prices are "sticky" if oligopolistic firms face kinked demand curves. Even if costs change substantially, such firms will not alter their prices because they fear that none of their competitors will follow price hikes, but all will match price cuts.

The Kinked Demand Curve

Prices in highly concentrated industries were once thought to be unresponsive to changes in costs or demands. The kinked demand curve model of oligopoly pricing sought to explain "stickiness" of oligopolistic prices as a natural result of noncollusive behavior.[3]

> *The **kinked demand curve model** assumes that other oligopoly firms maintain current prices if any firm raises its prices, but all firms match any price reductions by any single firm.*

How these assumptions affect pricing strategy is shown in Figure 9. At point *a*, the price is currently P_e, and q_e units of the good are sold by

each firm in this pure oligopoly. Demand curve D_0 represents the highly elastic demand curve facing a firm if other firms ignored its price changes. If the firm were alone in lowering its price, its sales would soar (a movement along D_0 to the right of q_e), but if it were to raise its price and the others did not follow, its sales would plummet (movement along D_0 to the left of q_e). When one firm raises its prices and others do not, consumers will shift to the competitors' products.

If rivals match all price changes, however, demand curve D_1 reflects the firm's less elastic options. If it slashes prices and all other firms do the same, the firm's sales grow only slightly. The firm's sales fall little if both it and its rivals boost prices. Along D_1 the firm loses few sales to other firms because their relative prices are constant. All firms merely gain or lose sales based on the elasticity of the industry's total demand. The respective marginal revenue curves for D_0 and D_1 are labeled MR_0 and MR_1.

3. In his Nobel Prize acceptance address, George Stigler discouraged the use of kinked demand curves because of insufficient empirical support for sticky prices predicted by the model. Nevertheless, the kinked demand curve model is one of the best models for illustrating oligopolistic interdependencies.

This model's assumptions imply that only part of each curve is relevant: Price cuts will be matched by rivals, but price hikes will not. Thus, the demand curve facing a firm is the thicker part of the D_0 curve for outputs less than q_e and the thicker portion of D_1 for outputs above q_e. Matching segments are emphasized similarly for marginal revenue curves. Note that this marginal revenue curve has a gap at output q_e between points b and c, corresponding to the "kink" in demand; hence the name "kinked demand curve."

The importance of this kink and the gap in the marginal revenue curve is shown in Figure 9. Profit maximizers produce where marginal revenue equals marginal cost, so q_e output is sold at price P_e as long as the marginal cost curve stays between MC_0 and MC_1. Thus, this model explains why prices might be sticky in oligopolistic industries even if costs change. Marginal cost can rise from point c to point b without affecting the price.

Kinked demand models seem reasonable, but critics point to some flaws. First, price rigidity may be no more frequent in oligopolies than other industries.[4] Concentrated industries appear to quickly pass along cost increases as they occur. After all, advertising, quality, and new product development may raise costs without significantly expanding market demand. If only one firm's profit is squeezed, it may be forced to maintain its current price. But if profits for all firms in an oligopoly shrink, all might follow a price hike; this yields a new kink at the higher price.

Second, kinked demand models fail to explain (a) why entry does not occur, (b) how oligopoly emerges, (c) how the equilibrium price, P_e, is initially established, or (d) how prices change. These problems have caused the model to be used sparingly by researchers. A major advantage of the kinked demand model is its simplicity in conveying the flavor of strategic business reactions and rivalry.

---

4. This was the finding of George Stigler, reported in "The Kinky Oligopoly Demand Curve and Rigid Prices," *Journal of Political Economy*, October 1947, pp. 432–449.

Cartels

Few Americans knew the term "cartel" before 1973–1974, when OPEC (Organization of Petroleum Exporting Countries), the best known cartel, became a household word.

A **cartel** *is an organization through which members jointly make decisions about prices and production.*

Cartels usually require outright collusion, although in a sufficiently concentrated industry (2 or 3 firms), tacit (unspoken) collusion is possible. Collusive price-fixing for most manufactured products is illegal in the United States, but it is permitted in many international markets.

Cartels operate primarily in natural resource markets, and, at various times, have controlled international markets for such basic materials as copper, tin, bauxite (aluminum ore), diamonds, chrome, phosphate, petroleum, coffee, and bananas. Most successful cartels are coordinated by the governments of major producing countries. Markets were formerly cartelized for sugar, rubber, nitrates, steel, radium, magnesium, and electric lights. Why do cartels seem to come and go? How do cartels set prices and production?

Cartel Requirements A successful cartel requires control over the bulk of output by a small group of cartel members. Cartels cannot maintain high prices if many fringe competitors are not members. A small group is more likely than a large group to agree about pricing and output strategies, because the members of any group have different goals and objectives.

The good must also be fairly homogeneous; numerous differentiated substitutes would require agreements on an extensive array of prices. After a cartel price is established, sales territories or production quotas must be set. Doing this for multiple goods and prices would be a formidable task. Mature technology is also a key for cartel success. If technology advances rapidly, constant changes in costs make it difficult for members to agree on prices. Moreover, the incentive to cheat on a cartel arrangement may be overwhelming if a firm discovers a new way to cut production costs.

Cartelization will be more successful the less elastic the market demand for the good. A cartel can simultaneously raise prices and boost total revenue if its market demand curve is relatively price inelastic. Less elastic demand also lessens problems of excess capacity as prices are increased. Finally, some method is needed to monitor member compliance and prevent cheating.

Cartel Pricing Policies   A cartel's members jointly decide what price to charge and how much to sell. Most cartels try to produce and price as a monopolist would. This **joint-profit maximization** approach is diagrammed in Panel A of Figure 10. The cartel sets price at P_0 and restricts its members' combined output to Q_0. This yields the largest possible total profit (shaded), but a crucial issue remains: sharing the cartel's output and profit among its members.

How to allocate production depends on the product and the market. In some cases, exclusive territories are assigned: Each firm agrees to service only its own territory. Where this approach is unworkable, output quotas may be established for each firm. OPEC uses this approach; every member country agrees to limit its crude oil sales to the quota set by the cartel leadership. These agreements are, however, routinely broken.

Cheating   Each cartel member has strong incentives to cheat. Suppose that you are one of five members of the cartel shown in Panel A of

FIGURE 10   Cartels and the Incentive to Cheat

A cartel is intended to permit firms in an industry to share monopoly profits (Panel A). However, each firm can increase its own profits by offering secret price concessions to other firms' customers. Thus, there is a powerful incentive for cartel members to cheat, and cartels tend to be unstable. When governments help in establishing or perpetuating cartels, however, any cheating is easier to control, so moderately stable cartels may result. Note that Panel B represents an individual member; output (q_0) is a fraction of total output (Q_0), a fact reflected by the scales on the x axes. Since we imply that only one member is cheating, in Panel A, $0q_0 + Q_0Q_1$ is equal to $0q_1$ in Panel B.

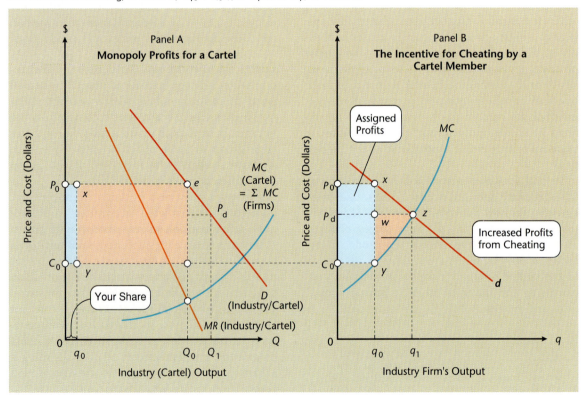

Figure 10 and are currently selling your equal share ($q_0 = Q_0/5$) of the total output Q_0 at the cartel price P_0. Your firm's marginal cost is shown in Panel B of Figure 10. At q_0 output, your profits equal $C_0 P_0 xy$ in Panel B, which also equals $C_0 P_0 xy$ in Panel A after adjusting for differences in scale between Panels A and B ($q_0 = Q_0/5$).

If you persuade your competitors to maintain the cartel price (P_0) but secretly offer a discounted price P_d to selected customers, your profits will grow from (a) pirating some of their customers and (b) servicing some of the demand that is unmet at this higher cartel price. The marginal revenue to you from cheating exceeds your marginal cost. Your profits will rise because (a) you are not giving price cuts to your assigned customers, (b) your competitors do not give price cuts to the customers they retain, and (c) you can sell to more buyers — the customers who will not buy at a cartel price of P_0, but who are willing to pay P_d for $Q_1 - Q_0$ amounts of output. Your profits will rise by the area ywz in Panel B, which is the difference between your marginal cost of producing extra output $q_1 - q_0$ and the price P_d you receive for each extra unit of production.

Instability Cheating on a cartel agreement can be profitable, but only if it is undetected. Cartels collapse if widespread cheating is uncovered; most members will cut prices and behave in a fairly competitive fashion, with the result that the profits that originally motivated formation of the cartel vanish. The fact that undetected cheating offers the prospect of great profits is one of the greatest threats to the stability of a cartel. Is cheating likely to go unnoticed? Nobel Prize–winning economist George Stigler has noted that:

The detection of secret price-cutting will of course be as difficult as interested people can make it. The price cutter will certainly protest his innocence, or, if this would tax credulity beyond its taxable capacity, blame a disobedient subordinate. The price cut will often take the indirect form of modifying some nonprice dimension of the transaction. The customer may, and often will,

divulge price reductions, in order to have them matched by others, but he will learn from experience if each disclosure is followed by the withdrawal of the lower price offer. Indeed the buyer will frequently fabricate wholly fictitious price offers to test the rivals. Policing the collusion sounds very much like the subtle and complex problem presented in a good detective story.[5]

Cheating is only one hazard to cartel stability. There are incentives to try to retain customer loyalty by granting price concessions where sales to individual buyers are large and infrequent. Huge economies of scale and high fixed costs may create irresistible pressure to slash prices during periods of slack demand so that overhead costs can be spread across larger output and sales. For example, cracks in OPEC's effectiveness appeared during the international recession of 1981–1983; worldwide consumption shrank, and an oil glut emerged. OPEC members routinely exceeded their quotas, offering crude oil at big discounts below the official $34-per-barrel price.

Perhaps the greatest threat to a cartel is that high prices and profits will attract new competitors or spur development of substitutes for the cartel's products. From World War II into the 1970s, for example, the Brazilian government restricted coffee exports to bolster its price. The result? Brazilian coffee lost much of its share of the world market when coffee plantations in Africa and Central America were started by profit seekers.

Profits in many industries would soar if competitors were free to collude about prices, enforce output quotas or territories, and bar the entry of potential rivals. Consequently, history is rich with attempts at cartelization that misfired because of cheating, inability to deter entry, or government prosecution. All cartels that have been successful for long have depended on laws, regulations, and intergovernmental cooperation to prevent cheating and deter entry. (It seems almost an economic law that only government-sanctioned cartels last more than a few months.)

---

5. George J. Stigler, *The Organization of Industry* (Homewood, IL: Richard D. Irwin, Inc., 1968), p. 44.

FOCUS 2

The Rise and Fall of OPEC

Crude oil prices ranged between $1.80 and $4.00 per barrel from World War II until the 1970s, while gasoline ranged from $0.22 to $0.35 per gallon, including taxes. The Organization of Petroleum Exporting Countries (OPEC), formed in the 1960s, was a sleeping giant that exercised little economic clout until 1974–1975. Figure 11 shows that when this giant cartel finally awoke, it did so with a vengeance.

During 1974–1975 alone, OPEC raised the price of crude oil from $4 to $10 per barrel. Output quotas were assigned to OPEC members, and with only limited cheating, these production limits were honored for a brief period. Price hikes continued, with a barrel of oil hitting the $20 mark by 1977, $30 in 1980, and finally peaking at an official price of $34 per barrel in 1982–1983. By 1987, however,

the spot price of oil had fallen about $10 per barrel, and gasoline had fallen from its high of $1.45 in 1981 to around $0.70 per gallon. After adjusting for inflation, the real prices of petroleum products were close to pre-OPEC levels. What happened?

Part of the answer is the demand side. The long-term growth of world oil consumption dropped sharply throughout this era. Most industrialized nations are oil importers, and skyrocketing oil prices slowed the rate of economic growth and precipitated high unemployment and substantial inflation in much of the world from 1974 to 1983. Growth in the demand for oil also shriveled because oil's high price stimulated energy conservation: More insulation was put into private residences, office buildings, and manufacturing facilities; automobiles and

airplanes were modified to achieve greater fuel efficiency; and industry adopted less energy-intensive technology.

The other key to the collapse of OPEC's high prices came from the supply side. The late 1970s were an era of feverish exploration for new sources of energy. Vast pools of oil were developed in such areas as Mexico, Alaska, and in the North Sea. Coupled with the decline in world energy demand, these swelling supplies of non-OPEC members caused OPEC to boost output quotas because member countries relied heavily on oil exports for their national income.

Cheating by OPEC members who exceeded their assigned quotas was relatively minor in the 1970s, but so many members were violating the OPEC agreements that by 1984 the spot price of oil was $4 to $8 below the official $34 price. Oil

The history of OPEC (outlined in Focus 2) and cartels in diamonds, coffee, and bananas are evidence that short-run success is possible. Major reasons for OPEC's shakiness in the 1980s (and Iraq's 1990 invasion of Kuwait) were rampant cheating by OPEC members and widespread discoveries of oil fields not controlled by OPEC.

Most cartels violate our antitrust laws, but

these laws largely exempt agricultural cooperatives, athletic groups, labor unions, such professional bodies as the American Medical Association, and export associations. Farmer organizations, the AFL-CIO, the AMA, and similar cartels all try to restrict output and hold prices up, primarily by limiting entry. The National Collegiate Athletic Association (NCAA) is

FIGURE 11 Oil and Gas Prices on a Roller Coaster

OPEC drove up the prices of oil and gasoline substantially from 1974 to 1981. By 1986, however, conservation, the development of non-OPEC sources of energy, and the growth of cheating on limits to production by OPEC members appeared to have doomed the success of this oil cartel.

Source: *Statistical Abstract of the United States 1991* and *Economic Report of the President 1991*.

flooded the world market, and the price plummeted. Although OPEC had enjoyed substantial success for almost a decade, the growth of external supplies and cheating had seriously undermined the OPEC cartel by 1986. Whether these forces have been fatal to the long-term effectiveness of the OPEC cartel remains to be seen.

OPEC drove up the prices of oil and gasoline substantially during 1974–1981. By 1986, however, conservation, the development of non-OPEC sources of energy, and the growth of cheating on limits to production by OPEC members appeared to have doomed the success of this oil cartel.

Source: U.S. Department of Commerce, Bureau of the Census, Statistical Abstract of the United States 1991, and Economic Report of the President 1991.

a legal buyers' cartel that prohibits paying workers (college athletes) more than room, board, and tuition. But every year, several schools are penalized by the NCAA for cartel violations.

Successful collusion requires a stable environment, but business conditions are unlikely to be stable. When products are significantly differentiated, or resource costs are volatile, or demands are fickle, or entry is easy, or competitors are numerous, or technology advances rapidly, or policing a cartel agreement is excessively costly, then the quiet cooperation that oligopolists would like may be replaced by strategic behavior as intense as championship chess and as hostile as war.

Evaluating Oligopoly

How do oligopolies compare with more competitive industries? Firms in oligopolistic industries have considerable market power, yielding economic inefficiency similar to that described for monopoly. In equilibrium, the marginal social benefit (price) of their products exceeds the marginal social cost. Compared with purely or even monopolistically competitive industries, output will tend to be lower, and at higher prices to consumers.

If oligopoly arises from economies of scale, however, it is possible that consumers pay lower prices than they would were the market more competitive. Furthermore, if research and development (R&D) leading to technological change requires massive outlays, small competitive firms may be unable to finance adequate innovation. Some economists suggest that society gains over the long run when short-run profits reaped by oligopolistic firms are plowed back into the development and innovation of newer and better products.

Evidence on the effects of oligopolies is mixed. Economies of scale are clearly responsible for the oligopolistic nature of some industries. In other instances, however, satisfactory economies of scale can be realized by smaller firms, and oligopoly is sustained by legal or strategic entry barriers. Finally, the evidence does not support the idea that large firms are especially responsible for new inventions and technological advances in our economy. If anything, it appears that the desire for increased market power has been the driving force behind the creation of most oligopolies.

In the next chapter, we investigate in more depth alternative strategies that firms may follow when they operate in interdependent industries.

Chapter Review: Key Points

1. Most U.S. markets fit neither the purely competitive nor the monopoly molds. Most industries are *monopolistically competitive* or *oligopolistic*.

2. *Monopolistic competition* occurs when entry into an industry is easy and there are large numbers of suppliers of slightly differentiated products. Demands for a pure competitor's products are perfectly elastic (horizontal at the market price), but the demands facing monopolistic competitors are negatively sloped but still highly elastic.

3. *Product differentiation* refers to differences that consumers perceive between close substitutes, which can be real or imagined. These perceptions are created by such things as advertising and promotion and/or by differences in the actual goods. Product differentiation is intended to expand the demand for a firm's output and to make demand less elastic.

4. Monopolistically competitive firms produce and sell levels of output that equate marginal revenue and marginal cost. The price is then determined by demand. This is similar to pure monopoly, but the level of short-run profits derived from market power is generally lower, given that numerous other firms sell close substitutes.

5. Entry is relatively easy in monopolistic competition, so accounting profits fall to normal levels (zero economic profits) in the long run. However, equilibrium output will be less and prices will be higher under monopolistic competition than in purely competitive markets. The *excess capacity theorem* refers to the fact that, unless they price discriminate, monopolistic competitors never operate at minimal average costs. Higher prices and lower levels of output are the costs of product differentiation.

6. An *oligopoly* is an industry comprised of a few sellers who recognize their mutual interdependence. Competitive strategies by one firm in the industry will normally be countered by the other sellers.

7. Economies of scale are among the causes of oligopolies. Some goods require substantial plant and equipment, so efficient production requires servicing a considerable por-

tion of total industry demand. Mergers also facilitate the creation of oligopolies by joining competitors into single firms. Finally, oligopolies may exist because of other types of entry barriers that deter new firms from entering the industry.

8. There are numerous oligopoly models, but they break down into two major categories: *collusive* and *noncollusive*. The noncollusive *kinked demand curve model* assumes that if one firm raises its prices, other firms will ignore the increase, while other firms in the industry will match any price cuts. The result is a demand curve for the firm that is kinked at the current equilibrium price. This irregularity leads to a discontinuity (gap) in the marginal revenue curve. Consequently, changes in costs may not lead to changes in prices. This theory forecasts "sticky" prices in oligopolistic industries, but price stickiness is not confirmed empirically. Kinked demand curve models also fail to explain how the original equilibrium price is established, how prices change, or how entry by new rivals is deterred.

9. A *cartel* is an organization established to facilitate collusion by firms in an industry. It sets price and output ceilings for all its members. Cartels must be concentrated in the hands of a few firms that control significant proportions of an industry's output. The product needs to be reasonably homogeneous because agreements regarding heterogeneous products would be complex and difficult to enforce.

10. Cartels try to *maximize joint profits* and then allocate territories or industry output quotas. The stability of any cartel is threatened by the profits potentially available through undetected price cuts, or "cheating," by potential new entrants who seek to share in profits, and by adverse legal action. Collusion is illegal in most markets in the United States.

11. Industry output will be less and prices will be higher under oligopoly than in pure or monopolistic competition. Some economists argue that monopoly profits for large firms are necessary to finance extensive research and development activities and facilitate technological advance. The evidence does not confirm this hypothesis.

Key Concepts

Ensure that you can define these terms before proceeding.

oligopoly
monopolistic competition
product differentiation
conscious interdependence
merger
kinked demand curve
cartels
joint-profit maximization

Problems and Questions

1. Are the following examples of persuasive or informative advertising?
   a. Newspaper want ads.
   b. "Coke's the one."
   c. "Merrill Lynch is 'bullish' on America."
   d. "Del Monte now offers more than twenty Mexican food products."
   e. "Harmony Homes—spacious mountain view living for as little as $59,950."
   f. "Allstate—the 'good hands' people."
   g. Coupons for new products in grocery store advertisements.
   h. "You could drive to the moon and back before the gas you'd save in a Toyota would be worth more than the money you'd save buying a Pontiac."
   i. "Buy a new Dodge before May 1 and get a $500 rebate from Chrysler."
   j. "Use Hoarse, the cough medicine more doctors recommend."

2. What differentiates monopolistic competition from pure competition? Name five industries that are monopolistically competitive.

3–5. Calculate concentration ratios for the four largest (CR_4) and eight largest (CR_8) firms in the following industries. Rank these industries from most to least concentrated. Are these CRs consistent?

3. The plate glass industry has annual sales of $4 billion. The ten largest glass producers had 1991 sales (in millions of dollars) equal to: Able = $725, Baker = $380, Charlie = $145, Darwin = $710, Eden = $68,

Foxtrot = $110, Gulf = $350, Hurricane = $911, India = $168, and Joker = $319.

4. Annual pencil sales are $600 million, shared (in millions of dollars) among all pencil makers as follows: Smudge = $13, Taxman = $243, Utmost = $122, Vexation = $114, Wax = $78, Xenon = $12, and Zebra = $18.

5. Annual sales of printing equipment total $7 billion, shared (in millions of dollars) as follows: 15 small specialty firms average $40, Korabi = $1,215, Lommox = $642, Mongo = $222, Nota = $98, Oryx = $789, Pogo = $2,130, Quzer = $166, Rastafa = $87, and 291 tiny firms split the remaining sales.

6. Suppose all advertising was informational and all product differentiation was "real" in a particular monopolistically competitive industry. Would technical or allocative inefficiencies continue to exist in long-run equilibrium?

7. How do price takers and price makers differ? Is the difference in the market power held by IBM and the corner grocer more quantitative than qualitative? What are the qualitative differences between these firms?

8. What ensures that firms in monopolistically competitive industries will not earn economic profits in the long run? What prevents the same result in oligopoly markets?

9. Until the 1960s, IBM had a stranglehold in the computer industry, and Xerox had a near monopoly in copying equipment. What has happened in these markets since then?

10. The term "invention" covers the research and development of a product or technique. "Innovation" means implementing an invention into production. Can you cite three major inventions made by organizations that were small at the time? Three major innovations by firms with oligopoly power?

11. One oligopoly model suggests that firms will attempt to capture as large a market share as possible by locating in the center of the market. This model suggests that people will not be served if they want substantially different products than the majority of people want. According to the developer of this model, Harold Hotelling, this accounts for such things as parallel programming by television networks, the middle-of-the-road images sought by politicians, the homogeneity of apple cider, the similarities between Protestant churches, and the phenomenon of four gas stations at the corners of busy intersections, among other things. How do you think his view that there is too little product differentiation stacks up against the view that monopolistic competition causes too much artificial product differentiation?

12. Some economists assert that oligopolistic industries are vulnerable to "hit-and-run" tactics if price and profits get too high. Other large firms can enter, earn short-run economic profits, and then leave if competition gets too severe. What actions can oligopolists take to reduce the likelihood of such threats? Would these activities lead to lower economic profits? Greater efficiency from oligopolies?

13. Standard models predict that if firms wield market power, price will exceed marginal cost and that there will therefore be inefficiency in equilibrium. These models assume that every good has only a single price, but the reality is that quantity discounts, coupons, and other marketing promotions create tremendous disparities in prices at all times. Does the pervasiveness of price discrimination counter much of the argument that monopolistically competitive or oligopolistic markets are inherently inefficient? Why or why not?

14. The U.S. automobile industry has always been considered an oligopoly. Is it still an oligopoly? What role does the increasing internationalization of our economy play in the way we classify industries? Does this give the monopolistically competitive structure a new role to play in economic analysis?

15. When trying to classify an industry as either monopolistically competitive or oligopolistic, when does the *many* of monopolistic competition become the *few* of oligopoly? Can you think of some objective way to measure this?

16. Name some of the conditions that would make it easier for a cartel to be successful. How likely are these conditions to be met? How might the firms comprising an oligopoly coordinate their activities without forming an illegal cartel?

CHAPTER

Strategic Behavior

Business leaders and, indeed, people in general, differ greatly in what they are able to accomplish with given amounts of resources. Consequently, small armies led by brilliant military strategists sometimes defeat large armies commanded by unimaginative generals. Skilled poker players may be consistent winners even if, on average, they are dealt poor cards, while mediocre players usually walk away from a game as losers despite average or better cards. And one firm may fail miserably, while an apparently similar firm prospers. Luck is sometimes a decisive factor, but even more frequently, correctly forecasting the behavior of your friends or rivals and then developing an effective strategy is the key to success or failure.

> **Strategic behavior** *entails ascertaining what other people are likely to do in a specific situation and then following tactics that maximize your gain or minimize any harm to you.*

The traditional approach for analyzing product markets described in the preceding three chapters provides a general recipe for analyzing an industry, but it largely ignores strategic behavior. This chapter describes recent developments in economic theory that allow us to explicitly take into account some of these strategic considerations.

The traditional approach appears deceptively simple. First, ascertain the type of environment in which a firm operates. (Is it purely competitive, purely monopolistic, monopolistically competitive, or oligopolistic?) This *market structure* almost rigidly determines each firm's *conduct* (output decisions and pricing behavior), which yields an industry's overall *performance* (e.g., its efficiency and profitability). This approach, termed the **structure-conduct-performance paradigm** (sometimes shortened to **S-C-P theory**), is graphed in Figure 1. A brief review of this approach is our first task in this chapter.

Three related recent challenges to the S-C-P model shape the organization of the rest of this chapter. Advocates of the *new industrial organization* charge that the S-C-P approach overemphasizes the number of active firms in an industry, while it neglects (*a*) how business interactions can be better modeled with modern *game theory*, (*b*) how differences in the quality of *information* among economic transactors shape business decisions and market structures, and (*c*) how *business strategies* often develop as imaginative responses to the specifics of different competitive environments. Before we investigate insights arising from these three perspectives, we will review some central results of the traditional approach.

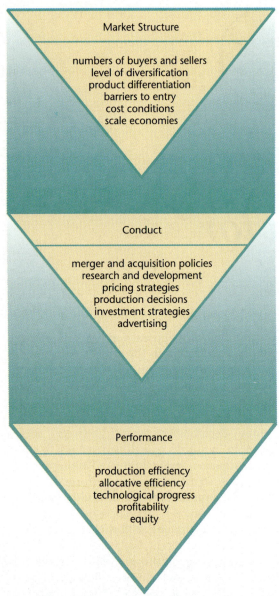

Market Structure

numbers of buyers and sellers
level of diversification
product differentiation
barriers to entry
cost conditions
scale economies

Conduct

merger and acquisition policies
research and development
pricing strategies
production decisions
investment strategies
advertising

Performance

production efficiency
allocative efficiency
technological progress
profitability
equity

FIGURE 1   The Structure-Conduct-Performance (S-C-P) Paradigm

This traditional *structure-conduct-performance* model of industrial organization is increasingly challenged by analysts who believe that it ignores (*a*) too many factors influencing behavior that are specific to an industry or its dominant firms, and (*b*) asymmetries of information that put transactors on different negotiating stances than would occur if all information was shared. This S-C-P approach is also indicted for overemphasis on the number of firms in an industry and inadequate attention to dynamic aspects of competition, including the ease of entry and exit.

Structure-Conduct-Performance[1]

Traditional S-C-P theory dictates three steps in analyzing an industry. First, it emphasizes properly categorizing an industry's market structure according to (*a*) the number of active competitors, (*b*) barriers to entry and exit, and (*c*) the extent of product standardization. Second, conventional models conclude that certain pricing and output decisions (conduct) predictably arise from market power or its absence. (Sparse competition, barriers to entry, or product heterogeneity create market power.) Finally, this theory suggests that the equilibrium price of any imperfectly competitive firm invariably exceeds marginal social cost; too little of the good is produced, creating allocative and productive inefficiencies.

Movement along the continuum of market structures from monopoly toward pure competition appears to yield more efficient resource allocations. Consequently, the structure-conduct-performance approach suggests that government policy to cure problems of industrial organization is straightforward—outlaw monopolies or near monopolies where possible, while tightly regulating market power that arises from economy of scale. (Our chapters on "Antitrust" and "Regulation" show that there are major practical problems with this conclusion even when these policies seem appropriate.)

The S-C-P paradigm may excessively focus on an industry's current characteristics, e.g., numbers of buyers and sellers, economies of scale, and the rate of technological advance. It concludes that collusion and profit rates are tightly linked to the number of firms in the industry. Economists undertook study after study correlating profit and concentration within an industry, and many then attributed any high profits to excessive concentration.

This approach caused most economists to ignore unique features of industries. Robert Solow, a Nobel Prize winner, has noted that "You can't

1. The structure-conduct-performance paradigm is outlined by R. E. Caves, one of its advocates, in *American Industry: Structure, Conduct, and Performance*, 2/ed. (Englewood Cliffs, NJ: Prentice-Hall, 1967), 16.

understand the history of the tire industry without recognizing that Harvey Firestone was a guy who cut prices merely to shake up the competition."[2] Many economists now argue that understanding the pressures in any industry requires focused study on the specifics of that industry.

Vigorous development increasingly requires a country to have some industries that compete effectively in world markets. The S-C-P approach diverted attention from vital questions that determine economic progress. These questions, in the words of Michael Porter,[3] include: "How can we explain why Germany is the home base for so many of the world's leading makers of printing presses, luxury cars, and chemicals? Why is tiny Switzerland the home base for international leaders in pharmaceuticals, chocolate, and trading? Why are leaders in heavy trucks and mining equipment based in Sweden? Why has America produced the preeminent international competitors in personal computers, software, credit cards, and movies? Why are Italian firms so strong in ceramic tiles, ski boots, packaging machinery, and factory automation equipment? What makes Japanese firms so dominant in consumer electronics, cameras, robotics, and facsimile machines?"

Studies drawn from S-C-P theory are relatively sterile in addressing such issues as the growth or decline of industries. Excessive concentration can clearly yield high profits, but so can such factors as rapid technological innovation, superior products, or unusually efficient managers. In the past two decades, economists have reexamined S-C-P assumptions, focusing attention instead on the specifics of strategic behavior within particular industries. This approach to studying industrial behavior is central to a school of thought whose advocates call it the *new industrial organization.*[4]

The New Industrial Organization

The new industrial organization shares with the earlier S-C-P approach a search for generalizations from one industry that apply to others. Although the conclusions of this new approach often differ from those of the earlier approach, many conclusions still overlap. Advocates of the new industrial organization[5] stress that: (*a*) a single firm's actions may affect industrial concentration, (*b*) dynamic decisions (decisions made over time) are invariably rational, and (*c*) differential information shapes firm behavior and market structure.

This first point leads to the idea that, either individually or jointly, firms often pursue strategies to bar entry into their industry; potential competition often determines incumbent firms' current pricing and output policies. For example, banks located close to each other may unite to oppose the chartering of a new bank, citing the low interest rates they charge, lack of "need" for another bank, their willingness and ability to accommodate all "creditworthy" applicants for loans, and their service to the community.

The second point is that firms, like all economic agents, make sequential rational decisions over time. What you will do in a particular situation depends on what you learned from experience after making decisions in similar situations. For example, if you have noted that car prices typically fall just before new models arrive at your local dealer in December, you may not buy in November, electing to wait for the end-of-year sales. Similarly, firms consider the previous reactions of their rivals when planning a business strategy. Dynamic game theory models of rational decisions extend the boundaries of earlier theory. We examine some of these conclusions in a moment and introduce several simple game theory models to give you a flavor of how it addresses some complex questions.

2. Quoted in "Truth in Teaching Microeconomics," a paper by Reuven Brenner presented at a conference at Middlebury College, 1989.

3. Michael E. Porter, *The Competitive Advantage of Nations* (New York: The Free Press, 1990).

4. Much of this revolution in industrial organization analysis derives from Thomas Shelling, *The Strategy of Conflict* (Cambridge, MA: Harvard University Press, 1960).

5. Bonanno, G. and Brandolini, D., *Industrial Structure in the New Industrial Economics* (Oxford, U.K.: Clarendon Press, 1990). See also Alexis Jacquemin, *The New Industrial Organization: Market Forces and Strategic Behavior* (Cambridge, MA: The MIT Press, 1987).

The third point recognizes that bargaining parties may have different information about potential transactions that often affect incentives and decisions. For example, a firm's manager may know that a huge layoff is scheduled as soon as a contract is completed, but try to keep workers from looking for other jobs through false reassurances that the firm has a pending new contract to be fulfilled. This type of *knowledge asymmetry* is common. Traditional models that treat information as free and perfect, or which assume that all transactors share the same information base, typically yield different conclusions than models recognizing asymmetric information.

Our next step is to describe game theory and look at a simple *prisoners' dilemma* model where both players move simultaneously. We then introduce a dynamic "product standards" game that illustrates the frequent benefits of being able to move first.

Game Theory

The absence of overt or tacit collusion leads to rivalrous behavior that business leaders think of as competition. Pure competition is an impersonal process in which firms adjust outputs to a market determined price. Oligopolists who compete in a noncooperative fashion have more weapons at their disposal, including adjustments of prices, outputs, product lines and capacity, advertising, and their rates of technological innovation. This diversity of possible strategies among oligopolists led to the development of game theory in 1944 by the mathematician John von Neumann and the economist Oskar Morgenstern.

Game theory *is the study of strategic interactions among interdependent decision makers.*

Game theory has been extended beyond oligopolistic behavior and is now applied to such areas as poker, courtship, athletic competition, collective bargaining, and national defense. A **game** requires pairing the costs and benefits of all possible strategies adopted by one **player** (participant) with all possible strategies adopted by an opponent. The **payoff** to each player depends on the strategies of other players, but players can select only their own strategy, not the strategies of other players. Then each set of possible outcomes is analyzed to ascertain an equilibrium, which occurs when every player optimizes, after adjusting for the likely strategies of other players.

Types of Games

Winners' gains exactly offset losses to losers in such **zero-sum games** as poker. Most examples of game theory in economics are **non-zero-sum games**. Gains typically exceed losses in **positive-sum games**; exchange according to comparative advantage is an example. Violence is generally a **negative-sum game**; victims of a mugging may suffer bodily damage in addition to monetary loss, while the mugger only gains the money. Net gains may be either positive or negative in some non-zero-sum games, depending on the strategies of the players. For example, all firms in a market can profit if all charge the same high price, but if all charge a low price, all their profits are low.

Prisoners' Dilemma

A classic noncooperative game known as the *prisoners' dilemma* is often applied to cases of business competition, and helps explain why cartel arrangements break down. Suppose that two armed robbers (Able and Charley) are jailed separately and cannot communicate. Each is told that if neither confesses, both will serve a year in prison. If only one confesses and helps to convict the other, the squealer will go free while the silent party will serve 10 years. If both confess, however, both will be sentenced to 4-year terms.

Figure 2 shows a *payoff matrix* describing each robber's options and payoffs. For example, if both hold out (don't confess), each spends a year in jail $(-1, -1)$. Similarly, their terms are for 4 years $(-4, -4)$ if both confess. What should each player do?

Equilibrium in this prisoners' dilemma occurs if both players follow their dominant strategies. A strategy is dominant if, no matter what strategy your opponents select, your payoff is maximized (or a negative payoff is minimized).

		Charley	
		Hold out	Confess
Able	Hold out	-1, -1	-10, 0
	Confess	0, -10	**-4, -4**

Sentences of Able, Charley

FIGURE 2   A Payoff Matrix for the Prisoners' Dilemma

In this game, Able and Charley cannot communicate and face these payoffs. If one party confesses and the other does not, the confessor goes free and the other party spends 10 years in jail. If both are silent, they both go to jail for 1 year; if both confess, they each spend 4 years behind bars. The result is that both will confess and spend 4 years in jail—no other choice is a dominant strategy for either player. The dilemma results from the payoffs shown and the fact that they cannot communicate. In this case, *confess-confess* is a Nash equilibrium because "confess" is each player's dominant strategy.

*A **dominant strategy** is a player's best response to any strategy other players might pick.*

Consider Able's dominant strategy. No matter which strategy Charley picks, Able gains by confessing, because he goes free if Charley holds out (compared to a year in jail if he, Able, holds out), while saving 6 years if Charley confesses (10 years − 4 years). In fact, both Able and Charley have dominant strategies—confess. Consequently, *confess-confess* is a **dominant strategy equilibrium,** because it is each player's dominant strategy. The dilemma facing prisoners is that they seem unable to cooperate so that each gets the shorter sentence—one year each in the case of Able and Charley. Refuting the "honor among thieves" stereotype, almost all prisoners succumb (as at the conclusion of the movie *Goodfellas*) and "rat" on their colleagues.

How does the prisoners' dilemma apply to oligopoly? Consider a cartel that sets output ceilings for each member. Every member will enjoy

reasonable profit if no firm cheats by exceeding its quota, but a lone cheater will gain even more profit. If cheating is rampant (and it will be if players follow dominant strategies), all members' profits suffer. The power of the prisoners' dilemma game is reflected in the collapse of OPEC. The dilemma OPEC members faced ultimately brought down energy prices. The prisoners' dilemma model also applies in such areas as bids at an auction, the nuclear arms race, and strikes by unions when collective bargaining breaks down.

Cooperation in Game Theory   One obvious question is, "Why don't both prisoners agree not to confess? Then, each spends only a year in jail." Since one robber could potentially go free by confessing when the other doesn't, whether communication beforehand would matter would depend on whether agreements to hold out are binding. Although both might agree not to rat on the other, both eventually confess unless each can enforce their agreement on the other. If, however, agreements are binding, the results of the game differ.

Cooperative games permit players to make binding agreements, and players may form coalitions. **Noncooperative games** *permit neither binding commitments nor coalitions.*

The prisoners' dilemma makes it clear that binding commitments change a game's equilibrium by changing the payoff matrix. For example, if Charley would murder Able if Able confessed and Able knows it, then Able's costs of confessing rise dramatically. This changes the payoffs, so the game is now different. How can players ensure that commitments are binding? Violence is a possibility, but agreements may also be made binding through such mechanisms as legally enforceable contracts, government regulations, or side payments (bribes) from one party to another.

Examples of cooperative games include (a) international trade, (b) collective bargaining, in which firms and unions bargain over employment conditions, and (c) plea bargaining between prosecutors and defense attorneys. Cooperative games break down, however, if a party can gain by violating what was supposed to be a binding agreement. The prisoners' dilemma, hostile corporate takeovers, or pure competition are all examples of noncooperative games.

Moving First

The sequence of moves is unimportant in a simple prisoners' dilemma. No matter which prisoner chooses first, Able always confesses because he knows that if he is silent, he will spend 10 years in jail if Charley follows dominant strategy, rather than 4 years if he (Able) confesses. But the sequence of moves is important in many games. For example, a chess player who starts with the white pieces has the first move — an advantage over an equally talented player who uses the black pieces.

Consider the case of IBM and Compaq in Figure 3. Both manufacturers must select either small (3.5") or large (5.25") disk drives as standard for their own computers, and both gain by using the same sizes. Their payoffs illustrate why making the initial decision or *first move* can be highly profitable for firms. If IBM (assume it goes first) installs 3.5" disk drives, so will Compaq. If Compaq selected first, IBM would install large drives to maximize its profit (payoff). The first firm to introduce its standard clearly sets the industry standard. Each of these equilibria is also an example of a Nash equilibrium.[6]

> A **Nash equilibrium** *is a strategy combination where no player has a net incentive to change unless other players change.*

In the final equilibrium, either both will use 3.5" or both will use 5.25" drives; each firm will avoid losses by sticking with its now profitable strategy. In the prisoners' dilemma, there was only one Nash equilibrium (confess-confess), but there are two in this case. The final equilibrium turns on which player moves first. Many games have multiple Nash equilibria, and game theorists have developed sophisticated decision rules

Payoffs to (Compaq, IBM)

FIGURE 3   The First Mover Advantage
The ability to set industry standards for disk drives depends on the payoffs and the ability to move first. Both manufacturers gain if they select the same size drives for their computers. If IBM moves first it will select small drives, while Compaq will select large if it can move first. Both *small-small* and *large-large* are Nash equilibria — neither firm has an incentive to change after one equilibrium (set of strategies) has been selected. In this game, the outcome depends on which firm moves first.

(beyond the scope of our inquiry) to determine which outcomes are most likely.

Dynamic Games

Real life games are seldom one-shot events like the prisoners' dilemma, but involve a sequence of choices over time. Consider the prisoners' dilemma repeated for a number of periods. How can we determine what would be a player's best set of choices over time?[7]

Both Able and Charley would like to cooperate and be silent, but without the ability to enforce agreements, both would ultimately confess. Both also know that in the last repetition of the game, both confessed, so each might as well confess in the next to last period, and so on, until both confess in round one! Thus, both Able and Charley will serve $4 \times n$ (the number of periods in the game) years in jail.

---

6. This section is based on Eric Rasmusen, *Games and Information: An Introduction to Game Theory* (Oxford, U.K.: Basil Blackwell, 1989).

7. We ignore the effect of time on the value of outcomes — a discount rate of zero is assumed. This simplification seldom affects the outcomes of games.

Dynamic (repeated) games lead to more sophisticated strategies than do one-shot games. These more sophisticated strategies can result in higher overall payoffs over time (or less jail time in the prisoners' dilemma). Two possibilities for infinitely repeated games are a *grim* strategy and *tit for tat*.

Grim Strategy   The opposite of being first is to wait for an opponent's first move. Although most boxing trainers urge their boxers to "be first," some boxers are natural counterpunchers who wait until their opponents make the first move. Similarly, many people may try to gather information in uncertain situations by letting the opponent move first. For example, people who are negotiating with a used car dealer often gain by refusing to answer the salesperson's "How much are you willing to pay for this car?" — insisting instead that the dealership state a "rock-bottom price" as a starting point for haggling.

Following a noncommittal policy is known as a grim strategy.

> A **grim strategy** *entails refusal to commit to a position until the other player commits to a position.*

Since some move is required in the first round, a prisoner following a grim strategy will begin in a "cooperative" (silent) mode. Prisoners who stick to grim strategies remain silent until the other person confesses but then confess in each subsequent round. If both steadfastly follow grim strategies, both receive minimum sentences. A grim strategy is at fault when two timid people, both of whom might like a deeper relationship, are each afraid to say, "I love you." Their romance is doomed if neither makes a first move. (A matchmaker may be the only solution.)

Tit for Tat   Extensive experiments suggest that, in repetitive games, most people ultimately tailor their interactions to their opponents' previous choices. Instead of sticking to a strategy based on how your opponent first commits, you might begin in a cooperative mode, but then repeatedly echo whatever your opponent did in the previous period.

> A **tit-for-tat strategy** *begins cooperatively. Thereafter, in any period, tit for tat entails echoing what the opponent did in the previous period.*

Tit for tat in everyday life means responding in kind to people's behavior. Whether they treat you well or badly, you treat them in precisely the same fashion. Tit for tat may not result in a stable equilibrium. For example, if one player begins tit for tat cooperatively, but another starts in a noncooperative mode, the players will infinitely flip-flop for as long as the game continues.

Asymmetric Payoffs

Game theorists have explored ways to avoid the "ratting" disaster in a prisoners' dilemma. *Reputation building* convinces opponents that past behavior is a good predictor of future behavior. Since the past entails only sunk costs, why wouldn't each party in a repeated prisoners' dilemma "let bygones be bygones" and make the best decision in each round? Firms, governments, and individuals often nurture reputations for toughness or hard bargaining. *Asymmetric payoffs* between parties are one possible motive for reputation building.

> In an **asymmetric payoff,** *the payoffs from cooperation for at least one party are higher than the payoffs to some other players.*

Silence equals cooperation in the prisoners' dilemma. A party preferring to cooperate only confesses if the other party does. Our example of asymmetric payoffs (Figure 4) involves consumers who decide to purchase only from sellers with "clean" environmental records. These consumers boycott polluters' products. The (0, 0) payoff connotes consumers' refusals to deal with sellers who have ever polluted. (Some critics called for a boycott of Exxon products as a response to the *Valdez* oil spill in Alaska.)

A reputation as a nonpolluter will ensure long-run returns, so nonpollution as a strategy means that consumers will continue to purchase products. Buyers only pick boycott as a defensive action when sellers cheat (save on pollution con-

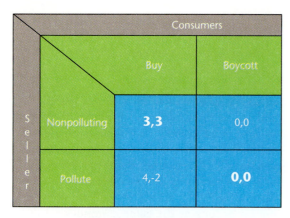

Payoffs to (Sellers, Consumers)

FIGURE 4 An Asymmetric Payoff Matrix

Some consumers will boycott the outputs of polluting firms — the 0, 0 payoff is the choice of consumers who boycott if the firm pollutes even *once*. Boycotts are strictly defensive — consumers prefer to buy. Pollute-boycott is one Nash equilibrium, but it is inferior to another possible equilibrium. If consumers and firms communicate, and if short-term effectiveness of increased pollution control is not excessively costly to the firm, the nonpollute-buy Nash equilibrium will be the most likely outcome; firms will cultivate reputations for "clean" production to maintain long-run viability in the industry.

trol costs) and pollute. While pollute-boycott is a Nash equilibrium, it is not a dominant strategy (the only outcome) as confessing is in the prisoners' dilemma. Reputation can be important in many models — including, for example, an oligopolist that builds a reputation for matching price cuts of opponents but not price increases, or *entry deterrence* decisions, in which a potential new entrant must judge the willingness of incumbent firms to fight market entry.

We have now sampled game theory through simple situations where information is symmetric — both players share the same information about the state of the world, strategies, and payoffs. But what happens when the information available to players differs? The next section examines the effects of asymmetric information.

Asymmetric Information

Transactors (people engaged in bargaining) seldom have equal knowledge.

Asymmetric information occurs when people have different levels of knowledge about a bargaining situation.

At times, knowledge asymmetries are not a problem. For example, a stereo dealer may have vast technical knowledge about woofers, tweeters, distortion, and so on, when all you care about is whether a stereo has a great sound. But, as Focus 1 indicates, asymmetric information can precipitate major mistakes and inefficiencies — even if markets are highly competitive.

Economists categorize problems of asymmetric information into two major groups: *moral hazard*, where an inadequately monitored party to a contract takes a hidden action that violates the other party's interests, and *adverse selection*, where, before a contract is finalized, one party conceals information that would make the contract unacceptable to the other. Moral hazard is present, for example, if a cashier skims cash paid for meals at a restaurant, or if a seller later decides to renege on a guarantee. Adverse selection, on the other hand, is at fault if only high-risk drivers buy car insurance, or if a firm buys merchandise on credit knowing that it will file for bankruptcy before paying. We will deal with inefficiencies arising from moral hazard before exploring problems of adverse selection.

Moral Hazard

Transactions for future performance create moral hazards that can frustrate expectations about costs and benefits. Inability to perfectly forecast and control future behavior is the key problem. For example, if you paid for knee surgery in advance, might a surgeon do sloppier work than if you will pay only if the knee responds satisfactorily? On the other hand, after your knee is repaired, might you delay payment and haggle over the surgeon's charges?

A **moral hazard** *occurs when one party to a contract can unexpectedly raise the costs or lower the benefits of the other party, who is unable to monitor or control the first party's actions.*

The Winners' Curse

If you play bridge, you know that failure to make a bid is most frequent after a hotly contested bidding sequence. This is an example of a *winners' curse*, which some economists argue haunts successful bidders whenever competition is vigorous. This recent theory suggests that certain competitive situations yield systematic errors—not in every case, but on average. Sales auctions are intended to elicit the highest possible price from buyers. Contract auctions are intended to elicit the lowest possible bids from suppliers—e.g., from construction companies. Proponents of the theory argue that the winners' curse afflicts all such highly competitive auctions.

Everyone makes mistakes, but is the direction of error systematic? If so, then people are evidently failing to learn from experience—a possibility most traditional economists are reluctant to accept. The essence of the winners' curse model is that

opportunities for gain are studied carefully by many people when a bidding situation is highly competitive, and that the average assessment of the qualities of an item for sale (or the costs likely to be incurred in fulfilling a contract) is probably more accurate than the assessment of the winning bidder.

Suppose, for example, that you were the high bidder for a 1989 Saab at a used car auction. The question is, why didn't other people match your bid? The answer, according to this model, is that other people knew that the car was worth less than you bid. A faulty engine, bad tires, or some other problem of which you are unaware (but they are not) must be present. Similarly, the argument goes, a contractor who wins a bid to build a section of highway in a remote area is probably unaware of how rocky the substrata is after the top layer of soil is removed or how costly it is to acquire certain

supplies locally. Thus, you probably paid too much for the Saab, and the contractor's bid was too low for building the road. If you suffer from the winners' curse, you can't win.

The counterargument is that vigorous competition sparks extensive consideration of the worth of a good, or the costliness of a contract. This is especially true when the stakes are high. Although some people will fail to acquire adequate information, and so will make incorrect bids, the idea that people are rational suggests that winning bids will be incorrect as often in one direction as in the other. In fact, if people try to avoid risk (and most do), the uncertainty driving the logic of the winners' curse should actually cause winning bids for sales items to generate extra consumer surplus, on average. Moreover, a winning contractor should reap extra profit, on average, because of willingness to absorb risk.

Moral hazards arise because choices tend to reflect personal costs and benefits; the effects on others are, at most, secondary considerations. No contract for future performance can cover every possibility, so most transactions rely heavily on *good faith* efforts. But time tends to blur promises

to diligently consider the interests of the other party to a bargain.

Suppose your instructor agreed to enter A's in the grade book right now for every student who promises to work hard this semester. Would most students follow through and study diligently? Could ignoring the effects on other people cause athletes with guaranteed contracts to engage in riskier outside activities — e.g., skiing or hang gliding? Is moral hazard present when parents provide Visa cards "for emergencies" to college students? Might drivers who always removed ignition keys after parking their uninsured cars tend to forget to lock them up if insurance covers losses from theft or vandalism? This is why insurance companies offer huge discounts for policies with high deductibles!

Opportunistic behavior after an arrangement is made is most severe if parties to a contract do not anticipate its renewal. Moral hazard is less important if both parties expect future agreements. Unexpectedly imposing costs or reducing the benefits of the other party causes it to rely less on good faith when a subsequent contract is negotiated. This reluctance will increase the bargaining costs of both parties. (We return to this point in a moment while discussing problems in the used car market.) If either party does not expect "repeat business," a related problem known as *adverse selection* can be severe.

Adverse Selection

Estimates of expected costs and benefits from a contract tend to be unbiased if each party shares fully all the information available before reaching a final agreement. Frequently, however, one side may conceal or distort information to strengthen its bargaining position. This can verge on fraud. For example, someone who already took a course might sell you an old text, knowing that the instructor is requiring use of a newer edition.

> **Adverse selection** *occurs when one bargaining party ultimately suffers unexpected disadvantages because the other party conceals information prior to a contract.*

You may have heard of pensioners who have been bilked of their life savings by "con artists"; confidence games are extreme examples of the problem of adverse selection. Operators of fly-by-night businesses often guarantee faulty goods, knowing that the guarantees are worthless. Some deadbeats try to build up records of paying small bills so that they can secure credit that will allow them to run up indebtedness that they never intend to pay. Similarly, a teacher fired from a previous job who wants employment may try to project a nurturing image, never revealing a personal history as a child abuser.

The problem of adverse selection is a major reason for laws that forbid fraud, and a standard approach in court cases that ambiguity in a contract will be interpreted to help the party who did not write the contract.

The Market for Lemons

Used car markets exemplify classic problems posed by asymmetric information.[8] Consider a simple model of information in used car markets. Suppose sellers with perfect information sell cars to one-time buyers with limited information. Buyers may know the proportion of lemons and good cars, but cannot distinguish lemons from "cream puffs." Adverse selection allows sellers of lemons to misrepresent their cars. Because buyers cannot ascertain quality in this model, both lemons and good cars sell for the same price!

Lemons will be overpriced while "cream puffs" are undervalued. But owners of good cars will not want to sell at these reduced prices, while owners of lemons are delighted to sell. The result of this oversimplified model is that only lemons are offered for sale, or a market fails to exist. The lesson here is that when quality is unknown to the buyer, equilibrium prices fall and fewer transactions occur, even though further gains from exchange could be realized. However, since markets for used cars thrive in most communities, what has this model ignored?

The answer is that alternative mechanisms have developed around this market to partially resolve problems of asymmetric information. Drivers who fear buying lemons in the open market may buy only from close friends, who presumably hope to maintain amicable relation-

---

8. Akerlof, George A., "The Market for 'Lemons': Quality Uncertainty and the Market Mechanism," *Quarterly Journal of Economics*, 1970, pp. 488–500.

ships. Publications such as *Consumer Reports* provide data on quality and frequency of repair for most vehicles. Firms such as "Lemon-Aide" emerge: experts who will, for $60, assess quality and look for hidden defects for potential buyers. Guarantees also help, but only if they are enforceable.

Federal law now requires "mileage certificates" on all cars, and some states have enacted defect-disclosure laws intended to protect consumers from unscrupulous dealers. Some economists argue, however, that most auto dealers have continuing relationships with their communities, making these laws unnecessary.

Adverse selection and moral hazard are most significant in markets dominated by one-time transactions. Although most employment contracts are repetitive across time, asymmetric information may still pose problems.

Efficiency Wages

Employer-employee conflicts that originate from asymmetric information include the *principal/agent problem* introduced in our chapter on "Theory of the Firm." Loafing on the job may occur, for example, if firms cannot closely monitor performance; the chance to loaf while drawing a paycheck is a moral hazard. A firm, on the other hand, may convert inconveniences to itself into burdens on its workers if, for example, it tries to maintain morale by concealing the fact that bad investments have gutted employee pension plans.

The existence of substantial and sustained unemployment in some labor markets clashes with standard theories of competitive labor markets, because wage reductions should quickly and automatically eliminate unemployment (surpluses of labor). One explanation for the apparent paradox of involuntary unemployment focuses on how firms try to tailor employment decisions to offset moral hazards.

The supply and demand for labor shown in Figure 5 yields equilibrium of q_L employment at wage w_L under standard assumptions. A worker not performing satisfactorily (shirking) could be fired, but if this labor market were purely competitive, this worker almost immediately finds

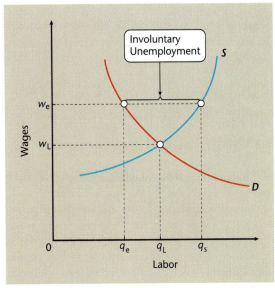

FIGURE 5 Efficiency Wages and Equilibrium Unemployment

Efficiency wages are set above market equilibrium to increase the costs of dismissal and reduce shirking by employees. Efficiency wages, if paid by all employers, increase the costs of being fired by creating a pool of unemployed, $q_s - q_e$; this increases costs for dismissed employees. Such attempts by employers to reduce shirking is one of several explanations for involuntary unemployment in labor markets.

another job at wage w_L. Thus, firing workers is ineffective as a disincentive against loafing or dishonesty.

Employers are aware that such moral hazards must be offset by other incentives. One solution is for the firm to engage in reputation building. A reputation as a firm that seldom lays off workers, even when business is slack, may attract excellent workers without requiring payments of premium wages. In this case, shirking, if discovered, would cause a worker to forfeit job security. On the other hand, a reputation as an unreliable employer that mistreats workers may stimulate shirking by workers. In such cases, the firm may be forced to expend more resources monitoring employee performance.

Another solution to curb shirking is for an employer to pay wages above prevailing market wages. A firm may start new employees at a low wage but, after the newly hired worker performs well, quickly raise the pay to a premium level.

These employees would lose their premium wages if fired, and would be less likely to be able to duplicate the salary and benefits of their existing jobs.

Efficiency wages *are wages higher than market clearing wages, and are intended to raise the costs of dismissal and reduce shirking by employees.*

This may seem paradoxical because, if all firms pay wages that exceed the market clearing wage, dismissal would not harm employees. Figure 5 suggests, however, that high efficiency wages (w_e) to control shirking reduce employment to q_e. Unemployment equals $q_s - q_e$ in this type of equilibrium, because q_s workers are willing to work at wage w_e. Dismissed employees will be at least temporarily unemployed, raising their costs of shirking. Similarly, employers find it difficult to "skim" the best workers from the labor pool while only paying a market clearing wage. Thus, involuntary unemployment may be partially explained by the employers' attempts to offset moral hazards by paying premium wages.

Results from our analysis of the "market for lemons" may partially apply to unemployed workers (and vice versa). Just as "lemons" are eagerly sold in the used car market, disproportionate numbers of "shirkers" may inhabit the pool of unemployed workers (and used cars may be "unemployed" for extended periods before they are sold).

Screening and Signaling

Employers (principals) and potential employees (agents) alike confront problems of adverse selection and moral hazard when negotiating. Moral hazard arises if workers shirk, or if firms fail to deliver on well-intentioned promises about job conditions after an employee is on board. Adverse selection is a problem if unemployed workers consciously exaggerate how diligently they will perform, or if firms paint overly rosy pictures of dreary dead-end jobs. How can potential adverse selections be countered?

Employers often set minimal job requirements to *screen* applicants. Education, experience, government licensing, recommendation letters, and promotion from within are all screening devices. Such screens compel potential employees to acquire skills, experience, or education to meet the requirements for the job offered by the employer.

Screening *occurs when a principal examines the qualifications of a potential agent before offering the agent a contract.*

Alternatively, agents (employees) knowing their own abilities may attempt to convey this to potential principals (employers) by obtaining education or certificates as signals observable by principals.

Signaling *involves behavior by agents to communicate special qualifications that will elicit the offer of a contract from a principal.*

Screening and signaling are attempts to finesse adverse selection. Just as lemons depress prices for all used cars, "lemon" workers would drive down all wages if screening and signaling were impossible. Unfortunately, screening stimulates résumé inflation and phony degrees from diploma mills. Even if employers closely check credentials, no barrier is ever 100 percent effective in screening out incompetence or dishonesty. Some critics also charge that overemphasis on formal credentials bars some workers from having appropriate access to some jobs. This complaint is discussed in Focus 2.

Economists increasingly recognize that lack of equal information among transactors poses problems. Although we have focused on how asymmetric information affects the efficiency of market systems, similar problems plague the use of other allocative mechanisms. Some governments, for example, often conceal vital information from their citizens. We have introduced game theory and surveyed consequences of asymmetric information among transactors. Our final task in this chapter is to address business strategies directed against both active and potential competitors.

Credentialism

Some critics of modern employment practices think that college degrees are artificial barriers to entry into many occupations. They believe that incompetent practitioners of many professions are protected from competition by people who might be extremely able but who lack the formal education required, either legally or by standard practice, to secure a job. IBM would not have hired either Steve Jobs or Steve Wozniak (the founders of Apple Computers) as computer engineers; neither had a college degree. Today, GE would not hire its founder, Thomas Edison, as a scientist; he lacked even a grade school education. Abe Lincoln could not practice law in most states today; he apprenticed as an attorney but never attended college. Socrates, Aristotle, Plato, and most of your professors lack the credentials now required to teach high school courses in the United States.

According to these critics, there are many people who could successfully do jobs not currently open to them because they lack the necessary degrees. Moreover, acquiring the degrees would waste their time, because degree programs allegedly fail to teach virtually anything required by many jobs. Do you think a management trainee in a department store should be compelled to have a degree? Many chain stores have such requirements. Degrees are no guarantee of competence, nor does the lack of formal education mean that someone is incompetent.

Business Strategies

No firm with market power enjoys long-run economic profits unless competitors are precluded from entry. The theory of *contestable markets* identifies potential competition as the key to market structure and performance.[9]

Contestable Markets

Contestable markets theory pivots on the idea that competitive vigor is less related to the number of firms currently in an industry than to the ease of market access by other firms if prospects for economic profit exist.

> **Contestable markets theory** *suggests that easy market entry can force even firms that are the sole current sellers of goods to produce the same output levels and set the same prices as would firms in pure competition.*

Conventional S-C-P analysis assumes that the number of firms in an industry determines the extent of market power and, thus, the prices charged for output. Contestable markets theory turns this assumption on its head, arguing that the prices buyers are willing to pay for given amounts of goods determine the numbers of firms in an industry if outsiders can always freely enter the market. One conclusion is that even if a

---

9. The theory of contestable markets is described in W. Baumol, J. Panzar, and R. Willig, *Contestable Markets and the Theory of Industry Structure* (New York: Harcourt Brace Jovanovich, 1982).

firm is the sole supplier in a market, that firm is forced to behave as if it were in competition if the market is "contestable." This theory identifies the absence of barriers to entry and exit as the motor that drives the allocative and productive efficiency of vigorous competition.

The purely competitive model suggests that external firms will try to share in any supernormal returns in an industry. Entry swells industry supplies over time and creates excess capacity at existing market prices, forcing prices down. This erodes profitability in the industry. Thus, forestalling entry or encouraging exit is an important way to maintain or create market power.

Many critics try to refute the "contestability" assumption by arguing that at least minor barriers to entry exist in virtually all markets. Some major barriers are natural (technological); others result from the conscious strategies of incumbent firms. Building excess capacity is one way firms try to deter entry. Unused excess capacity may not harm existing rivals. If used, however, it may drive some incumbent firms to exit. One example would be building a new plant that raised industry output until all existing rivals suffered losses. Such a new plant (whether used or not) would clearly deter potential new entrants. Excess capacity might be one prong of a predatory strategy.

Predatory Behavior

Predation is intended to drive rivals from the market, and uses such tactics as low prices, expanded output, aggressive advertising, introduction of close substitutes for rivals' products, rapid technological innovation, redesign of existing products to make them incompatible with rivals' products, or monopolizing access to essential resources.

> **Predatory behavior** *occurs when a firm attempts to drive rivals from the industry and deter entry. After rivals exit, the predator firm presumably will raise its prices to levels consistent with its market power.*

Predatory strategies are often hard to distinguish from normal competition and thus are difficult to enforce in a court of law. Firms use these policies to expand their market shares while lowering expected rates of profit to other incumbents or potential rivals.

Predatory behavior is forbidden by U.S. antitrust laws, and has been discussed for a century — John D. Rockefeller (founder of the original Standard Oil Company) was charged with predatorially monopolizing oil. Standard acquired a 90 percent market share of the petroleum business between 1870 and 1899. (No proof was ever offered, however, that prices were raised following the demise of competitors. Standard Oil may simply have been the least cost producer of oil.)

Monopoly profits attract potential entrants. Consider the monopolist shown in Figure 6. The entry of a rival would raise industry output, so prices and profits would fall. During a period of predation, an incumbent intent on again becoming a monopolist will, for example, set a predatory price of P_P, and try to fulfill industry demand Q_D while incurring losses equal to the shaded area. After its rival withdrew from the industry, the monopoly would reinstate price P_M.

Note that the predatory firm loses substantially more than its rival does, because the incumbent must accommodate all demand, while a rival is free to contract output to cut its losses. Presumably, the predatory firm expects to make up for this loss after regaining its monopoly position. One problem for this model is that boosting prices after rivals are driven from the market may be a self-defeating strategy because new entry would then be stimulated. Consequently, aggressive firms will try to adopt policies that deter entry or induce exit at the least cost. Some economists have concluded that firms will select strategies whose costs do not rise with market share — strategies that involve fixed expenditures. Examples include research and development (R&D) spending, institutional advertising intended to promote the brand name, and manipulation of regulatory policies.

Consider a predator and a rival who produce identical goods with constant marginal costs, selling output for price P_0 as shown in Figure 7. Suppose the predator offers a superior innovation (demand rises to D_1) with higher cost, MC_1,

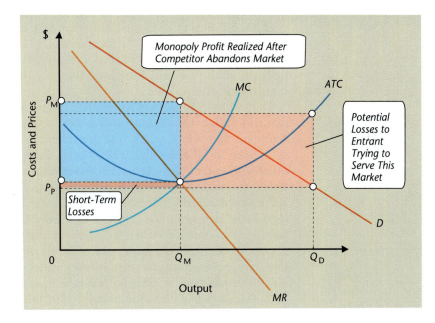

FIGURE 6   Predatory Pricing

Predatory pricing occurs when one firm lowers its price (to P_P in this case) to drive rivals from the industry. This incumbent firm is prepared to incur losses (equal to the small pink-shaded area) in the expectation that, with a future monopoly price of P_M, long run economic profit (the blue area) will recoup these losses.

Labels within the figure:

$ Monopoly Profit Realized After Competitor Abandons Market

Costs and Prices

P_M

MC

ATC

Potential Losses to Entrant Trying to Serve This Market

P_P

Short-Term Losses

D

0

Q_M

Q_D

Output

MR

which buyers value at P_1, where $P_1 > MC_1$. One predatory strategy is to price the innovation below P_1 but above MC_1; the rival sells nothing because buyers value the superior product by more than the price difference ($ac > ab$). The rival eventually exits, enabling the predator to price monopolistically.

Predators may manipulate pricing, timing, and innovation in ways almost impossible to make illegal. Low prices, for example, may signal potential competitors that entry would be a mistake. Dominant firms can also redesign product lines with components incompatible with rival products. For example, IBM might design new computers to be incompatible with add-ons from makers of PC clones. Computer makers and telecommunication firms have often attracted antitrust litigation (the focus of the next chapter) in this area of incompatibility. How superior innovations clobber rivals is illustrated in Figure 7.

Another tactic is product preannouncement. By announcing plans to enhance its product line soon, an incumbent may bar entry and make it harder for rivals to sell. Software is characterized by substantial demand-side economies of scale, so users often become locked into a given program. (A hackers' cliché: "The best program is the one you already know.") A sufficiently large user base can block sales of rival products. For example, Lotus 1-2-3 and dBase III, with huge market shares of spreadsheet and data base software, respectively, routinely preannounce enhancements. (Updates commonly run over 2 years late.) New entrants find it hard to gain a niche in these markets, despite the obsolete nature of both programs and the advances made by other software developers.

Predatory pricing works especially well if a firm (or a cartel) has significant cost advantages. OPEC, for example, set prices that significantly exceeded the marginal costs of oil for all OPEC member countries during 1974–1980. U.S. oil companies, assuming that oil prices would continue to climb, invested tremendous resources into developing relatively high-cost sources of domestic oil. When world oil prices plummeted in the early 1980s, many high-cost oil projects (e.g., conversion of oil shale in the Rocky Mountains) were abandoned, and U.S. oil companies absorbed enormous losses.

When oil prices subsequently rose, few oil companies even considered reopening their high-cost U.S. projects. They recognized that OPEC could simply cut prices to levels that would impose further losses on high-cost opera-

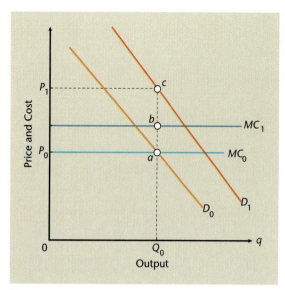

FIGURE 7   Nonprice Behavior to Deter Entry

Some economists argue that predatory behavior can occur from product innovation or by redesigns that make existing products incompatible with rival products. In this instance, the dominant firm (predator) introduces a new or revised product that has market demand of D_1 and the product is valued by consumers at P_1. Since rivals' products are inferior, a price below P_1 will potentially drive rivals from the industry, enabling the predator to raise prices. Economists have developed game theory scenarios using (a) rapid technological innovation, (b) duplicative products intended to absorb shelf space in stores and prevent access by competitors, and (c) advertising as predatory weapons. The major problem with these nonprice predatory models is our inability to distinguish predatory and normal competitive behavior.

tions. Thus, even if the current price would support a project, it was not pursued because of the potential for OPEC to undercut the price. The dynamics of this semipredatory situation also fit under the umbrella of *limit pricing* models.

Limit Pricing

The vigor of competition is largely determined by outsiders' ability to enter a market. A 1950s model of strategic behavior is limit pricing. The limit pricing model postulates an incumbent firm and potential entrants with the same cost curves (this simplifies the analysis). Further, new

entrants can expect to capture only that part of the market not satisfied by the incumbent. Thus, the new entrant believes that total industry output after entry will equal the incumbent's current output plus its own.

The average total cost curve and industry demand facing incumbents and potential entrants are shown in Figure 8. The incumbent has set a price of $8 and sells 200,000 units. If another firm enters, and the incumbent firm continues to produce 200,000 units, total output will rise and industry prices will fall. As Figure 8 shows, the demand curve facing a new entrant will be D_0 (the difference between industry demand and incumbent sales at each price), and the only equilibrium for this market will be 300,000 units sold at $5 (the incumbent sells 200,000 units and the entrant sells 100,000). Consequently, the incumbent firm can deter

FIGURE 8   Limit Pricing

If economies of scale are important, firms in an industry following a limit-pricing strategy would not realize profits over the long haul if prices were set to maximize short-run profits. New entrants might still be able to cover their average costs given the "residual" demands available to them. (The residual demand curve represents the demand remaining after existing firms have serviced their current customers.) If the industry establishes a price a bit below this level (less than $5), the residual demand available to potential entrants is inadequate to support a new firm.

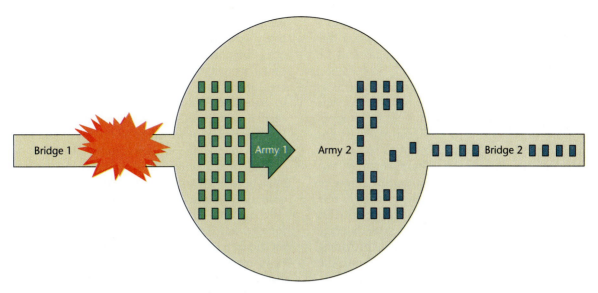

FIGURE 9   Burning Bridges and Sunk Costs

If Army 1 burns the bridge behind it, Army 2 will retreat from this island, because its leaders know that Army 1 now has no option but fighting, and Army 2 would rather give up the island than fight. (Hernado Cortez burned his ships after arriving in Mexico, intent that his Conquistadores would be motivated to conquer the Aztec empire.) Similarly, a firm heavily committed to an industry because of costly excess capacity may persuade potential rivals to look for greener pastures in other markets.

entry by setting a price slightly below $5 because any potential entrant would expect losses upon entry. At any price below $5, the residual demand of the new entrants would be below their average total cost curves, imposing losses to the new entrants. Notice that the limit price is not the monopoly price, but an incumbent firm can earn long-run economic profits with this strategy.

Sunk Costs as Entry Barriers

Economists express several reservations about this version of a limit price. First, why should potential entrants believe an incumbent will maintain old output levels after entry of a competitor? Both firms might gain if industry output were reduced. Second, if both have the same cost curves, what distinguishes potential entrants from incumbents? And if entrants have superior financial resources, why couldn't they force an incumbent to exit?

New developments in game theory have added a rich array of strategic possibilities to limit pricing models. Our earlier discussion of game theory demonstrated that the ability to

make binding commitments makes a threat more credible. Just how can an incumbent firm make its threat to continue producing 200,000 units seem credible?

One way to see the answer is to envision two armies trying to occupy an island connected by bridges from opposite sides, as shown in Figure 9. Each army will let the other have the island rather than fight. (Fighting is very costly!) If Army 1 immediately burns its bridge, Army 2 will allow Army 1 to occupy the island since Army 1 now only has one option left — to fight. This analogy suggests than an incumbent firm can commit to a large output by acquiring considerable excess capacity, signaling to any potential rivals that huge increases in output will punish any firm rash enough to enter the market.

Economists have recently begun to explore the role that sunk costs play in entry decisions.[10] An irreversible capital decision may be an effective deterrent to entry, the more slowly capital

---

10. John Sutton, "Endogenous Sunk Costs and Industrial Structure," in Bonanno, G. and Brandolini, D., *Industrial Structure in the New Industrial Economics* (Oxford, U.K.: Clarendon Press, 1990), 22–37.

depreciates and the more specific capital is to a particular firm. If a viable used market for capital exists, the less likely entrants will be deterred.

A reconsideration of limit pricing models is based on information asymmetry.[11] Incumbents do not charge low prices because of high capacity; low prices are used to signal potential entrants that demand is insufficient to sustain another firm or that the incumbent has low production costs. Some firms use low prices to acquire market share to learn the intricacies of a particular product line or business. This **learning-by-doing** approach can drive average costs down as experience is gained, providing firms with competitive advantages well into the future.

Accommodation Some economists have concluded that the costs to firms of limit pricing or predation far outweigh *accommodation* of entry. Several game theory models indicate that non-price techniques or buying rivals at premium prices avoid predation costs or allow greater

profits than occur under limit pricing.[12] Alternatively, entry may simply be accommodated without a fight, depending on the payoffs. For example, if a small, cheap hotel were built in a resort area, an existing resort might use the small hotel to handle overflow customers. The more the small hotel focused on specialized customers, the less threatening it would be to the resort and the greater the likelihood of accommodation.

Modern economists view prices, capacity, and innovation as weapons competitors use to acquire or maintain competitive advantages in specific markets. Most research in game theory is focused on dominant firm scenarios and asymmetric information models. Competitive advantages extend beyond product markets, so this analysis is increasingly used to investigate resource markets and firms' financial decisions.

Most advocates of the new industrial organization recognize that the older structure-conduct-performance paradigm provides some valid insights into how firms behave. Instead of totally scrapping the traditional approach, their research is intended to refine its insights and to correct what they perceive as its errors in charting a direction for government policy, especially antitrust laws. In the next chapter, we consider government attempts to curb market power through antitrust laws.

---

11. Milgrom, P. and J. Roberts, "Limit Pricing and Entry Under Incomplete Information: An Equilibrium Analysis," *Econometrica*, 1982, pp. 443–460. Also see Milgrom, P. and J. Roberts, "Information Asymmetries, Strategic Behavior and Industrial Organization," *American Economic Review Papers and Proceedings*, 1987, pp. 184–193.

---

12. McGee, J., "Predatory Pricing Revisited," *Journal of Law & Economics*, 1980, pp. 289–330.

Chapter Review: Key Points

1. *Strategic behavior* entails ascertaining what other people are likely to do in a specific situation, and then following tactics that maximize your gain or minimize any harm to you.

2. The *structure-conduct-performance* paradigm is the traditional formula for antitrust policy and industrial organization analysis. According to this approach, market structure (numbers of competitors, economies of scale, types of products) determines the conduct (pricing and output decisions) of firms, which in turn determines industry performance (efficiency and technological progress).

3. The *new industrial organization* questions whether market structure dominates pricing and output decisions, emphasizing instead (a) strategic behavior, which is analyzed with game theory, and (b) the effects of asymmetric information (differential information between bargaining parties).

4. *Game theory* is the study of strategic interac-

tions among interdependent decision makers, including those in oligopoly markets. *Payoff matrices* are constructed to examine how transactors minimize their losses or maximize their gains, given the most likely decisions of other players in a game.

5. A *dominant strategy* is a player's best response, no matter what strategy is pursued by the player's rivals.

6. In a *prisoners' dilemma*, the dominant strategy of each party results in inefficiency. Cooperation would allow both to gain, but lack of cooperation is the dominant strategy.

7. *Cooperative games* involve players who can make binding commitments, while *noncooperative games* do not permit such agreements. The ability to enforce agreements changes the equilibrium of most games.

8. A *Nash equilibrium* is a set of strategies where no player has an incentive to change, given that other players do not change. There may be multiple Nash equilibria for a game, but after one is selected by the players, that equilibrium will continue until the system experiences an external disturbance.

9. *Dynamic games* involve sequences of choices over time and result in a wide array of possible strategies. A *grim strategy* entails cooperating until your opponent fails to do so and then clobbering the opponent in every subsequent round. A *tit-for-tat* strategy responds in kind to whatever your opponent did in the previous round.

10. Models that recognize *asymmetric information* (different information among transactors) have different outcomes than do models that assume sharing of information.

11. A *winners' curse* occurs when asymmetric information results in systematic losses to "winners" in competitive bidding situations.

12. *Moral hazard* results when some arrangement provides incentives for one party to engage in *inefficient behavior* that raises costs or reduces benefits to the other party. *Adverse selection* occurs when one party to a bargain has superior information when the bargain is struck, resulting in unexpected losses to the other party.

13. The market for used automobiles (lemons) is one extreme example of asymmetric information where the expected result is uniformly low prices for all cars sold, no market at all, or only lemons offered for sale. The *principal/agent problem* is another case where inefficiencies arise from informational asymmetry. Firms cannot consistently monitor employee performance.

14. Wages paid to workers that exceed market clearing wages are called *efficiency wages*. Efficiency wages increase the costs of dismissal and are designed to reduce shirking (the moral hazard problem) by employees. Efficiency wages provide an explanation for involuntary unemployment in labor markets.

15. *Signaling* involves attempts by agents to communicate certain images to potential principals. *Screening* occurs when a principal sets minimum standards before employing an agent.

16. A *contestable market* is a market without substantial barriers to entry so that it mimics the competitive outcome.

17. *Predatory behavior* involves activity by firms to drive rivals from the market or to deter entry. Once rivals disappear, predators can set prices consistent with their market power. A problem with this model is that reentry would normally occur when the high price is resumed, unless the predator firm has significant cost advantages so that potential rivals expect reentry to prompt lower prices once again.

18. *Limit pricing* is a strategy intended to inhibit market entry. Limit pricing techniques include low prices that make it unprofitable for new entrants, or that signal that the market is insufficient for a new entrant. Low prices also convey the message that the incumbent firm is a low-cost (efficient) firm.

19. Economists have recently begun examining the role that sunk costs as precommitments to capacity have on deterring entry into markets. Game theory has opened up many avenues for future research and has changed our views on the relationship between strategic behavior and industrial structure.

Key Concepts

Ensure that you can define these terms before proceeding.

structure-conduct-performance paradigm
new industrial organization
game theory
dominant strategy
Nash equilibrium
grim strategy
tit for tat
moral hazard

adverse selection
lemons market
efficiency wages
screening and signaling
contestable markets theory
predatory behavior
limit pricing

Problems and Questions

1. Do the following situations reflect simple rational ignorance, moral hazard, or adverse selection?

   a. Your new car turns out to be a lemon.

   b. The dealer blames you for your new car's problems and refuses to honor verbal guarantees.

   c. You get an A in a course by turning in a plagiarized term paper.

   d. Balmy weather ruins your ski vacation.

   e. After you have saved money as a family for years, your spouse dies. You then marry a murderous fortune hunter and change your will so that your new spouse will inherit your fortune.

   f. You were laid off because you goofed off on the job after you worked long enough to become eligible for unemployment compensation.

   g. You pay a brilliant friend $100 to write a term paper, and your former friend does a sloppy job that causes you to fail a course.

   h. Soon after your silver anniversary you become embroiled in a nasty divorce because of irreconcilable differences.

   i. A sluggish housing market keeps you from selling, so you hire an arsonist and "sell" your house to the insurance company.

   j. An ambitious flim-flam artist gains control of a savings and loan association and makes loans to relatives that will predictably result in default.

2. Suppose your instructor guarantees that the student with the highest score at the end of this course will receive an A+. A classmate proposes that all students hand in blank paper for all written work, give answer "c" to all multiple choice questions, and answer "T" for all true/false questions. All students will have the same "highest" grade and everyone will get an A+. Why would you expect this scheme to backfire even if all students agreed to this strategy?

3. What role do you think moral hazard played in the current savings and loan crisis/scandal? How did the combination of deregulation and federal insurance on deposits interact to create the present situation? Should economists have been able to predict the outcome from the beginning?

4. Does the prisoners' dilemma game provide some insight into why police interrogate prisoners separately? What types of mechanisms (strategies) could criminals create to reduce the probability of the *confess-confess* equilibrium?

5. In the 1950s, teenagers sometimes played a game called "chicken." Drivers initially half a mile apart would drive their cars at each other at high speed. The first driver who turned to avoid a crash was castigated as a "chicken." What do you think was the most common result of this game? How does this game resemble the nuclear weapons race that has plagued relationships between the United States and the Soviet Union?

6. What evidence might you look for to discover whether some concentrated industry was contestable and vulnerable to competition?

7. Most capitalistic economies have an infinite horizon, with the possible exception of Hong Kong, which will soon be returned to China. Does the prisoners' dilemma explain Hong Kong's current brain drain as skilled labor emigrates to other nations? What would you choose to do if you owned a trading firm in Hong Kong with mobile assets?

8. Fill in Figure 10 with a two-person payoff matrix for a situation on "Wheel of Fortune" where (a) Bob racked up a potential score of $11,000, and, unfortunately, couldn't guess

the last consonant in the puzzle, but now knows the answer, while (*b*) Bruce, the current spinner, knows the answer, but only spun the wheel for $150 for the last consonant in the puzzle. Suppose that Susan, the next player in line, will win $1,900 if Bruce doesn't answer properly. If side payments were allowed, who would identify the quote correctly? What minimal side payments would be required? What would happen in this game if the same excellent players were on this show every night and could make binding agreements about how each would play?

9. Firms cannot predict exactly how productive or honest any prospective employee will be once hired. What are shortcomings of each of the following devices some employers use to screen job applicants? (*a*) Grades, diplomas, or degrees. (*b*) Letters of recommendation. (*c*) On-the-job training or work experience with other employers. (*d*) Impressions from interviews. (*e*) Tests of aptitudes, skills, or personality. (*f*) Lie detector examinations.

FIGURE 10   A Payoff Matrix for "Wheel of Fortune"

Which devices do you think are most effective? Which do you think are too heavily weighted by many employers? Which other mechanisms are (or should be) used to screen job applicants? What are their advantages? Shortcomings?

CHAPTER

Antitrust Policy

People of the same trade seldom meet together, even for merriment and diversion, but the conversation ends in a conspiracy against the public, or in some contrivance to raise prices.

Adam Smith, *The Wealth of Nations*, 1776

Political pressures for corrective action arise from the inefficiencies and perceived inequities of excessive market power. Government's options to combat abuses of market power include (*a*) regulation, (*b*) nationalization (governmental operation), and (*c*) antitrust laws.

Regulation is a complex issue addressed in a later chapter. Dismay with how nationalized industries operate has unleashed a broad trend toward *privatization* — state enterprises are being converted into private firms from China to the Soviet Union to Brazil to South Africa. (Critics charge that public officials abuse market power at least as much as private firms would, and too often are legally protected from competition.) Our focus in this chapter is government's third policy option — antitrust policy.

The structure-conduct-performance (S-C-P) theories presented earlier indicate that pure competition is the most efficient structure for an industry, and unregulated monopoly, the least. The preceding chapter, however, suggests that business tactics are not determined by structure alone. Antitrust policy is intended to diffuse

market power. Before we consider antitrust policies in depth, we will examine current U.S. industrial structure and discuss some implications for the economic performance of the hundreds of thousands of firms in our economy.

Dynamics within specific industries vary widely, but on average, performance verges on that of a monopoly as an industry's biggest firms gain larger market shares. *Size* is often equated with *market power*, but big industries may contain many huge firms, none of which has much market power. For example, the U.S. oil industry contains almost 17,000 oil producing companies, of which a dozen or so generate sales exceeding $1 billion. Even Exxon, the largest oil company, markets only about 11 percent of U.S. petroleum sales, or less than 5 percent of world production. Firms often achieve size because of economies of scale, superior technology, or managerial talent, but competition among giants appears increasingly vigorous.

Measuring Market Power

The structure-conduct-performance approach has led to attempts to quantitatively estimate the market power concentrated in the hands of a few firms in an industry.

The Lerner Index of Monopoly Power

Theory from our "Monopoly" chapter suggests that market power creates a gap between marginal cost and price. This led economist Abba Lerner to propose the **Lerner index of Monopoly Power** (LMP), which is:

$$LMP = \frac{\text{price} - \text{marginal cost}}{\text{price}}$$

The LMP is zero for pure competitors because price equals marginal cost. Marginal cost and price in Figure 1 are both $30 at competitive output q_e (point a); LMP = $(30 - 30)/30 = 0$. The exercise of market power increases the Lerner index because the equilibrium gap between price and marginal cost rises. Monopoly output and price in Figure 1 are q_M and $50 respectively (point b), so LMP = $(50 - 30)/50 = .40$. Lerner's reasoning was fine but, unfortunately, the marginal cost data required to calculate an LMP are not generally available.

FIGURE 1   The Lerner Index of Monopoly Power (LMP)

The Lerner Index of Monopoly Power (LMP) is equal to $(P - MC)/MC$. LMP for a competitive firm (output q_c at point a) would equal 0 [$(30 - 30)/30 = 0$]. For any firm with market power LMP > 0. For example, the monopolist in this figure selling q_M units at $50 would have an LMP of 0.40 [$(50 - 30)/50 = 0.40$].

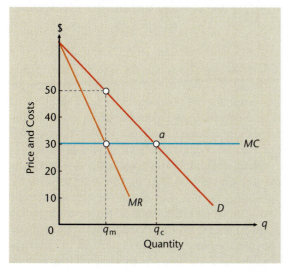

Market Concentration Ratios

Data are sporadically available (with a 3- to 5-year delay) to compute industry concentration ratios, which may help identify market power. A **concentration ratio** is the percentage of total industry sales, assets, employment, value added, or output accounted for by an industry's biggest four or eight firms, although any number of firms could be used. Formally, four-firm concentration ratios are defined as

$$CR_4 = \sum_{i=1}^{4} S_i$$

where S_i is the market share of the ith firm and $S_1 > S_2 > S_3 > S_4$.

Table 1 presents four-firm and eight-firm concentration ratios (CRs) for 24 U.S. industries. Concentration (CR_8 for 1982) declines as you move down the table. Changing industry concentration can be interpreted from data for changes in concentration ratios and for the number of firms in the industry. For example, market power among firms producing electronic computing equipment appears to have fallen sharply. Not only has its concentration ratio fallen, but the computer industry had five times as many firms in 1982 as in 1967. This undoubtedly reflects technological advances that are still taking place in computers.

Is Concentration Increasing?   The evidence on whether industrial concentration is increasing is mixed. Most economists cite figures like those in Table 1 to argue that, on average, domestic concentration ratios for most industries changed little between 1967 and 1982 — or between 1930 and the present. Relative stability of our industrial structure is supported by data for concentration ratios. Note that although the number of firms in many industries has increased, most giant firms have retained their market shares.

Critics often argue that market power within particular industries is less important than the increasing concentration of economic power accomplished primarily through mergers. Conglomerate mergers have allowed the largest

Table 1 *Concentration Ratios for Selected Industries, 1967–1982*

| | Percent of Shipments | | | | | |
Industry	Four Largest Firms 1967	Four Largest Firms 1982	Eight Largest Firms 1967	Eight Largest Firms 1982	Total Number of Firms 1967	Total Number of Firms 1982
Motor vehicles and car bodies	92	92	98	97	107	284
Cigarettes	81	(D)	100	(D)	8	8
Telephone, telegraph apparatus	92	76	96	83	82	259
Organic fibers, noncellulosic	84	77	94	91	22	44
Tires and inner tubes	70	66	89	86	119	108
Aircraft	69	64	89	81	91	139
Photographic equipment	69	74	81	86	505	723
Soap and other detergents	70	60	78	73	599	642
Motor vehicle parts and accessories	60	61	68	69	1,424	2,000
Blast furnaces and steel mills	48	42	66	64	200	211
Electronic computing equipment	66	40	83	57	134	685
Farm machinery and equipment	44	53	56	62	1,526	1,787
Petroleum refining	33	28	57	48	276	282
Construction machinery	41	42	53	52	578	817
Pharmaceutical preparations	24	26	40	42	791	584
Paper mills	26	22	43	40	203	135
Bread, cake, and related products	26	34	38	47	3,445	1,869
Periodicals	24	20	37	31	2,430	3,143
Radio & TV communications equipment	22	22	37	35	1,111	2,083
Newspapers	16	22	25	34	7,589	7,520
Sawmills and planing mills	11	17	15	23	10,016	5,810
Bottled and canned soft drinks	13	14	20	23	3,057	1,236
Commercial printing, letterpress	14	14	21	19	11,955	10,211
Commercial printing, lithographic	5	6	8	10	6,718	17,332

Source: U.S. Department of Commerce, Bureau of the Census, MC 82-5-7, 1982 Census of Manufacturers, April 1986.
Note: (D): Withheld to avoid disclosure.

American firms to steadily acquire a growing share of all U.S. manufacturing assets over the past half century. Figure 2 indicates that the top 200 firms (0.1 percent of all U.S. manufacturing corporations) control three quarters of all manufacturing assets, and this percentage has crept up slowly over the last half century.

Is Big Bad? Major debates also surround the issue of whether bigness and badness are synonymous in the case of a conglomerate. Virtually all giant firms operate in several industries, and nearly all operate across national boundaries. Thus, although concentration within specific industries may be relatively stable, giant multinationals are increasingly important players on the international economic scene. In addition to their huge shares of manufacturing assets (capital), these giants also account for growing proportions of employment, sales, and profits.

Giant conglomerates may not have as much market power as big firms that operate in only one industry, but they do have substantial economic clout and may exercise their power in the political arena. Multinational firms are of special concern because of their interests in international politics, but even giants are not immune to market forces. Many of our largest firms seem

70
60
50
40
Percent
30
20
10
0

1950   1960   1970   1980   1990

100 Largest Corporations   200 Largest Corporations

FIGURE 2   Proportion of Manufacturing Assets Held by the 100 and 200 Largest Corporations, 1950—1990
Source: Statistical Abstract of the United States, 1991.

firmly entrenched at the top, but Table 3 in our chapter on "Theory of the Firm" provides evidence of some turnover among these huge organizations.

Regulatory barriers to entry or restrictions on imports facilitate concentration, but significant economies of scale can make concentration unavoidable in some industries. High capital costs erect substantial entry barriers if profits are uncertain. Where economies of scale are substantial, high fixed costs combined with low marginal costs cause average costs to fall across a wide range of output. In the short run, average variable costs may reach their minimum (the shutdown point) at extremely low prices and high output levels. These economies of scale incite cutthroat competition during periods of slack demand. A price war often shrinks the numbers of firms in an industry when losers go bankrupt. Price wars also generate pressures for collusive price-fixing agreements, or for cries from the industry for government "bailouts" and protective regulations and controls.

A major deficiency of concentration ratios is ambiguity in categorizing industries. Firms must

be classified into industry groups whose products are easily substituted by consumers. Distinguishing between close and distant substitutes is difficult. One solution might be to examine the cross-elasticities of demand between products. Unfortunately, the data required to estimate cross-elasticities are rarely available.

Alone, even information on substitutability by consumers might be inadequate to define an industry; production substitutability must be considered as well. Markets are *contestable* if a number of firms use roughly the same types of plant and equipment to manufacture different products and if switching from one product line to another is easy. For example, the technology for photocopying might allow Xerox to shift easily into computer production, or such camera makers as Kodak or Polaroid might easily shift into manufacturing copying machines. Defendants in antitrust cases increasingly use contestability to rebut legal charges. Firms that can easily cross industry boundaries should be grouped as potential competitors.

Although Standard Industry Classification (SIC) codes attempt to classify industries, many

SIC codes are overly inclusive. For example, patented products with no close substitutes may be lumped with goods that are only roughly similar. For years, photocopying machines (dominated by Xerox) were categorized with other copying equipment. Are ditto machines, mimeographs, and printing presses really close substitutes for Xerox equipment?

Perhaps the major defects of SIC codes and concentration ratios are that they consider only domestic sales by U.S. producers. The extent of competition is understated if imports are ignored. General Motors, Ford, and Chrysler are obviously not nearly as dominant as the CR_4 for motor vehicles in Table 1 suggests. Even recognizing such difficulties, however, concentration ratios provide crude snapshots of shared market power.

The Herfindahl-Hirschman Index

Traditional theory suggests that concentrated industries are more likely to sustain economic profits. A Federal Trade Commission study revealed, however, that a single firm's market share is quite often the best predictor of its profits, regardless of concentration in the industry as a whole.[1] The study concluded that, on the average, each 10 percent rise in market share yields a 2 percent increase in profitability.

This evidence shifted the attention of the Justice Department's Antitrust Division to the **Herfindahl-Hirschman Index** (HHI) which estimates concentration by emphasizing the firms with the largest market shares, as measured by the formula:

$$HHI = \sum_{i=1}^{n} S_i^2$$

where S_i is the market share of the ith firm. The HHI places the greatest weight on the largest firms by squaring market shares.

The lone firm in a monopolized industry would have a market share $S_1 = 100$ percent, and the HHI = $100^2 = 10,000$. If, on the other hand, 100 firms each control 1 percent of sales, then the HHI would be 100. Thus, the HHI falls as the number of firms in an industry rises or as firms' sizes become more uniform. Consider a market where four firms have 20 percent each and 20 firms have 1 percent each, and a second market where one firm has 77 percent and 23 firms each have 1 percent. Four-firm concentration ratios in both industries would be 80 percent, but the HHI paints a different picture; 1,620 and 5,952, respectively. HHIs capture differences in concentration hidden by concentration ratios alone.

The Antitrust Division now uses price-elasticity measures and the HHI to screen proposed mergers. Mergers in relatively unconcentrated industries have been almost immune from legal challenges since 1982. In fact, as Table 2 indicates, most of the largest mergers in history have occurred in the past decade, in part because mergers in concentrated industries have also been permitted. These have included GE/RCA, Chevron/Gulf, Chrysler/AMC, British Petroleum/Standard Oil of Ohio, and Texaco/Getty Oil. Allowing such mergers was a radical shift from earlier periods when almost all major merger proposals were challenged.

Mergers and Market Power

Concentration increases when major competitors merge, whether measured by concentration ratios or a Herfindahl-Hirschman Index. Market power gained through merger may be socially undesirable if the firms are among the leaders of a concentrated industry. On the other hand, merger of small firms into one viable competitor in a concentrated industry can be socially beneficial if the merged firm is more able to compete with established giants. Ideally, public policy would prohibit all harmful mergers, but only them.

The Urge to Merge

One obvious motive for a merger is to eliminate a competitor and consolidate market power. A second motive may entail principal/agent prob-

---

1. "Attacking the Test that Curbs so Many Mergers," *Business Week*, November 16, 1981, p. 151.

Table 2 *The Largest Mergers and Acquisitions in U.S. History*

Firm Acquired	Acquiring Firm	$Billion	Year
1. RJR—Nabisco	Kohlbert, Kravis & Roberts	24.9	1988
2. Warner Communications	Time	13.9	1989
3. Gulf Oil	Chevron	13.3	1984
4. Kraft	Philip Morris	11.5	1988
5. Squibb	Bristol Meyers	11.5	1989
6. Getty Oil	Texaco	10.1	1984
7. Conoco	DuPont	8.0	1981
8. Standard Oil of Ohio	British Petroleum	7.9	1987*
9. Federated Dept. Stores	Campeau	7.4	1988
10. Marathon Oil	USX (U.S. Steel)	6.5	1981
11. Contel	GTE	6.2	1990
12. Beatrice Food	Kohlberg, Kravis & Roberts	6.2	1986
13. RCA	General Electric	6.2	1986
14. Superior Oil	Mobil Oil	5.7	1984
15. Pillsbury	Grand Metropolitan	5.7	1988
16. General Foods	Phillip Moris	5.6	1986
17. Safeway Stores	Kohlberg, Kravis & Roberts	5.3	1986
18. Farmers Groups	BAT Industries	5.2	1988
19. Southern Pacific	Santa Fe RR	5.2	1983
20. Southland	JT Acquisitions	5.1	1987

*For 45 percent share that British Petroleum did not already own. Source: *Fortune,* various issues, 1980–1991.

lems: Executives' desires for job security sometimes cause firms with abundant cash on hand to buy firms suffering cash-flow problems. This tactic makes the acquiring firm a less attractive target for a hostile takeover. Firms also merge to exploit cost savings arising from economies of information, marketing, advertising, production, or financing, or to pool complementary technologies or patents.

For example, several firms merged into Hal Roach Studios in 1987 to exploit a new "colorizing" technique for old black-and-white films. The merged firms included one holding rights to a "classics" library, another owned television stations spread across the nation, and a third distributed movies and television programming worldwide. The earnings potential for this vertically integrated firm vastly exceeded that of the sum of the individual firms.

The stock market quickly reevaluates the profit prospects of merged firms. The value of stock falls if most analysts perceive a merger as a bad deal, but if a merger enhances the expected future profitability of the surviving firm, the value of its stock will quickly exceed that of the total stock in the previous firms.

Promotional profits *are increases in the total value of the stock of the merged firms.*

Potential promotional profits to holders of large blocks of stock (often the promoters of merger) provide substantial incentives to merge competing firms.

Major Merger Movements

Four major waves of mergers have swept our economy in the last century. Each torrent of mergers arose out of the economic conditions and the legal climate of the times.

The First Wave: Horizontal Acquisition

John D. Rockefeller, Andrew Carnegie, Cornelius Vanderbilt, J. P. Morgan, and other tycoons engineered much of the first wave of mergers around the turn of the last century, aggressively trying to consolidate oil, steel, railroads, sugar, finance, and other industries. Corporate holding companies known as **trusts** permitted these men to gain control of vast amounts of capital. History is filled with colorful stories about their chicanery in trying to acquire the assets of competitors.

The vast majority of mergers and acquisitions during this period were horizontal mergers—absorbing direct competitors can be a short cut in attaining market dominance. Such giants as U.S. Steel, General Electric, and Standard Oil were formed. Abuse of the resulting market power appeared routine. Perceived offenses by these major companies fomented a general outcry for restrictions on trusts, leading to the passage of the Sherman Antitrust Act in 1890, which attempted to forbid horizontal mergers. Ironically, horizontal mergers continued until loopholes were tightened by the Clayton Act.

The Second Wave: Vertical Acquisition A second irony is that the second merger wave fol-

lowed passage of the Clayton Act in 1914, only ending when the Great Depression wilted corporate profits. Acquisitions during this period were primarily vertical, which entails gaining control over various stages of production from raw materials to finished manufacturing. Firms desiring to grow via merger were channeled toward vertical mergers, because horizontal mergers were squelched by bans on "monopolization or attempts to monopolize." Horizontal mergers were relatively trivial compared to the boom of monopolization that occurred during the first great merger wave.

The Third Wave: Conglomerates The stock market crash of 1929 vaporized prospects for promotional profits, and slack demands for output during the Great Depression curtailed mergers based on economies of scale. Figure 3 shows that the merger rate fell drastically and remained low until the third big wave appeared late in the 1950s, again, paradoxically, on the heels of major antitrust legislation—the Celler-Kefauver

FIGURE 3 Waves of Mergers and Acquisitions over the Past Century

Act of 1950. This third wave lasted into the early 1970s.

The bulk of the mergers during this period were conglomerate mergers, which combine firms from unrelated industries. For example, DuPont's (a chemical company) 1982 acquisition of Conoco Oil was a conglomerate merger. One famous conglomerate is International Telephone and Telegraph (ITT), which mushroomed in 1960. ITT's assets grew from roughly $900 million in 1960 to over $6 billion in 1970. About two-thirds of this 700 percent growth occurred through mergers with companies in unrelated industries.

The Fourth Wave: Corporate Raiding

Merger activity was subdued through the 1970s, but the perception that the Reagan administration was sympathetic to "corporate raiders" renewed interest in mergers. Antitrust guidelines announced in 1982 fostered conglomerate mergers and also allowed horizontal or vertical mergers that would have been challenged by earlier administrations. During the 1980s over 31,000 mergers and acquisitions with a total value of $1.34 trillion were consummated. Horizontal mergers among giant oil companies were especially common in the 1980s. The biggest deal of all time was the 1989 $24.7 billion leveraged buy-out of RJR Nabisco by Kohlberg, Kravis & Roberts, which was primarily financed by foreign banks.

The torrent of mergers during the 1980s was driven by a permissive political environment in Washington, creative financial techniques (e.g., junk bonds), and fallout effects from the ongoing internationalization of markets. Merger activity is stimulated by prosperity, especially if many stocks appear "undervalued" relative to expected profits. Recessions or a hostile political climate tend to stifle merger activity.

People try to insulate themselves from changes that disrupt their lives and job security. Mergers often entail closing obsolete plants. The magnitude of mergers and acquisitions created a backlash in many states. Lack of federal action to curb mergers fomented a wave of state laws to dampen their effects (see Focus 1). Merger activity waned as the economy slowed down during 1989 and 1990. This may be a temporary lull,

and an annual rate of mergers and acquisitions in the 3,000 to 4,000 range may resume in the 1990s, unless business conditions worsen significantly, or if voters' attitudes toward mergers become more hostile. Figure 4 summarizes the extent of takeover control statutes in the United States as of 1990.

The Urge to Purge

Some mergers are like unhappy marriages. Successful mergers tend to occur when (a) they involve firms in closely related businesses (horizontal mergers), (b) the price paid by the acquiring firms is not excessive, (c) an acquisition is financed with stock swaps or cash rather than debt (bond financing), and (d) executives from acquired firms continue to manage.[2]

A common merger problem is that good executive skills in one business may not be portable to another. Conflicting corporate "cultures" can make an acquisition almost worthless, as Exxon discovered when, in 1975, it attempted to expand into office automation. Over the next decade, Exxon poured over $2 billion into its QYX office products division. Exxon executives, accustomed to 3- to 5-year planning horizons in the oil business, could not make decisions quickly enough to keep pace with the rapidly changing pace of office automation. Exxon finally sold its office products division at a huge loss in 1985.

The 1980s witnessed both mergers and its flip side, *voluntary restructuring*—the jettisoning of bad acquisitions. Nearly 30 percent of all acquisition activity in the 1980s (roughly 10,000 deals) involved sell-offs of corporate assets. Many conglomerates are scaling back to "do what they do best." For example, ITT disposed of nearly 100 subsidiaries in the early 1980s. Beatrice, another giant conglomerate, went through a spasm of "demerger" in 1987 and 1988, trimming its operations to focus on its original area of expertise, processing food.

Corporate raiding has pressured management to see if undervalued plums can be disposed of at prices higher than those reflected in the price of

---

2. "Do Mergers Really Work?," *Business Week*, June 3, 1985, pp. 88–100.

State Actions on the Antitrust Front[*]

Many state governments are disturbed by relaxed antitrust enforcement at the federal level and have enacted antitakeover laws to restrain hostile takeovers in their jurisdictions. Today, over 40 states have various statutes to control hostile acquisitions. These statutes include the following types:

• **Control Share Acquisition Laws** require unaffiliated shareholder approval of voting rights for a stockholder whose interest exceeds some threshold level.

• **Nonstockholder Constitu-**

ency Laws enable directors to consider factors other than return to stockholders in takeover battles. These other factors include impact on employees, communities, the environment, and so on.

• **Business Combination/ Freeze-Out Laws** provide for waiting periods (3 to 5 years) before hostile acquirers can control assets of firms acquired.

• **Fair Price Laws** often force investors who acquire a threshold level of ownership (20 to 30 percent) to tender for (offer to buy) remaining shares at a "fair price."

Poison Pill Laws permit boards to enact shareholder provisions that deter hostile takeovers. These pills typically involve favorable asset purchasing provisions for existing stockholders in the event of a takeover.

• **Antigreenmail Laws** prevent boards from purchasing large blocks of company stock above market prices without stockholder approval.

[*]Jay B. Kasner and Jeremy A. Berman, "State Laws: Added Firepower for Boards to Resist Takeover Offers," Mergers and Acquisitions, July/August 1990, pp. 81–88.

the firm's stock. Firms unable to milk their assets for the highest possible returns are prime targets for corporate raiders and other disposal experts.

Public Policy Toward Business

Government policies about industrial structure have been directed along two broad lines. The first, regulation, has existed since the adoption of the U.S. Constitution: Article I, Section 8 (the "Commerce Clause") gives Congress the power "To regulate Commerce with foreign Nations, and among the several States . . . ." Any federal law might be considered regulation, but the term

usually entails some government body setting rules for a market about prices, outputs, or operating and managerial procedures. In such situations, government substitutes regulation for the forces of competition.

Antitrust is the second broad approach to dealing with industry structure. Several laws have amended the Sherman Antitrust Act of 1890. The antitrust approach ideally restructures industry to conform closely to the assumptions of pure or monopolistic competition. Mergers that would lead to unwarranted concentration would be prohibited. Where this is not possible, law and regulation ideally force an industry's performance to mimic the competitive ideal.

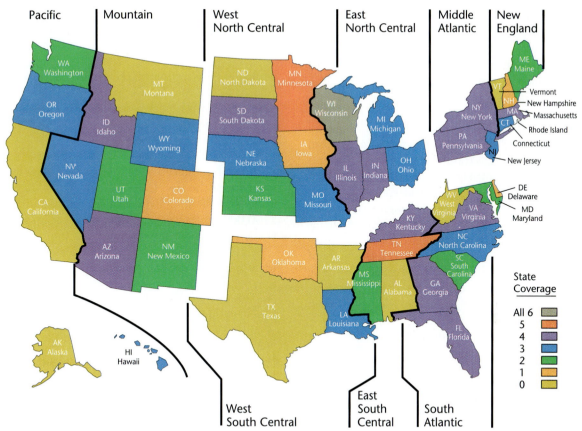

FIGURE 4 Takeover Control Statutes by States, 1990

The rest of this chapter is devoted to examining antitrust policies.

Antitrust Policy

The previous four chapters set the stage for a discussion of antitrust policies. A mix of antitrust policies and regulation may be used to combat business strategies that distort allocations because of asymmetric information (e.g., moral hazard or adverse selection). The rationale for vigorous antitrust actions to counter the effects of excessive market power is fairly simple. Pure competitors adjust output until the last unit sold provides benefits just equal to production costs. That is, marginal social benefits equal marginal social costs ($MSB = MSC$), so that the market operates in an economically efficient manner.

When firms exercise market power, the price of the last unit sold tends to exceed both its cost and the competitive price. Economic inefficiency is a problem when the price (marginal social benefit) charged by a firm exceeds marginal social cost. Therefore, purely competitive markets tend to be more allocatively efficient than those controlled by firms with market power. Moreover, consistent monopoly profit may result in concentrations of wealth and economic power that are incompatible with most social and political ideas of equity.

This analysis may seem straightforward, but as the last chapter suggested, major disagreements exist about whether large firms or noncompetitive strategies are inherently bad. One legal point of view is that monopoly is bad *per se*. The idea of a benevolent monopoly is discarded in favor of the argument that abuse invariably flows from substantial market power. A natural conclusion from this point of view is to stamp out market power through forced *divestiture*, the breaking up of large corporations into numerous independent small companies. For example, AT&T was forced to divest itself of all its local operating companies in the early 1980s.

The Argument for Bigness

Some defenders of modern corporate giantism argue that size is a tribute to the success of entrepreneurs and managers in serving consumers' needs in exceptionally efficient ways. Large corporations may also be a consequence of capital-intensive and highly complex modern technology. Other defenders contend that large enterprises are necessary to comply with the maze of federal, state, and local regulations governing modern business practice. Small firms have difficulty acquiring the capital needed to sustain these endeavors.

Public policy has generally presumed that market power should be curtailed. This presumption is based primarily on the economic theory you have learned in the last few chapters. The stated goals of antitrust policy are to outlaw monopolization of markets and to prohibit specific misconduct associated with market power. We need a brief overview of our major antitrust laws before evaluating the success of antitrust in the United States.

The Antitrust Laws

The thrust of each of the five major U.S. antitrust laws is to limit market power or to prohibit undesirable business practices. All were enacted in response to perceived business abuses—allegations against Standard Oil, the railroads, and others. Late in the last century, there was strong political support for a constitutional amendment to outlaw monopolies.

The Sherman Act Against this background, the Sherman Antitrust Act was enacted in 1890.

The two major provisions of the **Sherman Antitrust Act** are:

Section 1: Every contract, combination in the form of trust or otherwise, or conspiracy, in restraint of trade or commerce among the several States, or with foreign nations, is hereby declared to be illegal.

Section 2: Every person who shall monopolize, or attempt to monopolize, or combine or conspire with any other person or persons, to monopolize any part of the trade or commerce . . . shall be deemed guilty of a felony . . . .

Both sections then go on to spell out penalties for violation of the law. Corporations may be fined up to $1 million; individuals may be fined up to $100,000, or they can be imprisoned for up to 3 years, or both, at the discretion of the court.[3]

Section 2 has been especially hard to enforce. Identifying the market to prove "monopolization" requires scrutiny of both the market (geographic characteristics?) and the nature of the product (substitutability from the vantage points of both consumers and other potential producers). Once such questions are settled, the court must determine what constitutes a monopoly. Must a firm control 100 percent of a market to be guilty of monopolization? Should a 90 percent market share be illegal? 80 percent? 70 percent?

Section 2 also prohibits "attempts to monopolize." What conduct is intended to produce a monopoly? It seems strange from today's perspective, but early court cases often prosecuted union strikers as violators of the Sherman Act. These cases and other ambiguities in the Sherman Act led to passage of more specific antitrust laws.

The Clayton Act In 1914, The Sherman Act was amended by the **Clayton Act**, which spelled out particular offenses more precisely and introduced into law the phrase "where the effect [of various practices] may be to substantially lessen competition or tend to create a monopoly."

---

3. The Sherman Antitrust Act was originally passed in 1890. The fine for violating the act was raised from $5,000 to $50,000 in 1955 and then to $100,000 for individuals and $1,000,000 for corporations in 1976. The 1976 amendments also made Sherman Act violations (previously misdemeanors) into felonies and raised the maximum prison term from 1 year to 3 years.

According to the **Clayton Act**:

Section 2: It shall be unlawful for any person engaged in commerce . . . to discriminate in price between different purchasers of commodities of like grade and quality . . . .

Section 3: It shall be unlawful for any person engaged in commerce . . . [to require buyers to agree] . . . that the lessee or purchaser thereof shall not use or deal in the goods . . . of a competitor . . . of the lessor or seller . . . .

Section 4: [This technical section prohibits mergers where the effect is to "substantially lessen competition or tend to create a monopoly."]

Section 8: [This section forbids interlocking directorates, prohibiting any individual from being a director of competing corporations if any of the firms has capital in excess of $1 million.]

The courts have enumerated many specific standards for enforcement of the price discrimination section (Section 2). For example, price discrimination is permitted if a defendant can show that it does not reduce competition (e.g., discounts for senior citizens to movies and super-saver fares on airlines). Moreover, price discrimination is permitted for intangible properties or services, or where differences in costs account for different prices.

Courts constantly deal with such schemes such as *tie-in sales* under Section 3. (For a long time, IBM only leased its computers and forbade attaching its equipment to equipment produced by competitors. A.B. Dick tied sales of ink to its mimeograph machines.) New schemes are constantly hatched by firms trying to skirt the provisions of Section 3.

The Federal Trade Commission Act   The **Federal Trade Commission (FTC) Act** of 1914 created a commission, the FTC, to investigate and challenge any "unfair methods of competition . . . , and unfair or deceptive acts or practices in or affecting commerce." The act did not define "unfair practices," leaving the interpretation of the statute and the determination of what practices are unfair or deceptive up to the FTC, subject to review by the courts. The courts have severely restricted the scope of the FTC. Curtail-

ing business fraud and such deceptive practices as false and misleading advertising has been one area where it has been reasonably effective.

More recently, the FTC has turned its attention to restrictive state and local regulations and licensing practices that limit competition. For example, the FTC forced the American Medical Association (AMA) and the American Bar Association (ABA) and their local affiliates to quit setting fees, respectively, for medical and legal procedures. For decades, these organizations had enforced high fee structures by censuring doctors or lawyers who did not abide by the fee structures with "unprofessional conduct." The FTC's vigor in challenging perceived unfair business practices ebbs and flows with the political tides, but the FTC remains a watchdog guarding consumer interests.

The Robinson-Patman Act   Section 2 of the Clayton Act was amended by the **Robinson-Patman Act** in 1936. This act was designed to limit price discrimination in the form of special promotional allowances. Discounts were permitted only where justified by differences in costs or when introduced as "good faith" efforts to meet competition. Because quantity discounts have been attacked under the Robinson-Patman Act, many economists criticize the law as a protector of small firms from competition rather than a guarantor of competition. Huge differences exist between protecting competitors from failure and promoting competition.

The Celler-Kefauver Antimerger Act   The Clayton Act prohibited acquisition of a competitor's stock, but the Supreme Court distinguished between stock purchases and acquisition of assets (plant, equipment, and so on). Mergers were allowed if one firm acquired another's assets, even if through illegal acquisition of voting stock. Numerous mergers took this path during the 1930s and 1940s.

In 1950, the **Celler-Kefauver Antimerger Act** attempted to close this loophole by making it illegal to acquire either the stock or assets of a competitor. Additionally, the act erected special hurdles for mergers if there was a trend toward concentration in an industry. If two relatively small firms tried to merge to improve their com-

FOCUS 2

Von's Grocery — Only Numbers Matter!

The idea that competitive performance requires numerous competitors was once a hallmark of antitrust policy. Nowhere was this as evident as in the *United States v. Von's Grocery Company* (1966) case. Von's Grocery of Los Angeles acquired Shopping Bag Food Stores, combining the third and sixth largest local grocery chains for a total market share of 7.5 percent. The number of owner-operated single grocery stores had declined from 5,365 in 1950 to 3,590 in 1963. Over the same period, the number of chains nearly doubled.

The court held this merger illegal, observing that: "Congress feared that a market marked at the same time by both a continuous decline in the number of small businesses and a large number of mergers would slowly but inevitably gravitate from a market of many small competitors to one dominated by one or a few giants, and competition would thereby be destroyed. Congress passed the Celler-Kefauver Act to prevent such a destruction of competition." This Court simply counted heads and totally ignored the competitive changes that were taking effect.

A vigorous dissent by one judge argued that "local competition is vigorous to a fault, not only among chain stores themselves but also between chain stores and single-store operators." Over three-quarters of the acquisitions between 1961 and 1964 (including Von's) were "market extensions, involving neither the elimination of direct competitors in the Los Angeles market nor increased concentration of the market . . . . [The majority opinion is] . . . nothing more than a requiem for the so-called 'Mom and Pop' grocery stores — the bakery and butcher shops, the vegetable and fish markets — that are now economically and technologically obsolete in many parts of the country."

---

petitive position, the Celler-Kefauver Act (as interpreted) would prohibit such a merger even if this might improve competition (see the Von's Grocery case in Focus 2). Until recently, this act virtually eliminated horizontal and vertical mergers among major corporations. The basic contents of the five major acts are summarized in Table 3.

Exemptions from Antitrust Laws

The Sherman Antitrust Act made every "combination . . . in restraint of trade" illegal. As this act was interpreted by the courts, political pressures and economic realities arose that have virtually exempted several important groups from antitrust prosecution.

Agricultural Cooperatives   The Clayton Act exempted agricultural associations so that nonprofit cooperatives could be formed without violating the antitrust laws, although some constraints try to prevent cooperatives from setting their prices "unduly" high.

Labor Unions   National policy favors the right of workers to unionize and bargain collectively. The Sherman Antitrust Act, however, was originally used to stifle union activity. Sections 6 and 20 of the Clayton Act largely exempted collective bargaining by workers from antitrust actions.

Table 3 *Summary of Antitrust Laws*

Statute and Year of Enactment	Major Provisions
Sherman Antitrust Act (1890)	Prohibits contracts, combinations, and conspiracies in restraint of trade and forbids monopolization or attempts to monopolize.
Clayton Act (1914)	Prohibits certain forms of price discrimination, contracts that prevent buyers from dealing with sellers' competitors, acquisition of one corporation's shares by another if the effect will be to substantially lessen competition, and interlocking directorates between competing corporations.
Federal Trade Commission Act (1914)	Established the FTC to investigate unfair and deceptive business practices.
Robinson-Patman Act (1936)	Amended the Clayton Act (Section 2) to prohibit discounts and other special price concessions. Price discrimination is permissible only where it is: 1. based on differences in cost. 2. a good faith effort to meet competition. 3. based on differences in marketability of product.
Celler-Kefauver Antimerger Act (1950)	Amended Section 7 of the Clayton Act to plug the loopholes that permitted merger via acquisition of assets. In addition, the law prohibited mergers where there was a trend toward concentration.

Sports Organizations   Curiously, the courts have almost totally exempted professional baseball and have provided specialized exemptions for other amateur and professional sports organizations from antitrust actions on the strange doctrine that they are not in interstate commerce because sporting events are "entertainment, not business." Thus, the NFL, NBA, NCAA, AAU, and a variety of other associations in our multibillion-dollar sports industry are reasonably free to collude against their employees, potentially competitive organizations, or each other. These exemptions are, however, increasingly under attack in the courts. NFL players, for example, want antitrust laws applied to eliminate the NFL by-laws that limit each player's right to negotiate with teams other than those that "drafted" or traded for them.

Export Industries   The Webb-Pomerene Act of 1918 largely exempts from antitrust actions those associations that focus on export trade. Many nations encourage cartel formation for purposes of international trade. The Webb-Pomerene Act enables U.S. firms to engage in joint ventures when competing with foreign cartels. Export trade associations may legally act somewhat like cartels for American firms, but only in their international operations.

Regulated Industries and Insurance   Our "Regulation" chapter discusses how detailed regulation replaces market forces in some industries. Normally, the tighter is public regulation, the greater the exemption from antitrust laws. For example, public utilities are seldom challenged, because their rights to monopolize are recognized and their rate structures are regulated. Because regulatory agencies presumably express the public interest, exemption from antitrust laws seems sensible to allow the public to realize any gains from cooperation among regulated firms.

Some states set rate structures for certain types of insurance. Consequently, Congress and the courts have helped insurance companies squeeze under this national umbrella of protection from antitrust action. Huge settlements in suits for damages probably account for much of the high cost of insurance in our litigious society, but freedom to collude on rate structures may be another reason why so many complain about the high cost of insurance.

The Antitrust Laws in Practice

Current antitrust enforcement is based on the Sherman Act, as amended, but Sections 1 and 2 are rather broadly written. What are the meanings of *monopolize* and *attempts to monopolize*? What behavior is permitted, and what is prohibited? And how will oligopolists be treated? How will firms know if they can merge without the threat of prosecution?

Monopolization and Market Power

A literal interpretation of Section 1 of the Sherman Act would ban most major transactions. The Sherman Act was vague about what was legal and what was not, leaving that decision to the courts. Nor does Section 2 clearly define "monopoly." To make matters worse, the courts historically have been a bit schizophrenic in interpreting the Sherman Act.

The "Rule of Reason" In two early cases involving Standard Oil and the American Tobacco Company, the Supreme Court ruled that trusts (monopolies) could either be "good" or "bad" and suggested that the Sherman Act only outlaws "bad" restraints on trade.

> *The* **rule of reason** *approach attempted to distinguish good trusts from bad trusts, using such criteria as whether they set their prices to yield supernormal profits, or attempted to run competitors out of business.*

Both Standard Oil and American Tobacco were judged "bad" trusts and were subjected to **divestiture** — they were split into several firms.

Certain anticompetitive practices (refusals to deal and tie-in sales) were permitted if a firm proved that its conduct fit logically with other practices permitted by law. Whether a practice was held to be "reasonable" depended on such things as the percentage of the market affected, expected duration of the practice, and the relative strengths of the parties involved.

The *Per Se* Doctrine In the 1945 case of *U.S. v. Aluminum Co. of America* (*Alcoa*), the Supreme Court applied the **per se doctrine** to interpret antitrust laws. The Court reasoned that the Sherman Act does not condone "good" trusts and forbid "bad" trusts; it prohibits all monopolization and restraints on trade. Whether a firm abused its power or obtained its monopoly by reasonable methods was irrelevant. The fact of monopoly was sufficient. In this case, Alcoa was forced to sell some assets to other producers to enhance competition in the aluminum industry.

> *The* **per se doctrine** *asserts that certain contracts or combinations seem inherently so contrary to competition that they are illegal per se.*

The government needs only to show that such agreements were reached; whether competition has been harmed is immaterial. *Per se* violations include: (*a*) price-fixing agreements, (*b*) schemes to split customers into territories, (*c*) agreements between competitors to refuse to deal with certain suppliers or customers, and (*d*) "tie-in sales," where a dominant seller forces a buyer to purchase peripheral products in order to purchase the desired good.

After the *per se* approach was adopted, the courts also began trying to address what constitutes a monopoly by looking at such factors as the number, size, and strength of the firms in the market, the nature of the technology, and any economies of scale.

Oligopolies and Antitrust

Market power hinders allocative efficiency and may create inequity, regardless of whether this power is exercised by a monopolist or shared among firms in an oligopoly. However, the Sherman Antitrust Act outlaws *monopolies* and *attempts to monopolize*. To what extent do oligopolies represent "attempts to monopolize"? The kinked demand curve model suggests that stability in pricing might be one hallmark of oligopoly. When oligopolistic prices change, we would predict that all prices in the industry will change simultaneously and by roughly similar amounts due to the close relationships among the oligopolists.

Conscious Parallelism of Action Noncollusive oligopolistic interaction may cause identical behavior that is as effective in restraining trade as an overt cartel agreement among firms, but there are no witnesses or documents to prove conspiracy. The dilemma is clear — parallel oligopolistic actions are often allocatively harmful, but the parallel action results from oligopolistic interdependence; the Sherman Act requires proof of conspiracy.

The FTC developed the idea of conscious parallelism of action to deal with this problem. In several landmark cases, the Supreme Court inferred conspiracy from parallel action by competitors.

> **Conscious parallelism of action** *is an inference of "attempts to monopolize" from like changes in prices and outputs by competitors.*

This approach lasted several decades but was eventually overturned. Courts now examine the totality of conduct rather than looking only at parallel action, which is not illegal *per se*. Parallel business policies are recognized as potentially arising from (*a*) independent judgment, (*b*) noncompetitive behavior, or (*c*) the dynamics of competition. (Pure competition yields simultaneous price adjustments — a trait shared with numerous oligopoly models.) Clearer evidence of conspiracy is now required for a finding of an illegal attempt to monopolize.

Merger Policy

Some antitrust efforts are intended to squelch market power in its infancy. Strong antimerger policies evolved over the years, but many were abandoned in the early 1980s. The **Hart-Scott-Rodino Antitrust Improvement Act** of 1976 permits the Department of Justice to require (*a*) any information relevant to an investigation, and (*b*)

premerger notification by firms. The latter provision forces big firms to wait 30 to 50 days after notifying the government before consummating any merger. During the waiting period, the Department of Justice can evaluate the legality of proposed mergers, and it can immediately sue to block mergers it opposes. This approach helps avoid the messy puzzle often encountered in the dissolution of a company that has already been merged.

In 1982, the Justice Department announced merger guidelines to improve the predictability of federal merger policy. After noting that numerical standards must be tempered by judgment, the Department categorized mergers according to (*a*) the level of the Herfindahl-Hirschman index in the industry and (*b*) the change in the index that would occur because of the merger. (This change can be calculated simply by multiplying the percentage shares of the two firms and doubling the answer.[4]) The following guidelines then indicate the likelihood of a challenge to a horizontal merger based on the postmerger HHI:

1. HHI < 1,000: **Unconcentrated Industries**

   The Justice Department is unlikely to challenge any such merger.

2. 1,000 < HHI < 1,800: **Moderate Concentration**

   If the HHI increases less than 100 points, the Department will probably not challenge the merger. A challenge is more likely the greater the change in the HHI.

3. HHI > 1,800: **Highly Concentrated Industries**

   Increases in the HHI of less than 50 points will probably go unchallenged, but mergers raising the HHI more than 100 points will generally be challenged. Changes in the HHI of between 50 and 100 points will be resolved by assessing other factors.

---

4. The Justice Department noted that ". . . in calculating the HHI before the merger, the market shares of the merging firms are squared individually. Thus: $a^2 + b^2$. After the merger, the sum of those shares would be squared. Thus: $(a + b)^2$, which equals $a^2 + 2ab + b^2$. The increase in the HHI therefore is represented by $2ab$."

The other factors considered include such things as (a) whether one of the merging firms is a dominant leader in the industry, (b) ease of entry into the market, and (c) ease and profitability of collusion. Where one merging firm is the industry leader (has a market share exceeding 35 percent and is twice as large as the second largest firm), the merger is challenged.

Horizontal mergers that might have generated economies of scale or other benefits were once prevented by rigid enforcement of antimerger laws, as typified by the Von's Grocery decision. The Department of Justice now takes the position that, "Although they sometimes harm competition, mergers generally play an important role in a free enterprise economy. They can penalize ineffective management and facilitate the efficient flow of investment capital and the redeployment of existing productive assets. While challenging competitively harmful mergers, the Department seeks to avoid unnecessary interference with that larger universe of mergers that are either competitively beneficial or neutral."[5]

The Future of Antitrust Policy

The complexity and size of modern business has parallels in the complexity and costliness of modern antitrust actions, which may turn into multimillion-dollar affairs. For example, seemingly continuous litigation against IBM was abandoned in 1982. It had absorbed thousands of hours by hundreds of lawyers, 104,000 pages of transcripts, 726 court days, and many millions of dollars during the 1950s, 1960s, and 1970s. A similarly enormous case against American Telephone and Telegraph was finally settled out of court in 1982.

Major market structures often differ so much from the model of pure competition that some economists and policymakers advocate vigorous antitrust initiatives. Antitrust laws have been on the books for almost a century, however, with little perceptible effect on our industrial struc-

ture. Indeed, huge merger waves closely followed the Sherman Act (1890), the Clayton Act (1914), the Celler-Kefauver Antimerger Act (1950), and the Hart-Scott-Rodino Antitrust Improvement Act (1976). A few corporate giants of past years have been dismembered by antitrust actions (Standard Oil, American Tobacco, and Alcoa), but most (GM, DuPont, General Electric, IBM, etc.) have escaped the antitrust hatchet largely intact.

Most antitrust litigation is initiated by small companies with complaints about low prices charged by competitors. Most antitrust battles turn on narrow interpretations of legal technicalities, with the courts frequently trying to protect competitors instead of competition. George Stigler, after reviewing international data, found little evidence that market concentration differs between countries that have strong antitrust laws and those that do not.

Is Antitrust Passé?

The magnitude of antitrust action depends primarily on the political climate. Teddy Roosevelt gained a reputation as a "trust buster" at the turn of the century, but attacking market power has been on a back burner in most recent administrations.

The reasons for vigorous antitrust policies have probably diminished over time. Our economy is increasingly open, so competition from foreign producers makes more of our domestic markets contestable. Indeed, many economists now contend that the most effective "antitrust laws" are free trade agreements that smash barriers protecting corporate giants from foreign competition. The tendency for adventurous conglomerates to engage in "hit-and-run" entry and exit whenever profits differ among markets is another powerful competitive force.

The continuing trend toward ever greater concentration of assets in the hands of the few hundred largest American companies, however, is very discomforting to people disturbed by the potential political aspects of concentrations of economic power. They consider it unfortunate that antitrust policies leave conglomerate mergers untouched.

5. Merger guidelines issued by the U.S. Department of Justice, June 14, 1982.

In this part of the book, we have examined the structure-conduct-performance of firms in product markets, various possible business strategies, and the arsenal of antitrust weapons available to government in its attempts to control the abuse of market power. In the next part, our attention is transferred to economic interactions in markets for labor, land, capital, and entrepreneurial talent.

Chapter Review: Key Points

1. *Market power* exists whenever a firm can set the price of its output. (Market power and monopoly are not synonymous.) Market power builds a gap between price and marginal cost. The *Lerner index of Monopoly Power* (LMP) uses this fact to measure market power as $(P - MC)/P$. However, estimating MC with accounting data is almost impossible.

2. Market concentration ratios provide some evidence of monopolization or oligopolistic power. *Concentration ratios* are the percentages of total sales, output, or employment in an industry controlled by a small number of the largest firms in the industry.

3. Major difficulties are encountered in defining an industry. The existence of *close consumption substitutes* is one consideration; the ease with which potential competitors might enter an industry (*contestability*) is another. The Department of Commerce lumps firms into Standard Industrial Classifications (SICs) to try to solve this problem, but with only mixed success.

4. The *Herfindahl-Hirschman Index* (HHI) is the sum of squared market shares (ΣS_i^2). Squaring places more emphasis on big firms. The Justice Department now uses the HHI as a guide to the permissibility of mergers.

5. *Concentration* varies substantially between industries. Nearly 100 percent of all cigarettes produced and sold in the United States are produced by fewer than eight companies, but the eight largest printing companies produce only about one-tenth of all printing. However, roughly 70 percent of all manufacturing assets are controlled by the 200 largest American corporations. Concentration ratios grew dramatically in many industries before 1930, but the average has crept up only slowly, if at all, since then.

6. Big firms might be justified by enormous capital requirements or substantial economies of scale. In such cases, proper public policy may take the form of regulation. The major thrust of public policy where no such justifications for bigness exist has been to encourage competition through *antitrust actions*. The current level of concentration is testimony to the apparent failure of this policy.

7. One reason for merger is to increase the scope of a firm's operations so that economies of scale in information, marketing, advertising, production, or financial management may be exploited. The job security of executives is occasionally a motive, and raises the issue of the principal/agent problem. A third reason, by far the most important for policy, is that merger eliminates business rivals and facilitates economic concentration and market power. Increases in market power that result from merger may be reflected rapidly in higher prices for the merged companies' stock. This creates *promotional profit* for current stockholders.

8. The first major wave of mergers in the United States lasted roughly from 1890 until 1914 and was dominated by *horizontal* mergers—the absorption of competitors.

9. Most horizontal mergers were outlawed with the passage of the *Clayton Act*, so a wave of *vertical* mergers, lasting from 1914 until the 1929 stock market crash, resulted in further economic concentration. Vertical mergers unite suppliers of raw materials or intermediate goods with processors or other firms further along the production chain.

10. Merger activity died during the Great Depression, but revived in the mid-1950s. Because most vertical mergers were prohibited by the Celler-Kefauver Antimerger Act,

companies that were very dissimilar were merged into *conglomerates*.

11. Merger activities slowed down during the 1970s but reemerged strongly during the 1980s in a fourth wave that some people describe as "the golden age of dealmaking." Mergers slowed sharply in 1990, however, after (*a*) some "dealmakers" were prosecuted for manipulating stock values and trading on "insider" information, and (*b*) the economy sank into a recession.

12. The *Big Five Antitrust Laws* are summarized in Table 3.

13. Agricultural cooperatives, athletic organizations, labor unions, export trade associations, regulated industries, and insurance companies are largely exempt from antitrust action.

14. In applying the *Sherman Antitrust Act*, the courts have historically taken two different approaches. The rule of reason approach prohibits bad monopolies and permits reasonable restraints on trade, while the *per se doctrine* forbids all monopolies regardless of conduct.

15. Merger policy is now based on various factors, but if the postmerger HHI exceeds 1,800, the Department of Justice is likely to challenge the merger.

Key Concepts

Ensure that you can define these terms before proceeding.

Lerner index of Monopoly Power (LMP)	Federal Trade Commission (FTC) Act
concentration ratios	Robinson-Patman Act
Herfindahl-Hirschman Index (HHI)	Celler-Kefauver Antimerger Act
Sherman Antitrust Act	rule of reason
	per se doctrine
Clayton Act	conscious parallelism of action

Problems and Questions

Compute values for the Lerner Index of Monopoly Power (LMP) for problems 1–4. Rank these firms according to the amounts of market power your answers suggest.

1. Alpha Inc. Price = $100 Marginal Cost = $100

2. Beta Corp. Price = $0.60 Marginal Cost = $0.20

3. Gamma Ltd. Price = $12 Marginal Cost = $10

4. Delta Inc. Price = $5 Marginal Cost = $3

   Compute Herfindahl-Hirschman Indexes (HHI) for the industries described in problems 5–7 and indicate which of any possible mergers within each industry might be challenged under current Department of Justice antitrust guidelines.

5. Ten firms all share equally in total sales of silver eating utensils.

6. Percentages of total sales of automatic garage door openers are divided as follows: Macron = 40 percent, Contrails = 30 percent, Vulcan = 20 percent, and ten small firms each sell 1 percent of the total market.

7. The three largest tobacco companies respectively sell 51 percent, 29 percent, and 16 percent of all tobacco products. There are eight other tobacco firms, each accounting for $\frac{1}{2}$ percent of industry sales.

8. It has been argued that the emergence of large firms that wield sizable market power is an inevitable outcome of an unencumbered competitive process. Do you agree or disagree? Why?

9. According to standard theory, the major economic problem posed by the exercise of market power is economic inefficiency. Studies that have attempted to measure the "welfare loss" caused by monopoly have, however, yielded tiny estimates of loss. No serious empirical study suggests that more than 1 to 2 percent of GNP is lost because of market power, with most estimates being much less than 1 percent.[6] Is antitrust a waste of taxpayers' resources if these estimates are correct? Are there other socially important reasons to limit industrial concentration? If so, what are they?

---

6. The first such study (Arnold Harberger, "Monopoly and Resource Allocation," *American Economic Review* 44, May 1954, pp. 77–87) estimated this loss at only 1/10 or 1 percent of our GNP. No subsequent reputable study has estimated a loss exceeding 1 percent of GNP.

10. When the Oakland Raiders moved to Los Angeles in 1982, they touched a vital nerve of the National Football League. This move, which was subsequently upheld by the courts, weakened the NFL's influence over the movement of franchises and threatened to undercut the pooling of network television revenues (60 percent of NFL income). The NFL is now lobbying Congress for a blanket antitrust exemption. Do you think professional sports should be exempt from antitrust laws? Should owners of professional teams be permitted to move their teams at their discretion? NFL critics argue that the league "is more interested in limiting the number of teams and ensuring profits for the existing 28 owners." Do you agree?

11. The U.S. Department of Justice and the Federal Trade Commission are responsible for ensuring that industrial performance closely approximates the performance of the competitive ideal. Would it be feasible or even beneficial for these federal watchdogs to use the antitrust laws to impose competitive structures on all industries that are highly concentrated? Why?

12. In some concentrated industries, most notably cigarettes and breakfast cereals, the largest firms continually introduce new brands so fast that entry into the industry by smaller firms may be virtually impossible. Should these barriers to entry be permitted? Would consumers lose if existing firms were required to reduce the number of brands they market? Explain.

13. A decade ago, the computer industry was dominated by a few companies. Today, competition is fierce. What accounts for the change — government antitrust action? Is the same thing likely to occur in steel, aluminum, and other basic industries? Why?

14. In 1982, the Justice Department proposed to attack a horizontal merger if, after defining the relevant product market for the merged firm, a hypothesized price increase of 5 percent could be expected to be sustained for over a year. Is this a reasonable measure of increased concentration from a merger? Why?

15. Government antitrust actions have been notoriously large and expensive (the IBM and AT&T cases are examples). The typical *private* antitrust case involves about $50,000 in legal fees for each side, about 30 hours of top executives' time, and is usually completed within 2 years. Because private antitrust actions are relatively inexpensive, some have argued that the law should be liberalized to permit more private antitrust suits and curtail the federal government's role. Do you think this is a workable solution to the mounting costs of federal antitrust litigation? What problems might this pose?

Aspen Skiing Co. v. Aspen Highlands Skiing Corporation (1985)

 Firms with market power are convenient targets for private antitrust suits from smaller rivals. Is a company with considerable market power under an obligation to cooperate with its smaller business competitors or to enter into a joint operating agreement? Or must it refuse to deal with competitors? This recent Supreme Court decision examines these issues.

Aspen is a destination ski resort with a reputation for "super powder," "a wide range of runs," and an "active night life," including "some of the best restaurants in North America."

Between 1958 and 1964, three independent companies operated the Ajax, Highlands, and Buttermilk mountains. A fourth mountain, Snowmass, opened in 1967. In the early years, each company offered its own day or half-day tickets for use of its mountain. In 1962, however, the three competitors also introduced an interchangeable ticket. The 6-day, all-Aspen ticket provided convenience to the vast majority of skiers who visited the resort for weekly periods, but preferred to remain flexible about what mountain they might ski each day during the visit. It also emphasized the unusual variety of ski mountains available in Aspen.

As initially designed, the all-Aspen ticket program consisted of booklets containing six coupons, each redeemable for a daily lift ticket at Ajax, Highlands, or Buttermilk. The price of the booklet was often discounted from the price of six daily tickets, but all six coupons had to be used within a limited period of time—seven days, for example. The revenues from the sale of the 3-area coupon books were distributed in accordance with the number of coupons collected at each mountain.

In 1964, Buttermilk was purchased by Aspen Skiing Co. (Ski Co.), and, in 1967, Ski Co. opened Snowmass. In the 1971–1972 season, the coupon booklets were discontinued and an "around the neck" all-Aspen ticket was developed. This refinement on the interchangeable ticket was advantageous to the skier, who no longer found it necessary to visit the ticket window every morning before gaining access to the slopes.

Ski Co. and Highlands used random sample surveys to allocate the revenues from the 4-area, 6-day ticket. Highlands' share of the revenues from the ticket was 17.5 percent in 1973–1974, 18.5 percent in 1974–1975, 16.8 percent in 1975–1976, and 13.2 percent in 1976–1977. During these four seasons, Ski Co. did not offer its own three-area, multiday ticket in competition with the all-Aspen ticket. By 1977, multiarea tickets accounted for nearly 35 percent of the total market.

In the 1970s the management of Ski Co. increasingly expressed their dislike for the all-Aspen ticket. They complained that a coupon method of monitoring usage was administratively cumbersome. They doubted the accuracy of the survey and decried the "appearance, deportment, [and] attitude" of the college students who were conducting it. In addition, Ski Co.'s president had expressed the view that the 4-area ticket was siphoning off revenues that could be recaptured by Ski Co. if the ticket was discontinued. In 1978, Ski Co. offered Highlands a 4-area ticket provided that Highlands would agree to receive a 12.5 percent fixed percentage of the revenue. Highlands rejected the offer of the fixed percentage.

In its place, Ski Co. offered the 3-area, 6-day ticket featuring only its mountains. In an effort to promote this ticket, Ski Co. embarked on a national advertising campaign that strongly implied to people who were unfamiliar with Aspen that Ajax, Buttermilk, and Snowmass were the only ski mountains in the area.

Highlands finally developed an "Adventure Pack," which consisted of a 3-day pass at High-lands and three vouchers, each equal to the price of a daily lift ticket at a Ski Co. mountain. The vouchers were guaranteed by funds on deposit in an Aspen bank, and were redeemed by Aspen merchants at full value. Ski Co., however, refused to ac-cept them. Later, Highlands re-designed the Adventure Pack to contain American Express Travel-er's Checks instead of vouchers. Ski Co. accepted these in ex-change for daily lift tickets.

Without a convenient all-Aspen ticket, Highlands basically be-came "a day ski area in a desti-nation resort." Highlands' share of the market declined steadily.

In 1979, Highlands filed a complaint alleging that Ski Co. had monopolized the market for downhill skiing services at Aspen in violation of Section 2 of the Sherman Act.

Although Ski Co.'s pattern of conduct may not have been "bold, relentless, and preda-tory," the record in this case comfortably supports an infer-ence that the monopolist made a deliberate effort to discourage its customers from doing business with its smaller rival. The sale of its 3-area, 6-day ticket, particu-larly when it was discounted below the daily ticket price, de-terred the ticket holders from ski-ing at Highlands. The refusal to accept the Adventure Pack cou-pons in exchange for daily tickets

was apparently motivated en-tirely by a decision to avoid pro-viding any benefit to Highlands even though accepting the cou-pons would have entailed no cost to Ski Co. itself, would have provided it with immediate ben-efits, and would have satisfied its potential customers. Thus, the evidence supports an inference that Ski Co. was not motivated by efficiency concerns and that it was willing to sacrifice short-run benefits and consumer goodwill in exchange for a perceived long-run impact on its smaller rival.

Questions

1. This case seems to suggest that if a firm has market power and no valid business reason to refuse to deal with a competitor, it must do so or face treble damages under the Sherman Antitrust Act. Do you agree with this rule?

2. Suppose the four mountains in Aspen were owned by four separate firms, but one moun-tain was vastly superior to the other for skiing. Assume fur-ther that the firm owning the superior mountain refused to enter into a four-mountain, 6-day package with the other firms. Do you think this case would require cooperation or joint marketing of the four mountains?

3. Suppose that Aspen Skiing Company and Aspen High-lands Skiing Corporation de-cided to merge. What would happen to the HHI? Do you think the Justice Department would permit the merger? How are this case, Von's Gro-cery, and the current merger guidelines related? Is there a significant difference between the joint marketing arrange-ment required in this case and merger of the two firms?

4. Do these two firms have in-centives to enter into price competition? In effect, has the court ordered and immunized joint-profit maximization under the guise of protecting consumer convenience?

5. Should the court have only considered the Aspen ski mar-ket as the relevant market? Is there competition from other ski resorts in Colorado and the West?

6. Is the effect of this case to eliminate "making a higher profit and making life harder for your competitors" as valid business reasons? Is the Court correct when it states that Ski Co.'s acceptance of Adventure Pack coupons entailed no cost to Ski Co. itself?

PART 8

Resource Markets

Why are some people prosperous, while others are destitute? Our attention now turns to how similar interactions in resource markets affect the structure of resource payments and resource employment. This ultimately shapes the distribution of income and, at a more personal level, determines your own level of prosperity.

Most production costs are ultimately payments to resource suppliers. Demands and supplies of these resources share many characteristics of markets for consumer goods. Just as markets for consumer goods range from purely competitive to monopolistic, resource markets range from situations of diffused power to markets with single sellers or buyers.

A competitive approach to resource markets called *marginal productivity theory* is developed in Chapter 28. Firms' demands for labor depend on how much revenue each worker generates. This foundation for resource demands is blended with a theory of factor supplies to explain resource prices and allocations in competitive markets. We focus on competitive labor markets, but the forces of marginal productivity are exerted in competitive markets for all resources.

The use of economic power to alter wage structures and employment by large firms and such organizations as unions and employer associations are the subject of Chapter 29. Unions traditionally try to use their economic clout to raise wages, while firms traditionally try to maximize profits by holding wages and other production costs in check. In a static environment with little technological change, a large firm such as a big textile mill in a small Southern town may try to maximize profits by minimizing wages and other costs. Workers may react over time by combining into unions to bargain collectively for higher wages. However, in a growing economy with rapid technological change, this pessimistic view can be replaced with an optimistic view in which high profits go to creative firms with high-quality leading-edge products, which are generated by paying high wages to attract the best workers. This more dynamic view of the economic process envisions an endless stream of innovations coming from people as the key, not a boring stream of the same old standardized items coming from machines with people as mere robotized accessories. Human capital is central to this dynamic process, and investment in education becomes the key to prosperity.

Discussions of how markets for land, capital, and entrepreneurship determine rates of rent, interest, and economic profit await you in Chapter 30, which concludes with an overview of how marginal productivity operates to distribute total income among the owners of different resources.

CHAPTER

Competitive Labor Markets

All of us buy and consume goods. This requires most of us (children and retirees may be exempt) to generate income by selling resources—our labor, land, capital, or entrepreneurial talent. Your income is largely determined by the amounts and types of resources you control—and their prices. Technology combines with the extent of market competition to largely determine how resources are used and how well resource owners are compensated.

The competitive pressures in labor markets we analyze in this chapter operate, in varying degree, in all resource markets. The chapter begins with an exploration of firms' demands for labor when both labor markets and output markets are highly competitive. The choices people make about employment are our second area of concern; these choices underpin labor supplies. *Human capital theory*, our next topic, explains how people hone specialized skills to enhance their job opportunities. The resulting skill differentials influence both the demand side and the supply side of labor markets, which in turn determine equilibrium wages and employment.

Some people see current wage differentials as proof that life is unfair. Why do mediocre doctors make more than excellent plumbers? Why do outstanding teachers make less than second-rate lawyers? How disparate are wages according to gender, race, and age? Reasons for such

wage differentials are our final concerns in this chapter.

Derived Demands for Resources

Resource markets differ from markets for consumer goods primarily because resources usually satisfy human wants only indirectly, through production. Thus, people's *direct* demands for consumer goods create *derived demands* for resources—demands based on the resources' productive contributions to final consumer goods. In a sense, resource supplies are also largely derived, in that resource owners seek income to purchase goods—a worker, for example, trades labor for income with which to buy food and shelter.

Consumers' demands for goods yield **derived demands** *for the resources that produce those goods.*

This is why job opportunities for computer programmers and electronics engineers expand when industrial technology advances. Conversely, demands for teachers shrank when the post–World War II baby boom went bust and school enrollments dropped. Demands for teachers are now rebounding to accommodate the off-spring of the 1950's baby boomers.

The demand for final goods is one dimension of the demand for labor; the other is labor productivity, which depends on technology and the prices and availability of other resources. But how do profit-seeking firms translate these influences into a hiring decision? Recall that firms maximize profit by expanding output until marginal revenue equals marginal cost ($MR = MC$). A parallel condition specifies how firms maximize profits in labor markets: They hire additional labor and thus produce and sell more output until the last unit of labor adds as much to revenue as it adds to costs. This principle is the cornerstone for resource acquisitions in all resource markets.

The Demand for Labor

How do employers decide how many workers to hire? Would you employ someone for $8 per hour who could produce $10 worth of goods per day? Hardly. You would lose $54 for each 8-hour shift. But you would jump at the chance to hire a different worker who cost $8 hourly and generated $200 in daily output. Firms' demands for labor are related to worker productivity and the value of output.

Let's return to your Colorado gold mine and assume that labor is the only variable input; other influences on production are fixed. The law of diminishing marginal returns means that beyond some point, extra workers add less and less to total production. For simplicity, Table 1 ignores the possibility that specialization might initially yield increasing returns. The first miner hired generates 3 ounces of gold weekly. Employing a second raises total output to 5 ounces per week, for a gain of 2 ounces per week. This *marginal physical product of labor* (MPP_L) is listed in column 3 for up to 10 workers.

Marginal Revenue Product

Computing the marginal revenue product requires calculating the extra revenue from the gold each additional miner produces.

> **Marginal revenue product (MRP)** *is the extra sales revenue from the output* [$\Delta TR = \Delta (P \cdot q)$] *generated by an extra resource unit* (ΔL).

Regardless of market structure, all firms base hiring decisions about all resources on each factor's *MRP*, which can be calculated as either $\Delta Pq \div \Delta L$ or $MR \times MPP_L$ (marginal revenue times marginal physical product of labor). A re-

---

Table 1   *Data for Western Gold Mine*

(1) Number of Workers L	(2) Total Oz. of Gold Produced per Week q	(3) Marginal Physical Product of Labor MPP_L	(4) Price of Gold per Oz. $P = MR$	(5) Value of the Marginal Product of Labor $VMP = MRP$
1	3.0	3.0	$500	$1,500
2	5.0	2.0	500	1,000
3	6.8	1.8	500	900
4	8.4	1.6	500	800
5	9.8	1.4	500	700
6	11.0	1.2	500	600
7	12.0	1.0	500	500
8	12.8	.8	500	400
9	13.4	.6	500	300
10	13.8	.4	500	200

Note: This table assumes that other factors are fixed and that gold is sold in a competitive market.

source's *MRP* reflects its value to a firm, which is not always the same as its value to society as a whole.

Value of the Marginal Product How socially valuable is a resource? We showed earlier that a good's price approximates its marginal social benefit ($P \cong MSB$).[1] Similarly, a resource's marginal social benefit is the value (as measured by price) of its marginal physical product, calculated as $P \times MPP$.

> *The social value of the output produced by the marginal worker is known as the* **value of the marginal product (VMP)**.

In competition $P = MR$, so the marginal revenue product of labor ($MRP_L = MR \times MPP_L$) and the value of the marginal product are identical ($VMP_L = MRP_L$).

International markets set a competitive price for gold, which in Table 1 is assumed to be $500 per ounce (column 4). The value of the marginal product in column 5 is computed by multiplying columns 3 and 4. A pure competitor's demand for labor is based on the value of its marginal product. Note that VMP_L is influenced by both labor productivity (MPP_L) and the demand for the product (P). Labor's VMP_L curve in your gold mine is illustrated in Figure 1; this is your short-run demand curve for labor.

Marginal Factor Cost

The number of miners you will hire to maximize profits depends on what you must pay them.

> **Marginal factor cost (MFC)** *is the extra cost incurred in hiring an additional unit of a resource.*

Marginal factor costs are identical to wage rates (w) in purely competitive labor markets. All payments for labor (e.g., salaries and such fringe

---

1. This statement assumes that resource endowments are deemed equitable and that externalities are absent. We discuss complications caused by externalities and inequity in later chapters.

FIGURE 1 A Competitive Firm's Demand for Labor (Data for Western Gold Mine)

Firms hiring in competitive labor markets can hire as many workers as they want at the going wage rate, because the supply of labor is perfectly elastic. A competitive firm's short-run demand for labor is the value of the marginal product curve for labor (VMP_L). A competitive firm that hires competitively is in equilibrium when $VMP_L = w$ (the wage rate). This firm will not hire more than six workers because the cost of the seventh ($w = 600) exceeds the value of this last worker's output ($500). (*Note:* This figure is based on Table 1.)

benefits as health insurance and paid vacations) are considered *wages*.

The profit-maximizing rule for output decisions (expand until $MR = MC$) leads to the idea that more resources will be hired as long as the extra funds brought in by a resource (its *MRP*) are at least as great as the money taken away (its *MFC*). Thus, hire more of any input whenever $MRP \geq MFC$. For purely competitive firms operating in competitive labor markets, this translates into a rule: Hire until the VMP_L of the last worker employed equals that worker's marginal factor cost. Competitively set wage rates equal marginal factor cost, so profit maximization for pure competition requires that $VMP_L = w$.

Mining gold is hard, dirty work, so assume that a purely competitive labor market dictates that each miner be paid $600 weekly. At this wage, you hire six miners (point *e* in Figure 1), because the value of the marginal product of the sixth worker is also $600. You would not hire a seventh, because the extra $500 in revenue to you is less than the $600 cost of hiring. You would hire a seventh miner only if weekly wages were $500, an eighth miner at $400, and so on. But if wages rose to $700 weekly, the sixth miner, who generates only $600 in marginal revenue product, would be laid off.

We conclude that, all else equal, the value of the marginal product curve for labor is a competitive firm's demand curve for labor. Just as changes in commodity prices cause movements along demand curves for goods, changes in wages trigger movement along demand curves for labor. And, by way of summary, the VMP curve is based on the demand for output as reflected in its price (P) and technology (MPP). Price hikes that reflect growing demands for goods also increase demands for the resources producing those goods — the VMPs of the resources rise because $VMP = P \times MPP$. Thus, anything that boosts marginal productivity also increases the demand for the resource.

Shifts in Demands for Labor

Competitive demands for labor ($VMP_L = P \times MPP_L$) may shift in response to changes in (*a*) output prices, (*b*) prices of other resources, (*c*) technology, or (*d*) the inherent productivity of workers.

Output Prices Many people treat gold as insurance. Political unrest could boost international demands for gold. If gold's price rises to $1,000 per ounce, your demand for miners' labor (VMP_L) rises from D_0 to D_1 in Figure 2. The amount each miner produces is unaffected, but the value of each output level doubles because gold prices double. VMP_L increases, raising profit-maximizing employment at the $600 weekly wage from six miners to nine (point f).

If waning interest in gold then drives down its price to $100 per ounce, your demand for miners shrinks to D_2. You will close the mine because the VMP_L of no worker ever exceeds $300 per week, but each miner's wage is $600. Not only must you pay the fixed costs of owning the mine, but you would lose an additional $300 per week even if you retained only one employee. You are clearly better off to shut down and lose only your fixed costs any time gold falls below $200 per

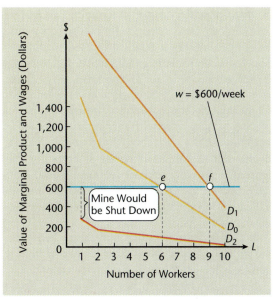

FIGURE 2 Shifts in the Demand for Labor

The value of the marginal product of labor equals the output price times the marginal physical product of labor ($VMP_L = P \times MPP_L$). Thus, changes in the price of output will shift the VMP_L curve, which is the competitive firm's short-run demand for labor.

ounce. (The VMP_L of the first miner is only $600 when gold is $200 per ounce.)

Prices of Other Resources Changes in the prices of other resources, and consequently in their utilization, can also shift demands for labor. Resources are frequently complementary. For example, miners' productivity tends to rise if lower capital costs induce investment in new capital equipment. Replacing dull picks and shovels with newer tools allows miners to recover more gold. Rising marginal physical products of labor would raise their VMPs and your demand for labor. Similarly, higher capital costs and reductions in capital per worker might reduce your demand for miners' services. In addition to their complementarity, however, resources are also substitutes for one another. For example, declines in capital costs or huge wage hikes could cause miners to be replaced by machinery. (Coal mining has been a declining industry for decades primarily because of aggressive wage hikes demanded by the United Mine Workers union.)

Technological Change Technological changes can directly raise demands for labor. You would hire more miners if newly invented machinery boosted each miner's productivity. But technological advances do not always raise demands for labor. Sophisticated new excavation equipment might replace some miners. The process of replacing human labor with machinery is known as **automation**. During the 1960s, some analysts feared that automation would structurally disemploy a growing pool of workers. These fears have proven groundless, because producing, repairing, and operating automatic machinery require labor.

Automation may cause temporary but traumatic dislocations of workers, even if falling demands for labor in some markets are offset by growing demands in other occupations. Some forecasters predict that industrial robots will increasingly take over routine assembly line work, and that employment will shift primarily toward service industries. Many auto workers lost their assembly line jobs when ''robots'' were introduced in the early 1980s, compounding the high unemployment in Detroit and other ''motor cities'' caused by slack sales worldwide during 1979–1983. In the long run, however, this automation may have saved more jobs than it destroyed. Without domestic automation, the growing comparative advantages of foreign automakers threatened the survival of the entire American auto industry and all its jobs.

The Quality of Labor Demands for labor rise when people work harder or acquire more productive skills. Education or on-the-job training can enhance labor productivity. Conversely, if miners began working less diligently, their *VMPs* and your demand for their labor would fall.

Elasticity of Demand for Labor

We have seen that the demand for labor is a derived demand and that employment varies inversely with the wage rate. But how much do wage changes affect employment?

The responsiveness of the amount of labor demanded (ΔL) to a change in wages (Δw)

is measured by the **elasticity of demand for labor,** *which is roughly*[2]

$$e_L = \frac{\%\Delta L}{\%\Delta w}$$

The elasticity of demand for labor is directly related to (*a*) the elasticity of demand for output, (*b*) labor's share of total costs, (*c*) the ease of substitution between labor and other resources, and (*d*) the time allowed for adjustments to changes in wages.

Price Elasticity of Demand for Output The more elastic the demand for a final output, the harder it is for a firm to raise prices to cover higher labor costs. For example, onion farmers individually could not pass on a raise to onion harvesters because the demand facing any single onion farm in perfectly elastic. A wage hike will lower the quantity of labor demanded substantially when higher wages cannot easily be passed on to consumers because the demand for the good is very elastic. Alternatively, if falling wages cause production costs and prices to drop, sales and employment will rise; the greater the elasticity of demand for the product, the more sales and employment rise. Thus, the more elastic (*inelastic*) the demand for the product, the more elastic (*inelastic*) the demand for labor.

Labor's Share of Total Cost A given wage change's effect on employment is positively related to wages as a proportion of total costs. For example, if wages are only 10 percent of total cost, a 20 percent wage hike raises total costs (and price) by roughly 2 percent. But if wages are 80 percent of total costs, a 20 percent wage hike exerts pressure for a 16 percent rise in price. For the same rise in wages, employment will be less affected in the first instance because smaller increases in output prices will cover the higher wage costs. Thus, the demand for labor is more elastic the greater labor's share of total cost.

The Ease of Factor Substitution The easier it is to substitute one resource for another, the

---

2. Precise computation of e_L requires using midpoint-based formulas as described in our chapter on elasticity.

greater the elasticities of demand for both resources. For example, if it is easy to switch from coal to oil or natural gas in generating electricity, then small changes in the relative prices of these fuels yield huge changes in the primary fuel used, and utility companies' demands for each fuel will be very elastic. Similarly, the demand for labor is very elastic if workers are easily replaced by machines, and vice versa, but the demand for labor tends to be more inelastic the more difficult it is to substitute other resources for labor.

Time Longer periods allow firms to adjust more completely to changing wages. Resource substitutions are easier and technological change also becomes more feasible. For example, soaring wage rates for coal miners during 1945–1965 stimulated automation and more efficient excavating techniques. Thus, the elasticity of demand for labor grows as the time horizon expands to allow more latitude about both technologies and resources. Table 2 summarizes the effects of these four factors on the elasticity of demand for labor.

The Supply of Labor

You should now have some ideas about ways in which productivity and output prices shape resource demands, and about some determinants of the elasticities of resource demands. We have assumed that a firm can hire all the labor it wants at a fixed wage, but demand is only one dimension of any resource market. Understanding labor markets requires us to examine supply as well.

The **supply of labor** *depicts the amount people are willing to work per time period at alternative wage rates.*

Labor supplies for individual markets and the economy as a whole are determined by

1. Population size and labor force participation rates.

2. Preferences of individuals about leisure versus income from work.

3. Rates and structures of wages.

4. *Human capital* — the education, training, and skills of potential workers.

These influences on labor supplies are considered next.

Population and Labor Force Participation

Almost 60 percent of our population participates in the labor force, but labor force participation varies by several characteristics, including age and gender, as shown in Figure 3. People aged 20 to 54 are, predictably, most likely to work for pay in the labor market.

A **labor force participation rate** *is the percentage of a given population that is in the work force, i.e., has a job or is looking for one.*

Social dynamics influence participation rates. Only 35 percent of women over 20 were in the

---

Table 2 *Influences on the Elasticity of Demand for Labor*

Demand for Labor Is

More Elastic if	Less Elastic if
1. Output demand is relatively elastic. (Vegetables)	1. Output demand is relatively inelastic. (Cigarettes)
2. Wages are a large percent of total cost. (Word processing)	2. Wages are a small percent of total cost. (Computer chips)
3. Resource substitution is easy. (Robots in manufacturing)	3. It is difficult to substitute resources. (Nursing care)
4. Firms have more time to adjust to wage changes. (Long run)	4. Time for adjustment is severely limited. (Immediate run)

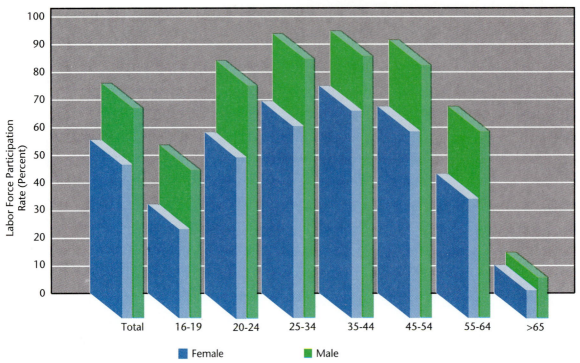

FIGURE 3   Labor Force Participation Rate by Age and Gender, 1990

Gender and age are only two of the many variables that influence participation in the labor force. Others include education, spouse's income or other family income, race, and the number and age of children in the family.

Source: *Statistical Abstract of the United States 1991*

work force in 1950. Today, 58 percent work for pay. Men's participation fell from 86 percent to roughly 76 percent over this same period. We need to examine some influences on individual labor supply decisions to explain trends of this type.

Labor-Leisure Choices

Suppose you are offered a job at $10 per hour and can set your own work schedule. Even if you are a full-time student, you might reduce your course load a bit to take advantage of such an offer. Assume that you decide to work 20 hours a week. If the offer were raised to $25 per hour, you might drop out of school altogether and work 40 or 50 hours per week. This means that your labor supply curve is positively sloped between wages of $10 and $25, as shown by curve *ab* in Figure 4.

Let's really get outrageous. If you were offered $100 per hour, would you work more than 50 hours weekly? Unlikely. At a very high wage, you might feel that you were making plenty of money with only 20 hours of work weekly. Two thousand dollars is a tidy sum, and if you work long hours, you might not have time to enjoy the fruits of your labor. Thus, in Figure 4 we show a *backward-bending* supply of labor for all wages above $25 per hour.

Why are individual labor supplies often negatively sloped at high wage rates? The key to answering this question is understanding that changes in wage rates alter the price of **leisure** — a good that is negatively related to the amount of labor supplied. You have less leisure time available the more you work.

Recall the income and substitution effects that we explored as separate aspects of people's responses to price changes for a good. The **substi-**

tution effect of a higher wage reduces your consumption of leisure activities relative to work because the higher your wage, the more income you surrender when you take off from work. As your wage rises, you tend to work more and consume less leisure time because the opportunity cost of free time has risen. There is, however, an offsetting **income effect:** The demand for leisure, as for any normal good, rises with income. Thus, your higher income causes you to want to "buy" more leisure by working less.

The income and substitution effects operate in opposite directions when the wage rate changes. At low wages, the substitution effect is generally more powerful than the income effect because total income is so low. Thus, a higher wage rate leads to the provision of more work because people tend to substitute work (and the potential for greater consumption) for leisure. When the substitution effect dominates the income effect, the labor supply curve is positively sloped. When your wages and total income are very high, however, the income effect tends to overpower the

FIGURE 4 The Individual's Supply of Labor

As the wage rate rises, it becomes increasingly costly not to work; therefore, the *substitution effect* induces people to work and reduce leisure. On the other hand, higher wages make greater incomes possible, and this *income effect* will cause people to want more leisure time to enjoy their income. If the substitution effect is more powerful than the income effect, the supply of labor is positively sloped. This tends to be the case when wages are low. However, at high wage rates, the income effect may overpower the substitution effect, in which case the supply of labor is backward bending.

substitution effect in your labor decision. This results in a backward-bending supply curve for your labor similar to the curve *bc* in Figure 4.

Wage Structures and Rates

A change in the wages of any member of a household may affect the labor supply decisions of other members. For example, if a primary worker's earnings failed to keep pace with inflation, other family members might enter the labor market to maintain the family's standard of living. Another possibility is that a wage hike for a primary breadwinner may induce other members to cut back their work effort as the family unit consumes more "household services" from other family members. If market wages rise for other household members, families may substitute in the opposite direction. Some economists argue that this effect is especially powerful if a family's entire income is subject to high tax rates. Focus 1 examines the effects of tax rates on labor supplies internationally.

Social roles, customs, and numerous other nonfinancial considerations also influence labor decisions. For example, the birth of a child may temporarily keep its mother at home. Desires for education or training also affect the timing and duration of individual participation in the labor force.

Supply and demand analysis normally assumes that each unit of the item considered is identical. Human labor, however, is far more variegated than are long-stemmed roses, bulldozers, or parcels of land. Some variations among people are innate and some are accidental, but many are cultivated to amplify differences in human productivity.

Human Capital

People are not born with the same potential intelligence or raw talent, but inherited differences are magnified or offset by acquired skills. Sharpening productive talents or acquiring new skills is called *investment in human capital.*

> **Human capital** *represents improvements made to the labor embodied in human beings.*

FOCUS 1

Labor Supply and Taxes: A Global View

Taxes, especially marginal income tax rates (the added income tax on additional income), inhibit people's willingness to put in additional hours or to work at all. Economists from Europe and the United States met recently to discuss how tax rates affect individual labor supplies. All economists applied the same research techniques to their respective countries to ascertain the extent to which income taxes have reduced labor supplies from families.

As Table 3 illustrates, the effect of progressive income tax rates on labor supplies was rather consistent across these countries. The magnitude of the negative effect of progressive income tax rates on the willingness of fe-

males to work is remarkable, and it became even more significant as the size of a woman's family expanded. These findings suggest that progressive income tax rates make it more difficult for society to achieve a balanced

labor force composed of equal numbers of men and women. In 1986, U.S. marginal tax rates were dropped to a maximum of 33 percent, at least partially explaining a recent surge in labor force participation by women.

Table 3 *Percentage Change in Labor Supplies Accounted for by Income Tax Rates by Gender (1983)*

Country	Men	Women	Maximum Marginal Rate
Sweden	−15	−29	58
France	0	−25	60
Italy	0	−20	72
United States	−2.6	−20	50

Source: "Special Issue on Taxation and Labor Supply in Industrial Countries," *The Journal of Human Resources*, Volume XXV, Number 3, Summer 1990. Note: All studies used data from the early 1980s.

Most of us spend years in school or in on-the-job training preparing ourselves to be more productive. Attention to our general health or migrating to find more suitable jobs also involves investment in human capital. Self-improvement fanatics may spend most of their lives acquiring human capital. We bring to our training or education certain natural aptitudes and strengths. Our abilities to perform certain tasks are honed as we invest in human capital.

Investment in Education Investment in new machinery or other physical capital requires sacrifices of potential current consumption so that

higher levels of future income and consumption can be realized. Acquiring new skills through education requires similar sacrifices. The time and money you sacrifice to attend college are examples.

College is partially a consumption experience for many students, offering football games, parties, and other social opportunities. Love of learning may also play a role, but most students perceive earning a degree as one step toward a higher income stream and access to "the good life." If you view your education primarily as an investment that should increase your future income, it is important to select your major carefully because some majors may merely make you a scholarly short-order cook.

Investments in human capital involve balancing higher lifetime earnings against the costs of acquiring valuable skills. As a college student, you must pay for tuition, books, and other out-of-pocket expenses, and you have less time available for current employment. Moreover, your first job as a new graduate may not yield the wage you might have earned had you moved directly from high school into the labor market and had 4 years of work experience. After a few years on the job, however, your income will probably exceed that of most high school graduates who went directly into the labor market.

Figure 5 graphs typical out-of-pocket costs and income forgone against lifetime earnings from a college degree. The top line in the figure reflects a typical earnings profile for college graduates over their working lives, while the lower line indicates average relative earnings for high school graduates who do not go to college. Area *A* represents out-of-pocket expenses, *B* is forgone earnings, and C is the gross returns to average college graduates. As long as your area C is sufficiently larger than *A* + *B* to cover a normal rate of return, you can benefit by investing in your education. (We detail this type of calculation two chapters hence.)

Your own prosperity depends on returns from your education, but society as a whole also shares in both the costs (through taxes) and benefits of much training and education. Education tends to make life more predictable and pleasant for everyone. For example, we all benefit from widespread literacy. Can you imagine the traffic snarls if most drivers could not read traffic signs? We also benefit by having well-educated voters. Moreover, well-educated people generally receive higher incomes, pay more taxes, and commit proportionally fewer crimes. Finally, more productive workers expand average standards of living by the extra output their higher productivity provides.

These are only a few of the benefits shared by educated people with society as a whole. These collective benefits justify some sharing of education costs through taxes. However, the share of gains going to others declines as we progress through the education system. Things we learn in grade school make us semicivilized. High school civilizes us even more, on average if not in every case. But more benefits derived from college are personal, either in the form of consumption now or higher income later.

Marginal productivity theory suggests that you will receive more income to the extent that a degree makes you more productive. The onset of

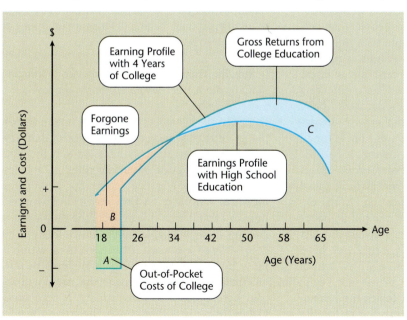

FIGURE 5 Payoffs from Investments in Education

High school graduates who immediately enter the work force will not incur the costs of education borne by their college-bound peers (area *A*) and will initially have higher incomes (area *B*). However, typical college-educated people eventually surpass the incomes of those who do not extend their formal education (area C).

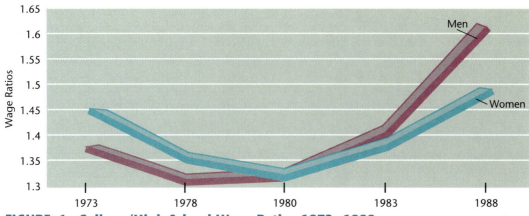

FIGURE 6 College/High School Wage Ratios 1973–1988

diminishing returns, however, implies that more education eventually yields successively smaller additions to your lifetime income. These reflections are supported by the private rate of return estimates developed by numerous economists over the last few years. Rates of return decline as individuals become more educated. For example, the personal rate of return from completing the last year of high school (9–11 to 12 years) is roughly 18 percent, while the average return from a college degree is now around 15 percent.

Figure 6 shows college/high school wage ratios for men and women during the past two decades. College/high school wage ratios reflect the average wage premium paid to people with college degrees compared to people with only high school diplomas. This wage premium is now 61 percent for men and 45 percent for women. Wage premiums fell during the 1970s, reflecting the rapid increase in college-educated "baby boomers" who outstripped the growth in demand for their services. Today, wage ratios for all college-educated people are growing.

One cautionary note: These returns reflect only private earnings and do not include social benefits and personal gratification from extended education. For example, the public benefits from the works of Einstein, Keynes, or most Nobel Prize winners probably could not have been produced by people with only high school educations.

Formal education is one way to acquire human capital. Education is a powerful device for the screening and signaling described in our "Strategic Behavior" chapter. Proficiency in some occupations is enhanced little by schooling, however, but grows immensely with experience and on-the-job training.

Work Experience Economists distinguish between general and specific training.

General training *increases a worker's marginal productivity equally for many firms.*

For example, general training on a computer raises a worker's potential productivity with many firms, and acting lessons may open up many roles to an actor.

Specific training *only increases the productivity of the worker where currently employed.*

For example, convicts learning to make license plates primarily increase their productivity for prison work, or actors rehearsing specific lines only perform better in certain roles.

General Training A firm invests in a worker's human capital only if it expects the employee to stay on the job long enough for the firm to recoup at least a normal return on its investment. How can a firm that invests large sums to train electronics technicians ensure that they will not quit before the firm's investment is recovered? Other firms are willing to pay the going wage for trained personnel. Firms will be reluctant to bear the costs of general training, so trainees typically bear these costs by temporarily accepting wages below the values of their marginal products. Apprenticeship programs are prime examples — apprentices pay for their general training by accepting wages far below those paid to fully trained workers.

The military uses a different approach. It guarantees substantial general training but requires recruits to legally commit to several years of service. This partially explains why the military harshly penalizes AWOL personnel or deserters. (Private employers cannot copy the military's example because slavery is illegal.)

Specific Training Although much of a technician's training is general, some portion normally represents specific training. Expertise gained when a technician works only on one firm's product often cannot be transferred to other companies; that training is specific to that employer. Firms can ignore competition for job-specific skills that lack value to other firms.

Firms consequently absorb the costs of specific training and share in the returns. Military weapons training or knowledge about a particular cost accounting system within a given firm or about a specific delivery route are examples. A firm tries to pay specifically trained workers more than its competitors would, but less than the values of the workers' marginal products. These slight wage premiums reduce worker turnover and ensure that, on average, firms secure returns on their investments in specific training.

Implicit Labor Contracts Employee turnover and quit rates are negatively related to wage premiums a firm pays employees with substantial specific training. Firms that invest heavily in specific training for their employees have strong incentives to retain them. Higher wages than other firms will offer are one way to reduce quit rates, but firms use many nonwage incentives as well. Many career employees do not pressure their employers for big raises during prosperous periods; in turn, these firms offer job security by not laying off such workers when business conditions soften. This behavior is known as an *implicit labor*

contract. Seniority rules and pension plans that tie benefits to longevity with a firm also cut turnover and enable firms to recoup their human capital investments.

Unfortunately, their shorter remaining work lives may exclude some older workers from job openings that require substantial specific training. This is one example of ways in which market outcomes may seem inequitable, and occasionally even cruel.

Wage Structures and Labor Supplies

Even if all individual supplies of labor were backward bending, the supply of labor facing any firm or industry in the long run would still be perfectly elastic or positively sloped. The explanation for this seeming paradox is actually very simple.

Suppose Accounting Associates of Atlanta (AAA), a major accounting firm, raises its wage offers slightly. No matter how content accountants happen to be, some will overcome inertia and leave their current jobs to take AAA's offer. More pay for the same work sounds pretty good, and the higher the pay, the more numerous will be the accountants available to meet AAA's labor requirements. AAA, an individual firm, is clearly faced with a positively sloped supply curve of accountants, even if the total supply of current accountants is backward bending. But how about the supply of workers facing the accounting industry? If wages for all accountants doubled, might backward-bending supplies of labor for all current accountants mean that less accounting gets done? *No!*

One reason is that some workers with accounting skills who are not presently using them would respond to higher pay by moving back into this line of work. Many young people seeking remunerative careers might also view accounting more favorably. These young people, plus established workers in areas with skills closely related to accounting (e.g., bookkeepers or financial planners), would view the jump in accountants' wages as a strong incentive to acquire more training in that field. Pay for accountants rose sharply in the 1970s and 1980s, and business colleges were flooded with accounting

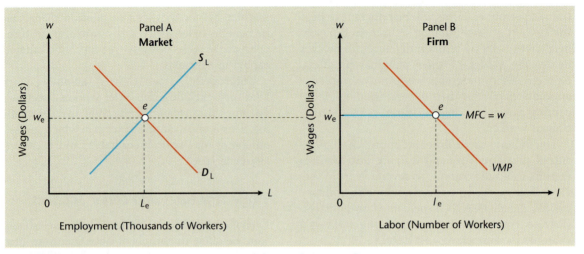

FIGURE 7 Equilibrium in the Competitive Labor Market

The wages determined in competitive labor markets (Panel A) determine the amounts of labor employed by competitive firms (Panel B), which expand their hiring until the value of the marginal product equals the wage rate ($VMP_L = MRP_L = MFC_L = w_e$).

majors. Similar adjustments occur in any industry with growing needs for any type of labor. Higher wages are magnets that attract extra labor services in the long run (just as economic profits attract entry and competition).

In summary, individual supplies of labor are normally positively sloped, but may bend backward at relatively high wage rates. Even if individual labor supply curves are negatively sloped, however, the supplies of labor facing firms or industries will be positively related to wage rates. The demand for labor depends on labor productivity, technology, the demand for the final product, and the levels of other productive resources employed. We are now in a position to merge labor market supplies and demands to see how equilibrium wages and employment are determined.

Labor Market Equilibrium

In a standard plot of some stories popular earlier in this century, Horatio Alger, a poor young country bumpkin, comes to the sinful "Big City." Through righteous thoughts and modest exertion, he wins fame and fortune. Unfortunately, righteousness, wishful thinking, or mod-

est exertion seldom secure high incomes. The Horatio Alger legend may occasionally come true, but marginal productivity theory probably more accurately reflects how labor markets will affect your future well-being.

Wages and Employment

Figure 7 depicts the interaction of labor supplies and demands for both an individual firm and all firms hiring from a given labor market. The market demand for labor, D_L, is only roughly the sum of individual firms' demands.[3] The market supply of labor, denoted S_L, is precisely the horizontal sum of individual labor supplies. Interac-

---

3. In deriving the market demand curves for consumer goods, we horizontally sum individual demands. In competitive factor markets, such summations of VMP curves are only a first approximation. Assume wages fell. Each firm in an industry would demand more labor and produce more output, but this added output could be sold only at lower prices. When the price of the good fell, each firm's VMP would shift to the left and less labor would be demanded, as you saw in the gold mine example. This effect reduces the market elasticity of the demand for labor, partially offsetting the employment effect of lower wages. Simple summation does not consider the effects of changes in factor costs on product prices. We leave an expanded discussion of this point to advanced classes.

tions of labor supply and demand determine the equilibrium level of wages (w_e) and employment (L_e).

Equilibrium processes resemble those in purely competitive markets for goods. If current wages are below equilibrium, shortages of labor create a tight job market, and employers will bid wages up in attempts to fill vacancies. During 1974–1984, wages rose sharply for anyone with expertise in petroleum or computers. "Head hunters" from employment agencies contacted some people every week or so to see if they were interested in changing jobs. Eventually, however, wages move toward equilibrium.

Wages above equilibrium create labor surpluses and unemployment. The unemployed will ultimately bid wages down as they try to secure jobs, but this can be a painful and time-consuming process. The recession of 1990–1991 depressed both the incomes of workers and local economies throughout the United States, especially in the Northeast.

Every firm that hires from a competitive labor market faces a labor supply curve that is horizontal at the existing market wage (w_e) and can hire as much labor as it wishes at that wage. Purely competitive firms hire only until the value of the marginal product of labor ($VMP_L = MRP_L$) equals marginal factor cost, which is the wage rate ($MFC_L = w$). In Figure 7, L_e workers are hired at a wage of w_e (point e in Panel A). Thus, the market clears when $VMP_L = MRP_L = MFC_L = w_e$; anyone qualified and willing to work at the prevailing wage is employed, while firms hire exactly as much labor as they choose. Purely competitive markets for capital, land, or entrepreneurial skills, which are explored two chapters hence, operate in a similar fashion.

Labor Market Efficiency

Adam Smith's "invisible hand" receives high marks for efficiency in purely competitive product markets. The demand curve for any good reflects society's marginal benefits, and the good's supply curve reflects society's marginal opportunity costs. If there are no externalities, resources are efficiently allocated where the demands and supplies for goods meet. These allocations reflect societal wants, given the prevailing structure of ownership rights to resources, which in turn largely determines the distribution of income.

Competitive resource markets are similarly efficient. The demand for labor reflects society's demands for the goods labor produces, because the VMP_L curve roughly portrays society's *marginal benefit* curve from employment. The labor supply curve facing an industry reflects the *marginal costs* to society of employing labor in that industry, because that labor might also be at leisure or employed in other industries. This is diagramed in Figure 8.

Society receives what it pays for when competitive labor markets are in equilibrium (point e) because the marginal social benefits and marginal social costs of employment are equal. Suppose employment were only at L_0. The marginal social benefits from additional employment and production equal w_1 (point a), while marginal costs are only w_0 (point b). A net social gain equal to distance ab can be realized by shifting an

FIGURE 8 Efficiency in Competitive Labor Markets

In a competitive world, labor markets operate efficiently. Demands for labor reflect the marginal social benefits (MSB_L) from particular employment, and labor supplies reflect the marginal social costs (MSC_L) of employment. In equilibrium, $MSB_L = MSC_L$, and there is efficiency.

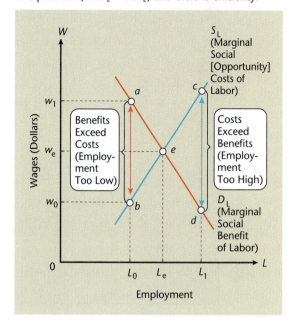

additional unit of labor into this industry. Thus, employment level L_0 is below the socially optimal level of employment in this industry. Conversely, if employment were L_1, the net loss to society from employment of the last worker would be distance cd.

Society's resources are allocated efficiently only when marginal social benefits and costs are equal, a result achieved in competitive labor markets because they are reflected, respectively, in the demands and supplies of labor. J. B. Clark, the first internationally prominent American economist, was the developer of the $VMP_L = w$ rule for efficiency in labor markets. His ideas still dominate analyses of resource markets.

Wage Differentials

It is no secret that one key to a high-paying job is expertise in a hot field demanded by many employers. The types of expertise in greatest de-

mand are constantly changing, in part because of the continuing growth of international trade. Focus 2 may help you pin down a strategy to help in coping with income and job instability caused by international trade.

You should recognize, however, that factors other than human capital can influence pay differentials enormously. In 1776, Adam Smith observed that if similarly valuable human capital is required in two jobs, then, all else equal, pay (including fringe benefits) will be lower for the job with working conditions that are more convenient, pleasant, slower paced, safer, more certain, or that require less responsibility. Figure 9 indicates how average pay varies across certain occupations.

Some jobs are so inherently obnoxious or dangerous that premium pay is necessary to attract workers. Suppose you had the option of greeting restaurant customers for $10 per hour or emptying grease traps for a restaurant chain at the same wage. Most of us would obviously choose to greet diners. This typical reaction shrinks the

FIGURE 9 Average Pay in Selected Jobs, 1990

Wage differentials reflect differences (*a*) in people (e.g., human capital, personality, employment discrimination), and (*b*) in the desirability of different types of work. This figure suggests how human capital and willingness to endure demanding, unpleasant, or dangerous conditions blend to generate wage differentials across various occupations.

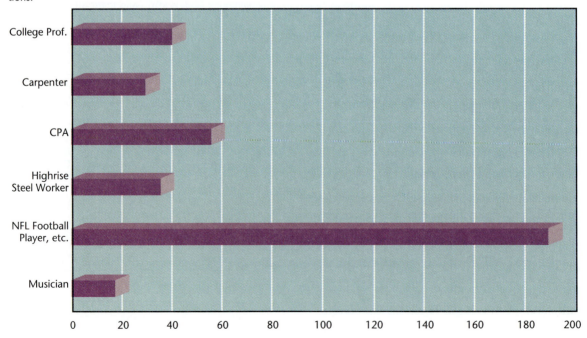

J. B. Clark (1847–1938)

John Bates Clark was the leading American economic theorist at the turn of the century. His position in American economics was similar to that of Alfred Marshall in British economics. Clark was an important innovator in economic theory even though he lacked the vigorous intellectual stimulation Marshall received at Cambridge.

Clark's complete writings were intended to restructure classical theories of value and distribution, but his most enduring contribution is found in the *marginal productivity theory of income distribution* set forth in *The Distribution of Wealth* (1899). Clark sought to prove that every unit of labor and capital is paid precisely the value it adds to total product—its marginal productivity. His model hinges on resource mobility, competition, and the law of diminishing returns.

Labor and capital are each interchangeable, according to Clark, so each worker or piece of capital is, in a sense, the last one. Clark reasoned that, although tasks within a firm differ in importance, if a worker engaged in an important task were removed, the remaining work would be reassigned so that all essential tasks would be done, leaving the least important tasks undone. This means that no single unit of labor is more important than any other.

Firms operate in a region of their production functions where diminishing marginal returns cause each worker added to a work force to raise total output by a smaller amount than did the previous worker. The employer will hire more workers as long as the last one hired contributes at least as much to total revenue as the cost of employing that worker. Because every worker is the marginal worker, and because the *last* worker hired adds to the employer's gross income an amount equaling the wage rate in a competitive labor market, all workers are paid the values of their marginal products.

Properly understood, Clark's marginal productivity theory is a rebuttal to Marx's charge that competitive capitalism systematically robs labor because workers contribute more to total product than the wages they receive. Clark maintained, on the contrary, that the payment to capital is also determined by its marginal productivity and that there is no "surplus value" expropriated from labor as alleged by Marx. Whatever amount of labor is employed, capital so shapes itself that each unit of equivalent labor is working with the same amount of capital. Thus, the product of every unit of capital is also equivalent to every other; when every unit is paid the value of its contribution to total product, there is no surplus to be expropriated. In short, each factor receives a payment determined by the product of its own final increment, and the reward to capital, no less than the reward to labor, is a necessary payment for its productivity.

Early economists were even more prone to take positions on normative issues than are economists today, many of whom pride themselves on their scientific objectivity (if such a thing is possible). Clark tried to use his positive findings to "prove" that payments of income according to contribution (marginal productivity) are inherently equitable. The fact that this idea is as controversial today as it was when Clark first pronounced and published his "proof" is testimony that normative issues cannot be resolved scientifically.

supply of grease-trap cleaners and expands supplies of labor for more pleasant jobs. Similarly, most people will perform more dangerous work only if they view the extra compensation for risk as appropriate. Thus, trash collectors tend to draw higher pay than ditch diggers, and specialists at putting out oil-rig fires receive premium wages relative to roofers. Even before *perestroika*, Soviet coal miners drew twice the pay of typical factory workers.

How Can You Compete in a Global Economy?

Armies of low-wage foreign workers haunt the dreams of many Americans. Are there ways to protect your financial future? Might pressures from international trade even boost your labor income? Fortunately, the answer is "Yes" to both questions. Before we try to outline a plan of action, however, you need some background information.

Chapter 2 and the last part of this book describe how standards of living everywhere are improved through specialization and exchange. International competition is also a powerful force to equalize prices globally, both for goods and for resources. Some economists describe a *law of one price*; others invoke a *factor price equalization theorem*.

A stereo sold in Belgrade must generate the same net revenue to a competitive producer (after transportation costs, taxes, etc.) as one sold in Quebec. International competition in certain labor markets also tends to equalize pay for, say, basketball players in Orlando and Rome (after adjusting for costs of living, regional preferences, etc.). But how does trade exert pressure to equalize wages for all comparable occupations in Barcelona, Melbourne, and San Diego?

One part of the answer is that, under fairly reasonable assumptions, free trade is almost a perfect substitute for resource mobility. A Soviet computer programmer does not need to physically relocate to Moscow, Idaho to compete with Idaho programmers. (*Tetris*, a computer game developed in the Soviet Union, is internationally popular.) Similarly, a French vintner can stay in Bordeaux while competing with California winemak-ers. Pressures from trade to equalize prices for goods also stimulate producers everywhere to adopt similar technologies. Microchip makers in Malaysia use the same basic technologies as chipmakers in Silicon Valley. This ultimately translates into similar marginal physical productivities of labor, and, consequently, wages.

A second type of international competition among workers arises from location decisions by multinational corporations. Consider a janitor in an Indiana plant that manufactures mirrors. If the company operating this plant could produce mirrors in Manila instead, then the Indiana janitor must compete for a job with a Filipino janitor. If the Indiana plant is relatively more costly, manufacturing will shift to the Philippines.

The third part of the answer is that workers compete with other

Regional wage differences arise from higher costs of living (New York City versus Atlanta), harsher climate (North Slope, Alaska versus Portland, Oregon), or less attractive scenery (Midland, Texas versus Boulder, Colorado). Some occupations offer stable employment (government service), while others confront workers with seasonal layoffs or uncertain futures (construction). Severe swings in employ-ment stimulate higher wages (steel work on sky-scrapers versus military enlistment). And people employed in occupations offering opportunities for tax evasion will be willing to accept lower "official" wages.

Some wage differentials arise from the condition of the firm or industry in which you are employed, or from local prosperity. Bigger firms tend to pay better than smaller firms, as do grow-workers within their national borders. If, say, U.S. bankers enjoy higher returns on their investments in human capital than U.S. lawyers do, then some Americans considering careers in law will switch to banking instead. These adjustments will continue until returns on comparable human capital investments are roughly equalized.

How does this analysis help answer the title question of this Focus? Competitive forces combine to equalize wages, interest rates, and rents for comparable land throughout the world. This means that if the resources you control are relatively scarce internationally, then your share of the gains from international trade (the increased purchasing power of your income) will exceed the average. But if your resources are even more abundant internationally than within your own country (e.g., unskilled labor), then your gains from trade will be less than average.

A sad reality is that unskilled Americans gain less from international trade than those with more human capital do, both absolutely and relatively, because they must compete with abundant numbers of unskilled foreigners. This may be the major reason why the share of earned income going to Americans at the bottom of the economic spectrum has declined over the past decade or so, while the share going to Americans toward the top of the spectrum has been rising.* (See the statistics in

*After transfer payments and in-kind redistributions (e.g., food stamps, medicare, subsidized housing), the share of total income (earned plus transfers) going to families in the bottom half of the income spectrum has increased consistently over the past 60 years or so.

our "Redistribution of Income" chapter.)

The world is full of bright industrious people. The trick is to tailor your resources so that they are relatively scarce in the rest of the world, even if relatively abundant in the United States. This usually entails acquisition of human capital. On average, Americans have better access to education than most people—although many foreigners are catching up quickly. Thus, the answer to our major question is almost a cliché: Get as much education as you can stand, and try to develop expertise that will be increasingly in demand as internationalization continues into the twenty-first century.

ing and more profitable industries. Stagnant local economies, on the other hand, at least temporarily tend to depress all wages. These problems are cured, in part, by labor mobility. In the long run, workers flow out of stagnant firms, industries, and regions, moving toward jobs in more prosperous work environments.

This chapter has focused on the effects of competition in labor markets, but many labor markets are far from competitive. Some imperfections originate in the private sector (e.g, employment discrimination or unions), but some also emerge from government policies (e.g., limits on the employment of youngsters, health and safety regulations, and minimum-wage laws). The next chapter explores some consequences of inadequate competition in resource markets and government policies for the labor market.

Chapter Review: Key Points

1. The demand for any resource is related to the (*a*) amounts of other factors employed, (*b*) production technology used, and (*c*) demand for the product. Because the demand for labor (or any factor) hinges on the demand for final products, it is a *derived demand*.

2. *Marginal revenue product* (MRP) is the firm's revenues generated by hiring the marginal unit of some input. In pure competition, this is the same as *VMP*. Any resource will be employed up to the point where the additional revenue competitive firms receive (the *value of the marginal product*, or *VMP*) just equals the cost of an additional unit of the resource (the *marginal factor cost*, or *MFC*). In competitive labor markets, the marginal factor cost (MFC) equals the *wage rate* (*w*), so pure competition in all markets means that $VMP = MRP = MFC = w$.

3. Increases (*decreases*) in the demand for the product, in labor productivity, or in the amounts of other resources used will normally increase (*decrease*) the *VMP* and demand for labor. Technological changes may either increase or decrease labor demands. *Automation* is the replacement of workers by new technologies.

4. The *elasticity of demand for labor* is directly related to (*a*) the *elasticity of demand for the final product*, (*b*) *labor's share of total costs* represented by the wage bill, (*c*) the ease of factor *substitution*, and (*d*) the *time for adjustment*.

5. The supply of labor depends on (*a*) wage rates and structures, (*b*) labor force participation, (*c*) the number of hours people are willing to work, and (*d*) the education, training, and skills of workers.

6. Workers experience both *income* and *substitution effects* when wage rates change. Increased wages cause labor to substitute work for leisure, because work expands consumption opportunities and leisure is more costly. However, higher wages mean that for a given amount of labor effort, workers will earn more income, and, if leisure is a normal good, they will want to consume more leisure and work less. If the substitution effect is larger than the income effect, supplies are positively sloped. Backward-bending labor supplies result when income effects dominate substitution effects.

7. While the individual's labor supply curve may be backward bending, the supply of labor to any industry will always be positively sloped. Industry supplies and demands for labor establish the *equilibrium wage*, as each firm hires additional units of labor until the value of the marginal product equals the market wage rate.

8. Competitive demand curves for labor represent the marginal benefits to society from additional employment, and supply curves reflect the marginal cost to society of using those resources. Employing labor to the point where $D_L = S_L$ is efficient because society's benefits from additional employment equal its costs. More or less employment than this yields inefficient resource allocations, because society gets more (or less) than it desires in an opportunity cost sense.

9. Labor quality improves through investments in *human capital, which* include formal education and on-the-job training. Education benefits both the individual and society at large. Training is classified as either general or specific: *General training* enhances a worker's productivity equally for many firms, while *specific training* only increases the worker's productivity for the current employer.

10. Turnover and quit rates are negatively related to the levels of specific training workers have received and to the wage premiums paid them. Firms that invest heavily in their employees have strong incentives to retain them and do so (*a*) by paying higher wages than other firms will offer, and (*b*) through special rules based on seniority or pension provisions that reward longevity with the firm.

11. The most important determinants of *wage differentials* are (*a*) human capital, and (*b*) working conditions. All else equal, premium wages are paid to compensate workers who endure less pleasant jobs.

Key Concepts

Ensure that you can define these terms before proceeding.

derived demand

marginal revenue product (*MRP*)

value of the marginal product (*VMP*)

marginal factor cost (*MFC*)

elasticity of demand for labor

supply of labor

human capital

general training

specific training

wage differentials

Problems and Questions

1. Marginal productivity theory suggests that people are paid according to the productive contributions of their resources, including labor. But such things as seniority rules clearly create situations where some people who are paid less are more productive than some people who are paid more. Do you think that the forces of marginal productivity generate a strong tendency for payment to be roughly proportional to contribution? Why or why not?

2. Some successful people like to brag that they started with nothing and owe "nothing to nobody." Marginal productivity theory suggests that technology and the amount of capital and the number of people we work with are powerful influences on our productivity and income. How are "rugged individualists" who believe they have "done it on their own" both supported and rebutted by marginal productivity theory?

3. Some 1930's radicals held that pay should be determined by how vital a job is to society. For example, people who maintain traffic lights or collect trash would be paid more than Hollywood stars or the promoters of such fads as Ninja Turtles. Do you think this argument has merit? Why, or why not?

4. Some highly intelligent, well-educated people work very hard and receive little in return. Is a Ph.D. in music who practices constantly and becomes the world's 211th-best oboe player entitled to more pay than a waiter is? Does capitalism undervalue artistry or esoteric knowledge? If so, how

should we determine appropriate incomes for people whom the market system spurns?

5. Distinguishing between labor and human capital can be extremely difficult. Are there any tasks that can be accomplished by raw labor untempered by some education or experience? If so, what are they?

6. In his book *Inequality*, Christopher Jencks argues that public education may lead to a meritocracy in which incomes differ greatly not because of inheritances of wealth but because of genetic differences. Does income often depend more on who you are than what you can do? Do you think public education facilitates social stability by providing nonviolent avenues for poor children to channel their energies toward becoming rich and powerful adults? Is a meritocracy fairer than an aristocracy based on birth?

7. Several studies, after adjusting for other individual characteristics, suggest that short men are paid less than tall men and that short men are less likely to be promoted. Other studies suggest that attractive people tend to receive higher pay and quicker promotions than do those who are considered either plain or beautiful. Are these results consistent with marginal productivity theory? Do you think these studies are correct? If so, what do you think accounts for these and similar findings?

8. Assume the following relationship holds for labor employed and lawns mowed per 10-hour day for your "Zippy" lawn service.

Labor	Lawns Mowed/Day
1	18
2	34
3	48
4	60
5	70
6	78
7	84
8	88
9	90

a. Compute the marginal physical product of labor for each additional unit of labor employed.

b. During the months of April and May you receive an average of $15 per lawn mowed, and labor costs $150 per worker per day. How many workers will you employ during these months?

c. Fierce competition from teenagers during June through August drops prices to $10 per lawn. If wages were stuck at $150 per day, how many employees would you lay off each summer? How much of a wage cut would your employees have to take to remain employed during June through August?

9. Your sports paraphernalia plant is facing labor cost increases of 20 percent because a new defense plant in your community is attracting workers and tightening the local labor market. You currently employ 50 workers and your wage elasticity of demand for labor is 1.10. How many workers will you continue to employ after the wage increases have taken effect?

10. Refer back to Table 1 in our "Production and Cost" chapter. Suppose that each ton of sand and gravel sells for $10, and that the figures shown are output per hour.

a. For wages ranging from $1 to $12 hourly, calculate the amounts of labor this firm would employ. (This is the firm's demand curve for labor.)

b. Repeat this operation assuming that sand and gravel sells for $8 per ton.

c. Assume each worker's marginal physical product increases by 20 percent because of a technological advance. How many workers would be hired if output sells for $10 per ton and the wage rate is $7 per hour?

Age Discrimination: Wayne R. Metz v. Transit Mix (1987)

Metz managed a concrete plant for Transit Mix in Indiana. During the three years prior to Metz's discharge, Transit experienced financial problems attributed to the decline in local construction. In November 1983, when Transit closed its plant and laid off Metz, it had not decided whether to close the Indiana facility permanently or only for the winter.

In February 1984, Transit sent the assistant manager of another plant (Burzloff) to inspect the Indiana plant. Burzloff took orders from the plant's regular customers while he was there and later requested that he be allowed to manage the facility. Transit approved, and in April 1984 discharged Metz.

At the time of his layoff, Metz had an annual salary of $26,000, or about $15.75 an hour. He was among the highest paid of Transit employees and, having worked for Transit for 27 years, was the company's second most senior employee. Burzloff was 43 and had worked for Transit for 17 years when he replaced the 54-year-old Metz as manager. Burzloff's salary as manager was about $8.05 an hour.

The Age Discrimination in Employment Act (ADEA) prohibits employers from discriminating on the basis of age. Its objective in part is to promote employment of older workers on the basis of ability rather than age. To permit recovery for an ADEA claim through indirect means, the plaintiff must first establish a *prima facie* case of employment discrimination. This requires showing that he or she (1) belongs to the protected class (age 40 or older), (2) was qualified for the position, (3) was terminated, and (4) was replaced by a younger person. The employer then has the burden of presenting evidence that the plaintiff's discharge was a result of "some legitimate, nondiscriminatory reason." If the defendant meets this burden, the burden shifts to the plaintiff to prove that the reasons proffered for discharge were merely a pretext for discrimination.

The ADEA has consistently been interpreted to prohibit an employer from replacing higher-paid employees with lower-paid employees to save money. Cost-cutting is not a legitimate, non-discriminatory reason for discharging an older employee while retaining younger, lower-paid employees.

Metz's salary reflected 27 years of service to Transit. When Transit decided that the company's poor performance no longer justified the salary given Metz, it replaced Metz without first asking Metz to take a pay cut.

We are, of course, aware that employers must control costs to remain competitive and that this imperative of survival inevitably creates conflicts with prohibitions against age discrimination. We think it would be unwise, however, to translate this imperative into a rule that an older employee can be fired and replaced by an equally proficient younger employee merely because the older employee happens to be earning more money.

EASTERBROOK, Circuit Judge, Dissenting

The earlier court found that Transit was not going to pay $26,000 to manage the Indiana plant because of inadequate business to support such a salary. We have held before that a firm may lay off employees of any age when economic conditions make that prudent. "Economic conditions" implies comparison of employees' wages with their product; a plant that is unprofitable at an average wage of $20 per hour may be a bonanza at an average wage of $10. If Transit had said: "We are losing money, in part because of your high salary, so we are closing that plant," Metz could not have complained.

Metz's victory today is Pyrrhic —not for him, but for older employees in general. The court tells employers to keep their

continued

plants closed. Throw overpaid employees out of work because their salaries are high but don't you dare hire anyone else at a lower salary. If that rule were widely followed, the Metzes of the world would be no better off, and the Burzloffs (also in the protected age group) would be worse off. They would be denied advancement, and other employees whom the Burzloffs would manage would never be hired. If Congress wants to hurt older workers, so be it. But judges should not go out of their way to injure protected groups.

The customary response is that no one is protected by the ADEA unless qualified for the job. An older employee whose skills have diminished is not qualified. Yet there are degrees of skill; an employee is not "qualified" one day and "unqualified" the next. The question is not "Is Jones qualified?" but "Can Jones do the job well enough to cover his wage?" A welder working on sheet metal at $10 per hour may be unqualified for a welding job paying $30 per hour in a nuclear plant where lives depend on the quality of the joint and other, better welders compete for the position. There is no "qualified welder" in the abstract, and there is no "qualified manager" either. To say that someone is "qualified" to manage the Knox plant is to say that he can add to the value of the enterprise at least the cost of his salary. If he cannot do this, he is unqualified for the particular job at the particular time. It is not possible to divorce the ability to do a job from the wage demanded. If the ADEA allows employers to make decisions based on performance—surely it does, even though performance is systematically related to age—then it also allows decisions based on the interaction of performance and wage. If the wage is too high for the performance, the employer may act.

If we apply this analysis rigorously, we will fundamentally change American business. A firm may not curtail its operations on the basis of high wages. A firm may not give lower-paid employees a wage increase without doing the same for higher-paid employees if wage discrimination is age discrimination. In times of corporate austerity, firms may no more reduce the salaries of their managers because that is age discrimination.

Would an employer, bent on slashing costs, find older employees' wages the most attractive target? This is a question about the profile of an employer's wage bill by the age of its employees. No evidence in this case shows that the wage-age profile at Transit has an upward slope. It is not appropriate to take judicial notice of a wage-age profile that creates a problem—

especially when the court is "noticing" something that is not true.

A growing literature on human capital suggests that there may be times when employers will pay wages that do not represent the employees' marginal products. For example, while receiving firm-specific training the employee may receive a wage exceeding his or her product; this is how the firm finances the training. Later the firm will recoup its investment by paying less than the marginal product. Other firms that give employees access to trade secrets or put them in positions of trust may try to cement the employees' loyalty (or honesty) with "golden handcuffs"—wages in excess of the employee's marginal product, a form of special compensation the employee forfeits if he leaves the firm. Still other firms may pay employees slightly less than their marginal product early in their careers, knowing that as each employee's productivity declines at the end of his career, the firm will be paying more than marginal product. This gives employees strong reasons to stick with their firms and be more productive throughout their careers, which in turn yields society the benefit of everyone's abilities.

Questions

1. This case outlines the general legal approach in analyzing cases where plaintiffs allege discrimination on the basis of race, sex, age, national origin, or handicap. Does this "prima facie" shifting of the burden of proof seem reasonable to you?

2. Will this decision lead to layoff provisions where only people in nonprotected classes will be laid off?

3. The ADEA is interpreted as prohibiting replacement of highly paid older workers with lower-paid younger employees. Since a large portion of the work force is between 40 and 65, does this rule effectively restrict firms to replacing workers between the age of 40 and 65 with workers who are older?

4. The majority opinion argues that Metz should have been asked to take a salary cut. Do you think the court would have ruled against Transit if it had asked Metz to accept a salary equal to that of a younger employee?

5. What options does the court leave to firms to remain competitive if high (over?) paid employees cannot be replaced with lower-paid people?

CHAPTER

Imperfect Competition in Labor Markets

Product markets range from pure competition to monopoly. Resource markets run a similar gamut. Our description of pure competition in labor markets in the previous chapter only obliquely addresses certain practical questions about work and pay. For example, relative wages and access to certain jobs may depend less on willingness and ability to excel on the job than on such things as (*a*) connections (e.g., are you a union member, or is your golfing buddy an executive for your potential employer?), (*b*) credentials (e.g., job experience, recommendations, or college degrees), (*c*) personality characteristics only loosely related to productivity (e.g., how can a shy but determined applicant compete for a job against a less diligent but charming extrovert?), and (*d*) a potential employer's market power in either resource or output markets.

You will study three basic types of imperfections in resource markets in this chapter: (*a*) relative to otherwise identical but purely competitive firms, firms with market power restrict output and thus demand fewer resources; (*b*) resource buyers with clout may reduce quantities demanded to depress resource prices; and (*c*) resource sellers with market power may boost resource prices by restricting the quantity available. Labor markets are especially plagued by noncompetitive influences: Government regulations abound, and powerful unions restrict sup-

plies to drive wages up, while powerful employers flex their economic muscle to drive wages down.

Our first concerns are problems posed from the demand side when employers exercise substantial market power, either as sellers of goods or as buyers of labor. Then we look at concentrated power from the supply side, among sellers of labor — primarily, labor unions. Finally, we survey the history and current status of American unionism.

Monopolists' Diminished Labor Demands

You already know that firms with market power raise prices and restrict output to maximize profit. The result for resource markets is that fewer resources are employed than when markets are competitive.

Suppose gold output trickled off in your Colorado mine, but that you discovered a rich vein of tantalite ore. Tantalum is used to line tanks for liquids, as an alloy in tungsten-carbide cutting tools, and in certain electronics applications. It is also quite rare, so assume that you gain substantial market power. Relevant portions of the demand for tantalum and your production function are listed in Table 1.

Tantalum output for various numbers of miners parallels that for gold production, but your market power means that the demand curve for tantalum slopes downward. For example (from columns 2 and 3 of Table 1), if you sell 50 pounds weekly, you can charge $90 per pound. Raising output to 110 pounds, however, requires a price cut to $50 per pound.

Market power depresses marginal revenue below price because added output is salable only if prices are cut for all units produced. You must now decide (1) what price to charge and how much to produce to maximize profits, and (2) how many workers to hire to get the job done. The answer to question 1 automatically answers question 2 because it takes a specific number of workers to produce the most profitable level of output.

Any firm maximizes profit when the revenue generated by the last worker hired (MRP) equals the wage outlays incurred by hiring the last worker (MFC). If all markets are purely competitive, this translates into the rule that the value of the marginal product ($VMP = MRP$) equals the wage ($MFC = w$), so $VMP = MRP = MFC = w$. A rule that profit is maximized when $VMP = w$ works only for pure competitors operating in competitive labor markets. The more general rule for maximum profits is that $MRP = MFC$. Market power causes the value of the marginal

product to exceed the marginal revenue product and reduces the amount of labor hired.

Let's apply this approach to your mine. Column 3 of Table 1 shows that hiring more workers raises output but lowers tantalum prices. Marginal revenue from tantalum mined by extra workers (column 5) is below its price. Each extra miner adds $MR \times MPP = MRP$ to your dollar sales volume (column 7 — the marginal revenue product of labor), but this is below the value of the marginal product (in $P \times MPP$ column 8). For example, the third miner raises tantalum output by 18 pounds (from 50 to 68 pounds per week), but its price falls from $90 to $80 per pound. The $10 price cut on the first 50 pounds of tantalum shrinks the revenue from hiring a third miner to only $940 (column 7) instead of the $1,440 (18 × $80) value of that third miner's marginal product (column 8).

Thus, because market power causes the price of output to exceed its marginal revenue, labor's value of the marginal product ($VMP = P \times MPP$) is greater than its marginal revenue product ($MRP = MR \times MPP$). The maximum profit rule requires that the marginal revenue product equals the marginal factor cost ($MRP = MFC$). Thus, profit is maximized for your tantalum mine when

$$VMP > MRP = MFC = w$$

Table 1 *Data for Tantalum Production*

Production Function						Demand for Labor	
(1)	(2)	(3)	(4)	(5)	(6) Marginal Physical Product of Labor MPP ($\Delta q/\Delta L$)	(7) Marginal Revenue Product of Labor MRP ($MR \times MPP$)	(8) Value of the Marginal Product of Labor VMP ($P \times MPP$)
Number of Workers L	Pounds of Tantalum Produced per Week q	Price of Tantalum per Pound P	Total Revenue TR ($P \times q$)	Marginal Revenue MR ($\Delta TR/\Delta q$)			
1	30	$100	$3,000	$100.00	30	$3,000	$3,000
2	50	90	4,500	75.00	20	1,500	1,800
3	68	80	5,440	55.22	18	940	1,440
4	84	70	5,880	27.50	16	440	1,120
5	98	60	5,880	0	14	0	840
6	110	50	5,500	−31.67	12	−380	600
7	120	40	4,800	−70.00	10	−700	400

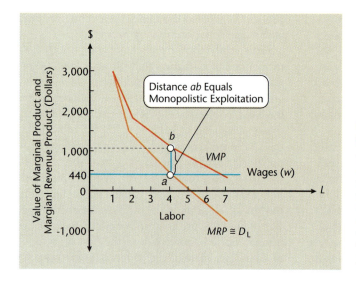

FIGURE 1 Equilibrium Employment for the Tantalum Monopolist

The value of the marginal product ($VMP = P \times MPP$)—the amount of revenue a competitive firm gains when it hires its last worker—is lower for a firm with market power, because $P > MR$. Hence, the marginal revenue product ($MR \times MPP$) is less than the value of the marginal product. Monopolistic exploitation is the difference between VMP and w (distance ab). (*Note:* The VMP and MRP shown are drawn from Table 1.)

The revenue the last worker adds (MRP) equals the cost of hiring (MFC), which in this case is the competitive wage rate w, but this wage rate is below the value of the marginal product. Your market power allows you to pay workers less than the marginal social value of their output and forces us to distinguish between the VMPs and MRPs of labor. $MRP = MR \times MPP$, so marginal revenue product also equals the change in total revenue realized by hiring one more unit of labor ($MRP = \Delta TR/\Delta L$). Both MRP and VMP (columns 7 and 8 from Table 1) are diagramed in Figure 1.

Suppose that you now hire labor from a competitive market at $440 weekly. To equate the MRP with the $440 wage, you would hire four workers (point a). Note that at point a, $MRP = MFC$ ($MRP = \$440 = MFC$). The fifth worker adds nothing to total revenue ($MRP = 0$) but would cost $440 per week—clearly a losing proposition.

Monopolistic Exploitation Resource suppliers who are paid less than the values of their marginal products are said to be *exploited*.[1]

---

1. *Exploitation* sounds like a very judgmental term, but it is the standard language of this analysis. The early work in this area was done by Marxist economists. This does not invalidate their analysis, but it does explain this inflammatory terminology.

If market power causes the value of the marginal product of labor to exceed the wage rate, the difference is known as **monopolistic exploitation**.

The fourth worker's VMP is $1,120 (point b), which is far above the fourth worker's MRP and wage of $440. The difference between the VMP and w (line ab, or $680) is called *the rate of monopolistic exploitation of labor*.

Monopsony in a Labor Market

Another source of exploitation arises if firms exert economic clout as resource buyers. No single firm's hiring noticeably affects wages in purely competitive labor markets. For example, in large cities the prevailing wages of secretaries, clerks, and delivery people are unaffected by any one firm's hiring. Contrast such markets with those for small towns where a coal mine dominates employment. Sole buyers of a good or resource are **monopsonists**.

A buyer has **monopsony power** *if restricting the amount of a good or resource purchased reduces the price the buyer must pay.*

A labor monopsonist is the sole employer in a specific labor market and faces the entire labor

Table 2 *Supply of Labor Data for a Firm with Monopsony Power*

(1) Labor L	(2) Weekly Wage w	(3) Total Labor Cost TC_L $(w \times L)$	(4) Marginal Factor (Labor) Cost MFC $(\Delta TC_L/\Delta L)$
1	$250	$ 250	$ 250
2	300	600	350
3	380	1,140	540
4	485	1,940	800
5	550	2,750	810
6	600	3,600	850
7	700	4,900	1,300
8	800	6,400	1,500

supply. Thus, its hiring decision determines the wage rate. A labor market in which a monopsonist pays all workers equally is outlined in Table 2. Hiring three workers requires the monopsonist to pay a wage rate of only $380 per week to this community's three most eager beavers. We will temporarily assume that wage discrimination is impossible to simplify this analysis. Thus, employing four local workers forces the monopsonist to raise its wage offer to $485 to attract the next, slightly less eager beaver to work, and necessitates a raise of $105 each to the preceding three workers.

The important result is that monopsony power raises marginal factor cost (MFC) above the wage rate. If this firm hires three workers at $380 per week, its labor costs are $1,140; these costs rise to $1,940 if the firm employs four workers at $485. Hiring a fourth worker without wage discrimination requires a wage increase to $485 per week to the original three workers, which boosts total labor costs by $800, not $485. Such wage increases cause the MFC to exceed the wage rate for each employment level. The MFC shown in column 4 of Table 2 is the change in total labor costs from hiring one extra worker. How does the excess of this MFC over the wage rate affect this firm's hiring? Figure 2 shows the labor supply and its MFC to this monopsonist.

A monopsonist's marginal factor cost curve is above the labor supply curve, just as a monopolist's marginal revenue curve is below the de-

mand curve it faces. The value of the marginal product from our gold mine of previous chapters is also shown, so Figure 2 depicts a monopsony selling a competitive output and $VMP = MRP$. This firm maximizes profit by hiring labor until

FIGURE 2 Equilibrium Wage and Employment for a Monopsonist

If the supply of labor facing a firm is positively sloped, then the wage increases that must be granted to all workers cause the marginal factor cost (MFC) curve to lie above the supply curve. This analysis ignores possible wage discrimination to simplify the analysis.

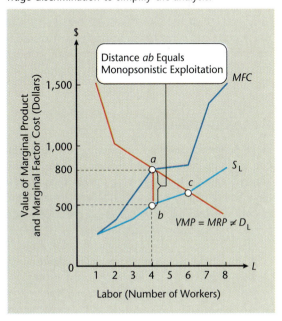

the $MRP = MFC$ at \$800 (point a in Figure 2) but only pays \$485 each to the four workers willing to work for that weekly wage (point b). Thus, $VMP = MRP = MFC > w$.

Monopsonistic Exploitation A labor monopsonist hires fewer workers and pays lower wages than a firm hiring in a competitive labor market. If this firm faced a \$600 wage from a competitive labor market, it would hire six workers (point c). Thus, the monopsonist pays workers less than a competitive employer would. Absent its monopsony power, this firm would hire four workers at a competitive wage of \$800 (point a). Monopsony power enables it to hire four workers for a \$485 wage, far below the values of their marginal product ($VMP = \$800$). The difference (\$315) is termed **monopsonistic exploitation** of labor.

> **Monopsonistic exploitation** *occurs when a firm exercises its clout in hiring labor; it equals the difference between the value of the marginal product of labor and its wage rate.*

Few pure monopsonists exist, although huge firms located in small communities may dominate local labor markets and exercise substantial monopsony power. For example, residents in small towns may rely heavily for employment on lumber mills in the Northwest, or textile mills in the Southeast. A more common type of monopsonistic exploitation occurs when firms control individual employees sufficiently to wage discriminate.

Wage Discrimination

Have you ever worked for a company that discouraged workers from sharing information about wages or salaries? Many firms that do not have standard pay scales treat salary information as confidential. This is a common practice when a firm practices *wage discrimination*.

> **Wage discrimination** *occurs when workers receive different pay that is inconsistent with their individual marginal productivities.*

This is possible only if a firm has some monopsony power, just as price discrimination for goods requires a firm to possess market power. This type of monopsony power may be exercised whenever any employee views a particular firm as offering special advantages such as location, job security, or opportunities for promotion.

The discussion in our "Monopoly" chapter showed that price discrimination may partially remedy the economic inefficiency created when firms exercise market power. Wage discrimination may similarly cure some of the inefficiency caused by monopsony power. For example, if the monopsonist shown in Table 2 and Figure 2 could perfectly wage discriminate, it would hire six workers (exactly the same as would a competitive firm) rather than the four it hires as a nondiscriminating monopsonist. However, it would respectively pay the first through sixth workers weekly wages of only \$250, \$300, \$380, \$485, \$550, and \$600 — the total weekly wage bill would be only \$2,565, instead of the \$3,600 that would be paid weekly by a purely competitive employer. The \$1,035 difference represents monopsonistic exploitation. Although this wage discrimination does facilitate efficiency, it is widely viewed as inequitable (more on this in a moment).

Employers who treat salary information as confidential argue that publicizing wage differentials just leads to bickering about which employee deserves what. Under this system, employees have little incentive to reveal their own pay but seek information about the pay of others. If you learned that someone made less than you did, you would probably be silent if their work was comparable to yours. If, however, someone with a comparable job made more than you, you might use the information to negotiate a raise. If you think about this for a moment, you will understand why many workers join employers in a conspiracy of silence when salary information is confidential. Although secrecy may reduce quibbling about salaries when pay scales are not standardized, the major advantage for employers is that confidentiality facilitates wage discrimination and monopsonistic exploitation.

Minimum-Wage Laws and Monopsony Power

The effects of minimum-wage laws in competitive labor markets are summarized in Panel A of Figure 3. The prevailing wage is $4 before the minimum wage is introduced into this competitive market, and 70 units of labor are employed (point *a*). When a $5 minimum wage is imposed by law, employment falls to 58 (point *b*), and unemployment increases to 40 units of labor (98 minus 58); more people want to work at the higher wage (point *c*).

The effect of a minimum wage may be quite different if firms exert monopsony power. Before enactment of a minimum wage in Panel B, fewer workers are employed (50) at a lower wage ($4) by the monopsonist (point *g*) than by

a comparable competitive firm (point *a*). Introducing the minimum wage alters the monopsonist's *MFC* by forcing the firm to pay at least $5 per hour, at which it can hire up to 98 workers. Average wages must rise to attract more than 98 workers, so the firm's *MFC* curve becomes *becdf*, and profit-maximizing employment is 58 workers at $5 per hour.

The result that minimum-wage laws may boost both employment and wages by monopsonistic firms is often cited as a benefit of these laws. Critics rebut this analysis with studies showing that the biggest effect of higher minimum wages is disemployment of inexperienced teenagers in competitive labor markets. Employment is also likely to fall if firms practiced systematic wage discrimination before passage of a minimum wage. (We showed how wage discrim-

FIGURE 3   Minimum-Wage Laws in Competitive and Monopsony Labor Markets

A minimum-wage law will cause unskilled workers to experience unemployment if the labor market is competitive, as shown in Panel A. Setting a minimum wage at $5 means that 40 individuals who want to work will be unable to find jobs (point *c* minus point *b*). It is theoretically possible, but unlikely, for a minimum wage to increase employment if there is substantial monopsony power in the labor market. In Panel B, a $5 minimum wage alters the monopsonist's *MFC* so that 40 new employees are hired; equilibrium employment moves from point *e* to point *c*.

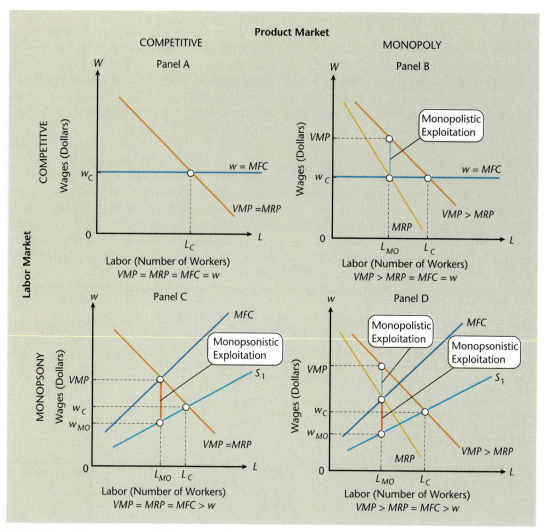

FIGURE 4 Summary of Wage and Employment Equilibria

The marginal value of labor to society is the *VMP* curve; the marginal social cost of labor is the competitively determined wage (*w*). In a competitive world (Panel A), there is no exploitation of labor, and economic efficiency exists because the marginal benefit to society of a specific employment just equals marginal social cost (*VMP* = *w*, so *MSB* = *MSC*). Monopolistic exploitation (Panel B) is accompanied by inefficiency because *VMP* > *MRP* implies that the marginal social benefit exceeds the monopolist's marginal private benefit from hiring extra workers (*MSB* > *MPB*, so *MSB* > *MSC*). Monopolistic exploitation (Panel C) is a situation where the monopsonists' marginal private costs are greater than the marginal social costs of employment (*MFC* > *MSC* = *w*), so again there is inefficiency. Panel D illustrates the case where the factors leading to inefficiency because of monopoly and monopsony power are combined.

ination raises employment by monopsonists. Minimum-wage laws may eliminate this effect.) Thus, minimum wages probably foster unemployment. In 1989, the United States followed the lead of several European countries by setting lower minimum "training" wages for teenagers than for adults. How much this will alleviate persistently high teenage unemployment is not yet clear.

A Summary of Imperfect Competition by Employers

Translation of the $MRP = MFC$ rule into equilibrium wages and employment depends on a firm's product and labor markets, as summarized in Figure 4. When product and labor markets are both competitive (Panel A), the firm hires efficiently where $VMP = w$. Panel B shows that when a monopolistic seller hires from a competitive labor market, workers are paid less than the values of their marginal products, and fewer

workers are hired than under competitive conditions. A monopsony labor market combined with a competitive product market is depicted in Panel C. Firms with monopsony power also hire fewer workers, at lower wages, than would pure competitors. Last, Panel D illustrates equilibrium employment and wages when a labor monopsonist has market power in the output market. Not surprisingly, a monopsonist/monopolist hires the fewest workers at the lowest wages and is the most exploitative — the difference $VMP - w$ is greatest.

Wage Differentials and Discrimination

The systematic earnings differentials displayed in Table 3 are evidence that wage discrimination is too often exercised on the basis of race, gender, or age. Differentials in human capital, willing-

Table 3 *Median Annual Earnings by Race, Gender, and Age (1988)*

	Median Weekly Earnings	Median Annual Earnings	Percent of All Workers Earnings		Median Weekly Earnings	Median Annual Earnings	Percent of All Workers Earnings
Men	449	23348	116.62	**Occupations**			
16–24 years	261	13572	67.79	Executive	682	35464	177.14
25 and over	487	25324	126.49	Professional	651	33852	169.09
				Technical	510	26520	132.47
Women	315	16380	81.82	Sales	488	25376	126.75
16–24 years	235	12220	61.04	Admin/Clerical	418	21736	108.57
25 and over	335	17420	87.01	Service	299	15548	77.66
				Mechanics	441	22932	114.55
White	394	20488	102.34	Construction	423	21996	109.87
Men	465	24180	120.78	Transportation	394	20488	102.34
Women	318	16536	82.60	Farm/Forest/Fish	234	12168	60.78
Black	314	16328	81.56	**All Workers**	385	20020	100.00
Men	347	18044	90.13				
Women	288	14976	74.81				
Hispanic	290	15080	75.32				
Men	307	15964	79.74				
Women	260	13520	67.53				

Source: U.S. Bureau of Labor Statistics, Bulletin 2307 and *Employment and Earnings,* January 1990.

FOCUS 1

Are Exploitation and Discrimination Caused by Capitalistic Greed?

Are large numbers of "greedy" business owners too obsessed with maximizing profit? Relative to most white males, are other groups of workers typically underpaid, given their productivity? You may be surprised to learn that it is logically inconsistent to respond positively to both of these questions. To see why, let's begin by examining how profit seeking affects situations where wages are less than workers' marginal revenue products.

Suppose you inherited a small fortune you wanted to turn into a large fortune, and were convinced that many people are exploited by being paid less than their labor is worth. One strategy might be to place a want ad in the local paper declaring, "If you are worth $12 hourly but are only paid $6 hourly, come to work for *My Company*—I will pay you $7 an hour." If, as a consequence, you avoided hiring

workers paid the values of their marginal products, hiring instead only workers that you can exploit to the tune of $5 hourly, your fortune should grow rapidly. But your success would incite mimicry, and you would soon see ads from competitors: "If *My Company* pays only $7 for $12 worth of your productivity, come to work for *Our Enterprise*. We'll pay you $8 per hour." But this would elicit even higher wage offers as competition to exploit profit opportunities grew. Ultimately, all the workers worth $12 an hour would be paid $12 an hour.

The conclusion that aggressive competition by profit-seekers should eliminate exploitation seems in conflict with research findings that women and members of other disadvantaged groups make only a fraction of the pay of white males with comparable education and expe-

rience. Only two logical reconciliations present themselves. Either (a) all workers are paid what they are worth, on average, and these wage gaps reflect real differences in productivity—not bigotry, or (b) competition for profits is too weak to eliminate wage differentials not justified by productivity.

Some people use this analysis to argue that profit seeking is vigorous, ensuring that people are uniformly paid what their labor is worth and that wage gaps by gender, ethnicity, or race merely reflect differences in the willingness and ability of people from different groups to accomplish various jobs. For example, women are asserted to have more career interruptions because of family obligations and to be less committed to their careers, while typical members of most minority groups are asserted to have inferior educa-

ness to endure unpleasant or dangerous job conditions, regional preferences, and circumstances peculiar to particular firms or industries were cited in the preceding chapter to explain occupational wage differentials. The pay differentials in Table 3 only partially reflect meaningful differences in occupational patterns, education, and training and experience. Wage gaps between those under and over 25 years of age are largely

explained by different levels of experience. Experience cannot account, however, for most of the wage differences by race and gender.

Occupational Crowding

History is replete with cases where women and members of minority groups were denied equal access to jobs or paid less than some white males tions and erratic work experience that has diminished their productivity.

A powerful counterargument suggests, however, that many people who make hiring decisions have agendas other than profit alone, and that this creates wage structures not based on performance alone. Many white male executives, for example, surround themselves with employees having shared interests (e.g., golf, the stock market, gourmet meals, or office politics). Some might try to defend their hiring practices with statements such as, "Surveys prove that productivity suffers because female supervisors make both men and women uncomfortable," or, "I hired my friend's son because I've known him since he was a baby, and I have confidence that he will do a great job." Nevertheless, even if conscious prejudice seldom governs employment policies, the results of hiring based on friendship or shared interests instead of capacity to do the job denies equal access to good jobs with high pay. This counterargument concludes that using criteria other than potential performance for hiring and promotions prevents realization of the productive potential of nonwhites and females.

An irony is that white males are probably not enriched by discriminatory practices, which cause economic inefficiency if jobs are filled by white males who are not the best applicants. Many potential gains available through specialization according to comparative advantage are lost, and the total value of output will be less than would occur if performance alone governed employment practices.

How can such inefficiencies and inequities be overcome? Ideally, people who make employment decisions for firms would become more profit oriented — not less! Focusing on productivity instead of group affinity would undoubtedly decrease wage differentials based on race, ethnicity, and gender.

Affirmative action plans are a controversial option. Preferential hiring of women and members of minority groups is intended to broaden access to jobs but, however well intended, sometimes creates its own set of inefficiencies and inequities. These plans too often degenerate into quotas that are filled, in part, by eroding reasonable qualifications for the job. This escalates a backlash from some white males "passed over" for employment or promotions. In our "Income Distribution" chapter, we discuss more of the pros and cons of some proposed remedies for discrimination in employment.

received for the same work. Focus 1 points out the fallacy that some people commit when they blame discrimination and exploitation on entrepreneurial greed.

Women may suffer especially from wage discrimination because many employers view women's work decisions as secondary to their husbands' career moves. Reasonable job security for women has been bait to facilitate wage discrimination. The resulting potential for exploitation is a powerful argument for recent "equal pay for equal work" laws, which may promote equity without hindering efficiency.

Some women want this law extended to raise wages for careers into which most women were once channeled — nursing, teaching, and clerical work. They argue that these workers are underpaid because of occupational crowding.

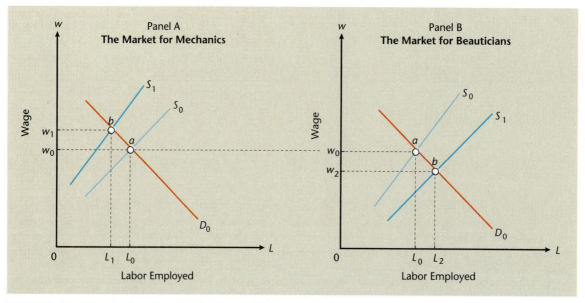

FIGURE 5   Discrimination and Wage Differentials (Salary Gaps)

Excluding women from certain occupations (e.g., work as auto mechanics) reduces the supply of labor and boosts wages in these markets, as shown in Panel A. At the same time, however, labor supplies are swollen and wages are relatively depressed in the occupation into which women are channeled (e.g., cosmetology), as indicated in Panel B.

Occupational crowding *occurs when women or members of other disadvantaged groups are pressured toward low-wage occupations.*

For example, nurses are typically far more educated and bear more responsibility than hospital janitors. Advocates of the *doctrine of comparable worth* are aghast that janitors tend to be paid more. Such apparent discrepancies in pay relative to the value of a job must be the result of sex discrimination, according to their reasoning. In fact, a recent study by the AFL-CIO concluded that "women's work pays best if it's done by a man."[2]

Figure 5 shows how occupational crowding can create pay differentials between men and women. Begin by assuming a lack of discrimination and that the vocations of auto mechanic and beautician require comparable training and effort. Both occupations would have salaries of w_0, and each market would employ L_0 units of labor

with roughly equal proportions of men and women.

Suppose that jobs as mechanics or similar work become closed to women, while cosmetology and a few other jobs remain open to all. The supply of mechanics shrinks by almost half when women are excluded, while a few male beauticians retrain as mechanics when mechanics' wages rise. Most women previously working as mechanics will move into such jobs as beautician. Supply curves shift to S_1 in Figure 5, reflecting fewer mechanics and more beauticians. An occupational wage differential of $w_1 - w_2$ results.

Decomposing Wage Differentials

A recent study by the Bureau of the Census[3] found that, on average

---

2. *Salaried and Professional Women: Relevant Statistics,* compiled by the AFL-CIO's Department for Professional Employees, 1988.

3. U.S. Bureau of the Census, Current Population Reports, Series P-70, No. 10, *Male-Female Differences in Work Experience, Occupation, and Earnings: 1984,* U.S. Government Printing Office, Washington, D.C., 1987.

1. Women are more likely to have "career interruptions" than men.

2. Women tend to have fewer years on their current jobs than men.

3. Women graduates cluster in education and nursing-related fields.

Over half of male college graduates (57 percent) majored in law, medicine, dentistry, science, math, business, economics, or engineering, compared to only 28 percent of women.

Women workers averaged roughly 70 percent of the pay for men in 1990. What proportion of this difference is strictly gender related, and what proportion is explained by work interruptions, less experience and tenure on the current job, level of education and major, or other factors that might affect productivity? Table 4 provides the results from the Bureau of the Census study that adjusted the actual wage difference for various characteristics of individuals.

For college graduates, experience variables account for nearly one-fourth of the wage differential. Education and field of study account for another one-eighth — nearly all of which was due to choice of major. Occupational structure accounted for roughly one-sixth of the total pay differential. These data demonstrate that occupational crowding is central to the male-female wage gap. Finally, such characteristics as marital status, region, union-nonunion, race, and presence of children accounted for almost 13 percent of the pay gap between men and women. All these factors explained almost two-thirds of the total wage gap, with much of it accounted for by occupational crowding.

Comparable Worth

"Equal pay for *comparable* work" is now legally required in more than a dozen states, and bills are pending in Congress and several other state

Table 4 *Accounting for Male-Female Wage Differentials*

Proportion of Male-Female Earnings Differential Accounted for by Differences in the Mean Values of the Independent Variables (Based on coefficients for males)

Characteristic	Not High School Graduates	High School Graduates	College Graduates
Experience[1]	.139	.222	.226
Schooling[2]	(NA)	.008	.127
Field of study	(NA)	(NA)	.116
Skilled trades[3]	.129	(NA)	(NA)
Occupational structure[4]	.303	.300	.174
Other characteristics[5]	.024	.071	.128
All characteristics	.595	.601	.655
Residual	.405	.399	.345

Source: U.S. Bureau of the Census, Current Population Reports, Series P-70 No. 10, *Male-Female Differences in Work Experience, Occupation, and Earnings,* 1984, U.S. Government Printing Office, Washington, D.C., 1987.

[1] Number of years with current employer, years in current occupation less years with current employer, years of work experience less years in current occupation, whether usually worked full time during work years, length of time between current and previous job.

[2] Type of high school program, number of math, science, and foreign language courses in high school, whether public or private high school (high school and college graduates); highest degree and field of study (college graduates).

[3] Whether in precision production, craft, or repair occupation.

[4] Percent of persons in occupation who are female.

[5] Marital status, type of geographic area, whether covered by a union contract, size of firm, class of worker, whether involuntarily left last job, race and Hispanic origin, disability and health status, presence of children.

legislatures.[4] Even in states where comparable worth is not the law, many firms are adopting job evaluation programs in quests for internal equity. The salary gap that comparable worth is expected to close varies by occupation and age.[5] But, as Table 4 shows, younger women now fare much better than older women. This is partially a reflection of better education and training, but it also reflects the growing number of young women majoring in business, computer science, law, medicine, and engineering.

Until recently, unequal access to remunerative employment did push many women into occupations that pay relatively little, but whether a law requiring "equal pay for comparable work" will achieve the goals of its advocates is debatable. The first problem in implementing this approach is ascertaining how much particular jobs should pay. Most markets to which this doctrine would apply are quite competitive, but we presumably cannot rely on market wage solutions. This means that officials from some government agency will need to consider the qualities of each job: Skill requirements, how pleasant the work environment is, and the relative risks to workers are only a few of the many factors that would need to be considered. Weighing education and classroom teaching duties against hot, sweaty, and dangerous work on a construction crew, for example, is unavoidably subjective. The slow and costly process of unraveling such complex issues would be unlikely to satisfy many people.

Suppose all these problems were resolved. The basic problem remains that wages have been depressed because of swollen supplies of nurses, teachers, and clerical workers. New legal requirements raising wages to above the equilibrium pay for holders of jobs that have historically been "women's work" will, unfortunately, have effects similar to those of a legal minimum wage. Many women currently employed in these occupations would lose their jobs, and there would be surpluses of secretaries, teachers, and nurses.

These surpluses would be translated into unemployment, in part because firms would have strong incentives to find substitutes as higher salaries were legally mandated. For example, office work would become even more automated. Receptionist slots would be pared to the bone. Electronic filing systems would be simplified to reduce routine clerical work. Business correspondence would become more standardized to minimize the need for individualized letters, and firms would rely even more heavily on negotiations by telephone. Nurses would find more of their tasks taken over by orderlies or technicians. Schools would be pressured to contain costs by increasing student/teacher ratios.

Likely consequences of wider adoption of the comparable worth approach would be higher unemployment rates among women, and widening inequality in the relative earnings of women. Thus, this approach might be like some policies we described in Chapter 4: Many members of the groups targeted for help may be harmed in unforeseen ways. Fortunately, this problem may cure itself as time elapses and women increasingly shun traditional "women's careers" to become doctors, lawyers, pilots, or engineers.

Effects of Wage Discrimination

Most studies of wage differentials between males and females and between blacks and whites come to similar conclusions: Roughly one-third of these differentials arise from employment discrimination, with experience and occupational crowding apparently accounting for most of the rest.[6] These differentials generate forces that can be self-perpetuating. For example, groups suffering from lower wages have less incentive to invest in education or on-the-job training because the rate of return from this investment will tend

---

4. "Comparable Worth: It's Already Happening," *Business Week*, 29 April 1986, pp. 52–56.

5. "The Truth About The Salary Gap(s)," *Working Women*, Jan. 1988, pp. 61–62.

6. See Orn B. Bodvarsson, "Using Reverse Regression to Estimate Salary Discrimination When the Wage-Setting Process is Costly," paper presented to the Southern Economic Association, November, 1990. Using detailed national data for 2,400 black and white men between the ages of 29 and 39, he found that in occupations where workers were paid commissions or on a piece rate basis, discrimination was nonexistent. The same conclusion was reached for professional and technical workers.

to be less. This problem is exacerbated if only inferior schooling is available, a problem facing many black students. Inferior schools are infamous for channeling students into crowded or unskilled occupations.

Unfortunately, the doctrine of comparable worth is questionable as a cure for problems caused by occupational crowding. The best remedy for such problems may be better career counseling and improved access to education.

You have seen how imperfect competition by employers and occupational crowding may distort labor markets. We will now examine the supply side and labor unions.

Labor Unions

Unions traditionally have been organized around a particular craft or industry. Plumbers, machinists, air-traffic controllers, and other workers organized on the basis of particular skills rely on **craft unions** to bargain with management. **Industrial unions,** on the other hand, organize all the workers in such industries as mining, steel, autos, and rubber.

Until their merger, the *American Federation of Labor* (AFL) consisted only of craft unions and competed with the *Congress of Industrial Organizations* (CIO), which covered only industrial unions. Jurisdictional strikes often erupted when both attempted to organize the same workers. For example, conflicts in chemical plants between the CIO's Oil, Chemical, and Atomic Workers Union and AFL craft unions representing electricians or machinists sometimes became violent. A treaty between AFL and CIO unions was finally consummated with their 1955 merger into the AFL-CIO.

Today, jurisdictional fights exist primarily between AFL-CIO unions and such independents as the Longshoremen. These disputes focus on which union will represent given workers and what goals to pursue. Job security and higher wages involve trade-offs. For example, the United Mine Workers Union traditionally sought huge wage hikes despite the resulting mass substitution of capital for labor and consequent dis-

employment of many union members. Other unions prize job security and so temper their demands for higher wages.

Union Security

Unions attempt to ensure job security for their members in part because union leaders seek security themselves. Special clauses in many union contracts are designed to strengthen the hands of union leaders as sole bargaining agents for their members. The strongest protection a union can have is a *closed shop* agreement with management.

> A **closed shop** *makes union membership a prerequisite for employment.*

The Taft-Hartley Act of 1947 outlawed this form of union security. *Open shops* are at the opposite pole from closed shops.

> *In an* **open shop,** *the firm employs workers regardless of union membership.*

Unions legally must negotiate for all workers in an organized firm, but dues or membership are optional. Thus, an open shop may permit nonunion free riders. Unions only control members, so firms may be able to nullify strikes by using nonunion workers (called *scabs* by union members) extensively, yet nonunion workers receive the same benefits as union workers.

The *union shop* is similar to a closed shop.

> **Union shop** *employers may hire either union or nonunion labor, but new employees must join the union within a specified period to keep their jobs.*

Under a union shop arrangement, union members can be expelled only for nonpayment of dues. This protects workers from being expelled (with loss of their jobs) for infractions such as disagreeing with the union leadership or violating union policies.

Besides abolishing closed shops, the Taft-Hartley Act allowed state **right-to-work laws** outlawing the union shop. Twenty-one states have

Table 5 *Important Events in American Labor History*

1778 — NY printers demanded wage hikes, but their organization dissolved after raises were granted.

1786 — Philadelphia printers gained a minimum weekly wage of $6 in the nation's earliest authenticated strike.

1806 — The Philadelphia Cordwainers went bankrupt after members were found guilty of conspiring to strike.

1834 — The National Trades Union formed the first national labor federation, but folded during the financial panic of 1837.

1842 — In *Commonwealth* v. *Hunt,* the Massachusetts Court held labor unions to be legal organizations. Massachusetts and Connecticut laws prohibited children from working more than 10 hours a day.

1862 — The "Molly Maguires," a secret society of Irish coal miners, were charged with acts of terrorism against mine bosses; 14 of their leaders were imprisoned and 10 were executed.

1869 — The Knights of Labor gained 700,000 followers by winning railroad strikes and advocating the 8-hour day.

1884 — A Bureau of Labor was formed in the Department of Interior, growing into the Department of Labor in 1913.

1886 — One policeman was killed and several were wounded in the Chicago Haymarket riot, arousing public opinion against unionism and retarding a drive for the 8-hour day. The American Federation of Labor (AFL) was founded.

1890 — The United Mine Workers first organized in Columbus, Ohio.

1894 — The American Railway Union's strike against the Pullman Co. was defeated when Federal troops enforced injunctions. Eugene V. Debs and other leaders were imprisoned.

1908 — The United Hatters' boycott of D.E. Loewe and Co. was held to be in restraint of trade under the Sherman Act.

1912 — Massachusetts passed a minimum wage for women and minors.

1914 — The Clayton Act limited use of injunctions in labor disputes and legalized union picketing.

1917 — A copper miners' strike ended when an Arizona sheriff deported 1,200 "wobbly" (Industrial Workers of the World) strikers. Union efforts to organize workers signing "yellow-dog" contracts were held to be illegal.

1921 — The Supreme Court held that nothing in the Clayton Act legalized secondary boycotts (*Duplex* v. *Deering*).

1933 — Frances Perkins became Secretary of Labor, the first woman named to the Cabinet.

passed such laws. Unions responded with **agency shop** agreements that require all employees to pay union dues. This arrangement has been defended as preventing nonunion workers from free riding: All workers represented by a union should share the costs of collective bargaining. Unions also exert control over workers through **check-off provisions** in contracts, which require firms to deduct dues from paychecks. These provisions make it easier for unions to collect dues and retain members. The Taft-Hartley Act prohibits firms from deducting union dues unless authorized by a majority of workers, but roughly 80 percent of union contracts now have check-off provisions.

Unions did not develop overnight. The path to modern collective bargaining was paved with strife between union organizers and business owners and managers who did not want to share power with labor. Some of the chronology of the union movement is detailed in Table 5. The next section examines the history of unions in this country.

The American Union Movement

A forerunner of modern unions was the Carpenters' Society of Philadelphia, established in 1724, which bargained for wage increases and organized charity work. An interesting note is that

1935 — The National Labor Relations (Wagner) Act established the right to organize unions. The Social Security Act was enacted. The Congress of Industrial Organizations (CIO) was formed.

1937 — GM recognized the United Automobile Workers and U.S. Steel recognized the Steel Workers as bargaining agents.

1946 — The Employment Act of 1946 required policies promoting "maximum employment, production, and purchasing power."

1947 — The Taft-Hartley Act forbade closed shops and secondary boycotts, and allowed states to pass "right-to-work" laws.

1949 — An amendment to the Fair Labor Standards Act (1938) directly limited child labor for the first time.

1955 — Merger of the American Federation of Labor and Congress of Industrial Organizations unified over 85 percent of all U.S. union members.

1959 — The Landrum-Griffin Act made certain activities by labor or management illegal.

1962 — Federal employees' unions were granted the right to bargain collectively with government agencies.

1963 — The Equal Pay Act of 1963 prohibited wage differentials based on sex.

1964 — The Civil Rights Act of 1964 barred job discrimination because of race, color, religion, sex, or national origin.

1965 — "Medicare" first provided partial coverage for those over 65 for most medical expenses.

1968 — The Age Discrimination in Employment Act made job discrimination against persons aged 40 to 65 illegal.

1970 — The first strike in Post Office history virtually paralyzed mail service. The Occupational Safety and Health Act set safety and health standards for the nation's workplaces.

1974 — The Social Security Act for the first time provided for automatic cost-of-living adjustments.

1975 — Interns and residents backed by the AMA struck 22 NY hospitals.

1981 — Air traffic controllers represented by PATCO illegally struck and many of these federal employees were fired.

1988 — The United Automobile Workers and General Motors attempt a new form of labor-management relations known as "jointness" and industrial democracy.

1990 — A 15-year decline in unionism had dropped union membership to fewer than one American worker in seven.

---

members who disclosed wages to nonmembers were fined.[7] During the early 1800s, numerous unions emerged and then faded away, but within a century, unions had become fixtures on the national scene.

Until the Great Depression, firms commonly fought union organizers with firings, violence, and **yellow-dog contracts**, by which workers agreed not to join any union. Employers also circulated **blacklists** of union "troublemakers." Finally, unions faced considerable legal adversity.

Judges sympathetic to business owners issued *injunctions* (or restraining orders) against numerous union acts, including strikes or boycotts. If a union violated an injunction, its leaders could be held in contempt of court and jailed.

In the Danbury Hatters' case in 1908, the Supreme Court declared unions to be in restraint of trade, violating the Sherman Antitrust Act.[8] The court ruled that a national boycott had cost the Lowe Hat Company $80,000 and applied the Sherman Act's triple damage clause to the United Hatters union. This case, more than any

---

7. William Miernyk, *The Economics of Labor and Collective Bargaining* (Lexington, MA: Heath, 1965), p. 14.

8. *Loewe v. Lawlor*, 208 U.S. 274 (1908).

other, forced unions into the political arena. The Clayton Act (1914) largely shielded unions from antitrust prosecution. Today, union weapons such as strikes and boycotts are legal.

Union growth during the 1920s was hampered when firms aggressively labeled unions as un-American, and yellow-dog contracts were standard operating procedure. A series of violent strikes fostered antiunion sentiment. Demands for skilled workers from craft unions fell as mass production spread. Prosperity also aggravated declines in union membership because booming wages and job security left industrial workers content.

The Great Depression softened the country's mood toward unionism. Believing they were on the brink of disaster, many workers collectively acted to buffer the chaos of the business cycle, and total union membership tripled between 1933 and 1940. Organizing drives were aided by passage of the Wagner Act in 1935. This prolabor legislation guaranteed the right to organize unions and made it an unfair labor practice for a firm to refuse to negotiate with a union supported by a majority of its workers.

Union membership as a percentage of the labor force continued to grow through the 1940s, but many aspects of the Wagner Act were perceived as biased in favor of unions. This dissatisfaction resulted in passage of the Taft-Hartley Act (1947), which outlawed secondary boycotts (refusals by union members of one firm to handle any intermediate products produced by other firms that were being struck) and jurisdictional strikes (where the only issue was which union would represent workers), and which also permitted states to pass right-to-work laws forbidding union shops.

Many antiunion people are obsessed that unions are increasingly powerful, but their influence is actually waning in the United States while rising in other developed nations (Figure 6). Union membership as a percent of the work force has fallen for three decades; fewer than one in seven workers now belong to a union.

Some researchers argue that American unions were far too successful in winning wage increases during the 1960s and 1970s compared to their foreign counterparts. This hampered the ability of American manufacturers to compete in world markets, prompting them to take harder lines against unions. In addition, a major problem facing union organizers is the growing importance of white-collar workers, who tend to be less interested in union membership. With this brief history in mind, we now turn our attention to collective bargaining and union strategies to raise wages for their members.

Unions and Collective Bargaining

Just as corporate managers represent stockholders' interests, unions represent many workers' interests (with similar principal/agent problems) while negotiating work contracts. Major union contracts cover thousands of workers. The relationships between firm managers and union leaders often blend public hostility and private symbiosis.

Union Strategies to Raise Wages

Unions provide a "collective voice" for workers and have succeeded in curtailing or reducing managerial abuses in many firms and industries. Most people, however, view increases in wages as the major role of a union.

Demands for labor are downward sloping, so wage hikes reduce the quantity of labor demanded and thus normally eliminate some jobs. Union negotiators must weigh this trade-off. If an industry is largely nonunion, demand for union labor may be relatively elastic, thus making unemployment a more likely prospect for union members when union wages are raised. Giant national unions try to protect their members by organizing entire industries. In cases of purely local labor markets (construction, for example), only local workers must be unionized to protect union jobs from nonunion competition. A union can choose from several strategies to raise wages once an industry is organized. Consider Figure 7. Without unionization, firms'

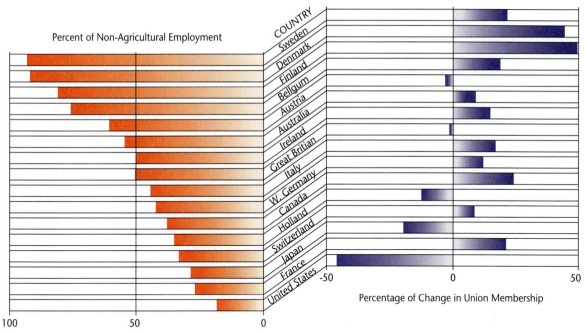

Percent of Non-Agricultural Employment

COUNTRY
Sweden
Denmark
Finland
Belgium
Austria
Australia
Ireland
Great Britian
Italy
W. Germany
Canada
Holland
Switzerland
Japan
France
United States

-50   0   50

Percentage of Change in Union Membership

100   50   0

FIGURE 6   Union Membership as a Percentage of the Nonfarm Work Force: Selected Countries, 1970–1987

Total union membership in the United States has been falling in recent years and union membership as a percentage of the work force has been declining for over three decades. These trends in the United States are counter to those occurring in several other developed nations.

Source: Bureau of Labor Statistics, *Employment and Earnings*, January 1988 and *The Economist*, August 1990.

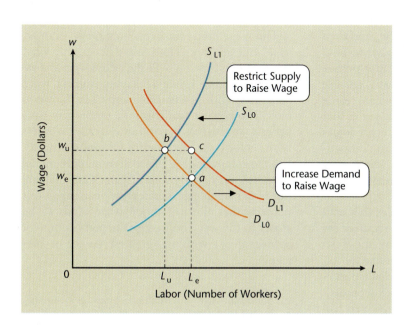

FIGURE 7   Various Union Strategies to Raise Wages

Unions can be instrumental in raising wages by either (*a*) reducing the supply of labor, or (*b*) increasing the demand for labor. The effective supply of labor can be reduced by imposing barriers to entry into an occupation—such as a requirement of union membership, extensive experience, or professional licensing. The demand for labor can be enhanced by improving labor productivity, by increasing the demand for output, or through contracts that require "featherbedding."

demands for labor would be D_{L0} and the supply of labor, S_{L0}, with resulting employment of L_e workers at a wage of w_e (point a).

Restricting the Labor Supply A first union strategy might be to try to shrink labor to this industry by shifting the labor supply curve leftward to S_{L1}, raising the union wage to w_u (point b). Thus, the union movement has supported policies such as child labor laws, restrictive immigration policies, compulsory retirement plans, laws to "protect" women from hard or hazardous work, and shorter work weeks. Most craft unions require lengthy apprenticeships to restrict competition from other workers. Some unions that dominate a particular labor market charge high initiation fees or simply limit new memberships to shift the supply of union labor to the left.

Rationing Work A union that controls all of an industry's work force might simply bargain for a wage of w_u. This creates a huge labor surplus and substantial unemployment or underemployment. The union then uses a *hiring hall* to spread the work available to its members. Rules to allocate jobs range from "first-come, first-served" to strict "seniority."

Stimulating the Demand for Union Labor If the union can negotiate a wage of w_u and then raise the demand for its members' labor to D_{L1}, they suffer only minor unemployment at point c (labor supply exceeds labor demand at wage rate w_u). Examples of this approach include using political clout to obtain local building codes that require labor-intensive construction technologies or lobbying for quotas to limit foreign competition for union members' services. Unions may also work with management to increase worker productivity.

Featherbedding refers to work rules that artificially boost the number of workers required for certain tasks. Although forbidden by the Taft-Hartley Act, it has been a union strategy to bolster demands for labor in several industries — railroads, printing, and shipping (dock workers). For example, long after coal engines were replaced by diesel, railroad unions insisted that

trains carry firemen, who rode along even though there were no coal fires to tend.[9] For years, New York musicians had a union contract requiring standby orchestras for every event at which out-of-state musicians played.

Just as oligopolists act strategically to cope with interdependencies in setting prices and output, negotiations between unions and management at times resemble a card tournament — or war. Several models have been developed to characterize this process.

Bilateral Monopoly

One early model of collective bargaining is called *bilateral monopoly*.

> **Bilateral monopoly** *assumes that a union is the sole agent for a firm's labor (a monopoly on the labor [supply] side), while the firm is the sole employer of union labor (a monopsony on the hiring [demand] side).*

The monopsonist employer depicted in Figure 8 would prefer to hire L_e units of labor at a wage rate of w_e. The union, on the other hand, would want the L_e units of labor to be paid at least w_u. Given the marginal revenue product (*MRP*) curve shown, wage rate w_u is the maximum that the firm would be willing to pay for L_e units of labor.

The wage limits for bargaining range from w_u to w_e, but this model fails to predict exactly what the wage settlement will be. Moreover, we assumed that the union seeks the highest wage consistent with full employment of its L_e members. The powers that control a union may have other goals, such as maximum wages for workers with seniority or job security for union officials. For these reasons, the bilateral monopoly model is useful primarily in specifying some general limits to bargaining. About all we can say at this point is that the negotiated wage tends to be closer to the wage desired by the party (union or management) with the greatest power or bargaining savvy.

---

9. Some states had laws requiring firemen on each train. Such a requirement was a part of the Arizona State Constitution until 1964.

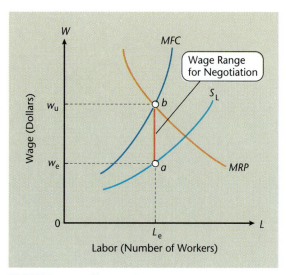

FIGURE 8   Bilateral Monopoly in Labor Markets

The early bilateral monopoly model of collective bargaining assumed that employers with monopsony power must deal with unions with market power as suppliers of labor. When a buyer with monopsony power confronts a seller with market power, price and quantity are determined by which side is the better negotiator or has more power.

Wage Setting and the Duration of Strikes

Bilateral monopoly models identify a range of wages within which union and management will agree but fail to specify a final wage. Moreover, these models ignore strikes. John Hicks, a Nobel Prize winner, developed a more robust model of collective bargaining, adapted in Figure 9.[10] The firm willingly offers a wage of w_0 without a strike, but the union insists on a wage of w_1, a difference so great that a strike begins at time zero (0).

Strikers ride financial and emotional roller coasters. After the euphoria of a brief vacation, reality begins knocking at workers' doors. Backlogged do-it-yourself projects are finished, and boredom sets in as a strike drags on. As unemployment checks and union benefits run out, strikers exhaust past savings and worry about their bills. These hardships press wage demands

---

10.   J. R. Hicks, *The Theory of Wages* (London: Macmillan, 1932), Chapter VII.

down along the union resistance curve in Figure 9 as time passes.

Over the same period, the firm's willingness to pay higher wages is traced out as the employer's concession curve. Few strikes are surprises, so most firms can meet predictable orders from stockpiled inventories. Managers often form skeletal work crews during a strike, but inventories evaporate and managers become exhausted; the operation grinds toward a halt, increasing firms' willingness to pay higher wages. The intersection of the employer's concession curve and the union resistance curve marks the end of this strike. The final wage settlement is at w_e, and the expected duration of this strike is S_e. As you can see, this simple model offers considerable insight into labor negotiations. Notice, however, that if both sides recognize in advance that the final contract will be for wage w_e, a strike is unnecessary. Thus, most strikes are accidental, reflecting miscalculations about the respective offers which will ultimately be acceptable to each side.

FIGURE 9   Hicks's Theory of Industrial Disputes

The onset of a strike (time 0) is a signal that union workers demand much higher wages than management is willing to pay. As time elapses, workers become willing to settle for less as their financial reserves evaporate, while management is increasingly willing to raise its offer as its inventories decline and stockholders and customers apply pressure to settle. Declining wage demands and rising wage offers intersect to signal the end of this particular strike at time S_1.

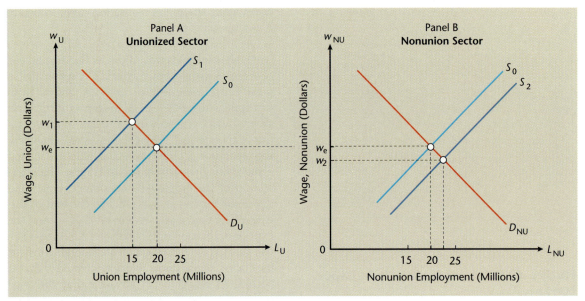

FIGURE 10   Union and Nonunion Wage Differentials

Restricting the supply of labor may cause union wages to rise (Panel A), but flows of labor into the nonunionist sector may cause nonunion wages to fall (Panel B).

We will now turn our attention to the effects of unions that extend beyond the unionized sectors of the economy.

Economic Effects of Labor Unions

[U]nions . . . receive more credit and at the same time more blame than they deserve.

Gary Becker[11]

In addition to concerns about the political power of large unions, opponents of unions worry about three possible economic effects of unions: (*a*) distorted wage structures, (*b*) inflationary pressure, and (*c*) disruption caused by strikes.

Union-Nonunion Wage Differentials

Most people believe that unions can raise their members' wages substantially over nonunion wages. Figure 10 shows how a **union-nonunion**

wage differential can develop. Assume that markets for union (*U*) and nonunion (*NU*) workers are initially identical, with 20 million workers employed in each sector at a wage of w_e. Total employment equals 40 million. The markets for union and nonunion workers are illustrated in Panels A and B, respectively.

If negotiation raised union members' wages to w_1, 5 million (20 million − 15 million) union workers would be disemployed. After all, one cost of higher wages is less employment. As these workers abandon the job market or seek nonunion jobs, the supply of union labor falls to S_1. Nonunion wages drop when some of the 5 million disemployed union workers are absorbed. The nonunion wage would shrink to w_2 as the nonunion labor supply swells to S_2, amplifying the wage differential. Note that total employment falls a bit, because some people disemployed from the union sector will be unwilling to work at this depressed nonunion wage rate.

Two surveys by H. Gregg Lewis (in 1963 and 1986) summarized more than 200 studies of the relative wage effects of unions during the period 1920–1979. Lewis placed the average wage gap in the 15 to 20 percent range, varying from a

11.   G. S. Becker, "It's Time to Scrap a Few Outmoded Labor Laws," *Business Week*, 7 March 1988, p. 18.

Depression-era high of almost half to a low of 2 percent following World War II.[12] Lewis's work suggests that wage gaps are greatest during economic downturns and least during periods of economic prosperity. He estimates that during 1967–1979, the average wage gap was 15 percent.

The erosion of unions during the 1980s, however, may mean that union-nonunion wage gaps have been falling. A recent study suggests that union-nonunion pay gaps fell by roughly 4 percentage points during the 1980s.[13] Lewis noted that this wage gap varies substantially, however, and appears to be affected by geographic region, the type of job, and such characteristics of typical workers as marital status, race, health, and age. This gap widens as an industry becomes relatively more unionized and narrows when unemployment in an industry grows, or if most firms in an industry are larger, or when typical workers are relatively more educated.

Many people think that unions have boosted most workers' wages. Numerous historical studies contradict this perception, finding that the extent of unionization does not affect labor's share in national income, either historically in the United States or between countries today. You should remember, also, that union wage premiums are created, in part, by depressing wages in nonunionized sectors of the economy.

Unions and Inflation

Some opponents of unions rant that curing inflation requires controlling "those *@&$%&! unions." Inflation is blamed on unions on the theory that they artificially boost wages through collective bargaining or strikes. Firms then pass these higher costs forward by charging higher prices, inspiring unions to demand higher wages to offset members' losses due to inflation, and so on. This high-wage/higher-price/higher-wage spiral is thought by many to be the principal cause of inflation in the United States.

Critics of this analysis point out that unions represent only one worker in seven and argue that union wage hikes can only raise prices modestly. If union labor absorbs 20 percent of all production costs and unions negotiate 10 percent wage hikes, output prices need only rise by 2 percent on the average. Moreover, they might point to Figure 10 and argue that union wage hikes are largely offset by resulting cuts in nonunion wages. Blaming rapid inflation on unions is ludicrous in the eyes of these critics.

One rebuttal is that this analysis ignores union strength in such key industries as steel, automobiles, chemicals, and crucial inputs for other sectors of the economy. Higher wage costs and prices for major intermediate goods ripple through the economy as upward price pressures on all outputs. Moreover, union wages set standards for many nonunion firms, which match collective bargaining agreements to avoid unionization of their workers. Finally, if higher wages create massive unemployment and the federal government responds with expansionary macroeconomic policies, there is a classic supply-side inflation cycle. The debate surrounding the impact of union wage increases on inflation will probably continue for as long as unions exist.

Losses from Strikes

Unions are blamed for innumerable economic woes. One question that arises is, "If unions represent only one worker in seven, how can they cause rapid inflation, economic chaos from strikes, and other social ills?" Economists lack consensus about unions, but most believe their impact is exaggerated. Strikes and the closed-door collective bargaining process make juicy material for the media. Publicity often makes union organizing and bargaining look like bloody battles. Collective bargaining is a frustrating process, but it works most of the time. Only about 2 to 4 percent of all negotiations result in strikes, and most of these last less than two weeks, as Figure 11 illustrates.

Although most strikes center on disagreements about wages, other major issues that cause strikes include (a) union organization and secu-

12. H. G. Lewis, *Unionism and Relative Wages in the United States: An Empirical Inquiry*, 1963, Chapter V, and *Union Relative Wage Effects: A Survey*, 1986, (both from Chicago: The University of Chicago Press).

13. K. E. Anderson, P. M. Doyle and A. E. Schwenk, "Measuring Union-Nonunion Earnings Differences," *Monthly Labor Review*, June 1990, pp. 26–38.

Panel A
Major Strikes

Total Major Strikes (Hundreds)

Workers Involved (Millions)

Panel B
Percentage of Labor Time Lost Because of Strikes

FIGURE 11   Number of Major Strikes and Percentage of Labor Time Lost, 1947–1987

Only a small percent of the work force is on strike during any given year, and most strikes are for short periods. Although some of the numbers in Panel A seem large, Panel B indicates that well under 1 percent of labor time is lost because of strikes.

Source: Bureau of Labor Statistics, *Current Wage Developments*, February 1988.

rity, (b) work rules, (c) overtime questions, (d) safety, (e) interunion and intraunion matters (e.g., assignment of work between competing unions, or sympathy strikes), and (f) job security disputes. Strikes may have significant costs beyond the income lost by the strikers. Firms incur higher costs in getting their products to customers during strikes, and some sales may be lost because of inability to meet deadlines. After a strike is settled, most firms recoup through increased shipments, and all that is suffered is delay. But this is not always the case. Strikes by farmworkers may leave crops rotting on the ground. Consumer goods, homes, and capital equipment go up in smoke when fire fighters strike. Strikes that reduce supplies cause consumers to bear the costs as higher prices and lower consumption.

The public has traditionally opposed strikes by public employees, especially nurses, teachers,

fire fighters, and police officers. Laws usually forbid strikes by public employees and substitute binding arbitration as a means of resolving conflicts. Strikes do occur, but many groups of public employees now mix collective bargaining with old-fashioned politics to pressure elected officials into meeting their demands.

This chapter has explored the effects on wages and employment when concentrated economic power is wielded in labor markets by resource buyers (market and monopsony) or resource sellers — primarily unions. The markets for land, entrepreneurship, and capital examined in the next chapter tend to be far more competitive, but you may find a few cases where some of the analysis of this chapter seems to apply. More normally, markets for nonlabor resources tend to operate according to the marginal productivity theory introduced in the previous chapter, but each does so in its own unique way.

Chapter Review: Key Points

1. The *marginal revenue product* (*MRP*) curve for a firm selling in an imperfectly competitive product market will be below the *value of the marginal product of labor* (*VMP*) curve. All firms will hire labor until the marginal revenue product equals the *marginal factor cost* (*MFC*) of labor. Because *MRP* < *VMP*, employees of firms with market power are paid less than the values of their marginal products. This difference is called *monopolistic exploitation*.

2. A *monopsonist* is the sole buyer of a particular resource or good. Labor monopsonists face an entire market supply of labor. If all workers are paid equally, a monopsonist's marginal factor cost curve will lie above the labor supply curve it faces. Relative to pure competitors, labor monopsonists pay lower wages and hire fewer workers. In addition, labor will be paid less than the value of its marginal product, a difference referred to as *monopsonistic exploitation*.

3. When competitive conditions prevail in both resource and product markets, the firm hires labor until $VMP = MRP = MFC = w$. When monopoly prevails in the product market, but the monopoly firm hires labor under competitive conditions, labor is hired up to the point where $VMP > MRP = MFC = w$. Given a competitive product market and monopsony power in the labor market, a firm will maximize profits by hiring labor until $VMP = MRP = MFC > w$. Finally, when a firm has both monopoly and monopsony power, labor is hired up to the point where $VMP > MRP = MFC > w$. Any difference between *VMP* and *w* represents *exploitation*, a term borrowed from Marxist jargon.

4. A minimum wage legally set above the equilibrium wage in competitive labor markets will raise unemployment. It is possible, but unlikely, that minimum wages might increase employment and wages simultaneously, but only where there is substantial monopsonistic exploitation of unskilled workers and wage discrimination is not practiced, an unlikely combination. A union wage hike might have the same effect. However, the markets where minimum-wage hikes raise existing wages are typically rather competitive. Thus, increased unemployment is the normal result when minimum wages are increased.

5. Unions have traditionally organized into craft or industrial unions. Craft unions were the bulwark of the *American Federation of Labor* (AFL); industrial unions comprised the *Congress of Industrial Organizations* (CIO). Frequent jurisdictional disputes over which organization would represent particular workers caused the two to merge into the AFL-CIO in 1955.

6. To protect their prerogatives as sole bargaining agents for workers, unions and their leaders use several kinds of agreements with organized firms. *Closed shops* require workers to be union members as a precondition for employment. At the other end of the spectrum, *open shops* permit union and nonunion members to work side by side. This arrangement is quite unsatisfactory to unions because nonmembers receive the benefits of collective bargaining but need not pay union dues. *Union shops* are compromises between closed and open shops. The employer can hire union or nonunion workers, but an employee must join the union within some specified period (usually 30 days) to retain the job. The Taft-Hartley Act of 1947 outlawed the closed shop and permitted individual states to pass right-to-work laws forbidding union shops. In many of these states, *agency shops* have been created to protect unions from free riders. Workers may choose not to belong to the union but must pay dues.

7. Unionism developed in a hostile environment. The Great Depression shifted public policy in favor of collective bargaining. As trade unionism grew, many felt that unions became corrupt and too powerful, and tighter organizing and financial reporting constraints were imposed on labor organizations. The union movement was relatively stable from roughly 1950 until 1980, but has declined as a percentage of the total labor force in the 1980s. The labor force increasingly consists of white-collar workers who are reluctant to join unions.

8. *Bilateral monopoly*, a very early model of col-

lective bargaining, describes the limits to the wage bargaining process but provides little predictive power. Sir John Hicks's bargaining model predicts both final wage settlements and the duration of strikes.

9. *Labor unions* have typically employed three methods to increase the wages of their members: (*a*) reductions of the supply of workers to an industry; (*b*) establishing higher wages and then parceling out the available work to members; and (*c*) policies designed to increase demands for union labor.

10. *Wage differentials* between union and non-union workers average roughly 10 to 15 percent. Some people blame inflation on excessive union wage demands. Large wage hikes in key industries may set the pattern for other industries. Higher wages may raise unemployment and induce public officials to pursue expansionary macroeconomic policies, further intensifying inflationary pressures. Since organized labor represents less than one worker out of seven, it is unlikely that unionism explains much inflation.

11. A small percentage of collective bargaining negotiations end in *strikes*, and most of these are short. Strikes often impose costs on individuals and firms that are not direct parties to labor negotiations. Strikes may cause shortages, shipping delays, or losses of perishable products.

12. Public employee unions frequently mix politics and collective bargaining to win their demands. Public officials negotiating contracts are seldom those who are responsible for developing government budgets; thus, they may have only weak incentives to resist union wage demands.

Key Concepts

Ensure that you can define these terms before proceeding.

monopolistic exploitation	labor unions
	bilateral monopoly
monopsony power	closed shop
monopsonistic exploitation	open shop
	union shop

Problems and Questions

1. Use this information about output and the demand for dehydrated water to answer the following questions:

Labor	Output	Price
0	0	—
1	60	200
2	100	180
3	136	160
4	168	140
5	196	120
6	220	100
7	240	80

a. Compute and graph the *MRP*s and *VMP*s of labor.

b. If labor is purchased from a competitive market and wage rates are $400 per unit, how many units of labor will you employ?

c. Given the employment equilibrium in question b, what is the extent of your monopolistic exploitation?

2. Suppose that all your competitors for the services of professional water dehydrators go bankrupt and you become a monopsonist faced by this labor supply schedule:

Labor	Wage Rate
0	—
1	200
2	300
3	400
4	800
5	1200
6	1500
7	1800

a. How many workers will you employ now that you are a monopsonist?

b. What is the extent of both monopolistic and monopsonistic exploitation in this instance?

3. Some economists insist that there are so many "greedy capitalists" that exploitation and wage discrimination are impossible. How might competitive drives for profits ensure that everyone is paid "what they're worth"? How do we account for wage differentials between sexes and races if vigorous competition leads to payment of the value of the marginal product?

4. Many firms view salary information as confidential. Can you cite reasons for this practice other than wage discrimination? Do you believe these other reasons are valid?

5. If most firms in certain highly competitive industries (e.g., textiles) monopolistically exploit their employees and wage discriminate, what would happen to employment if these firms were forced to quit these practices? Would their current workers be better off? Why or why not?

6. Some people think that wage structures are compressed relative to workers' productivities. In other words, people with high incomes tend to be underpaid relative to their productivity, while those at the bottom of the pay scale are overpaid relative to their productive contribution. Do you think these critics are correct? If so, what does this suggest about the extent of competition in labor markets? If you think that reality is the opposite of this idea, what features of the labor market cause overpayment of people with relatively high salaries and underpayment of people with relatively low wage incomes?

7. The standard model of monopsony leads to substantial underemployment relative to competition and raises the possibility that minimum-wage laws may expand employment. Can you use logic paralleling the discussion of price discrimination from our chapter on monopoly to show that perfect wage discrimination will cause a monopsonist to hire the same amount of labor as would be employed in a purely competitive labor market? What are the implications of this analysis for economic efficiency? . . . for equity? Do you think that firms having monopsony power also typically have the ability to wage discriminate? Which do you think is more common, pure monopsony power, or the ability to wage discriminate by paying workers in inverse proportion to their desperation for employment?

8. Some economists argue that by permitting collective bargaining, we condone monopoly despite Sherman Antitrust Act prohibitions of monopolies. Is there anything inherently more palatable about labor monopolies than about product monopolies? By encouraging

unions to expand through various laws protecting collective bargaining, are we creating what John Kenneth Galbraith has called "countervailing power," where big unions bargaining for workers offset the effects of concentrated industry? Is there any reason to suspect that the two forces, big labor and big business, will not combine like OPEC to gouge the little consumer? What forces, if any, keep this from happening?

9. In the 1980s, union membership declined steadily. What do you think accounts for the reduction in union membership during this period? Do you foresee labor unions recovering from this decline, or will it continue? Why do you think so?

10. Right-to-work laws presently forbid union shops in 21 states. How can unions in these states protect themselves from free riders? What arguments can you make in favor of right-to-work laws? Against? More than one student of labor relations has commented that the name *right-to-work* was a stroke of genius, that without it few people would vote for the legislation. Are right-to-work laws appropriately named? If not, what should these laws be called?

11. The Taft-Hartley Act outlaws the closed shop, yet in some industries or occupations it is almost impossible to find a job unless you belong to a union. Are these unions doing something illegal? How do you explain this apparent contradiction between the law and reality? Why would employers agree to hire only union members if they did not have to?

12. Some economists argue that the most effective union to date is the American Medical Association. Do you agree? Does the AMA operate like a labor union? In what ways? Name some other professional societies that perform the same functions as unions for their members. Should these associations be subjected to the same democratic standards and financial reporting standards that are applied to unions? How do you think medical doctors would feel if the AMA changed its name to United Medical Doctors of America, Amalgamated Brotherhood of Medical Doctors, or some similar moniker?

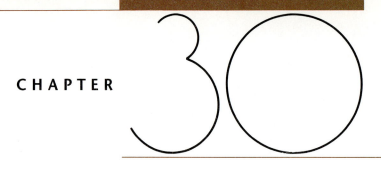

CHAPTER 30

Rent, Interest, Profits, and Capitalization

Great fortunes are usually based, not on wages, but rather on income from rents on land, interest on capital, or entrepreneurial profit. This chapter describes these nonwage sources of income. Most people rely primarily on wage income, which may explain why most people are not rich. (Michael Milken, who launched "junk bonds" as the hottest financial investment of the 1980s, may be one notable exception. His 1987 salary (including bonuses) was $550 million — the highest annual income ever recorded for one person. Of course, he wound up in jail for violating securities laws.)

Market forces shape the rates of rents, interest, and profit much as they determine workers' wages. The derived demands for all resources are based on output prices and each resource's marginal contribution in producing goods consumers want. This production entails transforming materials so that they become more valuable in form, space, time, or possession. Market prices direct these transformations.

Resources are also altered to enhance value. Human capital, for example, makes labor more valuable. Acquisition of human capital partially motivates your quest for a degree. Most workers try to learn skills that will increase wage incomes. Similarly, potential income gains motivate owners of nonlabor resources to carefully mold their assets. Investment in capital, for example, can

take myriad forms; whether new capital will be hand tools, buildings, measuring instruments, or industrial robots depends on which form of capital is expected to be most profit- able. Entrepreneurs try to develop special expertise in areas they forecast as profitable, and land owners plant their acreage or build shopping malls on it so that their land is most valuably used.

Markets for capital, land, and entrepreneurial talent tend to be even more competitive than labor markets. Geography and habit often limit workers' mobility, but investors compete in international markets, rapidly shifting financial capital between investments when even slight differentials arise in rates of return; economic capital follows soon thereafter. Entrepreneurs also respond quickly to the slightest whiff of a profit opportunity. Although land cannot move geographically, flows of other resources when higher resource payments beckon make land mobile between uses if not spaces.

Our first task in this chapter is an overview of how different mixes of resources affect the outputs of typical production processes. Second, we will examine the nature of economic rent and the role it plays in allocating resources. We then turn to explanations of how interest rates are determined and to the sources of economic profits. Finally, we investigate capitalization, which transforms predictable rents, interest, or profits into wealth. As you work through this chapter, keep in mind that markets for capital, entrepreneurship, and land are all relatively competitive and tend to conform to the principles of marginal productivity theory discussed earlier.

Resource Ratios and Productivity

The amounts and types of other resources used in a production process are major determinants of labor productivity. For example, even unskilled workers in the United States work with much more capital and consequently produce far more than their counterparts in, say, India. Thus, American trash collectors each process more garbage than Indian trash collectors because Americans use more trucks, crushers, and other equipment. The relatively high amount of capital per worker in industrialized countries is a major reason that workers in advanced nations enjoy higher wages on average than do workers in less developed economies.

The flip side of this is that capital productivity rises as the number of workers per machine grows. Large amounts of capital per worker in the United States mean that the amount of labor per unit of capital is low relative to less developed countries such as India. Thus, while output per worker is high in the United States relative to India, output per unit of capital is probably higher in India. In the United States, hand shovels are often idle on big construction projects; in India, a shovel typically is more productive and might be used for three shifts every day. The upshot of this is that labor productivity and wages tend to be higher the greater the capital-to-labor ratio, while interest payments and the productivity of capital tend to be higher the lower the capital-to-labor ratio.

This broad notion holds for virtually all resource ratios: (*a*) capital is more productive and highly paid the greater the amounts of labor, entrepreneurial talent, or land working with capital; (*b*) entrepreneurs will be more productive and highly remunerated the fewer the entrepreneurs attempting to use other given resources; and (*c*) land will be more productive and draw

higher rents the more capital and labor are used to work the land. For example, relative to vast desolate ranches on which a few cowhands try to keep track of a few scattered cattle, closely tended, small flower farms covered with greenhouses and automatic watering equipment produce much more value per acre.

The general principles of marginal productivity govern the markets for labor, land, capital, and entrepreneurial talent, but each market has unique characteristics. The last two chapters outlined some specifics of labor markets, so we will now examine these other markets.

Economic Rents

"Rent" usually conjures up payments to landlords or prices charged for temporary use of a videotape, or a truck at the local "Rent-All." As seems too often true, economists have taken a perfectly good word, "rent," and attached their own special meaning to it.

> **Economic rent** *is realized whenever the owner of any resource is paid more than the minimum necessary to elicit the quantity supplied of that productive resource.*

Thus, economic rent broadly applies to parts of many payments to resource owners.

Economic rents may have little to do with apartment leases or similar "rental" values. For example, many rock musicians spend years "paying their dues" — working for peanuts in smoke-filled bars and generally hustling just to get by. If they hit it big and begin to pull down seven figures annually, there is an enormous difference between their superstar incomes and the small amounts for which they were once willing to play music. Economists view such differences as economic rents. Land is about the only resource, however, that generates "pure" economic rents.

Pure Land Rents

One unique characteristic of land is its absolutely fixed supply. The land available to society cannot grow even if payments to landowners rise to

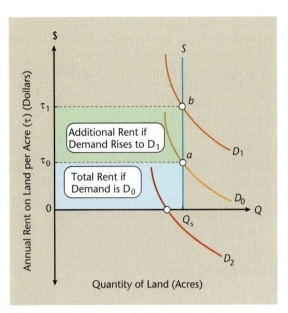

FIGURE 1   Economic Rent for Raw Land

The annual rental value of any factor that is fixed in supply is determined strictly by demand. Pure economic rents are realized only if supply is absolutely fixed, as is the case with locations or the physical characteristics of land.

infinity; the supply is perfectly inelastic at Q_s in Figure 1. If demand is D_0, rent per acre will be τ_0 and total rent is area $0Q_s a\tau_0$. If new technology enhanced land's physical productivity, or if higher output prices boosted the derived demand for land to D_1, rent per acre would rise to τ_1, yielding total rent equal to the area $0Q_s b\tau_1$. What will rent for raw land be if demand is D_2? Zero, and some land will be idle. All payments received for the fixed supply of land are pure rents determined solely by the strength of demand.

The clearest examples of pure economic rents are payments for use of unimproved land. Note that when people construct dikes or drain swamps, they create capital, not new land. (Recall that any improvement increasing the productivity of natural resources is classified as capital.) Consequently, the supply of land is perfectly inelastic, so changes in demand yield proportional changes in land rents. Demands and rental rates for different parcels of land differ according to their locations and their physical characteristics.

Location Rents   Why is a vacant square block in Manhattan worth more than an acre of prime Kansas wheat land? Transportation costs are a major reason. Looked at from a different perspective, the customer populations differ, causing different values. One facet of *location rents* is that if a seller can locate so that customers bear lower transportation costs than are incurred in buying from a competitor, the advantageously located seller can charge more for the goods and services it produces.

Suppose that you owned an isolated Kansas farm and replicated a chunk of downtown Manhattan on the north forty, including a hamburger stand. If you cut the price charged at your hamburger stand by half and put on an advertising campaign worthy of Ronald McDonald, your sales would fall far short of those by your New York rival. The reason is that for the average hamburger buyer, the total cost of a hamburger (including transportation costs) would be far less at the New York stand than at yours. New Yorkers would become regular customers only if you charged such a low price for hamburgers that transportation costs were overcome. Fat chance!

Another facet of location rents is that a firm is able to pay lower prices for inputs if it locates so that its input suppliers (workers, for example) gain from lower transportation costs than would be incurred in selling to a competing firm. When being in business at a particular location gives a firm the ability to charge more to its customers or to pay less to its suppliers, the owner of the location will become aware of these advantages and charge rents sufficiently high that only normal profits are received by the firm.

For example, suppose you leased a building in a run down area of Chicago to establish a fancy French restaurant. Then suppose that a huge luxury hotel unexpectedly located in the next block—business would boom and you might profit immensely in the short run. When your lease was up, however, your landlord would raise your rent to exploit the increased profitability of the location. Economic rents of this type, known as **location** (or *site*) **rents**, are illustrated in Figure 2. Actual rents per square foot for the most expensive shopping centers in selected cities are shown in the table included in this figure.

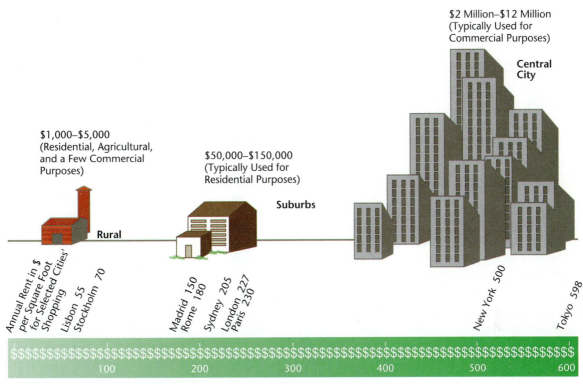

$2 Million–$12 Million
(Typically Used for
Commercial Purposes)

Central City

$1,000–$5,000
(Residential, Agricultural,
and a Few Commercial
Purposes)

$50,000–$150,000
(Typically Used for
Residential Purposes)

Suburbs

Rural

Annual Rent in $
per Square Foot
for Selected Cities'
Shopping

Lisbon 55
Stockholm 70

Madrid 150
Rome 180

Sydney 205
London 227
Paris 230

New York 500

Tokyo 598

$$
100   200   300   400   500   600

FIGURE 2   Value of Acre of Land, Depending upon Location
Market values and rental rates for land are influenced strongly by where a particular
parcel is located. As we move further and further from hubs of business activity, economic rents for land tend to decline.

Rents from Physical Characteristics Marginal productivities and the rental rates of parcels
of land reflect differences in fertility or the values
of minerals the parcels bear. Some land is not
used at all. Windswept deserts and arctic tundra
are examples of land so barren and remote that
its marginal productivity is effectively zero.

David Ricardo, who originated the theory of
pure rent, observed that marginal (barely useful)
land commands zero rent whenever equally productive parcels are vacant. For example, you
could always live "rent free" at an oasis in the
Sahara if at least one comparable oasis were vacant. If the owner tried to charge any positive
rent, you would move to a vacant oasis. The production cost saved by using more productive
land versus marginal land equals the rental value
per period of the more productive land.

Competition for cost reductions from particular sites permits a landowner to charge rent re-

flecting the productivity differences between
superior land and the marginal (zero rent) land.
Ricardo viewed land rent as an **unearned surplus**
because its fixed supply would be available even
at a zero price. Henry George gained fame by
arguing that this unearned surplus to landowners
could be taxed without creating economic ineffi
ciency.

Rents to Other Resources

The concept of economic rent originated with
David Ricardo's analysis of corn and the land
used to produce it. Economic rents are received,
however, whenever a resource owner is paid
more than the minimum necessary to induce a
given amount of the resource. Thus, many owners of scarce resources earn economic rents. The
economic rents received when resource supply
curves are imperfectly elastic are illustrated in

Henry George (1839–1897)

High birth rates and the arrival of millions of immigrants caused rapid growth of the nineteenth-century American economy. Fertile frontier lands were homesteaded, and urban land values boomed. Henry George and his followers believed landowners unjustly reaped major benefits from economic growth, which George perceived as rightfully belonging to society in general. In *Progress and Poverty* (1879), George proposed a **single tax** on land equal to the surplus that landowners were receiving and thought these revenues could finance all government spending. His reasoning is illustrated in Figure 3.

Equilibrium rent per acre before the land tax is τ_0 (point *a*). A tax equal to half of annual rent would cut the net rent per acre to landowners to τ_T. They cannot change the supply of land to drive its rental rate up. Attempts to raise rents would fail, because surpluses of vacant land would develop. Rent that can be charged land users is strictly demand determined, so landowners cannot avoid the full burden of a pure land tax.

How would a land tax affect allocation? If untaxed land were used optimally, the most profitable uses would remain so after imposing the tax. (If you are able to keep half of all rent, 50 percent of the *highest* possible economic rent is the best you can do.) Thus, land taxes seem allocatively neutral.

The central thrust of George's economics is that land rent can be taxed heavily without distorting production incentives. George felt that "nothing short of making land common property can permanently relieve poverty and check the tendency of wages to the starvation point." He proposed to do this not by directly nationalizing land, but by the roundabout method of taking away the unearned income that proprietors enjoyed from land rents.

Land nationalization schemes were common in George's day, but he generally opposed government intervention and proposed leaving land titles in individual ownership, merely taxing all land at 100 percent of its rental value. This levy should be, according to George, a single tax to replace all other taxes. *Progress and Poverty* became his era's best selling work on economics and the bible of the single-tax movement.

A single tax on land sounds appealing, but it suffers from several flaws: (*a*) potential revenue would probably not cover today's total government spending; (*b*) administration would be complex, because distinguishing the values of land from its improvements—clearing, irrigation, buildings—is quite difficult; (*c*) rent does provide resource owners with incentives to find users who most highly value the re-

sources; and (*d*) land is not the only resource that generates economic rents. A single tax on land rent would impose the full burden of paying for government on landowners. This seems unfair from the vantage point of current landowners.

George's single-tax movement reached its apex in his 1886 race for mayor of New York City. Running as the candidate of the United Labor Party, George finished second, but there was wide speculation that he might have won an honest ballot count. Henry George died during another run at the mayor's office in 1897, but left his imprint on economic reform movements at home and abroad.

FIGURE 3 Effect of a Tax on Land: Landowners Bear the Burden

Landowners alone bear the full burdens of land taxes, because the total amount competitive renters will pay to use land is determined strictly by its productivity. If landlords try to shift a land tax forward in the form of higher rental rates, surplus land will be available, along with pressures for rent reductions. For example, if landlords tried to raise their rental rate to τ_1, there would be surplus land. Equilibrium rents on land are always "all the market will bear."

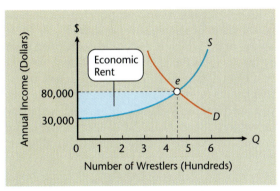

FIGURE 4 Economic Rent and Professional Wrestlers

Economic rents are realized whenever a supplier of a resource receives more than the minimum necessary to make the factor available to the market. Thus, the area above the supply curve but below the price line is economic rent, which is sometimes called the supplier's surplus. In markets for output, such areas represent producer surplus, which is the flip side of consumer surplus. Recall that consumer surplus is the area below a demand curve but above the price line. It is the difference between what a buyer would willingly pay for a specific quantity of a good and the amount actually paid because goods can be bought at a uniform price.

Figure 4, which portrays a positively sloped labor supply curve for professional wrestlers.

Equilibrium occurs at point *e* when 450 wrestlers work for annual incomes averaging $80,000, but only very reluctant wrestlers (those making up the labor supply near point *e*) are paid the bare minimums necessary for their services. Other wrestlers would work for less and so receive economic rents as surpluses above their minimum acceptance wages. For example, if Gorgeous George were willing to work for $50,000 annually (his actual salary is $80,000), his economic rent is $30,000. Total rents to wrestlers equal the shaded area above the supply curve but below the wage rate.

Rents and Efficiency

Economic rent is any surplus to a resource owner when income exceeds the opportunity cost of providing the resource to society as a whole. Economic rents are fairly common because most productive resources are at least partially fixed: their supplies are not perfectly elastic for the entire economy. This "fixity" generates economic rents.

People who view the income distribution as unfair often aim their displeasure at high incomes from interest, profit, or rent. Referring to multimillion-dollar-a-year sports figures or movie stars, they express sentiments such as "No one is worth more than $_____ ($1,000,000?) annually." Do rents serve any purpose beyond enrichment of the owners of land or specialized talents? If not, these surpluses can be completely taxed by government with no net loss to society. But both the short- and long-run consequences of taxing economic rents might actually cause inefficient allocations of resources.

Short-Run Allocation Even in the short run, the drive to maximize economic rent creates incentives for resource owners to use their productive resources in the most valuable ways possible and to maintain them properly. Suppose that you own a city block that will potentially rent for $1 million annually. If rents were taxed 100 percent, would incentives exist to seek the highest bidder so that the land would be put to its most valuable use? Absolutely not!

Henry George argued that land would be used efficiently even if 50 percent taxes on rent were imposed because "half is better than nothing." When we consider models that recognize transaction costs, however, his analysis stumbles. If the tax were 99.99 percent, for example, the $100 received if you found the $1 million bidder for use of your land would be unlikely to overcome your transaction costs. You might simply let your land lie idle. But what if the site tax were only 80 percent? Or 32 percent? Any tax rate, however low, reduces the incentive to incur transaction costs so that land is put to its most valuable use.

Some corporate CEOs, movie stars, musicians, novelists, and athletes realize incomes that seem outrageous. Much of such income is economic rent, so why not impose 100 percent taxes on annual incomes over $1,000,000? This question is partially answered if you ponder how you would react were you in this position. High income tax rates explain why many English actors and rock stars have immigrated to Switzerland and the United States.

Another problem is that parts of even extraordinary incomes are not pure rents. If emigration seems unattractive, why bother to be worth more than $1,000,000 annually? Established actors might study their lines less diligently or do fewer films. Might opera singers begin to smoke or fail to avoid colds? Would successful authors write as much? Would sports superstars play as hard or often? Would they willingly play in industrial towns, or might most gravitate to sunny resort areas? Some might still strive to excel out of personal pride, but after a certain point, we suspect that cold, hard cash motivates most people whose specialized skills earn large economic rents.

In summary, rents are important even in the short run, because they are incentives to maintain rent-generating resources, and because they are important in ensuring that those who most highly value scarce resources are able to use them.

Long-Run Allocation Many resources that draw economic rents because they are semifixed in the short run are far from fixed for the economy as a whole over the long haul. Prospects of high income motivate people to invest in assets that subsequently command economic rent. Today's opportunity costs become tomorrow's fixed costs, as resources jell into fixed assets. For example, medical students undergo years of expensive training in hopes of high economic rents once their M.D. degrees are in hand. Investors in buildings or capital equipment draw economic rents over the useful lives of these assets.

Would tomorrow's superstar athletes have as much incentive to polish their skills if the economic rents enjoyed by basketball's Michael Jordan, tennis's Steffi Graf, or football's Randall Cunningham were taxed away? *No!* Would the lawyers of the next generation be as skilled as F. Lee Bailey or Richard "Racehorse" Haynes if the incomes of top attorneys were limited because they are economic rents? From whence would come future Luciano Pavarottis, Danielle Steeles, or Bill Cosbys? The long-run effects of taxing all economic rent would be disastrous because there would be fewer incentives to invest in oneself or in capital equipment; the entire economy would stagnate.

It should come as no surprise that the annual rental value of any resource is tied closely to its selling price, which is the wealth associated with owning a resource or other asset. Before we discuss capitalization, which is the process of translating rents or other flows of income into wealth, you need an understanding of interest and profits, which also may be capitalized through the process described near the end of this chapter.

Interest

You may have deposits in a bank account that draw interest. Why does your bank pay interest? The answer seems obvious: Banks make loans at higher interest rates than they pay depositors. Most loans, however, are made to business investors who buy capital—machines or buildings. Thus, interest is ultimately a payment to providers of economic capital. Interest payments are somewhat roundabout in advanced economies, being spread among those who own capital directly and others whose saving and financial investment make it possible for society to accumulate economic capital.

Interest Rates

We will focus on interest payments to holders of financial capital to simplify our analysis. Similar reasoning applies to direct owners of economic capital.

> **Nominal interest rates** *are the percentage of monetary premiums paid per time period for the use of money.*

The ultimate lenders are those who save by spending less than their income. If you pay a dime annually for each dollar you owe on a car loan, the annual interest rate is 10 percent. (The people you truly owe are depositors in the lending institution.) Because of differences in borrowers and debt instruments—car loans, mortgages, government or corporate bonds, and so on—there are many nominal interest rates at any given time. These "IOUs" are a large component of our financial capital. Interest rates vary among these financial instruments because of:

1. *Risk.* Different borrowers have different probabilities of defaulting on their loans. Naturally, higher "risk premiums" in the interest rate are charged the greater the risk of default.

2. *Maturity.* Interest rates are generally higher the longer it will take to retire a loan, in part because lenders have sets of expectations that become increasingly uncertain as the time period considered becomes longer.

3. *Liquidity.* Better developed markets for specific debt instruments drive interest rates down, because the transaction costs incurred in buying or selling such IOUs will be lower. Competition among lenders to grant certain types of loans facilitates liquidity.

Interest rates commonly range from a government-subsidized 5 percent annually to a loan shark's 5 percent weekly. References to "the rate of interest" usually mean the nominal interest rate charged annually on long-term (20- to 30-year) riskless loans. Interest rates on negotiable long-term government bonds or those charged to "prime" borrowers are reasonable approximations of this concept.

Changes in the price level drive wedges between real interest rates and nominal interest rates.

> The **real interest rate** is the percentage of purchasing power annually paid by borrowers to lenders.

Real interest rates can be roughly computed by subtracting the percentage annual rate of inflation from nominal interest rates. For example, 14 percent nominal interest yields only about 6 percent real interest if annual inflation is 8 percent.

Markets for Financial Capital

Interest is a payment to providers of economic capital. Saving makes new capital supplies available; thus, the ultimate capital suppliers are sav-

ers. Just what factors determine the interest rate? After adjusting for inflation, the real interest rate depends on:

1. *Premiums savers require to delay gratification.* Most of us want goods now instead of later, unless we are rewarded for waiting. If 10 percent more goods are required to get typical savers to wait a year to consume their income, real interest rates gravitate toward 10 percent.

2. *Premiums required for sacrificing liquidity.* Less-liquid assets generate higher rates of return, or we would all hold cash.

3. *Productivity of new capital.* If new capital reproduces 12 percent of its value in new goods each year, interest rates tend toward 12 percent.

These three factors are reflected in the demands and supplies of *loanable funds.*

The total demand for loanable funds in the United States depends on the plans for borrowing by domestic consumers, government, business, and by foreigners. The supply depends on (*a*) plans for saving by individual households, (*b*) international flows of financial capital (by which foreign savers can make loans to U.S. borrowers, or vice versa), and (*c*) the monetary policy of the central bank.

Keep in mind that markets for loanable funds are affected by government deficits and debt, monetary policies, and international capital flows, but these are macroeconomic topics. The analysis of this section would not change in a meaningful way if we considered all the roles played by all the entities just listed. Therefore, for simplicity we will focus on household plans to save as sources of loanable funds and on business borrowing as a use of loanable funds.

Demands for Loanable Funds Some business borrowing is to cover current operating expenses, but we will concentrate on the investment plans that absorb the bulk of business borrowing. Firms construct buildings, buy machinery, or purposely increase inventories only if they expect to profit by doing so. Firms can finance these investments with funds from (*a*) retained earnings, (*b*) direct sales of the company's stock, or (*c*) sales of new bonds, or loans from financial institutions. Naturally, the depositors (savers) are the real lenders. The third approach is called *debt capital*. To simplify our analysis even further, we focus on debt capital in the remainder of this section. The thrust of our analysis would not change if we separately considered each form of financial capital. Keep in mind that financial capital is merely a tool used to secure purchasing power over a wide range of goods, including economic (physical) capital.

Business investors demand funds for a variety of investments, each of which is expected to yield profits to the borrower. Just as the demand for labor depends on labor's marginal productivity, the demand for capital depends on its marginal productivity. Capital's marginal productivity (its *MRP*) as a percentage of expenditures on capital is known as the **rate of return on investment** (*r*). Like the demands for other resources, the demand for capital is a derived demand.

The demand for capital goods generates demand for loanable funds to finance new investment. In Figure 5, this demand for loanable funds is expressed in terms of rates of return and real interest rates. One explanation for the negative slope of demand curves for capital and loanable funds is that greater investment causes more and more capital to be used with fixed amounts of land and labor. The law of diminishing marginal returns then causes successive doses of capital to be decreasingly productive.

An alternative approach is to recognize that firms rank potential investment projects from the highest expected rate of return to the lowest. Assuming that funds from retained earnings or new stock offerings are insufficient, these projects underpin the demand for loanable funds shown in Figure 5. Only a few projects will yield a 20 percent rate of return or greater ($1 billion worth in Figure 5). As the rate of return requirement falls, firms find that more projects are advantageous. If interest costs fall to 10 percent, $4 billion worth of projects are profitable (point *b*); $8 billion in new investments generate rates of return of at least 5 percent (point *c*).

Construction costs and equipment costs are

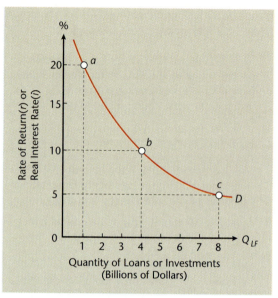

FIGURE 5 The Demand Curve for Debt Capital (Loanable Funds)

The diminishing rate of return to investment in new capital is mirrored in the downward slope of the demand curve for loanable funds.

obviously important determinants of business investment. Because the supply curves for capital goods are positively sloped, their costs and prices tend to rise during prosperity as demand for investment goods increases, choking off short-term surges in investment. Conversely, declines in the costs of investment goods during economic downturns slow the fall of investment spending.

Investors do most of the borrowing in this country, but consumers and all levels of government also borrow substantially. Consumer purchases of homes and automobiles fall sharply when interest rates rise. Although the federal government's borrowing seems unaffected by interest rates, state and local governments borrow more to finance schools, parks, and roads when their interest costs are less. Thus, when consumer, investor, and government demands for loanable funds are combined, the market demand curve slopes downward. As with all other markets, however, demand is only half of the story.

Supplies of Loanable Funds The supply of loanable funds is positively related to the price received (interest). The ultimate lenders (savers who supply loanable funds) receive interest for the use of their funds. The major alternative for saver/lenders is current consumption, but a few, who value liquidity highly or who expect a financial crash, may hoard their savings. High interest rates confront individuals with high opportunity costs of current consumption (or hoarding). As a result, many save (providing funds to the capital market) and use their future wealth (amount saved plus interest) for consumption at a later time.

Equilibrium Interest Rates Equilibrium in the financial capital market is shown in Figure 6. The initial demand for funds D_0 reflects the rates of return expected by business (plus consumer or government borrowing). It is negatively sloped, because investments become less profitable as interest rates rise. The initial supply curve S_0 is

FIGURE 6 The Market for Loanable Funds

Increases in saving will increase the supply of loanable funds and decrease the interest rate. Reduced anxiety about the future tends to expand both the demand and the supply of loanable funds.

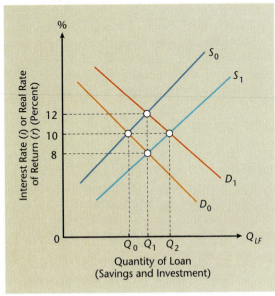

positively sloped because household saving grows as interest rates paid savers rise (the opportunity costs of current consumption rise).

The rate of return on new investment equals the interest rate in equilibrium, which occurs at the intersection of the demand (D_0) and supply (S_0) curves in Figure 6. The initial equilibrium rate of return and interest rate will be 10 percent, and the quantity of investment loans will equal Q_0. Suppose that expected returns on new capital investments rise so that the demand for loanable funds increases to D_1. Equilibrium interest and investment loans would rise to 12 percent and Q_1, respectively. Similarly, suppose households decide to delay consumption and save more. When families increase the rate at which they postpone consumption, the loanable funds available for investment rise, supply shifts from S_0 to S_1, and interest rates fall. Finally, when investors grow more optimistic, expected rates of return, interest rates, and financial investments all rise.

In summary, interest rewards households who save for deferring their consumption and for sacrificing liquidity. Interest is also a return to capital that depends on capital's marginal productivity. The interest rate charged on a particular financial instrument depends on its liquidity and length of time to maturity, and on lenders' perceptions of the probability of default.

Entrepreneurs and Economic Profit

Economic profit and a desire to change the world are the fundamental motivations of entrepreneurs who establish firms to innovate new products and technologies in a capitalist economy. Most people misunderstand this role of profit and substantially overestimate average profit both per sales dollar and as a return on invested capital. You know that a firm's accounting profit is the difference between total revenue and explicit costs, which pay for the use of resources not owned by the firm. Only after subtracting implicit costs (opportunity costs of resources owners provide to operate a firm) from accounting profit do we have pure economic profit, which is also a pure rent to the firm's owners.

Economic profit *is revenue exceeding all opportunity costs for resources.*

In a purely competitive and unchanging economy in which transaction costs were zero, economic profit would always be zero; implicit payments to sustain owner-provided resources would absorb all accounting profits. In reality, transaction costs are significant, and the future is uncertain. Many changes are wrought by entrepreneurial quests for profits. Moreover, monopoly power is commonplace. This leads to the major sources of pure economic profits: (*a*) monopoly power, (*b*) innovation, and (*c*) uncertainty.

Monopoly Profit

Monopoly power enables some firms to generate total revenue far in excess of the opportunity costs of the resources used. But can a monopolist continually enjoy economic profit? Transaction costs, uncertainty, and entry barriers create short-run profit opportunities. *Monopoly profit* may persist into the long run if barriers prevent entry by competitors, but profits will stimulate resource flows that eliminate monopoly profit in *contestable* markets.[1] If so, profit will have served its function by signaling where society desired greater production. If barriers preclude entry in the long run, economy-wide efficiency will not occur, but the drive for monopoly profit does encourage least-cost production.

The capitalization processes described in a moment suggest that profit is realized primarily by the owners when a firm secures a monopoly position. Predictable profits are capitalized in the long run into a higher market value (and thus higher opportunity costs) for ownership of the monopoly; subsequent owners can expect only normal profits.

Rewards for Innovation

Innovation is another source of profit.

Innovation *involves the development and implementation of a new product or production process or the opening of a new market.*

A firm is likely to profit if it is among the first to introduce a successful good or a more efficient technology. Profits fall when competitors mimic successful innovators. Thomas Edison, for example, became rich when he established General Electric as the outlet for his genius, but GE now faces hordes of competitors and realizes only normal profits.

Invention and innovation are not synonymous; each is a part of the process of change. Some highly successful inventions have been innovated by firms not directly associated with the inventor. You may never have heard of Gilbert Hyatt, but in 1990, the courts and the U.S. Patent Office recognized him as a primary inventor of modern computer chips. The microchip makers who launched a revolution in how we live by innovating his chips wound up paying him royalties only after extended bouts in court.

Joseph Schumpeter first expressed the innovation theory of profits to help explain the business cycle.[2] Entrepreneurs will attempt to capitalize on new profit opportunities created by a significant innovation, and their collective investments fuel economic booms. Once the advantages from the innovation are fully absorbed, however, investment declines, pushing the economy into a downturn to await another major innovation.

Risk Bearing and Uncertainty

If the likelihood of some occurrence is fairly predictable, many people will adjust in similar ways, so only normal rates of return can be expected. Buying insurance is one adjustment against life's possible hazards, or you might *self-insure* and take your chances. Some aspects of the future,

---

1. Our ''Strategic Behavior'' chapter describes how contestable markets differ from competitive markets.

2. Joseph A. Schumpeter, *Business Cycles: A Theoretical, Historical, and Statistical Analysis of the Capitalist Process* (New York: McGraw-Hill, 1939).

however, seem totally unpredictable. If fortune smiles, unexpected profit may be your reward for bearing the risk of just being in a line of business, or you may be clobbered if disaster unexpectedly strikes your industry.

The economist Frank Knight first distinguished risk from uncertainty.[3]

> **Risk** *exists when the probability of a given event can be estimated.*

For example, if a firm can reliably predict that, on average, a production process will yield 3 defective units out of 100, it can adjust for these risks by considering "losses due to defects" as a normal cost of doing business. Similarly, the probabilities of fire, certain accidents, or the death of a key executive can be fairly reliably predicted, and insurance is available. Again, these risks will be reflected in production costs and output prices.

Uncertainty, on the other hand, forces entrepreneurs to weigh imperfect information and base their decisions on subjective judgments.

> **Uncertainty** *occurs when a potential occurrence is so unpredictable that forecasts are unavoidably almost pure guesswork.*

According to Frank Knight, profits are rewards for bearing uncertainty. Entrepreneurs invest in an expectation of generating sufficient revenues to cover all costs, including allowances for all risks, but the unfolding of time may yield events beyond any entrepreneur's wildest hopes or fears. Uncertainty makes it impossible to predict economic profits or losses.

The Economic Role of Profits

Uncertainty, innovation, and monopoly power are major sources of economic profit, but what functions do profits perform? Economic profits signal that prices exceed average costs and indicate that social welfare can be improved by shifting resources from unprofitable to profitable endeavors. Conversely, industry-wide economic losses signal that too many resources are devoted to production of a particular good and could beneficially be shifted elsewhere.

Profits are also a stimulus for efficiency. Entrepreneurs' desires for profits will cause costs to be cut wherever possible, freeing resources for other uses. Competition forces profits down to normal levels as imitators mimic successful firms, whether success is derived from being in a certain product line or from using a more efficient technology. Competition also punishes relatively inefficient high-cost firms with economic losses.

Profits also reward the entrepreneurs who innovate new products and technologies in an uncertain business environment. The drive for entrepreneurial profit propels society along a path of economic growth and progress. Predictable rents, interest, or profits are translated into wealth through *capitalization* processes when resources that generate these income flows can be sold. In the next section, we examine the mechanics of how competition for income streams determines the market values of income-generating assets.

Capitalizing Income Streams

Suppose you manage a rock group called "Nuclear Winter," currently being booked as a warm-up act for more popular bands. The group's third album suddenly goes platinum and phones begin to ring. Promoters want "Winter" to headline upcoming concerts, but it is solidly booked for the next six months at $5,000 per appearance. Who will benefit from the group's popularity during the next six months? Promoters who contracted with your band prior to its hit album will profit by selling out their concerts even if they raise ticket prices. How long will these economic profits (which could also be considered rents) continue to be received by individual concert promoters?

Being a smart promoter yourself, you will quit

---

3. Frank H. Knight, *Risk, Uncertainty, and Profit* (Boston: Houghton-Mifflin, 1921).

booking "Winter" as an opening act and will raise its fee when you negotiate future contracts so individual concert promoters will earn only normal profits. This *capitalizes* rents from the group's popularity. The group's fee now reflects the higher ticket prices and attendance for each performance. If you held exclusive rights to book the group, you could sell the contract for a fat profit.

> **Capitalization** *is the transformation of future income streams into current value or wealth and quickly eliminates economic profits.*

Similar capitalization processes occur in farming. If international grain prices soar, farmers temporarily enjoy economic profits. But the price of farmland rises when expected profits are capitalized into higher land values. Even farmers who own their land find the opportunity cost of holding it rising, squeezing out the economic profit derived from farming. Their higher wealth naturally would keep them from mourning this fate.

Investors prefer more income to less, and they want it sooner rather than later. Thus, the capitalized value of an income stream will be larger (*a*) the greater the income stream, and (*b*) the more quickly income is realized. Truly understanding these relationships requires knowing how to calculate present values and rates of return.

Present Values

Economic investment generates future output and yields an income stream to the investor. The income stream per period as a percentage of the dollar outlay for a capital good is the **rate of return**. Determining whether an investment will be profitable requires calculating its *present value*, which is the value today of all expected future income.

> The **present value** *of an asset is the discounted value today of the expected income stream associated with the asset.*

Suppose you were offered a guaranteed $100 payable one year from today and that your savings account earned 6 percent interest annually. What is the most you would willingly pay for this IOU? Certainly less than $100. You can calculate the amount at which you will do equally well by having your funds in either the savings account or this IOU by answering the question: How much money would I have to put in the bank at a 6 percent annual interest rate so that when the interest earned in one year is added to the original amount, the total equals $100? This problem boils down to $1.06(PV) = \$100$, where *PV* stands for present value. If you divide both sides of this equation by 1.06 and then solve for $PV = \$100/1.06$, you have the answer. Similar questions can be answered for any interest rate, any time period, or any amount of money using the following formula:

Present Value

$$PV = \frac{Y_1}{(1+i)^1} + \frac{Y_2}{(1+i)^2} + \cdots + \frac{Y_n}{(1+i)^n}$$
$$= \sum_{t=1}^{n} \frac{Y_t}{(1+i)^t}$$

where:
Y_t = payment expected at time t.
i = annual interest rate or discount rate.
t = time period.
n = number of periods when payments are expected.
Σ = an arithmetic operator meaning "sum across."

If you use a 6 percent interest rate to discount the $100 payable one year from today, the $PV = \$100/1.06$, which equals $94.34. This amount in a savings account paying 6 percent interest would yield $94.34 \times (.06) = \$5.66$; at the end of the year your principal plus interest would total to $94.34 + $5.66, which is $100. If you had to wait two years for the $100, what is the most you would pay, assuming the interest rate is 6 percent? The answer is $89, because $\$100/[1+.06]^2 = \$89$. Naturally, an IOU paying $100 next year plus $100 two years hence would be worth $94.34 + $89.00 = $183.34.

State legislatures came under tremendous pressure during the 1980s to hold taxes in check. Many responded by enacting state lotteries. Federal "truth-in-lending" laws were enacted to help people avoid misunderstandings about interest rates and present values. Focus 1 indicates how misleading state lotteries are, because their advertising fails to reflect the importance of discounting future income streams.

Perpetuities The present value formula may appear formidable, but there is a shortcut in calculating present values if the annual income expected from an asset is fixed into the indefinite future at a constant Y_t. Such assets, known as **perpetuities,** are computed with the following equation:

Present Value for Perpetuities

$$PV = \frac{Y_t}{i}$$

Thus, if a parcel of land is expected to generate annual rent of $10,000 forever, and the interest rate is 10 percent (.10), the parcel's present value is $100,000. If a government bond promises to pay $1,000 annually forever to its owner, and the interest rate is 8 percent, it is worth $12,500. Bonds of this type, called *consols*, are issued by the Bank of England.

Rates of Return

While present value calculations are very important to financial analysts, investors are more often interested in rate of return analysis, which facilitates "quick and dirty" comparisons of alternative investments. If you are majoring in accounting or finance or are just interested in investment analysis, you should pay special attention to both present value and rate of return formulas — you will undoubtedly see them again.[4]

---

4. You may want to keep this book as a simple, clear introduction to this complex topic.

The **rate of return** *is the annual return to an asset expressed as a percentage of the asset's price.*

Investors usually have some idea of the income stream they might expect from an investment. We can determine the rate of return (r) by solving the following formula:

Rate of Return Calculation

$$P = \sum_{t=0}^{n} \frac{Y_t}{(1+r)^t}$$

where P equals the price of the investment good, r equals the annual rate of return, and all other variables are as defined earlier. Since we know price (P) and expected income in each time period (Y_t), the only unknown is r, the rate of return. For example, if an asset selling for $100 today will pay $110 a year from today, the rate of return is 10 percent. A $112 payment in a year yields a rate of return of 12 percent. Thus, the larger the expected income in each time period, the greater the rate of return for a given price.

Comparing Present Values and Rates of Return

How are present values and rates of return related to each other and to the capitalization process? If the present value is at least as great as the price ($PV \geq P$), then the expected rate of return is at least as great as the interest rate ($r \geq i$); you will invest because the asset appears profitable. You will not invest if an asset's price exceeds your estimate of present value because the expected rate of return will be less than the market rate of interest.

Generally, we know the price (P), the going interest rate (i), and the income expected each year (Y_t) when we evaluate an investment.

Break-Even Investments

$$PV = \sum_{t=0}^{n} \frac{Y_t}{(1+r)^t}$$

Are Lottery Tickets Sucker Bets?

Maybe we need "truth-in-winning" laws. Truth-in-lending laws force financial institutions to disclose all interest and miscellaneous costs to borrowers. But similar standards apply only inconsistently to state lotteries, magazine subscription "sweepstakes," and similar schemes aimed at people afflicted with get-rich-quick mentalities.

The sad reality is that winning $1,000,000 in a state lottery won't even come close to making you a millionaire. The biggest reason is that lottery commissions spread top prizes across 20 checks and 19 years of payments. (You get a first check when you win, and then one at the end of each of the next 19 years.) State governments effectively collect the interest on your winnings. Another consideration is taxes. State, federal, and local taxes usually absorb at least 40 percent of your prize. Thus, winning $1,000,000 usually generates annual checks of roughly $30,000 because taxes are withheld. Still a tidy sum, but what is this income stream worth today?

Suppose 10 percent is the standard interest rate. Your winnings are worth $30,000 + $30,000/1.10 + $30,000/(1.10^2) + ... + $30,000/(1.10^{19})$, or a grand total of $282,732. When interest rates and taxes are considered properly, it would take a cool $3,569,184 as an announced prize to yield a present value of $1,000,000 and truly make the winner a millionaire.

What are the odds against getting rich by buying lottery tickets? Typical state lotteries brag that they pay out half of their revenues in prizes. Most gloss over taxes and the length of time for payout. In fact, lottery commissions usually buy annuities from financial institutions to handle payoffs to winners across time. They pay roughly 30 percent of the face value of the announced winnings for these annuities. And then the states collect taxes on your winnings. Consequently, on average, "the house" collects roughly 75 percent to cover its expenses out of all revenues from lottery tickets.

On the other hand, roughly 3 percent of each bet, on average, goes to cover the operations of a gambling casino in Las Vegas or Atlantic City. For example, the average payout to craps players is $35 paid out for every $36 that gamblers bet. Casinos support their operations by collecting $1 out of each $36 bet. Unlike states that collect state income taxes from winners, however, casinos don't collect a "casino tax."

This analysis suggests that, if you cannot control the impulse to gamble, you are likely to do much better by dealing with private organizations instead of a state government. Lottery tickets are a terrible gambling strategy, shunned by economists, statisticians, or almost anyone with any sense about what payoffs should be to warrant a financial investment. Most lottery tickets are, unfortunately, sold to misguided dreamers and poor people who don't know about better investments.

When this equation holds, an investment is a *break-even* proposition. For example, if an investor could expect $224 a year hence, and the interest rate were 12 percent, a price of $200 makes an investment a break-even proposition. However, your assessment of the present value of an asset may be either higher or lower than the going price. Similarly, you may estimate the rate of return as either above or below the market interest rate.

Present value calculations solve for the current worth of an income stream by discounting expected future income with the market rate of interest, both of which we know. Rate of return analysis also assumes that we know how much income to expect in the future and when it will be received, but solves for an unknown *implicit* interest rate (r) while using the known current price to arrive at a solution.

Parallels in calculations of present values and rates of return may make it seem that maximizing one is equivalent to maximizing the other. Unfortunately, this perception can be misleading and result in misplaced investment priorities. Consider two one-time financial investments. Suppose that you have exactly $1,000 available. Your first option is a coupon for $10 guaranteed to quadruple to $40 in one day—a 300 percent return that is almost immediate. Unfortunately, buying the $10 coupon will prevent you from exercising your second risk-free option—your $1,000 will double in a day, yielding only a 100 percent return. Despite the fact that you must forgo the investment with the higher rate of return, doubling the $1,000 investment is clearly preferable to quadrupling a $10 investment over the same period.

Which of the following is more valuable as an investment? (*a*) A $5,000 investment in a Christmas tree lot will double your funds by generating a rate of return of 100 percent, but only for one month. (*b*) A $1 billion investment in a vitamin pill plant will generate a 1 percent net return per month forever. Even though the annualized return from the tree lot exceeds 1,200 percent (because of compounding), the investment in the pill factory is much more valuable. The key to sound investment is, "When in doubt, maximize present values—not rates of return."

Capitalization and Competition

There is tremendous competition for profits. If you are astute, several other astute investors will probably assess any given investment much as

you do. If present value appears to exceed price substantially, there may be bidding wars that rapidly drive the price toward present value. Even if you do manage to pick up what you view as a bargain, you certainly would not then sell it for less than its present value to you.

Thus, the equilibrium price of any asset is its present value. Moreover, competition causes the rate of return expected from any asset, after adjusting for risk, to equal the market rate of interest. The process that discounts expected future income by the interest rate to arrive at present value and price is *capitalization*.

How might you use your knowledge of the capitalization process? Assume you own 1,000 shares of a wildcat oil company earning $1 per share per year. If market conditions required a 10 percent rate of return, shares of stock would sell for $10. What if the firm hit a gusher expected to triple its annual earnings? Stock shares would quickly rise to roughly $30 after the gusher was announced. What rate of return would be expected by people who bought stock after this discovery? Roughly 10 percent, just as before. Similar capitalization processes determine the prices of all sorts of economic resources and financial investments.

We suggested earlier that any predictable income stream is quickly capitalized. Focus 2 describes how capitalization enriches people who establish successful enterprises.

One possible road to riches requires finding assets for which the current owners have underestimated future earning power. You can then purchase these assets relatively cheaply. When the true earning capacity of the assets becomes known, you can become rich by selling the assets for considerably more.

One roadblock that makes this a difficult avenue to wealth, however, is vigorous competition from many other bright bargain hunters. At times, attempts to discover bargains lead people who acquire *insider information* about financial securities to break the law. Ivan Boesky acquired notoriety and millions of dollars as an *inside trader*—trading (illegally) based on inside information he procured. Profit is likely for anyone who acts on information about events that will affect the values of assets in predictable ways—

FOCUS 2

Capitalization and the NFL

Professional football's domination by the National Football League (a cartel) went largely unchallenged from the league's establishment in 1920 until the 1960s. The NFL had 14 teams spread across the country in major cities by 1960. Several other cities sought NFL franchises, but established owners resisted growing pressure for expansion. (Cartel members recognize that increased output reduces prices.)

The sport's growing popularity and the advent of televised games (primarily on CBS and NBC) boosted revenue, attracting a group of wealthy fans who decided to compete with the NFL by launching the American

Football League. These entrepreneurs were prepared to suffer initial losses in hopes of ultimate success in competing with the NFL. Each prospective owner ventured $25,000 for a franchise to start a team, locating largely in population centers neglected by the NFL. The AFL negotiated TV contracts of its own (primarily with ABC), and quickly proved competitive, drawing sellout crowds in Denver, Buffalo, San Diego, and other "second-tier" markets. A bidding war for players ensued, and by 1965, the NFL capitulated to a merger.

Each $25,000 investment by an original AFL owner is now worth roughly $160 to 220 million. Does this huge increase

mean that investment in an NFL franchise today would be enormously profitable? Capitalization explains why the answer is *no!* The NFL, and then the AFL, were enormously profitable for their original owners. Huge profits are possible for the entrepreneurs who start sports franchises and watch them succeed. But people who subsequently buy pieces of paper called "franchises" for millions of dollars can expect only normal returns. Capitalization causes the prices of franchises to equal the present value of expected returns. Thus, a buyer of an established franchise can expect only normal returns on investment.

---

but only if they act before that information is widely publicized.

The Marginal Productivity Theory of Income Distribution

In our "Production and Costs" chapter, we showed that least cost production requires profit-maximizing firms to use combinations of resources so that the marginal physical products of particular resources are proportional to the prices of the resources. This concept translates

into the *principle of equal marginal productivities per dollar*:

$$\frac{MPP_L}{w} = \frac{MPP_K}{r} = \cdots$$

This is one application of the law of equal marginal advantage to production. Multiplying all *MPP*s by the price (*P*) of output reveals that competitive firms must operate so that the values of the marginal products of all resources ($VMP = P - MPP$) are proportional to their prices:

$$\frac{VMP_L}{w} = \frac{VMP_K}{r} = \cdots$$

But resource prices are equal to marginal factor costs if resource markets are competitive, and the market compels competitive firms to pay resource owners incomes equal to the resources' VMPs, so:

$$\frac{VMP_L}{MFC_L} = \frac{VMP_K}{MFC_K} = \cdots = 1$$

This suggests that a competitive market system tends to divide income according to the productive contribution of each individual's resources. Of course, product or resource markets are seldom purely competitive, but this brief review does identify some central tendencies for the distribution of income in a capitalist economy.

This *marginal productivity theory of income distribution* also points to a key for personal wealth. People will be relatively prosperous if they control a lot of resources that make valuable productive contributions to output. Incentives embedded in the structures of wages, rents, interest incomes from capital, and profits are signals about how to alter resources and allocate them so that they are used most valuably.

Marginal productivity theory encapsulates a lot of information about incentives in a market economy. For example, interest rate differentials may cause you to shift funds from a savings account into a money market fund. Higher interest rates may induce you to consume less and save more. If you enjoy art, economics, finance, and philosophy about equally well, pay differentials may channel you toward the more remunerative of these areas of study. Pay differentials are, for better or worse, signals about how society values (at the margin) having more people in particular occupations.[5] Consequently, musicians whose personal preferences run to classical may perform rock, and serious artists may be forced to live off of income generated by painting houses.

This theory cannot even hint, however, at the most equitable income distribution — a normative question that is addressed late in the next part of this book. We have now discussed markets for goods and resources, touching upon certain government policies along the way. The next part of the book details the microeconomic role of government in a market system. We will address various types of inefficiency and inequity whose causes range from inherent problems with market solutions to failures inherent in government decision making.

---

5. Artists and philosophers might use *paradox of value* arguments (from our "Consumer Choice" chapter) to argue that, just as water is absolutely more valuable (has more total utility) than diamonds (which have higher marginal values and prices), philosophy and the arts are absolutely more valuable to society than finance or economics. Relative prices and wage structures, however, are based on marginal valuations.

Chapter Review: Key Points

1. *Economic rent* exists whenever resource owners receive more than the minimum required for them to supply given amounts of the resource.

2. Land has a unique economic characteristic — it is fixed in supply. Thus, its supply curve is perfectly inelastic, and all payments for the use of land are pure rent. Land rents vary by location and particular physical characteristics, such as fertility or stores of minerals.

3. Land is not unique in generating economic rents. Any resource paid more than the minimum required to elicit its availability also generates economic rents.

4. "Single taxers" inspired by Henry George propose a 100 percent tax on land rent as a single tax to finance all government spending. They argue that taxing this unearned surplus would not distort the allocation of land and thus would not hinder economic efficiency. The *single-tax proposal* suffers from (*a*) inability to finance the entire public sector, (*b*) administrative problems in distinguishing land values arising out of improvements made by owners from rent as an unearned surplus, and (*c*) reduced incentives for landowners to put their land to the best possible uses if rent is taxed away.

5. Economic rent promotes economic effi-

ciency by providing resource owners with incentives to put their assets to the most valuable uses.

6. *Nominal interest rates* are the percentage annual premiums paid to borrow funds. Interest rates on financial instruments vary according to (*a*) risk, (*b*) maturity, and (*c*) liquidity. The interest rate normally means the rate on a long-term riskless bond.

7. In the long run, *real* (purchasing power) *interest rates* depend on (*a*) premiums required to induce savers to delay consumption, (*b*) desires for liquidity, and (*c*) the productivity of capital. These factors determine interest rates through markets for *loanable funds*.

8. *Pure economic profits* are the residual after adjusting accounting profits for the opportunity cost of resources provided by a firm's owners. Profit may arise from *monopoly power*, from bearing business *uncertainty*, or from *innovation*.

9. Profits are a driving force in a capitalist economy, channeling resources to their most productive uses and stimulating progress, as entrepreneurs innovate and endure business uncertainty. Profits induce efficiency; competitive firms that do not produce at the lowest possible cost will suffer economic losses.

10. *Present values* are the sums of the discounted values of future income that may be expected from owning an asset. The present value of an asset and its price will be identical in equilibrium. If the present value exceeds price, then the asset is a profitable investment because the expected rate of return exceeds the interest rate. *Capitalization* is the process whereby prices gravitate toward present values of assets.

Key Concepts

Ensure that you can define these terms before proceeding.

economic rent
nominal interest rates
real interest rates
economic profit

risk
uncertainty
innovation
capitalization

present value
rates of return

marginal productivity theory of income distribution

Problems and Questions

1. Jane, Lynn, and Tanya are all paid $100,000 annually as doctors in an urban medical clinic. The minimum salaries that each woman would have been willing to accept are, respectively, $35,000, $60,000, and $100,000. Calculate the individual economic rent derived by the three doctors. What is their total economic rent?

2. Patriotic Americans bought huge amounts of government "War Bonds" that promised only low nominal interest rates during World War II. Why might many of these savers have been dismayed when these bonds matured in the 1950s?

3. Calculate the real rate of interest given the following information:

Nominal Rate of Interest	Rate of Inflation
a. 12 percent	7 percent
b. 15 percent	4 percent
c. 6 percent	9 percent

4. What rate of interest would you charge a borrower if the expected rate of inflation is:

   a. 5 percent and you want a 6 percent real return?

   b. 8 percent and you want a 5 percent real return?

   c. −5 percent and you want a 7 percent real return?

5. If you have $20,000 to invest, which combinations of the following investment opportunities would be the best use of your funds? Rank these investments according to rates of return and according to present value. Why would you forgo the investment with the highest rate of return?

   a. A $20,000 investment yielding $25,000 in one year.

   b. A $12,000 investment yielding $16,000 in one year.

   c. An $8,000 investment yielding $8,500 in one year.

d. A $4,000 investment yielding $4,300 in one year.

e. A $4,000 investment yielding $4,500 in one year.

6. Draw sets of supply and demand curves for loanable funds to show the effects on current nominal interest rates of the following scenarios.

a. Investors become pessimistic about the future.

b. Households decide to hold more of their wealth in highly liquid assets.

c. Households opt for present consumption over future consumption.

d. Both households and investors begin expecting the cost of living to rise by 10 percent annually.

7. The federal government is by far the world's largest borrower. How might it use any monopsony power to hold down its interest costs? Construct a graph to show how this might occur.

8. Winnings from state lotteries are subject to federal, state, and local income taxes, and payments to big winners are typically spread across twenty-year periods without interest. Suppose you lived in an area where total income taxes were 40 percent, and you won $5 million in today's lottery.

a. How much would you receive (after taxes) in this first year's check?

b. If the interest rate were 10 percent annually, how much would someone be willing to pay you today for the rights to next year's check? For rights to the check you are scheduled to receive two years from today?

c. Write the formula you might use to calculate the present value of all your winnings. (To ensure that you understand capitalization processes, explain this formula in the simplest terms possible.)

d. Has winning this lottery made you a millionaire? (A millionaire has a current net worth (present value) of more than $1,000,000.)

9. Economic rents and economic profits are both "surpluses" in excess of opportunity costs from the vantage point of society as a whole. They are unnecessary to secure resources socially. Rent on the land used by any firm is a true opportunity cost to that firm, however, although economic profits are not. Can you reconcile the apparent contradiction that rents are often opportunity costs to the individual user but not to the entire society?

10. Land taxes may not cause gross misallocations of land, but property taxes are widely perceived as dissuading owners from improving land in an optimal fashion. High property taxes are also blamed for the deterioration of the urban cores of large cities. How elastic is the supply of improvements to land vis-à-vis the supply elasticity of land per se? How might land values be distinguished from improvements if land taxes replaced property taxes?

11. The Soviet Union, following Marx's theory that interest is a mechanism capitalists use to exploit workers, traditionally rejected using an interest rate to discount the future benefits from investment projects. Explain how ignoring interest rates might cause savings to flow into less than socially optimal investments.

12. Accounting profits generally exceed economic profits because accountants may fail to consider implicit costs. Can you think of activities that might generate "implicit revenues" so that economic profits would exceed accounting profits? Might this explain how firms in some competitive lines of business continually generate accounting losses but continue to operate?

13. Some people who start a successful enterprise encounter major difficulties in managing their companies once the firm is on its feet. For example, Steve Wozniak and Steven Jobs built Apple Computers from a tiny operation housed in a garage into a billion-dollar concern between 1976 and 1981, but professional managers and stockholders had banded together and ousted both from leadership of the company by 1985. What are the differences in the personalities required to be innovative entrepreneurs and to be professional managers? Is it likely that one person can embody both sets of attributes? Can you cite other cases in which people who were strong "starters" were

weak "finishers"? Where a strong starter established a series of successful companies, but was never able to maintain control once success was enjoyed? Where strong starters proved quite capable of effective management once an enterprise was successful?

14. Assume the federal government issues a bond that pays $1,000 per year forever. If the general level of interest rates is 10 percent, what will be the price of the bond when issued? After the bond is issued, if interest rates rise to 20 percent, what will happen to the price of the bond? What will happen if interest rates fall to 5 percent?

15. Big cash winners on TV game shows or in magazine subscription contests commonly are paid in installments over a period of years. Suppose you were a contestant on "Name That Tune" and won $100,000, receiving $20,000 today and $20,000 at the end of each of the next four years. If the interest rate was 10 percent, what would have been the present value of your winnings? Are there other reasons to believe that the values of prizes are overstated? What would you guess is the average percentage of overstatement?

Capitalizing on Insider Information
SEC v. Materia (1984)

*The Securities and Exchange Commission (SEC) forbids trading securities on the basis of **insider information**— knowledge not available to the general public about events that affect securities prices (e.g., lawsuits, new product development, or plans for mergers or takeovers). Insiders presumably could get a jump, allowing them to profit by buying or selling before information concerning profits was available to the public. The judge's ruling in the following case illustrates a typical case of insider trading.*

Our era aptly has been styled the "age of information." Francis Bacon recognized nearly 400 years ago that "knowledge is power," but only in the last generation has it risen to the equivalent of the coin of the realm. Nowhere is this commodity more valuable or volatile than in the world of high finance, where facts worth fortunes while secret may be rendered worthless once revealed.

Anthony Materia was employed by a printer of financial documents, including many concerning proposed tender (merger) offers. Because even a hint of an upcoming tender offer may send the price of the target company's stock soaring, the identity of a target is zealously guarded. It is customary, therefore, for offerors (or their law firms) to omit information that might identify a merger target until the last possible moment. Code names are used, blanks are left unfilled until the eve of publication, and misinformation may even be included in early drafts. In sum, a quick reading of preliminary paperwork would not reveal this confidential information.

In his job as a copyholder, Materia read clients' drafts aloud to a proofreader, who ensured that page proofs conformed to the copy received from the client. Despite scrupulous efforts to keep confidential information secret, Materia divined the identities of at least four tender offer targets between December 1980 and September 1982. He purchased stock within hours of each discovery, and within days — after the offer had been made public — he sold his holdings at substantial gains.

Determined to combat securities fraud, Congress enacted comprehensive yet open-ended statutes capable of adaptation and refinement. In recent years, developments in capital formation and novel means of effecting corporate combinations have spawned a new genre of confidential information. Courts are increasingly called upon to address a myriad of issues regarding the use of such data. We do not believe the drafters of the Securities Exchange Act of 1934 — envisaging as they did an open and honest market — would have countenanced the activities engaged in by Anthony Materia.

Questions

1. Will insider trading speed up the process of capitalizing changes in expected profits caused by an event that constitutes the insider information?

2. Most foreign stock exchanges do not forbid trading on insider information. Does trading securities on the basis of insider information merely determine who gains when stock prices rise or fall to reflect capitalization of expected changes in a firm's profitability? Or does insider trading, instead, provide opportunities for fraud, or unfair profits to the traders?

PART 9

Modern Microeconomic Issues

We have examined how markets tend to operate efficiently when (*a*) numerous potential buyers and sellers with freedom of entry and exit compete vigorously, (*b*) information is symmetric and widespread, (*c*) economies of scale are insignificant, and (*d*) external effects from transactions are negligible. Our primary concerns in this part of the book are assessments of market failures and the government policies intended to overcome them. *Market failures* arise from excessive market power, strategic behavior, or external (spillover) effects on parties not involved in particular transactions. Some analysts also classify "inequitable" income distributions as market failures.

The notion that government policies will efficiently cure market failures is often unrealistic. Political mechanisms may yield allocative results that are superior to those of the marketplace in some cases, but not in others. The magnitude of specific market failures should be weighed against the intensity of *government failure*, which occurs because public policies are often plagued by such problems as inadequate information, political pressures from special-interest groups, or inefficient incentive structures for government bureaucrats.

We will begin with a framework for examining policies. First, in Chapter 31, we develop a rationale for governmental action by investigating areas in which the market may fail to allocate resources acceptably. Then, we survey the American tax system, measuring both current taxes and recent tax reforms against principles of efficiency and equity. In Chapter 32, we focus on *public choice*, an approach offering insights into government failure by analyzing political behavior from an economic perspective. Chapter 33 deals with the economic role of government regulation. In Chapter 34, we examine issues about resource management and environmental quality. Problems of agriculture are our major concerns in Chapter 35. Finally, in Chapter 36, we address poverty and government redistributions of income.

Applying microeconomic tools to the areas covered in this part of the book should familiarize you with applied economic analysis, but we barely scratch the surface of the kinds of problems into which microeconomics can offer valuable insights. Looking at all possible problem areas would require a book twice as long as this one and a course twice as long as the one in which you are enrolled, exhausting your pocketbooks and the patience of your professors and our publishers. You will have opportunities to study many of these topics if you take further courses in economics.

CHAPTER

Market Failure and Public Finance

Business transactions would be much less certain if firms had rights to specify the meaning of "a pound," or to define all terms in any contracts signed. Thus, a pure laissez-faire system would be economically inefficient without some basic regulations. Government simplifies our lives by setting standards for money and weights and measures and by enforcing contracts. Certainty about the rules of business and clearly specified property rights facilitate efficiency.

The rationale for government action becomes even more powerful when the marketplace is perceived to fail despite a stable legal environment. Firms with monopsony power may exploit workers (e.g., a textile mill operated by abusive managers who dominate employment in a small town). Consumers may be exploited if firms exercise excessive market power (e.g., were electric rates for a public utility company unregulated). Another problem is that private markets cannot efficiently coordinate private decisions about the production and delivery of some broad types of goods, including such things as national defense, the administration of justice, or a cleaner environment.

In this chapter, we categorize types of *market failure* and identify appropriate government cor-

rections for certain types of failures. Once a need for government is recognized, we need to address who should pay for it and how. We will survey several types of taxes to assess how well our current system conforms to normative principles of taxation. In the next chapter, we explore political decision making and *government failure*. There, you will find some answers to why public policy so often deviates from the ideals we describe in this chapter.

Economic Roles for Government

A standard prescription for unstable, inequitable, or inefficient outcomes of markets is government action. In addition to maintaining a stable legal environment for economic activity, widely accepted goals for government now include

1. Ensuring full employment, a stable price level, and a secure and growing standard of living. (*Instability* is the first category of market failure.)

2. Facilitating equity through redistributions of income. (Potential *inequity* is a second broad type of market failure.)

3. Promoting market competition and allocating resources to meet public wants efficiently. (The third major type of market failure is potential *allocative inefficiency* because of excessive market power, or because certain goods will not be optimally provided in purely private markets.)

Stability, the first goal, is primarily a macroeconomic topic. Policies intended to achieve *equity*, the second goal, are addressed in a later chapter. Antitrust policies (covered in a previous chapter) promote *efficiency* through competition. Our focus in this chapter is how government allocates resources to provide for public wants.

Government in the United States now directly allocates roughly one-fifth of our national output in attempts to meet these goals. Another 15 percent is redistributed through *transfer payments*, which include such outlays as welfare payments and loans to farmers or students. Figure 1 provides estimates of the size and recent growth of total government activity.

Market Failure: Allocation

Competitive markets usually perform well when all parties to a transaction pay for benefits received and are compensated for costs they incur. For example, if you buy a warm coat for protection from cold winter days, the people who produce your coat are paid for this use of their resources. Unfortunately, securing payments for some types of goods is difficult, and identifying those who incur costs can also be a problem. No private firm, for example, could sell you cleaner air by using less-polluting production processes without simultaneously providing cleaner air for your neighbors. Nor could a neighbor privately buy national defense without protecting you.

Competitive markets allocate most standard goods so that marginal social benefits equal marginal social costs, as at point *a* in Figure 2. Allocative failure occurs when equilibrium marginal social benefits and costs diverge. Any market equilibrium except that at point *a* represents an allocative failure. Improper pricing and output

FIGURE 1 The Growth of Government Outlays

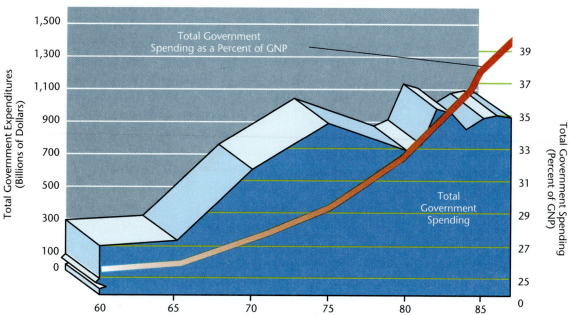

Source: *Economic Report of the President 1991.*

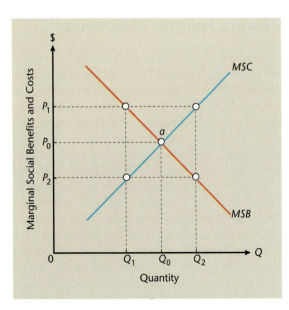

FIGURE 2 Socially Optimal Price and Quantity and Market Failure

Economic efficiency requires that marginal social cost equal marginal social benefits (*MSC* = *MSB* at point *a*). Market failure occurs when *MSC* and *MSB* diverge. For example, the *MSC* of increasing output from Q_0 to Q_2 units equals point *b*, while the *MSB* from the Q_2 unit equals only point *c*, entailing a net social loss that is avoidable by restricting output to Q_0 units. A symmetric failure to exploit all possible net social gains occurs if output is below Q_0 units.

occurs when private markets are afflicted with any of three basic types of problems.

Our "Monopoly" chapter showed how *market power* may create inefficiency, with suboptimal output and excessive prices. But even competitive markets may generate failures that seem to justify government action. *Externalities* (pollution is an example) can warp price signals so that production costs or our demands are inaccurately reflected. Another difficulty, the *public goods* problem, results when shared consumption is possible but people cannot be denied access to a good's benefits. National defense is an example.

Government may correct market failures by (*a*) promoting competition, (*b*) directly providing certain goods, or (*c*) modifying the composi-

tion of private outputs through taxes, subsidies, or regulations. (Some cynics argue that ideal adjustments are highly unlikely, because government is hopelessly inefficient, but only philosophical anarchists argue that government provision of certain goods never improves efficiency.)

Monopoly Power

Private firms with market power charge higher prices and produce less than the optimal output that would be produced in pure competition. Long-run average cost curves that decline across a wide range of output relative to market demand may make competition inefficient and yield a natural monopoly (utility companies are examples). Antitrust legislation (studied in a previous chapter) may curb monopoly power and promote competition, or regulation (two chapters hence) can steer natural monopolists toward efficient behavior.

Externalities

Some benefits or costs of certain activities *spill over* to parties not directly involved in the activity. These spillover benefits and costs are externalities.

> **Externalities** *are the benefits conferred or costs imposed on a "third party" not directly participating in negotiations that result in a transaction.*

This type of market inefficiency is common when market prices and outputs fail to reflect these third parties' preferences. For example, when farmers spray their crops, some pesticide may wash into nearby streams. If this pesticide is absorbed by microorganisms and works its way up the ecological chain, your fishing or health may deteriorate so that you partially bear the cost of using the pesticide. Most human activities generate externalities, some trivial and some of major concern. Cooking creates heat and smoke, every car emits noxious fumes, loud stereos annoy your neighbors, and so on. All forms of pollution — chemical, air, noise, and litter — are *negative externalities*.

Pollution and obnoxious billboards would be even more prevalent if markets were unregulated. Commuting would be more dangerous if drivers continually negotiated for the right-of-way, and big city traffic might suffer terminal gridlock. Deadly epidemics might decimate our populace if all immunizations were voluntary. You may have heard of "Typhoid Mary," a restaurant worker who infected thousands of people in her day.

Producers whose outputs generate negative externalities tend to ignore costs to others, so the prices charged reflect only the producers' private costs. Thus, pollution-generating goods tend to be overproduced and underpriced. Government uses a mix of regulations to control different pollutants, because absolutely prohibiting pollution would probably eliminate all production—most human activities, including production, generate at least trivial pollution. Trade-offs exist between the cleaner environment most of us would like and the higher levels of consumption most of us desire.

Positive externalities that spill over from an activity may also create inefficiency. Immunization against contagious diseases is one example. You are less likely to suffer from the flu if you are inoculated, and we who are your neighbors are less likely to catch it as well. But you tend to ignore our benefits when you decide whether to be immunized, and so are less likely to get a flu shot than is socially optimal. Thus, private market decisions result in underproduction and overpricing of goods that generate positive externalities, because the value to society exceeds the demand price individuals willingly pay when they are uncompensated for external benefits.

Let's consider negative externalities in more detail. Garbage accumulating around the Slob family's property is shown in Figure 3. Suppose this family ignores informal social pressure to maintain their home. When they decide how often to have trash hauled away, the Slobs ignore declines in the values of adjacent property, noxious odors, and exposing their neighbors to diseases. Unless they are compelled to consider these external costs, the Slobs will choose point a, leaving Q_0 garbage around their home, on average, at a private cost of P_0 per unit. Society might just legally require them to have all their trash hauled off instantly, but this would ignore benefits to the Slobs (or even ourselves) of being able to let the garbage pile up temporarily instead of having it removed at all times. After all,

FIGURE 3 The Costs and Benefits of the Slob Family's Garbage

Living next to a slob is never pleasant. In economic jargon, slobs impose external costs on their neighbors and would be less slovenly if they took their neighbors' discomfort into account. Note that the Slob family in our example has a positive demand for garbage lying around. If they didn't want to store garbage, they would pay more and have it hauled away.

the Slobs are members of society. What we would like is to ensure that they consider the effects on their neighbors from stockpiling trash.

The demand curve D reflects the Slobs' gains from littering their home, tidying up only occasionally instead of being fastidious at all times. The MSC curve reflects losses from litter suffered by both the Slobs and their neighbors, with the MC curve reflecting only the Slobs' marginal private cost. Suppose the Slobs could legally store trash. In this case, the vertical distance bc between the cost curves represents the amount neighbors would willingly pay the Slobs to reduce trash accumulation to socially optimal level Q_1. If neighbors could legally limit the Slobs' debris, this vertical distance is the price the neighbors would charge the Slobs for accumulating garbage. Note that the optimal amount of trash is not zero. After all, we all keep a little garbage on hand, even on the days when garbage is collected.

How to deal with externalities is addressed in detail in our chapter on environmental quality. It is time to examine the market failure that seems to require the most of government — the public goods problem.

Public Goods

A desire for more shoes can be cured by a trip to a shoe store. But suppose you want more public parks or a stronger national defense. If you voluntarily send a check to the National Park Service or the Department of Defense, even if they spend your money wisely you will not have appreciably better access to parks or be noticeably better defended. The problem is that these are examples of public goods. **Public goods** are both *nonrival*, because people can consume such goods simultaneously, and *nonexclusive*, because denying people access to such goods is prohibitively expensive.

*A **public good** can be enjoyed by numerous individuals at the same time (nonrivalry); once a public good is available, denying access to a consumer is prohibitively expensive (nonexclusion).*

Prisons are examples of public goods because keeping violent criminals behind bars makes the world safer for the rest of us. We need not compete with each other to use public goods once they are produced because public goods do not involve rivalry. Most goods are **private goods**, however; they are *rival* and *exclusive*.

Rivalry and Nonrivalry Consumption exhausts a *rival good* so that no one else can consume the same unit of it. No one else can consume a particular taco if you eat it first. You cannot use my raincoat if I am wearing it. Food and clothing are rival goods. We can, however, enjoy the same TV program without rivalry. When your TV receives signals, it does not affect the signals to mine. A police patrol can simultaneously protect both you and your neighbor from burglars. Police protection and TV broadcasts are examples of *nonrival goods*.

Exclusion and Nonexclusion Restaurants do not have to serve you unless you wear a shirt and shoes. A theater can require you to buy a ticket before seeing a film. Movies and meals are *exclusive goods*. But if the Air Force protects you from attacks by foreign enemies, your neighbor is automatically protected. The Air Force cannot easily protect you from attack while disregarding your neighbor. National defense is a *nonexclusive good*. Nonexclusion occurs whenever it is prohibitively expensive to prevent people from enjoying a good.

Government provides most public goods. Traffic lights smooth traffic patterns to hasten us to our destinations, cut accident rates, and prevent terminal gridlock in major cities. Other public goods include weather reports, cancer research, democratic government, and national defense. Once the military is maintained and ready, every person in the United States consumes defense services simultaneously, and we all receive this protection whether we pay taxes or not, and whether we want it or not!

Public provision does not, however, require public production. For example, NASA space probes use equipment built by private firms. Alan Shepard, the first American in space, reported that his last thought before his Gemini rocket was launched was that the rocket and his space capsule contained millions of parts, "all built by the lowest bidder."

Providing for Public Goods

Nonexclusive and nonrival goods differ markedly from private goods, so social demand curves for public goods require different construction than for market demand curves for private goods.

Private vs. Public Demands Recall that market demands for most goods are *horizontal* summations of individual demand curves — the quantities demanded at each price are summed. This is how the individual demands of Alan and Beth for lobsters, a private good, are summed in Panel A of Figure 4. The total demand for a public good, however, is a *vertical* summation of individual demand curves, as shown in Panel B. We all gain by having extra police patrols cruising our neighborhood at night, so our demand for this extra surveillance reflects the dollar amount we would collectively pay for it. A total demand curve for a public good is constructed by adding the funds we each would willingly pay for each possible amount of the good. (For simplicity, Alan's demands for patrols and lobsters are identical. Beth's individual demands are also identical. Different summation procedures, however, yield different total demands for these two goods.)

Optimal Public Goods How do we ascertain how much of a public good to provide? Alan's (*A*) and Beth's (*B*) individual demands for police patrols are shown together with their total demand curve in Panel B of Figure 4. We assume that neither is trying to be a free rider, so both reveal their demands for police patrols. The total demand is the vertical summation of Alan's and Beth's demands. Suppose that costs are $6 per patrol. If three patrols are provided each night, Alan values each patrol at $4, while Beth values each at $2. The $6 cost per patrol could be covered if each paid in proportion to their gains [($4 × 3) + ($2 × 3)].

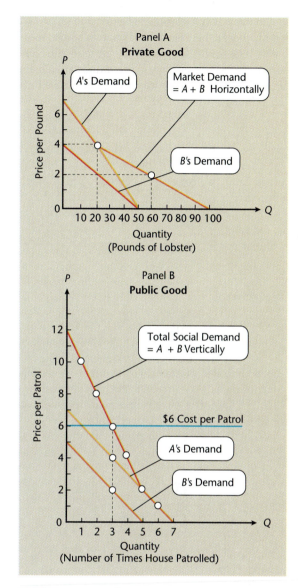

FIGURE 4 Market Demands for Private and Public Goods

We all face the same prices for private goods but buy different amounts, so the market demand is the horizontal sum of individual demands (Panel A). We all consume the same public goods but value them differently, so the total demand for public goods requires vertically summing individual demands (Panel B). Revenue adequate for optimal amounts of a public good are generated if each person pays his or her marginal benefit from the good (in dollars) times the amount of the good provided. In this case, three patrols nightly at $6 per patrol could be secured if Beth paid $6 and Alan paid $12.

Contrast this with optimal provision of private goods in Panel A; each individual pays the same price per unit, but each consumes different amounts. Alan consumes 35 pounds of lobster annually at $2 per pound, while Beth buys only 25 pounds at that price.

The preceding solution to public goods assumes that individuals willingly reveal their preferences. Further, it suggests that we could pay for these public goods by taxing individuals in proportion to "benefits received." This benefit approach is not, however, easily translated into the real world of taxes, nor is it the primary basis of taxation.

Taxation

Taxes are the price we pay for civilization.

Oliver Wendell Holmes, Jr.

Taxes finance most of government spending. Many Americans complain about high taxes, but Figure 5 indicates that residents in most developed economies pay relatively more.

Who should pay how much of which taxes? Equity is a slippery concept, but analyzing fairness in taxation is helped by precision about terms. Two somewhat contradictory principles broadly address equity in distributing tax burdens. The *benefit principle* favors taxes in accord with people's benefits from government spending; the *ability-to-pay principle* advocates taxes in accord with one's wealth or income.

Equity: The Benefit Principle

The benefit principle is an ancient doctrine that taxes should be in proportion to the benefits individuals receive from government.

> The **benefit principle of taxation** *taxes people in proportion to the marginal benefits they receive from a governmentally provided good.*

This principle conforms to a universal gut feeling that you should pay for what you get. Revenues just adequate for optimal provision in our police

patrol example can be secured by levying taxes so that people share costs in proportion to their marginal benefits.

Taxation according to marginal benefits is, unfortunately, impractical for most pure public goods. The public sector provides an incredible array of goods; collecting all the information required for appropriately different taxes is prohibitively costly. People cannot be excluded from enjoying the benefits whether they paid taxes or not. These characteristics of public goods lead to the free rider problem.

Free Rider Problems Suppose taxes were based strictly on your reported benefits from a public good. Some people might assert that they want little or none of it. Crafty types might even try to get tax credits by asserting that the good harms them. Once other people agree to buy a public good, free riders can enjoy it without cost.

> The **free rider** *problem arises when people evade paying for goods that are nonexclusive; they can use such goods without payment.*

A few people might voluntarily contribute funds for a nonrival good from which exclusion was impossible. The erratic success of public TV is one example. More commonly, however, voluntary contributions would be insufficient for private firms to accommodate our collective demands for public goods. There is little incentive to reveal your demands for police protection, space exploration, spraying against mosquitos, landscaping public roads, or maintaining courts and prisons if you will be taxed accordingly. Why not be a "free rider"? Widespread free riding may preclude some public goods. Private firms could not adequately market them, so government provides a variety of public goods and forces us to pay for them through taxes.

User Charges General tax revenues are used to pay for most goods provided by government, but the benefit approach to funding public goods is the basis for user charges that relate taxes to expected benefits. When a governmentally provided good has the exclusive characteristics of a private good, benefits can be approximated and

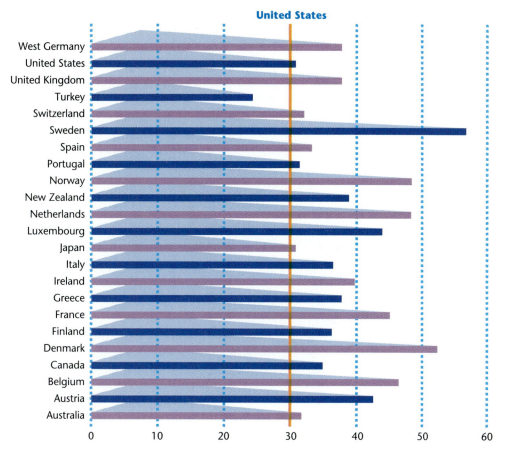

FIGURE 5 Tax Rates as Percentages of GDP—International
Sources: *CIA World FactBook 1990, Handbook of Economic Statistics 1990.* Calculations by authors.

users can be charged accordingly. Examples include bus fares and entry fees for public museums, zoos, parks, or toll roads. Gasoline taxes are also roughly proportional to benefits; owners of heavy trucks or drivers of huge gas hogs pay more gas taxes than do drivers of fuel-efficient compact cars, but they also put more wear and tear on the highways that gasoline taxes support.

Although the benefit principle of taxation is often inapplicable because individuals' preferences for public goods are concealed, general tax revenues are often used to fund activities where user charges could easily be applied. For example, should vegetarians pay for meat inspections? User charges imposed on meat-packers would be shifted forward to meat buyers. Similarly, federal

tests of new medicines could be billed to the pharmaceutical companies that want to market them. If airports, air traffic controllers, and airplane safety inspectors were paid for by carriers, these tax burdens would not be borne by people who benefit little from air transport.

Political and practical difficulties, however, are not the only drawbacks of benefit taxes. Benefit taxation may conflict with other types of concerns about equity.

Equity and Ability to Pay

An alternative to the benefit principle of taxation is the idea that taxes should be proportional to one's ability to pay.

The **ability-to-pay principle** *suggests that the "fairest" tax is one based on your financial ability to support government activities.*

Taxes can be related to income in three basic ways:

1. A tax is **progressive** if the percentage tax rate rises as income rises; higher incomes are taxed proportionally higher than lower incomes.

2. **Proportional** taxes are a fixed percentage of income. The "flat rate" tax proposal would institute a proportional tax.

3. A tax is **regressive** when the percentage of income paid as taxes declines as income rises.

The benefit and ability-to-pay principles, though apparently incompatible, may lead to similar policies. Rich people may benefit more than poor people do from such public goods as national defense or police and fire protection because rich people stand to lose more from disasters. They tend to drive more miles on public roads, and ring up more "frequent flyer" bonuses when flying out of publicly supported airports. Thus, both the benefit and the ability-to-pay principles may support the idea that the rich should pay more taxes than the poor.

Vertical Equity Vertical equity is the idea that a rich person should pay more taxes than a poor one for each to bear the same burden in supporting government.

Vertical equity *asserts that people better able to pay higher taxes should do so.*

Implementing vertical equity in any tax system involves deciding who should pay higher rates and then writing tax laws that actually collect this amount from the correct people. Wealth and income are normally viewed as good measures of one's ability to pay taxes. Progressive taxation is, however, unnecessary for vertical equity; even regressive tax systems might satisfy this equity principle as long as the rich paid more in absolute terms.

Horizontal Equity The Fourteenth Amendment to our Constitution (the Equal Protection clause) states, "nor shall any State deprive any person of life, liberty, or property, without due process of law; nor deny to any person within its jurisdiction the *equal* protection of the laws." This concept that "equals must be treated equally" is now known as horizontal equity.

Horizontal equity *requires that individuals who are equal in all important respects be treated equally.*

Implementing a horizontally equitable tax system first requires identifying what constitutes equal circumstances—income, wealth, age, or marital status? Then we must specify what equal treatment means. Does equal treatment mean equal tax rates, or equal tax payments over your lifetime?

Equity in our tax system requires both horizontal and vertical equity. Horizontal equity dictates that equals should pay equal taxes; vertical equity that "unequals" should be treated unequally. Vertical equity is at the heart of the ability-to-pay principle.

Tax Burdens and Efficiency

Apparent inequity in the tax system is a major concern, but economists focus their studies on inefficiency, an area permitting greater precision. In his *Wealth of Nations*, Adam Smith suggested that efficiency in taxation requires taxes to be certain (unavoidable) and convenient, and that collection costs be minimized relative to the tax yield.

Government's net tax revenues ideally would exactly equal costs incurred by taxpayers. Taxpayers' costs unavoidably exceed net government revenues, however, because of (*a*) government's *administrative costs* (e.g., operating expenses for the Internal Revenue Service), and (*b*) taxpayers' *compliance costs* (e.g., time absorbed in keeping records for taxes and filling out tax reports, or payments to tax lawyers and accountants).

Total costs of a tax, however, include other, more subtle costs, and ultimately equal the losses of disposable (after-tax) income and purchasing power to taxpayers. Consider an untaxed individual who enjoys a certain standard of living, including current levels of government services. Now impose a tax on that person.

The **total burden** *of a tax equals the amount of money that would have to be paid the individual on whom the burden falls to make that person just as well off with the tax as without it.*

Differences between total tax burdens and net government revenues reflect inefficiency.

Excess Burdens

If high state taxes on beer cause New Yorkers to drive to New Jersey to buy their brew, then the total tax burden includes not only the revenues actually collected by New York, but also the time and transportation costs to the New Yorkers who avoid the tax. If some of these commuters wind up dying in traffic accidents, or if they drunkenly kill other people, then this loss of life is also a part of the total burden of the tax. Excess burdens arise whenever people are made worse off than the losses imposed by the taxes actually collected from them.

The **excess burden** *of a tax is the difference between the total burden and the tax revenue collected by government.*

In addition to administrative and compliance costs, taxes impose excess burdens if they distort the prices faced by consumers, workers, savers, investors, or business decision makers.

In 1985, Kyoto, Japan began taxing visitors to Buddhist temples. The tax was strongly opposed by most temple priests as a violation of their religious principles. The priests initially let visitors in free rather than pay the tax, but they eventually closed the temple doors to visitors. The city collected no revenue, but tourists suffered (an excess burden). Finally, after negotiations broke down, the city abolished the tax.

Supply and demand analysis can allow us to scrutinize excess burdens. In Figure 6, S_0 and D_0 reflect the nontaxed supply and demand for quarts of milk. For simplicity, we assume constant production costs at P_0 per quart.

Suppose a tax of t per quart is imposed on milk. This tax shifts the supply curve to S_1 from the buyer's perspective. As buyers and sellers adjust to this tax, consumers watch the price of a quart of milk rise from P_0 to P_t, while the amount sold falls from Q_0 to Q_1. At Q_1 quarts monthly, the difference between the price paid by the buyer (P_t) and the price received by the seller (P_0) exactly equals tax t. Prior to the tax consumers paid $0P_0cQ_0$ for Q_0 quarts of milk, but would have willingly paid $0dcQ_0$. Thus, they enjoyed a consumer surplus of $P_0 dc$. The rise in the consumers' price to P_t shrinks consumer surplus by the area below the consumer demand curve but above the original price (P_0) and below

FIGURE 6 The Excess Burden of a Tax

Only under ideal circumstances will the losses of consumer surplus and economic rent (or producer surplus) due to a tax be fully offset by tax revenues. In the case shown here, the full burden of the tax is borne by consumers, who lose surplus P_0P_tbc while government gains revenue of P_0P_tba. There is a "deadweight" welfare loss of abc.

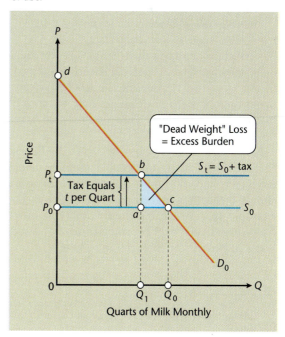

the new price (P_1). The consumer surplus lost equals the trapezoid P_0P_1bc.

Government, however, gains monthly revenues of t per bottle for Q_t quarts of milk, a total of area P_0P_1ba, which it can use to meet taxpayers' wants. The total loss of consumer surplus minus the gains to government equals area abc $(P_0P_1bc - P_0P_1ba)$. The triangle abc is a *deadweight loss* to society from this tax; it is an excess burden. These losses, however, may be more than offset by consumer surpluses from government services provided with the tax revenues. Of course, if government spending is inefficient, this excess burden may understate consumers' losses. Government ideally minimizes the excess burdens incurred in securing any given total of tax revenues.

Neutrality

The neutrality principle combines and extends Adam Smith's certainty, convenience, and economy principles. Ideally, the costs of transferring purchasing power from private hands into the public purse are minimized.

> A **neutral tax** *distorts neither consumer buying patterns nor the production methods used by firms. Its total burden just equals the tax revenue collected — there are no excess burdens.*

Tax neutrality requires that the tax directly cause only income effects, not substitution effects.[1] That is, a neutral tax does not induce behavior to avoid the tax; behavior changes only because of lost purchasing power. This requires that taxes be unavoidable.

No action by taxpayers (perhaps at the behest of their lawyers) should enable them to avoid payment, and the only impact on taxpayers should be declines in their purchasing power. For example, tax structures should not encourage fringe benefits in work contracts instead of direct wage payments, or financial investment in tax-

---

1. You may want to review the discussion of income and substitution effects from the chapter on consumer choice.

free municipal bonds rather than capital equipment. Nor should it encourage consumption of housing instead of groceries or automobiles. (Our tax system has done all these things.) Taxes that directly alter the relative benefits and costs facing consumers or business decision makers are nonneutral and inefficient. A neutral tax will be more certain, convenient, and economical than a nonneutral tax.

All taxes, unfortunately, induce substitution effects by directly altering relative prices, thereby changing the behavior of consumers and firms. As a result, taxes are often evaluated by their relative neutrality. Because all taxes are somewhat flawed, economists normally try to specify which are the most nearly neutral (those with the smallest excess burdens) and least inequitable in generating governmental revenues.

The Current Tax System

Old taxes are the best taxes.

A Legislator's Proverb

Current sources of tax revenues at the federal and state levels are indicated in Figure 7, which also identifies important areas of government spending. Just how efficient and equitable are the important taxes now used by our federal, state, and local governments?

Personal Income Taxes

One flaw of progressive personal income taxes is that rising marginal tax rates create disincentives that discourage investment and work effort. Another is that our complex Internal Revenue Code creates loopholes that allow individuals and corporations to legally avoid taxes. Tax *avoidance* is legal, but high marginal rates also provide huge incentives for tax *evasion* — the illegal nonpayment of taxes. Disincentives, tax evasion, and legal loopholes erode the tax base and cause legislators to raise tax rates. For example, if erosion of the base causes a tax rate of 50 percent to be applied to only half of potential untaxed

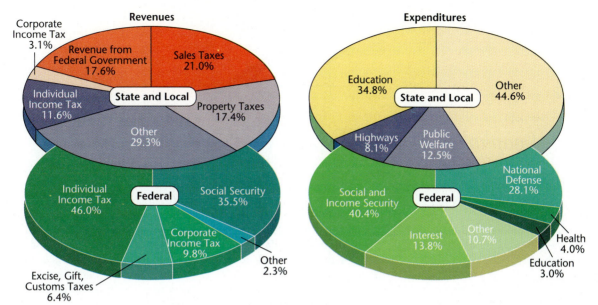

FIGURE 7   Revenue Sources and Expenditure Patterns for Federal, State, and Local Governments

The federal government relies almost exclusively on income and payroll taxes for revenues. State and local governments, on the other hand, get the bulk of their revenues from property and sales taxes, from user fees, and from the federal government through grants-in-aid. Federal expenditures are focused on those activities that are national in scope (national defense and Social Security), while state and local expenditures are for services that affect people within limited geographical areas.

Source: U.S. Bureau of the Census, *Statistical Abstract of the United States 1990* (110th ed.), Washington, D.C., 1990.

income, then the rate could be dropped to 25 percent if all income were taxed.

At first glance, our four-step progressive income tax system might seem an example of an ability-to-pay tax, but loopholes erode its progressivity. Families with salary income of $30,000 frequently pay more taxes than similar families with interest income from tax-free bonds of $50,000. This violates vertical and horizontal equity.

Several studies indicate, however, that even after allowing for the heavier exploitation of loopholes by high-income families than by low-income families, the incidence of our income tax is, on average, mildly progressive. Not all loopholes are designed only for the rich. For example, mortgage interest is deducted by more than 90 percent of all families who itemize deductions. Moreover, as Focus 1 indicates, the idea that loopholes offer huge advantages for those who

use them is grossly exaggerated, primarily because artificially stimulated competition causes overinvestment in tax-sheltered areas.

You know how complicated computing your federal tax liability can be if you have ever filed a Form 1040 (the long form). Some state income tax computations are even more complex. Most economists favor eliminating almost all exemptions, credits, and deductions except for necessary business expenses. Then tax rates could be lowered substantially and still yield the same tax revenues. This would eliminate much of the vertical and horizontal inequity in income taxes and would substantially reduce the economic inefficiency caused by preferential tax treatments for some sources of income.

For all the flaws of our income tax system, there seems to be widespread support for income taxation with some degree of progressivity. Few Americans favor abolishing the Sixteenth

Tax Loopholes: Private Benefits and Public Costs

Most people perceive tax loopholes as mechanisms that allow rich people to escape their fair shares of the tax burden. But do the rich really gain much from loopholes? Contrary to the implications of tidbits that frequently appear in the media (e.g., columns reporting that "Daddy Warbucks only paid $314.83 in taxes last year on his billion dollar income"), few people gain very much by using tax loopholes. Here is an example to show why.

Assume that most investors were in a 50 percent tax bracket, and that all investment markets were initially in equilibrium and could be expected to yield after-tax rates of return equal to 10 percent. Now suppose that the Turkey Farmers Association persuaded Congress to declare that frozen turkeys were vital to the national defense and that income from turkey farming should be exempted from all federal taxes.

This raises the after-tax rate of return from turkeys to 20 percent, and many investors could be expected to try to take advantage of this loophole. As money flowed into turkey farms, however, the resulting sharp drop in turkey prices would be paralleled by a decline in the rate of return from turkey farming. Simultane-ously, other investment areas would decline because of outflows of resources into turkey farming. In these nonfavored areas, the prices of goods would rise, and this would be paralleled by increases in rates of return for these goods. The law of equal marginal advantage implies that the final equilibrium would entail equal after-tax rates of return from all investments, including turkey farming.

Those who used this loophole would gain very little from it. Such loopholes ultimately only shift resources into tax-sheltered areas, which means that fewer resources are available to less favored industries than market forces alone indicate are optimal. Overall, tax loopholes reduce government revenues, but loophole users' gains are trivial. And the distorted structure of national output reflects loopholes instead of consumer preferences.

If loopholes ultimately provide so little gain to those who use them, then why do proposals to plug loopholes arouse such outrage? The answer is that closing a loophole can impose huge losses on people who currently use them. For example, many people have bought expensive houses because interest on mortgages is deductible from taxable income. This deductibility has artificially raised the demand for houses and pushed up real estate prices. Were this deduction eliminated, current homeowners would lose, not only because of higher taxes, but because housing prices might plummet as well.

Who gains from loopholes? In large measure, the gainers are those who acquire specialized resources before favorable tax laws are enacted. They can become wealthy when the values of tax-sheltered areas are capitalized. Another group that gains are the tax attorneys, CPAs, and "financial planners" who advise people who want to avoid taxes. But even this group gains very little because most are competent people who would have been successful in other areas had tax loopholes never existed.

Tax reform historically has meant providing relief to groups that seem overburdened because of loopholes enjoyed by too many other groups. This has caused incredible complexity in the tax codes as loopholes have piled on top of loopholes over time, a situation only partially remedied by the Tax Reform of 1986. In the next chapter, you will learn some reasons why public policy is often shaped in ways that make little economic sense.

Amendment, which authorized income taxes. The major bone of contention is how to simplify income taxes and make them fairer.

Tax Reform The 1986 Tax Reform Act represented the most complete revamping of our tax system in decades. Income taxes were eliminated for most low-income families, and the bill replaced the 15 tax brackets under the old system (ranging from 11 to 50 percent) with two basic brackets (15 and 28 percent), and a "temporary surcharge" (an extra 5 percent) that applied primarily to upper-middle-income taxpayers. Revisions in 1990 intended to help limit the soaring federal budget deficit converted this surcharge into a permanent third bracket of 33 percent that applied to higher incomes. Table 1 details the 1991 tax rates for various filing categories.

The 1986 tax reform was not intended to lower most people's taxes. Its major advantages are consistency and (alleged) simplicity. Major loopholes were closed, allowing sharp cuts in individual and corporate tax rates. *Consistency* (loophole closure) was expected to rebuild public confidence that people in similar circumstances pay similar taxes (horizontal equity), and that high-income families pay their "fair share" (vertical equity). *Simplicity* reduces the need to keep detailed accounting records. (Some studies report that such accounting absorbs resources equal to 1 to 2 percent of personal income.)

Most income is now taxed more uniformly, regardless of source. For example, capital gains from financial investments historically were taxed at around half the investor's normal marginal rate. This preferential treatment was dropped in 1986, although President Bush vainly sought to reinstate lowered taxes on capital gains during 1989–1991. His position, only weakly supported by most studies, is that favorable treatment of investment income will stimulate saving, investment, and economic growth.

Loophole closure refocused investments toward real values instead of a frantic search for loopholes. The new law, however, largely retained deductibility for real estate interest and property taxes, the two major "middle class" loopholes. Pressure from state and local governments also caused interest income from state and municipal bonds to remain tax exempt. Nevertheless, most public finance experts perceived the 1986 tax reform as a major step in the direction of efficiency and equity.

Social Security Taxes

You may be surprised to learn that the *Social Security* tax is expected to be the single largest source of federal revenues by the year 2000. Social Security taxes, unemployment compensation, and workmen's disability taxes are **payroll taxes**. That is, they are based primarily on the payrolls that firms pay. Try this multiple-choice question: The Social Security tax is borne by (*a*) workers, (*b*) employers, (*c*) consumers, (*d*) a 50/50 split between workers and employers, (*e*) a 50/50 split between workers and consumers.

The idea that Social Security taxes are split

Table 1 *Personal Income Tax Rates on Taxable Income (1991)*

Rates	Joint Return with Two Exemptions	Single Taxpayer with One Exemption	Head of Household with Two Exemptions	Married Filing Separately with One Exemption
15%	$0–32,450	$0–19,450	$0–26,050	$0–16,225
28%	32,451–78,400	19,451–47,050	26,051–67,200	16,226–39,200
31%	Over 78,401	Over 47,050	Over 67,200	Over 39,200

Source: *Standard Federal Tax Reports,* Commerce Clearing House, Inc, "Explanation of the Revenue Reconciliation Act of 1990," Vol. 77, No. 47, October 31, 1990.

Table 2 *Social Security Tax Hikes*

Year	Maximum Covered Base ($)	Tax Rate* (Percentage)	Maximum Amount of Tax*
1934	2,000	2.0	$ 40
1970	7,800	9.6	748
1975	14,100	11.7	1,650
1980	25,900	12.3	3,176
1985	39,600	14.1	5,584
1990	51,300	15.3	7,850

*Half of these rates and amounts are legally levied on employers; the other half are legally borne by employees.
Source: Social Security Administration, 1991.

50/50 by employers and employees is a myth. This is the legal incidence of the tax, which in 1991 required employers and employees each to pay 7.51 percent of the first $45,000 in wage income. Table 2 shows how this tax has changed over the years.[2] The simple fact is that the full tax is probably borne by workers. Here is an example to show why.[3]

Suppose that you work for ABC Corporation and your marginal revenue product is $800 weekly. If there are no other employment expenses to consider, competition forces ABC to pay you $800 weekly. Now suppose you insist that ABC send $50 to your Aunt Mary each week. The firm, however, will not retain your services unless you agree to allow them to deduct it from your check; if the law dictates that they send checks for $50 to the widowed aunts of all employees, they will cut wages correspondingly. It makes no sense to keep an employee worth only $800 if total employment costs exceed $800 weekly. Likewise, if money also must be sent to Uncle Sam because you are employed, you will bear this full burden: Your gross salary will shrink by the amount of the tax.

Social Security has been "pay-as-you-go" for decades. Thus, current workers' taxes cover benefits to retirees. Even the entry of baby boomers into labor markets did not ease the growing tax burden, as the ranks of older Americans have swollen. Burdens on younger workers may become horrendous when boomers begin reaching age 65 in 2011.

Critics are dismayed that 65-year-old retirees who draw $100,000 in investment income can extract transfers from 18-year-old dishwashers working for minimum wages. Among many reform proposals are (a) raising the minimum age for retirement benefits, (b) eliminating benefits to the wealthy, (c) having all revenues come from general revenues, and (d) replacing Social Security with a "negative income tax" plan whereby people receive payments if they earn below a certain level of income. (Negative income taxes are discussed in our "Redistribution" chapter.) Pressure will mount to modify the system as the population of older people continues to grow, raising payroll tax burdens.

Sales and Excise Taxes

Sales taxes are percentage taxes broadly levied on dollar sales volumes, primarily by state and local governments. If sales taxes cover all goods,

---

2. Of course, firms cannot pay taxes; only people can. To make this myth consistent, the firm's share is presumably forward-shifted to customers as higher prices.

3. Most studies conclude that the after-tax wage elasticity of the aggregate supply of labor is approximately zero. You might review our discussion of tax incidence in our "Elasticity" chapter to construct a formal proof that payroll taxes will, consequently, be borne primarily by labor.

they are reasonably neutral and efficient. Sales taxes are not neutral, however, to the extent that they exempt items such as food, housing, or labor services. They distort relative prices and economic behavior.

Excise taxes are selectively applied to items like telephone calls, utility bills, and gasoline. A 10 percent federal excise tax on car prices exceeding $30,000 was enacted in 1991. Some excise taxes, called *sin taxes* (e.g., on cigarettes and liquor), are especially popular ways to raise revenues. Again, price distortions create economic inefficiency.

Sales and excise taxes are widely attacked as regressive because the proportion of income spent on taxed goods is higher for the poor than for the rich. Consequently, such "basic necessities" as food are often tax-exempt. Those who attack tax regressivity often advocate soaking "rich" corporations. Unfortunately, this strategy may backfire.

Corporate Income Taxes

Corporate accounting profits are taxed at the rates shown in Table 3 and, when initially levied, are borne by stockholders. However, consumers bear much of this tax burden in the long run, because *corporate income taxes* apply to accounting profits, which are largely normal profits, not economic profits. This tax raises costs and ultimately prices, because normal profits are a long-run production cost. Moreover, even a tax on pure profit may ultimately be borne in part by consumers because aggregate investment is dampened; a reduced capital stock drives up prices in the long run.

The tax distorts prices to the extent that it is forward-shifted; that is, the prices of goods manufactured primarily by corporations are raised relative to the prices of goods most often produced by unincorporated firms. A sad irony is that if, relative to rich people, poor people devote larger shares of income to the mass-produced goods supplied by corporations, the tax burden is regressive. People who think that corporate income taxes "soak the rich" are probably wrong.

Table 3 *Corporate Tax Rates*

Taxable Income	Rate (Percentage)
$0–50,000	15
50,001–75,000	25
75,001–100,000	34
100,001–335,000	39
Over 335,000	34

Source: Internal Revenue Service, 1991.

People will buy corporate stock reluctantly if the tax is backward-shifted. (Firms cannot truly pay taxes; only people can — in this case, stockholders.) The corporate sector will shrink relative to noncorporate firms until after-tax rates of return are equalized.

The inefficiency of the corporate income tax makes it extremely unpopular among most economists. One proposed reform is to eliminate corporate income taxes and allocate corporate profits to stockholders, who would then pay normal personal income taxes on their shares of corporate profits. Economists from across the political spectrum differ little in their dislike of the corporate income tax, but politicians almost universally favor it because their constituents often see the tax as a way for the "little guy" to get even with Big Business.[4]

Property Taxes

The supply of land is perfectly inelastic. Thus, *land taxes* are relatively neutral — a tax on pure land rent has almost no effect on rental rates for land relative to other resources or goods. People often mistakenly apply this reasoning to property taxes, which are, however, among the least popular levies of all.

A **property tax** is based on the value of landholdings *plus* capital improvements. The supply of land is perfectly inelastic, but improvements

---

4. Former President Reagan casually proposed eliminating corporate income taxation in 1983, but adverse reactions from other politicians and the media quickly squelched the idea.

are very elastically supplied in the long run. Suppose you own prime land in an area with high property taxes. If you put a new building on it, you will pay higher taxes. Thus, the property tax is a disincentive to development. Similarly, if you are a slum landlord with tenants whose poverty limits the rents you can charge, will you repair or modernize your buildings if your tax bill jumps substantially as a consequence? *Unlikely!* Many students of the urban scene attribute part of the decay of central cities to high property taxes.

Inheritance and Gift Taxes

Federal inheritance tax rates are presented in Table 4. These taxes appear progressive, but note that the first $600,000 is tax-exempt. You might think that inheritance taxes could be avoided by giving your heirs the money, but *gift taxes* plug that loophole.

Extremely wealthy individuals avoid the inheritance tax in other ways. For one thing, they

Table 4 *Marginal Tax Rates for Federal Estate and Gift Taxes (1991)*

Taxable Net Estate or Gift ($ Thousands)	Marginal Tax Rates
$ 0– 10	18%
10– 20	20%
20– 40	22%
40– 60	24%
60– 80	26%
80– 100	28%
100– 150	30%
150– 250	32%
250– 500	34%
500– 750	37%
750–1,000	39%
1,000–1,250	41%
1,250–1,500	43%
1,500–2,000	45%
2,000–2,500	49%
Over 2,500	50%

Source: Internal Revenue Service, 1991.

can establish trusts that delay disbursements of estates until long after a person's death. For example, if you had assets of $200 million, you might leave the money to your grandchildren, with funds being paid out only when they reached age 35, allowing your children to live on the interest in the interim. This is only one of many loopholes that make the inheritance tax an "optional tax" in the words of some experts. One proposed reform of the income/inheritance tax systems is to merge them. That is, any inheritances or gifts would simply be treated as taxable income.

Tax Reform Proposals

Rankings of the fairness of various taxes yield similar responses from the general public and tax experts. Virtually no taxes are thought fair. Our overview suggests that badly flawed taxes have historically outweighed equitable and efficient taxes. Widespread discontent has led to major reform proposals to bring our tax system into closer harmony with widely accepted principles of taxation: Fairness or equity, economic neutrality, and simplicity.

Value-Added Taxes (VATs)

Our tax system has distorted incentives, stifled economic performance, and been so loaded with loopholes that large parts of it should probably be abandoned. Social Security and corporate income taxes are among possible targets for abolition. But what might replace revenues generated by these taxes? A favorite contender is the value-added tax.

Value-added taxes (VATs) *resemble sales taxes but apply only to differences between a firm's sales and its purchases from other firms.*

Thus, a VAT is a fixed percentage of a firm's payments for resources and is not applied to intermediate products the firm purchases from other firms.

A major virtue of the VAT is that it is reasonably neutral. Another is that tax evasion is extremely difficult, which partially accounts for its use in much of Europe. A drawback is that VATs are largely hidden; final customers may be unaware of the VAT embodied in the price of a product. A normative objection is that, like sales taxes, VATs may be somewhat regressive. Finally, VATs require more cumbersome accounting than sales taxes because VATs must be paid at several levels of output. Nonetheless, value-added taxes are probably more efficient and less inequitable than corporate income taxes, Social Security taxes, or a number of other levies in the government's tool box.

Flat Rate Taxes

Many critics claim that attempts to make income taxes highly progressive are self-defeating. They argue first that high marginal tax rates discourage investment and so, in the long run, actually hold down the incomes of most "working stiffs" — those whose productivity would be enhanced were they working with more capital. The obsolescence of British manufacturing and the comparatively slow growth of British wages from World War II through the 1970s are cited as examples of this problem. (The British economy began its recovery after tax rates were sharply reduced in the early 1980s.)

A second difficulty is that high marginal tax rates increase the payoff from lobbying for new loopholes. These loopholes reduce the true progressivity of the tax system to a mere shadow of the nominal rates. Few high-income individuals fail to exploit loopholes. Progressivity has been combined with complex loopholes so that even tax experts have often been uncertain as to how much they owed. A third problem is that high marginal tax rates are incentives for illegal tax evasion.

One proposed answer for all these problems is the *flat rate tax*. Some analysts have suggested that a flat income tax of roughly 20 percent with no exemptions or deductions would (*a*) generate more revenue than the current tax system, (*b*) eliminate most tax evasion, (*c*) cut the amount of paperwork required from firms and households, and (*d*) cure the ulcers and headaches common around April 15 of each year. Critics of this proposal, however, fear that a flat income tax system would be an inequitable retreat from society's fight against poverty.

Consumption Taxes

Other critics argue that the major flaw in our income tax system is that, in a shortsighted quest for greater equality, income taxes kill the goose that lays the golden eggs. These critics view disparities in consumption levels, not income, as the root of social inequity. They argue that resource use (*consumption*) is more appropriate as a measure of ability to pay than are potential claims to resources (*income*). Another drawback to taxing income is the severe disincentive to save and invest. The critics' solution is to allow all saving as a deduction from taxes, effectively replacing income taxes with a tax on consumption alone. Consequently, people with incomes of $1,000,000 per year would be taxed on the full amount if they spent it on Rolls-Royces, furs, jewelry, and other extravagances. Investing almost all of a $1,000,000 income, on the other hand, would result in negligible taxes.

A *consumption tax* could be as progressive as any income tax system, so problems of regressivity are not necessarily raised. Moreover, according to the advocates of this approach, the resulting increase in saving and investment would greatly enhance labor productivity, and technological breakthroughs would allow substantial economic growth.

We have looked at the types of government activities that can be rationalized as proper cures for market failures and have examined various tax structures. Questions about why government spending and taxes so frequently depart from the ideal have been addressed only peripherally, however. Many of these questions are answered when we look at the political dimensions of policy making. The next chapter examines political behavior from an economic perspective.

FOCUS 2

The Microeconomics of Federal Debt: The Enemy is Us

Polls indicate that an overwhelming majority of Americans want a smaller, but more efficient government. Paradoxically, when asked about specific government functions, we express desires for better schools with smaller class size, more frequent garbage collection, research to provide cures for cancer and AIDS, safer streets (with fewer potholes) monitored by more police officers, and on and on. A majority of Americans now favor a more active government role in providing "affordable" health care for all. But will a government medical care program reduce the 12 percent of our GDP now devoted to health care? Unlikely. Can we afford all the government services that most of us would like? There is mounting evidence that the answer may be NO.

During every national election, the airways are filled with political promises that, "If elected, I will get the federal deficit under control." Ross Perot articulated this message in his bid for the presidency in 1992. "We're $4 trillion in debt, and we don't have anything to show for it . . . we've got the worst of all worlds now: a declining industrial base, declining schools, and the most violent, crime-ridden country in the world. What did that $4 trillion buy?"* Perot withdrew abruptly after the Clinton-Gore

ticket won the Democratic nomination, but he had raised issues that Clinton and Bush continued to address during the presidential race.

Should taxes be raised to close the deficit? Being in favor of tax cuts has usually paved the way to election year victory (e.g., President Reagan (1980 and 1984) and President "Read my Lips—No New Taxes" Bush (1988), while hints that "tax hikes may be necessary" spells likely defeat (Walter Mondale in 1984, Michael Dukakis in 1988). The 1992 election showed how much this thinking changed.

How do victorious candidates propose to eliminate federal deficits without raising taxes? Apparently, most voters believe that promises to "cut wasteful spending" can be fulfilled. But we also tend to believe that "wasteful government spending" is that which benefits other people, not ourselves. For example, farmers may view $10 billion to support agriculture as warranted, while favoring cuts in programs that benefit the urban poor. People whose income depends on defense contracts tend to favor continued big defense budgets, despite the demise of the USSR

as much of a threat to world peace. Naturally, teachers and the parents of school-aged children want more money to flow into education. Most of us, however, fail to recognize that all of these demands for more government sum to the big government that we have, not smaller government that we perceive as the proper size to serve our individual needs.

Another problem that may, in part, account for our growing national deficit is that we dislike the specific taxes government relies on, and the hassle associated with filling out all the forms government imposes to monitor its collection processes. We'd like the burden imposed on other groups—tax "the rich" is a popular theme. But who are the rich folks we'd like to pay more taxes? Surveys addressing this question typically find that the answer depends on who is asked the question, with most people defining those who should pay more taxes by the receipt of roughly 20 percent more income than the respondent receives. In the next chapter, we use economic analysis to address political aspects of government. By the time you've finished it, you should have a better feel for why government spending increasingly lags the tax revenues to pay for it.

_____
*U.S. News & World Report, *July 27, 1992.*

Chapter Review: Key Points

1. The economic goals of government are to
   a. Provide a stable legal environment, promote competition, and provide efficiently for public wants.
   b. Stabilize income, employment, and prices.
   c. Redistribute income and wealth equitably.

2. When marginal social benefits and marginal social costs diverge, *market failure* occurs. In such cases, government may be used to provide the socially optimal quantities of some goods and to limit economic bads.

3. *Externalities* occur when private calculations of benefits or costs differ from the benefits or costs to society because third parties gain or lose from a transaction.

4. *Nonrivalry* means that a good is not used up when any individual enjoys it; a beautiful sunset is an example. *Nonexclusion* means that it is prohibitively expensive to deny access to a good. Note, however, that public provision does not require public production. Private firms often produce goods that government then distributes.

5. A good that is both nonrival and nonexclusive is a *pure public good*. Public goods will be less than optimally provided by the market system, if they are provided at all, because of attempts to *free ride*. A rival but nonexclusive good embodies *externalities* that often hinders the efficiency of market solutions.

6. The *benefit principle of taxation* suggests that people should pay taxes in proportion to the marginal benefits key receive from a governmentally provided good.

7. The demand for a pure public good is the *vertical summation* of individual demand curves because all can enjoy the good simultaneously, while demands for private goods are summed horizontally. Adequate revenue for optimal quantities of public goods is generated if people pay taxes equal to their marginal benefits from public goods multiplied by the amounts of these goods provided.

8. The *ability-to-pay principle of taxation* requires taxes in proportion to people's income, their wealth, or possibly their consumption. This principle is closely related to the idea that government policies should move the income distribution closer to equality than is the market distribution of income.

9. The principle of *horizontal equity* suggests that equals should pay equal taxes; *vertical equity* requires higher taxes on the wealthy than on the poor.

10. If the loss to a taxpayer exceeds the government revenue gained, there is an *excess burden* of taxation. *Neutral taxes* impose only income, not substitution, effects and impose no excess burdens.

11. The *personal income tax* system is nominally progressive, but various loopholes make it somewhat inefficient and inequitable.

12. *Social Security taxes* are the second largest and fastest growing sources of federal revenues. They and other *payroll taxes* may be borne primarily by workers. Moreover, they are regressive, typically declining proportionately as personal income rises.

13. *Sales taxes* are reasonably efficient but, like income taxes, are marred by numerous exemptions. Many *excise taxes* apply to "sin" or "wasteful luxuries." Unless they are based on a benefit principle of taxation (for example, public zoo ticket fees or gasoline taxes), they tend to cause inefficiency and be regressive. (Poor people smoke and drink as much, by volume, as rich people.)

14. The *corporate income tax* discriminates against the corporate form of business and against the goods produced primarily by corporations. In the long run, most of this tax is probably forward-shifted to consumers. Thus, in the minds of most experts, this tax tends to be both inefficient and inequitable.

15. *Property taxes* provide disincentives for improvement and are blamed by some for the deterioration of central cities.

16. *Inheritance* and *gift taxes* have high and progressive rates, but can be avoided because these tax laws are riddled with loopholes.

17. A *value-added tax* (VAT) is similar to a sales tax in that it is forward-shifted. VATs only

apply to the value added by each firm. VATs, *flat rate taxes*, and progressive *consumption taxes* (not income) have been proposed as replacements for corporate income taxes or Social Security taxes.

Key Concepts

Ensure that you can define these terms before proceeding.

externalities

public goods

rival versus nonrival goods

exclusive versus nonexclusive goods

benefit principle of taxation

ability-to-pay principle of taxation

vertical equity

horizontal equity

excess burdens

tax neutrality

value-added taxes (VATs)

Problems and Questions

Table 5 reflects the astounding coincidence that Matthew's demands for street lights (a public good) and dry cleaning (a private good) happen to be identical, and that Rachel's demands for lights and cleaning are also identical.

1. Use graph paper to construct individual and market demands for dry cleaning if these two people comprise the market. Assume that their individual demand curves are straight lines.

2. Now graph their individual and collective demands for street lights.

Table 5 *Quantities of Both Goods Wanted Each Month at These Prices*

Price	Matthew	Rachel
$8	0	6
7	3	7
6	6	8
5	9	9
4	12	10
3	15	11
2	18	12
1	21	13

3. What are the individual price elasticities of demand for dry cleaning if the price of this purely competitive private service is $2? How much would each person purchase per month? What is the market elasticity of demand for dry cleaning if the price is $2? If a dry-cleaning monopoly faced a constant $2 average total cost and marginal cost, how much would it charge per item? How much dry cleaning would each individual have done at this price?

4. Suppose that maintenance and replacement cost averages $6 per street light. What number of street lights would be optimal? If Matthew and Rachel are each charged for street lights in proportion to their respective marginal benefits, how will the total cost of street lights be shared?

5. Indicate which of the following goods seem to be pure private goods, which are pure public goods, which generate positive externalities, which generate negative externalities, and which are likely to be produced by natural monopolies. Some goods may be hard to classify; they may fall into more than one category because production creates one type of effect, while consumption creates a different type of effect.

   a. Deodorant soap

   b. Electricity generated by atomic power

   c. Lawn fertilizer

   d. Radishes

   e. Surf boards

   f. Garlic

   g. Cancer research

   h. Speeding tickets

   i. Kindergarten

   j. Heavy-metal concerts

6. Why will fewer apartment dwellers voluntarily install smoke alarms than would be socially optimal? Does this justify regulations requiring smoke alarms? Will the number of smoke alarms in private homes be optimal without government regulation? How might pressure from neighbors and insurance companies eliminate the need for such regulations?

7. Can you think of ways to induce people to

reveal their preferences for certain public goods so that they will not be free riders? Try this for such things as schools, highways, and national defense.

8. Figure 8 illustrates the market for candy corn. The market was initially in equilibrium at the intersection of D_0 and S_0. The federal government then levied a tax against candy corn producers, which resulted in supply decreasing to S_1. How much of a tax was levied per pound against candy corn producers? How much will the government collect in revenues as a result of the tax? How much is the decrease in consumer surplus from the tax? How much is the excess burden of the tax? Who bears the greatest proportion of the burden of the tax?

9. Consider such shared social institutions as public officials, our justice system and the rule of law, and regulations such as traffic laws. In what senses are these public goods (or public bads)? Does government regulation that attempts to ensure the quality or safety of certain products provide some security to consumers? If so, is this security a public good? Why or why not?

10. Should most taxes be progressive, proportional, or regressive? Why? Try to use eco-nomic reasoning to classify the following current taxes according to whether, as family incomes grow, the proportions of income absorbed by these taxes rise, remains constant, or falls.

   a. Personal income tax.

   b. Corporation income tax.

   c. Social Security tax.

   d. Sales and excise taxes.

   e. Property taxes.

   f. Inheritance taxes.

11. Many people support the sentiments of "tax resisters" who refuse to pay income taxes. If resistance became more widespread, what would happen to the tax burdens of those who conscientiously pay all of their legal tax liabilities? What are the effects (psychological and otherwise) on someone who pays taxes honestly when someone else defends cheating because "everybody does it"? Do honest people subsidize tax cheats?

12. Discuss the proposition that inheritance taxes should be eliminated and that inheritance should be treated just like regular income for purposes of income taxation.

13. What problems might arise if value-added taxes (VATs) were used to replace the revenues lost from reducing or eliminating Social Security or corporation income taxes? What benefits would result from implementing value-added taxes? Would it matter whether the VAT applied only to consumer goods and services or to both consumption and investment goods?

14. An increasingly popular proposal is to entirely replace the current tax system with a single, flat rate income tax. What are the virtues of this proposal? The drawbacks? The advocates of this approach have managed to tilt recent tax legislation in their favor. By how much have recent changes in income tax rates reduced the nominal progressivity of our tax structure? Have some loopholes been eliminated recently, so that the actual progressivity of taxes has been affected less? If so, what loopholes have been plugged? Which loopholes remain in place? (Answering this question may require some library research.)

FIGURE 8 The Market for Candy Corn

Public Choice

Eternal optimists may think that government can infallibly cure the market failures described in the preceding chapter, but government policies are also often marred by inefficiency and inequity. No allocative mechanism works perfectly. Selecting the best mechanism for the task at hand usually involves trade-offs. Choosing government to remedy market failures, for example, may mean that the flexibility of markets is lost, and that *government failure* creates a new set of problems.

Economists increasingly apply their insights to the processes of government.

Public choice *analysis examines political behavior from an economic perspective.*

Specialists in public choice believe that the motives behind people's behavior in the political arena differ little from those behind their performance in the private sector: Equal proportions of saints and greedy sinners are found among workers, voters, union leaders, bureaucrats, professors, business tycoons, or politicians. Government policy making cannot be divorced from such realities as lobbying by special-interest groups, the desires of incumbents to be reelected, or bureaucratic inertia.

Our first topic in this chapter is private political behavior. Why do so few people vote, and

why do so many seem oblivious to political issues? Then we investigate alternative voting systems. Is majority rule superior to unanimity or point voting in reflecting voters' preferences? Our next broad area is political competition—government as a mechanism through which special-interest groups compete for scarce resources. Finally, we look at government bureaucracy, focusing on ways in which individuals may serve their private interests when they lack profit motives for efficiency.

Private Citizens and Politics

Consumers "vote with dollars" for the things they want in private transactions, but each consumer has different numbers of dollar votes. In modern democracies, adult citizens (except convicted felons) have equal rights to vote, so their opinions theoretically carry equal weight. Then why do so many people seem indifferent about politics?

Rational Voter Apathy

An election-year cliché is that "every vote counts." If people were always rational and if the outcome of every election hung on every vote and was crucial for everyone, then all eligible citizens would vote. We would not hear TV commentators lamenting voter apathy after every election.

Fewer than 10 percent of adult U.S. citizens bother to go to the polls in most local elections. Even in hotly contested national elections, a 60 percent turnout is unusual. Many Americans evidently conclude that the personal benefits of voting are outweighed by the personal costs. The following is one explanation for why many people judge that voting is not worth the effort.

Suppose that opinion polls indicate that 70 million people plan to vote in the next presidential election and that voters are split 50/50 between the Republican and Democratic candidates. This split maximizes the probability that your vote would matter if presidents were elected by popular vote. What is the probability that a single vote would change the outcome of this election? The probability of an exact 50/50 split of the vote is identical with the probability of flipping a coin 70 million times and obtaining exactly 35 million heads and 35 million tails—infinitesimal. Even if only 1,000 people voted, the probability that you might be the tie breaker if you were the 1,001st voter is less than 1 percent. The probability that any single voter will be the tie breaker is, of course, much lower the larger the number of votes.

The transaction costs of voting are not trivial when you consider the time and resources used to register, walk or drive to the polls, wait in line, learn about candidates and issues, and so on. This raises the question of why so many people do vote. Although the costs of voting are low, the probability of one vote swinging any important election is nearly zero. Some people argue that "if you don't vote, you have no right to complain," but there is no law or religious commandment to that effect.

One possible explanation for widespread apathy is that most people living in democracies are reasonably content and are skeptical that the outcome of any election is likely to change their lives very much. People living in dictatorships often correctly believe, however, that democratic voting will allow people more control over their lives. People who defy thugs and bullets to vote are asserting their belief in the outcomes of voting as a group process. Few of them believe that each individual vote is highly likely to change the outcome of every election.

Why Many People Do Vote The preceding analysis makes it seem almost irrational to vote. Major elections, however, usually draw a majority of eligible voters. Some people may vote because political campaigns resemble spectator sports—the stakes are generally higher, but voting is a bit like cheering for your favorite football team or buying a ticket to a game. Others view voting as a democratic duty. Most voters like to think of themselves as good citizens or feel guilty if they don't vote. Just as no soldier alone is likely to win or lose a war, no single vote is likely to swing a major election. Nevertheless, most soldiers and voters derive pleasure from participating in group processes that shape history.

Apathetic nonvoters who contend that individual votes "don't matter" are statistically correct. It may even be fortunate that many people don't vote. Voting is most likely among people with intense political preferences, and least likely among people who are indifferent about politics, and who know relatively little about the issues.

Rational Political Ignorance

Better the devil you know than the devil you don't.

Unknown

Can you name even five people who were on the ballot in the last election? How much did you know about the candidates' positions on budget deficits? Immigration? Gun control? If you are typical, your answer to these and similar questions is, "Not much."

> **Rational ignorance** *occurs when people decide that the marginal costs of more information exceed its marginal benefits.*

Information is costly. The future is uncertain. Therefore, consumers and producers operate with only imperfect information about markets. They are, to some degree, *rationally ignorant.* Similarly, voters rely on information that is far from perfect. The personal payoff from in-depth knowledge about all the candidates and issues decided in any important election is trivial, and generally far less than the benefits of information about market choices. For example, textile import quotas now cost consumers billions of dollars annually. If your share is only $5 to $10 and the probability of influencing an election with your vote is negligible, then the time and effort required to learn about candidates' positions on import quotas so that you can vote wisely probably exceed the personal benefits from a more informed vote. There are, however, significant personal benefits in knowing about the quality and price of clothing you buy.

Election results share many attributes of public goods—your president is my president, we share the same sets of laws, and so on. This creates incentives for "free riders," who either don't vote or rely on other voters to acquire knowledge about the candidates and issues. Thus, we should not be surprised that many voters select candidates on the basis of charisma, a flashing smile and a shock of wavy hair, or an impression that a certain candidate is dependable, experienced, or reflective. Small wonder that every major political campaign abounds with public relations flacks.

We have examined why so many people fail to vote, and why so many who do vote are relatively ignorant about political issues. Let's survey some of the different methods by which candidates and proposals can be chosen.

Systems of Voting

Although single votes have little direct influence on elections, those of us fortunate enough to live in democracies can vote to collectively determine who will govern. But how accurately are voters' preferences reflected by election results? Does the system of voting matter?

Majority Rule

Any group of a dozen or more people will find it difficult to agree on almost anything. Group decisions tend to be middle-of-the-road compromises that are inconsistent with any individual's preferences.

Majority rule *voting systems require votes from 50 percent plus one of the voters.*

Whenever we vote and use a simple majority rule, we can be almost certain members on the minority side of the vote will perceive that their interests were harmed by the outcome of the election. (Otherwise, they would have voted with the majority; votes reflect expectations of gain, or fears of loss.) Majority voting may even result in economic inefficiency, since the minority's losses may outweigh all gains to the side able to swing a majority of votes.

Potential Inefficiencies Although majority voting can be efficient, the example in Table 1 points out the possibility of inefficient results. Proposal X is defeated even though its benefits outweigh the costs by $300, but Proposal Y passes despite costs ($2,000) exceeding benefits ($1,700) by $300.

Notice that if supporters of Proposal X shared their gains with the potential losers, all could gain from its passage; if opponents of Proposal Y compensated the potential gainers, all could gain from its defeat. Thus, passage of Proposal X and defeat of Y would both be efficient moves. Majority rule voting yields inefficiency on both proposals, however, because it is illegal to pay money for votes. This is one reason for secret ballots. Markets for votes might shrink the inefficiency inherent in many voting situations, but a market approach to voting is widely viewed as unethical or inequitable.

The basic problem is that *intensities of preference* are easily registered in markets, but not by a majority rule. You can buy more or fewer pizzas based on the intensity of your preferences, but even if you passionately care who is elected dogcatcher, your vote counts no more than that of someone who randomly casts a vote that offsets yours.

Potential Inconsistencies Majority rule voting can yield inconsistent results, especially if choices are narrowed by sequential elections (e.g., party primaries). It is, for example, common for analysts to claim that Republican Smith could beat any Democrat in a presidential elec-

Table 1 *Inefficient Outcomes under a Simple Majority Rule*

	A Beneficial Proposal (X) Is Defeated		Votes			An Excessively Costly Proposal (Y) Is Adopted		Votes	
Individual	Benefits	Tax Cost	Aye	Nay	Individual	Benefits	Tax Cost	Aye	Nay
A	$ 700	$ 400	X		A	$ 425	$ 400	X	
B	600	400	X		B	575	400	X	
C	350	400		X	C	450	400	X	
D	375	400		X	D	150	400		X
E	275	400		X	E	100	400		X
Total	$2,300	$2,000	2	3	Total	$1,700	$2,000	3	2

tion, but that he has no chance because loyal Republicans will nominate Mr. Jones, who cannot beat any Democrat. Table 2 illustrates this point by considering a three-party system. Assume that the voters are roughly divided into thirds between the Tory, Whig, and Populist parties, and that the ultimate winner must receive over 50 percent of the vote. If no one receives a clear majority, then there is a runoff election between the top two candidates.

Suppose that Tory voters despise Populists and will vote for Whigs if there are no Tories in a runoff election. Whig voters, however, vote for Populist Party candidates over Tory candidates in runoff elections. To complete this circle, Populist voters will support Tory over Whig candidates. Table 2 shows the potential results if no candidate receives a clear majority in an initial election. Tory candidates win against Whigs in runoff elections, who would win against Populists, who, in turn, would beat the Tories.

Some analysts believe that the possible inconsistencies apparent in these results of majority

rule voting may also foment instability, with parties taking turns being in power. This is known as the *voting cycle* phenomenon. An alternative explanation for voting cycles is that voters do not want any party to have a monopoly on political power. This may partially explain for example, why voters have elected Republican presidents in five of the six national elections since 1968, while Democrats have held fairly consistent majorities in both the U.S. Senate and the House of Representatives, as well as a majority of governorships. Nevertheless, voting cycles and the resulting flip-flops in policies often create chaos for long-range planning by consumers, workers, and investors. Unstable policies would be less of a problem if changes required unanimous votes.

Unanimity

Some decisions are deemed so important that society requires more than a simple majority vote; minority opinions are weighed more heavily in determining critical social policies. A con-

Table 2 *Potential Inconsistencies in Voting*

	Parties in Runoff		
	Tory vs. Whig	Whig vs. Populist	Populist vs. Tory
Tory voter preferences	Tory	Whig	Tory
Whig voter preferences	Whig	Whig	Populist
Populist voter preferences	Tory	Populist	Populist
Winner	**Tory**	**Whig**	**Populist**

stitutional amendment requires either a constitutional convention called by three-fourths of all state legislatures or their ratification of an amendment approved by two-thirds of the members of both the U.S. Senate and the House of Representatives. Similar congressional votes are required to override a presidential veto. In most states, a jury trying a criminal case must reach a unanimous verdict, or the case must be either retried or abandoned by the prosecutor. In such situations, requiring **unanimity** or near unanimity limits exploitation of a minority. Moreover, any legal changes under pure unanimity rules presumably would benefit everyone or they would never be adopted. Thus, any changes would clearly improve economic efficiency.

One difficulty with requiring unanimity is that individuals who, on balance, are relatively unaffected by some proposal could withhold their votes to "blackmail" potential gainers from the proposed change. In a sense, requiring unanimity gives everyone the power to say, "It's my ball, so we play by my rules or we don't play." Although some people might negotiate disproportionate gains for themselves simply because of their political leverage, no voter would ever expect to lose from any unanimous vote.

A far more serious problem is that a unanimity rule is biased in favor of the existing situation. Unanimity might operate well if an overwhelm-

ing majority view the current situation as equitable, but it totally blocks political remedies for inequity, leaving only informal negotiation, violence, or the market as avenues open for people to pursue what they perceive as justice. For example, a unanimity requirement precludes any redistribution of income or wealth other than one that is strictly voluntary. A final flaw is that even though a unanimity rule protects the existing rights of minorities, it also provides only crude indications of the intensity of people's preferences.

Point Voting

One proposal to reflect the intensities of preferences better than any "one person, one vote" rule is the use of point voting.

> **Point voting** *assigns equal numbers of points to all voters, which they can allocate among various issues as they see fit.*

Voters ideally would allocate their points in proportion to their intensities of preference: that is, in proportion to their net expected gains or losses from given proposals. Thus, if individuals A, B, C, D, and E each have 100 points to allocate between the proposals in Table 1, they would ideally vote as in Table 3. Proposal X

Table 3   *The Results from Table 1 if Determined by Ideal Voting**

	Proposal X					Proposal Y			
			Votes					**Votes**	
Individual	**Benefits**	**Tax Cost**	**Aye**	**Nay**	**Individual**	**Benefits**	**Tax Cost**	**Aye**	**Nay**
A	$ 700	$ 400	92		A	$ 425	$ 400	8	
B	600	400	53		B	575	400	47	
C	350	400		50	C	450	400	50	
D	330	400		9	D	150	400		91
E	320	400		20	E	100	400		80
Total	$2,300	$2,000	145	79	Total	$1,700	$2,000	105	171

*Ideal point voting would mean that all voters would apportion their votes based on net benefits (benefits − costs). For example, Individual A's net benefits from Proposal X are $300 ($700 − $400); net benefits for Proposal Y are $25 ($425 − $400). Thus, Individual A's voting pattern would be 92 votes $\left(\frac{\$300}{\$325} \times 100\right)$ for Proposal X and 8 votes $\left(\frac{\$25}{\$325} \times 100\right)$ for Proposal Y.

passes and Proposal Y fails; these results reverse the inefficient results under simple majority rule voting. Since Proposal X yields net benefits while Proposal Y's costs exceed its benefits, these ideal "point voting" results are preferable to the results of a simple majority rule.

A major flaw in point voting is that people might skew their voting points toward issues that they expected to be close, figuring that others would ensure the passage or failure of issues not expected to be close. For example, suppose that you favored more spending on both national defense and medical research. If you expected a landslide vote on a national defense proposal but a close vote on medical research, you would probably place all your votes for medical research. Point voting systems are flawed when, instead of voting their true preferences, people try to forecast the outcomes of elections and then vote strategically. Election results would conform neither to the majority's will nor to reasonable benefit/cost decision making.

No matter which voting system is used, most people view government as failing if election results do not reflect voters' preferences. All voting systems are somewhat flawed in this regard, but the overwhelming use of majority rule voting has evolved out of two centuries of experimentation with other voting systems. We have examined voting from the perspectives of citizens. The other side of this equation is how electoral processes mold the political campaigns and policies of the candidates and private interests who want to shape government policy.

Politicians and Parties

Politics is the art of compromise.

Unknown

Some candidates seek political office to mold policy to their ideals, hoping to make this a better world. Their constituents' interests are primary concerns. Political opportunists, on the other hand, may care far more about simply acquiring power and prestige. The first step on the path to election for either type of candidate is to project an image voters will support. One obstacle is that no one can be all things to all people.

Any position on almost any issue will offend some voters. These pressures force all serious candidates, whether idealists or opportunists, to adopt compromise positions in predictable ways on a wide range of issues.

"Lumpiness" in Voting

I voted for the lesser of two evils.

Unknown

When consumers operate in the marketplace, their purchases can be fine-tuned to closely match their tastes and preferences. Even with such "lumpy" purchases as automobiles, you can buy a slightly bigger or smaller car, more or fewer options, keep it longer than your neighbor does, or trade it in sooner. Such fine gradations are not available in the political arena.

You might prefer Madison's stands on education and welfare reform, for example, while favoring Monroe's views on international relations. Voting is a *lumpy decision*, somewhat akin to tie-in sales contracts that require buying some things you do not want to get the things you desire. Casting a vote involves trade-offs because you cannot vote for a set of positions other than those taken by one of the candidates.

This is one reason that most public figures either state their positions on controversial issues in inoffensive terms or waffle—avoiding direct answers to barbed questions aimed at them by reporters or their political opponents. Rational ignorance among voters and the complexity of most issues are two other reasons that politicians frequently sidestep taking a stand. A fourth is that most serious political candidates strive for a moderate image.

The Median Voter Model

Differences among candidates are often more form than substance. It seems that all favor a strong national defense, adequate welfare for the "truly" needy, a balanced budget, and low taxes—positions become as predictable as calls to support "motherhood, apple pie, and the flag." Why do party platforms and political speeches so often seem like xerox copies of one another?

The **median voter model** *suggests that the median voter must be captured to achieve a majority vote and helps explain why political parties and candidates so often seem interchangeable.*

The median voter model partially explains similarities among political parties and candidates. In Figure 1, we assume that the preferences and voting patterns of individuals can be ranked very simply and are normally distributed along a continuum from the extreme left (revolutionary communism, perhaps) to the extreme right (fascism?). Point *M* is in the precise center of this spectrum and identifies the median voter — exactly half of all voters lie to the left, with the other half being to the right of this position.

Suppose that two candidates are running for an office. The median voter can provide the margin of victory if the winner must receive 50 percent plus 1 vote. Thus, the candidate who adopts positions on the issues closest to point *M* will capture the median vote and win the election. Regardless of their initial positions (say, *L* and *R*, respectively), both candidates find that shifting their positions slightly toward point *M* boosts their standings in public opinion polls. Figure 1 also uses a slightly right-wing candidate to illustrate how movements toward the extremes lose votes, while shifts to the center gain votes. The same would be true of a left-wing candidate. As the candidates each try to maximize their expected votes, each creeps toward point *M*. Ultimately, their positions may be almost indistinguishable.

You might think that a new third candidate could win this race by entering at, say, point *L* in Panel A, leaving the original candidates to split the votes from halfway between points *L* and *M* all the way to the extreme right. But this third candidate would also find that moving toward point *M* increases support by voters. This suggests that, ultimately, virtually all serious candidates for election gravitate toward point *M*. Similar forces are at work in elections ranging from that for president of your local PTA to the U.S. presidency, pressuring not only political candidates, but political parties as well, to gradually adopt middle-of-the-road policies.

The dynamic world of politics is grossly oversimplified in this median voter model; otherwise, there would be no differences between candidates or party platforms. Among other reasons, differences exist because

1. Voters' opinions on the numerous issues in any election cannot be simply described from left to right, and their opinions are only loosely correlated. For example, there may be no predictable connections between people's opinions on welfare, the environment, international trade, and law-and-order issues.

2. Voter distributions change according to circumstances, so it is impossible for politicians to know exactly where the median voter is on any controversial issue at any point in time.

3. Some politicians do have strong personal beliefs about some issues.

FIGURE 1   How Candidates and Parties Are Pushed to the Middle of the Road

The "bell-shaped" curve is based on the assumption that voters are normally distributed from left-wing to right-wing political positions. A right-wing candidate at point *R* gains more by moving toward the political center at point *M*, but is likely to lose substantial support from a move from *R* to the more extreme R_1. These losses of votes will be maximized if this candidate's opponent moves to a position just to the left of the candidate's position. The respective potential losses and gains pressure right-wing candidates and parties to move toward middle-of-the-road positions. Naturally, similar pressures would cause a serious left-wing candidate to shift toward the political center at point *M*.

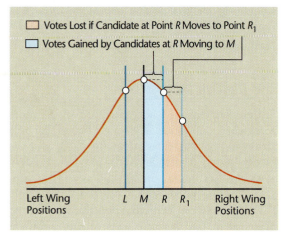

The median voter model also tends to break down because of low voter turnout and rational political ignorance. If a majority of eligible voters apathetically stay away from the polls, then the deciding votes in an election may be cast by well-informed political activists who belong to narrow special-interest groups. In spite of these qualifications, the median voter model helps explain the middle-of-the-road clustering of politicians and parties, which ignores the preferences of vast numbers of less moderate voters. It also hints at reasons for the dominance of the two-party system.

Two-Party Systems

That voters' preferences shift over time also helps explain *voting cycles* — why political control tends to swing between two parties in most democratic countries. Normally, one party locates slightly to the left of center, with the other being slightly right of center. Each then advertises itself as "the party of the future" and hopes that circumstances will move more voters in its direction.

The two parties, being reasonably comfortable with each other, then compete through expensive campaigns. A typical congressional campaign now requires a war chest of over $1 million; a recent U.S. Senate candidate in New York spent $14 million campaigning for a job that pays less than $100,000 annually — *and lost*. Campaign spending on television spots alone now exceeds $100 million in presidential election years. Such barriers frustrate third-party challenges to either dominant party. Another technique to bar entry is to make it difficult for a third party to get on the ballot. For example, the dominant parties may enact laws requiring that petitions be signed by huge numbers of voters before the third party can be on the ballot if it received less than 5 percent of the votes in a prior election.

Third parties tend to be launched from the extremes of the political spectrum and to be based on single issues. If a third party begins to attract more voters than either dominant party expected, the closest major party normally adopts a moderate version of the third party's position. If leaders of a third party seriously want political power, it tends to become more moderate and is eventually absorbed by the closest major party. Thus, mature democracies tend to operate under the control of two major parties. Third parties rarely displace major parties, and then only when a major party fails to respond to changes in voter preferences.

Two-party systems also tend to foster political stability. Italy has numerous parties, and there have been more governments than years since the end of World War II. As we have seen, politicians and political parties tend toward the middle of the road in an effort to capture votes. Once politicians are in office, can we expect them to shed their self-interest and work primarily for the common good of their constituents?

Political Allocation

Two things you never want to see made are sausages and laws.

Otto von Bismarck

Rational political ignorance, low voter turnouts, lumpiness in voting for a candidate, and the tendency for parties and politicians to cluster around middle-of-the-road positions are among the reasons that government policies only weakly mirror voter preferences. Lobbying and protracted negotiations among elected representatives are among the mechanisms that result in budgets and laws intended to balance the desires of *special-interest groups*, including those of voters. These mechanisms sometimes provide pressures for policies to more closely conform to voter preferences, but at other times they exacerbate problems inherent in political allocations of resources and incomes.

Logrolling

Economists generally favor most forms of voluntary exchange, because both sides expect to gain or no trade occurs.

Legislators commonly trade votes to obtain passage of proposals they favor, a process known as **logrolling**.

For example, one legislator might want more funding to clean up the environment, while another seeks higher agricultural price supports. Trading votes may enable both to get what they want. Logrolling may also be beneficial by allowing legislators to register their *intensities of preference*. Votes about matters upon which a legislator is reasonably indifferent are traded for votes on proposed legislation about which the lawmaker has strong feelings. This process can aid in the attainment of efficiency by allowing strongly held minority views to overcome weak opposition by the majority.

Economists recognize, however, that some exchanges may not be socially beneficial. An extreme case would be an agreement wherein you trade part of your loot from a bank robbery for my services as a lookout and getaway driver. Society's problem is that we are not the only people affected by this transaction — our victims' losses must be considered. Less dramatic but similarly damaging trades can take place through logrolling that results in pork barrel legislation.

Pork barrel legislation *uses tax revenues from taxpayers everywhere to fund projects that primarily benefit people in a narrower geographic area.*

Many federal projects generate benefits that are largely local. For example, Arizonans make up about 1 percent of our population and pay about 1 percent of federal taxes. Even if a canal system to convey water into dry parts of Arizona would cost $2 billion but generate benefits of only $1 billion, constituents would pressure Arizona's senators and representatives to support federal funds to build it. Arizonans would pay only 1 percent of the costs while receiving most of the benefits — a good deal for Arizonans, but a crummy deal for other voters.

Most pork barrel legislation is packaged with other pieces of pork and then tied to laws that are national in scope. Presidents cannot selectively veto parts of a law and so must either accept or veto the entire package. This is why some states have passed line-item veto legislation and why there is pressure to do this at the national level. Logrolling by lawmakers sympathetic to the goals of special interests is only one mecha-

nism that interest groups use to secure policies they favor.

Special Interests

Majority rule voting tends to slight minority interests, but determined political minorities are often able to impose policies weakly opposed by a majority of voters. For example, opinion polls consistently indicate that most Americans favor more restrictions on private firearms. Yet, for decades, the National Rifle Association has successful blocked national gun registration. Why? Typical voters care relatively little about gun control and are rationally ignorant of most candidates' positions on this issue. Thus, gun fanciers whose votes and contributions may be based on this issue alone make most politicians leery of pushing gun control. Similarly, people who feel strongly about abortion, prayer in schools, or protecting our steel industry from foreign competition may have disproportionally strong voices in determining certain social policies.

Voting is not the only way for special interests to accomplish their political goals. Money talks, and big money talks loudly. Campaign funds from a well-heeled minority may sway who gets elected, shading some politicians' positions on certain issues. Alternatively, campaign volunteers can beat the bushes to get other voters to support specific candidates. Money and bodies also may be used to propagandize for important minority issues. And then logrolling comes into play when politicians try to pass legislation favored by the interest groups that back them, including pork barrel projects for the folks in their home districts.

As we indicated earlier, one way that a democracy reflects intense preferences is for a minority to exert vigorous pressure and attain policies it favors. Much legislation enacted to benefit interest groups, however, may bear inefficiently high social costs.

Rent-Seeking

People are self-interested and try to manipulate allocative mechanisms to enrich themselves. In competitive markets, this normally entails trying to produce better goods at lower costs. This boosts society's production and potential consumption. Government can be similarly beneficial by setting rules to correct market failures, but economic legislation and regulation often seem tailored for special-interest groups. One problem with this is that the gains to special-interest groups are often less than the costs to the general public. Indeed, inefficiency in collective decision making arises primarily because costs are spread across a relatively anonymous, heterogeneous, and poorly informed public, while the benefits accrue to small cohesive groups.

> **Rent-seeking** *is the term applied to attempts by interest groups to manipulate public policy where the interest group's gains would be overshadowed by losses to the larger public.*

Recall that economic rent is any income received in excess of the minimum required to secure the resources that people make available. Figure 2 uses overly restrictive licensing of taxicabs to show why rent-seeking behavior is economically inefficient and reduces social well-being.

Suppose that the taxi market is initially in a competitive equilibrium, with supply S_0 being perfectly elastic at price P_0, and that demand is D_0. Consumer surplus equals triangle P_0ad, and cab companies cover all their costs, including a normal return on their investment. If major taxi operators thought that regulators could be persuaded to restrict competition, they could follow a rent-seeking strategy. They might cite horror stories to prove that some unwary tourists were gouged by unethical drivers as evidence of the evils of "cutthroat" competition. Suppose that taxi licenses were restricted to Q_1, and were granted only to solid, reputable companies. Cab fares would rise to P_1, shrinking consumer surplus to P_1ab. The loss of consumer surplus equals the trapezoid P_0P_1bd.

At first glance, society's "deadweight loss" appears to equal triangle cbd, with taxi companies reaping economic rent equal to P_0P_1bc. Rent-seeking, however, also absorbs resources directly, which shrinks the taxi firms' gains and increases the deadweight loss to society. Interest groups incur costs when seeking favorable laws or regulations and devote resources to mold public policies as long as the expected marginal gains

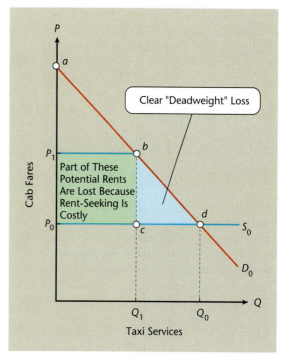

FIGURE 2 Why Rent-Seekers' Gains Are Less than the Resulting Social Losses

Suppose that rent-seeking cab companies persuade taxi regulators to follow overly restrictive licensing policies. If taxi services fall from Q_0 to Q_1, cab fares will rise from P_0 to P_1 and consumer surplus will shrink from P_0ad to P_1ab. There is a clear "deadweight" loss equal to cbd. Moreover, those who retain their cab licenses will not gain rents (profits) equal to P_0P_1bc. Some of the potential rents will be dissipated because of costs incurred in securing these political restrictions on market entry.

exceed the expected marginal costs. Consultants, lawyers, and professional lobbyists might be hired by the parties on all sides of an issue; time and money may be absorbed by hearings in front of regulatory boards or legislative committees. In some cases, unethical lawmakers or regulators who recognize the potential gains may demand bribes for favorable policies. None of these costs are incurred productively. The net result of rent-seeking behavior is a continuing social loss for as long as inefficient policies are in place, plus losses equal to the costs incurred by interest groups to secure favorable laws or regulations or to oppose unfavorable ones.

We have now discussed voting procedures, political campaigning, and the legislative process from a public choice perspective. Once laws are made, they must be administered. This brings us to the topic of government bureaucracy.

Bureaucracy

A government could print a good edition of Shakespeare's works, but it could not get them written.

Alfred Marshall

Whether private or public, large organizations develop extensive formal operating rules or managerial coordination becomes impossible. The resulting mountains of red tape cause many people to view bureaucracy as almost synonymous with mindless inefficiency.

Any large task-oriented organization is a **bureaucracy**.

The federal government is by far our largest employer. State and local governments also hire their share of workers, as shown in Table 4. Federal, state, and local governments employ over one-fifth of the U.S. labor force. Most government employees work in the agencies, or *bureaus*, that implement the laws passed by legislatures.

Many government bureaucrats work hard because they believe deeply in the mission of their agency. Economic theory suggests, however, that the best starting point for analysis of behavior is the assumption of self-interest. Anyone who has worked in a large organization knows that opportunities for raises and promotions are closely tied to the organization's fortunes; prosperity and growth yield larger personnel budgets in both public and private bureaucracies. Thus, we can expect career employees of any large organization to push for growth and to fight budget cuts.

Government agencies tend to have worse reputations than business bureaucracies. Major differences arise from different incentive structures. Divisions of private firms are usually profit centers, with growth depending on serving more customers better and at lower cost. Ascertaining efficiency is much harder in government bureaus that use tax revenues to cover costs. Legislators tend to consider whether a public service is provided adequately. If not, the standard solution is to boost funding. Thus, paradoxically, inefficiency may swell a bureau's budget. The opposite trend occurs in the private sector.

After reviewing 50 international studies of cost differences between publicly and privately provided services, Dennis Mueller, a public choice specialist, concluded, "The evidence that public provision of a service reduces the efficiency of its provision seems overwhelming."[1] In 40 out of 50 cases, public sector enterprises were significantly less efficient than their private counterparts, and in only 2 cases were public agencies relatively more efficient. Figure 3 presents a sample of the results of these studies.

Have you noticed that it is often easier to buy auto insurance than to get a license for a new car? That the time absorbed in buying 10 bags of groceries is often less than the time spent waiting in a line at the Post Office to buy a roll of stamps? Rewards for efficiency are few in government bureaucracies and may cause relative inefficiency because (*a*) services may be supplied to the public at the convenience of government employees rather than vice versa, and (*b*) government tends to pay relatively high prices for the things it buys. You may have read about outrageous cost overruns in Department of Defense

Table 4 *Government Employment*

	Millions of Government Employees		
	1970	**1975**	**1987**
Federal	5.0	4.6	4.8
Military	2.1	1.7	1.7
Civilian	2.9	2.9	3.1
State	2.8	3.3	4.1
Local	7.4	8.8	10.1

---

1. Dennis C. Mueller, *Public Choice II* (New York: Cambridge University Press, 1989).

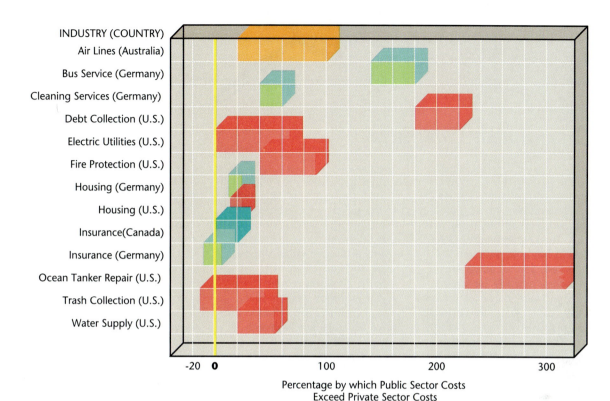

INDUSTRY (COUNTRY)
Air Lines (Australia)
Bus Service (Germany)
Cleaning Services (Germany)
Debt Collection (U.S.)
Electric Utilities (U.S.)
Fire Protection (U.S.)
Housing (Germany)
Housing (U.S.)
Insurance(Canada)
Insurance (Germany)
Ocean Tanker Repair (U.S.)
Trash Collection (U.S.)
Water Supply (U.S.)

-20 0   100   200   300

Percentage by which Public Sector Costs
Exceed Private Sector Costs

FIGURE 3 Public Versus Private Provision of Comparable Services

Many studies of public versus private provision of goods and services support the notion that efficiency declines when goods or services are provided publicly. The bars above represent ranges of costs. A value of 0 indicates that the service is provided at the same cost whether provided by a public or a private entity.

Source: Dennis C. Mueller, *Public Choice II* (New York: Cambridge University Press), 1989, pp. 262–265. Reprinted by permission of the publisher.

contracts. Focus 1 details some reasons for such apparent waste.

The basic problem, however, probably originates with the warped incentives common in many government bureaus. The tendency for *empire building* is only one of many types of bureaucratic behavior that emerge from inefficient incentive structures.

Empire Building

It is a commonplace observation that work expands so as to fill the time available for its completion. Politicians and taxpayers have assumed with occasional phases of doubt that a rising total in the number of civil servants must reflect a growing

volume of work to be done. Cynics, in questioning this belief, have imagined that the multiplication of officials must have left some of them idle or all of them able to work for shorter hours. But this is a matter in which faith and doubt seem equally misplaced. The fact is that the number of the officials and the quantity of the work to be done are not related to each other at all.

C. Northcote Parkinson[2]

Salary and status in a bureaucracy tend to be positively related to the numbers and levels of employees a manager supervises and the budget for

2. C. Northcote Parkinson, "Parkinson's Law," *The Economist*, November 1955.

FOCUS 1

Government Contracts

Military contracts for new weapons systems are almost uniformly plagued by mammoth cost overruns. The Department of Defense (DOD) has paid $400 for $17 hammers, $56 for $0.08 Allen wrenches, and $27 for screws that hardware stores sell for less than a dime. Prices for custom-built items in aircraft are even more startling: $600 armrests and toilet covers, $400 ashtrays, and $17,000 coffee pots. The U.S. Army abandoned its unserviceable Sergeant York battle tank after sinking almost $8 billion into the project.

Critics cite examples of this sort to indict defense contractors for price-gouging and to cite all of the bureaucrats who administered these contracts for incompetence. If the basic problems were this simple, the solution would be incredibly straightforward: Prosecute dishonest contractors and deny them future contracts, and hire competent administrators.

Such problems are not unique to the military. Government office buildings, flood control projects, highways, and nuclear plants also often entail sloppy work and cost overruns.

Some contracts require delivery of weapons systems years into the future, and inflation may drive up costs. For high-tech weapons, it takes 8 to 16 years to go from concept exploration to full-scale production and deployment. Many weapons systems are obsolete by the time they are battle ready. Contract specifications are often vague because designs are still on the drawing board. Bids on such projects cannot be ironclad.

The nature of government contracting, however, may make problems of this type unavoidable. Defense procurement, for example, is characterized by (a) all or nothing competition (if an aircraft company loses or does not bid on a new "stealth" bomber, it may not have another

opportunity for 20 years); (b) high technological demands and product precision uncertainty (many projects are vaguely specified initially, but have demanding requirements in the end); (c) unpredictable funding because of changing world events and the political nature of long-term contracts; and (d) heavy capital requirements.

A recent study summarized the precarious world of defense contracting:

The buyer can pressure the seller to reduce prices or threaten to stop purchasing altogether, leaving the seller with heavy capital outlays that reap no returns. Suppliers are clearly reluctant to make such investments for fear of exploitation. Inducements to do so include charging higher prices (to compensate for the risk) and writing long-term contracts with stiff penalty clauses for buyer withdrawal. . . . [D]efense transactions have an implicit third party. Not only are a producer and a military

which the manager is responsible. Thus, managers at all levels have incentives to acquire as many employees as possible, a practice termed **empire building.** In business, this usually requires showing that your division has extraordinary profit potential. In government bureaus, however, it normally requires persuading legislators of the enormity of the problem your agency

is supposed to cure. Thus, law enforcement officials predictably talk about organized crime and anarchy in the streets, educators decry teacher shortages and growing demands on our schools, admirals and generals stress world unrest, agriculture officials lament the plight of the family farmer—the ways bureaucrats try to build demands for their services seem endless.

buyer involved, but the U.S. Congress as well, with the latter intermittently withholding funding [to force] . . . changes in the procurement. Not surprisingly, with Congress reluctant to permit multiyear contracts, recourse to higher selling prices is a main inducement for firms to remain as defense contractors.*

Some problems with government contracting lurk in bureaucratic behavior. C. Northcote Parkinson, an English writer, developed "laws" of bureaucracy, one of which is "work expands to absorb the time available." As a project unfolds, specifications tend to grow excessively complex, which can be extremely costly. This occurs because many bureaucrats try to stay (or look) busy. One easy way to stay busy is to constantly write directives that detail the work of people you supervise. The 1985 DOD recipe for fruitcake is an unintentionally comic example—it took 18 pages. The recipe for a modern aircraft carrier runs to hundreds of thousands of pages. If the ratio of overspecification for fruitcake holds for U.S. Navy ships, the excess costs from this problem alone sum to billions of dollars. Doing business with the Pentagon is not easy. Reporting an oversight by DOD is thick and burdensome. So much so, that during 1982–1987 (the height of the Reagan defense buildup), the number of defense suppliers fell by two-thirds.†

Another problem is that contractors and contract administrators may share interests that violate the public interest. For example, many retired generals and admirals ultimately go to work for defense contractors. If you were about to retire as a high-ranking military officer, might you be "understanding" about exorbitant costs incurred by a contractor in accommodating your design changes—especially if that firm was a major employer of someone with your expertise?

We can only touch on some problems of government procurement; a detailed discussion would take volumes. DOD contract foibles have been on display recently, but many other types of government contracts seem executed at much higher costs than private contracts would be. The ultimate problem is inadequate incentives for efficiency. The costs of the resulting inefficiencies are borne by taxpayers.

*Donald L. Losman and Shu-jan Liang, The Promise of American Industry, (Westport, CT: Quorum Books), 1990, pp. 126–127.

†James Blackwell et al., Deterrence in Decay, Washington, D.C.: Center for Strategic and International Studies, May 1989, p. 31.

The Growth of Government

Few experts in any field ever conclude that their area will be of less concern in the foreseeable future. Thus, there are few credible witnesses to dispute claims that society needs to devote more resources in any number of directions. The result is that legislators, many of whom might want to slash taxes, are inundated with well-documented requests for more funding in support of almost all programs.

Pressing social problems seem to beget new programs that acquire lives of their own, even if the original problem fades away. Trying to identify areas to cut is often an exercise in frustration. Interest groups (including bureaucrats) become accustomed to programs that benefit them and always want more rather than less. Attempts to cut any spending category provoke intense lobbying. One common strategy used by bureau chiefs to combat proposed budget cuts is to assert that any cuts threaten a bureau's most popular services. This usually arouses loud support from the bureau's clients. This was one tactic used by some opponents of attempts to cut social spending in the early 1980s. Former President Reagan's supporters viewed cutting the *growth* of spending as a victory. The predictable result of the political processes described in this chapter? Government grows and grows, with no end in sight.

Public choice analysis identifies a number of problems inherent in political processes. Voting only crudely signals citizens' preferences and is flawed by apathy and rational ignorance, candidates base campaigns on image instead of substance, legislation is diverted from efficiently satisfying public wants by logrolling, pork barrel projects, and rent-seeking, and bureaucratization yields incentives for sloth and artificial growth.

Market Failure vs. Government Failure

We have discussed how markets operate and how they may fail. This part of the book focuses on the tasks of government and why it may fail to accomplish these tasks appropriately. Most economic issues can be placed on a continuum that stretches from problems efficiently resolved in markets on one end to issues that seem to require collective action at the other extreme. Whether a particular issue is best resolved in markets or through government is sometimes murky in the broad middle of this continuum. The answer may depend largely on the relative speed and precision with which these allocative mechanisms correct errors or adjust to changing circumstances.

Self-Corrections

On average, markets tend to respond quickly and efficiently to changes in consumer wants or mistakes made by business decision makers. For example, if markets fail to synchronize the plans of the buyers and sellers of a pure private good (thermal underwear or guacamole dip, for example), price adjustments tend to cure the resulting shortages or surpluses rather quickly. On the other hand, markets may never adequately provide such public goods as national defense, so these goods are provided through government.

Political adjustments are inherently slow in a democracy, however. When an elected official becomes extremely unpopular, voters must normally wait for the next election to "throw the rascal out"; coups or assassinations are undemo-

---

Table 5 *Market Failures vs. Political Failures*

Market Failure	Political Failure
1. Uncertainty about the future.	1. Uncertainty about the future.
2. Rational ignorance about consuming and investing.	2. Rational political ignorance.
3. Free riders for public goods.	3. Rational apathy and nonvoting.
4. Externalities and pollution.	4. "Tie-in sales" aspects of voting and inability to "fine-tune" spending patterns to voter preferences. All voting systems fail to reflect intensities of preference.
5. Monopoly power.	5. Disproportionate political power for special interests.
6. Inequity in the distributions of income and wealth	6. Majorities may inefficiently or inequitably vote against interests of minorities.
7. Fosters greediness and unhealthy competitiveness.	7. Fosters bureaucracy and empire building.

cratic. If a legislature enacts a disastrous policy, it may take years to repair the damage by changing the law. Once on the books, laws, regulations, and spending programs are hard to remove. Even though political solutions may be slow and inexact, government policy may be superior to private decision making when markets fail because of concentrated economic power, nonrivalry, nonexclusion, or inequity. Table 5 summarizes some failings of both the marketplace and government as allocative mechanisms.

We will examine some of the public policies that the government pursues to deal with various types of market failure in the next few chapters. As you read this material, keep in mind the simple lesson of the current chapter: Markets sometimes perform poorly, but so does government.

Chapter Review: Key Points

1. No allocative mechanism works perfectly. Just as markets fail in some cases, forces within all political systems can prevent government from reflecting the preferences of the people governed. *Public choice analysis* entails economic analysis of political behavior.

2. The probability that one vote will swing a major election is close to infinitesimal. Because the personal payoffs from voting are small, many people do not vote, nor do most find it personally worthwhile to inform themselves on a broad range of social issues. This is known as *rational political ignorance* and tends to be even more prevalent than the lack of information confronted when people make market decisions.

3. All voting systems are flawed in that economic efficiency may be lost through political decision making. *Majority rule* voting tends to impose losses on those taking minority positions; this is inefficient if their losses exceed the majority's gains. Majority rule may also lead to inconsistent or unstable political choices.

4. A *unanimity* rule ensures that all changes in laws are efficient, because everyone must expect to gain before acquiescing to a change. People who are reasonably indifferent about a policy change, however, might require excessive compensation for agreeing to the change from those who stand to gain much from the change. This would make changes in policies a very cumbersome and time-consuming process. Moreover, a unanimity rule assumes that the initial situation is equitable, which may be untrue.

5. *Point voting* would allow voters to indicate their preferences by allocating votes in proportion to how strongly they felt about some issues relative to others. This system is flawed, however, by the potential for strategic behavior; people might not vote their preferences per se, tending instead to weigh their votes according to how they expected others to vote.

6. Voting is a *lumpy* process; we cannot pick and choose among the political stances taken by the candidates for an office. The market permits us to fine-tune our decisions, but we generally can choose only a single candidate or platform when we vote.

7. Attempts to maximize their chances for election cause candidates and political parties to try to attract the *median voter*, whose vote tends to determine the outcomes of elections. Rational ignorance among voters causes many candidates to avoid taking stands on issues while attempting to project a moderate image. Political competition for the support of the median voter causes candidates and parties to cluster around *middle-of-the-road* positions and creates pressures for a *two-party system*.

8. *Logrolling* occurs when lawmakers trade votes. This allows legislators to register the intensities of their preferences, because they trade votes about which they care little for votes on things about which they feel strongly. Logrolling can, however, result in inefficient amounts of *pork barrel legislation*, which occurs when projects that have primarily local benefits are paid for by a broader taxpaying public.

Table 6 *Choices about National Priorities vs. Choices about Meals*

	Decision Makers		
	Xavier	**Yolanda**	**Zelda**
First Policy Choice	Stronger National Defense	Cleaner Environment	Controlling Inflation
First Choice of Meal	Ham	Roast Beef	Turkey
Second Policy Choice	Cleaner Environment	Controlling Inflation	Stronger National Defense
Second Choice of Meal	Roast Beef	Turkey	Ham
Third Policy Choice	Controlling Inflation	Stronger National Defense	Cleaner Environment
Third Choice of Meal	Turkey	Ham	Roast Beef

9. *Special-interest groups* may be overrepresented because of low voter turnouts, widespread rational political ignorance, and intense lobbying. However, intensities of preference may be better reflected in political decisions because of this overrepresentation.

10. *Rent-seeking* involves attempts by special-interest groups to manipulate government policies for private gain, even though the social costs of special laws or regulations would exceed the expected benefits to the interest group that seeks economic rents.

11. The efficiency of most government *bureaucracies* is hard to measure, and the absence of a profit motive reduces incentives for efficiency in the public sector. Managerial salaries and "perks" are often tied to the numbers of employees supervised and the size of the agency budget, which leads to *empire building* and further growth of government.

Key Concepts

Ensure that you can define these terms before proceeding.

public choice
rational ignorance
point voting
median voter model

logrolling
rent-seeking
bureaucracy
empire building

Questions and Problems

1. Why will "radical" candidates tend to moderate their positions if they want to increase their prospects for election?

2. Voting is inherently cruder than decision making in the marketplace.[3] Table 6 indicates how Xavier, Yolanda, and Zelda rank national priorities for defense, environmental quality, and controlling inflation. It also lists their preferences for the main course at their respective families' Thanksgiving dinners. Let's consider national priorities first. Who will be most disappointed if defense spending is slashed? If inflation soars because of increased spending on defense and higher environmental standards? If diverting resources to defense without stimulating inflation requires neglect of environmental quality? Is the first policy choice of at least one person doomed to receiving the lowest priority? Is a similar type of disappointment inevitable when it comes to what each family will have for Thanksgiving dinner? Why not?

3. It is illegal to buy votes in the United States. Can you explain why this ban on the sale of

---

3. A similar example was offered by Nobel Laureate Kenneth Arrow to demonstrate a theorem proving the impossibility of democratic choices being consistent with voter preferences.

votes is economically inefficient? Would it be desirable to make it legal for people to sell their votes? Why or why not?

4. Which voting system (a) plurality, (b) majority, or (c) unanimity — best preserves the rights of minorities? Why?

5. Several positions are sometimes filled through a single election. For example, the top three (or five, or seven) vote getters might be elected to a school board or as county commissioners. Why do some voters cast their ballots for fewer than the number of candidates who will gain office, even if they have preferences among those for whom they don't vote?

6. Table 7 lists the benefits and costs of a proposed public park to the citizens of Tiny Town. If majority rule voting is used, will the park initiative pass or fail? Will this outcome be efficient? Why? If point voting is used, will the park initiative pass? Will this outcome be efficient? Why?

7. Voting is optional in the United States, but it is illegal not to vote in some countries. Do you think making voting compulsory would reduce political apathy? How would compulsory voting affect the behavior of politicians? Would government policies be more or less in accord with voter preferences? Why?

8. Medical doctors are sometimes accused of building the demands for their services by exaggerating minor health problems and heightening the concerns of their patients. How might high-level government bureaucrats enhance the sizes and powers of their agencies through similar processes? What political institutions would they need to manipulate? Can you cite any cases where this type of thing seems to have occurred?

9. The market system and government are both allocative mechanisms. What are some advantages and disadvantages of each? In what areas now dominated by market forces should government assume a greater role, if any? In what areas should government allow market forces greater latitude? Why?

10. Since World War II, government transfer payments as percentages of national income have grown sharply, and federal spending on goods and services has fallen relative to state and local spending. What might be some explanations for these changes in patterns of government outlays?

11. One proposal to alter the current federal budgeting system is to allow taxpayers to specify the percentages of their income taxes to be allocated to each government budget category. Proponents of this unequal "point voting" system argue that this would eliminate lobbying by special interests for government programs requiring expenditures of tax revenues, and would result in budgets more closely attuned to taxpayers' desires. Do you think these arguments have merit? Can you mount other arguments for this proposal? Should the preferences of those who pay a lot of taxes be given more weight than the preferences of those who pay fewer or no taxes? What would you expect the effects to be on income redistribution programs were this proposal adopted? How might strategic behavior cause the budget to fail to truly reflect even taxpayers' preferences?

12. Votes generally fail to reflect the intensity of people's preferences about issues. What political mechanisms enable people to sway policies about which they feel strongly? Do you think these mechanisms improve the efficiency of policy making?

13. To what extent do you think that private bureaucrats are insulated from pressures for efficiency? Is this a serious problem?

Table 7 *Benefits and Costs for a Proposed Park*

	Benefits	**Costs**	**Points**
Amy	300	250	8
Bruce	150	250	5
Fitz	225	250	4
Skippy	400	250	12
Zan	200	250	10

CHAPTER

Government Regulation

That life grows ever more complex is a cliché. Complex societies are also regulated societies. At one time, you could count on your fingers the regulations governing most American industries. Today, you would need the appendages in a bushel basket of centipedes. Market failure is a rationale for some regulation, but how extensive should regulation be? Is excessive regulation too often a manifestation of government failure?

Business regulation is a massive task for government regulators, for the firms they oversee, and for hordes of lawyers and consultants from both sides. Concerns about pollution and the environment, discrimination, consumer and occupational safety and health, and a host of other social, economic, and political problems all contribute to the rising tide of business regulation. But business activity is not alone in being regulated. Consumer protection laws usually affect firms most directly, but regulations also limit consumers' options. Laws mandate school attendance until your mid-teens, prohibit self-prescription of penicillin or heroin, require stopping at red lights, forbid walking your dog without a leash and a shovel. . . .

Many observers charge that misguided regulation tramples our freedom and suffocates American business. Instead of providing a chicken for every pot, government's finger is in every pie.

Excessive regulation is blamed for reducing supplies and driving up production costs. This group blames unnecessary red tape that stifles productivity for much of the recent lag in our international competitiveness. Critics of a laissez-faire approach, on the other hand, advocate expanded regulation because they view competitive forces as weak, and misinformation, inequity, and instability as pervasive.

In this chapter, we will examine (a) the nature and extent of regulation, (b) market failures that may justify some regulations and government regulatory failures that may make the cure worse than the disease, and (c) cases for and against consumer protection.

The Growth of Government Regulation

Victims of a raw deal often react with, "There ought to be a law to . . . (prevent this type of cheating)." This is one reason why hundreds of federal, state, and local agencies now regulate business. Public utilities, for example, were engulfed by a wave of regulation in most states during 1912–1917. Figure 1 surveys the growth of major federal regulatory agencies, but only hints

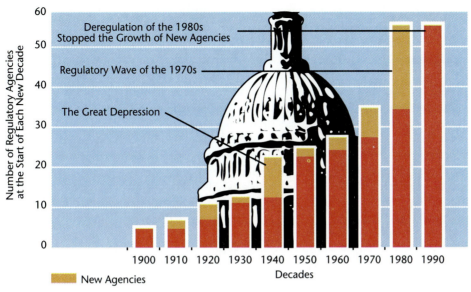

FIGURE 1   Number of Major Federal Regulatory Agencies

The power of the federal government to regulate commerce is established in the Constitution. This power was exercised little before the 1930s, but the 1960s and 1970s were an age of regulatory growth.

at regulatory growth in the 1960s and 1970s. State and local governments joined in the rush to regulate; the *Federal Register*, which lists new federal regulations, mushroomed from a few hundred pages annually to thousands of pages each month.

The Great Depression shattered support for moderate laissez-faire capitalism like a blow from a sledgehammer. Many new regulations in the 1930s were intended to smooth disruptions from business cycles and, perhaps mistakenly, increased government's controls over pricing and other competitive business practices in banking, public utilities, securities transactions, and labor contracts; farmers were supported, mortgage loans were guaranteed, and our welfare system was expanded.

The 1940s and 1950s were dormant decades for regulation, but a new wave erupted in the 1960s and 1970s. The doubling of new regulatory agencies shown in Figure 1 paradoxically occurred during a period when real disposable personal income rose by over 40 percent—one of the more prosperous periods in our history. What stimulated this burst of regulation? One theory of regulatory growth is that sophisticated

technology makes the simple rules of the past obsolete. Kenneth Boulding argues that just as an astronaut in a space capsule must follow a far stricter regimen than a cowboy on the prairie, so, too, must a space-age economy be controlled more tightly than the simpler economy of an earlier era.

Economist Robert Heilbroner has divided typical government relationships with industry into three phases. Its first role is as *promoter*; its second is as *regulator*; finally, it acts as a *guarantor*. He cites railroads as an example. Government actively promoted rail transport with right-of-way land grants and other subsidies late in the nineteenth century. Then railroads were closely regulated during the first half of this century. Finally, government now guarantees the railroads' existence. Much of the rail system has effectively been nationalized into Amtrak and Conrail. Similar scenarios have been played out in the nuclear, petroleum, and automobile industries (e.g., import restrictions against foreign cars).

Heilbroner's theory might extend to a fourth phase—*deregulation*. Many people seem tired of today's regulatory maze. The 1980 election of

Ronald Reagan signaled an abrupt halt to the creation of new regulatory agencies. He and his political allies found the voting public responsive when they argued that complex policies are often counterproductive.

Is it possible to reverse the upward trend of regulation? Perhaps, but most proposals to deregulate business have encountered fierce opposition. It seems paradoxical that, on a case-by-case basis, most individual regulations are fervently supported by large groups of people (including executives in regulated industries), despite public opinion polls suggesting that most people perceive regulation to be excessive.

Surprisingly, regulated industries spearhead much of the resistance to deregulation. For example, consumer groups and the liquor industry joined to vigorously resist proposals to thoroughly deregulate alcoholic beverage production. The support of regulated firms for regulation is evidence that it often acts as a barrier to entry against potential competitors.

Before we can judge whether our society is overregulated, we need a sense of how profoundly regulation shapes the U.S. economy. The IRS, FAA, FTC, FDA, EPA, and SEC are only part of the alphabet soup of well-known federal regulators. Table 1 lists some major federal regulatory agencies and describes their functions.

Why Is Business Regulated?

Some people view market systems as rife with fraud, discrimination, dangerous working conditions, and other maladies. In previous chapters, you saw how monopoly power may cause apparent inequity and economic inefficiency, which also arise from externalities or public goods problems. Regulation is one possible remedy for some market failures.

The **public interest theory of regulation** *is the idea that people need protection from business abuses. This theory assumes that regulation serves the public's interest by restricting harmful business activities.*

This rationale for regulation went unchallenged for years. When regulation has not operated in the public interest, a standard interpretation is that these imperfections are simply consequences of imperfect people doing their jobs as regulators in imperfect ways. Only recently has this explanation for regulatory peccadilloes been questioned.

After decades of studying the American economy, George Stigler identified numerous instances where regulation failed to guard public interests. He asked an obvious question: If the public interests are not being served, whose are? His answer turned previous theory on its head.

The **industry interest theory of regulation** *asserts that regulation is often tailored to serve the interests of regulated industries instead of those of the general public.*

This theory helps explain instances, for example, where regulatory barriers to entry protect existing firms from new competition.

The public choice approach described in the previous chapter offers a final possible explanation for regulatory behavior.

The **public choice theory of regulation** *emphasizes that bureaucrats produce complex regulations so that their power and budgets will grow.*

This perspective is a close relative of Stigler's industry interest theory. Public choice models frequently link special-interest laws and regulations with the interests of the bureaucrats who administer them. We will examine the traditional rationale for regulation — the public interest theory — before reviewing alternative interpretations.

The Public Interest and Business Regulation

The public interest theory of regulation centers on some possible market failures: externalities, monopoly power, and imperfect information.

Table 1 *Some Major Federal Regulatory Agencies*

Agency	Areas of Concern and Major Regulatory Function(s)
	Product Markets
Antitrust Division of the Justice Dept.	Promotes competition by enforcing federal antitrust laws.
Federal Communications Commission	Regulates broadcasting, telephone, and other communication services.
Federal Maritime Commission	Regulates foreign and domestic ocean commerce.
Federal Trade Commission	Protects consumers from unfair trade practices, false advertising, and overly restrictive licensing.
Interstate Commerce Commission	Regulates interstate surface transportation, including trucking, railroads, and water carriers.
	Labor Markets
Equal Employment Opportunity Commission	Investigates complaints of discrimination based on race, religion, sex, or age in hiring, promotion, firing, wages, testing, and all other conditions of employment.
National Labor Relations Board	Regulates and enforces collective bargaining agreements between companies and unions, and certifies elections of bargaining representatives.
	Financial Markets
Commodity Futures Trading Commission	Regulates futures trading on eleven U.S. futures exchanges.
Comptroller of the Currency	Supervises operations of over 4,700 national banks.
Federal Deposit Insurance Corporation	Examines, insures, and regulates banks.
Federal Home Loan Bank Board	Supervises and regulates savings institutions that specialize in financing of residential real estate.
Federal Reserve Board	Regulates banks and all financial institutions that offer draftable (checking) accounts.
Securities & Exchange Commission	Regulates all public securities markets to promote full disclosure.
	Energy and Environment
Corps of Engineers	Oversees construction along rivers, harbors, and waterways.
Environmental Protection Agency	Develops and enforces environmental standards for air, water, toxic waste, and noise.
Department of Energy	Oversees national energy policy.
Nuclear Regulatory Commission	Licenses and regulates civilian nuclear power facilities to protect public health and safety and the environment.
	Health and Safety
Consumer Product Safety Commission	Requires reporting of product defects and redesign and labeling to reduce unreasonable risks of injury from consumer products.
Federal Aviation Administration	Regulates aviation industry.
Food & Drug Administration	Protects against impure and unsafe foods, drugs, and cosmetics, and other potential hazards.
Occupational Safety & Health Administration	Regulates workplace safety and health conditions.
National Highway Traffic Safety Administration	Regulates motor vehicle safety through safety standards, uniform national speed limit, and protects consumers from vehicles with reset odometers.

Source: U.S. Office of the Federal Register, *The United States Government Manual* 1990–1991.

Problems of monopoly power and externalities are the foundations for much of business regulation. The idea that imperfect information adversely affects market solutions is used most to rationalize laws regulating consumer protection and labor markets.

Regulating Natural Monopolies

Using antitrust policy to lessen monopoly power by breaking up huge firms may inefficiently raise costs. If the minimum efficient scale of production (*MES*) is high relative to market demand, then at most a few firms can achieve the lowest possible production costs. Government provides highways, but most other natural monopolies (industries with such extensive economies of scale that only one firm can operate efficiently) are privately owned — e.g., electric generation, railroads, cable TV, and the distribution of natural gas. Requiring competition among small firms inefficiently denies the public the lower costs and prices available through economies of scale. But how can policymakers prevent natural monopolies from limiting output and raising prices?

The dilemma a natural monopoly poses is diagramed in Figure 2, which shows how economies of scale may allow only one firm to operate efficiently. If two firms each produced Q_m, average total costs for each firm would be AC_m. Since $2Q_M = Q_0$, limited demand drops the prices (P_0) these two firms could charge far below AC_m. Having two or more firms is unsustainable, because each would lose money until only one survived. If consumers bought from an unregulated monopoly, however, output would be limited to Q_m and sold at price P_m, possibly exceeding the price associated with some competition. Price exceeds marginal cost in this monopoly solution, so there is economic inefficiency.

The public interest is served best if only one firm exploits these economies of scale and then prices appropriately. A regulated uniform price restricted to a "fair price" P_r would yield normal profits, and consumers would pay less than the unregulated price P_m. However, socially optimal pricing and output requires that $P = MC$. Could a regulator reasonably require that the last unit Q_0 be sold at price P_0 so that efficiency is realized? If a price of P_0 is charged for each unit of output, the firm's revenue equals area $0P_0aQ_0$, which is inadequate to cover total costs equaling area $0P_1bQ_0$. No firm would be willing to stay in business if regulations forced such constant

FIGURE 2 The Dilemma of the Natural Monopolist

An unregulated monopolist will charge P_m, which is far above marginal cost (*MC*) and results in severe problems for the goals of efficiency and equity. The "fair price" P_r will just cover costs but still exceeds *MC* and so results in inefficiency. A uniform socially optimal price, P_0, would be efficient but would not cover average total cost (P_1). No firm would be willing to suffer losses consistently, which poses a dilemma for society. How can we secure efficiency and still ensure that investors in firms of this type receive fair rates of return?

losses. Fortunately, a form of price discrimination provides a way out of this quandary.

Block Pricing Block pricing techniques can efficiently generate sufficient revenues to cover all costs, including a normal rate of return for a regulated monopolist.

> *In a* **block pricing** *system the more you use of the regulated monopolist's product, the lower the price for extra units.*

For example, block pricing is used for electricity rates. You pay a hookup fee and then a minimum monthly charge. As you use more electricity, your total bill rises but the rate per extra kilowatt hour declines. Figure 3 replicates the cost and demand data in Figure 2 but shows that with block pricing, revenues (the entire shaded area) can cover costs (the entire crosshatched area). Because the price of the last unit equals its production cost in this example, marginal social benefit equals marginal social cost and this market operates efficiently. Notice that block pricing uses price discrimination to yield efficiency.

Block pricing is commonly used for public utilities (natural gas, electric, and telephone services), for railroads and other forms of regulated transportation, and for pipelines.

Rate Making In practice, utility regulation is a complex process that absorbs the efforts of thousands of people. **Rate making** (setting utility prices) requires the agency to select a base period for calculations (usually the preceding year). All the firm's operating costs, including depreciation and taxes, are then summed. A reasonable accounting profit, derived by multiplying the rate base by the percentage rate of profit allowed, is added to operating costs.

> *The* **rate base** *is the value of capital to which the profit rate applies. The regulator ideally adjusts* **rate structures** *so that total revenue covers all operating costs, including a normal profit.*

Desires for minimal rates must be weighed against allowing normal rates of return. This trade-off invariably provokes disagreements

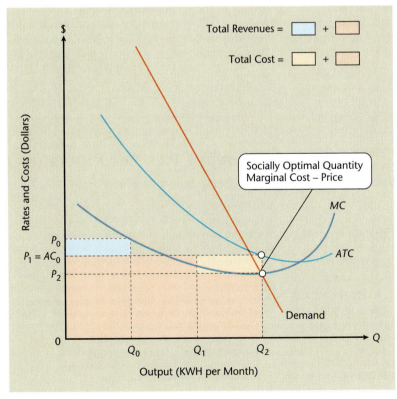

Total Revenues = ☐ + ☐

Total Cost = ☐ + ☐

Socially Optimal Quantity
Marginal Cost – Price

MC

ATC

P_0

$P_1 = AC_0$

P_2

Demand

0   Q_0 Q_1 Q_2 Q

Output (KWH per Month)

Rates and Costs (Dollars)

FIGURE 3   How Block Pricing Permits Revenues to Cover Costs and Facilitates Efficiency ($MSB = MSC$)

Block pricing, a form of price discrimination used by regulatory bodies to set rate structures, permits a firm to cover its costs and, at the same time, facilitates economic efficiency. For the first Q_0 units, you pay an average price of P_0, for units $Q_1 - Q_0$, price falls to P_1, and for the final $Q_2 - Q_1$ units, price equals P_2. The price charged for the last unit of output (approximately the marginal social benefit) equals the marginal social cost of production. Because $MSB = MSC$, we have economic efficiency.

about (*a*) appropriate values for items allowed in the rate base, (*b*) "fair" rates of return, and (*c*) how to structure rates. A utility has few incentives for efficiency if all "costs" are allowed. Executive limousines, private jets, resort homes, and similar luxuries would all become "costs." On the other hand, rates must adequately protect the financial health of the utility for it to attract investors. Finally, the regulatory commission must continually monitor the quality of service.

Practical Problems   Utility commissions normally target rates of return in the 8 to 12 percent range. Changes in fuel costs, demand, or efficiency can cause sustained deviations from the target return, prompting the regulatory commission to adjust the rates. When people are not especially concerned about their utility bills, regulated monopolies may operate inefficiently and still squeeze favorable rate structures from regulators. When higher costs arouse the public, however, utility companies may be unable to charge rates high enough to cover costs.

Some economists are skeptical that consumers gain from utility regulation. Regulation tends to become rigid and unresponsive to changing conditions. In fact, many of these economists argue that unregulated monopolies might outperform their regulated cousins. Nevertheless, the prospects for much deregulation in this area seem remote.

Control over pricing is the standard approach used to restrict the monopoly power of natural monopolies. Direct regulation, however, is generally used instead of the price system to manage externalities, which present a different type of market failure.

Externalities and Direct Regulation

Benefits or costs to a party not directly involved in an activity are *externalities*. Some forms of auto safety equipment convey externalities. Others do not. Seat belts and air bags, for example, protect only a car's occupants and could be sold just like air scoops, stereos, and so on. Drivers and their passengers are the primary beneficiaries of this equipment. It directly protects the individual buying it, and externalities are negligible.[1]

Shock-absorbing bumpers, on the other hand, generate externalities. The buyer gains, but other drivers do as well. Damages are reduced when a car with a shock-absorbing bumper collides with other cars. External benefits are bestowed on passengers of cars with regular bumpers, but payments for such external benefits are impossible to collect. Thus, private purchases of shock-absorbing bumpers will be less than socially optimal, so carmakers are now required to provide such bumpers. This is an example of a positive externality in which regulation governs the form of a good. Compulsory education and inoculations against communicable diseases also entail positive externalities.

Negative externalities spread costs beyond the transaction in question. If a firm discharges waste into a stream, people who use the stream for recreation pay part of the costs, even if they never buy the product. No firm will adequately control its waste voluntarily if cleaning up imposes costs not borne by its competitors. Competitors will undercut price premiums that cover the higher costs of nonpolluting firms. Government intervention may be necessary to compensate for these third-party costs. Direct regulation generally limits some forms of pollution and forbids other, more dangerous pollutants. We leave a detailed discussion of environmental policies to the next chapter.

Alternative Views of Regulation

The state—the machinery and power of the state—is a potential resource or threat to every industry in the society. With its power to prohibit or compel, to take or give money, the state can and does selectively help or hurt a vast number of industries.

George J. Stigler[2]

---

1. This argument ignores the effect on insurance rates of added injuries to occupants who do not wear protective restraints, and also assumes that harm to passengers consists only of medical costs.
2. George J. Stigler, "The Theory of Economic Regulation," *The Bell Journal of Economic & Management Science*, Spring 1971.

George Stigler (b. 1911–1992)

The politicians who invited George Stigler to a White House dinner after he was awarded a Nobel Prize in 1982 were dismayed when Stigler, during a press conference, described the economy as in a depression. His friends were not surprised. Stigler's record of advocating laissez-faire policies is matched by a reputation for being a straight shooter who calls them as he sees them.

The University of Chicago's "school" of economic thought has been known for its opposition to activist government policies throughout this century. Tall and lanky George Stigler shared stewardship over this tradition with his short, fellow Nobel Prize–winning friend, Milton Friedman, for almost half a century. Friedman is best known for his work in macroeconomics and monetary theory, while Stigler was a pioneer in the study of modern microeconomics.

Stigler's research provided evidence for the notion that genius often consists of an ability to see old ideas in new ways. He received his Ph.D. in 1938 from the University of Chicago and spent most of his career there, with occasional side tours to

Minnesota, Columbia, and the London School of Economics. He extended the frontiers of economic study in many areas, including industrial organization, the economics of information, and the sources and effects of government regulation. A hallmark of his work was rigorous hypothesis testing to ascertain which economic theories seem supported by real-world data.

Stigler fundamentally disagreed with those who view the market system as inherently defective because few markets conform to the assumptions of pure or perfect competition. Stigler found that industries characterized by monopolistic competition or oligopoly act much more competitively with respect to price, than most models of imperfect competition predict. In particular, he rejected the sticky prices assumed in the kinked demand curve model. Empirical work that found no relationship between price "stickiness" and market structure led him to urge the abandonment of kinked demand models.

Stigler was among the first to consider information as an economic good that consumers and firms alike pursue until its mar-

ginal benefits and marginal costs are equal. Stigler's seminal 1961 article fueled an explosion of research effort that helped launch the economics of information as a major subdiscipline of economics. He was also the first major modern economist to perceive that regulation is often instigated by the regulated. His extended studies of antitrust policies and regulation made him extremely skeptical that much government economic activity is in the public interest.

Another focus of his interest was the sociology of economics as a field of study. His essays on the development of economic theory and methodology are a staple of economists' reading lists. When Stigler challenged his grandson to name Adam Smith's best friend, the youngster is said to have responded, "You, Grandpa." (Most likely correct answer: David Hume.) Nevertheless, the boy's answer accurately reflected George Stigler's lasting enthusiasm for the ideas of the eighteenth-century Scottish moral philosopher and economist.

The public interest rationale for regulation prevailed until the 1970s, when George Stigler fundamentally changed the way most economists view much of economic regulation. If the public interest approach is correct, we would expect regulation primarily in highly concentrated industries (to regulate monopoly power), in industries with significant economies of scale, or in those exhibiting substantial externalities. But many regulations in such areas as taxi service, air transportation, trucking, and some professional licensing arrangements (barbering, for example) find little support in the public interest rationale.

Does Business Gain from Regulation?

The Constitution gives Congress power "to regulate commerce among the several states." The government can tax, compel resource allocations, or change the economic decisions of households and firms without their consent. The state can use these great powers to raise or lower profitability in any industry through four major mechanisms:

1. Direct subsidies to the industry, special tax breaks or punitive taxes, or advantageous or harmful operating regulations.

2. Restriction or encouragement of entry or exit (e.g., barriers on imports).

3. Subsidies, taxes, or limitations on complementary or substitute products.

4. Direct price-fixing policies (price floors or ceilings).

All four mechanisms have altered profitability in many industries. The merchant marine is heavily subsidized, as is education. Entry restrictions were effective in the airline industry, where the Civil Aeronautics Board (CAB) did not license a single new trunk line during the 40 years after its establishment in 1938. Another example is regulation of trucking by the Interstate Commerce Commission (ICC). In the 1960s and 1970s, applications for new truck lines averaged over 5,000 annually, while the number of firms in operation continually shrank.[3] Law and medi-

cine, too, are professions that benefit from restrictions on entry. Restrictions on the number of taxicabs that can operate in New York city have resulted in a $100,000 current value of taxi "medallions."[4]

Government policies also affect an industry's substitutes and complements. Laws banning the use of yellow food dyes that allowed margarine to mimic butter's appearance were enacted in the 1950s, when the dairy industry fought to hold its market for butter. Truckers vigorously support improvements to interstate highways. Naturally, railroads oppose their development. Construction unions have successfully opposed reforms to local building codes that block labor-saving technology. The consequence is that many building codes require outdated, labor intensive construction techniques that drive costs up but provide employment for union workers. Direct price-fixing is found in milk and cheese price supports and in many farm and tobacco subsidy programs.

Few of these regulation are in the public interest. Some advocates of regulation blame incompetent managers for failing to guard the public interest. Others argue that agencies are often "captured" by the regulated industry. Regulators need expertise, and what better source for expertise to help solve problems than from within the industry? Constant contact with industry experts frequently persuades regulators of industry positions. This helps explain why regulations often favor the industry rather than the public and why many states now fund consumer advocacy agencies.

Economic Models of Regulation

George Stigler concludes that public interest theories fail to explain most regulations because they assume that business opposes regulation. Assuming instead that firms seek regulations to serve their own interests yields inferences vastly different from those based on public interest theories. His *industry interest* theory views government as the supplier of regulatory services to an

---

3. *Ibid.*

4. Donald Dewey, *The Antitrust Experiment in America* (New York: Columbia University Press, 1990), p. 15.

industry. These services are paid for through lobbying or campaign contributions to policymakers who favor regulations the established firms want.

All firms seek monopoly power and abhor "cutthroat" competition; most would prefer to be part of a cartel. Cheating by members, however, causes unregulated cartels to disintegrate. One way to stabilize a cartel is through regulation of entry and prices. The major benefit of regulation to an industry is probably entry restriction.

Curiously, cartels are outlawed in some instances and implemented through law in others. Thus, railroads supported passage of the Interstate Commerce Act, early airlines favored establishment of the Civil Aeronautics Board, and so on. Regulated industries commonly mount major political offensives against proposed deregulation, but convictions of Teamster's Union officials in 1982 for trying to bribe a member of Congress to oppose trucking deregulation are evidence that firms are not the only beneficiaries of regulation.

Occupational licensing is a barrier to entry for barbers, lawyers, plumbers, dog groomers, realtors, doctors, travel agents. . . . You can be jailed or fined if you operate without a license. The call for licensing is often clothed in public interest rhetoric so that the public will not notice its pockets being picked. As higher earnings stimulate the supply of potential entrants into a profession, entry restrictions evolve that impose ever higher qualifications for new applicants. Higher standards frequently bar would-be members of a profession with credentials superior to those of "grandfathered" long-term practitioners. Of course, all this is done in the name of increasing professional quality for the public.

Regulation and Public Choice The public choice theory of regulation recognizes the importance of an industry's interests in shaping the regulatory environment. It augments the industry interest approach by pointing out that regulatory bureaucrats also have personal interests. Regulation may be excessively complex, for example, because this increases personnel requirements, feeding into empire building by heads of government agencies. Bureaucrats' power is enhanced when laws are broadly written so that

regulators have substantial discretion over the form of regulation. This elicits lobbying by regulated firms and provides a market for experts in the field, who switch jobs back and forth between an industry and its regulators.

Public choice theory combines with Stigler's industry interest theory to explain much of regulation. The voice of business is not the only input into regulatory processes, however, and in many cases, firms have conflicting interests. Real concerns about social well-being permeate both the political process and administrative agencies, and genuine public interest considerations may prevail.

In summary, rationales for government intervention in business activities emerge from several sources. Some regulations are responses to externalities. Other controls are based on economies of scale in production or the nature of the product itself. Some regulation arises from an industry's ability to promote its self-interest; some also serves the bureaucrats charged with administering the law, who gain power and larger budgets by expanding the scope and complexity of regulation. Each of these explanations seems to fit specific cases, but the overseeing of business is only part of the regulatory landscape. Consumers' activities are also shaped by governmental regulation.

Consumer Protection

Consumption is the sole end and purpose of all production; and the interest of the producer ought to be attended to only so far as it may be necessary for promoting that of the consumer.[5]

Adam Smith (1776)

Consumer protection is considered separately from business regulation because, even though firms are most directly regulated, consumers ultimately gain or lose from these rules. Who is regulated is unclear. Is the lawn mower industry regulated because it can sell only mowers with elaborate safety devices, or are consumers regulated because they are denied opportunities to

---

5. Adam Smith, *Wealth of Nations*.

buy cheaper but more dangerous mowers? Focus 1 indicates how profoundly even such standard consumer products as a hamburger are regulated.

If, as Adam Smith argued, business exists only to serve consumers' needs, then consumer protection laws may be a wasted effort; competitive firms fail if they serve consumers inadequately. But most people view fraud and other business abuses as widespread. No single approach addresses all the complex issues of consumer protection. Consider some arguments for and against consumer protection legislation.

Arguments Favoring Consumer Protection

Consumers are presumed capable of making reasoned choices to "vote" for the goods they want in a market economy. This assumption has much merit when simple goods are competitively produced. Consequently, the prevailing approach in this country for years was echoed by the doctrine of **caveat emptor:** "Let the buyer beware." Consumers alone felt the consequences for the use, misuse, safety, and overall quality of their purchases. Buyers bear the burden of proof when suing sellers for fraud or damage; the seller is presumed not liable unless proven guilty of fraud or some similar legal violation.

A landmark case in 1916 overturned the basic assumption of *caveat emptor*. Buick was held liable for injuries in *MacPherson v. Buick Motor Company* after a defective wooded wheel collapsed. The Supreme Court ruled that manufacturers are liable for negligently produced output. The field of product liability law grew from this case, and *caveat emptor* faded into the sunset. Experts in the field now often refer to the doctrine of **caveat venditor:** "Let the seller beware." Product liability has evolved into a complex field, but the pendulum has swung far in the direction of protecting consumers. With this legal coat of armor protecting the consumer, further regulation might seem unnecessary.

There are, however, other reasons to protect consumers. When externalities arise from consumption of a good, the private market may not "internalize" these benefits or costs properly.

The result is that too little is produced if externalities are positive, too much if externalities are negative. If unsafe lawn mowers harm third parties (via noise or property damage), these costs will not be borne solely by lawn mower owners. There will be more than an optimal number of hazardous and noisy lawn mowers.

Asymmetric Information The concept of *caveat emptor* implicitly assumes that consumers and producers share similar knowledge about product quality. This parity in knowledge may have been reasonably true in simpler times, but it is unrealistic for many complex modern products. This is the reason for laws requiring content labels on packaged foods and drugs, for "truth-in-lending" laws, and so on. Even with government requirements that producers reveal information, many products are so complicated that most consumers may not detect basic flaws. The time required for consumers to become technically knowledgeable about such things as cars and electronic equipment is obviously prohibitive.

The problems of **moral hazard** and **adverse selection** may also justify consumer protection. Moral hazard occurs when some parties (e.g., sellers) have incentives not to fulfill their duties under a contract. If you pay in advance for aluminum siding for your house, the firm that made the sale has an incentive to skip town or do a poor job.

Asymmetric information prior to a contract may induce adverse selection—one party may agree to terms that would be unacceptable if information were shared. For example, a pro basketball team might trade a player with a hidden drug problem, knowing he is unlikely to help his new team. Or lack of automotive safety might be disguised if problems were uncovered after production was under way. The Ford Pinto case is a notorious example.[6] Firms also commonly have better information than workers about on-the-

---

6. Ford was acquitted of criminal charges involving the dangerous placement of gas tanks in its Pinto. Nevertheless, Ford lost millions of dollars in suits brought by people maimed when rear-ended Pintos exploded.

Have It Their Way

Your Hamburger: 41,000 Regulations

PICTOGRAM ®

The hamburger, staple of the quick, inexpensive meal, is the subject of 41,000 federal and state regulations, many of those stemming from 200 laws and 111,000 precedent-setting court cases.

These rules, cited in a three-volume study by Colorado State University, touch on everything involved in meat production—grazing practices of cattle, conditions in slaughterhouses and methods used to process meat for sale to supermarkets, restaurants and fast-food outlets. Together, they add an estimated 8 to 11 cents per pound to the cost of hamburger.

The chart on this page gives just a sampling of the rules and regulations governing the burger you buy at the corner sandwich stand.

Pesticides—No more than 5 parts of the pesticide DDT per million parts of fat in the meat.

Bun—Enriched bun must contain at least 1.8 milligrams of thiamine, 1.1 milligrams of riboflavin and at least 8 but not more than 12.5 milligrams of iron.

Content—It must be fresh or frozen chopped beef and not contain added water, binders or extenders.

Growth promoters—Use of growth-stimulating drugs must end two weeks before slaughter.

Fat—No more than 30 percent fat content.

Pickle—Slices must be between ⅛ and ⅜ inches thick.

Lettuce—Must be fresh, not soft, overgrown, burst or "ribby."

Tomato—Must be mature but not overripe or soft.

Cheese—Must contain at least 50 percent milk fat and, if made with milk that is not pasteurized, must be cured for 60 or more days at a temperature of at least 35 degrees Fahrenheit.

Ketchup

Mayonnaise

Ketchup—To be considered Grade A fancy, it must flow no more than 9 centimeters in 30 seconds at 69 degrees Fahrenheit.

Mayonnaise—May be seasoned or flavored as long as the substances do not color it to look like egg yolk.

Inspections—As many as six inspections under Federal Meat Inspection Act can occur as meat is checked before and after slaughter and at boning, grinding, fabrication and packaging stages.

Source: Reprinted from U.S. News & World Report issue of Feb. 11, 1980. Copyright, Feb. 11, 1980, U.S. News & World Report.

job safety. Many people believe that imperfect information justifies regulation to control fraud, product safety, and occupational safety and health.

Under either *caveat emptor* or *caveat venditor*, people may buy or sell goods subject to legal recourse. Government, however, flatly prohibits production, sale, or purchase of some goods. Heroin, cyclamates, and flammable clothing for children are only a few examples. In these cases, consumers are considered unable to properly assess information. Curiously, some goods only suspected of being harmful, such as food colorings, are prohibited, while harmful substances like tobacco or alcohol are permitted. (Major reasons are the power of special-interest lobbying and wide acceptance of limited "rights" to smoke or drink — the prohibition of alcohol during the 1920s is regarded by most Americans as a failed experiment.)

Verifying advertisers' claims sometimes may require purchase and use, but a consumer can lose a bundle testing high-priced goods. Firms usually have information on rates of product failure. How can consumers protect themselves? Reasonable certainty regarding quality and safety can be provided by regulation. This certainty has the attributes of a public good and can be shared at zero marginal cost among consumers. For example, if medicine is uniformly of high quality because of regulation, your sense of security when taking a drug does not reduce my sense of security in taking the same medicine. This is another strong argument for government intervention.

Arguments Against Consumer Protection

Opponents of consumer protection laws point to consumers' losses of economic freedom because the range of available products is reduced. Competition alone, they argue, forces business to respond to consumer needs. Most concede, however, that markets do not operate infallibly. Any good may either exceed or fall short of expectations. Modern production techniques may limit defects, but imperfections always remain.

Consumers desiring safer products might obtain them by paying higher prices to cover the higher costs. Individuals differ in their willingness to incur risk, which should be reflected in the types of goods they consume. Consumer protection rules tend to destroy product diversity, one major benefit of the market system.

Opponents of consumer protection legislation also argue that the poor are hurt most by this form of government intervention. Poor people have very limited budgets, so they may have to buy goods of inferior quality if they are to consume at all. If regulation eliminates lower quality products, the poor may be effectively prohibited from consuming some kinds of goods. Wealthier groups can afford the added costs and generally buy higher quality goods in any event. For example, compulsory auto safety equipment drives up the relative prices of economy cars far more than those of luxury cars, which often have safety equipment as standard features — and even then, many people do not wear their seat belts, even where laws require their use. As a result, the rich are relatively less affected by consumer product safety legislation, while lower income groups bear its brunt.

Finally, opponents argue that safer products may not reduce accidents to the extent predicted. Some studies of how auto safety devices affect the overall accident and injury rate have produced startling results. Sam Peltzman concludes in one such study that enhanced vehicular safety leads to changes in drivers' behavior.[7] He argues that, housed in safer cars, some drivers become more reckless, causing more accidents, higher insurance rates, and increased pedestrian deaths. Traffic fatalities continue to rise despite mandatory safety equipment and lower speed limits. The evidence is incomplete, however, and considerable research remains before conclusive results can be obtained.

Consumer protection may be warranted when product externalities exist, when products are so technologically sophisticated that sellers have superior information about product quality, or when the price of a good is so high and purchases are so infrequent that a single loss to a consumer

---

7. Sam Peltzman, "The Effects of Automobile Safety Regulation," *Journal of Political Economy*, 1975, p. 667.

would spell disaster. Alternatively, consumer protection reduces freedom, may inhibit quick responses to consumer demands, reduces product choices, and may not accomplish the desired goal of safer products. These and other regulatory problems make the practical aspects of regulation challenging.

Other Regulations in Practice

Consumer regulations are diverse and varied, but they can be separated into a few categories. The earliest consumer protection statutes dealt with protecting the consumer from food, drugs, or cosmetics that were mislabeled, misbranded, or adulterated. A second group of laws protects consumers from unfair competition and false or misleading advertising. A third category deals with product safety, which was recognized as an important issue when the Consumer Product Safety Commission was established in 1972. In the labor market, several agencies protect workers from hazardous working conditions, discrimination based on sex or race, and abuses by management or unions of workers' fundamental right to collective representation. Another broad category of regulation hems in the financial and banking industry.

Perspectives on Regulation

Critics argue that red tape drives up the cost of living, and that the costs of bureaucratic rules governing business escalate every year. Both *direct* and *indirect* costs must be considered to evaluate this argument.

Direct Costs of Regulation

The direct costs of regulation include the *administrative costs* of operating regulatory agencies and the *compliance costs* incurred by regulated entities.

> **Direct costs of regulation** *include* (a) admin-istrative costs *to the government (employee salaries, office supplies, and other "overhead" expenses), and* (b) compliance costs *incurred*

by regulated entities (primarily the private sector, but also by other governmental units that must comply with regulations).

A 1981 study by Murray Weidenbaum (subsequently, Chair of the President's Council of Economic Advisors) and Robert DeFina estimated some direct costs of federal regulation.[8] They found that compliance costs were 20 times larger than administrative costs. Extrapolating their results to 1990, nearly $250 billion is now absorbed annually to meet federal regulations — roughly one-third of current U.S. private investment, or $1,000 per U.S. citizen. This $250 billion estimate probably understates total direct costs, because data were unavailable for nearly 20 major regulatory agencies.

Indirect Costs of Regulation

Government budget outlays have swollen as public demands for regulatory programs have grown. The costs of government go far beyond the national budget, however, because even programs with laudable objectives may generate indirect costs through their effects on workers, consumers, and other participants on the economic stage.

> **Indirect costs of regulation** *are undesirable changes in behavior in response to regulations, and resemble the excess burdens of taxation.*

Consider unemployment compensation. Many workers effectively receive paid vacations if they are laid off. Unemployment compensation is largely untaxed and is often as high as 80 percent of a worker's take-home wage. Thus, this program creates incentives for some people to work irregularly, sticking the burden on workers with stable jobs.

Similarly, government programs intended to protect family farmers instead enrich large corporate farms. The higher food prices consumers

---

8. M. Weidenbaum and R. DeFina, *The Rising Cost of Government Regulation* (St. Louis: Center for the Study of American Business, 31 Jan. 1981).

pay are largely overlooked when government costs are analyzed. These programs also create incredible surpluses of some farm goods. Every man, woman, and child in America would need to eat a box of cornflakes every day for a year to eliminate the corn now stored at government expense.

Taxes are also distortive. Many employee benefits are disguised as legitimate business expenses. Firms offer tax-free fringe benefits to their employees because, were these benefits paid in cash, employees' income taxes would rise. Thus, many employees join country clubs that they would not join if the firm were not paying their dues, drive company cars that are newer and grander than cars they would buy for themselves, and eat more elaborate lunches than they would if they were paying their own tabs.

Finally, business executives worry about how regulators might interpret a business decision. Consequently, they may not do what is necessary to innovate, cut costs, and service consumers at the lowest feasible prices. We have estimates of the direct costs of regulatory compliance, but how about the indirect costs of having talented people who look for loopholes around taxes or regulations instead of improving a firm's products?

Indirect costs are incurred whenever people adjust to policies in ways not intended by policymakers. It may be that regulations are complex because many people find ways to avoid simpler rules. The complicated lives we lead while adjusting to a maze of bureaucratic rules are among the indirect costs of government. When all direct and indirect costs of all federal, state, and local regulations are considered, regulation probably absorbs 5 to 10 percent of our national income. But costs are only one side of the regulatory equation; a balanced view would require estimates of the benefits of government regulation or deregulation. Unfortunately, data are not available that would permit scientific estimates of the benefits of regulation.

There seems to be a consensus that some regulation is necessary. But when has regulation gone too far? The president of Dow Chemical Company contends that one-third of the millions Dow spends on environmental, transportation, health and safety, and other forms of regulation is wasted. He cited a case where Dow spent $60,000 per plant to lower all railings from 42 inches to roughly 32 inches to meet Occupational Safety and Health Administration (OSHA) requirements. This was done even though Dow's studies had concluded that the 42-inch railings were considerably safer.[9] These examples and the study by Weidenbaum and DeFina attest to the costliness of regulation, which is ultimately reflected in lower business profits, less income to workers, and higher rates of unemployment. In the neighborhood of $200 to $400 billion is devoted to regulatory activity. Big government may create problems just as enormous as those posed by big business or big labor.

Deregulation and Reregulation

Numerous politicians have pledged to reduce government intervention in the private sector. The news media regularly report horror stories about overregulation. The past 15 years have ushered in substantial deregulation of trucking, airlines, banking, and a few other industries. Increased competition in these industries pushed prices down sharply. The economic pressures generated from airline deregulation led to many changes in the industry, including Continental Airlines' use of the federal bankruptcy statute to void its union contracts. (Focus 2 discusses airline deregulation in detail.)

Regulation often involves a complex combination of price and entry restrictions that can lead to higher prices and less service. Moreover, the competition among regulated firms tends to ignore pricing and be especially focused on advertising, product quality, or new product development. Regulation is often a compromise among conflicting public interest, industry interest, and bureaucratic objectives, which makes the results of deregulation somewhat unpredictable. Deregulation of the American Telephone and Telegraph Company taught us that deregulating the provision of a good or service often involves sub-

---

9. *Business Week*, April 4, 1977, p. 50.

FOCUS 2

The Airlines: Caveat Deregulator?

Few events from the Carter-Reagan eras generated more controversy than the Airline Deregulation Act of 1978. This act rolled back four decades of regulation that, according to the then Civil Aeronautics Board chairman, Alfred Kahn,* had

a. Resulted in higher air fares than without regulation.
b. Resulted in a serious misallocation of resources.
c. Encouraged carrier inefficiency.
d. Denied consumers a range of price/service options.
e. Created considerable excess capacity in the industry.

Although consensus among industry experts is lacking after a decade of deregulation, several facts are undisputed. First, after a brief flurry of new entrants like People Express, Southwest, and New York Air, most either went bankrupt or merged with other carriers. After an early expansion from 30 to 38 airlines, the industry has contracted, through 11 mergers and 16 acquisitions, so eight major carriers now control

*Reported in Alfred Kahn, "The Theory and Application of Regulation," Antitrust Law Journal, Vol. 177, 1986. Similar conclusions were reached by a Senate Subcommittee chaired by Sen. Edward Kennedy in 1976.

90 percent of revenue and passenger miles. Second, every major carrier has converted from linear route structures to national hub and spoke networks, resulting in greater carrier concentration at smaller airports. Third, average ticket prices, after adjusting for inflation, are down roughly 15 percent. And finally, airlines have lost billions since deregulation and have had an industry profit rate well below that in most other industries.

A Brookings Institute study estimates a $12 billion (in 1990 dollars) annual "improvement in the welfare of travelers with the largest proportion going to business travelers from increased flight frequency." Today, the industry is clearly more concentrated, but offers more flights at a lower cost. But not all travelers have enjoyed these reduced fares. Fares in 698 travel markets dominated by a single carrier are 14 percent higher than in competitive markets. Travel in the eight most concentrated hubs averaged nearly 20 percent more than the domestic average.†

The Department of Transportation notes that the hub and spoke systems "offer travelers convenient service to more desti-

†U.S. Department of Transportation, Secretary's Task Force on Competition in the U.S. Domestic Airline Industry, 1990, pp. 7–8.

nations than did the linear systems they replaced" and that hubs require a larger volume of frequent service to be efficient and this will naturally lead to greater concentration. Thus the economies of scale of hub and spoke networks require greater concentration, but enable carriers to use their labor and equipment more efficiently and provide better service to passengers. Figure 4 shows how one carrier, Northwest, has adapted its route structure to deregulation.

Critics contend that hub concentration is due not so much to the search for economies, but to the search for monopoly power to avoid the ruinous effects of unrestrained destructive competition. Airlines sell an instantly perishable product. Once a flight has left, the revenue lost from empty seats cannot be recovered. Seats do not sit in inventory like many other commodities. Since the marginal cost of filling empty seats approaches zero, any revenue represents a contribution to overhead and price discrimination is inevitable. By garnering pockets of monopoly power, price competition can be reduced. Figure 5 supports this contention that air carriers have used hub concentration as safe harbors and have used this power to raise fares.

Proponents of deregulation argue that airline markets are

Panel A

FIGURE 4 Northwest Airlines' Route Structure Before and After Deregulation

The deregulated competitive environment has resulted in all major carriers adopting a hub and spoke system (Panel B) to replace their previous linear systems. This new structure permits carriers to use their people and equipment more efficiently and provide a greater range of services to customers.

Source: U.S. Department of Transportation, *Secretary's Task Force on Competition in the U.S. Domestic Airline Industry*, 1990.

Dominant Carrier Share – 75% or more

Dominant Carrier Share – 50 – 75%

Dominant Carrier Share Less Than 50%

FIGURE 5 Changes in Average Fares for Large Hubs, 1979—1988

Source: U.S. Department of Transportation, *Secretary's Task Force on Competition in the U.S. Domestic Airline Industry*, 1990.

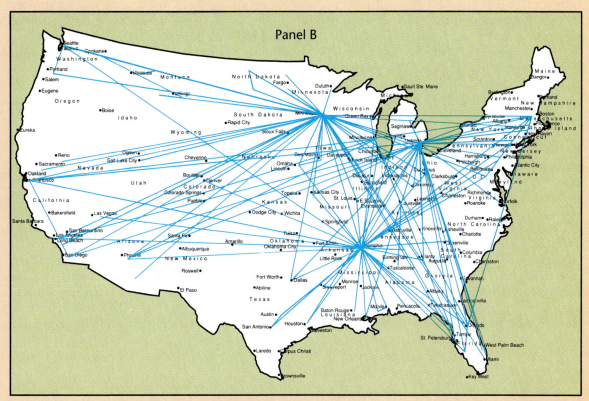

Panel B

contestable and that potential competition would keep fares in check. Recent studies suggest that the industry is not *perfectly* contestable, but the authors of one recent study conclude‡:

Limited contestability in many markets does not, however, support the conclusion that there is a need to reregulate the airlines. While the existence of market power may result in increased fares in some routes, it is not clear that these fares are higher than they would be under regulation. In addition, while fares on spoke-to-hub routes may be higher, there is a compensating gain to passengers. Service on many

routes is more frequent and the number of destinations served is larger because of the advantages of the hub and spoke system.

Finally, airline safety is a major issue with critics of deregulation. Destructive competition and the accompanying lower profits, they argue, create a natural tendency of management to cut corners with maintenance and safety. In the decade since deregulation, however, accidents each year per 100,000 flights have averaged half of the previous decade under regulation. Critics argue that this reduced accident rate is due to increased vigilance by the FAA and cockpit crews, and that increased monopoly power has reduced the pressure to cut corners.

The overall effect of deregulation of the airlines is the subject of an ongoing controversy. Con-

centration has increased, fares and profits are down, and airline safety seems secure. A decade may not be enough time for all answers to emerge. The industry can expect to be under a microscope for at least the next decade as calls for reregulation emerge from unions, companies, and some communities.

Sources: Steven Morrison and Clifford Winston, The Economic Effects of Airline Deregulation, *(Washington, D.C.: The Brookings Institution), 1986, Paul S. Dempsey,* Flying Blind: The Failure of Airline Deregulation, *(New York: Economic Policy Institute), 1990 and U.S. Department of Transportation,* Secretary's Task Force on Competition in the U.S. Domestic Airline Industry, *1990.*

‡Richard V. Butler and John H. Huston, "How Contestable are Airline Markets?," *Atlantic Economic Journal, June 1989, pp. 33–35.*

markets that may be quite different from each other. Deregulation that works well in one submarket may be less successful in another.

Problems of Deregulation That deregulation may be disruptive is evidenced by the turmoil and declines in national income throughout much of Eastern Europe (especially the USSR) as tightly regimented economies begin uneasy transitions toward less regulation. On a slightly smaller scale, almost every form of deregulation entails a certain amount of costly confusion. This is especially true when only one side of balanced sets of regulations are eliminated.

The recent U.S. savings-and-loan crisis is an example. Deregulation advocates failed to consider the *moral hazards* that arise if financial institutions are allowed to invest in almost any harebrained scheme while a government insurance program guarantees the first $100,000 of each account in insured institutions. The lesson of this calamity is not that this deregulation was a big mistake but, rather, that deregulation must be studied carefully so that such problems can be anticipated and remedied. The S&Ls that collapsed in the late 1980s probably would not have had as much money to play with if insurance on deposits had been eliminated for financial intermediaries that chose risky investment strategies and if this absence of insurance had been publicized.

Although deregulation has received a lot of publicity, every attempt at deregulation appears to be more than offset as new regulations are added to the books. For example, regulation increasingly governs public smoking, consumer protection laws for software purchases, and the use of "junk bonds" in corporate finance. The future might bring under the regulatory umbrella such wide-ranging issues as biogenetic research, euthanasia, no-drive days to reduce pollution, sexually transmitted diseases, and liquor promotions such as happy hours and twofers.

Deregulation generally stimulates competition, a fact that many people find discomforting. For example, almost every major airline crash generates calls for reregulation of the airlines. This reaction ignores the fact that deregulation affected the Civil Aviation Board's command over rate structures and ability to limit competition, not the FAA's control over safety issues. In fact, a recent study by the FAA indicates that airline safety has actually improved since U.S. skyways were deregulated. The number of passenger fatalities per 100 million miles flown dropped steadily from 1977 to 1990. In spite of such evidence, however, many people in the airline industry would like to see regulation reimposed.

We have some explanations for why political controversies surround regulation. One lesson is to be wary of advocates of regulation who try to persuade legislators that certain laws or rules are in the public interest. Self-interest is a strong incentive to develop arguments that may bamboozle the general public. Although many government activities do serve the public interest, the specifics of many of the government policies addressed in this part of this book are similarly shaped by special-interest groups.

Chapter Review: Key Points

1. The bulk of the regulatory agencies in this country were created during three decades. The first great surge occurred during the 1930s, when policymakers attempted to buffer the violent swings in the business cycle on our economic system. Well over half of all regulatory agencies, however, came into existence in the 1960s and 1970s. It is not obvious why regulation increased so dramatically during a period of relative prosperity and high economic growth.

2. The *public interest* theory of regulation focuses on some possible failures of the price system, including poor information, fraud, externalities, and monopoly power. Laissez-faire markets will not provide the socially optimal quantity of a product with externalities, so direct regulation is commonly used in an attempt to protect the public interest.

3. A *natural monopoly* involves substantial economies of scale, rendering direct compe-

tition impractical. Society has turned to regulation to prevent natural monopolies from reaping enormous profits and to move them toward socially efficient levels of output. The public interest may be served by requiring the firm to use *block pricing*, which uses price discrimination both to achieve efficiency and to equate total revenues from sales of the service with total costs of production, including a normal accounting profit.

4. Regulating public utilities is considerably more difficult than simple theory would suggest. Major problems arise in determining the *rate base*, a *"fair" rate of return*, and allowable costs. Regulatory agencies face a difficult task in balancing the interests of consumers and utility investors.

5. The *industry interest* view of regulation expressed by George Stigler suggests that industries can gain from regulation and therefore "demand" regulation from the government. As Stigler has noted, the state can, and often does, change the profitability of an industry through four main mechanisms: (*a*) direct taxes or subsidies, (*b*) restrictions on entry, (*c*) impacts on an industry's complementary or substitute products, and (*d*) direct price-fixing policies.

6. Stigler views the government as the supplier of regulatory services to various industries. The costs of obtaining favorable regulation include campaign contributions and lobbying expenses.

7. *Public choice theory* attributes much of the complexity of modern regulation to empire building by the heads of government agencies.

8. The law of product liability has evolved from an approach of *caveat emptor* — "Let the buyer beware" — to one of *caveat venditor* — "Let the seller beware." Direct mandates or prohibition of some transactions are also increasingly common. For example, new cars are required to have specific safety equipment; some new drugs are banned. *Caveat emptor* is most appropriate when both producers and consumers have roughly equal access to knowledge about the product. Today, however, producers commonly have considerably more information about

complex products than do consumers. It would be prohibitively costly for consumers to detect design and manufacturing flaws in most goods. In addition, modern corporations may use their massive financial and market power to manipulate consumers. Advertising claims are difficult for consumers to verify. Thus, government regulation is seen by many as the only practical solution to the problem of misrepresentation.

9. Opponents of *consumer protection* regulations argue that unregulated competition will force producers to respond to consumer needs, albeit imperfectly. Those individuals who want safer products will pay for them, and those willing to incur more risk will pay less. Furthermore, opponents argue that the poor are hurt most by consumer protection, which removes inferior but cheaper products from the market. For many of the poor, consumption opportunities are limited already, and removing the inferior (usually cheaper) products from the market may force them out of the market entirely.

10. Regulation is increasingly attacked as misguided and "nit-picky." Various deregulation schemes have been implemented in the 1980s. The next decade will probably bring continued reappraisal of the government's role as regulator, but whether this will translate into further reductions in regulation is highly speculative.

Key Concepts

Ensure that you can define these terms before proceeding.

public interest theory of regulation	rate base
	rate structure
industry (private) interest regulation	occupational licensing
	consumer protection
public choice theory of regulation	*caveat emptor*
	caveat venditor
natural monopoly	deregulation
block pricing	

Problems and Questions

1. Are the interests of the general public, the regulated industry, competing industries, or

government regulators most obviously served by the following types of regulations? Which industries gain and which lose in each case?

a. An AIDS vaccine is kept off the market for two years while the Food and Drug Administration tests it on animals to ascertain whether it is safe for humans.

b. Gasoline must contain 15 percent fuel-alcohol additives each winter in an attempt to reduce Denver's "Brown Cloud" of air pollution.

c. Penalties on clerks in stores are raised if they sell beer to minors.

d. Restaurants must be inspected every 180 days by the Department of Health.

e. Installation of new, safer toilet seats is mandated for every facility serving the public or employing more than six workers.

2. Should smokers who ultimately die because of their addiction be able to collect for damages from tobacco companies?

3. List three industries that would oppose government subsidies for expansion of public airports. List three that would favor such subsidies.

4. Assume the demand and cost curves depicted below accurately portray a natural monopoly. What would be the total annual

profits earned by this monopolist? At what price and output level would society's welfare be maximized? What would be the regulatory price? At this price, what would be the monopolist's annual profit?

5. The Occupational Safety and Health Act (OSHA) requires that workplaces be made as safe as possible (or more so, according to some critics), with little or no regard for costs. How would you expect OSHA regulations to affect the prices of goods previously produced under hazardous conditions relative to the prices of those that have always been produced in safe work environments? What would you expect to happen to wages in previously hazardous industries? In previously safe industries? What will happen to real wages economy-wide? To health insurance rates? Should it matter for the purposes of OSHA regulation whether the risks of particular occupations are well known or not? If so, why?

6. Under what circumstances should specific goods (for example, flammable clothing, saccharin, heroin, or marijuana) be prohibited? Under what circumstances should producers be liable for harmful or defective products? When, if ever, should the government provide information about consumer products instead of levying regulatory actions limiting or requiring access to goods (such as prescription drugs or automotive safety equipment, respectively)? When should consumers bear the consequences of faulty goods?

7. Suppose you were a Food and Drug Administration (FDA) official charged with licensing new drugs. There are two types of errors to which you might fall prey: (a) You might license a harmful drug, or (b) you might keep a very beneficial drug off the market. What do you think is the nature of the trade-off between these types of errors? Which of these two types of errors would you wish to minimize if your goal is (a) to maximize your prospects for job security or promotion, or (b) to maximize the public welfare? Are there natural checks in the marketplace if you make the first type of error? If you make the second type of error? What are the probable effects on research and development activities of pharmaceuti-

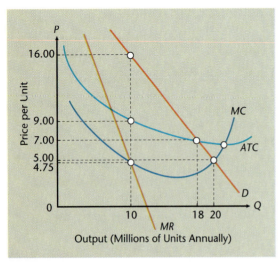

FIGURE 6 A Natural Monopoly

cal companies if you minimize the licensing of harmful drugs? If you minimize keeping good drugs off the market? In which direction do you think you would lean if you were a typical FDA official?

8. Some economists have developed proposals that they suggest will eliminate the need for public utility regulation, infuse an element of competition into situations of natural monopoly, ensure economic efficiency, and eliminate the problems of income distribution posed by monopoly power. The proposals take two forms. First, government licenses to provide such services as electricity, gas, or telephones could be sold to the highest dollar bidder. The proceeds from this license auction could then be rebated to the utility's customers. Alternatively, these monopoly licenses could be awarded to the firm that bids the lowest rate structure. Do you think these proposals provide economic efficiency? Equity? What problems could arise with implementation of these schemes?

9. Two surveys in 1986 revealed that, "a 2-to-1 majority of Americans believe the breakup of American Telephone and Telegraph was a bad idea, and few think telephone service has improved since the breakup. . . ." Twenty percent of those surveyed indicated they had considered canceling telephone service because of increased costs. Is this a case of the government "fixing something that wasn't broke"? What did the government hope to gain by splitting AT&T into eight separate companies? Are the current problems simply short-term corrections for a long history of monopoly?

10. In 1981, the Reagan Administration proposed almost total deregulation of the alcoholic beverage industry. Not only were consumer groups appalled by the proposal, but, paradoxically, the industry was appalled as well. The industry, it seemed, did not want "government off of its back." The industry went so far as to argue that the Federal Bureau of Alcohol, Tobacco, and Firearms is "a very lean, highly efficient organization . . . [providing] a very high return for its tax dollar . . . ." Why would the industry oppose deregulation? Are the tangled vines of federal regulation better than 50 sets of state regulations? Would consumers gain by deregulation of the alcoholic beverage industry?

Environmental Economics

"Three Billion Years Plus a Few Minutes"

ooze

cohesion, opulence

twinges, space, undulations

slithering, boring, hatching, germination

increase, complexity, blooming, coordination, cooperation

predation, parasitism, migration, competition, adaptation, selection

crowding, starvation, disease, populations, diversity, camouflage, mimicry

specialization, reduction, exclusion, conversion, blight, drought

pressure, defeat, decline, smoke, decimation

explosion, abuse, ignorance, teeming

contamination, residual, choking

silence, stillness

ooze

William T. Barry, from *Reflection*

Reprinted by permission of the author.

William Barry's poem hints that Earth may turn into a dead planet over the long haul. Is this inevitable? The drive to improve environmental quality seems to be racing with population growth and production processes that convert raw resources into waste. Population growth of 1.7 percent annually will push our number over 6 billion by the year 2000. The capacity to sustain life is already strained at the seams in places. As we try to stretch this capacity through extensive resource use, environmental decay and resource depletion rear their ugly heads. Mountains of garbage and problems like acid rain, nuclear waste, ozone depletion, oil spills, the greenhouse effect, and global warming increasingly encircle the globe.

Developed economies in Europe, North America, Japan, and the Soviet Union contain one-third of the world's population but use roughly four-fifths of all resources. (Eastern bloc countries produce relatively more pollution per unit of GNP than most economies that are more capitalistic.) Raw materials entering production–consumption systems are ultimately converted into goods, noxious gases, dirty water, solid wastes, heat, or radiation. Some resources seem about to vanish, so attaining a uniformly high quality of life may require either massive recycling or technological advances based on resources that are now unusable. Enhanced environmental quality entails sacrifice; by raising the explicit costs and prices of many goods, it foments social and economic disruption.

Categorizing externalities relative to other economic activities is our first task in this chapter. How property rights evolve, and how ambiguous property rights cause environmental problems are our next topics. Our attention then turns to types of externalities, and we describe how to determine optimal amounts of pollution. This chapter ends by examining alternative approaches to pollution and the current state of U.S. environmental policies.

Table 1 *Rivalness and Exclusion*

	Rival	Nonrival
	Pure Private Goods	**Excess Capacity**
Exclusive	Cola Candy bars Automobiles CDs	Theaters Airline flights Rapid transit trips Natural monopolies?
	Environmental Problems	**Pure Public Goods**

Nonexclusive	Congestion
	Overfishing
	Overuse of commons
	Pollution
	   Litter
	   Air
	   Water
	   Noise
		National defense
		Flood control projects
		Weather forecasts
		Infectious disease control

Market Failure and the Environment

Environmental problems usually reflect market failures that originate from the technical characteristics of certain goods, or in the nature of their production. We will look at some of these characteristics before considering environmental issues in detail.

Characteristics of Goods

The rival/nonrival and exclusive/nonexclusive relationships discussed in our "Public Finance" chapter are combined in goods in various ways. Table 1 summarizes four basic categories of economic activities.

Pure Private Goods Goods that are both rival and exclusive are **pure private goods** and tend to be efficiently provided by the marketplace. Most goods, from apples to zithers, are pure private goods.

Potential Excess Capacity A combination of nonrivalness and exclusiveness generally entails excess capacity. Theaters with empty seats or airline flights with unsold tickets offer examples of nonrival goods, but you can be excluded from flying or enjoying movies. Unless economies of scale are so significant that market power is concentrated (e.g., the monopoly problem), competitive markets normally provide these goods efficiently. However, crowding may diminish the enjoyment of some goods (e.g., theaters or public parks) when more and more people try to use them. Congestion and environmental decay often emerge when this occurs.

Environmental Problems Congestion and nonexclusion from the use of some scarce goods are keys to environmental breakdown. All allocative systems, including markets, almost uniformly fail when the costs of excluding a person who does not pay to use a good are prohibitive relative to the value of that good. A nonexclusive but rival good is typically overused, if it is provided at all.[1] If I enjoy scenery but also value the roadside as a garbage site, I may toss beer cans out my window as I drive down the highway. The resultant eyesore and the costs of cleaning up my litter are borne by taxpayers at large; my personal costs are trivial. (Most antilitter laws are only weakly enforced.)

---

1. Firms cannot profit from, and consequently will not produce, goods if people can enjoy the goods regardless of whether they pay.

Public parks on holidays and traffic congestion are examples of rival but nonexclusive activities. It sometimes seems that everyone wants to drive during the rush hour or on holidays. Limiting access to roads is seldom feasible, so many commuters sit idle, with their engines running and emitting air pollutants.

Abuse of the environment becomes rampant when both nonexclusion and rivalness for resource usage are present. In England, everyone once had access to certain fields for grazing that were held "in common," but these *commons* were often treated as though no one owned them. The **tragedy of the commons** occurs because individuals lacked the incentives to maintain the property that would exist if they owned it, so pasture land that was common property was typically overused and run down. Modern examples of the tragedy of the commons include the extinction of various species because of overfishing and "overwhaling" in international waters.

Despite the nonexclusivity of environmental quality, Focus 1 suggests that many Americans are increasingly so concerned about this issue that they incur personal costs to recycle the solid waste that threatens to bury us under mountains of garbage.

Pure Public Goods   A *pure public good* is both nonexclusive and nonrival. Weather forecasts on TV, for example, are nonrival, simultaneously benefiting all who want to make plans for picnics. Forecasts are also nonexclusive — preventing this information from spreading is virtually impossible. Private meteorologists can do little to prevent people from passing weather forecasts along. Hence, the U.S. Weather Service is the major source of basic weather information. Nonexclusivity makes it hard for private forecasters to survive.

Pollution as a Public Bad; Abatement as a Public Good

A public good, once produced, benefits many people, none of whom can be excluded from enjoying its use. *Pollution abatement* (reduction) generally fits this definition. Everyone in Los Angeles could enjoy a clearer view of the horizon if smog were eliminated. Thus, environmental quality is a public good. The public good and externality aspects of pollution and its control suggest that government might steer production and consumption toward optimal levels.

We dealt with public goods and excess capacity (e.g., natural monopoly) problems in previous chapters. Many economists view pollution as a problem that might be resolved if all natural resources were private property so that owners had incentives to manage these environmental resources properly.

The Evolution of Property Rights

The evolution of environmental policy in the United States is a textbook case of development of property rights to scarce resources, and of government involvement in this activity.

> **Private property rights** *assign individuals or organizations the rights to control access to certain resources or assets, including rights to charge for their use.*

Property rights usually develop in stages: (*a*) common access/nonscarcity, (*b*) common access/scarcity, (*c*) agency restrictions, and (*d*) fee-simple property rights.

Common access resources are available on a first-come, first-served basis. Vast buffalo herds that once roamed North America, for example, were treated by most Indian tribes as held "in common." Scarcity is not a problem until growth of population and output create overutilization. These resources are then quickly depleted or become congested or polluted. Buffalo were massacred as railroads and cities penetrated the American West. Other examples of the abuse of the commons include loud noises in residential neighborhoods, the extinction of passenger pigeons in the 1880s, or such activities as littering the highways.

Most modern economies are now beyond the common access/scarcity stage, because the greater productivity possible from restricted resource use causes abandonment of common-use policies. The enclosure movement in England and range wars between cattle ranchers and sheepherders in the old American West offer examples of conflicts during transitions from common use to limited use. We usually then move on to fee-simple property rights.

Fee-simple property rights allow the owner to use property in any fashion, including sale or destruction, as long as others' physical property (but not necessarily the financial value) is unaffected. (The term "fee-simple" means that monetary payments usually accompany transfers of ownership.) Evolution from common access/nonscarcity to scarcity (and overuse) of a resource usually leads to a system of property rights. Fee-simple property rights are basic for the attainment of economic efficiency in a competitive market economy. Market failure is common whenever fee-simple property rights seem impractical.

Property rights are efficient social remedies to externalities. Two major reasons why property rights sometimes fail to develop are that certain types of property rights might be (*a*) very costly to define and enforce, and (*b*) traded in ways that hinder the value of property owned by others. When definition and enforcement of rights to property are excessively costly, public control or legal conventions tend to govern allocation. Stoplights, nontransferable hunting licenses, pro rata shares of common-pool oil leases, and technological restrictions on ocean fishing are all cases where a system of fee-simple property rights appears so costly that reasonably efficient alternatives to markets have developed.

Political intervention is also common when one person's actions reduce the value — but not the physical characteristics — of another's property. Such cases involve *pecuniary* (monetary) externalities. If your job pays $10 an hour and I offer to do it for $5 an hour, your labor becomes less valuable. Thus, labor market access is legally restricted — immigration policies and child labor laws are examples. If you sell milk for $2 a gallon and I offer to sell it for $1 a gallon, the market value of your milk (and your dairy) declines.

Transactions in many markets are controlled after high-price producers secure laws limiting competition from low-price producers. Protecting pecuniary interests and not merely the physical rights of others tends to be inefficient; production costs are generally excessive. If an external effect is strictly pecuniary rather than physical, all parties pay the same prices, which efficiently tend to equal marginal social costs. For example, if growing competition from burger chains for the potato crop raises potato prices in grocery stores, the price hikes merely reflect greater social demands for potatoes.

Property Rights and Environmental Quality

Abuse of shared resources — clean air and water, scenic beauty, or peace and quiet — creates decay. Smog, foul water, litter, and airport noise are evidence that overuse of common property may fail to lead to efficient social institutions such as fully specified property rights. The debate continues about how much purity to seek and what techniques to use.

At one pole, some critics view "greedy capitalism" as the root cause of environmental decay, and economic analysis as irrelevant. Their position tends to be, "Forbid all pollution." The view that capitalism is the basic problem, however, is contradicted by recent revelations about environmental disasters in countries that once followed avowedly socialist policies. For example, the nuclear meltdown at Chernobyl in the Soviet Union reflected lack of environmental safeguards. Parts of Romania and Poland (Silesia) are among the most polluted regions on Earth, being covered with soot emitted because factories strove to meet output quotas set without regard for the environmental consequences.

At the opposite pole are those who believe that fully specified property rights harmonize economic activity. These people believe that if individuals are assigned full rights to control specific resources, a market economy will naturally achieve a healthy ecological equilibrium. We will examine both extreme views and some intermediate positions as well; but first, let us readdress externalities — the origin of many environmental problems.

FOCUS 1

Solid Waste Recycling

The problem with waste is that everyone wants you to pick it up and no one wants you to put it down.

William Ruckelshaus
(former EPA Director)

Americans will discard over 150 million tons of solid waste this year—enough to fill 80 lanes of garbage trucks extending from coast to coast. Nearly half of all states will fill their existing landfills by the year 2000. Stiff environmental regulations make average costs for new landfills nearly $60 million, but a NIMBY (Not In My Backyard) syndrome largely prevents their development. Figure 1 indicates the composition of this 150 million tons of garbage.

Moral suasion has swayed the American psyche favorably toward recycling as a remedy for environmental waste. Paper, plastics, metals, and glass are popular candidates for recycling. Aluminum cans represent a huge success cited by proponents of recycling. Virgin aluminum from bauxite is ten times more expensive than ingots from recycled

cans. The relatively high prices paid for scrap aluminum have resulted in more than half of all aluminum beverage cans being recycled.

Too many recycling efforts, unfortunately, merely alter the form and place of environmental decay. Filtering airborne or waterborne pollutants, for example, results in dirty filters and mounds of solid waste. Burning solid waste, in turn, increases air pollution. Most cities have abandoned experiments with incinerators, which reflected attempts to increase the longevity of existing landfill space and produce energy as a by-product. Los Angeles, for example, dropped its incinerator project after one study indicated that burning trash might cause one additional Californian to develop cancer each year.

Consider paper and cardboard,

which represent nearly 40 percent of all solid waste. Too few recycling paper mills are available to accomplish the recycling many municipalities now mandate—only eight mills are operating, and most are too remote from urban centers for cost-effective collection and transport. Buyer reluctance to use recycled newsprint—because it tears easily, disrupting tight deadlines by jamming high-speed presses—is another problem.

Paper bundles presented for recycling vary in quality. Recycling is impeded by "dirty" bundles—mixtures of newsprint, shopping bags, junk mail, cardboard, catalogs, phone books, magazines, and so on. Equipment cannot satisfactorily sort dirty bundles, necessitating human labor. "Clean" bundles fetch $12 per ton, but municipalities are charged $20 per ton for

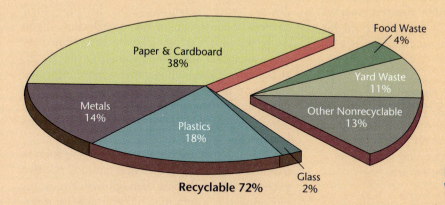

Paper & Cardboard
38%

Food Waste
4%

Yard Waste
11%

Metals
14%

Other Nonrecyclable
13%

Plastics
18%

Glass
2%

Recyclable 72%

FIGURE 1 Solid Wastes

the processing of dirty bundles. Teaching consumers who conscientiously try to recycle about the importance of keeping bundles clean is a key to making it economically viable. A million tons of dirty bundles of newsprint awaited recycling in 1991.

Switching packaging materials can be a complex and costly decision for firms. For example, in 1981, McDonald's switched from paper to plastic packaging in response to concerns about disappearing forests and pollution from paper mills. Then, in 1990, McDonald's received a black eye over its use of plastic foam containers. It has returned to paper, but can buy only "new" paper packaging— satisfactory decontamination of recycled paper is not feasible.

And policy flip-flops continue to be a problem. The latest word from the EPA is that paper containers are now considered more damaging than styrofoam.

Restructuring local government trash collection policies might enhance the success of recycling efforts. Most cities charge flat fees or pay for garbage collection through property taxes. To homeowners or tenants, adding additional cans for trash pickups entails only the cost of a new can and the effort required to move it to the curb. Some cities now use a per-can charge to encourage citizens to recycle and to be selective in the products they purchase. Residents who pay by their volume of trash tend to avoid relatively small products enclosed in large bulky

packages. Trash collection has declined by an average of 25 percent in cities where per-can fees have been instituted.

Per-trash-can fees, taxes on nonrecyclables, deposits on cans and bottles, and rewards for trash separation are only a few steps toward meeting the EPA goal of recycling 25 percent of our trash by 1995. Ensuring that recycling does not simply trade one form of pollution for a worse form of pollution is vital, as are appropriate incentives for consumers, firms, and government agencies. Perhaps even more important is persuading people that the time they spend recycling can help make our world cleaner and healthier.

Externalities

Competition tends to maximize both individual welfare and the public interest if only the parties *directly* involved in transactions are affected; marginal social benefits tend to equal marginal social costs.[2] But if external parties are physically (and not merely monetarily) affected, market prices and quantities usually fail to account for their preferences and social welfare may not be efficiently served.

> **Externalities** *occur when private calculations of costs or benefits differ from the costs or benefits to society. Externalities are present whenever third parties gain without paying for their marginal benefits, or lose without being compensated for the harm they endure.*

Of course, payments by external beneficiaries or compensation for external costs transforms a "third" party into a participant in a transaction, effectively "internalizing" the externality. For example, if my neighbors agreed to accept my offer of $1,000 to let me put a neon sign on my house, irritation about the neon sign would be internalized. And if such payments were necessary, the neighbors' preferences would be recognized, and I would be less likely to put up the sign. Only *uncompensated* externalities create inefficiency. Such externalities may emerge from either consumption or production.

External Benefits

Some *external benefits* originate in production. For example, a pharmaceutical firm might develop knowledge to cure some deadly disease. Legal monopolies on knowledge are prohibited, however, so the firm could not prevent competitors from using the knowledge. Only techniques uniquely embedded in some commodity or piece of equipment are patentable.

External benefits occur not only in production, but in consumption as well. If you landscape your yard, your neighbors may benefit without sharing in your expenses. Their property values rise, and they gain more attractive scenery, sweet-smelling flowers, and the like. If your family is inoculated against a contagious disease, your neighbors gain because their chances of contracting the disease decline. If you study economics in your spare time, you may enjoy a happier and more productive life. But if, at the same time, you become a more informed voter and better citizen, these gains are shared with people throughout this country. These are just a few examples of possible external benefits from consumption.

Without compensation to those who generate external benefits, activities that embody positive externalities may be less than optimal. For example, applied research may be profitable for a private firm, because specific applications are patentable, but basic research is seldom pursued privately, because the broad benefits of new knowledge cannot be marketed by the researchers. Similarly, children gain from education, but others also gain if education improves citizenship. If education were strictly private, it might be "overpriced," and far fewer people would extend their schooling. People would quit buying education as soon as another unit of learning cost more than they expected it to be worth to them. They would not consider gains to their neighbors when deciding how much education to obtain.

From the consumption side, suppose that planting flowering trees in your yard boosts both your personal satisfaction and the value of your property. Your demand for flowering trees is shown in Figure 2 as demand curve D_p. You can purchase all the trees that you desire for P_0 and will plant Q_0 trees. Your neighbors may enjoy the trees nearly as much as you do, and the value of their property may be enhanced by your trees.

Demand curve D_s incorporates your private demand plus the social benefits to your neighbors from your flowering trees. The marginal social benefits of your actions are the sum of any private benefits to you plus any external benefits enjoyed by other people. Getting these other

---

2. Perhaps naïvely, this statement assumes that the distribution of income is not a problem. We deal separately with issues of income distribution two chapters hence.

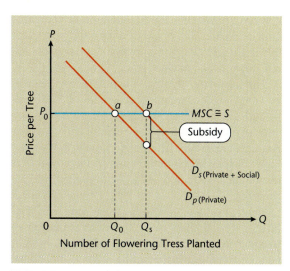

FIGURE 2 Positive Consumption Externalities

Positive consumption externalities cause private market demands (D_p) to understate the marginal benefits to society (D_s) of a good. Consequently, there will be underproduction and underconsumption of the good. A subsidy of *bc* per tree could be used to induce consumers to plant the socially optimal level of trees. (Of course, taxes or fines equal to *bc* for not planting trees could accomplish the same efficient result.)

people to pay for their benefits is unfortunately very difficult.

Maximum social welfare occurs when marginal social benefits and costs are equal, so optimal planting of trees would be Q_s. But you may not plant Q_s trees unless you are compensated for your investment beyond Q_0. This could be accomplished if the government subsidizes tree planting by *bc* dollars per tree. Without compensation covering the external benefits to your neighbors, you all will miss an opportunity to gain with no one losing. The reason is that in your private decision making, you tend to weigh your private costs and benefits much more heavily than any external benefits, which are usually ignored.

One cure for potential underproduction is communal arrangements, which may be either implicit or explicit. Implicit agreements occur when neighbors encourage each other to improve their properties through such things as informal and friendly competition — who has the nicest house, the prettiest lawn, and so on. Im-

plicit agreements tend to work best when only a few people are involved. Explicit agreements (community covenants or zoning) are more common when larger numbers must cooperate — all residents of some subdivisions may be required to have so many square feet of living space, or may be prohibited from painting their homes other than approved colors, or each may agree to spend a certain amount on landscaping, and so on. In general, as the number of people affected by an externality grows, restrictions on behavior tend to become more formal and less flexible.

External Costs

Pollution can arise from either consumption or production. Water pollution flows primarily from production processes; air and noise pollution result about equally from both. For example, both industrial wastes and the residues from washing dishes flow into sewer systems and then into our water supplies. Automobiles, smokestack industries, and coal-fired electric generation all contribute to the smog that engulfs many major cities and results in corrosive acid rain that falls on even some remote regions of our world. External costs are generated in many forms of production. Examples include noise pollution near airports, unsightly billboards and junkyards, and factories that belch noxious smoke.

Suppose farmers use pesticides on their artichoke crops and then irrigate their fields, washing some pesticide onto adjacent properties and into nearby streams because enforceable property rights to water are absent. If pesticide works its way up the ecological chain — harming your fishing and health — then you, who may never eat artichokes, partially bear the cost of artichoke production. Assume all farmers exude external costs of $2 per pound of artichokes when using chemical sprays. In Figure 3, the supply curve S_0 is based only on farmers' costs, but the marginal social cost is *MSC*, which is $2 higher.

Suppose artichoke farmers are now taxed $2 per pound if harmful pesticides are used, to cover all social costs of production. The price initially rises from $5 to $6 per pound, and annual output falls to 60,000 tons. Why the price rises and output falls is straightforward. There is a $2

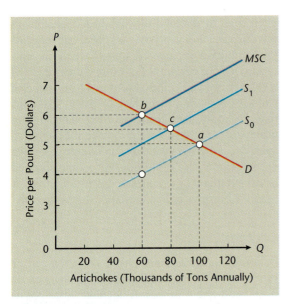

FIGURE 3   Pollution Costs: Market Equilibrium with External Costs

In economic parlance, most pollution is a problem of external costs of production. Suppose the market is initially at point *a*, where S_0 reflects only private costs. If the producers and consumers of polluting goods are forced to bear any external costs, their adjustments (*internalization*) may be to adopt nonpolluting (but more privately expensive) modes of production, as reflected in supply curve S_1 and the movement from *a* to *c*. If such changes in production processes are not feasible, production will fall more and price will rise more, as shown in the movement from *a* to *b*, when taxes are used to equate private and social costs. The full cost of cleanup is reflected in the marginal social cost (*MSC*) curve.

vertical shift of supply from S_0 to *MSC* when farmers' private costs rise $2 per pound. Farmers previously grew 100,000 tons at private costs of $5 per pound, which are now $2 per pound more for each output level when harmful sprays are used.

Unfortunately for artichoke growers, consumers would not continue to buy 100,000 tons if the price climbed to $7 per pound. The higher production costs will cause marginal farmers to fail, as consumers reduce artichoke consumption to 60,000 tons annually and the price rises to $6 per pound. Equilibrium moves from point *a* to point *b* in the short run, but farmers will look for ways to avoid this $2 pollution charge. Suppose that in the long run they discover nonpolluting

organic sprays costing $1 more than inorganic sprays. When they use the organic sprays to avoid the $2 tax, the supply of artichokes will rise from *MSC* to S_1.

The ultimate optimal output in Figure 3 is 80,000 tons of artichokes at a price of $5.50 per pound (point *c*). At this price, consumers buy and farmers sell what they want, and society's resources are used efficiently. Competitive markets fail to achieve such results if large numbers of people are harmed or large numbers of people pollute.

What can we conclude from this analysis? First, external costs cause the private market to oversupply the good because full costs are not borne by customers (point *a*). That is, the social costs of production (total private costs plus any external costs) are not charged to consumers. Second, if consumers pay full costs, less is produced and consumed (point *b*). Third, when a pollution charge is imposed, producers will seek ways to reduce their level of pollution if this reduces their total costs, which now include any external costs (point *c*).

Could any lone individual reduce pesticide pollution? You might pay farmers to stop or sue for damages. But lawsuits often involve transaction costs (attorney fees, etc.) that exceed the damage done. For example, individually suing all air polluters in Los Angeles would be very costly relative to the potential personal recompense for the harm done. People may seek legal remedies, however, when damages are extreme. The key is to force each firm to internalize (fully consider) the costs of pollution to innocent third parties.

Internalization *is the process of adjusting prices and output to reflect all external costs or benefits.*

If each buyer of a good pays full production costs, including environmental damages, then externalities are internalized, yielding optimal amounts of production and consumption.

Consider such problems as drunk and reckless drivers, loud neighbors who party until dawn, violent criminals, or litterbugs. These are market failures in the sense that consumption-based external costs are imposed on other people. Similar annoyances and dangers might be even more common in a pure laissez-faire society. Many analysts, however, view these as examples of government failure because one of government's basic tasks in a market economy is to protect broad legal rights to property, which may include rights to peaceful and tidy neighborhoods and safe streets. Society has tried to control tendencies to overproduce external "bads" through zoning, social regulation, or other legal sanctions.

Summary: External Benefits and Costs

Purely private markets produce too much (*too little*) of a good when external costs (*benefits*) are present. Externalities cause market failures, because people tend to weigh their private costs and benefits far more heavily than the costs borne or benefits received by outsiders. People maximize their personal welfare by equating the marginal private benefit from an action with its marginal private costs. This is quite rational, because trying to identify and negotiate with any potential third parties may be prohibitively costly, and because nonexclusivity for environmental quality would make such negotiations futile. Thus, market demands mirror marginal private benefits while market supplies reflect marginal private costs.

Society tries to compel decision makers to internalize externalities by assigning certain legal rights, through taxes or subsidies, or via mandates or prohibition. Pollutants are the most conspicuous examples of negative externalities. Firms ideally internalize any pollution costs, so consumers ultimately pay full production costs — private plus external costs. The growth and diverse characteristics of pollution have stimulated numerous public policies.

Alternative Solutions to Pollution

Nearly everyone recognizes that environmental decay must be controlled. That is where agreement ends. Extreme conservationists argue for a pristine environment and view the social benefits from abatement as overwhelming. To them, only technological limits should be allowed to constrain abatement; economic analysis is irrelevant.

Others argue for looser environmental standards and oppose many current regulations as overly stringent and costly.

Is Zero Pollution Optimal?

Optimal outputs require marginal social benefits and costs to be equated. This occurs when all pollution costs are internalized; if they are borne by the consumers and producers of goods whose production or use generates pollution, users and makers will weigh these costs and their decisions will be both personally and socially efficient.

Zero pollution sounds great, but your first question should be, "What would it cost?" If perfect purity were costless, we would all demand an immediate end to pollution — but the costs of 100 percent purity are prohibitive. Trade-offs exist between environmental quality on the one hand and goods required for even modest standards of living on the other. What is optimal pollution? Figure 4 provides an answer using cost–benefit analysis, which compares the costs and benefits of an activity — in this case, pollution abatement.

Panel A of Figure 4 depicts the total benefits and costs from pollution abatement. The total social benefit curve reflects the fact that an increasingly clean environment yields decreasingly valuable additional benefits as we approach 100 percent purity. This is reflected in a downward sloping marginal social benefit (*MSB*) curve in Panel B. Enormous gains may be realized from eliminating deadly pollutants, but as the environment grows increasingly clean, we become increasingly tolerant of minor residual pollutants. Virtually no one, for example, would be willing to swim in a sewer, but few refuse to swim in a reasonably clean public pool loaded with tiny children. Society's marginal benefit is the sum of all benefits to individuals from each reduction in pollution. Our "output" from pollution abatement translates into a given percentage reduction in pollution. Hence, as we move out along the horizontal axis, more abatement is achieved, and the environment becomes cleaner.

The total costs of abatement in Panel A rise as we expand efforts to reduce pollution. In Panel B, the positively sloped marginal social cost (*MSC*) of reducing pollution reflects diminishing

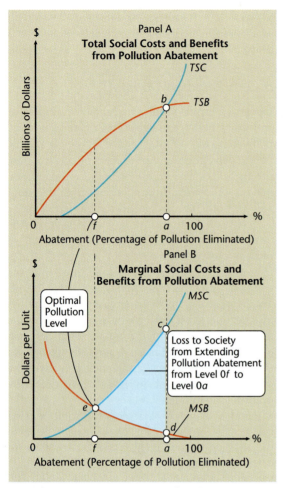

Panel A
Total Social Costs and Benefits from Pollution Abatement

Panel B
Marginal Social Costs and Benefits from Pollution Abatement

Optimal Pollution Level

Loss to Society from Extending Pollution Abatement from Level 0f to Level 0a

FIGURE 4   Determining the Optimal Level of Pollution

The total social benefits (*TSB*) from reducing pollution increase as we secure greater purity, but at a decreasing rate. Panel A also indicates that the total social costs (*TSC*) of purity rise at an increasing rate. This is reflected in Panel B in the increasing marginal social costs (*MSC*) and decreasing marginal social benefits (*MSB*) from cleaning up the environment. Optimal purity (or optimal pollution) occurs where the difference *TSB* − *TSC* is maximized, which is also where *MSC* = *MSB*. Purifying to the point where *TSC* = *TSB* results in a net social loss equal to area *dec* in Panel B.

marginal returns and increasing marginal costs. More ambitious attempts to reduce pollution entail ever greater sacrifices of resources. For example, the ash spewing from a chimney might be reduced by 20 percent by installing a crude chimney filter. (Big chunks are easy to screen.) Achieving a 40 percent reduction, however, requires a second filter with finer mesh to remove smaller particles, and this filter would require

more frequent replacement. Each subsequent filter to reduce pollution even further would have to be even finer and would require even more frequent replacement. Achieving zero pollution is virtually impossible. Maximizing social welfare requires that *MSB* = *MSC* at point *e* in our example. To extend abatement beyond the optimal level of pollution (0*f*) would waste resources because further reductions in pollution cost more than they are worth.

This analysis contradicts the notion that society should completely eliminate pollution regardless of costs. To push pollution control until the total benefits equaled the total costs (point *b* in Panel A) would mean that the last bit of cleanup effort would cost society *ac* (in Panel B), while yielding additional benefits of only *ad*. Society, by cleaning up beyond the optimal level of 0*f* percent to 0*a* percent receives additional benefits of *feda* (Panel B) but uses resources worth *feca* to complete the job, which wastes resources equal in value to shaded area *dec*.

Another implication is that optimal pollution levels will vary for different regions of the country depending on their respective benefits and costs. Regions particularly vulnerable to smog may want to impose especially stringent emissions standards. Densely populated areas (like Los Angeles) faced with severe auto pollution may choose to limit travel (no-drive days, commuter lanes) or to subsidize mass transit that would not be optimal in Wyoming. Focus 2 indicates that trade-offs between production and environmental quality may also affect the locations of certain industries.

The methods available to reduce pollution can be categorized according to their degree of intervention in the market process. The least interventionist is moral suasion, followed by various market techniques, then tax and subsidy incentives, and finally, outright government regulation and prohibition. We will examine each of these approaches.

Moral Suasion

Moral suasion lacks legal authority — its goals are to persuade offenders to voluntarily reduce offensive practices and to sensitize people to a problem.

FOCUS 2

Should We Export Pollution?

The aroma of Charles Dickens' London was a pungent mix of barnyard, fish market, and refinery. Almost 3 million Londoners relied on over 200,000 horses for basic transportation; wood and coal fires heated homes and provided energy for industry; raw sewage and kitchen slop flowed down open gutters into the Thames River. The drapes of Parliament were regularly drenched with water to prevent members from being overwhelmed by the stench.

London's atmosphere is now much more agreeable, primarily because environmental quality is a luxury good. Thus, London, Rome, and New York are cleaner than Bombay, Mexico City, or Hong Kong. High per capita income yields rules that banish dirtier forms of production. People living in less prosperous regions are less picky; they welcome even unpleasant industries that will provide jobs and income. For example, destitute local communities in the United States may lobby legislators to locate prisons nearby; some poor areas have been competing to be sites for radioactive waste dumps.

Political leaders whose major priorities are growth and development for their countries frequently tolerate lax safety and environmental standards to stimulate production or to attract industry. It is not surprising that the two most catastrophic industrial accidents ever recorded occurred in (*a*) Bhopal, India, when hundreds died and thousands became invalids after a toxic industrial gas was released, and (*b*) the Soviet Union, during the 1986 "meltdown" of a nuclear power plant at Chernobyl.

Environmental and safety standards tend to be lower in less developed countries. This suggests that environmental quality in the United States and other advanced economies would improve if we imported more goods that entail substantial pollution from poorer countries that seem more willing to tolerate wastes. Laws to forbid importing goods that were not produced under environmental regulations as stringent as those in the United States have, however, been proposed by several groups on a variety of grounds.

1. Environmentalists who are concerned that our entire planet is being polluted see exporting pollution as a short-sighted solution that will only delay and worsen an ultimate reckoning with the problem of environmental decay. (But not all pollution is ultimately global. Some is primarily local.)

2. Exporting dirty and dangerous industries is perceived as an immoral way to exploit the poverty of the less developed nations. (But are our morals preserved if our policies keep people in less developed countries impoverished?)

3. Domestic industries (and their workers), which must meet strict U.S. environmental standards, contend that allowing foreign competition that does not face similar standards is unfair. (A parallel of this view would be arguing that garbage dumps should be spread uniformly across land in country clubs and remote land that is barren.)

The ultimate question is whether developed countries that, because of their prosperity, demand high levels of environmental quality have any right to prohibit less prosperous countries from producing goods that entail substantial pollution. It may be that the comparative advantages of less advanced countries are strongly shaped by greater tolerance for environmental degradation.

Moral suasion *is social pressure to persuade people or institutions to act in some particular manner.*

For example, "Don't Be a Litterbug" campaigns reduce trash on public highways, and public hostility now restricts smoking to limited areas. Adverse publicity or threatened boycotts were the primary methods available early in the environmental movement, and may persuade some polluters to desist. Moral suasion has limited power, however, because many goods are marketed nationally, public information campaigns are expensive, and voluntary boycotts ask people to act against their own interests.

Effluent Charges and Subsidies

Many economists favor tax penalties or *effluent charges* to curb environmental decay. This modified use of the market relies on price incentives to optimally allocate resources when externalities are present. Government sets the fee (charge) on pollution or the reward for reducing pollution, and polluters are allowed to adjust without overt coercion.

Effluent Charges   The effluent charge approach is illustrated in Figure 5. Suppose that a

FIGURE 5   Effluent Charges

MC is the marginal cost of effluent control for this firm. Imposing an effluent charge of $1 per unit of effluent discharged on this firm will result in it incurring total control costs of $0E_0$ to reduce E_0 amount of effluents.

group of polluting manufacturers is located on a public lake that could also be used for recreation and fishing. Water pollution reduces the enjoyment derived from boating, skiing, fishing, and picnics.

Assume that community leaders estimate external costs per unit of effluent at $1 when only optimal pollution occurs. To attain optimal rates of discharge into the lake, the community charges the firms $1 per unit of discharge. The MC curve shows the firms' costs of reducing pollution. Given the $1-per-unit effluent charge, firms will reduce their effluents by E_0 units. The firms will not remove more than E_0 effluents because the removal cost (MC) exceeds the $1 effluent charge at quantities exceeding E_0.

Subsidizing Abatement   The government might use subsidies (the opposite of taxes) to encourage pollution abatement. Federal grants to pay for pollution control equipment have been used extensively to subsidize cleanups of state or local government sewage facilities. These sewer systems are now required to charge for their services based on measured use as a condition for receiving these federal funds.

Subsidies to private firms that reduce pollution ultimately subsidize the firms' customers, but are unlikely to be effective unless the subsidies make abatement profitable. Subsidies to encourage private pollution abatement could take such forms as grants to pay for equipment, tax credits, or rapid depreciation allowances. Substantial political opposition to subsidizing private pollution abatement has, however, sharply limited such subsidies.

Market Solutions

Many economists argue that environmental problems could easily be solved if appropriate property rights were available. Much private property is owned only in a limited way. For example, you may own a car, but there are numerous restrictions on how it can be used. Similar limits apply to ownership of land and buildings, guns, or ham radio equipment.

Lawsuits for Damages   One role of government in a market economy is enforcement of property rights. You could sue harmful polluters if property rights were assigned to protect you from being damaged by pollution. Lawsuits may work fairly well when pollution can be traced directly to a given polluter and the damage can be shown to be caused by that party's effluent. (The Atlas Chemical Industries' decision stated that the costs of pollution must be internalized by an industry.) But suppose that a firm had the right to pollute. Your only remedy might be to pay the firm to reduce pollution – if it were worth it to you.

Who has rights to use the environment? This was a crucial issue in the 1879 case of *Sturges v. Bridgman.*[3] Sturges, a doctor whose office abutted those already occupied by Bridgman, a confectioner, added an examination room next to the confectioner's kitchen. Noisy equipment kept the doctor from examining patients with a stethoscope in the new room, so he sued to prevent the confectioner from operating the equipment. An injunction was granted on the grounds that the machinery imposed external costs on the doctor. (Consider the possibility, however, that this injunction imposed external costs on the candy maker, who previously had the right to operate noisy equipment.)

Both private and public lawsuits to protect the environment have some advantages. First, victims of pollutants may be compensated for their losses – and they may not have other enforcement methods. Firms have incentives to clean up if the compensation paid exceeds the costs of cleaning up. Second, successful lawsuits alert other polluters to new liability limits, encouraging these firms to adopt cost-justified precautions to avoid future damage claims.

Using the courts to enforce rights to pollute or to be protected from pollution has several disadvantages. First, legal procedures are slow and costly. Cases tried today have been initiated, on average, two to four years earlier. Furthermore, such solutions are impractical if the damaged party lacks the resources to bring a suit. These solutions alone may leave society saddled with excessive waste. A slightly different problem is that if there are numerous polluters and "pollutees," it may be difficult to determine who harmed whom and to what degree. Lawsuits would face almost insurmountable difficulties in solving problems of fouled air in crowded industrial areas.

Legal remedies work best where the number of polluters is small and their victims are few and easily identified. But residents of Love Canal, New York and Times Beach, Missouri personally experienced the chaos of areas polluted by toxic chemicals. Fearful for their own health and that of their children, and faced by plummeting property values and a maze of red tape when they sought restitution, these victims learned how hard it can be to correct the harm done by even easily identified polluters.

Assigning Pollution Rights   A second approach that relies on market forces is for the public sector to sell licenses to discharge wastes.

Pollution rights *are licenses to discharge given amounts of waste products.*

Ronald Coase, a prominent economist, has shown that optimal pollution is identical no matter who is assigned the rights, polluter or harmed party, as long as those affected are easily identified, have roughly the same bargaining power (income), and can bargain without cost.[4] In this view, the environment is just another productive resource.

This bargaining process is reflected in Figure 6. The demand for *pollution rights, D_0,* is downward sloping. Pollution is Q_0 when the environment can be used freely as a garbage dump. Quotas might be auctioned if the community decided to allow only Q_e pollution. Business demands to pollute reflect the contribution of pollution to the revenues and profits of the firm. A firm willing to pay only P_a for each right to pollute (point *a*) undoubtedly can curtail pollution for P_a or less per unit of effluent. Businesses would be willing to pay P_e each for Q_e pollution rights. If

3. U.S. Supreme Court Case 11 Ch. D. 852 (1879). For a detailed analysis of this case, see Ronald Coase, "The Problem of Social Costs," *The Journal of Law and Economics*, Vol. III, October 1960.

4. Coase, R. H., "The Problem of Social Cost," *The Journal of Law and Economics*, Vol. III, 1960.

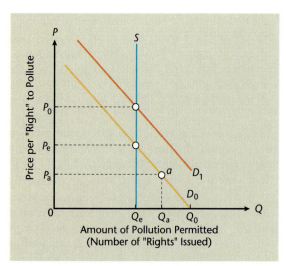

FIGURE 6   A Market for Pollution "Rights"

When the right to pollute is strictly limited and offered for sale on the open market, the demand D_0 for pollution rights depends on the marginal productivity of the environment as a receptacle for waste. Such a market will operate in much the same fashion as markets for other productive resources.

purity lovers would be hurt more than P_e by each unit of pollution, they could buy and retain the pollution rights. In this way, the initial sale of these rights would generate revenue for the community. If an auction were held and Q_e rights were sold, then excessive pollution ($Q_0 - Q_e$) would be eliminated.

What if other firms wanted to set up locally after the Q_e pollution rights had already been sold? They could buy rights from the owners of existing pollution rights. This might require buying an acutely dirty plant, shutting it down, and transferring its pollution rights to a new plant. Alternatively, a new firm could pay existing firms to install more antipollution equipment. Both techniques shift the demand for the right to contaminate from D_0 to D_1 in Figure 6. The value of pollution rights rises, but not the level of waste. Consumers of goods entailing pollution pay full production costs as higher costs of polluting are shifted forward.

This approach has several advantages. First, polluters have incentives to clean up. Little administration other than monitoring is required. And if the government decides later to reduce

pollution, it can repurchase existing rights — or if it became more accepting of pollution, it might sell even more rights as a revenue source. This approach can confer significant cost advantages to firms that implement relatively clean technologies. It may be a cheap and attractive alternative to direct regulation, and works reasonably well in a relatively enclosed environment, like a lake under the control of local authorities. But administration is more difficult when spillovers are more extensive. Another flaw is that some voters and politicians equate pollution with sin and are outraged at the idea of allowing economic reasoning to dominate what is for them a moral issue. Even these moralists, however, would probably agree that selling pollution rights is better than giving them away for free.

Regulations and Prohibition

Direct regulation is a politically popular remedy for environmental damage. Complete prohibition may be desirable in the case of extremely dangerous materials — e.g., plutonium or other powerful carcinogens. When total bans on certain pollutants are too costly relative to the benefits, the government limits noxious wastes through regulations and standards.

Regulation is costly to administer and provides firms no incentives to reduce pollution once a standard is met. Every stringent rule incites imaginative attempts to discover loopholes around it. This typically results in an incredibly complex patchwork of directives to prevent cheating or avoidance. In some instances, there may be no acceptable alternatives to direct regulation. We need to recognize, however, that the quality of life depends at least as much on production and economic growth as it does on purity, and that there are trade-offs between these goals.

Are Any Abatement Policies Optimal?

Each policy discussed so far has its particular advantages and disadvantages, summarized in Table 2. None is the "best" for all situations. Where a closed environment (a lake, for example) is polluted and few people are involved,

Table 2 *Summary and Evaluation of Some Environmental Policies*

Policy Option	Advantages	Disadvantages
Moral suasion	Least disruptive to market processes. Educates and sensitizes people to the nature of environmental problems. Permits individual choice.	Ineffective in reducing pollution levels.
Market solutions		
1. Lawsuits	Private lawsuits enable victims to recover.	It may be difficult to prove in a lawsuit who damaged whom. Lawsuits can be costly and expensive.
2. Pollution rights	Requires little government intervention. Reduces pollution to a given level depending upon the policy established. Relatively easy to administer.	Sometimes hard to develop "good" estimates of external costs for particular pollutants and polluters. "License" to pollute is politically unpopular. Typically requires a "closed" environment to administer effectively.
Taxes/Subsidies		
1. Effluent changes	Largest polluters have greatest incentives to reduce pollution. Generates revenue to further clean up environment.	Sometimes difficult to estimate appropriate charge. Monitoring compliance can be expensive, especially when large numbers of polluters are involved.
2. Subsidies	Relatively easy to administer.	Politically unpopular.
Direct regulation	Can be used to keep extremely harmful pollution below dangerous levels. Standards can preserve horizontal equity of the program. Politically most popular.	Once standard is met, polluter has no incentive to reduce pollution below standard (important if standard is above the socially optimal level). Administrative regulation often quite complex and cumbersome. Most interventionist in scope. Large bureaucracy is created to administer program. Does not generate its own revenue. Can become captive agency of particular special-interest groups. Generates incentives to creatively sidestep the regulation.

market approaches tend to be viable. Polluters and pollutees might simply be allowed to bargain with each other until they reach a solution. Effluent charges or subsidy schemes may also work efficiently. But these approaches break down where aspects of public goods arise. Standards and regulations may be appropriate if a problem is widespread and diverse. With extremely hazardous substances, complete prohibition may make the most sense.

Securing adequate energy supplies and bolstering economic growth are increasingly balanced against environmental protection and the quality of life as we move toward the twenty-first century. The history of environmental protection in the United States suggests that the Environmental Protection Agency increasingly relies on market solutions to environmental deterioration. Although regulation remains a major weapon, most studies suggest that market incentives instead of regulations provide cost savings of as much as 50 percent per unit of pollution abated.

U.S. Environmental Policies

We have examined various techniques to reduce pollution. As we noted earlier, political lags and other difficulties mean that sound economic policies are embraced only slowly, if at all, and transitions are often turbulent. Environmental protection in accord with modern economic analysis generally faces substantial obstacles, both technical and political.

Pollution Control in the United States

By the late 1960s, it was obvious that the United States had moved into the second phase of property rights: the tragedy of the commons. Environmental degradation was widespread, no longer affecting only isolated cities like Gary, Indiana, or Pittsburgh (which, incidentally, have made great strides toward improved air quality). Congress more formally delineated rights to use the environment by enacting environmental legislation for both water and air.

Arguments about environmental regulation can be rancorous. Environmentalists are often accused of shunning cost–benefit calculations in favor of rigid regulations requiring greater purity. Many environmentalists complain that bureaucrats fail to aggressively combat pollution. For example, turmoil at the EPA in the 1980s reflected outrage that regulators were "selling out" to polluting industries. This rhetoric has been counterbalanced: Firms faced with high costs of cleaning up oppose EPA regulations by loudly criticizing the ineptitude of environmental managers. In spite of this furor, environmental policy appears to follow a smooth and predictable path.

The first step in the movement away from common, unrestricted use of the environment required identifying the causes of such problems as air pollution. Smog was first noticed in the 1940s as a haze against the foothills east of Los Angeles. Although smog was first thought to be a passing thing, pressure gradually mounted to clean the persistent brown cloud. One problem was that no one could identify the nature of smog — where it came from or what its effects might be. By 1951, however, a Cal Tech study fingered auto emissions as the major culprit.

When the EPA was first charged with responsibility for environmental quality, it perceived mandatory cleanup by all polluters as the only practical approach. Pollution abatement was initially treated on a case-by-case basis, but uniform rules seemed necessary on two grounds. First, the EPA expected its mandates to be easily monitored. Second, uniform standards legally treat the affected parties equally, and are nondiscriminatory constitutionally, even if they dictate unequal burdens of pollution control.

During this period of uniform pollution control, society learned more about pollution and how to measure it, paving the way for marketable pollution rights to emerge. At the same time, political obstacles shaped mandatory rules and standards. Special-interest groups lobbied for rules to benefit them. Surprisingly, special-interest groups frequently pressed for increased environmental purity; it is a mistake to think that regulations harm all firms. Some are harmed and some are not. For example, control over pollution in steelmaking entails substantial economies of scale. Thus, big firms tend to advocate tough rules that drive their smaller competitors out of business. The demise of small firms promotes environmental quality. Firms in polluted regions want pollution control requirements to be as burdensome on firms in cleaner areas. This also enhances environmental protection, but at significant cost. In most cases, special-interest pressures have caused inefficient regulation.

Despite special-interest groups, there has been a steady movement toward more convenient and transferable environmental property rights. The EPA allowed the "bubble" concept to be implemented in many situations in the 1970s. "Bubble" refers to a performance standard imposed for the area surrounding a plant or a group of adjacent plants, as opposed to the standards that were originally imposed on each specific source within a plant.

*The **bubble concept** allows firms to transfer pollution rights between sources within a plant as long as a prescribed standard of environmental quality is met.*

There is a continuing evolution from the bubble concept to pollution rights that are marketable between plants. The gains from exchange that exist within a plant are also available between plants. Some permits to pollute are also now marketable.

*An **offset policy** allows a new firm to enter an overpolluted area by inducing other firms to reduce emissions. Air quality must show a net improvement, and the new firm must meet all individual standards imposed on existing firms.*

What this means is that a new entrant can bargain with existing firms, paying them either to shut down or to employ better pollution controls. For example, a California firm was permitted to build a 40,000-barrel-per-day oil terminal after paying $250,000 for an offset created when a local chemical plant closed.[5] In July 1991, trading for such offsets began in the Chicago Commodity Exchange. The 1990 Clean Air Act specifically permits coal-burning utilities to overcomply with sulfur dioxide standards and then sell their extra pollution rights.

Although market solutions have crept into the regulatory postures of agencies like the EPA, there are still many inefficiencies that exist only to enhance the wealth of special interests. For instance, the bubble concept applies only to old "grandfathered" plants, not new ones. New-versus-old disparities in environmental controls are a recurrent theme. Another example of special-interest effects is that the net improvement

in the environment necessary to qualify an offset as legal is a political football often kicked from one end of the field to the other. Firms with offsets for sale commonly try to influence regulators to require great improvements in environmental quality before allowing a new firm to enter a blighted area; this drives up the value of existing rights to pollute.

The Future of Environmental Protection

We can reasonably expect continuing improvements to environmental quality. As the EPA and the other regulatory agencies become more adept at their jobs, pollution control will cost less per unit, and a substitution effect will cause society to demand more purity. Increases in national income will also drive demand for environmental quality, which is a luxury good. This helps explain why such laws as the Clean Air Act of 1990 mandate improved environmental quality, but how far and how fast we are willing to go has limits. In 1990, the high costs expected with the sweeping "Big Green" initiative to set substantially higher environmental standards caused Californians to vote it down, and New Yorkers defeated a $2 billion environmental bond issue.

Markets for pollution permits will probably never be as unregulated as those for cars or land. Certain restrictions will be maintained in order to enhance the wealth of special-interest groups. Even the market for land is regulated. Zoning ordinances and other laws exist to protect the value of certain locations vis-à-vis others. It should not be surprising to find this same effect in air pollution rights. Finally, it seems unlikely that pollution taxes will ever be a widespread method of allocating the environment for the disposal of waste. In contrast, both uniform standards and marketable pollution permits endow the regulated firms with this value. It is unlikely that the political process will take this value from them.

To summarize the economics of environmental quality, we first must recognize that the environment is a scarce resource that has competing uses. Second, the political process weighs the cost of property rights definition and enforcement — and the profitability to special-interest

---

5. Tom Tietenberg, *Environmental and Natural Resource Economics*, 2/ed. (New York: HarperCollins, 1988), p. 351.

groups from property rights restrictions — against the inherent efficiency of private property ownership. Our experience in the environmental arena chronicles the changing equilibrium of these forces. As property rights become more completely defined and easily enforced, society is increasingly likely to use private property assignments to allocate use of our environment.

Chapter Review: Key Points

1. Goods that are purely rival and exclusive are *pure private goods*. Such goods (e.g., ice cream or umbrellas) are usually efficiently provided in a private market system. Goods that are nonrival but exclusive entail excess capacity and are also efficiently provided by markets unless elements of natural monopoly are present.

2. A good that is both nonrival and nonexclusive is a *pure public good*. Public goods will be less than optimally provided by the market system, if they are provided at all, because of attempts to *free ride*. A rival but nonexclusive good embodies *externalities* that often hinders the efficiency of market solutions. Pollution may be the problem if externalities are negative (costly); underproduction may result if externalities are positive (beneficial).

3. The four stages in the development of property rights are (*a*) common access/nonscarcity, (*b*) common access/scarcity, (*c*) agency restrictions, and (*d*) fee-simple property rights. *Fee-simple property rights* mean that you can do anything you want with your property so long as you do no physical damage to the property of others.

4. Positive *externalities* occur when an activity confers benefits on external third parties. Too few such activities are undertaken because private decision makers tend to ignore the external benefits.

5. Pollution situations in which damaged third parties are uncompensated, and hence unconsidered, are examples of negative externalities. Negative externalities impose costs on third parties. Too many activities generating negative externalities are undertaken, because private decision makers weigh the costs imposed on others too lightly, if at all.

6. Environmental quality is a public good, and controlling environmental pollution is costly. There are trade-offs between protecting the environment and producing goods that generate pollution, so the *optimal pollution* level is greater than zero.

7. *Pollution abatement* may occur through negotiation, *moral suasion* (jawboning and bad publicity), *effluent charges*, subsidies, lawsuits, the assignment of pollution rights, and government regulation. No single solution applies to all situations of negative externalities; they must generally be resolved on a case-by-case basis.

8. Pollution rights might be auctioned and then made transferable. The Environmental Protection Agency initially relied heavily on direct regulation through pollution ceilings, but is increasingly using *property rights* solutions to control environmental deterioration.

9. The *bubble concept* sets a pollution performance standard for a plant. A firm can transfer rights to pollute within or between plants inside the "bubble" as long as the standard is met.

10. The *offset policy* allows new firms that wish to produce in a polluted area to operate if they can induce existing firms to reduce air pollutants to offset the newcomer's emissions.

Key Concepts

Ensure that you can define these terms before proceeding.

property rights   pollution rights
externalities   bubble concept
internalization   offset policy
moral suasion

Problems and Questions

1. Draw a graph to show a negative externality (external costs) from a coal-burning electric utility. From society's viewpoint, will electricity be provided in optimal quantities at appropriate rates (price structures) if utility commissions fail to adjust for such negative externalities? Why? What sorts of solutions might equate marginal private costs and marginal social costs, and generate government revenue? What will happen to the price consumers pay for electricity if these solutions are implemented?

2. Far more species of plants and animals (e.g., dinosaurs) have become extinct than exist in the world today. Is concern about the potential extinction of certain species sufficient reason to bar economic development? A few years ago, for example, a subspecies of the snail darter (a minnow-like fish) was discovered in a river scheduled to be dammed. Construction of the multimillion-dollar dam was halted to preserve this subspecies. If you believe in "animal rights," do these rights extend to all species? For example, if you had the last samples on Earth of the viruses that generate smallpox or AIDS, would you reason that these species should be preserved?

3. Why are chickens, pigs, and cows in no danger of extinction despite their systematic slaughter to provide food for hungry people, while many edible wild animals are increasingly rare despite much lower "kill rates" (relative to total population) each year?

4. You are an ardent environmentalist who is shocked to learn that the government will soon begin selling rights to pollute. You and your friends express moral outrage that someone could be given the right to pollute at a time when environmental quality is threatened on many fronts. How might you, your friends, and others with similar views use the government's program to increase environmental quality?

5. Some analysts insist that external costs are so inherently bilateral that determining who is the polluter and who is the pollutee is hard. If a polluter is the one who imposes costs on others, then the people who benefit when regulation secures greater purity are the polluters, because they impose "cleanup" costs on firms and their customers. In this view, whether a firm should pay for pollution abatement or whether those who desire purity should "bribe" the firm to install pollution abatement equipment is entirely arbitrary. Moreover, the government need not interfere, because, in this view, the parties will privately bargain to reach an optimal solution. What problems do you see with this approach to environmental quality?

6. What motivates some firms to argue for stringent uniform standards of allowable pollution nationwide? Do you think it efficient to require firms to meet the same standards in metropolitan areas as in isolated areas? If not, which firms should face higher standards? Why?

7. Suppose you are deeply concerned about poor people's welfare. If you had access to a "magic button" that, when activated, would eliminate all pollution, should you push the button? Curiously, the answer may be *No!* You will need to draw material from the last few chapters to explain why you might not. Now suppose that a second "magic button" would eliminate all urban street crime. Should you push this button? Why or why not?

8. Figure 7 illustrates the marginal cost of pol-

FIGURE 7 Marginal Cost of Pollution Control for a Small Pulp Mill

lution control for a small pulp mill. Local authorities impose an effluent charge of 80 cents per gallon of effluent in an effort to reduce water pollution. How much effluent will the mill now discharge if it discharged 20,000 gallons daily prior to the effluent charge? Beyond what quantity of daily effluent will the mill pay the effluent charge? Why? If local authorities raise the charge substantially, say to $1.20 per gallon, will the amount of effluent the mill discharges drop substantially? Why?

9. Technological optimists believe that research and development will advance with sufficient speed that pollution, the energy crisis, and the rapid depletion of nonrenewable resources will be overcome through normal operations of the marketplace. Technological pessimists fear that technological advances will only hasten environmental decay and the depletion of resources. To them, only stringent regulations can forestall stripping the planet of resources and irremediably poisoning our environment. Into which camp do you fall? Why?

10. If your property or person is harmed by pollution, you can sue for damages. What are some of the shortcomings of using the civil courts to resolve the dangers posed by pollutants?

11. Nearly every large city contains neighborhoods whose residents complain loudly about noise from aircraft at a nearby airport. If the airport has been in existence for a long period, is forcing it to relocate an appropriate remedy? Would this be fair? Why or why not?

12. Suppose a smelly feedlot for cattle was located in a remote area long before a builder placed a housing development next to it. Should the right to be "smelly" inure to the feedlot owner, or should the right to "clean country air" be conferred on new home buyers? How could the real estate developer or the new home buyers reduce or eliminate the aroma of cattle if the feedlot had the right to stink up the area? How might the feedlot preserve the right to operate if homeowners were awarded rights to clean air? Why might the final amount of barnyard odor be the same in equilibrium regardless of which party was granted these rights to air quality?

13. Many critics of environmental policies charge that preserving every species and preventing extinction is too costly. John Sawhill, an economist and president of the Nature Conservancy, argues that preserving seemingly useless species may be essential. He argues that in the long run preserving a "genetic warehouse" may hold the key to our future well-being. Should all species be preserved no matter how high the cost? Is there an optimal rate of species extinction? We can probably estimate the marginal costs of preserving a species, but how could we estimate the marginal benefits, assuming they are unknown and will occur sometime in the future?

14. Suppose a tanker runs aground, spilling oil that spoils the beach. The community sues the ship's owners for cleanup costs, lost business, and such nonmarket benefits as enjoyment of the beach, fishing, and so on. How might you measure these nonmarket losses? If the tanker's owners were not required to pay nonmarket losses, might there be more than a socially optimal level of oil spills? Why or why not?

15. Some economists argue that the extinction of valuable, but endangered, animal species could be prevented through systems of private ownership. For example, ranches that now allow the hunting of rare game animals have powerful incentives to maintain breeding herds that should ensure the survival of certain rare species. Private ranches have been so successful in resurrecting the American bison that "buffalo steaks" are now served in some restaurants. African game preserves are now contemplating experiments to allow local citizens to harvest rhinoceros and elephants. The more endangered the species, the more valuable are its meat, tusks, horns, hooves, and so forth on world markets (as noted in the 1990 movie, *The Freshman*), and the more diligently will the "locals" assist game wardens in catching "poachers" who hunt illegally. Do you think this approach has merit? What special problems are posed for a "private property rights" approach to help preserve the blue whale, the bald eagle, the condor, or other migratory species?

The Economics of Agriculture

Farming conjures images of a simpler and more rewarding lifestyle. The hectic pace of modern life causes many suburbanites, who find watching their gardens grow a deeply satisfying, almost mystical experience, to long for farms of their own. This nostalgia, which largely ignores rural hardships, might be explained by the ability of many of us to trace our roots back to the land. Two centuries ago, 19 of 20 Americans relied on agriculture for income. Even though only 1 American in 50 now remains in farming, economic pressures for farmers to leave their land have not abated.

The major objectives of this chapter are to (*a*) survey the farm problem, (*b*) identify its causes, (*c*) evaluate past and present U.S. agricultural policies, and (*d*) note some possible future directions for agriculture policy.

The Farm Problem

Agriculture is often cited as the prime example of pure competition, but government is heavily involved in farming. American farmers comprise only about 2 percent of the U.S. population, but they easily feed us all and generate surpluses for export to help feed a hungry world. This agricul-

tural abundance contrasts sharply with the relatively low and erratic farm incomes depicted in Figure 1. Technological advances have boosted productivity faster in farming than in most other industries, but biological cycles and erratic weather cause wide swings in total agricultural output. Farm subsidies since the 1930s have absorbed enough funding to buy every square inch of agricultural land in the Western Hemisphere (including buildings and equipment), but pressures mount that will drive even more farmers into urban labor markets. Unraveling the paradoxes of American agriculture requires applying economic tools to a bewildering mix of historical forces and patchwork policies.

Low and Unstable Farm Income

Family farmers' woes predate the American Revolution. Figure 1 illustrates the basic problem. Per capita income for farmers has historically been both unstable and low relative to that for nonfarmers. From a modern peak of roughly 90 percent in 1973, U.S. farm income withered to about half the average urban income in the early 1980s but has slowly rebounded. Consequently, off-farm earnings from temporary or part-time work typically provide half the annual income of half of all farmers. An even more significant ad-

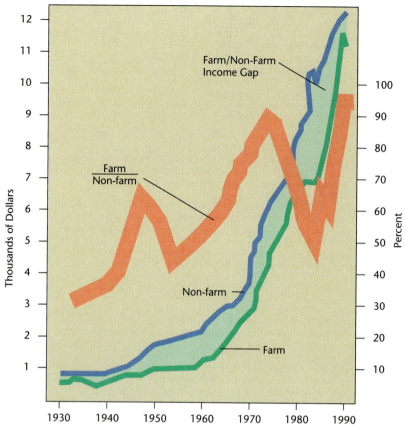

FIGURE 1   Per Capita Farm Income as a Percentage of Per Capita Nonfarm Income (thousands of dollars per capita and relative percentage)

Per capita income in agriculture is generally less than in the rest of the economy, and tends to be more erratic as well.

Sources: *Statistical History of the United States*, Bureau of the Census, Series A350-352, *Economic Report of the President*, 1991, and *Statistical Abstract of the United States 1990*.

justment to the enduring pressures of low and erratic income has been the exodus of farmers or their children from rural areas, as reflected in Figure 2.

Credit Problems   Credit is another recurring farm belt issue. Farming was mildly prosperous in the 1970s, so many farmers plunged into debt to buy land and new machinery and buildings. Consequently, land prices soared. Then, during 1980–1986, commodity prices and farm revenues collapsed; real market values of farm land fell roughly 30 percent. Figure 3 reflects the upward spiral in most farmers' debt-to-equity ratios. Rising real interest rates added to farmers' woes, and many could not pay their mortgages, so auctioneers' gavels signaled a wave of farm

foreclosures during 1984–1986. Failure rates in some farm communities rivaled those of the Great Depression. A few foreclosures provoked violence when neighboring farmers united in protest. Less well publicized, but almost as frequent, were failures of rural banks, which accounted for almost half of all bank failures during 1984–1986. These failures left many farming areas without convenient access to credit—another problem for farmers to surmount.[1]

A harsh drought in 1988 and rising international demands for grain elevated commodity

---

1.   Charles Calomiris, Glenn Hubbard, and James Stock, "The Farm Debt Crisis and Public Policy," *Brookings Papers on Economic Activity*, Vol. 2 (Washington, D.C.: The Brookings Institution, 1986), pp. 441–479.

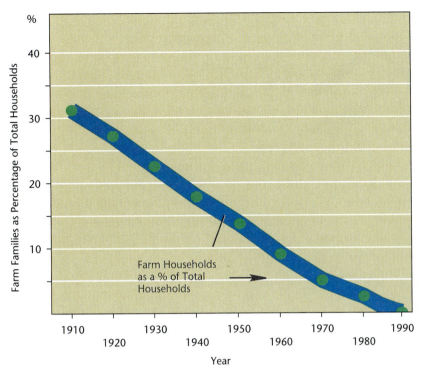

%

FIGURE 2 Leaving the American Family Farm, 1910–1990

This figure reflects the relative decline of agriculture as a way of American family life throughout this century, and the absolute decline since 1940.

Sources: *Statistical History of the United States*, Bureau of the Census, Series A350-352, *Economic Report of the President*, and *Statistical Abstract of the United States 1990*.

prices in the late 1980s. Higher commodity prices enabled most farmers to retire debt while land values slowly rebounded. This turnaround in commodity prices has helped ease farmers' credit problems, but the disastrous cycles of recent decades could easily be repeated if farmers resume heavy debt burdens in response to high commodity prices.

Competition and the Marginal Producer

A whiff of potential profit may induce firms suffering losses to hold on, and may attract new competitors who rely on resources ill-suited for the specific form of production. People make decisions at the margin, so some marginal firms teeter on the brink of failure in all competitive industries. For example, were a price floor on bananas set sufficiently high ($40 a pound?), there would probably be an Alaskan banana industry, and struggling Alaskan banana growers would be lobbying for higher price supports. Our farm problem resembles this far-fetched example because marginal farms are most threatened with extinction. Note, however, that a marginal farmer may not be on marginal land. If a farmer using good land fails because of credit problems, for example, the land will be taken over by another farmer.

Now that you have an overview of the farm problem, a brief look at the nature and structure of the agriculture industry is needed so that we can extend our analysis.

The Structure of Agriculture

Farms range from labor intensive small plots that grow exotic flowers, fruits, vegetables, or poultry to vast wheat farms densely covered with grain, to arid and isolated ranches that stretch from horizon to horizon, supporting only a few cattle per section.

Number and Sizes of Farm Properties

Stereotypes about how large typical farms may be are largely illusory. Variations in the scale of U.S. farm operations are indicated in Table 1.

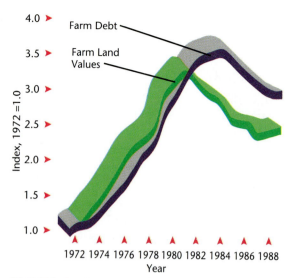

FIGURE 3   **Farm Land Values and Farm Debt, 1972–1990**

Modest agricultural prosperity combined with inflation to drive rural land prices up sharply during the 1970s. Farm debt escalated as well, in part to finance new equipment but primarily for land acquisitions by farmers who viewed low real interest rates as opportunities to expand. When rising interest rates and weak agricultural prices drove land prices and farm income down during 1980–1986, many farmers went even deeper in debt. In 1988 a severe drought led to an increase in commodity prices, which helped land values to rebound slightly and helped to ease farm debt.

Sources: Michael T. Belongia and R. Alton Gilbert, "The Farm Credit Crisis: Will It Hurt the Whole Economy?," Federal Reserve Bank of St. Louis *Review*, December 1985, p. 6, and *Statistical Abstract*, 1991.

Average (mean) farms cover more than 400 acres, but almost 60 percent cover fewer than 180 acres and account for less than one-eighth of all agricultural acreage. These smaller, "family" farms have been the primary focus of political rhetoric. At the other extreme, roughly one farm in seven exceeds 500 acres. Big farms tend to be corporate (stockholder owned), and collectively control about 70 percent of all acreage.

Most surveys of the farm problem ignore distinctions between farmers' incomes and their wealth. Persistently low farm income should drive down prices for farm property, but such adjustments occur slowly in agriculture. That the price of farm land remains comparatively high despite low incomes has led to a cliché that "farming is a way to live poor and die rich."

Table 1   *Number of Farms and Land in Agriculture (thousands)*

under 50 acres	595	28.6%
50–179 acres	645	30.9%
180–499 acres	478	22.9%
500–999 acres	200	9.6%
over 1,000 acres	169	8.0%
Total	**2,087**	**100%**

Source: *Statistical Abstract*, 1990.

Many farmers accept low income and rates of return on investment during their working years in hopes of accumulating assets that will support them during retirement. The resulting overinvestment in land contributes to oversupply and dampens the prices of farm commodities.

Farm Income and Wealth

Farm properties were worth roughly $600 billion in 1989, averaging $330,000 per farm — only 16 percent of which was mortgaged. Thus, average farm owners were worth about $285,000 in property alone, ignoring machinery and livestock. While urban incomes typically exceed those of farmers, average farm owners are wealthier than average nonfarmers.

Averages (means) can be misleading, however; the median farmer owns less than the 429 "average" acres, and an acre in Idaho is typically worth far less than one in Iowa or California. Larger farms account for disproportionate shares of total farm wealth, leaving many farmers impoverished relative to average urban families. Tenant farmers or sharecroppers, who pay 35 to 40 percent of their revenues to landowners, tend to be poor. Figure 3 indicates, moreover, that farm land values have yet to return to their previous levels, and many farmers must still contend with debt burdens incurred a decade earlier.

Causes of the Farm Problem

Politicians have done the most to encourage the production of food in all countries where the main medical problem is obesity, and most to discourage it in all countries where starvation remains a threat.

The Economist

Famine is epidemic in many less developed countries; cheap and abundant food supplies are a prerequisite for healthy economic growth. One primitive model of economic development uses this idea to argue for government policies that "squeeze" peasant farmers to free resources for industrial growth. Even though economists are increasingly skeptical of this model,[2] governments in less developed countries commonly hold agricultural prices below world market prices. The monetary prices of food are low in these countries, but shortages are rampant. Eastern European countries in the throes of trying to move toward greater reliance on markets (most prominently, the Soviet Union) provided numerous examples of such shortages during 1990 and 1991.

In the United States and most of Western Europe, however, this goal of cheap and abundant food has largely been met, leading to very different problems: excess output and depressed commodity prices. Overabundance and low prices stem largely from three factors: (*a*) rapid growth in agricultural productivity, (*b*) low price and income elasticities of demand for farm products, and (*c*) the relative immobility of agricultural resources.

Growth in Agricultural Productivity

Modern machinery, new strains of seed (the "Green Revolution"), crop rotation, scientific breeding programs, irrigation systems, and custom-blended fertilizers are among technological advances swelling agricultural yields while substantially shrinking rural labor requirements. Productivity growth in agriculture, illustrated in Figure 4, has been spectacular, and has been realized across the board. You might expect income to rise whenever you produce more. Rapid growth of output has not boosted farm revenues, however, because total food consumption is relatively insensitive to both its own price and consumer income.

<hr>

2. A powerful argument that exploiting peasants is likely to backfire is developed by Mancur Olson in "Agricultural Exploitation and Subsidization," *Choices*, Fourth Quarter 1990, pp. 8–11.

FIGURE 4   Farm vs. Nonfarm Output per Labor Hour (1977 base year)

Productivity growth in these indexed figures is reflected solely by the slopes of the curves, not their relative heights. Agricultural productivity growth exceeds the growth rates in manufacturing and services. Average farmers now produce 16 times as much as in 1930, while typical nonfarm workers produce only about 2.5 times more than in 1930.

Source: *Statistical Abstract*, 1990.

Demand Elasticities for Farm Products

Farm products, like other goods, conform to the law of demand: The quantity demanded is lower at higher prices and vice versa. However, the demand for agricultural products exhibits two characteristics that create problems for the farmer: It is relatively price inelastic and it grows only slowly over time. That demand is relatively price inelastic means that quantities adjust little when prices change. When goods are "necessities," the amounts people consume tend not to be significantly influenced by their prices. This implies that the proportion of income spent on these goods will grow if prices rise, or fall if prices decline.

The price elasticity of demand for various agricultural goods is shown in Table 2. The absence of good substitutes for all farm commodities

Table 2 *Some Price and Income Elasticities of Demand*

	Price Elasticities		Income Elasticity
	(A)	**(B)**	**(C)**
cotton (at farm)	0.1		
wheat (at farm)	0.02–0.2		
flour (retail)		0.80	−0.36
corn (at farm)	0.03–0.5	0.50	
apples (retail)	1.3		
peaches (retail)	1.5		
citrus (retail)	0.8		
oranges		0.66	
potatoes (retail)		0.11	
starchy roots			−0.20
beef (retail)	0.8–1.1		0.64
cattle (at farm)		0.68	
pork (retail)	0.7–1.0		
hogs (at farm)		0.46	
pig products			−0.20
lamb (retail)	1.8–2.3	1.78	
chicken (retail)	1.1–1.2	0.78	
all meat products (retail)	0.4–0.6		
milk		0.35	−0.50
eggs (retail)	0.3–0.4	0.32	0.37
butter (retail)	0.3–1.4	0.65	0.42
margarine (retail)	0.3–0.8		−0.20
sugar		0.24	
All Food (retail)	**0.2–0.5**		

Sources: (A) USDA, 1959. (B) P. George and G. King, *Consumer Demand for Food Commodities in the United States with Projections for 1980,* Giannini Foundation, 1971. © Heinz Kohler, *Intermediate Microeconomics,* New York: HarperCollins Publishers, 3/ed., 1990.

taken together causes their collective demands to be relatively inelastic: between .2 and .5. Taken singly, some farm products have relatively elastic demands, because there are many other farm products that are close substitutes for them — e.g., apples and pears and peaches and oranges, or pork and beef and lamb. If the price of apples, for example, increases drastically, people simply substitute in the direction of oranges or some other fruit.

Substitution is harder when the demand for a primary food or fiber is derived from a processed product. Cotton, wheat, and hops are examples. These commodities account for only small fractions of input costs in finished products (e.g., cloth, bread, and beer, respectively). Thus, a price change affects the final good's price relatively little, and the quantities demanded of these inputs are insensitive to price changes. The important point about the relatively inelastic demand for farm products is that when technological advances sharply boost farm outputs, consumers require huge price cuts before they will buy the extra output. This is a "catch-22" for farmers. If only one farmer harvests a bigger crop, that farmer gains. But when all farmers become more productive, they all lose, because the inelastic market demand causes prices and farm revenues to plummet.

Most agricultural products are also relatively income inelastic; column C of Table 2 reveals that several major farm outputs are even inferior goods. This means that farmers tend not to share in general prosperity, because even if our economy grows rapidly, the demand for farm output grows at a much slower pace. Total demand for farm goods is roughly proportional to population, but U.S. population growth rates are far below those of agricultural productivity.

The combined effects of low price and income elasticities and rapid productivity gains are illustrated in Figure 5. Assume the market is in initial equilibrium at point e_0 and equilibrium price and output are P_0 and Q_0, respectively. As the economy grows, farm demand also grows, but not as fast as the general economy. Thus, demand only shifts to D_1. During the same time, rising productivity shifts supply out to S_1. The end result is that farm prices and incomes plummet, while output rises to equilibrium point e_1.

Immobility of Farm Resources

Modern technology and large-scale farming now dominate American agriculture; even depressed

FIGURE 5   Why the Trend in Farm Revenues Is Down

When rapid growth in agricultural supplies (S_0 to S_1) is accompanied by only modest growth of the demands for agricultural goods (D_0 to D_1), the result is a sharp drop in farm revenues and financial catastrophe for many farmers. The relative price inelasticity of demand causes farm revenue to fall, so area $0ae_0c$ is much larger than area $0be_1d$.

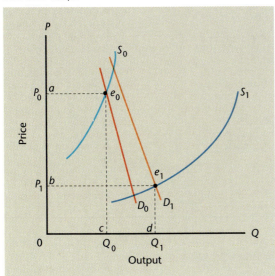

agricultural markets have not weakened farmers' personal incentives to adopt more efficient technology. Efficient new technology drives farmers to invest in highly specialized farm capital such as tractors and combines. Although agricultural productivity is enhanced, specialized farm capital is not easily transferred to other endeavors. Most resources in other sectors of the economy are not as specialized as those in farming, and therefore are more easily transferred between occupations. For example, computers are more easily transferred between occupations than are tractors. Capital is not the only immobile farm resource; skills learned in farming and operating farm equipment are not easily transferred to labor markets for other occupations.

Why Subsidize Agriculture?

Farmers advance several arguments for agricultural subsidies, including:

1. Working your own land is seen as a "more real" experience than the abstract work done by city folks. This leads to a view of the family farm as an especially worthy source of desirable social values.

2. Droughts, floods, blight, and insect infestations are cited as examples of extraordinary hazards unique to agriculture.

3. Farmers argue that, historically, much of American economic growth can be traced to resources freed up by productivity gains in agriculture.

4. Plentiful and relatively cheap food supplies have increased the health, longevity, and productivity of our labor force. These positive spillovers from agriculture justify public aid to farmers.

5. Agriculture is highly competitive; farmers cannot individually control crop prices, in contrast to most goods farmers buy (oil and gas, machinery, etc.), which are produced by firms with some market power.

6. Finally, national policies often unintentionally harm farmers, who believe that they are used as pawns when the government prohibits, for example, wheat exports to

the USSR or South Africa. Farmers also feel victimized by federal deficits and "tight" money policies that hike interest rates, or policies that raise the exchange rate of the dollar, sharply limiting agricultural exports.

Traditional Farm Programs

Congress has yielded to these arguments and tried numerous programs to restrict farm production and raise prices and incomes. Figure 6 indicates how subsidies to boost farm incomes have vacillated over time. Farm subsidy programs can be classified into

1. Crop restriction programs.

2. Purchase-loan price-support programs to boost farm prices.

3. Purchase-and-resale subsidy programs.

To understand these programs, you need to understand the concept of agricultural "parity." Parity conventionally stresses attempts to achieve fairness by placing bargaining parties on an equal footing. Agricultural parity refers to something a bit different.

The Concept of Parity

In the rich and mainly industrial countries farmers are paid too much, so they produce too much. In the poor and mainly agricultural countries farmers are paid too little, so they produce too little.

The Economist

The concept of parity pricing was introduced into law with the Agricultural Adjustment Act of 1933. The basic goal is to maintain the real purchasing power of the prices farmers receive for each unit of output. Thus, if during a 1909–1914 base period, a farmer could buy a certain amount of consumer goods with the revenue from one bushel of wheat, "parity" suggests that the same relationship should prevail in 1992. Thus, parity freezes the relationship between per-unit farm prices and the prices farmers typically pay. At times, Congress has paid lip service to the parity concept in setting agricultural policies, although this relationship has been relatively erratic, as Figure 7 indicates.

Most neutral analysts are skeptical about the idea that parity pricing is equivalent to fairness, because rapid productivity gains have slashed the amounts of inputs used per unit of farm output — average production costs declined even when input costs did not. The idea that agricultural

FIGURE 6   Federal Subsidies to Agriculture, 1950–1990

Sources: C. Zalauf, L. Tweeten, and T. Jackson, "Disequilibria," *Choices*, Fourth Quarter. 1989, pp. 32–35, and *Budget(s) of the U.S. Government, 1950–1991, USDA Financial Summary* 1991.

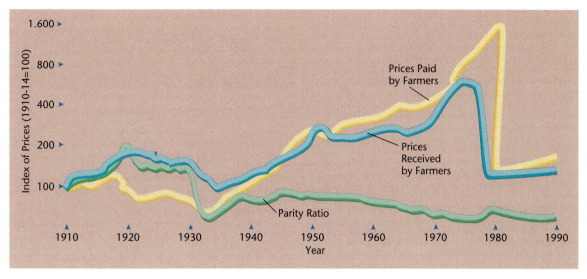

FIGURE 7   Parity Pricing

The idea that agricultural prices should maintain "parity" with other prices is an attempt to put a straightjacket on changes in relative prices as signals of society's changing priorities. Policy has only erratically been based on this concept.
Source: USDA.

prices should maintain parity with other prices is an attempt to put a straightjacket on changes in relative prices as signals of society's changing priorities. Nevertheless, the parity concept was a cornerstone of farm policy from 1933 through the 1960s. Many farmers adopted "100 percent parity" as a rallying cry during the early 1980s, when they sought more help from Washington and wanted price floors raised. Until the early 1970s, Congress generally maintained parity prices in the 70 to 90 percent range, although during World War II, price floors averaged 106 percent of the parity formula. More recently, however, only dairy farming has fallen under the parity concept.

Crop Limitation Programs

Programs intended to limit supply are based on the reasoning that a smaller output would command a higher price. Because the demand for farm output is price inelastic, then total farm revenue rises when smaller crops are sold at higher prices. Since less will be produced, total costs will be somewhat less, and therefore profits (net farm income) will rise. This analysis is shown graphically in Figure 8. The crop limita-

tion program only reduces total output from Q_0 to Q_1 while sharply boosting prices from P_0 to P_1.

FIGURE 8   Crop Limitation

Reducing supply boosts revenue whenever demand is relatively inelastic. If crop limitations reduce supply from S_0 to S_1, farm revenues grow by $abcd - degf$.

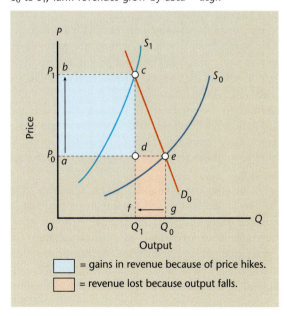

= gains in revenue because of price hikes.

= revenue lost because output falls.

Crop limitation programs raise a fundamental question: Whose crops will be limited? One approach is to restrict the amounts of particular commodities that each farmer can sell. Farmers who produce more than their quotas get angry when they cannot market their total crop at the inflated market price, but allowing them to do so would drive the market price down. One technique has been for government control boards (primarily at the state level) to allow only these quotas to be sold at the high price they initially set, with lower prices for any remainder. Dairy farmers, for example, typically are assigned quotas for fluid milk that can be sold at a relatively high price. A dairy can sell more than this quota, but only by accepting a lower price for milk that can legally only be made into cheese, ice cream, butter, or other processed milk products. (Is it either efficient or equitable for drinkers of whole milk to subsidize eaters of cottage cheese? This is effectively what happens.) At times, torrents of surplus products have caused farmers not to harvest their crops. At other times, state agricultural control boards have burned or dumped oranges, potatoes, and milk into empty fields. (Such policies are not unique to the United States. For example, thousands of tons of Brazilian coffee have been dumped in the ocean over the past half century.)

Another approach is for government to allot acreage. Only farmers with "allotment" rights are allowed to grow certain crops, and only specified amounts of land can be cultivated. Does this mean that if wheat farmers are allowed to plant, say, only half the land previously used to grow wheat, that wheat production will fall by half? *No!* Wheat farmers will continue to cultivate their better land; the less fertile half will lie fallow. Moreover, the resulting high price for wheat stimulates more intensive cultivation (e.g., more fertilizer and more thorough harvesting).

Allotment programs for grain, peanuts, soybeans, sugar beets, and cotton have frequently caused more crops to be grown with less total acreage. And of course, the total amounts of crops grown bear, on average, higher production costs than would be the case if farmers were allowed to use all their land. While not as flagrant as destroying harvested crops, these programs are also extremely inefficient. Dissatisfaction with various crop limitation programs led farmers to advocate a slightly different approach.

Purchase-Loan Price-Support Programs

Under a purchase-loan price-support program, the government guarantees farmers a higher price than would have prevailed otherwise. These artificially high prices are enforced through either outright government purchase of the surplus at the price floor, or the surplus may be kept off the market by a government loan program. Under a *storage and loan* program, farmers store their crops and obtain loans equal to the price floor, known as the "support" price. If the market price is below this support price, the farmer does not repay the loan and surrenders title to the crop to the government. But if the market price exceeds the support price, farmers pay off their loans and sell their output on the market at a higher price. For farmers, this is a "heads I win, tails you lose" proposition. The support price was linked to the parity price until the 1970s, when the parity concept was largely abandoned.

The nature of these programs is diagrammed in Figure 9. Equilibrium e would prevail without government intervention and yield price P_0 to the farmer. Since this is below the support price (P_1), the government must shift total demand (private + public demand) to D_1 to accommodate the current year's crop at the support price. Because only Q_1 could be sold to private individuals at support price P_1, government must purchase quantity $Q_0 - Q_1$. What is to be done with this surplus? Our government has provided these surplus commodities as foreign aid to developing nations, as the principal ingredient of the school lunch program, and as commodity supplements to the needy in the United States. Even so, farm surpluses have often filled silos and overflowed into mothballed ships or been dumped into mountains of grain along railroad sidings. Sometimes these surpluses simply rot.

These programs cause total farm income to rise by *abcd*, and we pay 0*fad* for food as consumers and *abcd* for surpluses as taxpayers. Do the gains to farmers offset the losses experienced by the rest of us? *No!* The reduction in food consumed ($Q_0 - Q_1$) had value to us (as consum-

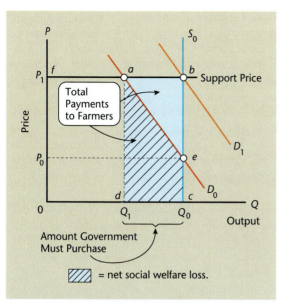

FIGURE 9 Using Loan Guarantees to Bolster Farm Prices

Purchase-loan price-support programs may boost farm incomes, but in an extraordinarily inefficient way. Resources are used to produce food and fiber that no one may ever use. At the margin, farmers' costs rise, so their net income is not enhanced by this program. Farmers collect $abcd$ as a guaranteed loan, but food worth $aecd$ to consumers is never used by anyone and is a deadweight loss to society.
(*Note:* We have simplified this graph and that in the next figure by assuming that supply is fixed. The results would not be substantially different were we to allow supply to be somewhat elastic in the relevant period.)

ers) equal to area $aecd$. This reduction in consumption is a loss to us without being a gain to the farmer. (We buy food and then are forced not to consume it, except for the parts that are used for school lunch programs, foreign aid, and supplements for the poverty stricken, e.g., cheese giveaways.) The area $aecd$ is a net social welfare loss from these programs.

The general effect of the program is clear — higher prices and incomes to farmers and higher consumer prices but less food. In addition to the inefficiency of this system of income redistribution from consumers to farmers, there are storage costs that must be borne by taxpayers.

Purchase-and-Resale Subsidy Programs

Direct purchase-and-resale programs are the most complicated of farm subsidies. They entail

paying a higher price than a free market would dictate to the farmer, and then reselling food to consumers at whatever price the market allows. Figure 10 depicts such a program. Again the farmer is guaranteed support price P_1, and total farm production is Q_0. Now, instead of storing the surplus necessary to achieve the support price, the commodity is sold to consumers at the equilibrium price P_0. The farmer receives price supports from the Department of Agriculture equal to the difference in prices $(P_1 - P_0)$ times the amounts of the commodity produced. This program is essentially the same as the purchase-loan-storage program except that government sells the commodity on the open market for what it will bring rather than dumping it abroad or letting it rot.

This program has the advantage over the other two of lower prices to consumers, so consumers are not clobbered by a double-edged sword of higher prices and higher taxes to support farm incomes. Although this program was economically more efficient than the other programs, it had one major flaw politically — direct payments to farmers permitted the public to see the extent

FIGURE 10 A Purchase-and-Resale Subsidy Program

Purchase-and-resale subsidy programs are more efficient than farm programs that remove produced goods from the market. There is still a welfare loss triangle equal to abc in this figure, however, because consumers value the extra goods produced as a consequence of this subsidy less than the costs incurred for the extra production.

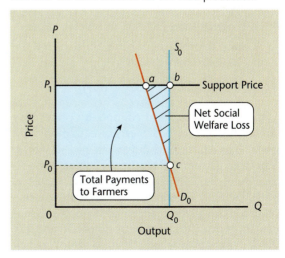

to which certain farmers were benefiting. Payments to individual farms and/or corporations exceeding $1,000,000 per year were not uncommon. Payments exceeding $100,000 annually were the norm for a large number of farmers. Getting paid not to produce while simultaneously receiving large subsidies became a political scandal. The result was restrictions by Congress on the total subsidies or payments any individual or corporation could receive.

Who Gained from Traditional Farm Programs? The bulk of farm subsidies have been paid to fewer than one-fifth of all farmers. The realization by Congress of such an unequal distribution of farm subsidies and the dramatic increases in farm prices in the early 1970s led to a reappraisal of past policies and a new farm bill in 1973. This bill set the future course of farm policy.

Farm Policies in the 1970s and 1980s

Traditional farm policies served the farmer relatively well until the early 1970s, when agriculture exports began to surge because of

1. A 1972 decision by the Soviet Union (continually repeated) to fill its domestic shortfall through imports from the United States.
2. Rising demands for livestock resulting from increased consumer incomes.
3. Poor agricultural harvests in several nations.
4. A sharp depreciation of the dollar in international currency markets.

Boom Years in the Early 1970s

In the early 1970s, farm commodity prices rose rapidly because of bad weather conditions and sparse harvests throughout much of the world. American farmers prospered, encouraging expansion of the competitive agriculture industry. By 1973, most organizations representing farmers urged the government to allow food production to expand to meet both domestic and expanded export markets. The focus of policy shifted from concerns about overproduction and low farm income to avoiding possible shortages, inflation from high farm prices, and using agriculture exports to reverse persistent deficits in our balance of payments. Farmers were anxious to cash in on booming demands for food and fiber and did not want outdated policies — primarily crop restriction programs — to hold them back. The Secretary of Agriculture at the time, Earl Butz, led the charge to accommodate farmers' wishes.

Agriculture and Consumer Protection Act of 1973 As a result, Congress enacted the Agriculture and Consumer Protection Act of 1973, which embodied a four-year program with the following features[3]:

1. *Target prices*: Price supports based on parity were replaced with target prices established by law. These target prices were guaranteed minimum price floors on basic agricultural commodities, and were established considerably below the peak farm prices of 1973 but above the support prices of previous years. When market prices were above these target prices, the government left agriculture to the free market. When prices fell below the target, direct payments to the farmer were based on normal yields and acreage.

2. *Agricultural production*: Although the previous crop limitation programs were extended, the Agriculture Department largely refrained from imposing crop limits and generally encouraged aggressive expansion by farmers.

3. *Subsidy ceilings*: The 1973 Act limited payments to $200,000 per individual farmer for all commodity programs combined.

The 1973 Act along with adverse domestic and global weather conditions provided the

---

3. This basic Act has been updated (1977, 1981, 1985, and 1990) and revised modestly, and there is a trend to tack in provisions to enhance environmental quality. Pesticides, for example, were increasingly controlled after Alar, an insecticide used in apple orchards, was identified as a carcinogen in 1989. Further testing of Alar, however, failed to prove the case against its use.

farmer with record or near record incomes. Per capita income for the farm population (including farmers' nonfarm earnings) actually exceeded that for the nonfarm population in 1973. Predictably, this agriculture bonanza was not shared equally among farmers. Most small farmers gained little ground during this period, but rural prosperity created by record prices and farm incomes throughout 1973–1976 added to strong inflationary pressures then being experienced in the economy. This made agriculture a hot political issue that precipitated consumer boycotts of many grocery store chains and some types of food, along with export embargoes on other agricultural products.

The agricultural prosperity during the 1970s (shown in Figure 11) yielded many secondary benefits for farmers. High incomes generated rapid capitalization of farm land, so farmers who owned their farms experienced huge gains in their wealth. Capital gains to farmers were nearly twice as great as the record total net farm income of this period. The result of this prosperity was reflected in farmers' balance sheets. Proprietors' equity almost doubled during 1970–1976, and farm mortgages fell from roughly 17

percent to 15 percent of the total value of farm land. The greatest enrichment of farmers during this period resulted from the skyrocketing price of farm land. Although propelled by rapid general inflation, farm land rose even faster than other prices. From less than $200 per acre in 1970, average prices per acre rose to over $700 by 1980.

Many farmers viewed this prosperity as a signal to expand and invested heavily in more, bigger, and better machinery and bought more high-priced acreage to cultivate. Some land that had previously lain fallow was planted and harvested. Many nonfarmers entered agriculture, expecting the prosperity to continue. The result was that both long-time farmers and new ones went deeply in debt in the hope of making fortunes. Unfortunately for most of those who followed this strategy, getting rich in farming is the exception rather than the rule.

Rural Hardships in the 1980s

The substantial gains in farm incomes and wealth recorded in the 1970s occurred in an era of relatively little government intervention. You might

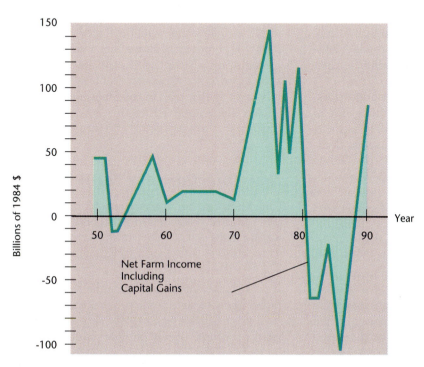

FIGURE 11 Net Farm Income Including Capital Gains

Agricultural incomes follow a boom-bust cycle that makes farming sometimes seem a bit like playing Russian roulette. The inclusion of capital gains to farmers makes income streams even more volatile.

Source: Calomiris, *BPEA*, p. 446.

think that farmers would consequently favor a hands-off policy, rather than government handouts. Nothing could be further from the truth.

Although the domestic demand for farm products has remained relatively strong, two factors combined to cause farm income to fall sharply: the erosion of export markets, and a worldwide rapid growth of agricultural harvests. By 1977, the dollar had depreciated to a record low on international money markets. This stimulated foreign demands for our farm exports. Then, when the dollar rose back toward peak levels in the early 1980s, and foreign crop failures were reversed, exports of U.S. agricultural products fell sharply. Several countries that had been major net importers of food products became net exporters during this period (e.g., China and Indonesia). Exports were also curtailed a bit by embargoes against some foreign governments (e.g., to protest apartheid in South Africa).

Even more significant were bountiful harvests that had swollen supplies and caused farm prices to fall substantially relative to production costs. The market prices of agricultural land also dropped, reflecting general gloom among farmers. From a peak of $823 in 1982, the average price per acre of farm land collapsed to $679 by 1985, precipitating a wave of farm foreclosures and bankruptcies throughout rural America. These slippages inflamed many farmers into calling for 100 percent parity, a return to older agriculture policies, and threats of strikes if their demands were not met.

Target prices and the acreage set-asides reestablished by the Food and Agriculture Act of 1977 did not provide major windfalls to farmers. These programs only postponed financial disasters that were brewing in the late 1970s. Target prices allowed market prices to achieve equilibrium levels and, if the prices were deemed too low, direct subsidies were paid to farmers who participated in the program. Even this program, however, left many farmers very unhappy. The reason? The prosperity of the early 1970s encouraged many people (primarily farmers' children) to enter the farming industry, while existing farmers expanded their operations by paying premium prices for land and machinery. When the future of any industry appears bright, many participants are willing to go deeply in debt so that they will share in the pie. High interest rates were more than offset by inflation during most of 1975–1979 and so did not discourage a flood of new financial investments in agriculture. When inflation began declining faster than interest rates fell during the early 1980s, farm income began declining. Consequently, land prices softened and many farmers found that their property was worth less than they had paid for it (and in some cases, less than its mortgaged value). Foreclosures were met with militant resistance by such organizations as the American Agriculture Movement.

The sharp decline in the international value of the dollar starting in 1986 helped to stimulate agricultural exports in the late 1980s. The bulk of the recent agricultural upturn, however, can be attributed to weather and an increased derived demand for grains. A severe drought in 1988 coupled with an increased world demand for meat has resulted in an upturn in commodity prices and farmers' outlooks.

Many observers of the business scene view the powerful swings from rural depression to prosperity and back again as a simple reflection of the market at work. Overly optimistic business forecasts often cause firms (including farmers) to bite off more than they can chew. The inevitable result is that many will be forced into bankruptcy. The power of farmers as a voting bloc is on the wane. Nevertheless, the importance of agriculture to the American economy means that it is unlikely that the United States will revert to a laissez-faire approach to the farm problem.

New Directions for Farm Policy

Targeted income maintenance may be required to save particular groups of farms [that are] deemed socially valuable.

Calomiris, Hubbard, and Stock

If policymakers intend to "save the family farm" rather than to enrich large, corporate farmers, then it is inefficiently costly for agricultural policies to continue to rely on unfocused price supports, acreage reduction programs, export subsidies, and other broad-gauge government transfer programs. These traditional approaches may be like trying to use a garage sale to bail out the savings-and-loan crisis. A more narrowly focused federal emphasis on ensuring that small farmers have access to credit markets (i.e., something like an expanded FHA loan guarantee program for small farmers) is one possibility. Another alternative is for the government to use a needs test in dispensing its transfers. Poor farm families alone would be subsidized.

One problem with this approach, however, is farmers' insistence that they seek, not welfare payments, but rather, just compensation for their contributions to society. Another problem is that explicitly setting welfare payments at higher levels for family farmers than for other impoverished Americans is politically unpalatable. If so, it may be the case that the only long-run cure for small and inefficient family farmers is to allow them to go out of business. There are no easy answers to the dilemmas confronted in redesigning agricultural policies.

Chapter Review: Key Points

1. The major problem for farmers is that income from agriculture has been relatively low and erratic for generations. No other sector of the economy has as consistently experienced tremendous productivity growth, so these low incomes are largely market signals that our society desires shifts of resources from agriculture into other forms of economic activity.

2. The demand for all farm products lumped together tends to be relatively price and income inelastic. Thus, much lower prices are required to clear markets when agricultural supplies grow significantly, and the widespread adoption of more productive agricultural technologies tends to drive farmers' revenues down sharply.

3. Farming is our largest industry, and it is among our most competitive. There are strong political pressures for the federal government to support farmers, however, for at least two reasons: (a) Many nonfarmers have great empathy for farming as a way of life, and (b) although a small minority, farmers have been active for a century in making their problems known to lawmakers.

4. The strong tendency for people to make decisions at the margin means that there will always be high-cost marginal producers who will be wiped out by slight reversals in the markets where they operate. No policy can prevent this from happening. The principal thrust of agricultural policy has been to restrict farm production to raise prices and farm revenues. These farm programs can be classi-

fied into (a) crop restriction programs, (b) purchase-loan price-support programs to boost farm prices, and (c) purchase-and-resale subsidy programs.

5. "Parity pricing" is based on the notion that the prices of farm products should not change relative to the prices farmers pay. A policy of 100 percent parity would enrich farmers who experience productivity gains and would freeze the incentives for efficient reallocations that are embedded in relative price changes.

6. Most policies intended to preserve the family farm have largely benefited large farming operations, many of which are corporate.

Key Concepts

Ensure that you can define these terms before proceeding.

marginal family farmers	parity
farm productivity	price supports
crop restrictions	target prices
allotments	subsidy ceilings

Problems and Questions

1. Show graphically how productivity growth reduces total revenue if demand is relatively price inelastic.

2. Although demands for farm products tend to

be relatively price and income inelastic, these demands tend to be roughly proportional to population. What does this imply about the coefficient of the population elasticity of these demands?

3. Suppose that both the short-run price elasticity of demand for wheat and its income elasticity are .3, and that its population demand elasticity is 1.0. If 120 million tons of wheat were sold in 1992 at a price of $6 per bushel, what will happen to wheat's price if, between 1992 and 1993, population grows 2 percent, income grows 3 percent, and good weather and new technology boost the amount of wheat marketed to 140 million bushels?

4. Suppose you were an extraordinarily efficient farmer who owned prime agricultural acreage. Would your income necessarily rise if the government guaranteed a price for some of your crops that was high enough to allow less efficient farmers to survive, and simultaneously restricted your output through an acreage allotment program? Why or why not?

5. Rapid growth of agricultural productivity over the centuries has meant that the proportion of population required in agriculture to feed the rest of us has consistently declined. Can you think of mechanisms other than relatively low farm incomes that would have accomplished the movement from rural areas into the urban work force?

6. If the value of the dollar on international currency markets is relatively high, U.S. agricultural exports tend to be constricted, as occurred during 1980 through 1984. When the dollar falls sharply, however, U.S. agricultural exports rise sharply, as they did during 1986 through 1988. Should the federal government buffer farmers against swings in their incomes that occur because of volatility in the international value of the dollar? Why or why not?

7. Richard McDougal, president of the American Cattlemen's Association, testified before the House Agriculture Committee that

Unfortunately for us, the best cure for low prices is low prices. That is, low prices bring about needed supply adjustments . . . . Similarly, the best cure for high prices is high prices. That is, high prices and profits bring supply increases, which then moderate prices to consumers.

Do you agree with this statement? Explain.

Mr. McDougal went on to testify:

Production of agricultural commodities is inherently cyclical . . . hundreds of thousands of individual producers make production decisions, in response to cost-and-price relationships . . . . Just as cattlemen overresponded to favorable returns in the late 1960s and early 1970s, wheat producers overresponded to . . . [high] prices in 1975.

Does this analysis seem basically correct to you? What would be the impact on the livestock industry of very high grain prices? Should we guarantee high prices to one group at the expense of other groups? Consider the trade-off between equity and efficiency!

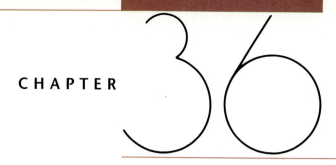

Income Distribution and Poverty

Most Americans wake up knowing that we will have full bellies and roofs to sleep under that night. But haunting images of starving children and the homeless regularly appear on television. About half of the world's people suffer from malnutrition and live in squalor. It is not surprising that poor people tend to be less healthy and die younger than those who command more resources. In the United States, slum dwellers consume much less than prosperous suburbanites do, and the incomes of migrant farmworkers fall far below the national average. Overseas, the opulence enjoyed by some wealthy people contrasts even more starkly with the lives of the impoverished.

Why is the relative prosperity that most Americans, Japanese, and Western Europeans enjoy so rare elsewhere? Why are some people poor, while others consume conspicuously and extravagantly? Do prosperous people have a duty to share with the less fortunate? If voluntary sharing seems inadequate, should government redistribute income and wealth? Do government redistributions of income provide disincentives to work among those receiving aid and those who ultimately provide aid?

Whether "money can buy happiness" is the first issue addressed in this chapter. We then present some alternative ethical criteria that ad-dress redistributing income and wealth. Then we examine the distribution of income and wealth in the United States. Finally, we identify influences on present distribution patterns, describe current American welfare programs, and look at proposed reforms. A majority of people in more fortunate circumstances favor aid to the poor, but are concerned that disincentives to work are embedded in welfare programs. We will consider whether aid programs provide for the needy without creating incentives to create a permanent underclass.

Prosperity and Happiness

Would most of us like more wealth than we have? Almost certainly. Jeremy Bentham, the utilitarian philosopher, offered two important propositions about wealth and utility. The first is widely accepted: All else equal, more income or wealth makes people happier. Bentham's second proposition is more controversial: On average, additional income means more to the poor than to the rich. That is, income itself may be subject to the law of diminishing marginal utility. We will deal with these issues in turn.

Does Money Buy Happiness?

Are the rich happier than the poor? Soap operas, pulp magazines, and bad novels often suggest that the price of being rich is a life of pain and suffering. Wouldn't most of us gladly risk such misery?

Numerous studies indicate that, on average, health and longevity are positively related to income and wealth. Prosperous people also tend to rate themselves as happier than people who are not, as the study reported in Figure 1 shows.

FIGURE 1   Income and Happiness

In Panel A, the percentage of people who rate themselves "pretty happy" seems unaffected by income. The response "very happy," however, is far more common for people with higher incomes, and relatively few of them are "not too happy." Many low-income people consider themselves "not too happy," while few are "very happy." This suggests that general satisfaction with life is positively related to income, as shown is Panel B.

Source: Drawn from a survey of Illinois residents, reported in N. M. Bradburn and D. Caplovitz, *Report on Happiness* (Chicago: Aldine, 1965). [Updated to 1990 dollars by authors.]

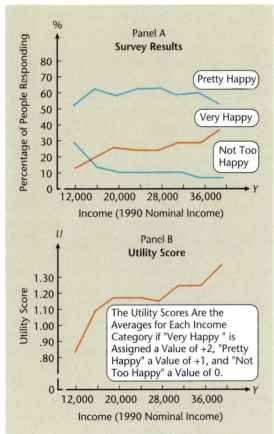

People were asked how happy they were. The responses shown in Panel A were assigned weights of +2 for "very happy," +1 for "pretty happy," and zero for "not too happy," leading to the *utility score* in Panel B. Utility scores climb as income rises, supporting Bentham's idea that higher income yields greater happiness, although there is a possibility of reverse causation—cheerful people may get better jobs and do better financially.

Do Extra Dollars Mean More to the Poor Than to the Rich?

This question cannot be answered objectively, because satisfaction is not measurable. People favoring greater equality might argue that extra dollars mean more to the poor because necessities generate more *utils* (imaginary measures of satisfaction) than do such luxuries as BMWs or jewelry. Defenders of current distributions could respond that income must mean more to the well-to-do, because most of them work hard for their income. The debate spins in circles, but a "best" income distribution cannot be scientifically ascertained. Wide differences in opinion exist about how income should be distributed.

Ethical Criteria for Distribution

When wealth is centralized, the people are dispersed. When wealth is distributed, the people are brought together.

The Analects of Confucius, Book 14

Ancient controversies surround fair divisions of income and output. Distribution has been thought unfair by most "have-nots"—and by many conscience-stricken "haves" as well. At least three schools of thought offer competing answers. One view is that income should be based on contribution; a second, that income should be distributed according to need; and a third, that income should be distributed equally.

The Contribution Standard

. . . he that will not work shall not eat.

John Smith, *The General Historie of Virginia*, 1624

Competition allocates income in proportion to the values of the marginal products and amounts of resources people supply. Marginal productivity theory underpins the *contribution standard*, whose advocates believe that rewarding contribution is both equitable and efficient. A contribution standard recognizes that income incentives encourage work effort, investment, and attempts to profit by serving other people's demands.

> The **contribution standard** *is the idea that income should be distributed according to the productivity of one's resources.*

This standard assumes that markets accurately gauge productivity. Thus, who gets how much is determined by impersonal market forces, without the favoritism inherent in centralized decision making. Income differences generated by a contribution standard are not a disadvantage, according to its champions, in part because people with high incomes save proportionally more, facilitating investment and economic growth. The rich and the poor alike gain according to the cliché, "A rising tide lifts all boats." Moreover, inequality is equitable if it results from smarter or harder work, longer hours, or higher rates of saving and investing.

A contribution standard uses "carrots" (income) to reward productivity, instead of the "sticks" (punishment for sloth) common under other systems. Should a cabdriver who works 60-hour weeks subsidize one who works only 30 hours? Should a factory worker who draws interest from savings squeezed from a slim paycheck share the interest with others who spend everything they make? Advocates of the contribution standard answer "No" to such questions, asserting that the standard is compatible with capitalism, sets efficient incentives for production and economic growth, and maximizes individual freedom.

Opponents of the contribution standard, however, wonder how well markets measure productivity. They argue further that the very young, the very old, and the handicapped among us must share in our income if our society is to be fair and humane.

The Needs Standard

From each according to ability, to each according to needs.

Louis Blanc

Some people lack physical or mental attributes or skills to be very productive, while wealthy heirs, by resource ownership alone, claim to be productive. Citing such perceived inequities, many opponents of a contribution standard favor ensuring that people's needs are met.

> The **needs standard** *asserts that income should be distributed "to each according to needs."*[1]

This slogan inspired Marxist revolutionaries for over a century, ultimately governing the nominal policies of countries containing one-third of humanity. Marxism's ongoing collapse in Eastern Europe and China is testimony to obstacles in implementing a needs standard.[2] Assessing needs is unavoidably imprecise and requires operation of an immense bureaucracy likely to favor political entrepreneurs. Production incentives are also a problem. How many people would work diligently if distribution were strictly by need? Is it proper to replace economic incentives with government coercion?

Trade-offs between efficiency and equity can be heart-wrenching. Most people agree that at least the basic needs of those who cannot provide for themselves must be accommodated, because

---

1. An interesting historical note is that Marx viewed distribution according to need as an objective to be implemented only after a "dictatorship of the proletariat" gave way to "pure communism." According to Marx, the most glaring inequity of capitalism is that workers are paid less than the value of their *average* products because exploitative capitalists steal any production in excess of subsistence wages. Thus, Marx was an advocate of a productivity standard, were productivity defined by averages rather than marginal products. After Marx's death, John Bates Clark developed marginal productivity theory and the argument that payments to owners of their resources' marginal products would absorb all production. It would be interesting, were it possible, to know what Marx's own reaction would have been to Clark's rebuttal of the exploitation doctrine.
2. Other aspects of an equality standard of distribution were introduced in Chapter 2.

Pie Makers vs. Pie Splitters: China and the USSR

Orthodox Marxists believe that a proper blend of "equality" and "need" is the only fair criterion for distributing income. They view capitalist-style "freedom" as a facade: Rich capitalists have freedom to exploit workers and hog most consumer goods, while the proletariats (working classes) only have freedom to suffer in silence. Capitalism's alleged efficiency has been vilified as an empty shell that masks extreme inequalities of income, manipulative advertising, and a general exploitation of consumers and workers.

This overall characterization of capitalist markets was an article of faith among the leaders who led Marxist revolutions and installed communism in the Soviet Union and China. Official hostil-ity to "exploitation" put a strange "supply-side" spin on economic activity. Restaurant employees' rights to stable jobs and income, for example, precede the rights of customers. Consequently, service is almost uniformly poor, because servers receive the same incomes regardless of whether customers are satisfied, and regardless of the restaurant's revenues. Under capitalism, consumer sovereignty yields a "demand-side" orientation. This means that restaurant employees who fail to render prompt and courteous service with good food experience low incomes and job instability.

Leadership groups led by the USSR's President Gorbachev and China's Deng Xiaoping have recently concluded that it is futile to try to reform the centralized bureaucracies that have coordinated economic activity, and that the fundamental orientation of Soviet and Chinese workers toward their jobs must change. These leaders have sought greater efficiency and growth through increased reliance on market forces.

Limited experiments with markets have succeeded in some targeted sectors. For example, China was a net importer of rice before farming was decentralized in 1980; it is now a major rice exporter on world markets. And much of the world's clothing is now produced by Chinese cooperatives. But many Soviet and Chinese ideologues and bureaucrats who feel attacked by market experiments have counterat-

we should not allow orphans, the aged, the severely handicapped, or society's misfits to starve. Whether capable but lazy people should be guaranteed the necessities of life is a separate issue. Focus 1 indicates how attempts to guarantee prosperity for everyone can backfire.

The Equality Standard

Dividing income equally avoids the great disparities in income that come about under the contribution standard and dispenses with the huge bureaucracy required for a needs standard.

The **equality standard** *asserts that income should be distributed equally across the population.*

All an equality standard requires is accurate national income accounting and a census of population: Divide national income by population, then mail each family a check for its share. Moreover, there is an economic rationale that under certain conditions an equal distribution of income generates the maximum economic welfare possible in a society.

tacked, focusing on the high incomes earned by ambitious entrepreneurs.

After decades of being conditioned that income differentials reflect exploitation, many Soviet and Chinese citizens cannot stand the idea that anyone deserves more income than anyone else. In the Soviet Union, for example, an inventor named Artyom Tarasov formed a cooperative called Tekhnika and earned almost 3 million rubles in 1988 by importing computers financed by exports of, among other things, recyclable industrial wastes.[*] The Interior Ministry began harassing Tekhnika and froze Tarasov's assets. In China, Guan Guangmei, a food store manager, was criticized in the Beijing media for making 20 times the income she paid employees.[†]

Hardliners in both countries have proposed narrow limits on income differentials in response to these and similar cases. Soviet bureaucrats, for example, have tried such ploys as 95 percent taxes on entrepreneurs—they are accustomed to governing economic activity, not by a rule of law, but rather, by administrative fiat.

Soviet and Chinese leaders are trying to reassure the nervous entrepreneurs who are emerging. Both USSR President Gorbachev and Chinese Premier Li Peng have indicated that ideology is less important than rapid economic development. Nevertheless, leaders in both countries are treading political high wires, trying to balance new incentives for productivity against the entrenched interests of bureaucrats whose jobs are threatened because they are inefficient.

The raging debates in China and the USSR over high incomes for entrepreneurs are evidence that rapid changes wrought by market forces make many people uncomfortable. This seems especially true in countries with long histories of official hostility that treats almost all market activities as criminal behavior.

[*]The New Russians, *Hedrick Smith* (New York: Random House, 1990), p. 287.

[†]*"Big Pay Can Be Big Pain in China,"* Chicago Tribune, 30 Dec. 1987, sec. 3.

Suppose you were the utilitarian ruler of a country with a fixed national income and were intent on maximizing social happiness. You suspect that some citizens would be reasonably happy with very little, while others would gain great happiness from higher monetary incomes. Unfortunately, you cannot measure any person's gain in happiness from a higher money income, nor can you objectively compare happiness between individuals. If you try to find out who would gain the most from more than an equal share, most people will exaggerate their needs, and some may lie to you. If you are convinced that each person gains from higher income but that, on average, the poor gain more than the rich, then expected happiness of the community is maximized if you simply divide all income equally.

Like distribution according to need, however, equal sharing of income erodes personal incentives for productivity. One ideal of socialism is to replace the selfish individuals assumed in conventional economic theory with people filled with desire to work for the betterment of all humanity. Attempts to educate masses of people into altruistic modes of behavior have uniformly failed, however, and enforced production quotas replaced income incentives for production in such countries as the Soviet Union and China. The collapse of this approach has caused a new generation of leaders in both countries to move toward more personal systems of rewards.

Inequality and Inequity

Life is unfair.

John F. Kennedy (1960)

People differ in natural ability and opportunity, in the times when and places where they were born, in age, race, sex, and religion. Most of all, they differ in luck. Some face discrimination, some are maimed or die in car wrecks or wars, and some are homely, demented, or physically or mentally impaired. Others are attractive, healthy, bright, buy winning lottery tickets, or are born with silver spoons in their mouths. Whether inequality is inherently inequitable is a normative issue that varies according to individual judgments and from case to case.

Some types of inequality may seem inequitable to some people, but simply cannot be eliminated. A genius cannot transfer IQ points to someone less intellectually gifted, for example, nor can a world-class sprinter give speed to us slowpokes. Other apparent inequities may be remedied through government policies or social reforms. The inequity of slavery ended with the Civil War, and discrimination by religion, race, or sex is now illegal in education, housing, and employment.

No society ever achieves a consensus that everyone is treated fairly because equity is unavoidably subjective. Suppose that everyone agreed with the idea of *horizontal equity*: Equals should be treated equally. Even this might do little to resolve equity because every person is somewhat unique. Advocates of the contribution standard argue that inequality of income or wealth is frequently justified by differences in the productivity of individuals' resources. Yet difficulties in specifying equity when people and circumstances differ have caused critics of a contribution standard to focus on inequality as evidence of inequity.

Distribution in the United States

Just how unequal is the U.S. income distribution? Table 1 shows pretax and pretransfer distributions of income since 1935. Although changes proceed only at a snail's pace, notice that the share of the middle 60 percent of recipients is now over half of all income. Moreover, because taxes are mildly progressive, while transfers tend to be regressive, Table 1 understates the share of net income received by people at the bottom and overstates the share of people at the top. Before we explore how much tax and transfer policies reduce inequality, we need to introduce a device for comparing distributions of income or wealth.

Lorenz Curves

It is hard to see changes in the income distribution and the extent of inequality from Table 1. Lorenz curves, developed by a German statistician, allow visual comparisons between distributions across time and between countries.

> A **Lorenz curve** *shows the cumulative percentage distribution of income or wealth in a society.*

Cumulative percentages of families and family incomes before taxes and transfers are on the axes of the Lorenz curve in Figure 2. Data (from Table 1) are sequentially summed to form the cumulative distribution listed below the figure. For example, if the bottom 20 percent and the second lowest 20 percent of the population respectively receive 5 percent and 11 percent of all income, then the lowest 40 percent of the population receives 16 percent of total income. And if the middle 20 percent gets 17 percent of total income, then the lowest 60 percent of the population receives 33 percent (5 + 11 + 17 = 33). And so on.

If the Lorenz curve were a diagonal like the straight line 0*e*, then income would be distributed evenly — each fifth of the population would receive one-fifth of income. If one family had all income while the rest of us had nothing, the Lorenz curve would be identical to the bottom and right-hand axes — line 0*fe*. The Lorenz curve for the United States is the curved line. The shaded

Table 1 *The Distribution of Income Before Taxes and Transfers, 1935–1990*

Family Group	Percent of Total Income					
	1935	**1950**	**1960**	**1970**	**1980**	**1989**
Lowest 20 percent	4.1	4.5	4.8	5.4	5.3	4.6
Second 20 percent	9.1	12.0	12.2	12.2	11.6	10.6
Middle 20 percent	14.1	17.4	17.8	17.6	17.5	16.5
Fourth 20 percent	20.9	23.4	24.0	23.8	24.0	23.7
Highest 20 percent	51.7	42.7	41.3	40.9	41.6	44.6
Top 5 percent	N/A	17.3	15.9	15.6	15.3	17.9

Sources: *Statistical Abstract of the United States,* 1986, 1990, and U.S. Bureau of the Census, *Money Income of Households, Families, and Persons in the United States* (Washington, D.C.: U.S. Government Printing Office), 1990.

area reflects inequality; the larger this area, the more unequal the income distribution.

A related measure of income concentration is the Gini index, a statistical measure derived from the Lorenz curve.

*The **Gini index** is the ratio of the area between the line of perfect equality (diagonal) and the Lorenz curve to the total area under the diagonal.*

In Figure 2, the Gini index would be the ratio of area *A* to area *A* plus area *B* or,

$$\text{Gini index} = \frac{A}{A + B}$$

The Gini index ranges from 0 (perfect equality) to 1 (perfect inequality).

Perfect equality can never be attained, if only because lifetime earnings patterns prevent continuously equal income distributions. Younger families typically earn less than more established families, primarily because of differences in work experience and past saving. Thus, even if every family had identical lifetime incomes, inequality would exist at every point in time because of typical age–earnings differences.

The Changing Distribution of Income

The state of economic development powerfully influences relative distributions of income, with more advanced countries tending to have greater income equality. For example, Figure 3 indicates that distribution is more equal in such countries as the United States, Japan, and West Germany than in such countries as Mexico, Turkey, Brazil,

FIGURE 2   Lorenz Curve (Income Before Taxes and Transfers)

Lorenz curves illustrate unequal distribution. In this figure, the cumulative shares of pretax income are shown (on the vertical axis) for ever larger proportions of the population, beginning at the bottom of the income ladder. The area between the Lorenz curve and the 45° reference line indicates the extent of inequality.

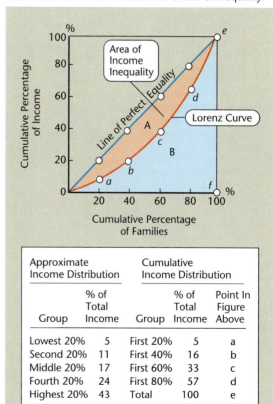

Approximate Income Distribution		Cumulative Income Distribution		
Group	% of Total Income	Group	% of Total Income	Point In Figure Above
Lowest 20%	5	First 20%	5	a
Second 20%	11	First 40%	16	b
Middle 20%	17	First 60%	33	c
Fourth 20%	24	First 80%	57	d
Highest 20%	43	Total	100	e

FIGURE 3 Gini Index Numbers for Selected Countries (1980–1983)

The Gini coefficients in this figure indicate that developing nations usually have problems because of both low income and severe inequality. Developed nations have more equally distributed incomes, but socialist nations report even greater equality. However, recent events in Eastern Europe suggest that improving the level of income may be more important than equality in the income distribution. Substantial evidence exists that equality of income is misleadingly reported for many socialist nations.

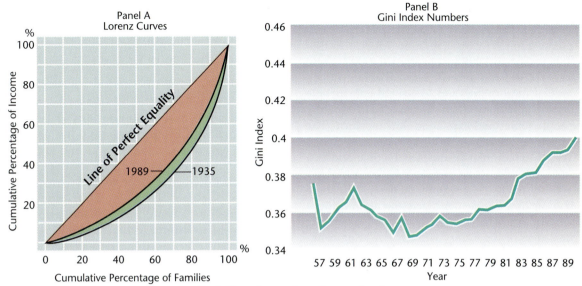

FIGURE 4 Lorenz Curves and Gini Indexes for the United States (1935–1989)

In the United States, there has been a gradual shift toward greater income equality in the last half century, but for the last two decades (Panel B), the pretax distribution has become somewhat more unequally distributed.

Source: U.S. Bureau of the Census, *Money Income and Poverty Status in the United States: 1989* (Washington, D.C.: U.S. Government Printing Office, 1990).

and Bangladesh. The average Gini coefficient for the developed nations shown is .337, while for the developing countries illustrated, it is .462 — nearly 40 percent more severe. Income as reported in the socialist nations was relatively evenly distributed, but research on the lifestyles of political kingpins and other favored groups in Eastern Europe, the USSR, and China suggests that the official statistics are unreliable.

The gradual shift toward greater equality in the United States is shown by the pretax Lorenz curves for 1935 and 1989 in Panel A of Figure 4. However, Panel B provides a little closer look at the changing distribution of pretax earnings in the United States over the last three decades. The Gini index has been rising steadily since the late 1960s, but the rate of change has not been constant. Between 1969 and 1979, the Gini ratio rose (income distribution became less equal) by 4.6 percent, but during the 1980s it jumped by 9.8 percent — over double the rate of change from a decade earlier.

Traditionally, U.S. Census Department sur-

veys focused on pretax incomes and fail to consider capital gains, tax payments, and benefits from government programs. A recent study by the Department of Commerce[3] concluded that "Taxes, government transfers, and other benefits have substantial effects on the level and distribution of income." After taxes, transfers, and capital gains are considered, the Gini index for 1989 drops by nearly 10 percent and the number of people below the poverty line drops by over 30 percent.

Taxes and transfer payments have resulted in a relatively more equal distribution of income. Some people, however, feel that redistribution schemes should focus on wealth instead of income, because income and prosperity are only roughly correlated.

---

3. U.S. Bureau of the Census, Current Population Reports, Series P-60, No. 169-RD, *Measuring the Effect of Benefits and Taxes on Income and Poverty: 1989* (Washington, D.C.: U.S. Government Printing Office, 1990).

The Distribution of Wealth

Wealth is the sum of financial assets and economic capital minus liabilities. Median household wealth in 1988 was nearly $36,000.[4] These assets include motor vehicles, real estate, stocks, mutual fund shares, and so on. Do poor people occasionally have high incomes? Do wealthy people sometimes experience low incomes? The surprising answer to both questions is "Yes." Wealth is cumulative unspent income and is a stock variable, while income is a flow variable.[5] Wealth tends to generate income, but some high-income people don't save and never achieve wealth; you may have read about high-rolling financiers or big lottery winners declaring bankruptcy. On the other hand, some wealthy people occasionally have low-income years. (Donald Trump had negative income of roughly $1 billion during 1989–1990.) This is common for retirees, among others. Most welfare programs are intended for people plagued by both little wealth and low income.

A 1991 Bureau of the Census study indicates that the lowest fifth of households had under 0.5 percent of assets in 1988, while the top 20 percent held 38 percent of wealth — excluding pension plans, jewelry, and household furnishings.[6] White families average 10 times as much wealth as African-Americans, and 8 times as much as Hispanics. Only 2 percent of minority families were classified as wealthy, while 14 percent of whites were in the richest bracket. The wealthy tend to be professional or self-employed and in stable homes. The poor tend to be uneducated and in broken homes. The major determinant of wealth, however, seems to be age. Typical heads of wealthy families are older than 55, while young families are often poor. Time allows you to acquire wealth — another good reason for preferring growing older to its alternative.

Determinants of Distribution

Now that you have seen snapshots of how income and wealth are distributed, we need to explore why some people are rich and some are poor. Many rich people inherit fortunes. (The most valuable talent anyone could have might be aptitude at parent selection.) Their productive assets generate income with no labor efforts by the owners, so heirs to fortunes generally land in high income brackets. Rent, interest, and corporate profit account for only about one-fifth of all income, but the bulk flows to the top 2 percent of the populace.

Income differentials also arise because, contrary to slogans and wishful thinking, we are not all created equal. Some of us are born with talents that especially suit us for remunerative careers. This is most obvious in entertainment or professional sports. Frustration will be your only reward if you cannot carry a tune but try to sing professionally, or stand less than 6 feet 8 inches tall and pursue a career as a center in the National Basketball Association. Levels of energy, motivation, amiability, and insight also separate individuals. Some people make choices that seem to doom them to poverty. For example, perpetual students in esoteric disciplines, most artists, actors, and musicians, and some ministers select occupations for psychic income, not financial remuneration. Discrimination based on race, sex, age, ethnic background, height, or general appearance also causes differences in the options available to otherwise equally gifted individuals.

Occupational restrictions may also keep qualified people out of some jobs. For example, doctors are the highest paid professionals, on average, but medical practice requires specialized education and the slots available in medical schools are limited. Some people step into management of a family business, while others bounce from job to job for years before settling into one that suits them. Finally, luck may play a major role in who gets a high-paying job and who

---

4. U.S. Bureau of the Census, *Household Wealth and Asset Ownership: 1988* (Washington, D.C.: U.S. Government Printing Office, 1990).

5. *Stock variables* are timeless, while *flow variables* lack meaning without a time period. A millionaire's assets exceed debts by at least $1 million, and time is irrelevant. It matters greatly, however, whether you make $100 hourly or weekly.

6. All studies of wealth, including this one, ignore human capital. In equilibrium, wealth and income are proportional if human capital is included in wealth.

doesn't — although some people seem to manufacture their own luck.

Poverty in America

Many people view poverty as evidence of the inequity of capitalism. In their minds, any economy generating over $6 trillion in output should not allow the squalor and deprivation seen in our urban ghettos and many rural communities. Critics of this position note that the poor in the United States are not nearly as destitute as the down and out in India, North Africa, or other less developed regions. Defenders of our current distribution also point out that most of the "poor" in this country have televisions, refrigerators, and other items considered luxuries in most other countries. Focus 2 points out that poverty is far from an absolute concept; our views of poverty depend on average standards of living in a society.

What Does Poor Mean?

Identifying the poor requires a definition of poverty. The 20 percent of our population with the lowest income is sometimes viewed as impoverished, but such an approach makes poverty incurable. Other definitions rely on estimates of the costs for families of various sizes and compositions of a "minimum" diet needed for life — soybeans, liver, lard, and other basic products. Such bland menus contain adequate nutrients, but would quickly bore anyone. You may have heard of the poverty line.

> The **poverty line** *is an index estimating the costs to secure minimal requirements for food, shelter, fuel, clothing, and transportation.*

This index is adjusted for family size, sex and age of the family head, number of minor children, and whether residence is rural or urban. Poverty thresholds in 1989 for various families are presented in Table 2. The poverty threshold for an average family of four now exceeds $12,000 in annual income.

Although historically one family in eight has been impoverished on average, there is tremen-

Table 2 *Poverty Threshold Levels by Size of Family and Sex of Head of Household, 1989*

Size of Family Unit	Threshold
One person (unrelated individual)	$ 6,311
15 to 64 years	6,452
65 years and over	5,947
Two persons	8,076
Householder 15 to 64 years	8,343
Householder 65 years and over	7,501
Three persons	9,885
Four persons	12,675
Five persons	14,990
Six persons	16,921
Seven persons	19,162
Eight persons	21,328
Nine persons or more	25,480

Source: Social Security Administration.

dous turnover among the poor. During a typical decade, more than 90 percent of the poor population changes; some people fall into poverty, replacing others who move above the poverty line. Despite policies designed to reduce inequality, roughly 1 to 2 percent of all people remain destitute year after year.

Profiles of Poverty

F. Scott Fitzgerald once said "The rich are different from you and me." Ernest Hemingway replied, "Yes, they are different. They have more money." This exchange can be turned upside down. Are the poor inherently different from the rich, or do they simply lack money?

Numerous studies indicate that certain personal characteristics are closely related to poverty. Some characteristics are not matters of choice: African-Americans, Hispanics, Native Americans, and new immigrants tend to be impoverished more often than are members of other population groups. The poor have relatively less education and labor participation, greater rates of illness and physical or mental disability, relatively more children, and heads of household who are more often female, very young, or very old, as reflected in Figure 5.

The most important determinant of income is the relationship of the family (or individual) to

Poverty: A Relative Concept

Friend: How's your spouse?
Economist: Relative to what?

An Unknown Pundit

This quip reflects a tendency among economists to measure almost everything relative to some alternative. *Poverty,* which is a "lack of wealth or material comfort," is no exception. People might agree that anyone without the physical means to sustain normal life is absolutely impoverished, but beyond that definition, poverty seems a relative concept that is determined by time and place. For example, many Americans below our official "poverty line" have amenities enjoyed only by the wealthy in less developed countries and seem prosperous relative to beggars and slum dwellers in some countries.

Consider how standards of living have changed over the centuries. The average lifespan of Europeans who survived childhood 1,000 years ago was less than 45 years. People in developed economies now typically live into their 70s because of advances in nutrition and medicine. Polio, cholera, smallpox,

diphtheria, and leprosy are now extinct or quite rare in developed economies. Canning and refrigeration make it possible to store food for long periods, and the growth of commerce has enriched diets throughout the world. Even the nobility of medieval times did not have access to things that many Americans who are classified as poverty-stricken take for granted: aspirin, fast-food restaurants, telephones, running water, automobiles, electric lighting, indoor plumbing, garbage collection, paved roads, public education and transportation, antibiotics, grocery stores, "painless" dentistry, television, and heating systems for their homes — this list could be extended for several pages.

Some Americans at society's bottom rungs — the homeless — do lead miserable lives, but for those in a position to receive food stamps and transfer payments, "life on the dole" is at least physically tolerable in most advanced economies. Suppose

that you had to choose between (*a*) the physical comforts of a typical U.S. family relying on welfare for all its income in 1991, and (*b*) the standard of living enjoyed by noble members of King Arthur's court. If you ignore the trappings of power enjoyed by feudal nobility, we suspect that you would be reluctant to trade the range of choices available to most poor Americans for life in a damp and drafty castle.

This does not mean that poor Americans have a soft life. There is no doubt that the most destitute people in our society are often homeless, cold, and hungry. Our point, instead, is that poverty is determined by cultural norms, of which material comforts are only one dimension. Wealth and income ultimately provide their holders with freedom, power, and deference from others. Poor people have relatively less power and fewer choices over their lives.

the labor market. Income opportunities are crucial if people are to be able to cure their own poverty. If jobs are the key, then government policies to maintain full employment might re-

duce poverty by providing job opportunities for the less fortunate. But high employment alone will not solve the problem of poverty. Unless discrimination is a barrier, job openings are gener-

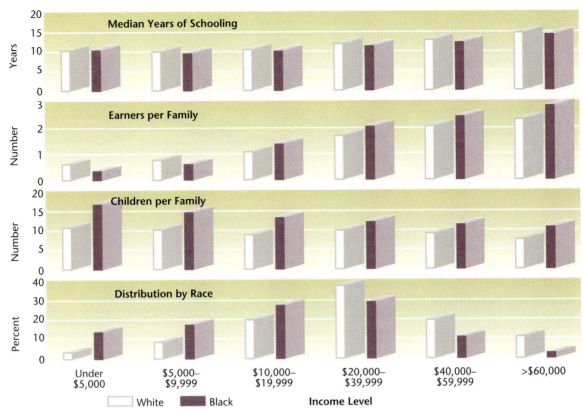

FIGURE 5 Family Characteristics by Income Level, 1984

Caucasian families with few children and more than one highly educated worker tend to have the highest incomes. Black families with numerous children, few workers, and low levels of education are commonly caught in poverty.

Source: U.S. Department of Commerce, Bureau of the Census, *Current Population Reports*, P-60, No. 156, April 1987.

ally won by those who are most willing and qualified to work. Many poor people lack the experience, training, and education a good job requires. Moreover, there are regional pockets of unemployment and poverty caused by the decline of some industries: Appalachian coal mining from the 1920s into the 1970s is an example. Centers for such "smokestack" industries as steel and automobiles experienced similar problems in the early 1980s, although these industries were slowly recovering until the recession of 1990–1991 weakened them once again.

Government as a Provider for the Poor

Private charity alleviates some poverty, but many people see government aid as the only real remedy for poor people's misery. Reducing poverty has aspects of a public good. You and I may both be distressed because people are hungry and homeless. If your private donations help ease this problem, I may feel less guilty about my failure to contribute; I encounter fewer panhandlers who ask for my "spare change" and see fewer stories about the poor on the news. Thus, I am less likely to contribute to charitable causes because I know that you do. Public good aspects of private giving mean that it is probably inadequate relative to society's desires to cure poverty. Government action may provide a more efficient solution.

The government attack on poverty has been two-pronged, stressing job opportunities where practical and instituting income maintenance

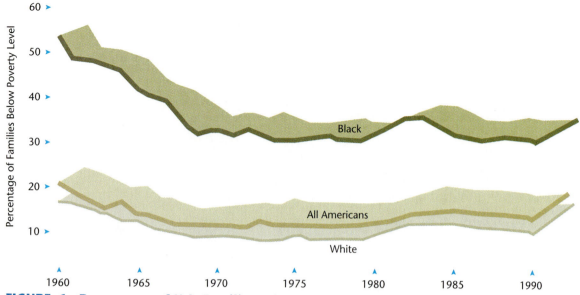

FIGURE 6 Percentage of U.S. Families Who Are Poor, 1960–1989

In 1990, roughly 13 percent of all families in the United States had incomes below the poverty level, but total figures can be misleading. For that same year, approximately 31 percent of all black families were impoverished, while only about one white family in ten was classified as "poor."

Social programs developed in the 1960s probably account for much of the gradual reduction in measured poverty that has occurred. The economic slumps of 1974–1975, 1980, and 1982–1983 were periods when the percentage of those living below the poverty line increased. The number of people living in poverty is substantially less when you include in-kind government transfers as income. Finally, these data indicate that black families on average are almost three times as likely to be poor as are their white counterparts.

Source: U.S. Bureau of the Census, *Money Income and Poverty Status in the United States: 1989* (Washington, D.C.: U.S. Government Printing Office, 1990).

programs for those who cannot or will not work. Rapid economic growth may provide the biggest boost to standards of living for those at the bottom of the economic ladder; Figure 6 indicates that the percentage of families below the poverty line dropped after President Johnson launched a "War on Poverty" in 1964. Federal funding for most welfare programs has grown continuously ever since, but over 30 million people remained below the poverty line in 1990. Poverty rates among black families have consistently been almost three times greater than those for white families.

A sharp jump in unemployment combined with reductions in the growth of social spending during the early 1980s worsened the plight of many people at the bottom of the income scale. This precipitated pressures for more federal funding from many who were concerned about poverty, but these pressures were offset somewhat by opponents of welfare spending. Opposition still continues from a growing chorus of critics who are skeptical that poverty can be cured by "throwing money at it." Their view, elaborated in Focus 3, is that welfare programs have yielded limited gains to some poor people and have fostered among many recipients an unhealthy dependence on government, while reducing work incentives among both taxpayers and welfare recipients.

Types of Poverty

Some analysts divide the poor into *involuntary* and *voluntary* groupings. Involuntary poverty occurs if people cannot provide for themselves;

FOCUS 3

Progress and Poverty Programs

Annual spending on social programs grew from $29.5 billion to more than $600 billion between 1960 and 1990, but the number of people living below the poverty line actually grew over this period. Architects of the "War on Poverty," begun in 1964, often assigned responsibility to society for poor people's woes and saw welfare programs as compensation for social injustice. Many people maintain similar attitudes today and advocate further expansion of these programs to remedy poverty. Some critics of our welfare system paradoxically blame much of current poverty on attitudes and programs instituted during the 1960s. Prominent among these critics are Thomas Sowell, an economist, and Charles Murray, a political scientist.

In his 1984 book *Losing Ground*, Murray cites evidence of deterioration in the quality of life among many groups that seem stuck at the bottom. Between 1960 and 1965, black students' academic aptitude test scores rose from 68 percent to 79 percent of the average scores of whites; 1965 was the peak year for both groups. The average

scores of black students on these tests had fallen to less than half of white norms by 1980. Annual rates of violent crime rose from 161 to 666 per 100,000 population between 1960 and 1988 (violent crime falls disproportionately on the poor). One black child in 5 was born to an unmarried mother in the 1950s; over half of all black infants today are illegitimate, and rates of white illegitimacy have risen from less than 1 in 50 to over 1 in 10. Four out of 5 white families include a married couple; the rate for black families has fallen sharply, to only 1 out of 2.

The basic problem, according to these critics, is that the rhetoric supporting many welfare programs implies that the poor bear no responsibility for alleviating their own poverty and that no stigma should be attached to being on welfare. This point of view means that the poor should not be expected to do anything for themselves; it is society's responsibility to lift people out of poverty.

These critics contend that such attitudes cause many poor people to feel like victims who cannot deal with their own prob-

lems, and who psychically cannot claim credit for their accomplishments. They become trapped in a culture of poverty. Few avenues of escape are open through which to gain any sense of personal pride. The result is that some welfare families may remain on welfare for generations—suspended in a childish state of dependence on a system that is encouraged by social workers.

What solutions are available? Few critics of the current welfare system favor abandonment of all welfare programs. Cutting all public assistance to zero would flood the nation's streets with many more millions of destitute and desperate people. Instead, most of these critics propose that programs be restructured to provide more incentives for poor people to work, to keep their families together, and to diligently pursue education and on-the-job training. Most of all, welfare programs should seek to instill in poor people a sense that they control their own destinies. In the words of Murray, "The lesson is not that we can do no good at all, but that we must pick our shots."

those who voluntarily choose poverty could earn adequate income but rely on welfare programs instead. One study suggests that welfare programs are so generous that by 1983, each additional $4,000 spent on welfare caused one additional family to voluntarily choose poverty.[7] How might higher welfare payments cause people to accept lower total income? Do you know workers who hate their jobs and would gladly quit working if society freely gave them half their current income? Similar choices may explain why some people choose to be poor.

Continuing debates between the advocates and opponents of welfare programs are mirrored in swings in social policies. Knowing some characteristics of typical poor families should help you understand why some people live on the ragged edge throughout their lives.

Alternative Views of Poverty

Some critics of welfare programs cite evidence that the poor tend to commit more crimes and be less able, less motivated, less mobile, more reproductive, and less educated than the general population. To these critics, the high incidence of poverty among certain racial or ethnic groups reflects failings of the cultural norms of these groups. There are, after all, prosperous members of every group. The success stories of many recent immigrants, especially from Southeast Asia, Jamaica, and Cuba, are cited as evidence that welfare is unnecessary. To these critics, the basic problem is failure to conform to the work ethic that has enabled other members of these same groups to succeed. These critics argue that many poor people are responsible for much of their own misery and that most welfare payments waste taxpayers' money because they reinforce the bad choices made by most of those who wind up poor.

A counterargument is that blaming the poor for their problems is misguided, that poor youngsters are obvious victims of poverty, and that immobility, nonparticipation in the labor force, and lack of education often reflect lack of opportunity or outright discrimination. Moreover, many of the aged poor have been poor all their lives, many large families were poor before they became large, and so on. If members of certain groups are denied equal chances to participate in the economy, those who lack skills or suffer from discrimination will remain poor. Studies suggest that racial discrimination may have accounted for as much as 40 percent of poverty in the 1960s, but more recent studies yield substantially lower estimates, an indication that discrimination may be abating.[8]

Economic Discrimination

Most of us agree that it is wrong to discriminate on the bases of sex, race, or other characteristics irrelevant to economic contribution or personal worth.

Economic discrimination *occurs when equivalent resources (labor) receive different payments (wages), even though their potential productive contributions are identical.*

There are many reasons for discrimination in labor markets. *Personal discrimination*, or *bigotry*, may play a major role, whether it is an employer's bigotry or the fear of bigotry from potential customers or other workers.[9] This may partially

7. "The New Structural Poverty: A Quantitative Analysis," by L. Gallaway, R. Vedder, and T. Foster, in *War on Poverty – Victory or Defeat?*, Hearings before the Joint Economic Committee, June 20, 1985 (Washington, D.C.: U.S. Government Printing Office, 1986).

8. See J. Haworth, J. Gwartney, and C. Haworth, "Earnings, Productivity, and Changes in Employment Discrimination During the 1960s," *American Economic Review*, March 1975, pp. 158–168, and J. Long, "Earnings, Productivity, and Changes in Employment Discrimination During the 1960s: Additional Evidence," *American Economic Review*, March 1977, pp. 225–227. Thomas Sowell in *Ethnic America* (New York: Basic Books, 1981) provides estimates that discrimination accounted for only about 10 percent of black/white wage differentials by the late 1970s. For a look at employee benefits and discrimination see B. F. Kiker and Sherrie Rhine, "Fringe Benefits and the Earnings Equation," *Journal of Human Resources*, 1987, pp. 126–137.

9. Discrimination may also occur because of customs or language. See Kevin Lang, "A Language Theory of Discrimination," *Quarterly Journal of Economics*, 1986, pp. 363–382.

account for the lower average wages of women and members of some minority groups.

Economic discrimination in labor markets takes several forms. Members of certain groups may suffer because

1. *Wage discrimination* causes them to be paid less than members of other groups are for equal work.
2. *Employment discrimination* excludes them from certain jobs.
3. *Occupational discrimination* bars them from certain occupations.
4. *Human capital discrimination* denies equal access to education or on-the-job training.
5. Outright *bigotry* fosters inequitable housing conditions, higher prices, and reduced medical care, for example.

Although bigotry stimulates the other four types of discrimination, it is not necessarily their only cause. Different groups, for example, may have different cultural norms about the values of education or hard work. Another problem is that different types of discrimination tend to reinforce each other. For example, low prospective wages yield reduced incentives for investment in human capital, ultimately widening income differences.

The battle against discrimination predates the American Revolution. From the time of President Lincoln's Emancipation Proclamation through the present, we have slowly marched toward an era in which government enforces a variety of civil rights legislation ensuring equal access to such things as education, housing, and employment opportunities.

Legal controversy has marked almost all policies intended to achieve equal opportunity — e.g., busing children to integrate our schools, and *affirmative action* plans imposed to overcome past occupational, wage, and employment discrimination. Although the path to equal opportunity has been rocky, there has been major progress on the civil rights front in the past few decades. Disagreements continue, however, about the extent to which discrimination accounts for income differentials between groups, what kinds of discrimination are involved, and

what policies will best remedy its effects.[10] One approach emphasizes welfare programs to compensate the victims of such earlier social policies as segregation or slavery, although extensive welfare programs are also advocated on other grounds.

Public Policies to Eliminate Poverty

Just who is "on" welfare? Who should receive welfare? How much? Such questions are meaningless without a definition of welfare.

Welfare *is received by anyone for whom the ratio of the personal benefits received (B) from government programs relative to the taxes paid (T) are greater than for average taxpayers.*

Thus, a person is on welfare if $B_i/T_i > B_0/T_0$, where B_i and T_i are the individual's benefits and taxes and B_0 and T_0 are the total benefits and taxes in the community or society. This can also be written as $B_i/B_0 > T_i/T_0$. For example, people are on welfare if they receive 2 percent of the total benefits from government programs ($B_i/B_0 = 0.02$) but only pay 1 percent of the taxes used to support government ($T_i/T_0 = 0.01$).

Our welfare system is an amalgam of many programs. In fact, people who are quite wealthy may be "on welfare." For example, some wealthy recipients contributed far less to Social Security than they receive after they reach retirement age. Most welfare recipients are, however, in low-income groups.

---

10. Thomas Sowell, for one (in his *Ethnic America* — see footnote 8), has argued that affirmative action has been more hindrance than help to members of minority groups. For example, he suggests that other people who encounter minorities in professional positions or high-level jobs commonly assume that these individuals gained their status not from competency, but to "fill some quota." A prospective employer may thus discount the previous experience of minority applicants who might otherwise be perfect for particular jobs and who would get these jobs were it not for the presumption that their previous experience was based solely on affirmative action requirements.

Aid to Families with Dependent Children

Aid to Families with Dependent Children (AFDC) is federally mandated, but administered by state and local governments. Explosive growth in AFDC rolls over the past two decades has been attributed to (*a*) relaxed requirements that increased the number of eligible families, (*b*) reductions in the social stigma from being on welfare, (*c*) work *disincentives* and pressures to dissolve families that are inherent in AFDC payment structures, and (*d*) payment differentials that cause the poor to flock into areas where welfare benefits are the most generous. The rapid growth in enrollment has created widespread concern that the AFDC system is out of control.

Panel A in Figure 7 illustrates the work disincentive effects of the original AFDC programs. Assume that if a given family has no earnings, the annual AFDC grant is $5,000 (point *a* in Panel

A). If the family earns up to an additional $5,000, the basic grant remains the same (point *b*). When the family's earnings exceed $5,000, however, AFDC grants are reduced dollar for dollar, so this poor family gains nothing by earning between $5,000 and $10,000 yearly (points *d* to *e*). Even worse, extra income is taxed and there may be losses of *in-kind subsidies* (Medicaid, food stamps, or public housing subsidies). This opens up the possibility that a welfare family's spendable income could fall faster than its earnings grew.

Poor families were often penalized for working, so many followed the path of least resistance. AFDC benefits are especially skimpy if families include an able-bodied male, which has pressured many males to abandon their wives and kids. Panel A shows that a 100 percent payment reduction on earned income over $5,000 is equivalent to a 100 percent marginal tax rate on

FIGURE 7 Work Disincentives and Welfare Programs

Can your take-home income fall if you earn more? When welfare programs are disjointedly tied to family income, the answer is "Yes." This incentive not to work is gradually being remedied, but Panel A reflects that this was a severe problem in the early 1970s. Under current regulations, the poor may face a marginal tax rate of 50 percent or more on additional income from employment, as shown in Panel B. While this still acts as a disincentive to work, it is much less severe than in the early 1970s when the adjusted marginal tax rate was often more than 100 percent for the working poor.

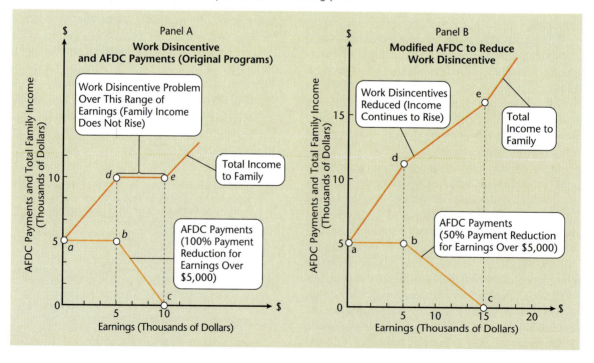

earned income. Families do not gain from higher earnings if the entire increase goes to the government. These disincentives in AFDC and similar programs have contributed to the "welfare mess," as it has been labeled by the media.

In the late 1970s, modest reforms of AFDC rules were aimed at cutting the implicit tax rate of over 100 percent faced by many poor families, but further changes during 1981–1983 reversed some of these reforms. Average "marginal tax rates" on AFDC benefits are now estimated at around 50 percent. Today's regulations are less distortive than earlier programs in this respect. Panel B of Figure 7 shows how lower implicit tax rates allow greater work incentives. As earnings exceed $5,000, benefits fall at a rate of only $.50 per $1, not dollar for dollar. Labor earnings now raise welfare families' spendable income; this was a rarity under the early system.

AFDC, unemployment compensation, and Social Security are among the many welfare programs that dispense cash grants. Other systems attempt to aid the poor through in-kind subsidies, including public housing, food stamps, Medicare and Medicaid, and various education, training, and rehabilitation programs. In-kind subsidies generally entail relatively high administrative costs and implicitly assume that recipients are incompetent to manage money were it given directly to them. Most economists are skeptical of this reasoning and view in-kind payments as inefficient. For example, it costs taxpayers roughly $1.12 to give a poor family a food stamp with a face value of $1. The $1 food coupon is worth less than $1 to most recipients because it cannot be used for purchases other than food. Cash grant programs will typically provide benefits to poor people that are closer to their costs to taxpayers. Thus, in-kind transfers are relatively inefficient forms of welfare.

Another problem area is that many government transfer programs are based on criteria other than poverty. If farmers, the elderly, families headed by single women, members of certain minority groups, or the disabled tend to be poor, it does not follow that separate programs are required for each group. Programs to aid the blind, the infirm, the aged, or members of minority groups do not exclude the wealthy handicapped, the wealthy aged, or wealthy minorities. Simi-

larly, there are affluent farmers, bankers, and TV station owners who are welfare recipients by our definition of welfare. They benefit from special subsidies or regulations bearing no relation to the taxes they pay.

Welfare Reform

Transfer payments of various types have been the fastest growing component of government outlays in the United States since World War II. A number of reforms have been proposed. Some are intended to cut the growth of transfer payments; other reforms would redistribute more income to the poor.

Workfare

The hardship of the Great Depression resulted in a national system of *unemployment compensation* administered by state agencies. Unfortunately, the side effects may be as undesirable as the broken families and idleness generated by AFDC. Sporadic employment patterns are encouraged, some income goes unreported, and some people who are not truly interested in work during some periods claim to be looking for jobs—causing unemployment statistics to be overstated and misdirecting macroeconomic policy making. Some who believe that the welfare system as a whole encourages idleness advocate **workfare** to replace welfare. Workfare programs require able-bodied people who seek unemployment compensation or other public assistance to do jobs for the local government units that dole out such benefits.

Consolidation

The current welfare system is mired in excessive regulations and income maintenance programs are fragmented among AFDC, unemployment compensation, Medicaid, food stamps, public housing, Social Security, and private charity. Ridding welfare programs of the work disincentives embedded in current policies is one major task of welfare reform; another is placing the welfare system under a single administrative umbrella, reducing duplication and costs. Some major programs are not based on income and thus benefit people who are not poor. There may be substantial gains from consolidation — both for taxpayers and for impoverished recipients. For these reasons, many economists favor a negative income tax approach to replace existing programs. Overall, we want the truly poor to get more aid, but where possible, we wish to preserve incentives for them to earn income on their own.

Family Allowance Plans

Many European nations and most British Commonwealth countries now have family allowance plans (FAPs).

> *Transfer payments from* **family allowance plans** *are based on the number of minor children in a family and are usually adequate to feed and clothe each child.*

Family allowance plans provide basic income floors, but the incomes from these plans are then taxed as normal income and the progressivity of income taxes shrinks the FAP subsidy as a family's income rises.

Poverty seems especially harmful to children, so family allowance plans were proposed by the Nixon, Ford, and Carter Administrations. A family allowance plan would be easier and cheaper to administer than the current welfare system. It would provide greater incentives for work than the many welfare programs that now confront the poor with very high implicit marginal tax rates; poor people's net incomes would always rise if they worked. Finally, it would eliminate situations where some poor people are technically ineligible for welfare but pay taxes to provide welfare to people who are better off. (For example, an impoverished family headed by a low-wage working male may pay taxes to provide AFDC for a family without a working head of household. Average AFDC payments often exceed the family income of the working male.) Insufficient income for a given family unit, including children, would be the sole criterion for net (after-tax) receipts of welfare.

Negative Income Taxes

Negative income taxes (NITs) are variants of family allowance plans.

> **Negative income tax** *plans attempt to balance the goals of equity and efficiency, and begin with an income floor. The level of assistance is reduced as additional income is earned by the family, but less than dollar for dollar.*

A typical NIT plan is diagrammed in Figure 8. The basic NIT floor on family income in this example is $6,000, and as the family earns an additional dollar, NIT benefits are reduced by $0.40. This negative income tax rate is 40 percent. When the family earns $15,000 on its own, NIT benefits are zero [$6,000 − ($15,000 × .40) = $0]. Beyond $15,000, the family pays positive taxes. Most economists envision these plans replacing all other income assistance plans. They would be administered through the Internal Revenue Service.

FIGURE 8   Negative Income Taxes

Negative income taxes (NITs) are proposals to replace most of the current welfare system with cash grants. In the example shown, the marginal tax rate is 40 percent, with a break-even income of $15,000. This means that welfare receipts would be 60 percent of any shortfall of income below $15,000 annually.

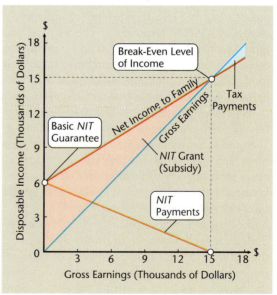

Conflicts within NITs Negative income taxes would be simple to administer and would eliminate the need to dovetail numerous programs, but like any form of income assistance, NITs must balance equity and efficiency. This entails setting support levels that preserve work incentives, provide equitable income floors, and minimize administrative costs. Equity considerations might dictate high support flows, while efficient work incentives require low negative marginal tax rates. The cost of a program escalates when these attributes are combined. For example, in Figure 8, if poverty levels for average families were considered to be $6,000, then the plan as diagramed would subsidize both the poor and some nonpoor; families with earnings between $6,000 and $15,000 continue to receive subsidies.

High basic income floors, low negative income tax rates, and low break-even income levels cannot coexist because, mathematically,

$$\text{break-even income} = \frac{\text{basic income floor}}{\text{negative income tax rate}}$$

Thus, break-even income rises when the income floor rises or the negative income tax rate falls. Tax revenues fall and the total cost of the program rises. Reduced disincentives for work may, however, cut costs by making many of the poor less reliant on the public dole. Moreover, if an NIT plan replaced the current hodgepodge of welfare programs, administrative costs should fall — allowing higher income floors and/or reductions in taxes.

There are other criticisms of NIT proposals, however. Some argue that NIT plans are too inflexible to solve many specific problems facing the poor. For example, older people may be unable to respond to work incentives, while youngsters need special care and assistance that parents may not provide. Others argue that in-kind services should supplement income assistance because many families may not wisely use the funds provided under an NIT plan. Proponents argue that an NIT package could provide both sufficient work incentives and an adequate income floor while replacing a bureaucratic, erratic, and expensive system with a consistent program.

In this chapter, we have looked at ethical criteria for the distribution of income, poverty the distributions of income and wealth in the United States, and programs to deal with poverty. Programs to provide for the poor may have inefficient incentive structures that discourage work effort, both for welfare recipients and for those whose tax dollars provide welfare. Placed in a public choice framework, bureaucrats may be more interested in increasing the number of people in their programs than in reducing reliance on welfare. The goals of equity and efficiency may both suffer as a consequence.

Chapter Review: Key Points

1. *Lorenz curves* are one way to portray inequality. Lorenz curves for income are graphical representations of the cumulative percentages of income received by given cumulative percentages of families. If the Lorenz curve is a straight-line diagonal, the income distribution is perfectly equal. Deviations from this diagonal reflect inequality in distribution.

2. A related statistical measure of income inequality is the *Gini index*. The Gini index is defined as the ratio of the area between the line of perfect equality and the Lorenz curve to the total area under the line of perfect equality. The Gini index varies from 0 (perfect equality) to 1 (perfect inequality).

3. Since 1935, income distribution in the United States has become markedly more equal, especially when capital gains, taxes, and transfer payments are considered. An examination of the pretax Gini coefficients, however, shows that pretax income has been growing more unequally distributed since the late 1960s, and this change was accelerated in the 1980s. Developed nations, in general, tend to have more equal distributions of income than do developing nations.

4. The Social Security Administration has developed income indices that define *poverty lines* for various family sizes, ages, and locations.

5. The causes of *poverty* are many and varied.

Relative to more prosperous families, the poor tend to have less education, fewer earners, and more children. These characteristics of the poor are not necessarily the causes of poverty. *Discrimination* may be an important factor. Persistent discrimination reduces incentives to invest in education and other marketable skills. Discrimination is often cited as the primary reason that a relatively large proportion of black families are in the lower income categories.

6. The major government program to fight poverty is *Aid to Families with Dependent Children* (AFDC). A floor on family income is established, but as the family earns additional income, reductions of AFDC benefits often pose extreme *disincentives* for work. Given the large number of different programs designed to help the poor, $1 increases in earned income sometimes result in more than $1 of lost benefits.

7. *Negative income tax plans* (NITs) have been suggested as solutions to the "welfare mess." Negative income tax proposals provide a floor on income; as additional income is earned, benefits are reduced but by less than the additional income earned. NIT proposals contain two essential elements: a basic income floor and a negative income tax rate. Increases in the floor or reductions in the negative tax rate increase the costs of the program. Equity considerations indicate needs for higher floors, while efficiency considerations point to needs for lower negative tax rates. Both goals cannot be satisfied with any one negative income tax plan.

8. Opponents of NIT proposals argue that guaranteed income floors will not solve all the problems of the poor. Proponents argue that providing sufficient income will solve the major problems. In general, NIT plans consolidate numerous programs under one administrative roof and might allow either reduced costs or increased benefits.

Key Concepts

Ensure that you can define these terms before proceeding.

contribution standard	Lorenz curves
needs standard	Gini index
equality standard	poverty line

economic discrimination

welfare

family allowance plan (FAP)

negative income tax (NIT)

Problems and Questions

1. Should society extend welfare to the less fortunate? Should the circumstances causing their poverty be considered? If so, how? Should cash grants be emphasized, or should society directly provide: (*a*) housing? (*b*) medical care? (*c*) food stamps? Why?

2. Should we seek equality of opportunity or equality of result?

3. Suppose that you were in charge of an overcrowded lifeboat filled with the survivors of a shipwreck. Unless some passengers leave the boat, all will perish. Would it be fair for you to allocate the spaces available to the highest bidders? Would this be efficient? If not, would it be fairer or more efficient were a few affluent passengers able to persuade a sufficient number of poorer people to relinquish their space by offering contracts guaranteeing prosperity for the volunteers' families? If not, what other allocative mechanism would be fairer or more efficient? Why?

4. Plot a Lorenz curve for each of the three countries for which income distribution data are provided in Table 3. Which country has the most unequal distribution of income? The most equal?

5. What would you expect to happen to the Lorenz curve for a country (*a*) if a more progressive tax system was instituted? (*b*) If

Table 3 *Income Distribution Data for Three Populations*

Family Group	Countries		
	A	B	C
Lowest 20 percent	10	12	18
Second 20 percent	15	15	19
Middle 20 percent	20	20	20
Fourth 20 percent	25	23	21
Highest 20 percent	30	30	22

education levels for all citizens became roughly equal? (*c*) If economic discrimination was significantly reduced?

6. In what sense are income and wealth exactly proportional in equilibrium? (Review the capitalization process discussed in a previous chapter for help on this question.)

7. Society devotes increasing amounts of resources to medical care for critical and sometimes incurable diseases or injuries. It is not unusual, for example, for the medical expenses of a very premature infant to exceed $1 million, and yet, even if it survives, the long-term consequences for the child are often tragic. Many parents cannot afford such outlays, and hospitals often simply treat these costs as overhead costs to be borne by other patients. Is this use of society's resources appropriate? What are some possible opportunity costs? Is this equitable? Why or why not?

8. Family assistance plans and negative income taxes presume that the poor lack money but not the skills to manage it. Administrative costs of these programs would be relatively low. Food stamp programs, Medicaid, and the provision of social workers seem predicated on the idea that poor people would not spend money properly if it were given to them. These programs bear high administrative costs. Do you think the poor are better off if their spending is closely supervised? If so, up to what proportion of government outlays for welfare could be spent for administrators and red tape before it would be better just to give money to the poor?

9. Which of the following negative income tax plans has the highest break-even level of income?

   a. Basic income floor of $6,000; a negative income tax rate of 50 percent.

   b. Basic income floor of $8,000; a negative income tax rate of 60 percent.

   c. Basic income floor of $4,500; a negative income tax rate of 30 percent.

10. a. A basic income floor of $5,000 and a negative income tax rate of 40 percent yields a break-even level of income equaling _____.

   b. If the break-even level of income is $9,000 and the negative income tax rate is 60 percent, what does the income floor equal? _____

   c. If the break-even level of income is $12,000 and the income floor is $7,200, what does the negative income tax rate equal? _____

11. In John Rawls' *A Theory of Justice* (Harvard, 1971), he proposes the following mental exercise as an approach for deciding how society might be made fairer. Suppose you were given a computer with a data bank containing every economic mechanism ever tried and every theory ever proposed to answer the questions of What? How? For whom? and When? You also have the advice of any social philosopher, living or dead. Your task is to design a just society, and you must address many issues, including distributing wealth and income. Your final overall plan will be instituted worldwide. The hook is that your position in the world will then be decided randomly — providing a powerful incentive for you to consider the final positions of all people. What are some changes you would make to current social institutions?

12. In *Anarchy, State, and Utopia* (New York: Basic Books, 1974), Rawls' colleague, Robert Nozick, argues that over time individuals acquire inalienable rights. His *entitlement theory of justice* is an ethical argument for the adage that "possession is nine-tenths of the law." In Nozick's view, you are entitled to your property unless it can be proven that you, or the people who transferred it to you, unethically acquired it. He concludes that government redistributions of wealth or income are ethically wrong, because they violate people's basic rights to choose how their property will be used. In his words, "There is no justified sacrifice of some of us for others." Do you think that historical events ethically justify the degree of inequality that now exists? Why or why not?

PART 10

The International Economy

International trade is growing faster than domestic production and income almost everywhere in the world. Virtually every aspect of daily life is affected—from the composition of our diets to the purchasing power of our income to the jobs we choose to issues of war and peace. We cannot remain oblivious to economic developments outside our national borders if we are to enjoy the relative prosperity of past generations of Americans. This is one reason this book is permeated with international issues and examples. Our purpose in this part of the book is to provide an integrated perspective on how international trade and finance affect standards of living around the world.

Gains from specialized production and exchange according to comparative advantage were introduced in Chapter 2. But other types of gains from trade may be even more important. These gains help explain why national economies are increasingly interdependent and prosperous, and why economic systems seem to be converging. Nevertheless, many people increasingly sing the protectionist's song—"Restrict imports of 'cheap' foreign goods." How almost everyone ultimately gains from international trade and why it is usually foolish to restrict trade are among the major topics we address in Chapter 37.

You can now buy stocks and bonds in American, Japanese, or Italian corporations through stock exchanges in Sydney, London, or Hong Kong (and soon, perhaps, Moscow and Beijing). International financial developments crucially affect, among other things, job opportunities and patterns of economic growth. This internationalization of capital markets has made currency exchange rates and "the value of the dollar" an issue not only for those fortunate enough to travel abroad, but for all of us. Capital flows and the advantages and disadvantages of the different means available to pay for imports and be paid for exports are at the heart of our discussion in Chapter 38.

Finally, the last chapter of this book examines various philosophies that underlie alternative economic systems, and how these philosophies have been put into practice. Recent events in Eastern Europe and China are evidence that systems and slogans that sound good in theory may be horrible in practice. In our modern world, everyone should know something about how other economies operate, and their advantages and disadvantages.

International Trade

Specialized production and exchange yield enormous benefits. The gain to both Hawaiians and Texans from trading sugar for oil is an obvious example. Similar advantages arise from transactions whether the people with whom we deal are Americans or foreigners. The exchange of goods and services across national boundaries is called *international trade*. Trade is generally a positive sum game; both sides expect to gain or they do not trade. International transactions are somewhat more complex than domestic trade, however, because of differences in currencies and national policies.

In this chapter, we discuss some advantages and possible disadvantages of commerce between traders separated by international borders. We also evaluate some arguments against free trade and consider the effects of policies that restrict trade.

The Size and Scope of Trade

International trade grows in importance year after year, ranging, among industrialized nations, from 8 to 12 percent of U.S. national income to roughly 30 percent in Great Britain. Few Americans, however, pay much attention to how international trade affects our daily lives. We drink Colombian coffee, cocoa from Ghana, or tea from Sri Lanka; wear Swiss watches and clothes made in China; watch TVs made in Japan; and burn gasoline refined from Arab oil in Hyundais, Fiats, or Toyotas. Most of our shoes, the graphite in our pencils, and even the elastic in our underwear come from abroad.

Foreign countries are markets for our production, so U.S. exports are one source of Aggregate Demand. Imports add to our Aggregate Supply; they are sources of consumption goods (e.g., Sony Walkman headsets) and investment goods (e.g., Korean steel I-beams). At the same time, they detract from Aggregate Demand, making marketing more difficult for the domestic producers who compete with imports. Consequently, macroeconomic policy must consider the impact of international trade on domestic inflation, unemployment, economic growth, and our GNP.

The importance of international trade in several major trading nations is shown in Figure 1. The sheer size of the United States makes it the world's single most important international trader; our exports and imports each exceeded $600 billion in 1991. Generally, however, trade is even more crucial to small countries than to large ones.

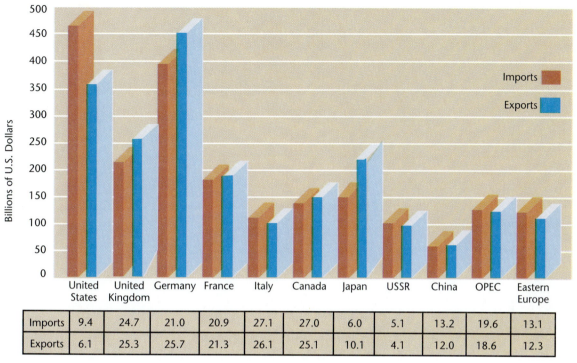

	United States	United Kingdom	Germany	France	Italy	Canada	Japan	USSR	China	OPEC	Eastern Europe
Imports	9.4	24.7	21.0	20.9	27.1	27.0	6.0	5.1	13.2	19.6	13.1
Exports	6.1	25.3	25.7	21.3	26.1	25.1	10.1	4.1	12.0	18.6	12.3

Percentages of GDP

FIGURE 1   Imports and Exports of Selected Countries as Percentages of GNP, 1990

Although the United States is a major trader, trade is less important to us as a percentage of GNP than it is to any other developed nation. Surprisingly, Japan is not especially dependent on foreign trade. Trade is especially vital, however, for such highly specialized countries as OPEC member nations. The major communist powers have not historically been significant traders, but this is likely to change dramatically in the 1990s.

Source: *Economic Report of the President*, 1991.

Why Do Nations Trade?

The United States has a highly skilled work force, an unmatched stock of capital equipment, and vast amounts of fertile land and raw materials. Even though our national income is more than twice that of our nearest competitor, U.S. exports and imports have each averaged 8 to 12 percent of national income in recent years. Figure 2 reveals which countries are our major trading partners. Why do Americans even bother to trade with the rest of the world?

All trade is motivated by expectations of gain — either increased income or reduced costs. The global value of income and output is maximized if the opportunity costs of producing everything everywhere are minimized. International trade is a mechanism for consumers to get goods at lower cost without having to travel to where the goods are produced, and for resource owners (e.g., labor) to receive higher income without having to relocate to wherever their outputs are most advantageously consumed. Efficient patterns of trade permit higher standards of living for people everywhere.

Curiously, we both import (to reduce costs) and export (to boost incomes) many goods that are close substitutes for each other. For example, while we are the world's biggest car importer, we are also its third largest car exporter. The com-

FIGURE 2   Major U.S. Trading Partners, 1990
(*Note:* All figures presented here are in billions of U.S. dollars.)
Source: *Economic Report of the President,* 1991.

position of U.S. foreign trade (indicated in Figure 3) is evidence that trade can be advantageous even when self-sufficiency is possible.

The Concept of Absolute Advantage

The notion of *absolute advantage* emerges from differences in the abilities of individuals and nations to produce goods from given resources. For example, one Arabian worker can get more oil out of 10 acres of Arab land than can one Georgian working 10 acres in Georgia. However, the Georgian might be able to raise more peanuts per acre than the Arab can. In this case, the Arab has an absolute advantage in oil production, while the Georgian has an absolute advantage in peanut growing. Obviously, each could gain from specialized production and trade. This notion led Adam Smith and other early economists to attempt to state a broad economic principle.

The **"principle"** of absolute advantage *asserts that nations gain by producing goods that require fewer domestic resources and exchanging their surpluses for goods produced abroad with fewer resources.*

This approach is incomplete, however, because it ignores the gains that may be available through trade even though one party has an absolute advantage in producing almost all goods (or, in a simple model, each of two goods).

Specialization and Comparative Advantage

Suppose U.S. workers can produce either four silk blouses or eight electric drills daily, while Chinese workers average only two silk blouses or one drill. An absolute advantage approach offers no way for Americans to gain from trade. The *law of comparative advantage* developed by David Ricardo (1772–1823) shows how trade can enrich people in both countries even if American workers have absolute advantages in both goods.

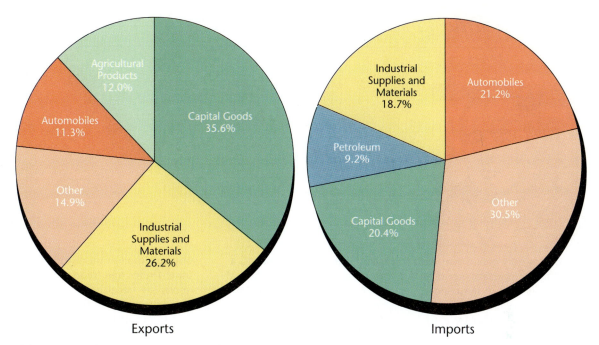

Exports

Imports

FIGURE 3 The Percentage Composition of U.S. Exports and Imports, 1990

The composition of our exports appears roughly balanced, except for net imports of fuels and minerals and net exports of machinery and agricultural products. Each of these broad categories, however, disguises a rich diversity of imports and exports.

Source: *Economic Report of the President*, 1991.

*The **law of comparative advantage**: mutually beneficial trade is always possible between nations whose pretrade relative costs and prices differ.*

Table 1 helps illustrate this key concept in international trade. Without trade, two drills are sacrificed to produce each silk blouse in the United States, while in China, each blouse costs only half of a drill. Imagine that you could cost-lessly move between these countries and that you initially had one blouse. You could begin by trading it for two U.S. drills and then trade the drills for four Chinese blouses, for which you would receive eight U.S. drills, and so on. China increasingly would specialize in blousemaking and the United States, in drill production. As long as the costs of blouses relative to drills did not change (price ratios of 2:1 in the United States and 1:2 in China), no one in either coun-

Table 1 *Outputs per Worker and Their Costs*

| Country | Electric Drills per Worker | Blouses per Worker | Pretrade Costs | | Free Trade Costs |
			Drills per Blouse	Blouses per Drill	
United States	8	4	2	1/2	1:1
China	1	2	1/2	2	1:1

David Ricardo (1772–1823)

David Ricardo's genius was illustrated in the practical world of affairs as well as in the realm of ideas. Disinherited by his wealthy Jewish father for marrying a Quaker at the age of twenty-one, Ricardo and his bride joined the Unitarian church, which at the time was viewed as a radical sect.

Ricardo successfully pursued a business career as a stockjobber and then as a loan contractor, and when he was forty-two, his accumulated wealth permitted him to retire from business. Bored with the idle life, he turned his attention to politics and intellectual pursuits. After a hesitant beginning as a writer on economic subjects, Ricardo etched his name on the pages of history by publishing a treatise, *On the Principles of Political Economy and Taxation*. He was not an accomplished writer, having a heavy-handed, obscure, and abstract style. Nevertheless, the force of his logic almost immediately attracted a close-knit band of gifted if dogmatic disciples.

Ricardo's appeal was based on his ability to cast a wide assortment of serious problems into simple analytical models that considered only a few strategic variables but yielded sweeping conclusions of a very practical nature. One example of Ricardo's penetrating insight concerns the doctrine of comparative costs. Earlier economists had taught that it pays a country to concentrate on the production of those goods it can produce more cheaply than any other country and to import those goods it can obtain at less cost than it could produce them at home. Ricardo developed the following not-so-obvious implication of this doctrine: Under free trade, not all goods are necessarily produced in countries where their absolute cost of production is lowest. He demonstrated that it could pay a country to import something, even though it could produce the same product with fewer resources at home. Ricardo's demonstration rests on the idea of relative efficiency, or comparative costs.

Ricardo's principle is developed in greater detail in the present chapter, but it is important to note that the core of all free trade arguments harks back to this Ricardian concept. Ricardo's discussion of land rent and his analysis of taxation were also pathbreaking works that place modern economists forever in his debt.

try would lose and you would gain. You might even become rich. Thus, this example shows how trade enhances efficiency.

The Terms of Trade Arbitragers (introduced in Chapter 4) can risklessly profit by buying low and selling high if relative price differentials between markets exceed the transaction costs incurred with intermarket transfers of goods. We need to add a bit more realism to our example, because vigorous competition would eliminate most of the economic profit from your attempts to arbitrage. Most of the potential gains would actually have been shared by Americans and

Chinese. Moreover, the prices of drills relative to blouses were artificially assumed constant in both the United States and China.

Arbitrage tends to equalize relative prices in all markets by boosting demand in the market with the lower price, driving that price up, and boosting supply in the market with the higher price, sending it down. In international trade, low-cost producers export, while high-cost producers face increased competition from imports. The phrase "*terms of trade*" refers to the prices of exported goods relative to imported goods:

$$\text{terms of trade} = \frac{\text{price of exports}}{\text{prices of imports}}$$

In our example, drills initially cost only half a blouse in the United States but two blouses in China, while blouses cost two drills in the United States but only half a drill in China. Intuitively, terms of trade should end up between the two countries' relative pretrade production costs at, say, a 1:1 price ratio in both countries. American consumers gain by buying "cheap" imported Chinese blouses while China's consumers gain by buying "cheap" imported U.S. drills. At the same time, U.S. drillmakers export at what they perceive is a premium price and Chinese blousemakers also perceive themselves as being paid premium prices for their exports. These types of cost savings and income growth are the foundations for the gains from trade.

Gains from Trade

Most gains from trade are distributed between producers of goods that are exported and consumers of goods that are imported. People everywhere, however, gain from trade in several ways. Gains from trade are realized internationally because of (*a*) specialization according to comparative advantage, (*b*) the uniqueness of certain resources, (*c*) gains from scale achievable through expanded markets, (*d*) the spread of technology, (*e*) accelerated capital formation, (*f*) accelerated innovation, and (*g*) improved international political stability.

Specialization Gains

People gain even if they could produce imported goods, because through specialization, their incomes and purchasing power rise. Access to export markets makes what people produce more valuable. Even those who do not work directly on exported goods ultimately have higher incomes because of increased demands in resource markets. Moreover, they are able to buy goods at lower opportunity costs than if they relied solely on domestic production.

> **Specialization gains** *from trade arise from producing and selling goods in which you have a comparative advantage, and buying other goods from other parties who can produce them at lower cost.*

In our example, U.S. drillmakers and blouse consumers would gain as the price of drills relative to blouses rose. (The U.S. price of blouses falls.) Similarly, Chinese blousemakers and drill buyers gain when the relative prices of blouses rise. Chinese blouse buyers and U.S. blouse producers might seem to lose, and so might Chinese makers and U.S. buyers of drills. In a moment we will show that these short-run gains from trade alone generally outweigh losses that arise because some people who compete with imports suffer disruptions to their lives and temporary losses of income.

Uniqueness Gains

Nature fails to provide local sources of some goods in certain regions. For example, diamonds, chromium, tin, petroleum, bauxite, and other minerals are not distributed smoothly across the earth's surface. Technology may also differ substantially between countries. International trade makes goods available that simply could not be produced domestically.

> The **uniqueness gains** *from trade arise from trading for goods that are not available from local sources.*

Uniqueness gains underpin trade for certain minerals and many foods, fibers, and animal products — such as bananas, coffee, silk, and frozen fish.

Gains from Scale

Adam Smith was the first economist to note that specialization is limited by the size of the market. Moving beyond domestic markets into international markets facilitates specialization that, in turn, allows expanded production. This occurs, in part, because least cost production for some goods requires output levels that exceed market demands within a single country.

> **Gains from scale** *occur when access to export markets stimulates production of larger amounts of goods at lower average costs.*

For example, Haiti would not, by itself, support an aluminum mill with sufficient capacity to produce at efficiently low costs. Nor is there sufficient demand for clocks in Switzerland alone to allow efficient production. Gains from scale include product diversity, which allows demands to be served that are skimpy in even the largest countries. Not even the U.S. market is large enough alone to justify research, development, and production of medicines to treat extremely exotic diseases; the U.S. market demand would be strictly below the average cost curve for production.

Long-Run Dynamic Gains

The purchasing power of national income grows immediately when imports expand, but long-run changes wrought by trade may be even more important than this short-run effect.

> **Long-run dynamic gains** *occur when trade accelerates economic growth and development.*

Long-run improvements occur when (*a*) trade spreads technology, or (*b*) higher income from trade accelerates capital formation, or (*c*) entrepreneurs are stimulated to innovate by profit

opportunities in export markets. These dynamic gains from trade are especially apparent in the rapid economic development of Japan and other Pacific Rim countries.

The Spread of Technology Trade spreads technology that would be known only locally if each country operated in isolation. Technological advances tend to be infectious — one researcher's discovery is improved upon by another, who stimulates a third, *ad infinitum*. Imagine how primitive life would be if every national group had to rediscover the wheel, electricity, and the advantages of indoor plumbing.

Capital Formation Dynamic gains also arise because trade boosts the value of national output, making it easier for people to save and invest. In less developed nations, higher real income from trade can enable people to move beyond bare subsistence; their increased saving allows new capital formation that can provide a way to break out of the vicious circle of poverty in which many countries are mired.

Innovation Vigorous competition stimulates entrepreneurial efforts to lower costs, improve existing products, and create entirely new products. International trade whets competitive instincts, in part by providing new markets that broaden profit opportunities. Experimentation with new forms of production and the innovation that results provide workers with a "learning-by-doing" environment, which sparks rapid economic growth and development.

International Political Stability

International trade also enhances international relations. To the extent that trade raises our standards of living, it also makes us more dependent upon the people of other nations, and they on us.

> **Political gains** *from trade arise when economic interdependency facilitates international political stability.*

Cessation of trade between warring countries

eliminates mutual benefits and is one cost of hostilities. Thus, interdependencies created by trade reduce the likelihood of war, because higher costs reduce the amounts demanded for any activity. Mutually beneficial trade is a powerful incentive for peaceful negotiation, just as mountain climbers attached by ropes may argue, but usually avoid potentially suicidal violence. International trade in military hardware (e.g., munitions sales to Iraq's Saddam Hussein before 1990) may be an exception to this general principle.

Net Gains from Specialization

Some types of gains from trade seem obvious. We turn now to demonstrating those gains that may seem less clear. Even short-run specialization gains alone generally confer *net* gains to the participants—even in the short run, total gains exceed all losses. Comparative advantage is a key to identifying these net gains.

Returning to our example where Chinese blouses were traded for American drills, we will use a simple short-run model suggesting who shares in the net gains from trade. We consider only two countries, but the logic holds if we consider any country vis-à-vis the rest of the world, or a host of goods instead of only two. In fact, the net gains available from trade rise as the number of traded goods rises and as the number of traders (people in different trading countries) grows.

We will begin with the following assumptions.

1. Production possibilities curves for both China and the United States have constant opportunity costs, but reflect different technologies.

2. Only two goods (drills and blouses) are produced and traded.

3. Goods, but not resources, can move freely between countries, while resources can move freely only between domestic industries.

4. All prices are perfectly flexible.

These simplifying assumptions may seem unrealistic, but they are used only to illustrate a point; most can be relaxed without changing the basic analysis.

Let us begin with aggregate production relationships for the United States and China similar to those outlined in Table 1. We will assume that workers in the United States can produce 400 million blouses or 800 million drills annually, or any combination in between, maintaining constant opportunity costs of two blouses per drill. Similarly, Chinese workers are able to produce 400 million drills or 800 million blouses annually, because we assume China's labor force is four times as large as ours.

Constant production costs yield linear production possibilities frontiers (*PPFs*) like those shown as solid lines in Figure 4. These frontiers can also be thought of as *consumption possibilities frontiers* (*CPFs*) because, without trade, neither country could sustain consumption beyond these boundaries. Suppose that both countries are originally producing and consuming at point *a* in both panels of Figure 4, which graphically reflects column 1 of Table 2. Finally, assume that the final trading ratio is one drill for one blouse.

The United States will specialize in the good with lowest domestic costs—drills, with annual production at 800 million units. Each drill now may be traded for a blouse, so a total of up to 800 million drills plus blouses might be consumed. The American *CPF* expands as shown in Panel A of Figure 4. Symmetrically, China will specialize in blouse production (800 million annually), and by trading blouses for drills, can expand its consumption to any combination of blouses and drills along the light *CPF* in Panel B.

A simplifying assumption reflected in Figure 4 and Table 2 is that after trade commences, each country consumes at point *b* in both panels. Table 2 outlines the specific gains from trade to each country. Americans consume an additional 100 million drills and 150 million more blouses. Similar gains are realized in China.

Note that people in both nations can consume more of both goods. This possibility exists with any specialization and exchange, whether within a country or internationally. An example at the

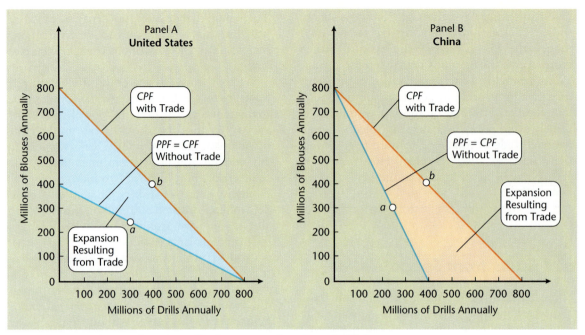

FIGURE 4   How Trade Expands Consumption Possibilities

Prior to trade, a country's sustainable consumption possibilities are limited by its production possibilities frontier. When trade commences, both trading partners experience
net gains from trade because, by specializing in those goods they produce at lowest
relative cost and by importing those things that they find costly to make themselves,
they can each consume more of all goods. Thus, their consumption possibilities expand
beyond their production possibilities, just as we gain individually by trading with others
instead of relying strictly on what we personally produce.

level of an individual family is the homebuilder
whose family has a nicer house than if it had to
produce not only its own home, but also its own
food, clothing, and all the other amenities of life.
Diversion into these other activities and away
from its area of expertise could easily cause the
family to live in a hovel.

Moving toward free trade resembles economic
growth generated by rapid technological advances. We can consume more even though no
more resources are available than previously;
even in the short run, both countries' gains from
free trade typically outweigh any losses. Gains
from trade are positively related to the diversity
in comparative advantages among the trading
groups.

The final terms of trade are 1:1 in our example, although they need not fall precisely at the
midpoint of no-trade prices. All prices are
shaped by both demand and supply. The pro-

duction possibilities frontiers we used address
only the supply side, but explicitly considering
demand would not change our conclusion that
trade confers net gains on all trading parties. People will not trade unless they expect to benefit.

Short-Run Gainers and Potential Losers

You may lose if the price of your output falls
relative to the prices of the things you buy. Thus,
economists talk about an "adverse change in the
terms of trade" whenever export prices fall relative to import prices. For example, an adverse
change in the U.S. terms of trade occurred when
the price of imported oil skyrocketed after Iraq
invaded Kuwait in 1990, while vigorous international competition precluded similar hikes in our
export prices.

When trade expands, changes in the relative
prices of imports and exports benefit some peo-

Table 2 *Specialization Gains from Trade*

Column 1 indicates that without trade, Americans initially consume 300 million drills and 250 million blouses. Once trade commences, Americans are able to consume 400 million of each, as listed in column 4. The gains from trade, listed in column 5, reflect the increases in American consumption of both types of goods. The Chinese enjoy similar net gains from trade.

Country Commodity	(1) Output and Consumption Before Trade (Millions)	(2) Production After Trade Commences (Millions)	(3) Exports (−) Imports (+) (Millions) Terms of Trade Are 1:1	(4) Consumption After Trade (Millions) (2) + (3)	(5) Gains from Trade (Millions) (4) − (1)
United States					
Drills	300	800	−400	400	100
Blouses	250	0	+400	400	150
China					
Drills	250	0	+400	400	150
Blouses	300	800	−400	400	100

ple and harm others, even though, on balance, the gains exceed any losses. Some individuals may suffer adverse changes in their individual "terms of trade" if trade exposes their output to competition from foreigners whose production costs are lower. A simple demand and supply model of the international blouse market will illuminate why some people dislike certain aspects of trade. We will abandon the confines of our "constant-cost" model and, for simplicity, assume that the dollar is the world currency; the complications of a multicurrency world are the subject of international finance.

Figure 5 depicts market demands and supplies for blouses in the United States (Panel A) and in China (Panel C). Without trade, U.S. blouse prices would be $80, or 2 drills. At every price below $80, there is an excess demand (XD) for blouses in the United States. Domestic producers are willing to supply fewer blouses than American buyers would purchase. This excess demand (the horizontal distance between the supply and demand curves) is graphed as XD_a in the center panel of Figure 5 and indicates how many blouses would be imported at various prices.

In China blouses would cost only $40 each, or half a drill, without the American market in which to sell. At prices exceeding $40, Chinese blousemakers are willing to sell more blouses

than Chinese consumers are willing and able to buy. This excess supply (XS) or surplus (the horizontal distance between the supply and demand curves) is graphed as XS_c in the center panel of Figure 5, and indicates how many Chinese blouses would be available for export at various prices greater than $40.

Equilibrium between our willingness to import and China's willingness to export occurs when our excess demand equals their excess supply. Blouses will sell for $60 in both the United States and China with free trade; annual Chinese output will rise to 11 million blouses, while U.S. output drops by 1 million blouses. Moreover, Chinese purchases of blouses decline by 1 million, while American blouse buying rises by 2 million annually.

Individual Gainers and Losers

Who gains from trade? Chinese blousemakers sell more blouses at higher prices. American blouse buyers also gain; the price of a blouse in the United States has dropped from $80 down to $60, and purchases have risen. Now, for possible short-run losers: American blousemakers may lose when the price falls to $60 (from $80), and Chinese blouse buyers may lose as the price rises to $60. Blouse ownership in China could decline because of the higher price, but higher Chinese

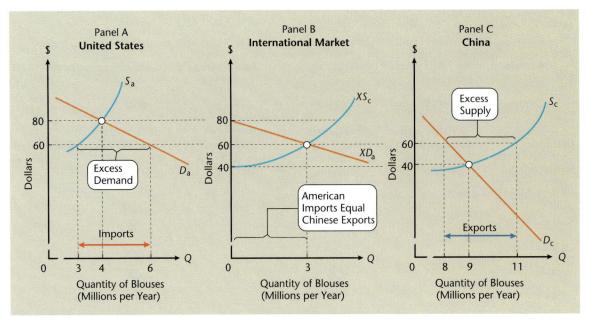

FIGURE 5   International Excess Demands and Supplies

Panel A shows that at prices for silk blouses below $80, the United States has excess demands. Panel C indicates that China has excess supplies of blouses at prices above $40. When American excess demands confront China's excess supplies in international markets (Panel B), imports and exports must be equal, and a price is determined that will prevail in both markets. (Excess supplies are the horizontal distances from demand to supply curves; excess demands are the horizontal distances from supply curves to demand curves.)

income would tend to boost purchases of blouses. The net effect is uncertain. American blouse output falls, but note that world blouse production has risen by 1 million units. Even former U.S. blousemakers tend to gain when they move into the production of drills, where the United States possesses a comparative advantage.

Because Americans are buying $180 million worth of blouses from China ($60 × 3 million), we will have "balanced trade" if we export $180 million worth of drills to China. We could build figures for the drill market similar to Figure 5 and would conclude that trade causes drill prices to fall in China, while drill prices rise in the United States; employment and output of the Chinese drill industry declines, but less than the U.S. drill industry grows. There will be more of both drills and blouses after trade commences.

Table 3 summarizes the gainers and possible short-term losers from trading drills for blouses, and vice versa. You should keep in mind, how-

ever, that this analysis only looks at short-run *specialization* gains and losses and that it only balances one import against one export. In a world of countless imports and exports, even those whose income falls because of lower-priced import competition for the good they produce also gain when they buy imports — including goods they personally produce — at lower prices. For

Table 3   *Gainers from Specialization and Potential Short-Run Losers from Trade*

People who purchase low-priced imports gain from trade, while people who rely on production of the good for income may lose in the short run.

Country	Gainers	Possible Losers
United States	Drill sellers Blouse buyers	Drill buyers Blouse sellers
China	Drill buyers Blouse sellers	Drill sellers Blouse buyers

example, competition from imported clothing may shrink textile workers' income, but they gain when they buy low-priced imports of oil, cars, VCRs, . . . , *and* clothes. When uniqueness, scale, dynamic, and political gains from trade are considered as well, it is hard to imagine anyone who ultimately loses from international trade.

Can we be fairly sure that gains to the four groups of winners more than offset the losses to the four groups of potential losers? We can. Trade expands global production of each good. Because both countries' consumption possibilities frontiers grow, gainers in each country could, but seldom do, compensate the losers from trade so that every man, woman, and child in both countries gained. If I gain $50 from a transaction that causes you to lose $20, we are both ahead if I share my gain by giving you $25.

Trade Adjustment Assistance

Most successful movements to restrict trade have been launched by groups who lose because they operate at comparative disadvantages when forced to compete with foreign producers. They are effective politically because they are strongly opposed to importing certain goods. Suppose that 100,000 people would lose $10,000 apiece annually if restrictions on textiles imports were eliminated (a total of $1 billion), while 200 million other Americans will shell out an average of an extra $10 a year for clothing (a total of $2 billion) if textile imports continue to be restricted. You have 100,000 people who will vote for or against politicians based largely on their platforms on textile quotas, and 200 million people who are, for the most part, oblivious to their personal losses and politicians' positions on trade.

Let us see why trade restrictions are inefficient and what might be done to ensure that everyone gains from free trade. In our example, if the 200 million consumers each contributed $6 annually to a relief fund for the 100,000 textile workers, each textile worker could receive $12,000 annually. If we set up the relief fund only with the precondition that textiles be freely imported, textile workers would gain ($2,000 each) and so would textile consumers ($4 each annually).

Clearly, this would be a move in the direction of economic efficiency: Everyone gains, and no one loses.

Examples like this have caused trade acts to include *trade adjustment assistance*, intended to provide retraining and financial assistance for workers displaced because of liberalized international trade. It is, unfortunately, very difficult to identify who loses from lower trade barriers. Congress seldom provides funding for this program; it is among the first items on the chopping block when politicians try to balance the budget. The end result has been rising sentiment for trade restrictions. Support for higher trade barriers is voiced by many unions and managers of industries facing foreign competition.

Arguments Against Free Trade

Goods tend to be produced at minimum opportunity cost and then traded by their producers for other goods that are subjectively more valuable to them. Thus, free trade tends to maximize the value of the world's production. Then why is free trade the exception instead of the general practice? The answer lies in arguments *against* free trade, and *for* import barriers against foreign goods. Some arguments are partially valid, but others verge on the irrational. All too commonly, irrational arguments prove persuasive or semivalid charges against free trade are applied incorrectly. It is also unfortunate that most trade barriers protect domestic industries in incredibly inefficient ways. We will begin by examining the weakest arguments for trade barriers and then work up the ladder to more telling thrusts against free trade.

Nationalism

Nationalistic "Buy American" campaigns (or pleas to shop at home-town merchants) entail asking or requiring people to act against their own interests. For example, costly advertising from Lee Iacocca (Chrysler's CEO) and the Garment Workers' union exhort us to preserve American jobs by buying domestic products instead of imports. Policymakers who yield to such chauvinistic arguments cut us off from gains from exchange in order to, for example, subsidize domestic producers or hold down foreigners' incomes. At times, such policies may generate psychic income — e.g., by defending "cultural identity" or "national heritage" — but higher costs or lower quality diminish our economic power. Thus, most trade restrictions are contrary to our real national interests.

The Exploitation Doctrine

Some people perceive trade as a zero sum game. They reason that if one trader gains, the other must lose. Thus, if we gain, we must be exploiting our trading partner. Such reasoning may hold for poker or roulette, but the gains from trade we just described indicate that people on both sides of an exchange gain. Transactions do not occur without expectations of gain. The belief that people in less developed countries lose absolutely and so are exploited when they trade with people in developed countries is clearly wrong.

A more sophisticated argument is that trade results in "relative oppression" because the stronger party's gains far outweigh benefits to the weaker trader. This argument is normally wrong because gains from trade are generally greatest in small countries — the less your trade affects the terms of trade offered by your trading partners, the greater your ability to exploit differences in the relative opportunity costs of production. For example, Monaco, a very small country, relies very heavily on trade and might be impoverished but for the world market. The United States and Germany, on the other hand, have wide internal markets and rich resource mixes. These giants rely less on trade than countries like Monaco or Switzerland. Imagine how destitute the United Arab Emirates might be without trade. Their natural resources consist largely of sand, oil, and more sand. Through trade, their per capita income now exceeds that enjoyed by typical Americans.

Retaliation

Many countries restrict imports from the United States, so why shouldn't we retaliate with barriers against their exports? This argument is often directed at Japan, which severely restricts imports of U.S. machinery and agricultural goods. One problem is that this notion ignores the harm done to U.S. consumers by retaliatory policies. When we restrict imports, we reduce the amounts of goods available to Americans and domestic prices rise.

Nevertheless, in some situations, our threat to retaliate against foreign governments' trade barriers can tip international negotiations so that their markets are opened to American exports. Just as workers' rights to strike must be exercised occasionally for the threat of a strike to have weight in union negotiations with management, the threat of retaliation against foreign trade barriers may be viable only if we occasionally do retaliate.

But retaliation is an effective negotiating tool only if it causes other countries to adopt freer trade policies, just as a strike harms union workers if it fails to yield a better work contract. And just as a permanent strike would harm workers, we normally compound the damage done by foreign trade restrictions if we retaliate with policies that are maintained in the long run. We may harm foreign producers, but we harm ourselves as well. In fact, some analysts argue that the worldwide depression of the 1930s was substantially worsened because of escalating retaliation by many major trading nations, and fear that a major trade war would cause another global depression.

Antidumping

The accusation that foreign producers compete unfairly by "dumping" is raised almost every time an American producer is undersold.

Dumping *occurs when a country exports at lower prices than those charged within the exporting country.*

Dumping might arise from international price discrimination, which entails charging desperate (domestic) buyers more than less desperate (foreign) buyers. In such a case, consumers in the country "dumped on" benefit from the discriminatory policy. Alternatively, a foreign government might try to create jobs by subsidizing exports. (Japan is commonly accused of such policies.) Finally, there may be "predatory" dumping, which means that a seller tries to establish a worldwide monopoly by driving competitors out of the market. Presumably, prices could then be raised to yield monopoly profits.

There is scant evidence of dumping, however, and if it does occur the customers who buy at lower prices are major beneficiaries. Congress has enacted laws against foreign producers dumping in U.S. markets. Should our government protect us from low prices? Dumping is legally inferred whenever imports are sold below cost. In one case, Mexican tomato growers were barred from U.S. markets because they were selling below cost. The sad fact was that a bumper crop had depressed the price so much that tomatoes sold below cost in Mexico. Mexican tomato growers had to sell the tomatoes before they spoiled. Banning U.S. imports simply compounded losses to Mexican farmers.

Infant Industries

Although loud clamoring for protection is now heard from "senile" industries, a slightly more valid but still misleading argument for trade restrictions is protection of *infant industries*. Shortly after the American Revolution, Alexander Hamilton argued that British industrial superiority only reflected a head start over American economic development, and that protection of infant industries from low-cost British competition was necessary for this country's industrialization.

Figure 6 shows what happens if production costs decline as industrialization proceeds. If the world price is P_w for some commodity and average production costs follow path AC_0 over time, eventually declining to P_w, then in the long run a protected infant industry will mature, be competitive in the world market, and not require protection. Notice, however, that if consumers buy constant quantities of the protected good in each period, they lose an amount equal to the orange area below AC_0 and above P_w. This loss is inefficient because these burdens are not offset by lower costs after the industry is established.

A path like AC_1 is necessary for the efficient establishment of a new industry. The discounted

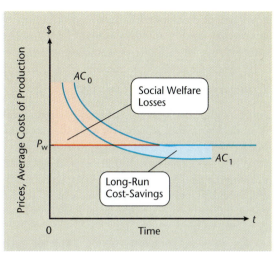

FIGURE 6   The Error in Infant Industry Arguments

The infant industry argument suggests that protection should be used so that immature industries can become competitive in the world market. However, tariffs or quotas designed to buffer infant industries from foreign competition will cause losses of social welfare (the orange area) unless they are offset by extraordinarily low costs (the blue area) in the long run. Of course, if such cost savings are possible, there is no need for protection, because profit-seekers will invest in this industry anyway.

value of the long-run lower costs (shaded blue) must exceed the initial losses (orange). Of course, if entrepreneurs perceive that in the long run they will achieve average production costs that are below world prices, they will build the new industry without protection. Even if the infant industry argument is occasionally semivalid, it would be better to subsidize the industry than to protect it with trade barriers.

The infant industry argument contains only the barest kernel of logic and is largely invalid, but it has been used by many less developed countries to justify protectionist policies; the almost uniform result is inefficient production and little or no growth in per capita income. For example, protection of a government-subsidized Indian automobile plant was rationalized by an infant industry argument in the 1970s. The factory ultimately produced only a few vehicles that resembled cheap Fiats, but average production cost exceeded that for a luxury Mercedes Benz. This high price tag illustrates how ignoring comparative advantages can lead to financial disaster. Indians would have been far better off if their government had focused on the production of goods that used labor (its abundant factor) more intensively and capital (its scarce resource) less.

Trade and Payments Deficits

Anxiety about imbalances of trade or payments is, in part, a throwback to a theory called *mercantilism*. Mercantilists argued that a country grows stronger by exporting more than it imports, drawing the balances in gold. Adam Smith discredited this theory by pointing out that real goods and resources are the true wealth of a nation, not money.

Nevertheless, concerns about trade or payments imbalances are sometimes legitimate. Some people advocate tariffs or quotas to reduce these deficits. The resulting misallocations are seldom worth any improvement in the balance of payments. When we run a trade deficit and there are net outflows of funds that "weaken the dollar," it is usually better to allow natural market adjustments to rectify the imbalance.

Moreover, there is the threat that other countries will retaliate if we impose trade barriers. Finally, shouldn't we be happy that foreigners are willing to sell us more than we sell them — if they are willing to take dirty green paper for the difference? Just as decapitation will cure the common cold, trade barriers may cure deficits in the balances of trade or payments, but better remedies are available.

Job Destruction

The view that imports reduce domestic employment is based on simpleminded logic: We will produce goods ourselves if we don't import them. One obvious fallacy: If imports reduce employment, exports expand it. In fact, one major study suggests that even more jobs are created in export industries than are lost because of imports.

Another problem is that import barriers invite retaliation that destroys jobs in export industries. In fact, trade barriers frequently trade good jobs for bad jobs. When imports threaten an industry's survival, the marketplace is signaling that the industry is relatively inefficient and may

be "senile." Trade barriers sustain comparatively inefficient industries and retard more efficient growth. Resource owners will ultimately be better paid if their resources are moved into areas in which they have comparative advantages.

Even if maintaining employment in certain industries is a national priority for some reason, trade barriers are incredibly inefficient ways to promote employment. The prices of the goods protected by import barriers rise far more than the incomes of protected workers do. Several studies indicate that "voluntary" limits on auto exports from Japan boosted U.S. carmakers' share of domestic sales by 6 to 8 percent, but raised American car prices by an average of $400 to $600, while Japanese import prices rose by between $2,000 and $3,800 apiece.[1] The result was that each American auto worker's job that was saved because of trade restrictions cost U.S. car buyers between $100,000 and $241,000. Table 4 presents a set of estimates of the costs of saving jobs through trade barriers.

These numbers may seem astounding, but trade barriers cause American consumers to lose in many ways, most of which are hidden.

1. Consumers subsidize U.S. industries and resource suppliers (e.g., workers) that lack comparative advantages in areas protected by trade barriers.

2. The market power of some domestic producers is protected, enabling them to restrict output and raise prices.

3. Nontariff trade barriers subsidize efficient foreign suppliers, substantially worsening our balance of payments.

4. These trade barriers effectively enable foreign producers to exercise monopoly power. The result is enrichment of foreign firms to the tune of billions of dollars each year. (It is ironic that U.S. trade policies to restrict imports provide foreign firms with huge monopoly profits, while our antitrust policies are only one aspect of an official policy of promoting domestic competition.)

---

1. Robert W. Crandall, "Import Quotas and the Automobile Industry: The Costs of Protectionism," *The Brookings Review*, Summer 1984, pp. 62–74.

Table 4 *Annual Cost for Protecting U.S. Jobs from Foreign Competition — 1979–1985*

Industry	Total Costs ($ Billions)	Cost per Job Saved ($ Thousands)
Automobiles	5.8	105–241
Book manufacturing	0.5	100
Dairy products	5.5	220
Fishing (tuna)	—	240
Glassware	0.2	200
Maritime	3.0	270
Shoes	—	30–46
Steel	6.8	114–750
Sugar	0.9	60
Textiles and apparel	27.0	40–45

Sources: G. Hufbauer, et al., *Trade Protection in the United States: 31 Case Studies* (Washington, D.C.: Institute for International Economics, 1986); Federal Trade Commission studies cited by Phil Gramm, "New Protection = Old Sophistry," *Wall Street Journal,* 4 Oct. 1985, p. 21.

To illustrate how inefficient trade barriers are as a way to protect jobs, consider policies that might provide jobs for 1,000 American diamond miners. The United States has a few sparse diamond fields. Barriers causing mediocre diamonds to cost $20,000 per carat could spur domestic diamond mining in some regions. South Africa and the Soviet Union, however, would realize huge profits by selling in U.S. markets. The high costs of trade barriers suggest that other policies to protect workers' incomes are more efficient. For example, Table 4 suggests that for most protected industries, one-time trade adjustment assistance of $50,000 per worker displaced by freer trade would be a bargain.

Harmful Income Redistribution

The United States is commonly perceived as having relatively less labor but more capital than the rest of the world. The *Hechscher-Ohlin* model of trade suggests that goods requiring heavy doses of a country's abundant resources will be exported and goods intensive in a country's scarcest resources will be imported. A corollary of this theory is that owners of resources that are more plentiful nationally than worldwide garner all short-run specialization gains from trade, while owners of resources that are relatively abundant internationally but scarce domestically suffer short-run losses from the specialization caused by freer trade.

This approach has been interpreted as suggesting that U.S. workers face stiffer competition from low-wage foreign labor because of trade, while American capital owners gain potential foreign customers. Thus, American wages are driven down by trade, while returns to capital rise; only capital owners enjoy the net specialization gains from trade.

Capital owners could more than compensate workers for income shrinkage caused by trade, but our institutions are not geared for such transfers (e.g., failure to fund trade adjustment assistance). Hence, working-class people suffer while the rich get richer. This theory may help explain some American labor unions' support for trade barriers. If we are truly concerned about income inequality, however, we should not ignore the gains to poor foreign workers when their products are exported, nor should we forget the uniqueness, scale, dynamic, and political benefits of trade.

The Hechscher-Ohlin model has often been misapplied by ignoring some major sources of U.S. comparative advantage. A partial rebuttal to the idea that capitalists gain from trade while American labor loses is that, more than other types of resources, the United States has relative abundances of rich farm land and labor that is adept with sophisticated technology. These resources are relatively scarce in the rest of the world, so American agricultural incomes and the incomes of highly skilled workers are enhanced by international trade. The post–World War II industrialization of Western Europe and Japan has shifted this country's gains from trade away from capitalists toward highly skilled workers and farmers. Less developed countries have also benefited enormously from increased competition among modern industrial powers for raw materials.

The Hechscher-Ohlin approach suggests that resource differentials largely determine the composition of imports and exports. Four decades of studies aimed at predicting the composition of trade from this model have, however, yielded mixed results. This prompted Michael Porter and his associates at the Harvard Business School to analyze trade patterns at a very detailed level. His conclusions are addressed in Focus 1.

Exploiting Monopoly/Monopsony Power

A country that is a major importer or exporter of a good can flex its muscle through trade restrictions to drive prices up or down. For example, a country having monopoly power might be able to impose an export tariff (tax) that would be borne in part by "foreign devils." If so, it is conceivable that the citizens of the exporting country would gain.

The monopolistic or monopsonistic unit may gain tremendously by manipulating its output or purchases (and consequently, prices), but only by imposing even greater losses on its customers or suppliers. For example, the Organization of Petroleum Exporting Countries (OPEC) jacked up oil prices by over 1,000 percent during the 1970s by agreeing to raise prices and restrict the outputs of member countries. They prospered for a period—but at the cost of worldwide economic recession that was especially hard on less developed countries. Brazil and Colombia, somewhat less successfully, combined to raise coffee prices, but only at considerable cost to coffee drinkers.

It would be naïve to expect altruism to deter countries from exercising economic clout. A country's leaders should nevertheless be leery of muscling around its trading partners, because abuse of monopoly or monopsony power invites retaliation and raises the specter of disastrous trade wars.

Diversity

Volatile demands or supplies can be devastating if a country specializes in only a few major outputs. Colombia's reliance on coffee is one example. Droughts, floods, or coffee blight can easily wipe out a year's income, or large harvests in Brazil might severely depress world prices. Diversification is one way of spreading the risk, just as farmers rotate their crops to "rest the soil" and spread their risks.

Protection of developing industries may encourage diversity, but at some cost in efficiency. These efficiency losses might be thought of as insurance premiums, but diversification could be encouraged at far less cost by production subsidies. On rare occasions diversification may be a valid goal for narrowly specialized countries, but not in the United States and other richly varied economies. Even small countries' diversification policies have often been so misdirected that opportunities for development were lost.

National Defense

Domestic access to certain products is crucial for our national defense, so we might want to protect such industries as aircraft or weapons from foreign competition. This argument is often misused and results in perverse policies. For example, the idea that we should not depend on foreign oil has been used for the past century to justify "Drain America First" policies that actually increased our long-run dependence on foreign oil suppliers.

We have only discussed import barriers to this point. National defense may provide more legitimate reasons for bans on exports of critical products and materials. Sales of scrap metal to Japan prior to World War II were clearly shortsighted. It would be equally foolish to allow terrorists or the Mafia to buy atomic weapons on a free market basis.

One final note: One major gain from trade is that mutual interdependence improves the prospects for peace. The costs of conflict increase, providing incentives to avoid war. Freer trade promotes international harmony and reduces the need for defense spending.

Trade Barriers

A number of mechanisms are used as barriers to free trade, but the most important are tariffs and quotas. Each can be imposed on either imports

FOCUS 1

Sources of Comparative and Competitive Advantages

Traditional models to explain why nations import certain goods and export others focus on different mixes of resources between countries. Australia, for example, has vast tracts of arable land but a relatively sparse population, while China is densely populated and much of its land is unsuited for agriculture. Thus, Australia predictably exports wool and grain to China, while importing such labor intensive goods as Chinese textiles.

The conventional model also implies that countries with relatively abundant natural resources should be prosperous, while those with fewer natural resources should be relatively poor—a prediction refuted by lower per capita incomes in such resource-rich countries as Mexico or Brazil when compared with the prosperity of such barren and overpopulated locales as Japan or Taiwan. Japan, for example, is a leading steel exporter despite its relative scarcity of fossil fuels and iron ore.

Such paradoxes raise questions about sources of comparative advantage. In the words of Michael Porter,[*] "How can we ex-

[*]Michael E. Porter, The Competitive Advantage of Nations (New York: The Free Press, 1990).

plain why Germany is the home base for so many of the world's leading makers of printing presses, luxury cars, and chemicals? Why is tiny Switzerland the home base for international leaders in pharmaceuticals, chocolate, and trading? Why are leaders in heavy trucks and mining equipment based in Sweden? Why has America produced the preeminent international competitors in personal computers, software, credit cards, and movies? Why are Italian firms so strong in ceramic tiles, ski boots, packaging machinery, and factory automation equipment? What makes Japanese firms so dominant in consumer electronics, cameras, robotics, and facsimile machines?"

Porter headed a research team that examined over a hundred industries spread across ten major countries. He concluded that basic resources (e.g., raw land and minerals) are much less important in explaining the international competitiveness of an industry than are advanced resources (sophisticated technology and a work force that is highly motivated and specialized, but adaptable). Comparative advantages arise primarily from how efficiently and effectively

these advanced resources are deployed.

Other important determinants of comparative advantage Porter identified include (a) robust domestic demand that allows an industry to get started, (b) internationally competitive suppliers and related industries, and (c) vigorous domestic competition that forces firms to achieve high quality for both products and customer service.

Porter found that government subsidies or protection from foreign competitors usually create only anemic industries that require continuous government support. He argues that international success for an industry is facilitated if government policies merely (a) encourage domestic rivalry, (b) invest heavily in human resource skills that enhance productivity, and (c) emphasize quality as a national priority. With this minimal sort of government intervention, areas of comparative advantage are then best decided in the international marketplace.

or exports, but restrictions on imports are far more common than export barriers.

Tariffs

In the United States, tariffs on exports are forbidden by the Constitution.

> A **tariff** is a special tax that applies only to goods traded internationally.

Import tariffs raise the domestic prices of goods and stimulate domestic production. The United States is a major trader in most goods, so U.S. tariffs also tend to drive down the incomes of foreign producers.

Suppose that we have a tariff on imported steel of $25 per ton, that the international price is $100 a ton, and that U.S. demands and supplies of steel are as depicted in Figure 7. Without the tariff, the United States domestic production would be 100 million tons annually, with imports equaling 60 million tons of steel (160 − 100). The $25-per-ton tariff allows American steelmakers to boost production to 120 million tons, but cuts domestic steel usage by 20 million

tons (to 140 million) while imports fall 40 million tons. As a result of the tariff, U.S. steel consumers now pay more for less steel. Government collects revenues from the tariff equal to the shaded area *abfe*, or $500 million ($25 × 20 million).

Nontariff Barriers

International negotiations to reduce trade barriers (e.g., *GATT*, the General Agreement on Trade and Tariffs) have tended to focus on tariffs. The result is growth of nontariff barriers to restrict free trade. For example, rigid U.S. regulatory standards have been used to limit automobile imports and drive up their prices. You might think this is appropriate, but a hint that safety or environmental standards are not always the real issue arises from the fact that Japanese standards drive up the prices of U.S. car exports to Japan even more. Both U.S. and Japanese carmakers have lobbied for regulations that are disadvantageous to foreign producers.

Quotas Quotas are the most common nontariff barriers to trade.

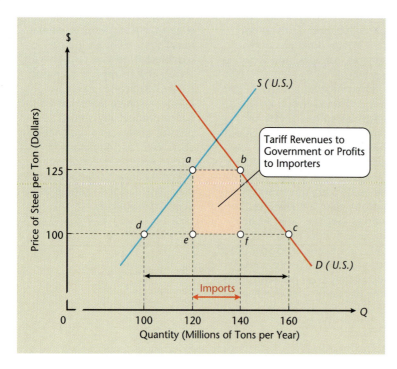

FIGURE 7 The Effects of Quotas and Tariffs

Quotas and tariffs both raise prices to consumers. In this example, a tariff of $25 per ton of steel will cut annual imports (*M*) from 60 million tons down to 20 million tons and will generate government revenues of $500 million. If a quota of 20 million tons is set, those granted import licenses will realize $500 million in profits, and consumers will still pay $125 per ton for steel.

Quotas *limit the amounts of goods that may be imported or exported.*

Both quotas and tariffs inefficiently raise the prices of imported goods so that potential gains from trade are not fully realized, but the side effects of quotas make them especially harmful. Let us investigate why this is so.

Suppose the $25 tariff in Figure 7 is replaced by an import quota of 20 million tons annually — the domestic price remains at $125 per ton, but government would collect no revenues. Importers who secured import licenses would collectively pick off profits of $500 million — 20 million tons of steel costing $100 per ton could be sold for $125 a ton. These potential profits make import licenses very valuable and provide substantial inducements for bribery and corruption.

Voluntary Export Restrictions In its international negotiations, the United States has traditionally been a cheerleader for freer international trade. Our actual policies, however, have been a bit schizophrenic. Fear of a trade war coupled with international treaties (instigated by the United States) to reduce tariffs have made it difficult for U.S. policymakers to bow to political pressures for protectionism by raising tariffs. This has diverted most industries that want protection from imports into lobbying for *voluntary export restrictions* (*VERs*). Our government threatens foreign industries with import barriers unless they restrict exports. *VERs* are "voluntary" only in the sense that you "voluntarily" give up when a robber points a gun at you and says "Your money or your life."

Japan imposed quotas on textile exports to the United States in the 1970s, and on its auto exports in the 1980s. We indicated earlier that restrictions on auto imports from Japan saved American auto workers' jobs at a cost of from $150,000 to $241,000 each. Curiously, the Japanese auto industry gained. The preceding analysis of quotas shows how. Limits on auto exports raised the prices Japanese firms received for exported vehicles and boosted their profits by billions of dollars. These profits would have been converted into U.S. tax revenues if tariffs had been used instead of quotas.

The Japanese reaction to this *VER* illustrates how regulation provokes unanticipated adjustments that may defeat its stated purpose. The goal of the *VER* was to protect American jobs and reduce the U.S. trade deficit, but it only limited the number of Japanese exports — not their value. Consequently, Japanese carmakers focused on exporting more luxurious lines — Toyota Land Cruisers, and the new Acura, Lexus, and Infiniti vehicles. Thus, some of the import pressure on economy cars was shifted to another market segment. But Yugos and Korean Hyundais were not subject to quotas, so they partially replaced the low-end Japanese exports in American garages. Even voluntary quotas have unpredictable results.

Another problem is that rigid quotas fail to accommodate changes in demand. Growth in demand can be met by imports with a tariff system, but not under import quotas. Finally, relative to tariffs, quotas retard the incentives of foreign producers to do research and innovation. Conclusion: From the perspective of the citizen/taxpayer, tariffs are preferable to quotas. However, either mechanism causes substantial economic inefficiency.

A Final Argument for Freer Trade

Perfect government policies might, in an ideal world, achieve any feasible set of goals we choose. Optimal trade barriers could efficiently exploit our own monopoly/monopsony power and counter that exercised by foreigners. Ideal barriers might also be constructed to protect American jobs, incomes, and infant industries, bolster our national defense, rectify trade and payments imbalances, and offset unfair practices by foreign governments.

In the real world, however, most trade barriers are enacted because of pressures from special interests. These barriers depress our national income, stimulate foreign retaliation and hostility against the United States, endanger jobs in export industries, and shrink competition for domestic firms that exercise monopoly power. Nor

FOCUS 2

Regional Economic Integration

Just as TV broadcasts and fast-food restaurant chains are slowly diminishing differences in regional dialects and in how towns look from Maine to Texas to Hawaii, advances in telecommunications and the gains from trade are blurring international borders and differences of language and culture. Groups of countries increasingly agree to follow common economic policies. OPEC, for example, sets oil prices for its 17 member countries (with erratic success). An even more significant trend is regional economic integration, whereby agreements tear down the trade barriers between neighboring countries. This may be a baby step toward free trade throughout the world.

The European Community

Germany, France, Italy, Belgium, the Netherlands, and Luxembourg launched the European Community (EC) in 1957. They have since been joined by the United Kingdom, Ireland, Denmark, Greece, Spain, and Portugal on a slow but steady path toward full economic integration. (See Figure 8.) Barriers restricting trade and capital flows have virtually disappeared. An official but still weak European Community government is at work on laws to govern commercial activity in all EC countries. The European Currency Unit (ECU) was established in 1979 to stabilize financial dealings among EC countries, and represents a giant step toward a common monetary system.

The North American Community

Trade between the United States and Canada flourished after most trade barriers and restrictions on resource flows were removed in 1989. Mexico is negotiating to join this economic union by 1994, although concerns about northward movements of more Mexican labor may somewhat limit any agreement's scope. Ongoing policies to "privatize" enterprises historically mismanaged by government bureaucracies have recently reawakened interest in Mexican stocks and bonds after a decade of pessimism caused by enormous international indebtedness.

Prospects

Japan and South Korea have similar "free trade" agreements, and they are negotiating with China and other Pacific Rim countries. Tariff barriers that restricted trade with the former USSR and other Eastern bloc countries are being dismantled, and negotiations are underway to reach accommodation with the EC and North American economic unions.

From a global perspective, regional economic integration has the disadvantage of erecting uniform trade barriers against outsiders. Nevertheless, the potential gains from even freer trade are so powerful that the next logical step is negotiated reductions of trade barriers between the emerging blocs of traders. There is reason to be optimistic that the full gains available from free trade throughout most of the world may ultimately be realized.

---

has the growth of nontariff barriers to trade prevented enormous and growing trade and payments deficits.

A major reason U.S. trade policies are so far from ideal is that specific trade barriers strongly affect the incomes of members of special-interest groups who are willing to work hard in the political arena for their passage. But members of the general public are politically apathetic about such things as import quotas on shoes, because

FIGURE 8 The European Community

their individual well-being is affected relatively little. The result is mounting pressure for protectionism that will inefficiently benefit the few at much higher cost to the broad public. Focus 2 points out, however, that recent international

agreements may pave the way for freer international trade.

International trade is a major source of economic development. At the same time, consumer demands grow and broaden as consumers' incomes grow, so trade tends to expand as the world economy grows. Trade also increases interdependence and improves international relations. In this chapter we have explored the gains from trade and exposed the fallacies behind most arguments against free trade. We hope you will remember these discussions when people debate trade policies.

Chapter Review: Key Points

1. International trade is important to people throughout the world. The smaller and less diversified an economy is, the greater is the importance of its international trade.

2. The *law of comparative advantage* suggests that there will be net gains to all trading parties whenever their pretrade relative opportunity costs and price structures differ between goods.

3. A country's *consumption possibilities frontier* (*CPF*) expands beyond its production possibilities frontier (*PPF*) with the onset of trade or with the removal of trade restrictions.

4. The *terms of trade* are the prices of exports relative to the costs of imports. An adverse change in the terms of trade lowers a country's *CPF*, while a favorable change in the terms of trade expands it.

5. Gains from trade arise because international transactions (*a*) provide unique goods that would not otherwise be available, (*b*) allow highly specialized industries to exploit economies of scale, (*c*) speed the spread of technology, and facilitate capital accumulation and entrepreneurial innovation, (*d*) encourage more peaceful international relations, and (*e*) facilitate specialization according to comparative advantage.

6. Domestic producers of imported goods may suffer short-term losses from trade, as do domestic consumers of exported goods. However, their losses are overshadowed by the specialization gains to the consumers of imports and the producers of exports. The gainers could always use parts of their gains to compensate the losers so that, on balance, no one loses. Moreover, *uniqueness, scale, dynamic,* and *political gains from trade* make it unlikely that anyone loses from trade in the long run.

7. Even the most valid of the arguments against free trade are substantially overworked. The arguments that are semi-valid include the ideas that (*a*) the income redistributions from trade are undesirable; (*b*) desirable diversity within a narrow economy is hampered by free trade; (*c*) national defense requires restrictions to avoid dependence on foreign sources, and (more validly) export restrictions to keep certain technologies out of the hands of potential enemies; and (*d*) major exporters of a commodity can exercise monopolistic power by restricting exports, while important consuming nations can exercise monopsonistic power through import restrictions.

8. Any exercise of international monopoly/monopsony power invites retaliation and causes worldwide economic inefficiency. Those who lose because of trade restrictions will lose far more than is gained by the "winners."

9. If trade is to be restricted, *tariffs* are preferable to *quotas* because of the higher tax revenues and the smaller incentives for bribery and corruption.

10. *Trade adjustment assistance* is one way that the gainers from trade might compensate the losers so that all would gain. However, the difficulty of identifying the losers and the failure to fund this program adequately have resulted in mounting pressures for trade restrictions.

Key Concepts

Ensure that you can define these terms before proceeding.

absolute advantage	dynamic gains
comparative advantage	gains from scale
uniqueness gains from trade	political gains
specialization gains	terms of trade
	dumping

infant industry
tariffs
quotas

voluntary export
restrictions

Problems and Questions

1. What would happen to standards of living in the United States if all foreign trade were prohibited? How significant do you think this would be? In what areas would the impact be the strongest?

2. How is smuggling related to import tariffs and quotas? (Positively, negatively, or not at all?) Does smuggling increase social welfare or decrease it? If your answer is that it depends on the types of goods smuggled, for which types of goods would smuggling increase welfare? What types of goods justify barriers against importation?

3. Suppose that workers in Java can each produce 10 tons of sugar or 200 shirts per year, while Cubans can each produce either 15 tons of sugar or 45 shirts annually. There are 10 million workers on each island.

   a. Use graph paper to draw *PPF*s for each country.

   b. What are the prices of these goods in each country without trade? Will the final terms of trade settle between these relative prices?

   c. Show graphically what happens to the *CPF*s of these islands if they begin trading and if the terms of trade settle at the exact midpoint of the initial price ratios without trade.

   d. Identify the groups that unambiguously realize short-run specialization gains from trade and the groups that might lose from trade.

4. What types of goods dominate our imports from Japan? What types of goods do you think we probably export to Japan? Are these patterns related to the types of resources that are relatively abundant or scarce in the two countries?

5. Name three goods for which U.S. dollar prices are likely to fall if trade barriers between Mexico and the United States are eliminated. Why would you not expect the prices of any goods that we export to Mexico to rise as a consequence of such an agreement?

6. How do a nation's endowments of labor, natural resources, and capital shape the outputs in which it has comparative advantages? What influence might weather have? Can you think of other determinants of a country's areas of comparative advantage?

7. Suppose England is abundantly endowed with capital but has a relative scarcity of labor, while India has abundant labor but sparse capital. Assume that tea production requires intensive labor inputs while woolens require relatively more capital. According to the Hechscher-Ohlin theory of trade, which goods will be imported and which exported in each country? Which resource owners gain from trade and which lose?

8. The Hechscher-Ohlin model of international trade has been extended to "prove" that international transactions tend to "equalize" factor payments (e.g., the purchasing power of wages and rates of return to capital). Since World War II, the rapid growth in labor incomes in Japan and Western Europe relative to that in the United States seems to support this theory. What mechanisms tend to equalize resource payments?

9. Most models of international trade assume that goods move across international borders but people and capital do not. Can you use the principles you have learned in this chapter to explain immigration patterns and international capital flows?

10. One critic of U.S. policies argues that "either we allow Mexican goods freer access to American markets or we allow Mexicans to immigrate into the United States more freely or we must send billions of dollars in foreign aid to Mexico to prevent a revolution that adopts anti-American policies." How does this argument mesh with ideas from this chapter?

11. Figure 9 illustrates the U.S. demand and supply for compact disc players. If the world price of compact disc players is $200, (*a*) How many disc players will the U.S. import? (*b*) How many disc players will the U.S. manufacture? If a $50 tariff is placed on

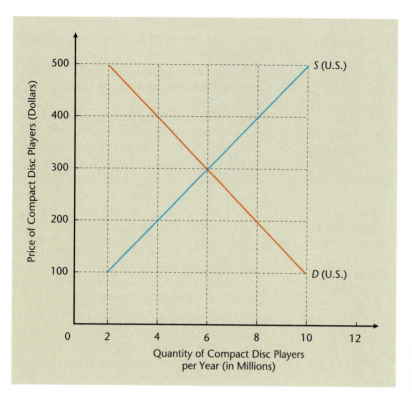

FIGURE 9   U.S. Supply and Demand for Compact Disc Players

each compact disc player, (c) What price will consumers pay for disc players? (d) How many disc players will the U.S. now manufacture? (e) How many disc players will the U.S. import? (f) How much will the government collect in revenues from the tariff?

12. Use Figure 9 to answer the following questions. (a) If the U.S. is currently importing 6 million compact disc players a year, what is the world price? (b) At this world price, how many disc players are manufactured in the U.S.? If the U.S. institutes an import quota of 4 million compact disc players annually, (c) What is the total number of disc players purchased by U.S. citizens annually? (d) By how much does U.S. production increase? (e) What is the potential total profit to importers as a result of the tariff? (f) How much revenue will the government collect from the imposition of the quota?

13. Restrictions on oil imports on the grounds of national security have undoubtedly led to greater domestic exploitation. Because petroleum is a depletable resource, this may account for our current increased, rather

than decreased, dependence on "unreliable foreign sources." What are alternatives to import restrictions as ways to assure the availability of oil in the event of national emergency? Would these mechanisms work as well to assure availability for goods other than nonrenewable resources?

14. Should American consumers pay higher prices because of trade barriers to protect the jobs of workers in "senile" industries? Do such policies in effect "protect consumers from lower prices"? What limits do you think there should be on free trade internationally? Are there valid reasons for protectionist policies?

15. The American steel, auto, and television receiver industries were all in bad shape even before the economy began to slump in the early 1980s. Plant closings in these industries led to calls for tariffs and quotas on steel, autos, and televisions. Do restrictions on trade make more sense in a slumping economy than in one that is prosperous? What are some disadvantages to using trade restrictions to bolster declining industries or a stagnant economy?

CHAPTER

International Finance

Would you enjoy a European vacation? Some lucky students can afford it and will go next summer, while others will wait a year or two, and still others will go only after they retire, if ever. A major influence on the cost of touring Paris or Rome is the dollar's *exchange rate* — its value relative to francs or lire. A high-valued dollar reduces our costs for a European tour and more of us fly overseas, but a lower exchange rate raises the cost of foreign travel so more of us stay home. Of course, a low-valued dollar makes America a bargain for foreign tourists, and the Grand Canyon, Disneyland, and similar spots will be more crowded than usual.

Most of us are more familiar with exchange rates than we are with other aspects of *international finance*, which covers such issues as (*a*) the economic consequences of flows of funds to finance international transactions, and (*b*) how these transactions are funded when some traders are based in countries that use dinars or pesos, for example, while their trading partners customarily deal in yen or dollars. How international trade and payments are related and the nature of balance of payments accounts are our first topics in this chapter.

How prices are set when traders use different currencies is our second concern. A key to this puzzle involves looking at different ways that

exchange rates between currencies can be determined. Exchange rates translate *all* wages and prices in one country's currency into their values in other countries' currencies. Our final task in this chapter is an overview of influences on the international value of the dollar during the past few years. This will complete the framework you need to interpret recent imbalances in countries' international payments.

Balances of Payments and Trade

Most Americans react with a yawn when they hear about the latest deficit in our balance of payments. The United States ran persistent deficits in its international trade and payments from the early 1980s into the 1990s. Few people can identify any personal ways in which they have been harmed by these deficits. Trade deficits or surpluses provide starting points for understanding international finance.

There is no special reason for inflows of dollars from sales of U.S. exports to match the outflows of dollars for our purchases of imports.

If the dollar value of merchandise imports exceeds that for exports of U.S. merchandise, *then the U.S. experiences a **balance of trade deficit**. But if the dollar value of our merchandise exports exceeds the monetary value of imports, there is a **balance of trade surplus**.*

Naturally, trade deficits in some countries are exactly balanced by trade surpluses in other countries — one country's imports are another's exports.

Balance of Payments Accounts

Accounting for international transactions in merchandise and services is the first step in building our balance of payments accounts.

*Our **balance of payments accounts** summarize flows of payments between the U.S. and foreigners with whom Americans deal.*

Transactions that cause Americans to send funds abroad drive this account toward a deficit; transactions generating inflows of funds move the balance of payments toward a surplus.

*A **deficit** occurs in our balance of payments if monetary outflows from the U.S. exceed money inflows; a **surplus** occurs if the inflows exceed outflows.*

Table 1 outlines the U.S. balance of payments account, which covers two major categories: the current account and the capital account. The *current account* deals with transfers and trade in goods and services. The *capital account* records transactions in such items as stocks, bonds, or real estate. These accounts are balanced by changes in the holdings of foreign currencies or net outflows of U.S. money — items (9) and (10) in this table.

The Current Account   Only merchandise shipments are considered when computing the balance of trade, but dollar for dollar, international transfers and sales of services have roughly equivalent macroeconomic effects. Transfer payments include such items as cash gifts between individuals in separate countries, and other unilateral transfers such as foreign aid or pension payments to workers who have retired abroad.

Many people intuitively believe that international trade occurs only in merchandise, not services. Nevertheless, a French tourist who exchanges francs for dollars and then gets a haircut in a Chicago barber shop before returning to Paris is effectively importing that haircut, and the barber is, perhaps unknowingly, an exporter. Foreign students in your class who pay their tuitions after exchanging their national currencies for dollars are "importing" education to their countries. How many of your professors do you think recognize that they are partially "exporting" their lectures?

The Capital Account   U.S. investments abroad historically accounted for most of our outflows of financial capital. Deposits to a Swiss bank account or purchases of stock on the Hong Kong exchange by Americans also cause outflows of funds. Similarly, if a Japanese firm builds an auto assembly plant in the United States, or buys U.S. Treasury bonds, funds flow into the United States.

The statistical discrepancy in these accounts is large because many transactions cannot be identified by type. Tracing funds used for such illicit transactions as drug smuggling (dollars for cocaine) is almost impossible, as is detecting what foreign tourists buy after they exchange their money for dollars.

Accounting records of foreign purchases of U.S. financial securities are also skimpy, as is true whenever countries do not closely monitor and control foreign transactions. Few governments keep close track of even huge investments of financial capital by foreigners, in part because the resources devoted to data collection have not kept pace with the growth of international flows of funds. The British government, for example, was recently dismayed to learn that its claim that Britain was "among the world's three biggest creditor nations" was no longer true by 1991, because the "statistical discrepancy" in its payments accounts had been attributable to net capital inflows for much of the 1980s.

After we sum all the transactions that draw money into the United States and subtract all transactions that send funds abroad, we have the balance of payments surplus or deficit, which summarizes net international transactions.

Table 1 *The U.S. Balance of Payments (1990 billions of dollars)*

	Receipts (+)	Payments (−)	Balance
Current Account			
(1) Merchandise Exports	+251		
(2) Merchandise Imports		−410	
Trade Balance			−159
(3) Net Investment Income	+14		
(4) Net Services		−3	
(5) Net Unilateral Transfers		−13	
Current Account Balance (1 + 2 + 3 + 4 + 5)			−161
Capital Account			
(6) Capital Outflows		−64	
(7) Capital Inflows	+203		
(8) Statistical Discrepancy		−17	
Official Reserves Transactions Balance (1 + 2 + 3 + 4 + 5 + 6 + 7 + 8)			+122
Method of Financing			
(9) Increases in U.S. Official Reserve Assets (−)		−9	
(10) Increase in Foreign Official Assets (+)	+48		
Total Financing of Surplus			+39
Sum of (1) through (10)			0

Source: *Survey of Current Business,* April 1991.

Imbalances of Payments

One consequence of the immense federal budget deficits of recent years has been persistent balance of payments deficits, a topic addressed in Chapter 14. We showed that if net private domestic saving $(S - I)$ was inadequate to cover any government deficit $(G - T)$, then the budget deficit will be financed by foreigners:

$$S + T - I - G = X - M$$

(Recall that M = imports, X = exports, S = domestic saving, I = investment, G = government outlays, and T = tax revenues.)

Our domestic saving and taxes have not covered domestic investment and government outlays in recent years $(S + T < I + G)$, so the United States has run large deficits in its current account $(X - M < 0)$. Many of this country's trading partners have used surpluses in their balances of trade (their current accounts) to purchase U.S. financial assets (Treasury bonds, corporate stocks and bonds, or real estate). Foreign financial investment in the United States has helped Americans to "live beyond" their current incomes in recent years.

The preceding government budget constraint can be rearranged to isolate the current account of the U.S. balance of payments:

$$X - M = (S - I) + (T - G)$$

Thus, reversing persistent deficits in our current account requires higher taxes or domestic saving (less consumption), or declines in government outlays or private investment—a harsh set of choices that international economists term the *absorption* problem. Americans must rely on inflows of foreign financial capital to sustain healthy domestic investment, or we must begin saving more or paying more taxes.

One way to attract foreign capital is through high interest rates that make investments in U.S. financial assets more attractive. International flows of funds are controlled by the forces of supply and demand operating in international money markets. The relative strengths of supplies and demands for a country's money are reflected in the relative prices of national currencies — their exchange rates.

Exchange Rates

Most international transactions require the currency of the buyer to be exchanged for the currency of the seller. For example, Americans usually want dollars, so foreign customers who buy from us must acquire U.S. dollars.[1] They express their demands for dollars by supplying their own currencies. Similarly, we demand foreign goods, make loans to foreigners, or invest abroad by supplying dollars, which translates into demands for foreign currencies. The relative demands and supplies of various currencies determine their relative prices, or exchange rates.

Suppose you buy a pound of Brazilian coffee. Your grocer will accept U.S. dollars to pay the wholesaler, who probably pays dollars to the importer. But most Brazilian coffee growers do not ultimately want dollars from the importer; they want Brazilian cruzeiros to pay their workers and suppliers. This means that dollars must be exchanged for cruzeiros. Thus, your coffee purchase is ultimately translated into a demand for cruzeiros in international money markets and, simultaneously, into a supply of dollars.

The price of one currency (cruzeiros) in terms of another (dollars) is called the **exchange rate.**

---

1. The U.S. dollar has historically been so universally convertible that foreigners often require dollar payments when they sell to other foreigners. OPEC, for example, states its oil prices in dollars. Thus, if the Czechs buy Saudi oil but lack sufficient Saudi dinars, the Saudis may be reluctant to accept Czechoslovakian korunas, requiring U.S. dollars instead. This creates an international transaction demand for dollars; few other currencies are used internationally as mediums of exchange, and none as commonly as the dollar. More about this in a moment.

If $1 can be exchanged for 200 cruzeiros, then the cruzeiro is priced at half a cent ($0.005) and the Brazilian exchange rate is 200. It takes 200 cruzeiros for a Brazilian to buy U.S. merchandise worth $1. Note that these exchange rates are reciprocals — if $1 = 200 cruzeiros, then one cruzeiro = 1/200th of a dollar.

The exchange rate translates all prices (including wages and interest rates) in one currency into their value in another currency. A low exchange rate of the dollar for the yen makes investment in the United States appeal more to Japanese investors, so Japanese financial capital will tend to flow into the United States. Huge federal budget deficits in the 1980s increased U.S. reliance on foreign capital. High real interest rates in the early 1980s made U.S. financial investments attractive to foreign investors, so huge capital inflows from abroad bolstered the dollar's exchange rate. However, our continuous need to attract ever more foreign capital caused the dollar's exchange rate to fall sharply during 1985–1988.

The dollar's recovery by 1991 allowed it to buy more yen. Thus, Japanese investors could receive more yen when selling their dollar assets; their investments were more profitable than expected. But Japanese investors will be out of luck if the dollar again falls on international markets. What looks like a good foreign investment if exchange rates are stable may be spectacular if the foreign currency's exchange rate rises, or a miserable dog if it falls. An exchange rate can rise through *appreciation* or *revaluation*, or fall through *depreciation* or *devaluation*.

Currency Appreciation and Depreciation

Exchange rates are like other prices in that changes in supplies and demands cause exchange rates to fluctuate unless governments control them. Table 2 shows cross exchange rates in May 1991 for nine major currencies. (In Table 4, you will see exchange rates for a much larger number of currencies, including the cruzeiro.)

There is **appreciation** *of a nation's currency if market forces cause foreign currencies to become cheaper.*

For example, if the cruzeiro's price fell from $0.004 to $0.002, a dollar would buy twice as many cruzeiros, and thus has appreciated.

Depreciation *of the domestic currency (e.g., dollars in the United States) means that foreign currencies have grown in value.*

A depreciated dollar buys fewer cruzeiros (and less coffee) than previously.

Revaluation and Devaluation

The flexible exchange rate system used between most countries since 1973 allows supplies and demands for currencies in international markets to set exchange rates. Before then, treaties established most exchange rates, but these agreements seldom survived if they were inconsistent with powerful market forces.

When fixed exchange rates are adjusted, the currency that appreciates is **revalued,** *and the depreciating currency is* **devalued.**

In an earlier era, many currencies were based on a *gold standard*, by which a government guaranteed to exchange a fixed amount of currency for a fixed amount of gold. Gold standards automatically yield fixed international exchange rates.

Even today, some exchange rates are fixed and occasionally must be adjusted. For example, exchange rates among European Community currencies are fixed, and tend to "float" in unison vis-à-vis other currencies. When the French economy suffered from high inflation and flight capital in 1983, however, the French franc was *devalued* relative to the German deutsche mark, the British pound, and all other EC currencies. The franc also *depreciated* relative to major currencies outside the EC. Realizing how market forces affect exchange rates is fundamental to understanding how the international economy operates.

Demands and Supplies of Currencies

Foreign money is collectively known as *foreign exchange*. Demands for foreign exchange resemble domestic demands for money. Most demands for foreign exchange are based on international transactions (in goods, services, or financial investments), but some key currencies (primarily

Table 2 *Foreign Exchange Rates — Cross Rates for Major Countries*

Key Currency Cross Rates Late New York Trading May 8, 1991

	Dollar	Pound	SFranc	Guilder	Yen	Lira	D-Mark	FFranc	CdnDlr
Canada	1.1526	1.9822	.78730	.59047	.00833	.00090	.66532	.19652	—
France	5.8650	10.087	4.0061	3.0046	.04241	.00457	3.3855	—	5.0885
Germany	1.7324	2.9794	1.1833	.88750	.01253	.00135	—	.29538	1.5030
Italy	1282.0	2204.8	875.68	656.76	9.270	—	740.01	218.58	1112.3
Japan	138.30	237.85	94.467	70.850	—	.10788	79.831	23.581	119.99
Netherlands ..	1.9520	3.3570	1.3333	—	.01411	.00152	1.1268	.33282	1.6936
Switzerland ..	1.4640	2.5178	—	.75000	.01059	.00114	.84507	.24962	1.2702
U.K.	.58146	—	.39717	.29788	.00420	.00045	.33564	.09914	.50448
U.S.	—	1.7198	.68306	.51230	.00723	.00078	.57723	.17050	.86760

Source: Telerate

This table showing cross exchange rates appears in the *Wall Street Journal* and other major newspapers almost every day. Note that the numbers below the blank diagonal are reciprocals of numbers above the diagonal. For example, the U.S. dollar's exchange rate for the Canadian dollar is shown in row 1, column 1, while the Canadian dollar's exchange rate for the U.S. dollar is in the last row, last column.

the dollar) are demanded for precautionary reasons or because they are viewed as stable assets. (Transaction, precautionary, and asset demands for money were discussed in Chapter 13.)

For simplicity, assume that the only two currencies are U.S. dollars ($) and German deutsche marks (DM). Our demand for deutsche marks is mirrored in our willingness to supply dollars. To see this, consider point *a* in both panels of Figure 1, which shows that if the exchange rate is one for one, we are willing to supply $1 billion for DM1 billion. When we can get DM2 for $1 (point *b* in Panel A), we are willing to supply $2 billion to get DM4 billion (each DM costs $0.50 at point *b* in Panel B). And so on. Comparing the matched points between Panels A and B will confirm that information in one is duplicated in the other.

Changes in exchange rates cause movements along international supply and demand curves for a currency, paralleling the way that price changes cause changes in quantities demanded or supplied along supply and demand curves for

goods. And, just as we assume certain influences constant to construct standard demand curves, isolating the effects of exchange rates on the quantity of dollars demanded to build the German demand curve for dollars requires holding constant (*a*) the prices of substitutes (foreign goods are the relevant substitutes), (*b*) foreign incomes, (*c*) foreign tastes and preferences, (*d*) expectations about exchange rate changes and relative inflation rates in both countries, and (*e*) the dollar prices of U.S. goods.

Symmetrically, we hold U.S. incomes, prices, preferences, expectations, and foreign prices in DM constant when drawing the U.S. supply curve of dollars. Changing any of these variables shifts the demand or supply of dollars. Table 3 summarizes how these variables affect the international demands and supplies of dollars.

Although we hold the dollar prices of American goods constant in the United States and the DM prices of German goods constant in Germany, the dollar prices of imports from Germany and the DM prices of our exports will

FIGURE 1   The U.S. Supply of Dollars and Its Mirror Image: The Demand for Foreign Exchange

The supply of American dollars on international money markets (Panel A) translates precisely into a demand for foreign currencies (Panel B).

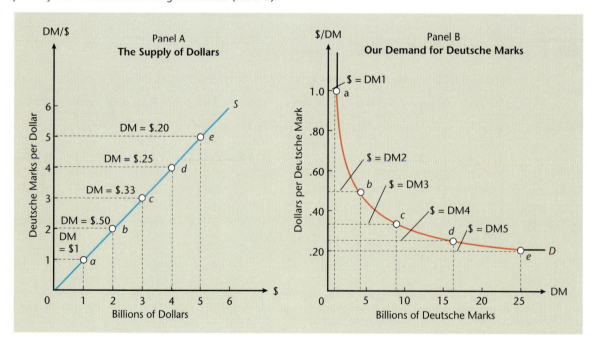

Table 3 *Shifts in International Demands and Supplies of a Currency**

Foreign Demands for Dollars Rise, Increasing the Dollar's Exchange Rate, If:

1. The domestic prices of goods in other countries rise.
2. The incomes of foreigners rise.
3. Foreigners' tastes for American products increase.
4. Foreigners expect the exchange rate of the dollar to rise.
5. The dollar prices of U.S. goods fall (e.g., deflation in the U.S.).
6. Investment in the U.S. appears more profitable (e.g., U.S. interest rates rise).

The Supply of U.S. Dollars on International Markets Increases, Lowering the Dollar's Exchange Rate, If:

1. The domestic prices of American outputs increase (e.g., inflation).
2. National Income in the United States increases.
3. Americans increasingly prefer imported goods.
4. Americans expect the exchange rate of the dollar to fall.
5. Inflation is expected abroad (e.g., we might expect prices for BMWs to rise).
6. Prices for imported goods fall (e.g., deflation abroad).
7. Foreign investments appear more profitable.

*Naturally, reversals of the movements listed here would reverse the effects on exchange rates as described.

change proportionally if exchange rates fluctuate. This is the key to why the demand and supply curves of dollars (or DM) slope down and up, respectively.[2]

The Supply of Currencies

The supply of dollars in Panel A of Figure 1 is based on Americans' offers to buy foreign currencies, which we then use to buy foreign goods and services or to invest abroad. This supply

2. Technically, this requires that international demands and supplies of goods be elastic, conditions that we assume are met throughout our exposition in this chapter.

curve slopes upward because it costs more dollars to invest abroad or to buy imports if foreign currency becomes more costly. Many previous American buyers of imports may drop out of the market or shift to substitutes (movements such as $e \rightarrow d \rightarrow c \rightarrow b \rightarrow a$). Conversely, if our exchange rate rises so we can buy more DM per dollar, we will be willing to supply greater quantities of dollars. This supply curve will shift if there are changes in American incomes or tastes, or in the prices of the foreign goods we import.

The Demand for Currencies

Our transaction demand for deutsche marks in Panel B of Figure 1 is really a demand by Americans to buy German goods and to invest overseas. We measure the price of the DM in terms of dollars, and this demand curve slopes down from left to right. If DM become more expensive in terms of dollars, the dollar prices of German goods and investments rise and Americans will buy fewer German goods and invest less abroad; instead, Americans will buy more American goods and invest more domestically. This means that they will demand fewer DM. When DM are cheaper, Americans will buy more of them because imports from Germany will be cheaper, as will dollar investments in Germany.

Equilibrium Exchange Rates

The supply curve of dollars is actually a "flipped over" demand curve for foreign currencies, as shown in Panel B of Figure 1. (Remember that exchange rates are the reciprocals of each other.) We offer (supply) dollars in order to buy foreign exchange, and ultimately, foreign goods. The demand curve for dollars is similarly a "flipped over" supply curve of the foreign currency.

This means that we can look at the same market with either set of curves. That is, our demand for foreign currency (Panel B) mirrors our supply of dollars (Panel A). Foreign demands for dollars (Panel A of Figure 2) are the supplies of foreign currencies (Panel B). We only need to look at one market in order to know precisely what is happening in the other. Henceforth, we will only look at the dollar market; no additional informa-

FIGURE 2   The Relationships Between Our Supply of Dollars and Demands for Foreign Exchange and Foreign Demands for Dollars and Supplies of Foreign Exchange

The markets for dollars (Panel A) and deutsche marks (Panel B) embody identical information. Our supply of dollars is a demand for deutsche marks, and the demand for dollars is expressed by the supply of deutsche marks. Thus, we only need to look at the market for one currency in order to know precisely the state of the market for the other currency.

tion is gained by looking at the market for DM (used here to represent all foreign currencies).

Interactions between these supply and demand curves determine equilibrium exchange rates and quantities of dollars and foreign currencies. In Figure 2, the equilibrium price of German DM is $0.50. This is the same as saying that the equilibrium price of the dollar is DM2. If the exchange rates of the dollar and deutsche mark are in equilibrium, this does not necessarily mean that the values of international transactions are offsetting so that there are no net flows of foreign exchange between countries.

Foreign Demands for Dollars

Among the reasons that the United States has been able to run persistent deficits in its balances

of payments are our size, our importance in world trade, and our history of political and economic stability. This has created transactions, precautionary, and asset demands for the dollar as a key international money, so that it is used for many international transactions even if no Americans are involved.

Transactions Demands   Foreigners have transactions demands for dollars not only to buy U.S. goods or invest in the United States, but also to transact with each other. For example, if Saudi Arabia exports oil to Brazil, it is unlikely that Brazilians will be able to pay with Saudi rials, and the Saudis may be unwilling to accept Brazilian cruzeiros. Use of the dollar solves this dilemma — Saudis will take dollars in exchange for their oil. The international acceptability of dollars causes Saudis, Brazilians, and other foreigners to seek dollars even if they have no plans to buy U.S. exports.

Precautionary and Asset Demands Rich foreigners who fear revolutions or chaos in their own countries may acquire dollars for precautionary reasons. Deposed dictators commonly flee their countries carrying suitcases filled with dollars (e.g., Ferdinand Marcos' departure from the Philippines). Foreign economic instability may also be a source of asset demands for dollars. For example, Israelis or South Americans may use dollar-denominated securities to hedge against rapid inflations in their own countries.

The point is that persistent deficits in the U.S. balance of payments may not be a sign of disequilibrium. Foreigners may want dollars more than they want the U.S. goods the dollars would buy. We are a major world banker, which means that we supply dollars the way other countries supply cars or cameras. In a sense, dollars may be the major U.S. export, and Americans gain substantially by the payments deficit. The production cost of dollars is trivial, and the U.S. economy gains tremendous *seignorage* (profit from printing money) in the process of supplying international money.

There are occasions, however, when imbalances of payments signal disequilibrium. We need to examine how foreign exchange markets can bring international supplies and demands of a currency into balance.

Curing Exchange Rate Disequilibria

Suppose that the exchange rate of the dollar for the DM is artificially held below equilibrium at, say, $0.25 per DM (DM4 per dollar) as shown in Figure 3 – relative to equilibrium, German DM are too cheap and dollars are too expensive. Situations like this offer one explanation for imbalances of international payments. In this example, there is a *surplus* of dollars on international markets, and the United States will experience a *deficit* of payments. Germany runs a compensating balance of payments *surplus*; if we constructed a graph depicting the DM market, it would show a *shortage* of DM internationally. Be sure that you

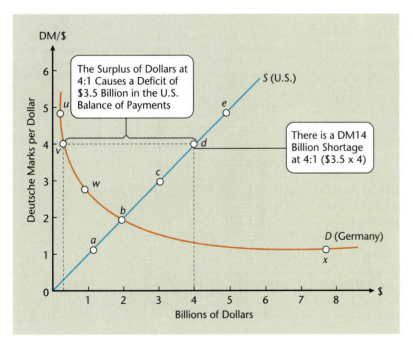

FIGURE 3 U.S. Balance of Payments Deficit Caused by Exchange Rates that Do Not Yield Equilibrium

An economic surplus of dollars leads to a deficit in the U.S. balance of payments. This implies that there is an offsetting economic shortage of deutsche marks and that Germany will experience a balance of payments surplus.

understand how surpluses of a currency imply that the issuing country experiences a balance of payments deficit, while a currency shortage implies a surplus in a country's balance of payments. This terminology is sometimes confusing.

Regardless of the cause of deficits or surpluses in a country's balance of payments, there are four basic ways of dealing with these imbalances. We can (*a*) allow changes in exchange rates, (*b*) adopt controls to ration foreign exchange, (*c*) follow macroeconomic policies to shift the supply or demand curves for foreign exchange, or (*d*) allow flows of money from deficit to surplus countries.

Each of these mechanisms has been widely used in some regions during some periods. Most payments, whether domestic or international, were made in currencies denominated in gold until World War I.

> *Fixed amounts of each currency exchange for given amounts of gold under an ideal* **gold standard** *so that all exchange rates are also fixed.*

A gold standard makes exchanging one currency for any other easy because their values in terms of gold are all fixed. An ounce of gold exchanges for an ounce of gold. But the supply of gold did not keep pace with the volume of transactions in rapidly growing economies, so countries everywhere in the world abandoned the gold standard and turned to *fiat* (paper) money.

Worldwide abandonment of gold-backed money in favor of fiat currencies raises the issue: What are the appropriate exchange rates between currencies? One answer to this question is given if governments intervene through *fixed exchange rate* agreements (price controls) or other regulations intended to stabilize exchange rates. Alternatively, it can be left to supply and demand. Since 1973, although some countries have linked their exchange rates to those of other countries (e.g., currencies in the European Community), most exchange rates have been *flexible* — governed largely by the forces of the marketplace.

Flexible (Floating) Exchange Rates

In Figure 4, there would be no deficits or surpluses if the DM rose to $0.50, which means $1 is only worth DM2 instead of DM4. As the price of the dollar fell and the price of foreign exchange rose, we would export more and import less, restoring equilibrium. This solution is called flexible (or *floating*) exchange rates and has been the dominant system used for over a decade.

> *A system of* **flexible exchange rates** *allows the relative prices of currencies to be set by market forces.*

Thus, international supplies and demands for various currencies have largely determined exchange rates since 1973.

One major objection to flexible exchange rates is that too much uncertainty may enter the sphere of international transactions because of exchange risk.

FIGURE 4 Flexible Exchange Rates: A Market Solution to Balance of Payments Deficits

If exchange rates are flexible, an economic surplus of dollars will cause the dollar to depreciate until the quantity of dollars demanded equals the amount supplied. Symmetrically, the deutsche mark will appreciate until equilibrium is reached. American balance of payments deficits and German balance of payments surpluses will be reduced or eliminated.

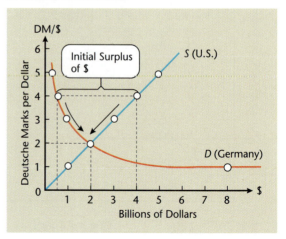

Exchange risk *arises because sellers lose if they agree to accept the buyers' national currency and it depreciates, while buyers lose if they agree to pay in the sellers' national currency and it appreciates.*

Uncertainty arises because buyers and sellers in international trade would each like the future payments stated in their own currencies to avoid possible losses.

Suppose, for example, that you were an importer of German cameras, and you contracted to buy 1,000 cameras to be delivered and paid for 120 days from today. If the contract specified payment in DM and the DM appreciated in the next four months, you would wind up paying more dollars for the deutsche marks due than you had expected. On the other hand, if dollar payments were specified and the DM appreciated, the exporter would receive fewer DM than expected. This exchange risk is a potent argument against flexible exchange rates.

Defenders of flexibility counter this objection by pointing out that importers and exporters can insure against exchange risk by dealing in forward markets that match future inflows against future outflows of dollars.

In a **forward market** *for currencies, sellers can contract to receive the currency desired in exchange for the currency received from buyers, or a buyer can contract to secure the currency desired by the seller.*

This insurance against exchange risk, however, involves transaction costs that are absent if exchange rates are absolutely fixed. An even more critical failing is that forward markets exist for only a few currencies, and even these are available for only limited future periods, as Table 4 illustrates. Critics also charge that flexible exchange rates encourage destabilizing speculation but, per our discussion in Chapter 4, it is unlikely that speculation is destabilizing in the long run.

Central bankers in many major countries are leery of perfectly flexible exchange rates. Consequently, central bankers often try to "manage the float," with, at best, mixed results. Although

flexible exchange rates adjust for surpluses and deficits automatically and have many of the desirable characteristics associated with market solutions, many governments reject flexible exchange rates, trying to resolve problems with international payments in other ways.

Macroeconomic Corrections

A balance of payments deficit will evaporate if the supply and demand curves shown in Figure 5 shift to intersect at an equilibrium exchange of DM4 instead of DM2. This cure for deficits or surpluses relies on macroeconomic adjustments.

Imbalances of payments caused by disequilibrium may be cured through **macroadjustments** *to Aggregate Demand that change nominal GNP (PQ).*

One option is for the deficit country to follow contractionary fiscal policies; domestic Aggregate Demand, including the demand for imported goods, will shrink. Another possibility is to reduce the money supply when a balance of payments deficit (a foreign exchange shortage) poses a problem. The resulting recessionary fall in output and/or deflation of domestic prices will cause us to import less. Either contractionary monetary or fiscal policies reduce the international supply of dollars shown in Figure 5.

Contractionary macroeconomic policies also induce lower prices for U.S. exports and encourage foreigners to buy more from us. The supply of foreign currency (DM) grows along with foreigners' demands for dollars in Figure 5. (Remember that the supply curve of DM mirrors the demand for dollars.) The original deficit in payments (distance *ab*) is eliminated as the economy moves from disequilibrium in the balance of payments (point *d*) to equilibrium (point *c*).

Some experts argue that deficits pose few problems; after all, deficit countries actually export money, which has a very low production cost, and receive goods and services embodying much higher production costs. These analysts recommend that the balance of payments surpluses in some countries be cured with expan-

Table 4 *Exchange Rates*

EXCHANGE RATES

Wednesday, May 8, 1991

The New York foreign exchange selling rates below apply to trading among banks in amounts of $1 million and more, as quoted at 3 p.m. Eastern time by Bankers Trust Co. and other sources. Retail transactions provide fewer units of foreign currency per dollar.

Country	U.S. $ equiv. Wed.	Currency per U.S. $ Wed.
Argentina (Austral)	.0001040	9616.03
Australia (Dollar)	.7837	1.2760
Austria (Schilling)	.08207	12.18
Bahrain (Dinar)	2.6532	.3769
Belgium (Franc)		
Commercial rate	.02808	35.61
Brazil (Cruzeiro)	.00391	256.08
Britain (Pound)	1.7205	.5812
30-Day Forward	1.7118	.5842
90-Day Forward	1.6972	.5892
180-Day Forward	1.6791	.5956
Canada (Dollar)	.8683	1.1517
30-Day Forward	.8659	1.1549
90-Day Forward	.8615	1.1607
180-Day Forward	.8557	1.1686
Chile (Peso)	.003052	327.69
China (Renmimbi)	.189226	5.2847
Colombia (Peso)	.001753	570.38
Denmark (Krone)	.1510	6.6240
Ecuador (Sucre)		
Floating rate	.000966	1035.00
Finland (Markka)	.24759	4.0390
France (Franc)	.17059	5.8620
30-Day Forward	.17011	5.8785
90-Day Forward	.16923	5.9090
180-Day Forward	.16805	5.9505
Germany (Mark)	.5774	1.7320
30-Day Forward	.5759	1.7365
90-Day Forward	.5729	1.7454
180-Day Forward	.5688	1.7580
Greece (Drachma)	.005284	189.25
Hong Kong (Dollar)	.12835	7.7910
India (Rupee)	.04950	20.20
Indonesia (Rupiah)	.0005208	1920.01
Ireland (Punt)	1.5515	.6445
Israel (Shekel)	.4405	2.2700
Italy (Lira)	.0007803	1281.61
Japan (Yen)	.007231	138.30
30-Day Forward	.007218	138.55
90-Day Forward	.007197	138.95
180-Day Forward	.007176	139.36
Jordan (Dinar)	1.5029	.6654

Country	U.S. $ equiv. Wed.	Currency per U.S. $ Wed.
Kuwait (Dinar)	z	z
Lebanon (Pound)	.001078	928.00
Malaysia (Ringgit)	.3627	2.7570
Malta (Lira)	3.0075	.3325
Mexico (Peso)		
Floating rate	.0003333	3000.00
Netherland (Guilder)	.5124	1.9515
New Zealand (Dollar)	.5895	1.6964
Norway (Krone)	.1483	6.7450
Pakistan (Rupee)	.0428	23.35
Peru (New Sol)	1.4503	.69
Philippines (Peso)	.03693	27.08
Portugal (Escudo)	.006739	148.40
Saudi Arabia (Riyal)	.26667	3.7500
Singapore (Dollar)	.5647	1.7710
South Africa (Rand)		
Commercial rate	.3585	2.7893
Financial rate	.3051	3.2780
South Korea (Won)	.0013805	724.35
Spain (Peseta)	.009341	107.05
Sweden (Krona)	.1617	6.1832
Switzerland (Franc)	.6835	1.4630
30-Day Forward	.6821	1.4661
90-Day Forward	.6793	1.4722
180-Day Forward	.6761	1.4790
Taiwan (Dollar)	.037010	27.02
Thailand (Baht)	.03905	25.61
Turkey (Lira)	.0002593	3857.01
United Arab (Dirham)	.2723	3.6725
Uruguay (New Peso)		
Financial	.000536	1865.00
Venezuela (Bolivar)		
Floating rate	.01841	54.32
SDR	1.34039	.74605
ECU	1.19047	. . .

Special Drawing Rights (SDR) are based on exchange rates for the U.S., German, British, French and Japanese currencies. Source: International Monetary Fund.

European Currency Unit (ECU) is based on a basket of community currencies. Source: European Community Commission.

z-Not quoted.

Note that forward rates are listed for only a few major countries, and that forward rates are not available for periods exceeding 180 days. The relative skimpiness of forward markets severely limits the ability of traders to avoid risk.

sionary macroeconomic policies, causing domestic prices to rise in surplus countries and the prices of their imports to fall; their surpluses of receipts from international trade would therefore be eliminated.

These sorts of *macroadjustments* are automatic under a gold standard, which was the policy of most developed countries in the half century preceding World War I. Payments deficits reduced a country's supply of gold money; surpluses increased it. But because macropolicy-based corrections require deflation and stimulate unemployment in countries experiencing a deficit, they tend to be unpopular with the people who live in those countries. Nor do most leaders of countries having excessive surpluses in their balances of payments welcome the suggestion

that expansionary or inflationary macroeconomic policies are in order.

Several foreign finance ministers, for example, urged the U.S. government to follow contractionary policies in the 1960s and 1970s to cure our chronic payments deficits. We offered counterproposals that their governments should pursue expansionary policies to cure their chronic surpluses, and they predictably ignored us. An interesting about-face occurred when contractionary U.S. monetary policies in the early 1980s dampened U.S. inflation and bolstered the international value of the dollar—foreign governments urged the Reagan administration to follow more expansionary policies to fight the worldwide recession that was, in part, attributable to our counterinflationary policies. A foreign diplo-

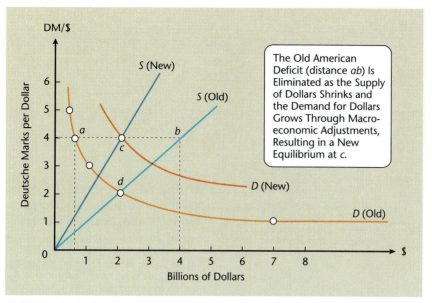

DM/$

The Old American Deficit (distance *ab*) Is Eliminated as the Supply of Dollars Shrinks and the Demand for Dollars Grows Through Macroeconomic Adjustments, Resulting in a New Equilibrium at *c*.

FIGURE 5   Using Macroeconomic Adjustment to Eliminate Deficits

Flows of funds from imbalances of payments tend to expand Aggregate Demands in surplus countries. If all countries are close to full employment, the prices of domestic goods in surplus countries will rise, making imports better buys. The resulting growth in imports will be reflected in rising demands for the currencies of deficit countries. At the same time, monetary outflows tend to reduce Aggregate Demand in deficit countries. There will be decreases in the prices of domestic goods relative to imports, and the international supplies of deficit countries' currencies will decline as imports fall. Thus, the exchange rate remains stable, with all adjustments coming in the form of higher prices in countries that initially experienced surpluses and lower prices in deficit countries. This solution poses no special problem if prices are perfectly flexible. If prices are rigid downward, however, macroeconomic adjustments may impose severe hardships.

mat compared dealing with the United States to "[S]haring a bed with an elephant; you must be careful when you nudge the beast to get it to roll over."

Exchange Controls

We might ration foreign exchange to cure deficits. At $0.25 per DM, only DM2 billion (at point *a* in Figure 6, worth $500 million) are available to Americans, but they would like to buy DM16 billion ($4 billion at point *b*) worth of German goods. The U.S. government could allocate the available DM2 billion among would-be importers through licenses, or it could curb some imports by using quotas or tariffs. Many Americans wanting to tour Germany or buy

German cameras or VWs would have to do without.

Such techniques are called *exchange controls* and are used in most underdeveloped countries today.

> **Exchange controls** *allow access to foreign exchange only to favored industries or individuals and make it illegal to exchange foreign for domestic currencies except through the government's banks at official exchange rates.*

Exchange controls are extremely inefficient and share many of the failings of quotas (described in the preceding chapter). Controls must be exercised through some government agency, and they create powerful incentives for smuggling,

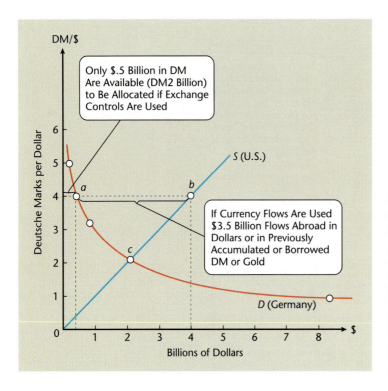

DM/$

Only $.5 Billion in DM Are Available (DM2 Billion) to Be Allocated if Exchange Controls Are Used

Deutsche Marks per Dollar

6
5
4
3
2
1
0

a
b
c

S (U.S.)

If Currency Flows Are Used $3.5 Billion Flows Abroad in Dollars or in Previously Accumulated or Borrowed DM or Gold

D (Germany)

1 2 3 4 5 6 7 8

Billions of Dollars

$

FIGURE 6   Using Exchange Controls to Prevent Currency Flows When Deficits Occur

Exchange controls can be used to artificially maintain the price of a currency above the equilibrium exchange rate, but this requires government rationing of the limited foreign exchange that is available. Alternatively, persistent balance of payments deficits may permit an exchange rate to be above equilibrium if the deficit country can borrow from surplus countries or draw down its stocks of gold or previously acquired foreign currencies.

bribery, graft, black marketeering, and general corruption.

Fixed Exchange Rates   Our earlier discussions of price controls indicated that if prices are fixed above their equilibrium values, there will be surpluses, while if the price of a good is held below its equilibrium value, there will be a shortage of that good. The same results hold for international currency markets.

If we have accumulated reserves of foreign exchange, or if we can beg, borrow, or steal reserves of foreign currencies from our friends and allies, we can rely on international flows of currencies or debt as the fourth and final solution to a balance of payments deficit.

> **Currency or debt flows** *can accommodate imbalances of international payments.*

In Figure 6, $0.5 billion dollars (DM2 billion) of our annual foreign exchange needs are met by regular inflows of foreign currency. How can we accommodate our remaining $3.5 billion (DM14 billion) outflow of funds? One system requires

an international agreement to "fix" exchange rates.

The Bretton Woods Agreement established the International Monetary Fund in 1944, along with a system of fixed exchange rates. (The International Monetary Fund lingers on, but the fixed exchange rate died of natural causes in 1973.) Under the Bretton Woods Agreement, most nations "pegged" the value of their currency to the dollar, which the United States agreed to redeem for gold at $35 per ounce. Because the values of all major currencies were pegged to the dollar (and thus, to gold), these currencies were "fixed" relative to each other as well.

The U.S. Treasury used some of the gold it had acquired over the previous century to pay parts of chronic deficits experienced from 1951 to 1973. Most of these deficits, however, were absorbed by foreign central banks when our trading partners bought the surplus dollars. Our theoretical willingness to redeem at least some dollars for gold and the willingness of our trading partners to absorb surplus dollars was a key to the fixed exchange rate system of this period.

*A system of **fixed exchange rates** requires governments to establish and maintain constant relative values for their currencies.*

Figure 7 shows how foreign governments (e.g., Germany) can ensure that our currency will never fall below certain values if they buy the dollars sent out as our balance of payments deficits. Similarly, we can set floors for the values of their currencies if we buy their money when they run deficits. In our example, the German government can supply DM or other currencies "on loan" to the United States and take the excess dollars off the market. This enables the two countries to maintain *fixed exchange rates*.

Persistent U.S. deficits will cause growing piles of American dollars to accumulate in German banks. The widespread acceptability of the dollar may enable Germans to use U.S. currency to pay for their imports, but then these dollars wind up consuming space in other foreign central banks.

There is a limit to the amount of dollars foreign governments will absorb. After a saturation point is reached, surplus dollars will return via the capital account of the U.S. balance of payments when foreigners begin buying Treasury bonds or corporate securities, U.S. firms, U.S. real estate, or foreigners may simply invest and establish production facilities in the United States.

Fixed exchange rates pose no special problems as long as exchange rates reflect the relative supplies and demands of currencies. In other words, fixed exchange rates do not cause any special problem as long as their values are the same as flexible exchange rates would be. Even if fixed exchange rates are initially in equilibrium, however, differences in macroeconomic policies or rates of economic growth between countries, or changes in tastes or technologies will cause the relative supplies and demands of currencies to change. Shortages and surpluses emerge amid persistent disequilibria in balances of payments

FIGURE 7   Fixing Exchange Rates Through International Agreement

A floor under the exchange rate of a deficit country can be guaranteed if surplus countries will buy unlimited amounts of the currency flowing from the country that experiences persistent deficits in its balance of payments.

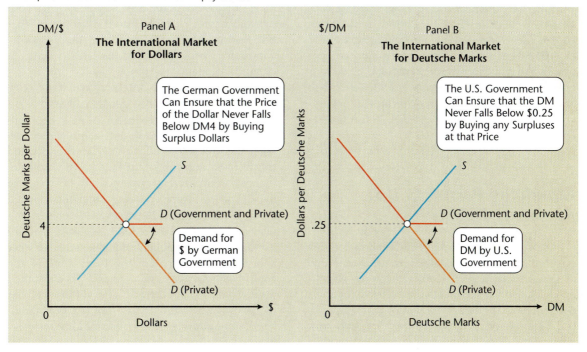

whenever fixed exchange rates fail to reflect the true demands and supplies of currencies.

In summary, there are four basic ways to deal with surpluses or deficits in balances of payments—change the price (float), ration (control), shift the curves (macroadjustment), or allow currency flows. Similar solutions apply equally to surpluses or shortages of wheat, gasoline, teachers, or skateboards. You can add a lot of frills, but this simple supply and demand analysis is what the complex world of international finance is really all about.

The Dirty Float: 1973 to ?

Most exchange rates have been flexible since 1973, but with some government intervention. In most markets for goods and services, surpluses or shortages are cured by price changes. Floating systems allow exchange rates to vary, so it would seem that U.S. balance of payments deficits (surpluses of dollars) should be cured automatically if they are signs of disequilibrium. But if imbalances of payments should vanish automatically, then why have U.S. payments deficits been so persistent?

We indicated earlier that one part of the answer is that foreigners have often wanted U.S. dollars even more than they wanted American goods. This suggests that our consistent deficits in international payments may be signs of economic and political health. Parts of U.S. deficits may be true symptoms of international imbalances, however, because governments everywhere have constantly intervened in foreign exchange markets.

Explaining Persistent U.S. Payments Deficits

If a country runs large and persistent deficits, foreign banks will accumulate substantial amounts of that country's currency when foreign suppliers exchange the payments they receive for their own money. Why have foreign private and central banks permitted the United States to run persistent balance of payments deficits?

The answer to this question is multifaceted. First, between 1946 and 1971, the dollar was the only major currency redeemable for gold, at least for purposes of international payments. Foreign central banks could present \$35 to the U.S. Treasury and demand one ounce of gold. It was illegal for Americans who were not jewelers, coin collectors, or dentists to own gold bullion, bars, or coins during this period. Any American gold not used industrially or in teeth or jewelry was used to back the dollar for international transactions.

The end of World War II saw the United States as the only major country with its manufacturing capacity intact. We supplied much of the world's needs and generally demanded payment in gold because most other currencies were either unstable or worthless. Hence, as we entered the 1950s, the United States had substantial gold on hand. The dollar was a nearly perfect substitute for gold for purposes of international payments because it was redeemable for gold.

This meant that our money was often viewed as at least as valuable as the American goods that might be bought with it by, say, the Italians; people in other countries would cheerfully accept dollars when they would not accept lire in payment for Italian purchases. In a sense, the convertibility of U.S. dollars into gold (under a "partial reserve system" much like that used by commercial banks) enabled the United States to create "international money."

After World War II, international trade grew far more rapidly than the quantity of gold available for international payments. The acceptability of the U.S. dollar as an international *key currency* made it possible for the U.S. Treasury and the FED to accommodate increasing world demands for an international medium of exchange by simply printing money. Americans gained through *seignorage* (differences between money's face value and its production cost) from this ability to print international money because we were able to export less than the total value of the goods we imported. In a sense, we consumed more than we produced. The difference was made up by the dollars we printed that circulated among foreign countries, seldom being redeemed for American output or resources. The international acceptability of the dollar was a major reason that the United States was able to run persistent and large deficits between 1951 and the present.

The relative prices of most currencies in international exchange markets presumably have been set by supply and demand since 1973. We may still run deficits under a floating exchange rate system, however, if foreigners commonly demand our dollars instead of American goods and services. Even so, foreign demand for dollars as insurance or as an internationally accepted means of payment does not completely explain the magnitudes of our balance of payments deficits throughout the 1970s.

The central banks and treasuries of a number of countries accumulated dollars during the 1970s to prevent the exchange rate of the dollar from falling even further or more rapidly than it did; the "float" has been a dirty float. Why would foreign governments (e.g., Japan) wish to maintain high prices for imports from the United States and concomitant low prices for Japanese products exported to Americans? Part of the answer is that employment and growth in the Japanese and some other economies are heavily dependent on their export industries. In addition, the Japanese farmers and manufacturers who compete with imports from the United States are very powerful politically.

When the Japanese central bank buys and holds the dollars paid for Japanese exports, the effect is the same as a tariff on their imports and a subsidy on their exports. This Japanese policy of acquiring growing amounts of dollars has resulted in subsidies to American consumers by Japanese consumers. Until Japanese taxpayers and voters catch on, we may continue to gain at their expense.[3] Curiously, our government pressured the Japanese government to adopt policies to eliminate the U.S. trade deficit with Japan. Can you figure out why?

In sum, the United States has been able to run balance of payments deficits fairly consistently for over three decades because:

1. Until the 1970s, fixed exchange rates under the Bretton Woods Agreement were adjusted only to cure "fundamental disequilibria." Most major trading countries found it advantageous to maintain the dollar's primacy until inflation in the 1960s and the vitality of some other currencies doomed the fixed exchange rate system that had been based on a sound dollar.

2. There has been a strong demand for the dollar for use as an international medium of exchange.

3. Dollar holdings have been viewed as "insurance" in unstable countries.

4. Such countries as Japan and Germany supported the dollar at artificially high exchange rates to boost U.S. demand for their exports. These policies increased employment and economic growth in these countries.[4]

The Dance of the Dollar

The dollar was indisputably the world's key currency from the end of World War II until the mid-1960s. Then the exchange value of the dollar declined relative to most major currencies during the 1970s, hitting its low in 1978. The dollar then recovered steadily until late 1985, as Figure 8 demonstrates. But why did the dollar fall during the 1970s? Why was it so strong in the early 1980s? And why did it weaken again after 1985, and then rise again in the 1990s? There are a number of explanations, all of them at least partially correct.

We know that the price of anything will fall if supply grows relative to demand, and vice versa. Some explanations for the fall of the dollar during the 1970s focus on reduced desires by foreigners to hold dollars; others focus on increased supplies of dollars in international markets. Al-

---

3. This support for the dollar can be viewed as a hidden subsidy that Japan, and more especially, Germany, used to induce the United States to provide defense services. Tens of thousands of American soldiers are stationed in Germany.

---

4. Throughout the 1970s, our government urged foreign governments to run budget deficits, increase their money supplies, and reduce trade barriers against American products, among other measures.

FIGURE 8   The Dance of the U.S. Dollar

The overall depreciation of the dollar relative to the average of other major currencies during the 1970s reflected the maturation of other currencies, the declining prestige of the United States, problems with inflation, the deterioration of our terms of trade as the prices of imports grew faster than the prices of our exports (e.g., oil imports versus machinery exports), rising concerns about the future of the dollar and of the American economy, and a host of other problems. The dollar's strong recovery during the early 1980s signaled a reversal of this downward spiral.

Source: *Economic Report of the President,* 1991.

though growing supplies and falling demands for the dollar (or vice versa) are interrelated, we will deal first with factors that alter international demands for dollars.

Inflation and Exchange Rates

There was substantial inflation during the 1970s, not only in the United States, but throughout the world. When our inflation abated in the early 1980s, the dollar surged upward in international exchange markets until 1985.

Relative Inflation   When prices increase faster in the United States than elsewhere, we buy more imports and supply more dollars internationally, but the demands for our exports and dollars fall. This line of reasoning leads to a classical explanation for falling exchange rates — relatively rapid inflation in the United States during the 1970s reduced foreign demands for dollars. Coupled with an increased supply of dollars, we have one part of the explanation for declining exchange rates. Then, as American infla-

tion abated in the early 1980s, the recovery of the dollar became stronger. Thus, relative inflation causes depreciation of a currency, while less than the average international rate of inflation causes exchange rate appreciation.

Expectations   An international perception during the 1970s was that more than any other major country, the United States was committed to expansionary, and consequently, inflationary policies. Increased income, whether real or inflated, boosts demands for imports. If other countries are not expected to follow similarly expansionary policies, there are growing pressures for balance of payments deficits.[5] U.S. inflation throughout the 1970s probably generated international expectations of continued inflationary policies and relative inflation in this country. Such expectations led foreigners to

_____

5.   This action reduces the exchange rate of the dollar and, by increasing the prices of our imports and decreasing the prices of U.S. exports, eliminates the deficits.

treat dollars as hot potatoes; their dollar holdings fell dramatically at times between 1974 and 1980.

There has been downward pressure on the dollar when international money managers have expected the United States to experience both continued relative inflation and substantial balance of trade deficits. When U.S. monetary growth began to slow in 1979, the dollar began its recovery. An American recession during 1981–1983 spread to the rest of the world as it choked off our demands for imports and constricted the international supply of dollars. High U.S. interest rates also attracted short-term financial investments by foreigners, further strengthening the dollar. It seems ironic that recessions bolster the dollar, but they do.

By 1985, the exchange rate of the dollar was so high that foreign finance ministers and American policymakers were alarmed. They agreed to follow policies to depreciate the dollar. Accordingly, foreign central banks sold dollars on international markets, increasing the supply to private financiers. Fear that the United States might begin following more expansionary macroeconomic policies caused many private financial institutions to be leery of holding many dollars. Coupled with record deficits in the U.S. balances of payments and trade that caused the international supply of dollars to swell, the dollar drifted down during 1985–1988. Nevertheless, the dollar had largely recovered by 1991.

Budget Deficits and Anemic Saving

We previously discussed how federal budget deficits and inadequate private domestic saving create pressure for borrowing from foreigners, which may take the form of foreign investments in the United States. (If $S + T < I + G$, then $X < M$.) But foreigners will invest in the United States only if this appears more profitable than investment elsewhere. If the exchange rate of the dollar appreciates, foreign investors gain, but if it depreciates, they lose. One way for foreigners to feel that investment in the U.S. is secure is for the exchange rate of the dollar to be so low that they think it likely that it will only rise.

Persistent federal budget deficits (our last surplus was experienced in 1969) create pressures for capital flows into the United States to offset current account deficits. But capital tends to flow into countries where, after adjustment for both normal business risks and exchange rate risk, the expected rate of return is the highest. Federal deficits pushed down the dollar in the late 1970s, and again during 1985 through 1988.

Portfolio Adjustments

For some time after World War II, the U.S. dollar and gold were viewed as the only stable international mediums of exchange. The world's supply of gold grew more slowly than the volume of international transactions. Consequently, institutions like central banks and international corporations were happy to use the dollars made available by our balance of payments deficits to meet their transaction demands for money and desires for liquid assets.

Economic instability in the United States beginning during the Vietnam conflict diminished confidence in the dollar. During the same period, numerous industrialized economies throughout the world matured or reached full recovery from World War II; their currencies became attractive parts of the portfolios of many countries' central banks, competing with the dollar as a reserve asset. The growing availability of good substitutes for dollars led financial institutions around the world to diversify, holding smaller proportions of their assets in dollars.

When the dollar began to depreciate a little during the mid-1970s, it fell off the pedestal that had caused so many countries to hold dollars. The huge proportion of international reserves held by foreign central banks in U.S. currency caused the "dollar overhang" to collapse. For example, in 1977 alone almost 60 percent of the dollars held by OPEC countries were exchanged for other currencies, intensifying pressure for the dollar to fall.

Several countries attempted in the late 1970s to price their exports (e.g., OPEC oil) on an index of such strong foreign currencies as the Swiss franc and German deutsche mark. These experiments temporarily weakened the dollar because it was less demanded for international transactions, but they ultimately failed, forcing renewed reliance on the dollar as the world's key currency and further bolstering the dollar's recovery in the early 1980s.

Oil and the Balance of Trade

During the 1970s our cumulative payments deficits added almost 30 percent to the total amount of dollars held abroad. Substantial parts of payments deficits over this period were attributable to oil imports. The international price of oil grew sharply when OPEC exercised its muscles during 1973–1981. Because American production technology is extremely energy intensive, higher oil prices only slowly reduced our oil imports. The dollar value of oil imports grew dramatically during the 1970s, worsening our balance of payments deficit. This—and our own increasing preferences for Japanese electronics, cameras, and cars—pushed down the exchange rate of the dollar. But by the early 1980s, our imports of crude oil were declining and the dollar began showing considerable strength in international financial markets.

The Monetarist Explanation

All the preceding factors provide parts of a solution to the temporary decline of the dollar. Predictably, some monetarists attribute the slide of the dollar to too rapid growth in the U.S. money supply (and declining rates of monetary growth were credited with its recovery). We will use the deutsche mark (DM) to explain the monetarist mechanism. The reasoning goes that if the supply of dollars grows relative to the demand for dollars faster than the supply of DM grows rela-

tive to the demand for them, then the dollar will depreciate relative to the deutsche mark.

The problem with this approach is that while it is unquestionably true, it has little explanatory value. In fact, during 1985–1988 the U.S. money supply grew less rapidly than the money supplies of virtually any other major country, yet the dollar danced downward relative to almost every major currency. Monetarists were unable to explain the declining demand for the dollar, other than by vague references to inflation. Then, the dollar's recovery during 1989–1991 was attributed to diminishing inflation.

In summary, among possible explanations for the decline of the dollar during the 1970s were

1. relative inflation of the dollar;

2. expectations that inflation in the United States would remain higher than elsewhere;

3. expected continuation of trade deficits;

4. persistent and growing federal budget deficits;

5. adjustments of international portfolios against the dollar;

6. modest depreciation caused the dollar to lose its "halo";

7. larger trade deficits caused by high oil prices;

8. too rapid monetary growth in the United States.

The recovery of the dollar in the 1980s apparently occurred because of reversals of a number of these factors. Each explanation seems logically plausible, yet none alone is a satisfactory explanation for the swings in the exchange rate of the dollar, and some are even contrary to the evidence.

Chapter Review: Key Points

1. Since we have no world currency, we must establish the value of each national currency in terms of all others. The *exchange rate* is the value of one currency in terms of another.

2. *Balance of payments* accounts record the flows of money into and out of a country and provide information about trade relationships among countries.

3. *Flexible*, or *floating*, systems of *exchange rates* permit the values of currencies to be set by market forces. If a country experiences a balance of payments *surplus* (*deficit*) under such a system, it is an indication that the country's citizens or government (*foreigners*) desire foreign (*domestic*) currencies.

4. A *fixed* exchange rate system imposes price ceilings and floors on currencies, often resulting in persistent disequilibria in balances of payments.

5. Explanations for the decline of the dollar in the 1970s range from relative inflation to expectations of continued inflation and payments deficits to federal budget deficits to the emergence of other strong international currencies to the cartelization of oil to too rapid monetary growth. Opposite trends then strengthened the dollar. Each of these explanations bears the germ of truth, but none alone is adequate to explain the dance of the dollar.

Key Concepts

Ensure that you can define these terms before proceeding.

balances of payments and trade surpluses and deficits

exchange rates

appreciation and depreciation

revaluation and devaluation

foreign exchange

gold standard

fixed exchange rates

flexible (floating) exchange rates

macroadjustments

exchange controls

currency flows

Questions and Problems

1. Calculate all possible exchange rates if a U.S. dollar ($) will buy 2 deutsche marks (DM), 1/2 of a British pound (£), 6 French francs (F), or 120 Japanese yen (¥).

2. One popular myth is that surpluses in the balances of trade and payments are good omens, while deficits are symptoms that a country may be suffering from economic anemia. Yet persistent U.S. balance of payments deficits during the past three decades may have been unavoidable simply because of the relative vigor of the American economy. How is this so? How have Americans gained from the trade deficit? From the payments deficit? How have they lost from these deficits? On balance, have the gains outweighed the losses?

3. Conventional theories of international finance suggest that imbalances of payments are signs of disequilibrium. A recent theory called "global monetarism," however, hypothesizes (among other things) that surpluses can be expected when people in some countries want more money more than they want more goods, while people in other countries have "too much" money and willingly trade some of their money for imports. How might persistent surpluses or deficits occur in equilibrium?

4. Global monetarists also favor fixed exchange rates, arguing that flexible rates make no more sense than reducing the price of the quarter relative to the penny if there are surpluses of quarters and shortages of pennies. What are the major differences, if any, between these situations? Do these economists have a point? What mechanisms are available to accommodate deficits or surpluses under fixed exchange rates? What are the implications of fixed exchange rates for the independence of macroeconomic policies?

5. After the dollar declined in the 1970s, foreign tourists found the United States an excellent place to shop for bargains. The United States quit being such a haven for foreign shoppers when the dollar recovered in the early 1980s. Then the decline of the dollar during 1985–1988 drew tourists to the United States, and foreign investment in the United States soared. Similarly, when the Mexican peso depreciated severely in 1982–1983, many Americans scurried to Mexico for bargains. Why do such bargains for foreigners sometimes emerge when a currency depreciates or is devalued? What does the existence of such bargains suggest about whether these currencies are temporarily overvalued or undervalued? What does your answer suggest about how balances of payments might change for these countries in the very near future?

6. Under what circumstances might depreciation or devaluation of a currency cause deficits in a country's balance of payments to worsen? How is your answer related to elasticities of demands and supplies for exports and imports? Why is any worsening of payments deficits likely to be strictly a short-term problem?

7. Recent growth of foreign investment in the United States alarms many Americans. There are calls to sharply limit foreign holdings of U.S. assets, but in periods when U.S. investment abroad has been vigorous, there are complaints that we are exporting jobs to low-wage countries. Can you offer arguments that justify both special limits on U.S. investment by foreigners and on foreign investments by Americans? Or should investors be allowed to place their capital wherever they think it will yield the largest profit?

Comparative Systems: The Shift Toward Capitalism

[In the USSR] the government pretended to be concerned about our welfare, and we pretended to work.

Russian émigré Yacov Smirnoff (now an American comedian)

Is capitalism doomed, as many of its opponents claim? Is socialism the wave of the future? Or, as most supporters of capitalism predict, is centralized socialism on the verge of collapse, so that capitalism will eventually dominate economic activity everywhere? Disagreements about human nature are at the core of this debate. Are people inherently competitive and driven by individual self-interest, or can our acquisitive habits be redirected toward universal cooperation as society matures?

As recently as 1989, few forecasters anticipated the imminent collapse of the Berlin Wall and German reunification, free elections in Poland, Bulgaria, Czechoslovakia, and the USSR, or the violent overthrow of the communist government in Romania. By 1991, even the hard-line government of Albania teetered on the brink of reform, and the withdrawal of subsidies from the Soviet Union threatened Fidel Castro's hold on Cuba. These changes are testimony to the pressures for privatization exerted by the increasingly vigorous forces of international competition.

Privatization *is the conversion of government activities into private firms or cooperatives.*

How different economic systems operate is the focus of this chapter. We begin with an overview of capitalism and libertarians, its strongest defenders. Anarcho-syndicalism, our second topic, shares with libertarianism a distaste for government, but is less enamored of capitalism. Then we survey several types of socialism, including Marxism. After a bird's-eye view of how different social philosophies have been expressed in contemporary economies, the chapter concludes with discussions of possible limits to economic growth and "Buddhist economics" — the idea that the ultimate solution to economic want is spiritual rather than physical.

This chapter will provide you with a sense of the spectrum of mechanisms that people have used to deal with scarcity. Such allocative mechanisms as brute force, tradition, random selection, queuing, and government continue to be used to resolve some economic problems in all societies, but one message comes through loud and clear: The market is increasingly accepted as the dominant means of allocating resources to foster economic growth. Major reasons for this ascendance are (*a*) the emphasis on efficiency emerging from the growth of international trade, and (*b*) advances in telecommunications that have globalized information about the successes and failures of alternative economic systems.

Perspectives on Capitalism

Although market higgling and haggling predate written history, the first systematic description of capitalism was in Adam Smith's *Wealth of Nations* (1776). This pathbreaking book spawned countless studies of market economies. Most developed economies rely heavily on the market system, but markets have historically played only minor roles in the lives of most of the world's population. In some countries, primitive economic conditions limited market transactions; in others, leaders opposed to capitalism outlawed most market activities. The collapse of central planning occurring in the Eastern bloc only hints at a worldwide evaporation of barriers to modern commercial activities.

Critics of capitalism argue that only greed and other base motives are nurtured by competition, which permeates everything from schools to athletics to business, and decry a consolidation of corporate power as an inevitable outcome of competition. Giant transnational corporations flourish, dominating world trade. Arguments for the superiority of competition assume that markets are easily accessible to potential competitors, which may apply in only a few sectors of most modern market economies.

Modern capitalism, according to its critics, is corrupt, unstable, inefficient, exploitative, dehumanizing, and outmoded. These critics view capitalism as pitting wealthy elites against the starving and powerless, and have predicted that it will soon "be swept into the dustbin of history." Capitalism's advocates naturally believe that these critics are wrong and cite many virtues of the price system, the two most important being freedom and efficiency.

The Recent Convergence Toward Capitalism

How competitive capitalism tends to foster economic innovation, efficiency, and growth is described elsewhere in this book. In the past four decades, primarily capitalist countries (e.g., the United States, Japan, South Korea, West Germany, Taiwan, Singapore, and Hong Kong) experienced average growth far surpassing that in almost all countries that are primarily socialist, especially those that relied most heavily on central planning (e.g., the USSR, China, and most of Eastern Europe). Consequently, a wave of privatization has swept through all countries intent on competing successfully in international markets; central planning has been declining sharply, especially since 1989.

The *status quo* never surrenders to change peacefully. The primary beneficiaries of central planning in Eastern bloc countries (e.g., bureaucratic planners, senior military officers, the secret police, and other communist party *apparatchiks*) are now fighting to retain their perks. Thus, disillusion with central planning has not caused capitalism to arise as official policy in the USSR and China. Instead, in hopes of managing change (while retaining power) and avoiding what they view as capitalism's excesses (e.g., huge incomes for top executives, with lower incomes for most workers), these countries' new leaders often discourage aggressive entrepreneurs, while they encourage intermediate measures (e.g., producer cooperatives) toward a market economy.

The "welfare state" system operating in Scandinavian countries is sometimes cited as a model for reform. Business firms might be privately owned and operated, with much of business profit then being taxed away to guarantee adequate incomes for all. Alternatively, "indicative planning" modeled after the French and Yugoslavian systems appeals to some who want to reform, but not abandon, central planning. These possibilities may merely offer pauses in a transition toward mixed capitalism as practiced in Germany, the U.S., or Japan. Almost all advanced nations (even the most capitalistic) are increasingly privatizing activities previously operated by government.

Later in this chapter, we address the history of central planning and the prospects for reform in the USSR and China. First, however, you need to understand why various economic philosophies have appealed so strongly to large numbers of business theorists, radical reformers, the clergy, and working-class intellectuals. A starting point is libertarianism, which advocates a laissez-faire market economy.

Libertarianism

Power corrupts, and absolute power tends to corrupt absolutely.

Lord Acton

Libertarians join anarchists in despising bureaucracy and government. Anarchists see giant corporations and big government as twin threats to freedom and as exploiters of labor. Libertarians focus more narrowly on problems posed by government. In the libertarian view, corporate abuses would evaporate if government did not suppress competitive behavior and foster concentrated economic power.

Libertarians, *the modern champions of laissez-faire capitalism, prize freedom as the most important social value, and advocate replacing government with the market system wherever possible.*

Libertarians see other goals as empty without freedom and constantly look for areas where government can be eliminated. Libertarians would forbid government provision of many goods (e.g., education, public parks and highways, and the postal service), and would abolish all welfare programs, as well as laws governing

1. Drugs, consensual sex between private individuals, and pornography.
2. Parental rights to control teenagers.
3. Wages and prices, including utility rates.
4. Professional licensing or such practices as a military draft.

Libertarians view most government action as hindering freedom and advocate markets as efficient and equitable cures for almost all social problems. They would restrict government to protecting private property rights and enforcing contracts. Although their numbers are small, many libertarian ideas have been central to the worldwide movement toward greater reliance on markets and shrinking reliance on government.

Anarcho-Syndicalism

There's no government like no government.

An Anarchist Slogan

One small group of capitalism's foes perceive corporate giants and government as parasites that exploit the working class. This group consists of anarchists, who would retain private property rights, and syndicalists, who seek collective worker ownership of nonhuman resources. Hatred of government is the glue that binds anarchism to syndicalism. Both groups are convinced that elite groups always control government. Under industrial capitalism, capitalists and professional managers control government; under centrally planned socialism, government is in the grip of an enormous bureaucracy. Anarchists and syndicalists believe that governments monopolize and institutionalize violence through imperialistic wars and police brutality. Hence, both groups would do away with the twin evils of corporate capitalism and state socialism.

Anarchism

Anarchists are popularly stereotyped as wild-eyed bomb throwers, but a little research reveals that their philosophy derives from the view that without government, worldwide violence and exploitation would be reduced.

Philosophical **anarchism** *counts on cooperation among people to ensure social harmony in the absence of government or law.*

Anarchists are not necessarily opposed to the market system, but view modern capitalism as a system in which professional corporate managers and government officials are in cahoots to exploit workers. Corporations exist only because of government recognition. In an idealized anarchy, the rights to what individuals produce could not be "stolen" by capitalists who rely on government to legitimize their exploitation of workers. Most anarchists would recognize private property rights and disavow social ownership of anything. In this position, anarchism is closer to libertarianism than to socialism.

But how might government be eradicated? Answers to this question range from pacifism to bloody revolution. William Godfrey, an English clergyman, and the Russian Prince Kropotkin thought that if we all just ignored government, it would dry up and blow away. The image of "anarchy" as synonymous with chaos and anarchists as bomb throwers originated with Mikhail Bakunin, who convinced his followers that random violence could precipitate the collapse of governments and capitalism. Instead, widespread fear of violence brought anarchism as a social philosophy into lasting disrepute.

Syndicalism

Many of the socialist reformers described in the next section have faith that their goals can be achieved peacefully through the ballot box. Syndicalists disagree, viewing the state as an oppressive vehicle manipulated by power-hungry plutocrats. Syndicalism was the brainchild of the French philosopher Georges Sorel (1847–1922), who viewed stupid wars, corruption, and gross mismanagement as inevitable consequences of government.

> **Syndicalism** *would abolish the state, corporate capitalism, and private ownership of non-human resources. Each industry would be owned by its workers and run by elected worker committees.*

Society would be reorganized into **syndicates**, which are, effectively, industry-wide trade unions. Thus, there would be an auto syndicate, a steel syndicate, an electronics syndicate, and so on. Syndicates would replace government and control the workplace, but would leave people alone in all other matters.

Syndicalism arrived in the United States in 1905 with the founding of the Industrial Workers of the World (IWW) by Daniel Deleon, Eugene V. Debs, and "Big Bill" Haywood, all of whom are legends in the history of American radicalism. Debs collected over a million votes as the Socialist candidate for president during World War I, even though he had been jailed for sedition by President Woodrow Wilson.

IWW members, known as *wobblies*, grew to more than 100,000 before World War I. They intended to overthrow capitalism by locking out managers and seizing factories. The IWW was especially powerful among Western miners, railroad workers, and merchant seamen, who participated in more than 150 violent strikes before succumbing to internal strife arising from lack of a coherent vision of how an economy should operate "after the revolution."

Today, syndicalist ideas find expression in Western Europe and North America in "profit sharing" plans and in union demands for voices in managerial decisions. In Eastern Europe, the trend toward decentralized socialism is somewhat syndicalist, Yugoslavia being especially distinguished by "worker-management." *Solidarity*, the organization led by Lech Walesa that gained control of the Polish government in 1990, has syndicalist goals.

Evolutionary Socialism

There may be more species of birds than of socialists, but not many.

> *The unifying theme of* **socialism** *is the call for social ownership of all nonhuman factors of production — capital and natural resources.*

This does not imply that socialism forbids owning your own toothbrush. Ideally, it does mean that land, factories, and all major capital equipment would be held in trust by government so that everyone could share equitably in national income.

Although centrally planned socialism is increasingly recognized as a failure, there are still schisms within the socialist camp about how far social ownership should extend and which groups should make social and economic decisions. Some socialists believe that socialism will evolve democratically through the ballot box. Another large but shrinking group insists that capitalists control political processes, leaving violent revolution as the only way to institute socialist goals. The most conspicuous of these are *com-*

munists, who tried to adapt the ideas of Karl Marx to the circumstances of the twentieth century. Before we explore Marxism, we will briefly outline other forms of socialism.

Utopian Socialism

Dreamers who have sought to improve our imperfect world are scattered across the pages of history. Sir Thomas More (1478–1535), a Catholic saint and martyr who served as an advisor to England's Henry VIII, was one such dreamer. More's famous book *Utopia* borrowed a Greek word meaning "noplace." Today, *utopian* commonly refers to unrealistic ideals. More blamed poverty, waste, and avarice on private property, and proposed the creation of "Utopia," where everyone would share everything.

> **Utopian socialism** *is the idea that collective ownership eliminates greed and promotes personal growth, cultural enrichment, and democracy.*

People would work for the common good in jobs of their choice. Prices would be superfluous, because there would be as much joy from giving as from receiving; supplying and demanding would be equally satisfying.

More's ideas were largely ignored until early in the nineteenth century, when social ferment and the prospect of revolution swept Europe. Utopian socialism bloomed. Prominent utopians of this period included the French philosopher Charles Fourier (1772–1837) and the philanthropist Robert Owen (1771–1858). Owen, though born into poverty, became wealthy as a Scottish cotton-mill owner while still in his twenties. Infatuated with the utopian vision, he financed several self-contained, communally owned villages in Scotland and the United States. Neat rows of houses, free education, better working conditions, and wages in proportion to hours worked attracted thousands of people to this grand experiment. But all utopian communities of this period were (predictably?) poorly managed and uniformly failed.

It seems ironic that some of Owen's dreams were integrated into public policies in many modern mixed economies. Free public education, socialized medicine in much of Europe and medical insurance in the United States, healthier working conditions, and substantial parts of our current welfare system can all be traced to utopian goals.

Fabian Socialism

Founded in England in 1884, the *Fabian Society* jettisoned the utopian ideal of small communities, urging instead nationalization of heavy industry and municipal ownership of public utilities. Otherwise, their agenda echoed many reforms proposed by utopians: universal suffrage, income redistribution, free education and medical care, and laws to ensure safe work environments, forbid child labor, and limit women's working hours.

The early Fabians included such prominent intellectuals as playwright George Bernard Shaw, science fiction writer H. G. Wells, historian G. D. H. Cole, and Sidney and Beatrice Webb, a married team of economists. This small band grew and, as it collected members who were active in the British union movement, evolved into the present Labour party, which dominated the British government from World War I until 1980. Many advocates of capitalism blamed the Labour party's policies of nationalization for technological obsolescence and the sluggish growth of the British economy. They credit massive privatization since 1980 for the modern resurgence of British industry.

Christian Socialism

It is easier for a camel to pass through a needle's eye than for a rich man to enter the Kingdom of Heaven.

The Gospel of Matthew

Many conservative theologians interpret Christianity as supporting the status quo and the sanctity of private property. These clerics cite the scripture to "render unto Caesar that which is Caesar's and unto God that which is God's" to justify existing distributions of wealth, status, and power. In this view, social struggle is a diversion from spiritual development.

The "social gospel" movement, launched over a century ago by a group of French Catholic priests who borrowed many utopian ideas, reflects a very different view.

Christian socialism *advocates charity and peaceful social reforms.*

Repudiating the violence advocated by revolutionary socialists, Christian socialism stresses the dignity of work and favors labor unions. It resembles Fabian socialism in its goals, even though most Fabians were atheists or agnostics.

Pope Leo XIII and Pope Pius XI affirmed Catholicism's support for the "social gospel." Protestant theologians who were Christian socialists included Paul Tillich and Reinhold Niebuhr. The "social gospel" remains a powerful force within the World Council of Churches, as a mainspring of the ecumenical movement, and in church-related social programs.

An offshoot of this movement is the "liberation theology" espoused by radical South American priests who favor violent revolution to overthrow repressive regimes. Their philosophy blends Christianity with elements of Marxism, but it is opposed by more conventional Christian socialists, while most Marxists view liberation theology as a refusal to recognize reality.

Marxism: Revolutionary Socialism

The history of . . . society is the history of class struggle.

Karl Marx

Few people have left footprints on history comparable to those of Karl Marx. In the century following his death, more than one-third of humanity came to be governed by professed Marxists.

A central tenet of **Marxism** *is the idea that socialism will replace capitalism only after a violent revolution.*

Although the last few years have boded poorly for Marxists, his ideas continue to have millions of followers.

History as Economic Dialectics

Marxists believe that all of history can be interpreted as resolutions to *contradictions* emerging from the competing interests of people in different economic classes. These interpretations are rooted in *dialectical* analysis, a method originated by the idealist philosopher, Georg Hegel.

According to Hegel, every concept or **thesis** has meaning only when pitted against its opposite, or **antithesis**. Thus, the idea of *long* means nothing until contrasted with *short*, and *rich* means nothing without *poor*. Clashes between a thesis and its antithesis yield a **synthesis** — new knowledge about an evolving reality. Thus, the notions of rich and poor yield the concepts of *income* and *wealth*, syntheses that advance our grasp of the human condition. Hegel believed history to be dominated by dialectical changes in ideas. Marx rejected Hegel's focus on ideas, insisting that dialectical processes among material interests are the keys to historical change. This is why Marxism is sometimes called **dialectical materialism**.

If cause and effect relationships embedded in dialectical processes never change, then precise explanation of the past permits perfect prediction of the future. Marx thought he had unveiled basic historical laws in the perception that social and cultural changes are determined by juxtaposing thesis and antithesis in how we produce, exchange, distribute, and consume goods. These *contradictions* (from the Marxist jargon) are rooted in conflicts between different socioeconomic *classes*.

According to Marxists, **class warfare** *is an inevitable step in the historical process that facilitates economic progress.*

For example, the Marxist view of the Industrial Revolution is that it pitted an aggressive new class of manufacturers against vested agricultural interests throughout Europe, but especially in England. The rise of industrialization led

Karl Marx (1818–1883)

Marx was a genius . . . the rest of us were talented at best.

Friedrich Engels

The ideas of Karl Marx have had a larger impact on the twentieth century than those of virtually any other social philosopher, indelibly marking several academic disciplines including philosophy, psychology, history, and economics. Nevertheless, his major work, *Das Kapital*, must be seen for what he meant it to be, a critique of capitalism. Although Marx's was clearly the dominant contribution, virtually all his work was done in collaboration with his friend, Friedrich Engels. Curiously, Engels lived comfortably on his income from owning and managing a factory.

Scholars disagree on the extent to which events in Marx's life colored his thoughts on society, but two characteristics of his personality and experience are prominent. One is that adversity often came his way. For example, although Marx earned a Ph.D. in philosophy from the University of Jena, no university would hire him. His inflammatory rhetoric and alliances with radicals deprived him of a stable income and led to his expulsion from Germany. Exile was to play an important role in his life. Later, Marx was also expelled by the governments of Belgium and France.

His family finally settled in England, which was far too tolerant of individual freedom to expel him. Marx sporadically eked out a living as a journalist, serving a short stint as a foreign correspondent to the *New York Herald-Tribune*. (Would the course of history have been altered if the newspaper had ever given him a raise?) Had it not been for occasional doles from Engels, the entire Marx household might have starved. As it was, they were destitute.

Another aspect of Marx's personality was ambivalence, which may have originated with his parents' conversion to Christianity from Judaism, more for social convenience than from conviction. During adulthood, his dual commitments to political action and scholarly understanding were often in conflict. Marx's scholarly passions frequently interfered with his political activism, while his political zeal crept into his writing. Consequently, partisan outbursts and scathing condemnations of class interests permeated all his scholarly works.

Despite his internal turmoil, or perhaps because of it, Marx left a lasting mark on the world. His ambitious attempt to synthesize all social knowledge since Aristotle was intended to extend understanding of the conditions of human development so that the movement to higher stages of development might be accelerated. His vision of this ultimate society, dimly sketched, was that of a communist system based on rational planning, cooperative production, and equality of distribution. Above all, it was to be a society freed from all political and bureaucratic hierarchies.

Those societies that we call Marxist today score very poorly on this last point, but for Marx the "withering away of the state" was critical. Perhaps the tendency of his followers to compromise on this matter was what may have led Marx to allegedly declare on his deathbed, "I am not a Marxist."

to entirely new government policies, including a resurgence of British imperialism. Laws were adopted that evicted most peasants from their land so that they were forced to work in factories. Exploited workers were then pitted against industrial magnates, whom they would eventually displace during a short but bloody revolution.

Marx viewed this sequence as inevitable. In dialectical terms, thesis (feudal agricultural interests) met antithesis (industrial entrepreneurs — the *bourgeoisie*), leading to synthesis (the triumph of industrialization) within which there was a contradiction (wretchedness of the working masses). This synthesis became the new thesis (industrial capitalism), which, in confronting its antithesis (workers, known as *proletarians*, resent exploitation), leads to a new synthesis (the *dictatorship of the proletariat*).

In Marxist analysis, each stage of development is necessary, and collapses only when it reaches maximum efficiency, paralleling the larvae-pupae-cocoon-adult maturation of a butterfly. Thus, Marxists declare that "capitalism contains the seeds of its own destruction." But why should the chain of events leading to the overthrow of capitalism be inevitable? Answering this question requires digging deeper into Marxist doctrine.

Wages and Value

What makes something valuable? Most modern economists use market forces to explain the relative prices of goods. Marxists view this as superficial and argue that a good's value is proportional to the labor socially necessary for its production. For example, if golf balls require twice the labor needed to produce ballpoint pens, then balls are worth twice as much as pens. This *labor theory of value* was the standard explanation of prices from the time of John Locke until late in the nineteenth century.

But what is "socially necessary labor," and what roles do land and capital play in production? Marx defined *socially necessary labor* to include not only direct labor time but also the labor used to produce the equipment used in production. Marxists view all commodities and capital as *embodied* labor. Thus, production that uses up capital simply transforms the labor embodied in capital into a different form of congealed labor.

Interestingly, Marxists perceive only "hands-on" working time as labor. Service workers and pencil pushers are not regarded as providing real labor. (Adam Smith had similar reservations about managers and service workers.) Nor is all hands-on work socially necessary. For example, your labor is not socially necessary if you make mud pies no one wants. This is basically a supply approach to value, but by specifying that only "socially necessary labor" counts, Marxists allow demand in through the back door.

If prices are proportional to the amounts of direct and embodied labor in products, what determines wages? Karl Marx relied on the *subsistence theory of wages* developed by earlier thinkers to answer this question. This theory holds that wages will barely cover biological needs, with minor adjustments to meet the social and customary needs of workers. Unlike most classical economists, Marx believed that unemployment, not population pressures, forces wages toward subsistence levels. When workers produce more than is required to meet a payroll, capitalists exploit workers by paying them less than the value of their production. These differences are termed *surplus values* in the Marxist idiom. Marxists view all payments of interest, rent, and profits as surplus value.

Surplus Value and Capital Accumulation

According to Marxist dogma, mature industrial societies divide people into two basic classes: capitalists and workers. *Workers*, also known as the *proletariat*, own nothing but their own labor. *Capitalists* control working conditions and hours. A "reserve army of the unemployed" will take the jobs of workers unwilling to accept the working conditions laid down by capitalists. Competition from this surplus labor compels workers to accept subsistence wages. By setting longer working hours than those necessary to cover the subsistence wage, capitalists "appropriate" surplus values from workers. For example, if a worker can produce the subsistence wage in 5 hours but is forced to work 10 hours, a capitalist employer can appropriate surplus value equal to 5 hours of labor time.

Workers cannot save because they only receive subsistence wages. Capitalists, however, receive more than is necessary for their subsistence and convert most of this "stolen" surplus value into capital. This exploitation enables capitalists to accumulate capital to protect their privileged positions and to avoid exploitation themselves. (Big fish eat little fish.) Because capital accumulation facilitates economic growth, capitalism is viewed as a necessary stage of development. Once society has accumulated sufficient capital, however, the capitalist "robber barons" are dinosaurs on their way to extinction.

Class Warfare

The proletarians have nothing to lose but their chains. They have a world to win. Workingmen of all countries unite!

Karl Marx and Friedrich Engels
The Communist Manifesto (1848)

Marxists view ever greater capital accumulations, and then concentration of its ownership as inevitable results of competition among capitalists for surplus values. Marx believed that capitalism was plagued by a number of contradictions. Concentrated wealth creates one contradiction: Who will buy the goods produced by growing stocks of congealed labor? Workers can afford little from their subsistence wages, while capitalists spend far less than the surplus values they appropriate as their incomes. This leads to "underconsumption" and declining rates of profit. In Marxist theory, this contradiction yields capitalist business cycles.

Orthodox Marxists believe that capitalism is dynamically unstable. This means that each cyclical decline will be worse than the previous one, while successive economic booms accelerate at unsustainable rates. This occurs, according to Marx, because some capitalists will be wiped out during each depression and will be forced to join the proletariat. Thus, capital will be controlled by a shrinking pool of entrepreneurs. The final stage predicted by Marxists, *monopolistic fi-*

nance capital, involves an incredible concentration of economic power held by financial trusts. During this stage, imperialist wars rage among capitalist nations. Finally, massive unemployment will trigger short but violent revolutions during which workers will seize control over the resources stolen from them over many generations.

Marxist Predictions

The works of Marx and his collaborator, Engels, were written over a century ago. At that time, the evils of the factory system seemed blatant, and the aroma of revolution wafted throughout Europe. Marx and Engels were not alone in predicting revolutions to overthrow the existing order. Their "dialectical materialism" did, however, generate several specific predictions about the road to revolution:

1. Ever greater unemployment and "immiseration" of workers.
2. Declining rates of profit.
3. Explosive business cycles.
4. Rising concentrations of economic power.
5. Increasingly aggressive imperialistic policies.
6. Bloody revolutions as capitalistic economies reach maturity.

Mature capitalism would fall to communism like rotten fruit. Class struggles would end when the proletariat overthrew capitalists and their middle-class lackeys, the *petit bourgeoisie*. A short "dictatorship of the proletariat" would follow, during which workers would share the full values of production (subsistence wages plus surplus values). Then government would wither away, as outdated as an adult's baby tooth. Communism would evolve as the final synthesis, characterized by a classless society in which people would live and work under the condition, "from each according to ability, to each according to needs." And everyone would live happily ever after. In the end, the communist ideal resembles More's *Utopia*.

Most Marxist predictions seem way off target. Unemployment rates vary over the business cycle, but there is no discernible upward trend over the past century, even though growing percentages of the world's people have moved into the industrial labor force. The purchasing power of wages has risen dramatically over time. Are workers increasingly miserable, when most have color televisions and paid vacations? As Joan Robinson, a modern Marxist, conceded, " 'You have nothing to lose but the prospect of a suburban home and a motor car' would not have been much of a slogan for a revolutionary movement."

Average rates of profit have varied widely over the past century, but without discernible long-run trends. Sporadic booms and busts have plagued capitalism, but with decreasing severity during the past half century. Marx was, however, almost alone in correctly predicting greater industrial concentration. Economic power did become more concentrated from 1850 to 1930, but more recent evidence of increased industrial concentration is hard to glean from the data.

Increased roles for government, including the development of the modern welfare state, apparently have placed a safety net under the living standards of the poor, dampened business cycles, and diminished the growth of concentration. Most of the evils of capitalism identified by Marxists have been at least partially cured by a broad role for government in the market system. Marx's assertion that "the state is nothing but the organized collective power of the ruling classes" is almost certainly wrong.

A significant rebuttal of Marxist predictions is that communist revolutions have bypassed most industrialized capitalist nations, occurring instead in feudal agricultural economies. The USSR, China, Cuba, Vietnam, Kampuchea, and other underdeveloped countries "went communist." Eastern Europe was largely industrialized before succumbing to Marxism after being destabilized during World War II. Imperialistic wars started by major capitalist nations largely ended around the turn of the last century. More recently, communist governments have suffered enormous reversals, being widely replaced by more democratic governments that tend to privatize much of government activity.

One famous Marxist slogan is, "Religion is the opiate of the masses." Paul Samuelson, a Nobel Prize winner, has paraphrased this as, "Marxism is the opiate of the Marxists." No matter how brutal some socialist regimes are (e.g., the USSR under Stalin or Cambodia under Pol Pot) or how poorly Marxian predictions fare, many Marxists persist in believing that worldwide communism is desirable.

Have ideal societies been implemented where Marxists gained control? Marx and Engels wrote thousands of pages on capitalism's ultimate collapse, but less than a hundred pages even hint at specific mechanisms to replace markets. When communist revolutions succeeded in feudal rather than industrialized countries, the new leaders were on their own. Alternatives to markets as ways to answer What? How? and for Whom? had to be invented. None of these alternatives fostered prosperity. In the next section, we examine how the two most powerful Marxist countries, the USSR and China, have recently launched reforms that rely heavily on market mechanisms.

Alternative Economic Systems

The conditions under which men produce and exchange vary from country to country, and within each country again from generation to generation. Political economy, therefore, cannot be the same for all countries and all historical epochs.

Friedrich Engels

Resource ownership under socialism and capitalism alike implies the right to receive the income generated by the resources and to decide how resources will be used. Ownership is collective in socialist economies, with government acting as trustee over capital and land. Conversely, both ownership of most resources and decision making are largely private in capitalist economies.

Even if ownership is primarily private, however, the government allocates most resources in all wartime economies and under Fascist regimes (Hitler, Mussolini, et al.). Alternatively, ownership may be collective but controlled at industry or local levels, where small groups perform entrepreneurial functions (e.g., syndicalism or decentralized socialism). All these alternative systems have been tried during some period of history.

The Soviet Economy in Transition

Mankind has not succeeded in creating anything more efficient than a market economy.

> The "500 Days" Blueprint to Restructure the USSR (Adopted by the Parliament of the Russian Republic, September 1990)

The failure of central planning to "deliver the goods" for Soviet citizens has fomented experiments with market incentives and demands for political reform, punctuated in 1990 by declarations of independence from 13 of 15 of the USSR's republics. Nevertheless, central planning remains official policy, in part because of Soviet history.

History The October Revolution of 1917 was led by V. I. Ulyanov (known as Lenin). Under Bolshevik communism, the Soviet economy floundered until the first *Five Year Plan* in 1929 under I. Djugashvili (known as Stalin). The Soviet economy averaged annual growth now estimated at 2 to 3 percent between 1929 and 1965, which is especially remarkable when the destruction of Soviet industry during World War II is taken into account.[1] Although Soviet economic growth has faltered in recent years, the distortions common under central planning make this early record even more impressive.

Central Planning Most of American business detests the idea of central planning. Ironically, central planning resembles planning within many corporate giants, and central planning bureaucracies are similar to the hierarchies of giant corporations.

---

1. Earlier estimates based on inflated statistics placed the growth rate at 3 to 6 percent over this period. Soviet statistics have frequently been based as much on their propaganda value as on reality.

Central planning *occurs when the government sets wages and prices and specifies output quotas in a detailed way.*

Planning in business firms is geared to maximize profit, but if a government directly controls resources and ignores profits, how does it determine what, how, and for whom to produce? In large, diversified economies, coordinating production and distribution is incredibly difficult, but this has not prevented attempts at central planning in the USSR, China, and some of their satellites.

Central planning requires detailed targets for every sector of the economy. After production quotas are set, the Soviet planning agency, *Gosplan*, must channel outputs across industries. For example, coal and iron ore are required for the steel industry to meet its quota. Chaotic coordination is common; production lines often sit idle while awaiting needed intermediate goods. After the central plan is set, "enterprise managers" are responsible for meeting quotas; their income now depends heavily on achieving these quotas. Quotas are set in specific *success indicators* such as number of units, product mix, weight, or value. Unfortunately, each indicator leads to a different type of distortion.

Suppose you were in charge of nail production and your quota was set in tons of nails. What would be the easiest way to beat your quota? By weight, spikes are easier to produce than small nails. If your quota were in units of nails, you might produce lots of tacks. Length? Long skinny nails. Value? All nails would use only the costliest steel. The result is that consumers' needs have been poorly met. Gold-filigreed sewing machines that did not work resulted when quotas were set by value. Similarly, quotas for square feet of housing generate warped floors and cracked walls, and required units of clothing invite sloppy sewing on shoddy material. Former Premier Khrushchev cited a case when the chandelier quota was expressed in tons. You can imagine what happened. Many failures of central planning occupied warehouse space for years and finally became landfill.

Why is similar gross misallocation relatively rare in market systems? The answer is that managers of capitalist firms know that profits require production to be cost efficient and to consist of goods that consumers demand. Otherwise, firms will go bankrupt.

Why has the USSR relied on central planning? Ideology is a partial answer. Many Marxists view markets as evil and central planning as necessary. Another part of the answer is that top planning bureaucrats zealously guard their power. (In 1990, President Gorbachev's top economist, Nikolai Petrakov, labeled bureaucrats' antagonism to market reforms as "scorched earth policies.") But the strongest explanation is that the USSR grew slightly, despite central planning's inefficiencies, and used bloated statistics to claim even faster growth than that of more capitalistic countries. Ultimately, news media that crossed international borders made it obvious to Soviet citizens that their standards of living were falling further and further behind those enjoyed by people elsewhere. Table 1 compares historical growth in the Soviet economy with growth in some other major countries.

Why did growth defy the handicaps of central planning? Most prices and wages are set within Gosplan. Setting high prices for consumer goods and holding wages down enabled planners to divert vast output to the military and heavy industry. It is paradoxical that surplus values extracted from workers were probably larger under central planning than they were in most capitalist economies. Massive military and investment spending severely depressed the living standards of most Soviet citizens.

Soviet consumers now enjoy slightly larger pieces of a much larger pie because of these earlier sacrifices, but ignoring the forces of supply and demand has invariably meant shortages of many goods and surpluses of others. Moreover, because of time spent acquiring information about availability and then waiting, the real costs of most goods far exceed their ruble prices; even high prices and low wages have not shortened the lines for goods, lines in which most Soviet adults have spent almost 10 percent of their lives.

Stagnation   For more than seventy years, leaders of the USSR tried to justify the sacrifices of their people by threats of invasion from capitalist

Table 1   *Per Capita GNP for Selected Countries (in Billions of 1985 U.S. Dollars)*

Per Capita GNP, 1985 U.S. Dollars

United States	$16,710
Sweden	10,600
France	9,280
United Kingdom	7,860
USSR	7,400
Yugoslavia	5,600
China	340

Per Capita GNP Growth for Selected Countries

	1961–1965	1966–1970	1971–1975	1976–1980	1981–1985
United States	3.1	1.9	1.2	2.3	1.4
Sweden	4.5	3.5	2.2	1.0	1.6
France	4.5	4.5	3.2	2.8	.7
United Kingdom	2.5	2.0	2.0	1.7	1.3
USSR	3.1	3.9	2.1	1.4	1.1
Yugoslavia	N/A	N/A	3.5	4.8	.4
China	N/A	5.5	3.3	4.7	8.0

Source: CIA, *Handbook of Economic Statistics,* 1986.

nations. This "external demon" theory allowed leaders from Lenin through Brezhnev to operate a costly police state. The desires of most Soviet consumers for a better life were ignored, while Communist Party officials, Olympic athletes, scientists, military officers, and high-ranking bureaucrats often lived luxuriously. For example, there are still fewer than three cars per 100 Soviet citizens, but in 1975, Premier Brezhnev, whose regime was infamous for nepotism and corruption, had a stable of 16 limousines, including a Cadillac, a Lincoln, a Mercedes Benz, and a Rolls-Royce.

Orthodox Marxists view inflation and unemployment as diseases unique to capitalism. Consequently, Soviet inflation was hidden by long queues for goods, while every citizen was guaranteed a job. Political favoritism, however, often determined pay, promotions, and access to many goods that most workers in capitalist countries take for granted. This compounded the inefficiency of central planning and depressed many Soviet workers; drunkenness and loafing on the job became common because incentives for productivity were minimal. Soviet economic performance began to lag far behind that in most countries based on mixed capitalism. Marx's dream of a "withering away of the state" turned into a nightmare of rigid bureaucracy controlled by a small clique. Years of reasonable growth (1929–1965) deteriorated into stagnation and unmet Five Year Plans.

Roberto Michels, an early sociologist, may have explained this bureaucratic inertia with an idea he termed *the iron law of oligarchy*. He observed that union leaders often used vertical hierarchies of underlings to protect their power, and that leaders' successors resembled themselves. He theorized that virtually all organizations from local PTAs to the United Nations follow this pattern. His theory clearly described most Soviet leaders until recently, with each generation of high-living bureaucrats being succeeded by another.

Faltering Reform The economic morass created under central planning has unleashed powerful forces that may ultimately result in a Soviet economic structure similar to, for example, that

in Germany, Sweden, or France. President Gorbachev's ascendance in 1985 brought a new generation to power. Under the banners of *perestroika* (economic and social reform) and *glasnost* ("openness"), these younger leaders began experimenting with market forces and political liberalization. For example, government by the Communist Party was a part of the Soviet constitution, but this monopoly was rescinded in 1990, and a multiparty election was held in the USSR for the first time in eight decades.

Gorbachev's attempted sweeping reforms met with mixed success during his first five years in power. By 1991, production was grinding down because of uncertainty about the speed and precise direction of these reforms, and most of the 15 Soviet republics were demanding significant autonomy. A powerful backlash from entrenched officials and the military forced Gorbachev to try to slow the pace of change.

Despite this recent reversal, reasonable long run predictions include democratization and massive privatization—the sale of state enterprises to private investors and market determination of wages and prices. Currency reform (e.g., international convertibility of the ruble) is also on the agenda. These predictions are based on the long-run effects of the expanding world economy and continued improvement in international flows of information. People everywhere try to emulate successful patterns. The failure of central planning is increasingly evident, and most of the Eastern European nations that have abandoned the system should soon experience increases in their rates of economic growth.

Another source of pressure for reform is that technological gains to allow the USSR to compete economically requires free flows of information among industrial managers and researchers. Dictatorships cannot survive without secrecy, which is inconsistent with the information required to compete in the emerging global economy.

Convergence The *convergence hypothesis*, first stated in the 1960s by a Soviet economist named Lieberman, suggests that capitalist economies will become increasingly socialistic, while centralized socialism increasingly will rely on market forces. Although growing regulation in the United States is sometimes cited as evidence for the convergence hypothesis, deregulation is also a strong trend. It appears that Lieberman's "convergence" is primarily in the direction of capitalism. Private markets are increasingly important in the USSR, despite crackdowns on "economic crime," which means illegally buying or selling things ranging from blue jeans to cars to industrial machinery. Without the grease of underground capitalism, the Soviet economy might grind to a halt. Our underground economy is probably tiny compared with Soviet underground markets, which have allowed a large number of ruble millionaires to buy their ways into the privileged life-styles of their country's ruling class.

The Chinese Experience

Mao Zedong established a stable but oppressive government after leading communist forces to victory in 1949 in China, which had a long history of famines, political turmoil, and oppression. China's new leaders initially viewed the USSR as a model and imported a host of Soviet policies, including central planning. Even after ideological schisms in the 1950s evolved into general hostility between the two countries, the Peoples' Republic of China remained a strong command economy. In many ways, there was less economic freedom in China than in the USSR. For example, Soviet workers typically had more choices about their employment.

Mao insisted that "the new man in China" selflessly work for the common good rather than personal advancement. He abhorred material incentives for work effort and was hostile toward technical experts and professional managers. Consequently, communal leaders and factory managers were often chosen because of loyalty to Mao instead of ability to do the job. According to Mao, the "new Chinese man" should be able to perform every type of work and all work is equally valuable. Thus, China often compounded the inefficiency of central planning with failures to specialize its work force.

The Peoples' Republic achieved moderate growth despite these problems, although there were severe downturns when Mao instituted "The Great Leap Forward" from 1958 to 1960 and "The Great Proletarian Cultural Revolution" from 1966 to 1969. During these periods, experts who had managed to get the economy going were purged. These disruptions caused great losses of Chinese lives, production, and income. (From 30 million to 100 million Chinese are estimated to have died prematurely between 1945 and 1985 because of oppressive or misguided policies.)

China has averaged 3 to 6 percent annual growth since the death of Mao and the ouster of his cohorts. A major reason is that experts and skilled professional managers eventually regained power after each purge. Deng Xiaoping, a practical leader determined to modernize China, began opening the Chinese economy up to market determination of prices and outputs in the 1980s. Central planning is gradually giving way to a decentralized form of socialism, with stress on worker cooperatives, especially in agriculture. China, which was forced to import grain throughout much of the reign of Mao, became a grain exporter in the mid-1980s, after farm communes were substantially privatized. China is also experimenting with allowing ambitious entrepreneurs to open their own small industrial firms.

Although China still officially follows egalitarian policies, party leaders obviously live far more comfortably than the Chinese masses. Lavish parties to entertain visiting foreign dignitaries hint at this luxury. Even so, the distribution of income and wealth may be a bit more equal in China than in capitalist economies or in the Soviet Union. Chinese communism has also nearly eradicated the once common evils of illiteracy, child prostitution, begging, and starvation. Medical care is widely available where once it was unknown. The Chinese are not litterbugs. Unlike many other underdeveloped countries, China is quite sanitary. But the revolution extracted massive costs in human life over a 25-year period, and restrictions on individual freedom are only slowly and erratically being phased out.

One major issue for the Soviet Union, and especially for China, is whether modernization in previously communist countries can occur without expanded freedom. During 1989, a "democracy movement" led by Chinese students and workers appeared to have tremendous momentum, but it was brutally suppressed by the Red Army. Continued domination by the Communist Party appears inconsistent with the information flows required for China to move forward as an economic power.

After Marco Polo visited the court of Kublai Khan, he described China to fifteenth-century Europeans as cruel and mysterious. China remains a mystery to Western economists because Chinese statistics are even more misleading and less available than Soviet statistics. As the nation becomes more modernized and open, better information about the Chinese economy should become available.

Decentralized Socialism, Indicative Planning, and Welfare States

Modified capitalism and centrally planned socialism, as practiced respectively in the United States and the Soviet Union, delineate a range of economic systems that leaves a vast middle ground. Private ownership of productive resources may be blended with substantial planning and extensive welfare systems, or social ownership of resources may be combined with market determinations of what is produced and how production occurs.

France and "Indicative Planning"   Although the French economy is primarily capitalistic, before 1982 it used planning far more than other modern Western economies.

*In a system of **indicative planning**, leaders of government, industry, and labor unions meet regularly to exchange information and to negotiate targets for industrial production.*

The French used this process to try to avoid specific shortages, surpluses, and production bottlenecks. For example, if housing was expected to boom, the lumber and brick industries were alerted, and construction unions were asked to step up their apprenticeship programs. Under indicative planning, a bumper crop of superior

wines might have cued officials to negotiate for reduced foreign tariffs on French exports.

The French government also maintained tight controls on investment. By setting up plans to coordinate economic activities, it normally secured voluntary compliance to the overall plan. However, when specific unions or industries failed to comply, the government showed little reluctance about using sanctions and price controls. Government remains very significant in the French economy, collecting 2 francs in taxes out of every 5 francs of GNP.

Planning initially expanded under the administration of François Mitterand, elected in 1981. Mitterand nationalized banking as well as some heavy industry. Although the French economy performed very well for a brief period after the inception of indicative planning, with fairly consistent growth and negligible unemployment from the mid-1950s until the mid-1970s, it faltered even more than did most other European economies in the early 1980s. This resulted in a return to greater reliance on markets during 1984–1991. Indicative planning has been reduced significantly, and government activities are increasingly privatized.

Sweden's Welfare State   Sweden is a typical Scandinavian economy. Severe poverty has been eliminated because the welfare system covers every Swede from the cradle to the grave.

*In modern **welfare states,** resources are largely privately owned, but high taxes and a massive welfare system mean that income is distributed across the society.*

Thus, the Swedish economy has been called "welfare capitalism."

Worker productivity in Sweden is unsurpassed, and per capita income now rivals that in the United States, in spite of reduced incentives that many people consider vital to hard work. Only about 5 percent of Swedish enterprises are government operated. More than 90 percent of all businesses are private; roughly 5 percent operate as producer or consumer cooperatives.

Many Americans view themselves as very heavily taxed, with roughly 30 percent of gross domestic product absorbed by taxes. In Sweden, taxes are nearly half of the country's GNP, the highest tax take of any industrialized capitalist economy. A surprisingly simple tax system relies heavily on a very progressive income tax structure to foot the bill for most social programs.

Swedish prosperity is unquestionably aided by the fact that the nation has avoided major wars for more than a century and that it allocates few resources to national defense. A long history of industrialization has fostered a well-developed work ethic. Collective bargaining is widespread, and negotiations between unions and management have generally been peaceful. Despite this success, the Swedish government is also moving slowly in the direction of reducing government activity and increasing reliance on the market system.

Great Britain   Rudyard Kipling's famous line, "The sun never sets on the British Empire," was true when he wrote it at the turn of the century. Since World War I, however, the British Empire's colonies have evolved into only a very loose confederation, and there are now several countries that exceed Great Britain as a world power. Mighty civilizations have risen and fallen before, but why did the world's first industrial giant fall by the wayside? Some observers attribute Britain's decline to World War I. Others point to a lack of coherent and consistent economic policy.

Just as the Middle East has spawned many important religions, Great Britain is the birthplace of most of the world's economic systems. Utopian and Fabian socialism, the welfare state, the roots of capitalist ideology, and Keynesian demand management policies all found British soil to be a fertile breeding ground. Marx researched most of the three volumes of *Das Kapital* in the British Museum.

The decline of Britain may have resulted from erratic policies that meandered among the ideas expressed by a variety of economic prophets. From John Locke's writings about private property until World War I, Britain was among the most capitalistic of countries. Then Fabian socialism gave birth to Labour governments that nationalized much of British industry.

Militant unionism and an unwillingness to promote new investment rendered much of British industry obsolete by 1980. Britain was reluctant to allow entrepreneurs to pursue the most profitable investments available; instead, political pressures channeled investment spending toward senile industries. The extensive and expensive British welfare system appears to have caused serious problems for work incentives, while high tax rates and threats of nationalization dampened new investment and technological innovations.

Highly progressive tax rates, especially on investment income, stymied entrepreneurship and left English workers using antique technology. But wealth was apparent on London streets. This paradox is explained by the fact that many wealthy English people chose to squander their money on furs and Rolls-Royces rather than engage in risky investments from which high taxes prohibited much of a rate of return.

Just as the Roman Empire dissolved and Italy emerged, the British Empire devolved into England. Italy and England followed similar paths in terms of economic power and international influence, but both now appear to be on the road to recovery. In 1980, Prime Minister Thatcher announced plans to resurrect the marketplace. Following the supply-side path initiated in the United States by former President Reagan, she slashed tax rates and privatized many of the industries nationalized earlier. John Major, who succeeded Thatcher in 1990, announced plans to continue her basic policies with relatively little modification. The future of Great Britain is now linked to the prosperity of the European Community.

Is Small Both Beautiful and Necessary?

Scarcity exists when people want more than is available. There are two basic ways to deal with the problem of scarcity. The first, emphasized in all of the economies we have described and by most economists of both capitalist and socialist persuasions, is to stretch resources as much as possible by maximizing production to try to accommodate human desires. The second approach is to try to reduce human wants to levels consistent with the resources at hand. Those who advocate this second path are opposed to both capitalist and socialist visions of the proper economic system.

One set of critics attack vast material production as an improper goal that leads us away from fulfilling our spiritual needs. These critics focus on inner peace and living in harmony with nature as more appropriate goals. According to them, "small is beautiful." Religious leaders who preach that materialism pits individual against individual and against the divine will are legion. The teachings of E. F. Schumacher, who developed what he calls *Buddhist economics*, are representative of this view.

Other critics of capitalism accept material production as desirable but argue that unchecked capitalism devours depletable resources and will leave nothing for future generations. These critics argue that there are natural *limits to growth* and view environmental despoliation as part of the price we pay for excessive economic development. They fear the onset of a new Dark Age in which human society will have "run out" of everything, and believe that if "small is beautiful," small is also necessary to our survival.

Buddhist Economics

Minimizing human wants is the central thrust of many idealists and religious people who recognize that people have fundamental material needs but who consider color televisions, flashy clothes, and sporty cars as distractions that impede spiritual development. Thus, things that many of us consider necessary for "the good life" are perceived as actually getting in the way of the good life favored by these idealists. Such critics believe that most of our material demands are foisted on us by capitalists who use the demands for their products to cajole people into working 40 hours a week or more.

Under capitalism, income, status, and worth depend on work, so we create work by creating artificial demands. Although many religions require their priests to take vows of poverty, certain aspects of Buddhism contain the most elabo-

rate strictures, which assert that the path to nirvana (enlightenment) requires only minimal material comforts. These critics think that socialists have bought the line, "more means better," although the socialist stress on replacing competition with cooperation is at least partly in keeping with the religious values underlying the Buddhist approach.

In a best-selling book, *Small Is Beautiful: Economics As If People Mattered*, E. F. Schumacher elaborated the economic ideas of Mohandas Gandhi, who led India to independence from Britain after World War II.[2] Schumacher has referred to these ideas as "Buddhist economics," although they also draw from Hindu teachings.

The idea that "small is beautiful" stresses curbing material want as the key to dealing with scarcity, and emphasizes local self-sufficiency, and small-scale, labor-intensive technology.

Gandhi rejected mass production and the sophisticated technology used in modern industrial states. He recognized that production in isolated villages is inevitably lower than it is in densely populated cities in which crowds of people work on hectic assembly lines, but felt that the benefits of the simple life were well worth the production foregone. Gandhi's philosophy is akin to Buddhism in its emphasis on the spiritual enrichment to human life available, in this case, by avoiding industrialization.

Limits to Growth

In the minds of critics who argue that economic growth must be controlled, the energy crisis of the 1970s and widespread pollution are coupled with computer forecasts that excessive desires for consumer "goodies" will soon deplete the natural resources of "Spaceship Earth." These critics, whose number includes such prominent economists as Kenneth Boulding, argue that cap-

---

2. E. F. Schumacher, *Small Is Beautiful: Economics As If People Mattered* (New York: Harper and Row, 1973).

italism encourages people in developed economies to seek ever higher consumption. In their view, this "cowboy" mentality promotes a disregard for the pollution generated by heavy industry and "anti-Earth gas guzzlers" and depletes the minerals, timber, and other resources necessary to sustain future generations.

They point out that known reserves of petroleum, coal, metallic ores, and other finite raw materials are insufficient to allow consumption by the populations of less developed countries to grow to the standards of living enjoyed by people in North America and Western Europe. Moreover, their projections suggest that even without economic growth, if raw materials continue to be depleted at current rates, most will be gone within two or three generations. Their solutions? Get natural, rid ourselves of plastic-oriented mindsets, and generally scale everything down.

Defenders of capitalism and growth try to rebut these arguments by suggesting that technological advances will permit continued growth, and that automatic changes in relative prices will force us to use natural resources more efficiently as they become scarcer. Moreover, they suggest that, as our technology advances, we will learn to use raw materials presently seen as worthless. Those who advocate limits to growth are generally pessimistic that technology will bail us out of the difficulties they foresee.

Chapter Review: Key Points

1. *Libertarianism* is a philosophy that rejects almost all but the simplest government activities. It strongly advocates laissez-faire capitalism.

2. *Anarchy* is the absence of government. *Syndicalism* is a system in which an industry's workers own the means of production, which are controlled by democratically elected worker councils. Syndicates are effectively trade unions that own their industries.

3. *Socialism* entails eliminating private ownership of nonhuman productive resources, which would be owned collectively.

4. *Marxism* is based on *dialectical materialism*, which suggests that the course of human history is determined by clashes between an economic *thesis* and its *antithesis* that yield a *synthesis*, or progression, for human life.

5. Marxism postulates conflicts between economic classes that emerge from the theft by capitalists of *surplus values*, which are the excesses of production over subsistence wages. These surplus values are translated into accumulations of capital.

6. Marx predicted (*a*) growing wretchedness and unemployment of the working class, (*b*) ever greater concentrations of capital, (*c*) declining rates of profit, (*d*) explosive business cycles, (*e*) increasingly aggressive imperialistic policies, and (*f*) bloody revolutions as capitalist economies reached full maturity. In most respects, except for the (now slowing) concentration of capital, these predictions seem erroneous.

7. The Soviet Union and the People's Republic of China have used *central planning* extensively and have managed moderate growth in their command economies by forcing consumption down in order to raise social saving and investment. These economies have been plagued with inefficiency; great loss of freedom has been just one cost of their rapid economic development. Now that pragmatic new leaders are at the helm, China and the USSR both seem increasingly willing to let market forces operate.

8. *Indicative planning* has been used in France to coordinate the activities of industries, unions, and government. Although not as bureaucratic as Soviet central planning, government has used strong legal and economic sanctions to ensure compliance with its plans.

9. Northern European nations such as Sweden have extensive welfare programs financed by heavy tax rates. However, industry is largely in private hands, and labor productivity is as high as anywhere in the world.

10. Perhaps the most radical criticisms of capi-

talism and all economies based on material production assume that the proper solution to scarcity is to curtail our material wants and to simplify the economy as much as possible, even if it requires large losses of production. Somewhat less radical critics argue that there are *limits to growth*, and that we must all learn to live with less.

Key Concepts

Ensure that you can define these terms before proceeding.

privatization

libertarianism

anarcho-syndicalism

utopian socialism

Fabian socialism

Christian socialism

dialectical materialism

communism (Marxism)

class warfare

central planning

indicative planning

welfare state

small is beautiful

Questions for Thought and Discussion

1. People work not only to receive wages and salaries, but also for the applause of their peers and the respect of their neighbors. Many business firms confer impressive-sounding titles on their employees, or recognize long service with the proverbial gold watch. Worker heroes in the Soviet Union are awarded "Stakhanovite" Medals if they consistently exceed their production quotas. "Self-criticism" and plaudits dished out in group therapy sessions shaped the personalities and work habits of Mao's "new man" in China. These are a few of the many techniques that have been tried in attempts to mold or reduce greed as motivation for work. Do you think human beings are inherently self-interested, or are we only conditioned to be greedy? If conditioning explains our greed, are the techniques we have described likely to be successful in reducing or channeling self-interested behavior? Can you think of other techniques that would reduce avaricious behavior? Do you think it would be better if we were all less greedy? Why or why not? How do your answers to these questions relate to which economic system you think operates most efficiently and most compatibly with human welfare?

2. Suppose you were the president of an extremely impoverished country. After reading this chapter, would you choose socialism, capitalism, or some other system as the best path to accomplish economic growth and development? Why?

3. The role of government would be extremely limited if a libertarian became president and if libertarians were elected to majorities in Congress. Assuming that they did not all resign as a means of reducing government, what are some of the institutions or regulations that libertarians would eliminate or modify?

Epilogue

Where do you go from here? A few of you may regret having taken economics; others may feel that the time it took to prepare for this course was well spent, but you have no intention of extending your formal training in economics. Still others may choose to take three or four more courses in this field. We can promise those of you who fit into any of these categories that you will encounter economic concepts repeatedly, regardless of the path your life takes.

But this epilogue is really addressed to those few students who find the analytical methods we use and the problems we tackle so intriguing that you are considering a career as an economist. We are grateful that there are so few of you; otherwise, the supply of economists might be so great that those of us who love economic reasoning would not be able to live comfortably while doing the work we like best. John Maynard Keynes once issued a challenge to aspiring economists that we would like to echo:

The study of economics does not seem to require any specialized gifts of an unusual order. Is it not, intellectually regarded, a very easy subject compared with the higher branches of philosophy and pure science? Yet good, or even competent economists are the rarest of birds. An easy subject, at which few excel! The paradox finds its explanation, perhaps, in that the master economist must possess a rare combination of gifts. He must be a mathematician, historian, statesman, philosopher — in some degree. He must understand symbols and speak in words. He must contemplate the particular in terms of the general, and touch abstract and concrete in the same flight of thought. He must study the present in the light of the past for the purposes of the future. No part of man's nature or institutions must lie entirely outside his regard. He must be purposeful and disinterested in a simultaneous mood; as aloof and incorruptible as an artist, yet sometimes as near the earth as a politician.

J. M. Keynes (1924)

Everyone who wishes to be an economist would do well to pursue the lofty goals implicit in Keynes's essay.

Glossary

Ability to Pay Principle The idea that the rich should pay more taxes than the poor. (See also Benefit Principle of Taxation.)

Absolute Advantage The idea that nations should produce goods which absorb fewer resources than in other countries, and exchange their surpluses for goods produced with fewer resources elsewhere; replaced by the Law of Comparative Advantage.

Absolute Price The monetary price of a good. (See also relative price.)

Activism The Keynesian notion that Aggregate Demand should be adjusted by government macroeconomic policy to offset shocks to Aggregate Demand or Aggregate Supply. "Finetuning" is an extreme version of this approach.

Administration Lag The period that passes before discretionary policy changes can be implemented; monetary policy can be implemented quickly through the FED's Federal Open Market Committee; fiscal policies entail long administration lags because discretionary changes in taxes or government expenditures require changing the law.

Administrative Costs of Regulation Include the salaries of government workers, inspectors, office supplies, etc. (See also compliance costs of government regulation.)

Adverse Selection Occurs when a party to a contract has been deceived about the qualities it expects to receive from a transaction.

Aggregate Demand Curve The negative relationship that exists between the general price level (P) and the quantity demanded (Q) of total national output.

Aggregate Expenditures The sum of consumption, investment, government purchases, and net exports ($C + I + G + [X - M]$).

Aggregate Expenditures Curve The relationship between Aggregate Expenditures and income; positively sloped because income induces spending. Sometimes known as a Keynesian cross diagram.

Aggregate Supply Curve A positive relationship between real national production (Q) and the absolute price level (P).

Aid to Families with Dependent Children (AFDC) A major program designed to alleviate poverty; originally this program was characterized by a payment structure which provided overwhelming incentives for recipients not to work.

Allocative Mechanisms Alternative modes for a society to use in deciding how inputs will be allocated among competing ends and how incomes and production will be distributed.

Anarchism The idea that government should be eliminated, leaving people largely free to do as they pleased. Anarchists believe that social harmony would evolve naturally through cooperative efforts. Most philosophical anarchists recognize the importance of private property rights and, hence, completely disavow social ownership.

Appreciation of a Currency When the exchange rate (price) of a currency increases as measured by its exchange rates with other currencies.

Arbitrage The risklessly profitable process of buying a good at a lower price in one market and selling the same good at a higher price in another market; forces relative prices of the same good toward equality in all markets.

Artificial Barriers to Entry Significant barriers to entry that are not caused by natural market forces. Government or existing firms erect these barriers to exclude competition.

Asset Demand for Money Exists because people (*a*) perceive money as riskless relative to alternative assets, (*b*) confront transaction costs in acquiring other assets that exceed their expected rate of return, and (*c*) expect the prices of alternative assets to fall in the near future.

Asymmetric Information When people have different levels of knowledge about a bargaining situation.

Automatic (Built-in) Stabilizers Government tax and spending mechanisms that automatically drive the federal budget into deficit when the economy slumps or into a surplus when inflationary pressures build; tend to stabilize economic activity.

Automation Technological advances that replace human labor by machinery.

Autonomous Expenditure Spending unrelated to income; occurs at zero income. Investment, government purchases, net exports, and part of consumer spending are all treated as autonomous in very simple Keynesian models.

Autonomous Spending Multiplier The number which, when multiplied by the sum of all autonomous spending, yields equilibrium income; in simple Keynesian models, this multiplier equals the reciprocal of the marginal propensity to save.

Average Fixed Cost (AFC) Total fixed cost (*TFC*) per unit of output (*Q*); *TFC/Q* graphs as a rectangular hyperbola.

Average Physical Product of Labor (APP$_L$) Production per worker; equals total output (*Q*) divided by labor (*L*); *Q/L*.

Average Propensity to Consume (APC) The proportion of disposable income consumed; $apc = C/Y_d$.

Average Propensity to Save (APS) The proportion of disposable income saved; $APS = S/Y_d$.

Average Revenue Revenue per unit of output; synonym for price in the absence of price discrimination; equals total revenue (*TR*) divided by output: *TR/Q*.

Average Revenue Product Revenue per unit of an input; is computed by dividing a given total revenue (*TR*) by the amounts of given resources (e.g., workers (*L*)) generating this revenue (e.g., *TR/L*).

Average Total Cost (ATC) Total cost incurred per unit of output; often termed *average cost* or *unit cost*; $ATC = AVC + AFC$.

Average Variable Costs (AVC) Variable cost per unit of output; equals *TVC/Q*. (See also variable costs.)

Bad Anything the consumption of which decreases human happiness.

Balance of Payments A record of the payments between a country and the countries with which it trades. Balance of payments deficits occur when a country's payments of money to foreigners exceed its receipts from foreigners. A balance of payments surplus occurs when a country's receipts from foreigners exceed its payments to foreigners.

Balance of Trade (deficit, surplus) The relationship between a country's annual exports and imports. A deficit in the balance of trade exists when the dollar value of a country's imports exceeds the value of its exports. A surplus in the balance of trade exists when the dollar value of a country's exports exceeds the dollar value of its imports. Differs from balance of payments because foreign investment flows and loans, etc., affect payments.

Barrier to Entry A significant obstacle of some sort that either discourages or prevents the entry of firms into an industry.

Barter Trading goods for other goods rather than money.

Basic Economic Problem Scarcity, which means that fewer goods are freely available than people want to consume.

Basic Economic Questions *What* economic goods will be produced, *how* will resources be used for which types of production, and *who* will get to use the goods?

Benefit Principle of Taxation The idea that individuals should be taxed in proportion to the marginal benefits that they receive from governmentally provided commodities and services. (See also ability to pay.)

Bilateral Monopoly Occurs when a monopoly supplier confronts a monopsonistic buyer.

Black Market Transactions that violate legal price ceilings.

Blacklisting Circulation by employers of lists to bar hiring of union organizers or other "troublemakers."

Block Pricing Price discrimination for utility rates.

Board of Governors The governing body of the Federal Reserve System. Six regular board members are appointed to staggered 14-year terms of office; the Chair is appointed to a 4 year term.

Bonds Promises by government or corporations to pay certain amounts of money by specific future dates.

Break-even Point The rate of output at which total revenue equals total cost.

Bretton Woods Agreement (1944) Established both the International Monetary Fund and a fixed exchange rate system with the dollar as the world's key currency. Other nations agreed to peg their currencies to the dollar.

Budget Deficits or Surpluses Occur, respectively, when government outlays exceed or fall below government revenues.

Budget Line A line showing various combinations of goods which cost the same amount as the consumer's income.

Bureaucracy A large organization with many employees, called bureaucrats; tends to be governed by many rules and regulations, called red tape.

Business Cycles Alternating periods of expansion and contraction in economic activity.

Business Firms Centers of production, they sell goods in output markets and buy services in resource markets.

Buyers' Market Occurs when the prevailing market price lies above the equilibrium price, resulting in a surplus.

Capital All physical improvements made to natural resources that facilitate production, including buildings and all machinery and equipment.

Capital Deepening When the percentage growth of the capital stock exceeds the growth rate of the labor force; real per capita output normally rises.

Capital Widening When the labor force and the capital stock experience identical percentage rates of growth.

Capitalism An economic system based on private property rights and emphasizing private, as opposed to governmental or collective, decision making. (See also laissez faire, socialism.)

Capitalization The process whereby income streams are transformed into wealth, resulting in the elimination of economic profits.

Cartel An organization of firms that jointly make decisions about prices and production for the entire group, usually attempts to charge monopoly prices and limit production to monopoly rates of output. OPEC is an example.

Caveat Emptor An ancient legal doctrine which suggests that buyers are the best judges of whether or not they receive full value from the goods they purchase, and that buyers should bear the consequences of their own decisions; it means "let the buyer beware."

Caveat Venditor A legal doctrine reflected in prohibitions against fraud and in sellers' legal liability for damages if unknown dangers lurk in a product; a Latin phrase meaning "let the seller beware."

Celler-Kefauver Antimerger Act (1950) This act made it illegal for major firms to acquire the stock or assets of their competitors.

Central Bank An institution whose function it is to make a nation's financial system operate as smoothly as possible; serves as the government's banker.

Central Planning or Centralized Decisionmaking Major economic decisions are made by some central authority, as in the Soviet Union.

Certificates of Deposit (CDs) Very long-term, high-value savings accounts issued by financial institutions.

Christian Socialism Emphasizes the virtues and dignity of work and advocates labor unionization; rejects the violent means to overthrow capitalism advocated by radical socialists and communists.

Circular Flow Model Shows interactions between households and firms. Households are centers for wealth holding and consumption, and buy goods from the firms that produce them; firms buy resources from households in order to produce goods and services.

Classical Theory A systematic study of the functioning of a market economy which concluded that, in the long run, the economy would always attain full employment at equilibrium GNP, assuming the validity of Say's Law and flexible wages, prices, and interest rates.

Clayton Act (1914) Specified offenses more precisely than did the Sherman Act (1890); the Clayton Act forbade price discrimination and interlocking directorates, exempted collective bargaining from antitrust actions, and exempted agricultural associations so that nonprofit corporations could be formed without violating antitrust laws.

Closed Shop A firm that has agreed to hire only union members; these agreements are illegal under the Taft-Hartley Act.

Collective Bargaining The process by which workers who are members of a labor union negotiate with an employer to set wages, hours, and working conditions.

Command Economy These economic systems resolve the basic economic questions through central planning; allocations of inputs and distributions of goods are coordinated by a bureaucracy.

Commodity Any tangible produced good that may be owned.

Commodity Money Has substantial value independently of what it will buy. Gold and silver coins are examples.

Common Stock Ownership shares in a corporation.

Communism An idealized classless society in which all people would live and work under the condition "from each according to ability, to each according to needs"; under communism, all nonhuman property would be owned collectively.

Comparable Worth The idea that jobs typically filled by women should generate wages equal to those paid to men with comparable skills.

Comparative Advantage, Law of Mutually beneficial trade can always take place between two countries (or individuals) whose pretrade cost and price structures differ.

Competition A process driving price close to opportunity cost. Pure competition requires: (*a*) numerous potential buyers and sellers; (*b*) homogeneous outputs or inputs, precluding nonprice competition; (*c*) each buyer and seller to be small relative to the market so that no single decision will influence the price of the item or service; and (*d*) an absence of long run barriers to entry or to exit. (See also contestable markets theory.)

Complementary Goods Goods that are consumed together, such as tennis racquets and balls; a negative cross-price elasticity of demand exists between complementary goods.

Compliance Costs of Government Regulation Costs incurred mainly by the private sector (and also by state and local governments) in the process of complying with regulations. (See also Administrative Costs of Regulation.)

Concentration Ratio The percentage of some aspect of market power (e.g., sales) wielded by the leading 4 or 8 firms in an industry.

Conglomerate A firm that operates in several different industries.

Constant Cost Industry The long run industry supply curve is horizontal; constant per unit production costs are incurred for every output level because the supplies of all the resources used are perfectly price elastic.

Consumer Equilibrium (the Cardinal Utility approach) A consumer maximizes total utility when the last cents spent on each good yield the same number of utils of satisfaction; no reallocation of spending will increase total utility.

Consumer Equilibrium (the Indifference Curve approach) Consumers maximize satisfaction upon reaching tangency between their budget constraint lines and the highest attainable indifference curves.

Consumer Price Index (CPI) A statistical comparison, over time, in the prices of goods bought by typical urban consumers; the base year equals 100, with subsequent changes in the price level reflecting inflation (over 100) or deflation (under 100).

Consumer Surplus A gain to consumers arising from differences between the amounts of money they would willingly pay to consume goods and the amounts that they must pay in order to consume the good; the area below their demand curves but above the price line.

Consumption Spending by households for goods used to gratify human wants; the major component of Aggregate Demand.

Contestable Markets Theory Suggests that all advantages of pure competition as a market structure are realized if freedom of entry and exit exists, and that the number of firms currently in a market is less important for efficiency than the threat of potential new entrants. (See also Competition.)

Contraction (Recession) A decline in economic activity; unemployment and inventories rise unexpectedly.

Contribution Standard The idea that income should be distributed according to the productivity of one's resources.

Corporation An organization formed under state law that is considered a legal person distinct and separate from its owners.

Cost-Push Inflation Upward price level movements that originate on the supply side of the economy; cost-push cycles of inflation generate clockwise adjustment paths of inflation versus real output.

Costs of Unemployment, Economic Include the opportunity costs of the output unemployed workers could have produced were they employed.

Credit A promise to pay at some future date is exchanged for money.

Cross Elasticity of Demand A measure of the responsiveness of the quantity demanded of one good to changes in the price of another; computed by dividing the percentage change in quantity demanded of a good by the percentage change in price of another good: $\%\Delta Q_x/\%\Delta P_y$; positive for substitute goods, but negative for complementary goods.

Crowding-Out Hypothesis The idea that increases in governmental spending inevitably cause reductions in private consumption or investment.

Crude Quantity Theory of Money A monetary theory that the price level is exactly proportional to the nominal money supply (M).

Currency Coins and paper money.

Cyclical Deficit The difference between government revenues and outlays that emerges because the macroeconomy is operating below its potential. (See also structural deficit.)

Cyclical Unemployment Unemployment that results from a recession.

Decentralized Decisionmaking When most decisions about what to produce, when and how to produce, and who gets to use output are determined in private markets.

Decentralized Socialism Economic systems characterized by social ownership of resources, but which rely on markets to resolve the economic problem by setting equilibrium prices and quantities.

Decrease in Demand An entire demand curve shifting downward and to the left; occurs only if one or more of the nonprice determinants of demand change. Less will be purchased at each possible price.

Decrease in Supply The entire supply curve shifts to the left; occurs only if one of the nonprice determinants of supply changes so that less will be available at each possible price.

Decreasing Cost Industry An industry for which the long-run supply curve is negatively sloped, reflecting declines in per unit costs as production in the industry increases.

Deflating Using a price index to adjust monetary values for changes that occur to the price level over time; dividing the nominal values of a time series for a variable by (1% of) the price level during the period in which the nominal variable occurs.

Deflationary Gap See recessionary gap.

Demand Purchases of a good that people are actually willing and able to make, given the prices and choices available to them.

Demand Curve A graph of the maximum quantities of a good that people are willing to purchase at various market prices.

Demand Deposits Funds kept in a financial institution that by law must be available upon the depositor's demand; checking accounts.

Demand, Law of The quantity demanded of an economic good varies inversely with its price.

Demand Price The highest price that buyers are willing and able to pay for a specific amount of a good or resource. Also known as subjective price. (See also supply price.)

Demand Schedule A table reflecting the maximum quantities of a given good or resource that will be purchased at various market prices.

Demand-Side or Demand-Pull inflation Hikes in the price level that originate from growth of Aggregate Demand; caused by excessively rapid increases in the growth rate of the nominal money supply or upward shifts in autonomous real expenditures; demand-pull inflation generates a counterclockwise adjustment path of inflation versus real output.

Depreciation The amount of capital used up during a period. Also known as the capital consumption allowance.

Depreciation of a Currency A decrease in the value of one currency measured in terms of its exchange rates with other currencies.

Depression A sharp and sustained decline in business activity.

Derived Demand The demand for a resource that exists because of its productivity; resource demands are derived from demands for output.

Devaluation of a Currency Occurs when exchange rates are either "pegged" or fixed under a gold standard and some government decides to decrease the gold content of its currency; not synonymous with depreciation of currency.

Development, Economic Qualitative changes in an economic system; economic development occurs when there are improvements in either the quality of life or the quality of goods, or both.

Dialectical Materialism Karl Marx's explanation of historical change; all massive social and cultural changes are determined by contradictions that exist in the ways that societies produce, exchange, distribute, and consume goods; for the most part, these contradictions are embedded in conflicts that exist between the different classes in society.

Diminishing Marginal Returns, Law of When additional equal units of a variable input are applied to fixed inputs, a point is inevitably reached where total output increases at a diminishing rate as additional units of the variable input are applied to the fixed inputs; diminishing marginal returns are pervasive even in the long run because it is virtually impossible to vary all influences on production both proportionally and simultaneously.

Diminishing Marginal Utility, Principle of Consumption of successive units of a good eventually causes an additional unit of the good to yield less satisfaction than that of the preceding unit.

Diminishing Returns, Law of The further any activity is extended, the more difficult (and costly) it is to extend it further.

Dirty Float Occurs when governments intervene in a "floating" foreign exchange market in order to stabilize exchange rates.

Discount Rate (d) The interest rate that the FED charges member banks when they borrow money from FED "discount windows."

Discretionary Fiscal Policy Deliberate changes in government spending and tax policies for economic stabilization purposes.

Discrimination, Economic Occurs when equivalent units of a resource receive different rates of remuneration even though their potential marginal contributions to total output are the same.

Diseconomies of Scale A firm's average costs rise as output rises.

Disequilibrium When the forces for change in a system are not in balance.

Disincentives Penalties that discourage an activity; often applied to government policies that discourage productive activities.

Disinflation A significant decrease in the rate of inflation, this normally creates pressures for recessions.

Disposable Personal Income (DPI) The after-tax income households receive in a given year; equals consumption plus saving (C + S).

Dissaving Negative saving; occurs when desired consumption exceeds income; families go in debt or draw down past savings to afford their purchases.

Distortion Costs of Inflation Losses from distorted decisions caused when inflation warps relative prices and reduces certainty.

Divestiture When court orders require large corporations to break down into smaller independent companies.

Division of Labor Specialization of labor by task, e.g., when one person designs a computer program, another writes the computer code, a third "debugs" the program, a fourth writes the user manual, a fifth copies the program to diskettes, a sixth packages and ships the programs, and so on.

Dominant Strategy In game theory, a player's best response, no matter what strategy other players might pick.

Double Coincidence of Wants A requirement of barter that you must locate someone who has what you want and who wants what you have to transact.

Dumping When a country sells an export for less than the price charged domestically for that good; may result from international price discrimination, which entails charging desperate domestic buyers more than indifferent foreign buyers; predatory dumping occurs when a country tries to drive competitors out of a market to establish a monopoly.

Durable Goods Consumer goods that are useful for more than one year.

Economic Growth Quantitative change in an economic system; occurs when a society acquires greater productive capacity that can be used for consumption or investment.

Economic Incidence of a Tax The final burden of a tax; that is, who actually pays the tax through lower purchasing power.

Economic (Capital) Investment Purchases of new output that can be used for further production. The four basic types of new capital are: (a) new business structures; (b) new residential structures; (c) new machinery and equipment; and (d) inventory accumulation.

Economic Profit The excess of revenues over the opportunity costs of the resources employed; these profits reward an entrepreneur if they exceed the minimum necessary to continue the firm's existence and are a premium for risk bearing and innovating.

Economic Rent Surpluses reaped by owners of a

resource if it is paid more than the minimum necessary to elicit the supply of the resource.

Economics The study of how individuals and societies allocate their limited resources in attempts to satisfy their unlimited wants.

Economies of Scale When long-run average costs fall as output rises.

Economies of Scope Cost savings realized because certain types of production are complementary.

Efficiency, Economic Occurs when the opportunity cost of some specific amount of a good is at its lowest possible value, and when maximum production from given resources and costs is achieved; implies that gains to anyone entail losses to someone else.

Efficient Markets Theory The idea that all possible gains that are foreseeable will be exploited by private individuals.

Efficiency Wages Wages that exceed market clearing wages which are intended to raise the costs of dismissal and reduce shirking by employees.

Egalitarianism The idea that everyone should have the same income.

Elasticity The sensitivity of one variable relative to some other variable. (See also income elasticity of demand, price elasticity of demand, price elasticity of supply.)

Eminent Domain Government's legal right to acquire property without the previous owner agreeing to the price government pays.

Empire Building Exaggerating the difficulty of the mission of a bureaucracy so that the budget of the agency will be expanded.

Employment Act of 1946 Established the Council of Economic Advisors and set priorities of full employment with price level stability, but provided few directives about how to achieve such goals.

Employment Discrimination Occurs when particular groups suffer a higher incidence of unemployment than other groups.

Entrepreneurship The organizing function which innovates new goods and production processes, and business uncertainty when it combines the services provided by other resources so that goods are produced.

Entry and Exit into an Industry If there are no barriers to entry and exit, entry into an industry by outside competitors or exit of existing firms continue until economic profits are zero; positive profits attract new entrants, while economic losses cause exit from an industry. Potential entry by competitors is the key to "contestable" markets theory.

Equal Distribution of Income Standard One ethical criterion for distributing income and wealth; assumes that an extra dollar means more to the poor than to the rich, and ignores the disincentives for production that occur when incomes are independent of productivity.

Equal Marginal Advantage, Law of Efficiency requires similar resources to be used to equally advantage. In consumption, the last cent spent on any good must yield the same satisfaction as the last cent spent on any other good. In production, the last cent spent on any resource must yield the same output as the last cent spent on any other resource.

Equal Marginal Productivities per Dollar, Principle of The last few cents spent on any resource must yield the same additional output as the last few cents spent on any other resource. This is a requirement for least cost production and maximum profit.

Equal Marginal Utilities per Dollar, Principle of The last few cents spent on any good yield identical amounts of satisfaction or utility; algebraically, this requires $MU_1/P_1 = MU_2/P_2 = \ldots = MU_m/P_m$, where the subscripts 1 through m-1 denote commodities and m denotes money.

Equation of Exchange $MV = PQ$, where M denotes the nominal money supply, V denotes the income velocity of money, P denotes an index for the general price level, and Q denotes real output; a tautology, since it is true by definition.

Equilibrium Exists when the pressures that bring about change in the market system are in balance. Macroeconomic equilibrium — when desired demand expenditure equals actual income or output. Microeconomic equilibrium — when the quantities of a good or resource demanded and supplied are equal.

Equilibrium (Market-Clearing) Price The market price that clears the market.

Equilibrium Quantity The quantity of a good marketed at the equilibrium price.

Equity Fairness, a normative concept; value judgments are inherent in specifying what is fair.

Escalator Clauses Contractual obligations specifying that future payments of money will be adjusted for price level changes.

Excess Burdens of a Tax The amounts by which the total burden of a tax exceeds government revenue yielded by the tax.

Excess Demand The amount by which the quantity demanded exceeds the quantity supplied when the prevailing market price lies below the market-clearing price; normally associated with shortages.

Excess Reserves (XR) the amounts by which banks' legal (total) reserves exceed their required reserves.

Excess Supply The amount by which the quantity supplied exceeds the quantity demanded when the prevailing market price lies above the market-clearing price; normally associated with surpluses.

Exchange Controls Legal limits on the ability to buy or sell foreign currencies; frequently stimulate black markets for foreign money.

Exchange Rate The value of one currency expressed in terms of another currency, or some combination of other currencies.

Excise Tax A per unit tax levied on a specific good.

Exclusive Good A good is exclusive if people can be denied access at a relatively low cost; if these people do not pay, they may be excluded from consuming the good.

Expansion (Recovery) The phase of the business cycle when economic activity begins to increase; employment rises, inventories fall unexpectedly.

Expected Rate of Inflation The percentage annual rate at which economic transactors expect the general price level to rise.

Expenditure Approach to Estimating GNP The sum of personal consumption, investment, government purchases of goods and services, and net exports: $GNP = C + I + G + (X - M)$.

Explicit Costs Outlays of funds to individuals or firms external to the producer; some examples are wages paid employees, rent payments, utility bills, and purchases of intermediate goods.

Exploitation Payment of wages less than the value of the marginal product of labor. May result from a firm's monopsony power as a hirer of labor, or because a firm has monopoly power.

Exports Goods manufactured in this country and purchased by foreigners.

External Supply Shocks These shocks, which originate outside the economy, shift the Aggregate Supply curve to the left; rising production costs create pressures for supply-side (cost-push) inflation and increasing unemployment.

Externalities Market failures that occur whenever some activity affects economic transactors who are not directly involved in the activity. Pollution is an example of a negative externality; education generates positive externalities to the extent that all of society gains from being a part of a more educated populace. External costs and benefits are largely ignored by individual decision makers.

Fabian Socialism This socialist theory advocates nationalizing only heavy industry; all other property would be privately owned, although extensive welfare programs would ensure that people's needs were met.

Family Allowance Plan (FAP) Many European nations countries now have family allowance plans based on the number of minor children in a family; these payments are usually adequate to feed and to clothe each child in the family and are made regardless of the family's income.

Featherbedding The employment of workers who are not in productive jobs; normally a result of union pressure or inefficient government regulation.

Federal Funds Market A privately operated network that enables banks to borrow or lend large amounts of money for very short periods.

Federal Open Market Committee (FOMC) The policymaking body within the Federal Reserve System.

Federal Reserve System (FED) Central bank of the United States; created by Congress in 1913 to buffer financial crises by acting as a bankers' bank and lender of last resort; the FED's primary role is conducting monetary policy.

Federal Trade Commission (FTC) Act (1914) Created the FTC and empowered it to challenge any "unfair methods of competition . . . , and unfair or deceptive acts or practices in or affecting commerce."

Fiat Money Money that is worthless as a commodity and which has value only because of its use as a medium of exchange.

Final Goods Goods bought by the consumers or investors who ultimately use them.

Financial Capital Securities; paper claims to goods or resources.

Financial Intermediation The process by which household saving is made available through financial institutions to those desiring to spend in excess of their income (especially investors).

Financial Investment Paper documents representing financial claims on assets, created when purchases of stocks, bonds, and real estate are made.

Fine-tuning Government attempts to make the economy function as smoothly as possible by frequently changing both monetary and fiscal policies to offset even minor fluctuations in economic activity.

Firm An entity that operates one or more plants and which buys productive resources from households.

Fiscal drag A tendency to generate budget surpluses in a growing economy, assuming that government spending and tax rates remain unchanged; arising because of our progressive income tax, fiscal drag retards growth of Aggregate Demand.

Fiscal Policy Policies for government spending or setting tax rates or revenues to either stimulate or contract economic activity; intended to offset cyclical fluctuations in economic activity.

Fisher Effect Adjustments of nominal interest rates as borrowers and lenders compensate for expected inflation in order to secure some equilibrium "real" rate of interest.

Fixed Costs The total of all costs not related to the level of production; fixed costs are also known as historical, sunk, or overhead costs, and are irrelevant for rational decision making.

Fixed Exchange Rates A system in which international agreements set the values of all currencies in terms of one another; the exchange rates of currencies are not allowed to respond to changes in the relative supplies and demands for the currencies; balance of payments surpluses and deficits occur in a fixed exchange rate system when equilibrium exchange rates differ from the fixed (pegged) exchange rates and can be eliminated only through adjustments of Aggregate Demands or Aggregate Supplies.

Flexible (Floating) Exchange Rates The major alternative to a system of fixed exchange rates; under this exchange rate system, markets for individual currencies determine their equilibrium and actual exchange rates.

Flexible Wages, Prices, and Interest Rates According to classical theory, full employment was guaranteed by the existence of perfectly flexible wages, prices, and interest rates. (See also Say's Law.)

Flow Variable An economic variable that is only meaningful if measured over a period of time; income and production are examples.

Foreign Exchange A stock of foreign currencies held as an asset.

Foreign Sector Substitution Effect Tendency to import more and export less in response to an increase in the price level, and to invest more abroad and less domestically because a higher price level normally entails higher domestic production costs. Partially accounts for the negative slope of the Aggregate Demand curve. (See also Wealth Effect and Interest Rate Effect.)

Forward (Futures) Markets Markets in which contracts to deliver currencies or products at some future date are bought and sold.

Fractional Reserve Banking System A banking system in which banks are legally required to hold only a fraction of their demand deposit liabilities in the form of reserves.

Free Enterprise System Agreements to trade are made by private buyers and sellers; ownership of resources is private, not social.

Free Good A good for which the quantity demanded fails to exceed the quantity available at a price of zero.

Free-Rider Problem Encountered in the consumption of public goods; refers to the lack of incentives for people to reveal their true preferences for public goods once these goods are provided; nonexclusive goods can be consumed at a zero price by those who contribute nothing to cover their production costs.

Frictional Unemployment Unemployment that exists because no one possesses perfect knowledge concerning job opportunities, nor free mobility between places of employment; lends a certain flexibility to the economy.

Functional Distribution of Income A breakdown of total income into the proportions paid to owners of various types of resources.

Functional Finance The view that balance in the economy is important and that imbalance in the federal budget is not important.

Future Goods Investments (postponed consumption) that boost productive capacity.

Gains from Scale Cost savings realized because international trade enables firms to become larger because they serve larger markets.

Gains from Specialization of Labor The extra output yielded when workers combine different types of expertise to perform a particular task.

Gains from Trade Improvements in human welfare because trading parties gain by acquiring (*a*) unique goods that they could not produce, (*b*) goods at lower costs than could be yielded by own-production, (*c*) transfers of technology (*d*) greater income that, through higher saving, stimulates investment, (*e*) gains from economies of scale made possible by larger markets, and (*f*) calmer relations with other people because of mutual interdependence.

Galloping Inflation Increases in the price level at double-digit or faster rates annually.

Game Theory A technique that requires assessing the potential gains and losses from all possible strategies by all participants in some activity so that the most likely combinations of choices and outcomes can be ascertained.

General Equilibrium Analysis A method of analysis that not only looks at the direct effects of some variables on others, but also at indirect effects and feedbacks among the economic variables.

General Training Training that increases the productivity of a worker equally for numerous possible places of employment.

GNP (Implicit Price) Deflator A price index composed largely of components from the **CPI** and **PPI**; used to adjust nominal GNP for changes in the price level.

GNP Gap The amount by which current GNP is below full-employment GNP.

Gold Standard Money may be exchanged at a fixed rate for gold; e.g., until 1969, one ounce of gold could be bought from the U.S. Treasury for $35, or sold to it for $35.

Good Anything which satisfies a human want and, in so doing, increases human happiness.

Gresham's Law Bad money drives out good.

Grim Strategy In game theory, entails refusal to commit to a position until other players commit to a position.

Gross National Product (GNP) The value of all production that takes place annually.

Herfindahl-Hirschman Index (HHI) The sum of the squares of the market shares of the firms in an industry; HHIs are now used as guidelines for antitrust actions.

Hoarding Holding money in idle cash balances; money that is hoarded is not spent on consumption or investment; causes velocity to fall.

Horizontal Combination A firm which has numerous plants producing identical or similar products.

Household Income Used for consumption, saving, or taxes.

Households Individual or family units that provide input services, and that are the ultimate storehouses of wealth; they purchase goods in the output markets, and they sell resources in input markets.

Human Capital Improvements made in the labor embodied in human beings; people invest in human capital so that their labor services become both more productive and more highly paid.

Human Capital Discrimination Reduces access by certain groups to schooling, on-the-job training, or to human capital investments.

Humphrey-Hawkins (Full Employment and Balanced Growth) Act (1978) Augments the Employment Act of 1946 by (*a*) identifying specific economic priorities; (*b*) directing the president to cstablish goals based on those priorities; and (*c*) creating procedures to improve the coordination and development of economic policy between the president, the Congress, and the Federal Reserve System.

Hyperinflation Increases in the price level at rates exceeding 50 percent per month.

Idle Cash Balances Money that is hoarded.

Impact Lag The period that passes before newly implemented changes in policy have an impact on economic activity; the impact lag of tax policy is short relative to that of monetary policy.

Implicit Contract Unspoken agreements between firms and workers that the firm will continue to provide jobs when economic conditions are poor if the employee does not demand huge wage increases during periods of prosperity.

Implicit Costs The opportunity costs of all resources that a firm's owner makes available for production without direct outlays of money; examples are the values of the entrepreneur's funds, labor, and land tied up in the firm.

Imports Goods produced in foreign countries and consumed or invested domestically.

Income Approach to Estimating GNP GNP is the sum of personal consumption, total savings, and total taxes (GNP = C + S + T).

Income Effect Changes in consumption patterns arising because price changes also change the purchasing power of money incomes; may be positive, negative, or zero.

Income Elasticity of Demand A measure of the responsiveness of the quantity demanded of a good to changes in real income; computed by dividing the percentage change in the quantity demanded of a good by the percentage change in real income: $\%\Delta Q_{xd} / \%\Delta Y$.

Income Velocity (V) of Money $V = PQ/M$; the number of times annually that the average unit of money changes hands during the process of purchasing GNP (PQ).

Incomes Policies Measures intended to curb inflation without reducing Aggregate Demand expenditures; these policies include jawboning, wage and price guidelines, and wage and price controls.

Increase in Demand When the entire demand curve shifts upward and to the right; more will be purchased at every price; occurs only if one of the nonprice determinants of demand changes.

Increase in Supply When the entire supply curve shifts rightwards; buyers will be offered more at every price; occurs only if a nonprice determinant of supply changes; causes equilibrium price to decrease.

Increasing Cost Industry An industry whose long-run supply curve is an upward sloping line; higher costs per unit are incurred as production in the industry increases.

Index Numbers Numbers used to make relative comparisons of a specific variable between time periods.

Indicative Planning France, whose economy is primarily capitalistic, has used indicative planning, which entails trying to coordinate economic activity by setting production targets for major industries.

Indifference Curve A line connecting the various combinations of two goods that yield the same total utility; the consumer is indifferent among the various bundles of goods along an indifference curve.

Indirect Business Taxes Various taxes that are viewed by business firms as costs of production; are not part of National Income since they are not resource payments. Examples are sales and excise taxes.

Induced Expenditures Expenditures that depend on income.

Industrial Policy Government uses subsidies, tax breaks, and protection from foreign competition to support "target industries" that have high productivity, strong "linkages", or future importance.

Industry All firms that compete in some product market.

Industry Interest Theory of Regulation Regulation of industry serves, not the public interest, but instead serves the particular interests of the regulated industries.

Infant Industry Argument for Tariffs The notion that emerging industries need to be protected from more efficient, established, foreign competitors.

Inferior Good A good for which the income elasticity of demand is negative; the demand for this type of economic good varies inversely with real income; technically, a good for which the income effect of a price change is negative.

Inflation Upward movements of the absolute price level.

Inflationary Gap The amount by which autonomous expenditures exceed those necessary for full employment income or output.

Informative Advertising Accurate information provided to consumers so that good economic choices can be made at lowered transaction costs; not a waste of resources.

In-Kind Transfers Welfare paid, not as cash, but rather as, e.g., food stamps, educational grants, or housing allowances.

Innovation In the 1930s, Joseph Schumpeter argued that progress in capitalist systems is driven by major innovations, including: (*a*) introduction of a new good, or new quality in a familiar product; (*b*) introduction of new technology; (*c*) opening of a new market; (*d*) discovery of a major source of raw materials; and (*e*) reorganization of a major industry.

Inputs Things used in the production process, such as labor and raw or semifinished materials.

Interest Payments per time period for the use of capital services.

Interest Rate Effect The Aggregate Demand curve slopes down in part because higher price levels increase the interest rate, which reduces purchases; dollar amounts required to finance a given investment grow, while the nominal supply of loanable funds available does not.

Intermediaries (Middlemen) Firms that convey goods from the ultimate producer to the ultimate user. Intermediaries are profitable only if they reduce transaction costs.

Intermediate Goods Semiprocessed goods used in the production of other economic goods.

International Trade Exchanges of goods across national boundaries; facilitates efficient uses of the world's scarce resources.

Investment Additions to real capital stock, i.e., all final purchases of capital equipment (machinery, tools, etc.), all residential or commercial construction, and changes in inventories.

Invisible Hand Adam Smith's term for automatic market adjustments toward equilibrium.

Involuntary Saving Occurs when government policies decrease consumption in order to stimulate capital accumulation; governments can force individuals to save a portion of their income through taxation, inflationary financing of government expenditures, or by setting low wages and high prices.

Jawboning Oratory used by policymakers to persuade people or institutions to act against their individual interests; especially common as an exhortation to hold prices below equilibrium levels.

Joint Profit Maximization A cartel of oligopolistic firms tries to share the profits that a monopoly would make if it controlled the industry.

Key Currency An international medium of exchange; use of the U.S. dollar as an international medium of exchange was a major reason the U.S. has been able to run persistently large balance of payments deficits since 1951.

Keynes Effect The initial decreases (*increases*) in both the nominal interest rate and the real interest rate brought about by faster (*slower*) growth of the nominal money supply.

Keynesian Fiscal Policy Policies designed to combat the problems associated with inadequate Aggregate Demand.

Keynesian Government Growth Ratchet The tendency for government to grow because policymakers cut taxes and expand spending during economic downturns but do not raise taxes or cut spending during inflationary episodes.

Keynesian Investment Schedule The idea that investment demand is insensitive to movements of the interest rate, but that it is very sensitive to changes in expectations.

Keynesian Liquidity Preference The idea that the demand for money is extremely sensitive to interest rate movements and may even become horizontal at very low interest rates.

Keynesian Model A framework used to describe how output responds to changes in Aggregate Demand; generally ignores price level changes.

Keynesian Monetary Transmission Mechanism The idea that changes in the nominal money supply affect consumer spending only indirectly; money → interest rate → investment → income represents the chain of events emanating from a change in the money supply's rate of growth.

Keynesian Theory Specifies that macroeconomic adjustments involve changes in quantities below full employment and that price level changes only become the major adjustment mechanism after Aggregate Demand exceeds a full employment level.

Keynes' Fundamental Psychological Law of Consumption Consumption expenditures increase as income rises, but by a smaller amount.

Kinked Demand Curve Model An oligopolistic pricing model that explains noncollusive oligopolistic behavior and predicts stickiness or rigidity of prices in oligopolistic industries.

Labor Labor services are typically measured in terms of the total amount of time worked during a given interval.

Labor Force Participation Rate (LFPR) The proportion of a population in the labor force; computed by dividing the labor force by the total population (or sub-population).

Labor Theory of Value The idea that the value of anything is exactly proportional to the labor time socially necessary for its production; this approach was the standard economic explanation of price until late in the 1800s and is still an article of faith among orthodox Marxists.

Labor Unions A worker organization that negotiate labor contracts with firms' managers to set wages and the conditions of work.

Laffer Curve A figure showing that very high tax rates may so discourage productive efforts that fewer tax revenues are collected than if tax rates were substantially lower.

Laissez-Faire This philosophy embraces the notion that a market system operates most efficiently when government minimizes its activity in the economy; according to this philosophy, governments should provide national defense and police protection, specify property rights, and enforce contracts drawn up between economic agents—and little or nothing else. (See also capitalism, socialism.)

Land Includes all natural resources, such as unimproved land, minerals, water, air, timber, wildlife, and fertility of the soil.

Legal Barriers to Entry Governmentally erected barriers to entry into an industry; these barriers maintain monopoly power by legally prohibiting or limiting competition from other firms; barriers include patents, copyrights, and licensing or bonding restrictions.

Legal Incidence of a Tax Falls on the party who legally must pay the tax to government, but the economic burdens may be shifted to others.

Legal Reserves Total bank reserves; the sum of bankers' required reserves and excess reserves.

Lemons Market The notion that adverse selection will cause the market for used cars to be dominated by bad used cars (lemons) because asymmetric information causes good used cars ("creampuffs") and lemons to sell for the same prices. Sometimes generalized to other markets, e.g., labor markets.

Lerner Index of Monopoly Power (LMP) An estimate of monopoly power using the percent by which price of output exceeds marginal cost; monopoly power is then measured as: $(P - MC)/P$.

Libertarianism A philosophy based on the notion that individual freedom is the most important social goal; libertarianism emphasizes the inherently coercive nature of government, and urges reliance on the free market system to resolve nearly every human problem.

Limit Pricing Occurs when firms that possess monopoly power set a profitable price that is low enough to discourage potential entrants.

Liquidity How easy (costless) it is to turn an asset into cash; the transaction costs entailed with the purchase or sale of an asset is directly related to its illiquidity.

Liquidity Preference The total demand for money in a Keynesian model; derived by summing the transactions, precautionary, and asset (speculative) demands for money.

Liquidity Trap The horizontal portion of the Keynesian liquidity preference curve; occurs only when economic transactors choose to hold all increases in the nominal money supply in idle cash balances; it is doubtful if perfect liquidity traps have ever existed.

Logrolling When legislators trade votes.

Long Run (LR) A period of sufficient duration for all feasible resource adjustments to any event to be completed.

Long-Run Average Cost Curve (LRAC) A curve showing the minimum average costs of producing each level of output after adjusting all resource inputs, including the size of the plant.

Long Wave Theory of Business Cycles A theory of long (50–60 year) waves in economic activity was developed in the 1920s by a Russian economist named Kondratieff.

Lorenz Curve A Lorenz curve shows the degree of inequality that exists in distributions of income or wealth in a particular society.

M1 = currency + demand deposits in commercial banks + all interest paying checkable accounts.

M2 = M1 + short term time deposits.

M3 = M2 + long-term deposits (Certificates of Deposit or CDs).

Macroeconomic Equilibrium Occurs when Aggregate Supply and Aggregate Demand are equal; causes the economy to be stationary.

Macroeconomics The branch of economics concerned with aggregate variables such as the levels of total economic activity, unemployment, inflation, the balance of payments, economic growth and development, the money supply, and the federal budget.

Majority Rule When the winning side of a vote must capture 50 percent plus one vote.

Malthusian Prognosis Reverend Thomas Malthus, an early nineteenth century English economist, promulgated the dismal notion that all workers were doomed to live a subsistence existence; in formulating his forecast, Malthus neglected to consider birth control and the favorable impact of technological advances on the world's ability to produce food.

Marginalism The idea that virtually all decisions

are based on the effects of small changes from a current situation.

Margin Requirements A FED tool that sets the legal minimum percentage down payments required for purchases of stock.

Marginal Cost = Marginal Revenue (MC = MR) A condition required for maximum profits. Typically, $MR > MC$ for units prior to the $MR = MC$ level of output, so extra output boosts profit or cuts losses. Higher output levels than the $MR = MC$ level entail $MR < MC$ and would not be produced.

Marginal Cost (MC) The change in total cost associated with producing an additional unit of output; computed by dividing the change in total cost (ΔTC) by the change in output (ΔQ): $MC = \Delta TC/\Delta Q = \Delta TVC/\Delta Q$.

Marginal Physical Product of Labor (MPP$_L$) The additional output produced by an additional unit of labor; computed by dividing the change in total output (ΔQ) by the change in labor (ΔL): $\Delta Q/\Delta L$.

Marginal Propensity to Consume (MPC) The change in saving brought about by a small change in disposable income ($MPC = \Delta C/\Delta Y_d$).

Marginal Propensity to Save (MPS) The change in saving brought about by a small change in disposable income ($MPS = \Delta S/\Delta Y^d$).

Marginal Resource (or Marginal Factor) Cost (MRC) The additional cost incurred in purchasing the services of an additional unit of a productive input; computed by dividing the change in total cost of production (ΔTC) by the change in input (ΔN): that is, $\Delta TC/\Delta N$; also computed by dividing the change in total variable costs of production (ΔTVC) by the change in input (ΔN): that is, $\Delta TVC/\Delta N$.

Marginal Revenue (MR) The additional revenue associated with selling an additional unit of output; computed by dividing the change in total revenue by the change in output: $MR = \Delta TR/\Delta Q$.

Marginal Revenue Product (MRP) The additional total revenue generated by an added unit of a variable input; computed by dividing the change in total revenue (ΔTR) by the change in input (ΔN): that is $\Delta TR/\Delta N$; or by multiplying marginal revenue by the marginal physical product of a resource: that is, $MR \times MPP_n$.

Marginal Social Benefits (MSB) Computed by summing the marginal private benefits and the marginal external benefits, if any, from consuming additional units of commodities or services.

Marginal Social Costs The sum of marginal private costs and any marginal external costs incurred in producing additional units of a good.

Marginal Utility (MU) The added utility or satisfaction derived by a consumer from the consumption of an additional unit of a good.

Market Mechanisms that enable buyers and sellers to strike bargains and to transact.

Market Demand Curve A graphic representation totalling all individual demand curves; it is derived for the most goods by horizontally summing all individual demand curves.

Market Economies Systems that rely on market interaction of supplies and demands to resolve the economic problem; the price system is used to coordinate the diverse plans of consumers and producers.

Market Equilibrium When neither shortages nor surpluses exist because at the prevailing price, the quantities demanded and supplied are equal.

Market Failure When the market resolution of an economic problem is inefficient, inequitable, or unstable.

Market Period An interval too short to allow changes in decisions about amounts of output, so that only prices may be varied.

Market Price The price that is confronted in the market whether we buy or not.

Market Supply Curve A figure derived by horizontally summing all individual supply curves.

Market System See Capitalism, Free Enterprise System.

Maximizing Behavior *Homo sapiens* are perceived as human calculators who strive to maximize pleasure and to minimize pain.

Measure of (Net) Economic Welfare (MEW) A welfare measure obtained after deducting from GNP items that do not contribute to economic welfare and adding items that do, but which are not counted in GNP.

Measure of Value and Unit of Account The function performed by money as a common denominator through which the relative prices of goods are stated; reduces the information costs associated with exchange.

Median Voter Model Suggests that the median voter must be captured to achieve a majority of the vote, and attempts to explain why political parties and candidates tend to be so similar, and why two parties tend to dominate electoral processes.

Medium of Exchange The most important service that money provides; refers to standard items used to execute transactions.

Menu (Repricing) Costs of Inflation The costs in time and effort incurred in redesigning rate schedules and repricing goods.

Mercantilism A discredited economic doctrine that fostered imperialism and advocated surpluses in a country's balance of trade.

Merger The joining of two or more firms into a single firm.

Microeconomics The branch of economics that focuses on individual decision making, the allocation of resources, and how prices, production, and the distribution of income are determined.

Mid-Point Bases Used in elasticity calculations to avoid ambiguity in measuring percentage changes to variables. An average of the beginning and ending period is used as the base from which relative changes are measured.

Minimum Efficient Scale (MES) of Production The smallest output level that allows a firm to reach the lowest possible long run average cost.

Mixed Economies Societies in which some allocations rely on the market system while others rely government or some other allocative mechanism.

Model The structure of a theory.

Monetarism The idea that erratic growth in the money supply is the major cause of macroeconomic instability.

Monetarist Monetary Transmission Mechanism The idea that changes in the growth rate of the nominal money supply affect private spending directly; an increase in the money supply yields a proportional rise in nominal GNP: $MS \rightarrow (C + I) \rightarrow Y$ is the causal chain emanating from a change in the monetary growth rate.

Monetary Base or High-Powered Money (MB) The total of bank reserves plus currency held by the nonbanking public.

Monetary Growth Rule The idea that the economy will be relatively stable if the money supply is set to grow at a low fixed percentage rate regardless of short run economic conditions.

Money Illusion Decision makers suffer from money illusion if their decisions are based on movements of the monetary values of economic variables rather than on the real values of the variables.

Money Multiplier (m_p, m_a) Potentially equals the reciprocal of the reserve requirement ratio ($m_p = 1/rr$) – the number which, when multiplied by a change in total reserves, yields the potential change in the money supply. Actually, $m_a = MS/MB$ because of currency holdings of the public, excess reserves, and other leakages.

Monopolistic Competition An industry in which many firms sell slightly differentiated goods and there is freedom of entry or exit; monopolistic competition resembles pure competition, but goods are heterogeneous and each firm possesses a bit of monopoly power.

Monopoly The lone seller of a good that has no close substitutes.

Monopoly Power Possessed whenever a seller can force prices up by restricting output.

Monopsonist The sole buyer of a particular good or resource.

Monopsony Power Possessed whenever a buyer can force price down by restricting purchases.

Moral hazard When a contract creates an incentive for opportunistic behavior that raises the costs or lowers the benefits to the other party.

Moral Suasion See "Jawboning."

Multiplier Effect The total change in spending that results when new autonomous spending boosts income which, in turn, is spent, creating more income, and so on. See also Autonomous Spending Multiplier.

Nash Equilibrium A strategy combination in game theory where no player has a net incentive to change unless other players change.

National Banks Banks chartered by the Comptroller of the Currency and that must be members of the Federal Reserve System.

National Debt The value of government bonds in the hands of the public or foreigners.

National Income (NI) A measure of economic activity computed by summing all resource incomes; equals the sum of wages and salaries, rents, interest, and the corporate and noncorporate incomes of firms.

Natural Barriers to Entry Significant barriers to entry that result from the nature of the economic good or from the cost structure inherent in its production.

Natural Monopoly A market in which only one seller can most efficiently produce an economic good; the production process is characterized by tremendously large fixed costs and relatively small variable costs; emerges where the market demand is small relative to the economies of scale.

Natural Rate Theory The notion that the economy is inherently stable and that unemployment and real interest will coincide with their natural rates in the long run; according to this theory, traditional Keynesian policy goals are unattainable because attempts to drive down unemployment or real interest rates more than can be reconciled with people's preferences are self-defeating in the long run.

Negative Externality When a market transaction imposes costs on third parties not directly involved in any aspect of the exchange.

Negative Income Taxes (NIT) Negative income tax plans represent attempts to reconcile equity and efficiency considerations in resolving the problems posed by income inequality and poverty; the negative income tax plan maintains incentives for recipients to work to earn additional income.

Net Investment Gross investment minus depreciation; represents net additions to an economy's capital stock or productive capacity.

Net National Product (NNP) The net value of commodities and services produced in the economy after adjusting for the fact that we have used up productive capacity; equals GNP minus depreciation; also equals National Income (**NI**) plus indirect business taxes.

Neutral Tax Imposition of a neutral tax distorts neither consumer buying patterns nor the methods used by firms in the conduct of their business; in other words, the imposition of a neutral tax does not distort relative prices by inducing substitution effects.

New Classical Macroeconomics Modern theories that extend classical theories of competitive markets; normally supports laissez faire macroeconomic policies.

New Industrial Organization (new I-O) In contrast to the more traditional Structure-Conduct-Performance (SCP) approach, new I-O de-emphasizes the numbers of competitors in an industry, and stresses (*a*) how economic interactions can be better modeled with *game theory*, (*b*) how *asymmetric information* among transactors shapes business decisions and market structures, and (*c*) how *strategies* develop in response to the specifics of different competitive environments.

Nominal Rate of Interest The average annual percentage monetary premium paid for the use of money.

Nominal Values The current dollar values of economic variables.

Nondiscretionary Fiscal Policy See Automatic Stabilizers.

Nondurable Goods Goods that are used up in less than one year.

Noneconomic Costs of Unemployment Include the psychological trauma of being unemployed and the social unrest unemployment engenders.

Nonexclusive Good A good is nonexclusive if a person can enjoy it without paying for the right to consume; the result when it is relatively expensive to prevent individuals from consuming a good.

Nonrival Good A good is nonrival if consumption of the good by an individual does not prevent consumption of the same unit of that good by other people.

Normal Good Any good with a positive income elasticity of demand.

Normal Profits A normal cost of production; income that entrepreneurs must receive to make production worthwhile to them.

Normative Economics Deals with values and addresses what should be rather than what is.

Occam's Razor The "principle of parsimony," which suggests that the simplest workable theories are also the best and most useful.

Occupational Discrimination Exclusion of certain groups from particular occupations.

Oligopoly A market in which several large firms control most of an industry's output. The few firms that comprise the industry must each consider other firms' reactions before setting its policies; mutually interdependent behavior is the unique characteristic of oligopoly; the importance of predictability leads to cooperation between firms. Pure oligopolies produces homogeneous outputs, while impure oligopolies produce slightly differentiated outputs.

Open Market Operations When the FED's Open Market Committee buys and sells U.S. bonds; these operations determine the size of the money supply by altering the amounts of reserves in the banking system.

Open Shop A firm that employs workers without considering union membership.

Opportunity Cost The value of the next best opportunity to a good or to some activity.

Opportunity Cost of Money Keynesians view the true price of money as the interest rate, since the closest alternatives to money as an asset are stocks, bonds, and other assets that pay interest. Monetarists argue, instead, that the true price of money is the reciprocal of the absolute price level—the purchasing power of money—since money is a substitute for all other goods and assets.

Outputs Transformed materials; the results of production.

Paradox of Thrift The possibility suggested by Keynes that an increase in saving at all income levels (depicted by an upward shift of the saving function) may cause equilibrium income or output to decrease, and could result in less saving rather than more.

Parity The idea that government subsidies should be used to ensure that agricultural goods' prices are stable relative to other prices.

Partial Equilibrium Analysis A method of economic analysis which looks at the direct effects of some chosen variables on others, assuming other influences constant.

Partnership An unincorporated firm formed by two or more persons.

Passive Policy Setting permanent policies (e.g., a monetary growth rule) and allowing the market system to adjust to any temporary shocks to the economy.

Patents Legal barriers to entry that extend to their holders a renewable right to produce an economic good for 17 years and that prohibits the production of the good by other firms; intended to promote research and development of new goods and technologies.

Payoff Matrix In game theory, a table that matches sets of gains or losses when "players" choose from the options available to them. The payoff to any player from selecting a particular option depends on the option(s) selected by other players.

Peak (Boom) The phase of the business cycle when a preponderance of measures of economic activity are at their high points.

Per Capita Income A crude measure of economic well-being computed by dividing National Income by the population.

Perfectly Price Elastic Demand or Supply Curves Horizontal lines at the current market price; perfectly price elastic demand or supply curves have a price elasticity of infinity at every point.

Permanent Income (Wealth) The average income expected over one's lifetime; according to Milton Friedman, permanent income explains a person's patterns of consumption and money holdings.

Perpetuity A bond that will pay a fixed amount of money each year until it is purchased by the government that issued it.

Personal Discrimination Bigotry; generates inequitable housing conditions, higher prices for comparable goods, reduced medical care, and other problems.

Persuasive (Competitive) Advertising Designed to persuade or to mislead consumers rather than to inform them; entails a waste of resources.

Phillips Curve An inverse statistical relationship between the rate of change of the general price level and the rate of unemployment; in 1959, A. W. Phillips, an English economist, reported an empirical foundation for the idea that policymakers faced a permanent trade-off between unemployment and inflation; during the 1970s, the Phillips curve proved highly unstable.

Planned Injections Equal to Planned Withdrawals A condition necessary for macroeconomic equilibrium. Injections include all forms of autonomous spending; withdrawals represent such dilutions from spending streams as saving or taxation.

Planned or Intended Investment The amount of investment that business firms desire to make at each income level, assuming that business expectations remain unchanged.

Planned or Intended Saving The amounts of saving desired at each income level, assuming that savers' expectations remain constant.

Plant A production facility with a specific location, it may be involved in processing, fabrication, assembly, wholesale, or retail.

Plurality When the outcome of an election is

determined by which side gets the most votes; a majority is unnecessary.

Point Voting When each voter is assigned a certain number of votes and can cast them among various electoral issues depending on the intensity of preferences.

Political Business Cycles Swings in economic activity that occur when macroeconomic policies are manipulated to improve incumbents' chances of reelection. The economy booms before elections, and stagnates after them.

Pollution In economic parlance, a negative externality.

Pollution Abatement Programs Techniques used to reduce pollution.

Pork Barrel Legislation that yields benefits that are primarily local, but where funding is by the national government.

Positive Economics Value-free descriptions of and predictions about testable relationships among economic variables.

Positive Externality Occurs when a market activity bestows benefits on economic transactors who are not direct parties to the activity.

Potential GNP What an economy could produce at high rates of utilization of all resources; full employment GNP approximates potential GNP.

Precautionary Demand for Money The amount of money that economic transactors desire to hold to cover unexpected expenses; is positively related to income or wealth.

Present Value The present value of any asset is the value now of the income stream expected from the asset, discounted by the interest rate; the demand price of the asset.

Pretrade Costs The rate of exchange that exists domestically between two goods prior to international trade; also referred to as the domestic terms of trade; given by the slope at each point along the production possibility frontier.

Price Ceiling A maximum legal price set at the behest of buyers.

Price Discrimination Occurs when essentially the same good is sold at different prices, and price differentials do not reflect different production costs; perfect price discrimination absorbs all potential consumer surplus derived from consuming a good.

Price Elasticity of Demand (or Supply) Measures of the responsiveness of the quantity demanded (**supplied**) of a good to changes in the price of the good; roughly computed by dividing percentage changes in quantities demanded (**supplied**) of a good by the percentage changes in its price: $\%\Delta Q_{xd}/\%\Delta P_x$ (or $\%\Delta Q_{xs}/\%\Delta P_x$). To see how these percentage changes are calculated, however, see Mid-Point Bases. (See also Elasticity, Income Elasticity of Demand.)

Price Floor A minimum legal price set at the behest of sellers.

Price Taker or Quantity Adjuster A competitive buyer or seller whose actions do not affect prices; they can choose only among quantities.

Principal/Agent Problem When an agent (e.g., an employee) pursues personal goals that conflict with the principal's (e.g., the employer's) contractual rights.

Prisoners' Dilemma A noncooperative "game" in which every player's dominant strategy imposes losses on all other players. The result is that all players lose relative to the payoffs available if all players followed cooperative strategies.

Private Debt Debts owed by consumers or business firms.

Private Ownership System Resources are privately owned.

Privatization The conversion of a government activity into a private business.

Product Differentiation When consumers perceive differences in competing goods; real differences in similar products may be related to durability, styling, or other physical characteristics; imaginary differences result from advertising or the imaginations of consumers; firms use product differentiation to try shift the demands for their products to the right and to decrease the price elasticity of the demands for their goods.

Production Occurs when materials are transformed in ways that make them more valuable.

Production Function The technical relationship that exists between inputs and outputs; allows all inputs to vary as different rates of production are achieved; not synonymous with total product curve.

Production Possibility Frontier (PPF) A curve showing the various combinations of goods that an economy could produce, assuming a fixed technology and full employment and efficient resource utilization.

Profit The excess of a firm's total revenues over total cost; accounting profits consider only the explicit costs incurred by a firm; economists view total costs in terms of opportunity costs, which include both explicit and implicit costs; is a return to entrepreneurs for bearing uncertainty and innovating.

Progressive Taxes Tax rates which vary directly with income, so that the proportion of income devoted to taxes rises as income rises.

Promotional Profits The increases in the values of stock controlled by individuals who engineer a merger.

Property Rights Legal rights that people possess over property; the broadest of property rights are *fee-simple* property rights that allow individuals: (*a*) to use goods in any manner so long as other people's property rights are not violated; (*b*) to exchange these property rights for others; and (*c*) to deny the use of their goods to others.

Property Tax A tax based on the value of capital improvements and land.

Proportional Taxes Tax rates that do not vary with income; the same percentage of income is collected in taxes regardless of the income level.

Proprietors Individuals in business for themselves.

Psychic Income Value of nonmonetary satisfaction gained from an activity.

Psychological Theories of the Business Cycle Focus on the herd instincts of human beings coupled with prolonged periods of optimism and pessimism.

Public Choice Economic interpretations of political behavior.

Public Debt Created when government spends more than it collects in tax revenue; the public debt grows when government sells bonds to the public in order to finance a deficit.

Public Good A public good is a good which can be consumed by more than one individual at a time (nonrivalry) and whose consumption cannot be denied a consumer who desires it (nonexclusion) once the good is provided.

Public Interest Theory of Regulation This theory suggests that government should control unethical business practices and regulate businesses plagued by such market failures as: (*a*) externalities, or (*b*) monopoly power derived from economies of scale.

Quantity Demanded The amount of a good purchased at a given price.

Quantity Supplied The amount of a good supplied at a given price.

Quantity Theory of Money The idea that the dominant determinant of the price level is the money supply. An extreme version attributes all inflation to excessive monetary growth.

Queuing Allocating goods or resources on a first come/first served basis. This tends to result in queues (lining up for access).

Quota A quantitative restriction on trade, the imposition of quotas raises the prices of imported goods and causes failure to fully realize potential gains from international trade.

Rate Base The value of a regulated firm's capital stock to which an acceptable, or fair, rate of return applies.

Rate of Return The annualized average size of the income stream per time period as a percentage of the dollar outlay for an investment.

Rational Expectations The notion that markets operate so efficiently that policy goals will not be achieved, even in the short run, unless the timing and the effects of demand-management policies come as surprises to the public.

Rational Ignorance Decision makers will search for information only as long as the expected benefit exceeds the expected cost and, thus, people may choose to be rationally ignorant of much information.

Real Business Cycles Some new classical macroeconomists contend that external shocks to Aggregate Supply are permanent, and do not represent merely temporary departures from a long run trend of economic growth. Concludes that activist policies are unwarranted.

Real Rate of Interest The annual percentage premium of purchasing power paid by a borrower to a lender for the use of money; the amount of extra goods, expressed in percentage terms, that can be enjoyed if consumption is delayed; computed by adjusting the nominal interest rate for the rate of general price change.

Real Values The current dollar value of economic variables after adjustment for price level changes. (See also deflating.)

Recession Modern name for a depression.

Recessionary Gap A deficiency in autonomous expenditure that, if filled, would be multiplied so that full employment output was achieved.

Recognition Lag Arises because policymakers'

perceptions about current economic conditions are clouded, and time and effort are required to gather, compile, process, and interpret data to gain some feeling for any widespread changes in economic activity; applies equally to both monetary and fiscal policies.

Regressive Taxes Tax rates which vary inversely with income, so that tax payments decline relative to income as income rises.

Reindustrialization See **Industrial Policy.**

Relative Price Price of a good in terms of another good. (See also Absolute Price.)

Rent Payments per time period for the services of land. (See also Economic Rent.)

Rent-Seeking Attempts by special interest groups to shape public policies to their advantage, even though such policies may impose excessive costs on the general public.

Required Reserves (RR) The reserves that banks are legally required to hold against their deposits.

Reserve Requirement Ratio (rr) The fraction of its deposit liabilities that a bank must hold in reserves.

Reserves The amounts of money held in a bank's vault or on deposit at the FED to meet withdrawals of deposits.

Resources Land, labor, capital, and entrepreneurship.

Ricardian Equivalence The idea that people will adjust so that whether government spending is financed by taxes or bonds is irrelevant.

Risk The likelihood of an event for which a probability can reasonably be estimated. (See Uncertainty.)

Rival Good A good is rival if consumption of a unit of the good by one individual exhausts that particular unit so that another individual cannot consume it.

Robinson-Patman Act (1936) Strengthened the Clayton Act's limits on price discrimination; however, it permitted discounts if they could be justified by differences in costs of production or if they were introduced as "good faith" efforts to meet competition.

Rule of Reason The rule of reason approach to the Sherman Act permitted certain restrictive practices of a firm despite their anticompetitive effects if the firm could prove that its conduct was based on sound business practice and was secondary to its primary business practices.

Rule of 72 The time required for some variable to double is calculated by dividing its percentage annual growth rate into 72. This approach adjusts for compounding (e.g., interest on interest).

Sales Tax A percentage tax that is typically levied on the sales value of most commodities and/or services.

Saving The change in one's total wealth over some period of time.

Say's Law "Supply creates its own demand"; that is, the very act of producing a product creates an equivalent amount of demand, since people do not work for the sake of work alone; named after the classical economist, Jean Baptiste Say.

Scarce Good A good for which the quantity demanded exceeds the amount available at a zero monetary price.

Scarcity A state the results because resources are limited and cannot accommodate all of our unlimited wants.

Screening When a principal examines the qualifications of a potential agent before offering the agent a contract.

Seasonal Unemployment Unemployment that varies with the season.

Seignorage The profits made by governments when they coin or print money.

Sellers' Market When the prevailing market price lies below the equilibrium price, resulting in a shortage.

Services Intangible economic goods.

Sherman Antitrust Act (1890) Our first antitrust law; specifies that "every contract, combination in the form of trust or otherwise, or conspiracy, in restraint of trade or commerce among the several States, or with foreign nations, is hereby declared illegal"; and, according to the second section, "every person who shall monopolize, or attempt to monopolize . . . shall be deemed guilty of a felony."

Shifted Backward A tax is shifted backward when its economic incidence falls on owners of resources supplied to the firm.

Shifted Forward A tax is said to be shifted forward when the economic incidence of the tax falls on the consumer.

Shirking A principal/agent problem that occurs when an agent (e.g., an employee) fails to perform satisfactorily because the principal (e.g., an employer) cannot adequately monitor the agent's performance.

Shocks An external shock (e.g., war or bad weather) causes macroeconomic disequilibrium by disrupting Aggregate Supply.

Shortage Occurs if some people cannot buy all of an economic good for which they are willing to pay the going price.

Short Run (SR) An analytic period of time in which at least one resource is fixed so that firms can neither enter nor leave the marketplace — a firm can shut its plant down, but it cannot leave the industry.

Shutdown Point The price/output combination at which total revenue equals total variable costs; in the short run, the firm must at least cover the variable costs of production; if it cannot, then it will shut down and minimize its losses by incurring only fixed costs.

Signaling Behavior by agents to communicate special qualifications that will elicit the offer of a contract from a principal.

Socialism A system characterized by collective ownership of property and government allocation of resources. (See also Capitalism, Laissez Faire.)

Socially Necessary Labor The Marxist concept that includes not only direct labor time, but also the labor time used to construct factories and to produce capital equipment; Marxists view all commodities and capital as congealed labor.

Special Interest Groups Groups that can gain from public policies that may not be in accord with the interests of other groups or society as a whole.

Specialization When different resources (e.g., people's labor) are used to produce different goods. This is most advantageous when resources are allocated so that every good is produced at the lowest possible opportunity cost.

Specific Training Training that a firm provides a worker that only increases the productivity of the worker for that firm.

Speculative Demand for Money Inversely related to the interest rate; refers to the amount of money that economic transactors desire to hold at alternative interest rates for the purpose of speculating against movements in the prices of stocks or bonds.

Speculators Intermediaries who buy a good in the hope of selling it at a higher price at a later point in time. Profitable speculation tends to reduce price volatility and the risks to others of doing business.

Spillovers (Externalities) When benefits or costs are bestowed upon third parties who are not part of a transaction; produce false price signals and lead to nonoptimal decisions.

Stabilization Attempts to use macroeconomic policy to achieve full employment, price stability, and economic growth.

Stagflation The simultaneous occurrence of high rates of inflation and high rates of unemployment; stagflation, or inflationary recession, occurs during both demand-induced and supply-induced cycles of inflation when Aggregate Supply declines relative to Aggregate Demand.

Standard Industry Classification (SIC) Codes Categories developed by the Bureau of Census in order to classify industries.

Standard of Deferred Payment Money performs this function by being acceptable for contractual obligations involving future payments.

State Banks Banks that are chartered by state governments; they have the option of becoming members of the Federal Reserve System.

Statutory (Legal) Incidence of a Tax Falls on the party responsible for paying the tax, but a tax's economic incidence may be shifted.

Stock See Common Stock.

Stock Variable An economic variable that can be measured holding time constant.

Store of Value Money is a store of value in that, except for inflation, it is a relatively riskless way of holding wealth.

Strategic Behavior Tactic used by existing firms to preclude entry by potential competitors into an industry.

Strategic Behavior Ascertaining how other people ("players" in game theory) are likely to behave, and then following tactics to maximize your gain or minimize any harm to you.

Structural Deficit The budget shortfall that would result because of the design of current government tax and outlay programs, were the economy operating at its capacity. (See also Cyclical Deficit.)

Structural Unemployment Unemployment that arises because workers do not possess the skills required for existing job opportunities.

Structure-Conduct-Performance Paradigm The

theory that *market structure* almost rigidly determines each firm's *conduct* (output decisions and pricing behavior), which yields an industry's overall *performance* (e.g., its efficiency and profitability).

Subsistence Theory of Wages A classical explanation of how wage rates were determined; this theory suggests that wages would be sufficient to meet the biological needs of workers, with only minor adjustments to meet the social and customary needs of workers.

Substitute Goods Goods that are substituted one for another in consumption; positive cross price-elasticities of demand exist between substitute goods.

Substitution Effect the change in the pattern of consumption brought about by a change in the relative price structure; the substitution effect of a price change is always negative, for consumers will always substitute cheaper goods for more expensive goods; the substitution effect is generally so powerful that it serves as the theoretical underpinning for the law of demand.

Superior (Luxury) Good A good for which the income elasticity of demand is greater than one; that is, the demand for this kind of economic good is very sensitive to real income changes.

Supply The amounts of goods or resources that producers or owners are willing to sell in the market under various conditions.

Supply Curve A graphic representation of the maximum quantities of a good or resources that producers or owners are willing to supply at various market prices.

Supply, Law of The quantity of an economic good supplied varies directly with the price of the economic good.

Supply Price The lowest price at which sellers are willing to make a specific quantity of a good available. (See also Demand Price.)

Supply-Side Economics A "New Classical" reemphasis on the importance of the effects of government policies on Aggregate Supply; rebuts Keynesian emphasis on Aggregate Expenditures.

Surplus, or Excess Supply The excess of the quantity supplied over the quantity demanded at a given price.

Surplus Value The difference between the total value of what workers produce and what workers are paid for their labor services; surplus value is expropriated by the capitalists, according to Marxists; surplus value is the sum of rent, interest, and profits.

Survival Principle The idea that the most efficient firms in an industry are those that remain viable over time; the optimal size of firms is indicated by the size of the firm that survives in an industry over time.

Syndicalism A revolutionary sociopolitical theory that advocates the overthrow of government and the reorganization of society into syndicates, which are effectively industrywide trade unions.

Taft-Hartley Act (1947) This legislation amended the Wagner Act and made certain labor union practices unfair, outlawed the closed shop, and permitted individual states to pass "right-to-work" laws that ban union shops.

Tariff A tax on internationally traded goods; the imposition of tariffs raises the prices of imported goods and prevents full realization of potential gains from international trade.

Team Production Most complex forms of production cannot be accomplished efficiently (or at all) by lone individuals or families. Firms coordinate team production to (*a*) reduce transaction costs, and (*b*) exploit economies of scale.

Technological Change Occurs when a given stock of productive inputs produces a greater quantity of output, or when a given amount of output can be produced with fewer productive inputs; refers to greater efficiency in market processes, improved knowledge concerning the use of productive inputs in production, the advent of completely new production processes, improvements in the quality of human and nonhuman resources, and new inventions and innovations. The idea of progress is tightly bound up in the process of technological change.

Terms of Trade The prices of exported goods relative to imported goods after international trade has commenced.

Theory A testable hypothesis concerning the way in which observable facts are related.

Tie-In Sales Attempts by firms to exploit their market power by using tie-in sales agreements that require customers to buy another product as a condition for buying the monopolized good.

Tit-for-Tat In game theory, a strategy that begins cooperatively. Thereafter, in any period, tit-for-tat entails echoing what the opponent did in the previous period.

Total Burdens of a Tax The amounts of money that individuals would have to be paid to make them just as well off with the tax as without.

Total Cost All costs to the firm of producing a particular rate of output; computed by multiplying the quantity of a good produced by the per unit cost of producing the good.

Total Product Curve The technical relationship that exists between production and various levels of one input, assuming that other resources are held constant.

Total Revenue The dollar value of a firm's sales; computed by multiplying the quantity of a good sold by its per unit price.

Total Revenue Minus Total Cost (TR − TC) Approach The profit maximizing firm will produce the rate of output at which total revenue most greatly exceeds total cost.

Trade Adjustment Assistance Provides retraining and financial assistance for workers disemployed because of liberalized international trade.

Transaction Costs The costs associated with gathering information about products and transporting goods and people geographically or between markets.

Transaction Demand for Money The amount of money that economic transactors desire to hold in order to execute expected transactions; is positively related to income and wealth.

Transfer Payments Transfers of income from one set of households to another set through such programs as welfare payments, social security, and food stamps.

Trap of Underdevelopment Less developed countries typically remain underdeveloped for the following reasons: (a) high rates of population growth that result in low per capita incomes; (b) negligible capital accumulation because of low saving rates fostered by low per capita incomes; (c) rather primitive products are purchased by consumers; and (d) low rates of labor productivity.

Trough (Depression) Phase of the business cycle when most measures of economic activity are at their low point.

Unanimity A requirement that all voters agree before new policies are implemented.

Uncertainty When a reasonable estimate cannot be made of the probability that some event will occur. (See also Risk.)

Unemployment When an individual wants work but is without a job.

Unintended Inventory Changes A balancing item for the economy, these changes in inventories resolve any differences between the planned saving and planned investment functions and assure that actual saving and actual investment are equal at all times.

Union Shop A firm that will hire nonunion workers, but joining the union is a requirement for continued employment.

Uniqueness Gains Arise because exchange allows traders to secure goods not available from local sources in reasonable quantities at reasonable prices.

Usury Law A legal ceiling on the interest rates that lenders may charge borrowers.

Util An imaginary unit of measurement of satisfaction.

Utilitarianism A philosophy developed in England during the 1800s by Jeremy Bentham, an eccentric English philosopher and social reformer; this school of thought embraced the notion that satisfactions or utilities of individuals could be measured, and it sought "the greatest happiness for the greatest number."

Utopian Socialism All property would be collectively owned and all decisions would be democratic.

Value Added The excess of a firm's revenues over the amount it pays to other firms for intermediate goods; used to calculate GNP and, in much of Europe, as a major base for taxes.

Value-Added Approach to Estimating GNP GNP equals the sum of the values added to economic goods at each level of production.

Value of Money The purchasing power of money, which is determined by the interaction of the supply of and demand for money.

Value of the Marginal Product (VMP) The value to society of the output produced by an additional unit of a variable input; computed by multiplying the price of output (P_x) by the marginal physical product of a unit of input (MPP_N): that is, $VMP = (P_x) \times (MPP_N)$.

Variable Costs Costs that vary with the level of production; variable costs are also known as direct costs or prime costs, and are the only costs that rational decision makers consider.

Vertical Combination A firm having different plants producing products at different production levels within an industry.

Voluntary Saving The voluntary decisions of individuals to defer consumption until some future date.

Voluntary Unemployment The frictional unemployment that exists when everyone who wants to work at the prevailing wage rate has a job or can find one rapidly.

Wage-Price Controls Legal restrictions most often used to keep prices from coinciding with their equilibrium levels.

Wage Discrimination Occurs when members of a particular group are paid less than are members of other groups for doing equal work.

Wages Payments per time period for labor services.

Wagner Act (1935) Guaranteed labor the right to organize independent unions and made a company's refusal to negotiate with an elected union an unfair labor practice.

Wealth The discounted present values of income streams that are paid to the owner of an asset.

Wealth Effect The Aggregate Demand curve slopes down, in part, because higher price levels reduce the purchasing power of such financial assets as money or bonds, and vice versa.

Webb-Pomerene Act (1918) Exempts export trade associations from antitrust litigation.

Winners' Curse A theory that vigorously competitive situations are likely to impose losses on the winning bidder because the winning bidder is probably ignorant of information possessed by other bidders.

Yellow-Dog Contracts Contracts that were widely used by business firms during the anti-union years to prevent the formation of labor unions by their employees; as a condition of employment, workers were forced to sign a yellow-dog contract, which was an agreement not to join a labor organization.

Zero Economic Profit The long run equilibrium state of pure competition. All opportunity costs are covered by revenues, but there will be no net resource movements because no better opportunities exist elsewhere.

Name Index*

* Some names recur so frequently in this book (e.g., Adam Smith, John Maynard Keynes, and Milton Friedman) that not all references to them in the text are cited here.

Subject Index

Plant, 466
Point voting, 728
Policy doses, 384–385
Policy lags, 380–384; administrative, 382; destabilizing effects, 383; impact, 382–383; recognition, 382
Political behavior, economics of, Chapter 32; and business cycle, 347, 388
Political Business Cycles, 347, 388
Political stability (gains from trade), 832–833
Pollution, 764–766, Chapter 34; alternative solutions to, 773–779; bubble concept, 781; as an external cost, 704, 771–772; as a public bad, 766; effluent charges, 776; is optimal zero? 773–774; lawsuits for damages, 776; market solutions to, 776; offset policy, 781; regulation, 778; 'rights', 777; subsidizing abatement, 776; and trade, 775
Population, 400; and business cycles, 104; and diminishing returns, 400; and Malthus, 104, 401–402; S curves and growth, 104; and the work force, 400; in underdeveloped countries, 402–403
Population growth, 401
Pork barrel legislation, 732
Portfolio adjustments (international trade), 869
Positive economics, 17
Positive externality, 705, 748
Positive relationship, 26
Positive-sum-games, 586
Potential GNP, 207
Potential money multiplier, 250
Poverty, 809–817; in agriculture, 785–788; in America, 811–817; and discrimination, 816–817; involuntary, 814–816; line, 811; profiles of, 811–813; programs, 815; as a public bad, 813; public policy to eliminate, 817–819; as relative concept, 812; types of, 814–816; voluntary, 814–816; War on, 814
Precautionary demand for money, 281, 859
Predatory pricing behavior, 596–598
Prehistory, 409
Present value, 282, 690, 692; and lotteries, 692
Present consumption versus future growth, 42, 404
Price, 10; absolute, 11; change and income effects, 58, 446, 460–462; demand, 57; equilibrium, 72; as incentives/disincentives, 13; as information, 12–13; of life, 12; marginal revenue, 517; and marginal utility, 445; market, 57, 72; as rationing devices, 13; relative, 11; short run, 514; as signals, 393; stickiness, 291; subjective, 57–58; and substitution effects, 58, 446, 460–462; supply, 66; versus quantity adjustments, 199; and wage controls, 86
Price ceiling, 86–87
Price/cost dynamics, 114
Price consumption curve, 460
Price controls, 86, 392

Price discrimination, 551; arbitrage, 552; and efficiency, 556; profits from, 551; requirements for, 551
Price elasticity of demand, 421
Price elasticity of supply, 429
Price floor, 88
Price index numbers, 134
Price leadership, 570
Price level, 108, 134–136 (See also Inflation); adjustments, 199; and Classical monetarism, 287; and Classical theory, 175, 395; crude monetary theory of, 287; and Keynesian theory, 178, 395
Price maker, 508
Price and quality, 453
Price rigidity (stickiness), 291, 361, 575
Price system, 13, 52
Price taker, 508, 511
Primitive culture, 409
Principal, 468
Principal/agent problem, 468, 593; shirking, 593
Principle of absolute advantage, 828
Prisoners' dilemma, 586–587
Private budget constraints, 311; corporations, 311
Private good, 706, 765
Private property rights, 48–49
Private sector, 32
Privatization, 327, 465, 604, 873
Producer cooperatives, 470
Producer Price Index (PPI), 138
Product differentiation, 563
Production, 6, 464, 482, Chapter 22; economic costs of, 491–493; least cost, 495; team, 466
Production efficiency, 13–14
Production function, 482
Production possibilities and trade, 44–45, 833–834
Production possibilities frontier, 38, 833; and choices between present and future, 40; and crowding out; and diminishing returns, 40; and economic growth, 40–43; and international trade, 44–45, 833–834; and opportunity costs, 40; resources, 40; scarcity, 40; technology, 42
Productive capacity: See Production possibilities frontier
Productive inefficiency (market power), 566
Productive resources, 6
Productivity: See Marginal physical product
Productivity and inflation, 357
Profit maximization for competitive firm, 515–516
Profit maximization for a monopolist, 543–546
Profits, 7, 474, Chapters 21 and 30; and costs, 525; economic, 7, 474, 68; and fiscal policy, 222; and innovation, 68; as market signals, 524–525; in Marxian economics, 880; maximization, 474, 517; and monopoly, 68, 543–545; in national income, 156–157; normal, 475, 526; payment to entrepreneurship, 7, 68; and price discrimination, 551–553; promotional,

609; and risk, 7, 689; role of, 526, 689; and uncertainty, 7, 689
Progressive tax, 710
Proletarians, 880
Promotional profits, 609
Property rights, 766
Property rights and environment, 767
Property rights, fee-simple, 767
Property tax, 717–718
Proportional tax, 710
Proprietors' income, 156
Proprietorship, 469
Protectionism, and inefficiency, 843
P* (P-star), 306
Psychic income, 475
Psychological theories of the business cycle, 107–108
Public choice, 724, Chapter 32; macro, 388
Public choice theory of regulation, 744, 751
Public debt, 309, 320, 720, Chapter 14; benefits of, 325; burdens on future generations, 323; foreign holding, 320–321; interest on, 321–323; must it be repaid? 323–325; recent growth, 309–310; remeasuring, 325–328
Public finance, Chapter 31
Public goods, 706, 707
Public interest theory of regulation, 744
Public sector, 32
Public utilities: See Natural monopoly
Pure competition, 510, Chapter 23 (See also Competition); evaluation of, 530–532; long run, 526; supply curve, 522
Pure monopoly, Chapter 24 (See also Monopoly)
Pure oligopoly, 567
Pure public good, 766

Quadrants (mathematical), 24
Quality and Prices, 453
Quantity adjusters, 508, 511 (See also Price takers)
Quantity vs. price adjustment (macro), 199
Quantity theory of money, 284, 295
Queuing, 46, 884
Quotas:; as barriers to trade, 844–845; in production (USSR), 883

Racial discrimination: See Discrimination
Raiders, corporate, 570–571, 611–612
Random selection, 46
Rate of interest: See Interest rate
Rate of return, 111, 173, 186, 295, 686, 690, 691
Rate structure of utilities, 747–748
Rational choice and information, 449
Rational expectations, 372–375, 395; limitations, 374–375
Rational ignorance, 451–452, 725–726
Rational self interest, 8
Real business cycles, 375–378
Real money, 295
Real rate of interest, 368–369, 685
Real values, 136
Real wages, 342, 345

National Income and Related Statistics, 1968-1991

Basic GDP / GNP Accounts	1968	1969	1970	1971	1972	1973	1974	1975	1976	1977
GROSS DOMESTIC PRODUCT	889.3	959.5	1010.7	1097.2	1207.0	1349.6	1458.6	1585.9	1768.4	1974.1
Personal Consumption Expenditures*	552.5	597.9	640.0	691.6	757.6	837.2	916.5	1012.8	1129.3	1257.2
Gross Private Domestic Investment*	137.0	153.2	148.8	172.5	202.0	238.8	240.8	219.6	277.7	344.1
Government Purchases*	197.7	207.3	218.2	232.4	250.0	266.5	299.1	335.0	356.9	387.3
Net Exports*	5.5	5.6	8.5	6.3	3.2	16.8	16.3	31.1	18.8	1.9
SUM TO: Gross National Product*	892.7	963.9	1015.5	1102.7	1212.8	1359.3	1472.8	1598.4	1782.8	1990.5
MINUS: Depreciation Allowance*	73.9	81.4	88.8	97.5	107.9	118.1	137.5	161.8	179.2	201.5
EQUALS: Net National Product*	818.7	882.5	926.6	1005.1	1104.8	1241.2	1335.4	1436.6	1603.4	1789.0
MINUS: Indirect Business Taxes*	79.6	84.4	94.0	107.0	110.7	118.5	131.9	147.5	162.2	171.2
EQUALS: National Income*	739.1	798.1	832.6	989.1	994.1	1122.7	1203.5	1289.1	1441.4	1617.8
MINUS: Social Security Contributions	50.4	57.9	62.2	68.9	79.0	97.6	110.5	118.5	134.5	149.8
MINUS: Corporate Income Taxes*	39.4	39.7	34.4	37.7	41.9	49.3	51.8	50.9	64.2	73.0
MINUS: Undistributed Corp. Profits*	29.4	25.2	17.9	26.4	34.4	37.0	20.2	37.1	46.4	62.3
PLUS: Transfer Payments*	87.2	97.6	113.6	129.0	142.8	162.9	189.1	230.8	255.1	274.8
EQUALS: Personal Income*	707.2	772.9	831.8	894.0	981.6	1101.7	1210.1	1313.4	1451.4	1607.5
MINUS: Personal Taxes*	97.7	116.0	116.2	117.3	142.0	152.0	171.8	170.6	198.7	228.1
EQUALS: Disposable Income*	609.6	656.7	715.6	776.8	839.6	949.8	1038.4	1142.8	1252.6	1379.3
REAL GNP (in $1982 Billions)	2365.6	2423.3	2416.2	2484.8	2608.5	2744.1	2729.3	2695.0	2826.7	2958.6
Per Capita Disposable Income ($1982)	$8,728	$8,828	$8,992	$9,234	$9,569	$10,095	$9,852	$9,834	$10,098	$10,336
Percent Change in Real Per Capita DI	3.1	1.1	1.9	2.7	3.6	5.4	-2.4	-0.2	2.7	2.
Money and the Price Level										
Consumer Price Index (1982-4=100)	34.8	36.7	38.8	40.5	41.8	44.4	49.3	53.8	56.9	60.6
Percentage Inflation Rate	4.2	5.5	5.7	4.4	3.2	6.2	11	9.1	5.8	6.
Supply of Money, M1*	197.5	204	214.5	228.4	249.3	262.9	274.4	287.6	306.4	331.
Population / Labor Force										
Population (Millions)	200.7	202.7	205.1	207.7	209.9	211.9	213.8	216.0	218.0	220.
Civilian Labor Force (Millions)	78.7	80.7	82.8	84.4	87.0	89.4	91.9	93.8	96.2	99.
Unemployment (Millions)	2.8	2.8	4.1	5.0	4.9	4.4	5.2	7.9	4.4	7.
Percent Unemployment / Total Labor	3.5	3.4	4.8	5.8	5.5	4.8	5.5	8.3	7.6	6.
International Trade										
Exports*	54.8	60.4	28.9	72.4	81.4	114.1	151.5	161.3	177.7	191.
Imports*	49.3	54.7	60.5	66.1	78.2	97.3	135.2	130.3	158.9	189.
The Federal Budget										
Federal Government Receipts*	153.0	186.9	192.8	187.1	207.3	230.8	263.2	279.1	298.1	355.
Federal Outlays*	178.1	183.6	195.6	210.2	230.7	245.7	269.4	332.3	371.8	409.
Federal Surplus (+) or Deficit (-)*	-25.0	3.2	-2.8	-23.0	-23.4	-14.9	-6.1	-53.2	-73.7	-53.

* Billions of Dollars

** 1991 data are preliminary